fifth edition

intermediate
ACCOUNTING
comprehensive volume

Harry Simons, MA, CPA

Professor of Accounting
University of California, Los Angeles

Consulting Editor

Jay M. Smith, PhD, CPA

Professor of Accounting
Brigham Young University

Published by

A61 **SOUTH-WESTERN PUBLISHING CO.**

CINCINNATI   WEST CHICAGO, ILL.   DALLAS   NEW ROCHELLE, N.Y.
BURLINGAME, CALIF.   BRIGHTON, ENGLAND

ISBN: 0-538-01610-8

Library of Congress Catalog Card Number 72-122517

1 2 3 4 5 6 7 8 9 10 11 12 K 0 9 8 7 6 5 4 3 2

Printed in the United States of America

preface

The fifth edition of *Intermediate Accounting — Comprehensive Volume* is a text for a year course to follow the introductory study in accounting. This edition, as earlier editions, seeks to serve the needs of two groups: (1) economics, business, or management students who do not plan to go beyond the intermediate course, and (2) accounting students who expect to continue with the study on an advanced level. Each of these groups must be familiar with the objectives of accounting and with the principles that have evolved in response to these objectives. Each of these groups must possess a full understanding of the nature of the basic accounting statements as well as the limitations that are involved in their preparation. With such a background, the student who does not specialize in accounting can properly interpret the statements and reports that emerge from the accounting process; the accounting major makes important progress in his chosen field and can look forward to achieving a full accounting competence and ultimate admission into the accounting profession.

Important advances have taken place in both the theory and practice of accounting in the period since the last edition of *Intermediate Accounting*, and the fifth edition represents a major revision of the earlier work. Discussions in the text focus in particular upon the challenges to principles and practices in recent years and to the responses that have been made to these challenges. There is further discussion of the problems that assume high current significance and to the alternatives that must be evaluated in ultimately reaching answers to these. Particular emphasis is placed on such matters as the changing nature of contemporary principles and practices, the increased application of present-value concepts in the valuation process, the analysis for recording purposes of the highly complex transactions that arise in an economic environment that becomes ever more complex, and the modifications and refinements that are employed in developing accounting information that is designed to provide maximum value to its user.

Special reference is made in the discussions to the significant contributions to accounting theory and its application in the last decade by professional and research groups. Reference is made to the many publications of the American Institute of Certified Public Accountants, including the series of Accounting Research Studies and also the Statements and the Opinions of the Accounting Principles Board. The contributions in the form of special studies and committee reports by the American Accounting Association receive prominent attention. Discussions include reference to the latest tax laws and other legislation affecting current practice. Terminology, statements, and forms that are currently found in practice are used in the illustrations. Questions, exercises, and problems sections have been revised and many new materials have been added including problems that have been given in recent years in the Uniform Certified Public Accountant Examination.

Although the basic form of the work is continued in the fifth edition, changes that have taken place in theory and practice are fully expressed and illustrated. A summary of the basic changes that were made follows.

■ The introduction and review of fundamental processes has been expanded to five chapters. The expansion was regarded as necessary in view of the different introductory courses that have been taken by students entering the intermediate study. Some introductory courses are limited to one semester; other introductory courses, although offered over a year, place heavy emphasis upon the managerial aspects of accounting, information systems, and computer methods and data processing. The expansion of the opening section of the text permits a full review of the concepts and principles underlying accounting and their application in the accounting process. Full recognition is made of the development of the conceptual structure of accounting and of those groups that have contributed importantly to this development. The accounting process from the recording phase to the summarizing phase is fully explained and illustrated. Changes in the form and content of the basic financial statements receive special emphasis. Students with a strong accounting background will be able to expand their understanding of the fundamental processes and add to their security in applying these; students without such a background will be able to acquire a firm foundation in basic theory and important experience in the application of such theory.

■ The different classes of assets are considered in the order in which they appear on the balance sheet. Valuation procedures for each class of assets receive particular attention. Special consideration is given to the specific matters that follow. A full discussion of the alternative valuation procedures for marketable securities is provided. Challenges to the traditional concepts for the valuation of inventories are described. Changes in recent years that provide for the use of alternate valuation methods for holdings in affiliated companies receive full attention. In discussing business acquisitions, recording processes applying "purchase" and "pooling of interests" approaches are distinguished, and the accounting procedures under each approach are described and evaluated. In recording property acquisitions, the provisions for recognizing the income tax investment credit are described. Present and proposed departures from cost in the valuation of property items are fully discussed. In considering intangible assets, new concepts in the valuation of goodwill receive full attention. Special focus is also directed to the criteria that are to be considered in reporting long-term leases on the financial statements. The problems that will find their solutions in the future are also suggested.

■ The classes of liabilities are considered in the order in which these appear on the balance sheet. Valuation problems in the recognition of liabilities, both short-term and long-term, receive special recognition. The consideration of long-term liabilities includes discussion of the wide variety of debt arrangements that have assumed importance in recent years. Special attention is directed to convertible bonds and to special obligations that are accompanied by other securities representing potential equity items. The nature of accounting for pension plans is described and the recognition of pension liabilities in present practice is described and illustrated.

■ The alternate positions that are recognized upon the redemption of capital stock and upon the reacquisition of shares of treasury stock are described and illustrated. The preparation of the income statement, the retained earnings statement, and the balance sheet are illustrated. A full description is provided of earnings per share measurements that have become an integral part of income statement reporting. In accordance with the position taken by the American Institute of Certified Public Accountants, the statement of changes in financial position (the funds statement) is recognized as one of the basic financial statements. The nature and use of this statement is described, the broadened interpretation of funds is recognized, and the preparation of the statement using both working capital and cash definitions for funds is illustrated. The conventional work sheet approach is employed in preparing the statement but alternative approaches are recognized and described.

■ The conventional approaches to the analysis and interpretation of the balance sheet, the income statement, and the funds statement are described and illustrated. Summaries accounting for the variation in gross profits and summaries offering break-even analysis are explained and illustrated, and the special contributions that these can make to the user of financial data are indicated. The development of such analyses has been simplified. Chapters on statements from incomplete data and on the correction of statements have been continued and expanded to offer a complete coverage of these matters as well as to provide the student with a comprehensive review of the materials presented earlier. The final chapter on the preparation of statements adjusted to reflect changing price levels has been revised in accordance with present valuation and presentation practices. The emphasis on continuity that must be found in adjusted statements prepared in successive periods has been continued in this revision.

Those who are familiar with earlier editions of this work will recognize that the original form and nature of presentations are preserved in the new edition. First, the theoretical setting is given for the subject to be discussed. The alternative views and approaches that may be taken are then explored and evaluated. Finally, the opinions that are expressed by leading authorities are indicated and the generally accepted position is defined. The accounting process is viewed here not as a static process but as one that must respond to changes in the economic, political, and social environment.

Each chapter concludes with a set of questions, exercises, and problems. Questions provide a review of theory. Exercises offer practice in applying theory to specific problems. Problems require that a student apply his entire background to broader situations. The first few problems in each chapter offer practice in applying the concepts that are developed in the chapter presentation; remaining problems are of a more comprehensive nature and call for greater skill. Almost all of the chapters conclude with problems adapted from the CPA examination that have been selected because they represent a high challenge to the student, at the same time contributing importantly to his accounting growth and maturity.

The author wishes to thank the American Institute of Certified Public Accountants and the American Accounting Association for permission to quote from their various publications and pronouncements.

Harry Simons

contents

Contents

chapter 1

basic accounting concepts and principles

Accounting is a service activity. Its function is to provide quantitative information, primarily financial in nature, about economic entities that is intended to be useful in making economic decisions — in making reasoned choices among alternative courses of action.[1]

Several important concepts are included in this recent definition of accounting by the Accounting Principles Board, the spokesman for the accounting profession. Accounting is a *service activity*. It is intended to fulfill a *useful function* in our society by offering to provide service to various segments of the economic community that are directly or indirectly involved with business entities. It is primarily concerned with *quantitative financial information* that describes the activities of a business, rather than qualitative, judgmental evaluations of those activities. The output of the accounting system is intended to serve as an aid to users who must make *decisions* between alternative actions that are available to them. To the extent that accounting information fulfills these goals, the accounting system is fulfilling its major purpose.

Users of accounting information

Users of accounting information may be divided into two major categories: external users and internal users. *External users* are those groups or individuals who are not directly concerned with the day-to-day operations of the business, but who are indirectly related to the business. They include absentee owners, creditors, potential owners and creditors, labor union representatives, and governmental agency employees. *Internal users* include all levels of management personnel within a business entity who are responsible for the planning and control of operations.

---

[1]*Statements of the Accounting Principles Board, No. 4*, "Basic Concepts and Accounting Principles Underlying Financial Statements of Business Enterprises" (New York: American Institute of Certified Public Accountants, 1970), par. 40.

Several branches of accounting have evolved to meet the needs of these groups. Two of the most important branches have been identified as financial accounting and managerial accounting. *Financial accounting* systems are primarily designed to provide financial statements to external users for their decision processes, although internal users also have access to such statements and use them in many of their decisions. *Managerial accounting* systems are primarily designed to supplement the financial accounting information for internal users, thus assisting them in reaching certain operating decisions. As businesses have become more complex, the availability of relevant information provided on a timely basis has become highly important to both classes of users. In order to meet this information need, companies have found it necessary to establish improved information systems. The increasing availability and use of business computers have resulted in vastly improved information systems that can provide more relevant and timely data than was possible heretofore.

This text is primarily concerned with financial accounting and thus places particular emphasis on the needs of the external users.

General objectives of financial accounting

Financial accounting has been described as a system that provides "a continual history quantified in money terms of economic resources and obligations of a business enterprise and of economic activities that change these resources and obligations."[1] This history has become increasingly important to the external user as the complexities of business organization and operations have made it more difficult to determine the position of a company and the results of its operations. The corporate form of business organization has contributed to this difficulty.

By its very nature the corporate form calls for extended and accurate accounting. It has permitted the accumulation of large amounts of resources by a single entity. In large corporations the investment and management groups are separated. Ownership interests are liquid and readily transferable. The number of investors having any first-hand knowledge of the activities of the companies in which they have an interest is small. Accounting becomes a major source of information concerning corporate financial status and progress for the investor. Accounting also becomes an indispensable source of information for other absentee groups that are interested in the company.

If important economic decisions must be made by absentee owners, creditors, and other external users from statements produced by the

---
[1]*Ibid.*, par. 41.

financial accounting system, these statements should meet several general objectives. They should:

1. Provide reliable information about economic resources and obligations.
2. Provide reliable information about changes in net resources resulting from profit-directed activities.
3. Provide financial information that assists in estimating the future earning potential of the entity.
4. Provide reliable information about changes in net resources from sources other than profit-directed activities (for example, transactions between the enterprise and its owners).
5. Provide disclosure of other information relevant to statement users' needs.[1]

The latter objective is open-ended, and requires continual study of the needs of external users. The financial statements that are designed to meet the needs of the external user and that should meet the objectives listed above are frequently referred to as *general purpose statements*.

Accounting and the attest function

A special responsibility of some accountants is to attest to the reliability and fairness of accounting statements that are prepared for external users by other accountants. Many persons regard this as the most important role that the accountant can assume, a role that gives him professional status. The accountant who performs this role is called an *auditor*. He examines and reviews the statements prepared under the direction of management and issues his opinion as to how fairly the data in the statements are presented. The auditor thus adds some greater degree of confidence to the various segments of the business community who utilize and rely on such statements.

The need for accounting principles

If accounting data were used only within a company, management could prescribe the rules and procedures to be followed. If the rules and procedures were consistently and accurately applied, the resulting information could be used in the decision process without change. But many external users of financial statements use accounting reports in a comparative way. Company A is compared with Company B; Industry X is compared with Industry Y. As a result of such use, standards and guidelines are necessary so that accounting information can be compiled and reported in a manner that will enable comparisons to be made. These standards and guidelines are referred to most commonly as "generally accepted accounting principles."

---

[1] *Ibid.*, par. 77–81.

Accounting principles are not static or unchanging. Many of them do not have universal acceptance, and there are frequently alternative procedures for recording identical events. Before an accountant can either prepare financial statements for external use or engage in an audit of management's external statements, he must have a working knowledge of these generally accepted accounting principles. The person who relies upon the financial statements in making decisions also needs to understand these principles so that he can better understand the nature of the statements as well as their limitations.

Professional associations concerned with accounting principles

There have been numerous attempts by individuals and by professional and governmental organizations to establish fundamental accounting concepts and principles. These efforts have met with varying degrees of success. Before discussing some of the more important of these attempts, reference to the different accounting bodies who share the responsibility in developing principles is essential.

American Institute of Certified Public Accountants (AICPA). The American Institute of Certified Public Accountants is the professional organization of practicing *certified public accountants* in the United States. The organization was formed in 1887 and was originally named the American Institute of Accountants. A monthly publication, *The Journal of Accountancy*, was first issued by the Institute in 1905, and it communicates with its members concerning the problems of accounting and the challenges and responsibilities faced by the profession.

Certified public accountants are licensed by the various states. Although a uniform examination is prepared by the AICPA and administered twice each year throughout all of the states and territories, the individual states still set the educational and experience requirements for certification. Some states issue a CPA certificate upon passing the examination without any required experience; others require one to four years of experience before a certificate is issued. A number of states now require a bachelor's degree in business with an emphasis in accounting as a requirement for taking the examination. Other states, however, have lesser educational requirements. For some time the AICPA has exerted considerable pressure among the states for standardizing educational and experience requirements. In recent years, the Institute has recommended that the states require a college program that includes a "common body of knowledge" specified by a special AICPA committee and eliminate the experience requirement for certification.

There are two groups within the states that assume responsibility for the professional activities of certified public accountants: (1) state boards and (2) state societies. The members of a *state board of accountancy* are normally appointed by the governor of the state. The state board is responsible for determining and regulating the admission requirements of new members into the profession. This responsibility includes administering the examination and evaluating the candidate's education and experience prior to the issuance of a certificate. Once a state board has approved issuance of a certificate, it must further determine that the appropriate regulations governing the use of the certificate are followed by those who are recognized as CPA's. These boards, therefore, have the power to issue and to revoke the CPA certificate.

The *state societies of certified public accountants* are responsible for meeting the professional organizational needs of the members in each state. State societies are presently independent organizations; however, they maintain close relationships with the staff of the AICPA. National committee assignments of the Institute, for example, are generally initiated by the state societies.

Neither the Institute nor the state societies can issue or revoke a certificate. They may admit and suspend members from their respective organizations based upon their own rules and regulations; however, they cannot prevent one from using the "CPA" designation.

American Accounting Association (AAA). The American Accounting Association was known as the American Association of University Instructors in Accounting from 1918 until 1935, when its name was changed to its present designation. The AAA is primarily an organization for accounting educators, although others are admitted to membership. Student associate memberships are available. A quarterly journal, the *Accounting Review*, is sponsored by the AAA. Articles in the *Accounting Review* generally discuss matters of accounting theory as compared with articles in the *Journal of Accountancy* that are primarily concerned with matters of accounting practice. AAA Committee reports and discussions of these reports are communicated to AAA members through the *Accounting Review*.

Although the AAA now has a permanent executive secretary, its officers and committees rotate each year among the members. The AAA does not claim to serve as a majority voice for the educators. Its major role is to serve as a forum within which individual educators can express their views either individually or in special appointed committees. It also assists individual members in financing research projects whose purpose is to add new understanding in the field of accounting.

Securities and Exchange Commission (SEC). The Securities and Exchange Commission was created by an Act of Congress in 1934. The primary role of the SEC is to regulate the issuance and trading of marketable securities by corporations to the general public. This body has established reporting requirements for corporations that issue securities to the public to insure adequate disclosure of pertinent facts concerning the activities of the issuing companies. The regulations of the SEC also require independent verification of annual financial statements, and the SEC reviews both the reports and the supporting verification to ascertain compliance with the law. The principal governing acts of the SEC are the Securities Act of 1933 and the Securities Exchange Act of 1934. Although the SEC has the power to issue regulations defining how corporations should report financial affairs to shareholders, it has for the most part relied upon the accounting profession, through the AICPA, to perform this function. In recent years, the SEC has taken some actions that have moved the profession to accelerate its efforts to improve accounting practices and to achieve greater uniformity in reporting.

Other organizations. Although the three organizations discussed here have traditionally exercised considerable influence upon the establishment of accounting principles, the influence of other groups has also been felt recently. The *Financial Executives Institute (FEI)*, formerly the Controllers' Institute, is a national organization composed of financial executives employed by large corporations. The FEI membership includes treasurers, controllers, and financial vice-presidents. The FEI publishes a monthly journal, *The Financial Executive*, and has sponsored several research projects relating to financial reporting problems. One of its more prominent studies was conducted in the late 1960's. This study considered the manner in which a company operating in a number of industries should report the financial progress attained by different company segments. Both the AICPA and the SEC have utilized this research in formulating their pronouncements on this subject.

Another influential group is the *National Association of Accountants (NAA)*. This organization is more concerned with the use of accounting information within the enterprise than with external reporting, and thus has directed its research primarily toward cost accounting and information systems. It's monthly publication, *Management Accounting*, deals mainly with problems involving information systems and the use of accounting data within the organization. Because the corporation's information system can provide information for both internal and external users, the NAA is concerned about the relationship of accounting principles for internal reporting to those for external reporting.

Several societies of financial analysts have been formed. The most prominent of these groups is the *Financial Analysts Federation*. Admittance to this group is based upon a qualifying examination. Because financial analysts are a major user of external accounting reports, they are very much concerned with the present status of financial reporting. Members of this group have often been quite critical of corporate financial reporting practices and have continued to request increased disclosure of pertinent financial data.

Development of accounting principles

Accounting was originally defined by the Committee on Terminology of the AICPA as follows:

> Accounting is the art of recording, classifying, and summarizing in a significant manner and in terms of money, transactions and events which are, in part at least, of a financial character, and interpreting the results thereof.[1]

The reference to accounting as an art does not rule out the fact that the accountant's work is practiced within a framework of fundamental doctrine. This body of doctrine consists of certain principles and practices that have won acceptance within the profession because of both their logic and their proved usefulness. These principles in effect represent the response of the accounting profession to the needs and expectations of the various user groups requiring financial information. Again it should be emphasized that when reference is made to accounting principles, it must be understood that the term is not used to suggest natural laws of universal applicability but rather that body of standards that as of the time are considered to be good accounting practice. This concept is well described in APB Statement No. 4 that describes basic concepts and principles as follows:

> Present generally accepted accounting principles are the result of an evolutionary process that can be expected to continue in the future. Changes may occur at any level of generally accepted accounting principles. . . . Generally accepted accounting principles change in response to changes in economic and social conditions, to new knowledge and technology, and to demands of users for more serviceable financial information. The dynamic nature of financial accounting—its ability to change in response to changed conditions — enables it to maintain and increase the usefulness of the information it provides.[2]

Development of principles by the AICPA. Through the groups named earlier in this chapter, fundamental theory is subject to constant reexamination and critical analysis so that it may better serve the needs of the users of financial information. The AICPA, as spokesman for the accounting profession, has played the most significant role in developing these principles. It was not until the early 1930's, however, that this

---

[1] *Accounting Terminology Bulletin No. 1*, "Review and Résumé" (New York: American Institute of Certified Public Accountants, 1953), par. 9.

[2] *Statements of the Accounting Principles Board, No. 4, op. cit.*, par. 208 and 209.

role began to emerge. From 1932 to 1934, an Institute committee worked with the New York Stock Exchange in an attempt to establish some basic standards. From this committee came a short list of "accepted accounting principles" designed to improve financial reporting. The Institute continued to study financial reporting through various committees, and in the late thirties formed the Committee on Accounting Procedure (CAP). The primary responsibility of this committee was to prepare Accounting Research Bulletins (ARB's) that would establish more detailed guidelines for reporting corporate financial activity. Between 1939 and 1958, fifty-one bulletins were issued. These bulletins covered a variety of matters. In some instances the conclusions of newly-released bulletins were not consistent with those issued in the past. Furthermore, no serious attempt was made to relate the various topics studied into an integrated theory of accounting, although a consolidation of the first 42 bulletins was issued in 1953 as Bulletin No. 43.

During this same time period, a subcommittee of the Committee on Accounting Procedure continued to examine the terminology that was used in financial statements. The first terminology committee had been formed in 1920 by the Institute. Several of the ARB's issued between 1939 and 1952 dealt primarily with terminology. When the Accounting Research Bulletins were consolidated in 1953, the terminology bulletins were also consolidated into Terminology Bulletin No. 1. Between 1953 and 1958, three additional terminology bulletins were issued.

The progress of the AICPA in improving reporting practices through almost twenty years of publishing bulletins was not regarded by all parties as entirely satisfactory. Critics, both inside and outside of the profession have felt that there was a lack of means for sufficient research and documentation in the study and deliberations of the committees leading to the publication of the bulletins. Many of the bulletins, it was claimed, were either overly permissive or overly vague, which permitted the accountant wide discretion in applying the position taken in the bulletins. Some members of the profession preferred this flexibility; in fact, some felt that it was absolutely necessary. Other members were of the opinion that the lack of a strong theoretical foundation and the resulting large number of alternative principles that were regarded as equally acceptable tended to undermine seriously the potential usefulness of financial statements.

The critics' voices became more influential, and a new organization was initiated by the AICPA in 1959. In place of the Committee on Accounting Procedure, the Institute adopted a dual approach in the development of accounting principles. One part of the program created the *Accounting Research Division* (*ARD*) with a full-time director of accounting research. Research projects are developed by the staff and others who are asked to assist the staff. The results of the research projects are published in a series of *Accounting Research Studies* (*ARS*). The second part of the program provided that these studies were to be used by the profession as a whole and more specifically by a special board of the AICPA referred to as the *Accounting Principles Board* (*APB*). The APB consists primarily of practicing accountants who review all evidence available on a given subject and are authorized to issue "Opinions" that serve to replace or supplement preceding recommendations. Initially, the Board was composed of 21 members. However, the number of members and the composition of the membership has varied since its creation.

Before an APB opinion is issued in final form, an exposure draft is made available to a wide variety of interested parties. This procedure has resulted in extensive discussion within the profession of proposed opinions, and in some cases opinions have been substantially revised after comments on the exposure draft have been reviewed by the Board. However, some problems have not been fully understood until after the issuance of an opinion. In some instances, this made it necessary for the Board to issue opinions that rescinded or amended all or parts of an opinion that had been released earlier.

The influence of the Accounting Principles Board was greatly enhanced in 1964 when the Council of the Institute unanimously adopted a set of recommendations which stated in effect that departures from the APB Opinions must be disclosed either in the footnotes to the financial statements or in the audit reports prepared by members of the AICPA. Among the specific recommendations adopted by the Council were the following:

... "Generally accepted accounting principles" are those principles which have substantial authoritative support.

... Opinions of the Accounting Principles Board constitute "substantial authoritative support."

... "Substantial authoritative support" can exist for accounting principles that differ from Opinions of the Accounting Principles Board.

... No distinction should be made between the Bulletins issued by the former Committee on Accounting Procedure on matters of accounting principles and the Opinions of the Accounting Principles Board. Accordingly, reference in this report to Opinions of the Accounting Principles Board also apply to the Accounting Research Bulletins.

... The failure to disclose a material departure from an Accounting Principles Board Opinion is deemed to be substandard reporting.

... The Committee on Professional Ethics and the Institute's legal counsel have advised that the present By-Laws and Code of Professional

Ethics would not cover an infraction of the above recommendations. Whether the Code of Professional Ethics should be amended is a question which should be studied further.[1]

As a result of the profession's response to these recommendations, AICPA positions as reflected in their official pronouncements have been applied to financial reporting almost universally.

The Board has in some situations authorized the issuance of "Statements." These statements, which concern accounting matters, do not carry the authority of an Opinion. Statements have been considered necessary when the Board is of the opinion that it does not have sufficient evidence to recommend specific action but believes that certain analyses or observations on accounting matters should be brought to the attention of its membership. For example, Statement No. 2 issued in 1967 urged accountants to report segmented income information for single companies operating in various segments of the economy.[2] Statement No. 3 issued in 1969 suggested that accountants consider issuing supplemental price-adjusted statements to accompany the basic financial statements.[3] Statement No. 4, issued in 1970, was a statement on the "Basic Concepts and Accounting Principles Underlying Financial Statements of Business Enterprises." The objectives of this statement were (1) "to provide a basis for enhanced understanding of the broad fundamentals of financial accounting," and (2) "to provide a basis for guiding the future development of financial accounting."[4]

Statement No. 4 is the first publication of the Board that establishes a general framework for the development of generally accepted accounting principles. In this statement the APB defines the environment of accounting as faced by the profession today, and divides the basic concepts of accounting into (1) objectives, (2) basic features, (3) basic elements, (4) pervasive principles, (5) modifying conventions, (6) broad operating principles and (7) detailed accounting principles. Members of the Board who prepared the statement benefited from earlier research studies of the Accounting Research Division and from publications of the American Accounting Association.[5] Many of the definitions, terms, and

---

[1]*Opinions of the Accounting Principles Board, No. 6*, " Status of Accounting Research Bulletins" (New York: American Institute of Certified Public Accountants, October, 1965), Appendix A.

[2]*Statements of the Accounting Principles Board, No. 2*, "Disclosure of Supplemental Financial Information by Diversified Companies" (New York: American Institute of Certified Public Accountants, 1967).

[3]*Statements of the Accounting Principles Board, No. 3*, "Financial Statements Restated for General Price-Level Changes" (New York: American Institute of Certified Public Accountants, 1969).

[4]*Statements of the Accounting Principles Board, No. 4, op. cit.*, par. 2.

[5]Special credit was given by the Accounting Principles Board to ARS No. 1, *The Basic Postulates of Accounting* by Moonitz, ARS No. 3, *A Tentative Set of Broad Accounting Principles* by Sprouse and Moonitz, and ARS No. 7, *Inventory of Generally Accepted Accounting Principles for Business Enterprises* by Grady.

concepts contained in Statement No. 4 are incorporated into the material presented in the remainder of this text.

The history of the statements and pronouncements by the AICPA is an interesting one and adds strength to the observation that accounting is an evolving art.

Development of principles by the AAA. The American Accounting Association has also had as one of its major objectives the development of accounting principles. The general approach of the executive committee of the Association has been to establish broad basic principles upon which financial reporting should be based. Five basic statements under a variety of titles have been issued by special committees appointed by the AAA. These statements have not attempted to cover all possible aspects of accounting theory. Rather, these statements have directed attention to areas where the committees, acting for the Association, have felt that serious objections could be raised to existing practices. The statements were issued in 1936, 1941, 1948, 1957, and 1966. A number of statements of a supplementary nature were issued relative to both the 1948 and 1957 statements. Although each of the AAA statements made some impact upon the profession, frequently their conclusions were regarded by many accountants as too theoretical for practical use.

The 1966 statement, *A Statement of Basic Accounting Theory*, broke tradition from the earlier statements. Not only was it much longer and broader in scope, but it purported to develop a more cohesive framework underlying accounting data. The members of the committee that prepared the statement attempted to specify what constituted accounting data. They established four standards that, in their opinion, should be found in all accounting information: (1) relevance, (2) verifiability, (3) freedom from bias, and (4) quantifiability.[1] Using these standards as a foundation, they also proposed certain communication guidelines and indicated how accounting information for both internal and external use could be developed in terms of these standards. A number of the concepts introduced in this statement were incorporated in Statement No. 4 of the Accounting Principles Board.

Development of principles by the SEC. The Securities and Exchange Commission has made extensive contributions to the development and the expression of accounting doctrine by issuing rules and regulations relating to the reports to be filed by registrants and by rendering opinions on matters of theory and practice in its official decisions, reports,

---

[1] *A Statement of Basic Accounting Theory* (Evanston, Illinois: American Accounting Association, 1966), p. 8.

and its Accounting Series Releases. The issuance of the Accounting Series Releases by the Commission was announced as a "program for the publication, from time to time, of opinions on accounting principles for the purpose of contributing to the development of uniform standards and practices in major accounting questions."[1]

The number of Accounting Series Releases now exceeds one hundred. Their major role has been to point out problems that require some action by the AICPA and to encourage research in establishing more universally acceptable accounting principles.

Summary of developments by professional organizations. The progress that has been made in defining the body of doctrine that is applicable to contemporary reporting has been highly important both to the accounting profession and to those who use the services offered by the profession. The practitioner, aware of standards that have general support, is afforded guidance as well as a sense of security in his performance. The product of accounting is improved and at the same time tends to achieve greater uniformity and comparability. The reader of the financial report, familiar with the standards that have been applied in its preparation, can view it with added confidence and compare it with other reports prepared within a common framework.

Generally accepted accounting concepts and principles

Major objectives of this text are to present the theory that underlies current accounting practice, to explain the alternative methods that are presently acceptable for recording transactions, and to develop the analytical ability that is required for one to evaluate the strengths and weaknesses of both present and proposed accounting alternatives. The theory in support of specific accounting procedures is discussed in the appropriate sections of the text. However, there are a number of basic concepts and principles that should be understood before the different classes and types of transactions are reviewed. These basic concepts and principles have had alternative terms applied to them: assumptions, standards, conventions, basic features, objectives, postulates, and axioms. Many frameworks of theory have been prepared that attempt to classify concepts and principles into various categories. The first serious attempt by the Accounting Principles Board to do this resulted in the publication of Statement No. 4. In several of these frameworks, some concepts and principles are identified as being more basic than others. The APB referred to the primary factors that financial accounting should possess

---

[1] *Accounting Series Releases*, United States Securities and Exchange Commission, p. iii.

as *qualitative objectives*.[1] Other accounting concepts and principles are descriptive of conventions that have developed over time and that are partly dictated by the environment in which accounting functions.

In the remaining pages of this chapter, the reasoning that forms the basis for several of the more important concepts and principles will be presented. The discussion is divided into: (1) *basic qualitative objectives* as outlined in Statement No. 4, and (2) *other basic concepts and principles*. The concepts and principles discussed in the second category are presented in alphabetical sequence to avoid any implication of priority in the theoretical framework. The set of principles included in this chapter is not intended to be an exhaustive one. Additional concepts and principles considered less general will be discussed in subsequent chapters.

Basic qualitative objectives. In order for accounting information to be useful, it must have certain qualities or characteristics. Seven qualities are identified by the APB in Statement No. 4 as being basic if financial accounting is to fulfill its service objectives. These qualities are:

1. Relevance
2. Understandability
3. Verifiability
4. Neutrality
5. Timeliness
6. Comparability
7. Completeness

The objectives listed are related to the broad ethical goals of society, goals of truth, justice, and fairness. These objectives must be achieved in financial reporting if the statements generated by the accounting system are to achieve maximum usefulness.[2]

Relevance. The Accounting Principles Board identifies relevance as the primary qualitative objective. Information must be relevant to its intended use. If it is not relevant, it is useless regardless of how well it meets the other objectives. The objective of relevance is to select methods of measuring and reporting that will aid those individuals who rely upon financial statements to make decisions. Many critics of financial statements have argued that traditionally prepared statements are irrelevant to many decisions that must be made. An increasing amount of research is being conducted to evaluate this criticism. What information is required by those who must make a decision? How can

---

[1]Similar concepts were labeled "standards" by the special committee of the American Accounting Association in *A Statement of Basic Accounting Theory.*

[2]*Statements of the Accounting Principles Board, No. 4, op. cit.*, par. 85 and 86.

current practice be changed to improve the relevance, and thus the usefulness, of accounting information?

In its statement in 1966, the American Accounting Association comments on the importance of the concept of relevance as follows:

> The accounting function should, under many circumstances, provide information with a high degree of relevance to a specific intended use although it may have little relevance to any other. When this is done, care must be taken to disclose the limitations of the information to prevent the possible assumption of universal relevance. To have information used for purposes for which it has no relevance is likely to be worse than having no information at all. Not only may decisions be influenced wrongly, but the user may be diverted from an effort to acquire relevant information.[1]

Understandability. In order for financial information to be useful in a decision process, it must be expressed in terminology that is understandable to the user. Business transactions and activities have become increasingly complex. It is not always possible to describe complex transactions in simple terms; therefore, the user of the statements must attain a minimum level of competence in understanding the terminology used in accounting statements. However, the accountant has a basic responsibility to describe business transactions clearly and concisely.

Verifiability. Accountants seek to base their findings on facts that are determined objectively and that can be verified by other trained accountants. The APB in listing verifiability as an objective states, "verifiable financial accounting information provides results that would be substantially duplicated by independent measurers using the same measurement methods."[2]

All accounting measurements, however, cannot be completely free from subjective opinions and judgments. Cash receipts and disbursements can be adequately supported by vouchers, and cash on hand is determined by count; full support and verification for this element and its changes are available. Findings here can be readily verified. Purchases of goods and services, as well as sales, are also generally well supported by evidence and subject to verification. There are a number of areas in accounting, however, where determinations must be based in part upon judgment, estimate, and other subjective factors. The recognition of depreciation is an example of the latter. But the degree of estimate can be minimized by the attempt to develop evidence that will lend objective support to conclusions. Verifiable determinations are encouraged as a means of reducing possible error, bias, or intentional distortion, and achieving an accounting that can be accepted with confidence.

---

[1] *A Statement of Basic Accounting Theory, op. cit.*, p. 9.

[2] *Statements of the Accounting Principles Board, No. 4, op. cit.*, par. 90.

Neutrality. Financial statements should not be biased in favor of one group to the detriment of another. This objective may conflict with the basic objective of relevance; however, the presumption of the Accounting Principles Board is that external financial reports are general purpose statements that meet the common needs of a wide variety of users. Specialized needs must be met in other ways. The qualitative objective of neutrality is similar in concept to the American Accounting Association standard "freedom from bias" and to the all-encompassing principle of "fairness" advocated by a national CPA firm.

The following observations were made concerning freedom from bias in the AAA statement:

> The standard of freedom from bias is advocated because of the many users accounting serves and the many uses to which it may be put. . . . It is conceivable that biased information could properly be introduced if it would aid one group without injuring the position of any other, but this conclusion cannot be reached with certainty in external reporting, where all potential users must be considered. Thus, bias should be avoided in external general purpose reports.[1]

In a similar fashion, the concept of fairness is described by one national CPA firm as follows:

> . . . the one basic accounting postulate underlying accounting principles may be stated as that of fairness — fairness to all segments of the business community (management, labor, stockholders, creditors, customers and the public), determined and measured in the light of the economic and political environment and the modes of thought and customs of all such segments — to the end that the accounting principles based upon this postulate shall produce financial accounting for the lawfully established economic rights and interests that is fair to all segments.[2]

Neutrality, freedom from bias, and fairness to all parties are terms that together describe an important qualitative objective of financial accounting information.

Timeliness. The meaning of the qualitative objective of timeliness is almost self-evident. However, it is so vital to the concept of usefulness that it must be explicitly included. Information furnished after a decision has been made is of no value. All accounting systems should be established to provide information to all users in a timely manner. In meeting this objective, financial statements must be prepared prior to the time an accountant can be absolutely certain as to the results of an entity's

---

[1] *A Statement of Basic Accounting Theory, op. cit.,* p. 11.

[2] *The Postulate of Accounting — What It Is — How It Is Determined, How It Should Be Used* (Arthur Andersen & Co., 1960), p. 31.

operations. The entity is an ongoing enterprise with many interacting activities. Thus, any attempt to measure the success of an entity at some point in time before its dissolution must rely heavily on estimates. Unless such estimates are made and reported, it is not possible for users to judge the success or failure of the entity during a given period. Decisions by investors, creditors, governmental authorities, management, and others rely on these estimates. By convention, the year has been established as the normal period for reporting. In recent years, annual statements, as well as statements covering shorter intervals such as quarters, have been provided by entities to satisfy the needs of those requiring financial information.

Comparability. Comparability may be regarded as intra-comparability, or comparability within a single enterprise, and inter-comparability, or comparability between enterprises.

Consistency is an important ingredient of intra-comparability. In view of variations such as the different procedures for cost allocation in measuring depreciation, the different approaches for pricing inventories in developing cost of goods sold, and the different forms and classifications for the presentation of operating and financial data, methods that are adopted should be consistently employed if there is to be continuity and comparability in the accounting presentations. In analyzing statements one constantly seeks to identify and evaluate the changes and trends within the enterprise. Conclusions concerning financial position and operations may be materially in error if, for example, reducing-charge depreciation is applied against the revenue of one year and straight-line depreciation against the revenue of the next year, or if securities that are owned are reported under long-term investments in one year and under current assets in the following year. Consistency in the application of accounting procedures is also recognized as a means of insuring integrity in financial reporting; the use of alternate procedures in succeeding periods opens the doors to possible manipulation of net income and asset and equity measurements.

This is not to suggest that methods once adopted should not be changed. A continuing analysis of the business activities, as well as changing conditions, may suggest changes in accounting methods and presentations that will lead to more informative statements. Such changes should be incorporated in the accounting system and statements. But the financial statements should be accompanied by a clear explanation of the nature of the changes and their effects, where they are material, so that current reporting can be properly interpreted and related to past reporting.

Inter-comparability, or comparability between enterprises, is more difficult to achieve than comparability within a single enterprise. A primary objective of external financial accounting reports is to provide information that will permit a comparison of one company with another. This concept of comparability requires that like things be accounted for in the same manner on the financial statements. Basic similiarities and differences in the activities of companies should be clearly apparent from the financial statements. They should not be influenced by selection and use of different accounting methods.

One of the greatest unsolved problems in accounting is the present acceptance of alternative accounting methods under situations that do not appear to be sufficiently different to warrant different practices. Much current research in accounting is directed toward identifying circumstances that justify the use of a given method of accounting. If such research is successful, alternative methods can be eliminated where circumstances are found to be the same. In the meantime, current practice requires a disclosure of the accounting methods that are used. Although this disclosure does not generally provide enough information for a user to convert the published financial information from one accounting method to another, it does provide information that will assist the user to determine the degree of inter-company comparability. The Accounting Principles Board recognizes the importance of comparability and its related concept of consistency, and in Statement No. 4 declares:

> The Board ranks comparability among the most important of the objectives of financial accounting, . . . and is attempting to narrow areas of difference in accounting practices that are not justified by differences in circumstances.[1]

Completeness. The last qualitative objective enumerated by the Accounting Principles Board is completeness. This requires that all financial accounting data that meet the other six qualitative objectives be reported. This objective is frequently referred to in accounting literature as *full disclosure.* Completeness, however, does not mean disclosure of just any data. Too much data may be valueless to users if it does not meet the basic requirements of relevance, understandability, verifiability, neutrality, timeliness, and comparability. Excessive detail, descriptions, and qualifications may actually serve to obscure certain significant facts and relationships and thus impair financial presentations. A better term for full disclosure is *adequate disclosure* — disclosure that is adequate to the needs of the users.

---

[1]*Statements of the Accounting Principles Board, No. 4, op. cit.,* par. 105.

The importance that is attached to adequate disclosure is underlined in the Code of Professional Ethics of the AICPA. Rule No. 2.02a of this code provides in part:

> In expressing an opinion on representations in financial statements which he has examined, a member or associate may be held guilty of an act discreditable to the profession if he fails to disclose a material fact known to him which is not disclosed in the financial statements but disclosure of which is necessary to make the financial statements not misleading . . .

The objective of completeness calls not only for disclosure of all financial facts but also for the presentation of such facts in a manner that will lead to their proper interpretation. Care should be taken in developing data classifications, arrangements, and summaries, and in employing exhibits and supporting and supplementary schedules.

It may be possible to provide all significant financial information within the body of the financial statements through the use of descriptive account titles and supporting data developed in parenthetical form. Frequently, however, certain matters can better be handled by means of (1) special notes to accompany the statements, or (2) explanations in the auditor's report accompanying the statements. Whenever the data are not included in the statements, the statements should refer to such supporting material as representing an integral part of financial reporting.

Other concepts and principles of accounting. A number of other concepts and principles of accounting have become widely accepted. These have not been regarded as being as basic as the qualitative objectives just discussed. They are frequently found to be the result of a combination of both theory and practice. As further knowledge is gained concerning the purposes and uses of accounting statements, new concepts and principles may become accepted. This is the evolving process that characterizes the art of accounting.

The following accounting concepts and principles are discussed in the remaining pages of this chapter:

1. Conservatism
2. Continuity of life — the going concern
3. Entity
4. Historical cost
5. Income determination
6. Materiality
7. Quantifiability
8. Stable monetary measure

Conservatism. Alternative approaches may frequently be indicated in resolving certain problems relative to the measurement of financial position and progress.   When alternatives exist, accountants have generally felt that they can serve business best by adopting a "conservative approach" — choosing the alternative with the least favorable effect upon owners' equity.

The doctrine of conservatism is illustrated in the application of practices such as the following: increases in the values of assets and anticipated gains are normally ignored until realized by means of sale; declines in asset values and anticipated losses, however, are normally recognized before a sale occurs. Inventories, for example, are normally valued at cost or market, whichever is lower. A market value in excess of cost is ignored or shown only parenthetically, recognition of the gain awaiting realization through sale; a decrease in market value, however, although not yet incurred through sale, is recognized. Again, certain expenditures are charged in full against current revenue despite the possibility of future benefits. For example, a large-scale advertising campaign may contribute to future revenues; however, in view of the indeterminate character of the contribution, conservatism would suggest no deferral but rather the recognition of the entire amount as expense.

A conservative approach in the measurement process is desirable. However, the deliberate and arbitrary understatement of asset values or overstatement of liabilities simply to achieve conservatism on the balance sheet is hardly the appropriate application of this concept. There are instances when, as a means of arriving at conservative appraisals of business worth or business debt-paying ability, inventories have been deliberately understated, property and intangible assets have been reported at nominal amounts, and reserves for possible losses and future contingencies have been established and reported among the liabilities. Conservatism expressed in this manner results in financial statements that no longer serve to report a revenue-expense matching process. The understatement of inventories to achieve a conservative working capital position carries with it an understatement of current income; the current understatement of inventories results further in the understatement of cost of goods sold and the overstatement of net income in the next period. The arbitrary reduction of property items to report a conservative asset position results in the understatement of depreciation charges and in the overstatement of net incomes in subsequent periods; balance sheet conservatism here has been accompanied by a contrary effect on subsequent income statements. The recognition of fictitious liabilities to achieve a conservative owners' equity results in the misrepresentation of financial position until such balances are canceled; if payment of expenses in the future is applied against such liability balances, net incomes of these periods will be overstated. Departures from sound measurement procedures to accomplish balance sheet conservatism serve to distort net income and net asset and owners' equity measurements.

The concept of balance sheet conservatism carries over from an earlier day when the accounting process was considered to be concerned largely with the preparation of a statement of financial condition for creditors and owners. The income statement occupied a supporting role by linking successive balance sheets, income measurement being determined by the values assigned to assets. But with a growing recognition of the importance of income both as a progress and a value indicator, the income statement has now become the center of attention. With emphasis upon accuracy in earnings measurement, there has come a regard for the balance sheet as "the connecting link between successive income statements and as the vehicle for the distribution of charges and credits between them."[1] Conservatism is now accepted as a moderating and refining influence to be applied to the matching process as a whole.

Continuity of life — the going concern. When the future is unpredictable, one can only assume a continuity of existence and a business environment to follow that is similar to that in which the enterprise finds itself currently. The business unit thus is viewed as a *going concern* in the absence of evidence to the contrary. The continuity assumption is support for the preparation of a balance sheet that reports costs that are assignable to future activities rather than realizable values that would attach to properties in the event of voluntary liquidation or forced sale. The continuity assumption calls for the preparation of an income statement that reports only such portions of costs as are allocable to current activities. Obviously, the assumption of a going concern may be invalidated by future experience. Financial statements, then, should be regarded as of a provisional nature, with support for their conclusions still to be found in the events of the future. If business termination were anticipated, a *quitting concern* assumption would be called for; the implications of such change of status would then require recognition.

In applying the assumption of continuity, the intent of management must frequently be recognized in problems of valuation and presentation. For example, if it is the policy of management to trade in automotive equipment at three-year intervals even though such equipment may have a materially longer life, the intent of management governs the allocation of cost. Or if management has taken steps to replace a currently maturing bond issue with a new issue, the maturing issue continues to be reported as noncurrent since it will make no claim upon current assets.

---

[1]*Accounting Research Bulletin No. 1*, "General Introduction and Rules Formerly Adopted" (New York: American Institute of Certified Public Accountants, September, 1939), p. 2.

Entity. The accountant normally views the business enterprise as a specific entity separate and distinct from its owners and any other business unit. It is the entity and its activities that assume the focus of his attention. The unit owns resources contributed by creditors and by its owners, whether sole proprietor, partners, or stockholders. The boundaries of the accounting entity may not be the same as the legal boundaries. The entity concept is most directly in conflict with the proprietorship concept under which the individual owner receives the focus of attention, and the owner's personal assets are not legally separated from the assets he has invested in his business ventures.

Historical cost. Accounting as it is practiced today is founded upon the *cost valuation principle*. The amount of money actually exchanged in a transaction is the amount used as a basis for the recognition of goods or services acquired. Cost represents a value that is regarded as definite and immediately determinable, and thus also satisfies the objectives of verifiability and neutrality. Its use is supported as a means of closing the doors to possible error, bias, or even intentional misstatement, and achieving an accounting that can be accepted with confidence.

The exclusive use of cost as opposed to alternative current value measurements has been questioned with increasing frequency in recent years. Several committees of the American Accounting Association have suggested that supplementary statements be provided to reflect current values for items such as inventory and long-lived assets. In its 1966 statement, the AAA recommended that multi-valued reports be adopted that would provide both historical cost data that had been verified by market transactions and current values that went beyond completed transactions to reflect the effects of the environment and possessed a high degree of relevance.[1] Advocacy of the current value approach has not been limited to committees of the American Accounting Association. A number of practitioners in recent years have maintained that adequate disclosure is not being made when there is no use of current values.[2]

There can be little doubt that regardless of what additional data may be disclosed on the financial statements, cost data will continue to maintain the central prominence in financial statements for many years to come.

Income determination. As has been previously emphasized, one of the chief functions of financial statements is to provide information that

---

[1] *A Statement of Basic Accounting Theory, op. cit.*, pp. 30 and 31.

[2] For example, a practitioner, Howard Ross, a partner in Touche, Ross, & Co., published a book in 1969 entitled *Financial Statements — A Crusade for Current Values*. In this book, Mr. Ross is in agreement with the multi-valued statement approach advocated by the 1966 AAA Statement.

will aid users in evaluating the effectiveness of an entity in meeting its objectives. The income statement has been increasingly used to provide information that will aid in this evaluation. The income statement is divided into two main categories: net inflows of resources from the profit-directed activities of an enterprise that are referred to as *revenue*; and net outflows of resources from the profit-directed activities of an enterprise that are referred to as *expense*. *Net income* is the difference between these two categories.

The revenue for a period is generally determined independently from expense by application of the concept of *revenue realization*. Essentially, the realization of revenue is a timing problem. Revenue could be recognized at a number of points during the production and sales cycle of a product. The realization principle, however, provides that before revenue is realized (1) the earning process must be complete or virtually complete, and (2) an arms-length market exchange must have taken place.[1] Based upon these criteria, revenue is generally recognized at *the point of sale*, that is, at the point when an arms-length transaction between two willing and competent parties has been completed. Other points in the cycle are sometimes used because of the special nature of the transactions.

Expenses for a period are determined by their recognition either directly against revenue or indirectly against revenue by association with the time period involved. This process has frequently been referred to as *the matching process*. Many allocations of cost are arbitrary because of the artificiality of attaching a cost to each unit of revenue and because of the uncertainty that remaining unallocated costs will contribute to the realization of future revenue.

It should be emphasized that since the point in time for the recognition of revenue and expense is identical with the point in time that changes in assets and liabilities are recognized, income determination is directly interrelated with asset valuation. Because of the importance that is attached to net income, a more detailed discussion of income determination is included in Chapter 3.

Materiality. Financial reporting is concerned only with information that affects the decisions to be made by users of the financial statements. Contrary to the belief of many readers of financial statements, the amounts reported in the statements are often not exact. For many decisions such exactness is not required. There is, of course, a point at which information that is incomplete or inexact does affect a decision. This point defines the boundary between information that is material and

---

[1]*Statements of the Accounting Principles Board, No. 4, op. cit.,* par. 150.

information that is immaterial.   At the present time, there are few guidelines to assist the accountant in applying the concept of materiality. The accountant must exercise his judgment as to whether a failure to disclose amounts that are inexact or certain data that are incomplete will affect the decisions of the users of financial statements.

The American Accounting Association Committee on Concepts and Standards Underlying Corporate Financial Statements comments on materiality and offers a criterion for judging materiality in the following statement:

> In the selection of classifications, in planning the extent of summarization, in giving emphasis to or omitting information, and in determining periodic net income, materiality is often a deciding factor. Materiality, as used in accounting, may be described as a state of relative importance.   The materiality of an item may depend on its size, its nature, or a combination of both.   An item should be regarded as material if there is reason to believe that knowledge of it would influence the decisions of an informed investor.[1]

Additional research is presently being conducted by the AICPA to assist in defining and applying the materiality concept to situations encountered by accountants in their practice.

Quantifiability.   There are many kinds of information that are of interest to a person who wishes to be fully informed about a business. Such information includes not only matters that can be readily measured, such as the number of machines in operation, the wages paid to employees, and the amount of raw materials used, but also more subjective facts, such as the attitudes of the employees about their employer and their work, the motivation of management to achieve previously stated objectives, and the effectiveness of the research department. What types of information, or parts thereof, should be measured and presented by the accountant if he is to fulfill his responsibility?

Generally, accounting attempts to reduce information to a common denominator so that facts may be conveniently summarized. The monetary measure has traditionally been accepted as that common unit and is generally used in most financial reporting.   The statement by the American Accounting Association in 1966 urged that the money concept be broadened to include nonmonetary information that could be quantified.   Measurements in terms of pounds, yards, and months could also be included as accounting information if they meet the other prescribed standards.   However, if the information is to be included in the body of the financial statements, the data must be converted to monetary terms to permit aggregation.   Parenthetical remarks and footnotes, however,

---

[1] *Accounting and Reporting Standards for Corporate Financial Statements and Preceding Statements and Supplements* (1957 rev.; Madison, Wisconsin: American Accounting Association), p. 8.

may contain data measured in nonmonetary units and, indeed, must be provided if the principle of full disclosure is to be realized.

Stable monetary measure. The dollar is the common money denominator of financial accounting in the United States. Value changes in the dollar are assumed to be unimportant. Accounting systems are designed to account for the use of given units of money, that is, their inflow and their outflow. Thus, the accounting systems tend to produce statements that summarize stewardship functions of management. Changes in the value of the monetary unit fail to assume importance when a historical cost principle is adopted that regards only the accounting for original dollars as important. However, many accountants have felt uncomfortable about the relevance of accounting information that is insensitive to changes in the value of the measuring unit. Although all accounts shown on the balance sheet are labeled "dollars," they are not dollars of equal purchasing power. Accountants add these various dollars together as though the monetary units were stable. But when the value of the dollar fluctuates greatly over time, the stable monetary unit assumption obviously loses its validity.

Some countries, recognizing the need for reporting in a stable unit, have adopted some form of *price-level accounting*. Although price-level accounting has been proposed from time to time by accountants in the United States, a strong movement to require price-level adjusted data has not materialized. In 1969 the Accounting Principles Board issued Statement No. 3 in which it concluded that statements adjusted for changes in the purchasing power of the dollar should be provided as supplements to the conventional financial statements. The nature of the problems that are involved in such restatements are presented in Chapter 28.

QUESTIONS

1. What types of economic decisions would be made by each of the following users of financial accounting statements? For each decision, indicate specifically the type of information that would be required.

    (a) A nonmanagerial stockholder who owns 75% of the outstanding common shares.

    (b) A financial analyst for a large mutual investment fund.

    (c) A prospective investor in the stock of a leading automobile manufacturer.

    (d) An insurance company that has loaned the reporting firm $25 million for ten years at 7%.

2. Name three governmental agencies that require periodic financial reports from business firms, and indicate the uses that these agencies make of the reports.

3. What kinds of financial accounting reports would be most useful in assisting a user to "estimate the future earnings potential of an entity"?

4. For whom should the general purpose external financial statements be prepared? What kinds of decisions are made on the basis of financial statements?

5. A large manufacturing corporation with thousands of stockholders throughout the country is studying its financial statements with the idea of eliminating unnecessary duplication in them. It has been suggested that such duplication might be eliminated by preparing a single set of statements to be used by department heads, top management, and the stockholders. Evaluate the desirability and practicality of this practice.

6. The owner of a business, planning to sell it, has requested his CPA to prepare statements for the information of prospective buyers. "Don't use your regular statements," he instructs the CPA, "because I want to get as much as I can. Make the business look as good as possible." Would it be proper for the CPA to prepare statements that are different from those he ordinarily prepares for the client at the end of the year? If so, what form would they take?

7. Why is an attest function necessary in our economic environment?

8. Mr. Lowe, president of Lowe Enterprises, Inc., has read much in the business literature about the controversies over accounting principles. He does not understand why the development of principles is important. Explain why it is important for the accounting profession to have a set of principles.

9. "Prescribed principles are hindrances to creative and flexible financial reporting. More misleading information is likely to be communicated as the rules of accounting become more rigid." Comment upon these thoughts.

10. Summarize the essential differences between the methods used by each of the following organizations in formulating accounting principles: (a) the American Accounting Association, (b) the American Institute of Certified Public Accountants, (c) the Securities and Exchange Commission.

11. Why is relevance considered the most basic of the qualitative objectives?

12. How can the quality of verifiability be measured?

13. What is the difference between consistency and comparability?

14. Some accountants have suggested that budgets and profit plans should be reported to external users. Evaluate this type of forecast statement in terms of each of the seven qualitative objectives.

15. Which of the qualitative objectives is most likely violated by each of the following situations? (Briefly support your answers.)

  (a) A prospective purchaser of a company receives only the conventional financial statements.

(b) An investor examines the published annual reports of all companies in the steel industry for the purpose of investing in the most profitable one.
(c) A company uses the prefix "reserve" for a contra asset, a liability, and a retained earning appropriation.
(d) A company reports all of its land, buildings, and equipment on the basis of a recent appraisal.
(e) Management elects to change its method of inventory valuation in order to overcome an unprofitable year from operations. Such a change enables the company to report a gradual growth in earnings.

16. Why is the concept of conservatism considered to have both favorable and unfavorable connotations?

17. If the entity concept were not applied, how would financial reporting differ for a sole proprietorship?

18. The historical cost concept has been seriously challenged. What deficiencies does it have, and what alternative measurement methods have been proposed to overcome these weaknesses?

19. What conditions must exist before revenue is recognized as having been earned?

20. Why is the materiality concept a difficult one to apply?

21. It has been suggested that current market values be used to report temporary investments on the balance sheet. What currently accepted principles are violated with this approach?

22. Identify the accounting principle or principles that are applied in each of the following situations:
(a) A company uses the lower of cost or market for valuation of its physical inventory.
(b) An inventory delivery on the last day of the year was omitted from the physical inventory. No adjustment was made on the books for the omission.
(c) During the year, inflation of 5% took place. No adjustment for this change is made on the books.
(d) Product development costs are deferred as assets to be written off against future income.
(e) Albert Haws owns a laundry, a restaurant, and a bookstore. He has separate financial statements prepared for each of the businesses.
(f) The Metropolitan Construction Company prepares an annual statement reflecting the profitability of its construction contracts in process.

EXERCISES

1. The Weber Corporation, whose stock is wholly owned by W. E. Weber, reports on its balance sheet on December 31, 1972, the following:

Fixed assets. $200,000
Less accumulated depreciation 16,000 $184,000

Analysis of this account indicates that land and buildings were acquired at the beginning of 1971 for $30,000 and $120,000 respectively; buildings had an estimated life of 20 years. In November of 1972, a real estate tax bill indicated a tax for 1973 based on land valued at $40,000 and buildings valued at $160,000 respectively. Weber authorized that land, buildings, and the accumulated depreciation be adjusted in accordance with such values. (a) Indicate what changes, if any, you would make in reporting the assets on the balance sheet. (b) Give the theoretical support for your conclusions.

2. J. W. Wilson is impressed with his accountant's defense of conservatism in accounting and therefore suggests that the accountant currently make the adjustments indicated below. State your position on each item and give theoretical support for your position.

(a) Inventories are reported at a cost of $56,000. Wilson would report these at the lower of cost or market, $52,500.

(b) Goods that have been unsaleable for a five-year period have been excluded from the inventory and have been set aside in the warehouse with the hope that someone might offer to buy them. The goods are carried at $7,500 and Wilson would write these off.

(c) An account receivable for $750 is carried with a customer that Wilson has not seen for more than a year. Wilson would write this balance off.

(d) Leasehold improvements of $15,000 were made by Wilson. However, such improvements will ultimately revert to the owner of the property on termination of the lease, and Wilson would write off the full cost currently.

(e) Cash surrender value on life insurance with a balance of $3,850 is reported among the assets. Since Wilson does not expect to make any claim on the policy until the maturity, he believes that this balance should be written off.

(f) Goodwill of $12,500 had been recorded on the books currently when Wilson acquired a branch unit and paid this amount in excess of tangible assets acquired because of exceptionally high earnings of the branch unit. Mr. Wilson believes that this asset is one that cannot be sold and therefore should be written off.

(g) Wilson is being sued for breach of contract in the amount of $7,500. No liability has yet been established on the books for this item. Although the court has not yet rendered a final decision, Wilson believes that the statements should reflect this potential liability. Wilson's attorney is uncertain as to the outcome of the suit.

(h) All goods are sold with a warranty for repairs and replacements for a six-month period. In the past expenses for repairs and replacements were recorded at the time they were incurred. Wilson estimates that expenses for repairs and replacements still to be incurred on goods sold during the last half of the year will total $5,000, and he believes that a liability for this amount should be reported.

3. The following items were reported in the machinery account on the books of the Bellows Company in 1973. What position would you take on each item? Give theoretical support for your conclusions.

Date	Description	Debit	Credit
January 3	Costs of dismantling and removing old machine...	$ 1,200	

Date	Description	Debit	Credit
January 5	Proceeds from disposal of old machine......		$4,000
January 10	Invoice price of new machine..............	$40,000	
January 16	Freight charges paid on delivery of new machine.................................	1,500	
February 12	Costs of installing new machine............	8,500	
February 12	Costs of labor, spoilage, etc. in test runs prior to actual use of machine..................	1,500	

PROBLEMS

1-1. For each of the items enumerated below, give the letter item that indicates the accounting concept or principle that is applied.

A. Conservatism
B. Continuity of life — the going concern
C. Entity
D. Historical cost

E. Income determination
F. Materiality
G. Quantifiability
H. Stable monetary unit

(1) Adjustments are made to the allowance for doubtful accounts at the end of each year at 2% of credit sales for the year. *E*

(2) A delivery truck acquired at the beginning of the year is reported at 80% of cost; its trade-in value at this time would be only 50% of cost. *B D*

(3) Inventories are reported at the lower of cost or market. *A*

(4) Periodic payments of $2,500 per month for services of P. J. Jones who owns all of the stock of the company are reported as salary; additional amounts paid to Jones are reported as dividends. *C*

(5) An advance collection for services is reported as a current liability. *E*

(6) A liability is established at the end of each year for the estimated cost of repairs and replacements for units sold currently that may prove to be defective. *E*

(7) All payments out of petty cash are charged to Miscellaneous Expense. *F*

(8) The Jones Co. held 100 shares of stock in another company that had been acquired and was reported at $40 per share. During the year the stock was split 2 for 1 but no entry was made on the books other than reporting the additional number of shares received. After the split, the stock had a market value of $35 per share. *A - A*

(9) An adjoining piece of land had been acquired four years ago for $40,000 and is being reported as an investment at this amount. Price indexes have shown a 20% increase for the four-year period; a real estate broker has indicated that he could find a buyer who would pay $75,000 for the property. *D*

1-2. J. C. Paxton opened a retail store at the beginning of 1971. From informal records that he maintained, he prepared a comparative income statement for 1972 and 1971 as reproduced at the top of the next page.

	Year Ended	
	Dec. 31, 1972	Dec. 31, 1971
Sales..........................	$ 81,200	$ 65,000
Cost of goods sold............	46,500	52,500
Gross profit...................	$ 34,700	$ 12,500
Selling and general expenses...	26,500	24,000
Net income (loss).............	$ 8,200	$ (11,500)

You are called in to review Paxton's records, and in the course of the review you find the following:

(a) Paxton has included in sales only amounts collected from customers. He had receivables from customers on December 31, 1971, of $1,650 and on December 31, 1972, of $2,600.

(b) Paxton has reported all purchases of goods for resale each year as cost of goods sold. He did not take an inventory at the end of each year since he states amounts would be approximately the same. You determine that the inventories had a cost of approximately $18,000 at the end of 1971 and at the end of 1972.

(c) Advertising charges were assigned to the year in which the specific charges were incurred. Advertising charges totaled $6,000 of which $4,500 was incurred in the first year in view of the heavy promotion to inform the public of the store opening.

(d) Acquisitions of furniture and fixtures were recognized as charges to general expense each year, since Paxton believed that acquisitions would be more or less continuous during the life of the business. Furniture and fixtures acquisitions were $4,500 in 1971 and $3,600 in 1972. Furniture and fixtures had an estimated life of 10 years.

(e) Paxton withdrew $400 per month in 1971 and $500 per month in 1972 and charged general expenses for such drawings. Paxton insisted that the time and effort that he spent in the business were worth double the amounts withdrawn and that such charges were very conservative.

(f) Paxton contributed certain supplies to the business that he had salvaged from a previous operation. He indicated that these had an original acquisition cost of approximately $800, had a replacement cost as of the beginning of 1971 of $1,200, but that since the expenditure had been made prior to 1971, he had recognized no charge on the transfer to the new business. The supplies had been fully consumed in approximately equal amounts in 1971 and 1972.

Instructions: Prepare a corrected comparative income statement. In supporting schedules for each balance, indicate any changes that were made and the accounting concept or principle that you would use to support such changes.

1-3. The J. L. Cory Company does not maintain a formal set of accounting records. However, a description of all transactions is kept in chronological order. For the month of June the following summary of transactions was provided by management to their public accountant:

(a) Total sales on account, $64,500.

(b) Cash receipts totaled $82,500, including $58,000 from customers, $4,000 from rent received in advance (July–October) on a warehouse owned by the company, and the balance from a loan from the Mid-Central Bank on a six-months note.

(c) Purchases of merchandise on account, $65,000.

(d) A physical inventory of merchandise at June 30 disclosed a value of $23,000, an increase of $6,000 from the beginning of the month.

(e) Cash disbursements for the month were listed as follows:

(1) Payments for purchases of merchandise on account, $45,000.

(2) Payment of a one-year fire insurance policy dated June 1, $1,200.

(3) Payments for supplies, $6,200 (60% of these supplies are still on hand on June 30).

(4) Payments for salaries, $1,850. An additional $300 is owed at June 30.

Instructions: (1) Prepare an income statement from the above list of transactions. What accounting concepts and principles are illustrated by the preparation of this statement?

(2) What additional information would be necessary to more completely apply the income determination principle?

1-4. L. A. Workman has drawn up a financial statement for his business on December 31, 1972, employing valuation procedures as follows:

Cash $15,000 (includes cash in the bank, $13,600, and customers' checks that could not be cashed but that Workman feels will ultimately be recoverable, $1,400.)

Marketable securities $45,000 (represents the value on December 31 of securities reported at the beginning of 1972 at a cost of $34,500.)

Value of insurance policy $15,000 (the sum of the payments made on a life insurance policy that requires further payments through 1982. The cash surrender value of the policy at the end of 1972 is $4,600.)

Furniture and fixtures $45,000
Less accumulated
  depreciation   45,000
Book value $ —0— (represents furniture and fixtures acquired in 1965 that have been fully depreciated although they are still in use.)

Intangible assets $40,000 (recorded in 1972 when a competitor offered to pay Workman this amount for the lease entered into when the company was formed and which still has 5 years to run at a rental that is 5% of net sales.)

Sundry payables $1 (recorded as a result of a suit of $50,000 against Workman for breach of contract; the attorney for Workman has offered to pay $15,000 in settlement of the suit but this has been rejected; it is the opinion of the attorney that the suit can be settled by payment of $25,000.)

Instructions: Indicate what change, if any, you would make in reporting each of the items listed above. In each case indicate any theoretical failure that is indicated in the present reporting and the theoretical support for the suggested change.

financial statements -
the balance sheet

The principles applied in the preparation of financial statements have been presented in the preceding chapter. It is important to recognize that the financial statements are the objective of such principles. An accounting system is established to provide the various reports and analyses for internal and external users. Traditionally, however, only one set of statements has been made available to external sources. This set normally consists of (1) a *balance sheet* that reports the financial position of the business at a certain date, (2) an *income statement* that describes the change in the owners' equity arising from operations since the position of the enterprise was last stated, and (3) a *statement of changes in financial position* that describes the change in the financial resources that has taken place since the position of the enterprise was last stated. When the change in owners' equity is not fully explained by the income statement, a supplemental statement referred to as the *statement of changes in owners' equity*, or for the corporation, the *retained earnings statement*, is usually provided to offer a full reconciliation of the difference. These statements have become accepted as general purpose statements. They are intended to be relevant to a broad variety of external users. Although there has been some discussion about the need to prepare special purpose statements that would be directed to specific external users, there has not been any significant movement in this direction in practice.

The balance sheet is discussed in this chapter. The income statement will be discussed in the following chapter. The statement of changes in financial position, as well as a number of supplementary analytical statements, is described in later chapters.

Content of the balance sheet

The *balance sheet*, also variously called the *statement of financial position* and the *statement of condition*, reports the assets, liabilities, and owners' equity of the business unit at a given date. The financial position is the cumulative result of all transactions of the business from its beginning. Since the balance sheet is basically historical, reporting the position growing out of a series of recorded transactions, only a thorough understanding of the principles and practices that are followed in the recording process offers an appreciation of the nature of the statement. Some of the basic concepts of balance sheet content, form, and presentation are considered in this chapter. Discussions of the individual asset, liability, and owners' equity items in later chapters will serve to develop more fully the nature of the balance sheet.

The balance sheet is an expansion of the basic accounting equation, Assets = Liabilities + Owners' Equity. The character and the amount of the assets are exhibited. The liabilities and owners' equity normally bear no relationship to specific assets and hence are presented as balances related to the assets as a whole.

For accounting purposes, assets include those costs that have not been applied to revenues in the past and are considered to afford economic utility in the production of revenues in the future. Assets, then, include both monetary assets such as cash, marketable securities, and receivables, and those costs that are recognized as recoverable and hence properly assignable to revenues of future periods, such as inventories, prepaid insurance, equipment, and patents.[1]

Liabilities measure the economic obligations of the enterprise to the creditor group. The method for settlement of liabilities varies. Liabilities may call for settlement by cash payment or settlement through goods to be delivered or services to be performed.[2]

Owners' equity measures the interest of the ownership group in the total resources of the enterprise. Such interest arises from investments by

---

[1] The authors of Accounting Research Study No. 3 define assets as " . . . expected future economic benefits, rights to which have been acquired by the enterprise as a result of some current or past transaction." Robert T. Sprouse and Maurice Moonitz, *A Tentative Set of Broad Accounting Principles for Business Enterprises*, Accounting Research Study No. 3 (New York: American Institute of Certified Public Accountants, 1962), p. 8. The Accounting Principles Board simply defines assets as " . . . economic resources of an enterprise that are recognized and measured in conformity with generally accepted accounting principles." *Statements of the Accounting Principles Board, No. 4*, "Basic Concepts and Accounting Principles Underlying Financial Statements of Business Enterprises" (New York: American Institute of Certified Public Accountants, 1970), par. 132.

[2] Liabilities are defined by Sprouse and Moonitz in ARS No. 3 as " . . . obligations to convey assets or perform services, such obligations resulting from past or current transactions and requiring settlement in the future." *loc. cit.* The Accounting Principles Board defines liabilities as ". . . economic obligations of an enterprise that are recognized and measured in conformity with generally accepted accounting principles." *Statements of the Accounting Principles Board, No. 4, loc. cit.*

owners, and the equity changes with the change in net assets resulting from operations. An ownership equity does not call for settlement on a certain date; in the event of business dissolution, it represents a claim on assets only after creditors have been paid in full. The method of reporting the owners' equity varies with the form of the business unit. Business units are typically divided into three categories: (1) *sole proprietorships*, (2) *partnerships*, and (3) *corporations*.

Balance sheet items are generally classified in a manner that will facilitate the analysis and the interpretation of financial data. Information of primary concern to all parties is the business unit's solvency — its ability to meet current obligations. Accordingly, assets and liabilities are classified as (1) *current* or *short-term* items and (2) *noncurrent, long-term*, or *fixed* items. When assets and liabilities are classified, the difference between current assets and current liabilities may be determined. This is referred to as the company's *working capital* — the liquid buffer available in meeting financial demands and contingencies of the future.[1]

Current assets and current liabilities

There have been important changes in the criteria for designating items as current or noncurrent in recent years. Originally, the "current" designation was applied to cash and those assets that would be realized in cash within one year and to liabilities that would be due within one year. This definition would call for the exclusion of inventories and receivables not expected to be converted into cash within one year and the exclusion of prepaid expenses that do not produce cash. Liabilities maturing after one year from balance sheet date would likewise be excluded from the current category. However, both the American Institute of Certified Public Accountants and the American Accounting Association have recommended a broadening of the definition of current items to emphasize a company's ability to meet its claims in the course of current operations rather than in the event of liquidation. Accordingly, current items are held to embrace those items relating to the particular company's "normal operating cycle." These groups conceive ordinary operations to involve the circulation of resources within the current group. Cash is converted into inventories, inventories into receivables, and receivables ultimately into cash again. Assets falling within this cycle are considered current. Prepaid expenses are included in the current grouping since they represent substitutes for expenditures that otherwise would

---

[1]"Working Capital" is used in this text to denote the excess of current assets over current liabilities. Sometimes this excess is referred to as "net working capital," the term "working capital" then being used to denote total current assets.

require the use of current resources within the operating cycle. Current liabilities are conceived as those items making a claim against assets classified as current, and consist of: (1) payables for goods and services purchased, and (2) collections in advance of the delivery of goods or the performance of services sold.

The position of the AICPA Committee on Accounting Procedure on current assets follows:

> ... For accounting purposes, the term *current assets* is used to designate cash and other assets or resources commonly identified as those which are reasonably expected to be realized in cash or sold or consumed during the normal operating cycle of the business. Thus the term comprehends in general such resources as (a) cash available for current operations and items which are the equivalent of cash; (b) inventories of merchandise, raw materials, goods in process, finished goods, operating supplies, and ordinary maintenance material and parts; (c) trade accounts, notes, and acceptances receivable; (d) receivables from officers, employees, affiliates, and others, if collectible in the ordinary course of business within a year; (e) installment or deferred accounts and notes receivable if they conform generally to normal trade practices and terms within the business; (f) marketable securities representing the investment of cash available for current operations; and (g) prepaid expenses such as insurance, interest, rents, taxes, unused royalties, current paid advertising service not yet received, and operating supplies. Prepaid expenses are not current assets in the sense that they will be converted into cash but in the sense that, if not paid in advance, they would require the use of current assets during the operating cycle.[1]

The Committee further suggests that the one-year period be used as a basis for current asset classification in those instances where the average operating cycle is less than twelve months, but where the operating cycle exceeds twelve months, as in the case of the tobacco, distillery, and lumber industries, that the longer period be used.

In accordance with the foregoing concept of current assets, the Committee lists the following items as noncurrent:

(a) Cash and cash claims restricted to use for other than current operations, designated for the acquisition of noncurrent assets, or segregated for the liquidation of noncurrent debts.

(b) Advances or investments in securities, whether marketable or not, made for the purposes of control, affiliation, or other continuing business advantage.

(c) Receivables not expected to be collected within twelve months arising from unusual transactions such as the sale of capital assets or advances to affiliates, officers, or employees.

---

[1]*Accounting Research Bulletin No. 43*, "Restatement and Revision of Accounting Research Bulletins" (New York: American Institute of Certified Public Accountants, 1953), Ch. 3, par. 4. The American Accounting Association Committee on Concepts and Standards Underlying Corporate Financial Statements supports the Institute's conclusions on working capital in its Supplementary Statement No. 3, "Current Assets and Current Liabilities," 1951.

(d) Cash surrender value of life insurance policies.

(e) Land and other natural resources.

(f) Depreciable assets.

(g) Long-term prepayments fairly chargeable to the operations of several years.

Current liabilities are described as follows:

> The term *current liabilities* is used principally to designate obligations whose liquidation is reasonably expected to require the use of existing resources properly classifiable as current assets, or the creation of other current liabilities. As a balance sheet category, the classification is intended to include obligations for items which have entered into the operating cycle, such as payables incurred in the acquisition of materials and supplies to be used in the production of goods or in providing services to be offered for sale; collections received in advance of the delivery of goods or performance of services; and debts which arise from operations directly related to the operating cycle, such as accruals for wages, salaries, commissions, rentals, royalties, and income and other taxes. Other liabilities whose regular and ordinary liquidation is expected to occur within a relatively short period of time, usually twelve months, are also intended for inclusion, such as short-term debts arising from the acquisition of capital assets, serial maturities of long-term obligations, amounts required to be expended within one year under sinking fund provisions, and agency obligations arising from the collection or acceptance of cash or other assets for the account of third persons.[1]

The current liability classification, however, does not include the following items, since these do not require the use of resources classified as current:

(a) Obligations due at an early date that are to be discharged by means of the issuance of new obligations in their places. There should, however, be parenthetical disclosure of the reason for continuing to report such items as noncurrent.

(b) Debts that are to be liquidated from funds that have been accumulated and are reported as noncurrent assets.

(c) Loans on life insurance policies made with the intent that these will not be paid but will be liquidated by deduction from the proceeds of the policies upon their maturity or cancellation.

(d) Obligations for advance collections that involve long-term deferment of the delivery of goods or services.

Current assets are normally listed on the balance sheet in the order of their liquidity. These assets, with the exception of marketable securities and inventories, are usually reported at their estimated realizable values. Thus, current receivable balances are reduced by allowances for estimated doubtful accounts. Marketable securities are generally reported at cost. Inventories may be reported at cost or on the basis of "cost or market, whichever is lower."

---

[1] *Ibid.,* Ch. 3, par. 7.

Few problems are generally found in the valuation of current liabilities. Payables can usually be determined or accrued accurately.
Some items may require estimates as to the amounts that will ultimately
be paid. The claims, however determined, if payable currently, must
be included under the current heading.

The importance of a satisfactory working capital position cannot be
minimized. A business may not be able to survive in the absence of a
satisfactory relationship between current assets and current liabilities.
Furthermore, its ability to prosper is largely determined by the composition of the current asset pool. There must be a satisfactory balance
between liquid assets in the form of cash and temporary investments, and
receivables and inventories. Activities of the business center around
these assets. Cash and temporary investments, representing immediate
purchasing power, are used to meet current claims and purchasing,
payroll, and expense requirements; receivables are the outgrowth of
sales effort and provide cash in the course of operations; merchandise is
also a source of cash as well as the means of achieving a profit. Management in setting policies with respect to selling, purchasing, financing,
expansion, and dividends must work within the limitations set by the
company's working capital position.

Noncurrent assets and noncurrent liabilities

Assets and liabilities that do not qualify for presentation under the
current headings are classified under a number of noncurrent headings.
Noncurrent assets are generally listed under separate headings such as
Investments, Land, buildings, and equipment, Intangible assets, and Other assets.
Noncurrent liabilities are listed under separate headings such as *Long-
term debt, Deferred revenues,* and *Other liabilities.*

Investments. Investments held for such long-term purposes as regular
income, appreciation, or ownership control are reported under the heading "Investments". Examples of items properly reported under this
heading are long-term stock, bond, and mortgage holdings; securities of
affiliated companies as well as advances to such companies; sinking fund
assets consisting of cash and securities held for the redemption of bonds
or stock, the replacement of buildings, or the payment of pensions; land
held for future use or sale; the cash surrender value of life insurance; and
other miscellaneous investments not used directly in the operations of
the business. Long-term investments are normally reported at cost.

Land, buildings, and equipment. Properties of a tangible and relatively permanent character that are used in the normal business operations are reported under the heading "Land, buildings, and equipment."

Land, buildings, equipment, machinery, tools, furniture, fixtures, and vehicles are included under this heading. Buildings and equipment items are normally reported at cost less accumulated depreciation.

Intangible assets. The long-term rights and privileges of a non-physical character acquired for use in business operations are reported under the heading "Intangible assets." Included in this class are such items as goodwill, patents, trademarks, franchises, copyrights, formulas, leaseholds, and organization costs. Intangible assets are normally reported at cost less amounts previously amortized.

The term *fixed assets* is frequently applied to all of those long-term properties that are used in the production of goods and services. As thus used, fixed assets would consist of two groups — *fixed tangible assets* represented by land, buildings, and equipment and *fixed intangible assets* represented by the items named above.

Other long-term assets. Those noncurrent assets that cannot be reported satisfactorily under any of the previous classifications may be listed under the general heading "Other long-term assets" or may be listed separately under special descriptive headings. Such assets include cash funds representing deposits received from customers, deposits made with vendors to secure contracts, and long-term advances to officers.

Prepayments for services or benefits to be received over a number of periods are properly regarded as noncurrent. Among these are such items as plant rearrangement costs and developmental and improvement costs. These long-term prepayments are frequently reported under a *deferred costs* or *deferred charges* heading. However, objection can be raised to a deferred costs designation since this designation could be applied to all costs assignable to future periods including inventories, buildings and equipment, and intangible assets. The deferred costs heading may be avoided by reporting long-term prepayments within the other long-term assets section or under separate descriptive headings.

Deferred Income Taxes Expense may be shown under "Other long-term assets" or may be reported separately. Income taxes are considered to be prepaid when paid on a computed income that is more than the income reported on the financial statements. The tax difference must be a temporary one caused by a *timing* difference — a difference in the period in which revenue or expense is recognized on the tax return and on the books. Under these circumstances, matching of income taxes expense with revenue requires that the taxes paid on taxable income in excess of the book income be deferred and recognized as an addition to taxes paid in the period when the income is ultimately recognized on the books.

Contingent assets. Circumstances on the balance sheet date may indicate the existence of certain rights or claims that could materialize as valuable assets upon the favorable outcome of certain events. In the absence of a legal right to the properties at this time, these can be viewed only as *contingent assets*. Contingent assets may be reported by a special note or by appropriate comment under a separate contingent assets heading following the other asset classifications. Tax claims, insurance claims, and claims against merchandise creditors may warrant such treatment. Reference to contingent assets is rare in practice.

Long-term debt. Long-term notes, bonds, mortgages, and similar obligations that will not require the use of current funds for their retirement are generally reported on the balance sheet under the heading "Long-term debt." Sometimes the term *fixed liabilities* is used to refer to the long-term obligations.

When an amount borrowed is not the same as the amount ultimately required in settlement of the debt and the debt is stated in the accounts at its maturity amount, a debt discount or premium is reported. The discount or premium should be related to the debt item; a discount, then, should be subtracted from the amount reported for the debt, and a premium should be added to the amount reported for the debt. The debt is thus reported at its present value as measured by the proceeds from its issue. Amortization of the discount or premium brings the obligation to the maturity amount by the end of its normal term. When a note, a bond issue, or a mortgage formerly classified as a long-term obligation becomes payable within a year, it should be reclassified and presented as a current liability.

Deferred revenues. Cash may be received or other assets recognized for goods and services that are to be supplied in future periods. Such transactions are recognized in the accounts by charges to assets and credits to accounts reporting the advance payments. The latter balances are properly carried forward until the company meets its responsibilities through the delivery of goods or the performance of services. If, in subsequent periods, the expenses of providing the goods and services are less than the obligations that are discharged thereby, earnings will be recognized; on the other hand, if expenses are greater than the obligations that are discharged, losses will be incurred. Examples of transactions that call for revenue deferral and recognition as long-term obligations include fees received in advance on long-term service contracts, and long-term leasehold and rental prepayments. These prepayments are normally reported on the balance sheet under the heading of *Deferred revenues* or *Deferred credits*.

The deferred revenues heading is considered objectionable by some accountants on the grounds that it fails to suggest the liability character of the items that are listed thereunder. The use of a heading such as *Advances by customers and other parties* might well clarify the nature of the items that are listed.

All prepayments for goods and services are frequently reported under the deferred revenues heading, including those calling for settlement in the near future. However, the noncurrent classification is appropriate only when an item represents no significant claim upon current assets. When significant costs are involved in satisfying a claim and these costs will be met from the company's current assets, the prepayment should be recognized as a current liability. The obligation arising from the receipt of cash in advance on magazine subscriptions, for example, is properly recognized as a current liability in view of the claim that it makes upon current assets.

Other long-term liabilities. Those noncurrent liabilities that cannot be reported satisfactorily under the long-term debt or deferred revenues headings may be listed under the general heading "Other long-term liabilities" or may be listed separately under special descriptive headings. Such liabilities include obligations to customers in the form of long-term refundable deposits, long-term obligations to company officers or affiliated companies, matured but unclaimed bond principal and interest obligations, and amounts payable under pension plans.

Deferred Income Taxes Payable may be shown under "Other long-term liabilities" or may be reported separately. Income taxes are considered to have accrued when taxes are paid on a computed income that is less than the income reported on the financial statements. The difference, as in the case of the deferred income taxes expense previously mentioned, must be a temporary one caused by a timing difference. In this case, however, the timing difference has resulted in postponing income taxes until a later period. Timing differences may occur, for example, in recognizing depreciation on the tax return and on the books, and also in recognizing revenue on installment sales and on long-term construction contracts. A matching of income taxes expense with revenue requires that taxes that are postponed be accrued and recognized as a subtraction from taxes paid in the period when the income is ultimately recognized on the tax return.

Contingent liabilities. Past activities or circumstances may have given rise to possible future liabilities, although legal obligations do not exist on the date of the balance sheet. Such possible claims are known as *contingent liabilities* and are normally reported by a note or appropriate comment under a separate contingent liability heading. Possible obligations resulting from the discounting of customers' notes, accommodation endorsements on obligations of other parties, pending lawsuits, and taxes and other charges in dispute are examples of contingent liabilities.

Careful distinction should be made between the contingent liabilities just described and liabilities that exist but that cannot be definitely measured in amount on the balance sheet date. For example, an income tax liability may have accrued although the exact amount of the obligation is not yet determinable; or payments may have to be made ultimately to employees under retirement plans although the costs of such plans cannot be finally determined. These claims must be arrived at by estimate but they cannot be ignored in setting forth the financial condition. The estimated liability for income taxes is payable currently and hence is properly reported under the current heading; the estimated liability for pensions is not payable currently and hence is reported under a noncurrent heading.

Owners' equity

In the case of a sole proprietorship, the owner's equity in assets is reported by means of a single capital account. The balance in this account is the cumulative result of the owner's investments and withdrawals as well as past earnings and losses. In the partnership, capital accounts are established for each partner. Capital account balances summarize the investments and withdrawals and shares of past earnings and losses of each partner and thus measure the partners' individual equities in the partnership assets.

In the corporation, the difference between assets and liabilities is referred to as the *stockholders' equity*, the *shareholders' equity*, or simply, *capital*. In presenting the stockholders' equity on the balance sheet, a distinction is made between the equity originating from the stockholders' investment, referred to as *paid-in capital*, and the equity originating from earnings, referred to as *retained earnings*. In certain instances the stockholders' equity includes *appraisal capital* resulting from asset revaluation. Sometimes the term *surplus* is applied to all corporate capital balances other than capital stock. Thus, paid-in capital other than that portion representing capital stock is designated *paid-in surplus* or *capital surplus*, retained earnings is designated *earned surplus*, and appraisal capital is designated *appraisal surplus*.

Paid-in capital. Paid-in capital is generally reported in two parts: (1) *capital stock* representing that portion of the contribution by stockholders that is assignable to the shares of stock-issued; (2) *additional paid-in capital* representing investments by shareholders in excess of the amounts assignable to capital stock as well as invested capital from other sources.

Capital stock outstanding that has a par value is shown on the balance sheet at par. Capital stock that has no par value is stated at the amount received on its original sale or at some other value as set by law or as assigned by action of the board of directors of the corporation. When more than a single class of stock has been issued and is outstanding, the stock of each class is reported separately. *Treasury stock*, which is stock issued but subsequently reacquired by the corporation, is subtracted from the total stock issued or from the sum of paid-in capital and retained earnings balances. The capital stock balance is viewed as the *legal capital* or *permanent capital* of the corporation.

A premium received on the sale of par-value stock or the amount received in excess of the value assigned to no-par stock is recognized as additional paid-in capital. Additional paid-in capital may also arise from transactions other than the sale of stock, such as from the acquisition of property as a result of a donation or from the sale of treasury stock at more than cost. The additional paid-in capital balances are normally added to capital stock so that the full amount of the paid-in capital may be reported. When stock is sold at less than par, capital stock is shown at par and the discount is reported as a subtraction item in arriving at paid-in capital.

Retained earnings. The amount of undistributed earnings of past periods is reported as *retained earnings*. An excess of dividends and losses over earnings results in a negative retained earnings balance called a *deficit*. The balance of retained earnings is added to the paid-in capital total in summarizing the stockholders' equity; a deficit is subtracted from paid-in capital.

Portions of retained earnings are sometimes reported as restricted and unavailable as a basis for dividends. Restricted earnings are designated as *appropriations*. Appropriations are frequently made for such purposes as sinking funds, plant expansion, contingencies, and the reacquisition of capital stock. When appropriations have been made, retained earnings on the balance sheet consists of an amount designated as *Appropriated* and a balance designated as *Unappropriated* or *Free*.

Appraisal capital. An increase in asset balances to conform with values established by an independent appraisal of assets is accompanied by an increase in *appraisal capital*. Appraisal capital is added to paid-in capital and retained earnings balances in arriving at the total stockholders' equity.

Offsets on the balance sheet

A number of balance sheet items are frequently reported at gross amounts that call for the recognition of offset balances in arriving at proper valuations. Such offset balances are found in asset, liability, and owners' equity categories. In the case of assets, for example, an allowance for doubtful accounts is subtracted from the sum of the customers' accounts in reporting the net amount estimated collectible; accumulated depreciation is subtracted from the related buildings and equipment balances in reporting the costs of the assets still assignable to future revenues. In the case of liabilities, bonds reacquired, or *treasury bonds*, are subtracted from bonds issued in reporting the amount of bonds outstanding; a bond discount is subtracted from the face value of bonds outstanding in reporting the net amount of the debt. In the case of stockholders' equity in the corporation, a discount on capital stock is subtracted from the par value of capital stock in reporting paid-in capital; a deficit is subtracted from paid-in capital.

The offsets described above are required in the proper reporting of particular balance sheet items. Offsets are improper, however, if applied to asset and liability balances or to asset and owners' equity balances even when there is some relationship between the items. For example, a company may accumulate cash in a special fund to discharge certain tax liabilities; but as long as control of the cash is retained and the liabilities are still outstanding, the company should continue to report both the asset and the liabilities. Or a company may accumulate cash in a special fund for the redemption of preferred stock outstanding; but until the cash is applied to the reacquisition of the stock, the company must continue to report the asset as well as the owners' equity item. A company may have made advances to certain salesmen while at the same time reporting accrued amounts payable to others; a net figure cannot be justified here, just as a net figure cannot be justified for the offset of trade receivables against trade payables.

Balance sheet terminology

The accounting profession has engaged in a continuing effort to define the terms used in accounting. It has also directed attention to those terms that have been subject to misinterpretation because of an accounting use that differs from their popular use. Such efforts have been accompanied by a movement to modify terminology where modification might contribute to a better understanding of accounting.

Net worth and surplus. As early as 1941 the American Institute of Certified Public Accountants raised the question of more informative designations in reporting stockholders' equity. The use of *net worth* to designate stockholders' equity was challenged on the grounds that "a balance sheet does not purport to reflect and could not usefully reflect the value of the enterprise or of equity interests therein." The need for designations that would emphasize *investment* rather than *value* was recognized. The use of the term *surplus* was also found to be objectionable on the grounds that its popular use to indicate "excess," "residue," "that which remains when use or need has been satisfied," was hardly in agreement with its accounting use. As indicated earlier, "surplus" as employed in an accounting sense has been used to suggest investment by owners, as in *paid-in surplus*; accumulated earnings, as in *earned surplus*; and unrealized profits, as in *appraisal surplus*. To clarify reporting, the AICPA Committee on Terminology in 1949 and again in 1953 recommended the discontinuance of the term "surplus" in the balance sheet presentation of the stockholders' equity, and the substitution of terms clearly indicating the sources from which capital was derived.[1]

Reserves. The use of the term "reserves" and classification problems relating to reserves have been subject to special inquiry and challenge. The term *reserve* is popularly interpreted to mean property that is held or retained for some special purpose. For accounting purposes, such property would be referred to as a deposit, a temporary investment, or a sinking fund. The reserve designation, however, has been employed in the following conflicting ways on the balance sheet:

(1) As a valuation account — Reserve for Bad Debts, for example, to reduce a receivable balance to the estimated amount collectible.

(2) As a liability whose amount is uncertain — Reserve for Federal Income Taxes, for example, to indicate the amount of income taxes estimated to be payable.

(3) As an appropriation of retained earnings — Reserve for Bond Retirement Fund, for example, to represent an appropriation of retained earnings corresponding to the assets that have been segregated and that are to be used for bond retirement.

The AICPA Committee on Terminology in 1953 recommended certain limitations in the use of the reserve designation. Since the generally accepted meaning of the term "reserve" relates only to appropriations of retained earnings, the Committee recommended that its use be limited to items within this class. The Committee further suggested that asset offsets be referred to by such titles as "less estimated losses on collection"

---

[1]See *Accounting Terminology Bulletin No. 1*, "Review and Résumé" (New York: American Institute of Certified Public Accountants, 1953), par. 65–70. The American Institute has continued to use the term "surplus" in some of its pronouncements. The Committee on Accounting Procedure states in its preface to *Accounting Research Bulletin No. 43*, "Although the committee has approved the objective of finding a better term than the word *surplus* for use in published financial statements, it has used *surplus* herein as being a technical term well understood among accountants, to whom its pronouncements are primarily directed."

and "less accrued depreciation," and that a liability involving an estimate be reported as either an "estimated liability" or a "liability of
estimated amount."[1]

The use of "reserve" as an asset valuation account, a liability, and
an owners' equity balance should be discouraged. But even more objectionable is the practice of listing such diverse reserve elements under a
common heading "Reserves" usually reported between the liabilities
and the owners' equity sections on the balance sheet. This practice
results in a distortion of asset, liability, and owners' equity balances,
making necessary a full analysis of the reserves and their identification
with the appropriate balance sheet section in arriving at a summary of
assets and related equities. Further, the use of such titles as "Miscellaneous Reserves," "General Reserves," and "Contingency Reserves" within
a reserves section frequently makes accurate identification of the reserve
item impossible. The American Accounting Association Committee on
Concepts and Standards Underlying Corporate Financial Statements
has taken a firm stand on this matter, recommending elimination of the
"reserves section" on the balance sheet and the presentation of its elements as deduction-from-asset, or liability, or retained earnings amounts.[2]

The term "net worth" is rarely found in modern practice. However,
the terms "surplus" and "reserve" are still found, although there has
been significant movement towards acceptance of the recommendations
mentioned.[3] Most of the illustrations in the text employ the statement
forms and terminology recommended by leading accounting authorities.
However, alternate forms and terms are used in some text questions,
exercises, and problems, since these are still encountered in practice.
It must be pointed out that in communicating the business story, movement toward more readily understood terminology is only one phase of
the problem. The person who uses the statement must be educated so that
he understands the nature of accounting, the service that it can legiti-
mately perform, the limitations to which it is subject, and the kind of
analysis and interpretation that is appropriate under these circumstances.

[1]*Ibid.*, par. 57–64.

[2]*Accounting and Reporting Standards for Corporate Financial Statements and Preceding Statements and Supplements*, "Supplementary Statement No. 1, Reserves and Retained Income" (Madison, Wisconsin: American Accounting Association, 1957), p. 19.

[3]*Accounting Trends & Techniques* published annually by the AICPA, summarizes and analyzes the accounting practices that are found in the financial reports released each year by 600 industrial companies. In the AICPA list of 600 survey companies, the number using the term "surplus" in reporting paid-in capital ("capital surplus," for example), was 158 in 1970 as compared with 375 in 1948; the number using the term "surplus" in reporting ac-cumulated earnings ("earned surplus," for example) was 32 in 1970 as compared with 501 in 1948. The term "reserve" was used in reporting accumulated depreciation by 33 com-panies in 1970 as compared with 118 companies in 1960. *Accounting Trends & Techniques*, (25th ed.; New York: American Institute of Certified Public Accountants, 1971), pp. 122, 137, 139.

Form of the balance sheet

The form of the balance sheet varies in practice. Its form may be influenced by the nature and size of the business, by the character of the business properties, and, in some instances, by requirements set by regulatory bodies. The balance sheet is generally prepared in *account form*, assets being reported on the left-hand side and liabilities and owners' equity on the right-hand side. It may also be prepared in *report form*, with assets, liabilities, and owners' equity sections appearing in vertical arrangement.

The order of asset and liability classifications also varies. For example, where emphasis is placed upon a company's working capital position and liquidity, asset and liability groups, as well as the items within such groups, may be presented in the order of liquidity. This is the usual presentation for a mercantile company or a manufacturing company. A balance sheet in account form with financial data reported in the order of liquidity is illustrated on pages 46 and 47.

When readers of a balance sheet are concerned primarily with such factors as total land, buildings, and equipment and the method of financing such property, and when a satisfactory condition as to solvency is assumed, as in the case of a public utility, for example, the order of presentation may emphasize property investment and the financing of such investment. Class headings on the balance sheet may be reported in the following order:

Land, buildings, and equipment	Paid-in capital
Intangible assets	Retained earnings
Investments	Long-term debt
Other long-term assets	Deferred revenues
Current assets	Other long-term liabilities
	Deferred revenues

When the report form is used, liability and owners' equity totals may be added together to form an amount equal to the asset total. In other instances total liabilities are subtracted from total assets, and owners' equity is reported as the difference. A variation of the report form referred to as the *financial position form* has found some favor. This form emphasizes the current position and reports a working capital balance. The financial position form is illustrated at the top of page 48. (Individual assets and liabilities are omitted in the example.)[1]

---

[1]Analysis of the reports of the AICPA list of survey companies with fiscal years ending within the calendar year 1970 showed that 26 companies used the financial position form. This was down from the total of 79 companies that used this form in 1959. *Accounting Trends & Techniques, op. cit.,* p. 51.

Anderson
Balance
December

Assets			
Current assets:			
Cash in bank and on hand.........................		$ 36,500	
Marketable securities (reported at cost; market value, $71,500)...		70,000	
Notes receivable, trade debtors*..................	$ 15,000		
Accounts receivable.............................	50,000		
	$ 65,000		
Less allowance for doubtful accounts.............	5,000	60,000	
Claim for income tax refund......................		9,000	
Creditors' accounts with debit balances.............		750	
Advances to employees...........................		1,250	
Accrued interest on notes receivable...............		250	
Inventories (at lower of cost or market)............		125,000	
Prepaid expenses:			
Supply inventories...........................	$ 3,000		
Insurance...................................	4,250	7,250	$310,000
Investments:			
Cash and securities in preferred stock redemption fund		$ 22,500	
Cash surrender value of officers' life insurance policies.		7,500	30,000

Land, buildings and equipment:	Cost	Accumulated Depreciation	Book Value	
Land................................	$ 80,000		$ 80,000	
Buildings............................	150,000	$ 35,000	115,000	
Equipment...........................	100,000	45,000	55,000	
	$330,000	$ 80,000		250,000

Intangible assets:		
Organization costs................................	$ 6,500	
Goodwill...	18,500	25,000
Other long-term assets:		
Advances to officers..............................	$ 15,000	
Customer deposits................................	5,000	20,000
Total assets......................................		$635,000

---

*The company is contingently liable on customers notes of $25,000 that have been discounted at the bank.

Account form

Related balance sheet items are frequently combined so that the balance sheet may be prepared in condensed form. For example, land, buildings, and equipment may be reported as a single item; raw materials, goods in process, and finished goods inventories may be combined; and investments may be reported in total. Consolidation of similar items within reasonable limits may actually serve to clarify the business position and data relationships. Supporting detail for individual items, when considered of particular significance or when required by law, may be supplied by means of special summaries referred to as *supplementary schedules.*

Corporation
Sheet
31, 1972

Liabilities			
Current liabilities:			
Notes payable, trade creditors...................		$ 14,250	
Accounts payable.............................		12,500	
Dividends payable............................		5,000	
Advances from customers......................		5,750	
Estimated income taxes payable.................		27,000	
Accrued liabilities:			
Salaries and wages payable....................	$ 1,000		
Taxes payable...............................	1,500	2,500	$ 67,000
Long-term debt:			
5½% First-mortgage bonds due December 31, 1976..		$100,000	
Less unamortized bond discount.................		5,000	95,000
Deferred revenues:			
Unearned lease income.......................			20,000
Other long-term liabilities:			
Deferred income taxes payable..................			3,000
Total liabilities.................................			$185,000

Stockholders' Equity			
Paid-in capital:			
Common stock, $5 stated value, 100,000 shares authorized, 50,000 shares issued and outstanding.......	$250,000		
Paid-in capital from sale of common stock at more than stated value..................................	45,000	$295,000	
Retained earnings................................		155,000	
Total stockholders' equity.........................			450,000
Total liabilities and stockholders' equity..............			$635,000

balance sheet

Balance sheet data are generally presented in comparative form. With comparative reports for two or more dates, information is made available concerning the nature and the trend of financial changes taking place within the periods between balance sheet dates. When a statement is presented in a special form, the heading should designate the nature of the form that is provided, as for example, "Condensed Balance Sheet," or "Comparative Balance Sheet."

Along with the movement towards more descriptive terminology has come the attempt to improve the manner of presentation of financial data. Parenthetical remarks and notes are frequently employed to

Anderson Corporation
Statement of Financial Position
December 31, 1972

Current assets..		$310,000
Less current liabilities..................................		67,000
Working capital..		$243,000
Add:		
Investments...		30,000
Land, buildings, and equipment..........................		250,000
Intangible assets..		25,000
Other long-term assets..................................		20,000
Total assets less current liabilities......................		$568,000
Deduct:		
Long-term debt less unamortized bond issue costs..............	$95,000	
Deferred revenues.......................................	20,000	
Deferred income taxes payable...........................	3,000	118,000
Net assets..		$450,000
Stockholders' equity:		
Paid-in capital..		$295,000
Retained earnings.......................................		155,000
Total stockholders' equity...............................		$450,000

Financial position form of balance sheet

explain or to supplement the basic financial data. Careful classification of items under descriptive headings and the presentation of data in comparative form provide more meaningful statements. Presentations in condensed forms and the elimination of the number of cents or dollars, figures being stated to the nearest dollar or hundreds of dollars, clarify relationships and facilitate analysis.

Some companies provide simplified statements that attempt to offer basic financial data in a nontechnical and explanatory manner. The development of original forms by different companies is a movement away from one objective of the profession, which is to encourage uniformity so that statements may be generally comparable. Furthermore, it is questionable whether the simplified statements have received a better response from users or have proved to be any more informative than statements prepared in the conventional manner.

A variety of different balance sheet forms are found in practice. Several selected statements are given in the appendix of this textbook. These should be studied carefully, for they offer suggestions as to the different approaches that may be taken in the development of statements summarizing financial status.

QUESTIONS

1. How would you define assets, liabilities, and owners' equity?

2. What is the relationship between the balance sheet and the income statement?

3. Why are the definitions for *current* assets and *current* liabilities regarded as important for proper balance sheet reporting?

4. Explain the two positions that have been taken in distinguishing items as current and noncurrent. Which position do you support? Why?

5. (a) Give examples of expense prepayments that are properly reported as (1) current items and (2) noncurrent items. What factors govern in the determination of the appropriate classification? (b) Give examples of revenue prepayments properly reported as (1) current items and (2) noncurrent items. What factors govern here?

6. Browne Liquidators, Inc., insists on reporting the cash surrender value of life insurance on company officials as a current asset in view of its immediate convertibility into cash. Do you support this treatment?

7. Indicate under what circumstances each of the following can be considered noncurrent: (a) cash, (b) receivables, (c) investments in securities, (d) inventories.

8. Under what circumstances would bonded indebtedness due in six months be reported as a noncurrent item?

9. (a) What objections can be made to the use of the heading "Deferred costs"? (b) What objections can be made to the use of the heading, "Deferred revenues"?

10. What justification is there for treating intangible items as assets on the balance sheet?

11. Explain how the deferred income taxes payable balance meets the commonly accepted definition of liabilities.

12. Why is a premium or discount on bonded indebtedness reported as an addition to or subtraction from the face value of the bond liability?

13. What major classifications may be applied to (a) assets, (b) liabilities and (c) owners' equity items? Indicate the data that are reported within each classification.

14. Give an example of (a) a contingent asset, (b) a contingent liability, and (c) a contingent owners' equity item.

15. Distinguish between the following: (a) contingent liabilities and estimated liabilities, (b) appropriated retained earnings and free retained earnings, (c) capital surplus and appraisal surplus.

16. What two basic sequences may be employed in listing assets, liabilities, and owners' equity on the balance sheet? What factors govern in making a choice between the two?

17. (a) What objections are raised to the use of the terms (1) reserve, (2) net worth, and (3) surplus? (b) What suggestions have been made with respect to these terms in attempts to improve financial reporting?

18. Indicate those balance sheet items that may require the presentation of parenthetical remarks or footnotes if the reader of the statement is to be adequately informed.

EXERCISES

1. Indicate the balance sheet classification for each of the following accounts. In the case of doubtful items, indicate what additional information would be required.

(a) Retained Earnings
(b) Accrued Vacation Pay
(c) Cash Sinking Fund for Payment of Bonds Payable
(d) Retained Earnings Appropriated for Contingencies
(e) Receivables — U. S. Government Contracts
(f) Investment in Bonds
(g) Accrued Interest on Investment in Bonds
(h) Treasury Stock
(i) Unclaimed Payroll Checks
(j) Accumulated Depreciation
(k) Accrued Interest on Bonds Payable
(l) Dividends Payable on Preferred Stock
(m) Raw Materials
(n) Unearned Subscription Income
(o) Employees Income Taxes Payable

2. State how each of the following accounts should be classified.

(a) Accumulated Patent Amortization
(b) Income Taxes Payable
(c) Accumulated Depletion
(d) Retained Earnings Appropriated for Contingencies
(e) Allowance for Doubtful Accounts
(f) Liability for Pension Payments
(g) Marketable Securities
(h) Paid-In Capital from Sale of Stock at More Than Stated Value
(i) Unamortized Bond Issue Costs
(j) Goodwill
(k) Deficit
(l) Advances to Salesmen
(m) Customers Accounts with Credit Balances
(n) Creditors Accounts with Debit Balances
(o) Cash Representing Miscellaneous Refundable Deposits
(p) Prepaid Rental Expense
(q) Accrued Interest on Notes Receivable
(r) Subscription Income Received in Advance
(s) Treasury Stock
(t) Deferred Income Taxes Expense
(u) Tools
(v) Deferred Income Taxes Payable
(w) Loans to Officers
(x) Leasehold Improvements
(y) Patents

3. Indicate how each of the following items should be classified on the balance sheet:

   (a) Cash surrender value of life insurance.
   (b) Sinking fund cash for retirement of bonds.
   (c) Bonds payable in six months out of sinking fund cash.
   (d) Note receivable that will be collected in 10 annual installments.
   (e) Cash deposited with broker on option to buy real estate.
   (f) Land held as future plant site.
   (g) Warehouse in process of construction.
   (h) Cash fund representing customers' deposits on returnable containers.
   (i) Cash fund representing sales tax collections.
   (j) Goods in process that will require more than one year for completion.

4. The bookkeeper for Olsen-Oakes, Inc., submitted the following balance sheet as of June 30, 1972:

Olsen-Oakes, Inc.
Balance Sheet
June 30, 1972

Cash	$15,000	Accounts payable — trade	$25,000
Receivables — trade	25,000	Stockholders' equity	70,000
Inventories	40,000		
Goodwill	15,000		
	$95,000		$95,000

Reference to the records of the company indicated the following:

   (a) Cash included a check for $700 that was returned by the bank marked "maker unknown"; it is doubtful whether payment will ever be recovered on this check.

   (b) State and local taxes of $1,200 were accrued on June 30. However, $1,200 had been deposited in a special cash account to be used to pay these and neither cash nor the accrued taxes were reported on the balance sheet.

   (c) Goods costing $1,500 were shipped to customers on June 29 and 30, at a sales price of $2,200. Goods shipped were not included in the inventory as of June 30. However, receivables were not recognized for the shipments since invoices were not sent out until July 3.

   (d) The corporation had been organized on January 1, 1972, by exchanging 6,500 shares of no-par stock with stated value of $10 per share for the net assets of the partnership of Olsen and Oakes.

Prepare a corrected balance sheet as of June 30, 1972.

5. From the following chart of accounts, prepare a balance sheet in account form showing all balance sheet items properly classified. (No monetary amounts are to be recognized.)

Accounts Payable
Accounts Receivable
Accrued Interest Receivable
Accrued Salaries
Accumulated Depreciation — Building
Accumulated Depreciation — Equipment
Advertising
Allowance for Decline in Value of Marketable Securities
Allowance for Doubtful Accounts
Appraisal Capital
Bond Fund
Bonds Payable
Buildings
Cash in Bank
Cash on Hand
Common Stock
Cost of Goods Sold
Deferred Income Taxes Expense
Depreciation Expense — Buildings
Dividends
Dividends Payable
Doubtful Accounts Expense
Equipment
Estimated Warranty Expense Payable
FICA Taxes Payable
Gain on Sale of Land
Gain on Sale of Marketable Securities
Goodwill
Income Summary
Income Taxes
Income Taxes Payable

Interest Income
Inventory
Investment in Bonds
Land
Land Improvements
Leasehold Improvements
Loss on Purchase Commitments
Marketable Securities
Miscellaneous General Expense
Notes Payable
Notes Receivable
Notes Receivable Discounted
Paid-In Capital from Sale of Common Stock at More Than Stated Value
Paid-In Capital from Sale of Treasury Stock
Patents
Pension Fund
Petty Cash
Premium on Bonds Payable
Prepaid Insurance
Prepaid Taxes
Property Taxes
Purchases
Purchases Discount
Retained Earnings
Retained Earnings Appropriated for General Contingencies
Sales
Sales Salaries
Travel Expense

PROBLEMS

2-1. Prepare a properly classified balance sheet for the Cummings Sales Corp. from the following account balances as of March 31, 1972:

Accounts Payable	$42,900	Buildings	$150,000
Accounts Receivable	53,000	Cash in Banks	14,500
Accrued Interest on Notes Receivable	200	Cash on Hand	1,200
Accumulated Depreciation — Buildings	70,000	Cash Surrender Value of Life Insurance Policies	8,500
Accumulated Depreciation — Machinery and Equipment	20,000	Claim for Income Tax Refund	2,500
Advances from Customers on Contracts in Progress	6,500	Common Stock, $20 par	300,000
Allowance for Doubtful Notes and Accounts	2,100	Employees Income Taxes Payable	1,820
		Finished Goods	21,000
		Franchises	21,000
		Goods in Process	39,400

Income Taxes Payable.......	$ 12,300	Preferred Stock, $5 par.......	$150,000
Interest Payable............	1,000	Premium on Common Stock..	30,000
Investment in Stock of Subsidiary Company.........	125,000	Prepaid Insurance...........	2,250
		Property Taxes Payable......	2,100
Investment in Undeveloped Properties...............	106,000	Raw Materials..............	16,900
Land......................	65,000	Retained Earnings (debit balance)...................	63,470
Machinery and Equipment...	72,000	7% Serial Bonds Payable (due March 1, 1973)...........	10,000
Misc. Accrued Expenses......	3,700		
Misc. Supplies Inventories....	3,100	7% Serial Bonds Payable (due in 1974 and thereafter).....	100,000
Notes Payable (current)......	25,000		
Notes Payable (due 1977)....	25,000	Temporary Investments in Marketable Securities......	21,200
Notes Receivable...........	11,200		
		Tools.....................	5,000

2-2. From the account balances given below for the Snow Corporation, as of December 31, 1972, prepare a balance sheet with information properly classified:

Accounts Payable...........	$ 49,600	Employees Income Taxes Payable....................	$ 1,200
Accounts Receivable........	96,000	Equipment.................	51,000
Accrued Interest and Property Taxes...................	5,420	FICA Taxes Payable........	700
		Goodwill..................	45,000
Accrued Salaries...........	750	Income Taxes Payable.......	9,800
Accumulated Depreciation — Buildings................	51,000	Interest Receivable.........	900
		Inventories................	126,900
Accumulated Depreciation — Equipment...............	14,000	Land......................	45,000
Advances to Officers........	15,000	Land for Future Plant Site....	39,000
Allowance for Doubtful Accounts..................	13,000	Notes Payable.............	32,000
		Notes Receivable...........	25,000
8% Bonds Payable, due Sept. 1, 1981....................	125,000	Paid-In Capital from Sale of Common Stock at More Than Stated Value.......	75,000
Bond Sinking Fund.........	60,000	Patents...................	25,000
Buildings..................	135,000	Preferred Stock, $100 par.....	110,000
Buildings and Equipment Relocation Costs............	12,000	Premium on Bonds Payable...	5,000
Cash......................	23,900	Premium on Preferred Stock..	6,500
Cash Dividends Payable......	21,000	Prepaid Taxes, Insurance, and Miscellaneous Services.....	3,400
Cash Surrender Value of Life Insurance................	6,240	Rent Receivable............	2,200
		Retained Earnings..........	48,570
Common Stock, $50 Stated Value....................	150,000	Supplies...................	2,100
Deferred Income Taxes Payable....................	21,200	Temporary Investments in Marketable Securities......	28,000
		Unearned Lease Income.....	1,900

2-3. The following balance sheet was prepared by the accountant for Northwest Plywood, Inc. Prepare a corrected statement in good form using account titles that meet the recommendations of the AICPA.

Northwest Plywood, Inc.
Balance Sheet
June 30, 1972

Assets

Cash...	$ 25,500
Marketable securities (includes 10% ownership in stock of Oregon Timber, Inc., at cost of $125,000).............	206,000
Inventories (net of amount still due suppliers of $63,500).	559,400
Prepaid expenses (includes a deposit of $10,000 made on future delivery of special inventories)...............	32,100
Fixed assets (excluding $50,000 of equipment still in use, but fully depreciated).............................	220,000
Goodwill (based upon estimate of President of Northwest Plywood, Inc.)..................................	50,000
Total assets.................................	$1,093,000

Liabilities and Stockholders' Equity

Notes payable ($65,000 due in 1974)..................	$ 110,000
Accounts payable (not including amount due to suppliers of inventory — see above)........................	95,000
Reserve for pensions payable.........................	80,000
Reserve for building expansion........................	75,000
Reserve for depreciation — fixed assets.................	73,000
Taxes payable......................................	25,300
Bonds payable (net of discount of $30,000).............	170,000
Reserve for deferred income taxes......................	83,000
Common stock (20,000 shares @ $10 par)..............	200,000
Premium on common stock...........................	50,500
Reserve for contingencies............................	15,000
Retained earnings — unappropriated...................	116,200
Total liabilities and stockholders' equity...........	$1,093,000

2-4. The Big D Ranch summarizes its financial position in the following letter to their accountant. Based upon this information, prepare a properly classified balance sheet as of December 31, 1972.

January 20, 1973

Dear Gordon:

The following information should be of value to you in preparing the balance sheet for Big D Ranch as of December 31, 1972. The balance of cash as of December 31 as reported on the bank statement was $18,200. There were still outstanding checks of $6,420 that had not cleared the bank and cash on hand of $2,590 was not deposited until January 4, 1973.

Customers owed the company $23,900 at December 31. We estimate that 10% of this amount will never be collected. We owe suppliers $8,000 for poultry feed purchased in November and December. About 40% of this feed was used before December 31.

Because we think the price of grain will rise in 1973, we are holding 10,000 bushels of wheat and 5,000 bushels of oats until spring. The market value at December 31 was $1.60 per bushel of wheat and $.85 per bushel of oats. We estimate that both prices will increase 10% by selling time. We are not able to estimate the cost of raising this product.

Big D Ranch owns 2,000 acres of land. Two separate purchases of land were made as follows: 1,500 acres at $150 per acre in 1959, and 500 acres at $300 per acre in 1965. Similar land is currently selling for $500 per acre. The balance of the mortgage on the two parcels of land is $165,000 at December 31; 10% of this mortgage must be paid in 1973.

Our farm buildings and equipment cost us $176,400, and on the average are 50% depreciated. If we were to replace these buildings and equipment at today's prices, we believe we would be conservative in estimating a cost of $300,000.

We have not paid 1973 property taxes of $5,500 that were billed to us in late November. Our estimated income taxes for 1972 are $12,500. A refund claim for $2,800 has been filed relative to the 1970 income tax return. The claim arose because of an error that was made on the 1970 return.

The operator of the ranch will receive a bonus of $3,500 for 1972 operations. It will be paid when the entire grain crop has been sold.

As you will recall, we issued 14,000 shares of $10 par stock upon incorporation. The ranch received $255,000 as net proceeds from the stock issue. Dividends of $35,000 were declared last month and will be paid on February 1, 1973.

The new year appears to hold great promise. Thanks for your help in preparing this statement.

Sincerely

Douglas Hansen
President — Big D Ranch

2-5. The following account balances appear in the ledger of Jayco, Inc., on June 30, 1973:

	Dr.	Cr.
Accounts Payable — Trade		$ 54,800
Accounts Receivable — Trade	$ 95,000	
Accrued Interest Receivable	2,000	
Accrued Salaries and Wages		3,200
Advance to Affiliated Company	20,000	
Allowance for Sales Discount		1,500
Allowance for Doubtful Accounts		5,000
Allowance to Reduce Inventories to Lower of Cost or Market		10,200
Bonds (payable in installments of $21,000 on September 1 of each year)		126,000
Cash Surrender Value of Life Insurance	5,600	
Employees Income Taxes Payable		3,100
Estimated Employee Retirement Benefits		66,500
First National Bank — Fund for Employee Retirement Benefits	69,000	
First National Bank — General Account	16,900	
First National Bank — Payroll Account	12,000	
FICA Taxes Payable		700
Income Taxes Payable	16,500	
Inventories	231,500	
Investment in Affiliated Company	210,000	
Marketable Securities	21,300	
Office Supplies	4,150	
Prepaid Insurance	1,725	
Returnable Containers	17,500	
Unamortized Organization Costs	25,000	
Unamortized Bond Issue Costs	6,200	

Instructions: Select the current assets and the current liabilities and present these as they would appear on a balance sheet prepared in financial position form.

2-6. The bookkeeper for the Town Corporation prepares the following condensed balance sheet. A review of the account balances disclosed the data listed below.

Town Corporation
Balance Sheet
December 31, 1973

Current assets.	$109,200
Less current liabilities.	60,000
Working capital.	$ 49,200
Add other assets.	90,880
	$140,080
Deduct other liabilities.	4,200
Investment in business.	$135,880

An analysis of the current asset grouping revealed the following:

Cash.	$ 9,200
Trade accounts receivable (fully collectible).	26,000
Notes receivable (notes of customer who has been declared bankrupt and is unable to pay anything on his obligations)	2,000
Marketable securities, at cost (market value, $5,150).	10,100
Inventory.	57,700
Cash surrender value of insurance on officers' lives.	4,200
Total current assets.	$109,200

The inventory account was found to include the cost of supplies of $620, a delivery truck acquired at the end of 1973 at a cost of $4,200, and fixtures at a depreciated value of $20,800. The fixtures had been acquired in 1970 at a cost of $25,000.

The total for other assets was determined as follows:

Land and buildings, at cost of acquisition on July 1, 1971.	$124,000
Less balance due on mortgage, $32,000, and accrued interest on mortgage, $1,120 (mortgage is payable in annual installments of $8,000 on July 1 of each year together with interest for the year at that time at 7%).	33,120
Total other assets.	$ 90,880

It was estimated that the land, at the time of purchase, was worth $60,000. Buildings as of December 31, 1973 were estimated to have a remaining life of 17½ years.

Current liabilities represented balances that were payable to trade creditors. Other liabilities consisted of withholding, payroll, real estate and other taxes payable to the federal, state, and local governments. However, no recognition was given to accrued salaries, utilities, and other miscellaneous items totaling $700.

The company was originally organized in 1969 when 10,000 shares of no par stock with a stated value of $5 per share were issued in exchange for business assets that were recognized on the books at their fair market value of $110,000.

Instructions: Prepare a corrected balance sheet in financial position form with the items properly classified.

2-7. The bookkeeper for the Benjamin Corporation submits the following condensed balance sheet. A review of the account balances reveals the data listed below. Using the balance sheet and the related data, prepare a corrected balance sheet reporting individual asset, liability, and capital balances properly classified.

Benjamin Corporation
Balance Sheet
June 30, 1973

Current assets...............	$ 61,000	Current liabilities.............	$ 31,650
Other assets.................	159,150	Other liabilities..............	22,500
		Capital.....................	166,000
	$220,150		$220,150

An analysis of current assets discloses the following:

Cash...	$ 12,000
Marketable securities held as temporary investment.....	14,000
Trade accounts receivable...........................	13,500
Inventories, including advertising supplies of $500......	21,500
	$ 61,000

Other assets include:

Land, buildings, and equipment, cost $165,000, depreciated value....................................	$136,000
Deposit with a supplier for merchandise ordered for August delivery....................................	1,300
Goodwill recorded on the books to cancel losses incurred by the company in prior years....................	21,850
	$159,150

Current liabilities include:

Accrued payrolls....................................	$ 1,750
Accrued taxes......................................	1,000
Accrued rent.......................................	3,000
Trade accounts payable, $22,600, less a $1,700 debit balance reported in the account of a vendor to whom merchandise had been returned after the account had been paid in full.......................................	20,900
Notes payable......................................	5,000
	$ 31,650

Other liabilities include:

7% mortgage on land, buildings and equipment, payable in semiannual installments of $2,250 through June 30, 1978..	$ 22,500

(*continued*)

Capital includes:

10,000 shares of preferred stock, $10 par...............	$100,000
40,000 shares of common stock at stated value..........	66,000
144,150	$166,000

Common shares were originally issued for a total consideration of $100,000, but the losses of the company for past years were charged against the common stock balance.

2-8. The balance sheet below is submitted to you for inspection and review. In the course of the review you find the data listed below. Using the balance sheet and the information that follows, prepare a corrected balance sheet with accounts properly classified.

Reed Corporation
Balance Sheet
December 31, 1973

Assets		Liabilities and Stockholders' Equity	
Cash........................	$ 20,000	Accrued liabilities.............	$ 1,000
Accounts receivable...........	72,000	Loan payable.................	22,500
Inventories..................	88,000	Accounts payable.............	58,500
Prepaid insurance............	5,000	Capital stock................	100,000
Land, buildings, and equipment.	130,000	Surplus.....................	133,000
	$315,000		$315,000

(a) The possibility of bad debts on accounts receivable has not been considered. It is estimated that bad debts will total $2,000.

(b) $20,000 representing the cost of a large-scale newspaper advertising campaign completed in 1973 has been added to the inventories, since it is believed that this campaign will benefit sales of 1974. It is also found that inventories include merchandise of $6,500 received on December 31 that has not yet been recorded as a purchase.

(c) Prepaid insurance consists of $400, the cost of fire insurance for 1974, and $4,600, the cash surrender value on officers' life insurance policies.

(d) The books show that land, buildings, and equipment have a cost of $210,000 with depreciation of $80,000 recognized in prior years. However, these balances include fully depreciated equipment of $30,000 that has been scrapped and is no longer on hand.

(e) Accrued liabilities of $1,000 represents accrued salaries of $3,000, less noncurrent advances of $2,000 made to company officials.

(f) Loan payable represents a loan from the bank that is payable in regular quarterly installments of $2,500.

(g) Tax liabilities not shown are estimated at $4,500.

(h) Deferred income taxes payable arising from timing differences in recognizing income totals $9,500. These taxes were not included in the balance sheet.

(i) Capital stock consists of 5,000 shares of 6% preferred stock, par $10, and 10,000 shares of common stock, stated value $5.

(j) Capital stock had been issued for a total consideration of $125,000, the amount received in excess of the par and stated values of the stock being reported as surplus.

chapter 3

financial statements -
the income statement

The *income statement*, also variously called the *earnings statement*, the *statement of profit and loss*, and the *statement of operations*, summarizes business activities for a given period and reports the· net income or loss resulting from operations and from certain other defined activities. The importance of measuring and reporting income, as well as the nature and the content of the income statement, is described in the sections that follow.

Importance of measuring and reporting income

The measuring and reporting of business income has acquired steadily increasing importance and, at present, accountants generally regard this as one of their most important responsibilities.[1] Reference is made to the income statement by many different groups who need to evaluate the results of business activities. Reference is also made to this statement by those who desire to determine the worth of a business, for it is business earnings that ultimately validate asset values. The measurement of income has presented many problems to the accountant because of the absence of a precise definition for "income," and he has had to exercise judgment on a great many matters in arriving at such measurement.

A major part of accounting research has been directed toward the matter of *income determination*. This represents a shift in the attention of

---

[1]For example, APB Statement No. 4 states: "The information presented in an income statement is usually considered the most important information provided by financial accounting because profitability is a paramount concern to those interested in the economic activities of the enterprise." *Statements of the Accounting Principles Board, No. 4,* "Basic Concepts and Accounting Principles Underlying Financial Statements of Business Enterprises" (New York: American Institute of Certified Public Accountants, 1970), par. 12.

accountants from the balance sheet to the statement reporting periodic flow of revenues and expenses. Historically the balance sheet was considered to be the primary statement. It was used by the creditors to evaluate the liquidity of a company and by the owners to evaluate the financial position of a company and the changes that had taken place in such position. Early pronouncements by the American Institute of Accountants emphasized the balance sheet and the valuation, presentation, and verification of items reported on this statement.

A number of factors have contributed to the growing importance of the income statement. Primary factors have been the income tax laws, the absentee ownership of corporations, and the increased internal use of accounting information.

Income tax laws. Since 1913 when the 16th Amendment to the Constitution was passed, taxes on income at both national and state levels have become very significant. This has created a need for every business entity to establish some system for the measurement of income. Various tax regulations have become increasingly specific as to what constitutes income for tax purposes. In the majority of cases these regulations follow practices that are currently being applied by accountants in preparing general financial statements. However, there are some troublesome areas that arise because the objective of income measurement for the government is related to its regulatory and financial responsibilities. These may not coincide with procedures that are considered appropriate in measuring the profitability of a specific enterprise over a limited time span. Serious questions can often be raised when certain tax regulations become the accepted procedures for financial accounting.

Absentee ownership of corporations. The growth of the corporate form of ownership has created a large group of absentee owners. It is estimated that there are over 30 million stockholders of American corporations. The stockholders of most corporations have very little contact with the operations of the companies in which they have holdings except through the published reports that they receive periodically. Although they can attend annual stockholders meetings, very few of them actually do. The stockholders regard their involvement as a financial one and evaluate their investment in comparison with other financial alternatives. Because of these conditions, the average stockholder looks for financial data that can help him in evaluating his investment. The net income figure, as well as related income or earnings per share data, is widely reported in newspapers and financial services. Although there

is much theorizing among observers of the stock market as to the degree to which the market value of stock is affected by periodic reports of earnings, it is clear that the stockholder is interested and does pay close attention to this measure of profitability. Stockbrokers often refer to the relationship between stock prices and current earnings and use the measurement of price times earnings to reflect the profitability of the entity.

Increased internal use of accounting information. Not only has there been an increase in interest in the income statement by outside users, but the same can also be said for the primary internal user — management. Years ago an intuitive feel as to how well things were going in an enterprise was often possible for most proprietors; but today the complexity of modern business makes it impossible for one man to acquire such an intuitive feel. Managements of large and growing corporate enterprises dealing in many different product areas need to have profitability information to answer questions relating to past programs, present programs, and projected programs. Questions arise such as: How effective was our past advertising policy? Should we make or buy certain component parts for our end-line products? Should we add to our product lines? Information systems within the enterprise must be prepared to answer these questions and often do so in the context of some version of the income statement.

Nature of income

The accountant must be familiar with the concepts involved in income determination. The relationship between the income statement and the balance sheet makes it impossible to completely separate them in discussion. Implications for balance sheet valuations are frequently embodied in the concepts of income.

With the increasing attention being given to the income statement, it is only natural that certain questions have been raised concerning income: What purpose should it serve in our economy? How can it best serve this purpose? Unfortunately these questions, though frequently asked, have not been satisfactorily answered. A senior partner for a national accounting firm has raised the following questions: What is the purpose of the income statement? Are we trying to show venture results? Or are we trying to show the earning power of a company's productive facilities?[1] And other questions could be raised such as: Is our function limited to that of a historian reporting on the past? Or are we trying to

---

[1]Leonard Spacek, "The Treatment of Goodwill in the Corporate Balance Sheet," *Journal of Accountancy* (February, 1964), p. 35.

provide the best guide for estimating future earning power?[1]   All of these questions are appropriate ones; however, all of the answers may not be provided by the same income statement.   Some of the purposes, perhaps, are being satisfied better by present accounting methods than others.   Before examining the concepts that underlie present income measurement and reporting, some of the other concepts that are suggested by accounting and economic literature deserve attention.

The valuation (indirect) method of income determination

It has been suggested earlier that a business entity commences activities in the attempt to increase its net assets through profitable operations.   This increase in net assets is referred to by many economists as a change in the "well-offness" of the entity, alternately referred to as the "income" of the firm.   This is indeed an appealing concept.   Income normally connotes something desirable in our economy and thus is reasonably represented by such net asset increase.   This suggests that one way to determine income is to value the net assets of an entity at two different times and compute the change that has occurred.   If the change is positive after adjustment for any investment or withdrawal of assets by the owners, there has been *income*.   If the change is negative, there has been a *loss*.   Because income is determined by comparing net assets at two different times, this method of income determination is referred to as the *valuation method*, or *indirect method*.

The valuation method is the method most commonly used by the economists in their discussion of income.   One of the most quoted economists in accounting literature, J. R. Hicks, defined income as the maximum value which an entity can distribute during a period and still expect to be as well-off.[2]   Although net assets is accepted as the indicator of importance, it is necessary to arrive at a precise definition of the meaning of *value of net assets*.   Is it the historical cost of the net assets reduced by some amount for their use?   Is it the current value of the net assets determined by replacement or market values?   Is it the historical cost of the net assets adjusted for the change in price levels since original acquisitions?   All of these, as well as other concepts, may be regarded as satisfying the general term, value of net assets.   Another question that

---

[1]As indicated in Chapter 1, the general objectives of financial accounting that were enumerated by the APB in Statement No. 4 include both of these general concepts.   Objective 2 emphasizes the provision of reliable information about changes in net resources that result from profit-directed activities, and objective 3 emphasizes the provision of financial information that assists in estimating the earning potential of the enterprise.   *Statements of the Accounting Principles Board, No. 4, op. cit.*, par. 78 and 79.

[2]J. R. Hicks, *Value and Capital* (2d ed.; Oxford University Press, 1946).

must be resolved is what is to be included in net assets. Should intangible items such as goodwill, patents, and leaseholds be included in assets? Should estimated payments relating to warranties and pensions be included in liabilities?

For many years economists, and recently some accountants, have approached these difficult questions by attempting to define net assets in terms of the present value of the cash benefits that net assets are expected to provide. These parties maintain that we should arrive at *future cash flows* in amount and time, and with the use of appropriate discount rates determine the present worth of these streams of future benefits. Net assets as thus computed can be compared as of different points in arriving at income. Although this concept has some theoretical merit, it has had minor influence upon practice. We live in an uncertain world with limited knowledge of future cash flows. Expectations as to these future flows vary among those individuals related to the company. With limited knowledge of the future, what should be accepted as the appropriate discount rates to apply to cash flows in arriving at asset values? Because of these uncertainties the accountant has turned to more direct ways of defining income.

The matching (direct) method of income determination

The method of income determination that has proved most acceptable to the accountant has been the *matching method*, or *direct method*. The matching method involves the determination of the amount of revenue that has been earned by an entity during a given period and the amount of expired costs that are applicable to that revenue. The difference between these two items is recognized as *net income*. If users were willing to wait until the end of the life of a business unit for the full results of its operations, it would be an easy matter to compute the total revenue and total expense of the business and the resulting net income or net loss. However, users of the income statement, seeking to judge the progess of an entity, need periodic measurements of business profitability. In fact, users seem increasingly interested in receiving financial statements more frequently than at the traditional annual intervals. Interim statements are being provided by an ever increasing number of companies. Thus, the element of timing, both for revenue and expense, becomes ever more significant. Rather than concentrating on asset valuations, the center of attention is thus transferred to a discussion of *revenue realization* and *expense recognition*. It should be recognized, however, that because the financial statements are fundamentally interrelated, the point in time at which revenues and expenses are recognized is also the time when changes in amounts of net assets are recognized.[1]

Nature of revenue.   The Accounting Principles Board defines *revenue* as:

> ... gross increases in assets or gross decreases in liabilities recognized and measured in conformity with generally accepted accounting principles that result from those types of profit-directed activities of an enterprise that can change owners' equity.

Revenue, in the view of the APB, is derived from three general activities:

1. Selling products.
2. Rendering services and permitting others to use enterprise resources, which result in interest, rent, royalties, fees, and the like.
3. Disposing of resources other than products — for example, plant and equipment or investments in other entities.[2]

Revenue, as defined by the APB, does not include assets acquired by purchase, proceeds from borrowing, investment by owners, or adjustments of revenue of prior periods.

Although this description of revenue defines the activities that produce revenue, it does not specify the time period in which the revenue should be recorded and recognized in the income statement. A general realization rule has evolved which states that revenue should be recorded when two conditions are met: (1) the earning process is complete or virtually so, and (2) an exchange has taken place. This rule has led to the conventional recognition of revenue at a specific point in the earnings process — when assets are sold or services are rendered.[3] However, there are sufficient deviations from the general rule to justify a closer look into the nature of revenue.

The first type of activity described by the APB as producing revenue is the sale of products. The cycle of revenue-producing goods as it passes through an entity can be a long one. The beginning point is not well defined, but let it be assumed that it begins with the development of proposals for a certain product by an individual or by the research and development department of a business unit. From the idea stage, the future product is carefully described in plans and engineering specifications. Bills of material are prepared, a production schedule is agreed upon, and raw materials are ordered, delivered, and placed into production. Labor and factory overhead are added to the raw materials as the product proceeds through the manufacturing process. Once com-

---

[1]This interrelatedness is recognized and described in *Statements of the Accounting Principles Board, No. 4, op. cit.*, par. 136 and 147.
[2]*Ibid.*, par. 134 and 148.
[3]*Ibid.*, par. 150 and 151.

pleted, the product is transferred to the finished goods warehouse. The product is listed in company catalogs, it is promoted in advertising campaigns, and it moves through the company's distribution system to the final sale. Frequently sales are on a credit basis, and after a period of time collections are made on the accounts. The product may be sold with a warranty for necessary repairs or replacements. The cycle thus extends from the original idea to the end of the warranty period. All of these steps are involved in the realization of the sales revenue. If there is a failure at any step, revenue may be seriously curtailed or possibly completely eliminated. And yet, there is only one aggregate revenue amount for the entire cycle, the sale price of the goods. The question then is: When should revenue be recognized?

Answers to the question of when revenue should be recognized can be divided into two broad categories: (1) at one specific point in the cycle, or (2) at two or more points in the cycle.[1] The prevailing practice provides for recognition of revenue at one specific point in the cycle. Of course, determining the specific point presents a problem. Applying the previously mentioned guidelines, revenue from sale of products is recognized at the *point of sale*, usually interpreted to mean the time of delivery to customers. It is felt that prior to the sale, there has not been an arm's-length determination of the market value of the goods. This makes any objective measure of revenue subject to dispute. In addition, most businessmen feel that the critical event is the sale of an item, and that the earning process is not complete until the sales commitment has been substantially fulfilled. The same guidelines dictate that revenue from services is recognized *when services have been performed and are billable*, and that revenue from permitting others to use enterprise resources is recognized *as resources are used* or *as time passes*.

There are two notable exceptions to the general rule. One exception to the rule of recognition of revenue at the point of sale is found, for example, when market values are firmly established and the marketability of a given product is assured. Revenue in such instances is recognized at the *point of completed production*. Examples of products that meet these criteria are certain precious metals and farm products with assured sales prices. In other instances, when uncertainty exists as to the collectibility of a receivable arising from the sale of goods or services, recognition of revenue may be deferred to the *point of actual cash collection*. The *installment sales method* of accounting is an example of the application of this practice. Although the installment sales method of deferring

---

[1]This subject was considered by a special AAA Committee on Realization which was established in 1964 and published its conclusions in 1966. Some of their comments on point of revenue realization are included in this section. *Accounting Review* (Evanston, Illinois: American Accounting Association, April 1965), pp. 312-322.

revenue beyond the point of sale is accepted as an alternate method for purposes of income taxation, it is not generally accepted for financial statement purposes "unless the circumstances are such that the collection of the sale price is not reasonably assured."[1]

The second exception is found when revenue is recognized at two or more points in the cycle. Although conceptually one can maintain that revenue is being earned continuously throughout the cycle, the measurement of revenue under such a concept may become impractical. It also raises special questions, such as: Should revenue of an equal amount be assigned to each phase of the cycle? Or should revenue be recognized in proportion to the costs incurred in each phase of the cycle? In certain cases, however, the production phase of the cycle carries over more than one accounting period and some allocation of revenue over the period is considered essential to meaningful statements. Construction contracts for buildings, roads, and dams that may take several periods to complete are often of this nature. The *percentage-of-completion* method of accounting for inventory values is used to meet these special conditions. This method requires a firm contract of sale prior to construction and an ability to estimate with reasonable accuracy the costs remaining to be incurred on the project. Portions of the total estimated revenue are recognized as the project progresses.

Thus revenue recognition occurs at certain specifically defined points in the revenue-producing cycle. Prior to these points, all valuations are stated in terms of cost. After these points, use is made of *estimated* or *actual realizable values*. Discussion will certainly continue within the accounting profession as to the validity and acceptability of alternative points of revenue recognition. However, regardless of the point of revenue selected, the relationship that has been defined between revenue and expenses will still hold.

Nature of expenses. The Accounting Principles Board defines *expenses* as:

. . . gross decreases in assets or gross increases in liabilities recognized and measured in conformity with generally accepted accounting principles that result from those types of profit-directed activities of an enterprise that can change owners' equity.

The APB states further that expenses are:

. . . costs that are associated with the revenue of the period, often directly but frequently indirectly through association with the period to which the revenue has been assigned.

---

[1]*Opinions of the Accounting Principles Board*, *No. 10*, "Omnibus Opinion — 1966" (New York: American Institute of Certified Public Accountants, 1967), par. 12.

Costs, then, are either associated with past revenues and charged to retained earnings as prior period adjustments, or associated with current revenues and reported as expenses. Expenses are classified in Statement No. 4 as follows:

1. Costs directly associated with the revenue of the period.
2. Costs associated with the period on some basis other than a direct relationship with revenue (such as time, for example).
3. Costs that cannot, as a practical matter, be associated with any other period.[1]

The Accounting Principles Board uses the terminology of *gains* and *losses* to refer to the results of transactions that involve revenue and expenses from other than sales of product, merchandise, or service. Expenses, as defined by the APB, do not include repayments of borrowing, expenditures to acquire assets, distributions to owners (including the acquisition of treasury stock), or corrections of expenses of prior periods. The terms revenue and expenses will be used in this text in the manner in which they are defined by the Board.

A primary difficulty in income determination is the decision as to how various expenses are, in fact, to be associated with revenues. It has not been possible to prescribe exact rules for *association*, or *matching*.[2] Certain guidelines for the recognition of expenses to be deducted from revenues in arriving at net income or loss have evolved through time. When the accountant is faced with an absence of guidelines, he will have to exercise judgment. The APB defines three expense recognition principles as being of special significance: (1) *associating cause and effect*, (2) *systematic and rational allocation*, and (3) *immediate recognition*.[3]

Associating cause and effect. Some costs can be associated directly with specific revenue. When this association is possible, the cost is recognized as an expense of the period in which the revenue is recognized. Thus, if an inventory item on hand at the end of a period represents a source of future revenue under the point of sale principle, the cost of producing the item is deferred to a future period and it is reported as an asset. Certain costs, such as labor and materials, can be directly related to the cost of producing the inventory item. Other costs, such as manufacturing overhead, may be assumed to be associated with an inventory item on some logical basis such as the number of labor hours or the number of machine hours required to produce the item. Judgment

---

[1]*Statements of the Accounting Principles Board, No. 4, op. cit.*, par. 135 and 155.

[2]Recent APB pronouncements have been more specific in establishing guidelines for making these associations. Critics of this trend have stated their fear that accounting may become a set of rigid rules if such a trend continues.

[3]*Statements of the Accounting Principles Board, No. 4, op. cit.*, par. 157–160.

plays an increasingly more important part as the association becomes less direct.

Care must be taken to assure that proper recognition is made of all costs already incurred, as well as those yet to be incurred relative to any revenue currently recognized.

Systematic and rational allocation. In the absence of a direct cause and effect relationship, a different basis for expense recognition is commonly used. Here the attempt is made to associate costs in a systematic and rational manner with the periods that are benefitted. In arriving at such expense recognition, estimates must be made of the timing pattern of the benefits that are received from the individual costs and systematic allocation methods developed. The methods that are adopted should appear reasonable to an unbiased observer and should be followed consistently.

Some of the costs allocated to a period become immediate expenses and are associated with current revenue. Other costs "attach" to inventories and other similar assets on some logical basis, and thus are associated with future revenue by being deferred as assets. Examples of costs that are associated with periods in a systematic way include costs of buildings and equipment, patents, insurance, and taxes.

Immediate recognition. Those costs that cannot be related to revenue either by associating cause and effect or by systematic and rational allocation, must be recognized as expenses of the current period or written off as prior period adjustments. Because of specific restrictions on the classes of items that qualify as prior period adjustments, most of the asset balances or costs currently incurred are recognized as expenses in the period when no discernible future revenues can be associated with them, and their deferral cannot be supported.

Effects of changing price levels

Thus far, reference has been made to the use of historical cost association. There is nothing in income determination that requires that historical costs be used. When current costs of replacement of goods and services that are in resources and commitments of the entity differ from historical transaction-based costs, such current costs could be matched against currently generated revenues. This approach was suggested by Sprouse and Moonitz in Accounting Research Study No. 3 and was also implicit in the recommendations of the American Accounting Association in their *Statement of Basic Accounting Theory.* In the latter publication, the study committee advocated the use of multi-valued statements; both the balance sheet and the income statement would show in one column historical costs, and in a second column, current costs. When it is maintained that the primary purpose of the income statement is to enable the user to predict future income, it would follow that current costs will more closely suggest the costs that will be experienced in the future.

Although there has been increasing discussion of the use of current costs, accountants generally do not appear ready to move away from the more secure and objective historical cost structure.

One of the principal causes of deviation between historical and current costs in the United States is the steady decline in the value of the dollar. As indicated in Chapter 1, accountants operate on the "as if" assumption. They account for activities as if the value of the dollar were stable. To the extent that this assumption is not valid, effects will be far reaching on all financial statements. Particular care will be necessary in interpreting comparative statements. When price levels have been changing, for example, income statements comparing operations for several years may lead to conclusions that are inaccurate; reported sales increases may, in real terms, represent decreases.

The question of price-level changes has been discussed by accountants for many decades. In some countries adjustments are regularly made on the financial statements to reflect changes in the *general price index*. Such adjustments are applied to historical costs, and therefore are not necessarily measures of current cost. The staff of the research division of the AICPA has studied this issue carefully and in 1963 issued Accounting Research Study No. 6. In this study they recommended that supplementary statements should be used to reflect the effects of the changing price levels. The Accounting Principles Board in Statement No. 3 issued in 1969 indicated their full support for this position. As yet, however, there has been very little acceptance of this recommendation in published annual reports.

Special problems in the preparation of the income statement

The importance of the revenue-expense relationships and the significance that attaches to the earnings and earnings power of the entity for the user of the income statement have been described in the first part of this chapter. In view of the importance attached to these matters, the question continually arises: How can these matters be expressed on the income statement in the most informative and useful form?

For many years a great deal of attention has been applied to the answers to two broad questions:

(1) What concepts should be applied to income reporting? Should income reporting recognize all transactions affecting the owners' equity

with the exception of dividends and transactions between the entity and its owners, or should income reporting also exclude transactions that would impair the net income figure as an indicator of current earnings from operations and future earnings power?

(2) What concepts should be applied to the recognition of income taxes? Should income taxes expense be recognized as a single charge against earnings, or should it be identified with the several classifications that are recognized for the period — income before extraordinary items, extraordinary items, and prior period adjustments? Furthermore, should income taxes be reported at the amount actually payable for the period, or should taxes be recognized at an amount other than that payable when there are timing differences that occur in reporting income on the financial statements and on the income tax return?

Current operating performance and all-inclusive reporting. The presentation of *extraordinary gains and losses* has been the subject of much controversy through the years. It was not until 1966 that the statement presentation of extraordinary items was specifically defined by the Accounting Principles Board. In Opinion No. 9, the APB went on record as clearly favoring the preparation of an income statement that included extraordinary items. Prior to this opinion, there were two generally accepted forms that could be used for the income statement, and the selection of the form was determined by the manner in which the business unit preferred to recognize extraordinary items. One form, referred to as the *current operating performance statement*, provided for reporting that was limited to normal and recurring operating items; extraordinary and nonrecurring items were recorded directly in retained earnings and reported on an accompanying statement that summarized all of the changes in the owners' equity for the period. An alternate form, known as the *all-inclusive income statement*, provided for the presentation of extraordinary items on the face of the income statement after reporting the normal operating items. In employing the first form, the final amount was generally designated "net income"; in the second form, the final amount was designated by some as "net income," by others as "net income and extraordinary items." Because both of these income statement forms were being used in practice, there was a lack of consistency in reporting by different enterprises, and there was a real danger of misinterpretation of the results of operations by statement users.

The current operating performance statement. The current operating performance statement found its support in the following arguments:

(1) The income statement should show as clearly as possible what the company was able to earn under normal conditions for the period so

that sound comparisons can be made with similar summaries for prior periods as well as with summaries of other companies.

(2) Use of the all-inclusive statement may result in misleading inferences as to the level of sustained earning power since many persons reading the statement may be unable to eliminate those items that distort operating results. The reader, unfamiliar with the full story behind the items indicated, is less qualified than the accountant to determine what items should be rejected in measuring the basic earning power of the enterprise.

The American Institute of Certified Public Accountants had issued a number of pronouncements on the manner of reporting extraordinary items prior to APB Opinion No. 9. In Bulletin No. 43, the Committee on Accounting Procedure had defined net income and had suggested standards for the determination of extraordinary items to be excluded from net income as follows:

> . . . it is the opinion of the committee that there should be a general presumption that all items of profit and loss recognized during the period are to be used in determining the figure reported as net income. The only possible exception to this presumption relates to items which in the aggregate are material in relation to the company's net income and are clearly not identifiable with or do not result from the usual or typical business operations of the period.[1]

In recommending the exclusion of extraordinary items in reporting net income, the Committee also expressed a strong preference for reporting these on the retained earnings statement rather than on the income statement. The Committee was of the opinion that even when the latter are listed in a separate section following a net income determination on the income statement, misconceptions might arise as to whether the earnings for the period are represented by the amount actually designated as net income or by the final and often more prominent amount reported after recognition of the extraordinary items. When reporting is to take the all-inclusive form, the Committee cautioned that special care be taken to report clearly and unequivocally the net income figure and to describe precisely the final figure on the statement for what it represents, for example, "net income and special items," "net loss and special items," or "profit on sale of subsidiary less net loss."[2]

---

[1]*Accounting Research Bulletin No. 43*, "Restatement and Revision of Accounting Research Bulletins" (New York: American Institute of Certified Public Accountants, 1953), Ch. 8, par. 11.

[2]*Ibid.*, par. 13. It may be observed that the Committee on Accounting Procedure in 1948 had recommended that the income statement be prepared in "current operating performance" form. However, this stand was modified and the "all-inclusive" form was termed "acceptable" in 1951, after the Securities and Exchange Commission in its revised Regulations S-X ruled that items of profit and loss given recognition in the accounts during a period but not included in the determination of net income or loss be reported as additions to or deductions from such net income or loss on the income statement.

The all-inclusive statement. Those supporting the all-inclusive statement offered the following arguments in support of their position:

(1) A statement purporting to show operating results for a fiscal period should provide the full story of activities so that annual statements since the start of the enterprise will offer the total income history for the life of the enterprise. Whether gain or loss is the product of one year or of several years, it deserves recognition on the income statement so that the total business and management performance may be evaluated. The all-inclusive statement is simple to prepare, is not subject to variations in judgment as to treatment of special items, is easy to understand and less subject to misunderstandings, and can be accepted with confidence as a complete report of the administration of business properties.

(2) The current operating performance statement carries with it a number of difficulties and dangers:

a. The reader of financial statements untrained in accounting may be unaware of the fact that an income statement can be prepared in a manner incomplete as to activities of the period, and by failing to analyze the change in retained earnings will not have a full appreciation of current activities as well as the long-run earning capacity of the enterprise.

b. Permitting the omission of extraordinary items opens the doors to possible manipulation of current earnings by burying significant information in retained earnings.

c. Use of distortion as a criterion for the omission of items means the adoption of standards for normalizing income rather than measuring income.

d. Differences in judgment will be found in the treatment of borderline cases.

e. The presentation of earnings data in this form carries with it implications as to future earnings. However, the past is only of limited help in forecasting; furthermore, unusual events are a part of the past and should be considered in arriving at estimates concerning the future.

Present recommended practices. The Accounting Principles Board in 1966 in Opinion No. 9 recommended important changes toward the all-inclusive concept of income reporting. Ordinary operations, as well as extraordinary items, are to be presented on the income statement. Income before extraordinary items is reported as a separate total within the body of the statement. The last line of the statement that reports the sum of ordinary operations and extraordinary items is to be designated "net income."

The APB recognized that the distinction between ordinary operating items and extraordinary items will require the use of judgment by the accountant. However, to assist the accountant in making the distinction, the Board indicated that if an item is to qualify as extraordinary, (1) it should be of a character significantly different from the typical or customary business activities of an entity, (2) it would not be expected to recur frequently and would not be considered as a recurring factor in any evaluation of the ordinary operating processes of the business, and (3) it would be material in relation to operating results.

The Board offers examples of extraordinary items, assuming that they qualify under the criteria above. These are:

1. The sale or abandonment of a plant or a significant segment of the business.
2. The sale of an investment not acquired for resale.
3. The write-off of goodwill due to unusual events or developments within the period.
4. The condemnation or expropriation of properties.
5. A major devaluation of a foreign currency.[1]

The Board also includes examples of items that would not be considered extraordinary but which would be included in the normal operating results regardless of size.

1. Write-downs of receivables, inventories, and research and development costs.
2. Adjustments of accrued contract prices.
3. Gains or losses from fluctuations of foreign exchange.[2]

Prior period adjustments have also been the subject of much discussion in connection with the current operating performance and all-inclusive approaches. Prior period adjustments were usually handled in the same manner as extraordinary items and reported either in the retained earnings statement or in the income statement. In Opinion No. 9 the Board sets up specific criteria for the recognition of items as prior period adjustments and provides that only adjustments that meet these criteria may be excluded from the determination of net income and reported as direct changes in owners' equity accounts. Prior period adjustments are limited to those material adjustments that:

1. Can be specifically identified with business activities of a prior period, and
2. Are not attributable to economic events occurring subsequent to the date of the financial statements for the prior period, and
3. Are determined primarily by persons other than management, and
4. Were not susceptible of reasonable estimation prior to their final determination.[3]

In addition to stating the above criteria which must be present before an item is considered an adjustment of a prior period, the Board includes some examples of items that are included within the criteria and some that are not.

---

[1] *Opinions of the Accounting Principles Board, No. 9,* "Reporting the Results of Operations" (New York: American Institute of Certified Public Accountants, 1966), par. 21.

[2] *Ibid.,* par. 22.

[3] *Ibid.,* par. 23.

Examples of items that meet prior period adjustment criteria and thus are excluded from net income are:

1. Material, nonrecurring adjustments or settlements of income taxes, of renegotiation proceedings, or of utility revenue under rate processes.
2. Settlements of significant amounts resulting from litigation or similar claims.

In most cases involving such adjustment, the opinion of the reporting auditor would probably have been qualified in the prior period because of uncertainty.

Examples of items that do not meet the prior period adjustment criteria are:

1. Changes in estimated remaining lives of fixed assets.
2. Relatively immaterial adjustments of provisions for liabilities (including income taxes).
3. Adjustments related to realization of assets, for example, the collectibility of accounts receivable, the ultimate recovery of deferred charges, or the realizability of inventory arising from economic events occurring subsequent to the date of the financial statements for the prior period.[1]

Accounting changes. In Opinion No. 9, the Board did not answer certain questions concerning the manner of reporting a change in accounting principle or accounting estimate or the manner of reporting the correction of an error in previously issued financial statements. A key question involved in reporting changes is whether the effects of the change should be applied retroactively, currently, or prospectively. If retroactive treatment is followed, the change may be reported either by restating financial statements of prior periods or by reporting the full effect of the change as a special cumulative item in the current income statement. The restatement of prior period financial statements for some changes is frequently difficult, if not impossible, because of the unavailability of data. In addition, a policy of restating prior period statements may confuse the reader and may also erode his confidence in financial statements. On the other hand, if the effects of the change are reported currently and prospectively, trend summaries of operations and other analytical computations could be misleading to statement users.

In 1971, in Opinion No. 20 on accounting changes, the Board gave a full statement of its position on these matters and provided guidelines for the reporting procedures to be employed in each instance.

Change in accounting principle. There will be occasions when a company will adopt a generally accepted accounting principle that is different from the one used previously. The term "accounting principle"

---

[1]*Ibid.*, par. 24.

includes not only principles and practices but also the methods of apply-ing them. The following are specifically named as examples of such changes: a change in the method of inventory pricing, such as from the last-in, first-out method to the first-in, first-out method; a change in the method of depreciation for previously recorded assets, such as from the double-declining-balance method to the straight-line method; a change in the method of accounting for long-term construction contracts, such as from the completed-contract method to the percentage-of-completion method; a change in accounting for research and development expendi-tures, such as from recording these as expense when incurred to deferring these and amortizing the cost.

The Board states that there is the presumption that an accounting principle once adopted should not be changed in recording events and transactions of a similar type. Consistent application of accounting principles is important to the user of financial statements in the satis-factory analysis and evaluation of comparative data. The presumption of use of the same principle may be overcome, however, if the use of an alternate principle can be supported as preferable. The Board comments,

> ... The issuance of an Opinion of the Accounting Principles Board that creates a new accounting principle, that expresses a preference for an accounting principle, or that rejects a specific accounting principle is sufficient support for a change in accounting principle. The burden of justifying other changes rests with the entity proposing the change.[1]

When a change in principle can be supported, the Board generally takes the position that the effect of the change should be included in net income of the period in which the change is made. Assets and liabilities as of the beginning of the period would be restated to report the balances that would be found if the new principle had been applied in past periods; the accompanying charge or credit recognizing the cumulative effect of such change in principle upon past earnings would be recorded separately and reported on the income statement for the current period following "extraordinary items." Other revenue and expense balances for the period would be reported on the basis of the newly adopted principle.[2]

---

[1]*Opinions of the Accounting Principles Board, No. 20,* "Accounting Changes" (New York: American Institute of Certified Public Accountants, 1971), par. 16.

[2]The Board specifies that in a few instances of accounting principle change, "the advan-tages of retroactive treatment in prior period reports outweigh the disadvantages." Accord-ingly, in these instances, the Board concludes, the change in net assets should be accompanied by a charge or credit directly to the owners' equity. The changes that are to be accorded this special treatment are limited to (1) a change from the last-in, first-out method of inventory pricing to another method, (2) a change in the method of accounting for long-term construc-tion-type contracts, and (3) a change to or from the "full cost" method of accounting that is used in the extractive industries. *Ibid.,* par. 27.

Change in accounting estimate. Accounting Principles Board Opinion No. 20 recognizes that changes in accounting estimates are necessary consequences of the periodic financial presentations. Judgments relative to future events and their effects may require modification as additional experience or more information is gained. Changes in estimates, as previously concluded in APB Opinion No. 9, should be recognized in the current and subsequent periods. A change in the method of depreciation of an asset, for example, would be treated as a change in accounting principle; a change in the estimated remaining life of an asset would call for a change in current and subsequent charges for depreciation. Although a change in an estimate does not require the restatement of the account balances, a description on the income statement of the change and its effect upon income and earnings per share should generally be provided.[1]

Correction of errors in prior period financial statements. The Board recognizes that there will be occasions when account balances will require correction as a result of the discovery of errors that were made in previously issued statements. Such errors may arise from mathematical mistakes, the misuse or omission of certain data, mistakes in the application of accounting principles as well as failures to apply generally accepted principles. When a correction of an error made in the past is required, the Board takes the position that the effect of such change should be reported as a prior period adjustment. Assets and liabilities as of the beginning of the period, then, would be restated to corrected balances; the accompanying charge or credit recognizing the cumulative effect of such error upon past earnings would be reported directly in the owners' equity.[2]

Recognition of an item as a prior period adjustment indicates that prior period statements used for comparative reporting require restatement in terms of the information currently available. In view of the qualifications that are applied in defining items as prior period adjustments in Opinions No. 9 and No. 20, such adjustments are expected to be rare. This, of course, is the objective of the Board who seek to avoid the dilution of public confidence resulting from the restatement of financial statements of prior periods.

Allocation of income tax expense. Earnings of the corporation are generally subject to federal, state, and local income taxes. At one time it was considered acceptable practice to report income tax expense as a

---

[1]*Ibid.*, par. 31–33.
[2]*Ibid.*, par. 36–37.

single charge against earnings, and to report taxes at the amount actually payable. Both of these concepts have been challenged, and significant changes in such procedures have been recognized.

Intraperiod tax allocation. Current practice requires that income tax expense be allocated and assigned to income from ordinary operations and to amounts reported as extraordinary items and as prior period adjustments. The results of normal activities, extraordinary items, and prior period adjustments together with the income tax consequences related to each of these can then be clearly reported. This concept is referred to as *intraperiod tax allocation.*

In APB Opinion No. 11, the Board observed,

> ... The income tax expense attributable to income before extraordinary items is computed by determining the income tax expense related to revenue and expense transactions entering into the determination of such income, without giving effect to the tax consequences of the items excluded from the determination of income before extraordinary items. The income tax expense attributable to other items is determined by the tax consequences of transactions involving these items.[1]

It should be observed that in applying these concepts, when either ordinary or extraordinary items result in a loss, thus serving to reduce the taxes that would otherwise be payable, tax allocation is still required if the two types of activities are to be satisfactorily presented and evaluated. However, allocation here involves the assignment of a tax charge that is larger than the actual tax payment to the positive balance accompanied by a tax credit counterbalancing the excessive tax charge to the negative balance. Favorable activities of the period, then, carry their normal tax burden; unfavorable activities which served to reduce the taxes that otherwise would have been payable are summarized in terms of their net effect upon the owners' equity.

Interperiod tax allocation. Current practice also provides that adjustments be made to the charge for income taxes when there are timing differences between book income and taxable income. Some differences arise because certain revenue items are not taxable and certain expense items are not deductible for tax purposes. These differences are permanent ones and the resulting tax advantage or disadvantage is likewise permanent. Other differences, however, are timing differences — differences arising because the periods in which revenue and expense items are recognized on the books are not the same as the periods in which these items are recognized on the tax return. Because of the generally

---

[1]*Opinions of the Accounting Principles Board, No. 11,* "Accounting for Income Taxes" (New York: American Institute of Certified Public Accounts, 1967), par. 52.

accepted view that income taxes are an expense of doing business and not a division of net income, the Accounting Principles Board has stated that the appropriate matching of revenues and expenses requires the application of *interperiod tax allocation* procedures. APB Opinion No. 11 states:

> Interperiod tax allocation is an integral part of the determination of income tax expense, and income tax expense should include the tax effects of revenue and expense transactions included in the determination of pretax accounting income.[1]

Interperiod tax allocation procedures call for the adjustment of the income tax expense balance to the amount applicable to book income. Charges or credits are made to the expense account accompanied by entries to Deferred Income Taxes Expense or to Deferred Income Taxes Payable. The nature of timing differences and the entries that are required in recording the interperiod allocation of income taxes are described and illustrated in the next chapter.

Content of the income statement

The income statement as currently presented in practice generally consists of a series of sections that develop the net income for the period. Such sections include (1) revenue from the sale of goods and services, (2) cost of goods sold and expenses of providing services, (3) operating expenses, (4) other revenue and expense items, (5) income taxes relative to income before extraordinary items, and (6) extraordinary gains and losses net of income taxes. In the income statement for the corporation, the summary of net income is followed by a special presentation of earnings per share for the period on the residual equity, common stock, computed on the basis of the data that are reported on the income statement.

Sales. *Revenue from sales* reports the total sales to customers for the period. This total should not include additions to billings for sales and excise taxes that the business is required to collect on behalf of the government. Such billing increases are properly recognized as a current liability. Sales returns and allowances and sales discount should be subtracted from gross sales in arriving at net sales revenue. When the sales price is increased to cover the cost of freight to the customer and the customer is billed accordingly, freight charges paid by the company should also be subtracted from sales in arriving at net sales. Freight charges that are not absorbed by the buyer are recognized as selling expenses.

Cost of goods sold. When merchandise is acquired from outsiders, the cost of goods relating to sales of the period must be determined. *Cost*

---

[1] *Ibid.*, par. 12a.

of merchandise available for sale is first determined. This is the sum of the beginning inventory, purchases, and all other buying, freight, and storage costs relating to the acquisition of goods. A net purchases balance is developed by subtracting purchases returns and allowances and purchases discount from gross purchases. *Cost of goods sold* is calculated by subtracting the ending inventory from the cost of merchandise available for sale.

When the goods are manufactured by the seller, the *cost of goods manufactured* must first be calculated. Cost of goods manufactured replaces purchases in the summary just described. The determination of cost of goods manufactured begins with the cost of goods in process at the beginning of the period. To this is added the cost of materials put into production, the cost of labor applied to material conversions, and all of the other costs for services and facilities utilized in manufacturing, including factory superintendence, indirect labor, depreciation and other costs relating to factory buildings and equipment, factory supplies used, patent amortization, and factory light, heat, and power. The total thus obtained represents the cost of goods completed and goods still in production. The goods in process inventory at the end of the period is subtracted from this total in arriving at the cost of the goods finished and made available for sale.

Operating expenses. *Operating expenses* are generally reported in two categories: (1) selling expenses and (2) general and administrative expenses. Selling expenses include such items as sales salaries and commissions and related payroll taxes, advertising and store displays, store supplies used, depreciation of store furniture and equipment, and delivery expenses. General and administrative expenses include officers and office salaries and related payroll taxes, office supplies used, depreciation of office furniture and fixtures, telephone, postage, business licenses and fees, legal and accounting services, contributions, and similar items. Charges related to the use of buildings, such as rent, depreciation, taxes, insurance, light, heat, and power, should be allocated in some equitable manner to manufacturing activities and to selling and general and administrative activities. In the case of the merchandising concern, charges relating to buildings are generally reported in full in the general and administrative category.

Other revenue and expense items. Other revenue and expense items include items identified with financial management and other miscellaneous recurring items not related to the central operations. Other revenue includes earnings in the form of interest and dividends, and miscellaneous earnings from rentals, royalties, and service fees. Other expense includes interest expense and other expenses related to the miscellaneous revenue items reported.

Income taxes relative to income before extraordinary items. The income tax expense should report the taxes on revenue and expense transactions that are included in the computation of pretax income. This will require application of the income tax allocation procedures described earlier. In reporting the taxes, the components that are included in their determination should be disclosed. Parenthetical remarks or notes in the income statement may be considered appropriate in defining the nature and purpose of the allocations.

Extraordinary gains and losses net of income taxes. Any items that qualify as extraordinary gains and losses are listed in this section. These items are adjusted for income taxes as determined by the allocations described earlier.

Form of the income statement

The income statement traditionally has been prepared in either *multiple-step* or *single-step* form. An example of the income statement in multiple-step form is presented on page 81 and in single-step form on page 82. In each case, the presentation is made in accordance with the recommendations in APB Opinions No. 9 and No. 11. In the multiple-step form, the ordinary operations are first summarized and designated as income before extraordinary items; this is followed by a listing of the extraordinary items. Revenue and expense items are grouped to provide different income measurements as follows:

1. *Gross profit on sales* (or *gross margin*) — the difference between sales and the costs directly related to such sales.
2. *Operating income* — gross profit on sales less operating expenses.
3. *Income before income taxes* — operating income increased by other revenue items and decreased by other expense items.
4. *Income before extraordinary items* — income less the income taxes applicable to ordinary income.
5. *Net income* — income before extraordinary items plus or minus extraordinary items and applicable income taxes.
6. *Earnings per common share* — the presentation of earnings per common share in terms of income before extraordinary items, extraordinary items, and net income.[1]

The single-step form as described in APB Opinion No. 9 is in reality a modified single-step form because of the required separation of ordinary

---

[1]APB Opinion No. 15 calls for the presentation of earnings per common share data on the face of the income statement. If dilution of earnings is possible because of the existence of convertible securities or stock options or warrants, separate earnings figures disclosing potential dilution must also be shown. This subject is discussed in detail in Chapter 22.

Anderson Corporation
Income Statement
For Year Ended December 31, 1972

Revenue from sales:			
Sales..		$510,000	
Less: Sales returns and allowances..................	$ 7,500		
Sales discount..............................	2,500	10,000	$500,000
Cost of goods sold:			
Merchandise inventory, January 1, 1972.............		$ 95,000	
Purchases....................................	$320,000		
Freight in....................................	15,000		
Delivered cost of purchases.......................	$335,000		
Less: Purchases returns and allowances..... $1,000			
Purchases discount............... 4,000	5,000	330,000	
Merchandise available for sale......................		$425,000	
Less merchandise inventory, December 31, 1972.......		125,000	300,000
Gross profit on sales................................			$200,000
Operating expenses:			
Selling expenses:			
Sales salaries.................................	$ 30,000		
Advertising expense	15,000		
Depreciation expense — selling and delivery equip....	5,000		
Miscellaneous selling expense....................	10,000	$ 60,000	
General and administrative expenses:			
Officers and office salaries.......................	$ 48,000		
Taxes and insurance...........................	20,000		
Miscellaneous supplies expense...................	5,000		
Depreciation expense — office furniture and fixtures..	5,000		
Doubtful accounts expense.......................	2,500		
Miscellaneous general expense...................	15,000	95,500	155,500
Operating income................................			$ 44,500
Other revenue and expense items:			
Interest income................................	$ 3,000		
Dividend income...............................	10,000	$ 13,000	
Interest expense................................		7,500	5,500
Income before income taxes........................			$ 50,000
Income taxes:			
Current tax charge, $27,000 less $5,000 applicable to gain			
on sale of investments reported below.............		$ 22,000	
Tax charge arising from timing difference in computing			
depreciation.................................		3,000	25,000
Income before extraordinary items....................			$ 25,000
Extraordinary items:			
Gain on sale of investments.......................		$ 20,000	
Less applicable income taxes......................		5,000	15,000
Net income.......................................			$ 40,000
Earnings per common share:			
Income before extraordinary items..................			$ .50
Extraordinary items.............................			.30
Net income.......................................			$ .80

Multiple-step income statement

Anderson Corporation
Income Statement
For Year Ended December 31, 1972

Revenues:		
Net sales..	$500,000	
Other revenue — interest and dividends........................	13,000	$513,000
Expenses:		
Cost of goods sold...	$300,000	
Selling expense..	60,000	
General and administrative expense............................	95,500	
Interest expense...	7,500	
Income taxes (including deferred taxes of $3,000)..............	25,000	488,000
Income before extraordinary items................................		$ 25,000
Extraordinary gain on sale of investments (net of income taxes of $5,000)		15,000
Net income...		$ 40,000
Earnings per common share:		
Income before extraordinary items............................		$ .50
Extraordinary income...		.30
Net income..		$ .80

Single-step income statement

and extraordinary items. However, as illustrated, all ordinary revenue items and expense items are listed and summarized without separate headings for cost of goods sold, gross profit, and other revenue and expense items.

Many accountants have raised objections to the multiple-step income statement form. They point out that the various income designations have no universal meaning and may prove a source of confusion to the reader. Quoting such designations in the absence of a complete income statement may prove ambiguous or actually misleading. They further maintain that multiple-step presentation implies certain cost priorities and an order for cost recoveries. But there is no such order and there can be no earnings unless all costs are recovered. These persons support the single-step form that minimizes sectional labeling. The single-step form has won wide adoption in recent years.

The income statement is frequently prepared in condensed form and simply reports totals for certain classes of items, such as cost of goods sold, selling expenses, general expenses, other revenue and expense, and extraordinary items. This was done in the single-step statement above. Additional detail may be provided by the use of supporting schedules.

It may be observed that the use of condensed income statements by large units engaged in a number of diversified activities has been severely criticized recently by the Securities and Exchange Commission and many investment analysts. There have been a great number of mergers of large enterprises in recent years, with a large diversity of products and services provided by each unit. Income statements prepared in condensed form may tend to disguise the important trends operating within the individual segments of the conglomerate. In a special study conducted for the Financial Executives Institute in 1967–68, Professor Robert K. Mautz recommended that divisionalized income statement reporting be required when the operations of a segment of a corporate entity accounted for more than 15 percent of the total business of the entity. The SEC accepted this recommendation but reduced the percentage to 10 percent. In an advisory statement in 1967, the Accounting Principles Board urged diversified companies to review carefully their various operations and to consider reporting revenue, expenses, and earnings by separable industry segments. Some voluntary movement toward more operating detail is beginning to be made.

When goods are manufactured by the seller, the cost of the goods manufactured must be determined before the cost of goods sold can be computed. If a summary of cost of goods manufactured is to accompany the financial statements, it should be presented as a schedule in support of the amount reported on the income statement. Assuming that the merchandise available for sale in the example on page 81 was obtained by manufacture rather than by purchase, cost of goods sold on the income statement would be presented as shown below. The supporting schedule is shown on page 84.

Cost of goods sold:
Finished goods inventory, January 1, 1972......................	$ 40,000	
Add cost of goods manufactured per manufacturing schedule......	310,000	
Merchandise available for sale................................	$350,000	
Less finished goods inventory, December 31, 1972...............	50,000	$300,000

Frequently only the cost of goods sold is reported on the income statement. If a schedule of the cost of goods sold is to be provided, it should summarize the cost of goods manufactured as well as the change in finished goods inventories. Instead of reporting beginning and ending inventories, it is possible simply to report inventory variations for the period in arriving at the cost of materials used, cost of goods manufactured, or cost of goods sold. For example, an increase in the finished goods inventory would be subtracted from the cost of goods manufactured in arriving at the cost of goods sold; a decrease in the finished goods inventory would be added to the cost of goods manufactured in arriving at the cost of goods sold.

The statement of changes in owners' equity

When the only change in the owners' equity arises from earnings for the period, the balance sheet prepared at the end of the period may

Anderson Corporation
Manufacturing Schedule
For Year Ended December 31, 1972

Goods in process inventory, January 1, 1972............			$ 25,000
Raw materials:			
Inventory, January 1, 1972........................		$ 30,000	
Purchases..	$105,000		
Freight in..	10,000		
Delivered cost of raw materials.....................	$115,000		
Less: Purchases returns and allowances....... $1,000			
Purchases discount.................. 4,000	5,000	110,000	
Total cost of raw materials available for use..........		$140,000	
Less inventory, December 31, 1972..................		40,000	100,000
Direct labor..			140,000
Manufacturing overhead:			
Indirect labor.................\....................		$ 20,000	
Factory superintendence....\.....................		14,500	
Depreciation expense — factory buildings and equipment		12,000	
Light, heat, and power............................		10,000	
Factory supplies expense..........................		8,500	
Miscellaneous factory overhead....................		15,000	80,000
Total goods in process during 1972....................			$345,000
Less goods in process inventory, December 31, 1972......			35,000
Cost of goods manufactured.........................			$310,000

Manufacturing schedule

report in the owners' equity section the balance of the equity at the beginning of the period, the change arising from earnings for the period, and the resulting balance at the end of the period. Normally, however, more than the earnings must be recognized in explaining the change in equity, and a *statement of changes in the owners' equity* is prepared to accompany the financial statements. In the case of the corporation, if transactions affecting the stockholders' equity have been limited to changes in retained earnings, a *retained earnings statement* is prepared. This statement reports the beginning balance for retained earnings, earnings for the period, prior period adjustments net of taxes, and dividend declarations. A retained earnings statement to accompany the income statement prepared on page 81 is shown on the following page.

The income statement and retained earnings statement may be prepared in *combined* form. In preparing the combined statement, net income data are first listed and summarized. The net earnings for the period is then combined with the retained earnings balance at the beginning of the period. This total is adjusted for prior period adjustments and for dividend declarations in arriving at the retained earnings balance at the end of the period. Data can be presented in either multiple-step or single-step form. The combined statement listing data

Anderson Corporation
Retained Earnings Statement
For Year Ended December 31, 1972

Retained earnings, January 1, 1972..............................		$144,000
Add net income per income statement...........................		40,000
		$184,000
Deduct: Prior period adjustment — correction of inventory overstatement, net of income tax refund of $9,000.................	$ 9,000	
Dividends declared.....................................	20,000	29,000
Retained earnings, December 31, 1972..........................		$155,000

Retained earnings statement

in single-step form can be prepared in the following form (details for revenues and expenses have been omitted).

Anderson Corporation
Income and Retained Earnings Statement
For Year Ended December 31, 1972

Revenues...		$513,000
Expenses..		488,000
Income before extraordinary item..		$ 25,000
Extraordinary gain on sale of investments (net of income taxes of $5,000).......		15,000
Net income..		$ 40,000
Retained earnings, January 1, 1972......................................		144,000
		$184,000
Deduct: Prior period adjustment — correction of inventory overstatement, net of income tax refund of $9,000............	$ 9,000	
Dividends declared.................................	20,000	29,000
Retained earnings, December 31, 1972....................................		$155,000

Combined income and retained earnings statement

Prior to the issuance of APB Opinion No. 9, the combined income and retained earnings statement was frequently prepared because it offered a means of reporting both ordinary operations and extraordinary items on the same statement while still offering a clear distinction between the two classes of data. Now that the extraordinary items are clearly set forth on the income statement, the popularity of this form may decline. However, the combined statement may still be preferable when prior period adjustments are reported.

Some companies depart from the conventional forms of income reporting in the attempt to display revenue and expense data in simplified or more popular and readable form. Data may be presented in narrative or graphic form to help the reader grasp significant relationships. A variety of income statements and related retained earnings statements are included in the appendix of this textbook.

QUESTIONS

1. An article in a financial journal was titled "What are Earnings? The Growing Creditability Gap." What do you think was meant by this title?

2. There has been a shift from the balance sheet to the income statement as the statement of primary accounting importance. What reasons can you offer for this change in emphasis?

3. What are the major differences between the valuation and matching methods of income determination? Which is most commonly followed in practice?

4. What concepts of "well-offness" might be applied in the valuation method of income determination? What do you prefer and why?

5. What factors determine the timing of revenue recognition?

6. A manufacturer of farm implements sells its products to dealers who in turn sell them to farmers. To induce dealers to carry an adequate stock, the dealer is not required to pay for merchandise received until 30 days after sale to the customer. In addition, the dealer is permitted to return unsold merchandise at any time within nine months from the time it is received. The dealer holds title to the merchandise while it is in his hands. In some years, the returns were low; in others years they have amounted to 25% of the shipments. Bad debts are low. No interest is charged dealers on the balances in their accounts. At what point should the manufacturer recognize revenue?

7. At harvest time, a wheat producer moves his wheat to a grain elevator and receives a warehouse receipt for it. His decision to sell wheat is based on his need for cash and on his forecast of the market. At what point should the producer recognize revenue?

8. Why is the process of matching costs in income determination so difficult?

9. Do you think matching of revenue and expense is more difficult to apply in a machine assembly plant than in a CPA firm? Why?

10. Distinguish between (a) costs, (b) expenses, and (c) losses.

11. Small loan companies often experience operating losses in the operation of newly opened branch loan offices. Such results can usually be anticipated by management prior to making a decision on expansion. An accounting firm has recommended that the operating losses of newly opened branches should be reported as deferred charges during the first twelve months of operation or until the first profitable month occurs. Such deferred charges would then be amortized over a five-year period. Would you support this recommendation?

12. "Income and expense are classified primarily by ship and voyage, each voyage of each ship being considered as a separate venture. The net income or loss is computed for each voyage, rather than on the basis of income and expenses received and incurred during an arbitrary period of time such as a month or a year.... The practice followed by steamship companies is to treat all revenues from uncompleted voyages as deferred income and all expenses applicable to uncompleted voyages as deferred expenses . . . the revenue and expenses of a steamship company . . . will be those applicable only to voyages terminating within the period." (NAA Bulletin, November 1958) (a) What alternative approaches can you suggest for the above described practice? (b) Evaluate the practice described.

13. What items on the income statement are most significantly affected by price-level changes?

14. What theoretical support exists for interperiod tax allocation?

15. How would you distinguish between ordinary items and extraordinary items for income statement presentation?

16. What factors determine whether an item can be reported as a prior period adjustment?

17. The APB has adopted the concept that extraordinary items should be recognized on the income statement. What reasons can you give to support the view that extraordinary items should be recorded directly in retained earnings?

18. (a) What objections can be made to the multiple-step income statement? (b) What objections can be made to the single-step statement?

EXERCISES

1. List each of the following as an asset, expense, extraordinary loss, or a prior period adjustment:
- (a) Loss on sale of long-term investments.
- (b) Loss on sale of securities by security dealer.
- (c) Write-off of goodwill and patents in the interest of conservatism.
- (d) Installation costs for new machinery.
- (e) Payments representing organization costs.
- (f) Costs of rehabilitating plant just purchased.
- (g) Cost of grading land for construction.
- (h) Additional federal income tax assessment for prior years.
- (i) Landscaping costs upon completion of new building.
- (j) Charges on suits arising from breach of contract in a prior period.
- (k) Purchase and retirement of bonds outstanding at an amount in excess of their book value.
- (l) Contributions to United Fund.
- (m) Loss from flood.
- (n) Loss on sale of shopworn merchandise.

2. Give the section of the income statement in which each of the following items is reported:
- (a) Gain on sale of land.
- (b) Purchases discount.
- (c) Charge for doubtful accounts in anticipation of failure to collect receivables.
- (d) Loss from long-term investments written off as worthless.
- (e) Loss from a strike.
- (f) Income tax refund.
- (g) Loss from inventory price decline.
- (h) Depletion.
- (i) Sales discount.
- (j) Dividends received on long-term investments.
- (k) Income taxes for current period.
- (l) Charge for omission of depreciation in prior periods.
- (m) Collection of life insurance policy upon death of officer.
- (n) Vacation pay of employees.
- (o) Payment in settlement of damage suit for breach of contract arising in current period.

3. Indicate how you would report each of the following items:

(a) A loss resulting from spring floods.

(b) Write-off of the balance of deferred personnel training costs; original write-off was expected to be five years, but balance for the last three years is being written off in the third year.

(c) Amortization of goodwill balance.

(d) Additional income taxes levied on prior period tax return.

(e) Collection of accounts receivable previously written off.

(f) Settlement of patent infringment suit brought against the company in prior period.

(g) Gain on refunding of long-term debt.

(h) Loss regarded as not material arising from sale of securities.

4. Indicate which of the following items involves the realization of revenue or gain. Give the reasons for your answer.

(a) Land acquired in 1952 at $15,000 is now conservatively appraised at $40,000.

(b) Stock acquired as an investment at $40 per share now has a market value of $52.

(c) Timberlands show a growth in timber valued at $40,000 for the year.

(d) An addition to a building was self-constructed at a cost of $3,600 after two offers from private contractors for the work at $4,650 and $5,000.

(e) Certain valuable franchise rights were received from a city for payment of annual licensing fees.

(f) A customer owing $4,600, which was delinquent for one year, gave securities valued at $5,000 in settlement of his obligation.

(g) Merchandise, cost $1,000, is sold for $1,600 with a 50% down payment on a conditional sales contract, title to the merchandise being retained by the seller until the full contract price is collected.

(h) Cash is received on the sale of gift certificates redeemable in merchandise in the following period.

5. Changes in account balances for the Sloan Sales Co. during 1972 were as follows:

	Increase (Decrease)
Cash...	$ 35,000
Accounts receivable..	5,000
Merchandise inventory.....................................	40,000
Buildings and equipment (net)...........................	120,000
Accounts payable...	(25,000)
Bonds payable..	100,000
Capital stock...	75,000
Additional paid-in capital.................................	5,000

Dividends paid during 1972 were $15,000. Calculate the net income for the year assuming there were no transactions affecting retained earnings other than the dividend payment.

6. E and E, Inc., shows a retained earnings balance on January 1, 1972 of $130,000. For 1972, the net income was $30,000 before income taxes and the following special items:

Gain on sale of long-term investments, $10,000.
Refund of income tax payments by federal government for 1971, $15,000.
Omission of depreciation charges of prior years, $10,000.
A claim has been filed for an income tax refund of $4,000 in connection with the above item.

Income taxes for 1972 were $14,400, that includes $2,500 resulting from the gain on the sale of the investments. Dividends of $12,000 were declared by the company during the year. Prepare the income statement for E and E, Inc., beginning with "income from operations before income taxes," and prepare an accompanying retained earnings statement.

7. The selling expenses of F and M, Inc., for 1972 are 10% of sales. General expenses, excluding doubtful accounts, are 25% of cost of sales but only 15% of sales. Doubtful accounts are 2% of sales. The beginning merchandise inventory was $62,000 and it decreased 25% during the year. Income for the year before income taxes of 40% is $52,000. Prepare an income statement, giving supporting computations.

PROBLEMS

3-1. The following data were taken from the ledger of the Royal Co. at the end of 1972:

Retained earnings,		Selling and general expenses	$22,000
January 1	$ 16,250	Federal and state income	
Sales	250,500	taxes, 1972	30,300
Purchases	180,000	Additional federal income	
Increase in inventory, 1972.	12,000	taxes assessed for prior	
Purchases discount	3,000	years	4,400
Sales discount	3,600	Adjustments in income of	
Dividends declared	40,000	prior years — additions	
Interest expense	500	to building reported as	
Dividends received	1,200	repairs	12,000

Instructions: Prepare a multiple-step income statement accompanied by a retained earnings statement.

3-2. The Lundgren Co. on July 1, 1971, reported a retained earnings balance of $762,500. The books of the company showed the following account balances on June 30, 1972:

Sales	$1,090,000
Inventory: July 1, 1971	80,000
June 30, 1972	82,500
Sales returns and allowances	15,000
Purchases	768,000
Purchases discount	12,000
Gain on sale of long-term investments	40,000
Dividends declared on common stock	65,000

Selling and general expenses..........................	$125,000
Income taxes: Applicable to ordinary income..........	99,750
Applicable to gain on sale of investments..	10,000
Collection of income tax refund for prior years..........	26,000

Instructions: Prepare a single-step income statement accompanied by a retained earnings statement.

3-3. The Nordic Supply Co. prepares a multiple-step income statement. The statement is supported by (1) a manufacturing schedule, (2) a selling expense schedule, and (3) a general and administrative expense schedule. Prepare an income statement with supporting schedules using the data for the year ended April 30, 1972 listed below.

Income taxes for the current year were as follows:

Applicable to ordinary income.......................	$16,925
Applicable to gain on sale of land....................	2,000
Total income taxes................................	$18,925

Inventory balances at the end of the fiscal period as compared with balances at the beginning of the fiscal period were as follows:

Finished goods.................................	$7,900 increase
Goods in process..............................	4,500 increase
Raw materials.................................	3,000 decrease

Other account balances include the following:

Advertising Expense.......	$ 6,500	Indirect Labor...........	$ 24,000
Delivery Expense.........	12,200	Interest Expense..........	10,200
Depreciation Exp.—Mach..	5,600	Misc. Factory Costs.......	6,000
Direct Labor.............	66,000	Misc. General Expense....	3,200
Dividend Income.........	300	Misc. Selling Expense.....	2,150
Dividends Declared.......	30,000	Officers Salaries..........	16,200
Doubtful Accounts Exp....	1,600	Office Salaries...........	13,000
Factory Heat, Light,		Office Supplies Expense...	3,200
Power................	18,900	Raw Materials Purchases..	76,000
Factory Maintenance......	2,600	Raw Materials Returns....	2,000
Factory Superintendence...	20,000	Royalty Income..........	2,70
Factory Supplies Expense..	4,000	Sales....................	361,000
Factory Taxes............	14,000	Sales Discount...........	4,000
Freight In on Raw Mat'ls..	2,500	Sales Returns and Allow....	4,700
Gain on Sale of Land.....	8,000	Sales Salaries............	25,000

3-4. The following balances were taken from the books of Edina Supply Corporation on December 31, 1972:

Cash Dividends Declared..	$ 48,000	Purchases Discount......	$ 22,350
General and Administra-		Purch. Returns and	
tive Expense...........	176,000	Allow................	11,150
Interest Income..........	13,500	Sales...................	1,650,000
Interest Expense.........	21,250	Sales Discount..........	28,250
Loss on Retirement of		Sales Returns and	
Company Bonds.......	95,750	Allow................	16,570
Merchandise Purch.......	940,500	Selling Expense........	178,500

Income taxes for 1972 amounted to $100,000; however, the income taxes applicable to net income, exclusive of the loss on the retirement of the company bonds, amounted to $147,875.

Merchandise inventory: January 1, 1972............... $190,000
                          December 31, 1972............ 150,000
Retained earnings: January 1, 1972.................. 482,000

Instructions: Prepare a combined statement of income and retained earnings for the year ended December 31, 1972. (Summarize income in multiple-step form.)

3-5. Fidelity Investment Company started in business at the beginning of 1972. It purchased 100 shares of Dorsey, Inc., and 100 shares of Hoyt Stores, Inc. Data on these investments on a per share basis are as follows:

	Dorsey	Hoyt
Cost..	$60.50	$82.25
Net income reported — 1972..................	7.00	7.50
Dividend paid — 1972......................	6.00	5.00
Market value — 12/31/72....................	54.25	79.75

Fundamental Investment Company and American Shares, Inc., also started business at the beginning of 1972. Each company purchased 100 shares of Hume Manufacturing Co. and 100 shares of Kovar Electronics, Inc. Data on these investments, also on a per share basis, are as follows:

	Hume	Kovar
Cost..	$50.75	$90.25
Net income reported — 1972..................	4.00	6.00
Dividend paid — 1972......................	3.00	none
Market value — 12/31/72....................	56.25	94.00

American Shares, Inc., sold its shares of Kovar Electronics, Inc., on December 31, 1972, at the market value shown above. At the same time it purchased 200 shares of Magnatronics, Inc., for $9,350. The other companies continued to hold their original investment.

Instructions: (1) Compute the net incomes for the three companies, using each of the following approaches to revenue recognition for each company (no expenses are to be recognized in computing your answers):
(a) Dividends received (plus gain on sales, if any).
(b) Net income reported by company whose stock is owned.
(c) Dividends received adjusted by any change in the market value of the stock.
(2) Evaluate each of the approaches as to its informational value to investors.

3-6. The York Corporation was organized on March 21, 1972, 15,000 shares of no-par stock being issued in exchange for land, buildings and equipment valued at $60,000 and cash of $15,000. Data below summarize activities for the initial fiscal period ending December 31, 1972:
(a) Net income for the period ending December 31, 1972, was $12,000.
(b) Raw materials on hand on December 31 were equal to 25% of raw materials purchased in 1972.

(c) Manufacturing costs in 1972 were distributed as follows:

Materials used...... 50%

Direct labor........ 30%

Manufacturing over-
head............. 20% (includes depreciation of building, $2,500)

(d) Goods in process remaining in the factory on December 31 were equal to $33\frac{1}{3}\%$ of the goods finished and transferred to stock.

(e) Finished goods remaining in stock were equal to 25% of the cost of goods sold.

(f) Operating expenses were 30% of sales.

(g) Cost of goods sold was 150% of the operating expenses total.

(h) Ninety percent of sales were collected in 1972; the balance was considered collectible in 1973.

(i) Seventy-five percent of the raw materials purchased were paid for; there were no expense accruals or prepayments at the end of the year.

Instructions: (1) Prepare a balance sheet, an income statement, and a supporting manufacturing schedule. (Disregard income taxes.)

(2) Prepare a summary of cash receipts and disbursements to support the cash balance reported on the balance sheet.

3-7. Kwik-Bild Corporation sells and erects shell houses. These are frame structures that are completely finished on the outside but are unfinished on the inside except for flooring, partition studding and ceiling joists. Shell houses are sold chiefly to customers who are handy with tools and who have time to do the interior wiring, plumbing, wall completion and finishing, and other work necessary to make the shell houses livable dwellings.

Kwik-Bild buys shell houses from a manufacturer in unassembled packages consisting of all lumber, roofing, doors, windows and similar materials necessary to complete a shell house. Upon commencing operations in a new area, Kwik-Bild buys or leases land as a site for its local warehouse, field office and display houses. Sample display houses are erected at a total cost of from $3,000 to $7,000 including the cost of the unassembled packages. The chief element of cost of the display houses is the unassembled packages, since erection is a short low-cost operation. Old sample models are torn down or altered into new models every three to seven years. Sample display houses have little salvage value because dismantling and moving costs amount to nearly as much as the cost of an unassembled package.

Instructions: (1) A choice must be made between (a) expensing the costs of sample display houses in the period in which the expenditure is made, and (b) spreading the costs over more than one period. Discuss the advantages of each method.

(2) Would it be preferable to amortize the cost of display houses on the basis of (a) the passage of time or (b) the number of shell houses sold? Explain.

(AICPA adapted)

chapter 4

the accounting process

The basic accounting concepts and principles underlying financial statements and the form and content of these statements were described in the first three chapters. Certain procedures must be established by every business unit to provide the data that are to be reported on the financial statements. These procedures are frequently referred to as the *accounting process*.

The accounting process is composed of two parts: (1) the *recording phase* and (2) the *summarizing phase*. During the fiscal period it is necessary to engage in a continuing activity — the recording of transactions in the various books of record. At the end of the fiscal period the recorded data are brought up to date and summarized and the financial statements are prepared. The recording and summarizing phases of the accounting process are reviewed in this chapter. The accounting process as it is applied to a particular business unit is illustrated in the next chapter.

The recording phase

Accurate statements can be prepared only if transactions have been properly recorded. A transaction is an action that results in a change in the assets, the liabilities, or the owners' equity of a business. There are two general classes of transactions that require accounting recognition: (1) *business transactions*, or transactions entered into with outsiders; and (2) *internal transactions*, or accountable transfers of costs within the business. Among the latter, for example, are the transfers of materials, labor, and manufacturing overhead costs to goods in process and transfers of goods in process to finished goods, in manufacturing activities.

Accounting records. The accounting records of a business consist of: (1) the original documents evidencing the transactions, called *business* *papers* or *vouchers;* (2) the media for classifying and recording the transactions, known as the *books of original entry* or *journals;* and (3) the media for summarizing the effects of transactions upon individual asset, liability, and owners' equity accounts, known as the *ledgers* or *ledger records.*

The manner in which the accounting records are organized and employed within a business is referred to as its *accounting system.* The various recording routines in such a system are developed to meet the special needs of the business unit. Recording processes must be designed to provide information accurately and efficiently, while at the same time, serving as effective controls in preventing mistakes and guarding against dishonesty.

Business papers. Normally a business paper or voucher is prepared as a first record of each transaction. Such a document offers detailed information concerning the transaction and also fixes responsibility for such information by naming the parties identified with the transaction. The business papers are support for the data that are to be recorded in the books of original entry. Copies of *sales invoices* or *cash register tapes,* for example, are the evidence in support of the sales record; *purchases invoices* support the purchases or invoice record; *debit* and *credit memorandums* support adjustments in debtor and creditor balances; *check stubs* or *duplicate checks* provide data concerning cash disbursements; the corporation *minutes book* supports entries authorized by action of the board of directors; *journal vouchers* prepared and approved by appropriate officers are a source of data for adjustments or corrections that are to be reported in the accounts. Documents underlying each recorded transaction provide a means of verifying the accounting records and thus form a vital part of the information and control system.

Books of original entry. Transactions are analyzed from the information provided on the business papers. They may then be recorded in chronological order in the appropriate books of original entry. Transactions are analyzed in terms of accounts to be maintained for (1) assets, (2) liabilities, (3) owners' equity, (4) revenues and gains, and (5) expenses and losses. Classes (4) and (5) are temporary owners' equity accounts summarizing net income data for the current period. The analysis is expressed in terms of *debit* and *credit.* Asset, expense, and loss accounts have left-hand or debit balances and are decreased by entries on the right-hand or credit side. Liabilities, owners' equity, revenue, and gain accounts have credit balances and are decreased by entries on the debit side.

Although it would be possible to record every transaction in a single book of original entry, this is rarely done. Whenever a number of transactions of the same character take place, special journals may be designed in which such transactions can be conveniently entered and summarized. Special journals eliminate much of the repetitive work involved in recording routine transactions. In addition, they permit the recording function to be divided among accounting personnel, each individual being responsible for a separate record. Such specialization often results in greater efficiency as well as a higher degree of control.

Some examples of special journals are the *sales journal*, the *purchases journal*, the *cash receipts journal*, the *cash disbursements journal*, the *payroll register*, and the *voucher register*. Regardless of the number and nature of the special journals, there are certain transactions that cannot appropriately be recorded in the special journals, and these are recorded in the *general journal*.

Sales on account are recorded in the sales journal. The subsequent collections on account, as well as cash sales and other transactions involving the receipt of cash, are recorded in the cash receipts journal. Merchandise purchases on account are entered in the purchases journal. Subsequent payments on account, as well as all other transactions involving the payment of cash, are recorded in the cash disbursements journal or in the *check register*. A *payroll record* may be employed to accumulate payroll information including special payroll withholdings for taxes and other purposes; in certain instances, this record may be used as a book of original entry providing the debits to salaries and wages and the credits to accrued payroll and other liability accounts.

Column headings in the various journals specify the accounts to be debited or credited and account titles and explanations may be omitted in recording routine transactions. A "miscellaneous" column is usually provided for transactions that are relatively infrequent and account titles are specially designated in recording such transactions.

The use of special columns facilitates recording and also serves to summarize the effects of a number of transactions upon individual account balances. The subsequent transfer of information from the books of original entry is thus simplified as this process is performed with the aggregates of many transactions rather than with separate data for each transaction. Certain data must be transferred individually — data affecting individual accounts receivable and accounts payable and data reported in the "miscellaneous" columns — but the volume of transcription is substantially reduced.

Transactions that do not occur frequently enough to justify a special journal are recorded in the general journal. The general journal provides debit and credit columns and space for designating account titles and it can be used in recording any transaction. A particular business unit may not need certain special journals, but it must have a general journal.

Accounts and the ledger. Information as reported on a business paper and analyzed, classified, and summarized in terms of debits and credits in the books of original entry is transferred to accounts in the ledger. Such transfer is referred to as *posting.* The accounts then summarize the full effects of the transactions upon assets, liabilities, and owners' equity and are used as a basis for the preparation of the financial statements.

Accounts are sometimes referred to as *real* (or *permanent*) accounts and *nominal* (or *temporary*) accounts. The balance sheet accounts are referred to as real accounts; the income statement accounts are referred to as nominal accounts. If during the course of the accounting period a balance sheet or an income statement account balance represents both real and nominal elements, it may be described as a *mixed account.* The store supplies account, for example, is composed of two elements: (1) the store supplies used, and (2) the store supplies still on hand. There is no need to analyze mixed accounts until financial statements are prepared. At this time the real and nominal portions of each mixed account must be determined.

When accounts are set up to record subtractions from related accounts reporting positive balances, such accounts are termed *offset, contra,* or *negative accounts.* Allowance for Doubtful Accounts is an offset to Accounts Receivable and is a negative asset account. Sales Returns and Allowances is an offset to Sales and is a negative revenue account. Certain accounts that are related to others and are to be added to them are sometimes referred to as *adjunct accounts.* Examples of these are Freight In that is added to the purchases balance and Paid-in Capital from Sale of Capital Stock at More Than Stated Value that is added to the capital stock balance.

The real and nominal accounts required by a business unit vary depending upon the nature of the business, its properties and activities, the information to be provided on the financial statements, and the controls to be employed in carrying out the accounting functions. The accounts to be maintained by a particular business are usually expressed in the form of a *chart of accounts.* Such a chart lists in systematic form the accounts with identifying numbers or symbols that are to form the framework for summarizing business operations.

It is often desirable to establish separate ledgers for detailed information in support of balance sheet or income statement items. The *general ledger* then carries summaries of all of the accounts appearing on the financial statements, while separate *subsidiary ledgers* afford additional detail in support of general ledger balances. For example, a single accounts receivable account is usually carried in the general ledger, and individual customers' accounts are shown in a subsidiary *accounts receivable ledger;* the capital stock account in the general ledger is normally supported by individual stockholders' accounts in a subsidiary *stockholders ledger;* selling and general and administrative expenses may be summarized in a single general ledger account, individual expenses being carried in a subsidiary *expense ledger.* The general ledger account that summarizes the detailed information reported elsewhere is known as a *controlling account.*

Whenever possible, individual postings to subsidiary accounts are made directly from the business paper evidencing the transaction. This practice saves time and avoids errors that might arise in summarizing and transferring this information. A business paper also provides the basis for the journal entry that authorizes the postings to the controlling account in the general ledger. In many instances business papers themselves are used to represent a book of original entry. When this is done, business papers are assembled and summarized, and the summaries are transferred directly to the appropriate controlling accounts as well as to the other accounts affected in the general ledger. Whatever the procedure may be, if postings to the subsidiary records and to the controlling accounts are made accurately, the sum of the detail in a subsidiary record will agree with the balance in the controlling account. A reconciliation of each subsidiary record with its related controlling account should be made periodically, and any discrepancies that are found should be investigated and corrected.

The use of subsidiary records results in a number of advantages: (1) the number of accounts in the general ledger is reduced, thus making the general ledger more useful as a basis for preparing reports; (2) errors in the general ledger are minimized because of fewer accounts and fewer postings; (3) the accuracy of the posting to a large number of subsidiary accounts may be tested by comparing the total of the balances of the accounts with the balance of one account in the general ledger; (4) totals relating to various items are readily obtained; (5) specialization of accounting duties and individual accounting responsibilities is made possible; and (6) daily posting is facilitated for accounts that must be kept up to date, such as customer and creditor accounts.

The voucher system. A relatively large organization ordinarily provides for the control of purchases and cash disbursements through adoption of some form of a *voucher system.* With the use of a voucher system, checks may be drawn only upon a written authorization in the form of a *voucher* approved by some responsibile official.

A voucher is prepared, not only in support of each payment that is to be made for goods and services purchased on account, but also for all other transactions calling for payment by check including the cash purchases, the retirement of debt, the replenishment of petty cash funds, payrolls, and dividends. The voucher identifies the person authorizing the expenditure, explains the nature of the transaction, and names the accounts that are affected by the transaction. Vouchers related to purchases invoices should be compared with receiving reports. Upon verification, the voucher and the related business papers are submitted to the appropriate official for final approval. Upon such approval, the voucher is numbered and recorded in a *voucher register*. The voucher register is a book of original entry. Charges on each voucher are classified and summarized in appropriate columns and the amount to be paid is listed in an Accounts Payable or Vouchers Payable column. After a voucher is entered in the register, it is placed in an unpaid vouchers file together with its supporting papers.

Checks are written in payment of individual vouchers. The checks are recorded in a check register as debits to Accounts Payable or Vouchers Payable and credits to Cash. Charges to the various asset, liability, or expense accounts, having been recognized when the payable was recorded in the voucher register, need not be listed in the payments record. When a check is issued, payment of the voucher is reported in the voucher register by entering the check number and the payment date. Paid vouchers and invoices are removed from the unpaid vouchers file, marked "Paid," and placed in a separate paid vouchers file. The balance of the payable account after the credit for total vouchers issued and the debit for total vouchers paid should be equal to the sum of the unpaid vouchers as reported in the voucher register and as found in the unpaid vouchers file. The voucher register, while representing a book of original entry, also serves as a subsidiary ledger affording the detail in support of the accounts or vouchers payable total, and the need for a ledger reporting the individual payable accounts is eliminated.

From manual operation to electronic data processing. As a business grows in size and complexity, the recording process becomes more involved and means are sought for improving efficiency and reducing costs. Some business units may find that a system involving primarily manual operations is adequate in meeting their needs. Others may find that recording requirements can be handled effectively only through mechanical devices or elaborate electronic data processing equipment.

In a manual accounting system all operations are carried on by hand. Original documents — invoices, checks, and other business papers —

are written out, and the data they contain are transferred by hand to the journals, the ledgers, and the trial balance. Many small businesses rely solely on manual methods of processing accounting data.

As the volume of record keeping expands, machines may be added to the system. Machines to supplement manual operations often include posting machines, accounting machines, and billing machines. By using special papers, these machines are able to prepare original documents and journal and ledger records at one time, thus saving the work of transferring data. They also can perform a few routine arithmetic operations, such as adding journal columns and computing ledger balances.

Companies requiring great speed and accuracy in processing large amounts of accounting data may utilize an electronic system. The heart of the electronic system is a *computer* that is capable of storing and recalling vast quantities of data, performing many mathematical functions, and making certain routine decisions based on mathematical comparisons. The system normally includes various other machines that can "read" data from magnetic tapes or punched cards and print information in a variety of forms, all under the control of the computer.

The installation of an electronic system normally entails many basic changes in the business papers and the accounting records that are used. Data on original documents must be transferred by *input* preparation equipment to magnetic tapes or punched cards so that the computer can read them at high speeds. For this purpose, the business papers may be encoded with magnetic characters or punch holes which allow the input equipment to process this information directly, reducing the amount of human intervention in the process.

Complete accounting records equivalent to journals, ledgers, and subsidiary files may be maintained on reels of magnetic tape, on magnetic discs, or in the electronic "memory" of the computer. The computer can search through these to recall any needed information almost instantaneously. But in such form these records cannot be read by humans, so information must be printed by *output* devices for use outside of the electronic system.

Under the direction of a series of instructions called a *program*, the computer performs the desired operations at electronic speeds. The program may be changed in a short time to make the computer perform different functions. As a result the computer is extremely versatile and may be used in practically every phase of the accounting process.

For example, the computer can prepare the weekly payroll. It may have information stored in its memory concerning hourly wages, accumulated wages for the year to date, tax status, and deductions for each employee. Upon reading the current week's employee hours, the computer calculates all wages and deductions, adjusts the cumulative wage record for each employee, aggregates wages and deductions so that proper ledger balances can be determined, and directs the automatic printer to prepare payroll checks.

The computer system may maintain accounts with customers. It can print invoices, analyze sales data, adjust inventory records, and prepare lists of goods to be reordered. Accounts with creditors may also be maintained by the system. It can determine the accuracy of purchases invoices, calculate discounts, print checks for the proper amounts when payments are due, and adjust cash and accounts payable records.

Despite their tremendous capabilities, electronic systems cannot replace skilled accountants. In fact, their presence places increased demands on the accountant in directing the operations of the system to assure the use of appropriate procedures. Although all arithmetical operations can be assumed to be done accurately by the computer, the validity of the output data depends upon the adequacy of the instructions that are given it. Unlike a human accountant, a computer cannot think for itself but must be given explicit instructions in performing each operation. This has certain advantages in that the accountant can be sure that every direction will be carried out precisely. On the other hand, this places a great responsibility on the accountant to anticipate any unusual situations that might require special consideration or judgment. Particular techniques must also be developed for checking and verifying data recorded in electronic form.

The remainder of this chapter is concerned with the summarizing activities that are required in preparing periodic financial statements. The exact manner in which these activities are carried out may vary somewhat, depending upon the degree of mechanization of the particular accounting system. The underlying objectives of these procedures are the same, however, whether the operations are performed manually or with a high-speed computer.

The periodic summary

The accounting routine at the close of the fiscal period is frequently referred to as the *periodic summary* and normally consists of the following steps in the order stated:

1. *A trial balance of the accounts in the ledger is taken.* The trial balance offers a summary of the information as classified and summarized in the ledger, as well as a check on the accuracy of recording and posting.

2. *The data required to bring the accounts up to date are compiled.* Before financial statements can be prepared, all of the accountable information that has not been recorded must be determined.

3. *A work sheet is prepared.* By means of the work sheet, data in steps (1) and (2) are summarized and classified.

4. *Financial statements are prepared from the work sheet.* Statements that summarize operations and that show the financial condition are prepared from the information supplied on the work sheet.

5. *Accounts are adjusted and closed.* Accounts in the ledger are brought up to date. Balances in nominal accounts are then closed into appropriate summary accounts. The results of operations as determined in the summary accounts are finally transferred to the appropriate owners' equity accounts.

6. *A post-closing trial balance is taken.* A trial balance is taken to check the equality of the debits and credits after posting the adjusting and closing entries.

7. *Accounts are reversed.* Accrued and prepaid balances that were established by adjusting entries are returned to the nominal accounts that are to be used in accounting for activities involving these items in the new period.

The last step is not required but is often desirable as a means of facilitating recording and adjusting routines in the succeeding period.

The adjusting and closing procedures require particular attention, and these are described in the following sections.

The summarizing phase — adjusting the accounts

The division of the life of a business into periods of arbitrary length creates many important problems for the accountant who must summarize the financial operations for a certain period and report on the financial position at the end of this period. Transactions during the period have been recorded in real and nominal accounts. At the end of the period, mixed accounts require adjustment. At this time, too, other financial data not recognized currently must be entered in the accounts in bringing the books up to date. The special problems that arise in bringing the accounts up to date and in summarizing their effects are considered under the following headings:

Asset depreciation and cost amortization
Probable uncollectible accounts
Accrued expenses
Accrued revenues
Prepaid expenses (expenses paid in advance)
Deferred revenues (revenues received in advance)
Inventories

Asset depreciation and cost amortization. Charges to operations for the use of land, buildings, and equipment items and intangible assets must be recorded at the end of the period. In recording asset depreciation or amortization, operations are charged with a portion of the asset cost and the carrying value of the asset is reduced by that amount. A reduction in an asset for depreciation is usually recorded by a credit to a valuation account. Adjustments at the end of a period for depreciation and amortization may be made as follows:

Depreciation of Machinery......................	12,500	
Accumulated Depreciation — Machinery........		12,500
Amortization of Patents.......................	1,500	
Patents......................................		1,500

Probable uncollectible accounts. Provision is ordinarily made for the probable expense that will result from failure to collect receivables. In recognizing the probable expense arising from the policy of granting credit to customers, operations are charged with the estimated expense, and receivables are reduced by means of a valuation account. When there is positive evidence that receivables are uncollectible, receivables are written off against the valuation account. To illustrate the adjustment at the end of the period, assume that receivables of $5,000 are estimated to be uncollectible. An adjustment is made as follows:

Doubtful Accounts Expense......................	5,000	
Allowance for Doubtful Accounts................		5,000

Accrued expenses. During the period, certain expenses may have been incurred although payment is not to be made until a subsequent period. At the end of the period, it is necessary to determine and record the expenses that have not yet been recognized. In recording an accrued expense, an expense account is debited and a liability account is credited.

At the beginning of the new period, the adjustment may be reversed by a charge to the liability and a credit to the expense. The reversing entry makes it possible for the accountant to record the expense payments in the new period in the usual manner, the entry on the credit side of the expense account absorbing that part of the payments recognized as expense in the prior period. If a reversing entry is not made, expense payments will have to be analyzed as to (1) the amount representing payment of an accrued liability, and (2) the amount representing expense of the current period.

Accounting for accrued expense illustrated. To illustrate accounting for an accrued expense when (1) reversing entries are made and (2) reversing entries are not made, assume that accrued salaries on December 31 are $350. Payment of salaries for the week ending January 4 is $1,000. Adjustments are made and the books are closed annually on December 31. The entries that may be made are shown at the top of the following page.

Accrued revenues. During the period, certain amounts may have been earned although collection is not to be made until a subsequent

	(1) Assuming Liability Account Is Reversed	(2) Assuming Liability Account Is Not Reversed

December 31
Adjusting entry to record accrued salaries.
	Salaries........ 350
	   Salaries Payable 350
		Salaries......... 350
		   Salaries Payable. 350

December 31
Closing entry to transfer expense to the income summary account.
	Income Summary. xxx
	   Salaries...... xxx
		Income Summary.. xxx
		   Salaries....... xxx

January 1 Reversing entry to transfer balance to the account that will be charged when payment is made.	Salaries Payable.. 350 Salaries...... 350	No entry

January 4
Payment of salaries for week ending January 4.
	Salaries...... 1,000
	   Cash...... 1,000
		Salaries Payable. 350
		Salaries........ 650
		   Cash........ 1,000

period. At the end of the period, it is necessary to determine and record the earnings that have not yet been recognized. In recording accrued revenue, an asset account is debited and a revenue account is credited.

At the beginning of the new period, the adjustment may be reversed by a charge to revenue and a credit to the asset. The reversing entry makes it possible for the accountant to record the revenue receipts in the new period in the usual manner, the entry on the debit side of the revenue account absorbing that part of the receipts recognized as revenue in the prior period. If a reversing entry is not made, receipts will have to be analyzed as to (1) the amount representing collection of an accrued asset, and (2) the amount representing revenue of the current period.

Accounting for accrued revenue illustrated. To illustrate accounting for accrued revenue when (1) reversing entries are made and (2) reversing entries are not made, assume that on December 31, accrued interest on bonds held as an investment is $100. Adjustments are made and the books are closed annually on December 31. The entries that may be made are as follows:

	(1) Assuming Asset Account Is Reversed	(2) Assuming Asset Account Is Not Reversed

December 31
Adjusting entry to record accrued interest.
	Accrued Interest
	  on Investment in
	  Bonds........ 100
	   Interest Income. 100
		Accrued Interest
		  on Investment in
		  Bonds......... 100
		   Interest Income. 100

December 31
Closing entry to transfer revenue to the income summary account.
	Interest Income.. xxx
	  Income
	   Summary.... xxx
		Interest Income... xxx
		  Income
		   Summary..... xxx

	(1) Assuming Asset Account Is Reversed	(2) Assuming Asset Account Is Not Reversed

January 1
Reversing entry to transfer balance to the account that will be credited when collection is made.
	Interest Income.. 100
	  Accrued Interest
	    on Investment
	    in Bonds.... 100
		No entry

May 1
Collection of interest for six-month period.
	Cash............ 300
	  Interest Income. 300
		Cash............ 300
		  Accrued Interest
		    on Investment
		    in Bonds..... 100
		  Interest Income. 200

Prepaid expenses. During the period, charges may have been recorded on the books for commodities or services that are not to be received or used up currently. At the end of the period it is necessary to determine the portions of such charges that are applicable to subsequent periods and hence require recognition as assets.

The method of adjusting for prepaid expenses depends upon how the expenditures were originally entered in the accounts. The charges for the commodities or services may have been recorded as debits to (1) an expense account or (2) an asset account.

Original debit to an expense account. If an expense account was originally debited, an asset account is debited for the expense applicable to a future period and the expense account is credited. The expense account then remains with a debit balance representing the amount applicable to the current period.

The balance in the asset account is ordinarily returned to the expense account at the beginning of the new period by a reversing entry. This is desirable since expenditures of the same character will continue to be recorded in the expense account, and the expense account at the end of the next period should show all of the relevant data for determining the adjustment at that time.

Original debit to an asset account. If an asset account was originally debited, an expense account is debited for the amount applicable to the current period and the asset account is credited. The asset account remains with a debit balance that shows the amount applicable to future periods. In this instance, no reversing entry is needed since expenditures for the same purpose will continue to be recorded in the asset account.

Accounting for prepaid expense illustrated. To illustrate the two methods of accounting, assume that a 3-year insurance policy, dated July 1, is purchased for $900. Adjustments are made and the books are closed annually on December 31. The required entries are shown at the top of the following page.

	(1) Assuming Charge Is Made to an Expense Account	(2) Assuming Charge Is Made to an Asset Account

July 1
Payment of premium
	Insurance Expense 900
	   Cash......... 900
		Prepaid
		  Insurance....... 900
		   Cash.......... 900

December 31
Adjusting entry to record:
(1) unexpired portion.
(2) expired portion.
	Prepaid
	  Insurance...... 750
	Insurance
	  Expense..... 750
		Insurance Expense. 150
		Prepaid
		  Insurance..... 150

December 31
Closing entry to transfer expense to the income summary account.
	Income Summary. 150
	Insurance
	  Expense..... 150
		Income Summary.. 150
		Insurance
		  Expense...... 150

January 1 Reversing entry to transfer balance to the account that will be charged with subsequent expenditures.	Insurance Expense 750 Prepaid Insurance.... 750	No entry

Deferred revenues. During the period, cash or other assets may have been received from customers in advance of fulfillment of the company's obligation to deliver goods or services. In recording the transactions, assets are debited and accounts reporting such receipts are credited. The latter balances must be analyzed at the end of the period to determine the portions that are applicable to future periods and hence require recognition as liabilities.

The method of adjusting for deferred revenues depends upon how the receipts for undelivered goods or services were originally entered in the accounts. The receipts may have been recorded as credits to (1) a revenue account or (2) a liability account.

Original credit to a revenue account. If a revenue account was originally credited, this account is debited and a liability account is credited for the revenue applicable to a future period. The revenue account remains with a credit balance representing the earnings applicable to the current period.

The balance in the liability account is ordinarily returned to the revenue account at the beginning of the new period by a reversing entry. This is desirable since receipts of the same character will continue to be recorded in the revenue account, and the revenue account at the end of the next fiscal period should show all of the relevant data for determining the adjustment at that time.

Original credit to a liability account. If a liability account was originally credited, this account is debited and a revenue account is credited for the amount applicable to the current period. The liability account remains with a credit balance that shows the amount applicable to future periods.   In this instance, no reversing entry is needed since receipts of the same character will continue to be recorded in the liability account.

Accounting for deferred revenue illustrated.   To illustrate the two methods of accounting, assume that on October 1, $600 is collected representing rents for a period of one year from this date. Adjustments are made and the books are closed annually on December 31. The required entries are as follows:

	(1) Assuming Credit Is Made to a Revenue Account	(2) Assuming Credit Is Made to a Liability Account

October 1
Collection of rents.
	Cash............ 600
	   Rental Income . 600
		Cash............ 600
		   Rent Received
		     in Advance ... 600

December 31
Adjusting entry to record:
  (1) unearned portion.
  (2) earned portion.
	Rental Income... 450
	   Rent Received
	    in Advance .. 450
		Rent Received in
		   Advance....... 150
		   Rental Income .. 150

December 31
Closing entry to transfer revenue to the income summary account.
	Rental Income... 150
	   Income
	    Summary.... 150
		Rental Income.... 150
		   Income
		    Summary..... 150

January 1
Reversing entry to transfer balance to the account that will be credited with subsequent receipts.
	Rent Received in
	   Advance...... 450
	   Rental Income . 450
		No entry

Inventories.   When perpetual or book inventory records are not maintained, physical inventories must be taken at the end of the period to determine the inventory to be reported on the balance sheet and the cost of goods sold amount to be reported on the income statement. When perpetual or book inventories are maintained, the ending inventory and the cost of goods sold balance appear in the ledger and no adjustment is required. The two practices are described for the merchandising enterprise and for the manufacturing enterprise in the following paragraphs.

Physical inventories — the merchandising enterprise.   In a merchandising enterprise, the beginning inventory and the purchases account may be closed into the income summary account. The ending inventory is then recorded by a debit to the inventory account and a credit to the income summary account. The asset account now reports the inventory balance at the end of the period; the income summary account shows the cost of goods sold. To illustrate, assume the following facts: merchandise on hand, January 1, 1972, $95,000; purchases, 1972, $330,000; merchandise on hand, December 31, 1972, $125,000.   The entries required to close the beginning inventory and to record the ending inventory are as follows:

To close the beginning inventory:	Income Summary............	95,000	
	Merchandise Inventory.......		95,000
To record the ending inventory:	Merchandise Inventory.........	125,000	
	Income Summary...........		125,000

After Purchases has been closed into Income Summary, the inventory and income summary accounts appear as follows:

Merchandise Inventory

Beginning inventory	95,000	To Income Summary	95,000
Ending inventory	125,000		

Income Summary

Beginning inventory	95,000	Ending inventory	125,000
Purchases	330,000		

(Balance: Cost of goods sold, $300,000)

Physical inventories — the manufacturing enterprise. In a manufacturing enterprise, three inventories are recognized: raw materials, goods in process, and finished goods. If cost of goods manufactured is to be summarized separately, beginning and ending raw materials and goods in process inventories are recorded in a manufacturing summary account, and beginning and ending finished goods inventories are recorded in the income summary account. To illustrate, assume the following data:

Inventories, January 1, 1972: Raw materials, $30,000; Goods in process, $25,000; Finished goods, $40,000.

Charges incurred during 1972: Raw materials purchases, $110,000; Direct labor, $140,000; Manufacturing overhead, $80,000.

Inventories, December 31, 1972: Raw materials, $40,000; Goods in process, $35,000; Finished goods, $50,000.

The entries to close the beginning inventories and to record the ending inventories follow:

To close the beginning inventories:	Manufacturing Summary.........	30,000	
	Raw Materials...............		30,000
	Manufacturing Summary.........	25,000	
	Goods in Process.............		25,000
	Income Summary.............	40,000	
	Finished Goods..............		40,000
To record the ending inventories:	Raw Materials.................	40,000	
	Manufacturing Summary.......		40,000
	Goods in Process..............	35,000	
	Manufacturing Summary.......		35,000
	Finished Goods................	50,000	
	Income Summary...........		50,000

After manufacturing costs are closed into the manufacturing summary account, the balance in this account summarizes the cost of goods manufactured. The cost of goods manufactured is transferred to the income summary account and the latter then reports cost of goods sold. Inventory and summary accounts will appear as follows:

Finished Goods

Beginning inventory	40,000	To Income Summary	40,000
Ending inventory	50,000		

Goods in Process

Beginning inventory	25,000	To Manufacturing Summary	25,000
Ending inventory	35,000		

Raw Materials

Beginning inventory	30,000	To Manufacturing Summary	30,000
Ending inventory	40,000		

Manufacturing Summary

Beginning Raw Materials Inventory	30,000	Ending Raw Materials Inventory	40,000
Beginning Goods in Process Inventory	25,000	Ending Goods in Process Inventory	35,000
Raw Materials Purchases	110,000	Cost of Goods Manufactured to Income Summary	310,000
Direct Labor	140,000		
Manufacturing Overhead	80,000		
	385,000		385,000

Income Summary

Beginning Finished Goods Inventory	40,000	Ending Finished Goods Inventory	50,000
Cost of Goods Manufactured	310,000		

(Balance: Cost of goods sold, $300,000)

Perpetual inventories — the merchandising enterprise. When the perpetual inventory plan is maintained, a separate purchases account is not used. The inventory account is charged whenever goods are acquired. When a sale takes place, two entries are required: (1) the sale is recorded in the usual manner, and (2) the merchandise sold is recorded by a debit to Cost of Goods Sold and a credit to the inventory account. Subsidiary records for inventory items are normally maintained. Detailed increases and decreases in the various inventory items are reported in the subsidiary accounts, and the costs of goods purchased and sold are summarized in the inventory controlling account. At the end of the period, the inventory account reflects the inventory on hand; the cost of goods sold account is closed into Income Summary. These accounts appear as follows:

Merchandise Inventory

| Beginning inventory | 95,000 | To Cost of Goods Sold | 300,000 |
| Purchases | 330,000 | | |

(Balance: Ending inventory, $125,000)

Cost of Goods Sold

| Cost of Goods Sold | 300,000 | To Income Summary | 300,000 |

Income Summary

| Cost of Goods Sold | 300,000 | | |

Even if a perpetual inventory system is not used, a closing procedure similar to the foregoing may be preferred. Purchases can be closed into the inventory account. The inventory account would then be reduced to the ending inventory figure and Cost of Goods Sold charged with the inventory decrease. Cost of Goods Sold is closed into Income Summary.

Perpetual inventories — the manufacturing enterprise. When perpetual inventories are maintained by a manufacturing enterprise, materials purchases are recorded by charges to Raw Materials. Materials removed from stores for processing are recorded by debits to Goods in Process and credits to Raw Materials. Labor and manufacturing overhead costs, also, are charged to Goods in Process. Finished Goods is debited and Goods in Process is credited for the cost of goods completed and transferred into the finished goods stock. The entry to record a sale is accompanied by an entry to record the cost of goods sold, Cost of Goods Sold being debited and Finished Goods credited. At the end of the period, inventory accounts report ending balances; Cost of Goods Sold is closed into Income Summary. Normally raw materials, goods in process, and finished goods inventory accounts are controlling accounts, individual changes in the various inventory items being reported in the respective subsidiary ledgers. Frequently such procedures are maintained as a part of a system designed to offer detailed information concerning costs. Perpetual inventory accounts, together with the other accounts affected in the closing process, will appear as follows:

Finished Goods

| Beginning inventory | 40,000 | To Cost of Goods Sold | 300,000 |
| Cost of goods manufactured | 310,000 | | |

(Balance: Ending inventory, $50,000)

Goods in Process

Beginning inventory	25,000	To finished goods	310,000
Raw materials received for processing	100,000		
Direct labor	140,000		
Manufacturing overhead	80,000		

(Balance: Ending inventory, $35,000)

Raw Materials

Beginning inventory	30,000	Raw materials transferred to goods	
Raw materials purchases	110,000	in process	100,000

(Balance: Ending inventory, $40,000)

Cost of Goods Sold

Cost of Goods Sold	300,000	To Income Summary	300,000

Income Summary

Cost of Goods Sold	300,000	

Even if the perpetual inventory system is not used, a closing procedure similar to the foregoing may be preferred. The raw materials purchases account can be closed into the raw materials inventory account. The inventory account would then be reduced to the ending inventory balance, and Goods in Process would be debited. Direct labor and manufacturing overhead accounts are closed into Goods in Process. Goods in Process is then reduced to the ending inventory figure and Finished Goods in debited. Finished Goods is finally reduced to its ending balance and a cost of goods sold account is opened and debited for the inventory decrease. Cost of Goods Sold is closed into Income Summary.

The summarizing phase — closing the accounts

After the accounts have been adjusted and the ending inventories recorded, nominal accounts are closed into the income summary account. In a sole proprietorship and partnership, the balance in the income summary account is transferred to owners' equity accounts. In a corporation, when there have been earnings, provision must be made for income taxes before activities can be summarized. Income Taxes is debited and Income Taxes Payable is credited. The charge for taxes is closed into Income Summary, and the balance in the summary account is transferred to Retained Earnings.

Closing the accounts with provision for intraperiod tax allocation. When nominal accounts include extraordinary items, income taxes should be allocated between ordinary operations and the extraordinary items. Separate nominal accounts may be established to report taxes applicable to ordinary operations and taxes applicable to the individual extraordinary items. When prior period adjustments have been recorded directly in the retained earnings account, taxes related to net income are reported in appropriate taxes expense accounts, and any taxes that are related to the prior period adjustments are recorded directly in Retained Earnings. Intraperiod tax allocation results in a full matching of revenue and expenses and provides summaries that are meaningful and directly comparable with similar summaries of the past.

The entries given below illustrate the allocation of income taxes between ordinary operations and extraordinary items. Assume that income taxes on a corporation's taxable income are 50%; however, taxes on gains from the sale of assets qualifying as long-term capital gains are limited to 25%. In example (1) below, it is assumed that a company has income from ordinary operations of $100,000 that is taxable and also an extraordinary gain from the sale of an investment of $50,000 that qualifies as long-term capital gain. In example (2) it is assumed that a company has income from ordinary operations of $200,000 that is taxable and also an extraordinary loss from fire of $50,000 that is fully deductible for tax purposes.

Summary of Transactions for the Year	Entries to Record Tax Provision

(1) Ordinary income.......... $100,000
    Extraordinary gain, qualifying
      as long-term capital gain..... 50,000
                               $150,000
	Income Taxes Applicable to
	   Income Before Extraordin-
	   ary Items.............. 50,000
	Income Taxes Applicable to
	   Extraordinary Gain...... 12,500
	   Income Taxes Payable ... 62,500

Taxes applicable to ordinary in-
   income: $100,000 × 50%..... $ 50,000
Taxes on extraordinary gain,
   $50,000 × 25%............. 12,500
Tax liability.................. $ 62,500	

(2) Ordinary income.......... $200,000
    Extraordinary loss, fully
      deductible................ 50,000
                             $150,000
	Income Taxes Applicable to
	   Income Before Extraordin-
	   ary Items..............100,000
	Income Tax Credit Appli-
	   cable to Extraordinary
	   Loss................. 25,000
	   Income Taxes Payable... 75,000

Taxes applicable to ordinary in-
   come: $200,000 × 50%....... $100,000
Taxes applicable to net income
   after fire loss: $150,000 × 50%. 75,000
Tax credit related to fire loss..... $ 25,000	

To illustrate the application of the foregoing procedures in the accounts of a company at the end of a period, assume that nominal accounts after adjustment report the following balances:

Debits		Credits	
Cost of goods sold.........	$300,000	Sales....................	$500,000
Operating expenses.......	155,500	Other revenues...........	13,000
Other expenses..........	7,500	Extraordinary gain........	20,000
	$463,000		$533,000

The total income tax liability on the total income of $70,000 ($533,000 − $463,000) is estimated at $30,000. Assume that the extraordinary gain qualifies as a long-term capital gain resulting in a tax limited to 25% of the gain, or $5,000. Charges are made to Income Taxes Applicable to Income Before Extraordinary Items, $25,000, and Income Taxes Applicable to Extraordinary Gain, $5,000, and Income Taxes Payable is credited for $30,000. In addition, a claim for an income tax refund of $9,000 is filed as the result of an overstatement of the ending inventory of the prior period. A charge is made to an asset account, Claim for Income Tax Refund, for $9,000, and Retained Earnings is credited for this amount.

When the entries for taxes have been recorded, nominal accounts may be closed to Income Summary and Income Summary closed into Retained Earnings; these accounts will appear as follows:

Income Summary

Cost of Goods Sold	300,000	Sales	500,000
Operating Expenses	155,500	Other Revenues	13,000
Other Expenses	7,500	Extraordinary Gain	20,000
Income Taxes Applicable to Income Before Extraordinary Items	25,000		
Income Taxes Applicable to Extraordinary Gain	5,000		
Net Income to Retained Earnings	40,000		
	533,000		533,000

Claim for Income Tax Refund

Claim for income tax refund on prior period adjustment	9,000	

Income Taxes Payable

	Estimated income taxes on net income	30,000

Retained Earnings

Dividends	20,000	Balance, January 1	144,000
Prior period adjustment — overstatement of ending inventory	18,000	Net income for year	40,000
		Income taxes credit relating to prior period adjustment	9,000

Closing the accounts with provision for interperiod tax allocation. It was stated in the preceding chapter that when there are timing differences between book income and taxable income, adjustments are required that provide for the assignment of income tax charges to book income at the amount that is regarded as applicable to that income rather than at the amounts actually to be paid. Timing differences calling for the application of interperiod tax allocation procedures are classified and the entries in each case illustrated in the following sections.[1]

---

[1]It was assumed in the illustration previously given in this chapter that book income and taxable income were the same.

Book income before taxes is less than taxable income. (1) *Revenue is deferred for book purposes but is currently recognized for tax purposes.* Assume that a company collects advance rents for a three-year period and recognizes such collection as deferred revenue. For income tax purposes, however, the rents must be recognized as revenue and are taxed in the period they are received. If income taxes are recognized on the books at the amounts actually payable, the current period is penalized by a charge for taxes on revenue not currently recognized while subsequent periods are correspondingly favored by the absence of taxes on revenue that emerges from the balance originally deferred. Interperiod tax allocation procedures call for reducing the charge for taxes by the portion related to the taxable income that exceeds book income; this portion of the tax charge should be assigned to future periods concurrent with the recognition of the deferred revenue as realized.

(2) *Expense is currently recognized for book purposes but is deferred for tax purposes.* Assume that a company charges initial organization costs to revenues of the first year of operations. For income tax purposes, however, these costs must be capitalized and are amortizable over a period of not less than 60 months. The charge for taxes currently payable, then, will exceed the tax charge applicable to book income because of the expense that is not recognized for tax purposes; taxes in subsequent periods will be correspondingly less than the taxes applicable to book income because of deductions that are recognized for tax purposes but that do not appear on the books. Here, as in the preceding example, the charge for taxes in the first year should be reduced by the portion related to the taxable income that exceeds book income; this portion of the tax charge should be assigned to future periods concurrent with the recognition of organization costs as a deduction for tax purposes.

Circumstances such as the above require recognition of a deferred taxes expense balance that is assignable to later periods when book income will exceed taxable income. Assume that book and taxable incomes for a corporation for a three-year period are as follows:

	Book Income Before Income Taxes	Taxable Income
1970	$100,000	$120,000
1971	100,000	90,000
1972	120,000	110,000
	$320,000	$320,000

Assume also that throughout this period the tax rate is 50%. Entries to record the taxes to be paid each year as well as the allocation of taxes between periods are listed on the following page.

1970: To record accrued taxes on tax- Income Taxes 60,000
       able income, 50% of $120,000.   Income Taxes Pay. .   60,000

       To defer portion of income tax Deferred Income Taxes
       estimated to be applicable to   Expense 10,000
       subsequent periods, 50% of   Income Taxes   10,000
       $20,000, taxable income in ex-
       cess of book income.

1971: To record accrued taxes on tax- Income Taxes 45,000
       able income, 50% of $90,000.   Income Taxes Pay. .   45,000

       To recognize portion of tax ex- Income Taxes 5,000
       pense deferral as an addition to   Deferred Income
       current tax charge, 50% of   Taxes Expense . . .   5,000
       $10,000, book income in excess
       of taxable income.

1972: To record accrued taxes on tax- Income Taxes 55,000
       able income, 50% of $110,000.   Income Taxes Pay. .   55,000

       To recognize balance of tax ex- Income Taxes 5,000
       pense deferral as addition to   Deferred Income
       current tax charge, 50% of   Taxes Expense . . .   5,000
       $10,000, book income in excess
       of taxable income.

A comparison of book results in the absence of tax adjustments with results when adjustments are made is given below:

	Book results unadjusted			Book results adjusted		
	Income Before Income Taxes	Income Taxes	Net Income	Income Before Income Taxes	Income Taxes	Net Income
1970..	$100,000	$ 60,000	$ 40,000	$100,000	$ 50,000	$ 50,000
1971..	100,000	45,000	55,000	100,000	50,000	50,000
1972..	120,000	55,000	65,000	120,000	60,000	60,000
	$320,000	$160,000	$160,000	$320,000	$160,000	$160,000

Note that in the unadjusted results, income taxes were $15,000 lower in 1971 than in 1970 even though income before income taxes was identical in both years. The adjusted results properly match the income taxes against revenue and reflect equal taxes for equal reported book income.

Book income before taxes is more than taxable income. (1) *Revenue is currently recognized for book purposes but is deferred for tax purposes.* Assume that a company engages in a long-term construction contract requiring three years for its completion and for book purposes recognizes income on a percentage-of-completion basis. For income tax purposes, however, the company elects to report the full contract income and pay income taxes in the year of contract completion. If income taxes are recognized on the books at the amounts actually payable, periods in which the contract is still in progress and in which portions of the income are recognized are favored through the absence of income taxes, and the period in which the contract is completed is correspondingly penalized by a charge for taxes on the entire contract income. Interperiod tax allocation procedures call for increasing the charge for taxes payable by the amount of taxes on the portion of book income that exceeds taxable income; the tax charge in the period in which the contract is completed, then, can be limited to the amount applicable to the income recognized on the books in the period of completion.

(2) *Expense is deferred for book purposes but is currently recognized for tax purposes.* Assume that a company acquires property with a five-year life and reports depreciation on the books on a straight-line basis or at the rate of 20 percent per year. For income tax purposes, however, it elects to recognize depreciation by the sum-of-the-years-digits method and reports annual charges for the five-year period of 5/15, 4/15, 3/15, 2/15, and 1/15 of cost. Charges for taxes payable in the first and second years, then, are less than the charges applicable to book income because depreciation recognized on the tax return exceeds that per books; taxes that are payable in the fourth and fifth years are correspondingly greater than the taxes applicable to book income because depreciation per books exceeds the depreciation recognized for tax purposes. In applying interperiod tax allocation procedures, charges for taxes in the first two years should be increased by taxes on the portions of the book income that exceed taxable income; tax charges in the fourth and fifth years, then, can be limited to the amounts that are applicable to the income recognized per books.

These circumstances require the recognition of a deferred income tax liability balance that will relieve tax charges of later periods when taxable income will exceed book income. Assume that book and taxable incomes for a corporation are as follows for a three-year period:

	Book Income Before Income Taxes	Taxable Income
1970	$100,000	$ 80,000
1971	100,000	110,000
1972	120,000	130,000
	$320,000	$320,000

Assume a 50% tax rate as in the earlier examples. Entries to record the taxes to be paid each year, as well as the allocation of taxes between periods, are listed below and on the following page.

1970: To record accrued taxes on taxable income, 50% of $80,000.

Income Taxes	40,000	
Income Taxes Pay..		40,000

To accrue income taxes estimated to be applicable to income not currently reported,
50% of $20,000, book income
in excess of taxable income.

Income Taxes....... 10,000
  Deferred Income
    Taxes Payable...   10,000

1971: To record accrued taxes on taxable income, 50% of $110,000.

Income Taxes....... 55,000
  Income Taxes Pay..   55,000

To apply portion of tax accrual
as a reduction in current tax
charge, 50% of $10,000, tax-
able income in excess of book
income.

Deferred Income Taxes
  Payable........... 5,000
  Income Taxes.....   5,000

1972: To record accrued taxes on taxable income, 50% of $130,000.

Income Taxes....... 65,000
  Income Taxes Pay..   65,000

To apply balance of tax accrual
as a reduction in current tax
charge, 50% of $10,000, tax-
able income in excess of book
income.

Deferred Income Taxes
  Payable........... 5,000
  Income Taxes.....   5,000

A comparison of book results in the absence of tax adjustments with results when adjustments are made is given below:

	Book results unadjusted			Book results adjusted		
	Income Before Income Taxes	Income Taxes	Net Income	Income Before Income Taxes	Income Taxes	Net Income
1970..	$100,000	$ 40,000	$ 60,000	$100,000	$ 50,000	$ 50,000
1971..	100,000	55,000	45,000	100,000	50,000	50,000
1972..	120,000	65,000	55,000	120,000	60,000	60,000
	$320,000	$160,000	$160,000	$320,000	$160,000	$160,000

Financial reports on cash versus accrual basis

In the preceding pages of this chapter, adjustments were made at the end of the period in an attempt to measure accurately revenues and expenses of the fiscal period. In the case of revenues, amounts *earned* rather than amounts collected, and in the case of expenses, amounts *incurred* rather than amounts paid, were recognized and given effect in the measurement of net income. Statements recognizing revenues in the period when earned and expenses in the period when incurred are said to be prepared on the *accrual basis*. For most businesses, satisfactory measurement of operating results can be achieved only through accounting on the accrual basis.

Statements are said to be prepared on a *cash basis* when revenues and expenses are recognized only upon the receipt and the disbursement of cash. In the case of a pure cash basis, revenues from the sale of goods and services are recognized only at the time collections from customers are made; expenses are recognized only when payments are made for equipment, goods, services, and other operating items. There is no recognition of bad debts since revenue is not recognized unless cash is received; there is no recognition of depreciation since the entire cost of the equipment is recognized as expense at the time of payment.

The federal government permits the filing of income tax returns on the accrual basis or on the cash basis. But the cash basis for tax purposes is actually a combination cash-accrual basis, since it is recognized that the application of a strictly cash approach as described could result in serious distortions in net income measurement. Furthermore, a strictly cash approach could offer a means of shifting significant amounts of revenues and expenses from one year to another by control of cash receipts and disbursements. The following requirements must be observed by a taxpayer reporting on a cash basis:

1. When goods are sold, income from sales must include full recognition of sales on account, and cost of goods sold must include full recognition of purchases on account and also inventories. In the case of merchandising or manufacturing companies, then, the gross profit on sales is the same on the cash basis and the accrual basis. But professional men or companies selling services may disregard receivables from clients and recognize as revenues only amounts actually collected.

2. When receivables must be recognized, the taxpayer is given the option of recognizing as bad debts expense either (a) those amounts actually written off as uncollectible during the period or (b) amounts anticipated to be uncollectible established through satisfactory valuation procedures.

3. In the case of acquisitions of land, buildings, and equipment items and intangible assets, deductions are allowed only to the extent of the depreciation or amortization allocable to the current period.

4. The reporting policy that is adopted must be employed consistently each period.

Use of the cash basis, then, generally means the use of a hybrid system, with sales, purchases, depreciation, and doubtful accounts being reported as on the accrual basis, but with remaining revenue and expense items being measured by cash receipts and disbursements. The cash basis offers certain advantages in simpler and more economical accounting. A summary of operations prepared on the cash basis may be acceptable when failure to recognize accruals and prepayments results in relatively minor misstatements that are largely counterbalanced in periodic reporting. But when accruals and prepayments are material in amount and vary significantly from period to period, satisfactory net income measurement would call for the adoption of the accrual basis.

From transactions to statements

Preceding pages have stressed the importance of financial reports in modern economic society. The usual procedures for recording transactions and the sequence of events incident to the preparation of such reports have been briefly reviewed. The treatment applied to these transactions and events was referred to as the accounting process.

The accounting process includes the entire field of analyzing, classifying, recording, and summarizing. It includes the successive steps that constitute the accounting cycle. It starts with the first written record of the transactions of the business unit and concludes with the final summarized financial statements.

The significance of the accounting process and its applicability to every business unit, regardless of size, in our economic society must be appreciated. Although the procedures may be modified to meet special conditions, the process that has been reviewed here is basic in accounting for every business unit.

QUESTIONS

1. What is the accounting function supplied by (a) the business paper? (b) the book of original entry? (c) the ledger?

2. Distinguish between: (a) real and nominal accounts, (b) general journal and special journals, (c) general ledger and subsidiary ledgers.

3. What advantages are provided through the use of (a) special journals, (b) subsidiary ledgers, and (c) the voucher system?

4. (a) What business papers are used in posting debits and credits to customer and creditor accounts? (b) Would it be better practice to post to these accounts from books of original entry? Explain.

5. What are the major advantages of electronic data processing as compared with manual processing of accounting data?

6. The computer will ultimately take the place of the accountant. Do you agree?

7. List and describe the steps in the periodic summary. State why each step is necessary.

8. Define a mixed account. Should any accounts remain mixed after the adjusting entries have been posted? Explain.

9. Explain the nature and the purpose of (a) adjusting entries, (b) closing entries, and (c) reversing entries.

10. The accountant for Spring Company enters adjusting entries directly to the ledger without preparing formal adjusting entries in the general journal. Evaluate this practice.

11. (a) State a general rule that may be applied in determining when to reverse adjusting entries. (b) Give examples for both accrued revenue and accrued expense items where exceptions to the rule can be supported.

12. Payment of insurance in advance may be recorded in either (a) an expense account or (b) an asset account. Which method would you recommend? What periodic entries are required under each method?

13. The receipt of rentals in advance may be recorded in either (a) a revenue account or (b) a liability account. Which method would you recommend? What periodic entries would be required under each of these methods?

14. Distinguish between adjusting the inventory account for a merchandising enterprise using a physical inventory system and one using a perpetual inventory system.

15. What is the purpose of a separate manufacturing summary account?

16. The bookkeeper for the Walls Co. does not reverse accrued and prepaid balances at the beginning of the period. At the end of the period he charges or credits these accounts to bring them to the appropriate balances as of the end of the fiscal period, and the offsetting debits and credits are made to the related revenue and expense accounts. Revenue and expense accounts at the end of the year thus report receipts and disbursements and the adjustments resulting from variations in the accrued and prepaid balances. Evaluate this procedure.

17. The bookkeeper for the Young Corporation does not adjust the revenue and expense accounts at the end of the period but makes closing entries in the usual manner, leaving certain revenue accounts with debit balances and certain expense accounts with credit balances. He claims that this saves the effort required in adjusting and reversing accounts, adjusting, closing, and reversing being accomplished at the same time. Do you agree?

18. Describe the entries that would be made in recognizing the income taxes for the period in each case below:
   (a) There are earnings from ordinary operations and an extraordinary loss that is less than such earnings.
   (b) There are earnings from ordinary operations and a credit for a prior period adjustment that was recorded directly in Retained Earnings. An amended tax return has been filed.
   (c) There is a loss from ordinary operations, an extraordinary gain that is greater than the loss, and a debit for a prior period adjustment that was recorded directly in Retained Earnings. A claim for tax refund has been filed.

19. In adopting tax allocation procedures for timing differences between financial and taxable income, what adjustments are made when (a) book income before taxes is less than taxable income, and (b) book income before taxes is more than taxable income? In your opinion, what timing differences are most commonly found?

20. Under what circumstances will a Deferred Income Taxes Payable balance be reduced to a zero balance? Why do most companies report an increasing balance in this account?

21. (a) Distinguish between reporting on a cash basis and reporting on an accrual basis. (b) What are the advantages and disadvantages of reporting on a cash basis?

EXERCISES

1. On March 15, 1972, J. L. Jensen paid insurance for a three-year period beginning April 1. He recorded the payment as follows:

Prepaid Insurance.............................	1,080	
Cash..		1,080

(a) What adjustment is required on December 31? What reversing entry, if any, would you make? (b) What nominal account could be debited instead of Prepaid Insurance? What adjustment would then be necessary? What reversing entry, if any, would you make?

2. Eldon Lytle received rent of $2,400 for one year beginning March 1. He recorded the transaction as follows:

Cash..	2,400	
Rent Received in Advance......................		2,400

(a) What adjustment is required on December 31? What reversing entry, if any, would you make? (b) What nominal account could have been credited instead of Rent Received in Advance? What adjustment would then be necessary? What reversing entry, if any, would you make?

3. In analyzing the accounts of Don Norton, the adjusting data listed below are determined on December 31, the end of an annual fiscal period. (a) Give the adjusting entry for each item. (b) What reversing entries would be appropriate? (c) What sources would provide the information for each adjustment?

(1) The prepaid insurance account shows a debit of $600, representing the cost of a 3-year fire insurance policy dated July 1.

(2) On October 1, Rental Income was credited for $800, representing income from subrental for a 4-month period beginning on that date.

(3) Purchase of advertising materials for $700 during the year was recorded in the advertising expense account. On December 31 advertising materials of $150 are on hand.

(4) On October 1, $750 was paid as rent for a 6-month period beginning on that date. The expense account, Rent, was debited.
(5) Miscellaneous Office Expense was debited for office supplies of $400 purchased during the year. On December 31 office supplies of $75 are on hand.
(6) Interest of $60 is accrued on notes payable.

4. The following information is taken from the records of the Basin Company:

	Balance January 1, 1972	Balance December 31, 1972	Transactions During 1972
Accruals:			
Interest receivable.............	$200	$240	
Wages payable................	475	500	
Interest payable..............	375	300	
Cash receipts and payments:			
Interest on notes receivable......			$ 620
Wages.......................			32,000
Interest on notes payable........			465

Compute the interest income, the wages expense, and the interest expense for the year.

5. Account balances before and after adjustment on December 31 follow. Give the adjustment that was made for each account.

Account Title	Before Adjustment Dr.	Before Adjustment Cr.	After Adjustment Dr.	After Adjustment Cr.
(a) Merchandise Inventory........	$31,500		$35,000	
(b) Allowance for Doubtful Accounts	1,500			$ 6,000
(c) Accumulated Depreciation.....		$16,000		18,500
(d) Sales Salaries................	24,200		24,650	
(e) Income Taxes................	4,800		5,450	
(f) Royalty Income.............		7,000		7,500
(g) Interest Income.............		550		600

6. Changes in account balances and other data for the Leslie Co. are described below, but in each case certain transactions that took place during the period are not stated. Give the entry to record the missing data affecting each account.

(a) Sales salaries: accrued, /1/72, $1,800; accrued, 12/31/72, $2,400; sales salaries for the period, $29,000.
(b) Interest income: accrued 1/1/72, $250; accrued 12/31/72, $500; interest income for the period, $4,000.
(c) Allowance for doubtful accounts: balance 1/1/72, $600; balance, 12/31/72, $1,550; increase at end of period by adjustment, $5,100
(d) Rental income received in advance: balance, 1/1/72, $1,800; balance, 12/31/72, $850; rental income for the period, $7,000.
(e) Supplies on hand: balance, 1/1/72, $2,600; balance, 12/31/72, $1,850; supplies expense for the period, $12,000.

(f) Delivery equipment: balance, 1/1/72, $7,100; balance, 12/31/72, $7,800; equipment sold during the period, $13,000 (cost).

(g) Accounts receivable: balance, 1/1/72, $22,000; balance, 12/31/72, $26,500; collections on accounts during the period, $230,000; bad accounts written off during the period, $4,400.

(h) Accounts payable: balance 1/1/72, $18,000; balance, 12/31/72, $16,500; purchases on account during the period, $155,000; purchases discounts taken during the period, $1,600.

7. Upon inspecting the accounts for the Robinson Co. before they are closed at the end of 1972, you find the following data. What entries are required to correct the accounts?

(a) A sale of merchandise for $800 had been made on December 31, 1971. The merchandise, cost $600, was delivered to the customer on this date and was not included in the ending inventory. However, the sale was not recorded until the remittance was received on January 10, 1972.

(b) 100 shares of Phillips Company stock were sold at $60 per share on July 7, 1972. The bookkeeper debited Cash and credited the investment account for proceeds from the sale, $6,000. The investment account shows that 200 shares of this stock were originally acquired at a cost of $15,000.

(c) Raw materials, cost $500, received on December 31, 1971, had been included in the inventory of raw materials taken on that date. However, the materials were recorded as a purchase on January 4, 1972, when the invoice was received.

(d) Equipment, cost $6,000, acquired on July 1, 1968, depreciated on a 5-year basis, was destroyed by fire on May 1, 1972. Cash was debited and Equipment was credited for $1,000, the proceeds from an insurance policy.

8. Some of the accounts that appear in the ledger of the Thorn Manufacturing Co. on November 30, the end of a fiscal year, follow:

Finished Goods	$ 70,000	Direct Labor	$130,000
Goods in Process	70,000	Manufacturing Overhead	100,000
Raw Materials	60,000	Sales	900,000
Raw Materials Purchases	340,000	Operating Expenses	150,000

Physical inventories on November 30 are: raw materials, $70,000; goods in process, $60,000; finished goods, $40,000. The federal income tax liability is computed at 50% of net income.

Assuming no further adjustments, give the entries required to adjust and close the accounts according to two different methods.

9. The Logan Co. reported for 1972 taxable net income of $160,000 and an extraordinary gain of $40,000 from the retirement of bonds outstanding at less than book value that was fully taxable. Assume income tax rates for 1972 of 50%. (a) Give the entry that would be made in recording the income taxes for 1972. (b) Assuming that the bond retirement had resulted in a loss of $40,000 that was fully deductible for tax purposes, give the entry that would be made in recording the income taxes for 1972.

10. The Otto Corporation accrues certain revenue on its books in 1970 and 1971 of $3,500 and $4,000 respectively, but such revenue is not subject to income taxes until 1972. Book income before taxes and taxable income for the three-year period, then, are as follows:

	Book Income	Taxable Income
1970.	$14,000	$10,500
1971.	16,500	12,500
1972.	15,000	22,500

Assume that the rate applicable to taxable income is 30% in each year. What entries would be made at the end of each year to recognize the tax liability and to provide for a proper allocation of taxes in view of the differences in book and taxable income?

11. From the following information, compute the cash collections from customers of the Conlin Company for 1972.

Sales.	$352,500
Accounts receivable, January 1.	32,600
Accounts receivable, December 31.	24,000
Doubtful accounts expense.	5,000
Allowance for doubtful accounts, January 1.	10,000
Allowance for doubtful accounts, December 31.	9,000

12. Smith and Snow, attorneys, summarize income on a cash basis. Their net income for 1972 is calculated at $15,900. What net income would they have shown for the year if income had been calculated on the accrual basis and the following adjusting data were recognized?

	Jan. 1, 1972	Dec. 31, 1972
Receivables from clients.....	$12,000	$9,250
Office supplies on hand.......	310	360
Unearned retainer income......	1,600	3,000
Miscellaneous accrued expenses...	450	200

PROBLEMS

4-1. The trial balance of Allman, Inc., shows among other items the following balances on December 31, 1972, the end of a fiscal year:

Accounts Receivable.	80,000	
4½% Panorama City Bonds.	50,000	
Buildings.	90,000	
Accumulated Depreciation — Buildings.		31,500
Land.	100,000	
6% First-Mortgage Bonds Payable.		100,000
Rental Income.		26,000
Office Expense.	2,000	

The following facts are ascertained on this date upon inspection of the records of the company:

(a) It is estimated that approximately 2% of accounts receivable may prove uncollectible.

(b) Interest is receivable semiannually on the Panorama City bonds on March 1 and September 1.

(c) Buildings are depreciated at 2½% a year; however, there were building additions of $30,000 during the year. The company computes depreciation on asset acquisitions during the year at one half the annual rate.

(d) Interest on the first-mortgage bonds is payable semiannually on February 1 and August 1.

(e) Rental income includes $1,500 that was received on October 1, representing rent on part of the buildings for the period October 1, 1972, to September 30, 1973.

(f) Office supplies of $600 are on hand on December 31. Purchases of office supplies were charged to the office expense account.

Instructions: (1) Prepare the journal entries to adjust the books on December 31, 1972.

(2) Give the reversing entries that may appropriately be made at the beginning of 1973.

4-2. The following information is available with respect to transactions of Galaxy Publishers, which began operations in 1972:

(a) Cash collections on annual subscriptions to their monthly magazine during the last six months of 1972 were as follows:

July	$10,800	October	$ 6,500
August	7,000	November	8,500
September	6,200	December	10,000

The subscriptions are effective as of the start of the month following receipt of the subscription.

(b) Payments for insurance coverage were made as follows:

Policy Date	Coverage (years)	Premium
July 1	3	$750
September 30	1	110
October 1	3	450
November 30	1	240

(c) The annual real and personal property tax paid on December 5, 1972, was $1,820. The bill covers the city's fiscal year beginning July 1, 1972.

(d) Advertising materials of $900 were purchased from July 1 to December 31. No materials were on hand on July 1. Approximately one third of the materials purchased remains on hand on December 31.

Instructions: (1) Assuming that original entries for revenue and expense items in each of the above transactions were made to real accounts, give the necessary adjusting entries at the end of the 6-month period. (Give schedules following journal entries to show how the amounts were calculated.)

(2) Assuming that original entries for revenue and expense items in each of the above transactions were made to nominal accounts, give the necessary adjusting entries.

(3) State which of the entries in parts (1) and (2) may appropriately be reversed at the beginning of 1973.

4-3. The bookkeeper for the Clark Co. has submitted an income statement for the year ended December 31, 1972, with results as follows:

Income from operations.	$110,900
Gain on sale of investments.	21,000
Net income. . . . . *Entre credit*.	$131,900

Accounts have not yet been closed, and a review of the books discloses the need for the following additional adjustments:

(a) The account, Office Expense, shows the cost of all purchases of office supplies for the year. At the end of 1972 there are supplies of $600 on hand.

(b) The allowance for doubtful accounts shows a debit balance of $200. It is estimated that 3% of the accounts receivable as of December 31 will prove uncollectible. The accounts receivable balance on this date is $29,100.

(c) The ledger shows a balance for accrued salaries and wages of $1,800 as of December 31, 1971, which was left unadjusted during 1972. No recognition was made in the accounts at the end of 1972 for accrued salaries and wages which amounted to $1,950.

(d) The ledger shows a balance for accrued interest on investments of $375 as of December 31, 1971, which was left unchanged during 1972. No recognition was made in the accounts at the end of 1972 for accrued interest on investments which amounted to $440.

(e) The prepaid insurance account was debited during the year for amounts paid for insurance and shows a balance of $1,200 at the end of 1972. The unexpired portions of the policies on December 31, 1972, total $560.

(f) A portion of a building was subleased for 3 months, November 1, 1972, to February 1, 1973. Unearned Rental Income was credited for $1,200 and no adjustment was made in this account at the end of 1972.

(g) The interest expense account was charged for all interest charges incurred during the year and shows a balance of $1,900. However, of this amount, $250 represents charges applicable to 1973.

(h) Provision for income taxes for 1972 is to be computed at a 50% rate. However, the income taxes applicable to the sale of investments are limited to 25% of the gain.

Instructions: (1) Give the entries that are required on December 31, 1972, to bring the books up to date. (In recording income taxes, provide a schedule to show how the corrected net income subject to tax was determined.)

(2) Prepare a revised summary of the results from 1972 activities.

4-4. The bookkeeper for the Terry Co. prepares no reversing entries and records all revenue and expense items in nominal accounts during the period. The following balances, among others, are listed on the trial balance at the end of the fiscal period, December 31, 1972, before accounts have been adjusted:

Accounts Receivable	$38,000
Allowance for Doubtful Accounts (cr.)	250
Accrued Interest on Investments	700
Discount on Notes Payable	75
Prepaid Real Estate and Personal Property Taxes	450
Merchandise Inventory	25,200
Accrued Salaries and Wages	1,000
Discount on Notes Receivable	700
Unearned Rental Income	375

Inspection of the company's books and records reveals the following information as of December 31, 1972:

(a) Uncollectible accounts are estimated at 3% of the accounts receivable balance.

(b) The accrued interest on investments totals $600.

(c) The company borrows cash by discounting its own notes at the bank. Discount on notes payable at the end of 1972 is $400.

(d) Prepaid real estate and personal property taxes are $450, the same as at the end of 1971.

(e) The merchandise inventory is $26,900.

(f) Accrued salaries and wages are $1,075.

(g) The company accepts notes from the customers giving its customers credit for the face of the note less a charge for interest. At the end of each period any interest applicable to the succeeding period is reported as a discount. Discount on notes receivable at the end of 1972 is $375.

(h) Part of the company's properties had been sublet on September 15, 1971, at a rental of $750 per month. The arrangement was terminated at the end of one year.

Instructions: Give the adjusting entries that are required to bring the books up to date.

4-5. The bookkeeper for the Backman Corporation submits an income statement for the year ended December 31, 1972, which reports the following:

Income from ordinary activities	$72,400
Deduct loss from theft	19,600
Net income	$52,800

An inspection of the books before they are closed reveals the following accounting errors and omissions:

(a) A balance of $1,200 for accrued salaries established at the end of 1971 was left unchanged during 1972, with no recognition of accrued salaries as of December 31, 1972, which totaled $1,525.

(b) A balance of $400 for accrued interest on customer notes established at the end of 1971 was left unchanged during 1972, with no recognition of accrued interest as of December 31, 1972, which amounted to $275.

(c) Prepaid Insurance was debited for insurance premiums paid during 1972 and was left at the end of 1972 with a balance of $440. The unexpired insurance balance at the end of 1972 was $150.

(d) On December 1, 1972, part of a building was sublet by the company for 6 months; $900 was collected and was recorded as Rental Income. No adjustment was made in this balance at the end of 1972.

(e) On November 1, 1972, the company borrowed cash on a $7,500 one-year non-interest-bearing note. The note was discounted by the bank at 8%. The discount was reported as Interest Expense. No adjustment was made for this item at the end of 1972.

(f) Bonds of $100,000 are outstanding. Interest at 6% is payable semi-annually on February 1 and August 1. No entry was made for accrued interest as of December 31, 1972.

(g) Income taxes for 1972 are to be calculated at 50% of taxable income. (The loss from theft is fully deductible from other taxable income in arriving at the net income subject to tax.)

Instructions: (1) Give the entries that are required on December 31, 1972, to bring the books up to date. (In recording income taxes, provide a schedule to show how the balance of income from ordinary activities subject to tax was determined.)
(2) Prepare a revised summary of the results from 1972 activities.

4-6. The Walker Co. shows book income before income taxes and taxable income for 1971 and 1972 as follows:

	Book Income	Taxable Income
1971.....................	$ 93,800	$142,400
1972.....................	115,200	104,400

The reason for the discrepancies is found in the fact that the company, organized in the middle of 1971, wrote off against revenue of that year organization costs totaling $54,000. For federal income tax purposes, however, the organization costs can be written off ratably over a period of not less than 60 months. For income tax purposes, then, the company deducted 6/60 of the costs in 1971 and 12/60 of the costs in 1972. Income taxes are to be calculated at 50% of taxable income.

Instructions: Give the entries that would be made on the books of the company at the end of 1971 and 1972 to recognize the income tax liability and to provide for a proper allocation of taxes in view of the differences in book and income tax reporting.

4-7. Income data of the Rigby Company for the first five years of its operations are summarized below:

	1968	1969	1970	1971	1972
Sales.	$1,000,000	$1,200,000	$1,200,000	$1,250,000	$1,250,000
Cost of goods sold.	650,000	750,000	750,000	775,000	775,000
Gross profit on sales.	$ 350,000	$ 450,000	$ 450,000	$ 475,000	$ 475,000
Operating expenses.	160,000	225,000	220,000	240,000	235,000
Income before income taxes.	$ 190,000	$ 225,000	$ 230,000	$ 235,000	$ 240,000

Cost of goods sold includes depreciation on land, buildings, and equipment items that was calculated by the straight-line method. However, for income tax purposes, the company employed "accelerated depreciation" methods providing for higher charges in the early years of asset life and correspondingly lower charges in the later years. Depreciation charges on the books as compared with charges that were recognized for income tax purposes during the five-year period were as follows:

	1968	1969	1970	1971	1972
Depreciation per books.	$140,000	$155,000	$165,000	$165,000	$165,000
Accelerated depreciation per tax return.	260,000	240,000	190,000	140,000	95,000

All of the revenue of the company is taxable; all of the expenses are deductible for income tax purposes. Income tax rates in each year were 50% of taxable income.

Instructions: (1) Give the entries that would be made by the company for the years 1968 through 1972 to record the accrual of income taxes if income is charged with income taxes allocable to such income.

(2) Prepare a comparative income statement for the Rigby Company for the five-year period assuming the use of interperiod tax allocation procedures.

(3) Prepare a comparative income statement for the Rigby Company for the five-year period assuming that interperiod tax allocation procedures were not used and charges for income taxes were recognized at the amounts actually becoming payable each year.

4-8. You have been asked by the Regis Supply Company to review their books and to indicate what effect income tax allocation procedures will have on their statements. The following reconciliations of book and taxable income are made available to you for the three years 1970–72.

	1970	1971	1972
Book operating income.................	$100,000	$ 50,000	$200,000
Add:			
Nondeductible expense for tax purposes...		50,000	
Excess of book depreciation over tax depreciation..........................			10,000
Deferred revenue taxable in period of collection.........................	20,000	6,000	20,000
	$120,000	$106,000	$230,000
Less:			
Excess of income on installment sales over income reportable for tax purposes....	25,000	36,000	20,000
Excess of tax depreciation over book depreciation............................	10,000	20,000	
Taxable income.......................	$ 85,000	$ 50,000	$210,000

Instructions: Assume tax rates are 50% on taxable income. For each of the three years prepare journal entries to record the income taxes expense and liability.

4-9. The Mid-West Manufacturing Company prepared the following reconciliation between taxable and book income for 1972:

Income per tax return.............................	$2,050,000
Add excess depreciation taken on tax return as compared with books.......................................	100,000
	$2,150,000
Less:	
Capital gain on sale of land reported as an extraordinary item on income statement......................	100,000
Estimated expenses of future warranties not allowable for tax purposes until expenses are actually incurred.	170,000
Advance rental income taxable in period of receipt...	50,000
Operating income per books........................	$1,830,000

A prior period adjustment of $150,000 was charged directly against retained earnings. An income tax refund claim has been filed for this adjustment. Ordinary tax rates apply to this adjustment.

Instructions: (1) Assuming an ordinary tax rate of 50%, and a tax on capital gains of 25%, prepare the required journal entries to record the tax liability at December 31, 1972.

(2) Prepare the income statement for 1972 beginning with "Income before income taxes."

4-10. The income statement for the Marvel Electric Co. for the year ended December 31, 1972, was as follows:

Marvel Electric Co.
Income Statement
For Year Ended December 31, 1972

Sales.....................................			$1,200,000
Cost of goods sold:			
Materials purchased..................	$360,000		
Add decrease in materials inventory....	20,000	$380,000	
Direct labor.........................		110,000	
Manufacturing overhead..............		140,000	
		$630,000	
Add decrease in goods in process inventory............................		20,000	
		$650,000	
Deduct increase in finished goods inventory.............................		15,000	635,000
Gross profit on sales....................			$ 565,000
Selling and general expenses............			205,000
Income before income taxes............			$ 360,000
Deduct income taxes (income taxes, $155,000 plus credit applicable to extraordinary loss, $25,000)......................			180,000
Income before extraordinary items........			$ 180,000
Less loss on bond retirement (net of $25,000 income tax credit)..................			25,000
Net income........................			$ 155,000

Instructions: Give the journal entries to close the accounts at the end of 1972.

chapter 5

the accounting process illustrated

The accounting process as described in the preceding chapter is composed of a number of steps in well-defined sequence. To review, these steps consist of:

1. Making a first record of each transaction on an appropriate business paper or form.
2. Recording the transactions in chronological order in the books of original entry.
3. Posting the transactions as classified and summarized in the journals to the appropriate accounts in the ledgers.
4. Preparing a trial balance of the accounts in the general ledger and reconciling supporting data in the subsidiary ledgers with respective controlling accounts.
5. Compiling the data to bring the accounts up to date.
6. Preparing the work sheet.
7. Preparing the financial statements and supporting schedules.
8. Adjusting and closing the accounts.
9. Preparing a post-closing trial balance.
10. Reversing the adjustments that established accrued and prepaid revenue and expense balances.

The entire course of the accounting process is illustrated in the example that appears on the following pages. The books of original entry for a hypothetical manufacturing company, the Mitchell Corporation, are described. Data in the journals are transferred to the ledger, and the procedures involved in the periodic summary at the end of a fiscal year are then illustrated.

Books of original entry

The Mitchell Corporation maintains the following books of original entry: a sales journal, a sales returns and allowances journal, a cash receipts journal, a voucher register, a cash payments journal, and a general journal.

Sales journal. The sales journal as summarized at the end of the month appears as follows:

Sales Journal

Cash Dr.	Accounts Receivable Dr.	Date	Description	Sales Cr.	Sales Taxes Payable Cr.
250 00	780 00	31 31	Sales on account for day... Cash sales for day.......	750 00 240 00	30 00 10 00
8,800 00	24,500 00	31	Total................	32,000 00	1,300 00
(√)	(116)			(41)	(218)

One entry is made to record the sales on account for each day. Accounts Receivable is debited; Sales and Sales Taxes Payable are credited. Debits are posted to the individual customer's account in the accounts receivable ledger directly from the sales invoices.

One entry is also made for the cash sales for each day. Cash is debited and Sales and Sales Taxes Payable are credited.

Sales returns and allowances journal. The sales returns and allowances journal appears as follows:

Sales Returns and Allowances Journal

Date	Description	Accounts Receivable Cr.	Sales Returns and Allowances Dr.	Sales Taxes Payable Dr.
31	Sales returns and allowances for day......................	26 00	25 00	1 00
31	Total....................	520 00	500 00	20 00
		(116)	(041)	(218)

One entry is made to record the sales returns and allowances for each day. Sales Returns and Allowances and Sales Taxes Payable are debited; Accounts Receivable is credited. Credits are posted to the individual customer's account in the accounts receivable ledger directly from the credit memorandums.

Cash receipts journal. The cash receipts journal appears as follows:

Cash Receipts Journal

Cash Dr.	Sales Discount Dr.	Date	Account Credited	Post. Ref.	Sundry Accounts Cr.	Sales Cr.	Accounts Receivable Cr.
6,565 00		31	Notes Receivable.	113	6,500 00		
			Interest Income. .	72	65 00		
10,000 00		31	Notes Payable . . .	211	10,000 00		
1,020 00	20 00	31	K. T. Nelson.	√			1,040 00
250 00		31	Sales.	√		250 00	
48,460 00	255 00	31	Total.	√	16,565 00	8,800 00	23,350 00
(111)	(042)				(√)	(√)	(116)

One entry is made each day for the total amount collected on accounts receivable. In this entry Cash and Sales Discount are debited and Accounts Receivable is credited. Credits are posted to the individual customer's account in the accounts receivable ledger from a separate list of receipts on account maintained by the cashier.

In order to maintain the cash receipts journal as a complete record of all cash received, an entry for cash sales is made each day. This entry is also made in the sales journal so that the sales journal provides a complete record of sales. To avoid double posting of the transaction, the total of the Cash Dr. column in the sales journal and the total of the Sales Cr. column in the cash receipts journal are checked and are not posted. As a result, the debit to Cash for cash sales is posted from the cash receipts journal as a part of the total of the Cash Dr. column, and the credit to Sales for cash sales is posted from the sales journal as a part of the total of the Sales Cr. column.

Voucher register. The voucher register maintained by the company appears across the top of pages 134 and 135.

The company does not maintain an expenses control account and therefore a number of separate columns are provided for expenses in the voucher register. The total of each amount column is posted to the corresponding account, with the exception of the Payroll Dr. column and the Sundry Accounts Dr. and Cr. columns.

The debits to the various accounts for salaries and wages are posted directly from the payroll records. The total of the amounts thus posted equals the total of the Payroll Dr. column in the voucher register.

(left page)   Voucher Register

Date	Vou. No.	Payee	Paid Date	Ck. No.	Accounts Payable Cr.	Raw Materials Purchases Dr.	Freight In Dr.	Payroll Dr.	
21	31 5154	First National Bank	12/31	4207	8,120				21
22									22
23	31 5155	Payroll	12/31	4208	1,780			2,000	23
24									24
25	31 5156	Midwest G. & E.			1,700				25
26	31 5157	Jack's Hardware			300				26
27	31 5158	Jarris Supply Co.			1,200	1,200			27
28	31 5159	Petty Cash	12/31	4210	160				28
29	31	Total			37,020	6,800	400	15,300	29
					(213)	(51)	(52)	Posted to accounts as indicated by payroll records	

The debits posted from the payroll records to the various salaries and wages accounts for the month of December are as follows:

Direct Labor...	$ 6,500
Indirect Labor.......................................	1,900
Sales Salaries and Commissions......................	2,100
Delivery Salaries....................................	800
Factory Superintendence.............................	1,700
Officers Salaries....................................	1,400
Office Salaries......................................	900
	$15,300

One payroll record is kept for direct labor, indirect labor, sales salaries and commissions, and delivery salaries; another, for factory superintendence, officers salaries, and office salaries. The first group is paid weekly; the second, semimonthly. The entry for the payroll on December 31 in the voucher register is for the second group only.

General debits reported in the voucher register for December total $14,010 and are composed of the following items (the first five items represent vouchers recorded prior to December 31 and are not shown in the partial record):

Employees Income Taxes Payable (November)............	$ 2,000
FICA Taxes Payable (November).......................	440
Sales Taxes Payable (November)......................	720
Prepaid Insurance...................................	250
Building Maintenance and Repair.....................	480
Notes Payable.......................................	8,000
Interest Expense — Other............................	120
Factory Heat, Light, and Power......................	1,700
Tools...	300
	$14,010

For Month of December, 1972   (right page)

Factory Supplies Dr.	Misc. Factory Overhead Dr.	Adver-tising Expense Dr.	Misc. Selling Expense Dr.	Misc. Del. Expense Dr.	Office Supplies Dr.	Misc. Gen. Exp. Dr.	Sundry Accounts			
							Account	P. R.	Dr.	Cr.
							Notes Payable	211	8,000	
							Interest Expense—Other	83	120	
							Employees Inc. Taxes Pay.	214		200
							FICA Taxes Pay.	215		20
							Factory Ht., Lt., & Power	624	1,700	
							Tools	131	300	
	20		60		80					
400	300	800	200	180	750	220	Total		14,010	2,340
(1110)	(626)	(632)	(633)	(642)	(1111)	(653)			(√)	(√)

General credits reported in the voucher register for December represent payroll income tax and federal social security tax withholdings. These are summarized for the month as follows:

Employees Income Taxes Payable...................... $ 2,130
FICA Taxes Payable................................   210
                                                    $ 2,340

Cash payments journal. The cash payments journal is illustrated below. This cash payments journal accounts for all of the checks that are issued during the period. Checks are issued only in payment of vouchers that have been properly approved. In entering a check, the payee is designated together with the number of the voucher authorizing the payment. The cash payments record when prepared in this form is frequently called a *check register.*

Cash Payments Journal

Date	Check No.	Account Debited	Vou. No.	Accounts Payable Dr.	Purchases Discount Cr.	Cash Cr.
31	4207	First National Bank....	5154	8,120 00		8,120 00
31	4208	Payroll...............	5155	1,780 00		1,780 00
31	4209	Pat Hay..............	5006	500 00	10 00	490 00
31	4210	Petty Cash...........	5159	160 00		160 00
31		Total...............		29,480 00	160 00	29,320 00
				(213)	(71)	(111)

General journal. The general journal with the entries for the month of December is given on page 136. This general journal is prepared in three-column form. A pair of columns is provided for the entries that are to be made to the general ledger accounts. A "detail" column is provided for the individual debits and credits to subsidiary records that accompany entries affecting general ledger controlling accounts.

Journal

Date		Description	Post. Ref.	Detail	Debit	Credit
1972 Dec.	1	Notes Receivable...................	113		6,000 00	
		Accounts Receivable..............	116			6,000 00
		T. A. Wellman...................	AR	6,000 00		
		Received note from customer.				
	12	Allowance for Doubtful Accounts.......	0116		120 00	
		Accounts Receivable..............	116			120 00
		B. B. Bartlett...................	AR	120 00		
		To write off uncollectible customers account.				
	22	Accounts Payable..................	213		200 00	
		Case and Downs, Inc..............	AP	200 00		
		Raw Materials Returns and Allow....	051			200 00
		Materials returned to supplier.				
	31	Payroll Taxes Expense.............	625		210 00	
		FICA Taxes Payable..............	215			210 00
		To record employer's taxes payable for month under Federal Insurance Contributions Act (social security legislation).				
	31	Payroll Taxes Expense.............	625		200 00	
		State Unemployment Taxes Payable..	216			200 00
		To record employer's tax payable for month under State Unemployment Insurance plan.				
	31	Payroll Taxes Expense.............	625		30 00	
		FUTA Taxes Payable.............	217			30 00
		To record employer's tax payable for month under Federal Unemployment Tax Act.				

Posting and preparation of trial balance

Data in the journals are transferred to the accounts in the ledger at the end of December, and a trial balance is then taken. In order to conserve space here, the complete ledger of the Mitchell Corporation is not reproduced. Instead, the information that would appear in the ledger has been summarized in tabular form on page 137. The tabulation shows: (1) a trial balance of the accounts in the ledger on November 30, (2) the effects upon account balances of the information transferred from the books of original entry for the month of December, and (3) a trial

Account Title	Trial Balance November 30, 1972		Transactions December, 1972		Trial Balance December 31, 1972	
	Debit	Credit	Debit	Credit	Debit	Credit
Cash	22,770		(CR) 48,460	(CP) 29,320	41,910	
Petty Cash	200				200	
Notes Receivable	6,500		(J) 6,000	(CR) 6,500	6,000	
Accounts Receivable	57,490		(S) 24,500	(SR) 520		
				(CR) 23,350	52,000	
				(J) 6,000		
				(J) 120		
Allowance for Doubtful Accounts		730	(J) 120			610
Finished Goods	36,000				36,000	
Goods in Process	21,000				21,000	
Raw Materials	17,000				17,000	
Factory Supplies	5,100		(VR) 400		5,500	
Office Supplies	2,050		(VR) 750		2,800	
Prepaid Insurance	4,750		(VR) 250		5,000	
Bailey, Inc. Common Stock	24,300				24,300	
Land	40,000				40,000	
Buildings	42,500				42,500	
Accumulated Depreciation—Buildings		6,800				6,800
Machinery and Equipment	64,000				64,000	
Accumulated Depreciation—Machinery and Equipment		9,300				9,300
Office Furniture and Fixtures	5,000				5,000	
Accumulated Depreciation—Office Furniture and Fixtures		1,600				1,600
Delivery Equipment	8,000				8,000	
Accumulated Depreciation—Delivery Equip.		3,600				3,600
Tools	9,700		(VR) 300		10,000	
Patents	6,500				6,500	
Goodwill	40,000				40,000	
Notes Payable		18,000	(VR) 8,000	(CR) 10,000		20,000
Accounts Payable		20,370	(CP) 29,480	(VR) 37,020		27,710
			(J) 200			
Employees Income Taxes Payable		2,000	(VR) 2,000	(VR) 2,130		2,130
FICA Taxes Payable		440	(VR) 440	(VR) 210		420
				(J) 210		
State Unemployment Taxes Payable		530		(J) 200		730
FUTA Taxes Payable		250		(J) 30		280
Sales Taxes Payable		720	(VR) 720	(S) 1,300		1,280
			(SR) 20			
6% First-Mortgage Bonds		100,000				100,000
6% Preferred Stock, $100 par		50,000				50,000
Common Stock, $20 par		150,000				150,000
Treasury Stock — Common	30,000				30,000	
Premium on Preferred Stock		2,000				2,000
Retained Earnings		50,450				50,450
Sales		333,000		(S) 32,000		365,000
Sales Returns and Allowances	4,500		(SR) 500		5,000	
Sales Discount	2,845		(CR) 255		3,100	
Raw Materials Purchases	78,600		(VR) 6,800		85,400	
Raw Materials Returns and Allowances		1,900		(J) 200		2,100
Purchases Discount		2,020		(CP) 160		2,180
Freight In	4,300		(VR) 400		4,700	
Direct Labor	69,700		(VR) 6,500		76,200	
Indirect Labor	20,700		(VR) 1,900		22,600	
Factory Superintendence	18,300		(VR) 1,700		20,000	
Building Maintenance and Repairs	2,520		(VR) 480		3,000	
Factory Heat, Light, and Power	18,780		(VR) 1,700		20,480	
Payroll Taxes Expense	8,660		(J) 210			
			(J) 200			
			(J) 30		9,100	
Property Taxes Expense	7,300				7,300	
Miscellaneous Factory Overhead	3,000		(VR) 300		3,300	
Sales Salaries and Commissions	21,900		(VR) 2,100		24,000	
Advertising Expense	7,300		(VR) 800		8,100	
Miscellaneous Selling Expense	2,000		(VR) 200		2,200	
Delivery Salaries	8,200		(VR) 800		9,000	
Miscellaneous Delivery Expense	1,920		(VR) 180		2,100	
Officers Salaries	14,600		(VR) 1,400		16,000	
Office Salaries	9,100		(VR) 900		10,000	
Miscellaneous General Expense	2,080		(VR) 220		2,300	
Interest Income		635		(CR) 65		700
Dividend Income		300				300
Royalty Income		1,750				1,750
Interest Expense — Bonds	5,000				5,000	
Interest Expense — Other	2,230		(VR) 120		2,350	
	756,395	756,395	149,335	149,335	798,940	798,940

balance as of December 31 formed by combining the trial balance of November 30 and the transactions for December.

The letters in the parentheses preceding each amount in the transactions columns of the tabulation indicate the books of original entry on the previous pages from which the information was obtained. The identification letters are: Voucher Register (VR); Cash Receipts Journal (CR); Cash Payments Journal (CP); Sales Journal (S); Purchases Journal (P); Sales Returns and Allowances Journal (SR); and General Journal (J). These are the letters that are customarily used to indicate the sources of the information that is posted.

Compilation of adjusting data

In considering the adjustments that are required in preparing statements at the end of 1972, it is found that the accounts do not show the following information:[1]

(1) A dividend of $1.50 per share, payable January 15, 1973, to stockholders of record December 31, 1972, was declared on Bailey, Inc., common stock. The Mitchell Corporation holds 200 shares of Bailey, Inc., common stock as a long-term investment.

(2) Dividends on Mitchell Corporation's stock were declared and are payable on January 10, 1973, to stockholders of record December 26, 1972, as follows:

> Regular quarterly dividend of $1.50 on 500 shares of 6% preferred stock outstanding, $100 par.
>
> Forty cents per share on 6,000 shares of common stock outstanding, $20 par (7,500 shares of stock were originally issued; 1,500 shares were reacquired and are held as treasury stock.)

The following adjusting data as of December 31, 1972, were compiled upon thorough examination of the company's books and records:

Physical Inventories:
> (6) Finished goods, $49,000.
> (7) Goods in process, $28,000.
> (8) Raw materials, $20,000.
> (9) Factory supplies, $1,200.
> (10) Office supplies, $700.

Doubtful Accounts:
> (11) The allowance for doubtful accounts is to be increased by $1,800.

Depreciation and Amortization:
> (12) Buildings depreciation, 4% a year.
> (13) Machinery and equipment depreciation, 5% a year.
> (14) Office furniture and fixtures depreciation, 10% a year.

---

[1]The adjusting data are numbered to correspond to the numbers given the adjustments on the work sheet on pages 140 to 143. Numbers (3), (4), and (5) do not appear in this list because the data for these adjustments, representing transfers of beginning inventories, already appear on the work sheet trial balance.

(15) Delivery equipment depreciation, 20% a year.

(16) Tools on hand are valued at $7,500.

(17) Patents are to be reduced by $500, the amortization for the year.

Accrued Expenses:

(18) Salaries and wages:
   Direct labor, $1,400.
   Indirect labor, $300.
   Sales salaries and commissions, $400.
   Delivery salaries, $200.

(19) Accrued interest on bonds payable, $1,000.

(20) Accrued interest on notes payable, $600.

Prepaid Expenses:

(21) Prepaid insurance, $2,600

(22) Prepaid property taxes, $300.

Accrued Revenue:

(23) Accrued interest on notes receivable, $200.

Deferred Revenue:

(24) Royalties received in advance, $350.

Income Taxes:

(25) Provision of $10,000 is to be made for federal and state income taxes.

Building expenses, insurance expense, and taxes are to be distributed as follows: to manufacturing operations, 85%; to general and administrative operations, 15%.

Retained earnings of the company were $52,700 on January 1, 1972, and have been affected only by dividends declared on preferred stock prior to recording the foregoing data.

Preparation of the work sheet

The adjusting data must be combined with the information on the trial balance in bringing the accounts up to date. This may be done and the financial statements developed through the preparation of a work sheet. In the construction of a work sheet, trial balance data are listed in the first two amount columns. The adjusting entries are listed in the second pair of columns. Sometimes a third pair of columns is included to show the trial balance after adjustment. Account balances as adjusted are carried to the appropriate statement columns. A work sheet for a manufacturing enterprise usually includes a pair of columns for (1) manufacturing schedule accounts, (2) income statement accounts, and (3) balance sheet accounts. A similar work sheet form would be used for a merchandising enterprise except for the absence of manufacturing schedule columns.

The work sheet for the Mitchell Corporation is shown on pages 140 to 143.

Mitchell
Work
For Year Ended

	Account Title	Trial Balance		Adjustments		
		Debit	Credit	Debit	Credit	
1	Cash	41,910				1
2	Petty Cash	200				2
3	Notes Receivable	6,000				3
4	Accounts Receivable	52,000				4
5	Allow. for Doubtful Accounts		610		(11) 1,800	5
6	Finished Goods	36,000		(6) 49,000	(3) 36,000	6
7	Goods in Process	21,000		(7) 28,000	(4) 21,000	7
8	Raw Materials	17,000		(8) 20,000	(5) 17,000	8
9	Factory Supplies	5,500			(9) 4,300	9
10	Office Supplies	2,800			(10) 2,100	10
11	Prepaid Insurance	5,000			(21) 2,400	11
12	Bailey, Inc., Common Stock	24,300				12
13	Land	40,000				13
14	Buildings	42,500				14
15	Accum. Depr. — Buildings		6,800		(12) 1,700	15
16	Machinery and Equipment	64,000				16
17	Accum. Depreciation — Machinery and Equipment		9,300		(13) 3,200	17
18	Office Furniture and Fixtures	5,000				18
19	Accum. Depreciation — Office Furniture and Fixtures		1,600		(14) 500	19
20	Delivery Equipment	8,000				20
21	Accum. Depr. — Del. Equip.		3,600		(15) 1,600	21
22	Tools	10,000			(16) 2,500	22
23	Patents	6,500			(17) 500	23
24	Goodwill	40,000				24
25	Notes Payable		20,000			25
26	Accounts Payable		27,710			26
27	Employees Inc. Taxes Payable		2,130			27
28	FICA Taxes Payable		420			28
29	State Unempl. Taxes Payable		730			29
30	FUTA Taxes Payable		280			30
31	Sales Taxes Payable		1,280			31
32	6% First-Mortgage Bonds		100,000			32
33	6% Preferred Stock, $100 par		50,000			33
34	Common Stock, $20 par		150,000			34
35	Treasury Stock — Common	30,000				35
36	Premium on Preferred Stock		2,000			36
37	Retained Earnings		50,450			37
38	Sales		365,000	(2) 3,150		38
39	Sales Returns and Allowances	5,000				39
40	Sales Discount	3,100				40
41	Raw Materials Purchases	85,400				41
42	Raw Mat. Returns and Allow.		2,100			42
43	Purchases Discount		2,180			43
44	Freight In	4,700				44
45	Direct Labor	76,200		(18) 1,400		45
46	Indirect Labor	22,600		(18) 300		46
47	Factory Superintendence	20,000				47
48	Bldg. Maintenance and Repairs	3,000				48
49	Factory Heat, Light, and Power	20,480				49
50	Payroll Taxes Expense	9,100				50
51	Property Taxes Expense	7,300			(22) 300	51
52	Misc. Factory Overhead	3,300				52
53	Sales Salaries and Commissions	24,000		(18) 400		53
54	Advertising Expense	8,100				54
55	Miscellaneous Selling Expense	2,200				55

Corporation
Sheet
December 31, 1972

	Manufacturing Schedule		Income Statement		Balance Sheet		
	Debit	Credit	Debit	Credit	Debit	Credit	
1					41,910		1
2					200		2
3					6,000		3
4					52,000		4
5						2,410	5
6					49,000		6
7					28,000		7
8					20,000		8
9					1,200		9
10					700		10
11					2,600		11
12					24,300		12
13					40,000		13
14					42,500		14
15						8,500	15
16					64,000		16
17						12,500	17
18					5,000		18
19						2,100	19
20					8,000		20
21						5,200	21
22					7,500		22
23					6,000		23
24					40,000		24
25						20,000	25
26						27,710	26
27						2,130	27
28						420	28
29						730	29
30						280	30
31						1,280	31
32						100,000	32
33						50,000	33
34						150,000	34
35					30,000		35
36						2,000	36
37						47,300	37
38				365,000			38
39			5,000				39
40			3,100				40
41	85,400						41
42		2,100					42
43		2,180					43
44	4,700						44
45	77,600						45
46	22,900						46
47	20,000						47
48	2,550		450				48
49	20,480						49
50	7,735		1,365				50
51	5,950		1,050				51
52	3,300						52
53			24,400				53
54			8,100				54
55			2,200				55

(*continued*)

Work Sheet (Concluded)

	Account Title	Trial Balance		Adjustments		
		Debit	Credit	Debit	Credit	
56	Delivery Salaries	9,000		(18) 200		56
57	Miscellaneous Delivery Expense	2,100				57
58	Officers Salaries	16,000				58
59	Office Salaries	10,000				59
60	Miscellaneous General Expense	2,300				60
61	Interest Income		700		(23) 200	61
62	Dividend Income		300		(1) 300	62
63	Royalty Income		1,750	(24) 350		63
64	Interest Expense — Bonds	5,000		(19) 1,000		64
65	Interest Expense — Other	2,350		(20) 600		65
66	Dividends Receivable			(1) 300		66
67	Div. Pay. on Preferred Stock				(2) 750	67
68	Div. Pay. on Common Stock				(2) 2,400	68
69	Income Summary			(3) 36,000	(6) 49,000	69
70	Manufacturing Summary			(4) 21,000	(7) 28,000	70
71				(5) 17,000	(8) 20,000	71
72	Factory Supplies Expense			(9) 4,300		72
73	Office Supplies Expense			(10) 2,100		73
74	Doubtful Accounts Expense			(11) 1,800		74
75	Depreciation Exp. — Buildings			(12) 1,700		75
76	Depr. Exp. — Mach. and Equip.			(13) 3,200		76
77	Depr. Exp. — Office Furn. and Fix.			(14) 500		77
78	Depreciation Exp. — Del. Equip.			(15) 1,600		78
79	Depreciation Exp. — Tools			(16) 2,500		79
80	Amortization of Patents			(17) 500		80
81	Accrued Salaries and Wages				(18) 2,300	81
82	Accrued Interest on Bonds Pay.				(19) 1,000	82
83	Accrued Interest on Notes Pay.				(20) 600	83
84	Insurance Expense			(21) 2,400		84
85	Prepaid Property Taxes			(22) 300		85
86	Accrued Interest on Notes Rec.			(23) 200		86
87	Royalties Received in Advance				(24) 350	87
88	Income Taxes			(25) 10,000		88
89	Income Taxes Payable				(25) 10,000	89
90		798,940	798,940	209,800	209,800	90
91	Cost of Goods Manufactured					91
92						92
93	Net Income					93
94						94

The adjustments to the inventory accounts should be particularly noted. Items (4) and (5) are entered as debits to Manufacturing Summary and as credits to Goods in Process and Raw Materials respectively. These entries transfer the beginning inventory costs to the manufacturing summary account. Entries (7) and (8) are debits to Goods in Process and Raw Materials respectively and credits to Manufacturing Summary. These entries record the goods in process and raw material inventories at the end of the fiscal period and reduce manufacturing costs by the

Work Sheet (Concluded)

	Manufacturing Schedule		Income Statement		Balance Sheet		
	Debit	Credit	Debit	Credit	Debit	Credit	
56			9,200				56
57			2,100				57
58			16,000				58
59			10,000				59
60			2,300				60
61				900			61
62				600			62
63				1,400			63
64			6,000				64
65			2,950				65
66					300		66
67						750	67
68						2,400	68
69			36,000	49,000			69
70	21,000	28,000					70
71	17,000	20,000					71
72	4,300						72
73			2,100				73
74			1,800				74
75	1,445			255			75
76	3,200						76
77			500				77
78			1,600				78
79	2,500						79
80	500						80
81						2,300	81
82						1,000	82
83						600	83
84	2,040		360				84
85					300		85
86					200		86
87						350	87
88			10,000				88
89						10,000	89
90	302,600	52,280					90
91		250,320	250,320				91
92	302,600	302,600	397,150	416,900	469,710	449,960	92
93			19,750			19,750	93
94			416,900	416,900	469,710	469,710	94

amount of the ending inventories. Both the debit and the credit amounts reported in the manufacturing summary account are carried to the manufacturing schedule columns. The manufacturing schedule columns then include all of the data that are required in computing cost of goods manufactured. The cost of goods manufactured is now transferred to the debit column of the Income Statement so that the net income for the period may be computed.

Adjustment (3) is a debit to Income Summary and a credit to Finished Goods, whereas adjustment (6) is a debit to Finished Goods and a credit to Income Summary. Entry (3) transfers the beginning finished goods inventory to Income Summary; entry (6) records the finished goods inventory at the end of the period and reduces cost of goods available by the amount of the ending inventory. Both the debit and credit amounts in the income summary account are carried to the income statement columns. The income statement columns then include all of the data that are required in computing cost of goods sold.

A number of methods may be used in recording inventory data on the work sheet. A simple procedure would be the following:

Account Title	Trial Balance		Adjustments		Manufacturing Schedule		Income Statement		Balance Sheet	
	Dr.	Cr.	Dr.	Cr.	Dr.	Cr.	Dr.	Cr.	Dr.	Cr.
Finished Goods 1/1, 1972	36,000						36,000			
Goods in Process 1/1, 1972	21,000				21,000					
Raw Materials 1/1, 1972	17,000				17,000					
Finished Goods 12/31, 1972								49,000	49,000	
Goods in Process 12/31, 1972						28,000			28,000	
Raw Materials 12/31, 1972						20,000			20,000	

In this example, beginning inventories in the trial balance are carried to the manufacturing schedule and the income statement columns; ending inventories are listed separately as credits in the manufacturing schedule and the income statement columns and as debits in the balance sheet columns without inclusion in the adjustments columns. An even simpler procedure would be to report the ending inventory balances on the same lines used for beginning inventories; beginning balances would then be carried as debits to the manufacturing schedule and the income statement columns, while ending balances would be entered directly as credits in the manufacturing schedule columns and as debits in the balance sheet columns. Although procedures for recording adjustments directly in the statement columns are acceptable, adjusting entries are still required in the journal to bring accounts up to date and to transfer revenue and expense account balances to the appropriate summary account. It is generally desirable to assemble all adjusting data and to summarize this information in informal journal form before making formal entries in the general journal. When such a procedure is followed, it may prove convenient to recognize adjustments on the working papers in exactly the same form that is to be followed in recognizing the adjustments in the journal. This procedure was followed on the work sheet on pages 140 to 143 even though this involves more work than a direct method of adjustment as described.

It was indicated earlier that building expenses, insurance expense, and taxes are allocated 85% to manufacturing activities and 15% to general and administrative activities. The percentages used in the distribution of the charges were developed by means of an analysis of expenses during the period. The building maintenance and repairs account is shown on the trial balance at $3,000; 85% of $3,000, or $2,550, is entered in the manufacturing schedule columns and 15%, or $450, is entered in the income statement columns. The charges for payroll taxes expense, property taxes expense, depreciation of buildings, and insurance expense are similarly distributed on the work sheet.

Preparation of financial statements

The financial statements are prepared using the work sheet as the basic source of data for the presentations.

Balance sheet. The balance sheet of the Mitchell Corporation, shown on pages 146 and 147, is prepared from the balance sheet columns on the work sheet. A number of items reported in the balance sheet columns of the work sheet have been combined for balance sheet presentation. Such a procedure may be followed when items can be combined under a descriptive title and when amounts involved for the individual items are not material. Items that have been combined include: accrued interest and dividends receivable; office supplies, prepaid insurance, and prepaid taxes; income tax withholdings, FICA taxes payable, state unemployment taxes payable, federal unemployment taxes payable, and state sales taxes payable; accrued interest on notes payable and bonds payable; and dividends payable on preferred stock and common stock. The retained earnings balance on the balance sheet is composed of retained earnings reported in the trial balance columns, minus the charge to retained earnings for dividends shown in the adjustments columns, plus the net income reported in summarizing the work sheet.

Income statement. The income statement is prepared from the income statement columns on the work sheet. The income statement is presented on page 148.

Manufacturing schedule. The manufacturing schedule is prepared from the manufacturing schedule columns of the work sheet and is shown on page 149.

Retained earnings statement. The retained earnings statement is prepared from the balance sheet columns on the work sheet and is shown on page 149.

Adjusting and closing the accounts

Upon completing the work sheet and statements, entries are made in the journal to bring the accounts up to date and to close the accounts. Before closing the accounts, any current, correcting, and adjusting entries are recorded. Although such entries may first have been prepared in informal form in the course of preparing the work sheet, these are now entered formally in the journal. Closing entries may be conveniently prepared by using as a basis for the entries the balances as shown in the manufacturing schedule and income statement columns of the work sheet. The following entries are required for the Mitchell Corporation:

Mitchell
Balance
December

Assets

Current assets:			
Cash on hand and in bank................................		$42,110	
Notes receivable......................................		6,000	
Accounts receivable............................$52,000			
Less allowance for doubtful accounts.............. 2,410		49,590	
Accrued interest and dividends receivable....................		500	
Inventories:			
Finished goods................................$49,000			
Goods in process............................. 28,000			
Raw materials................................ 20,000			
Factory supplies.............................. 1,200		98,200	
Prepaid expenses:			
Office supplies, insurance, and property taxes..............		3,600	$200,000
Investments:			
Bailey, Inc., common stock			24,300

Land, buildings, and equipment:	Cost	Accumulated Depreciation	Book Value
Land.............................	$ 40,000	—	$40,000
Buildings.........................	42,500	$ 8,500	34,000
Machinery and equipment............	64,000	12,500	51,500
Office furniture and fixtures..........	5,000	2,100	2,900
Delivery equipment.................	8,000	5,200	2,800
Tools............................	7,500	—	7,500
Total land, buildings, and equipment...	$167,000	$28,300	

Total land, buildings, and equipment...			138,700
Intangible assets:			
Patents...		$ 6,000	
Goodwill...		40,000	46,000
Total assets...			$409,000

Current Entries

December 31, 1972

(1)	Dividends Receivable...............................	300	
	Dividend Income.................................		300
	To record announcement of $1.50 dividend on investment in 200 shares of Bailey, Inc., common stock.		
(2)	Retained Earnings..................................	3,150	
	Dividends Payable on Preferred Stock................		750
	Dividends Payable on Common Stock................		2,400
	To record declaration of dividends payable on January 10 to stockholders of record December 26.		

(The adjusting and closing entries are presented on pages 150 to 152.)

Corporation — Exhibit A
Sheet
31, 1972

Liabilities

Current liabilities:		
Notes payable...	$20,000	
Accounts payable..	27,710	
Income taxes payable....................................	10,000	
Miscellaneous sales, payroll, and withholding taxes payable......	4,840	
Accrued salaries and wages................................	2,300	
Accrued interest on notes and on bonds payable..............	1,600	
Dividends payable on preferred and common stock	3,150	$ 69,600
Long-term debt:		
6% First-mortgage bonds, due November 1, 1980		100,000
Deferred revenues:		
Royalties received in advance..............................		350
Total liabilities...		$169,950

Stockholders' Equity

Paid-in capital:			
Capital stock:			
6% Preferred stock, $100 par, 500 shares issued and outstanding...................................		$ 50,000	
Common stock, $20 par (7,500 shares issued).............................	$150,000		
Less treasury stock (1,500 shares reacquired, carried at par).............	30,000		
Common stock, 6,000 shares outstanding........		120,000	
Premium on preferred stocks......................		2,000	$172,000
Retained earnings...		67,050	
Total stockholders' equity....................................			239,050
Total liabilities and stockholders' equity.......................			$409,000

Mitchell Corporation — Exhibit B

Income Statement

For Year Ended December 31, 1972

Revenue from sales:			
Sales..		$365,000	
Less: Sales returns and allowances...................	$ 5,000		
Sales discount...............................	3,100	8,100	$356,900
Cost of goods sold:			
Finished goods, January 1, 1972.....................		$ 36,000	
Cost of goods manufactured (Schedule B-1)...........		250,320	
Total cost of finished goods available for sale..........		$286,320	
Less finished goods inventory, December 31, 1972.......		49,000	237,320
Gross profit on sales.................................			$119,580
Operating expenses:			
Selling expenses:			
Sales salaries and commissions.....................	$24,400		
Advertising expense..............................	8,100		
Miscellaneous selling expense......................	2,200		
Delivery salaries.................................	9,200		
Depreciation expense — delivery equipment..........	1,600		
Miscellaneous delivery expense....................	2,100	$ 47,600	
General and administrative expenses:			
Officers salaries.................................	$16,000		
Office salaries...................................	10,000		
Office supplies expense...........................	2,100		
Doubtful accounts expense........................	1,800		
Depreciation expense — buildings..................	255		
Depreciation expense — office furniture and fixtures....	500		
Insurance expense...............................	360		
Building maintenance and repairs..................	450		
Payroll taxes expense............................	1,365		
Property taxes expense...........................	1,050		
Miscellaneous general expense.....................	2,300	36,180	83,780
Operating income....................................			$ 35,800
Other revenue and expense items:			
Interest expense — bonds..........................	$ 6,000		
Interest expense — other..........................	2,950	$ 8,950	
Interest income..................................	$ 900		
Dividend income.................................	600		
Royalty income..................................	1,400	2,900	6,050
Income before income taxes...........................			$ 29,750
Income taxes..			10,000
Net income...			$ 19,750

Mitchell Corporation — Schedule B-1
Manufacturing Schedule
For Year Ended December 31, 1972

Goods in process inventory, January 1, 1972			$ 21,000
Raw materials:			
Inventory, January 1, 1972		$ 17,000	
Purchases	$85,400		
Freight in	4,700		
Delivered cost of raw materials		$90,100	
Less: Raw materials returns and allowances	$2,100		
Purchases discount	2,180	4,280	85,820
Total cost of raw materials available for use		$102,820	
Less inventory, December 31, 1972		20,000	82,820
Direct labor			77,600
Manufactured overhead:			
Indirect labor		$ 22,900	
Factory superintendence		20,000	
Building maintenance and repairs		2,550	
Factory heat, light, and power		20,480	
Payroll taxes expense		7,735	
Property taxes expense		5,950	
Factory supplies expense		4,300	
Depreciation expense — buildings		1,445	
Depreciation expense — machinery and equipment		3,200	
Depreciation expense — tools		2,500	
Amortization of patents		500	
Insurance expense		2,040	
Miscellaneous factory overhead		3,300	96,900
Total goods in process during 1972			$278,320
Less goods in process inventory, December 31, 1972			28,000
Cost of goods manufactured			$250,320

Mitchell Corporation — Exhibit C
Retained Earnings Statement
For Year Ended December 31, 1972

Retained earnings, January 1, 1972		$52,700
Add net income per income statement		19,750
		$72,450
Deduct: Dividends on preferred stock	$3,000	
Dividends on common stock	2,400	5,400
Retained earnings, December 31, 1972		$67,050

Adjusting Entries
December 31, 1972

(3)	Income Summary..................................	36,000	
	Finished Goods................................		36,000
	To transfer beginning finished goods inventory to Income Summary.		
(4)	Manufacturing Summary...........................	21,000	
	Goods in Process..............................		21,000
	To transfer beginning goods in process inventory to Manufacturing Summary.		
(5)	Manufacturing Summary...........................	17,000	
	Raw Materials................................		17,000
	To transfer beginning raw materials inventory to Manufacturing Summary.		
(6)	Finished Goods..................................	49,000	
	Income Summary..............................		49,000
	To record ending finished goods inventory.		
(7)	Goods in Process................................	28,000	
	Manufacturing Summary........................		28,000
	To record ending goods in process inventory.		
(8)	Raw Materials..................................	20,000	
	Manufacturing Summary........................		20,000
	To record ending raw materials inventory.		
(9)	Factory Supplies Expense	4,300	
	Factory Supplies..............................		4,300
	To record cost of factory supplies used.		
(10)	Office Supplies Expense...........................	2,100	
	Office Supplies................................		2,100
	To record cost of office supplies used.		
(11)	Doubtful Accounts Expense........................	1,800	
	Allowance for Doubtful Accounts.................		1,800
	To provide for doubtful accounts.		
(12)	Depreciation Expense — Buildings..................	1,700	
	Accumulated Depreciation — Buildings............		1,700
	To record depreciation on buildings.		
(13)	Depreciation Expense — Machinery and Equipment......	3,200	
	Accumulated Depreciation — Machinery and Equipment.		3,200
	To record depreciation on machinery and equipment.		
(14)	Depreciation Expense — Office Furniture and Fixtures...	500	
	Accumulated Depreciation — Office Furniture and Fixtures		500
	To record depreciation on office furniture and fixtures.		
(15)	Depreciation Expense — Delivery Equipment	1,600	
	Accumulated Depreciation — Delivery Equipment......		1,600
	To record depreciation on delivery equipment.		
(16)	Depreciation Expense — Tools	2,500	
	Tools.......................................		2,500
	To record depreciation on tools.		
(17)	Amortization of Patents...........................	500	
	Patents......................................		500
	To record amortization of patents.		

(18) Direct Labor	1,400	
Indirect Labor	300	
Sales Salaries and Commissions......................	400	
Delivery Salaries....................................	200	
Accrued Salaries and Wages........................		2,300
To record accrued salaries and wages.		
(19) Interest Expense — Bonds...........................	1,000	
Accrued Interest on Bonds Payable.................		1,000
To record accrued interest on bonds.		
(20) Interest Expense — Other...........................	600	
Accrued Interest on Notes Payable.................		600
To record accrued interest on notes payable.		
(21) Insurance Expense..................................	2,400	
Prepaid Insurance..................................		2,400
To record expired insurance.		
(22) Prepaid Property Taxes.............................	300	
Property Taxes Expense............................		300
To record prepaid taxes.		
(23) Accrued Interest on Notes Receivable................	200	
Interest Income...................................		200
To record accrued interest on notes receivable.		
(24) Royalty Income....................................	350	
Royalties Received in Advance......................		350
To record royalties received in advance.		
(25) Income Taxes......................................	10,000	
Income Taxes Payable.............................		10,000
To record estimated income taxes payable.		

Closing Entries
December 31, 1972

Manufacturing Summary.................................	260,320	
Raw Materials Returns and Allowances...................	2,100	
Purchases Discount.....................................	2,180	
Raw Materials Purchases............................		85,400
Freight In...		4,700
Direct Labor.......................................		77,600
Indirect Labor.....................................		22,900
Factory Superintendence............................		20,000
Building Maintenance and Repairs....................		2,550
Factory Heat, Light, and Power.....................		20,480
Payroll Taxes Expense..............................		7,735
Property Taxes Expense.............................		5,950
Miscellaneous Factory Overhead.....................		3,300
Factory Supplies Expense...........................		4,300
Depreciation Expense — Buildings....................		1,445
Depreciation Expense — Machinery and Equipment........		3,200
Depreciation Expense — Tools.......................		2,500
Amortization of Patents............................		500
Insurance Expense..................................		2,040
To close manufacturing accounts into Manufacturing Summary.		
Sales...	365,000	
Interest Income.......................................	900	
Dividend Income......................................	600	
Royalty Income.......................................	1,400	
Income Summary...................................		367,900
To close revenue accounts into Income Summary.		

(continued)

Closing Entries (Concluded)

Income Summary..	361,150	
Manufacturing Summary............................		250,320
Sales Returns and Allowances......................		5,000
Sales Discount...................................		3,100
Building Maintenance and Repairs..................		450
Payroll Taxes Expense............................		1,365
Property Taxes Expense...........................		1,050
Sales Salaries and Commissions....................		24,400
Advertising Expense..............................		8,100
Miscellaneous Selling Expense.....................		2,200
Delivery Salaries................................		9,200
Miscellaneous Delivery Expense....................		2,100
Officers Salaries................................		16,000
Office Salaries..................................		10,000
Miscellaneous General Expense.....................		2,300
Interest Expense — Bonds.........................		6,000
Interest Expense — Other.........................		2,950
Office Supplies Expense...........................		2,100
Doubtful Accounts Expense........................		1,800
Depreciation Expense — Buildings..................		255
Depreciation Expense — Office Furniture and Fixtures......		500
Depreciation Expense — Delivery Equipment..............		1,600
Insurance Expense...............................		360
Income Taxes...................................		10,000
To close expense accounts into Income Summary.		
Income Summary.....................................	19,750	
Retained Earnings.............................		19,750
To transfer the balance in Income Summary to Retained Earnings.		

Preparation of post-closing trial balance

After the adjusting and closing entries are posted, a post-closing trial balance is prepared to verify the equality of the debits and credits. The post-closing trial balance is given on the opposite page.

Reversing the accounts

The adjustments establishing accrued and prepaid balances may now be reversed. The reversing entries follow:

January 1, 1973

Accrued Salaries and Wages...............................	2,300	
Direct Labor.....................................		1,400
Indirect Labor...................................		300
Sales Salaries and Commissions....................		400
Delivery Salaries................................		200
Accrued Interest on Bonds Payable...........................	1,000	
Interest Expense — Bonds.........................		1,000
Accrued Interest on Notes Payable...........................	600	
Interest Expense — Other.........................		600
Property Taxes Expense.................................	300	
Prepaid Property Taxes...........................		300
Interest Income.......................................	200	
Accrued Interest on Notes Receivable.....................		200
Royalties Received in Advance...........................	350	
Royalty Income...................................		350

Mitchell Corporation
Post-Closing Trial Balance
December 31, 1972

Cash..	41,910	
Petty Cash...	200	
Notes Receivable..	6,000	
Accounts Receivable.......................................	52,000	
Allowance for Doubtful Accounts...........................		2,410
Dividends Receivable......................................	300	
Accrued Interest on Notes Receivable......................	200	
Finished Goods..	49,000	
Goods in Process..	28,000	
Raw Materials...	20,000	
Factory Supplies..	1,200	
Office Supplies...	700	
Prepaid Insurance...	2,600	
Prepaid Property Taxes....................................	300	
Bailey, Inc., Common Stock................................	24,300	
Land..	40,000	
Buildings...	42,500	
Accumulated Depreciation — Buildings......................		8,500
Machinery and Equipment...................................	64,000	
Accumulated Depreciation — Machinery and Equipment........		12,500
Office Furniture and Fixtures.............................	5,000	
Accumulated Depreciation — Office Furniture and Fixtures..		2,100
Delivery Equipment..	8,000	
Accumulated Depreciation — Delivery Equipment.............		5,200
Tools...	7,500	
Patents...	6,000	
Goodwill..	40,000	
Notes Payable...		20,000
Accounts Payable..		27,710
Income Taxes Payable......................................		10,000
Employees Income Taxes Payable............................		2,130
FICA Taxes Payable..		420
State Unemployment Taxes Payable..........................		730
FUTA Taxes Payable..		280
Sales Taxes Payable.......................................		1,280
Accrued Salaries and Wages................................		2,300
Accrued Interest on Bonds Payable.........................		1,000
Accrued Interest on Notes Payable.........................		600
Dividends Payable on Preferred Stock......................		750
Dividends Payable on Common Stock.........................		2,400
6% First-Mortgage Bonds...................................		100,000
Royalties Received in Advance.............................		350
6% Preferred Stock, $100 par..............................		50,000
Common Stock, $20 par.....................................		150,000
Treasury Stock — Common...................................	30,000	
Premium on Preferred Stock................................		2,000
Retained Earnings...		67,050
	469,710	469,710

The post-closing trial balance is frequently prepared after the reversing entries have been posted. When such practice is followed, a check is offered on the accuracy of adjusting, closing, and reversing the accounts.

Interim statements

Statements are prepared at least once a year, and at that time the accounts in the ledger are adjusted and closed. Many business units, however, require statements during the fiscal year at one-month, three-month, or six-month intervals. Such statements may be prepared for management and internal use, or they may also be made available to stockholders as a means of keeping this group informed on financial progress during the year.

When interim statements are desired, they are prepared by means of a work sheet. The accounts in the ledger may be adjusted but they are not closed. In preparing the work sheet, balances in the ledger are first listed in trial balance form. Because accounts have not been closed since the end of the previous year, nominal accounts reflect balances to date. Adjustments are listed on the work sheet to bring the account balances up to date, and adjusted balances are carried to the appropriate statement columns. Financial statements are then prepared from the work sheet.

For example, in preparing the interim statements at the end of March, the adjusting data are reported on the working papers just as though the fiscal period were one quarter. Inventories and accrued and prepaid items as of March 31 are recorded. Amortization and depreciation for a three-month period are stated. The balance sheet prepared from the work sheet reports the financial position as of March 31; the income statement reports cumulative results for the three months ended March 31. To obtain an income statement for the month of March alone, it is necessary to subtract revenue and expense balances on the income statement for the two-month period ended February 28 from cumulative balances reported on the income statement for the three-month period ended March 31. Inventory figures as of February 28 and March 31 are reported, and an income statement for the month of March is then available. By following the procedure just outlined, monthly statements, as well as cumulative income statements, can be made available.

QUESTIONS

1. The Peck Co. maintains a sales journal, a sales returns and allowances journal, a voucher register, a cash receipts journal, a cash payments journal, and a general journal. For each account listed below and at the top of the next page indicate the possible journal sources of charges and credits.

Cash   Merchandise Inventory
Marketable Securities   Land and Buildings
Notes Receivable   Accumulated Depreciation
Accounts Receivable   Notes Payable
Allowance for Doubtful Accounts   Vouchers Payable

Accrued Expenses
Capital Stock
Retained Earnings
Sales
Sales Returns and Allowances
Sales Discount

Purchases
Freight In
Purchases Returns and Allowances
Purchases Discount
Salaries
Depreciation

2. Describe the kind of work sheet that would be employed for:

(a) A merchandising company.
(b) A manufacturing company.
(c) A departmentalized business, the gross profit to be ascertained for each department.
(d) A manufacturing organization with retail sales departments, an operating income to be determined for each department.

3. When would you recommend the preparation of working papers with a pair of columns reporting an adjusted trial balance?

4. Describe two methods that may be followed in adjusting the accounts for the ending inventories on the work sheet of a manufacturing company.

5. The accountant for the Dayton Co. in adjusting the accounts on the working papers charges or credits the beginning inventory to adjust it to the ending balance, with an offsetting credit or charge to an inventory variation balance. The inventory as adjusted is carried to the balance sheet column and the variation balance is carried to the appropriate income statement column. Appraise this procedure.

6. The accountant for the M. A. Tyler Store, after completing all adjustments except those for the merchandise inventories, makes the entry reported below to close the beginning inventory, to set up the ending inventory, to close all nominal accounts, and to report the net result of operations in the capital account.

Merchandise Inventory, December 31, 1972	18,000	
Sales	200,000	
Purchases Discount	2,000	
Merchandise Inventory, January 1, 1972		20,000
Purchases		140,000
Selling Expense		20,000
General and Administrative Expense		15,000
Interest Expense		1,500
M. A. Tyler, Capital		23,500

(a) Would you regard this procedure acceptable?
(b) What alternate procedure could be followed in adjusting and closing the accounts?

7. The Bradshaw Corporation prepares financial statements and adjusts and closes the accounts at the end of each month. The Carter Corporation prepares financial statements monthly, but adjusts and closes the accounts only at the end of each year.

(a) Will the reports of each company be the same?

(b) Can a cumulative "year-to-date" income statement be made available for the Bradshaw Corporation? How?

(c) Can income statements covering single months be made available for the Carter Corporation? How?

(d) Which procedure, monthly or annual closing, do you consider preferable? Why?

8. State the effect upon the balance sheet and the income statement of each of the following errors:

(a) Accrued expenses are overstated at the end of the period.

(b) Deferred revenues are understated at the end of the period.

(c) Prepaid expenses are understated at the end of the period.

(d) Accrued revenues are overstated at the end of the period.

(e) The inventory is understated at the end of the period.

(f) Depreciation on an equipment item is overlooked at the end of the period.

EXERCISES

1. Using a voucher register and cash payments journal similar to those illustrated on pages 134 and 135, record the following transactions:

(a) Voucher No. 1305 was issued for the purchase of raw materials of $1,500 from T. C. Holmes.

(b) Voucher No. 1306 was issued for the purchase of machinery of $2,250 from Bell Bros.

(c) Voucher No. 1307 was issued for freight charges of $60 payable to Central R.R. on shipment from T. C. Holmes. Check No. 409 was issued in payment of freight charges.

(d) Voucher No. 1308 was issued for payment of note of $5,000 and interest of $150 to State Bank. Check No. 410 was issued in payment of note and interest.

(e) Check No. 411 was issued to T. C. Holmes for $1,470 in payment of invoice less discount of 2%.

(f) Voucher No. 1309 was issued for the payroll for the week totaling $660, less income taxes withheld, $105, and less FICA taxes withheld, $30. Check No. 412 was issued for payroll less deductions.

2. Using sales and cash receipts journal forms as illustrated on pages 132 and 133, together with a general journal, record the following transactions:

(a) A sale on account is made to J. A. Berry for $600 plus sales taxes, $24.

(b) A check for $612 is received from Berry representing payment of his invoice less a sales discount of $12.

(c) Cash sales for the day are $915, on which sales taxes of $20 are collected.

(d) Cash of $1,000 is received on a 60-day, 8% note for this amount issued to the bank.

(e) Furniture and fixtures, cost $700, book value $250, are sold for cash of $75.

(f) A dividend check for $60 is received on shares of stock owned.

3. Prepare an income statement for P. M. Brown for the month of June from the following cumulative data:

	January 1 to May 31	January 1 to June 30
Sales.....................................	$66,000	$80,000
Less: Sales returns and allowances..........	$ 1,500	$ 1,800
Sales discount.......................	1,200	1,450
	$ 2,700	$ 3,250
Net sales.................................	$63,300	$76,750
Cost of goods sold:		
Merchandise inventory, January 1.........	$14,000	$14,000
Purchases...............................	$36,000	$44,000
Less purchases discount.................	700	850
	$35,300	$43,150
Merchandise available for sale............	$49,300	$57,150
Less merchandise inventory, May 31.......	16,000	19,300
Cost of goods sold.....................	$33,300	$37,850
Gross profit on sales.....................	$30,000	$38,900
Operating expenses:		
Selling expenses........................	$10,500	$12,800
General and administrative expenses.......	6,800	8,200
Total operating expenses................	$17,300	$21,000
Operating income.......................	$12,700	$17,900
Other revenue — interest income............	350	400
	$13,050	$18,300
Other expense — interest expense..........	250	250
Income before extraordinary item...........	$12,800	$18,050
Extraordinary gain from sale of investments..		1,050
Net income..............................	$12,800	$19,100

4. Accounts of Modern Products Co. at the end of the first year of operations show the following balances:

Cash..	$ 17,000	
Investments................................	20,000	
Machinery..................................	50,000	
Factory Buildings............................	80,000	
Land.......................................	40,000	
Accounts Payable...........................		$ 30,000
Common Stock..............................		200,000
Premium on Common Stock.................		40,000
Sales.......................................		300,000
Raw Materials Purchases....................	140,000	
Direct Labor...............................	100,000	
Manufacturing Overhead....................	72,500	
Operating Expenses........................	52,000	
Income on Investments......................		1,500
	$571,500	$571,500

At the end of the year physical inventories are: raw materials, $40,000; goods in process, $30,000; finished goods, $30,000. Prepaid operating expenses are $1,500 and accrued manufacturing overhead is $500. Accrued income on investments is $300. Depreciation for the year on buildings is $2,000, apportioned $1,500 to the factory and $500 to general operations. Depreciation of machinery is $2,500. Federal and state income taxes for the year are estimated at $10,000. Give the entries to adjust and close the books.

5. Upon inspecting the books and records for the Morey Manufacturing Co. for the year ended December 31, 1972, you find the following data. What entries are required to bring the accounts up to date?

(a) A receivable of $200 from V. N. White is determined to be uncollectible. The company maintains no allowance for such losses.

(b) A creditor, the Williams Co., has just been awarded damages of $2,200 as a result of breach of contract during the current year by Morey Manufacturing Co. Nothing appears on the books in connection with this matter.

(c) A fire destroyed part of a branch office. Furniture and fixtures that cost $20,000 and had a book value of $12,000 at the time of the fire were completely destroyed. The insurance company has agreed to pay $10,000 under the provision of the fire insurance policy.

(d) Advances of $1,000 to salesmen have been recorded as Sales Salaries.

(e) Machinery at the end of the year shows a balance of $24,500. It is discovered that additions to this account during the year totaled $7,000, but of this amount $4,000 should have been recorded as repairs. Depreciation is to be recorded at 10% on machinery owned throughout the year, at one half this rate on machinery purchased during the year.

6. H. V. Hoyt fails to adjust the accounts for the following items in closing the books on December 31, 1972. Assume that the omissions are never discovered but that adjustments are properly made at the end of 1973. What effect does each omission have on the net incomes for 1972 and for 1973?

(a) Sales salaries accrued, $30.

(b) Prepaid advertising, $200. Advertising Expense was debited for advertising payments.

(c) Depreciation of office machine, $50.

(d) Accrued interest on notes receivable, $20.

(e) Office supplies inventory, $100; Office Supplies, an asset account, was charged for purchases of office supplies and has a balance of $300.

7. The Blender Sales Co. shows a credit balance in the income summary account of $21,600 after the revenue and expense items have been transferred to this account at the end of a fiscal year. Give the remaining entries to close the books, assuming:

(a) The business is a sole proprietorship; the owner, P. B. Blender, has made withdrawals of $9,000 during the year and this is reported in a drawing account.

(b) The business is a partnership; the owners, P. B. Blender and T. Z. Blender, share profits 5:3; they have made withdrawals of $10,000 and $8,000 respectively and these amounts are reported in drawing accounts.

(c) The business is a corporation; the ledger reports additional paid-in capital, $200,000, and retained earnings, $30,000; dividends during the year of $12,000 were charged to a dividends paid account.

8. M. J. Porter began operations in 1972 with cash of $20,000. Sales for the year were $60,000, and collections from customers during the year were $36,000. Accounts receivable on December 31 are believed fully collectible. Purchases for the year were $44,000, and payments on account during the year were $27,500. All sales were made at double the cost of the merchandise. Operating expenses were all paid in cash. The income statement reported net income for 1972 of $10,000. (a) Prepare a balance sheet as of December 31, 1972. (b) Submit a summary of cash receipts and disbursements for the year.

9. Sales for the Symetric Products Co. were $150,000 for 1972. The beginning inventory was 30% of the cost of goods sold. The ending inventory was 40% of the beginning inventory. Selling expenses were 10% of sales and absorbed 30% of the gross profit on sales. Income before income taxes was 8% of sales. Income taxes were 50% of income before taxes. Prepare an income statement for 1972.

PROBLEMS

5-1. The following data are assembled from the books and records of the Mondale Corporation:

(a) The company borrowed $30,000 from the bank on November 10, issuing a note that is payable in 90 days with interest at 9%.
(b) The company paid $1,620 for a fire insurance policy covering a three-year period beginning October 1, 1972. The charge was made to Prepaid Insurance.
(c) A $9,000 note dated November 20, 1972, and due in 90 days with interest at 9% was received from a customer in payment of account.
(d) The company received $2,400 representing rent for parking privileges granted to a neighboring business for the period July 1, 1972–June 30, 1973. The credit was made to Unearned Rental Income.

Instructions: (1) Give the adjusting journal entries as of November 30, 1972, assuming that the books are adjusted monthly but are closed at the end of each calendar year.
(2) Give the adjusting journal entries as of December 31, 1972, assuming that the books are adjusted monthly but are closed at the end of each calendar year.
(3) Give the adjusting journal entries as of December 31, 1972, assuming that the books are adjusted and closed only at the end of each calendar year.

5-2. Data from the books of the Garrison Company are compiled as follows:

(a) On August 1, payment of $3,600 was made for a fire insurance policy covering a three-year period beginning on this date. The charge for the premium was made to a real account.

(b) 8% first-mortgage bonds of $1,000,000 were issued on October 1, 1972. Interest is payable semiannually on April 1 and October 1.

(c) Rent of $1,050 was received from a tenant occupying part of a building. The rent covers the period November 15, 1972, to February 28, 1973, and was reported as Rent Received in Advance.

(d) The company purchased $15,000 U.S. 6% Treasury Bonds on April 1. Interest on the bonds is payable semiannually on February 1 and August 1.

Instructions: (1) Give the adjusting journal entries as of November 30, 1972, assuming that the books are adjusted monthly but are closed at the end of each calendar year.

(2) Give the adjusting journal entries as of December 31, 1972, assuming that the books are adjusted monthly but are closed at the end of each calendar year.

(3) Give the adjusting journal entries as of December 31, 1972, assuming that the books are adjusted and closed only at the end of each calendar year.

5-3. Account balances taken from the ledger of the Randall Supply Corporation on December 31, 1972, follow:

Accounts Payable	$ 30,000	Land	$ 58,000
Accounts Receivable	56,000	Long-Term Investments	10,500
Advertising	4,000	Mortgage Payable	40,000
Accumulated Depreciation		Notes Payable—Short Term	12,500
— Buildings	16,500	Office Expense	13,400
Allowance for Doubtful Ac-		Purchases	115,400
counts	1,150	Purchases Discount	950
Buildings	60,000	Retained Earnings, Dec. 31,	
Capital Stock, $10 par	150,000	1971	11,700
Cash	20,000	Sales	205,000
Dividends	12,000	Sales Discount	4,500
Freight In	3,000	Sales Returns	2,800
Insurance Expense	1,200	Selling Expense	41,200
Interest Expense	2,200	Supplies Expense	3,500
Interest Income	550	Taxes — Real Estate, Pay-	
Inventory, Dec. 31, 1971	54,000	roll, and Other	6,650

Adjustments on December 31 are required as follows:

(a) The inventory on hand is $75,600.

(b) The allowance for doubtful accounts is to be increased to a balance of $2,500.

(c) Buildings are depreciated at the rate of $3\frac{1}{3}\%$ per year.

(d) Accrued selling expenses are $3,200.

(e) There are supplies of $650 on hand.

(f) Prepaid insurance relating to 1973 and 1974 totals $600.

(g) Accrued interest on long-term investments is $200.

(h) Accrued real estate, payroll and other taxes are $750.

(i) Accrued interest on the mortgage is $400.

(j) Income taxes are estimated to be 50% of the income before income taxes.

Instructions: (1) Prepare an eight-column work sheet.

(2) Prepare a balance sheet, income statement, and retained earnings statement.

(3) Prepare adjusting, closing, and reversing entries.

5-4. The account balances taken from the ledger of Arnold Moore and Frank Nielson at the end of the first year's operations on December 31, 1972, and the data for adjustments are given below:

Accounts Payable	$12,600	Personal — Arnold Moore	
Accounts Receivable	3,100	(debit)	$ 2,400
Capital — Arnold Moore	10,000	Personal — Frank Nielson	
Capital — Frank Nielson	8,150	(debit)	900
Cash	9,650	Purchases	82,000
Interest Expense	500	Purchases Discount	2,300
Interest Income	350	Purchases Ret. and Allow.	1,650
Miscellaneous General Ex-		Sales	85,000
pense	12,600	Sales Salaries	8,000
Notes Payable	6,000	Store Furniture	3,700
Notes Receivable	2,000	Store Supplies	600
		Taxes	600

Data for adjustments, year ended December 31, 1972:

(a) Inventories: merchandise, $24,100; store supplies, $280.
(b) Depreciation of store furniture, 10% a year. Additions to store furniture were made on March 1 costing $900.
(c) Accrued advertising, $95.
(d) Taxes paid in advance, $200.
(e) Accrued taxes, $215.
(f) Accrued interest on notes payable, $75.
(g) Accrued interest on notes receivable, $105.
(h) 5% of the accounts receivable are expected to prove uncollectible.
(i) Moore and Nielson divide earnings in the ratio 3:2.

Instructions: (1) Prepare an eight-column work sheet.
(2) Prepare an income statement, a statement of changes in partners' capital accounts, and a balance sheet.
(3) Prepare adjusting, closing, and reversing entries.

5-5. The following account balances are taken from the books of the Hales Manufacturing Co. on December 31, 1972, the end of the first year of operations:

Cash	$ 30,875	Indirect Labor	$ 25,500
Accounts Receivable	92,800	Heat, Light, and Power	10,500
Factory Supplies	1,200	Maintenance and Repairs	7,200
Office Supplies	700	Miscellaneous Factory	
Land, Buildings, and Equip-		Overhead	3,500
ment	205,000	Sales Salaries and Commis-	
Accounts Payable	86,000	sions	24,000
6% Bonds Payable	150,000	Advertising	18,000
Common Stock, $20 par	100,000	Miscellaneous Selling Ex-	
Sales	470,000	pense	22,000
Sales of Raw Materials (at		Office Salaries	19,500
cost)	26,100	Miscellaneous General and	
Raw Materials Purchases	250,200	Administrative Expense	4,625
Freight In	7,000	Interest Expense — Bonds	4,500
Direct Labor	105,000		

The following adjustments are to be made on December 31:

(a) Inventories:

Finished goods....	$22,000	Factory supplies... $	500
Goods in process...	14,000	Office supplies....	250
Raw materials.....	26,000		

(b) Provision for doubtful accounts, 1% of sales of finished product.

(c) Depreciation, 8%, chargeable ½ to manufacturing, ¼ to selling, ¼ to office.

(d) Accrued wages and salaries:

Direct labor.......	$ 4,200
Indirect labor.....	500
Sales salaries.....	300

(e) A dividend of $1 per share had been declared December 28, 1972, and is payable January 10, 1973.

(f) Bond interest payment dates are March 1 and September 1.

(g) Income taxes for 1972 are estimated at $13,000.

Instructions: (1) Prepare a ten-column work sheet.

(2) Prepare a balance sheet, an income statement, a manufacturing schedule, and a retained earnings statement.

(3) Prepare the adjusting, closing, and reversing entries.

5-6. The following account balances are taken from the general ledger of the Blaine Manufacturing Co. on December 31, 1972, the end of its fiscal year. The corporation was organized January 2, 1966:

Cash on Hand and in Banks.	$ 35,625	Shipping Dept. Equip.....	$ 12,000
Notes Receivable.........	18,500	Accumulated Depreciation	
Accounts Receivable......	56,000	— Shipping Dept. Equip.	7,200
Allowance for Doubtful Ac-		Patents..................	27,500
counts................	650	Notes Payable...........	20,000
Finished Goods — Janu-		Accounts Payable.........	45,700
ary 1, 1972............	40,500	6% First-Mortgage Bonds.	100,000
Goods in Process — Janu-		6% Preferred Stock, $100	
ary 1, 1972............	42,000	par...................	100,000
Raw Materials — Janu-		Common Stock, $100 par..	100,000
ary 1, 1972............	24,000	Premium on Common	
Factory Supplies..........	17,000	Stock................	10,000
Shipping Supplies.........	8,500	Retained Earnings........	125,000
Office Supplies...........	6,200	Sales....................	560,000
Tools....................	20,000	Sales Ret. and Allow......	10,000
Patterns and Dies.........	30,000	Sales Discount...........	7,000
Land....................	20,000	Raw Materials Purchases..	110,200
Buildings................	125,000	Freight and Cartage In....	8,800
Accumulated Depreciation		Purchases Ret. and Allow..	3,000
— Buildings...........	18,000	Purchases Discount.......	3,400
Machinery and Equipment.	160,000	Direct Labor.............	108,000
Accumulated Depreciation		Indirect Labor..........	32,000
— Machinery and Equip.	30,000	Plant Superintendence.....	20,000
Office Furniture and Fix-		Maintenance and Repairs	
tures.................	15,000	of Buildings............	6,300
Accumulated Depreciation		Maintenance and Repairs	
— Office Furn. and Fix.	9,000	of Machinery...........	7,000

Heat, Light and Power (Factory).............	$ 11,000	Officers Salaries..........	$ 25,000
Taxes...................	10,200	Office Salaries............	14,000
Misc. Factory Overhead...	3,600	Insurance Expense........	8,500
Sales Salaries............	35,000	Postage, Telephone, and Telegraph............	1,400
Sales Commissions........	12,300	Misc. Office Expense......	1,500
Traveling Expense........	8,500	Interest Income..........	800
Advertising Expense.......	23,125	Interest Expense — Bonds.	3,500
Shipping Dept. Salaries....	6,000	Interest Expense — Other..	1,000
Misc. Shipping Dept. Exp..	1,000		

The following adjustments are to be made on December 31, 1972, before the books are closed:

(a) Inventories:
Finished goods, $49,500; goods in process, $60,200; raw materials $36,600; factory supplies, $2,700; shipping supplies, $2,500; office supplies, $1,000.

(b) Depreciation and amortization:
Shipping department equipment, $12\frac{1}{2}\%$.
Office furniture and fixtures, 10%.
Machinery and equipment, 5%. New machinery and equipment costing $60,000 was installed on March 1, 1972.
Buildings, 4%. Additions to the buildings costing $50,000 were completed June 30, 1972.
Patents were acquired on January 2, 1966. A charge for patent amortization for 1972 is to be made at 1/17 of the original patents cost.
A charge for patterns and dies amortization for 1972 is to be made at 15% of the balance in the patterns and dies account.
A charge for tools used during the year is to be made at 25% of the balance in the tools account.

(c) The allowance for doubtful accounts is to be increased to a balance of $3,200.

(d) Accrued expenses:
Salaries and wages: direct labor, $1,400; indirect labor, $300; sales salaries, $400; shipping department salaries, $200.
Interest on bonds is payable semiannually on February 1 and August 1.
Interest on notes payable, $50.
Property taxes, $2,000.

(e) Prepaid expenses: insurance, $2,500.

(f) Accrued revenue: interest on notes receivable, $500.

(g) The following information is also to be recorded:
(1) It is discovered that sales commissions of $1,200 were charged in error to the account Shipping Department Salaries.
(2) On December 30 the board of directors declared a quarterly dividend on preferred stock and a dividend of $1.50 on common stock, payable January 25, 1973, to stockholders of record January 15, 1973.
(3) Income taxes for 1972 are estimated at $30,000.
Taxes, expired insurance, and building expenses are to be distributed as follows: to manufacturing operations, 60%; to selling operations, 25%; to general operations, 15%.
The only charges to retained earnings during the year resulted from the declaration of the regular quarterly dividends on preferred stock.
The balance of Retained Earnings on January 1, 1972 was $129,500.

Instructions: (1) Prepare a ten-column work sheet. There should be a pair of columns for trial balance, adjustments, manufacturing schedule, income statement, and balance sheet.

(2) Prepare (a) a balance sheet, (b) an income statement supported by schedules showing the cost of goods manufactured, selling expenses, and general and administrative expenses, and (c) a retained earnings statement.

(3) Prepare all of the journal entries necessary to give effect to the foregoing information and to adjust and close the books of the corporation.

(4) Prepare the reversing entries that may appropriately be made.

5-7. Mr. L. T. Knowles has been in business for almost a year and believes he has been quite successful. He asks you to help him determine how much he has made so far. You obtain the following data from an analysis of Mr. Knowles' check stubs and from the information he provides.

Amount invested January 15:	
Cash	$ 15,000
Inventory	40,000
	$ 55,000
Less amount still due to suppliers for purchase of inventory	8,000
	$ 47,000

Cash receipts:	
From customers	$185,000
From loan by R. V. Knowles	25,000

Cash disbursements:	
To suppliers	$135,000
For wages to employees	30,000
For miscellaneous expenses	15,000

Other information at December 31:	
Amounts due from customers	$ 22,000
Amounts payable to suppliers	18,000
Inventory on hand	35,000
Prepaid expenses	2,800
Office supplies	200

Instructions: Prepare an income statement and a balance sheet for Mr. Knowles as of December 31.

5-8. A balance sheet for the Spencer Supply Company on January 1, 1972, reports the following balances:

Cash		$17,250	Accounts payable		$10,500
Accounts receivable..	$6,000		Salaries payable		300
Less allowance for			Taxes payable		200
doubtful accounts	350	5,650	C. H. Spencer, capital		30,600
Inventories		15,100			
Prepaid insurance		100			
Furniture	$4,200				
Less accumulated					
depreciation	700	3,500			
		$41,600			$41,600

Transactions for 1972 are summarized below:

Sales on account.	$105,000
Purchases on account.	70,000
Sales returns (credits were made to customers' accounts). . .	1,500
Cash collected on accounts receivable.	97,000
Discounts allowed on accounts collected.	1,200
Uncollectible accounts written off against allowance.	200
Cash paid on accounts payable.	60,000
Discounts taken on accounts paid.	800
Operating expenses paid.	22,500

Withdrawals for personal use:

Merchandise (cost).	$ 2,000	
Cash.	16,000	18,000

Cash borrowed from the bank on a note dated November 1, 1972, and payable 6 months from this date together with interest at 8%.	6,000

In addition to the foregoing information, the following data are to be considered on December 31: inventories, $20,000; prepaid insurance, $250; accrued salaries, $550; and accrued taxes, $400. Depreciation of furniture for the year is $350. The balance in the allowance for doubtful accounts is to be increased by $150.

Instructions: Prepare an income statement, a balance sheet, and a statement of changes in the owner's equity account for the year ended December 31, 1972. ("T" accounts or working papers should be used in developing statement data.)

5-9. The Chapman Sales Co. is organized on January 2, 1972, selling its total authorized stock of 6,000 shares for cash at par, $60,000. Transactions for the next six months follow:

Payments for equipment.	$ 30,000
Sales on account.	181,000
Purchases on account.	172,000
Cash borrowed on long-term notes.	40,000
Operating expenses paid.	42,000
Purchases returns and allowances (charges were made to creditors' accounts).	3,000

A cash dividend of $2,000 is declared in June, payable July 15. On June 30, there are accounts receivable of $40,000 that have not been collected; sales discounts of $1,200 were allowed on accounts collected. On June 30, there are also accounts payable of $30,000 that have not been paid. An allowance for doubtful accounts of $650 is to be established on accounts receivable on hand. The merchandise inventory on this date is $62,900. Depreciation for the six months is estimated at $900. In addition, adjustments are to be made for the following prepaid and accrued items as of June 30:

Prepaid insurance.	$1,000
Advances to employees.	550

(Insurance and advances were recorded as operating expenses during the period.)

Accrued interest on notes payable......................... $1,250
Accrued salaries..   350
Accrued payroll and property taxes........................   650

The income taxes for 1972 are estimated at 50% of the net income.

Instructions: Prepare an income statement, a balance sheet, and retained earnings statement for the six-month period ended June 30, 1972. (T accounts or working papers should be used in developing statement data.)

5-10. The Forbes Company commenced operations on July 1, 1972. The following shows the gross debits and credits in each account of the ledger as of December 31, 1972, except for goods in process and finished goods inventory accounts. The company uses a cost system for its manufacturing operations.

	Transactions		Trial Balance December 31, 1972	
	Dr.	Cr.	Dr.	Cr.
Cash........................	$464,000	$370,000	94,000	
Notes Receivable..............	20,000	12,000	8,000	
Accounts Receivable...........	340 000	302,000	38,000	
Finished Goods................	compute	compute	30,000	
Goods in Process..............	compute	compute	14,000	
Raw Materials.................	125,000	118,000	7,000	
Supplies......................	18,000	14,000	4,000	
Prepaid Insurance.............	1,900	1,500	400	
Land, Buildings, and Equipment..	95,000	0	95,000	
Mortgage Payable..............	0	50,000		50,000
Accrued Mortgage Interest......	0	750		750
Accrued Wages................	145,100	147,000		1,900
Capital Stock..................	0	150,000		150,000
Vouchers Payable..............	325,000	365,500		40,500
Sales........................	0	360,000		360,000
Cost of Goods Sold.............	250,000	0	250,000	
Selling Expense................	27,500	0	27,500	
Administrative Expense.........	29,000	0	29,000	
Financial Expense.............	6,250	0	6,250	
			603,150	603,150

You are also given the following information:

(a) The ending goods in process inventory consists of the following: materials — $6,000; direct labor — $4,500; and manufacturing overhead — $3,500.
(b) Insurance premiums apply two thirds to the factory and one third to the office.
(c) The cost of the finished product is made up of: materials 40%, labor 40%, and manufacturing overhead 20%.

Instructions: Set up skeleton ledger "T" accounts. Show therein the entries making up the transactions included in the figures shown on the trial balance. Key each entry (debit and offsetting credit) by use of a number, and on a separate sheet give an explanation and support for each entry.

(AICPA adapted)

chapter 6

cash and temporary investments

The first part of this book has established a foundation for a careful analysis of the specific balance sheet classifications. The order of presentation will follow that of the conventional balance sheet, beginning with the most liquid assets, cash and temporary investments, and proceeding with the other asset items, the liabilities, and the owners' equity.

Cash

Cash is the most active item on the accounting statements. The movement of cash completes almost all purchases and sales transactions. Purchases of goods and services normally result in cash payments; sales normally result in cash receipts. Cash, more often than any other asset, is the item involved in business transactions. This is due to the nature of the business transactions which include a price and conditions calling for settlement in terms of the medium of exchange.

In striking contrast to the activity of cash is its unproductive nature. Since cash is the measure of value, it cannot expand or grow unless it is converted into other properties. Excessive balances of cash on hand are often referred to as "idle cash." Efficient cash management requires that available cash be continuously working in one of several ways — for example, as part of the operating cycle or as a short-term or long-term investment.

Composition of cash

Cash is represented by those monetary as well as nonmonetary items that are immediately available to management for business purposes. Cash includes commercial and savings deposits in banks and elsewhere that are available upon demand, and money items on hand that can be used as a medium of exchange or that are acceptable for deposit at face value by a bank. Cash on hand would include petty cash funds, change funds, and other regularly used and unexpended monetary funds, together with nonmonetary items consisting of personal checks, travelers' checks, cashiers' checks, bank drafts, and money orders.

"Acceptance at face value on deposit" is a satisfactory test in classifying as cash the items that may be found in the cash drawer. It is assumed that deposits in a bank are made regularly and that deposits become the basis for disbursements by the depositor. Although postage stamps may in some instances pass for mail payments of small amounts, they are not accepted for deposit and should be classified as office supplies. Postdated checks are in effect notes receivable and should not be recognized as cash until the time they can be deposited. Checks deposited but returned by the bank because of insufficient funds in the debtor's account are receivables. Cash-due memorandums for money advanced to officers and employees are receivable items, in some instances less satisfactory receivables than those of trade customers. Paper left at a bank for collection represents a receivable until collection is made and the amount is added to the depositor's account. Stocks, bonds, and United States securities, although immediately convertible into cash, cannot be used as a means for making payments, hence do not constitute cash but should be recognized as investments.

Deposits in foreign banks subject to immediate and unrestricted withdrawal qualify as cash. Such balances should be converted into their U. S. dollar equivalents as of the date of the balance sheet. However, cash in foreign banks that is blocked or otherwise restricted as to use or withdrawal and cash in closed banks should be designated as claims or receivables of a current or noncurrent character and should be reported subject to allowances for losses on their realization.

Cash balances that have been specifically designated by management for special purposes may be separately reported. But those cash balances that are to be applied to some current purpose or current obligation are properly reported in the current section on the balance sheet. For example, cash funds for employees' travel, for payment of current interest and dividends, or for payment of taxes or other obligations included in the current liabilities may be separately reported but are still classified as current.

Cash restricted as to use by agreement should be separately designated and reported. Such cash should be reported as a current item only if it is to be applied to some current purpose or obligation. Cash representing refundable deposits collected from customers, for example, requires separate reporting. Classification of the cash balance as current or noncurrent should parallel the classification applied to the liability.

Cash balances that are not available for current purposes require separate designation and classification under a noncurrent heading on the balance sheet. The noncurrent classification applies to items such as the following: time deposits not currently available as a result of withdrawal restrictions; cash deposits on bids or options that may be applied to the acquisition of noncurrent assets; and cash funds held by trustees for plant acquisitions, bond retirement, and pension payments.

Since the concept of cash embodies the standard of value, no valuation problem is encountered in reporting those items qualifying as cash.

Control of cash

The term *internal control* has been broadly defined by the Committee on Auditing Procedure of the AICPA as ". . . the plan of organization and all of the coordinate methods and measures adopted within a business to safeguard its assets, check the accuracy and reliability of its accounting data, promote operational efficiency, and encourage adherence to prescribed managerial policies."[1] This definition may be considered to embrace both *accounting controls* and *administrative controls*. Accounting controls dealing with the safeguarding of assets and the reliability of records are expressed in the form of systems of authorization and approval, separation of duties concerned with record keeping and reporting from those concerned with operations and asset custody, physical controls over assets, and internal auditing. Administrative controls dealing with operational efficiency and adherence to managerial policies are expressed in the form of statistical analyses, time and motion studies, performance reports, employee training programs, and quality controls.[2]

Obviously, the system of internal control must be developed with appropriate regard to the size and nature of the particular unit that is to be served. Its design should provide the maximum contributions practicable considering the special risks that are faced as well as the costs of providing controls. The increased use of data processing equipment for processing accounting transactions has not eliminated the need for carefully designed control systems. As new equipment is acquired and introduced into the system, the establishment or modification of controls should be considered.

In any system of internal accounting control, special emphasis must be placed on the procedures for handling and accounting for cash.

---

[1]*Internal Control — Elements of a Coordinated System and Its Importance to Management and the Independent Public Accountant* (New York: American Institute of Certified Public Accountants, 1949), p. 6.

[2]*Statement on Auditing Procedure No. 33*, "Auditing Standards and Procedures" (New York: American Institute of Certified Public Accountants, 1963), Ch. 5, par. 5.

Problems in cash control. Because of the characteristics of cash — its small bulk, its lack of owner identification, and its immediate transferability — it is the asset most subject to misappropriation. Losses can be avoided only by careful control of cash from the time it is received until the time it is spent.

Control over business cash normally requires as a minimum the separation of cash custodial functions and cash recording functions. When the same persons have access to cash and also to the cash records, the business becomes vulnerable to the misappropriation of cash and to the manipulation or falsification of cash records. The following are representative of the practices that have been found under these circumstances: (1) cash receipts from sales, from recoveries of accounts previously written off, from refunds on invoice overpayments, and from other sources are understated, the unrecorded cash being pocketed; (2) receivables are not entered on the books and cash collected on such receivables is withheld; (3) customers' accounts are credited for remittances but Sales Returns or Doubtful Accounts Expense is charged and the cash is withheld; (4) checks for personal purposes are charged to business expense; (5) invoices, vouchers, receipts, payroll records, or vouchers once approved and paid are used in support of fictitious charges, and endorsements on checks issued in payment of such charges are subsequently forged; (6) the cash balance is misstated by erroneous footings in the cash receipts and disbursement records, cash equivalent to the misstatement being withheld.

Two additional practices, *check kiting* and *lapping*, may be found when those who handle cash also maintain the cash records of the business.

Check kiting occurs when at the end of a month a transfer of funds is made by check from one bank to another to cover a cash shortage, and the entry to record the issue of the check is held over until the beginning of the new period. A cash increase in the customer's balance is recognized by the second bank in the current month as a result of the receipt of the check but a corresponding decrease in the customer's balance is not recognized by the first bank because the check has not yet been presented for payment. When the bank statements are received, the balance in the bank in which the check was deposited shows an increase. At the same time, the balance shown in the bank on which the check was drawn remains unchanged. A cash shortage is thus temporarily concealed.

Lapping occurs when a customer's remittance is misappropriated, the customer's account being credited when cash is collected from another customer at a later date. This process may be continued with further misappropriations and increasing delays in postings. To illustrate lapping, assume that on successive days cash is received from customers A, B, and C in amounts of $75, $125, and $120. A's payment is misappropriated. A is subsequently credited with $75 out of B's payment and the difference, $50, is misappropriated. B is credited for $125 upon C's $120 payment and $5 is returned on the amounts originally "borrowed." The shortage at this point is $120, the unrecorded credit to C's account. This procedure can be continued with but slight delay in recording any customer's payment. The embezzler usually intends to return the money and avoid the strain of lapping after he has made a "profit on his investments." Unable to make restitution, he may resort to a fictitious entry charging Doubtful Accounts Expense or some other expense account and crediting the customers' balances to bring these up to date.

When, during the course of the day, cash records and summaries report a cash total that differs from the amount available for deposit and it is assumed that cash has been lost or errors have been made in making change, an adjustment is made to a cash short and over account. The balance in this account may be reported as a financial management item in summarizing net income. However, a cash shortage resulting from employee defalcation should be charged to an account with the employee or the bonding company liable for such losses. Failure to recover the shortage requires the recognition of a loss from this source.

Attributes of cash control systems. A system of accounting control over cash funds should serve to disclose cash discrepancies as well as to fix responsibility for any possible misappropriations or mistakes in handling and recording cash. When misuse of funds or errors are indicated, it is only fair to members of an organization that the causes be determined and the responsibility be fixed so that innocent parties may be spared any embarrassment. Responsibilities for the handling and recording functions should be specifically defined and scrupulously observed and carried out.

The system for the control of cash must be adapted to the particular business that it is to serve. It is not feasible to attempt to describe all of the features and techniques that might be employed in businesses of various kinds and sizes. In general, however, systems of cash control deny access to the records to those who handle cash. This reduces the possibility of improper entries to conceal the misuse of cash receipts and cash payments. The misappropriation of cash is greatly reduced if two or more employees must conspire in the embezzlement. Further, systems normally provide for separation of the receiving and paying functions.

The basic characteristics of a system of cash control are listed and described below:

1. Specifically assigned responsibility for handling cash receipts.
2. Separation of handling and recording cash receipts.
3. Daily deposit of all cash received.
4. Voucher system to control cash payments.
5. Internal audit at irregular intervals.

Specifically assigned responsibility for handling cash receipts. A fundamental principle in controlling any asset is that it be specifically assigned to one person. This principle is especially vital in the area of cash. If more than one person must have access to the same cash fund at different times, a reconciliation of the cash on hand should be made each time the responsibility is shifted. Any shortage or questionable transaction can then be identified with a particular person.

Separation of handling and recording cash receipts. An adequate system normally requires that cash from sales and cash remittances from customers be made available directly to the treasurer or the cashier for deposit, while records related to such transactions, as well as records related to bank deposits, be made available directly to the bookkeeping division. It is also desirable that comparisons of bank deposits with the book records of cash be made regularly by a third party who is engaged neither in the cash handling nor in the cash recording functions. Frequently, for example, a clerk opens the mail, prepares lists of remittances in duplicate, and then sends the cash and one copy of the list of remittances to the cashier and the second copy of the list to the bookkeeping division. Readings of cash registers are made by some responsible individual other than the cashier at the end of the day. The cash, together with a summary of the receipts, is sent to the cashier; a summary of the receipts is also sent to the bookkeeping division. Although deposits in the bank are made by the cashier or treasurer, entries on the books are made from lists of remittances and register readings prepared by individuals not otherwise involved in handling or recording cash. Members of the accounting or auditing staff compare periodic bank statements with related data on the books to determine whether the data are in agreement. If customers' remittances are not listed and the cash is misused, statements to customers will report excessive amounts and protests will lead to sources of the discrepancies; if cash receipts listed are not deposited properly, the bank record will not agree with cash records.

Daily deposit of all cash received. The daily deposit of all cash received prevents sums of cash from lying around the office and being used for other than business purposes. Officers and employees have less opportunity to borrow on IOU'S. Both the temptation for misappropriation of cash and the risk of theft of this item are avoided. The bank now protects company funds and releases these only upon proper company authorization. When the full receipts are deposited daily, the bank's record of deposits must agree with the depositor's record of cash receipts. This double record provides an automatic check over cash receipts.

Voucher system to control cash payments. The use of the voucher system to control cash payments is a desirable feature of cash control. Vouchers authorizing disbursements of cash by check are made at the time goods or services are received and found acceptable. Entries in the voucher register recording the expenditures and the authorizations for payment are made by the bookkeeping division. Checks are also prepared here and are sent, together with the documents supporting the disbursements, to the person specifically authorized to make payment, normally the official designated as treasurer. This person signs and issues checks only after careful inspection of the vouchers supporting and authorizing payments. The bookkeeping department, upon notification of the issuance of checks, makes appropriate records of this fact. Receiving and paying functions of the business are maintained as two separate systems. In each instance, custodial and recording activities are exercised by different parties.

Internal audit at irregular intervals. Internal audits at irregular and unannounced intervals may be made a part of the system of cash control. A member of the internal auditing staff verifies the records and checks upon the activities of those employees handling cash to make sure that the provisions of the system are being carried out. Such control is particularly desirable over petty cash and other cash funds where cash handling and bookkeeping are generally combined.

Double record of cash. The preceding section listed the daily deposit of all cash received as an important factor in the control of cash. If all cash receipts are deposited daily, then the bank record of deposits will agree with the depositor's record of cash receipts. As a complementary device, all cash payments should be made by check, the bank then maintaining a record for checks that will agree with the depositor's record of cash payments. Two complete cash summaries are thus available, one in the cash account and the other on the monthly bank statement. In addition to the advantages resulting from organized and consistent routines applied to cash receipts and disbursements, a duplicate record of cash maintained by an outside agency is made available as a check upon the accuracy of the records kept by the company.

Maintenance of the double record of cash involves two special business and accounting procedures described in the following sections: (1) the adoption of a system of cash disbursements from a petty cash fund, and (2) reconciliation of the bank balance with the cash account balance at regular intervals.

Imprest system of cash funds. Immediate cash payments and payments that are too small to be made by check may be made from a petty cash fund. Under the *imprest system* the petty cash fund is created by drawing a check to Petty Cash for the amount of the fund. In recording the establishment of the fund, Petty Cash Fund is charged and Cash is credited. The cash is then turned over to a cashier or some person who is to be solely responsible for payments made out of the fund. The cashier generally requires a signed receipt for all payments made. Such receipts may be printed in prenumbered form. Frequently a bill or other memorandum is submitted when a payment is requested. A record of petty cash payments may be kept in a *petty cash journal*.

Whenever the amount of cash in the fund runs low and also at the end of each fiscal period, the fund is replenished by writing a check equal to the payments that have been made. In recording replenishment, expenses and other appropriate accounts are charged for petty cash disbursements and Cash is credited. Replenishment is necessary whenever statements are to be prepared since petty cash disbursements are recognized on the books only when the fund is replenished.

The request for cash to replenish the fund is supported by a summary and analysis of the signed receipts that were required at the time of the payments from the fund. This analysis is the basis for the charges that are recognized on the books when the replenishing check is issued. The signed receipts, together with appropriate supporting documents, are filed as evidence supporting petty cash disbursements.

The cashier of the petty cash fund is held accountable for the total amount of the fund in his care. He must have on hand at all times cash and signed receipts equal in amount to the original balance of the fund. He should be discouraged from cashing employees' checks from petty cash or otherwise engaging in a banking function. If a banking function is to be undertaken, it should represent a separate activity with a fund established for this purpose. Inasmuch as the cashier normally keeps the petty cash records, the rule of separating the recording and handling of cash is not here enforced.

The imprest system may be employed not only for petty cash but for other cash funds in a large organization. For example, a branch office or agency may be allowed a fund that is subsequently replenished for amounts equal to disbursements out of the fund. Evidence concerning payments out of the fund is submitted with the request for replenishment, and fund disbursements are recorded on the books at the time of fund replenishment.

The petty cash operation should be maintained apart from other cash funds employed for particular business purposes. For example, a business may require funds for making change. Certain sums of coins and currency are withheld from deposit at the end of each day to be carried forward as the change funds for the beginning of business on the next day. A separate account should be established to report a cash supply always on hand. Also, special funds or bank accounts may be established for payrolls, dividend distributions, and bond interest payments. Each fund would call for a separate accounting.

Reconciliation of bank balances. When daily receipts are deposited and payments other than those from petty cash are made by check, the bank's statement of its transactions with the depositor can be compared with the record of cash as reported on the depositor's books. A comparison of the bank balance with the balance reported on the books is usually made monthly by means of a summary known as a *bank reconciliation statement*. The bank reconciliation statement is prepared to disclose any errors or irregularities existing in either the records of the bank or the records of the business unit. It is developed in a form that points out the reasons for discrepancies in the two balances. It should be prepared by an individual who neither handles nor records cash. Any discrepancies should be brought to the immediate attention of appropriate company officials.

An understanding of the reciprocal relationship that exists between the records of the depositor and of the bank is necessary in the preparation of the reconciliation statement. All debits to the bank on the books of the depositor should be matched by credits to the depositor on the books of the bank; all credits to the bank on the books of the depositor should be matched by debits to the depositor on the books of the bank. To illustrate, cash from sales is recorded on the books of the depositor by a debit to the account with the bank, for example, Cash — State First National Bank, and a credit to Sales; the bank upon receiving the deposit debits Cash and credits the account with the depositor. A check in payment of an account is recorded on the books of the depositor by a debit to Accounts Payable, and a credit to the account with the bank; the bank upon clearing the check debits the account with the depositor and credits Cash.

When the two records are compared, certain items may appear on one record and not on the other, resulting in a difference in the two balances. Most of these differences result from timing lags, and are thus normal. These differences in depositor and bank balances may be classified as follows:

(1) *Debits on the depositor's records without corresponding credits on the bank records.* For example, a deposit recognized on the depositor's records on the last day of the month may have been mailed, put into an after-hours depository, or held for transfer to the bank on the next day, and does not appear on the bank statement.

(2) *Credits on the depositor's records without corresponding debits on the bank records.* For example, checks that were drawn and are recognized on the depositor's records may not yet have cleared and do not appear on the bank statement.

(3) *Debits on the bank records without corresponding credits on depositor's records.* For example, the bank may have charged the depositor's account for bank services, checkbooks, interest, returned customers' checks, and other items, but the depositor has not been notified of these charges before receiving his bank statement and these do not appear on his books.

(4) *Credits on the bank records without corresponding debits on the depositor's records.* For example, the bank may have credited the depositor's account for amounts collected on his behalf, but the depositor has not been notified of these before receiving his bank statement and these do not appear on his books.

If, after considering the items mentioned, the bank statement and the book balances cannot be reconciled, a detailed analysis of both the bank's records and the depositor's books may be necessary to determine whether errors or other irregularities exist on the records of either party.

There are two common forms of the bank reconciliation statement. One form is prepared in two sections, the bank statement balance being adjusted to the corrected cash balance in the first section, and the book balance being adjusted to the same corrected cash balance in the second section. The first section, then, contains items that the bank has not recognized as well as any corrections for errors that were made by the bank; the second section contains items that the depositor has not yet recognized and any corrections for errors that were made on the depositor's books.

The other form begins with the bank statement balance and reports the adjustments that must be applied to this balance to obtain the cash balance on the depositor's books. The second form, then, simply reports the items that account for the discrepancy between the bank and book balances. The first form is illustrated on the following page; the second is shown on page 178.

Mason, Inc.
Bank Reconciliation Statement
November 30, 1972

Balance per bank statement, November 30, 1972..............		$2,979.72
Add: Receipts for November 30 not yet deposited...	$658.50	
Charge for interest made to depositor's account		
by bank in error.....'...................	12.50	671.00
		$3,650.72
Deduct outstanding checks:		
No. 1125.................................	$ 58.16	
No. 1138.................................	100.00	
No. 1152.................................	98.60	
No. 1154.................................	255.00	
No. 1155.................................	192.07	703.83
Corrected bank balance...............................		$2,946.89
Balance per books, November 30, 1972.....................		$2,552.49
Add: Proceeds of draft collected by bank November 30 ($500 face less $1.50 bank charges)...	$498.50	
Check No. 1116 for $46 recorded by depositor as $64 in error........................	18.00	516.50
		$3,068.99
Deduct: Bank service charges....................	$ 3.16	
Customer's check deposited November 25 and returned marked uncollectible......	118.94	122.10
Corrected book balance...............................		$2,946.89

Reconciliation of bank and book balances to corrected balances

Although the first form of bank reconciliation may be considered preferable because it develops a corrected cash figure and shows separately all of the items requiring adjustment on the depositor's books, some accountants prefer to use the second form, which is consistent with the nature of the reconciliation that is required for many other accounts.

After preparing the reconciliation, the depositor should record any items appearing on the bank statement and requiring recognition on his books as well as any corrections for errors discovered on his own books. The bank should be notified immediately of any bank errors. The following entries are required on the books of Mason, Inc., as a result of the reconciliation just made:

Cash..	498.50	
Miscellaneous General Expense..................	1.50	
Notes Receivable............................		500.00
To record collection of a $500 time draft by the bank on which bank charges were $1.50.		

Mason, Inc.
Bank Reconciliation Statement
November 30, 1972

Balance per bank statement, November 30, 1972...............			$2,979.72
Add: Receipts for November 30 not yet deposited...		$658.50	
Charge for interest made to depositor's account by bank in error.......................		12.50	
Bank service charges......................		3.16	
Customer's check deposited November 25 and returned marked uncollectible............		118.94	793.10
			$3,772.82
Deduct: Outstanding checks:			
No. 1125..................	$ 58.16		
No. 1138..................	100.00		
No. 1152..................	98.60		
No. 1154..................	255.00		
No. 1155..................	192.07	$703.83	
Check No. 1116 for $46 recorded by depositor at $64 in error................		18.00	
Proceeds of draft collected by bank on November 30........................		498.50	1,220.33
Balance per books, November 30, 1972......................			$2,552.49

Reconciliation of bank balance to book balance

Cash.......................................	18.00	
Advertising................................		18.00
To record correction for check in payment of advertising that was recorded as $64 instead of the actual amount, $46.		
Accounts Receivable.........................	118.94	
Miscellaneous General Expense.................	3.16	
Cash.......................................		122.10
To record customer's uncollectible check and bank charges for November.		

After these entries are posted, the cash account will show a balance of $2,946.89. This is the amount to be reported on the balance sheet. These adjustments are clearly distinguishable when using the first form of bank reconciliation. They are shown separately as adjustments on the books. If the second form is used, adjustments can be determined only after careful analysis of all reconciling items.[1]

---

[1]A customer's check that is returned by the bank when it cannot be cashed may be redeposited when it is assumed that a deposit was made by the customer to cover the check. When a charge is made to the customer's account upon the return of a check, the redeposit would be recorded as a normal collection of a receivable. When a check is returned by the bank and redeposited in the same period, some systems provide for no entry to be made; the omission does not affect the cash balances but it does affect the total receipts and disbursements reported by the bank.

The bank reconciliation is frequently expanded to incorporate a proof of both receipts and disbursements as separate steps in the reconciliation process. Two reconciliation forms may be employed here as in earlier examples. One form develops corrected balances for both receipts and disbursements of the bank and the depositor, as illustrated below. The other form, as illustrated on page 180, reports the items that account for the discrepancies in receipts and disbursement balances reported on the two sets of records.

Opening balances, increases, decreases, and closing balances as reported on both the bank statement and the depositor's books are first listed. A reconciliation as of the end of the preceding period after the depositor's books have been brought up to date is then provided in the first column. Receipts are reconciled in the second column and disbursements in the third column. With proof of receipts and disbursement

Mason, Inc.

Reconciliation of Receipts, Disbursements, and Bank Balance

November 30, 1972

	Beginning Reconciliation October 31	Receipts	Disbursements	Ending Reconciliation November 30
Balance per bank statement...	$5,895.42	$21,212.40	$24,128.10	$2,979.72
Receipts not deposited:				
October 31..............	515.40	(515.40)		
November 30...........		658.50		658.50
Outstanding checks:				
October 31..............	(810.50)		(810.50)	
November 30...........			703.83	(703.83)
Charge for interest made by bank in error...........			(12.50)	12.50
Corrected bank balance.....	$5,600.32	$21,355.50	$24,008.93	$2,946.89
Balance per books..........	$5,600.32	$20,857.00	$23,904.83	$2,552.49
Bank service charges........			3.16	(3.16)
Customer's check deposited November 25 found to be uncollectible			118.94	(118.94)
Proceeds of draft collected by bank on November 30		498.50		498.50
Check No. 1116 for $46 recorded by depositor at $64 in error.................			(18.00)	18.00
Corrected book balance.....	$5,600.32	$21,355.50	$24,008.93	$2,946.89

Reconciliation of bank and book balances to corrected balances

Mason, Inc.

Reconciliation of Receipts, Disbursements, and Bank Balance

November 30, 1972

	Beginning Reconciliation October 31	Receipts	Disbursements	Ending Reconciliation November 30
Balance per bank statement...	$5,895.42	$21,212.40	$24,128.10	$2,979.72
Receipts not deposited:				
October 31..............	515.40	(515.40)		
November 30............		658.50		658.50
Checks outstanding:				
October 31..............	(810.50)		(810.50)	
November 30............			703.83	(703.83)
Bank service charges........			(3.16)	3.16
Customer's check deposited Nov. 25 found to be uncollectible.................			(118.94)	118.94
Proceeds of draft collected by bank on November 30.....		(498.50)		(498.50)
Charge for interest made by bank in error............			(12.50)	12.50
Check No. 1116 for $46 recorded by depositor at $64 in error.................			18.00	(18.00)
Balance per books..........	$5,600.32	$20,857.00	$23,904.83	$2,552.49

Reconciliation of bank balance to book balance

data, adjustments relating to ending balances may now be reported in the final column and the closing bank and book balances proved.

In order to complete this type of reconciliation, each adjustment must be carefully analyzed. Two columns are always affected for each adjustment. For example, receipts of $515.40 on October 31, 1972, were received by the bank in November and are therefore included in the total bank receipts of $21,212.40 for November. However, the deposit was recorded on the books as a receipt in October and is not included in the book receipts of $20,857.00 for November. The reconciliation accounts for this by deducing the in-transit receipts from the total bank receipts.

Often the parentheses in the disbursements column are reversed, and the total disbursement is shown with parentheses to indicate a deduction when adding horizontally. Using this reverse procedure requires that a careful analysis be made of the reconciling items because whenever an item is to be added vertically to the disbursement total it must be enclosed in parentheses, while an item to be deducted is not enclosed in parentheses.

The expanded reconciliation procedure normally reduces the time and effort required to find errors made by either the bank or the depositor. In developing comparisons of both receipts and disbursements, the areas in which errors have been made, as well as the amounts of the discrepancies within each area, are immediately identified and checking procedures can be directed and narrowed accordingly. This procedure is frequently used by auditors when there is any question of possible discrepancies in the handling of cash.

Misrepresentation of current condition. Although a system of internal control may provide for the effective safeguarding of cash, careful examination of the records is still necessary at the end of the accounting period to determine whether transactions have been satisfactorily recorded and cash and the current position of the business are properly presented. Certain practices designed to present a more favorable financial condition than is actually the case may be encountered. Such practices are sometimes referred to as "window dressing." For example, cash records may be held open for a few days after the close of the fiscal period and cash received from customers during this period reported as receipts of the preceding period. An improved cash position is thus reported. If this balance is then used as a basis for drawing predated checks in payment of accounts payable, the ratio of current assets to current liabilities is improved. For example, if current assets are $30,000 and current liabilities are $20,000 providing a current ratio of 1.5 to 1, recording payment to creditors of $10,000 will produce balances of $20,000 and $10,000, a current ratio of 2 to 1. The current ratio is also improved by writing checks in payment of obligations and entering these on the books even though checks are not to be mailed until the following period. Or the current position, as well as earnings and owners' equity, is overstated by predating sales made at the beginning of the new period. A careful review of the records will disclose whether any improper practices have been employed. If such practices are discovered, the accounts should be corrected.

Cash planning

Cash planning within a company does not take place without management effort. Many companies which are basically sound in organization and product control frequently have financial problems because management does not understand the basic importance of cash planning. A full knowledge of the techniques of budgeting and forecasting is essential to sound financial control.

Business budget. Management, in meeting its responsibilities and in achieving successful business operations, needs to develop intelligent objectives and means for the realization of such objectives. The instrument that management employs to express its objectives and to define the guides and controls for achieving these is the business *budget*. A comprehensive operating budget offers an integrated and detailed plan for the future. Standards are set for sales, production, and expenses. The inflow and outgo of cash are planned. Statements are prepared reporting the estimated earnings and financial position in terms of projected operations, financing, and earnings distributions. With a well-organized master plan for integrated and coordinated action by all parts of the organization, operations may be channeled toward achievement of individual and collective goals. Continuous comparisons are made between the standards that have been set by the budget and the results actually achieved through operations. Variations between budgetary standards and actual results are evaluated, and adjustment and revision of the standards are made when appropriate.

Although the budget expresses the objectives set by top management and those in charge of operations, its preparation, as well as subsequent analyses indicating the degree to which objectives have been realized, is normally the responsibility of the controller and his staff. The accounting staff is technically qualified to organize and present operational plans in the most satisfactory form. The accountants, too, are best qualified to develop the analyses that are required by management in evaluating the past and setting plans for the future.

Cash forecast. An important part of any budget is the forecast and planning of cash. Cash is the beginning and the end of all business activity, and any plans for the future must be directly related to cash. Even in the absence of a comprehensive budgetary program, attention must be directed to cash, its expected movement, and methods for its proper utilization and control, if financial chaos is to be avoided. Adequate cash must be readily available for all current needs; at the same time, any cash in excess of current needs and reasonable reserves must be profitably employed.

The preparation of a *cash forecast* requires estimates of future cash receipts and cash disbursements. In projecting the cash flow, it is necessary to refer to forecasts and plans that have been made by management relative to sales, inventory acquisitions, operational costs, and plant and equipment acquisitions. Appropriate consideration must also be given to commitments with creditors and owners and probable actions of the board of directors that will affect the cash position.

Cash receipts and disbursements may not be matched in the months to come as the result of a number of factors, the most important of which are the following:

1. Purchases and payments to creditors predate sales and collections from customers. Cyclical factors call for heavy seasonal expenditures that are recovered only at some later date.
2. Acquisition of plant and equipment items are made at various intervals.
3. Long-term debt is retired at various intervals.

With a full consideration of these factors, management may set plans for establishing and maintaining a satisfactory cash balance. In meeting the requirements of (1) above, steps may be taken to provide for a supply of cash through short-term borrowing or through the conversion of marketable securities held for such purposes. Upon the recovery of cash through sales, excess cash may be applied to the payment of loans, to the acquisition of marketable securities, to the increase of the cash balance, or to the payment of dividends. In meeting the requirements of (2) and (3), planning may be directed towards the acquisition of cash through long-term borrowing, through the issuance of additional stock, or through the accumulation of cash from the normal operations of the business unit.

Illustration of cash forecast. A cash forecast prepared in statement form as a part of a budgetary program is illustrated on page 184. The illustration covers only a part of a year. Ordinarily the forecast would be developed for a period of a year.

The statement is usually accompanied by schedules that offer detailed support for the various data summarized thereon. Although the example makes reference to a number of schedules, only the schedules in support of collections on trade accounts receivable and payments on trade accounts payable are illustrated.

Management, in requesting a line of credit or special short-term financing that is to be liquidated through normal operations, may be required to submit forecasts that go beyond cash and embrace the entire working capital position. The budget for operations as a whole may be employed in developing the working capital forecast; in the absence of such a comprehensive budget, special analyses are necessary in developing such a presentation.

Illustration of cash and current position forecast. A combined cash and current position statement covering a four-month period is illustrated on page 186. It is assumed that the forecast is submitted with an application for a bank loan to finance inventories during a seasonal peak period; the loan is to be paid off at the end of the season.

Carver Co.

Cash Forecast

For Three Months Ending December 31, 1972

	October	November	December
Cash sales.................................	10,000	15,000	25,000
Collections on accounts receivable (see schedule)..	50,000	61,000	80,500
Other receipts (interest and dividend income, see schedule).............................	2,500	2,000	3,000
	62,500	78,000	108,500
Merchandise payments (see schedule)...........	68,600	44,100	19,600
Expense payments (see schedule)..............	25,000	27,500	30,000
Other payments (acquisition of furniture and equipment, see schedule)...................	7,500		
	101,100	71,600	49,600
Cash increase (decrease) for month............	(38,600)	6,400	58,900
Cash balance at beginning of month...........	16,500	7,900	14,300
Cash requirements:			
Obtained through loans....................	10,000		
Obtained through sale of marketable securities..	20,000		
	7,900	14,300	73,200
Cash applications:			
To payment of loans......................			(25,000)
To purchase of marketable securities.........			(35,000)
Cash balance carried into succeeding month......	7,900	14,300	13,200

Cash Forecast

Schedule Reporting Collections on Accounts Receivable*

For Three Months Ending December 31, 1972

	Estimated Sales	October	November	December
August.........................	40,000	4,000		
September......................	50,000	40,000	5,000	
October........................	60,000	6,000	48,000	6,000
November......................	80,000		8,000	64,000
December......................	105,000			10,500
Total monthly collections.........		50,000	61,000	80,500

*Terms of sale — no cash discounts, payments due by the tenth of the month following sale. It is assumed that collections on charge sales will be made as follows:

Month of sale...................................... 10%
First month following sale........................... 80%
Second month following sale......................... 10%

Cash Forecast

Schedule Reporting Payments on Accounts Payable*

For Three Months Ending December 31, 1972

	Estimated Purchases	Purchases Discounts	Net Purchases	October	November	December
September..	60,000	1,200	58,800	19,600		
October....	75,000	1,500	73,500	49,000	24,500	
November..	30,000	600	29,400		19,600	9,800
December..	15,000	300	14,700			9,800
Total monthly payments.....................				68,600	44,100	19,600

*A 2% cash discount is allowed by vendors on payments made within 10 days from date of purchase. It is assumed that discounts will be taken on all purchases, payments to be made as follows:

Month of purchase.................................. $66\frac{2}{3}\%$
Month following purchase (first 10 days)............. $33\frac{1}{3}\%$

The forecast indicates that cash will be available to meet the terms of the loan. It also indicates that working capital will increase during the four-month period from $45,000 (current assets, $67,500, less current liabilities, $22,500) to $72,500 (current assets $90,000, less current liabilities, $17,500), an increase of $27,500. The revenue and expense columns on the statement offer support for this change: revenues are expected to generate working capital of $204,000 while cost of sales and expenses will consume working capital of $176,500. To arrive at an estimate of the net income for the period, however, depreciation, as well as other charges and credits arising from asset and liability changes outside of the working capital pool, would have to be recognized.

Temporary Investments

A company with an excess of available cash may deposit such funds as a time deposit or under a certificate of deposit at a bank, or it may purchase securities. Income will thus be produced that would not be available if cash were left idle. Investments made during seasonal periods of low activity can be converted into cash in periods of expanding operations. Asset items arising from temporary conversions of cash are commonly reported in the current asset section of the balance sheet under the heading, Temporary Investments.

Securities that are purchased as temporary investments should be marketable on short notice. There should be a day-to-day market for them, and the volume of trading in the securities should be sufficient to

E. J. Barnes Sales Co.
Forecast of Cash and Current Position[1]
For Four Months Ending December 31, 1972

	Current Assets				Current Liabilities			Income Summary	
	Cash	Receivables and Accruals	Merchandise	Total	Payables and Accruals	Bank Loan	Total	Expenses	Revenues
Balances, September 1........	$12,000	$21,500	$34,000	$67,500	$22,500		$22,500		
September:									
Bank loan..............	40,000					$40,000			
Sales and cost of goods sold..		45,000	(30,000)					$30,000	$45,000
Purchases..............			42,000		42,000				
Expenses...............					6,500			6,500	
Collections............	30,500	(30,500)							
Payments..............	(50,000)				(50,000)				
	$32,500	$36,000	$46,000	$114,500	$21,000	$40,000	$61,000		
October:									
Sales and cost of goods sold..		30,000	(20,000)					20,000	30,000
Purchases..............			50,000		50,000				
Expenses...............					5,000			5,000	
Collections............	42,000	(42,000)							
Payments..............	(51,000)				(51,000)				
	$23,500	$24,000	$76,000	$123,500	$25,000	$40,000	$65,000		
November:									
Sales and cost of goods sold..		54,000	(36,000)					36,000	54,000
Purchases..............			20,000		20,000				
Expenses...............					8,500			8,500	
Collections............	34,800	(34,800)							
Payments..............	(43,500)				(43,500)				
	$14,800	$43,200	$60,000	$118,000	$10,000	$40,000	$50,000		
December:									
Sales and cost of goods sold..		75,000	(50,000)					50,000	75,000
Purchases..............			15,000		15,000				
Expenses...............					10,500			10,500	
Collections............	58,200	(58,200)							
Income tax liability.......					(28,000)				
Payment of bank loan......	(40,000)				10,000	(40,000)		10,000	
Balances, December 31......	$ 5,000	$60,000	$25,000	$90,000	$17,500		$17,500	$176,500	$204,000

[1]Note: In expressing transactions on the forecast, Sales are expressed as an increase in Receivables and an increase in Revenues; Cost of Goods Sold, as a decrease in Merchandise and an increase in Expenses; Purchases as an increase in Merchandise and an increase in Payables and Accruals; Collections as an increase in Cash and a decrease in Receivables and Accruals; and Expenses as an increase in Payables and Accruals and an increase in Expenses.

absorb a company's holdings without materially affecting the market price. Although there may be no definite assurance that the securities will be disposed of without loss, it is essential that any possible loss resulting from such disposal be kept at a minimum. Securities that have a limited market and fluctuate widely in price are not suitable for temporary investments. The prices of United States government securities tend to be relatively stable and the market for these securities is quite broad. Because of these factors, short-term government securities are widely favored despite their relatively low yield.

Composition of temporary investments

Investments qualify for reporting as temporary investments as long as (1) there is a ready market for converting such securities into cash and (2) it is management's intention to sell them if the need for cash arises. Such investments may be converted into cash within a relatively short period after being acquired, or they may be carried for some time. In either case, however, they are properly shown under the current heading. The following types of investments do not qualify as marketable securities and should not be included in the current section: (1) reacquired shares of the company's own stock, (2) securities acquired for control of a company, (3) securities held for maintenance of business relations, and (4) other securities that cannot be used or are not intended to be used as a ready source of cash.

Recording purchase and sale of marketable securities

Stocks and bonds acquired as temporary investments are recorded at cost, which includes brokers' fees, taxes, and other charges incurred in their acquisition. Shares are normally quoted at a price per single share; bonds are quoted at a price per $100 face value although they are normally issued in $1,000 denominations. The purchase of 100 shares at $5\frac{1}{8}$, then, would indicate a purchase price of $512.50; the purchase of a $1,000 bond at $104\frac{1}{4}$ would indicate a purchase price of $1,042.50.

When bonds are acquired between interest payment dates, the bond price is increased by a charge for accrued interest to the date of purchase. Such a charge should not be reported as part of investment cost. Two assets have been acquired — bonds and accrued interest — and the purchase price may be reported in two separate asset accounts. Upon the receipt of bond interest, the accrued interest account is closed and Interest Income is credited for the excess. Instead of recording the interest as an asset, Interest Income may be charged for the accrued interest paid. The subsequent collection of interest would then be credited in full to Interest Income. The latter procedure is usually more convenient.

To illustrate the entries for the acquisition of securities, assume that $100,000 in United States treasury bonds are purchased at 104¼ on April 1. Interest is 5% payable semiannually on January 1 and July 1. Accrued interest of $1,250 would thus be added to the purchase price. The entries to record the purchase of the bonds and the subsequent collection of interest under the alternate procedures would be as follows:

Asset approach:

Apr. 1	U.S. Treasury Bonds.....................	104,250	
	Accrued Interest Receivable............	1,250	
	Cash.................................		105,500
July 1	Cash.................................	2,500	
	Accrued Interest Receivable..........		1,250
	Interest Income.....................		1,250

Income approach:

Apr. 1	U.S. Treasury Bonds..................	104,250	
	Interest Income.....................	1,250	
	Cash.................................		105,500
July 1	Cash.................................	2,500	
	Interest Income.....................		2,500

When bonds are acquired at a price that is more or less than their maturity value and it is expected that they will be held until maturity, periodic amortization of the premium or accumulation of the discount with corresponding adjustments to interest income is appropriate. However, when bonds are acquired as a temporary investment and it is not likely that the bonds will be held until maturity, such procedures are normally not necessary.

When an investment is sold, the difference between the sales price and the value at which it is carried is reported as a gain or loss on the sale.

Valuation of marketable securities

Three different methods for the valuation of marketable securities have been advanced: (1) cost, (2) cost or market, whichever is lower, and (3) market.

Cost. Marketable securities held as temporary investments are most commonly carried at cost. The recognition of either gain or loss is deferred until the asset is sold, and at this time investment cost is matched against investment proceeds. The cost basis is consistent with income tax procedures that recognize neither gain nor loss until there is a sale or exchange.

Cost or market, whichever is lower. When using the lower of cost or market method, if market is lower than cost, security values are written down to the lower value; if market is higher than cost, securities are maintained at cost, profits awaiting confirmation through sale. In applying the lower of cost or market procedure, marketable securities may be reported at cost at one time and at market at another time, securities being valued regularly at the lower of the two alternate values.

The AICPA Committee on Accounting Procedure accepts the use of a lower market only under special conditions. The Committee states:

> In the case of marketable securities where market value is less than cost by a substantial amount and it is evident that the decline in market value is not due to a mere temporary condition, the amount to be included as a current asset should not exceed the market value.[1]

The lower of cost or market for the valuation of marketable securities has not been widely used in practice, probably because of the difficulty in defining "substantial amount" and also in determining whether declines were due to a "mere temporary condition."[2] Because the stock market has generally risen over the past, an aggregate condition of a market lower than cost has been relatively uncommon. Under conditions of sustained market decline, such situations would become more numerous. Serious challenge can be made when marketable securities that have declined substantially are reported at cost. The inclusion of market prices either in parenthetical comments or in a footnote is not a satisfactory answer. Such disclosure is not reflected in total assets and total owners' equity on the balance sheet, in earnings on the income statement, and in book value and earnings per share analyses that are given in the statistical reports of the many financial publications made available to the investor.

The lower of cost or market rule may be employed in two ways: (1) it may be applied to securities in the aggregate, or (2) it may be applied to the individual items. To illustrate, assume marketable securities with costs and market values on December 31, 1971, as follows:

	Cost	Market	Lower of Cost or Market on Individual Basis
1,000 shares of Carter Co. Common.	$20,000	$16,000	$16,000
$25,000 Emerson Co. 7% Bonds....	25,000	26,500	25,000
$10,000 Gardner Co. 6% Bonds.....	10,000	7,500	7,500
	$55,000	$50,000	$48,500

[1]*Accounting Research Bulletin No. 43*, "Restatement and Revision of Accounting Research Bulletins" (New York: American Institute of Certified Public Accountants, 1953), Ch. 3, par. 9.

[2]In the AICPA list of 600 survey companies, the number of companies reporting marketable securities at the lower of cost or market was 14, and the number reporting at cost was 225. *Accounting Trends & Techniques* (25th ed.; New York: American Institute of Certified Public Accountants, 1971), p. 53.

The lower of cost or market value on an aggregate basis is $50,000; on an individual basis, $48,500. It would appear that sufficient conservatism is exercised in reporting securities at $50,000, the amount that would become available upon conversion of all the securities.

Recognition of the decline in value on the books calls for the reduction of the asset and a charge to a loss account; however, the loss is not recognized for income tax purposes and the basis of the securities for measurement of gain or loss continues to be cost. Cost can be preserved on the books by the use of a valuation account to reduce the securities to market. The following entry may be made for this example:

Recognized Decline in Value of Marketable Securities.......................................	5,000	
Allowance for Decline in Value of Marketable Securities.................................		5,000

The balance sheet would show:

Marketable securities, at cost...................	$55,000	
Less allowance for decline in value of marketable securities.................................	5,000	
Securities at market value, December 31, 1971....		$50,000

This information could also be reported:

Marketable securities at market (cost $55,000)....	$50,000

The $5,000 loss may be reported on the income statement as a charge related to financial management.

When securities have been reduced to the lower of cost or market, adjustments are normally considered to be necessary in future periods only in the event of further declines. Having established a lower basis, this is considered as replacing cost for further comparisons with market. A market in excess of such substitute for cost is thus ignored until sale of the asset takes place.

Assume in the preceding example that the securities are sold in 1972 for $53,500. An entry is made as follows:

Cash..	53,500	
Allowance for Decline in Value of Marketable Securities.................................	5,000	
Marketable Securities — Carter Co. Common...		20,000
Marketable Securities — Emerson Co. 7% Bonds		25,000
Marketable Securities — Gardner Co. 6% Bonds		10,000
Gain on Sale of Marketable Securities.........		3,500

Neither the $5,000 loss nor the $3,500 gain is recognized for income tax purposes; instead, a $1,500 loss is reported on the tax return for 1972 when securities that cost $55,000 are sold for $53,500.

It was assumed in the entry that all of the securities were sold requiring full cancellation of the allowance. Assume, however, that only some of the holdings are sold. If the lower of cost or market had been applied on an individual basis, the allowance would be composed of amounts related to specific securities, and sale of a security would be accompanied by a charge to the allowance for the amount related to the security sold. When the lower of cost or market is applied on an aggregate basis and there can be no identification of the allowance with specific securities, losses are normally charged against the allowance until this balance is canceled. Further losses would be reported in nominal accounts. At the end of the period, if the aggregate market for securities on hand is less than their cost, an allowance for the decline would be established once more.

To illustrate, assume securities valued at the lower of cost or market at the end of 1971 as shown on page 189, but sale in 1972 of only the Carter Co. stock for $17,000. The following entry would be made:

Cash.	17,000	
Allowance for Decline in Value of Marketable Securities	3,000	
Marketable Securities — Carter Co. Common.		20,000

This entry leaves the valuation account with a balance of $2,000.

Assuming that the market value of the remaining securities remains unchanged at $34,000 at the end of 1972, they would still be reported at cost $35,000, less the allowance for decline carried over from the preceding period, $2,000, or $33,000.

On the other hand, assume sale of the Carter Co. stock for $14,000. The sale would be recorded as follows:

Cash.	14,000	
Allowance for Decline in Value of Marketable Securities.	5,000	
Loss on Sale of Marketable Securities.	1,000	
Marketable Securities — Carter Co. Common.		20,000

The total loss on the sale of Carter Co. stock was $6,000 ($20,000 − $14,000). Of this amount, $5,000 was recognized in 1971 when the security was reported at its lower market value and $1,000 is recognized in 1972 when the stock is sold.

Assuming again that the remaining securities have a market value of $34,000 at the end of 1972, the following entry would be required in reporting these at the lower market:

Recognized Decline in Value of Marketable Securities.	1,000	
Allowance for Decline in Value of Marketable Securities.		1,000

Market. In using market, current market prices are recognized as affording an objective basis for the valuation of marketable securities. Securities on the balance sheet are reported at their current values whether higher or lower than cost. Owners' equity on the balance sheet thus reflects not only the gains and losses on securities sold but also the changes in values of securities held. In applying market, it would be possible to recognize changes in security values by adjusting asset account balances and recognizing gain and loss from such asset restatement. However, to preserve investment cost data for income tax purposes, asset increases may be reported in special asset accounts; decreases may be reported in special valuation accounts. Furthermore, if it is felt that any increase in retained earnings should await sale of securities, appraisal capital may be credited.

To illustrate the procedure that may be followed, assume that at the end of 1972 securities costing $50,000 have quoted values of $60,000. The securities are sold in 1973 for $62,000. An unrealized gain is reported at the end of 1972. This is canceled when the securities are sold in 1973 and the effect of the sale is reported in the income statement. The entries are:

December 31, 1972

Marketable Securities — Increase to Current Market Value..................................	10,000	
Appraisal Capital — Increase in Marketable Securities to Current Market Value.........		10,000

March 5, 1973

Cash..	62,000	
Appraisal Capital — Increase in Marketable Securities to Current Market Value................	10,000	
Marketable Securities (at cost)..............		50,000
Marketable Securities — Increase to Current Market Value...........................		10,000
Gain on Sale of Marketable Securities.........		12,000

Although changes in market values must be disregarded for general income tax purposes, regulations do permit recognized dealers in securities to value periodic security "inventories" at cost, cost or market, whichever is lower, or market. The valuation procedure that is adopted must be applied consistently in successive tax reportings.

Evaluation of methods. Valuation at cost finds support on the grounds that it is an extension of the cost principle; the asset is carried at cost until a sale or exchange provides an alternative asset and confirms a gain or loss. The cost method offers valuation on a consistent base from period to period. It is the simplest method to apply and adheres to income tax requirements. However, certain objections to cost can be raised. The use of cost means that investments are carried at amounts that are more or less than values that can be objectively established at the date of the balance sheet, and the integrity of both balance sheet and income statement measurements can be challenged.

The AICPA has recognized the need for market information and, while adhering to its support of cost under normal circumstances, recommends that market value be included as supplementary information for the reader. A growing practice among reporting companies is to exclude specific market valuations and to insert the phrase "at cost which approximates market."[1] What degree and direction of latitude is covered in "approximates" is unclear and thus still leaves considerable doubt in the reader's mind as to what market really is and may lead him to conclusions that are significantly in error. The use of cost also means that identical securities are reported at different values because of purchases at different prices. A further objection is that management in controlling the sale of securities can determine the periods in which gains or losses are to be recognized even though such changes may have accrued over a number of periods.

The lower of cost or market procedure provides for the recognition of market declines and serves to prevent the mistakes that might arise in analyzing statements when these are not reported. The lower of cost or market is supported as a conservative procedure. But this approach is challenged on a number of grounds. It can be maintained that the recognition of price increases is no less important than the recognition of price decreases in stating financial condition and the result of operations. Valuation at the lower of cost or market may be the most complicated method to apply in the accounts. It fails to provide consistency in valuation — cost at the end of one period may be replaced by a lower of cost or market at the end of the next. As indicated earlier, in certain instances the lower of cost or market procedure may be overly conservative, providing valuations that are less than the aggregate lower market. Also, among its limitations, the lower of cost or market does not conform with income tax requirements and requires the maintenance of supplementary tax records. Furthermore, with timing differences in the recognition of losses on the books and losses on the income tax returns, there may be a need for interperiod tax adjustments.

When the market value for marketable securities is less than cost, little objection is made to recognizing the decline on the financial statements; consistency would call for recognizing market value when this is

---

[1]This phrase is used by 55% of the companies with marketable securities included in the 1971 edition of *Accounting Trends & Techniques, ibid.*

more than cost. With valuation at market, those referring to the financial statements can satisfactorily appraise the relationship of monetary assets and current assets to current liabilities; they can properly evaluate managerial decisions and activities relative to purchases, sales, and holdings of marketable securities. However, valuation at market is not as simple to apply as the cost method. It is also challenged as a departure from the cost principle and as lacking in conservatism. Furthermore, market is not acceptable for general income tax purposes and requires the maintenance of supplementary records for tax reporting. This method may also involve the need for interperiod tax adjustments in view of the timing differences of gains and losses on the books and on the income tax returns.

It would appear that in providing the fairest and most useful financial presentations, a company's monetary assets — cash and near-cash items — should be reported at their net realizable values. Accordingly, with evidence indicating a value for marketable securities that differs from cost, the recognition of such value in reporting the asset would appear to be justified. However, until such practice receives general acceptance, disclosure of market values as supplemental information should be rigidly enforced. The vague term "approximates market" is not sufficient. The Securities and Exchange Commission requires that the following rules be applied in reporting securities as a current asset in statements that are filed with the Commission:

> Include only securities having a ready market. . . . State the basis of determining the amount at which carried. The aggregate cost, and aggregate amount on the basis of current market quotations, shall be stated parenthetically or otherwise.[1]

Presentation of Cash and Temporary Investments on the Balance Sheet

For statement purposes, cash may be reported as a single item or it may be summarized under several descriptive headings, such as cash on hand, commercial deposits, and savings deposits. Since current assets are normally reported in the order of their liquidity, cash is listed first, followed by temporary investments, receivables, and inventories. When temporary investments are pledged for some particular purpose,

---

[1]Regulation S-X. This regulation is issued by the Securities and Exchange Commission and states the basic rules as to form and content that are to be observed in the preparation of reports that are required to be filed with the Commission under federal laws. The Commission has released a number of other instruction books and regulations that give the different rules and procedures adopted by the Commission.

the nature and the purpose of such a pledge should be disclosed parenthetically or by note.

Cash and temporary investments may be reported on the balance sheet in the following manner:

Current assets:

Cash on hand and demand deposits in banks............................			$ 46,000
Special cash deposits (to pay interest and dividends).........................			24,000
Temporary investments:			
Time deposits in banks...............		$100,000	
Marketable securities:			
U.S. Government obligations at cost (quoted market price, $148,500; $50,000 in bonds has been pledged as security on short-term bank loan).	$150,000		
Other stocks and bonds at cost (quoted market price, $44,200)............	35,000	185,000	
Total temporary investments............			285,000

Cash overdrafts

A credit balance in the cash account resulting from the issuance of checks in excess of the amount on deposit is known as a *cash overdraft* and should be reported as a current liability. An overdraft may not necessarily embarrass a company if a number of checks are outstanding and deposits are made to cover the checks before they are actually cleared. When a company has two balances with a single bank, there can be no objection to the offset of the overdraft against an account with a positive balance; failure by the depositor to meet the overdraft will actually result in bank action to effect such offset. However, when a company has accounts with two different banks and there is a positive balance in one account and an overdraft in the other, both an asset balance and a liability balance should be recognized in view of the claim against one bank and an obligation to the other; if recognition of an overdraft is to be avoided, cash should actually be transferred to cover the deficiency.

Offset of securities against tax liabilities

As a general rule the offset of assets against liabilities has been regarded as improper in the absence of a legal right of offset. The AICPA in the past has recognized an exception to this rule for specially issued government securities that could be used to pay federal income tax liabilities not due until the year following their accrual. However, in

recent years treasury regulations have provided for a gradual accelera-
tion of income tax payments and today tax payments are required quarterly based upon a company's estimated earnings and the amount of
taxes accruing on such earnings. Under the circumstances, the need for
the issuance of special securities that can be applied to the payment of
income taxes has disappeared. In 1966 the APB restated the rule of
offset to reflect these changes:

1. It is a general principle of accounting that the offsetting of assets and
   liabilities in the balance sheet is improper except where a right of
   setoff exists. Accordingly, the offset of cash or other assets against the
   tax liability or other amounts owing to governmental bodies is not
   acceptable except in the circumstances described in paragraph 3
   below.

2. Most securities now issued by governments are not by their terms designed specifically for the payment of taxes and, accordingly, should
   not be deducted from taxes payable on the balance sheet.

3. The only exception to this general principle occurs when it is clear
   that a purchase of securities (acceptable for the payment of taxes) is
   in substance an advance payment of taxes that will be payable in the
   relatively near future, so that in the special circumstances the purchase is tantamount to the prepayment of taxes. This occurs at times,
   for example, as an accommodation to a local government and in some
   instances when governments issue securities that are specifically designated as being acceptable for the payment of taxes of those governments.[1]

If the conditions described in Paragraph 3 do exist, the current tax
liability will be reduced by the investments made in the securities.
Assume that the tax liability at year end is $25,000 and special securities
are purchased at a cost of $19,000 which will be used to liquidate the
liability. The liability section of the balance sheet would reflect these
facts as follows:

Income taxes payable...........................	$25,000	
Less government securities purchased for the payment of taxes..........................	19,000	$6,000

[1]*Opinions of the Accounting Principles Board*, *No. 10*, "Omnibus Opinion — 1966" (New
York: American Institute of Certified Public Accountants, 1967), par. 7.

QUESTIONS

1. State how each of the following items should be reported on the balance sheet: (a) demand deposits with bank, (b) blocked cash deposits in foreign banks, (c) payroll fund to pay off accrued salaries, (d) change funds on hand, (e) cash on deposit in escrow on purchase of property, (f) cash in a special cash account to be used currently for the construction of a new building.

2. (a) Explain check kiting and lapping. (b) Mention at least six other practices that result in misappropriations of cash in the absence of an adequate system of internal control.

3. (a) What are the major advantages in the use of imprest petty cash funds? (b) What dangers must be guarded against when petty cash funds are used?

4. (a) What two methods may be employed in reconciling the bank and the cash balances? (b) Which would you recommend? Why? (c) Name at least two other circumstances that call for the preparation of reconciliations.

5. The following items were included as Cash on the balance sheet for the Mitchell Co. How should each of the items have been reported?
(a) Customers' checks returned by the bank marked "Not Sufficient Funds."
(b) Customers' postdated checks.
(c) Cashier's note with no due date.
(d) Postage stamps received in the mail for merchandise.
(e) Postal money orders from customers awaiting deposit.
(f) Receipts for expense advances to buyers.
(g) Change funds.
(h) Notes receivable that are in the hands of the bank for collection.
(i) Special bank account in which sales tax collections are deposited.

6. The Kern Co. engaged in the following practices at the end of a fiscal year:
(a) Sales on account from January 1–January 5 were predated as of the month of December.
(b) Checks in payment of accounts were prepared on December 31 and were entered on the books, but they were placed in the safe awaiting instructions for mailing.
(c) Customers' checks returned by the bank and marked "Not Sufficient Funds" were ignored for statement purposes.

Explain what is wrong with each of the practices mentioned and give the entries that are required to correct the accounts.

7. (a) What purposes are served by preparing a reconciliation of receipts and disbursements? (b) Why would this form be used by auditors?

8. (a) What is the nature of a budget? (b) What is a cash forecast? (c) Describe the preparation of the cash forecast and indicate problems that are encountered in maintaining a satisfactory cash status.

9. Some people have suggested that cash forecasts should be made available to the general public by including them as part of the generally available financial statements. What is your view on this matter?

10. On reconciling the cash account with the bank statement, it is found that the general cash fund is overdrawn $436 but that the bond redemption account has a balance of $5,400. The treasurer wishes to show cash as a current asset at $4,964. Discuss.

11. The Z Co. shows in its accounts a cash balance of $66,500 with Bank A, and an overdraft of $1,500 with Bank B on December 31. Bank B regards the overdraft as in effect a loan to the Z Co. and charges interest on the overdraft balance. How would you report the balances with Banks A and B? Would your answer be any different if the overdraft arose as a result of certain checks that were deposited and proved to be uncollectible and the overdraft was cleared promptly by the Z Co. at the beginning of January?

12. The Oak Hills Country Club maintained a $1,500 change fund. It was used to cash members' checks and to pay miscellaneous bills under $50. The fund was used by any of four girls in the office (including the bookkeeper), depending upon which one was free when a need arose. At the close of each day, all cash collected from the cash registers in the club was merged with the fund and with collections on account received from members. All checks and sufficient cash to equal daily receipts were deposited, and the remainder was returned to the fund. (a) What system weaknesses do you observe? (b) How would you correct them?

13. Define temporary investments. Distinguish between temporary investments and marketable securities.

14. (a) What positions are held with respect to the valuation of marketable securities? (b) What arguments can be advanced in support of each and which position do you feel has greatest merit?

15. One of the arguments advanced for using market as the valuation procedure for temporary investments is that it assists in a "proper evaluation of managerial decisions and activities relative to purchases, sales, and holdings of marketable securities." Give an example that would support this statement.

16. What two methods may be used to record the payment for accrued interest on bond investments? Which method do you feel is preferable?

17. The Brooks Co. reports marketable securities on the balance sheet at the lower of cost or market. What adjustments are required on the books at the end of the year in each case below:
   (a) Securities are purchased in 1970 and at the end of 1970 their market value is more than cost.
   (b) At the end of 1971 the market value of the securities is less than cost.

(c) At the end of 1972 the market value of the securities is greater than at the end of 1971 but is still less than cost.

(d) At the end of 1973 the market value of the securities is more than the amount originally paid.

18. Under certain conditions it is proper to offset either assets against liabilities or liabilities against assets. Comment upon the following practices of the Wells Company.

(a) An overdraft of $300 in the payroll fund kept with Farmers and Mechanics Bank is offset against the savings account balance kept with the same bank.

(b) Treasury bills of $50,000 are offset against Income Taxes Payable. The taxes are due sixty days from the statement date and there is nothing special about the treasury bills.

(c) A mortgage of $130,000 is offset against the buildings account of $180,000 to reflect a net equity in the buildings of $50,000.

(d) Advances to employees of $500 are offset against Accrued Salaries of $1,100.

EXERCISES

1. In auditing the books of Hendrickson, Inc., for 1972, you find that a petty cash fund of $250 is maintained on the imprest basis, but the company has failed to replenish the fund on December 31. Replenishment was made and recorded on January 15, 1973, when a check for $185 was drawn to petty cash for expenses paid. Your analysis discloses that $125 had been spent out of petty cash in 1972. What entry would be made in correcting the records, assuming that the books for 1972 have been closed?

2. An examination on the morning of January 2 by the auditor for the Designed Fencing Company discloses the following items in the petty cash drawer:

Currency and coin....................................		$ 15.16
IOU's from members of the office staff...................		45.00
An envelope containing collections for a football pool, with office staff names attached...........................		10.00
Petty cash vouchers for:		
Typewriter repairs...........................	$4.00	
Stamps.....................................	5.00	
Telegram charges............................	6.50	15.50
Employee's check postdated January 15..................		50.00
Employee's check marked "N.S.F.".....................		70.00
Check drawn by Designed Fencing Company to Petty Cash...		99.00
		$304.66

The ledger account discloses a $300 balance for Petty Cash. (a) What adjustments should be made on the auditor's working papers in order that petty cash may be correctly stated on the balance sheet? (b) What is the correct amount of petty cash for the balance sheet? (c) How could the practice of borrowing by employees from the fund be discouraged?

3. The following data are assembled in the course of reconciling the bank balance as of December 31, 1972, for Justin Lumber Co. What cash balance will be found on the company books, assuming no errors on the part of the bank and the depositor?

Balance per bank statement..........................	$1,512.60
Checks outstanding.................................	1,805.00
December 31 receipts recorded but not deposited........	320.00
Bank charges for December not recognized on books......	7.50
Draft collected by bank but not recognized on books.....	615.00

4. The Midwest Steel Co. receives its bank statement for the month ending June 30 on July 2. The bank statement indicates a balance of $231. The cash account as of the close of business on June 30 has a credit balance of $123. In reconciling the balances, the auditor discovers the following:

Receipts on June 30, $1,860, were not deposited until July 1.
Checks outstanding on June 30 were $2,215.
The bank has charged the depositor for overdrafts, $10.
A canceled check to S. S. Dohr for $56 was entered in cash payments in error as $65.

Prepare a bank reconciliation statement. (Use the form that reconciles bank and depositor figures to corrected cash balance.)

5. The following information was included in the bank reconciliation for Panama Corporation for June. What was the total of the outstanding checks at the beginning of June? Assume all other reconciling items are listed below:

Checks and charges returned by bank in June, including a June service charge of $15............................	$34,692
Service charge made by bank in May and recorded on books in June	10
Total of credits to Cash in all journals during June.........	38,477
Customer's N.S.F. check returned as a bank charge in June (no entry made on books)............................	200
Customer's N.S.F. check returned in May and redeposited in June (no entry made on books in either May or June)....	500
Outstanding checks at June 30........................	16,490
Deposit in transit at June 30.........................	1,200

6. Sales on account for the Meadows Company for March amount to $10,000 and they are estimated to increase by $4,000 in each succeeding month. Terms of the sales are 2/10, E.O.M. It is estimated that no collections will be made in the month of the sale, 80% will be collected within the discount period, 10% after the discount period in the month following the sale, and 7% in the second month following the sale. What are the estimated cash collections from customers for the month of July?

7. The Oliver Corporation completed the transactions in marketable securities listed below during 1972. What are the entries to record the transactions?

    (a) Purchased $10,000 Norton Co. 7% bonds paying 96½ plus accrued interest of $40.
    (b) Purchased 300 shares of Belnap Co. common stock at 21.
    (c) Received semiannual interest on Norton Co. bonds.
    (d) Sold 100 share lot of Belnap Co. common at 22½.
    (e) Sold $5,000 Norton Co. bonds at 95 plus accrued interest of $15.

8. Marketable securities are acquired by the Micro Co. during 1972 at a cost of $15,000. Marketable securities are to be reported on the balance sheet at the lower of cost or market. (a) What entry would be made at the end of the year assuming that the securities have a market value of $12,500? (b) What entry would be made at the end of the next year assuming: (1) that the market value of the securities has declined to $12,000? (2) The market value has recovered to $14,000? (3) The market value is $16,000?

9. Griswold Corp. acquires marketable securities in 1971 at a cost of $80,000. Market values of the securities at the end of each year are as follows: 1971, $70,000; 1972, $60,000; 1973, $63,000. Give the entries that would be made at the end of 1971, 1972, and 1973 and indicate how the securities would be reported on the balance sheet at the end of each year under each of the following assumptions:

    (a) Securities are reported at cost.
    (b) Securities are reported at the lower of cost or market.
    (c) Securities are reported at market.

10. At the end of 1972, The Talbot Company reports account balances relating to cash and temporary investments as follows:

Petty Cash.	$ 350
Cash in First National Bank — General.	32,349
Cash in First National Bank — Payroll.	(1,200)
Cash in Farmers Security Bank.	25,362
Cash on Deposit with Metropolitan Utilities.	300
Cash in University State Bank.	(2,100)
Marketable Securities.	135,600

An examination of the accounts discloses that marketable securities of $15,000 were special tax anticipation securities issued by the municipality that the Talbot Company can apply against the tax liability of $21,000. Show the account balances as they would appear within the current asset and current liability sections of the balance sheet.

PROBLEMS

6-1. The cash account of Dearborn Co. disclosed a balance of $4,557.55 on October 31, 1972. The bank statement as of October 31 showed a balance of $4,292.16. Upon comparing the statement with the cash records, the following facts were developed:

(a) The Dearborn Co.'s account had been charged for a customer's uncollectible check amounting to $623.20 on October 26.

(b) A two-month, 8%, $1,000 customer's note dated August 25, discounted on October 12, had been protested October 26, and the bank had charged the Dearborn Co. for $1,216.33, which included a protest fee of $3.00.

(c) A customer's check for $290 had been entered as $190 both by the depositor and the bank but was later corrected by the bank.

(d) Check No. 661 for $497 had been entered in the cashbook as $479, and check No. 652 for $32.90 had been entered as $329. The company uses the voucher system.

(e) There were bank service charges for September of $15.77.

(f) A bank memo stated that M. South's note for $500 and interest of $25 had been collected on October 29, and the bank had made a charge of $5.00 on the collection. (No entry had been made on the books when the note was sent to the bank for collection.)

(g) Receipts of October 29 for $1,325.10 were deposited November 1.

The following checks were outstanding on October 31:

No. 620........	$ 72.95	No. 673........	$ 75.16
632........	362.10	675........	110.29
670........	710.15	676........	393.26
671........	293.00		

Instructions: (1) Construct a bank reconciliation statement, using the form where both bank and book balances are brought to a corrected cash balance. (Use the form illustrated on page 177.)

(2) Give the journal entries required as a result of the information given above. (Assume that the company makes use of the voucher system.)

6-2. Analysis of the December bank statement for Suburban Enterprises, Inc., discloses the following information:

(a) Statement balance at December 31, 1972, was $27,220.

(b) Check issued by Suburban Machinery, Inc., for $415 was charged to Suburban Enterprises, Inc., in error.

(c) December bank charges were $30.

(d) Deposit of $600 was erroneously credited to Suburban Enterprises, Inc., account by the bank.

(e) Outstanding checks at December 31, 1972, were $7,290. They included a $300 check outstanding for 8 months to Amco Products which was canceled in December and a new check issued. No entry was made for the cancellation.

(f) Receipts on December 31 were $3,300. Receipts were deposited on January 2.

(g) An error in addition was made on the December 23 deposit slip. This slip showed a total of $2,120. The correct balance as credited to our account by the bank was $2,020. A count of cash on hand showed an overage of $100 as of December 31.

(h) The Cash in Bank balance in the general ledger as of December 31, 1972, was $23,175.

Instructions: (1) Prepare a bank reconciliation statement which reconciles the bank balance with the balance per books. (Use the form illustrated on page 178.)

(2) Give all of the entries required on the books at December 31, 1972.

6-3. The following data were assembled in preparing a bank reconciliation for the Swanson Company on June 30, 1972:

Bank statement, May 31 — balance $5,390 after bank service and collection charges of $40 not previously reported to the depositor and recorded on the books in June.

Cash balance, May 31 — balance $4,890 after outstanding checks of $1,260 not shown on bank statement and receipts for May 31, $720 not deposited as of end of the month.

Bank statement, June 30 — balance $7,270, which recognizes deposits of $9,800, checks cleared through the account, $7,860, and bank service and collection charges of $60 not previously reported to the depositor.

Cash balance, June 30 — balance $6,395, which recognizes receipts of $9,655 for June and checks written of $8,110 in June. However, receipts for June 30 of $575 have not been deposited as of this date; checks of $300 that were written prior to June and checks of $1,210 that were written in June have not yet been cleared by the bank.

Instructions: (1) Prepare a reconciliation of receipts, disbursements, and the bank balance for June. (Use the form illustrated on page 180.)

(2) Give any entries that may be required on the books of the company.

6-4. The following information is related to King-Richards, Inc.:

	1972	
	August	September
Bank statement balance — at month end....	$ 4,000	$ 4,860
Cash account balance — at month end......		3,833
Bank charges for N.S.F. check returned (normally written off in month following return)................................	80	160
Outstanding checks — at month end........	1,200	1,930
Deposits in transit — at month end.........	500	850
Bank service charges (normally recorded in month following bank charge)............	8	11
Check #411 was erroneously recorded in the company checkbook and journal as $286; the correct amount is $268. (This check was not outstanding on September 30.).......		268
Drafts collected by bank (not recorded by company until month following collection).....	400	300
Total credits to cash account..............	29,705	34,605
Total deposits on bank statement..........		35,000

The oustanding checks on September 30 include a company check for $200 that was certified by the bank on September 18.

All disbursements were made by check.

Instructions: Prepare a reconciliation of receipts, disbursements, and the bank balance for the month of September, 1972. Use the form illustrated on page 179.

6-5. A bank statement for Apex, Inc., shows a balance as of December 31, 1972, of $2,392.62. The cash account for the company as of this date shows an overdraft of $347.37. In reconciling the statement with the books, the following items are discovered:

(a) The cash balance includes $150 representing change cash on hand. When the cash on hand is counted, only $129.25 is found.

(b) The cash balance includes $200 representing a petty cash fund. Inspection of the petty cash fund reveals cash of $160 on hand and a replenishing check drawn on December 31 for $40.

(c) Proceeds from cash sales of $295 for December 27 were stolen. The company expects to recover this amount from the insurance company and has made no entry for the loss.

(d) The bank statement shows the depositor charged with a customer's N.S.F. check for $47.36, bank service charges of $15.65, and a check for $49 drawn by Apex Gear, Inc., and incorrectly cleared through this account.

(e) The bank statement does not show receipts of December 31 of $832.50, which were deposited on January 3.

(f) Checks outstanding were found to be $4,329.50. This includes the check transferred to the petty cash fund and also two checks for $57 each payable to M. K. Miller. Miller had notified the company that he had lost the original check and had been sent a second one, the company stopping payment on the first check.

Instructions: (1) Prepare a bank reconciliation statement, using the form in which both bank and book balances are brought to a corrected cash balance. (Use the form illustrated on page 177.)

(2) Give the correcting entries required by the foregoing.

(3) List the cash items as they should appear on the balance sheet on December 31.

6-6. The balance of $49,000 in the cash account of the Abner Company consists of these items:

Petty cash fund..	$ 200
Receivable from an employee...........................	100
Cash in bond sinking fund.............................	4,500
Cash in a foreign bank unavailable for withdrawal........	10,000
Cash in First State Bank..............................	30,000
Currency on hand.....................................	4,200

The balance in the marketable securities account consists of:

U.S. Treasury bonds..................................	$ 10,420
Voting stock of a subsidiary company (70% interest)......	122,000
Advances to a subsidiary company (no maturity date specified)..	30,000

A note receivable from a customer...................... 10,000
The company's own shares held as treasury stock........ 5,000
Stock of Western Telephone Co......................... 14,000

Instructions: Calculate the correct "Cash" and "Marketable Securities" balances and state in what accounts and in what sections of the balance sheet the other items would be properly reported.

6-7. Insulation Sales Co. made the following investments in marketable securities in 1971:

Sheffield Hardware...............	400 shares @ 45 3/4	$18,300
Berryman Instruments...........	500 shares @ 22 5/8	11,312
Superior First-Mortgage 6% Bonds..	30 $1,000 bonds at par	30,000
		$59,612

Berryman Instruments was sold at the end of 1973 for $8,500. The market values of the securities at the end of 1971, 1972, and 1973 were as follows:

	1971	1972	1973
Sheffield Hardware..................	$19,500	$15,900	$17,250
Berryman Instruments...............	10,200	8,600	
Superior First-Mortgage 6% Bonds.....	31,000	31,500	30,100

Instructions: Give whatever entries are required in 1971, 1972, and 1973 for the valuation and for the sale of securities, and show how the securities would be reported on the balance sheet prepared at the end of 1971, 1972, and 1973 under each of the following assumptions:

(1) Securities are valued at cost.
(2) Securities are valued at the lower of cost or market. (aggregate basis)
(3) Securities are valued at market.

6-8. Berman, Inc., carries marketable securities on the books at the lower of cost or market on the aggregate basis. On December 31, 1971, the balance sheet showed:

Marketable securities, at cost....................	$42,900	
Less allowance for decline in value of marketable securities................................	2,360	$40,540

The following analysis was made in establishing the allowance.

	No. of Shares or Face Value	Cost	Market
Utah Gas Co. Common.........	400 shares	$20,500	$18,000
Bennett Mfg. Common..........	150 shares	5,100	4,500
Conway, Inc., 6's	$19,000	17,300	18,040
		$42,900	$40,540

On June 30, 1972, the shares of Bennett Mfg. were sold for $4,000. On December 31, 1972, Utah Gas Co. shares were quoted at $42 per share; Conway, Inc., 6's were quoted at $960 per thousand-dollar bond.

Instructions: Give the entries that are required to record the sale of securities in 1972 and to adjust the valuation account at the end of 1972.

6-9. The Leslie Novelty Co. asks the controller to prepare a cash forecast for the first three months of 1973. The following information is assembled in developing the forecast:

Sales:		Purchases:	
January.....	$50,000	January......	$42,000
February....	60,000	February....	45,000
March......	75,000	March.......	36,000

All sales are made on a credit basis as follows: 2% cash discount if paid by the tenth of the month following the sale; credit period 30 days from end of month in which sale is made. Past experience has shown that 70% of the billings are collected within the first ten days of the month following the sale and credited with the discount, 20% of the billings are collected during the remainder of the month following sale, and 10% are collected in the second month following sale.

All purchases are made on terms of 2/10, n/30, and the company follows the practice of taking all discounts on the tenth day following the invoice date. It is assumed that purchases will be distributed evenly throughout the month, purchases for the last third of the month being paid in the first third of the succeeding month.

Selling and general and administrative expenses, excluding depreciation, will be paid as incurred and are anticipated as follows: fixed expenses, $7,000 per month; variable expenses, 15% of gross sales.

The following balances taken from a trial balance on December 31 are to be considered in developing the cash summary:

Cash......................................		$ 2,620
Accounts receivable:		
November...............................	$ 7,600	
December...............................	100,000	107,600
Accounts payable:		
December..............................		17,000
Bank loan due January 15, 1973.............		12,500
Estimated federal income tax for 1973 (The company expects to make a quarterly payment of $19,500 on 3/15/73).....................		39,000

Instructions: Prepare a forecast of the cash position by months supported by receipts and payments schedules in forms similar to those illustrated on pages 184 and 185.

6-10. The balance sheet of Jones and McCabe, Inc., shows the following balances for cash and temporary investments within its current asset section as of December 31, 1972:

Current assets:	
Cash...	$ 76,429
Temporary investments...........................	173,291
Total current assets.............................	$249,720

In examining the books, the following information is revealed with respect to the current assets:

Cash consists of a demand deposit of $16,337 at the First Security Bank; a time deposit of $5,500 that cannot be withdrawn until after April 1, 1974; customers' checks not yet deposited, $500, and customers' returned N.S.F. checks, $200; a demand deposit of $9,184, which is unavailable, being in a bank in a foreign country at war; an overdraft of $192 in the Merchants Bank; a time deposit of $4,500 in a building and loan savings association that is closed; advances of $1,675 to officers; sinking fund cash of $16,525; a pension fund of $22,000 for employees; and a petty cash fund of $200, of which $65 is cash, $45 is in the form of employees' IOU's, and $90 is supported by the receipts for expenses paid out of the fund.

The following securities are included under the temporary investments heading:

	Cost	Market Value (Including Accrued Interest)
Jones and McCabe, Inc., Treasury Stock...	$ 6,920	$ 7,358
Eastern Corporation Common Stock (temporary holding)....	3,490	3,250
Prairie Company, 6% bonds (interest payable March 1 and Sept. 1). Face value, $8,000. Acquired on Sept. 1, 1972 (temporary holding).....	8,190	8,300
5% United States Treasury Bonds (interest payable on March 1 and September 1). Face value, $30,000. Purchased with pension sinking fund cash. Acquired September 1, 1972......	30,600	30,750
Dick Co. Common Stock (temporary holding).....	7,235	5,500
Tonka Co. Common Stock (stock of subsidiary company).....	112,000	106,300
ACC Corp. Preferred Stock (temporary holding).....	4,900	6,300

Instructions: Show cash and temporary investments as these items should properly appear in the current assets section of the balance sheet. Provide schedules to indicate how foregoing balances are determined and what disposition is to be made of items not appropriately shown under the cash and temporary investment headings. Assume that marketable securities are reported at cost or market, whichever is lower, by means of a valuation account.

6-11. You have completed your examination of the cash on hand and in banks in your audit of the Hoosier Company's financial statements for the year ended December 31, 1972, and noted the following:

(a) The company maintains a general bank account at The National Bank and an imprest payroll bank account at The City Bank. All checks are signed by the company president, Douglas Hoosier.

(b) Data and reconciliations prepared by Donald Hume, the company bookkeeper, at November 30, 1972, indicated that the payroll account had a $1,000 general ledger and bank balance with no in-transit or outstanding items, and the general bank account had a $12,405 general ledger balance with checks outstanding aggregating $918 (#1202 for $575 and #1205 for $343) and one deposit of $492 in transit.

(c) Your surprise cash count on Tuesday, January 2, 1973, revealed customers' checks totaling $540 and a National Bank deposit slip for that amount dated December 30, 1972, were in the company safe and that no cash was in transit to the bank at that time. Your examination of the general account check book had revealed check #1219 to be the first unused check.

(d) Company general ledger accounts are prepared on a posting machine and all transactions are posted in chronological sequence. The ledger card for the general bank account is reproduced below.

(e) The December statements from both banks were delivered unopened to you. The City Bank statement contained deposits for $1,675; $1,706;

LEDGER

General Bank Account

The National Bank

DATE	FOLIO	DEBITS	CREDITS	BALANCE
11/30/72			BALANCE FORWARD	12,405
12/01/72		496		12,901
12/05/72	1206		1,675	11,226
12/06/72	1207		645	10,581
12/06/72		832		11,413
12/08/72	1208		1,706	9,707
12/08/72		975		10,682
12/08/72	1209		2,062	8,620
12/08/72	1210		3,945	4,675
12/11/72	1211		6,237	(1,562)
12/12/72		8,045		6,483
12/15/72		9,549		16,032
12/15/72	1212		1,845	14,187
12/21/72	RT		241	13,946
12/21/72	1213		350	13,596
12/21/72	1214		2,072	11,524
12/22/72		1,513		13,037
12/23/72	1215		2,597	10,440
12/27/72	1216		1,739	8,701
12/29/72		540		9,241
12/29/72		942		10,183
12/29/72	1217		1,987	8,196
01/03/73	1218		1,120	7,076
		22,892	28,221	

$1,845; and $2,597 and 72 paid checks totaling $7,823. The National Bank statement is reproduced below.

THE NATIONAL BANK

ACCOUNT NUMBER
133-0602

Hoosier Company   (General Account)
123 Main Street
City

DATE
12/31/72

BALANCE FROM LAST STATEMENT	NUMBER OF CHECKS	TOTAL AMOUNT OF CHECKS THIS MONTH	NUMBER OF CREDITS	TOTAL AMOUNT OF CREDITS THIS MONTH	SERVICE CHARGE	BALANCE ON ABOVE DATE
12,831	15	22,480	9	23,858		14,209

DATE MO. DAY	CHECKS AND OTHER DEBITS		DEPOSITS — CREDITS	BALANCE
12 01			492	13,323
12 06	1,675	267RT	496	11,877
12 06	575		832	12,134
12 08			975	13,109
12 11	1,706	654		10,749
12 12			8,045	18,794
12 14	2,062			16,732
12 15			9,949	26,681
12 18	6,237	1,845		18,599
12 19	241RT	546RT	546CM	18,358
12 22	2,072		1,513	17,799
12 27	2,597			15,202
12 28	4DM		1,010CM	16,208
12 29	12DM	1,987		14,209

D - DRAFT   RT - RETURN CHECK   SC - SERVICE CHARGE
OD - OVERDRAFT   CM - CREDIT MEMO   DM - DEBIT MEMO

(f) A special bank statement was secured by you personally from both banks on January 8, 1973, and The National Bank statement is reproduced below.

BALANCE FROM LAST STATEMENT	NUMBER OF CHECKS	TOTAL AMOUNT OF CHECKS THIS MONTH	NUMBER OF CREDITS	TOTAL AMOUNT OF CREDITS THIS MONTH	SERVICE CHARGE	BALANCE ON ABOVE DATE
14,209	3	6,034	2	1,482		9,657

DATE MO. DAY	CHECKS AND OTHER DEBITS		DEPOSITS — CREDITS	BALANCE
1 03	1,739	3,945	540	9,065
1 05	350		942	9,657

(g) You determine that the bank statements are correct except that The National Bank incorrectly charged a returned check on December 19 but credited the account the same day.

(h) On December 28 a 60-day, 6%, $1,000 note was collected by The National Bank for Hoosier for a $4 collection fee.

(i) The $12 debit memo from The National Bank was a charge for printed checks.

(j) Check #1213 was issued to replace check #1205 when the latter was reported not received by a vendor. Because of the delay in paying this account Hoosier Company was no longer entitled to the 2% cash discount it had taken in preparing the original check.

Instructions: Prepare a proof of cash for December for Hoosier's general bank account in The National Bank. Your proof of cash should show the computation of the adjusted balances for both the bank statement and the general ledger account of The National Bank for cash in bank November 30, December receipts, December disbursements and cash in bank December 31. The following column headings are recommended:

Description	Beginning Reconciliation November 30	December Receipts	December Disbursements	Ending Reconciliation December 31

(AICPA adapted)

6-12. Modern Products Corporation, a manufacturer of molded plastic containers, determined in October, 1972, that it needed cash to continue operations. The corporation began negotiating for a one-month bank loan of $100,000 which would be discounted at 9% per annum on November 1. In considering the loan, the bank requested a projected income statement and a cash budget for the month of November.

The following information is available:

(a) Sales were budgeted at 120,000 units per month in October 1972, December 1972, and January 1973, and at 90,000 units in November 1972. The selling price is $2 per unit. Sales are billed on the 15th and last day of each month on terms of 2/10, net 30. Past experience indicates sales are even throughout the month and 50% of the customers pay the billed amount within the discount period. The remainder pay at the end of 30 days, except for those anticipated to be uncollectible which average ½% of gross sales.

(b) The inventory of finished goods on October 1 was 24,000 units. The finished goods inventory at the end of each month is to be maintained at 20% of sales anticipated for the following month. There is no work in process.

(c) The inventory of raw materials on October 1 was 22,800 pounds. At the end of each month the raw materials inventory is to be maintained at not less than 40% of production requirements for the following month. Materials are purchased as needed in quantities of 25,000 pounds per shipment. Raw materials purchases of each month are paid in the following month on terms of net 30 days.

(d) All salaries and wages are paid on the 15th and last day of each month for the period ending on the date of payment.

(e) All manufacturing overhead and selling and administrative expenses are paid on the 10th of the month following the month in which incurred. Selling expenses are 10% of gross sales. Administrative expenses, which include depreciation of $500 per month on office furniture and fixtures, total $33,000 per month.

(f) The standard cost of a molded plastic container, based on "normal" production of 100,000 units per month, is as follows:

Materials — ½ pound	$ .50
Labor	.40
Variable overhead	.20
Fixed overhead	.10
Total	$1.20

Fixed overhead of $10,000 includes depreciation on factory equipment of $4,000 per month.

(g) The cash balance on November 1 is expected to be $10,000.

Instructions: Prepare the following for Modern Products Corporation assuming the bank loan is granted. (Do not consider income taxes.)

(1) Schedules computing inventory budgets by months for the following: (a) Finished goods production in units for October, November and December, (b) Raw materials purchases in pounds for October and November.

(2) A cash forecast for the month of November showing the opening balance, receipts (itemized by dates of collection), disbursements, and balance at end of month.

(AICPA adapted)

chapter 7

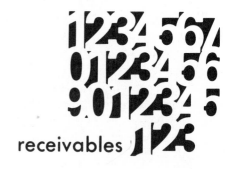

receivables

In its broadest sense, the term *receivables* is applicable to all claims against others, whether these are claims for money, for goods, or for services. For accounting purposes, however, the term is employed in a narrower sense to designate claims that are expected to be settled by the receipt of money.

Usually, the chief source of receivables is found in the normal activities of the operating cycle of the business. Business today is largely based on credit. Goods and services are sold on account, the collection of the accounts following some time after the sales. In the meantime, the seller has claims against the buyers. Other receivables arise as a result of such diverse activities as advances made by a company, the sale of properties and equipment items, and the sale of capital stock.

Composition of receivables

Receivables are composed of two classes: (1) those supported by formal promises to pay in the form of notes, referred to as *notes receivable*, and (2) those not so supported, referred to as *accounts receivable*. Accounts receivable may be divided into groupings as follows: (a) receivables from customers, (b) receivables from others, and (c) accrued receivables. Receivables should be established in the accounts only when supportable claims exist and it can be assumed that the claims will be realized.

Notes receivable. A note is an unconditional written promise by one party to another to pay a certain sum of money at a specified time. The note may be negotiable or nonnegotiable. It is negotiable or legally transferable by endorsement and delivery only if it provides for payment to the order of the second party or bearer. Such notes are commonly accepted by commercial banks for discount; hence they are considered more liquid than are other classes of receivables.

The term "notes" is commonly used to include not only promissory notes but also time drafts and trade acceptances. If time drafts and trade acceptances are material in amount, they may be summarized separately.

The notes receivable designation for reporting purposes should be limited to negotiable short-term instruments that are acquired from trade debtors and that are not yet due. When a written instrument fails to meet these requirements, it should be reported separately under an appropriately descriptive title. For example, notes arising from loans to customers, officers, employees, and affiliated companies should be reported separately.

Accounts receivable. As previously indicated, accounts receivable broadly include all receivables other than those supported by some form of commercial paper. Although it would be appropriate to refer to open accounts with customers arising from the sale of goods and services as "Trade Debtors" or "Trade Receivables" to distinguish these from other receivables, it has become established practice to use the designation "Accounts Receivable" to represent these claims. Accounts receivable for reporting purposes should be limited to trade accounts that are expected to be converted into cash in the regular course of business. The account balances, for example, should not include receivables arising from charges for containers if such charges will be canceled when containers are returned.

A receivable arising from the sale of goods is generally recognized when the title to goods passes to the buyer. However, the point at which title passes may vary with the terms of the sale, but it is general practice to recognize the receivable when goods are shipped to the customer. Receivables should not be recognized for goods shipped on approval where the shipper retains title to the goods until there is a formal acceptance, or for goods shipped on consignment where the shipper retains title to the goods until they are sold by the consignee. Under these circumstances only a memorandum entry is appropriate until title to the goods passes.

Receivables for services to customers are properly recognized when the services are performed. When work under a contract has not been completed at the end of the period, the amount due as of the balance sheet date will have to be calculated. Receivables should be recognized for the portion of work completed under construction contracts and for reimbursable costs and accrued fees on cost-plus-fixed-fee contracts.

Ordinarily, detailed records of customer transactions and customers' balances are carried in subsidiary records. Entries to subsidiary records may be made from original business papers evidencing the transactions.

With machine methods, subsidiary records are frequently maintained simultaneously with the preparation of invoices and remittance records.

Nontrade receivables should be summarized in appropriately titled accounts and should be reported separately. The following are examples of the receivables that should be carried separately: claims arising from the sale of securities or property other than goods or services; advances to stockholders, directors, officers, employees, and affiliated companies; deposits with creditors, utilities, and other agencies; purchase prepayments; deposits to guarantee contract performance or expense payment; claims for losses or damages; claims for rebates and tax refunds; subscriptions for capital stock; and dividends receivable.

Certain revenues for services or goods accrue with the passage of time and are most conveniently recognized when collections are made. At the end of the period, it is necessary to calculate the amounts accrued since the last collections and to establish appropriate accrued receivables. Accrued interest is recognized on assets such as bank deposits, notes, bonds, and annuities. Rentals may accrue on real estate holdings. Royalties and patent fees may accrue on certain rights and properties. For some business units accrued receivables may be small in total; for others, they may involve large amounts.

It was indicated in an earlier chapter that the current asset classification as broadly conceived comprehends all receivables identified with the normal operating cycle. Installment and other deferred collection contracts are current regardless of their terms. But receivables arising outside of the inventory-to-cash cycle qualify as current only if they are expected to be collected within one year. For classification purposes, each nontrade item requires separate analysis to determine whether it is reasonable to assume that it will be collected within one year. Noncurrent receivables are reported under the Investments or Other Assets caption, whichever may be considered appropriate.

Amounts due from officers, directors, and major stockholders arising out of sales and subject to the usual credit terms are normally considered current; however, when claims have arisen from transactions other than sales and current recovery is not assured, such items are properly classified as noncurrent. Sales to affiliated companies give rise to current claims, but advances are generally regarded as long-term in nature. Deposits on materials and merchandise ordered will soon represent inventories and are reported as current, but deposits on utility contracts are reported as long-term. Deposits for machinery and equipment ordered are noncurrent in view of the ultimate application of the deposit. Claims from the sale of assets other than merchandise and calling for periodic collections over a period exceeding one year require special analysis to determine the portion of the claim to be reported as current and the portion to be reported as noncurrent.

Subscriptions to capital stock are current only if they are currently collectible; when current collection is not probable or when payments may be deferred indefinitely, such balances are reported as noncurrent assets or in some instances more appropriately as subtractions from capital balances so that no more than the amount actually paid in by stockholders and subscribers is reported as paid-in capital.

When income tax refund claims or other claims have been granted and collection is expected within one year, they qualify for current presentation. When claims are still being processed and recovery is assured although the period required for such processing is uncertain, they are shown under a noncurrent heading. Certain claims may be in dispute. When a claim does not involve a material amount and there is little likelihood of recovery, no reference needs to be made to it on the balance sheet. On the other hand, if a material amount is involved and there is prospect of a favorable settlement, the claim is properly viewed as a contingent receivable and should be disclosed by a special note or by an appropriate comment under a separate contingent asset heading. If a contingent receivable becomes an actual receivable, an asset account is established and a special gain account is credited.

Creditor and customer accounts with contra balances require special attention. These balances are found by an analysis of subsidiary ledger detail. For example, assume that the accounts payable controlling account reports a balance of $10,000. Inspection of subsidiary account detail reveals accounts with credit balances of $10,500 and accounts with debit balances of $500. The nature of the debit balances should be investigated. If the debit balances have arisen as a result of overpayments or returns and allowances after payment, they are reportable as current assets in view of the claims that they represent for cash or merchandise from vendors. Such balances are properly reported under a title such as "Creditors' Accounts with Debit Balances" or "Sundry Claims." If debit balances represent advance payments on the purchase of raw materials or merchandise, these too are current assets reportable under some descriptive title such as "Advances on Purchase Contracts." In either case, Accounts Payable is reported at $10,500. Although both an asset and a liability are reported, no adjustment to the controlling account or the subsidiary ledger detail is required. Debit balances in the subsidiary ledger are carried forward and are ultimately canceled by purchases or cash settlement.

Customer ledger detail needs similar analysis. Customers' accounts with credit balances may result from overpayments, from customer returns after full payment, or from advance payments by customers. Such credits should be recognized as current liabilities, and accounts receivable should be reported at the sum of the debit balances in the subsidiary ledger.

It may be pointed out that when contra balances in customer and creditor accounts are not material in amount, they are frequently disregarded and only the net receivable or payable balance is reported on the balance sheet.

Valuation of receivables

Theoretically, receivables arising from the sale of property, goods, or services should be reported at their net realizable or cash value. This would suggest that receivables should be reduced by any interest implicit in their face amount, uncollectible items that may be anticipated in the course of their collection, and unearned finance or interest charges that are reported in their face amounts.

Reporting receivables at present values. When a sale is made at an amount that is collectible at some future date, the amount collectible may be regarded as consisting of both a sales price and a charge for interest for the period of the payment deferral. In the absence of an established exchange or sales price, the *present value* of the receivable should be determined by reducing the face amount of the receivable by an interest rate that is regarded as appropriate under the circumstances for the period that payment is deferred. The process of arriving at the present value of a sum is generally referred to as *discounting* the sum; the interest rate that is approximated for this period is generally referred to as the *imputed rate*. The difference between the face value of the receivable and its present value is recognized as a discount. A sale when collection is deferred is recorded by a debit to a receivable account, a credit to a discount on the receivable, and a credit to sales at the present value as reported for the receivable.[1] This discount is amortized as a credit to interest income over the life of the receivable; in preparing a balance sheet, any unamortized discount is reported as a direct subtraction from the face amount of the receivable.

Although the proper valuation of receivables calls for the procedure just described, exceptions to this procedure may be appropriate in special instances because of certain special limitations or practical considera-

---

[1] An interest rate provided by terms of the receivable that is higher or lower than a rate regarded as appropriate under the circumstances would call for similar analysis and the recognition of a premium or discount on the receivable.

tions. The Accounting Principles Board in Opinion No. 21 on interest on receivables and payables has provided guidelines for the recognition of present values and the accounting that is subsequently to be employed, but the Board indicates that this process is not to be regarded as applicable under all circumstances. Among the exceptions, it includes the following important groups:

> . . . receivables and payables arising from transactions with customers or suppliers in the normal course of business which are due in customary trade terms not exceeding approximately one year.[1]

Accordingly, short-term notes and accounts receivable arising from sales may be properly recorded at the amounts that are collectible in the customary sales terms.

Estimated uncollectible accounts. Almost invariably some of the receivables arising from sales will prove uncollectible. Uncollectible amounts will have to be anticipated if the charge for them is to be related to the period of the sale and receivables are to be stated at their estimated realizable amounts.

The amount of receivables estimated uncollectible is recorded by a charge to expense and a credit to an allowance account. The terminology for these account titles has changed somewhat over time. The term "Allowance for Doubtful Accounts" has largely replaced the earlier term of "Reserve for Bad Debts" following the recommendation of the AICPA terminology bulletin regarding restrictive use of the term "Reserve." Other possible secondary terms besides Doubtful Accounts which may be used are Losses, Uncollectible Accounts, or Bad Debts. The expense terminology usually is consistent with the secondary term, and thus becomes Doubtful Accounts Expense, Uncollectible Accounts Expense, or Bad Debts Expense. The charge for doubtful accounts may be reported as a deduction from sales on the theory that it is net sales — sales after uncollectibles — that must cover current charges and yield a profit. Instead of being treated as a contra-sales balance, however, the bad debts item is usually regarded as emerging from a failure of management, and, hence, is reported as a selling, general and administrative, or financial charge, depending upon the division that is held responsible for approving sales on account. The allowance account is then reported as a subtraction from accounts receivable. Use of the

---

[1]*Opinions of the Accounting Principles Board, No. 21*, "Interest on Receivables and Payables" (New York: American Institute of Certified Public Accountants, 1972), par. 3(a). It may be noted that the primary objective of the Opinion was not to suggest new principles but simply to clarify and refine the manner of applying existing principles.

allowance account avoids premature adjustments to individual receivable accounts while making possible a continuing control of subsidiary ledger detail by the accounts receivable account in the general ledger.

When positive evidence is available concerning the partial or complete worthlessness of an account, a charge is made to the allowance and the receivable is credited. Positive evidence of worthlessness is found in the bankruptcy, death, or disappearance of a debtor, failure to enforce collection legally, or a barring of collection by the statute of limitations. Write-offs should be supported by evidence of the uncollectibility of the accounts from appropriate parties, such as courts, lawyers, or credit agencies, and should be authorized in writing by appropriate company officers.

Bases for estimating charge for doubtful accounts. The estimate for doubtful accounts may be based upon (1) the amount of sales or (2) the amount of receivables. When sales are used as the basis for calculation, the problem of estimating the charge for doubtful accounts is viewed as one involving primarily the proper measurement of income. When receivables are used as the basis for calculation, the problem is viewed as one involving primarily the proper valuation of receivables. The methods employed under each of these bases are described in the paragraphs that follow.

Adjustment for doubtful accounts based on sales. The charges for doubtful accounts of recent periods are related to sales of such periods in developing a percentage of the charge for doubtful accounts to sales. This percentage may be modified by expectations in the light of current experience. Since doubtful accounts occur only with credit sales, it would seem logical to develop a percentage of doubtful accounts to charge sales of past periods. This percentage would be applied to charge sales of the current period. However, since extra work may be required in maintaining records of cash and credit sales or in analyzing sales data, the percentage is frequently developed in terms of total sales. Unless there is considerable fluctuation in the proportion of cash and credit sales periodically, the total sales method will give satisfactory results.

The *sales percentage method* for anticipating doubtful accounts is widely used in practice because it is sound in theory and simple to apply. Although normally offering a satisfactory approach to income measurement by providing equitable charges to periodic revenue, the method may not offer a "cash realizable" valuation for receivables. This shortcoming can be overcome by analyzing receivables at different intervals and correcting the allowance for any significant excess or deficiency.

Adjustment for doubtful accounts based on receivables. There are two methods of establishing and maintaining an allowance for doubtful accounts when receivables are used as the base for the adjustment:

1. The allowance is raised to a certain percentage of receivables.
2. The allowance is raised to an amount determined by aging the accounts.

Raising allowance to a certain percentage of receivables. The uncollectible accounts experiences of recent periods are related to accounts outstanding in such periods and these data are considered in terms of special current conditions. An estimate of the probable uncollectibles is developed and Doubtful Accounts Expense is charged and Allowance for Doubtful Accounts credited for an amount that brings the allowance to the desired balance. To illustrate, assume receivables of $60,000 and a credit balance of $200 in the allowance account at the end of the period. Doubtful accounts are estimated at 2% of accounts receivable, or $1,200. The following entry brings the allowance to the desired amount:

Doubtful Accounts Expense....................... 1,000
    Allowance for Doubtful Accounts...............   1,000

Although this method provides a satisfactory approach to the valuation of receivables, it may fail to provide equitable period charges to revenue. This is particularly true in view of the irregular determinations of actual uncollectibles as well as the lag in their recognition. After the first year, periodic provisions are directly affected by the current reductions in the allowance resulting from a recognition of uncollectible accounts originating in prior periods.

Raising allowance to an amount determined by aging the accounts. The most commonly used method for establishing an allowance in terms of receivables is that which involves *aging receivables*. Individual accounts are analyzed to determine those that are not yet due and those that are past due. Past-due accounts are classified in terms of the length of the period past due. An analysis sheet used in aging accounts receivable is shown on page 220.

It is desirable to review each overdue balance with some appropriate company official and to arrive at estimates concerning the degree of collectibility of each item listed. An alternative procedure is to develop a series of estimated loss percentages and to apply these to the different receivable classifications. The calculation of the allowance on the latter basis is also illustrated on page 220.

Doubtful Accounts Expense is now debited and Allowance for Doubtful Accounts is credited for an amount that will bring the allowance

Parker and Pope
Analysis of Receivables — December 31, 1972

Customer	Amount	Not Yet Due	Not More Than 30 Days Past Due	31–60 Days Past Due	61–90 Days Past Due	91–180 Days Past Due	181–365 Days Past Due	More Than One Year Past Due
A. B. Andrews..	$ 450				$ 450			
B. T. Brooks...	300					$ 100	$ 200	
B. Bryant......	200			$ 200				
L. B. Devine...	2,100	$ 2,100						
K. Flood......	200							$ 200
M. A. Young...	1,400	1,000		100	300			
Total.........	$47,550	$40,000	$3,000	$1,200	$ 650	$ 500	$ 800	$1,400

Parker and Pope
Estimated Amount of Uncollectible Accounts — December 31, 1972

Classification	Balances	Uncollectible Accounts Experience Percentage	Estimated Amount of Uncollectible Accounts
Not yet due...................	$40,000	2%	$ 800
Not more than 30 days past due.	3,000	5%	150
31–60 days past due...........	1,200	10%	120
61–90 days past due...........	650	20%	130
91–180 days past due..........	500	30%	150
181–365 days past due.........	800	50%	400
More than one year past due....	1,400	80%	1,120
	$47,550		$2,870

account up to the required balance. Assuming uncollectibles estimated at $2,870 as shown in the tabulation and a credit balance of $620 in the allowance before adjustment, the following entry would be made:

Doubtful Accounts Expense........................ 2,250
    Allowance for Doubtful Accounts................ 2,250

The aging method provides the most satisfactory approach to the valuation of receivables at their cash realizable amounts. Furthermore, data developed through aging receivables may be quite useful to management for purposes of credit analysis and control. On the other hand, application of this method may require considerable time and may prove expensive. The method still involves estimates, and the added refinement that is achieved by the aging process may not warrant the additional cost.

Also, it should be noted that here, as in the preceding instance, charges based upon the recognizable impairment of asset values rather than upon sales may fail to provide equitable periodic charges against revenue.

Corrections in allowance for doubtful accounts. As previously indicated, the allowance for doubtful accounts balance is established and maintained by means of adjusting entries at the close of each accounting period. If the allowance provisions are too large, the allowance account balance will be unnecessarily inflated and earnings will be understated; if the allowance provisions are too small, the allowance account balance will be inadequate and earnings will be overstated.

Care must be taken to see that the allowance balance follows the credit experience of the particular business. The process of aging receivables at different intervals may be employed as a means of checking the allowance balance to be certain that it is being maintained satisfactorily. Such periodic reviews may indicate the need for a correction in the allowance as well as a change in the rate or in the method.

When the uncollectible accounts experience approximates the anticipation of the losses, the allowance procedure may be considered satisfactory and no adjustment is required. When it appears that there has been a failure to estimate uncollectible accounts satisfactorily, resulting in an allowance balance that is clearly inadequate or excessive, an adjustment is in order. Since publication of APB Opinion No. 9, such an adjustment is to be reported on the income statement, usually as an addition to or subtraction from Doubtful Accounts Expense.

The recognition of current period receivables as uncollectible by charges to the allowance may result in a debit balance in the allowance account. A debit balance arising in this manner does not indicate that the allowance is inadequate; charges to the allowance simply predate the current provision for uncollectible accounts, and the adjustment at the end of the period should cover uncollectibles already determined as well as those yet to be recognized.

Occasionally, accounts that have been charged off as worthless are unexpectedly collected. The original entry whereby the customer's account was written off against the allowance should be reversed so that the customer's record may be complete. The receipt of cash is then recorded in the usual manner.

Uncollectible account recognition in period of discovery. Many small businesses may feel that the accounting refinement to be gained by anticipating uncollectibles hardly warrants the additional work required. Certain large businesses may encounter serious problems in developing reliable estimates of uncollectibles. These units, then, instead of anticipating uncollectible accounts, may prefer simply to recognize them in the periods in which accounts are determined to be uncollectible. When the loss is not anticipated by the establishment of an allowance, uncollectible accounts are written off by a charge to Uncollectible Accounts Expense or Bad Debts and a credit to the customer's account. Because the loss is now certain, and the write-off is made directly to the customer's account rather than to an allowance, the term Doubtful Accounts Expense is not appropriate. If an account written off is unexpectedly recovered in the same period, the entry to record the loss may be reversed and the collection recorded in the usual manner. If recovery is made in a subsequent period, it is necessary to restore the receivable balance and to credit a nominal account such as Recoveries of Accounts Written Off in Prior Periods; the collection is then recorded in the usual manner. The balance of Recoveries of Accounts Written Off in Prior Periods may be reported as a subtraction from Uncollectible Accounts Expense in arriving at the net charge for uncollectibles made currently.

Although theory supports the anticipation of uncollectibles so that current revenue may carry its full burden of expenses, the recognition of uncollectibles in the period of their discovery is widely practiced because of its simplicity and convenience. Either method can be used for income tax purposes. However, the method that is elected must be employed consistently on successive tax returns.

Anticipation of discounts and other charges in valuation of receivables. The foregoing discussion has been restricted to the provision for uncollectible items. Conditions of sales and collections may suggest the anticipation of other charges that will emerge in the realization of accounts receivable and hence should properly be matched against current revenue.

For example, if customers generally take cash discounts in making remittances, it may be argued that reporting revenue and receivables in terms of customer billings involves some overstatement of these balances. Under these circumstances, it may be desirable to anticipate the discounts by a charge to Sales Discount and a credit to Allowance for Sales Discount. Allowance for Sales Discount would be subtacted from Accounts Receivable so that receivables are reported at their estimated cash realizable value. Discounts on the collection of old accounts in the new period can be charged against the allowance account. However, it would be more convenient to transfer the allowance to the sales discount account by a reversing entry at the beginning of the new period. All discounts can then be charged to the sales discount account.

Similar recognition may be suggested for probable allowances yet to be made to customers for shipment shortages and defects, for price adjustments, and also for probable losses on sales returns. Claims that customers may make for freight charges that they pay on the receipt of goods or on the return of goods may call for consideration. Probable future expenses involved in the realization of accounts such as billing and collection expenses and attorneys' fees may likewise warrant consideration. It may be pointed out that the anticipation of charges for the items just mentioned is seldom found in practice and is not allowed for income tax purposes. When these charges are not anticipated and the volume of activities and experiences with respect to such charges does not vary significantly from period to period, the recognition of such charges in the period in which they are finally determined will have little effect upon periodic net income, although the receivables balance may include some minor overstatement.

The preceding discussion has considered charges relating to the realization of accounts receivable. The realization of notes receivable may involve similar charges. When sales are used as a basis for estimating future charges, allowances may be considered applicable to both accounts receivable and notes receivable received from customers. When accounts receivable are analyzed and used as a basis for developing related allowances, notes receivable would require similar treatment.

Unearned finance charges included in receivables. In many instances, the amount charged to the customer on sales contracts includes finance, interest, and other charges. These charges are actually earned with the passage of time and should be recognized as unearned at the time of the sale. The Accounting Principles Board in Opinion No. 6 makes the following observation:

> Unearned discounts (other than cash or quantity discounts and the like), finance charges and interest included in the face amount of receivables should be shown as a deduction from the related receivables.[1]

The entry at the time of sale should establish the unearned customer charges, and periodic adjustments should then be made to recognize the amounts earned. To illustrate, assume that installment sales contracts of $27,500 for a month that include finance charges of $2,500. Installment sales would be reported as follows:

Installment Accounts Receivable..................	27,500	
Sales..		25,000
Unearned Customer Finance Charges...........		2,500

[1] *Opinions of the Accounting Principles Board, No. 6*, "Status of Accounting Research Bulletins" (New York: American Institute of Certified Public Accountants, October, 1965), par. 14.

As collections are made on installment accounts, finance charges would be recognized as earned and entries would be made charging the unearned balance and crediting Revenues from Customer Finance Charges. In preparing a balance sheet, any unearned balance would be reported as a deduction from the related receivable.

Use of receivables in cash planning

A business may require cash for current purposes that exceeds the amount on hand and the amount to become available in the normal course of operations. The business may use accounts receivable or notes receivable as a basis for a cash advance from a bank or a finance company. These procedures are described in the sections that follow.

Customers' accounts as a source of cash. In order to obtain immediate cash, accounts receivable owned by the business may be (1) pledged, (2) assigned, or (3) sold.

Pledge of accounts receivable. Advances are frequently obtained from banks or other lending institutions by pledging accounts receivable as security on the loan. Ordinarily, collections are made by the borrower who is required to use this cash in meeting his obligation to the lender. The lender may be given access to the borrower's records to determine whether remittances are being properly made on pledged accounts.

Assignment of accounts receivable. Finance companies may agree to advance cash over a period of time as accounts receivable are assigned to them. The assignments carry a guarantee on the part of the assignor that he will make up any deficiency if the accounts fail to realize required amounts. Assignments thus represent, in effect, sale of accounts on a *recourse* basis. The cash advanced by the finance company is normally less than the assigned accounts by a percentage that is considered adequate to cover uncollectible items, returns and allowances, offsets, and amounts subject to dispute. When amounts actually recovered on assigned accounts exceed the sum of the advance and the finance company's charges, such excess accrues to the assignor. Charges made by the finance company frequently consist of a commission on the amount advanced, plus interest on the unrecovered balance of the advance computed on a daily basis. Assignments are usually made on a *non-notification basis*, customers remaining uninformed concerning the assignment; customers, then, make their payments to the assignor who is then required to turn the collections over to the assignee. When assignments are on a *notification basis*, customers are instructed to make their payments directly to the finance company.

Sale of accounts receivable. Certain dealers or finance companies purchase accounts receivable outright on a *without recourse* basis. This is known as accounts receivable *factoring*, and the buyer is referred to as a *factor*. Customers are notified that their bills are payable to the factor, and this party assumes the burden of billing and collecting accounts. In many instances, factoring may involve more than simply the purchase and collection of accounts receivable. Factoring frequently involves a continuing agreement whereby a financing institution assumes the credit function as well as the collection function. Under such an arrangement, the factor grants or denies credit, handles the accounts receivable bookkeeping, bills customers, and makes collections. The business unit is relieved of all of these activities. The sale of goods provides immediate cash for business use. Because the factor absorbs the losses from bad accounts and frequently assumes credit and collection responsibilities, the charge that he makes exceeds the interest charge involved in borrowing cash or the commission and interest charges involved in the assignment of receivables. In some instances the factor may withhold a portion of the purchase price for possible future charges for customer returns and allowances or other special adjustments. Final settlement is made after receivables have been collected.

Accounting procedures for accounts receivable financing. No special accounting problems are encountered in the pledge or the sale of receivables. When receivables are pledged, the books simply report the loan and the subsequent settlement. Disclosure should be made on the balance sheet by parenthetical comment or note of the receivables pledged to secure the obligation to the lending agency. When receivables are sold outright, Cash is debited, receivables and related allowance balances are closed, and an expense account is charged for factoring charges. When part of the purchase price is withheld by the factor, a receivable is established pending final settlement.

The assignment of accounts receivable is comparable to the discounting of customers' notes and similar accounting may be employed. To illustrate, assume that the Bronson Co. on March 1 assigns accounts receivable of $25,000 to the Weber Finance Co. and receives $19,500 representing an advance of 80% of receivables less a commission on the advance of $2\frac{1}{2}\%$. Collections are to be made by the assignor who is to deposit such receipts intact to the credit of the assignee. The entries on the books of the assignor and assignee are given on the following page.

It will be observed that the assignor makes two entries at the time of assignment: one entry sets the assigned accounts receivable apart under separate control; a second entry establishes a credit representing the

Transaction	Entries on Assignor's Books (Bronson Company)	Entries on Assignee's Books (Weber Finance Co.)

March 1
 	
Bronson Co. assigned accounts receivable of $25,000 to Weber Finance Co. receiving $19,500 representing an advance of 80% of receivables less a commission on the advance of 2½%.
	Accounts Rec.
	Assigned...... 25,000
	  Accounts
	    Receivable.. 25,000
	
	Cash.......... 19,500
	Assignment
	Expense...... 500
	  Equity of
	  Weber
	  Finance Co.
	  in Assigned
	  Accounts.... 20,000
		Bronson Co.
		  Accounts..... 25,000
		  Equity of
		  Bronson Co.
		  in Assigned
		  Accounts ... 5,000
		  Commission
		  Income..... 500
		  Cash....... 19,500

March 31
 	
Bronson Co. collected $15,000 on assigned accounts. This amount together with interest at 8% for one month on this amount, or $100, was remitted to Weber Finance Co.
	Cash.......... 15,000
	  Accounts Rec.
	  Assigned.... 15,000
	
	Equity of
	Weber Finance
	Co. in Assigned
	Accounts...... 15,000
	Interest Expense 100
	  Cash....... 15,100
		Cash.......... 15,100
		  Bronson Co.
		  Accounts.... 15,000
		  Interest
		  Income..... 100

March 31
 	
Sales returns and allowances granted by Bronson Co. on assigned accounts during March totaled $1,000.
	Sales Returns
	and Allow.... 1,000
	  Accounts Rec.
	  Assigned.... 1,000
		Equity of
		Bronson Co.
		in Assigned
		Accounts...... 1,000
		  Bronson Co.
		  Accounts.... 1,000

May 31
 	
Bronson Co. collected $8,500 on assigned accounts. Balance due, $5,000, together with interest at 8% for three months on this amount, or $100, was remitted to Weber Finance Co. in final settlement; $3,500 was retained. Remaining account balances relative to assignment were closed.
	Cash.......... 8,500
	  Accounts Rec.
	  Assigned.... 8,500
	
	Equity of
	Weber Finance
	Co. in Assigned
	Accounts...... 5,000
	Interest Expense 100
	  Cash....... 5,100
	
	Accounts
	Receivable.... 500
	  Accounts
	  Receivable
	  Assigned.... 500
		Cash.......... 5,100
		  Bronson Co.
		  Accounts.... 5,000
		  Interest
		  Income..... 100
		
		Equity of
		Bronson Co.
		in Assigned
		Accounts...... 4,000
		  Bronson Co.
		  Accounts.... 4,000

equity in the receivables of the assignee, accompanied by charges to Cash for the cash received, and to Assignment Expense for the charges made by the assignee. Thereafter, as cash is collected on assigned accounts, the assigned receivables balance is reduced and cash is remitted to the assignee reducing his equity. Entries are made to reduce the assigned receivables balance for such items as returns, allowances, and write-offs.

Upon final settlement with the assignee, any balance in Accounts Receivable Assigned is returned to the unassigned accounts control. The equity of the assignor in the accounts is always the remaining balance in the assigned accounts less the equity of the assignee.

On the books of the assignee, the advance of cash is recorded by a charge to an asset account for the total receivables assigned, a credit to an account with the assignor for the latter's equity in this total, a credit to Commission Income for the charges made, and a credit to Cash for the cash paid. As cash is received, Cash is debited and assigned accounts and interest income are credited. Reductions in assigned accounts involving charges that are to be absorbed by the assignee are recognized by reductions in the assignor's equity. Upon final settlement, any balance remaining in the assignor's equity in assigned accounts is offset against the assigned receivables balance.

If a balance sheet is prepared before the finance company has received full payment, the assignor recognizes the difference between the total accounts assigned and the portion required to cover the claim of the finance company as an asset. Disclosure is also made of the responsibilities to the finance company if assigned accounts do not realize enough to liquidate the loan. The assignee in preparing a balance sheet would report his interest in assigned accounts as an asset.

To illustrate, if in the preceding example balance sheets are prepared on March 31, information relating to assigned accounts may be reported as shown below.

Bronson Company

Current assets:

Accounts receivable–unassigned		$50,000
Company's equity in assigned accounts receivable:		
Assigned accounts.	$9,000	
Less equity of Weber Finance Co. in assigned accounts (company is contingently liable as guarantor of assigned accounts)	5,000	4,000
Total accounts receivable		$54,000

Weber Finance Company

Current assets:

Bronson Co. accounts	$9,000	
Less equity of Bronson Co. in assigned accounts	4,000	$5,000

When collections are made by the finance company, procedures similar to those illustrated can still be employed. In such instances, however, entries are made by the assignor when information is received from the finance company concerning collections, interest charges, and the return of accounts in excess of claims.

Management may employ accounts receivable financing as a temporary or emergency matter after exhausting the limited line of unsecured credit that may be available from a lending institution. On the other hand, management may engage in accounts receivable financing as a continuing policy. Recent years have witnessed an increasing number of factoring arrangements involving the full delegation of credit and collection responsibilities to specialists. Financial assistance to business through the factoring of open accounts today runs into billions of dollars.

Customers' notes as a source of cash. Cash may be obtained by selling customers' notes to a bank or to some other agency willing to accept such instruments. If a customer's note is non-interest-bearing, cash is received for the face value of the note less a charge for interest, known as *discount*, for the period from the date the note is discounted to the date of its maturity. If the note is interest-bearing, the maturity value of the note is first determined. The amount that is received from the bank is the maturity value of the note less discount calculated on this maturity value from the date the note is discounted to its maturity.

To illustrate entries for a non-interest-bearing note, assume that such a 90-day, $1,000 note dated December 1 is received from a customer, and the note is discounted on December 16 at 8%. The following entries are then made:

Dec. 1 Notes Receivable....................	1,000.00	
Accounts Receivable...............		1,000.00
Dec. 16 Cash.............................	983.33	
Interest Expense....................	16.67	
Notes Receivable...................		1,000.00
Interest: $1,000 \times .08 \times 75/360$, or 16.67.		

It should be observed that theoretical objections can be raised to the foregoing entries on the grounds that interest expense emerges from the failure to recognize a sales discount implicit in the acceptance of the note. If money is worth 8%, settlement of the account by a $1,000, 90-day, non-interest-bearing note may be regarded as settlement by note with a cash equivalent value of $980.39 ($1,000 ÷ 1.02). The following entry, then, is appropriate:

Notes Receivable.............................	1,000.00	
Sales Discount..............................	19.61	
Accounts Receivable.......................		1,000.00
Discount on Notes Receivable...............		19.61

The difference of $19.61 is regarded as a sales discount granted in receipt of the negotiable instrument.

Assuming that the note reported at $980.39 is sold for $983.33, the difference would be recognized as interest income. If the note is reported on the balance sheet before its sale or collection, an adjustment should be made to recognize the accrual of interest at 8% to the balance sheet date. The interest accrual is recorded by a debit to Discount on Notes Receivable and a credit to Interest Income; the balance of the discount should be subtracted from notes receivable in reporting the asset on the balance sheet. As indicated earlier, however, discounted values may be disregarded in recording short-term accounts and notes arising from sales to customers in the normal course of business. The sale of a receivable prior to its maturity date, then, involves the recognition of a charge to interest expense for the difference between its carrying value and the amount realized; collection of the receivable at its maturity is recognized as no more than recovery of the balance originally reported.

To illustrate the accounting for an interest-bearing note, assume that the note received from a customer in the previous example provides for the payment of interest at 8% at its maturity and that it is discounted at 8%. Under these circumstances, the following entries are appropriate:

Dec. 1	Notes Receivable....................	1,000.00	
	Accounts Receivable...............		1,000.00
Dec. 16	Cash.............................	1,003.00	
	Notes Receivable..................		1,000.00
	Interest Income...................		3.00

Maturity value of note: $1,000 + interest ($1,000 × .08 × 90/360), or $1,020.
Discount: $1,020 × .08 × 75/360, or $17.00.

When a person endorses a note "without recourse," he is relieved of any liability for the inability of the maker of the note or any prior endorser to pay the note upon its maturity. When he endorses a note without making any qualification, he becomes liable to subsequent holders of the note if it is not paid at maturity. However, if he is held liable on the note, he has the right to recover amounts he has paid from the maker of the note or prior endorsers who failed to comply with its terms.

Normally, endorsement without qualification is required in discounting a note, and the endorser becomes contingently liable on the note. Under these circumstances Notes Receivable Discounted instead of Notes Receivable may be credited when the note is discounted. Pending final settlement on the note, Notes Receivable would be regarded as a contingent asset. Notes Receivable Discounted, in turn, would be an accompanying contingent liability. When the person who holds the note at maturity receives payment from the maker, both payment and recovery contingencies are ended, and Notes Receivable Discounted can be applied against Notes Receivable.

The use of the notes receivable discounted account gives the same final result as that obtained when Notes Receivable is credited for notes that are discounted. Since data concerning the contingent liability are of concern only on the balance sheet date and these can be determined readily at the end of the period from an examination of the detailed record of notes discounted, the extra work involved in maintaining a notes receivable discounted account may not be warranted. When a notes receivable discounted balance is carried in the accounts, this balance is subtracted from notes receivable in reporting the notes receivable balance. Information concerning the contingent liability is provided on the balance sheet by means of a parenthetical remark or note or by special reference under a separate contingent liabilities heading.

If a note is not paid when it is due, the holder of the note must give the endorser prompt notice of such dishonor. The endorser is then required to make payment to the holder. Payment consists of the face value of the note plus interest and plus any fees and costs relating to collection. The full amount paid is recoverable from the maker of the note, and Accounts Receivable, Notes Receivable Dishonored, or Notes Receivable Past Due may be charged. If Notes Receivable Discounted was credited at the time the note was discounted, this balance, together with the original notes receivable balance, should be canceled. Subsequent recovery on the note is recorded by a charge to cash and a credit to the account with the debtor; failure to recover any portion of the balance due would call for writing off the unpaid balance.

Presentation of receivables on the balance sheet

Normally, the receivables that qualify as current items are grouped for presentation in the following classes: (1) notes — trade debtors, (2) accounts — trade debtors, (3) other receivables, and (4) accrued receivables. Reporting should disclose those notes that are nonnegotiable. The detail reported for other and accrued receivables depends upon the relative significance of the various items included. When trade accounts or installment contracts are properly reported as current but involve collections beyond one year, particulars of such deferred collections should be provided. Valuation accounts are deducted from the individual receivable balances or combined balances to which they relate. Notes receivable may be reported gross with notes receivable discounted shown as a deduction from this balance, or notes may be reported net with appropriate reference to the contingent liability arising from notes discounted. Accounts receivable assigned may be reported gross with the interest of the assignee in such balance shown as a subtraction item, or the company's interest in receivables may be reported net; here too, appropriate reference would be made to the contingent liability involved. When receivables are supported by pledges of collateral to assure their collectibility, the nature of the pledge and the fact that the receivables are wholly or partly secured should be disclosed. On the other hand, when receivables have been pledged or otherwise hypothecated on obligations of the company, these facts, too, should be disclosed and reference made to the obligation that is thus secured.

Current receivable items as they might appear on the balance sheet are shown below:

Receivables:

Trade notes and drafts receivable (notes of $20,000 have been pledged to secure bank borrowing)..........................	$ 39,500	
Less discount on notes receivable.........	1,500	$ 38,000
Trade accounts receivable (including installment contracts of approximately $30,000 not due for 12–18 months).................	$112,000	
Less allowance for doubtful accounts and repossession charges.....................	2,500	109,500
Miscellaneous notes and accounts, including short-term loans to employees of $6,500....		12,000
Accrued receivables.......................		4,500
Total receivables...........................		$164,000

QUESTIONS

1. The Proctor Corporation shows on its balance sheet one receivable balance that includes the following items: (a) advances to officers, (b) deposits on machinery and equipment being produced by various companies for the Proctor Corporation, (c) traveling expense advances to salesmen, (d) damage claims against transportation companies approved by such companies, (e) estimated federal income tax refunds, (f) accrued interest on notes receivable, (g) overdue notes, (h) receivables from a foreign subsidiary company, (i) subscriptions receivable on a new bond issue, and (j) creditor overpayments. Suggest the proper treatment of each item.

2. Soon after C. & R., Inc., had mailed statements to customers on the first of the month, three complaints were received stating that credit has not been given for checks mailed at least a week before the end of the previous month. Upon investigating the complaints, it was found that the proper credits had been made to the customers' accounts on the second and third of the current month. Is there need for any further investigation?

3. The Beller Co. includes in its current receivable total an investment in a joint venture with the Carter Corporation. Officials of the Beller Co. justify this practice on the grounds that the assets of the joint venture are all in current form. Comment on this practice.

4. The Baker Manufacturing Co. ships merchandise on a consignment basis to customers, title to such goods passing only at the time the goods are sold by the consignees. The Baker Manufacturing Co. charges accounts receivable for the cost of the goods shipped until sales are reported, when it increases the receivable accounts with the consignee to the regular billing price. Goods on consignment appear on the balance sheet as receivables. (a) Would you approve such practice? (b) Suggest an alternative procedure.

5. (a) What are the advantages of recording Accounts Receivable gross before sales discount rather than net of the discount? (b) How are a company's financial statements affected by using the gross rather than the net method of recording?

6. Suggest several methods for reporting income tax refund claims approved or under review and the circumstances supporting the appropriate use of each method.

7. An analysis of the accounts receivable balance of $8,702 on the books of Burke, Inc., on December 31 reveals the following:

Accounts from sales of last three months (appear to be fully collectible)	$7,460
Accounts from sales prior to October 1 (of doubtful value.........	1,312
Accounts known to be worthless.............................	320
Dishonored notes charged back to customers' accounts...........	800
Credit balances in customers' accounts.......................	1,190

(a) What adjustments are required? (b) How should the various balances be shown on the balance sheet?

8. (a) Give three methods for the establishment and the maintenance of an allowance for doubtful accounts. (b) What are the advantages and the disadvantages of each method? (c) Which do you feel is the preferable method?

9. Why is the collection of an account written off in a previous year not an adjustment to retained earnings?

10. In what ways is the title "Allowance for Doubtful Accounts" a superior title for the receivable valuation account than "Reserve for Doubtful Accounts"?

11. The Allowance for Doubtful Accounts of the Lucky Peak Corporation had a debit balance of $350 at the end of the current fiscal year. An aging schedule prepared by the treasurer disclosed that on the basis of prior periods experience, $3,600 of the current accounts would probably prove uncollectible. What adjustment is required to record the above data?

12. The bookkeeper for Wells, Inc., believes he can show a more accurate valuation of notes and accounts receivable by aging the notes and accounts and establishing an allowance on this basis than he can by crediting the allowance account with a percentage of net sales on account. Do you agree? Give the advantages of each procedure.

13. How would you determine the percentage to use for the various age categories of receivables under the "percentage of receivables" method of estimating doubtful accounts?

14. List and explain the nature of at least four deductions that may be applied under certain circumstances in the valuation of accounts receivable.

15. If unearned customer finance charges for installment receivables are carried as a separate valuation account balance, what difficulties do you foresee in calculating a proper allowance for doubtful accounts?

16. In what section of the income statement would you report (a) doubtful accounts expense, (b) sales discounts, (c) recovery of accounts written off in prior periods?

17. The Crosby Corporation sells home air-conditioning units. The cash price of such units is $1,500; the price on a deferred payment plan is $1,800. Those acquiring the units on the deferred payment plan sign a note that provides for payments of $100 per month for eighteen months.

How would you recommend that the deferred payment sales and subsequent collections be reported in the accounts?

18. (a) Distinguish between the practices of (1) pledging, (2) assigning, and (3) selling accounts receivable. (b) Describe the accounting procedure to be followed in each instance.

19. The Parker Co. enters into a continuing agreement with Mercantile Finance, Inc., whereby the latter company buys without recourse all of the trade receivables as they arise and assumes all credit and collection functions. Describe the advantages that may accrue to the Parker Co. as a result of the factoring agreement.

20. B. M. Lowell, who has been recording a contingent liability on notes receivable discounted, has noticed that he has been held liable on nearly as many customers' checks as he has on notes. He suggests setting up a "checks endorsed" account to show his contingent liability on checks. Is this advisable? Why?

21. The Beaner Company discounts at 8% the following three notes at the Security First Bank on July 1 of the current year. Compute the proceeds on each note using 360 days to a year.

  (a) A 90-day, 9% note receivable for $10,000 dated June 1.
  (b) A 6-month, 7% note receivable for $14,000 dated May 13.
  (c) A 4-month note payable dated July 1 with face value of $5,000.

22. Indicate several methods for presenting information on the balance sheet relating to (a) notes receivable discounted, and (b) accounts receivable assigned.

EXERCISES

1. The accounts receivable controlling account for the Abbott Co. shows a debit balance of $34,550; the allowance for doubtful accounts shows a credit balance of $1,600. Subsidiary ledger detail reveals the following:

Trade accounts receivable in 30 days..........................	$12,000
Installment receivables, due 1 month–18 months hence (including unearned finance charges of $500)...........................	3,500
Trade receivables from officers, due currently....................	1,250
Customers' accounts reporting credit balances arising from sales returns..	150
Advance payments to creditors on purchase orders...............	3,000
Advance payments to creditors on orders for machinery...........	5,000
Customers' accounts reporting credit balances arising from advance payments...	1,000
Accounts known to be worthless...............................	450

Trade accounts on which post-dated checks are held (no entries were
   made on receipt of checks)................................. $ 500
Advances to affiliated companies............................. 10,000

Show how this information would be reported on the balance sheet.

2. The trial balance before adjustment for the Moore Sales Co. shows
the following balances:

	Dr.	Cr.
Accounts Receivable..............	36,000	
Allowance for Doubtful Accounts.....	600	
Sales.........................		215,000
Sales Returns and Allowances........	1,000	

Give the adjustment for estimated doubtful accounts, assuming:

(a) The allowance is maintained at 2% of accounts receivable.
(b) The allowance is to provide for doubtful accounts of $680 arrived at by
   aging accounts.
(c) The allowance is to be increased by ½ of 1% of net sales.

3. Dexter Sales Co. assigns accounts of $60,000 to the Williams
Finance Co. guaranteeing these accounts and receiving an 80% advance
less a flat commission of 2% on the amount of the advance. Accounts of
$45,000 are collected and remittance is made to the finance company.
Bad accounts of $2,000 are written off against an allowance for doubtful
accounts; remaining accounts are collected and settlement is made with
the finance company together with payment of $1,200 for interest. What
entries are required on the books of Dexter Sales Co. and on the books of
Williams Finance Co. to record the assignment and the subsequent
transactions?

4. The Bond Co. decides to employ accounts receivable as a basis for
financing. Its current position at this time is as follows:

Accounts receivable	$30,000	Cash overdraft..........	$ 750
Inventories.............	45,000	Accounts payable	32,000

Prepare a statement of its current position, assuming that cash is obtained as indicated in each case below:

(a) Cash of $20,000 is borrowed on short-term notes and $18,000 is applied
   to the payment of creditors; accounts of $25,000 are pledged to secure
   the loan.
(b) Cash of $20,000 is advanced to the company by High Finance Co., the
   advance representing 80% of accounts assigned to it; assignment is made
   on a "with recourse" basis, and amounts collected in excess of the loan
   balance and charges accrue to the Bond Co.
(c) Cash of $20,000 is received on the sale of accounts receivable of $22,500
   on a "no recourse" basis.

5. Tom James received from Bob Williams, a customer, a 60-day, 8%
note for $3,000, dated November 6, 1971. On December 6, James had
Williams' note discounted at 4% and recorded the contingent liability.

The bank protested nonpayment of the note and charged the endorser with protest fees of $2.75 in addition to the amount of the note. On January 29, 1972, the note was collected with interest at 10% from the maturity date on the face value of the note. What entries would appear on James' books as a result of the foregoing?

6. Prior to 1973, the Johnson Company followed the percentage-of-sales method of estimating doubtful accounts. The following data is gathered by the accounting department.

	1969	1970	1971	1972
Total sales.................	$350,000	$400,000	$700,000	$1,200,000
Charge sales.................	200,000	320,000	650,000	1,200,000
Accounts receivable (end-of-year balance).................	62,000	78,000	120,000	250,0000
Allowance for doubtful accounts (end-of-year balance)........	1,000	5,000	3,000	20,000
Accounts written off..........	9,000	4,000	16,000	7,000

(a) What amount was charged to expense for 1970, 1971, and 1972?
(b) Compute the balance in the valuation account at the beginning of 1969 assuming there has been no change in the percentage of sales used over the four-year period.
(c) What explanation can be given for the fluctuating amount of write-off?
(d) Why do the actual write-offs fail to give the correct charge to expense?

7. The Hammond Lumber Company follows the procedure of charging doubtful accounts for 1% of all new sales. The following balances were found in using this method:

Year	Sales	Allowance for Doubtful Accounts (end-of-year balance)
1969	$3,530,000	$ 43,000
1970	3,800,000	71,000
1971	4,200,000	100,000
1972	4,395,000	132,000

(a) Compute the amount of accounts written off for the years 1970, 1971, and 1972.
(b) The external auditors are concerned with the growing amount in the allowance account. What action do you recommend that the auditors should take?
(c) What arguments might Hammond use to justify the balance in the valuation account? Allowance for Doubtful Accounts is the only accounts receivable valuation account used by Hammond.

8. On September 15, each note listed below is discounted by the bank at 8% for Red Owl Stores, Inc. Give the cash proceeds on each note.

(a) Customer's 60-day, $1,000, non-interest-bearing note dated August 16.
(b) Customer's 60-day, $1,500, 6% note dated August 31.
(c) Customer's 90-day, $1,276.20, 5% note dated September 10.
(d) Customer's 90-day, $1,512, 9% note dated August 1.

9. On June 1, 1972, J. P. Weller receives a $2,000 note from a customer on an overdue account. The note matures on August 30 and bears interest at 7%. On July 1, Weller discounts the note at 8% and applies the proceeds to the payment of creditors. On August 30, the customer is unable to make payment to the bank and the bank charges Weller's account for the maturity value of the note plus a $3 protest fee. On September 29, Weller accepts the customer's offer to cancel his liability with marketable securities valued at $2,050. Give all of the entries on Weller's books to record the foregoing.

PROBLEMS

7-1. Accounts receivable for the Toone Co. were reported on the balance sheet prepared at the end of 1972 as follows:

Accounts receivable..................		$53,100	
Less: Allowance for doubtful accounts.	$2,570		
Allowance for sales discount	830	3,400	$49,700

The company sells goods on terms of 3/10 e.o.m, n/30. At the end of the year accounts receivable are aged and the following percentages are applied in arriving at an estimate of the charge for doubtful accounts:

	Estimated Loss
Accounts not more than two months overdue..........	8%
Accounts more than two months but not more than six months overdue.......................................	25%
Accounts more than six months but not more than one year overdue......................................	60%
Accounts more than one year overdue................	100%

At the end of the year the company also anticipates sales discounts on all receivables not yet due for payment.

In 1973 the following transactions took place:

Sales on account.......................................	$362,852
Cash collected on account.............................	345,100
Cash discounts allowed................................	4,952
Sales returns and allowances..........................	2,320
Accounts written off..................................	1,720
Accounts previously written off but recovered...........	350

At the end of the year overdue accounts are as follows:

Accounts not more than two months overdue............	$7,200
Accounts more than two months but not more than six months overdue.......................................	2,100
Accounts more than six months but not more than one year overdue..	1,400
Accounts more than one year overdue..................	2,360

Instructions: (1) Give the entries required to record the transactions listed above and also to adjust the accounts.

(2) Calculate the balances for accounts receivable and the related allowances as of December 31, 1973, and show these as they will appear on the balance sheet.

7-2. The balance sheet for the Mathias Co. on December 31, 1972, includes the following receivable balances:

Notes receivable including accrued interest of $300.......	$32,600	
Less notes receivable discounted.....................	14,500	$18,100
Accounts receivable................................	$72,100	
Less allowance for doubtful accounts.................	5,100	67,000

Transactions during 1973 included the following:

(a) Sales on account were $525,100.
(b) Cash collected on accounts totaled $452,000, which included accounts of $93,000 on which cash discounts of 2% were allowed.
(c) Notes received in payment of accounts totaled $79,000.
(d) Notes receivable discounted as of December 31, 1971, were paid at maturity with the exception of one $8,000 note on which the company has to pay $8,090, which included interest and protest fees. It is expected that recovery will be made on this note in 1973.
(e) Customers' notes of $50,000 were discounted during the year, proceeds from their sale being $48,500. Of this total, $34,500 matured during the year without notice of protest.
(f) Customers' accounts of $7,090 were written off during the year as worthless.
(g) Recoveries of doubtful accounts written off in prior years were $850.
(h) Notes receivable collected during the year totaled $19,000 and interest collected was $1,250.
(i) On December 31, accrued interest on notes receivable was $630.
(j) Aging the accounts on December 31, 1972, revealed the need for an allowance for doubtful accounts of $4,800.
(k) Cash of $20,000 was borrowed from the bank, accounts receivable of $25,000 being pledged on the loan. Collections of $13,000 had been made on these receivables (included in the total given in transaction [b]) and this amount was applied on December 31, 1972, to payment of accrued interest on the loan of $400, and the balance to partial payment of the loan.

Instructions: (1) Prepare journal entries summarizing the transactions and information given above.

(2) Prepare a summary of current receivables for balance sheet presentation.

7-3. The following transactions affecting the accounts receivable of Lipstron Corporation took place during the year ended January 31, 1972:

Sales (cash and credit)...............................	$243,610
Cash received from credit customers (customers who paid $120,540 took advantage of the discount feature of the corporation's credit terms, 2/10, n/30)...............	125,609
Cash received from cash customers....................	82,748

Accounts receivable written off as worthless..............	$ 2,001
Credit memoranda issued to credit customers for sales returns and allowances...................................	23,402
Cash refunds given to cash customers for sales returns and allowances......................................	6,879
Recoveries on accounts receivable written off as uncollectible in prior periods (not included in cash amount stated above)	4,182

The following two balances were taken from the January 31, 1971 balance sheet:

Accounts receivable..................................	$39,227
Allowance for doubtful accounts......................	3,986

The corporation provides for its net uncollectible account losses by crediting Allowance for Doubtful Accounts for 1½% of net credit sales for the fiscal period.

Instructions: (1) Prepare the journal entries to record the transactions for the year ended January 31, 1972.

(2) Prepare the adjusting journal entry for estimated uncollectible accounts on January 31, 1972.

7-4. Economy Retailers assigns accounts of $40,000 to the A.A.A. Finance Co., receiving a 90% advance less a commission of 3% on the amount of the advance. Accounts of $20,000 are collected, this amount being forwarded to the finance company plus interest of $200. Accounts of $18,000 are collected; the balance owed is paid to the finance company, including interest of $280; of the remaining accounts receivable assigned, 75% is considered collectible and the balance is written off against Allowance for Doubtful Accounts.

Instructions: Prepare the entries required on the books of Economy Retailers to record the foregoing transactions.

7-5. The Broman Garment Company has run into financial difficulties. It decides to improve its working capital position by factoring one third of its accounts receivable and assigning one half of the remaining receivables to the local bank. Details of these arrangements were as follows:

Accounts receivable, 12–31–72.....$210,000	(before financing)
Allowance for doubtful accounts, 12–31–72...................	500 (credit)
Estimated uncollectibles, 12–31–72.	2% of accounts receivable balance
Factor discount rate.............	15% of gross receivables financed
Assignment withholding rate......	10% of gross receivables financed
Assignment service charge rate.....	2% amount advanced

Instructions: (1) Prepare the journal entries to record the receipt of cash from (a) factoring, and (b) assigning the accounts receivable.

(2) Prepare the journal entry to record the necessary adjustment to Allowance for Doubtful Accounts.

(3) Prepare the accounts receivable section of the balance sheet as it would appear after these transactions.

(4) What entry would be made on the company books of the Broman Garment Co. when factored accounts have been collected?

6-7-8

7-6. J. P. Loesch completed the following transactions, among others:

Oct. 1. Received a $5,000, 60-day, 9% note dated October 1 from S. L. Sorenson, a customer.
    20. Received a $1,500, 90-day, non-interest-bearing note dated October 19 from E. L. Manwaring as settlement for unpaid balance of $1,470.
    21. Had Sorenson's note discounted at the bank at 7%.
Nov. 3. Had Manwaring's note discounted at the bank at 8%.
    21. Received from B. C. Marshall, a customer, a $3,000, 90-day, 8% note dated November 1, payable to Marshall and signed by the Beneficial Corporation. Upon endorsement, gave the customer credit for the maturity value of the note less discount at 7%.
    25. Received a $3,000, 60-day, 6% note dated November 24 from G. H. Robinson, a customer.
Dec. 1. Received notice from the bank that Sorenson's note was not paid at maturity. Protest fees of $2.50 were charged by the bank.
    16. Received payment from Sorenson on his dishonored note, including interest at 9% on the face value of the note from the maturity date.

Instructions: (1) Give the journal entries to record the above transactions, showing contingent liabilities in the accounts. (Show data used in calculations with each entry.)
   (2) Give the adjusting entries that would be necessary on December 31.
   (3) Indicate the adjustments that may appropriately be reversed.

7-7. The following are some of the transactions completed by W. C. Thompson over a three-month period:

May 10. Received from P. M. Cory, a customer, a $2,000, 60-day, 9% note dated May 9.
    11. Received from B. L. Campbell on account, a $3,000, 90-day, 8% note dated May 10.
    20. Had Campbell's note discounted at the bank at 10%.
    24. Had Cory's note discounted at the bank at 10%.
June 3. Received a $1,950, 30-day, non-interest-bearing note dated June 1 from N. P. Gill, crediting the customer's account at face value.
     7. Had Gill's note discounted at the bank at 8%.
    28. Received from M. L. Wade, a customer, a $300, 60-day, 6% note dated June 13 and made by the William's Company. Gave the customer credit for the maturity value of the note less discount at 8%.
    29. Received a $2,700, 15-day, 7% note dated June 29 from L. Smith, a customer.
July 10. Received notice from the bank that Cory's note was not paid at maturity. Protest fees of $2.50 were charged by the bank.
    22. Received a $12,000, 60-day, 8% note dated July 22, from R. S. Russell, a customer.
    27. Received payment on Smith's note, including interest at 10%, the legal rate, on the face value from the maturity date.

Instructions: (1) Give the entries to record the above transactions showing the contingent liabilities in the accounts. (Show data used in calculations with each entry.)
   (2) Give the necessary adjusting entries on July 31.
   (3) Indicate the adjustments that may appropriately be reversed.

7-8. The Regis Company wishes to discount two notes receivable arising from the sale of merchandise. Both notes have a face amount of $100,000 and are due in one year. Note A carries no provision for interest and was reported at its present value using an interest rate of 6%. Note B is to be paid with interest at 6%. The bank rate in discounting notes is 6%.

Instructions: Prepare the necessary journal entries to record the discounting of the notes under each of the following assumptions. Notes receivable are originally recorded at their present values assuming a 6% interest rate.

(1) Assuming that the notes were discounted immediately upon receipt.

(2) Assuming that the notes were discounted nine months prior to maturity.

7-9. On December 31, 1972, the notes receivable account of the Angus Company consisted of the following notes:

Trade notes receivable, considered good:	
Due in 12 months or less............................	$ 72,000
Due in more than 12 months........................	12,000
Trade notes receivable, considered 80% collectible:	
Due in 12 months or less............................	41,000
Trade notes receivable, considered worthless.............	2,100
Trade notes receivable, considered good, and discounted with the First National Bank (with offsetting credits to Notes Receivable Discounted). Of these notes, $21,000 have been paid..	65,000
Notes receivable accepted on sale of diesel equipment (fixed asset), $18,000. This amount was payable $500 monthly; and the purchaser was considered a good credit risk......	18,000
Note receivable of Dale Angus, president, payable on demand. This note was received in payment of his subscription to 1,000 shares of common stock of Angus Company at par. Upon receipt of this note, the corporation issued a certificate of capital stock for 1,000 shares.............	100,000
	$310,100

Instructions: Indicate how each of the company's notes receivable would be classified on the balance sheet of December 31, 1972.

7-10. Current assets for the Klein Company are listed as follows on the balance sheet prepared on December 31, 1972:

Current assets:	
Cash...	$ 11,600
Marketable securities.......................................	32,575
Notes receivable...	16,900
Accounts receivable..	74,485
Merchandise inventory.....................................	82,300
	$217,860

An examination of the books revealed the following information concerning the current assets:

Cash included:

Petty cash funds (of which $490 is cash, $130 is in the form of employees' IOU's, and $30 is in the form of postage stamps)	$ 650
Customers' checks not yet deposited	2,100
Demand deposit at the First National Bank	8,200
An overdraft at the Central City Bank	(300)
Customer's non-interest-bearing note (due January 2, 1973) deposited at the First National Bank for collection	950
	$11,600

Marketable securities included:

Glendale Company Common (a subsidiary company), reported at cost	$16,155
Klein Company Preferred (treasury stock), reported at cost	12,100
9% Hamilton Company Bonds (interest payable January 1 and July 1), $4,000 face value, purchased September 1, 1972 as a temporary investment, reported at cost plus accrued interest to date of purchase	4,320
	$32,575

Notes receivable included:

Customers' notes (due in 1973)	$ 8,750
Glendale Company note (due March 1, 1973)	6,000
Note receivable from sale of equipment (due July 1, 1974)	6,150
Notes receivable discounted (customers' notes)	(4,000)
	$16,900

Accounts receivable included:

Creditors' accounts with debit balances	$ 1,000
Customers' accounts (regular)	37,770
Dividends receivable on investments	500
Deposit on equipment (ordered for delivery in December, 1974)	1,000
Installment accounts receivable ($17,800 due in 1973; $9,200 due in 1974)	27,000
Interest receivable on bond investment	120
Interest receivable on notes	270
Receivables from consignees (representing the merchandise at cost transferred to consignees and still unsold on December 31, 1972)	2,100
Refundable income taxes of prior periods (believed to be collectible in 1973)	1,250
Travel advances to employees	975
Subscriptions receivable on capital stock (due in 1974)	4,500
Allowance for doubtful accounts (on regular and installment accounts)	(2,000)
	$74,485

Merchandise inventory (representing a physical count of goods on hand), at cost	$82,300

Instructions: Revise the current asset section of the balance sheet presenting individual items appropriately included therein in a proper manner. Prepare schedules stating what disposition was made of those items excluded in the revised presentation.

7-11. The Bondale Corporation sold equipment on the installment basis. A balance sheet prepared December 31, 1971, indicated the following information under the heading "Notes and accounts receivable."

Installment notes assigned to MPT Corporation, including amounts due after one year........	$190,268	
Less amounts due MPT....................	82,967	$107,301
Installment notes, unassigned, including amounts due after one year.......................		407,071
Accounts receivable.........................		59,155
		$573,527
Less:		
Unearned interest on installment notes.......	$ 92,305	
Allowance for doubtful accounts............	66,200	158,505
Net balance.................................		$415,022

During 1972, the following transactions occurred:

(a) New installment sales of $1,500,000 were made during the year. Included in these notes was $125,000 of accrued interest.

(b) $550,000 of these notes were assigned to MPT Corporation. Proceeds from MPT amounted to $450,000; an interest charge of $25,000 was made for the advance and added to the amount owed MPT.

(c) Interest earned on installment loans during 1972 amounted to $142,000.

(d) Collections on assigned notes were $520,000 of which $375,000 was paid to MPT.

(e) Assigned notes for $26,500 were written off as uncollectible; $1,500 unearned interest charge was included in the accounts written off.

(f) Estimated uncollectible notes as of December 31, 1972, were $69,200 exclusive of unearned interest charges.

Instructions: Prepare journal entries for 1972 to record the above summarized transactions.

7-12. The Eastern Gas Company follows the practice of cycle billing in order to minimize peak work loads for its clerical employees. All customers are billed monthly on various dates, except in those cases when the meter readers are unable to enter the premises to obtain a reading.

The following information for the year ended September 30, 1972, is presented by the company:

		Customers Billed		Customers
Cycle	Billing Period	Number	Amount	Not Billed
1	Aug. 7–Sept. 5 (inclusive).....	2760	$13,800.00	324
2	Aug. 12–Sept. 10 (inclusive).....	3426	13,704.00	411
3	Aug. 17–Sept. 15 (inclusive).....	3265	14,692.50	335
4	Aug. 22–Sept. 20 (inclusive).....	2630	12,492.50	370
5	Aug. 27–Sept. 25 (inclusive).....	3132	13,311.00	468

You are further advised that all customers have been billed for prior periods and that the company's experience shows that charges for those customers whose meters were not read average the same amount as the charges for the customers billed in their cycle. In addition, the company assumes that the customers' usage will be uniform from month to month.

Instructions: Compute the unbilled revenues of the company as of September 30, 1972, arising from cycles No. 1 and No. 3. (*Do not* compute revenues from cycles 2, 4 and 5.) (AICPA adapted)

7-13. The Comity Loan Company is engaged in the consumer finance business. Prior to 1972 the company followed the direct write-off method of recording uncollectible loans. The company also provided a reserve for uncollectible loans by an appropriation of retained earnings.

During 1972 the Comity Loan Company decided to change to the allowance method of recognizing losses due to uncollectible loans. Permission was received to use this method for income tax purposes. The books, however, were continued on the write-off method for the full year of 1972. An analysis of the company's loss experience showed that 4% of the loans receivable at the end of each year prove uncollectible and are written off in the following year.

The following are condensed trial balances:

The Comity Loan Company
Trial Balances
December 31, 1972 and 1971

	December 31, 1972		December 31, 1971 (Post-closing)	
Cash........................	49,300		86,500	
Loans receivable..............	712,500		687,500	
Other assets..................	27,000		25,000	
Liabilities other than income taxes		520,700		543,500
Income taxes payable..........		21,300		20,000
Capital stock.................		100,000		100,000
Retained earnings.............		108,000		108,000
Reserve for uncollectible loans...		27,500		27,500
Dividends paid...............	10,000			
Interest income...............		165,000		
Operating expenses............	49,500			
Uncollectible loans written off...	13,400			
Interest expense...............	59,500			
Income taxes.................	21,300			
	942,500	942,500	799,000	799,000

Instructions: (Assume that the current income tax rate is 50%).

(1) Prepare the formal journal entries at December 31, 1972, to record the change in accounting methods for 1972.

(2) Prepare a formal income and retained earnings statement for the year ended December 31, 1972.

(AICPA adapted)

7-14. Hoffman Factors, Inc., was incorporated December 31, 1971. The capital stock of the company consists of 100,000 shares of $10 par value each, all of which was paid in at par. The company was organized for the purpose of factoring the accounts receivable of various businesses requiring this service.

Hoffman Factors, Inc., charges a commission to its clients of 2% of all receivables factored and assumes all credit risks. Besides the commission, an additional 10% of gross receivables is withheld on all purchases and is credited to Client Retainer. This retainer is used for merchandise returns, etc., made by customers of the clients for which a credit memo would be due. Payments are made to the clients by Hoffman Factors, Inc., at the end of each month to adjust the retainer so that it equals 10% of the unpaid receivables at the month's end.

Based on the collection experience of other factoring companies in this area, officials of Hoffman Factors, Inc., have decided to make monthly provisions to Allowance for Doubtful Accounts based on $\frac{1}{4}\%$ of all receivables purchased during the month.

The company also decided to recognize commission income on only the factored receivables which have been collected; however, for bookkeeping simplicity all commissions are originally credited to Commission Income and an adjustment is made to Unearned Commissions at the end of each quarter based on 2% of receivables then outstanding.

Operations of the company during the first quarter of 1972 resulted in the following:

Accounts receivable factored:

January	$200,000
February	400,000
March	300,000

Collections on the above receivables totaled $700,000.

General and administrative expenses paid during the period:

Salaries	$5,000
Office rent	900
Advertising	500
Equipment rent	1,600
Miscellaneous	1,000

On February 1, 1972, a three-month 6% bank loan was obtained for $500,000 with interest payable at maturity.

For the first three months of the year, the company rented all of its office furniture and equipment; however, on March 31, 1972, it purchased various equipment at a cost of $5,000, liability for which had not been recorded as of March 31.

Instructions: (1) Give all of the entries necessary to record the above transactions and to close the books as of March 31, 1972. (Disregard all taxes.)

(2) Prepare a balance sheet and an income statement as of March 31, 1972.

(AICPA adapted)

chapter 8

inventories - cost procedures

The term *inventories* is a designation for goods that are held for sale in the normal course of business, as well as for goods that are in production or are to be placed in production. Practically all tangible items fall into this classification at one time or another. Gasoline, oil, and automotive supplies are included in the inventory of a service station; crops and livestock are included in the inventory of a farmer; machinery and equipment are included in the inventory of a manufacturer producing such items for sale. It is the sale of inventories that normally provides a business with its chief source of revenue.

Inventories represent one of the most active elements in business operations, being continuously acquired, converted, and resold. A large part of a company's resources is frequently tied up in goods that are purchased or manufactured. The cost of such goods must be recorded, grouped, and summarized during the period. At the end of the period, costs must be allocated to current activities and to future activities. Such allocation normally occupies a central role in the measurement of periodic operating results as well as in the determination of financial position. Failure to allocate costs properly can result in serious distortions of financial progress and position.

Accounting for inventory costs presents a number of theoretical and practical problems. Members of the accounting profession have directed much thought to these problems in recent years, but there is still no general agreement on many important matters. This and the next two chapters consider these problems.

Classes of inventories

The term *merchandise inventory* is generally applied to goods held by a merchandising concern, either wholesale or retail, when such goods have been acquired in a condition for resale. The terms *raw materials, goods in process,* and *finished goods* refer to the inventories of a manufacturing concern. The latter items require description.

Raw materials. *Raw materials* are those tangible goods that are acquired for use in the productive process. Raw materials may be obtained directly from natural sources. Ordinarily, however, raw materials are acquired from other companies and represent the finished products of the companies from which they were purchased. For example, newsprint is the finished product of the paper mill but represents raw material to the printer who acquires it.

Although the term raw materials can be used broadly to cover all of the materials used in manufacturing, this designation is frequently restricted to materials that will be physically incorporated in the products being manufactured. The term *factory supplies,* or *manufacturing supplies,* is then used to refer to auxiliary materials, that is, materials that although necessary in the productive process are not directly incorporated in the products. Oils, fuels, cleaning supplies, etc., fall into this grouping since these items are not incorporated in a product but simply facilitate production as a whole; paint, nails, bolts, etc., although physically embodied in the final product, are normally of such minor significance as to warrant inclusion within the auxiliary grouping. Raw materials that can be directly associated with the production of certain goods are frequently referred to as *direct materials*; factory supplies are referred to as *indirect materials.*

Although factory supplies may be summarized separately, they should be reported as a part of the company's inventories since they will ultimately be applied to the productive process. Factory supplies should be distinguished from other supplies that make contributions to the delivery, sales, and general administrative functions of the enterprise. Such other supplies should not be reported as part of the inventories but as prepaid expenses.

Goods in process. *Goods in process,* alternately referred to as *work in process,* consists of materials partly processed and requiring further work before they can be sold. This inventory is considered to be made up of three cost elements: (1) *direct materials,* (2) *direct labor,* and (3) *manufacturing overhead* or *burden.* The cost of materials that can be directly identified with the goods in production is included under (1). The cost of labor that can be directly identified with goods in production is included under (2). The portion of manufacturing overhead assignable to goods still in production forms the third element in cost.

Manufacturing overhead consists of all manufacturing costs other than direct materials and direct labor. It includes factory supplies and labor not directly identified with the production of specific products. It also includes general manufacturing costs such as depreciation, maintenance, repairs, property taxes, insurance, and light, heat, and power, as well as a reasonable share of the managerial costs other than those relating solely to the selling and administrative functions of the business. Overhead may be designated as *fixed, variable,* or *semivariable.* Overhead charges that remain constant in amount regardless of the volume of production are referred to as fixed. Depreciation, insurance, rent, and property taxes normally fall into this category. Charges that fluctuate in proportion to the volume of production are called variable. Indirect materials, indirect labor, and repairs vary with production. Some charges vary, but the variations are not in direct proportion to the volume. These charges have both fixed and variable components and are designated as semivariable items. Factory supervision is an example of a semivariable item when it is fixed within a certain range of production but changes when production is not within this range.

Finished goods. *Finished goods* are the manufactured products awaiting sale. The cost of the finished product consists of the direct materials, direct labor, and manufacturing overhead costs assigned to it. Finished parts that were purchased and that are to be used in the production of the finished product are normally classed as raw materials; finished parts that are held for purposes of sale may be reported as finished goods.

Inventories in the measurement of income

When goods that are purchased or manufactured are all sold within a fiscal period, the determination of the gross profit on sales is a simple matter. The total cost of goods purchased or manufactured is also the cost of goods sold that is properly chargeable to revenue. Such a situation, however, is seldom found in practice. Normally a part of the goods acquired remains on hand at the end of the period. A value must be assigned to these goods. This value is subtracted from the total merchandise acquisition costs and is carried into the subsequent period to be charged against future revenue. Adequate records are required in providing cost data for statement purposes. Such records are also required for the proper internal control of goods on hand.

Two classes of questions arise in the determination of the inventory to be reported on the statements: (1) what items are properly included in the inventory? and (2) what values are to be assigned to such items?

Inventory systems

Quantities of inventories on hand are ascertained either through a *periodic system* that calls for *physical inventories* at the end of each period, or a *perpetual system* that calls for *perpetual* or *book inventories.*

The periodic system requires counting, measuring, or weighing goods at the end of the period to determine the quantities on hand. Values are then assigned to such quantities in arriving at the portion of the recorded costs to be carried forward.

The perpetual inventory system requires the maintenance of records that offer a running summary of inventory items on hand. Individual accounts are kept for each class of goods. Inventory increases and decreases are recorded in the individual accounts, the resulting balances representing the amounts on hand. In the manufacturing organization, a perpetual system applied to inventories calls for recording the full movement of goods through individual accounts for raw materials, goods in process, and finished goods. Perpetual records may be kept in terms of quantities only or in terms of both quantities and costs.

When the perpetual system is employed, physical counts of the units on hand should be made at least once a year to confirm the balances that are found on the books. The frequency of physical inventories will vary depending upon the nature of the goods, their rate of turnover, and the degree of internal control. A plan for continuous counting of inventory items on a rotation basis is frequently employed. Variations between the book record and the amounts actually on hand resulting from errors in recording, shrinkage, breakage, theft, and other causes should be recognized, and the book inventories should be brought into agreement with the physical count with offsetting charges and credits to an inventory adjustment account. The explanation for the discrepancy will determine whether the inventory adjustment balance should be regarded as an adjustment to cost of goods sold, as an operating expense, or as an extraordinary item on the income statement. Normal adjustments for shrinkage and breakage are recorded as adjustments to cost of goods sold. Abnormal shortages or thefts may be reported separately as operating expenses or as extraordinary losses.

Practically all large trading and manufacturing enterprises, as well as many relatively small organizations, have adopted the perpetual inventory system as an integral part of their record keeping and internal control. This system offers a continuous check and control over inventories as well as immediate data concerning inventory position. Purchasing and production planning are facilitated, adequate supplies on hand are assured, and losses incurred through damage and theft are fully disclosed. The additional costs of maintaining such a system are usually well repaid by the services that are provided to management through its adoption.

Items to be included in inventory

As a general rule, goods should be included in the inventory of the party holding title. The "passing of title" is a legal term designating the point at which ownership changes. There are instances where the legal rule may be waived for practical reasons or because of certain limitations that are found in its application. When the circumstances are such that the rule of passing of title does not need to be observed, there should be appropriate disclosure on the statements of the special practice that is followed and the factors that support such practice. Application of the legal test under a number of special circumstances is described in the following paragraphs.

Goods in transit. When terms of sale are "f.o.b. shipping point," title passes to the buyer with the loading of goods at the point of shipment. Application of the legal rule to a year-end shipment calls for recognition of a sale and an accompanying decrease in goods on hand on the books of the seller. On the other hand, the buyer should recognize such *goods in transit* as a purchase and an accompanying inventory increase even though there is no physical possession at this time. A determination of the goods in transit as of the year-end is made by a review of the incoming orders during the early part of the new period. The purchases records may be kept open beyond the fiscal period to permit the recognition of goods in transit as of the end of the period, or goods in transit may be recorded by means of an adjusting entry. Although no objection to the application of the legal rule can be raised by a seller, the buyer, in the interests of expediency, may prefer to ignore such a rule and employ "receipt" as a basis for the recognition of a purchase and the related inventory increase. The latter approach is not objectionable when amounts in transit are not material and the inclusion of such items before their receipt and acceptance offers practical difficulties.

When terms of a sale are "f.o.b. destination," application of the legal test calls for no recognition of the transaction until goods are received by the buyer. In this case, it is the seller who may prefer to ignore the legal rule and employ "shipment" as a basis for booking a sale and the accompanying inventory decrease. In view of the practical difficulties involved in ascertaining whether goods have reached their destination at year-end, application of a "shipment" rule is not objectionable under normal circumstances.

Segregated goods. When goods are prepared on special order and segregated for shipment, title may pass with such segregation. When goods are segregated at the end of the period and title has passed, the vendor may properly recognize a sale and exclude *segregated goods* from his inventory, while the vendee may properly recognize both a purchase and an inventory increase. Frequently, one encounters many practical problems in arriving at the portion of the inventory that is segregated as well as perplexing legal problems in defining the precise status of such goods. These difficulties normally lead to the adoption of a policy whereby entries for both sale and purchase await formal shipment of goods by the vendor.

Goods on consignment. Goods are frequently transferred to dealers on a consignment basis, the consignor retaining title to such goods until their sale by the consignee. Until the goods are sold and cash or a receivable can be recognized, the goods should continue to be reported as a part of the inventory of the consignor. *Consigned goods* are properly reported at the sum of their cost and the handling and shipping costs involved in their transfer to the consignee. The goods may be separately designated on the balance sheet as "Merchandise on Consignment." The consignee does not own the consigned goods; hence he reports neither consigned goods nor an obligation for such goods on his financial statements. Other merchandise owned by a business but in the possession of others, such as goods in the hands of salesmen and agents, goods held by customers on approval, and goods held by others for storage, processing, or shipment, should also be shown as a part of the ending inventory of the owner.

Conditional and installment sales. Conditional sales and installment sales contracts may provide for a retention of title by the seller until the sales price is fully recovered. Under these circumstances, it would be possible for the seller to continue to show the goods to which he has title, reduced by the buyer's equity in such goods as established by collections from the latter; the buyer, in turn, can report an equity in the goods accruing through payments that have already been made. However, when the possibilities of returns and default are negligible, the test of passing of title is generally relinquished and the transaction is recorded in terms of the expected outcome: the seller, anticipating completion of the contract and the ultimate passing of title, recognizes the transaction as a regular sale involving deferred collections; the buyer, intending to comply with the contract and acquire title, recognizes the transaction as a regular purchase.

The Accounting Principles Board has supported this policy by discouraging use of the installment sales method for book purposes.

Inventory valuation

In viewing the inventory in its dual position as (1) a value that is reported on the income statement in developing charges properly applicable to current revenue and (2) a value reported on the balance sheet that represents the charges properly assignable to future revenues, cost has been accepted as the primary basis for inventory valuation. A marked change in the value of the inventory between the purchase date and the date of inventory raises the question as to whether some recognition should be given to current inventory replacement values. With a rise in prices, accountants generally answer this question in the negative, insisting that income must await sale of the goods; with a decline in prices, however, there is wide support for recognizing such decline by applying the "cost or market, whichever is lower" valuation procedure. In a few special instances full departure from cost and the use of a sales price or a modified sales price basis is considered acceptable.

Income measurement rather than balance sheet valuation is generally regarded as the major criterion in accounting for inventories. The American Institute of Certified Public Accountants has taken this position. The AICPA has also held that although inventories should be reported at cost in keeping with the cost principle, modifications in cost may be appropriate under certain circumstances. The Committee on Accounting Procedure, in discussing inventory pricing, has expressed the following view:

> . . . In accounting for the goods in the inventory at any point of time, the major objective is the matching of appropriate costs against revenues in order that there may be a proper determination of the realized income. Thus, the inventory at any given date is the balance of costs applicable to goods on hand remaining after the matching of absorbed costs with concurrent revenues. This balance is appropriately carried to future periods provided it does not exceed an amount properly chargeable against the revenues expected to be obtained from ultimate disposition of the goods carried forward.[1]

In contrast with this position, the American Accounting Association's Special Committee on Inventories has felt that market value for inventories is also very important, and that multi-column statements should be prepared that report both cost and market valuations. This view was

---

[1] *Accounting Research Bulletin No. 43*, "Restatement and Revision of Accounting Research Bulletins" (New York: American Institute of Certified Public Accountants, 1953), Ch. 4, par. 4

also supported in the AAA's *A Statement of Basic Accounting Theory*.[1] There has been little support of these recommendations within the AICPA up to the present.

Inventory cost methods

The principal inventory valuation methods and their special applicabilities will be considered in detail. Attention is directed in this chapter to the measurement of cost when cost is required for inventory valuation as well as when cost is to be used as the first step in the development of a lower of cost or market value.

Determination of cost. The determination of the cost of the inventory may be no simple matter. First, it involves a determination of the expenditures that actually entered into the cost of the goods that were acquired. Second, it involves the application of a method for relating the different costs of the goods acquired to periodic revenue.

Inventory cost consists of all expenditures, both direct and indirect, relating to inventory acquisition, preparation, and placement for sale. In the case of raw materials or goods acquired for resale, cost includes, in addition to the purchase price, buying, freight, receiving, storage, and all other expenditures incurred to the time goods are ready for sale. Certain expenditures can be traced to specific acquisitions or can be allocated to inventory items in some equitable manner. Other expenditures may be relatively small and difficult to allocate. Such items are normally excluded in the calculation of inventory cost and are thus charged in full against current revenue.

The charges to be included in the cost of manufactured products have already been mentioned. Proper accounting for materials, labor, and manufacturing overhead items and their identification with goods in process and finished goods inventories may be best achieved through adoption of a cost accounting system designed to meet the needs of the business unit. Overhead at a predetermined rate may be assigned to goods being produced during the period. At the end of the period, when the actual overhead is determined, appropriate adjustments are made for any amount of underapplied or overapplied overhead. Certain costs relating to the acquisition or the manufacture of goods may be considered abnormal and may be excluded in arriving at inventory cost. For example, costs arising from idle capacity, excessive spoilage, and reprocessing are normally considered extraordinary items chargeable to

---

[1] *A Statement of Basic Accounting Theory* (Evanston, Illinois: American Accounting Association, 1966), p. 11.

current revenue. Only those portions of general and administrative costs that are clearly related to procurement or production should be included in inventory cost.

In practice, companies take different postions in classifying inventoriable costs. For example, costs of the purchasing department, costs of accounting for manufacturing activites, and costs of pensions for production personnel may be found either as parts of inventoriable costs or as direct deductions from revenue.

Discounts as reductions in cost. Discounts that are treated as a reduction of cost in recording the acquisition of goods should similarly be treated as a reduction in the cost assigned to the inventory. *Trade discounts* are discounts that convert a printed price list to the prices actually to be charged to the particular buyer. Cost, then, is list price less the trade discount; purchases should be reported at such cost with no accounting recognition given to the discount, and the inventory should be stated on an equivalent basis. *Cash discounts* are reductions in prices allowed only upon payment of invoices within a limited period. Inventory treatment depends upon whether cash discounts are regarded as a reduction in cost or as a source of revenue. If cash discounts are treated as a subtraction from purchases, the inventory balance should be correspondingly reduced; if cash discounts are reported as other revenue, inventories should be reported at invoice cost without reference to the discounts taken.

Treatment of purchases discounts as revenue is frequently found in practice and is defended on the grounds that the buyer takes special measures in liquidating a claim in advance of its due date to secure such discounts. There may be expenses attached to raising capital for the advance liquidation of debts. Financial management is charged with such expenses; discounts earned, then, may be properly credited to financial management and matched against such expenses.

Serious objection, however, can be raised to the foregoing practice wherein revenue arises from the act of buying. Sound accounting provides for income recognition from the sale of goods or services, not from their purchase. The buyer is offered goods at a net or cash price, and no more than this actually needs to be paid. Settlement is almost invariably made on a cash basis in view of the difference between the cash discount and the cost of borrowing money to make prompt payment. In fact, when settlement is not made within the discount period, a failure on the part of financial management is indicated either through carelessness in considering payment alternatives or through financial inability to avoid the extra charge.

Treatment of purchases discounts taken as a subtraction from purchases recognizes the discounts as an adjustment in purchase price. But this practice offers only partial recognition of the cost view just developed. Full agreement with the preceding analysis calls for recording purchases net and recognizing any amounts paid in excess of these amounts as Purchases Discounts Lost, a financial management expense item. When such a practice is to be followed, two methods may be employed: (1) accounts payable may be reported net or (2) accounts payable may be reported at the gross invoice price with a payable offset balance or liability valuation account reporting the purchases discounts available. The two methods are illustrated below.

Transaction	Accounts Payable Reported Net	Accounts Payable Reported Gross
Purchase of merchandise priced at $2,500 less trade discount of 30%–20% and a cash discount of 2%: $2,500 less 30% = $1,750 $1,750 less 20% = $1,400 $1,400 less 2% = $1,372	Purchases (or Inventory).....1,372 Accounts Payable........ 1,372	Purchases (or Inventory)...1,372 Allowance for Purchases Discount .... 28 Accounts Payable........ 1,400
(a) Assuming payment of the invoice within discount period.	Accounts Payable.....1,372 Cash........... 1,372	Accounts Payable.....1,400 Allowance for Purchases Discount ...... 28 Cash.......... 1,372
(b) Assuming payment of the invoice after discount period.	Accounts Payable.....1,372 Purchases Discounts Lost........ 28 Cash.......... 1,400	Accounts Payable.....1,400 Cash.......... 1,400 Purchases Discounts Lost........ 28 Allowance for Purchases Discount 28
(c) Required adjustment at the end of the period assuming that the invoice was not paid and the discount period has lapsed.	Purchases Discounts Lost........ 28 Accounts Payable........ 28	Purchases Discounts Lost........ 28 Allowance for Purchases Discount 28

Although recording purchases net and recognizing cash discounts lost as an expense is of obvious merit, it has failed to gain wide adoption. Chief objection is made on practical grounds. Use of this method calls for converting gross amounts stated on invoices into net amounts relating to individual acquisitions and using converted values throughout the accounting for inventories. This is normally less convenient than accounting in terms of gross invoice charges.

Specific identification of costs with inventory items. Revenue may be charged for goods sold on the basis of identified costs of the specific items sold. Such practice calls for the identification of a cost with each item acquired. When perpetual inventories are maintained, the sale of goods calls for the transfer of articles and their identified costs to the cost of goods sold. When a system of physical inventories is maintained, goods on hand require identification with specific invoices. In each instance, costs related to units sold are reported as cost of goods sold and costs identified with goods on hand remain to be reported as the ending inventory.

Although such identification procedure may be considered a highly satisfactory approach in matching costs with revenues in view of its objectivity and adherence to empirical fact, the practice may be difficult or impossible to apply or may be considered inadequate in view of special existing conditions. When an inventory is composed of a great many items, some being similar items acquired at different times and at different prices, cost identification procedures may prove to be slow, burdensome, and costly. When identical items have been acquired at different times, their identities may be lost and cost identification thus denied. Furthermore, when units are identical and interchangeable, this method opens the doors to possible profit manipulation through the choice of particular units for delivery. Finally, marked changes in costs during a period may warrant charges to revenue on a basis other than past identifiable costs.

Traditional cost flow methods

When specific identification procedures are considered inappropriate, it is necessary to adopt some assumption with respect to the flow of costs that is to be associated with the movement of goods. Three methods, each with a different assumption as to an orderly flow of costs, have achieved widest application. These are: (1) *first-in, first-out*, (2) *weighted average*, and (3) *last-in, first-out*.

First-in, first-out method. The first-in, first-out method (*fifo* method) is based on the assumption that costs should be charged out in the order in which incurred. Inventories are thus stated in terms of most recent costs. To illustrate the application of this method, assume the data shown at the top of the next page.

January	1	Inventory	200 units at $10	$ 2,000
	12	Purchase	400 units at 12	4,800
	26	Purchase	300 units at 11	3,300
	30	Purchase	100 units at 12	1,200
	Total		1,000	$11,300

A physical inventory on January 31 shows 300 units on hand. The inventory would be considered to be composed of the most recent costs as follows:

Most recent purchase, Jan. 30	100 units at $12	$1,200
Next most recent purchase, Jan. 26	200 units at 11	2,200
Total	300	$3,400

If the ending inventory is recorded at $3,400, cost of goods sold is $7,900 ($11,300 − $3,400), and revenue is charged with the earliest costs.

When perpetual inventory accounts are maintained, a form similar to that illustrated below is kept to record the cost of units issued and the cost relating to the goods on hand. The first column is used for memorandum entries reporting amounts ordered. Remaining columns show the quantities and values relating to goods acquired, goods issued, and balances on hand. It should be observed that identical values for physical and perpetual inventories are obtained when fifo is applied.

COMMODITY X (FIFO)

Ordered	Date	Received		Issued		Balance	
Memo-	Jan. 1					200 at $10	2,000
randum	12	400 at $12	4,800			200 at $10	2,000
						400 at $12	4,800
Entries	16			200 at $10	2,000		
				300 at $12	3,600	100 at $12	1,200
	26	300 at $11	3,300			100 at $12	1,200
						300 at $11	3,300
	29			100 at $12	1,200		
				100 at $11	1,100	200 at $11	2,200
	30	100 at $12	1,200			200 at $11	2,200
						100 at $12	1,200

Weighted average method. The weighted average method is based on the assumption that goods should be charged out at an average cost, such average being influenced by the number of units acquired at each price. Inventories are stated at the same weighted average cost. Assuming the cost data in the preceding section, the weighted average cost of a physical inventory of 300 units on January 31 would be as follows:

January	1	Inventory	200 units at $10	$ 2,000
	12	Purchase	400 units at 12	4,800
	26	Purchase	300 units at 11	3,300
	30	Purchase	100 units at 12	1,200
		Total	1,000	$11,300

Weighted average cost: $11,300 ÷ 1,000, or $11.30.
Ending inventory: 300 units at $11.30 = $3,390.

If the ending inventory is recorded at a cost of $3,390, cost of goods sold is $7,910 ($11,300 − $3,390), and revenue is charged with a weighted average cost.

Calculations above were made for costs of one month. Calculations could be developed in terms of data for a quarter or for a year.

When perpetual inventories are maintained but the costs of units issued are not recorded until the end of a period, a weighted average cost for the period may be calculated at that time and the accounts may be credited for the cost of total units issued. Frequently, however, costs relating to issues are recorded currently, and it is necessary to calculate costs on the basis of the weighted average on the date of issue. This requires the calculation of a new weighted average cost immediately after the receipt of each additional lot of merchandise. This method, which involves successive average recalculations, is referred to as a *moving average method*. The use of this method is illustrated below.

On January 12 the new unit cost of $11.33 was found by dividing $6,800, the total cost, by 600, the number of units on hand. Then on

COMMODITY X (MOVING AVERAGE)

Ordered	Date	Received		Issued		Balance	
Memo-	Jan. 1					200 at $10.00	2,000
randum	12	400 at $12	4,800			600 at $11.33	6,800
Entries	16			500 at $11.33	5,665	100 at $11.35	1,135
	26	300 at $11	3,300			400 at $11.09	4,435
	29			200 at $11.09	2,218	200 at $11.09	2,217
	30	100 at $12	1,200			300 at $11.39	3,417

January 16, the dollar balance, $1,135, represented the previous balance, $6,800, less $5,665, the cost assigned to the 500 units issued on this date. New unit costs were calculated on January 26 and 30 when additional units were acquired.

It should be observed that with successive recalculations of cost and the use of such different costs during the period, the cost identified with the ending inventory will differ from that determined when cost is assigned to the ending inventory in terms of the average cost for all goods available during the period. A physical inventory and use of the weighted average method resulted in a value for the ending inventory of $3,390; a perpetual inventory and use of the moving average method resulted in a value for the ending inventory of $3,417.

Last-in, first-out method. The last-in, first-out method (*lifo* method) is based on the assumption that the latest costs should be the first that are charged out. Inventories are thus stated in terms of earliest costs. Assuming the cost data in the preceding section, a physical inventory of 300 units on January 31 would have a cost as follows:

Earliest costs relating to goods, January 1	200 units at $10	$2,000
Next earliest cost, January 12	100 units at $12	1,200
Total	300	$3,200

If the ending inventory is recorded at a cost of $3,200, then cost of goods sold is $8,100 ($11,300 − $3,200), and revenue is charged with the latest costs.

When perpetual inventories are maintained but the cost of units issued is not recorded until the end of the period, the most recent costs relating to the total units issued may be determined and the inventory account credited for this cost. Cost, then, is the same as reported above. Frequently, however, costs relating to issues are recorded currently, and it is necessary to calculate costs on a last-in, first-out basis using the cost data shown on the date of issue. This is illustrated on the next page.

It should be noted that in applying lifo, physical and perpetual inventory values are not usually the same. In the example, a cost of $3,200 was obtained for the periodic inventory, whereas $3,300 was obtained when costs were calculated as goods were issued. This difference is due to the fact that it was necessary to charge out 100 units at $10 in the issue of January 16. The ending inventory thus reflects only 100 units of the beginning inventory.

With large and diversified inventories, application of the lifo procedures just illustrated may prove extremely burdensome. To reduce

COMMODITY X (LIFO)

Ordered	Date	Received		Issued		Balance	
Memo-	Jan. 1					200 at $10	2,000
randum	12	400 at $12	4,800			200 at $10	2,000
						400 at $12	4,800
Entries	16			400 at $12	4,800		
				100 at $10	1,000	100 at $10	1,000
	26	300 at $11	3,300			100 at $10	1,000
						300 at $11	3,300
	29			200 at $11	2,200	100 at $10	1,000
						100 at $11	1,100
	30	100 at $12	1,200			100 at $10	1,000
						100 at $11	1,100
						100 at $12	1,200

clerical work and to simplify the valuation process, procedures referred to as *unit lifo* are frequently employed. Goods making up the inventory are first segregated into a number of groups or pools based on their similarity in type if purchased or their similarity in degree of processing if manufactured. Having made the choice to adopt lifo as of a certain date, the number of units within each pool and the total costs of such units are determined. Average unit costs for goods within each pool are then calculated, units being regarded as all having been acquired at the same time. At the end of a period, units in each pool equal to the beginning number are assigned the beginning unit costs. An increase in the number of units in an inventory pool during a period is regarded as an incremental layer, and such incremental layer is valued at current costs applied on the basis of (1) actual costs of earliest acquisitions within the period (lifo), (2) the average cost of acquisitions within the period, or (3) actual costs of the latest acquisitions within the period (fifo). Increments in subsequent periods form successive inventory layers. A decrease in the number of units in an inventory pool during a period is regarded as a reduction in the most recently added layer, then in successively lower layers, and finally in the original or base quantity. Once a specific layer is reduced or eliminated, it is not restored.

To illustrate the valuation process, assume inventory pools and changes in pools as listed on the next page. The inventory calculations that follow are based on the assumption that average costs are used in valuing annual incremental layers.

Inventory pool increments and liquidations:

	Class A Goods	Class B Goods	Class C Goods
Inv., Dec. 31, 1970	3,000@$6	3,000@$5	2,000@$10
Purchases — 1971	3,000@$7	2,000@$6	3,000@$11
	1,000@$9		
	7,000	5,000	5,000
Sales — 1971	3,000	1,000	3,500
Inv., Dec. 31, 1971	4,000	4,000	1,500
Purchases — 1972	1,000@$8	2,000@$6	3,000@$11
	3,000@$10		
	8,000	6,000	4,500
Sales — 1972	3,500	2,500	2,000
Inv., Dec. 31, 1972	4,500	3,500	2,500

Unit-lifo inventory valuations:

	Class A Goods		Class B Goods		Class C Goods	
Inv., Dec. 31, 1970:	3,000@$6	$18,000	3,000@$5	$15,000	2,000@$10	$20,000
Inv., Dec. 31, 1971:	3,000@$6	$18,000	3,000@$5	$15,000	1,500@$10	$15,000
	1,000@$7.50[1]	7,500	1,000@$6	6,000		
	4,000	$25,500	4,000	$21,000	1,500	$15,000
Inv., Dec. 31, 1972:	3,000@$6	$18,000	3,000@$5	$15,000	1,500@$10	$15,000
	1,000@$7.50	7,500	500@$6	3,000	1,000@$11	11,000
	500@$9.50[2]	4,750				
	4,500	$30,250	3,500	$18,000	2,500	$26,000

[1]Cost of units acquired in 1971, $30,000, divided by number of units acquired, 4,000, or $7.50.

[2]Cost of units acquired in 1972, $38,000, divided by number of units acquired, 4,000, or $9.50.

Effects of traditional cost flow procedures compared. In using the first-in, first-out procedure, inventories are reported at or near current costs. In using last-in, first-out, inventories that do not change significantly in quantity are reported at more or less fixed amounts that relate back to the earliest purchases. Use of the average method generally provides inventory values that closely parallel first-in, first-out values, since purchases during a period are normally several times the opening inventory balance and average costs are thus heavily influenced by current costs. When the prices paid for merchandise do not fluctuate significantly, the alternative inventory methods may provide only minor differences on the financial statements. However, in periods of steadily rising or falling prices, the alternative methods may produce relatively material differences. Differences in inventory valuations on the balance sheet are accompanied by differences in earnings on the income statement for the period.

Use of first-in, first-out in a period of rising prices matches oldest low-cost inventory with rising sales prices, thus expanding the gross profit margin. In a period of declining prices, oldest high-cost inventory is matched with declining sales prices, thus narrowing the gross profit margin. On the other hand, use of last-in, first-out in a period of rising prices relates current high costs of acquiring goods with rising sales prices, and in a period of falling prices, low costs of acquiring goods with declining sales prices.

Average methods that provide inventory costs that are closely comparable with first-in, first-out costs offer operating results that approximate first-in, first-out results.

The application of the different methods in periods of rising and falling prices is illustrated in the example that follows. Assume that the Home Sales Co. sells its goods at 50 percent in excess of prevailing costs from 1969 to 1972. The company sells its inventories and terminates activities at the end of 1972. Sales, costs, and gross profits using each of the three methods are shown in the tabulation on page 262.

Although the different methods give the same total gross profit on sales for the four-year period, use of first-in, first-out resulted in increased gross profit percentages in periods of rising prices and a contraction of gross profit percentages in a period of falling prices, while last-in, first-out resulted in relatively steady gross profit percentages in spite of fluctuating prices. The weighted average method offered results closely comparable to those obtained by first-in, first-out. Assuming operating expenses at 30 percent of sales, use of last-in, first-out would result in a net income for each of the four years; first-in, first-out would result in larger net incomes in 1969 and 1970, but net losses in 1971 and 1972. Inventory valuation on the last-in, first-out basis tends to smooth off the peaks and fill in the troughs of business fluxuations.

Evaluation of traditional cost flow procedures. Fifo assumes a procession of costs that are assignable to revenue in exactly the same order in which they were incurred. The average method assumes a complete commingling of costs for units acquired with costs for units on hand, such commingled costs being assignable to revenue. Lifo assumes that first costs are identified with the inventory, subsequent costs bypassing the inventory and being assignable to revenue.

Fifo can be supported as a logical and realistic approach to the flow of costs when it is impractical or impossible to achieve cost identification with goods as these move forward. An assumed cost flow is achieved which closely parallels the actual physical flow of goods. Revenue is charged with costs considered applicable to those goods involved in the

	FIFO			WEIGHTED AVERAGE			LIFO[1]		
1969:									
Sales, 500 units @ $9			4,500			4,500			4,500
Inventory, 200 units	@ $5	1,000		200 @ $5	1,000		200 @ $5	1,000	
Purchases, 500 units	@ $6	3,000		500 @ $6	3,000		500 @ $6	3,000	
		4,000			4,000			4,000	
Ending Inv., 200 units	@ $6	1,200	2,800	200 @ $5.71 ($4,000÷700)	1,142	2,858	200 @ $5	1,000	3,000
Gross Profit on Sales			1,700			1,642			1,500
1970:									
Sales, 450 units @ $12			5,400			5,400			5,400
Inventory, 200 units	@ $6	1,200		200 @ $5.71	1,142		200 @ $5	1,000	
Purchases, 500 units	@ $8	4,000		500 @ $8	4,000		500 @ $8	4,000	
		5,200			5,142			5,000	
Ending Inv., 250 units	@ $8	2,000	3,200	250 @ $7.35 ($5,142÷700)	1,838	3,304	200 @ $5⎫ 50 @ $8⎭	1,400	3,600
Gross Profit on Sales			2,200			2,096			1,800
1971:									
Sales, 475 units @ $10.50			4,988			4,988			4,988
Inventory, 250 units	@ $8	2,000		250 @ $7.35	1,838		200 @ $5⎫ 50 @ $8⎭	1,400	
Purchases, 450 units	@ $7	3,150		450 @ $7	3,150		450 @ $7	3,150	
		5,150			4,988			4,550	
Ending Inv., 225 units	@ $7	1,575	3,575	225 @ $7.13 ($4,988÷700)	1,604	3,384	200 @ $5⎫ 25 @ $8⎭	1,200	3,350
Gross Profit on Sales			1,413			1,604			1,638
1972:									
Sales, 625 units @ $7.50			4,688			4,688			4,688
Inventory, 225 units	@ $7	1,575		225 @ $7.13	1,604		200 @ $5⎫ 25 @ $8⎭	1,200	
Purchases, 400 units	@ $5	2,000	3,575	400 @ $5	2,000	3,604	400 @ $5 ⎰	2,000	3,200
Gross Profit on Sales			1,113			1,084			1,488

The foregoing transactions are summarized below:

Year	Sales	FIFO Cost of Goods Sold	FIFO Gross Profit on Sales	FIFO Gross Profit % to Sales	WEIGHTED AVERAGE Cost of Goods Sold	WEIGHTED AVERAGE Gross Profit on Sales	WEIGHTED AVERAGE Gross Profit % to Sales	LIFO Cost of Goods Sold	LIFO Gross Profit on Sales	LIFO Gross Profit % to Sales
1969	4,500	2,800	1,700	37.8%	2,858	1,642	36.5%	3,000	1,500	33.3%
1970	5,400	3,200	2,200	40.7	3,304	2,096	38.8	3,600	1,800	33.3
1971	4,988	3,575	1,413	28.3	3,384	1,604	32.2	3,350	1,638	32.8
1972	4,688	3,575	1,113	23.7	3,604	1,084	23.1	3,200	1,488	31.7
	19,576	13,150	6,426	32.8%	13,150	6,426	32.8%	13,150	6,426	32.8%

realization of revenue; ending inventories are reported in terms of most recent costs — costs that fairly present the latest acquisitions and that may equitably be assigned to revenues of the subsequent period. Fifo affords no opportunity for profit manipulation; assignment of costs against revenue is determined by the order in which costs are incurred.

---

[1]Totals in the illustration are calculated to the nearest dollar.

The average cost approach, too, can be supported as realistic and as paralleling the physical flow of goods particularly where there is an intermingling of identical inventory units. Unlike the other methods, the average approach provides the same cost for similar items of equal utility. The method does not permit profit manipulation. Limitations ascribed to the average method are inventory values that perpetually contain to some minor degree the influence of earliest costs and inventory values that may lag significantly behind current prices in periods of rising or falling prices.

The cost assignment resulting from the application of lifo cannot normally be considered in harmony with a movement of goods through the business. One would seldom encounter a practice of priorities for the use or transfer of goods representing latest acquisitions. Sequences involved in the physical movement of goods are disregarded so that charges may be made to revenue in terms of most-current costs, that is, costs that are more nearly representative of the cost of replacing the gap in the inventory resulting from sales.[1]

However, it is argued that lifo offers a more accurate statement of earnings accruing to the ownership group than alternate methods. When fifo is used in a period of rising prices, for example, earnings are reported that are not fully available to owners but rather must be applied in part or in whole to higher-cost inventory replacement; in a period of falling prices, earnings are reported that fail to show the full resources accruing to owners from sales activities plus the amounts made available through lower cost inventory replacement. Lifo, on the other hand, by charging revenue with latest costs, avoids the recognition of "paper profit or loss" on an inventory that the company must continue to hold as long as it operates as a going concern. This aspect of the measurement process may be illustrated as follows:

	Inventory Cost	Sales Price	Latest Purchase Price	Fifo "Profit"	Lifo "Profit"	Dollars Available After Unit Replacement
With rising prices:	$10	$15	$12	$5	$3	$3
With falling prices:	$10	$12	$ 8	$2	$4	$4

Under lifo, that portion of sales proceeds that is required for the replacement of the inventory at higher costs receives recognition as net income only when it is freed through a subsequent replacement of inventories at lower costs. Lifo is acceptable for income tax purposes. Its

---

[1] It may be noted that some accountants would go beyond lifo and charge revenue with the replacement cost of goods sold (next-in, first-out, or *nifo*) rather than with latest acquisition costs.

use for tax purposes in a period of rising prices serves to postpone taxes until earnings are reflected in a company's net monetary assets.

Although arguments for lifo as a means of achieving satisfactory income measurement are impressive, one must consider the deficiencies of this method as applied to the recognition of inventory position for balance sheet purposes. The lifo inventory consists of an assembly of congealed costs or cost layers dating back to original acquisitions — costs that may differ materially from current prices. Such inventory costs enter into the determination of working capital and may seriously distort this measurement. Inventory position is also a determinant of total assets and capital. Adoption of lifo in a period of rising prices results in inventory understatement, a practice that is normally rationalized as acceptable on conservative grounds. Adoption of lifo in a period of falling prices results in inventory overstatement; here, it is fair to assume, there would be strong pressure for special action to write down inventory balances to replacement cost.

In certain instances, the use of lifo may produce highly unrealistic operating results. Assume, for example, that special conditions make it necessary for a company to liquidate a significant part or an entire inventory carried at costs that are materially different from current costs. Under these circumstances, the lifo gross profit margin would not be the steady percentage offered by the recurring application of current costs to current revenues but instead a highly distorted figure resulting from the need to charge off original inventory costs. Two specific examples may clarify this weakness.

(1) Many companies who rely upon steel as a basic raw material for their production processes use the lifo inventory method. Assume that during an extended steel strike many manufacturing companies find their steel stock dwindling as their fiscal year-end approaches. Unless they can restock their inventories, they will be forced to use lower priced inventory costs to match against current revenue, thus creating a substantial current profit. Assume, for instance, that company sales for the year are $6,000,000 and that the cost of goods sold using current year prices is $5,000,000, but using a mixture of current year and earlier years lower priced lifo layers, the cost of goods sold is $4,000,000. The resulting increase in profit is effected only because of the inability of the company to replace its normal stocks.

(2) The failure to protect lifo layers may be caused by a timing error in requesting shipments of purchases. Assume that a lumber company normally received its lumber by ship, but that at year-end orders were mishandled and a boat load was not received as planned. The com-

pany, in failing to record the boat load of lumber as a current year purchase, would have to apply older lifo cost against sales. The resulting profit could lead to conclusions that would not be justified by the facts.

Lifo may also invite profit manipulation practices. For example, purchases, though required to maintain an inventory position, may be postponed at the end of the period so that costs of prior periods may be used in measuring net income. On the other hand, purchases may be made at the end of the period, though goods are not required, so that costs of such latest purchases may be used in arriving at net income.

Last-in, first-out has been widely adopted largely because of its ability to smooth the profit curve and its income tax advantages in a period of steadily rising prices. However, it is not the effects of a procedure but its merit as a means of sound measurement that should determine its acceptance for general accounting purposes. Depreciation and amortization charges, for example, could be recorded in accordance with the ability of revenue to absorb such charges in smoothing the profit curve. Such practices would not lead to measurements of what actually took place; instead, they would serve to obscure measurements and thus contradict the aim of accounting to report financial activities fairly.

It is interesting to note that the American Institute of Certified Public Accountants and the American Accounting Association differ in the criteria that each would consider in the choice of method for assigning costs. The AICPA views income measurement as the primary factor in making a choice. The Committee on Accounting Procedure has stated as follows:

> Cost for inventory purposes may be determined under any one of several assumptions as to the flow of cost factors (such as first-in first-out, average, and last-in first-out); the major objective in selecting a method should be to choose the one which, under the circumstances, most clearly reflects periodic income.[1]

The American Accounting Association, however, has questioned the adoption of a cost flow assumption that is unrelated to the actual movement of goods. Its Committee on Concepts and Standards Underlying Corporate Financial Statements made the following statement:

> (1) Ideally, the measurement of accounting profit involves the matching precisely of the identified costs of specific units of product with the sales revenues derived therefrom.

---

[1]*Accounting Research Bulletin No. 43, op. cit.*, Ch. 4, statement 4.

(2) Where conditions are such that precise matching of identified costs with revenues is impracticable, identified cost matching may be simulated by the adoption of an assumed flow of costs.

(3) A flow assumption can be *realistic*, in that it reflects the dominant characteristics of the actual flow of goods; thus it may reflect the actual dominance of first-in, first-out (FIFO), average, or last-in, first-out (LIFO) movement. A flow assumption can be *artificial*, on the other hand, in that it premises a flow of costs that is clearly in contrast with actual physical movement.

(4) The LIFO flow assumption now has wide usage although in very few, if any, instances of its application can the assumption be justified on the ground that it corresponds even approximately with the actual flow of goods. *Artificial LIFO* has appeal to some during periods of markedly changing price levels as a means of approaching a matching of current cost (dollar costs adjusted to reflect changes in the general purchasing power of the monetary unit) with current revenues; however, grave doubt exists as to whether the accuracy of such artificial matching is sufficient to justify the resultant departure from realism. Present use of the method should be considered a transitory step which may ultimately be supplanted by better methods of accomplishing the intended result."[1]

As indicated before, a later committee of the AAA focused their attention on the alternative methods for valuing inventories and recommended that multi-column statements be used that would include a column for current replacement cost. In justifying their conclusions, the committee stated that:

. . . replacement cost is the best of the several available inventory measurements. To aid interpretation, both historical and replacement costs of inventories should be disclosed in an integrated set of financial statements.[2]

Support for lifo must be found in its merit as a means of charging current revenue with current costs. But lifo can be challenged on the grounds that it is no more than an artifice resorted to because of failures of accounting theory to provide a satisfactory and cohesive approach to the problem of price-level changes. In supporting the alternative methods one can insist that it is historical costs, as best determined, that should be used to measure cost of goods sold. Net income emerges from a comparison of revenues with those costs that made such revenues possible. In periods of changing prices, such accounting needs to be supplemented by special analyses in arriving at conclusions concerning economic gain, changes in resources, and the availability of resources for continued operations and for distribution to owners.

---

[1] *Accounting and Reporting Standards for Corporate Financial Statements and Preceding Statements and Supplements*, "Supplementary Statement No. 6, Inventory Pricing and Changes in Price Levels" (1957 rev.; Madison, Wisconsin: American Accounting Association), pp. 36–37.

[2] "A Discussion of Various Approaches to Inventory Measurement, Supplementary Statement No. 2," *Accounting Review* (July, 1964), p. 700.

Other cost procedures

The methods previously described for arriving at inventory cost are the ones most widely used. Several other procedures are sometimes encountered and deserve mention.

Cost of latest purchases. Sometimes goods are valued at cost of the latest purchase regardless of quantities on hand. When the inventory consists largely of recent purchases, this method may give results closely approximating those obtained through specific cost identification or first-in, first-out procedures with considerably less work. However, when the quantities of goods on hand are significantly in excess of the latest quantities purchased and major price changes have taken place, use of latest costs may result in significant cost misstatement.

Simple average of costs. Goods on hand are sometimes valued at a simple average of all of the costs for the period without regard to the number of units acquired on each purchase. With significant differences in quantities acquired, the disregard of the weight factor may result in unrepresentative costs.

Base stock method. A few companies employ the *base stock*, or *normal stock*, method. This method assumes that a minimum stock is a normal and permanent requirement of the business; current purchases are means of satisfying current sales requirements, and hence their cost is properly applicable to revenues. The base stock inventory is regarded as fixed as to quantity and fixed as to price. The price is frequently the lowest cost experienced for the stock by the business unit. At the end of the period the amount of goods on hand is determined. The base stock quantity is valued at the original base cost. An amount in excess of the base stock quantity is regarded as a temporary inventory increase and is valued at current costs, applied on a first-in, first-out, average, or other basis. A reduction in the base stock quantity is viewed as an amount temporarily "borrowed" to meet sales requirements, and this is charged to sales at current replacement value in view of the cost to be incurred in restoring the inventory deficiency.

To illustrate use of the base stock method, assume a base stock of 100,000 units at $1 per unit that has increased to a total of 120,000 units. If the current cost is $1.60 per unit, the inventory would be valued as follows:

Base stock..................	100,000 units @	$1.00	$100,000
Add base stock quantity excess at current cost........	20,000 units @	$1.60	32,000
Inventory value..............	120,000 units..........		$132,000

Assume an inventory of only 90,000 units, and a current cost for units of $1.60. The inventory would be valued as follows:

Base stock...................	100,000 units @	$1.00	$100,000
Deduct base stock quantity			
deficiency at current cost.....	10,000 units @	$1.60	16,000
Inventory value..............	90,000 units..........		$ 84,000

Instead of reporting $84,000, the inventory may be left at $100,000 by establishing an allowance for the deficiency with a credit balance of $16,000. Initial purchases in the next period of $16,000 would be applied against the allowance to cancel this balance.

As indicated above, the base stock is regarded as a permanent asset; operations are charged with the costs of maintaining the normal stock. Results obtained through the base stock method are closely comparable with those obtained by the last-in, first-out method and the arguments for and against last-in, first-out can be applied here. Charges to revenue are costs currently experienced. The inventory, normally reported at the lowest value in the experience of the organization, may be seriously understated in terms of current prices. Use of the base stock method is not permitted for income tax purposes.

Standard costs. Manufacturing inventories are frequently reported at *standard costs*, which are predetermined costs based upon representative or normal conditions of efficiency and volume of operations. Differences between actual costs and standard costs for materials, labor, and manufacturing overhead give rise to *standard cost variances* indicating favorable and unfavorable operational or cost experiences. Excessive materials usage, inefficient labor application, excessive spoilage, and idle time, for example, produce unfavorable variances, and these would be separately summarized in variance accounts.

Standard costs are developed from a variety of sources. Past manufacturing experiences may be carefully analyzed; time and motion studies, as well as job and process studies, may be undertaken; data from industry and economy-wide sources may be referred to. Standards should be reviewed at frequent intervals to determine whether they continue to offer reliable cost criteria. Changing conditions will call for adjustment in the standards, so that at the balance sheet date, standard costs will reasonably approximate costs computed under one of the recognized bases.

Direct costing. A practice that has been widely debated for many years is referred to as *direct costing, marginal costing*, or *variable costing*. Inventories under direct costing are assigned only the variable costs that are incurred in production — direct materials, direct labor, and the variable components of manufacturing overhead. Fixed costs are treated as periodic charges and assigned to current revenue. Only costs that can be directly related to output, then, are assigned to goods and charged to the period in which the goods are sold; costs that are a function of time and that are continuing regardless of the volume of output — for example, supervisory salaries, depreciation, and property taxes — are charged against revenue of the period in which they are incurred.

These differences may be illustrated as follows:

	Full Costing		Direct Costing	
Sales.....................		$200,000		$200,000
Variable cost of goods sold....	$110,000		$110,000	
Fixed cost of goods sold.......	55,000		62,500	
Total cost of goods sold.....		165,000		172,500
Gross profit................		$ 35,000		$ 27,500
Inventory value:				
Variable costs.............		$ 15,000		$ 15,000
Fixed costs...............		7,500		———
Total cost of inventory....		$ 22,500		$ 15,000

With conventional *full costing* or *absorption costing* applied to inventories, a high earning rate may emerge in a period of high production even though sales are declining. With direct costing, cost of goods sold varies directly with sales and a high earnings rate emerges in a period of high sales; changes in the volume of production have no effect upon earnings. For example, assume in the illustration above that, although sales remained the same, production had been greater and as a result the ending inventory was double the amount shown. Variable costs identified with the inventory would then amount to $30,000. Under full costing, a different allocation of fixed costs would now be appropriate. Assuming that $12,500 in fixed costs is allocated to the inventory reducing the fixed costs assigned to operations by $5,000, the gross profit would increase to $40,000. Under direct costing, the gross profit would remain unchanged at $27,500.

Support for direct costing is made on the grounds that it provides more meaningful and useful data to management than full costing. Direct costing enables management to appraise the effects of sales fluctuations on net income. Sales, current and potential, can be evaluated in terms of out-of-pocket costs to achieve such sales. The direct costing approach becomes a valuable tool for planning and control and offers management highly useful approaches to cost, price, and volume relationships.

Although no objection can be raised to the use of direct costing when it is used for internal reporting and as a means for assisting management in decision-making, objection can be raised to the extension of direct costing procedures to the annual financial statements. It is fair to maintain that in measuring financial position and the results of operations, inventories must carry their full costs including a satisfactory allocation of the fixed overhead costs. Fixed costs, no less than variable costs, are incurred in contemplation of future benefits and should be matched against the revenues that are ultimately produced through such efforts. Inventories, then, when arrived at by direct costing procedures for internal reporting, should be restated in terms of full costing whenever financial statements are to be prepared.[1]

Cost apportionment by relative sales value method. Mention needs to be made of a special accounting problem that arises when different commodities are purchased for a single sum. Such purchase calls for the apportionment of the cost to the units acquired in some equitable manner. This cost apportionment should recognize the utility that is found in the different units. Ordinarily, the estimated sales value of the different units provides the best measure of respective utilities, and accordingly cost is allocated on the basis of such estimated sales value. This procedure is referred to as the *relative sales value method*. Costs derived through apportionment in terms of sales value are charged to revenue as units are sold.

To illustrate application of the relative sales value method, assume the purchase by a realty company of 60 acres of land for $220,000. The costs of grading, landscaping, streets, walks, water mains, lighting, and other improvements total $300,000. The property is divided into three groups of lots as follows: Class A, 100 lots to sell for $2,000 each; Class B, 200 lots to sell for $2,500 each; and Class C, 20 lots to sell for $5,000 each. The total cost of the property, $520,000, is apportioned to the lots on the basis of their relative sales values. The cost apportionment is made as follows:

Class A lots, 100 at $2,000.............................	$200,000
Class B lots, 200 at $2,500.............................	500,000
Class C lots, 20 at $5,000.............................	100,000
Total sales value of Class A, B, and C lots..............	$800,000

---

[1]The Committee on Accounting Procedure of the American Institute of Certified Public Accountants although approving the exclusion of "idle facility expense, excessive spoilage, double freight and rehandling costs" in inventory costing, nevertheless observes, "As applied to inventories, cost means in principle the sum of the applicable expenditures and charges directly or indirectly incurred in bringing an article to its existing condition and location." It later states, "It should also be recognized that the exclusion of all overheads from inventory costs does not constitute an accepted accounting procedure." *Accounting Research Bulletin No. 43, op. cit.*, Ch. 4, statement 3 and par. 5. Direct costing is not acceptable on statements submitted to the Securities and Exchange Commission, and is not acceptable for federal income tax purposes.

	Total	No. of Lots	Cost Assigned to Each Lot
Cost apportioned to Class A lots:			
200,000/800,000 × $520,000 =	$130,000	100	$1,300
Cost apportioned to Class B lots:			
500,000/800,000 × $520,000 =	325,000	200	$1,625
Cost apportioned to Class C lots:			
100,000/800,000 × $520,000 =	65,000	20	$3,250
Total....................	$520,000		

The sale of a lot of any class results in a constant gross profit of 35% of sales.[1] Sale of a Class A lot would be recorded as follows:

Contracts Receivable............................	2,000	
Real Estate — Lot A-56.........................		1,300
Gross Profit on Sale of Real Estate...............		700

Products that are manufactured simultaneously by a common process are referred to as *joint products*. When it is impractical or perhaps impossible to identify raw material and processing costs with the individual products produced, such costs may be assigned to the different products in a manner similar to that just illustrated. The sales value of each product is determined, and the total production cost is then allocated according to the relative sales values of the respective products.

Products of relatively little value that are produced in the course of manufacturing the primary products are referred to as *by-products*. By-products are frequently valued at their sales prices or at sales prices less expenses of disposal, and costs identified with the primary products are reduced by the amounts assigned to the by-products. Total costs are thus identified with the entire output; earnings, however, emerge only upon the sale of the primary products.

Effects of errors in recording inventory position

Failures to report the inventory position accurately result in misstatements on both the balance sheet and the income statement. The effects of inventory errors on the financial statements prepared at the end of the fiscal period are indicated in the summary that follows.

(1) Overstatement of the ending inventory through errors in the count of goods on hand, pricing, or the inclusion in inventory of goods not owned or goods already sold:

---

[1]The same cost allocation can be developed by calculating the percentage of total cost to total estimated sales value, and applying such percentage to the sales price for the individual unit. In the example, cost is 65% of the total estimated sales value of the properties (520,000 ÷ 800,000). Each lot, then, is assigned a cost equal to 65% of its sales value: Class A lots have a cost of 65% of $2,000, or $1,300; Class B lots a cost of 65% of $2,500, or $1,625; Class C lots a cost of 65% of $5,000, or $3,250.

Current year:
  Income statement — overstatement of the ending inventory will
    cause the cost of goods sold to be understated and the net income
    to be overstated.
  Balance sheet—the inventory will be overstated and the owners' equity
    will be overstated.

Succeeding year:
  Income statement — overstatement of the beginning inventory will
    cause the cost of goods sold to be overstated and the net income
    to be understated.
  Balance sheet — the error of the previous year will have been
    counterbalanced on the succeeding income statement and the
    balance sheet will be correctly stated.

(2) Understatement of ending inventory through errors in the count
of goods on hand, pricing, or the failure to include in inventory goods
purchased or goods transferred but not yet sold:

Misstatements indicated in (1) above are reversed.

(3) Overstatement of ending inventory accompanied by failure to
recognize sales and corresponding receivables at end of period:

Current year:
  Income statement — sales are understated by the sales price of the
    goods and cost of goods sold is understated by the cost of the
    goods relating to the sales; gross profit and net income are thus
    understated by the gross profit on the sales.
  Balance sheet — receivables are understated by the sales price of the
    goods and the inventory is overstated by the cost of the goods that
    were sold; current assets and owners' equity are thus understated by
    the gross profit on the sales.

Succeeding year:
  Income statement — sales of the preceding year are recognized here
    in sales and cost of sales; gross profit and net income, therefore,
    are overstated by the gross profit on such sales.
  Balance sheet — the error of the previous year is counterbalanced on
    the succeeding income statement and the balance sheet will be
    correctly stated.

(4) Understatement of ending inventory accompanied by failure
to recognize purchases and corresponding payables at end of period:

Current year:
  Income statement — purchases are understated, but this is counter-
    balanced by the understatement of the ending inventory; gross
    profit and net income are correctly stated as a result of the counter-
    balancing effect of the error.
  Balance sheet — although owners' equity is reported correctly, both cur-
    rent assets and current liabilities are understated.

Succeeding year:
  Income statement — the beginning inventory is understated, but this
    is counterbalanced by an overstatement of purchases, as purchases
    at the end of the prior year are recognized currently; gross profit

and net income are correctly stated as a result of the counterbalancing effect of the error.

Balance sheet — the error of the previous year no longer affects balance sheet data.

Discoveries of inventory errors call for careful analyses of the effects of such errors and the preparation of entries to correct real and nominal accounts in order that both current and future activities may be accurately stated.

If the error is not discovered until a suceeding period, the correction to be made will depend upon the materiality of the item. As discussed in Chapter 3, the Accounting Principles Board has recommended that adjustments for prior periods that involve a change in the estimates used to record expenses and revenues should be recognized in the income statement rather than be made to the retained earnings account. Inventory errors of the nature described above that are not material in amount should also be corrected in this manner.

However, errors that do not arise from estimates and that are material under the circumstances should be corrected by entries directly to Retained Earnings. The inventory errors described in this section are of this type and, if material, should be recorded as prior period adjustments. If trend statistics are included in the annual reports, prior years' balances should be adjusted to reflect the correction of the error. Because of present-day audit techniques, it is probable that material inventory counting and cut-off errors will occur only rarely.

QUESTIONS

1. (a) What are the three cost elements entering into goods in process and finished goods? (b) What items enter into manufacturing overhead? (c) Define fixed overhead, variable overhead, and semivariable overhead and give an example of each.

2. (a) What charges may be considered to compose the cost of raw material acquisitions? (b) Which of these charges are normally included as a part of raw material cost for inventory purposes? (c) Which of these are normally excluded? Why? What disposition would be made of such items?

3. What are the advantages of using the perpetual inventory system as compared with the periodic system?

4. State how you would report each of the following items on the financial statements:

⤴(a) Manufacturing supplies.

  (b) Goods on hand received on a consignment basis.

  (c) Materials of a customer held for processing.

  (d) Goods received without an accompanying invoice.

  (e) Goods in stock to be delivered to customers in subsequent periods.

  (f) Goods in hands of agents and consignees.

ᴀᶜᴿ(g) Deposits with vendors for merchandise to be delivered next period.

  (h) Goods in hands of customers on approval.

  (i) Defective goods requiring reprocessing.

5. The Miller Company has followed the practice of recording all consignment sales as current period sales and has not carried goods on consignment as inventory. Under what conditions would this practice have no effect upon income?

6. Under what normal conditions would an accounting failure to recognize incoming merchandise in transit that was shipped FOB shipping point have no effect on the income statement?

7. Under what normal conditions is merchandise in transit reported as inventory?

8. The Alpha Co. records purchases discounts taken as revenue. The Beta Co. records purchases discounts lost as expense. (a) How does the accounting for purchases and inventory valuation for each company differ? (b) What are the arguments in favor of each practice? (c) Which practice do you favor? Why?

9. What are the advantages of using the cost method of inventory valuation? Do you see any disadvantages?

10. Trade discounts are frequently used to avoid extra catalog printing costs. Describe in what way trade discounts could affect these savings.

11. What objections can be raised to inventory valuation by specific cost identification procedures?

12. Compare the positions that are taken by the AICPA and the AAA relative to cost flow assumptions that may be considered valid in arriving at inventory cost.

13. Compare the effects of the use of fifo and lifo upon net income measurement in a period of rapidly rising prices.

14. Why did the AAA Committee on Inventories refer to lifo as an "artificial" pricing system?

15. The Wallace Co. decides to adopt unit lifo as of the beginning of 1972, and determines the cost of the different lines of merchandise carried as of this date. (a) What three different methods may be employed at the end of each period in assigning costs to quantity increases in specific lines? (b) What procedure is employed at the end of each period for quantity decreases in specific lines?

16. What is the difference between a weighted average and a moving average cost method? Which may be preferred and why?

17. (a) Describe the base stock method. (b) How does this method differ from inventory valuation by lifo?

18. (a) What type of company is likely to use standard costs? (b) What precautions are necessary in the use of standard costs?

19. (a) Of what value is direct costing? (b) Would you approve of this cost procedure for financial statement purposes?

20. Under what circumstances would you recommend use of cost apportionment by the relative sales method.

21. State the effect of each of the following errors made by Fields, Inc., upon the balance sheet and the income statement (1) of the current period and (2) of the succeeding period:

(a) The company fails to record a sale of merchandise on account; goods sold are excluded in recording the ending inventory.
(b) The company fails to record a sale of merchandise on account; the goods sold are included, however, in recording the ending inventory.
(c) The company fails to record a purchase of merchandise on account; goods purchased are included in recording the ending inventory.
(d) The company fails to record a purchase of merchandise on account; goods purchased are not recognized in recording the ending inventory.
(e) The ending inventory is understated as the result of a miscount of goods on hand.
(f) The ending inventory is overstated as the result of inclusion of goods held on a consignment basis and never recognized as a purchase.

22. The Magic Mfg. Co. reviewed its in-transit inventory and found the following items. Indicate which items should be included in the inventory balance at December 31, 1972. Give reasons for the treatment.

(a) Merchandise costing $2,350 was received on January 3, 1973, and the related purchase invoice recorded January 5. The invoice showed the shipment was made on December 29, 1972, FOB destination.
(b) Merchandise costing $625 was received on December 28, 1972, and the invoice was not recorded. You located it in the hands of the purchasing agent; it was marked on consignment.
(c) A packing case containing a product costing $816 was standing in the shipping room when the physical inventory was taken. It was not included in the inventory because it was marked "Hold for shipping instructions." Your investigation revealed that the customer's order was dated December 18, 1972, but that the case was shipped and the customer billed on January 10, 1973. The product was a stock item of your client. *(continued)*

(d) Merchandise received on January 6, 1973, costing $720 was entered in the purchase register on January 7, 1973. The invoice showed shipment was made FOB supplier's warehouse on December 31, 1972. Since it was not on hand at December 31, it was not included in inventory.

(e) A special machine, fabricated to order for a customer, was finished and in the shipping room on December 31, 1972. The customer was billed on that date and the machine excluded from inventory although it was shipped on January 4, 1973.

(AICPA adapted)

EXERCISES

1. Transactions of the Maynard Co. relating to goods purchased during December are summarized below:

Purchases were $15,000, terms 2/10, n/30.
Accounts of $12,500 were paid, including accounts of $11,500 paid within the discount period.

Give the entries to record purchases and invoice payments in December, assuming that:

(a) Accounts payable are recorded at invoice price and purchases discounts earned are summarized in the accounts.
(b) Accounts payable are recorded net and purchases discounts lost are summarized in the accounts.
(c) Accounts payable are recorded at invoice price and purchases discounts lost are summarized in the accounts.

2. The Baden Co. buys all of its merchandise from the Warren Manufacturing Co. and is allowed a trade discount of 15% – 10% – 5% and a cash discount of 3%. Purchases during January are $81,000 before discounts. Two thirds of the merchandise acquired is sold in January. At what value should the ending inventory be reported if the cash discount is treated as: (a) a reduction in purchases? (b) other revenue?

3. Changes in Commodity Y during January are:

Jan.	1	Balance	400 units @ $7	Jan. 10	Sale 300 units @ $12
	12	Purchase	200 units @ 8	30	Sale 200 units @ 14
	28	Purchase	200 units @ 9		

(a) Assuming that perpetual inventories are maintained and that accounts are kept up to date currently, what is the cost of the ending inventory for Commodity Y using: (1) fifo; (2) lifo; (3) average?
(b) Assuming that perpetual inventories are not maintained and that a physical count at the end of the month shows 300 units to be on hand, what is the cost of the ending inventory using each of the three methods listed in part (a)?

4. The Wilson Manufacturing Company record for Material No. 25A follows:

Sept.	1	Balance	100 units at $10	$1,000
	10	Received	200 units at 9	1,800
	20	Received	50 units at 12	600
	28	Received	100 units at 11	1,100

At the end of the month, 150 units are on hand. Give the cost of the ending inventory, assuming that it is calculated by each of the following methods: (a) first-in, first-out, (b) weighted average, (c) last-in, first-out, (d) cost of latest purchase, (e) simple average of costs.

5. The Woods Company decided to use unit lifo in valuing its inventories beginning in 1971. Commodity Z, included in its inventory on January 1, 1971, consisted of 6,000 units at a total cost of $6,600. Purchases and sales of Commodity Z during the next three years were as follows:

	Purchases		Sales	
	No. of Units	Amount	No. of Units	Amount
1971	25,000	$29,000	23,500	$38,000
1972	30,000	38,400	34,000	57,500
1973	32,500	39,000	28,000	49,200

Calculate the value to be assigned to Commodity Z at the end of 1971, 1972, and 1973.

6. The Adventurous Realty Co. acquires land for $70,000 and incurs additional costs of $38,600 in improving the land. The land is divided into lots that are classified as follows:

Class	No. of Lots	Sales Price per Lot
100	20	$2,400
200	35	2,000
300	42	1,500

(a) What is the cost of each lot to the company?
(b) What entry should be made if five Class 200 lots are sold on contract?

7. The Daud Store shows the following information relating to Commodity A which it handles:

Inventory, January 1	100 units @ $5
Purchases, January 10	300 units @ $6
Purchases, January 20	400 units @ $7
Sales, January 8	50 units
Sales, January 18	200 units
Sales, January 25	400 units

What is the value of the inventory at the end of January assuming cost is determined on the basis of a moving average?

8. (a) Gray Corporation uses direct costing for internal reporting. It has been suggested that use of direct costing on the balance sheet would understate income because of the complete write-off of fixed costs. Compute the effect on net income for 1972 of using direct costing to value the inventory as compared with full costing. Assume that there is no change in work in process between the beginning and the end of the year, and that the fifo cost flow method is used.

Inventory, January 1, 1972.................20,000 units
    Variable costs.............................$6.00 per unit
    Fixed costs (if inventory valued at full costs)....$2.00 per unit
Units produced in 1972......................140,000
Total fixed costs...........................$280,000
Inventory, December 31, 1972...............25,000 units
    Variable costs...........................$6.50 per unit

(b) What is the effect on net income if the ending inventory consisted of only 10,000 units?

9. Annual earnings for the Webster Co. for the period 1969–1973 appear below. However, a review of the records for the company reveals inventory misstatements as listed. Calculate corrected net earnings for each year.

	1969	1970	1971	1972	1973
Reported net income (loss)..	$19,500	$20,000	$2,000	$(4,500)	$15,000
Inventory overstatement, end of year.................	1,500		2,800		1,600
Inventory understatement, end of year............				4,000	

10. The errors listed below were made by the Marshall Sales Corporation in 1972. Give the entry required in 1973 to correct each error. Assume that the company arrives at its inventory position by physical count and that the books for 1972 have been closed. Assume that all amounts are material.

(a) The company failed to record a sale on account of $210 at the end of 1972. The merchandise had been shipped and was not included in the ending inventory. The sale was recorded in 1973 when cash was collected from the customer.

(b) The company failed to recognize $400 due from a consignee as a result of goods sold by this party at the end of 1972. The consignee had failed to report the sale of consigned goods and the company included their cost of $260 in inventory as Goods on Consignment.

(c) The company failed to recognize a purchase on account of $1,350 at the end of 1972 and also failed to include the goods purchased in the ending inventory. The purchase was recorded when payment was made to the creditor in 1973.

(d) The company failed to make an entry for a purchase on account of $60 at the end of 1972, although it included this merchandise in the inventory count. The purchase was recorded when payment was made to the creditor in 1973.

(e) The company overlooked goods of $360 in the physical count of goods at the end of 1972.

PROBLEMS

8-1. The Ringwood Corporation uses raw material A in a manufacturing process. Information as to balances on hand, purchases, and requisitions of material A are given in the following table:

	Quantities			
Date	Received	Issued	Balance	Unit Price of Purchase
Jan. 11	——	——	100	$1.50
Jan. 24	300	——	400	1.56
Feb. 8	——	80	320	——
Mar. 16	——	140	180	——
June 11	150	——	330	1.60
Aug. 18	——	130	200	——
Sept. 6	——	110	90	——
Oct. 15	150	——	240	1.70
Dec. 29	——	140	100	——

Instructions: What is the closing inventory under each of the following pricing methods?

(1) Perpetual fifo   (4) Periodic fifo
(2) Perpetual lifo   (5) Periodic lifo
(3) Moving average   (6) Weighted average

8-2. Records of the Barker Sales Co. show the following data relative to Commodity YIP:

Balance: Jan. 1—325 units at $25.50   Sales: Jan. 2—300 units at $35.00
Purchases: Jan. 3—300 units at 26.00   18—200 units at 35.70
                 12—350 units at 27.00   29—150 units at 36.00
                 24— 75 units at 26.50

Instructions: Calculate the inventory balance and the gross profit on sales for the month on each of the following bases:

(1) First-in, first-out. Perpetual inventories are maintained and costs are charged out currently.
(2) First-in, first-out. No book inventory is maintained.
(3) Last-in, first-out. Perpetual inventories are maintained and costs are charged out currently.
(4) Last-in, first-out. No book inventory is maintained.
(5) Moving average. Perpetual inventories are maintained.
(6) Weighted average.

8-3. Lehman's, Inc., sells a single commodity. Purchases, sales, and expenses for May, June, and July are summarized as follows:

	Purchases	
	Units	Cost per Unit
May 1–15.........................	2,000	$3.50
16–31.........................	3,000	3.75
June 1–15........................	1,500	4.25
16–30.........................	2,000	4.75
July 1–15........................	——	——
16–31.........................	2,000	4.25

	Sales Units	Sales Price per Unit	Operating Expenses
May..........................	2,000	$6.75	$2,700
June..........................	3,200	7.50	4,100
July..........................	3,100	7.75	3,700

Instructions: Prepare a comparative income statement summarizing operations for the months of May, June, and July for each case below:

(1) Assume that monthly inventories are calculated at cost on a first-in, first-out basis.

(2) Assume that monthly inventories are calculated at cost on a last-in, first-out basis.

(3) Assume that monthly inventories are calculated at cost on a weighted average basis. (Unit costs are calculated to the nearest cent.)

8-4. The Larson Mfg. Co. was organized in 1970 to produce a single product. Its production and sales records for the period 1970–1973 are summarized below:

	Units Produced No. of Units	Production Costs	Sales No. of Units	Sales Revenue
1970	320,000	$ 86,400	200,000	$122,500
1971	310,000	130,200	290,000	175,000
1972	270,000	129,600	290,000	203,000
1973	220,000	99,000	200,000	150,000

Instructions: Calculate the gross profit for each of the four years assuming that inventory balances are calculated in terms of:

(1) First-in, first-out.   (2) Last-in, first-out.

8-5. The Buffalo Products Company reports its inventories at lifo. Inventories are composed of three classes of goods. Values are assigned to each class as follows: units equal to the number on hand when lifo was adopted are assigned average costs as of this date; annual incremental layers thereafter are assigned the average cost for the period. Lifo was adopted in 1970. The inventory on January 1, 1973, and purchases and sales for 1973 were as follows:

Inventory, January 1, 1973

	Model A Units	Amount	Model B Units	Amount	Model C Units	Amount
1970 balance...	40,000@$.10	$ 4,000	20,000@$ .60	$12,000	5,000@$3.00	$15,000
1971 increment.	20,000@$.15	3,000	1,500@$1.00	1,500		
1972 increment.	10,000@$.17	1,700			2,000@$3.25	6,500
Total...	70,000	$ 8,700	21,500	$13,500	7,000	$21,500
Purchases, 1973	250,000	$50,000	60,000	$61,200	12,500	$42,500
Sales, 1973	265,000	$79,500	64,500	$96,750	12,000	$48,000

Instructions: Prepare a statement reporting sales, cost of goods sold (including purchases and inventory detail), and gross profits for each class of goods handled and for combined activities as of December 31, 1973. Provide supporting schedules to show how the ending inventory balances are developed for each class of goods.

8-6. First-in, first-out has been used for inventory valuation by the Crowley Co. since it was organized in 1970. Using the data that follow, redetermine the net incomes for each year on the assumption of inventory valuation on the last-in, first-out basis:

	1970	1971	1972	1973
Reported net income...........	$ 17,500	$ 30,000	$ 32,500	$ 45,000
Reported ending inventories — fifo basis...................	61,500	102,000	126,000	130,000
Inventories — lifo basis........	59,000	75,100	95,000	105,000

8-7. The Nelson Construction Company purchased 50 acres of land in the suburbs of a large city with the intention of improving, subdividing, and selling it in one acre lots. The purchase price for the tract of land was $210,000. The lots are given numbers and similar lots are grouped numerically. Lots 1–15 are choice lots and did not require extra improvements. They will sell for $8,000 each. Lots 16–30 required some extra improvements costing $34,000. They will sell for $7,000 each. Lots 31–50 required extensive drainage and clearing costing $40,000. They will sell for $6,500 each.

Instructions: Using the relative sales method, allocate the purchase and improvement costs to the various lots.

8-8. The ending inventories for the XYZ Company are shown in its accounts as follows:

1971....................$14,000
1972.................... 17,000
1973.................... 15,000

During an audit of the XYZ Company, it was discovered that the ending inventories should have shown the following amounts:

1971....................$10,000
1972.................... 19,000
1973.................... 20,000

Instructions: Prepare the necessary correcting entries at December 31, 1973, assuming that 1973 accounts are not yet closed.

8-9. The Leavitt Metal Products Co. adjusted and closed its books at the end of 1972, the summary of 1972 activities showing a net loss of $8,000. The following errors, made in 1972, all regarded as material, are discovered upon an audit of the books of the company made in March, 1973:

(a) Merchandise, cost $3,000, was recorded as a purchase at the end of 1972 but was not included in the ending inventory since it was received on January 3, 1973.

(b) Merchandise, cost $700, was received in 1972 and included in the ending inventory; however, the entry recording the purchase was made on January 4, 1973, when the invoice was received.

(c) 800 units of Commodity Z, costing $5.36 per unit, were recorded at a per unit cost of $3.56 in summarizing the ending inventory.

(d) Goods in the hands of a consignee costing $4,000 were included in the inventory; however, $2,400 of such goods had been sold as of December 31, and the sale was not recorded until January 31, 1973, when the consignee made a full remittance of $3,200 on this item.

(e) Merchandise, cost $600, sold for $760 and shipped on December 31, 1972, was not included in the ending inventory; however, the sale was not recorded until January 12, 1973, when the customer made payment on the sale.

Instructions: (1) Compute the corrected net income or loss for 1972.
(2) Give the entries that are required in 1973 to correct the accounts assuming the company uses the periodic inventory method.

8-10. The Erdman Manufacturing Company produces one principal product. The income from sales of this product for the year 1972 is expected to be $200,000. Cost of goods sold will be as follows:

Materials used	$ 40,000
Direct labor	60,000
Fixed overhead	20,000
Variable overhead	30,000

The company realizes that it is facing rising costs and in December is attempting to plan its operations for the year 1973. It is believed that if the product is not redesigned, the following results will be obtained:

Material prices will average 5% higher and rates for direct labor will average 10% higher. Variable overhead will vary in proportion to direct labor costs. If the sale price is increased to produce the same rate of gross profit as the 1972 rate, there will be a 10% decrease in the number of units sold in 1973.

If the product is redesigned according to suggestions offered by the sales manager, it is expected that a 10% increase can be obtained in the number of units sold with a 15% increase in sale price per unit. However, a change in the product would involve several changes in cost.

A different grade of material would be used, but 10% more of it would be required for each unit. The price of this proposed grade of material has averaged 5% below the price of the material now being used, and that 5% difference in price is expected to continue for the year 1973. Redesign would permit a change in processing method enabling the company to use less-skilled workmen. It is believed that the average pay rate for 1973 would be 10% below the average for 1972 because of that change. However, about 20% more labor per unit would be required than was needed in 1972. Variable overhead is incurred directly in relation to production; it is expected to increase 10% because of price changes and to increase an additional amount in proportion to the change in labor hours.

Instructions: Assuming the accuracy of these estimates, prepare statements showing the prospective gross profit if:

(1) The same product is continued for 1973.

(2) The product is redesigned for 1973.   (AICPA adapted)

8-11. You have been engaged for the audit of the Y Company for the year ended December 31, 1972. The Y Company is engaged in the wholesale chemical business and makes all sales at 25% over cost.

Shown below are portions of the client's sales and purchases accounts for the calendar year 1972:

Sales

Date	Reference	Amount	Date	Reference	Amount
12/31	Closing entry	$699,860	Balance forward		$658,320
			12/27	SI#965	5,195
			12/28	SI#966	19,270
			12/28	SI#967	1,302
			12/31	SI#969	5,841
			12/31	SI#970	7,922
			12/31	SI#971	2,010
		$699,860			$699,860

Purchases

Date	Reference	Amount	Date	Reference	Amount
Balance forward		$360,300	12/31	Closing entry	$385,346
12/28	RR#1059	3,100			
12/30	RR#1061	8,965			
12/31	RR#1062	4,861			
12/31	RR#1063	8,120			
		$385,346			$385,346

RR = Receiving report.
SI = Sales invoice.

You observed the physical inventory of goods in the warehouse on December 31, 1972, and were satisfied that it was properly taken.

When performing a sales and purchases cutoff test, you found that at December 31, 1972, the last receiving report that had been used was No. 1063 and that no shipments had been made on any sales invoices with numbers larger than No. 968. You also obtained the following additional information:

(a) Included in the warehouse physical inventory at December 31, 1972, were chemicals that had been purchased and received on receiving report No. 1060 but for which an invoice was not received until 1973. Cost was $2,183.

(b) In the warehouse at December 31, 1972, were goods that had been sold and paid for by the customer but that were not shipped out until 1973. They were all sold on sales invoice No. 965 and were not inventoried.

(c) On the evening of December 31, 1972, there were two cars on the Y Company siding:

   1. Car #AR38162 was unloaded on January 2, 1973, and received on receiving report No. 1063. The freight was paid by the vendor.
   2. Car #BAE74123 was loaded and sealed on December 31, 1972, and was switched off the company's siding on January 2, 1973. The sales price was $12,700 and the freight was paid by the customer. This order was sold on sales invoice No. 968.

(d) Temporarily stranded at December 31, 1972, on a railroad siding were two cars of chemicals enroute to the Z Pulp and Paper Co. They were sold on sales invoice No. 966 and the terms were FOB destination.

(e) Enroute to the Y Company on December 31, 1972, was a truckload of material that was received on receiving report No. 1064. The material was shipped FOB destination and freight of $75 was paid by the Y Company. However, the freight was deducted from the purchase price of $975.

(f) Included in the physical inventory were chemicals exposed to rain in transit and deemed unsalable. Their invoice cost was $1,250, and freight charges of $350 had been paid on the chemicals.

Instructions: (1) Compute the adjustments that should be made to the client's physical inventory at December 31, 1972. (2) Prepare the adjusting entries that are required as of December 31, 1972.

(AICPA adapted)

8-12. You are engaged in an audit of The Wayne Mfg. Company for the year ended December 31, 1972. To reduce the work load at year end, the company took its annual physical inventory under your observation on November 30, 1972. The company's inventory account, which includes raw material and work in process, is on a perpetual basis and the first-in, first-out method of pricing is used. There is no finished goods inventory. The company's physical inventory revealed that the book inventory of $60,570 was understated by $3,000. To avoid distorting the interim financial statements, the company decided not to adjust the book inventory until year end except for obsolete inventory items.

Your audit revealed the following information regarding the November 30th inventory:

(a) Pricing tests showed that the physical inventory was overpriced by $2,200.

(b) Footing and extension errors resulted in a $150 understatement of the physical inventory.

(c) Direct labor included in the physical inventory amounted to $10,000. Overhead was included at the rate of 200% of direct labor. You determined that the amount of direct labor was correct and the overhead rate was proper.

(d) The physical inventory included obsolete materials recorded at $250. During December these obsolete materials were removed from the inventory account by a charge to cost of sales.

Your audit also disclosed the following information about the December 31st inventory:

(e) Total debits to certain accounts during December are listed below:

	December
Purchases	$24,700
Direct labor	12,100
Manufacturing overhead expense	25,200
Cost of sales	68,600

(f) The cost of sales of $68,600 included direct labor of $13,800.

(g) Normal scrap loss on established product lines is negligible. However, a special order started and completed during December had excessive scrap loss of $800, which was charged to Manufacturing Overhead Expense.

Instructions: (1) Compute the correct amount of the physical inventory at November 30, 1972.

(2) Without prejudice to your solution to part (1), assume that the correct amount of the inventory at November 30, 1972, was $57,700. Compute the amount of the inventory at December 31, 1972.

(AICPA adapted)

chapter 9

inventories - special valuation
procedures

Although inventories are typically valued at their cost, there are situations in which deviations from cost appear warranted. Some of these deviations are regarded as generally accepted; others are under careful study within the profession. These special valuation procedures will be described and discussed in this chapter.

Inventory valuation at cost or market, whichever is lower

Replacement costs for goods that are held may fall below original acquisition costs, suggesting sales prices that are less than those anticipated when the goods were purchased. Such circumstances are considered to justify departure from cost and the use of the lower replacement costs in valuing the inventory. Recognition of an inventory decline identifies the loss with the period in which it was incurred; goods are reported at an amount that measures the contribution carried into the next period. This practice is referred to as valuation at *cost or market, whichever is lower,* or valuation at the *lower of cost or market.*

"Market" in "cost or market" is generally interpreted to be inventory replacement cost by purchase or manufacture. The Federal Income Tax Regulations offer the following definition:

> Under ordinary circumstances and for normal goods in an inventory, "market" means the current bid price prevailing at the date of the inventory for the particular merchandise in the volume in which usually purchased by the taxpayer. . . .[1]

Replacement cost includes freight, duties, and other costs incidental to the acquistion of goods.

Modification in the lower of cost or market rule. The rule of valuation at the lower of cost or market was originally applied to achieve

---

[1]Income Tax Regulations; Sec. 1.471-4. (a)

"balance sheet conservatism" and called for the inventory write-down to a lower market or replacement cost under all circumstances. In shifting the emphasis from the balance sheet to the income statement, accounting authorities now take the position that departures from inventory cost are appropriate only when the utility of the goods is no longer equal to cost and future revenue should be freed from a portion of the cost burden. Support for inventory reductions must thus be found in achieving appropriate charges to the revenue of subsequent periods and not in providing conservative balance sheet values.

Authorities do not agree on the procedure to be followed in achieving the foregoing objective. The American Institute of Certified Public Accountants would apply certain significant limitations in the application of the conventional cost or market rule. The AICPA Committee on Accounting Procedure defines "market" as follows:

> As used in the phrase *lower of cost or market*, the term *market* means current replacement cost (by purchase or by reproduction, as the case may be) except that:
>
> (1) Market should not exceed the net realizable value (i.e., estimated selling price in the ordinary course of business less reasonably predictable costs of completion and disposal); and
>
> (2) Market should not be less than net realizable value reduced by an allowance for an approximately normal profit margin.[1]

The foregoing sets a ceiling for the market value at sales price less costs of completion and disposal and a floor for such market at sales price less both the costs of completion and disposal and the normal profit margin. The ceiling limitation is applied so that the inventory is not valued at more than its net realizable value, that is, the estimated selling price less the cost of completion and disposal; failure to observe such limitation would result in charges to future revenue that exceed the ultility carried forward and an ultimate loss on the sale of the inventory. The floor limitation is applied so that the inventory is not valued at less than its net realizable value minus a normal profit; valuation at the floor still assures the recognition of a normal profit on the sale of the inventory in future periods.

To illustrate, assume that a certain commodity sells for one dollar; selling expenses are twenty cents; the normal profit is twenty-five cents. The lower of cost or market as limited by the foregoing concepts is developed in each case as shown in the illustration that follows.

---

[1]*Accounting Research Bulletin No.* 43, "Restatement and Revision of Accounting Research Bulletins" (New York: American Institute of Certified Public Accountants, 1953), Ch. 4, statement 6.

			Market			
Case	Cost	Replace-ment Cost	Floor (Estimated Sales Price Less Selling Expenses and Normal Profit)	Ceiling (Estimated Sales Price Less Selling Expenses)	Market (Limited by Floor and Ceiling Values)	Lower of Cost or Market
A	$.65	$ .70	$.55	$.80	$.70	$.65
B	.65	.60	.55	.80	.60	.60
C	.65	.50	.55	.80	.55	.55
D	.50	.45	.55	.80	.55	.50
E	.75	.85	.55	.80	.80	.75
F	.90	1.00	.55	.80	.80	.80

A: Market is not limited by floor or ceiling; cost is less than market.
B: Market is not limited by floor or ceiling; market is less than cost.
C: Market is limited to floor; market is less than cost.
D: Market is limited to floor; cost is less than market.
E: Market is limited to ceiling; cost is less than market.
F: Market is limited to ceiling; market is less than cost.

The dollar line below graphically illustrates the floor and ceiling range. B and A replacement costs clearly are within bounds and therefore are defined as market. D and C are below the floor and thus the market is the floor; E and F are above the ceiling and market therefore is the ceiling.

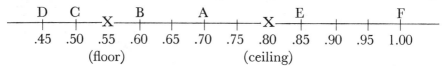

The Committee on Concepts and Standards Underlying Corporate Financial Statements of the American Accounting Association also viewed inventory valuation as a function of the income measurement problem but recommended the following procedure:

> . . . The residual cost should be carried forward in the balance sheet for assignment in future periods except when it is evident that the cost of an item of inventory cannot be recovered, whether from damage, deterioration, obsolescence, style change, over-supply, reduction in price levels, or other cause. In such event the inventory item should be stated at the estimated amount of sales proceeds less direct expense of completion and disposal.[1]

"Market" is abandoned as a test of subsequent utility in the above. Also, an inventory decline is ignored as long as cost is recoverable. In the example shown above, only case F would call for the recognition of a lower "market"; the market ceiling of eighty cents would be applicable here instead of the cost of ninety cents.

It may be observed that both authorities modify the "lower of cost or market" rule to a "lower of cost or residual useful cost" approach.

[1]*Accounting and Reporting Standards for Corporate Financial Statements and Preceding Statements and Supplements*, "Supplementary Statement No. 6, Inventory Pricing and Changes in Price Levels" (1957 rev.; Madison, Wisconsin: American Accounting Association), p. 36.

However, although the American Accounting Association would set a single criterion — sales proceeds less cost to complete and dispose — as a means for arriving at a residual cost to be carried forward and assigned to future revenue, the American Institute would recognize replacement costs but would establish significant limitations in their use.

Methods of applying lower of cost or market procedure. The lower of cost or market procedure may be applied to each inventory item, to the major classes of inventory items, or to the inventory as a whole. Application of this procedure to the individual inventory items will result in the lowest inventory value. However, application to inventory groups or to the inventory as a whole may provide a sufficiently conservative valuation with considerably less effort. For example, assume that balanced stocks of raw materials are on hand, some of which have gone down and others have gone up. When such raw materials are used as components of a single finished product, a loss in the value of certain materials may be considered to be counterbalanced by the gains that are found in other materials, and the lower of cost or market applied to this category as a whole may provide an adequate measure of the utility of the goods.

The illustration below shows the valuation procedure applied to (1) individual inventory items, (2) independent classes of the inventory, and (3) inventory as a whole.

	Quantities	Unit Cost	Market	Totals		Cost or Market, Whichever Is Lower		
				Cost	Market	(1) If Applied to Individual Inventory Items	(2) If Applied to Inventory Classes	(3) If Applied to Inventory as a Whole
Material A..........	4,000	$1.20	$1.10	$ 4,800	$ 4,400	$ 4,400		
Material B...........	5,000	.50	.40	2,500	2,000	2,000		
Material C..........	2,000	1.00	1.10	2,000	2,200	2,000		
				$ 9,300	$ 8,600		$ 8,600	
Goods in Process D...	10,000	1.60	1.40	$16,000	$14,000	14,000		
Goods in Process E....	12,000	1.00	1.20	12,000	14,400	12,000		
				$28,000	$28,400		28,000	
Finished Goods F.....	3,000	2.00	1.70	$ 6,000	$ 5,100	5,100		
Finished Goods G.....	2,000	1.50	1.60	3,000	3,200	3,000		
				$ 9,000	$ 8,300		8,300	
				$46,300	$45,300			$45,300
Inventory valuation...						$42,500	$44,900	$45,300

In valuing manufacturing inventories, raw materials declines are applicable to the raw materials inventory and also to raw materials costs in goods in process and finished goods inventories. Declines in direct labor and manufacturing overhead costs also affect the values of goods in process and finished goods, but these are usually ignored when they are relatively minor.

The method that is chosen for reducing an inventory to a lower market should be applied consistently in successive valuations. A lower market value assigned to goods at the end of a period is considered to be its cost for purposes of inventory valuation in subsequent periods; cost reductions once made, then, are not restored in subsequent inventory determinations.

For federal income tax purposes, taxpayers, except those who use lifo, may value their inventories at either cost or the lower of cost or market. Tax requirements provide for the application of cost or market to individual items; however, this rule may not be rigidly enforced when it involves certain practical difficulties. The valuation method that is elected must be applied on successive tax returns.

Evaluation of lower of cost or market procedure. Inventory valuation at the lower of cost or market is commonly employed in practice. However, such valuation is subject to serious criticism.

Valuation of inventories at the lower of cost or market can be challenged on the grounds that it violates the cost concept. Is it proper to distinguish between "favorable" and "unfavorable" costs and to adjust the latter to provide a more satisfactory showing in the period when these produce revenue? There would normally be no modification in charges for depreciation because of a decline in the replacement cost of buildings and equipment; nor would there be a modification in charges for bond interest because bonds can be issued at a lower interest rate. Then, should cost of goods sold be reduced in response to a decline in the replacement value of merchandise? Income measurements involve actual and not "fair" or "ideal" costs and revenues, some costs emerging currently from policies and transactions that date back to the time the company was organized.

Objection to valuation at the lower of cost or market is also raised on the grounds that it produces inconsistencies in the measurements of both the financial position and the operations of the enterprise. Market decreases are recognized but increases are not; with changes in the direction of market prices, a lower of cost or market valuation at the end of one year may be followed by a strictly cost valuation at the end of the next. Furthermore, serious income distortions may emerge when assumptions of future lower sales prices fail to materialize. To illustrate, assume that activities summarized in terms of cost provide the following results over a three-year period:

	1971		1972		1973	
Sales.................		$200,000		$225,000		$250,000
Cost of goods sold:						
Beginning inventory...	$ 60,000		$ 80,000		$127,500	
Purchases...........	120,000		160,000		90,000	
	$180,000		$240,000		$217,500	
Less ending inventory..	80,000	100,000	127,500	112,500	92,500	125,000
Gross profit on sales.....		$100,000		$112,500		$125,000
Operating expenses.....		80,000		90,000		100,000
Net income...........		$ 20,000		$ 22,500		$ 25,000
Rate of income to sales..		10%		10%		10%

Assume, now, that estimates as to the future utility of ending inventories indicated market values as follows:

1971	1972	1973
$75,000	$110,000	$92,500

If sales remained the same for the three years, inventory valuation at the lower of cost or market would provide the following results:

	1971		1972		1973	
Sales.................		$200,000		$225,000		$250,000
Cost of goods sold:						
Beginning inventory...	$ 60,000		$ 75,000		$110,000	
Purchases...........	120,000		160,000		90,000	
	$180,000		$235,000		$200,000	
Less ending inventory..	75,000	105,000	110,000	125,000	92,500	107,500
Gross profit on sales.....		$ 95,000		$100,000		$142,500
Operating expenses.....		80,000		90,000		100,000
Net income...........		$ 15,000		$ 10,000		$ 42,500
Rate of income to sales..		7.5%		4.4%		17.0%

Reduction of an inventory below cost reduces the net income of the period in which the reduction is made and increases the net income of a subsequent period. In the example just given, total net income for the three-year period is the same under either set of calculations. But the reduction of inventories to lower market values reduced the net income for 1971 and for 1972 and increased the net income for 1973. The fact that inventory reductions were not followed by decreases in the sales prices resulted in net income determinations that varied considerably from those that might reasonably have been expected from increasing sales and costs that normally vary with sales volume.

Application of the lower of cost or market procedure requires careful analysis of the underlying market conditions and care in arriving at the values to be used.

Application of lower of cost or market in the accounts. If beginning and ending inventories are reported on the income statement at amounts that are less than cost as a result of inventory pricing at the lower of cost or market, the cost of goods sold determination will include the effects of fluctuations in inventory replacement values. With unusual and substantial adjustments resulting from application of the cost or market rule, it is normally desirable to show these separately so that the reader of the income statement is fully informed on these matters and is able to make comparisons of operating results for successive periods.

Two procedures may be followed in separately setting forth the effects of market fluctuations in inventory values. One procedure calls for the periodic recognition of the effect upon incomes of an ending inventory reduced to a lower valuation. A second procedure calls for the periodic recognition of the effect upon incomes of both beginning and ending inventories adjusted to a lower of cost or market basis. The illustration on pages 294-295 compares the failure to recognize separately the effects of market fluctuations in inventory values with use of the alternative procedures indicated above.

In the first example, cost of goods sold each year reflects both goods sold and the effects of inventory declines. In the second example, the ending inventory for each year is reported on the basis of cost, and the inventory decline receives separate recognition. Beginning inventories are reported in terms of the inventory cost utility carried into the current period, a lower of cost or market value for a preceding period thus being used as the beginning cost in measuring cost of goods sold. In the third example, cost of goods sold is reported in terms of original cost. Inventory fluctuations are screened out of this section and the net effect of such fluctuations is reported separately as a loss or a gain. An inventory valuation account is adjusted periodically in reporting the ending inventory at a lower of cost or market basis. A decline in an ending inventory exceeding that related to a beginning balance calls for an increase in the valuation account and recognition of a loss; a decline in an ending inventory less than that related to a beginning balance calls for a decrease in the valuation account and recognition of a gain.

Inventories are frequently valued at the lower of cost or market as in the first example with no separate analysis of the effect of inventory fluctuations in the accounts. Such practice, although failing to provide a full analysis of operations, is normally the most convenient procedure. Periodic recognition of the loss on the ending inventory as in the second example offers a satisfactory approach to matching sales with the costs that may be considered applicable thereto while providing a separate analysis of current market declines. The allowance procedure with recognition of the net effect of inventory price fluctuations, the third example, finds support on the following grounds:

1. Price fluctuations relating to the inventory of both the prior year and the current year are removed from the cost of goods sold section. This may be considered particularly desirable when reductions in inventory replacement values are not necessarily followed by reductions in inventory sales prices; cost of goods sold and gross profit are stated in terms of cost.

2. When perpetual inventories are maintained, recognition of only the net periodic fluctuations through the valuation account avoids the need for detailed changes in subsidiary inventory records.

Lower of cost or market and lifo. Inventory values under lifo represent original cost and cost layers that remain after assigning most recent costs to revenue. In a period of falling prices, replacement costs may drop below costs identified with lifo inventories. With a practice that seeks to match current costs against current revenues, the reduction of inventory costs to a lower market would appear to be inappropriate. To adjust lifo inventories either up or down with corresponding adjustments to income would nullify the objectives sought in the adoption of lifo. However, modern accounting practice places no limitations upon application of the lower of cost or market procedure, and reductions in inventory replacement value are normally recognized by reductions in the lifo inventory. Unlike reductions when other inventory methods are employed and the lower of cost or market balances at the end of one period enter cost of goods sold in the next, reductions in lifo balances result in inventory valuations at the lowest market experienced by a company since its adoption of lifo.

Federal income tax regulations permit the use of lifo subject to certain conditions. Lifo is acceptable for tax purposes only if this method is used on the periodic financial statements. However, any reductions in lifo costing to a lower of cost or market basis that may be made in the accounts are not recognized for tax purposes. Furthermore, upon adopting lifo, any write-down to a lower of cost or market value in the closing inventory of the preceding year will have to be restored and both book inventory and taxable income for such year restated. In electing lifo for tax purposes, the taxpayer must weigh the possible advantages

(1) Failure to Recognize Separately Effects
of Fluctuations in Inventory Value

December 31, 1972:
Entries to record ending inventory:
  Inventory at cost.... $60,000
  Inventory at lower of
    cost or market.....   52,000
	Merchandise Inventory.. 52,000
	  Income Summary...... 52,000

Income statement for 1972:

Sales.........................		$240,000
Cost of goods sold:		
Beginning inventory....	$ 50,000	
Purchases............	130,000	
Cost of goods available.	$180,000	
End. inv. (lower of		
cost or market)........	52,000	128,000
Gross profit on sales....		$112,000
Operating expenses.....		100,000
Net income...........		$ 12,000

December 31, 1973:
Entries to close opening inventory.
Entries to record ending inventory:
  Inventory at cost.... $75,000
  Inventory at lower of
    cost or market.....   70,000
	Income Summary...... 52,000
	  Merchandise Inventory. 52,000
	
	Merchandise Inventory.. 70,000
	  Income Summary..... 70,000

Income statement for 1973:

Sales.........................		$280,000
Cost of goods sold:		
Beg. inv. (lower of		
cost or market)........	$52,000	
Purchases............	163,000	
Cost of goods available.	$215,000	
End inv. (lower of		
cost or market)........	70,000	145,000
Gross profit on sales.............		$135,000
Operating expenses.............		100,000
Net income....................		$ 35,000

against the reporting requirements and the denial of inventory write-downs for tax purposes.

A change from fifo to lifo will affect the comparability of the financial statements in the year of the change. In addition to meeting income tax requirements in the accounts, a company will also need to calculate the

(2) Recognition of Loss in Ending Inventory	(3) Recognition of Effect of Fluctuations on Beginning and Ending Inventories

Merchandise Inventory.   52,000
Loss on Reduction of
  Inventory to Market..   8,000
   Income Summary ...   60,000

Merchandise Inventory..   60,000
  Income Summary.....   60,000

Loss on Reduction of In-
  ventory to Market.....   8,000
  Allowance for Inventory
   Decline to Market....   8,000

Column (2):

Sales.........................		$240,000
Cost of goods sold:		
Beginning inventory...	$ 50,000	
Purchases...........	130,000	
Cost of goods available	$180,000	
Ending inventory (cost)	60,000	120,000
Gross profit on sales............		$120,000
Operating expenses.............		100,000
		$ 20,000
Loss on reduction of inv. to market		8,000
Net income..................		$ 12,000

Column (3):

Sales.........................		$240,000
Cost of goods sold:		
Beginning inventory....	$ 50,000	
Purchases............	130,000	
Cost of goods available.	$180,000	
Ending inventory (cost)	60,000	120,000
Gross profit on sales............		$120,000
Operating expenses.............		100,000
		$ 20,000
Loss on reduction of inv. to market		8,000
Net income....................		$ 12,000

Income Summary.....   52,000
  Merchandise Inventory   52,000

Merchandise Inventory.   70,000
Loss on Reduction of In-
  ventory to Market....   5,000
   Income Summary ...   75,000

Income Summary......   60,000
  Merchandise Inventory.   60,000

Merchandise Inventory..   75,000
  Income summary......   75,000

Allowance for Inventory
  Decline to Market.....   3,000
  Gain from Decrease in
   Inventory Allowance..   3,000

Column (2):

Sales.........................		$280,000
Cost of goods sold:		
Beg. inv. (lower of		
cost or market).......	$ 52,000	
Purchases...........	163,000	
Cost of goods available	$215,000	
Ending inventory (cost)	75,000	140,000
Gross profit on sales............		$140,000
Operating expenses.............		100,000
		$ 40,000
Loss on reduction of inv. to market		5,000
Net income..................		$ 35,000

Column (3):

Sales.........................		$280,000
Cost of goods sold:		
Beginning inventory		
(cost)................	$ 60,000	
Purchases............	163,000	
Cost of goods available.	$223,000	
Ending inventory (cost).	75,000	148,000
Gross profit on sales............		$132,000
Operating expenses		100,000
		$ 32,000
Gain from decrease in inv. allow...		3,000
Net income....................		$ 35,000

---

effect of the change in inventory methods upon net income and provide this information on the financial statements in parenthetical or note form. Readers of the statements will thus be afforded a summary of operations in terms of lifo as well as data enabling them to compare operations with those of the preceding period. In supplying these data, calculations of the ending inventory in terms of lifo and also in terms of the method originally employed will be required. Such calculations need to be made only in the year of the change.

To illustrate the effects of a change to lifo, assume the following data for the Morrow Co. that has valued inventories at fifo but adopts lifo in 1972:

Article	Inventory, Dec. 31, 1971		Purchases, 1972		Inventory, December 31, 1972			
					Fifo		Lifo	
	Units and Cost per Unit	Fifo Total Cost	Units and Cost per Unit	Total Cost	Units and Cost per Unit	Total Cost	Units and Cost per Unit	Total Cost
A	20,000 @ $1.90	$ 38,000	50,000 @ $1.80	$ 90,000	25,000 @ $1.80	$ 45,000	20,000 @ $1.90	$ 38,000
							5,000 @ $1.80	9,000
B	9,000 @ $2.50	22,500	30,000 @ $2.20	66,000	8,000 @ $2.20	17,600	8,000 @ $2.50	20,000
C	15,000 @ $4.00	60,000	40,000 @ $4.40	176,000	17,000 @ $4.40	74,800	15,000 @ $4.00	60,000
							2,000 @ $4.40	8,800
D	16,000 @ $4.50	72,000	25,000 @ $5.10	127,500	15,000 @ $5.10	76,500	15,000 @ $4.50	67,500
		$192,500		$459,500		$213,900		$203,300

The income statement that follows summarizes cost of goods sold in terms of lifo and explains by special note the effect upon net income of the change in the method of inventory valuation.

Morrow Co.
Income Statement
For Year Ended December 31, 1972

Sales..		$750,000
Cost of goods sold:		
Merchandise inventory, January 1, 1972 (cost upon the adoption of lifo)..	$192,500	
Purchases...	459,500	
Cost of goods available for sale.......................	$652,000	
Less merchandise inventory, December 31, 1972, on lifo basis	203,300	448,700
Gross profit on sales.....................................		$301,300
Operating expenses......................................		200,000
Income before income taxes..............................		$101,300
Income taxes..		47,200
Net income (see note below).............................		$ 54,100

Note: Inventories in prior years were reported on a first-in, first-out basis, and income before income taxes was calculated in accordance therewith. The inventory on December 31, 1972, on a first-in, first-out basis would be valued at $213,900, or $10,600 more than the value on a last-in, first-out basis; income under the method formerly followed would be greater than that reported above by $5,300 ($10,600 less income taxes at 50%).

Assume in the example that the inventory at the end of 1971 with a cost on a first-in, first-out basis of $192,500, had a market of only $185,000 and had been reported at the latter value. Upon adopting lifo for financial and income tax purposes in 1972, entries would be required to restore the inventory write-down to market and to recognize the additional income taxes applying to the income restatement for 1971. The income statement for 1972 would include the following special item:

Extraordinary gain:		
Cumulative effect on prior years (to December 31, 1971) arising from restatement of inventory of December 31, 1971, from a lower of cost or market value to cost in adopting lifo method.......	$7,500	
Less additional income taxes for 1971 applicable to restatement of inventory.	3,750	$3,750

Deteriorated goods, trade-ins, repossessions

A decline in market conditions may not be the only factor suggesting the use of values that are less than cost for inventories. There may be goods on hand that are deteriorated, obsolete, damaged, or shopworn. If such goods are unsalable, they should be excluded from the inventory. If the goods are salable but only at reduced prices, the lower of cost or market criterion should be applied in their valuation. When inventory cost shrinkages are significant, they should not be buried in cost of goods sold but should be reported under appropriate expense or loss headings. Thus, physical deterioration of goods arising from normal activities would be reported either as a special cost of goods sold item or as a selling expense, whichever might be considered more appropriate under the circumstances.

When goods are acquired in secondhand condition as a result of repossessions and trade-ins, they should be recorded at their estimated "cash purchase price." However, when this is difficult or impossible to define, the consistent application of "floor" values — amounts which, after increase by reconditioning charges, will permit the recognition of normal profits — would be appropriate. Sales efforts are required in the sale of repossessions and trade-ins just as in the sale of new items; recording the goods at floor values will permit the recognition of normal profits when goods are sold.

Losses on purchase commitments

Commitments are frequently made for the future purchase of goods at fixed prices. When price declines take place subsequent to such commitments, it is considered appropriate to measure and recognize such losses on the books just as losses on goods on hand.[1] A decline is recorded by a charge to a special loss account and a credit to an accrued liability account such as Accrued Losses on Purchase Commitments. Acquisition of the goods in a subsequent period is recorded by a credit to Accounts Payable, a charge canceling the accrued liability, and a charge to Purchases for the difference.

For example, assume that Travis Manufacturing Company entered into a purchase contract for $120,000 of materials to be delivered in March of the following year. At the end of the current year, the market price for this order had fallen to $100,000. The entry to record this decline and subsequent delivery of the materials would be as follows:

```
Dec. 31 Loss on Purchase Commitments...............   20,000
             Accrued Loss on Purchase Commitments.....             20,000


Mar.  1 Accrued Loss on Purchase Commitments.......   20,000
        Purchases................................  100,000
             Accounts Payable........................            120,000
```

The loss is thus assigned to the period in which the decline took place, and a subsequent period is charged for no more than the economic utilities of the goods it receives. Current loss recognition would not be appropriate when commitments can be canceled, when commitments provide for price adjustments, when hedging transactions prevent losses, or when declines do not suggest reductions in sales prices. Losses that are expected to arise from future sales commitments are not normally recognized as a charge against income. They may be recognized by footnote desclosure or by an appropriation of retained earnings.

Valuation at sales price

In special instances there is support for reporting goods at sales prices less costs to be incurred in their sale even though such values may exceed cost. Valuation at sales price must be regarded as exceptional treatment since earnings are recognized prior to time of sale. Such valuation can be justified only when it is a regular trade practice and arises from either (1) assured market conditions that make possible the immediate sale of the goods at stated prices, or (2) standard products, a

---

The AICPA Committee on Accounting Procedure states (*Accounting Research Bulletin No. 43, op. cit.,* Ch. 4, statement 10): "Accrued net losses on firm purchase commitments for goods for inventory, measured in the same way as are inventory losses, should, if material, be recognized in the accounts and the amounts thereof separately disclosed in the income statement." It may be observed that when such losses are recognized for book purposes but cannot be reported currently for income tax purposes, interperiod tax allocation may be required.

ready market, plus the inability to arrive at reasonable assignments of costs. Inventories such as gold, silver, and certain other metals may be accorded this exceptional treatment in view of their immediate marketability at a fixed sales price. Similar treatment may be accorded a farmer's inventory in view of the difficulty of arriving at satisfactory costs. When inventories are reported at more than cost, the special valuation procedure should be disclosed on the financial statements.

The Committee on Accounting Procedure of the AICPA sanctions the departure from cost and the recognition of realizable values in the accounts under the circumstances mentioned.[1] Departures from cost are also accepted for income tax purposes in special cases. Dealers in securities and in cotton, grain, and other commodities are permitted to value inventories at cost, the lower of cost or market, or at market value. The method that is elected must be used each period. Farmers are permitted to use a valuation procedure known as the *farm-price method*. This method provides for the valuation of inventories at current market prices less direct costs of marketing. If the farm-price method is adopted, it must be applied to the entire inventory with the exception of livestock. Livestock may be valued under either the farm-price method or the *unit-livestock-price method*. The latter is an adaptation of the standard cost method, providing for a classification of animals and the application to animals within each class of standard unit prices representing the normal costs of production. For example, a cattle raiser may estimate a cost of $75 to produce a calf and $50 a year to raise the calf to maturity. Animals would be classified and valued as follows: calves, $75; yearlings, $125; two-year olds, $175; mature animals, $225.

Valuation at market

There has been increasing support, particularly in recent years, for reporting inventories on the financial statements at their net realizable values or current replacement costs. Such valuation would recognize gains as well as losses when market or replacement costs differ from the costs of purchase or production. Earnings would emerge in two stages: (1) part of the earnings would be related to the periods in which goods are acquired, processed, and held; (2) the balance of the earnings would be related to the period in which goods are sold. Supporters of valuation at market insist that such valuation is necessary if inventories and working capital are to be fairly stated on the balance sheet. They also maintain that valuation at market is necessary if net income is to be measured in a fair and consitent manner.

---

[1]*Accounting Research Bulletin No. 43, op. cit.*, Ch. 4, statement 9.

A strong appeal for inventory valuation at market was made by Robert T. Sprouse and Maurice Moonitz in Accounting Research Study No. 3, "A Tentative Set of Broad Accounting Principles for Business Enterprises." Two statements by committees of the American Accounting Association have also stressed the need for these values. In 1964, an AAA Committee on Concepts and Standards for Inventory Measurement indicated that, although no single method for pricing inventory quantities had been found, the majority of Committee members felt that replacement cost was the best of the several available measurements. They concluded that the best solution to current reporting was a "simultaneous presentation of statements based on historical (acquisition) cost and the best estimate of 'current value' in order to disclose adequately the status and progress of the enterprise."[1]

In 1966, a special committee of the AAA, who were authorized to produce a basic statement of accounting theory, also recommended the acceptance of multi-valued reports that included current replacement cost data. The committee also indicated means of obtaining current-cost data. The committee concluded by stating:

> . . . techniques presently used to determine current replacement cost produce information which is sufficiently verifiable, quantifiable, and free from bias to justify their use in stating inventories of merchandise, materials, and supplies at their current replacement cost.[2]

Despite such support there has been little tendency among practitioners to accept inventory valuation at market. This procedure has been challenged chiefly on the grounds that it represents a departure from the cost concept and would violate the accounting standards of verifiability and objectivity. Further research seems necessary before these questions can be resolved.

Uncompleted contracts — profits based on degree of completion

A special valuation problem is encountered in those instances where a contractor engages in certain construction work requiring months or perhaps years for completion and the projects are found in various degrees of completion at the end of the contractor's fiscal period.

It is possible for a contractor engaged in a long-term project to carry such "work in process" at cost until it is completed, accepted by the customer, and the full profit can be calculated. This practice, referred

---

[1]"A Discussion of Various Approaches to Inventory Measurement, Supplementary Statement No. 2," *Accounting Review* (July, 1964), p. 700.

[2]*A Statement of Basic Accounting Theory* (Evanston, Illinois: American Accounting Association, 1966), p. 74.

to as the *completed-contract method*, is in conformity with the concept that revenue is not realized until a sale is completed and there can be formal recognition of new assets; revenue emerges from sales, not production.

However, the application of a sales basis concept of revenue for long-term contracts may lead to serious distortions of periodic achievement. If profit recognition is to await contract completion, the full profit will be related to the year in which the project is completed even though only a small part of the earnings may be attributable to productive effort in that period. Previous periods receive no credit for their productive efforts; as a matter of fact, they may be penalized through the absorption of selling, general and administrative, and other overhead costs relating to construction in progress but not considered chargeable to the construction inventory. Authorities are in general agreement that circumstances such as those described may justify departure from the sales standard as a basis for the recognition of revenue. Accordingly, they would support a valuation procedure that provides for an accrual of profit over the life of the contract in some equitable and systematic manner.

The AICPA Committee on Accounting Procedure comments on the point at which profit should be recognized as follows:

> It is recognized that income should be recorded and stated in accordance with certain accounting principles as to time and amount; that profit is deemed to be realized when a sale in the ordinary course of business is effected unless the circumstances are such that collection of the sales price is not reasonably assured; and that delivery of goods sold under contract is normally regarded as the test of realization of profit and loss.
>
> It is, however, a generally accepted accounting procedure to accrue revenues under certain types of contracts and thereby recognize profits, on the basis of partial performance, where the circumstances are such that total profit can be estimated with reasonable accuracy and ultimate realization is reasonably assured.[1]

A satisfactory approach to periodic profit recognition on long-term construction contracts may be achieved by use of the *percentage-of-completion method*. Use of the percentage-of-completion method calls for the selection of either of the following approaches:

(1) The degree of completion is developed by comparing costs already incurred with the most recent estimates as to total estimated costs to complete the project. The percentage that costs incurred bear to total estimated costs is applied to the estimated net profit on the project in arriving at the earnings to date. Profit is thus recognized in terms of a *percentage-of-cost completion*.

---

[1] *Accounting Research Bulletin No. 43, op. cit.*, Ch. 11, sect. A, par. 11 and 13.

(2) Estimates of the progress of a project in terms of the work performed are obtained from qualified engineers and architects. Such estimates are applied to total contract price, and costs incurred to date are subtracted from estimated revenue in arriving at current earnings.

To illustrate the application of the percentage-of-completion method using the first approach, assume that a dam is to be constructed over a two-year period commencing in September, 1971, at a contract price of $750,000. Summaries of construction progress and the estimated earnings for each year calculated on a degree of completion basis follow:

1971:	Contract price.................................		$750,000
	Less estimated cost:		
	Cost to date.................................	$ 50,000	
	Estimated cost to complete project..............	550,000	600,000
	Estimated total income........................		$150,000
	Estimated income — 1971:		
	50,000/600,000 × $150,000................		$ 12,500[1]
1972:	Contract price.................................		$750,000
	Less estimated cost:		
	Cost to date.................................	$450,000	
	Estimated cost to complete project..............	175,000	625,000
	Estimated total income........................		$125,000
	Estimated income to date:		
	450,000/625,000 × $125,000.................		$ 90,000
	Less income recognized in 1970.................		12,500
	Estimated income — 1972......................		$ 77,500
1973:	Contract price.................................		$750,000
	Less total cost:		
	Cost of prior periods..........................	$450,000	
	Current cost to complete......................	167,500	617,500
	Total income.................................		$132,500
	Less income recognized to date ($12,500 + $77,500).		90,000
	Estimated income — 1973......................		$ 42,500

---

[1]The same estimated earnings are developed if the relationship of cost incurred to total estimated cost is applied to the total contract price in arriving at the contract price considered earned, and this balance is then reduced by cost incurred to date. Calculations in the example would be:

Contract price considered earned: 50,000/600,000 × $750,000..............	$62,500
Cost to date...	50,000
Estimated income — 1971...	$12,500

In the preceding example, recognition of profit only upon project completion would have resulted in income of $132,500 in 1973. In the series of entries below recognition of profits on the basis of degree of completion is compared with recognition of profits only upon project completion based upon the facts in the example just given.

Transaction	Income Recognition by Percentage-of-Completion Method		Income Recognition by Completed-Contract Method	
1971: Costs of construction.	Construction in Progress.... 50,000 Materials, Cash, etc. ...	50,000	Construction in Progress.... 50,000 Materials, Cash, etc. ...	50,000
Advances from customer on contract.	Cash......... 60,000 Customer Advances....	60,000	Cash......... 60,000 Customer Advances....	60,000
Recognition of income for year.	Construction in Progress.... 12,500 Recognized Income on Long-Term Construction.	12,500		
1972: Costs of construction.	Construction in Progress.... 400,000 Materials, Cash, etc. ...	400,000	Construction in Progress.... 400,000 Materials, Cash, etc. ...	400,000
Advances from customer on contract.	Cash......... 425,000 Customer Advances....	425,000	Cash......... 425,000 Customer Advances....	425,000
Recognition of income for year.	Construction in Progress.... 77,500 Recognized Income on Long-Term Construction.	77,500		
1973: Cost of construction in completing contract.	Construction in Progress.... 167,500 Materials, Cash, etc. ...	167,500	Construction in Progress.... 167,500 Materials, Cash, etc. ...	167,500
Completion of contract: (a) Recognition of income for year.	Construction in Progress.... 42,500 Recognized Income on Long-Term Construction..	42,500	Construction in Progress.... 132,500 Income on Construction.	132,500
(b) Advances including payment in settlement.	Cash......... 265,000 Customer Advances....	265,000	Cash......... 265,000 Customer Advances....	265,000
(c) Approval of completed projects by customer.	Customer Advances..... 750,000 Construction in Progress...	750,000	Customer Advances..... 750,000 Construction in Progress....	750,000

Assume in the example that profits are measured on a percentage-of-completion basis using the second approach on page 302, and engineers and architects provide estimates of physical completion of the project at the end of each year as follows: 1971, 8%; 1972, 73%; 1973, 100%. Estimated earnings to be recognized in the accounts would be as follows:

Year	Revenue	Costs	Income
1971	8% × $750,000................. $ 60,000	$ 50,000	$ 10,000
1972	(73% × $750,000) − $60,000....... 487,500	400,000	87,500
1973	$750,000 − ($60,000 + $487,500)... 202,500	167,500	35,000
	$750,000	$617,500	$132,500

It should be observed that the practice of recognizing earnings on a job still in progress is a departure from normal valuation procedures and should be applied only when the circumstances are considered to warrant exceptional treatment. Estimates of the costs to complete a project or the degree of project completion should be developed from adequate data supplied by qualified architects and engineers. When reliable estimates cannot be obtained or when possible future contingencies may operate to reduce or cancel what appear to be accruing profits, conservatism requires the recognition of profit only upon project completion.[1] In the event that estimates indicate an ultimate loss on the contract, the full amount of such loss should be recognized in the accounts.

Financial statements should disclose the valuation method that is used for construction in progress as well as the full implications of such a method. When sales or transfers of partnership interests or of capital stock are involved, the status of contracts in progress and the degree of recognition of profits on such contracts in the asset and the capital sections assume vital significance.

In preparing the balance sheet, Construction in Progress summarizing construction costs and recorded income on construction to date is properly recognized as a current asset. The credit balance in the account with the customer summarizing advance and progress payments is properly reported as a subtraction from the construction in progress balance. An excess of customer advances over the balance in the asset

---

[1]The American Institute Committee on Accounting Procedure makes the following statement relative to the method to be employed: "The committee believes that in general when estimates of costs to complete and extent of progress toward completion of long-term contracts are reasonably dependable, the percentage-of-completion method is preferable. When lack of dependable estimates or inherent hazards cause forecasts to be doubtful, the completed-contract method is preferable." *Accounting Research Bulletin No.* 45, "Long-Term Construction-Type Contracts" (New York: American Institute of Certified Accountants, 1955), par. 15.

account should be recognized as a current liability. Advances from customers representing loans or deposits should be reported as liabilities.

When a building, installation, or construction contract covers more than one year, federal income tax regulations permit the taxpayer to recognize profits on a percentage-of-completion basis over the life of the project or in the year when the project is completed and accepted. Salaries, taxes, and other expenses not directly attributable to the contract must be deducted in the year in which incurred.

Consistent application of the method of accounting chosen is required for tax purposes, a change from the percentage-of-completion method to the completed-contract method, or a change from the completed-contract method to the percentage-of-completion method, requiring special permission. It should be observed that the use of different methods for financial statements and for income tax purposes will require the application of interperiod tax allocation procedures.

QUESTIONS

1. What reasons are given to support the use of cost when an inventory has a market value that is less than cost? What reasons are given to support the use of the lower of cost or market? Would you support the use of market values whether lower or higher than cost? Why?

2. Define "market" for purposes of inventory valuation at "cost or market, whichever is lower."

3. Objection has been raised to the use of the term "market" in the phrase "cost or market, whichever is lower." Can you recommend a more satisfactory term?

4. The use of cost or market, whichever is lower, is an archaic continuation of conservative accounting. Comment on this view.

5. Distinguish between the approaches that are adopted by the American Institute and the American Accounting Association in arriving at a lower than cost basis for inventory valuation. Which do you support? Why?

6. (a) Describe the application of the lower of cost or market valuation to (1) each inventory item, (2) inventory classes, (3) the inventory as a whole. (b) State the conditions that would indicate the use of each of these methods.

7. What conditions might suggest caution in the application of the rule of cost or market, whichever is lower? Why?

8. (a) State two procedures that might be used in the accounts for the separate recognition of inventory fluctuations arising from inventory valuation at the lower of cost or market. (b) What is the alternative to such separate recognition? (c) Would you recommend such special procedures in the accounts? Why?

9. There has been increasing support for the use of market values in reporting inventories on the financial statements. What are the major arguments that are raised in supporting such use?

10. The inventory of the Prince Co. on December 31, 1971, had a cost of $85,000. However, prices had been declining and the replacement cost of the inventory on this date was $70,000. Prices continued to decline and in early March, 1972, when the statements were being drawn up, the replacement cost for the inventory was only $55,000. How would you recommend that the inventory be reported on the statements for 1971?

11. The Berg Corporation began business on January 1, 1971. Information about its inventories under different valuation methods is shown below. Using this information you are to choose the phrase which best answers each of the following questions.

| | | | Inventory | |
| | | | | Lower of |
	Lifo Cost	Fifo Cost	Market	Cost or Market*
December 31, 1971	$10,200	$10,000	$ 9,600	$ 8,900
December 31, 1972	9,100	9,000	8,800	8,500
December 31, 1973	10,300	11,000	12,000	10,900

*Fifo cost.

(a) The inventory basis that would result in the highest net income for 1971 is:
    (1) Lifo cost, (2) Fifo cost, (3) Market, (4) Lower of cost or market.

(b) The inventory basis that would result in the highest net income for 1972 is:
    (1) Lifo cost, (2) Fifo cost, (3) Market, (4) Lower of cost or market.

(c) The inventory basis that would result in the lowest net income for the three years combined is:
    (1) Lifo cost, (2) Fifo cost, (3) Market, (4) Lower of cost or market.

(d) For the year 1972, how much higher or lower would net income be on the fifo cost basis than on the lower of cost or market basis?
    (1) $400 higher, (2) $400 lower, (3) $600 higher, (4) $600 lower, (5) $1,000 higher, (6) $1,000 lower, (7) $1,400 higher, (8) $1,400 lower.

12. The Bedford Co. has recognized inventory costs by the fifo method and periodically values the inventory at the lower of cost or market. In 1972 it decides to change to lifo. How should the change be effected in the accounts? What special disclosure would you make on the financial statements in the year of the change?

13. What advantages do you see to the use of multi-valued statements? Do you support their usage?

14. How does the accounting treatment for losses from purchase commitments differ between actual losses which have already occurred and losses which may occur in the future?

15. How should inventory items received as trade-ins be valued?

16. How should repossessed goods be valued for inventory purposes? Give reasons for your answer.

17. Distinguish between the farm-price method and the unit-livestock-price method of inventory valuation.

18. (a) Describe the percentage-of-completion method for recognition of profits on long-term construction contracts. (b) What problems are involved in the application of this method? (c) How would you report the following account balances? (1) Construction in Progress; (2) Customer Advances on Construction in Progress; (3) Deposits by Customers on Construction Contracts.

19. J. M. Livasy, a building contractor, states, "I do not use the percentage-of-completion method. It is just too difficult to apply." What problems are associated with valuation of inventories by the percentage-of-completion method? How cay they be overcome?

20. Under what conditions would the use of the percentage-of-completion method for long-term construction contracts involve income tax allocation procedures?

EXERCISES

1. The Midland Supply Co. uses the first-in, first-out method in calculating cost of goods sold for the three products that it handles. Inventories and purchases of these products during January and the market price of these products on January 31 are as follows:

	Commodity A	Commodity B	Commodity C
Inventory, Jan. 1......	2,000 units @ $ 6.00	3,000 units @ $10.00	4,500 units @ $ 1.00
Purchases, Jan. 1–15...	2,000 units @ 6.50	4,500 units @ 10.50	2,000 units @ 1.20
Jan. 16–31..	1,000 units @ 7.50		
Inventory, Jan. 31.....	2,000 units	2,500 units	4,000 units
Market, Jan. 31.....	$7.50 per unit	$9.50 per unit	$1.15 per unit

Calculate: (a) the cost of the inventory at the end of January; (b) the cost of goods sold for January; (c) the balance to be provided by means of an allowance account to reduce the inventory as of January 31 to a basis of cost or market, whichever is lower, as applied to the individual items.

2. Determine the proper carrying value of the following inventory if priced in accordance with the recommendations of the AICPA on inventory pricing.

Item	Cost	Replacement Cost	Net Realizable Value	Net Realizable Value Less Normal Profit
A	$1.75	$1.80	$1.95	$1.78
B	.68	.65	.70	.66
C	.29	.27	.35	.30
D	.83	.83	.81	.76
E	.79	.74	.79	.72
F	1.19	1.15	1.12	1.05

3. The Hughes Manufacturing Co. has the following items in its inventory on December 31, 1972:

	Quantities	Unit Cost	Market
Raw Material A................	2,000	$1.10	$1.00
Raw Material B................	7,000	2.40	2.50
Raw Material C................	6,000	3.00	3.20
Goods in Process #1............	8,000	3.75	3.80
Goods in Process #2............	4,000	5.00	5.10
Finished Goods X..............	3,000	7.00	7.20
Finished Goods Y..............	2,500	8.00	7.50

Calculate the value of the company's inventory using cost or market, whichever is lower, assuming that this valuation procedure is applied:

(a) To individual inventory items.
(b) To each class of inventory.
(c) To the inventory as a whole.

4. The Reese Company summarizes inventory data at the end of 1972 and 1973 as follows:

	1972	1973
Invoice cost.....................................	$22,000	$25,000
Lower of cost or market......................	19,500	23,000

What entries are required (a) at the end of 1972 in recording the ending inventory and (b) at the end of 1973 in closing the beginning inventory and recording the ending inventory, assuming each of the following accounting procedures:

(1) The company calculates cost of goods sold in terms of inventories at the lower of cost or market without separate recognition of the effect of inventory market fluctuations.
(2) The company makes periodic recognition of the loss in the ending inventory resulting from valuation at the lower of cost or market.
(3) The company makes periodic recognition of the effects of market fluctuation identified with beginning and ending inventories through valuation at the lower of cost or market.

5. The Olson Products Co. entered into a 6-month $750,000 purchase commitment for a supply of its major raw material on October 1, 1972. On December 31, 1972, the market value of this material has fallen so that current acquisition of the ordered quantity would cost $625,000. It is anticipated that a further decline will occur during the next three months and that market at date of delivery will be approximately $525,000. What entries would you make on December 31, 1972, to recognize these facts?

6. Gamble Enterprises, Inc., summarizes operations for 1972 as follows:

Sales...	$620,000
Cost of goods sold..............................	440,000
Gross profit....................................	$180,000
Operating expenses.............................	80,000
Income before income taxes......................	$100,000
Income taxes...................................	50,000
Net income.....................................	$ 50,000

First-in, first-out was used in calculating cost of goods sold. However, in view of rising costs throughout 1972, management decides to restate operations for 1972 with inventories reported on a last-in, first-out basis. Inventories on a fifo basis were as follows: January 1, 1972, $65,600; December 31, 1972, $86,200. Inventories at December 31, 1972, restated at lifo are $74,100. Assume that the federal income tax rate is 50%. Prepare a revised income statement for 1972.

7. Curtis Construction Co. reports its income for tax purposes on a completed-contract basis and income for financial statement purposes on a percentage-of-completion basis. A record of construction activities for 1972 follows:

	As of December 31, 1971			January 1, 1972– December 31, 1972	
	Contract Price	Costs Incurred	Percent Completed	Costs Incurred	Percent Completed During 1972
Project A	$1,450,000	$715,000	65%	$505,000	35%
Project B	1,200,000	850,000	75%	310,000	25%
Project C	1,650,000	350,000	25%	1,030,000	70%
Project D	900,000			515,000	60%
Project E	215,000			35,000	15%

General and administrative expenses for 1972 were $80,000.

(a) Calculate the income before income taxes for 1972 to be reported for financial statement purposes. (b) Calculate the income for 1972 to be reported for income tax purposes. (c) Calcualte the amount to be reported as deferred income taxes payable. Assume a 40% income tax rate.

PROBLEMS

9-1. Stanley, Inc., carries five products. Units on hand, costs, and market prices of these items on January 31, 1972, are as follows:

	Units	Cost per Unit	Current Market Price per Unit
Product 100............	3,900 units	$2.50	$2.30
101............	1,650 units	4.20	4.60
102............	4,800 units	3.00	3.10
103............	3,200 units	5.20	5.05
104............	1,600 units	1.65	1.60

Instructions: Prepare a statement to show the calculation of the inventory for statement purposes on the basis of cost or market, whichever is lower, as applied to individual products.

9-2. The Young Bros. Mfg. Co. manufactures parts for drilling wells. They use the fifo inventory method and follow the practice of valuing the inventory at the lower of cost or market. Severe competition has resulted in a sale price reduction at year end of 10% on all completed parts and a decrease of 20% in the replacement cost of raw materials. At the end of the current fiscal year, the following cost information pertained to the closing inventories:

Raw materials.......................................	$35,000
Goods in process:	
Raw materials....................................	25,000
Labor...	30,000
Overhead..	15,000
Finished goods (replacement cost $51,000)...............	60,000

Instructions: Make the adjustment necessary to record the ending inventory at the lower of cost or market applied to each *class* of inventory. (Assume normal markup of 30% of manufacturing costs for these parts. Selling costs are 10% of manufacturing costs)

9-3. Carbonic Machines carries three classes of inventory items. Inventory data as of December 31, 1972, are summarized below.

		Per Unit	
	Quantity	Cost	Replacement Cost
Raw materials			
A..............	200	$ 8.00	$ 8.60
B..............	400	10.40	10.20
C..............	50	16.80	16.20
D..............	600	10.00	9.60
E..............	150	5.00	5.20
Goods in process			
#1..............	100	16.00	14.50
#2..............	290	5.50	5.00
#3..............	110	3.00	3.30

	Quantity	Per Unit Cost	Per Unit Replacement Cost
Finished goods			
W.............	3,000	3.40	3.65
X.............	6,500	3.00	3.25
Y.............	1,900	2.30	2.20
Z.............	15,000	1.50	1.65

Instructions: Prepare summaries to develop inventory valuation at the lower of cost or market, assuming this valuation procedure is applied:

(1) To individual inventory items.
(2) To separate inventory classes.
(3) To the inventory as a whole.

9-4. The Stuart Sales Co. sells three products. Inventories and purchases during February and the market prices of these goods on February 28 are as follows:

	Product A	Product B	Product C
Inventory, Feb. 1.............	200 units @ $ 65	200 units @ $110	60 units @ $145
Purchases, Feb. 1–28..........	60 units @ 50	120 units @ 105	60 units @ 130
Total available for sale........	260	320	120
Sales, Feb. 1–28..............	50 units @ 95	40 units @ 145	10 units @ 220
	130 units @ 100	110 units @ 135	40 units @ 210
Total sales..................	180	150	50
Units on hand, Feb. 28........	80	170	70
Market values per unit, Feb. 28..	$50	$95	$140

Selling, general, and administrative expenses for February were $15,300.

Instructions: (1) Prepare an income statement for February, assuming that the ending inventory is valued at cost on a first-in, first-out basis.

(2) Prepare an income statement for February, assuming that the inventory is reduced to cost or market, whichever is lower, applied to individual products, and the inventory loss is reported separately on the income statement. (First-in, first-out is used in arriving at cost.)

9-5. The Superior Appliance Company began business on January 1, 1971. The company decided from the beginning to grant allowances on merchandise traded in as part payment on new sales. During 1972 the company granted trade-in allowances of $42,690. The wholesale value of merchandise traded in was $27,250. Trade-ins recorded at $26,000 were sold for their wholesale value of $18,000 during the year.

The following summary entries were made to record annual sales and trade-in sales:

Accounts Receivable.........................	293,260	
Trade-In Inventory..........................	42,690	
Sales.....................................		335,950

Cash..	18,000	
Loss on Trade-In Inventory...................	8,000	
Trade-In Inventory........................		26,000

When a customer defaults on his accounts receivable contract, the appliance is repossessed. During 1972 the following repossessions occurred:

	Original Sales Price	Unpaid Contract Balance
On 1971 contracts............	$25,000	$13,500
On 1972 contracts............	16,000	12,500

The wholesale value of these goods is estimated by the trade as follows:

(a) Goods repossessed during year of sale are valued at 50% of original sales price.

(b) Goods repossessed in later years are valued at 25% of original sales price.

Instructions: (1) At what value should Superior Appliance carry the trade-in and repossessed inventory at December 31, 1972?

(2) Give the entry that should have been made to record the repossessions of 1972.

(3) Give the entry that is required to correct the trade-in summary entries.

9-6. Jax, Inc., carries five items in their inventory. The following data are relative to such goods at the end of 1972:

	No. of Units	Cost	Per Unit Replace-ment	Per Unit Estimated Sales Price	Per Unit Cost to Sell	Per Unit Normal Profit
Commodity A	1,000	$ 2.90	$ 3.05	$ 5.00	$ 1.20	$ 1.25
Commodity B	1,200	3.95	3.05	6.00	.80	1.00
Commodity C	2,000	5.50	4.90	8.00	.90	2.00
Commodity D	3,000	7.00	7.50	9.00	1.20	1.75
Commodity E	250	12.30	12.00	12.00	1.00	3.00

Instructions: Calculate the value of the inventory under each of the following methods:

(1) Cost.

(2) The lower of cost or market without regard to market "floor" and "ceiling" limitations, applied to the individual inventory items.

(3) The lower of cost or market without regard to market "floor" and "ceiling" limitations applied to the inventory as a whole.

(4) The lower of cost or net realizable value applied to the individual inventory items.

(5) The lower of cost or market recognizing "floor" and "ceiling" limitations applied to the individual inventory items.

9-7. Comparative income summaries for the Martin Company appear on the next page. Inventories have been reported periodically at cost.

An analysis discloses that replacement costs for inventories on hand at the end of each year had been as follows:

	1971	1972	1973
Inventory at market...............	$12,500	$14,500	$23,000

	1971		1972		1973	
Sales...............		$67,500		$82,500		$88,500
Cost of goods sold:						
Beginning inventory.	$10,000		$13,000		$17,500	
Purchases.........	40,000		46,000		50,000	
	$50,000		$59,000		$67,500	
Less ending inv.....	13,000	37,000	17,500	41,500	22,000	45,500
Gross profit on sales...		$30,500		$41,000		$43,000
Selling and gen. exp...		20,000		23,500		25,000
Net income.........		$10,500		$17,500		$18,000

Instructions: Prepare a set of comparative income statements on each of the following assumptions:

(1) Inventories are recorded in the cost of goods sold section on the basis of cost or market, whichever is lower.

(2) Inventories are recorded at cost in the cost of goods sold section but at the lower of cost or market for balance sheet purposes, a charge being reported periodically on the income statement reporting the loss identified with the ending inventory.

(3) Inventories are recorded at cost in the cost of goods sold section but at the lower of cost or market for balance sheet purposes, the effect of fluctuations in price on beginning and ending inventories being reflected as a special item on the income statement.

9-8. The Nielsen Company decides in 1972 to change its inventory method from first-in, first-out to last-in, first-out on both its federal income tax returns and its financial statements. The inventory was reported on the tax returns and on the statements at the end of 1971 at $429,350 calculated on a first-in, first-out basis.

The inventory at the end of 1972 is calculated on both a first-in, first-out basis and a last-in, first-out basis. Valuations are as follows:

At first-in, first-out............................	$410,000
At last-in, first-out.............................	$369,400

The following data, in addition to the information listed above, are to be recognized in preparing an income statement for 1972:

Sales (net of returns and allowances).....................	$3,950,000
Purchases (net of returns and allowances)	2,625,000
Selling, general, and administrative expenses..............	755,400
Other income — interest and dividends...................	11,300
Other expenses — interest.............................	36,800

Provision for federal income taxes for 1972 is to be made at a rate of 50%.

Instructions: Prepare an income statement for 1972 that summarizes cost of goods sold in terms of the newly adopted lifo method and reports the effects upon net income of the change in the inventory method.

9-9. John Erickson is a contractor for the construction of large office buildings. At the beginning of 1973 he had three buildings in progress. The following data describe the status of these buildings at the beginning of the year.

	Contract Price	Costs Incurred to 1/1/73	Estimated Costs to Complete 1/1/73
Building 1............	$5,400,000	$2,000,000	$2,800,000
Building 2..........	8,400,000	5,200,000	2,300,000
Building 3..........	3,150,000	800,000	2,000,000

During 1973 the following costs were incurred:

Building 1	$2,000,000 (estimated cost to complete as of 12/31/73, $800,000)
Building 2	2,500,000 (job completed)
Building 3	1,000,000 (estimated cost to complete as of 12/31/73, $1,500,000)
Building 4	500,000 (contract price, $2,500,000; estimated cost to complete at 12/31/73, $1,500,000)

Instructions: (1) Compute the gross profit in 1972 if Mr. Erickson uses the percentage-of-completion method.

(2) Compute the gross profit for 1972 if Mr. Erickson uses the completed-contract method.

9-10. Vik Construction Co. uses the percentage-of-completion method of determining net income in its accounting records and reports but elects to use the completed-contract method for income tax purposes. Percentage of completion is measured by the ratio of costs incurred to date to estimated total costs of completion, and the company's record in estimating total costs has been excellent. General and administrative expenses are recognized as periodic costs.

Contracts in process over a four-year period are summarized as follows:

Contract	Year Completed	Contract Price	Total Direct Cost
A	Year 1	$800,000	$710,000
B	Year 2	420,000	390,000
C	Year 4	980,000	930,000
D	Year 3	340,000	280,000
E		580,000	550,000 (estimated)
F		610,000	540,000 (estimated)

General and administrative expenses incurred and the completion record by contract are shown below:

	Year 1	Year 2	Year 3	Year 4
General and administrative expenses.	$40,000	$30,000	$35,000	$30,000

	Year 1	Year 2	Year 3	Year 4
Completion record:				
Contract A.	100%			
Contract B.	30%	70%		
Contract C.		10%	50%	40%
Contract D.		20%	80%	
Contract E.			20%	60%
Contract F.				90%

Instructions: (1) Determine for each year (a) income before income taxes per books, and (b) net taxable income.

(2) Assuming income tax allocation procedures are to be applied and the tax rate is 50%, prepare journal entries to record the accrual of income taxes for Year 1 and Year 2.

9-11. The Crossover Bridge Company obtained a construction contract to build a highway and bridge over the Mississippi River. It estimated at the beginning of the contract that it would take three years to complete the project at an expected cost of $50,000,000. The contract price was $60,000,000. The project actually took four years, being accepted as completed late in 1972. The following information describes the status of the job as of the close of each production year.

	1969	1970	1971	1972	1973
Costs incurred.	$12,000,000	$14,000,000	$18,000,000	$10,000,000	
Estimated cost to complete.	38,000,000	26,000,000	11,000,000		
Collections on contract.	12,000,000	3,000,000	30,000,000	10,000,000	$ 5,000,000

Instructions: (1) What is the income for each of the years 1969-1973 under (a) the percentage-of-completion method, (b) the completed-contract method?

(2) Give the entries for each year assuming that the percentage-of-completion method is used.

9-12. Bud Leeke is a plumbing contractor who is operating as a sole proprietorship.

It is the regular practice of the business at the time a contract is received to set up the full contract price by a charge to Accounts Receivable and a credit to Unearned Contract Sales. As work progresses on an individual contract, progress billings are sent to customers. No entry is made on the books for such progress billings. Collections are entered as a credit to Accounts Receivable. *Income is recognized on a completed-contract basis for statement purposes.*

No charge is made to work in process for general overhead expenses until a contract is completed and closed out to completed contracts. At that time 10% is added to direct costs as an allocation of general expenses. There are no inventories of materials since they are purchased only as needed for contracts.

The following balances are shown on the books as of December 31, 1972:

	Debit	Credit
Cash	$ 5,200	
Accounts receivable	125,500	
Work in process	118,250	
Fixed assets (net)	21,000	
Accounts payable		$ 5,100
Unearned contracts		144,000
Leeke, capital		67,850
Contract sales		400,000
Cost of sales	308,000	
Expenses	67,000	
Expenses absorbed		28,000
	$644,950	$644,950

The following schedule of accounts receivable and work in process has been prepared by the bookkeeper.

	Accounts Receivable	Direct Costs	Contract Price	Amount Billed
Easy Co.	$ 46,500	Closed		
Louis Building Co.	——	$ 7,500	$ 9,000	$ 9,000*
Joseph & Sons, Inc.	1,000	17,500	15,000	15,000*
Goss Wreckers	2,000	8,250	14,000	13,000
Bealey Co.	11,000	35,000	41,000	30,000
Davis Co.	65,000	50,000	65,000	30,000
	$125,500	$118,250	$144,000	$ 97,000

*Completed contracts not closed on books.

Instructions: Prepare a formal balance sheet as of December 31, 1972, and an income statement for the year. Support all items requiring adjustments with appropriate schedules or computations in good form.

(AICPA adapted)

9-13. The Metro Construction Company commenced doing business in January, 1972. Construction activities for the year 1972 are summarized as follows:

Project	Total Contract Price	Contract Expenditures to Dec. 31, 1972	Estimated Additional Costs to Complete Contracts	Cash Collections to Dec. 31, 1972	Billings to Dec. 31, 1972
A	$ 310,000	$187,500	$ 12,500	$155,000	$155,000
B	415,000	195,000	255,000	210,000	249,000
C	350,000	320,000	——	300,000	350,000
D	300,000	16,500	183,500	——	4,000
	$1,375,000	$719,000	$451,000	$665,000	$758,000

The company is your client. The president has asked you to compute the amounts of revenue for the year ended December 31, 1972, that would be reported under the completed-contract method and the percentage-of-completion method of accounting for long-term contracts.

The following information is available:

(a) All contracts are with different customers.
(b) Any work remaining to be done on the contracts is expected to be completed in 1973.
(c) The company's accounts have been maintained on the completed-contract method.

Instructions: (1) Prepare a schedule computing the amount of income (loss) by project for the year ended December 31, 1972, to be reported under (a) the completed-contract method, and (b) the percentage-of-completion method.

(2) Prepare a schedule under the completed-contract method computing the amounts that would appear in the company's balance sheet at December 31, 1972, for (a) costs in excess of billings, and (b) billings in excess of costs.

(3) Prepare a schedule under the percentage-of-completion method that would appear in the company's balance sheet at December 31, 1972, for (a) costs and estimated earnings in excess of billings, and (b) billings in excess of costs and estimated earnings.

(4) The company adopted the percentage-of-completion method for financial reporting purposes and the completed-contract method for income tax purposes. Assume that income before provision for taxes for the year ended December 31, 1972, under the percentage-of-completion method is $80,000 and the taxable income is $20,000. The income tax rate is 50%. Prepare the journal entry that you would recommend to record the income tax liability at December 31, 1972.

(AICPA adapted)

chapter 10

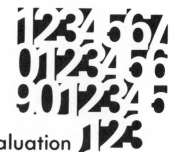

inventories - estimating procedures in valuation

Estimates are frequently employed in developing inventory quantities and inventory costs. Certain estimating procedures must be applied when inventories are lost by fire or other casualty. Estimating procedures are frequently employed in arriving at inventories of the mercantile enterprise when such procedures can offer satisfactory measurements without the counting and costing routines that would otherwise be necessary. Estimating procedures are also necessary in the manufacturing enterprise when detailed cost records are not kept. Widely used estimating procedures and the circumstances under which they are employed are described in the following pages.

Gross profit method

Estimates of merchandise on hand may be developed by means of the *gross profit method*. In using the gross profit method, the company's gross profit percentage is applied to sales in developing cost of goods sold; cost of goods sold is subtracted from the cost of goods available for sale in arriving at an estimated inventory balance.

The gross profit method of arriving at an inventory is applicable in the following instances:

1. When inventories are required for interim statements, or for the determination of the week-to-week or month-to-month inventory position, and the cost of taking inventories would be excessive for such purposes.

2. When an inventory has been destroyed by fire or other cause and the specific data required for its valuation are not available.

3. When it is desired to test or check on the validity of inventory figures determined by other means. Such application is referred to as the *gross profit test*.

The gross profit percentage that is used in reducing sales to a cost of goods sold balance must be a reliable measure of current sales experience. In developing a reliable rate, reference is usually made to past rates and these are adjusted for variations that are considered to exist currently.

Past gross profit rates may require adjustment when they are affected by inventory valuations expressed in terms of the lower of cost or market; rates affected by reductions applied to beginning or ending inventories may not be regarded as applicable under current experiences. Past gross profit rates may also require adjustment when inventories are valued at last-in, first-out, and significant fluctuations in inventory position and in prices have affected gross profits in a manner that is not representative of current experiences. Current changes in cost-price relationships or in the sales mix of specific products will further create need for modifying past rates.

The calculation of cost of goods sold depends upon whether the gross profit percentage is developed and stated in terms of sales or in terms of cost. The procedures to be followed in each case are illustrated below:

Example 1 — Given: Gross profit as a percentage of sales. Assume that sales are $100,000 and goods are sold at a gross profit of 40% of sales.

If gross profit is 40% of sales, then cost of goods sold must be 60% of sales:

Sales.....................	100%	Sales........................	100%
Cost of goods sold..........	?	=Cost of goods sold.............	60%
Gross profit...............	40%	Gross profit..................	40%

Cost of goods sold, then, is 60% of $100,000, or $60,000. Goods available for sale less the estimated cost of goods sold gives the estimated cost of the remaining inventory. Assuming that the cost of goods available for sale is $85,000, this balance less the estimated cost of goods sold, $60,000, gives an estimated inventory of $25,000.

Example 2 — Given: Gross profit as a percentage of cost. Assume that sales are $100,000 and goods are sold at a gross profit that is 60% of their cost.

(a) If sales are made at a gross profit of 60% of cost, then sales must be equal to the sum of cost, considered 100%, and the gross profit on cost, 60%. Sales, then, are 160% of cost:

Sales.....................	?	Sales........................	160%
Cost of goods sold..........	100%	=Cost of goods sold.............	100%
Gross profit...............	60%	Gross profit..................	60%

To find cost, or 100%, sales may be divided by 160 and multiplied by 100, or sales may simply be divided by 1.60. Cost of goods sold, then, is $100,000 ÷ 1.60, or $62,500. This amount is subtracted from the cost of goods available for sale in arriving at the estimated inventory.

(b) The cost of goods sold can be developed through an alternate calculation. If sales are 60% above cost, then the cost relationship to sales must be 100/160, or 62.5%.

Sales............	160%	But in terms	Sales............	100.0%	
Cost of goods sold.	100%	of sales as	Cost of goods sold.	62.5%	(100/160)
Gross profit......	60%	100%	Gross profit......	37.5%	(60/160)

Cost of goods sold, then, is 62.5% of $100,000, or $62,500.

Example 3 — Given: Sales as a percentage increase above cost. Assume that sales are $100,000 and goods are sold at 20% above cost. This is the same as saying that the gross profit is 20% of cost, and the answer would be developed as in Example 2 above. Sales, then, would be divided by 1.20, as in (a) above, or multiplied by .83⅓ (100/120), as in (b) above, in arriving at the estimated cost of goods sold.

When various lines of merchandise are sold at different gross profit rates, it may be possible to develop a reliable inventory value only by making separate calculations for each of the different lines. Under such circumstances, it is necessary to develop summaries of sales, goods available, and gross profit data for the different sections of the inventory.

Use of gross profit method for monthly inventory calculations. The gross profit method may be employed in developing a series of inventory values. For example, assume that the merchandise turnover is to be determined for a retail store whose gross profit calculation is as follows:

Sales.....................................		$500,000
Cost of goods sold:		
Inventory, January 1....................	$ 20,000	
Purchases.............................	310,000	
Cost of goods available for sale............	$330,000	
Inventory, December 31..................	30,000	
Cost of goods sold......................		300,000
Gross profit on sales.......................		$200,000

If only these data are available, the average inventory is $25,000, the sum of the beginning and ending balances divided by 2. The merchandise turnover, the number of times the average inventory has been replenished during the fiscal period, is then found to be 12 times, calculated as follows:

$$\frac{\text{Cost of goods sold}}{\text{Average inventory (using year-end balances)}} = \frac{\$300,000}{\$25,000} = 12$$

A more representative average inventory may be obtained by analyzing sales and purchases and computing monthly inventories by the gross profit method. These calculation are at the top of the next page.

	A Purchases	B Sales	COST OF GOODS SOLD			E Inventory Increase or (Decrease) (A−D)	F Inventory (F+E)
			C Cost as a Percentage of Sales	D Cost of Goods Sold (B×C)			
January 1							$ 20,000
January	$ 20,000	$ 30,000	60%	$ 18,000		$ 2,000	22,000
February	20,000	30,000	60	18,000		2,000	24,000
March	20,000	30,000	60	18,000		2,000	26,000
April	20,000	30,000	60	18,000		2,000	28,000
May	30,000	40,000	60	24,000		6,000	34,000
June	30,000	40,000	60	24,000		6,000	40,000
July	30,000	60,000	60	36,000		(6,000)	34,000
August	30,000	40,000	60	24,000		6,000	40,000
September	40,000	40,000	60	24,000		16,000	56,000
October	40,000	50,000	60	30,000		10,000	66,000
November	20,000	50,000	60	30,000		(10,000)	56,000
December	10,000	60,000	60	36,000		(26,000)	30,000
	$310,000	$500,000	60%	$300,000		$ 10,000	$476,000

The average inventory is calculated from the monthly inventory balances, and the merchandise turnover is determined as follows:

$$\frac{\text{Total of inventories}}{\text{Number of inventories}} = \frac{\$476,000}{13} = \$36,615$$

$$\frac{\text{Cost of goods sold}}{\text{Average inventory (using monthly balances)}} = \frac{\$300,000}{\$36,615} = 8.2$$

This figure is more accurate than the turnover that was developed on the basis of the year-end inventories which were unusually low and unrepresentative.

Use of gross profit method for computation of fire loss. A common application of the gross profit method occurs when a physical count of an inventory is impossible because of its physical destruction. For example, assume that on October 31, 1972, a wholesale distributing company had a fire in a warehouse which totally destroyed the contents, including many accounting records. Remaining records indicated that the last physical inventory was taken on December 31, 1971, and that the inventory at that date was $329,500. Microfilm bank records of canceled checks disclosed that during 1972 payments to suppliers for inventory items were $1,015,000. Unpaid invoices at the beginning of 1972 amounted to $260,000, and circularization of suppliers indicated a balance due at the time of the fire of $315,000. Bank deposits for the ten months amounted to $1,605,000. All deposits came from customers for merchandise except for a loan of $100,000 obtained from the bank during the year. Accounts receivable at the beginning of the year were $328,000, and an analysis of the available records indicated that accounts receivable on October 31 totaled $275,000. Gross profit percentages on sales were computed for the preceding four years as follows:

$$1968.\ldots\ldots\ldots\ldots\ldots\ldots\ldots.28\%$$
$$1969.\ldots\ldots\ldots\ldots\ldots\ldots\ldots.25$$
$$1970.\ldots\ldots\ldots\ldots\ldots\ldots\ldots.23$$
$$1971.\ldots\ldots\ldots\ldots\ldots\ldots\ldots.24$$

From these facts, the inventory in the warehouse at the time of the fire could be estimated as follows:

Estimate of sales January 1 to October 31, 1972

Collection of accounts receivable ($1,605,000 − $100,000)..	$1,505,000
Add accounts receivable at October 31, 1972..........	275,000
	$1,780,000
Deduct: Accounts receivable at January 1, 1972........	328,000
Estimate of sales January 1 to October 31, 1972........	$1,452,000
Average gross profit percentage on sales for past 4 years..	25%
Average cost percentage on sales for past 4 years........	75%
Estimate of cost of goods sold to October 31, 1972 ($1,452,000 × 75%).............................	$1,089,000

Estimate of inventory on October 31, 1972

Inventory January 1, 1972.........................		$ 329,500
Add: Payments to suppliers — 1972........	$1,015,000	
Amounts payable to suppliers, October 31, 1972..........	315,000	
	$1,330,000	
Deduct accounts payable to suppliers, January 1, 1972...............	260,000	
Estimate of purchases January 1 to October 31, 1972....		1,070,000
Goods available for sale..............................		$1,399,500
Estimate of cost of goods sold for 1972................		1,089,000
Estimated inventory, October 31, 1972................		$ 310,500

Retail inventory method

The *retail inventory method* is widely employed by retail concerns, particularly by department stores, as a means of arriving at reliable estimates of the business unit's inventory position whenever desired. When this method is employed, records of goods purchased are maintained in terms of costs and also at marked retail prices. The goods on hand at retail may be calculated at any time by subtracting sales for the period from the total goods available at retail. Cost and retail pricings of goods available are used in developing the percentage that cost bears to retail, and this percentage is applied to the goods on hand at retail in arriving at the estimated cost of such goods.

The determination of a company's inventory at the end of a month by using the procedure described follows:

	At Cost	At Retail
Inventory, January 1.........................	$30,000	$45,000
Purchases in January.........................	20,000	35,000
Goods available for sale......................	$50,000	$80,000
Deduct sales for January.....................		25,000
Inventory, January 31, at retail sales price.......		$55,000
Inventory, January 31, at estimated cost: $55,000× 62½% (percentage of cost to sales price, $50,000 ÷ $80,000)[1]...............................	$34,375	

It should be observed that the effect of the above procedure is to provide an inventory valuation in terms of average cost. No cost sequence is recognized; the percentage of cost to retail for the ending inventory is the same as the percentage of cost to retail for goods sold.

Use of the retail inventory method offers the following advantages:

1. Estimated interim inventories can be obtained without a physical count.
2. When a physical inventory is actually taken for periodic statement purposes, it can be taken at retail and then converted to cost without reference to individual costs and invoices, thus saving time and expense.
3. Checks are afforded on the movement of goods, since physical counts at retail should compare closely with inventories calculated at retail.

A physical count of the inventory to be reported on the annual statements is required at least once a year. Relatively significant discrepancies between a physical inventory and the inventory position as derived from book calculations should be investigated. Such inquiry may lead to sources of inventory misappropriations. Retail inventory records should be adjusted for variations shown by the physical count

---

[1]Instead of calculating the percentage that total cost bears to total retail price and then applying this percentage to the ending inventory at retail, it is possible to compute the cost of the inventory by a single arithmetical calculation as follows:

$$50,000/80,000 \times \$55,000 = \$34,375.$$

so that records reflect the actual status of the inventory for purposes of future estimates and control.

Markups and markdowns. The earlier inventory calculation assumed that after the goods were originally marked at retail prices, no further changes in such prices were made. Frequently, however, because of changes in the price level, changes in consumer demand, or other reasons, original retail prices are changed. The following items must ordinarily be considered in employing the retail method:

1. *Original retail* — the established sales price, including the original increase over cost variously referred to as the *markon* or *initial markup*.
2. *Additional markups* — increases that raise sales prices above original retail.
3. *Markup cancellations* — decreases in additional markups that do not reduce sales prices below original retail.
4. *Markdowns* — decreases that reduce sales prices below original retail.
5. *Markdown cancellations* — decreases in the markdowns that do not raise the sales prices above original retail.

The difference between cost and retail as adjusted for the changes described above is referred to as the *maintained markup*.

To illustrate the use of the above terms, assume that goods originally placed for sale are marked at 50% above cost. Certain merchandise costing $4 a unit, then, is marked at $6, which is termed the original retail. This increase in cost is variously referred to as a "50% markon on cost" or a "$33\frac{1}{3}$% markon on sales price." In anticipation of a heavy demand for the article, the retail price of the goods is subsequently increased to $7.50. This represents an additional markup of $1.50. At a later date the price is reduced to $7. This is a markup cancellation of 50 cents and not a markdown since the retail price has not been reduced below the original sales price. But assume that goods originally marked to sell at $6 are subsequently marked down to $5. This represents a markdown of $1. At a later date the goods are marked to sell at $5.25. This is a markdown cancellation of 25 cents and not a markup since sales price does not exceed the original retail.

In determining the goods on hand without a physical inventory, a record of each of the foregoing adjustments is required. The beginning inventory and purchases at retail are increased by net markups and decreased by net markdowns to arrive at goods available for sale at retail. Subtractions from goods available at retail are then made for sales, discounts to employees, inventory breakage, spoilage, and other losses. The ending inventory at retail as thus calculated may now be reduced to cost by applying the percentage that cost bears to retail.

In obtaining the cost percentage, the cost of goods available for sale (including any freight in) is normally related to the original retail plus the net markups, without taking into account the net markdowns. Calculation of the inventory in this manner is illustrated below.

	At Cost	At Retail
Beginning inventory....................	$ 8,600	$ 14,000
Purchases..............................	69,000	110,000
Freight in.............................	3,100	
Additional markups.....................		13,000
Markup cancellations...................		(2,500)
Goods available for sale..............	$ 80,700	$134,500
Deduct: Sales.........................		$108,000
Markdowns......................		4,800
Markdown cancellations.........		(800)
		$112,000
Ending inventory at retail............		$ 22,500

Ending inventory at estimated cost:

$22,500×60% (percentage of cost to retail before markdowns, $80,700÷$134,500)........ $ 13,500

Failure to recognize markdowns in calculating the cost percentage results in a lower cost percentage and consequently a lower inventory figure than would otherwise be obtained. Markdowns may be made for special sales or clearance purposes, or they may be made as a result of market fluctuations and a decline in the replacement cost of goods. In either case their omission in calculating the cost percentage is justified. This is illustrated in the two examples that follow:

Example 1 — Markdowns for special sales purposes: Assume that merchandise which cost $50,000 is marked to sell for $100,000. To dispose of part of the goods immediately, one fourth of the stock is marked down $5,000 and is sold. The cost of the ending inventory is calculated as follows:

	At Cost	At Retail
Purchases.............................	$50,000	$100,000
Deduct: Sales.........................		$ 20,000
Markdowns......................		5,000
		$ 25,000
Ending inventory at retail............		$ 75,000

Ending inventory at estimated cost:
$75,000×50% (percentage of cost to retail before markdowns, $50,000÷$100,000)..................... $37,500

If cost, $50,000, had been related to sales price after markdowns, $95,000, a cost percentage of 52.6 percent would have been obtained, and the inventory, which is three fourths of the merchandise originally acquired, would have been reported at 52.6 percent of $75,000, or $39,450. The inventory would thus be overstated and cost of goods sold understated. A markdown relating to goods no longer on hand would have been recognized in the development of a cost percentage to be applied to the inventory. Reductions in the goods available at sales price resulting from shortages, damaged goods, or employees' discount should likewise be disregarded in calculating the cost percentage.

Example 2 — Markdowns as a result of market declines: Assume that merchandise which cost $50,000 is marked to sell for $100,000. With a drop in replacement cost of the merchandise to $40,000, sales prices are marked down to $80,000. One half of the merchandise is sold. The cost of the ending inventory is calculated as follows:

	At Cost	At Retail
Purchases..	$50,000	$100,000
Deduct: Sales..		$ 40,000
Markdowns......................................		20,000
		$ 60,000
Ending inventory at retail....................................		$ 40,000
Ending inventory at estimated cost:		
$40,000 × 50% (percentage of cost to retail before markdowns, $50,000 ÷ $100,000).....................................	$20,000	

If cost, $50,000, had been related to sales price after markdowns, $80,000, a cost percentage of 62.5 percent would have been obtained and the inventory would have been reported at 62.5 percent of $40,000, or $25,000. Although this procedure reduces the inventory to cost, ignoring markdowns results in a cost percentage that reduces the inventory to a lower of cost or market basis. The use of the 50 percent cost percentage in the example reduces the inventory to $20,000, a balance that will provide the usual gross profit in subsequent periods if current prices prevail.

Discounts, returns, and allowances. Purchases should be shown net of cash discounts when discounts are regarded as a reduction of purchase cost rather than financial income. Purchases returns and allowances should also be shown as a deduction from purchases. A purchase return affects both the cost and the retail computations, while a purchase allowance affects only the cost total unless a change in retail price is made as a result of the allowance. Sales returns and allowances are proper adjustments to gross sales; however, sales discounts are not recognized since retail prices for goods purchased are recorded at gross amounts.

Limitations of retail method. It should be recognized that the calculation of a cost percentage for all of the goods carried is valid only when goods on hand can be regarded as a representative slice of the total goods handled. Varying markon percentages and sales of high- and low-margin items in proportions that differ from purchases will require separate records and the development of separate cost percentages for the different classes of goods. For example, assume that a store operates three departments and that for July the following information pertains to these departments:

	Dept. A		Dept. B		Dept. C		Total	
	Cost	Retail	Cost	Retail	Cost	Retail	Cost	Retail
Beginning inventory	$20,000	$ 28,000	$10,000	$15,000	$16,000	$ 40,000	$ 46,000	$ 83,000
Purchases.........	57,000	82,000	20,000	35,000	20,000	60,000	97,000	177,000
	$77,000	$110,000	$30,000	$50,000	$36,000	$100,000	$143,000	$260,000
Cost percentage...		70%		60%		36%		55%
Sales...........		80,000		30,000		40,000		150,000
Inventory at retail.		$ 30,000		$20,000		$ 60,000		$110,000
Inventory at cost ..		$ 21,000		$12,000		$ 21,600		$ 60,500
				($54,600)				

Because of the range in cost percentages from 36% to 70% and the difference in mix of the purchases and ending inventory, the ending inventory balance, using an overall cost percentage, is $5,900 higher ($60,500 − $54,600), than when the material departmental rates are used. When material variations occur, separate departmental rates should be computed and applied.

The retail method is acceptable for income tax purposes, provided the taxpayer maintains adequate and satisfactory records in support of inventory calculations and applies the method consistently on successive tax returns.

Dollar-value lifo procedures

Lifo valuation described in Chapter 8 included reference to unit lifo. Unit-lifo procedures called for a determination of the number of physical units comprising the inventory and the application of last-in, first-out costing to such quantities. Although unit-lifo procedures reduce the clerical routines, these still may be tedious, involved, and costly. Alternative procedures referred to as *dollar-value lifo*, using dollar values identified with the inventory rather than physical units as a basis for computing the lifo inventory, can simplify the valuation process significantly.

These procedures are widely used in practice and are acceptable for income tax purposes.

General procedures — dollar-value lifo. Dollar-value lifo views all goods in the inventory or in the separate pools to which it is to be applied as homogeneous. Inventories are taken in terms of current replacement prices. Beginning and ending inventory values are then converted by means of appropriate price indexes to base-year prices, prices at the time the lifo method was adopted. The difference between beginning and ending balances as converted is regarded as a measure of the inventory quantity change for the year. An inventory increase is recognized as an inventory layer to be added to the beginning inventory, and such increase is converted at the current price index and added to the dollars identified with the beginning balance. An inventory decrease is recognized as a shrinkage to be applied to the most recent or top layer and to successively lower layers of the beginning inventory, and such decrease is converted at the price indexes applying to such layers and subtracted from the dollars identified with the beginning inventory.

The following example illustrates dollar-value lifo calculations.

January 1, 1970 — date of adoption of dollar-value lifo:
January 1, 1970 inventory at base prices (cost) $38,000

December 31, 1970 — end of first year:
(a) December 31, 1970 inventory at year-end prices. $54,000
(b) December 31, 1970 inventory at base prices. $45,000
(c) January 1, 1970 inventory at base prices. $38,000
(d) 1970 inventory increase at base prices, $45,000 − $38,000 (b−c). . . . . $ 7,000
(e) Price index applying to 1970 layer, $54,000 ÷ $45,000 (a÷b).   120
(f) 1970 layer increase, $7,000 × 1.20 (d × e). . . . . $ 8,400
(g) December 31, 1970 inventory at dollar-value lifo, $38,000 + $8,400 (c+f). . . $46,400

	Base Prices	Index	Cost
Inventory composition: 1970 layer.	$ 7,000	120	$ 8,400
Base quantity.	38,000	100	38,000
	$45,000		$46,400

December 31, 1971 — end of second year:
(a) December 31, 1971 inventory at year-end prices. $66,000
(b) December 31, 1971 inventory at base prices. $50,000
(c) January 1, 1971 inventory at base prices. $45,000
(d) 1971 inventory increase at base prices, $50,000 − $45,000 (b−c). . . . . $ 5,000
(e) Price index applying to 1971 layer, $66,000 ÷ $50,000 (a÷b).   132
(f) 1971 layer increase, $5,000 × 1.32 (d×e). . . . . $ 6,600
(g) December 31, 1971 inventory at dollar-value lifo, $46,400 + $6,600 (1970g+f). $53,000

	Base Prices	Index	Cost
Inventory composition: 1971 layer.	$ 5,000	132	$ 6,600
1970 layer.	7,000	120	8,400
Base quantity.	38,000	100	38,000
	$50,000		$53,000

December 31, 1972 — end of third year:
(a) December 31, 1972 inventory at year-end prices........................... $56,000
(b) December 31, 1972 inventory at base prices.............................. $40,000
(c) January 1, 1972 inventory at base prices................................ $50,000
(d) 1972 inventory decrease at base prices, $50,000 − $40,000 (c−b).......... $10,000
(e) 1972 decrease: 1971 layer, $5,000 × 1.32 $6,600
                   1970 layer, $5,000 × 1.20   6,000...................... $12,600
(f) December 31,1972 inventory at dollar-value lifo, $53,000 − $12,600 (1971g−e). $40,400

	Base Prices	Index	Cost
Inventory composition: 1970 layer......................	$ 2,000	120	$ 2,400
Base quantity....................	38,000	100	38,000
	$40,000		$40,400

December 31, 1973 — end of fourth year:
(a) December 31, 1973 inventory at year-end prices........................... $55,000
(b) December 31, 1973 inventory at base prices.............................. $44,000
(c) January 1, 1973 inventory at base prices................................ $40,000
(d) 1973 inventory increase at base prices, $44,000 − $40,000 (b−c)............ $ 4,000
(e) Price index applying to 1973 layer, $55,000 ÷ $44,000 (a÷b)............. 125
(f) 1973 layer increase, $4,000 × 1.25 (d×e)................................ $ 5,000
(g) December 31, 1973 inventory at dollar-value lifo, $40,400 + $5,000 (1972f+f). $45,400

	Base Prices	Index	Cost
Inventory composition: 1973 layer......................	$ 4,000	125	$ 5,000
1970 layer......................	2,000	120	2,400
Base quantity...................	38,000	100	38,000
	$44,000		$45,400

The following items should be observed in the example:

December 31, 1970 — With an ending inventory of $45,000 in terms of base prices, the inventory has gone up in 1970 by $7,000; however, the $7,000 increase is stated in terms of the pricing when lifo was adopted and needs to be restated in terms of year-end prices which are 120% of the base level.

December 31, 1971 — With an ending inventory of $50,000 in terms of base prices, the inventory has gone up in 1971 by another $5,000; however, the $5,000 increase is stated in terms of the pricing when lifo was adopted and needs to be restated in terms of year-end costs which are 132% of the base level.

December 31, 1972 — With an ending inventory of $40,000 in terms of base prices, the inventory has gone down in 1972 by $10,000; however, the $10,000 decrease is stated in terms of pricing when lifo was adopted and needs to be restated in terms of the pricing of the inventory layers that are eliminated or reduced. The decrease is applied first to elimination of the 1971 $5,000 layer and next to the reduction of the 1970 $7,000 layer; decreases are restated in terms of the percentages at which these layers were included in the inventory cost — for 1971, 132% of the base level, and for 1970, 120% of the base level.

December 31, 1973 — The ending inventory of $44,000 in terms of the base prices indicates an inventory increase for 1973 of $4,000; this increase requires restatement in terms of year-end prices which are 125% of the base level.

It is assumed in the example that, instead of referring to industry or government sources for price indexes, indexes are most satisfactorily developed by comparing the prices of goods on hand at the end of each period with the prices assigned to such classes at the time of the adoption of lifo. In developing inventory values, goods may first be subdivided into reasonably homogeneous groupings and samples selected within these groupings; price relatives for the selected samples may then be employed in arriving at values assigned to groups and ultimately to the aggregate of goods on hand. In developing a value for the ending inventories in terms of base year prices after the first year, two steps may be employed: (1) a balance for the inventory in terms of beginning-of-year prices may be developed; (2) this balance may be converted to a base year value by dividing it by the index expressing the price change from the time of adoption of lifo until the beginning of the current year. To illustrate, in the example the price index was 120 at the end of 1970 and 132 at the end of 1971, or 10% above the 1970 level. If the December 31, 1971 inventory is found to be $66,000 on an end-of-year pricing basis and $60,000 at a beginning-of-year pricing basis, a base price valuation of $50,000 is arrived at by dividing $60,000 by 1.20, the cumulative price change from the time of adoption of lifo to January 1, 1971.

Retail-lifo procedures. Dollar-value lifo procedures just described can be applied to the retail inventory method in developing inventory values that reflect a last-in, first-out valuation approach. *Retail lifo* requires that index numbers be applied to inventories stated at retail in arriving at the quantitative changes in inventories. When the quantitative changes have been developed, ending inventories are restated in terms of the retail base amounts, and the layers involved in their composition and related cost percentages are applied to such values. The retail-lifo process calls for the following modifications in the conventional retail procedures that were described earlier:

1. The lifo inventory is composed of a base cost and subsequent cost layers that have not been assigned to revenues. With costs for prior periods to remain unchanged, only the cost of a current incremental layer requires calculation. Beginning inventory values, thus, must be disregarded in calculating a cost percentage applicable to a current inventory increase.

2. Markdowns, as well as markups, are recognized in calculating the cost percentage applicable to goods stated at retail. Markdowns were not recognized in arriving at the cost percentage when the objective was to arrive at a lower of cost or market valuation. However, with lifo measurements calling for inventory valuation in terms of cost, the recognition of both markups and markdowns becomes appropriate.

3. Upon adoption of retail lifo, an inventory valued at the lower of cost or market must be restated in terms of cost. This cost and the related retail assigned to such cost is regarded as the base inventory. Thereafter, periodic purchases and the retail values assigned to such purchases are recognized in arriving at the cost percentages that are applicable to incremental inventory layers.

Retail-lifo procedures are illustrated in the example that follows. Year-end price indexes expressed in terms of prices as of January 1, 1970, are: 1970, 105; 1971, 110; 1972, 112; 1973, 108. Retail for purchases is stated net of markups and markdowns.

	Retail	Index	Cost Percentage	Cost
January 1, 1970 — date of adoption of retail lifo:				
January 1, 1970 inventory................	$ 60,000	100	60	$ 36,000
December 31, 1970 — end of first year:				
Purchases.............................	$200,000		62	$124,000
December 31, 1970 inventory at retail......	$ 69,300			
December 31, 1970 inventory at retail base prices, $69,300÷1.05..................	$ 66,000			
1970 inventory increase at retail base prices, $66,000 − $60,000.....................	$ 6,000			
1970 layer increase — 1970 index, 105; 1969 cost percentage, $124,000 ÷ $200,000, or 62%................................	$ 6,000	105	62	$ 3,906
December 31, 1970 inventory at retail lifo, $36,000+$3,906.....................				$ 39,906
Inventory composition: 1970 layer...........	$ 6,000	105	62	$ 3,906
Base quantity.........	60,000	100	60	36,000
	$ 66,000			$ 39,906
December 31, 1971 — end of second year:				
Purchases.............................	$210,000			$134,400
December 31, 1971 inventory at retail......	$ 77,000			
December 31, 1971 inventory at retail base prices, $77,000÷1.10..................	$ 70,000			
1971 inventory increase at retail base prices, $70,000 − $66,000.....................	$ 4,000			
1971 layer increase — 1971 index, 110; 1970 cost percentage, $134,400 ÷ $210,000, or 64%................................	$ 4,000	110	64	$ 2,816
December 31, 1971 inventory at retail lifo, $39,906+$2,816.....................				$ 42,722
Inventory composition: 1971 layer...........	$ 4,000	110	64	$ 2,816
1970 layer...........	6,000	105	62	3,906
Base quantity.......	60,000	100	60	36,000
	$ 70,000			$ 42,722
December 31, 1972 — end of third year:				
Purchases.............................	$180,000			$117,000
December 31, 1972 inventory at retail......	$ 77,280			
December 31, 1972 inventory at retail base prices $77,280÷1.12..................	$ 69,000			
1972 inventory decrease at retail base prices, $70,000 − $69,000.....................	$ 1,000			
1972 decrease — 1970 layer..............	$ 1,000	110	64	$ 704
December 31, 1972 inventory at retail lifo, $42,722 − $704......................				$ 42,018
Inventory composition: 1971 layer...........	$ 3,000	110	64	$ 2,112
1970 layer...........	6,000	105	62	3,906
Base quantity.........	60,000	100	60	36,000
	$ 69,000			$ 42,018

	Retail	Index	Cost Percentage	Cost
December 31, 1973 — end of fourth year:				
Purchases...........................	$220,000			$132,000
December 31, 1973 inventory at retail......	$ 78,300			
December 31, 1973 inventory at retail base prices, $78,300 ÷ 1.08..................	$ 72,500			
1973 inventory increase at retail base prices, $72,500 − $69,000.....................	$ 3,500			
1973 layer increase — 1973 index, 108; cost percentage, $132,000 ÷ $220,000, or 60%..	$ 3,500	108	60	$ 2,268
December 31, 1973 inventory at retail lifo, $42,018 + $2,268......................				$ 44,286
Inventory composition: 1973 layer...........	$ 3,500	108	60	$ 2,268
1971 layer...........	3,000	110	64	2,112
1970 layer...........	6,000	105	62	3,906
Base quantity........	60,000	100	60	36,000
	$ 72,500			$ 44,286

Inventory valuation in a manufacturing concern

Manufacturing may take the *process* form, certain homogeneous products being produced by continuous processing methods, or it may take the *job order* form, a variety of products being produced according to special orders and specifications. In either form of manufacturing, when an organization does not maintain a cost accounting system that provides costs for goods in process and for goods completed, it becomes necessary to estimate the costs to be assigned to these inventories at the end of the fiscal period. The nature of the analysis that is required in estimating costs is described and illustrated in the section to follow. These examples assume the production of a single product by one continuous process.

Costs of manufacturing are summarized in materials, labor, and other manufacturing overhead accounts. These costs must be assigned to the goods that are still in production at the end of the period and to goods that were completed and placed in stock during the period. Costs assigned to goods completed during the period must then be related to the goods remaining on hand at the end of the period and to goods that were sold during the period.

In the manufacture of certain commodities, the raw materials required in their production are added at various stages during the course of production. In the manufacture of other commodities, all of the required raw materials are applied at the very beginning of production. In allocating manufacturing costs between goods remaining in production at the end of the period and goods completed during the period, the following information must be available:

1. The degree to which total *materials* requirements are met in the goods in process inventory.

2. The degree to which total *processing costs*, consisting of labor and manufacturing overhead, are met in the goods in process inventory.

The accounting problems that arise in the allocation of costs will
be illustrated by means of two examples: the first assumes that materials
are added uniformly throughout the period of production; the second
assumes that all of the required materials are put into process at the
beginning of production.

Example 1:   Materials are added uniformly throughout the period of production.

Assume the following inventories on December 31:

Finished goods — 3,000 units, cost $5.75 per unit, or $17,250.

Goods in process — 1,600 units, estimated 75% completed, cost $6,920.

Activities in January are summarized as follows:

6,000 units were started during the month raising the number in production to 7,600.

5,600 units were completed and transferred to finished stock during the month, 1,600
that had been partly completed at the beginning of the month and 4,000 that
were started and completed during the month.

2,000 units remaining in process at the end of the month were 30% completed.

4,500 units were shipped to customers during the month, 3,000 that had been completed in the prior period and 1,500 that were completed in January.

Manufacturing costs for January are summarized as follows:

Materials..	$ 6,000
Direct labor..	15,000
Manufacturing overhead.......................................	9,000
	$30,000

The estimates of the degree of completion of goods in process in beginning
and ending inventories express the estimated quantity of all of the elements of
manufacturing cost — raw materials and processing costs — required in the
final product.

It is first necessary to calculate the productive effort in the form of *equivalent
units*, representing a measure of the whole units of work performed in the factory
during the month. This may be done as follows:

Number of units completed in January............................	5,600
Deduct equivalent whole units in process on January 1, 1,600 units esti-
mated 75% completed, or.......................................	1,200
	4,400
Add equivalent whole units in process on January 31, 2,000 units esti-
mated 30% completed, or.......................................	600
Equivalent whole units of work performed in January...............	5,000

Manufacturing cost in January, $30,000, divided by the number of units of
work performed, 5,000, gives $6.00, the cost for each unit of work performed.
Using the first-in, first-out method, costs of goods completed, goods in process
inventory, goods sold, and finished goods inventory are determined as follows:

Cost of Goods Completed and Transferred from Factory to Stock:

$$
5{,}600 \text{ units}
\begin{cases}
1{,}600
\begin{cases}
\text{75\% completed in December, cost.} & \$\ 6{,}920 \\
\text{25\% completed in January, cost} = \$6.00 \times 400 \text{ equivalent} \\
\quad \text{units } (1{,}600 \times .25). & 2{,}400
\end{cases} \\[2em]
\underline{4{,}000} \text{ started and completed in January, cost \$6.00 per unit.} \quad 24{,}000 \\[1em]
\overline{5{,}600} \text{ units produced, cost \$5.95 per unit } (\$33{,}320 \div 5{,}600). \quad \$33{,}320
\end{cases}
$$

Cost of Goods in Process Inventory:

2,000 units, 30% completed in January, cost $6.00×600 equivalent units (2,000×.30). $3,600

Cost of Goods Sold:

$$
4{,}500 \text{ units}
\begin{cases}
\text{3,000 units on hand, December 31, cost \$5.75 per unit.} & \$17{,}250 \\
\text{1,500 units completed in January, cost \$5.95 per unit.} & 8{,}925 \\[1em]
\qquad\qquad\text{Total} & \$26{,}175
\end{cases}
$$

Cost of Finished Goods Inventory:

4,100 units completed in January, cost $5.95 per unit. $24,395

Manufacturing activities described above may be summarized in the accounts as follows:

GOODS IN PROCESS

Dec. 31 Balance, 1,600 units, 75% completed	6,920	Jan. 31 Cost of goods completed, 5,600 units	33,320
Jan. 31 Raw materials used	6,000		
31 Direct labor	15,000		
31 Manufacturing overhead	9,000		

(Balance in the account at the end of the month, $3,600, represents the cost of 2,000 units of goods in process inventory, 30% completed.)

FINISHED GOODS

Dec. 31. Balance 3,000 units	17,250	Jan. 31 Cost of goods sold, 4,500 units	26,175
Jan. 31 Cost of goods completed, 5,600 units from Goods in Process	33,320		

(Balance in the account at the end of the month, $24,395, represents the cost of 4,100 units of finished goods inventory.)

COST OF GOODS SOLD

Jan. 31 Cost of goods sold, 4,500 units	26,175

Example 2: Materials are put into process at the beginning of production.

Assume in the preceding example that materials are put into process at the beginning of production and that estimates of degree of completion of goods in process express only the estimated processing costs required in the final product. Here, in assigning costs to the inventories, it is necessary to calculate separately the materials cost and the processing cost required in the final product. Materials and processing costs are calculated as follows:

Materials costs: $6,000 divided by number of units started during month, 6,000, or $1.00 per unit.

Processing costs: $24,000, divided by equivalent whole units performed during month, 5,000, or $4.80 per unit.

Using the first-in, first-out method, costs for goods completed, goods in process inventory, goods sold, and finished goods inventory are calculated as follows:

Cost of Goods Completed and Transferred from Factory to Stock:

	1,600 { 75% completed in December, cost (materials and 75% of processing cost)	$ 6,920
	25% completed in January, processing cost, $4.80×400 equivalent units (1,600×.25)	1,920
5,600 units	4,000 units started and completed in January:	
	Materials cost at $1.00	4,000
	Processing cost at $4.80	19,200
	5,600 units produced, cost $5.72 per unit ($32,040÷5,600)	$32,040

Cost of Goods in Process Inventory:

2,000 units, 30% completed in January: Materials cost at $1.00	$ 2,000
Processing cost at $4.80×600 equivalent units (2,000×.30)	2,880
	$ 4,880

Cost of Goods Sold:

4,500 units	{ 3,000 units on hand, December 31, cost $5.75 per unit	$17,250
	1,500 units completed in January, cost $5.72 per unit	8,580
	Total	$25,830

Cost of Finished Goods Inventory:

4,100 units completed in January, cost $5.72 per unit [($32,040−$8,580)÷ 4,100 units]	$23,460

Inventories on the balance sheet

It is customary for business units to report trading as well as manufacturing inventories as current assets even though in some instances it may take considerable time before parts of such inventories are realized in cash. Among the items that are generally reported separately under the inventories heading are merchandise inventory or finished goods, goods in process, raw materials, factory supplies, goods and materials in transit, goods on consignment, and goods in the hands of agents and salesmen. Inventories are normally listed in the order of their liquidity.

Purchase orders should not be treated as additions to inventories, nor should sales orders be treated as deductions as long as title to goods has not passed. When goods have been formally set aside and the title is transferred, purchases or sales may be recognized with proper recognition of the effect of such transactions on the inventory position. Any advance payments on purchase commitments should not be included in inventories but should be reported separately. Such advances are preferably listed after inventories in the current asset section since they still await entry into the inventory phase of the operating cycle.

A number of parenthetical remarks or notes may be required in disclosing the valuation procedures employed. The basis of valuation (such as cost or lower of cost or market), together with the method of arriving at cost (lifo, fifo, average, or other method), should be indicated. The reader of a statement may assume that the valuation procedures that are indicated have been consistently applied and financial statements are comparable with those of past periods. If this is not the case, a special note should be provided stating the change in the method and the effects of the change upon the financial statements.

When the inventory method provides values that are materially less than current replacement costs, parenthetical disclosure of replacement costs should be offered. The use of lifo and base stock methods, for example, may result in serious distortions of working capital measurements. Data concerning replacement costs should be given if the reader of the statement is to be adequately informed on financial position.

An inventory allowance to reduce an inventory to a lower of cost or market basis is reported as a subtraction from the inventory at cost. However, an appropriation of retained earnings to preserve earnings within the business for possible future market decline in the inventory value is reported as a part of the stockholders' equity. If the decline fails to materialize, the appropriation balance is no longer required and is returned to the retained earnings account. If the decline does materialize, the appropriation is still returned to the retained earnings account where it will absorb the inventory loss that is ultimately carried to the latter account through net income.

If significant inventory price declines take place between the balance sheet date and the date the statement is actually prepared, mention of such declines should be made by parenthetical remark or note. When relatively large orders for merchandise have been placed in a period of widely fluctuating prices but the title to such goods has not yet passed, such commitments should be described by special note. Information should also be provided concerning possible losses on purchase commitments. Similar information may be appropriate for possible losses on sales commitments.

When inventories or sections of an inventory have been pledged as security on loans from banks, finance companies, or factors, the amounts pledged should be mentioned parenthetically in the inventory section of the balance sheet.

Inventory items may be reported as follows:

Inventories (valuation on the basis of cost or market, whichever is lower, cost being obtained by the first-in, first-out method):

Finished goods:		
On hand (goods of $100,000 have been pledged as security on loan of $75,000 from First State Bank)	$300,000	
On consignment..............	15,000	$315,000
Finished parts.................		25,000
Goods in process..............		300,000
Raw materials:		
On hand.....................	$210,000	
In transit from suppliers........	30,000	240,000
Factory supplies...............		12,000
Total inventories...............		$892,000

Prepaid expenses

It has been indicated that the current assets classification is composed of: (1) monetary assets — cash, temporary investments, and receivables; and (2) nonmonetary assets — inventories and prepaid expenses. Prepaid expenses representing rights to services have sometimes been referred to as "service receivables." However, these cannot be classified with receivables for they will not be converted into cash but rather will be applied to revenue of the operating cycle. This quality indicates a closer relationship to inventories and a more satisfactory designation as "service inventories." But prepaid expenses do not qualify as "items of tangible property held for sale" and hence should not be included as a part of a company's inventories. Prepaid expenses should be separately shown below inventories on the balance sheet.

Prepayments may be found for such items as insurance, rents, taxes, advertising, royalties, and supplies. When payment is made in advance of the receipt of a service or when supplies are acquired and not fully utilized, recognition of a prepayment is in order. Such prepayment should be assigned to future revenue in accordance with the expiration of the service or the consumption of the supplies. A discussion of several prepayments that are commonly found in business operations follows.

Unexpired insurance. Payments in advance are frequently made for insurance against fire and other hazards. Whenever statements are prepared, analysis of the insurance premiums is required to determine the portions chargeable to current revenues and the portions related to future periods to be reported as unexpired. With the maintenance of a number of insurance policies, a special record referred to as an *insurance register* may be maintained to offer detail relative to insurer, insurance coverage, periods covered, premiums, and premium allocations to periodic revenue.

Prepaid rent.   Rents for land, buildings, and for the use of motor vehicles and equipment are frequently paid in advance.   Periodically, determinations must be made of the rents chargeable to current revenues and the rents assignable to future revenues. The basis for the original charges — time, utilization, or other factors — should be used in establishing the prepaid balances.

Prepaid taxes, licenses, and fees.   Prepayments are frequently involved in taxes, licenses, and fees.   Such charges should normally be spread over applicable periods as indicated by the governmental authority concerned.

Operating supplies.   A business unit frequently acquires office, store, advertising, shipping, and other miscellaneous supplies.   The balances that remain on hand and are usable in subsequent periods should be reported as assets. The same procedures that are applied for the control, accounting, and valuation of inventories may be applied to supplies when these are found in large quantities and involve relatively significant costs.

QUESTIONS

1. Give certain instances in which estimates of inventory costs are necessary or appropriate and state what procedure would be followed in developing satisfactory estimates of such costs.

2. Distinguish between: (a) gross profit as a percentage of cost and gross profit as a percentage of sales; (b) markup cancellation and markdown; (c) the gross profit method of calculating estimated inventory cost and the retail inventory method of calculating estimated inventory cost.

3. What is your understanding of the meaning of the "gross profit test"?

4. What effect would the use of the lifo inventory method have upon the applicability of the gross profit method of valuing inventory?

5. How can a company verify that the use of the gross profit percentage approximates the cost of the inventory?

6. How can the retail inventory method be considered a perpetual inventory method?

7. Define (a) initial markup, (b) additional markup, (c) markup cancellation, (d) markdown, (e) markdown cancellation, and (f) maintained markup.

8. How should the cost percentage be calculated in the retail inventory method in arriving at a lower of cost or market valuation?

9. How are sales discounts recognized in using the retail inventory method?

10. A merchant taking inventory by the retail method maintains no separate record of markup cancellations and markdown cancellations. Instead he includes the former in markdowns and the latter in markups, as "these represent price decreases and increases respectively." How will this procedure affect his inventory at (a) retail? (b) cost?

11. What are the major advantages of dollar-value lifo?

12. Describe the application of dollar-value lifo procedures.

13. What valuation procedure is applied for an increase in inventory using dollar-value lifo? What procedure is applied for a decrease?

14. What kind of an enterprise will benefit most from the adoption of dollar-value lifo?

15. Describe retail lifo. What modifications in the conventional retail procedures are required in adopting and applying retail lifo?

16. (a) What is meant by the term "equivalent units"? (b) Does this term apply only to processing costs or is it applicable to raw material costs as well?

17. Some processing operations result in a loss of production units through evaporation. How should these lost units be accounted for in company ending inventory balances?

18. How would you recommend that the following items be reported on the balance sheet?

    (a) Unsold goods in the hands of consignees.
    (b) Purchase orders outstanding.
    (c) Advance payments on purchase commitments.
    (d) Raw materials pledged by means of warehouse receipts on notes payable to bank.
    (e) Raw materials in transit from suppliers.
    (f) An allowance to reduce the inventory cost to market.
    (g) An appropriation of retained earnings for possible future inventory declines.
    (h) Materials received from a customer for processing.
    (i) Merchandise produced by special order and set aside to be picked up by customer.
    (j) Raw materials set aside and to be used in connection with plant rehabilitation activities.
    (k) Finished parts to be used in the assembly of final products.
    (l) Janitorial supplies.

EXERCISES

1. Assume sales for a period of $100,000. What is the cost of goods sold under each assumption below?

(a) Gross profit on sales is 20%.
(b) Gross profit on cost of sales is 60%.
(c) Goods are marked up ¼ above cost.
(d) Gross profit on cost of sales is 150%.
(e) Goods are marked up 200% above cost.
(f) Gross profit on sales is 18%.
(g) Gross profit on cost is 18%.

2. (a) What is the percentage of profit on the basis of cost when the gross profit margin is 20% of selling price? 40% of selling price? 65% of selling price?

(b) What is the percentage of profit on the basis of sales price when the gross profit percentage is 25% of cost? 33⅓% of cost? 50% of cost? 100% of cost?

3. The sales and purchases data for the Anderson Co. follow:

	Sales	Purchases
January	$50,000	$40,000
February	60,000	40,000
March	65,000	50,000

The merchandise inventory at cost on January 1 was $20,000. Goods are sold at a gross profit of 20% on sales. Compute the monthly inventory balances for interim statement purposes.

4. G. L. Morgan requires an estimate of the cost of goods lost by fire on March 7. Merchandise on hand on January 1 was $60,000. Purchases since January 1 were $45,000; freight in, $5,000; purchases returns and allowances, $3,000. Sales are made at 20% above cost and totaled $42,000 to March 7. Goods costing $12,250 were left undamaged by the fire; remaining goods were destroyed. (a) What was the cost of goods destroyed? (b) What would your answer be if sales are made at a gross profit of 20% of sales?

5. R. S. Russell takes an inventory at cost on January 15, 1973, which is $25,000. His statements are based on the calendar year, so you find it necessary to establish an inventory figure as of December 31, 1972. You find that during the period January 2–15, sales were $80,000; sales returns, $1,500; goods purchased and placed in stock, $73,000; goods removed from stock and returned to vendors, $1,000; freight in, $500. Compute the inventory cost as of December 31, assuming that goods are marked to sell at 25% above cost.

6. From the information that follows for the Chance Co., compute by the gross profit method the value to be assigned to the inventory as of

September 30, 1972, and prepare an interim statement summarizing operations for the nine-month period ending on this date. Disregard income taxes.

	1/1/71–12/31/71	1/1/72–9/30/72
Sales (net of returns).	$1,250,000	$750,000
Beginning inventory.	210,000	365,000
Purchases.	1,076,000	530,500
Freight in.	58,000	36,000
Purchases discounts.	15,000	7,500
Purchases returns.	20,000	6,500
Purchases allowances	4,000	2,500
Ending inventory.	365,000	
Selling and general expenses.	225,000	160,000

7. Records for the Brooks Dept. Store disclose the following data:

	At Cost	At Retail
Merchandise inventory, Jan. 1.	$ 40,000	$ 60,000
Purchases, Jan. 1–Dec. 31	180,000	
Sales, Jan. 1–Dec. 31.		205,000
Sales returns, Jan. 1–Dec. 31.		5,000

A physical inventory taken on December 31 shows merchandise on hand valued at retail at $120,000. Compute the estimated cost of the ending inventory.

8. From the following information, compute the cost of inventory shortage for the Ajax Discount Stores for 1972. The company uses normal retail inventory procedures.

	Cost	Retail
Inventory, January 1, 1972 (cost ratio — 80%). . .	$ 9,600	
Purchases.	59,000	$74,000

Total sales for year amounted to $70,000. Markups were $6,000; markup cancellations were $1,500; markdowns, $3,000; freight in, $2,085; sales discounts, $2,000; and purchases discounts, $1,000. The physical inventory on December 31, 1972, was $15,000 (prices as shown on sales tags on items).

9. If the retail-lifo inventory method had been used in Exercise 8, what cost percentage would be used for 1972?

10. Yellow Dwarf, Inc., employs dollar-value lifo for periodic inventories. The inventory on January 1, 1972, was reported at $80,000; the inventory on December 31, 1972, was $93,500. The December 31 inventory at January 1 prices was $85,000. What cost would be assigned to the ending inventory?

11. You assemble the following information for the Burkes Department Store which computes its inventory at retail lifo:

	Cost	Retail
Inventory, January 1, 1972	$117,000	$150,000
Purchases	200,000	250,000
Increase in price level for year		5%

Calculate the cost of the inventory on December 31, 1972, assuming that the inventory at retail is (a) $147,000, (b) $168,000.

12. Compute the equivalent production figures for each case below:

(a) Started in process 10,000 units; completed and transferred 8,000 units; in process end of period, 2,000 units one-half completed.

(b) Started in process 25,000 units; completed and transferred 18,000 units; completed and on hand 3,000 units; in process end of period, 4,000 units three-fourths completed.

(c) Started in process 7,500 units; in process end of period, 1,000 units three-fourths completed, and 500 units two-fifths completed. No lost units.

(d) Opening inventory, 8,000 units three-eighths completed; started in process 20,000 units; completed and transferred 18,000 units; closing inventory, 5,000 units one-half completed and 5,000 units three-fourths completed.

(e) Opening inventory, 3,000 units one-third completed and 4,500 units one-half completed; started in process 30,000 units; closing inventory, 1,500 units one-fifth completed and 4,000 units three-fourths completed. No lost units.

13. The Babco Manufacturing Co. produces a cleanser product. During October materials of $22,000 were requisitioned for use in the factory. Other manufacturing costs in October were: labor, $40,000; overhead, $25,000. During October 15,000 units were completed and transferred to finished stock. On October 1 there were 8,000 units in process in the factory, estimated ¾ completed: estimated cost, materials — $16,800, and labor and overhead — $40,000. On October 31 there were 4,000 units in process, estimated ¼ completed. Degree of completion indicates the estimated portion of the total necessary cost to produce except for materials. All materials are put into production at the beginning of the process. There were no lost units. What is the cost of goods completed in October and cost of the ending goods in process inventory? Assume that the first-in, first-out method is used in calculating inventory costs.

14. Calculate the prepaid expenses of the Litho Manufacturing Co. as of October 31, 1972. The following data are available to you.

(a) Litho acquired a fire insurance policy covering a three-year period beginning May 1, 1970. The amount paid for the policy was $750.

(b) Property taxes of $2,200 were billed on July 15 for the city's fiscal year July 1, 1972, to June 30, 1973. Full payment was made on October 15, 1972.

(c) A 3-year equipment rental contract required a $225 deposit which was paid on July 1, 1972, when the equipment was obtained. Monthly rental charges are $75. The October payment has not yet been made, although previous monthly charges have been paid.

PROBLEMS

10-1. Quarterly purchases and sales for Hansen Electrical, Inc., are listed below. The corporation began 1972 with a merchandise inventory of $44,500. Goods have been sold at a uniform markup of 33⅓%.

	Purchases	Sales
January 1–March 31	$30,520	$38,600
April 1–June 30	30,900	51,620
July 1–September 30	50,200	58,300
October 1–December 31	27,000	72,000

Instructions: (1) Compute the inventory for the end of each quarter.
(2) Compute the merchandise turnover rate for the year based upon quarterly data.

10-2. The records of the appliance department for Shoppers' Delight Discount Store show the following data for the month of April:

Sales	$201,500	Purchases returns (at cost	
Sales returns	2,000	price)	$ 1,500
Additional markups	20,000	Purchases returns (at sales	
Markdowns	24,000	price)	2,300
Markdown cancellations	3,500	Markup cancellations	4,000
Freight on purchases	4,500	Beginning inventory (at cost	
Purchases (at cost price)	68,000	price)	116,000
Purchases (at sales price)	91,300	Beginning inventory (at	
		sales price)	170,000

Instructions: Compute the inventory at a conservative cost using the retail inventory method.

10-3. Compute the December 31, 1972, inventory for Home Manufacturing Corp. under the dollar-value lifo method. Business was started in 1967.

Date	Price Index	Inventory At Year-End Prices
12/31/67	100	$ 15,000
12/31/68	120	30,000
12/31/69	150	45,000
12/31/70	125	35,000
12/31/71	140	56,000
12/31/72	200	100,000

10-4. The Ellis Department Store decided in December, 1971, to adopt the dollar-value lifo method for calculating the ending inventory for 1972 and each year thereafter. Ellis feels that the published price indices are too general for his use; therefore, he intends to compute an index of price changes by sampling his stock of goods. The inventory at December 31, 1971, was $32,000 and this is considered the base cost for purposes of applying the dollar-value technique.

The following data have been accumulated as the basis for inventory valuation:

Description	Inventory Quantities (sample items)		Inventory Prices (end of year)		
	1972	1973	1971	1972	1973
A	40	40	$10.00	$12.70	$12.00
B	80	100	12.00	13.78	13.92
C	30	50	8.00	9.00	7.74
D	100	100	14.00	14.50	18.21
Total inventory cost at end-of-year prices..............			$32,000	$39,960	$44,730

Instructions: Compute the dollar-value lifo inventory for 1972 and 1973.

10-5. Warren-West, Inc., has adopted the retail-lifo method for stating its inventories. The following data are available for a four-year period ending December 31, 1973.

			Cost	Retail
1970	Inventory, January 1.................		$ 58,500	$ 90,000
	Purchases..........................		$155,000	$250,000
	Sales..............................			$230,000
	Price index (1/1/70 = 100)...........			110
1971	Purchases..........................		$145,000	$220,000
	Sales..............................			$237,250
	Price index (1/1/70 = 100)...........			106
1972	Purchases..........................		$156,000	$260,000
	Sales..............................			$250,150
	Price index (1/1/70 = 100)...........			108
1973	Purchases..........................		$201,600	$320,000
	Sales..............................			$305,000
	Price index (1/1/ 70= 100)...........			112

Instruction: Calculate the inventories to be reported at the end of 1970, 1971, 1972, and 1973.

10-6. The Roberts Department Store provides you with the following information for 1972:

	Cost	Retail
Beginning inventory.........................	$ 72,000	$ 90,000
Sales.......................................		183,000
Markups (net)...............................		15,000
Sales discount..............................		1,000
Markdowns (net).............................		8,000
Purchases...................................	148,000	193,000
Freight in..................................	7,000	
Purchases allowances........................	3,000	
Purchases discounts.........................	2,000	
Price level — beginning of year (base)........	100	
Price level — 1972..........................	107	

Instructions: (1) Determine the conventional retail cost percentage for the inventory.

(2) Calculate the retail value of the physical inventory at the end of the period assuming there was no shrinkage.

(3) Using retail-lifo procedures, compute retail and cost values for the inventory at December 31, 1972. Give your computations.

10-7. The Warner Co. began operations in December, 1970, and decided to use retail lifo in arriving at inventory values. On December 31, 1970, the inventory at retail was $45,000; its cost was $25,200. The following data are available for the period 1971–73.

	1971		1972		1973	
	Cost	Selling Price	Cost	Selling Price	Cost	Selling Price
Purchases.............	$117,000	$212,000	$155,000	$270,000	$162,500	$278,500
Freight in.............	4,800		7,440		5,500	
Markups (net).........		4,750		6,450		6,500
Markdowns (net).......		6,750		14,450		5,000
Sales.................		213,000		251,080		285,220

Price indexes for the line of goods sold by the company as of the end of each year as reported by an industrial publication were as follows:

1970..........120.0	1972..........129.6
1971..........126.0	1973..........127.2

Instructions: Calculate the inventories to be reported at the end of 1971, 1972, and 1973.

10-8. The Gopher Sports Shop values its inventory on the retail-lifo basis. At December 31, 1971, the inventory was valued as follows:

Lifo Layer Year	Cost	Retail	Price Index for Year
1965	$4,920	$8,200	100
1967	3,160	4,515	105
1969	4,480	8,961	103
1970	1,500	2,000	110
	$14,060	$23,676	

The following data were also compiled.

December 31, 1971 inventory at 1971 retail prices.........	$ 25,780
Purchases — cost.....................................	145,200
Purchases — selling price.............................	224,615
Freight in...	3,300
Sales returns..	3,740
Sales discount.......................................	650
Markups..	1,580
Markup cancellations.................................	360
Markdowns..	835
Gross sales..	234,000
Price index for 1972.................................	108

Instructions: Based upon the above information for 1972, compute (1) the 1972 cost ratio, and (2) the inventory amount that would be reported on the balance sheet at December 31, 1972.

10-9. Southside Iron Works, Inc., produces a single product. On December 1, 1972, inventories of the company were as follows:

Raw materials $10,000
Goods in process (800 units, approximately 60% completed) . . 25,800
Finished goods (300 units) 17,500

During December materials of $35,000 were purchased and materials of $40,000 were requisitioned for use in the factory. Costs during December were: labor, $38,000; other manufacturing costs, $12,000. During the month of December, 1,500 units were placed in finished stock and 1,100 units were sold at $70 per unit. At the end of the month, 1,200 units were in process, approximately 40% completed. Selling, general, and administrative expenses for the month were $12,000. Degree of completion indicates the estimated portion of the total cost to produce. The first-in, first-out method is used in calculating cost.

Instructions: Prepare an income statement accompanied by a manufacturing schedule. Provide summaries in support of inventory values used.

10-10. The Hughes Manufacturing Company uses the process cost system. The following quantity schedule for the month of January was obtained from the company records. All material costs are added at the beginning of the process.

	Department A	Department B
Quantity Schedule:		
Beginning inventory	2,500	1,500
Started in process	12,500	—
Received from prior departments	—	13,000
Total	15,000	14,500
Transferred to next department	13,000	10,500
Closing in-process inventory	2,000	4,000
	15,000	14,500
Cost Summary:		
Beginning goods in process	$ 2,485	$ 4,420
Cost for month:		
Materials	15,000	2,080
Labor	4,800	7,700
Overhead	5,280	5,500
Stage of completion — beginning inventory . . .	3/5	2/3
Stage of completion — ending inventory	1/4	3/8

Instructions: (1) Compute the equivalent whole units produced in January for each department.

(2) Compute the cost of the ending goods in process inventory for each department using the first-in, first-out method.

10-11. The Clean-Eze Soap Company manufactures 4 varieties of soap, all of which go through 4 departments, Mixing, Processing, Grinding, and Packaging. The Processing Department summarized quantity and cost data for March, 1972, as follows:

Processing Department Results — March, 1972

Quantity Schedule

Pounds in beginning inventory............................	100,000
Pounds received from Mixing Department during March......	850,000
Pounds of raw materials added............................	150,000
	1,100,000

Pounds transferred to Grinding Department..................	900,000
Pounds completed and on hand awaiting transfer to Grinding Department...	80,000
Ending goods in process inventory........................	120,000
	1,100,000

Cost Schedule

Cost of units transferred in from Mixing Department..........	$70,000
Materials..	10,200
Labor...	21,000
Overhead...	19,000

Composition of Beginning Inventory

Cost from Mixing Department — 100,000 pounds transferred in	$3,200
Materials (50% complete as to materials)....................	1,820
Labor (40% complete as to labor).........................	920
Overhead (40% complete as to overhead...................	1,790
Total value of goods in process inventory..................	$7,730

Composition of Ending Goods in Process Inventory

75% complete as to materials
50% complete as to labor and overhead

Instructions: (1) Compute the equivalent whole units of production for (a) preceding department costs, (b) materials costs, and (c) processing costs. (2) Compute the balance of the goods in process inventory as of the end of March using the fifo cost flow method.

10-12. The Borow Corporation is an importer and wholesaler. Its merchandise is purchased from a number of suppliers and is warehoused by Borow Corporation until sold to consumers.

In conducting his audit for the year ended June 30, 1973, the company's CPA determined that the system of internal control was good. Accordingly, he observed the physical inventory at an interim date, May 31, 1973, instead of at year end.

The following information was obtained from the general ledger:

Inventory, July 1, 1972	$ 87,500
Physical inventory, May 31, 1973	95,000
Sales for 11 months ended May 31, 1973	840,000
Sales for year ended June 30, 1973	960,000
Purchases for 11 months ended May 31, 1973 (before audit adjustments)	675,000
Purchases for year ended June 30, 1973 (before audit adjustments)	800,000

The CPA's audit disclosed the following information:

Shipments received in May and included in the physical inventory but recorded as June purchases	$ 7,500
Shipments received in unsalable condition and excluded from physical inventory. Credit memos had not been received nor had chargebacks to vendors been recorded.	
Total at May 31, 1973	1,000
Total at June 30, 1973 (including the May unrecorded chargebacks)	1,500
Deposit made with vendor and charged to purchases in April 1973. Product was shipped in July 1973	2,000
Deposit made with vendor and charged to purchases in May 1973. Product was shipped, FOB destination, on May 29, 1973, and was included in May 31, 1973, physical inventory as goods in transit	5,500
Through the carelessness of the receiving department a June shipment was damaged by rain. This shipment was later sold in June at its cost of $10,000.	

In audit engagements in which interim physical inventories are observed, a frequently used auditing procedure is to test the reasonableness of the year-end inventory by the application of gross profit ratios.

Instructions: Prepare the following schedules:
(1) Computation of the gross profit ratio for 11 months ended May 31, 1973.
(2) Computation by the gross profit method of cost of goods sold during June 1973.
(3) Computation by the gross profit method of the inventory at June 30, 1973.

(AICPA adapted)

10-13. Your new client has not prepared financial statements for three years since December 31, 1970. He used the accrual method of accounting and reported income on a calendar year basis prior to 1971. During the three years since December 31, 1970, his cash receipts and cash disbursements records were maintained and sales on account were entered when made, directly into an accounts receivable ledger. However, no general ledger postings have been made since the December 31, 1970 closing.

Your examination has disclosed balances at the beginning and the end of the three-year period as follows:

	December 31,	
	1970	1973
Aging of accounts receivable —		
Less than 1 year old......................	$ 7,700	$14,100
1 to 2 years old...........................	600	900
2 to 3 years old...........................		400
Over 3 years old..........................		1,100
Total accounts receivable.................	$ 8,300	$16,500
Inventories.................................	$ 5,800	$ 9,400
Accounts payable — merchandise purchases......	$ 2,500	$ 5,500

You have satisfied yourself as to the accuracy of the balances shown above. Other information available to you is as follows:

	1971	1972	1973
Cash received on account —			
Applied to —			
Current year's collections........	$74,400	$80,900	$104,400
Accounts of the prior year........	6,700	7,500	8,400
Accounts of two years prior......	300	200	1,000
Total......................	$81,400	$88,600	$113,800
Cash sales.........................	$ 8,500	$13,000	$ 15,600
Disbursements for merchandise purchases.........................	$62,500	$70,600	$ 86,900

No account balances have been written off as uncollectible during the three-year period. The ratio of gross profit to sales remains constant from year to year.

Instructions: Prepare a schedule showing sales, cost of goods sold, and gross profit for each of the years 1971, 1972 and 1973. Support the schedule with computations in good form. (AICPA adapted)

10-14. The operations of a department of a retail store that uses the retail method of inventory determination are given in the figures presented below:

Opening inventory — cost...............................	$14,250
Opening inventory — sales price...........................	19,105
Purchases — cost.......................................	33,771
Purchases — sales price...................................	46,312
Purchases allowances....................................	1,093
Freight in...	845
Departmental transfers (debit) — cost......................	100
Departmental transfers (debit) — sales price.................	140
Additional markups......................................	1,207
Markup cancellations....................................	274
Inventory shortage — sales price...........................	704
Sales (including sales of $4,460 of items that were marked down from $5,920)..	37,246

Instructions: Set up a computation showing the ending inventory at sales price and at cost as determined by the retail method. (AICPA adapted)

10-15. Under your guidance, as of January 1, 1972, the Little Corner Sporting Goods Store installed the retail method of accounting for its merchandise inventory.

When you undertook the preparation of the store's financial statements at June 30, 1972, the following data were available:

	Cost	Selling Price
Inventory, January 1.....................	$26,900	$ 40,000
Markdowns.............................		10,500
Markups...............................		19,500
Markdown cancellations..................		6,500
Markup cancellations....................		4,500
Purchases..............................	86,200	111,800
Sales..................................		122,000
Purchases returns and allowances..........	1,500	1,800
Sales returns and allowances..............		6,000

Instructions: (1) Prepare a schedule to compute the inventory on June 30, 1972, using the retail method of accounting for inventories. The inventory is to be valued at cost under the lifo method.

(2) Without prejudice to your solution to part (1), assume that you computed the inventory on June 30, 1972, to be $44,100 at retail and the ratio of cost to retail to be 80%. The general price level has increased from 100 at January 1, 1972, to 105 at June 30, 1972.

Prepare a schedule to compute the inventory on June 30, 1972, at the June 30 price level under the dollar-value lifo method.

AICPA (adapted)

10-16. Lopez Department Store converted from the conventional retail method to the retail-lifo method on January 1, 1972, and is now considering converting to the dollar-value lifo inventory method. Management requested during your examination of the financial statements for the year ended December 31, 1973, that you furnish a summary showing certain computations of inventory costs for the past three years.

Available information follows:

(a) The inventory at January 1, 1971, had a retail value of $45,000 and a cost of $27,500 based on the conventional retail method.

(b) Transactions during 1971 were as follows:

	Cost	Retail
Gross purchases........................	$282,000	$490,000
Purchases returns......................	6,500	10,000
Purchases discounts....................	5,000	
Gross sales............................		492,000
Sales returns..........................		5,000
Employee discounts....................		3,000
Freight in.............................	26,500	
Net markups...........................		25,000
Net markdowns.........................		10,000

(c) The retail value of the December 31, 1972 inventory was $56,100, the cost percentage for 1972 under the retail-lifo method was 62%, and the regional price index was 102% of the January 1, 1972 price level.

(d) The retail value of the December 31, 1973 inventory was $48,300, the cost percentage for 1973 under the retail-lifo method was 61%, and the regional price index was 105% of the January 1, 1972 price level.

Instructions: (1) Prepare a schedule showing the computation of the cost of inventory on hand at December 31, 1971, based on the conventional retail method.

(2) Prepare a schedule showing the computation of the cost of inventory on hand at the store on December 31, 1971, based on the retail-lifo method. Lopez Department Store does not consider beginning inventories in computing its retail-lifo cost ratio. Assume that the retail value of the inventory on December 31, 1971, was $50,000.

(3) Without prejudice to your solution to part (2), assume that you computed the inventory on December 31, 1971, (retail value $50,000) under the retail-lifo method at a cost of $28,000. Prepare a schedule showing the computations of the cost of the 1972 and 1973 year-end inventories under the dollar-value lifo method.

(AICPA adapted)

10-17. The E.A.P. Company is engaged in manufacturing. Its products are made principally from one raw material, and in order to insure uninterrupted production, it normally maintains a substantial inventory of the raw material. Because of advancing prices, the company in 1960 adopted the last-in, first-out method of pricing out its material requisitions, and thereafter valued its inventory at the prices shown by its perpetual inventory records.

As of December 31, 1971, the inventory consisted of 380,000 pounds carried on its books at an average price of $.90 per pound. The market price on December 31, 1971, was $1.50 per pound. As of December 31, 1972, the inventory was 420,000 pounds with a market price of $1.60 per pound. This was carried at the prices shown on the stock records, $270,000 pounds of this being valued at $.90 per pound and the remainder at prices which averaged $1.54 per pound. The purchases during the year were also made at an average price of about $1.54 per pound.

The operating accounts for the year ended December 31, 1972, included the following:

Sales.	$2,100,000
Goods in Process Inventory, 1/1/72.	146,600
Finished Goods Inventory, 1/1/72.	90,000
Direct Labor.	344,000
Cost of Materials Used.	1,217,000
Manufacturing Overhead.	302,000
Goods in Process Inventory, 12/31/72.	180,000
Finished Goods Inventory, 12/31/72.	100,000

On March 30, 1973, the warehouse in which the raw material inventory was stored was badly damaged by fire. The stock records were destroyed, but from other records the following figures were obtained:

Sales to March 30	$820,000
Purchases of materials	551,425
Direct labor	132,405
Manufacturing overhead	117,604
Goods in process inventory, March 30	175,000
Finished goods inventory, March 30	105,000
Salvage value of damaged materials	25,000

The purchase price of raw material during the three months had averaged $1.61 per pound with the price on March 30, at $1.62 per pound. The sales price during the period had varied only with the current material, labor and overhead cost existing at date of acceptance of the order, as is normal in this business.

Instructions: Calculate the amount of a claim for fire loss, assuming full insurance coverage. Show all computations to support the claim.

(AICPA adapted)

10-18. You have been retained by a fire insurance adjustor to examine the records salvaged from a fire which almost completely destroyed the office and warehouse of A, B and C, partners in a wholesale jobbing business.

Your report, directed to the adjustor, must include an estimate of the inventory value as of the date of the fire, January 2, 1973.

The merchandise handled by the firm is divided into three lines or classes of goods, designated as X, Y and Z. Classes X and Y each consist of a number of items which are bought and sold without change of form; Class Z consists of one item only for which raw material is bought and put through a manufacturing process.

The following records and data are found to be available:

(a) Duplicate sales invoices and credit memos, the totals of which are as follows:

	Sales	Credit Memos
Year 1970	$122,785	$6,585
Year 1971	110,942	7,582
Year 1972	87,451	4,160

A check of the numbers discloses that approximately 9% of the duplicate sales invoices for 1972 are missing.

(b) Duplicate bank deposit slips without any missing dates:

Year 1970	$108,066
Year 1971	96,008
Year 1972	91,150

Duplicate bank deposit slips were found to represent receipts from accounts receivable and cash sales only. You learn on inquiry that the partnership has made a practice of paying some expenses out of cash receipts not deposited. The amount of such payments cannot be determined.

(c) Purchase invoice files, accompanied by adding machine tapes purporting to show the total purchases for each year, with totals as follows:

Year 1970. . . . . $131,616
Year 1971.   117,935
Year 1972.   76,158

(d) Inventory sheets, taken by the management as of January 1, 1970:

Class X. . . . . $ 58,500
Class Y.   28,080
Class Z.   17,550
        — finished, 4/7 of which is raw material.   16,380

The management stated that about 17% was added to the cost of merchandise and raw materials in the 1970 inventory to cover freight and handling. A comparison of some of the inventory prices with purchase invoices at about the date of the inventory confirmed this statement. You find, however, that 2% of *net purchases* is sufficient to cover freight and handling into the warehouse and allow this percentage in *all cost computations*.

You ascertain also that 17% has been added to the cost of direct labor and overhead in the January 1, 1970 finished goods inventory, and that the overhead is 50% of the direct labor.

(e) Upon examination of the contents of the purchase invoice files you find that credit memos representing allowances on purchases have been listed on the adding machine tapes as invoices and included in the totals, as follows:

Year 1970. . . . . $7,548
Year 1971.   7,225
Year 1972.   6,120

All suppliers of merchandise and materials are circularized with a request for an itemized statement of account for the last three years, and these statements show additional credit memos in the following amounts:

Year 1970. . . . . $1,751
Year 1971.   3,128
Year 1972.   5,610

(f) Raw materials for Class Z are purchased in carload lots, and the invoices for the three years show total purchases of $33,000. You find that the shop foreman has kept a record showing that raw materials, of which the invoice cost was $34,000, have been put in process in the three years, and that the proportions of direct labor and overhead to materials cost have been approximately maintained.

(g) Analysis of a considerable number of sales invoices, selected in such a way as to give a fair sample of the entire file, and comparison with the computed cost of each item, give results which are summarized as follows:

	Percent of Net Sales	Percent of Gross Profit to Net Sales
Class X.	45%	10%
Class Y.	26%	15%
Class Z.	29%	21%

Instructions: Prepare computation of approximate inventory at January 2, 1973, including a schedule showing separately the raw materials and finished goods in Class Z. (Do not carry out any computations farther than the nearest dollar.)   (AICPA adapted)

chapter 11

investments - stocks

A company must invest funds in inventories, receivables, land, buildings and equipment, and other assets in order to engage in the sale of goods and services. But a portion of its available funds may be applied to assets not directly identified with primary activities. Assets that occupy an auxiliary relationship to central revenue-producing activities are referred to as *investments*. Investments are expected to contribute to the success of the business either by exercising certain favorable effects upon sales and operations generally, or by making an independent contribution to business earnings over the long term.

Classification of investments

From the standpoint of the owner, investments are either temporary or long-term. As suggested earlier, investments are classified as current only where they are readily marketable and it is management's intent to use them in meeting current cash requirements. Investments that do not meet these tests are considered *long-term* or *permanent investments* and are reported on the balance sheet under a separate noncurrent heading. The purpose to be served by the investment governs its classification.

Long-term or permanent investments include a variety of items. For discussion purposes, long-term investments will be classified in four groups: (1) investments in stocks, both preferred and common; (2) investments in bonds, mortgages, and similar debt instruments; (3) funds for bond retirement, stock redemption, and other special purposes; and (4) miscellaneous investments including real estate held for appreciation or for future use, advances to affiliates, interests in life insurance contracts, ownership equities in partnerships and joint ventures, and interests in trusts and estates. The accounting problems relating to long-term investments in stocks are considered in this chapter, those relating to the other long-term investments are considered in the next chapter.

Investments in stocks

Although long-term investments in corporate stocks may involve the risk of price decline, they may afford significant rewards in the form of periodic revenue and price appreciation. Frequently investments in stock are made to secure certain continuing business advantages. For example, stock ownership may be a means of obtaining suppliers for required materials and services or outlets for sales products. Here the income factor of the investment is only incidental to the other considerations. In certain instances, ownership of a controlling interest in the voting stock of a company may be sought. With control, activities of the related companies may be integrated towards the achievement of greater earnings. A company exercising control over another through majority ownership of its voting stock is called a *holding*, or *parent, company;* the company controlled is referred to as a *subsidiary company.*

Investments may be made in preferred or common stock. Preferred stock has certain preferences as to dividends and frequently as to assets upon dissolution. Sometimes preferred stock is convertible at the option of the stockholder into some other security, usually common stock. When this is the case, the preferred stock may be exchanged for common stock if corporate activities prove sufficiently profitable to make the common stock the more attractive equity.

The accounting procedures that are outlined on the following pages are equally applicable to short-term and long-term investments except when variations in treatment are indicated. Furthermore, the procedures would be employed by individual investors with single holdings in stock as well as by banks, investment companies, insurance companies, and other financial enterprises with many holdings.

Stock transactions. Shares of stock may be acquired on the New York Stock Exchange, the American Stock Exchange, and other exchanges in the different regions of the country. Stock that is not listed on the exchanges is acquired "over the counter" through stockbrokers. Stock may also be acquired directly from an issuing company or from a private investor.

When stock is purchased for cash, it is recorded at the amount paid, including brokers' commissions, taxes, and other fees incidental to the purchase. When stock is acquired "on margin," the stock should be recorded at its full cost and a liability should be recognized for the unpaid balance; to report only the amount invested would be, in effect, to offset the obligation to the broker against the investment account. An agreement or *subscription* entered into with a corporation for the purchase of stock is recognized by a charge to an asset account for the security to be received and a credit to a liability account for the amount to be paid. A charge for interest on an obligation arising from a stock purchase should be reported as expense. When stock is acquired in exchange for properties or services, the fair market value of such considerations or the value at which the stock is currently selling, whichever may be more clearly determinable, should be used as a basis for recording the investment. In the absence of clearly defined values for assets or services exchanged or a market price for the security acquired, appraisals and estimates are required in arriving at cost.

When two or more securities are acquired for a lump-sum price, this cost should be allocated in some equitable manner to the different acquisitions. When market prices are available for each security, cost may be apportioned on the basis of the relative market prices. When there is a market price for one security but not for the other, it may be reasonable to assign the market price to the one and the cost excess to the other. When market prices are not available, it may be necessary to postpone cost apportionment until support for an equitable division becomes available. In certain instances it may be desirable to carry the two securities in a single account and to treat the proceeds from the sale of one as a subtraction from total cost, the residual cost then to be identified with the other. To illustrate the foregoing procedures, assume the purchase of 100 units of preferred and common stock at $75 per unit; each unit consists of one share of preferred and two shares of common. Market prices at the time the stock is acquired are $60 and $10 per share for preferred and $10 per share for common. The investment cost is recorded in terms of the relative market values of the securities, as follows:

Investment in Preferred Stock....................	5,625	
Investment in Common Stock....................	1,875	
Cash..		7,500

Value of preferred: 100×$60 $6,000
Value of common: 200×$10   __2,000__ $8,000

Cost assigned to preferred: 6,000/8,000×$7,500 = $5,625.
Cost assigned to common: 2,000/8,000×$7,500 = $1,875.

If only a value for preferred of $60 is available, the investment may be recorded as follows:

Investment in Preferred Stock....................	6,000	
Investment in Common Stock....................	1,500	
Cash..		7,500

Cost of preferred and common..........	$7,500
Cost identified with preferred (market)	6,000
Remaining cost identified with common	$1,500

If the division of cost must be deferred, the following entry is made:

Investment in Preferred and Common Stock.........	7,500	
Cash..		7,500

The joint investment balance may be closed when a basis for apportionment is established and costs can be assigned to individual issues.

When stock is subject to special calls or assessments and such payments are made to the corporation, these are recorded as additions to the costs of the holdings. Pro rata contributions by the stockholders to the corporation to enable it to eliminate a deficit, to retire bonds, or to effect a reorganization, are also treated as additions to investment cost.

For federal income tax purposes, the sale of securities gives rise to a *capital gain* or *capital loss*. Such gain or loss is the difference between the cost of the securities sold and their sales proceeds. When securities are sold from lots acquired at different dates and prices and the identity of the lots cannot be determined, the cost of the securities must be calculated on a first-in, first-out basis. Tax laws further provide that capital gains and losses must be classified in terms of the holding period of the securities sold: if the period from the date the securities were acquired to the date they were sold is not more than six months, a *short-term* gain or loss is recognized; if the holding period exceeds six months, a *long-term* gain or loss is recognized. Certain tax advantages are granted to taxpayers with an excess of long-term capital gains over capital losses: (1) only 50 percent of such excess is included in gross income subject to tax; (2) under certain circumstances this portion of income is subject to less than the normal tax rates, thus providing a further tax advantage related to this source of income.

In accounting for securities on the books, care should be taken to preserve costs of the individual purchases as well as the dates of purchases and sales. Although the use of an average cost might be supported when securities have been acquired at different prices and identification is not possible, first-in, first-out is acceptable and is normally employed. The use of tax procedures in the accounts permits the preparation of the income tax returns from the books without the analyses and adjustments that would otherwise be necessary and also provides the taxpayer with data that he requires in planning the sale of securities in a manner that will offer him maximum tax advantages.

Stock valuation. Reference was made in an earlier chapter to the valuation of securities held as a temporary investment. Management's intent to use securities as a source of cash offers support for the recognition of current market values. But when management intends to hold securities, market values do not assume the significance that they would otherwise have. As in the case of other long-term assets, securities held as a long-term investment may be reported at cost. In making the statements more informative, costs should be supplemented by parenthetical disclosure of the aggregate market value of the securities. In those cases in which an investment consists of a significant part of a company's outstanding voting stock, special accounting procedures may be applicable. A full discussion of this matter is given on pages 371 to 375.

When a material and apparently permanent decline in the value of securities held as a long-term investment takes place, recognition of the loss is necessary if financial position is not to be misrepresented. For example, assume that stock is held in a company that has discontinued dividends or that faces the possibility of creditor control as a result of continued losses, or assume that stock is held in a company in a foreign country where war has broken out. With cost no longer considered recoverable, the investment should be written down. The reduction of an investment is accomplished preferably by a valuation account so that cost is preserved for income tax purposes.

Dividends. The receipt of cash dividends by a stockholder is recorded by a debit to Cash and a credit to Dividend Income. Three dates are generally included in the formal dividend announcement: (1) date of declaration, (2) record date, and (3) date of payment. The formal dividend announcement may read somewhat as follows: "The Board of Directors at their meeting on November 5, 1971, declared a regular quarterly dividend on outstanding common stock of 50 cents per share payable on January 15, 1972, to stockholders of record at the close of business, December 29, 1971." The stockholder becomes aware of the dividend action upon its announcement. But if he sells his holdings and a new owner is recognized by the corporation prior to the record date, the dividend is paid to the new owner. If the stockholder retains his holdings until the record date, he will be entitled to the dividends when paid. After the record date, stock no longer carries a right to dividends and sells "ex-dividend."[1] Accordingly, a stockholder is justified in recognizing the corporate dividend action on the record date. At this

---

[1]Stock on the New York Stock Exchange is normally quoted ex-dividend or ex-rights two full trading days prior to the record date because of the time required to deliver the stock and to record the stock transfer.

time a receivable account may be debited and Dividend Income credited. Upon receipt of the dividend, Cash is debited and the receivable credited.

There are some who would accrue dividends in the same manner as interest when the declaration of a regular dividend at a certain date is virtually assured by the nature of the security, the position and earnings of the company, and the policies of the board of directors. The recognition of accrued dividends under such circumstances is not objectionable if disclosure is made on the statements that such special practice is followed.

Federal income tax regulations provide that dividends are taxable only when unqualifiedly made subject to the demand of the stockholder. Hence, even though preparing the tax return on an accrual basis, the taxpayer recognizes dividends as revenue only when these become available. Ordinarily, the taxpayer maintains his books in accordance with the tax rule and recognizes revenue when the dividends are received.

Property dividends. Dividends that are distributed in the form of assets other than cash are referred to as *property dividends*. The corporation in distributing earnings by means of a property dividend normally credits the asset account for the cost of the asset distributed and charges retained earnings. The stockholder charges an asset account and credits dividend income. The stockholder, however, recognizes the dividend in terms of the value of the property item at the date of its distribution. To illustrate, assume that the Wells Corporation with 1,000,000 shares of common stock outstanding distributes as a dividend its holdings of 50,000 shares of Barnes Co. stock. The distribution of one share of Barnes Co. stock on every 20 shares of Wells Corporation held is made when Barnes Co. shares are selling at $16. A stockholder owning 100 shares of Wells Corporation stock would make the following entry in recording the receipt of the dividend:

Investment in Barnes Co. Stock.........................	80	
Dividend Income....................................		80
Received 5 shares of Barnes Co. stock, market price $16 per share, as a dividend on 100 shares of Wells Corporation stock.		

Income tax requirements for the receipt of a stock dividend are the same as described above.

Stock dividends. A company may distribute a dividend in the form of additional shares that are the same as those held by its stockholders. Such a dividend does not affect company assets but simply results in the transfer of retained earnings to invested capital. The increase in total shares outstanding is distributed pro rata to individual stockholders. The receipt of additional shares by stockholders leaves their respective equities exactly as they were; although the number of shares held by individual stockholders has gone up, there are now a greater number of shares outstanding and proportionate interests remain unchanged. The division of equities into a greater number of parts cannot be regarded as giving rise to revenue. To illustrate, assume that Eagle Corporation has 10,000 shares of common stock outstanding. The total of the stockholders' equity is $330,000; the book value per share is $33. If a 10% stock dividend is declared, an additional 1,000 shares of stock will be issued and the book value per share will decline to $30. A stockholder who held 10 shares with a book value of $330 (10 × $33) will hold 11 shares after the stock dividend, with the book value remaining at $330 (11 × $30).

The market value of the stock may or may not react in a similar manner. Theoretically the same relative decrease should occur in the market value as occurred in the book value; however, there are many variables influencing the market price of securities. If the percentage of the stock dividend issued is comparatively low (under 20–25%), there is generally less than a pro rata immediate effect on the stock market price. This means that while a stockholder after receiving a stock dividend will have no greater interest in the company, his investment may have a greater market value.

Because there is no effect on the underlying book value of the investment, only a memorandum entry needs to be made by the stockholder in recognizing the receipt of additional shares. Original investment cost applies to a greater number of shares, and this cost is divided by the total shares now held in arriving at the cost per share to be used upon subsequent disposition of holdings. The new per-share cost basis is indicated in the memorandum entry.

When stock has been acquired at different dates and at different costs, the stock dividend will have to be related to such different acquisitions. Adjusted costs for shares comprising each lot held can then be developed. To illustrate, assume that H. C. Smith owns stock of the Banner Corporation acquired as follows:

	Shares	Revised Cost per Share	Total Cost
Lot 1.....	50	$120	$6,000
Lot 2.....	30	90	2,700

A stock dividend of 1 share for every 2 held is distributed by the Banner Corporation. A memorandum entry on Smith's books to report the number of shares now held and the cost per share within each lot would be made as follows:

> Received 40 shares of Banner Corporation stock, representing a 50% stock dividend on 80 shares held. Number of shares held and costs assigned to shares are now as follows:

	Shares	Revised Cost per Share	Total Cost
Lot 1	75 (50 + 25)	$80 ($6,000 ÷ 75)	$6,000
Lot 2	45 (30 + 15)	60 ($2,700 ÷ 45)	2,700

These costs assume significance upon the sale of shares. The sale of the 75 shares comprising Lot 1, for example, would be charged with a cost of $6,000. The sale of only part of the shares identified with this lot would call for use of a cost of $80 per share. If shares sold are identified as those of Lot 2, cost would be recognized at $60 per share. Assuming that 100 shares are sold at $100 and stock is unidentifiable as to lot, the following entry would be made in giving effect to cost calculated on the first-in, first-out basis:

Cash	10,000	
Investment in Banner Corporation Stock		7,500
Gain on Sale of Banner Corporation Stock		2,500

Sold 100 shares, cost calculated on the first-in, first-out basis as follows:

75 shares at $80	$6,000
25 shares at $60	1,500
Total cost assigned to sale	$7,500

The foregoing analysis assumes maintenance of cost data in the investment accounts in accordance with income tax requirements. The use of an average cost on the books would result in a charge of $72.50 for each share sold ($8,700 ÷ 120). However, $72.50 cannot be used for tax purposes, and analysis by lot as illustrated would still be required in calculating the taxable gain or loss.

When stock of a class different from that held is received as a stock dividend, such a dividend, too, should not be regarded as revenue. As in the case of a like dividend, a portion of the retained earnings relating to the original holdings is formally labeled invested capital. All owners of the stock on which the dividend is declared participate pro rata in the distribution and now own two classes of stock instead of a single class. A book value is now identified with the new stock, but this is accompanied by a corresponding decrease in the book value identified with the original holdings. A similar position can be taken when an investor receives dividends in the form of bonds or other contractual obligations of the corporation.

One difference between the receipt of stock of the same class and securities of a different class needs to be noted. When common stock is received on common, all shares are alike and original cost may be equitably assigned in terms of the total number of units held after the dividend. When different securities are received whose value is not the same as that of the shares originally held, it would not be proper to assign an equal amount of original cost to both old and new units. Instead, equitable apportionment of cost would require use of the relative market values of the two classes of securities. To illustrate, assume the ownership of 100 shares of Bell Co. common stock acquired at $100 per share. A stock dividend of 50 shares of $25 par preferred stock is received on the common stock held. On the date of distribution the common stock is selling for $65 and the preferred stock for $20. The receipt of the dividend and the apportionment of cost is recorded as follows:

Investment in Bell Co. Preferred Stock 1,333.33
   Investment in Bell Co. Common Stock 1,333.33
      Received 50 shares of preferred stock as a dividend on 100 shares of common. Cost of common apportioned to common and preferred shares on the basis of relative market values of the two securities on the date of distribution:

      Value of Preferred   50 × $20 . . . . $1,000
      Value of Common   100 × $65   6,500
                                     $7,500

      Cost assigned to preferred: 1,000/7,500 × $10,000 = $1,333.33 (cost per share: $1,333.33 ÷ 50, or $26.67)

      Cost assigned to common: 6,500/7,500 × $10,000 = $8,666.67 (cost per share: $8,666.67 ÷ 100, or $86.67)

For federal income tax purposes, receipt by a stockholder of shares of any kind, common or preferred, as a stock dividend is nontaxable except when the distribution is made in lieu of cash. The distribution is regarded as having been made in lieu of cash if (1) it is made in discharge of preference dividends for the current year or for the preceding taxable year, or (2) the stockholder is given the option of receiving cash or other property instead of stock. When a stockholder receives a nontaxable stock dividend, the basis for calculating the gain and loss on share dispositions for both the new and the old shares is the same for tax purposes as that described above. Upon the disposal of shares received as a nontaxable stock dividend, the holding period, for purposes of reporting the gain or loss as a short-term or long-term item, begins with the date of acquisition of the original shares that formed the basis for cost. When a stock dividend is taxable, the new stock is reported as income at its fair market value at the date of its distribution, and this value becomes its basis; the old stock retains its original basis. The acquisition date for stock received as a taxable stock dividend is the date of its distribution.

Stock splits. A corporation may effect a *stock split* by reducing the par or the stated value of capital stock and increasing the number of shares outstanding accordingly. For example, a corporation with 1,000,000 shares outstanding may decide to split its stock on a 3-for-1 basis. After the split the corporation will have 3,000,000 shares outstanding; each stockholder will have three shares for every share originally held. However, each share will now represent only one third of the interest previously represented; furthermore, each share of stock can be expected to sell for approximately one third of its previous value.

The stock split requires no change in capital stock and retained earnings balances on the corporate books; however, the stockholders' ledger is revised to show the increased number of shares identified with each stockholder. Accounting for a stock split on the books of the investor is the same as that for a stock dividend. With an increase in the number of shares, each share now carries only a portion of the original cost. When shares have been acquired at different dates and at different prices, the shares received in a split will have to be associated with the original acquisitions and per-share costs for each lot revised. A memorandum entry is made to report the increase in the number of shares and the allocation of cost to the shares held after the split.

The income tax requirements for stock splits are the same as described above.

Stock rights. A corporation that wishes to raise cash by the sale of additional stock must first offer existing stockholders the right to subscribe to the new stock. This privilege attaching to stock is called the *preemptive right* and is designed to enable a stockholder to retain his respective interest in the corporation. For example, assume that a stockholder owns 50 percent of a company's outstanding stock. If the stock is doubled and the additional shares are offered and sold to other parties, his interest in the company would drop to 25 percent. With the right to subscribe to his pro rata share of any new offering, the stockholder can maintain his proportionate interest in the corporation. It should be noted, however, that preemptive rights generally apply only to the issue of the same kind of stock held by the stockholders. The statutes of some states allow the corporation to limit stockholders' preemptive rights by suitable provisions in the corporate charter.

Because of the possibility of failure to dispose of an entire new offering by sale to holders of rights, many corporations follow the policy of having the offering underwritten by an investment house. With such an arrangement, the underwriters agree to purchase at a fixed price all of the shares that are not sold through the exercise of rights.

In order to make subscription privileges attractive and to insure sale of the stock, it is customary for corporations to offer the additional issues to its stockholders at less than the market price of the stock. Certificates known as *rights* or *warrants* are issued to stockholders enabling them to subscribe for stock in proportion to the holdings on which they are issued. One right is offered for each share held. But more than one right is generally required in subscribing for each new share. Rights may be sold by stockholders who do not care to exercise them.

As in the case of cash and other dividends, the directors of the corporation in declaring rights to subscribe for additional shares designate a record date that follows the declaration date. All stockholders on the record date are entitled to the rights. Up to the record date, stock sells "rights-on," since parties acquiring the stock will receive the rights when they are issued; after the record date, the stock sells "ex-rights," and the rights may be sold separately by those owning the rights as of the record date. A date on which the rights expire is also designated when the rights are declared. Rights that are not exercised are worthless beyond the expiration date.

Accounting for stock rights. The receipt of stock rights is comparable to the receipt of a stock dividend. The corporation has made no asset distribution; stockholders' equities remain unchanged. However, the stockholders' investment is evidenced by shares originally acquired and rights that have a value of their own since they permit the purchase of shares at less than market price. These circumstances call for an allocation of cost between the original shares and the rights. Since the shares and the rights have different values, an apportionment should be made in terms of the relative market values as of the date that the rights are distributed. A separate accounting for each class of security is subsequently followed. The accounting for stock rights is illustrated in the example that follows.

Assume that in 1968 W. C. Warner acquires 100 shares of Superior Products no-par common at $180 per share. In 1972 the corporation issues rights to purchase 1 share of common at $100 for every 5 shares owned. Warner thus receives 100 rights — one right for each share owned. However, since 5 rights are required for the acquisition of a single share, the 100 rights enable him to subscribe for only 20 new shares. Warner's original investment of $18,000 now applies to two assets, the shares and the rights. This cost is apportioned on the basis of the relative market values of each security as of the date that the rights are distributed to the stockholders. The cost allocation may be expressed as follows:

$$\text{Cost assigned to rights:} \quad \frac{\text{Market Value of Rights}}{\text{Market Value of Stock Ex-Rights} + \text{Market Value of Rights}} \times \begin{array}{l}\text{Original} \\ \text{Cost of} \\ \text{Stock}\end{array}$$

$$\text{Cost assigned to stock:} \quad \frac{\text{Market Value of Stock Ex-Rights}}{\text{Market Value of Stock Ex-Rights} + \text{Market Value of Rights}} \times \begin{array}{l}\text{Original} \\ \text{Cost of} \\ \text{Stock}\end{array}$$

Calculation of the cost assigned to stock by the application of the formula above is not actually required; original cost less the cost assigned to rights gives the cost allocable to the original holdings.

Assume that Superior Products Common is selling ex-rights at $121 per share and rights are selling at $4 each. The cost allocation would be made as follows:

To rights: $\dfrac{4}{121 + 4} \times \$18,000 = \$576$ ($\$576 \div 100 = \$5.76$, cost per right)

To stock (balance): $\$18,000 - \$576 = \$17,424$ ($\$17,424 \div 100 = \$174.24$, cost per share)

The following entry may be made at this time:

Superior Products Stock Rights. 576
    Investment in Superior Products Common Stock.   576
        Received 100 rights permitting the purchase of 20 shares at $100. Cost of stock was apportioned on the basis of the relative market values of stock and rights on the date rights are distributed.

A corporation issuing rights generally notifies individual stockholders of the portion of cost to be applied to rights. While stockholders' cost assignments to rights will vary as a result of the different amounts that were originally paid for stock, the cost apportionment formula is the same in each case. Instead of notifying stockholders of an assignment of $\frac{4}{125}$ of the original cost to rights, as above, the corporate notice would normally instruct stockholders to calculate rights cost at 3.2% of their respective investment cost $(4 \div 125)$.

The cost apportioned to the rights is used in determining the gain or the loss arising from the sale of rights. Assume that the rights in the preceding example are sold at $4\frac{1}{2}$. The following entry would be made:

Cash. 450
Loss on Sale of Superior Products Stock Rights. 126
    Superior Products Stock Rights.   576
        Sold 100 rights at $4\frac{1}{2}$.

If the rights are exercised, the cost of the new shares acquired consists of the cost assigned to the rights plus the cash that is paid in the exercise of the rights. Assume that, instead of selling the rights, Warner exercises his privilege to purchase 20 additional shares at $100. The following entry is made:

Investment in Superior Products Common Stock...... 2,576
    Superior Products Stock Rights..................   576
    Cash.......................................   2,000
        Exercised rights acquiring 20 shares at $100.

Upon exercising the rights, Warner's records show an investment balance of $20,000 consisting of two lots of stock as follows:

Lot 1 (1968 acquisition) 100 shares
    ($17,424 ÷ 100 = $174.24, cost per share as adjusted)... $17,424
Lot 2 (1972 acquisition) 20 shares
    ($2,576 ÷ 20 = $128.80, cost per share acquired through
    rights)..   2,576
Total... $20,000

These costs provide the basis for calculating gains or losses upon subsequent sales of the stock.

When rights are received on stock that was acquired through several purchases at different costs, special care is required in tracing costs. Rights must be related to the different stock lots owned. Cost of each lot is then allocated between the stock and the rights emerging from the ownership of the particular lot. These costs are used in the future sale or exercise of the various lots of stock rights.

Frequently the receipt of rights includes one or more rights that cannot be used in the purchase of a whole share. For example, assume that the owner of 100 shares receives 100 rights; 6 rights are required for the purchase of 1 share. Here the holder uses 96 rights in purchasing 16 shares. He may allow the remaining 4 rights to lapse, he may sell the rights and report a gain or a loss on such sale, he may supplement the rights held by the purchase of 2 more rights making possible the purchase of an additional share of stock.

If the owner of valuable rights allows them to lapse, it would appear that the cost assigned to such rights should be written off as a loss. This can be supported on the theory that the issuance of stock by the corporation at less than current market price results in some dilution in the equities identified with original holdings. However, when changes in the market price of the stock make the exercise of rights unattractive and the rights cannot be sold, any cost of rights reported separately should be returned to the investment account.

Frequently no entry is made at the time of acquisition of rights, the reduction in the cost attaching to the original stock being made at the time the rights are sold or exercised. Although the transfer of cost through a stock rights account is not shown, investment balances would be the same after the sale or the exercise of rights as they would be with the entries illustrated previously.

For income tax purposes the procedures that have been illustrated are not applicable under all circumstances. When the fair market value of rights is less than 15 percent of the fair market value of the old stock, the basis of the rights is considered to be zero and the old shares retain their original cost unless the taxpayer formally elects to apportion original cost between the two securities. In the absence of such election, then, sale of rights would give rise to a taxable gain for the full sales price; exercise of rights would result in a basis for the new stock of no more than the purchase price. When the taxpayer elects apportionment or when the value of the rights is 15 percent or more of the market value of the old stock, the stock cost must be allocated between original stock and rights according to their relative market values. Tax accounting for stock and rights under these circumstances would follow procedures previously illustrated. The holding period for stock acquired through rights starts from the date that the rights are exercised. For tax purposes a loss cannot be claimed when rights are allowed to lapse; cost of the stock remains unchanged in the absence of the sale or exercise of rights.

Theoretical value of stock rights. Reference is frequently made to the *theoretical value* of stock rights. This is the value at which it is expected rights will sell on the market. The theoretical value may be calculated (1) when stock is still selling rights-on or (2) after the date rights have accrued to owners and stock sells ex-rights.

Calculation of theoretical value of rights when stock sells rights-on. The theoretical value of rights when stock sells rights-on may be calculated by the following formula:

$$\frac{\text{Value of Stock Rights-On Minus Subscription Price}}{\text{Number of Rights Required to Purchase 1 Share Plus 1}} = \text{Value of 1 Right}[1]$$

Assume that in the preceding example the common stock of Superior Products sells rights-on at $125 and that after the rights are sold separately a share can be bought for $100 plus 5 rights. By the use of the foregoing formula, the theoretical value of the rights is:

$$\frac{\$125 - \$100}{5 + 1} = \$4\frac{1}{6}$$

---

[1]The derivation of this formula may be observed from the following. Assume that the common stock of Superior Products sells rights-on at $125, but that it can be purchased later at $100 plus 5 rights.

Before rights sell separately:	1 share+1 right =$125
After rights sell separately:	1 share=$100+5 rights
The first equation is	1 share+1 right =$125
After transposition, the second equation is	1 share−5 rights=$100
	6 rights =$25
By subtracting the second equation from the first	
Then	1 right =$4⅙

The theoretical value of the stock, or the value at which the stock is expected to sell ex-rights, is $125 − $4⅙, or $120⅚. The foregoing values would result in similar costs for the purchase of rights and the payment of the exercise price ($100 + [5 × $4⅙]) as for the purchase of shares outright ($120⅚). However, the market may fail to provide such close cost correspondence when the stock and the rights are first quoted separately. In the example on page 365 it was assumed that the stock opened at $121 ex-rights, while rights sold for $4.

Calculation of theoretical value of rights after stock sells ex-rights. When stock sells ex-rights, the difference between the market value of the stock and the amount at which the stock can be acquired from the company through exercise of rights is the value attached to the number of rights required for such exercise. The theoretical value of the rights when the stock sells ex-rights may be expressed in formula form as follows:

$$\frac{\text{Value of Stock Ex-Rights Minus Subscription Price}}{\text{Number of Rights Required to Purchase 1 Share}} = \text{Value of 1 Right}$$

Assuming that the stock previously mentioned drops from $121 to $115, one would expect the rights to move down correspondingly from $4 to $3 as follows:

$$\frac{\$115 - \$100}{5} = \$3$$

Liquidating dividends. When a company consumes natural resources in its operations, sales revenue includes earnings as well as a recovery of the cost of such natural resources. When natural resources are limited and irreplaceable, the company may choose to distribute full proceeds becoming available from operations. Dividends paid, then, represent in part a distribution of earnings and in part a distribution of invested capital. Distributions involving both earnings and invested capital may also be found when a company makes full distribution of the proceeds from the sale of certain properties such as land or securities, or when a distribution represents the proceeds from business liquidation. Dividends representing a return of invested capital are known as *liquidating dividends*.

A stockholder receiving a dividend that consists of both a distribution of earnings and a return of invested capital credits revenue for the amount representing earnings and the investment account for the amount representing invested capital. To illustrate, assume that Lucky Mines, Inc., pays a dividend of $500,000, 60% representing a distribution of earnings and 40% representing a distribution of the cost recovery of certain wasting assets. A stockholder receiving a dividend of $1,200 makes the following entry:

Cash...	1,200	
Dividend Income.............................		720
Investment in Lucky Mines, Inc., Stock.............		480

Information regarding the portion of dividends representing earnings and the portion representing invested capital is reported to the stockholder by the corporation making the distribution. This report may not accompany each dividend check but instead may be provided annually and may cover the total dividends paid during the year. If dividends have been recorded as revenue during the year, the revenue account is charged and the investment account is credited when notification is received of the amount that is to be recognized as a distribution of invested capital.

When liquidating dividends exceed investment cost, excess distributions are reported as a gain from the investment. If liquidation is completed and the investment cost is not fully recovered, the balance of the investment account should be written off as a loss.

Sale of stock. When stock is sold, the investment account should be credited for the carrying value of the shares, which is original cost adjusted for any past stock assessments, liquidating dividends, stock dividends, splits, or rights. If stock transactions have been properly recorded in the past, adjusted cost is readily available; if there have been past accounting failures, appropriate account correction will be required. The difference between cash or the fair market value of other assets received and the adjusted cost of the shares is reported as a gain or loss on the sale.

Redemption of stock. Stock, particularly preferred issues, may be called in for redemption and cancellation by the corporation under conditions set by the issue. The call price is ordinarily set at a figure higher than the price at which the stock was originally issued, but this call price may be more or less than the cost to the holder who acquired the stock from another person after its original issue. When stock is surrendered to the corporation, an entry is made charging Cash and crediting the investment account. Any difference between the cash proceeds and the investment cost is recorded as a gain or a loss. For example, assume that an investor acquires 100 shares of Y Co. 6 percent, $100 par preferred stock at 97. These shares are subsequently called in at 105. The redemption is recorded on the stockholder's books by the following entry.

Cash..	10,500	
Investment in Y Co. 6% Preferred Stock.........		9,700
Gain on Redemption of Y Co. Preferred Stock....		800
Received $10,500 on call of Y Co. preferred stock, cost $9,700.		

Exchange of stock. When shares of stock are exchanged for other securities, the investor opens an account for the newly acquired security and closes the account of the security originally held. The new securities should be recorded at their fair market value or at the fair market value of the shares given up, whichever may be more clearly determinable, and a gain or loss is recognized on the exchange for the difference between the value assigned to the securities acquired and the carrying value of the shares given up. In the absence of a market value for either old or new securities, the carrying value of the shares given up will have to be recognized as the cost of the new securities. To illustrate, assume that the Z Co. offers its preferred stockholders two shares of no-par common stock in exchange for each share of $100 par preferred. An investor exchanges 100 shares of preferred stock carried at a cost of $10,000 for 200 shares of common stock. Common shares are quoted on the market at the time of exchange at $65. The exchange is recorded on the books of the stockholder by the following entry:

Z Co. Common Stock..........................	13,000	
Z Co. Preferred Stock..........................		10,000
Gain on Conversion of Z Co. Preferred Stock.....		3,000
Acquired 200 shares of common stock valued at		
$65 in exchange for 100 shares of preferred stock		
costing $100.		

Recognition of a gain or a loss on a security exchange can be supported on the grounds that the exchange closes the transaction cycle relating to the original asset and opens a new cycle, the newly acquired asset requiring valuation in terms of current market. However, there are some who object to the recognition of gain or loss on the exchange of stock for other securities. These hold that there is no actual realization of gain or loss as there would be upon the outright sale of stock; one asset has been replaced by a similar asset, the exchange requiring a transfer of cost from the asset originally held to the one newly acquired.

It may be observed that under federal income tax laws an exchange, whether in the form of securities or other properties, gives rise to a taxable gain or loss. But exceptions are made to this general rule and no gain or loss is recognized under circumstances that suggest that the new property is substantially a continuation of the old investment. In the case of exchanges of securities, the following exceptions are made: the exchange of common for common and preferred for preferred of the same corporation; the exchange of preferred for common pursuant to a conversion privilege in the preferred; and exchanges in a statutory corporate reorganization. Neither gain nor loss is recognized in these instances, nor is a change in basis recognized. The cost or other basis of the old security becomes the basis for the new; the acquisition date of the old security also becomes the acquisition date of the new. Other exchanges of securities are taxable, including stock for bonds, preferred for common (except under the condition above), common for preferred, bonds for bonds (unless of the same corporation and substantially identical), or common of one corporation for common of another. A gain or loss is established by the difference between the fair market value of the security received on the date of the exchange and the basis of the security exchanged. The basis of the new security is the fair market value recognized on the exchange; the acquisition date of the new security is the date of the exchange.

Investments representing substantial interest in voting stock

If an investment represents a substantial interest in the voting stock of the investee company, a deviation from the traditional cost method is required. A substantial interest is present if a majority ownership is held, but it may also be present when there is less than a majority ownership of the outstanding voting stock.

Ownership of majority interest in stock. The acquisition of a majority interest in the stock of another company which results in what is normally termed a *parent-subsidiary* relationship, raises the question of whether this calls for special accounting. This question arises in view of the control that is exercised over such events as payments of dividends by the subsidiary and the effects that favorable and unfavorable operations of the subsidiary can have upon the welfare of the parent. The latter effects are magnified when the investment constitutes a material part of the total assets of the acquiring or parent organization.

There are two positions that have been taken with respect to carrying investments in subsidiaries: (1) investments have been carried on a cost or a modified cost basis, comparable to investments in companies not so controlled, and (2) investments have been carried in a manner that reflects the degree of success or failure of the controlled unit. The first method emphasizes the legal factors in the relationship by recognizing only investment cost and is referred to as the *cost method;* the second method emphasizes the economic factors in the relationship by recognizing changes in the parent's equity in the subsidiary and is referred to as the *equity method*.

Cost method. When the cost method is used, the investment account reports the original cost of the investment in the subsidiary. Increases and decreases in the capital of the subsidiary resulting from earnings and losses are disregarded on the books of the parent. Dividends representing distributions of subsidiary earnings are recorded by credits to Dividend Income. Earnings of a subsidiary, then, are recognized only as these are distributed in the form of dividends.

The foregoing practices are normally subject to two important modifications representing departures from a strictly legal approach:

(1) Dividends that represent distributions of subsidiary earnings accumulated prior to the date on which the parent company acquired control are recorded by the parent not as dividend income but as reductions in the investment balance. Such dividends represent, in effect, a partial return of investment or the equivalent of a liquidating dividend, since the asset transfer is accompanied by the shrinkage of subsidiary net asset and owners' equity balances below acquisition amounts. The source of dividends, whether out of earnings accumulated prior to stock acquisition or after stock acquisition, could be ignored when holdings were small, all dividends received being recognized as revenue; but when holdings in stock are significant, it becomes important that dividends that impair the values in support of the investment balance be recognized as reductions in the investment.

(2) Recognition in the accounts should be made for a decline in the value of an investment when such decline is viewed as permanent. A write-down of an investment balance may be considered appropriate, for example, when unsuccessful operations of the subsidiary have seriously and presumably permanently impaired the value of the investment.

Equity method. When the equity method is used, the investment account reports investment cost modified by changes in the parent's equity in the subsidiary after subsidiary acquisition. Subsidiary net income increasing subsidiary net assets is recognized by the parent by a charge to the investment account and a credit to a separate income account; a subsidiary net loss reducing subsidiary net assets is recognized by a credit to the investment account and a charge to a separate loss account. Dividends reducing subsidiary net assets are recognized by a decrease in the investment balance. Thus, under the equity method a parent recognizes its share of the earnings or losses of a subsidiary in the periods for which they are reported in the financial statements of the subsidiary rather than in the periods in which earnings are distributed as dividends. The legal separation of the two companies is overlooked, and the economic reality of the controlling relationship is reflected in the accounts. One modification in the above procedure requires mention. A decline in the value of an investment that is viewed as permanent and indicates the inability of the investor to recover the carrying value of the investment would require a write-down of the investment to the lower value as in the case of the cost method.

Under the equity method, the investment in common stock is usually shown as a single amount in the balance sheet. Similarly, the parent's share of the subsidiary's income or loss is shown as a single amount in the income statement. An exception to this general rule may be necessary if extraordinary items are included in the subsidiary's net income. Such items should be recognized separately unless they would be immaterial in the income statement of the parent.

To illustrate the use of the cost and equity methods, assume the following for the Redco Corporation:

Transaction	Cost Method of Carrying Investment		Equity Method of Carrying Investment	
cember 31, 1970 — Investment in Blue Earth Co., 00 shares at $25 per re. The Blue Earth Co. s 2,500 shares outstanding; interest of the parent, n, is 80%.	Investment in Blue Earth Co...500,000 Cash...........	500,000	Investment in Blue Earth Co...500,000 Cash..........	500,000
cember 31, 1971 — Net ome reported by Blue rth Co. ome before extraordinary tems........... $50,000 raordinary ains........... 25,000 t income $75,000	No entry		Investment in Blue Earth Co... 60,000 Share of Income Before Extraordinary Items — Blue Earth Co.......... Share of Extraordinary Items — Blue Earth Co..........	40,000 20,000
uary 31, 1972 — Receipt dividends of $16,000 from e Earth Co., representing % of $20,000 dividend tribution.	Cash............ 16,000 Dividend Income	16,000	Cash............ 16,000 Investment in Blue Earth Co.	16,000
cember 31, 1972 — Net s reported by Blue Earth $30,000	No entry		Share of Net Loss— Blue Earth Co... 24,000 Investment in Blue Earth Co.	24,000

The investment in Blue Earth Co. at December 31, 1972, is reported at $520,000 under the equity method as compared with $500,000 under the cost method. This is explained by the fact that during the two-year period, retained earnings of the subsidiary has increased by a net amount of $25,000 and the investment account of the parent reflects 80 percent of such increase, or $20,000.

In recent years the equity method of reporting investments has received increasing support by the Accounting Principles Board. In 1966 the APB declared that investments in unconsolidated subsidiaries should be reported in consolidated statements by the equity method.[1] This was followed in 1971 by Opinion No. 18 that stated that the use of the equity method should be extended to include investments in subsidiaries on the parent company's financial statements when they are prepared for issuance to stockholders as the financial statements of the parent company only.[2] Opinion No. 18 also reaffirmed the position that the full economic implications to the parent of subsidiary ownership and operations can normally be presented only through the preparation of consolidated statements. Assets and liabilities of the subsidiary replace the investment account and are combined with assets and liabilities of the parent, and changes in retained earnings of the subsidiary are combined with retained earnings of the parent in developing a consolidated balance sheet; revenue and expense balances of the subsidiary are combined with similar balances of the parent in developing a consolidated income statement. Statements are prepared as though parent and subsidiary were a single entity. Financial position and progress are reported for affiliated units from an overall economic point of view, and the legal realities underlying the relationships are disregarded. The detailed problems involved in the development of consolidated statements are beyond the scope of this discussion.[3]

Ownership of less than a majority interest in stock. The accounting Principles Board in Opinion No. 18 also provided that the use of the equity method be extended to include investments that constitute less than a majority of the outstanding stock. The Board stated:

> The Board concludes that the equity method of accounting for an investment in common stock should also be followed by an investor whose investment in voting stock gives it the ability to exercise significant influence over operating and financial policies of an investee even though the investor holds 50% or less of the voting stock.[4]

This position calls for an interpretation of the term "significant influence." The APB suggests that the ability to exercise such influence may be indicated in several ways, such as representation on the board of directors, participation in policy making processes, material intercompany transactions, interchange of managerial personnel, or technological

---

[1]*Opinions of the Accounting Principles Board, No. 10,* "Omnibus Opinion — 1966" (New York: American Institute of Certified Public Accountants, December, 1967), par. 2-4. Application of this method is sometimes referred to as "one-line consolidation" since the economic implications of subsidiary activities are reflected only in the investment account and retained earnings of the parent.

[2]*Opinions of the Accounting Principles Board, No. 18,* "The Equity Method of Accounting for Investments in Common Stock" (New York: American Institute of Certified Public Accountants, March, 1971), par. 14.

[3]A full discussion of the preparation of consolidated statements is found in *Advanced Accounting* by Simons and Karrenbrock.

[4]*Opinions of the Accounting Principles Board, No. 18, op. cit.,* par. 17.

dependency. Another important consideration is the extent of ownership by an investor in relation to the concentration of other shareholdings. The Board recognizes that these factors will not always be clear and judgment will be required in assessing the status of each investment. To achieve a reasonable degree of uniformity in the application of its position, the Board set 20 percent as an ownership standard: the ownership of 20 percent or more of the voting stock of an investee carries the presumption, in the absence of evidence to the contrary, that an investor has the ability to exercise significant influence over the investee; conversely, the ownership of less than 20 percent leads to the presumption that the investor does not have the ability to exercise significant influence unless such ability can be demonstrated. Applying these guidelines, an investment of less than 20 percent would generally be carried at cost.

Entries on the books would be made in the same manner as entries for majority holdings as illustrated earlier. Disclosure in parenthetical or note form should be made on the financial statements concerning such matters as the accounting method used for the investment, the percentage of ownership represented by the shares held, and, when available, the quoted market value of the shares.

Investments and tax accounting

Previous discussions have indicated that federal income tax laws may call for the use of a certain method when a number of methods, including the one prescribed, may be considered theoretically sound for financial reporting purposes. In other instances tax laws call for the use of methods that differ from those that might warrant application on theoretical grounds. Normally the procedures that are to be required in the calculation of taxable income are applied in the accounts so that analysis of income and its restatement for tax purposes may be avoided. Such practice may be supportable when tax methods are acceptable or when their application offers measurements that do not differ materially from those obtained through the use of alternative methods considered sounder under the circumstances. But the use in the books of tax methods that result in significant misstatements of net income and financial position cannot be condoned. In the event of conflict between proper reporting procedures and required income tax procedures, financial statements should be developed in terms of the former, and supplementary records should be maintained to accumulate the data required for income tax reporting. Interperiod income tax allocation procedures may also be required on the books in recognizing the tax effect of such differences.

QUESTIONS

1. Distinguish between temporary and long-term investments.

2. How should each of the following be classified on the balance sheet?
   (a) Stock held for purposes of controlling the activities of a subsidiary.
   (b) Listed stock rights that are to be sold.
   (c) Stock that is intended to be transferred to a supplier in cancellation of an amount owed.

3. How would you record an investment in stock when it is acquired: (a) by exchange for an asset whose value is known? (b) by exchange for an asset whose value is not known, stock for patents, for example?

4. The Parker Co. accepts 2,000 shares of Murdock common stock in full payment of a claim of $12,000 against the latter company. State how this transaction would be recorded on the books of the Parker Co., assuming that (a) Murdock stock is closely held and no market value is available; (b) Murdock stock is quoted on the market at $5; (c) Murdock stock is quoted on the market at $6.50 bid, $7.50 asked.

5. How would you record the purchase of stock and bond units acquired for a lump sum when (a) only one of the securities is quoted on the market? (b) both securities are quoted? (c) neither security is quoted?

6. R. S. Doug purchases 1,000 shares of Abbott Motors at $90 a share in November, paying his broker $65,000. The market value of the stock on December 31 is $125 a share; Doug has made no further payment to his broker. On this date he shows on his balance sheet Abbott Motors Stock, $100,000, the difference between market value and the unpaid balance to the broker. Do you approve of this report? Explain.

7. What reasons may be offered for the infrequent use of property dividends by the corporation?

8. Distinguish between a stock dividend and a stock split. Under what circumstances should a company use one as compared with the other?

9. Some accounting writers have suggested that certain stock dividends should constitute income to the recipients. What is the basis for this view?

10. In the formula for computing the theoretical value of a stock right, when the stock sells rights-on, "1" is added to the number of rights required to purchase one share. Why?

11. If stock rights lapse and are not used, what disposition should be made of the investment cost allocated to the rights?

12. B. A. Beard receives $400 representing a dividend of $4.00 per share on Atlas Securities Co. stock, accompanied by a statement that $1.56 represents a distribution of income and $2.44 represents a dividend in partial liquidation. (a) What is the meaning of this statement? (b) What entry should Beard make in recording the dividend?

13. State how each of the following situations should be treated on the books and on the income tax return:
    (a) Announcement of dividends on stock and arrival of "record" date.
    (b) Sale of part of security holdings acquired in three lots.
    (c) Receipt of stock dividend of common on common.
    (d) Receipt of stock dividend of preferred stock on common.
    (e) Exchange of 1 share of common for 3 shares in a stock split-up.
    (f) Receipt of stock rights and their sale.
    (g) Surrender of preferred stock at a redemption price that is less than cost.
    (h) Receipt of a dividend of 1 share of Z Co. stock for every 10 shares of Y Co. stock held.
    (i) Receipt of dividends from a subsidiary company 90% owned.

14. (a) Define: (1) parent company, (2) subsidiary company. (b) How much stock ownership is required to exercise control?

15. What conflict, if any, exists between the equity method of reporting subsidiary company earnings on parent company statements and the entity theory?

16. "The equity method provides for the recognition of revenue prior to its realization, and therefore such revenue should be reported as unrealized and as a part of appraisal capital." "The equity method provides for the recognition of revenue in a manner that meets the objectives of accrual accounting, and therefore such revenue is properly included in income and thus retained earnings." Which position would you support? Why?

17. Under what conditions may an investor that owns less than a majority interest in the stock of an investee exercise significant control over the investee's operating and financial policies?

EXERCISES

1. Custom Display Corp. acquired 100 shares of Anderson Co. stock at 15. At a later date a stock dividend of 25 shares was received which was sold at 12. Proceeds from the sale were recorded as revenue. What correction in the accounts would you make assuming: (a) the transaction took place currently and accounts are still open? (b) the transaction was recorded in the previous period and accounts are closed?

2. The Billings Co. holds stock of Alloy Co. acquired as follows:

1970	100 shares	$5,600
1971	100 shares	4,900
1972	50 shares	2,300

Give the entries that would be made upon the sale of 150 shares in 1973 at $53 per share assuming that cost is determined by (a) the first-in, first-out method, (b) the weighted average cost, (c) identification of lots sold as 1971 and 1972 purchases.

3. Max Garrett holds stock of Skarnes, Inc., acquired as follows:

| Jan. 2, 1970 | 100 shares at $40 | $4,000 |
| Mar. 30, 1971 | 100 shares at $46 | 4,600 |

In 1972 Garrett receives a 50% stock dividend. He then sells 150 shares at 35. What entry would be made to record the sale? (Assume the use of the first-in, first-out method in recording the sale of shares.)

4. Therald Larson owns 200 shares of Weinman Co. common acquired at $50 per share. Give the cost basis per share for his investment holdings if:

(a) He receives a common stock dividend of 1 for 4.
(b) Common stock is exchanged in a 5-for-1 split.
(c) He receives a preferred stock dividend of 1 share for every 4 shares of common held; common is selling ex-dividend at $60; preferred is selling at $160.
(d) He receives a property dividend of 1 share of Hennepin Co. common, market price $7, for every 5 shares held.

5. The Davis Co. issues rights to subscribe to its stock, the ownership of 4 shares entitling the stockholder to subscribe for 1 share at par, $10. (a) Assuming that stock is quoted rights-on at $12.50, what is the theoretical value of a right? (b) Assuming that stock is quoted ex-rights at $12.50, what is the theoretical value of a right?

6. The Ryan Manufacturing Co. wishes to finance an expansion program through the issue of new stock. Accordingly, it offers its stockholders the opportunity to subscribe to new stock at $132 per share up to 50% of their holdings. The value of the stock on July 1 is $150 per share. Stock sells ex-rights on the market on July 2. H. R. Patton owns 100 shares of Ryan Manufacturing Co. stock acquired at a cost of $6,000. (a) What is the theoretical value of Patton's rights when these are received? (b) Assuming that the theoretical value is used as a basis for cost apportionment, what entry would be made if Patton sells his rights for $365? (c) What entry would be made if Patton exercises his rights?

7. On April 1, D. L. Hastings purchased 1,000 shares of Willis Corp. common stock, par $5, at $32. On July 7 Hastings received a stock dividend of 1 share for every 4 owned. On September 10 he received a cash dividend of 60 cents on the stock and was granted the right to purchase 1 share at $10 for every 4 shares held. On this date stock had a market value ex-rights of $15, and each right had a value of $1; stock cost was allocated on this basis. On December 12, Hastings sold 450 rights at $1.50 each and exercised the remaining rights. What entries will appear on Hastings' books as a result of the foregoing?

8. R. L. Dewey owns 100 shares in Adair Advertising, Inc., acquired in 1963 at a cost of $5 per share. Beginning in 1968, Dewey received dividends of $2 per share each year, the corporation notifying him that a portion of this amount represented earnings and the balance a liquidating dividend, the allocation to be made as follows:

	Income	Depletion Proceeds—Liquidating
1968............	$.712	$1.288
1969............	.63	1.37
1970............	.591	1.409
1971............	.83	1.17
1972............	.61	1.39

(a) What entries should Dewey have made each year in recording the dividends? (b) How would you report the investment on Dewey's balance sheet at the end of 1972?

9. The Bolin Co. acquires 425,000 shares of Wenger, Inc., in 1971 at a total cost of $1,600,000. Wenger, Inc., has 500,000 shares outstanding. What entries would be made by the Bolin Co. in 1972 for the following data?

(1) Wenger, Inc., announces net income of $30,000 for the first six months and pays a cash dividend of 5 cents per share.
(2) Wenger, Inc., announces a net loss of $15,000 for the second six months and distributes a 5% stock dividend.
(3) The Bolin Co. acquires an additional 26,250 shares of Wenger, Inc., stock at 5.

PROBLEMS

11-1. Transactions of Paul A. Bancroft during 1972 included the following:

January 20   Purchased 400 shares of Barton Co. at $75 plus brokerage charges of $600.

June 10   Received a 50% stock dividend.

November 1   Received stock rights permitting the purchase of one share at $60 for every 4 shares held. On this date rights were being traded at $3 each and stock was being traded at $72 per share.

November 18 Exercised 400 rights which pertained to the stock acquired on January 20, and sold remaining rights at 2 less brokerage charges of $6.

December 28 Sold 100 shares from the holdings acquired on January 20 at 68¼ less brokerage charges of $53.

Instructions: (1) Give journal entries to record the foregoing transactions. (Give computations in support of your entries.)

(2) Give the investment account balance on December 31, 1972, and the shares and costs making up this balance.

11-2. Following is a list of all the items in the investments account of Braun Equipment Co.

Apr. 10, 1972 — 1,000 shares of Hewlett, Inc., common stock purchased..	$37,950
June 25, 1972 — 8,200 shares of Adler-Vale Co. preferred stock purchased..	$41,000
Nov. 26, 1972 — 1,000 shares of Hewlett, Inc., common stock sold..	$25,900
Dec. 31, 1972 — Balance.......................................	$53,050

The fair market value of Adler-Vale Co. preferred stock on December 31, 1972, the date of your audit, as reflected by stock exchange quotations, was $7 per share. In view of this fact, the president of the company recommends that the book balance of $53,050 be allowed to stand since it is less than the market value of the remaining stock. The president explains that the account represented a relatively permanent investment of cash, and that in view of this single purpose, appreciation logically offsets the loss.

Instructions: (1) How would the investment be reported on the balance sheet according to presently accepted principles of accounting?

(2) If there were no constraints on the valuation to be used, would your answer be different? Why?

11-3. Tow, Inc., purchased common stock of Admiral Company as follows:

    March 8, 1972..................... 50 shares at $57.60 per share
    May 16, 1972.....................100 shares at $72.00 per share

Admiral Company issued a 20% common stock dividend on December 11, 1972, when market price was $68 per share. It issued common stock rights on December 28, 1972; each right entitled the holder to subscribe to one share at $60 for each four shares held. At the date of issue of the rights, market values were: per right, $4; per share ex-rights, $76.

On January 5, 1973, Tow, Inc., sold 76 of the rights which had been received on the stock purchase of May 16, 1972, at $5 each. The remaining rights were exercised on this date.

Instructions: (1) Prepare journal entries on books of Tow, Inc., to record the receipt of the stock dividend and the receipt of the stock rights.

(2) Compute the gain or loss on the sale of rights.

(3) Compute the number of shares in each lot and the cost basis of each lot on January 6, 1973, assuming market values are used to assign costs to rights.

11-4. R. A. Nelson owns 600 shares of Crawford, Inc., acquired on May 1, 1968, for $30,000.

During 1971 and 1972 the following transactions took place with respect to this investment:

Mar. 1, 1971   Received cash dividend of forty cents and stock dividend of 25%.

Oct. 15, 1971   Received stock rights offering the purchase of 1 share at $70 for every 5 shares held. At this time stock was quoted ex-rights at $95 and rights were quoted at $5; stock cost was apportioned on this basis. Rights were exercised.

Mar. 1, 1972   Received a cash dividend of forty cents and a stock dividend of 20%.

Dec. 5, 1972   Received stock rights offering the purchase of 1 share at $68 for every 5 shares held. At this time stock was quoted ex-rights at $78 and rights were quoted at $2; stock cost was apportioned on this basis. Rights were sold at $3, less brokerage charges of $75.

Instructions: (1) Give journal entries to record the foregoing transactions.

(2) Give the investment account balance as of December 31, 1972, including shares and costs in support of this balance.

11-5. The Lang Co. has the following securities on hand on January 1, 1972:

Investment in Midway Co. 6% Preferred, par $40, 75 shares. . $ 2,700
Investment in Toronto Iron Common, 500 shares. $30,250

During 1972 the following transactions were completed relative to investments:

Jan. 23   Purchased 150 shares of Taylor Co. common for $9,600.

Feb. 1   Received a cash dividend of 50 cents and stock dividend of 10% on Toronto Iron common.

Apr. 12   Purchased 200 shares of Taylor Co. common for $16,000.

May 20   Received the semiannual dividend on Midway Co. 6% preferred.

July 1   Taylor Co. common was split on a 2-for-1 basis.

Aug. 11   Received a dividend of $2 on Taylor Co. common.

11   Received a cash dividend of 50 cents and a stock dividend of 10% on Toronto Iron common.

Oct. 10   Sold 200 shares of Taylor Co. common for $9,100, and also sold the 75 shares of Midway Co. 6% preferred for $5,500.

28   Received rights on Taylor Co. common to subscribe for additional shares as follows: 1 share could be acquired at $40 for every 4 shares held. On this date stock was selling for 48 and rights were selling at 2; stock cost was apportioned on this basis.

Nov. 15   Sold all of the Taylor Co. rights for $805.

Dec. 20   Received a special year-end dividend on Toronto Iron common of $2.

Instructions: (1) Assuming the use of first-in, first-out in assigning costs to sales, give journal entries to record the foregoing transactions. (Give calculations in support of your entries.)

(2) Give the investment account balances as of December 31, 1972, including the number of shares and costs comprising such balances.

11-6. The following balances appeared in the ledger of the Cannon Company on December 31, 1969:

Investment in Dale Co. Common, par $100, 250 shares...... $24,000
Investment in Dale Co. 6% Preferred, par $100, 50 shares... $ 4,250

The Cannon Company uses the first-in, first-out method in accounting for stock transactions. In 1970, 1971, and 1972 the following transactions took place relative to the above investments:

Jan. 20, 1970 Holders of Dale Co. 6% preferred were given the right to exchange their holdings into an equal number of Dale Co. common, and the Cannon Co. made such exchange. Common shares on the date of exchange were quoted on the market at $126 per share.

Dec. 28, 1970 Received cash dividends of $3 per share on Dale Co. common.

July 30, 1971 Received additional shares of Dale Co. common in a 4-for-1 stock split. (Par value of common was reduced to $25.)

Dec. 28, 1971 Exercised option to receive one share of Dale Co. common for each 30 shares held in lieu of a cash dividend of $1.50 per share held. The market value of Dale Co. common on the date of distribution was $50 per share. Dividend income was recognized at the value of the shares received.

July 1, 1972 Received a stock dividend of 10% on Dale Co. common.

Oct. 15, 1972 Received warrants representing right to purchase at par 1 share of Dale Co. common for every 4 shares held. On date of warrants issue, the market value of shares ex-rights was $37, and of rights was $3; cost of the stock was allocated on this basis.

Oct. 30, 1972 Exercised 440 rights identified with the first lot of stock acquired and sold remaining rights at $2.50 per right less brokerage charges of $30.

Dec. 31, 1972 Sold 220 shares of Dale Co. common at $43 per share less brokerage charges of $110.

Instructions: (1) Prepare journal entries to record the transactions in Dale Co. holdings.

(2) Prepare a schedule showing the balance of Dale Co. common held by Cannon Company on December 31, 1972.

11-7. You have instructed the bookkeeper for Darrell Fabrics, Inc., to record all proceeds from security transactions directly in the investment accounts so that all of this data will be summarized there and will be available for analysis and proper disposition at the time of your audit. You find the following data in the account summarizing the investment with Brown Mfg. Common:

Brown Mfg. Common

1/12/71 Purchased 120 shares at 50.............. 6,000		2/15/72 Cash dividend...... 700	
7/15/71 Purchased 80 shares at 52.............. 4,160		3/25/72 Proceeds from sale of 20 rights at 4....... 80	
3/20/72 Payment on purchase of 60 shares through exercise of 180 rights. 3,300		12/20/72 Proceeds from sale of 120 shares at 62.... 7,440	

Further analysis discloses that rights were received in March, 1972, permitting the purchase of 1 share of stock at $55 for every 3 shares held. In May the company was informed that 5% of original stock cost was applicable to the rights.

Instructions: (1) Assuming the use of first-in, first-out in calculating cost on sales, give individual entries for each correction required in the investment account on December 31, 1972.

(2) Give the corrected balance for the investment account on December 31, 1972, and the shares and costs making up this balance.

11-8. The Russell and Mattsen Corporations each have 150,000 shares of no-par stock outstanding. Wilson, Inc., acquired 120,000 shares of Russell stock and 130,000 shares of Mattsen stock in 1968. Changes in retained earnings for Russell and Mattsen for 1972 and 1973 are as follows:

	Russell Corp.	Mattsen Corp.
Retained earnings (deficit), Jan. 1, 1972....................	$ 70,000	$(16,000)
Cash dividends, 1972...............	(40,000)	———
	$ 30,000	$(16,000)
Net income, 1972..................	70,000	75,000
	$100,000	$ 59,000
Cash dividends, 1973...............	———	(21,000)
	$100,000	$ 38,000
Net income (loss), 1973.............	(35,000)	(18,000)
Retained earnings, Dec. 31, 1973....	$ 65,000	$ 20,000

Instructions: Give the entries required on the books of Wilson, Inc., for 1972 and 1973.

11-9. On January 1, 1971, St. Paul Products acquired 30% (10,000 shares) of the common stock of Robbinsdale Belt Co. for $530,000. The following information appeared in financial statements prepared by Robbinsdale Belt Co. for 1971.

Income before extraordinary items.............		$130,000
Add extraordinary gains......................		35,000
Net income.................................		$165,000
Less: Cash dividends paid....................	$75,000	
Market value of stock dividends issued — 1,000 shares (transferred to paid-in capital section of balance sheet)..............	25,000	100,000
Increase in retained earnings — 1971..........		$ 65,000

Instructions: (1) Prepare all of the journal entries required during 1971 on the books of St. Paul Products for the investment in shares of the Robbinsdale Belt Co. under (a) the cost method, and (b) the equity method.

(2) Compute the amount that St. Paul Products would report at the end of 1971 for its investment in Robbinsdale Belt Co. under (a) the cost method, and (b) the equity method.

11-10. Smitters Corp. has various long-term investments and maintains its books on the accrual basis. The books for the year ended December 31, 1972, have not been closed. An analysis of the investment account for the year follows:

Smitters Corp.
Analysis of Investment Account
Year Ended December 31, 1972

			Account per Books	
1972	Transactions	Folio	Debit	Credit
Jan. 1	5,000 shares Backand Oil Co...........		$ 5,000	
	1,000 shares General Corp.............		33,500	
	50 shares, 6% Pfd. Grey Steel.........		6,000	
Feb. 10	Purchased 5,000 shares, Wash Motors...	CD	15,000	
Mar. 1	Cash dividend, Grey Steel.............	CR		$ 300
May 15	Sold 800 rights, General Corp.........	CR		1,200
May 16	Exercised 200 rights, General Corp. to purchase 50 shares, General Corp......	CD	2,250	
Aug. 5	Sold 200 shares, Wash Motors.........	CR		2,500
Sept. 18	Sold 100 shares, General Corp.........	CR		3,350
			$61,750	$ 7,350

Your work papers for the year ended December 31, 1971, show the following securities in the investment account:

Date of Acquisition	Number of Shares	Type of Security	Name of Issuer	Amount
Jan. 2, 1964	5,000	Common stock, no par value	Backand Oil Co.	$ 5,000
Apr. 1, 1965	1,000	Common stock, $100 par value	General Corp.	33,500
Nov. 15, 1965	50	6% preferred stock, par value $100	Grey Steel	6,000
				$44,500

After inquiry the following additional data were obtained:

(a) The General Corp. on May 12 issued warrants representing the right to purchase, at $45 per share, one share for every four shares held. On May 12 the market value of the stock rights-on was $50 and ex-rights was $49. Smitters Corp. sold 800 rights on May 15 when the market price of the stock was $51. On May 16, 200 rights were exercised.

(b) On June 30 Wash Motors declared a reverse stock split of 1 for 5. One share of new $.50 par value common was exchanged for 5 shares of old $.10 par value common.

(c) The sale of 100 shares of General Corp. stock was part of the 1,000 shares purchased on April 1, 1965. The stock was sold for $65 per share.

(d) The government of Backand in early 1972 confiscated the assets of the Backand Oil Co. and nationalized the company. Despite the protest of the United States government, the Backand government has refused to recognize any claims of the stockholders or management of the Backand Oil Co.

Instructions: Prepare a work sheet showing the adjustments to arrive at the correct balance in the investment account at December 31, 1972. The work sheet should include the names of other accounts affected by the adjustments or reclassifications. (Formal journal entries are not required. Supporting computations should be in good form.)

(AICPA adapted)

11-11. Raymond Black, whose fiscal year for accounting purposes ends on March 31 each year, holds common stock of the Ryan Corporation. A summary of transactions concerning these holdings is given below. (Several cash dividend transactions are omitted, and the problem requirements relate only to the data given.) Mr. Black uses the specific identification method in accounting for his stock transactions.

Transactions

June 12, 1965   Purchased 50 shares of Ryan Common ($100 par) at a total cost of $4,600.

Dec. 15, 1965   Paid assessment of $5 per share to Ryan Corporation.

Apr. 15, 1968   Converted 50 shares of Ryan Preferred into the same number of common shares in accordance with conversion privilege. The preferred shares had cost $4,900 and their market value was $96 per share. Market value of common was $101 at that time.

Nov. 2, 1969   Received cash dividend of 50 cents per share on Ryan Common.

May 7, 1970   Received additional shares of Ryan Common in a 2-for-1 stock split. (Par value was reduced to $50.)

June 2, 1970   Purchased 100 shares of Ryan Common at a total cost of $5,300.

Nov. 4, 1970   Exercised option to receive one share of common for each 10 shares held in lieu of a cash dividend of $5.40 per share held. The fair market value of a share was $54.

Nov. 2, 1971   Received ordinary stock dividend equal to 20% of common shares held.

Jan. 4, 1972   Received warrants representing right to purchase at par 1 share of Ryan Common for each 10 shares of common held. On date of issue of warrants, market price of shares ex-rights was $58 and of rights, $2.

Jan. 15, 1972 Exercised 100 rights applicable to the block of shares purchased on June 2, 1970 and sold all remaining rights. Net proceeds from sale of rights amounted to $1.80 per right.

Mar. 12, 1972 Sold 60 shares of Ryan Common for $3,240 net proceeds. Shares were identified as 50 of those purchased on June 2, 1970 and 10 purchased on January 15, 1972.

Instructions: Prepare a schedule (or schedules) showing clearly the computation of:

(1) The remaining cost of Ryan Corporation common shares held by Mr. Black on March 31, 1972.

(2) The total dividend income from date of acquisition of the first block of shares through March 31, 1972.

(3) The gain or loss on sales made of Ryan Corporation securities.

(AICPA adapted)

11-12. During your audit of the financial statements of The Newbold Corporation for the year ended December 31, 1972, you determine that a portion of the company's funds have been invested in securities.

The company's books are maintained on the accrual basis. A transcript of the investments account follows:

The Newbold Corporation
Work Sheet to Adjust the Investments Account
December 31, 1972

			Account per Books		
1972	Transactions	Folio	Debit	Credit
Jan. 3	Purchased 100 shares, National Motors.	CD	$ 4,500	
5	Purchased 100 shares, Major Electronics.	CD	500	
Mar. 31	Cash dividend, National Motors.......	CR		$ 50
Apr. 5	Sold 100 shares, National Motors......	CR		4,800
6	Purchased 100 shares, Ace Investment...	CD	2,300	
6	Purchased 100 shares, General Utility...	CD	2,400	
May 1	Received 100 stock rights, General Utility	J	100	
July 2	Purchased 10 shares, General Utility...	CD	130	
15	Purchased 50 shares, Acme Laboratories	CD	1,900	
18	Purchased 20 shares, The Newbold Corporation.........................	CD	3,000	
Aug. 15	Sold 10 shares, The Newbold Corporation............................	CR		1,550
Dec. 8	Received 2 shares, Acme Laboratories..	J	80	
8	Cash dividend, Acme Laboratories.....	CR		20
15	Cash dividend, Ace Investment........	CR		90
31	Cash dividend, General Utility........	J	120	
			$15,030	$ 6,510
	Balance per books..................			8,520
			$15,030	$15,030

The following information and data were developed from your audit procedures:

(a) The 100 General Utility rights were recorded at the May 1 quoted price on the stock exchange. (The credit in the journal entry was to Miscellaneous Income.) The stock was quoted at $19 per share ex-rights on May 1. For each 5 rights held, one share of General Utility stock could be purchased at $13 per share. The company exercised rights to buy 10 shares on July 2 when the market price was $16 per share. The rights expired on August 15.

(b) The Newbold Corporation purchased 20 shares of its own stock from the estate of a deceased stockholder. The stock has a par value of $100 and was originally issued for $115 per share. Ten of the twenty shares were sold to an officer of the company for $155 per share.

(c) In August Major Electronics was reorganized. The original issue of stock was eliminated. New common stock was issued to bondholders and other creditors.

(d) During December Acme Laboratories declared a 5% stock dividend. In lieu of fractional shares cash was distributed based on the current market price of $40 per share. (The credit in the journal entry was to Miscellaneous Income.)

(e) The Ace Investment Co. letter accompanying its annual dividend check gave the following composition of the dividend:

$.80 Derived from income from investments
  .10 Return of stockholders' capital
$.90 Total dividend.

(f) On December 15 General Utility declared a cash dividend of $1 per share payable on January 15, 1973, to stockholders on record of December 29, 1972. (The credit in the journal entry was to Miscellaneous Income.)

(g) The securities are kept in a safe deposit box. You examined the securities on January 8, 1973, after determining from the bank's records that the last entry to the box was on December 8. All securities were examined and properly accounted for.

Instructions: Prepare a work sheet showing the adjustments to arrive at the corrected balance in the investments account at December 31, 1972, and other adjustments or reclassifications arising from your audit of the account. Your work sheet should include the names of the other accounts affected by the adjustments or reclassifications. (Formal journal entries are not required.) The books have not been closed.

(AICPA adapted)

chapter 12

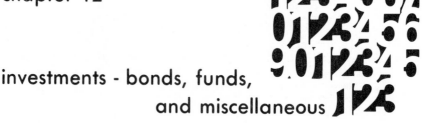

investments - bonds, funds, and miscellaneous

In addition to investment in stocks, many organizations may find other types of investment opportunities. Each class of investment has special characteristics that affect recording or valuation. The discussion of investments in this chapter will include bonds, funds, and miscellaneous items.

Bonds

Bonds and related obligations such as long-term notes and mortgages are means of raising capital used by trading, manufacturing, transportation, real estate, and utility enterprises as well as by the various governmental units — federal, state, and local. Investments in securities evidencing such obligations are made by the individual investor. Business units acquire securities of this class both for short-term and long-term investment purposes. Large blocks of these securities are held by insurance companies, banks, trust companies, various investment organizations, and educational and charitable institutions. Such securities also make up a large part of the holdings of pension, bond retirement, and other funds maintained by corporations. Bonds and long-term notes provide for the payment of interest at periodic intervals and principal sums at stated maturity dates. The probability of fluctuation in price during the time these securities are held is generally less than that in the case of stock, and the receipt of revenue is more regular and assured.

Kinds of bonds

A bond issue arises from a group contract known as an *indenture* between the borrowing corporation and investors. The bond issue is usually divided into a number of individual bonds of $1,000 denomination or face value. Bond interest payments are usually made at semi-annual intervals by the corporation or by an agent designated by the company. When all of the bonds mature on a single date, they are called *term bonds*; when bonds mature in installments, they are known as *serial bonds*.

Bonds issued by private corporations are classified as *secured* or *unsecured*. Secured bonds provide protection to the investor in the form of a mortgage covering the company's real estate and perhaps other property, or a pledge in the form of certain collateral. A *first-mortgage bond* represents a first claim against the property of a corporation in the event of the company's inability to meet bond interest and principal payments. A *second-mortgage bond* is a secondary claim ranking only after the claim of the first-mortgage bonds or senior issue has been completely satisfied. A *collateral trust bond* is usually secured by stocks and bonds of other corporations owned by the issuing company. Such securities are generally transferred to a trustee who holds them as collateral on behalf of the bondholders and, if necessary, will sell them to satisfy the bondholders' claim.

Bonds that are not protected by the pledge of certain property are frequently termed *debenture bonds*. Holders of debenture bonds simply rank as general creditors with other unsecured parties. The risk involved in such securities varies with the financial strength of the debtor. Debentures issued by a strong company may involve little risk; debentures issued by a weak company whose properties are already heavily mortgaged may involve considerable risk.

When another party promises to make payment on bonds if the issuing company fails to do so, the bonds are referred to as *guaranteed bonds*. A parent company, for example, may guarantee payment of the bonds issued by its subsidiaries.

Obligations known as *income bonds* have been issued when business failure has resulted in corporate reorganization. Such bonds require the payment of interest only to the extent of a company's current earnings. Income bonds may be cumulative or noncumulative. If cumulative, interest that cannot be paid in one year is carried over as a lien against future earnings; if noncumulative, no future lien arises from inability to meet interest payments.

The investor acquiring governmental obligations looks to the taxing authority of the issuing unit for the measure of its ability to raise money to meet debt service requirements. Certain government obligations are identified with government-owned enterprises, and principal and interest payments are made from the revenues accruing from such operations. These are known as *revenue bonds*.

Bonds may provide for their conversion into some other security at the option of the bondholder. Such bonds are known as *convertible bonds*. The conversion feature generally permits the owner of bonds to exchange his holdings into common stock. The bondholder is thus able to exchange his claim into an ownership interest if corporate operations prove successful and conversion becomes attractive; in the meantime he maintains the special rights of a creditor.

Other bond features may serve the issuer's interests. For example, bond indentures frequently give the issuing company the right to call and retire the bonds prior to their maturity. Such bonds are termed *callable bonds*. When a corporation wishes to reduce its outstanding indebtedness, bondholders are notified of the portion of the issue to be surrendered, and they are paid in accordance with call provisions. Interest does not accrue after the call date.

Bonds may be classified as (1) *registered bonds* and (2) *bearer* or *coupon bonds*. Registered bonds call for the registry of the owner's name on the corporation books. Transfer of bond ownership is similar to that for stock. When a bond is sold, the corporate transfer agent cancels the bond certificate surrendered by the seller and issues a new certificate to the buyer. Interest checks are mailed periodically to the bondholders of record. Bearer or coupon bonds are not recorded in the name of the owner, title to such bonds passing with delivery. Each bond is accompanied by coupons for individual interest payments covering the life of the issue. Coupons are clipped by the owner of the bond and presented to a bank for deposit or collection. The issue of bearer bonds eliminates the need for recording bond ownership changes and preparing and mailing periodic interest checks. But coupon bonds fail to offer the bondholder the protection found in registered bonds in the event bonds are lost or stolen. In some cases bonds provide interest coupons but require registry as to principal. Here, ownership safeguards are afforded while the time consuming routines involved in making interest payments are avoided.

Bond yield

The yield that is offered on the purchase of bonds varies with the safety of the investment. When the financial condition and earnings of a corporation are such that payment of interest and principal on bonded indebtedness is assured, the interest rate that the company must offer to dispose of a bond issue is relatively low. As the risk factor increases, a higher interest return is necessary to attract investors. The interest rate stated on the bonds is known as the *contract rate* or *nominal rate*. Although bonds provide for the payment of interest at a certain rate, this rate may not be the same as the prevailing or *market rate* for bonds of similar quality at the time the issue is sold. Furthermore, the market rate constantly fluctuates. It is these factors that result in the difference between bond face values and the prices at which the bonds sell on the market.

The purchase of bonds at face value implies agreement between the bond rate of interest and the prevailing market rate of interest. If the bond rate exceeds the market rate, the bonds will sell at a premium; if the bond rate is less than the market rate, the bonds will sell at a discount. The premium or the discount is the discounted value of the difference between the contract rate and the market rate of the series of interest payments. A declining market rate of interest subsequent to issuance of the bonds results in an increase in the market value of the bonds; a rising market rate of interest results in a decrease in their market value. The nominal rate corrected for the premium or the discount on the purchase gives the actual yield on the bonds, known as the *effective rate*.

Bond tables are available in determining the price to be paid for bonds if they are to provide a certain yield. A part of such a table is illustrated below.

VALUES TO THE NEAREST CENT OF 5% BOND FOR $1,000,000,
INTEREST PAYABLE SEMIANNUALLY

Yield	8 Years	$8\frac{1}{2}$ Years	9 Years	$9\frac{1}{2}$ Years	10 Years
4.00	$1,067,888.55	$1,071,459.36	$1,074,960.16	$1,078,392.31	$1,081,757.17
4.25	1,050,415.84	1,053,038.76	1,055,607.11	1,058,122.02	1,060,584.60
4.50	1,033,281.58	1,034,994.21	1,036,669.15	1,038,307.24	1,039,909.28
4.75	1,016,478.63	1,017,317.34	1,018,136.60	1,018,936.85	1,019,718.53
5.00	1,000,000.00	1,000,000.00	1,000,000.00	1,000,000.00	1,000,000.00
5.25	983,838.87	983,034.22	982,250.16	981,486.14	980,741.68
5.50	967,988.57	966,412.23	964,878.08	963,385.00	961,931.87
5.75	952,442.57	950,126.43	947,875.02	945,686.54	943,559.21
6.00	937,194.49	934,169.41	931,232.43	928,381.00	925,612.63
6.25	922,238.11	918,533.92	914,941.98	911,458.89	908,081.35
6.50	907,567.32	903,212.90	898,995.54	894,910.94	890,954.90
6.75	893,176.17	888,199.44	883,385.19	878,728.11	874,223.08
7.00	879,058.83	873,486.79	868,103.18	862,901.63	857,875.97

Assume, for example, that a $1,000, 10-year, 5% bond, interest payable semiannually, is bought to yield 4.50%. Reference to the column, "10 years" and the required yield line "4.50%," shows the value to be $1,039.91; if the bond is bought to yield 5.50%, it would be worth only $961.93.

This table can also be used to determine the effective rate on a bond acquired at a certain price. To illustrate, assume that a $1,000, 5% bond due in 10 years is selling at $975. Reference to the column "10 years" shows that a return of 5.50% is provided on an investment of

$961.93, while a return of 5.25% is provided on an investment of $980.74. The actual yield can be computed by interpolation. An interest decrease of .25% is found in the price increase of $18.81 ($961.93 to $980.74). Payment of $975.00, or $13.07 in excess of $961.93, reduces the 5.50% earnings rate by 13.07/18.81 of .25%, or .174%. The effective yield, then, is 5.50% less .174%, or 5.326%.

Bond acquisition

Bonds may be acquired directly from the issuer or they may be purchased on the open market through securities exchanges or through investment bankers.

An investment in bonds, whether short-term or long-term, is initially recorded at cost, which includes brokerage fees and any other costs incident to the purchase. Bonds acquired in exchange for assets or services are recorded at the fair market value of such consideration. When bonds and other securities are acquired for a lump sum, an apportionment of such cost among the securities is required. Purchase of bonds on a deferred payment basis calls for recognition of both the asset and the liability balances.

The purchase, as well as the sale of bonds, when made between interest payment dates requires calculation of the accrued interest which is added to the bond price. The amount paid for accrued interest on a purchase is subtracted from subsequent interest collections in measuring interest income; the amount received for accrued interest on a sale is recognized as interest income for the portion of the period that the bonds were held. In the calculation of accrued interest on bonds other than those issued by the United States Government, each month is considered to have 30 days. For example, the purchase on September 10 of bonds that pay interest on January 1 and July 1 requires calculation of interest for two months and 9 days or 69/360 year. In the case of U.S. Government bonds, the exact number of days must be determined and the year is considered to have 365 days in calculating the fractional part of the annual interest that has accrued. In the preceding example, then, calculation of accrued interest would be made for 71/365 year.

Amortization and accumulation procedures

When bonds are acquired as a temporary investment, investment cost is maintained in the accounts without adjustment. Interest is reported at amounts actually received. Upon disposition of the bonds, original cost is applied against net sales proceeds in arriving at the gain or the loss on the sale. If a similar procedure were to be followed on long-term bonds and these were held until maturity, a loss would emerge if bonds had been acquired at a premium and a gain if bonds had been acquired at a discount. But such "gains" and "losses" are in effect adjustments in interest of prior periods. Bonds are acquired at a premium in recognition of an interest rate that exceeds the rate prevailing at the time of bond purchase; hence interest income is properly viewed as consisting of the interest received less the portion of the receipt that may be considered to be a recovery of the premium originally paid. Bonds are acquired at a discount in view of an interest rate that is less than the prevailing rate; here interest income is properly viewed as interest received increased by a portion of the bond discount that will be realized at bond maturity. Although the attempt to refine income measurement by recognizing the change in bond value over its life is not warranted in the case of bonds acquired as a temporary investment, systematic adjustment for this factor is desirable when bonds are acquired as long-term holdings.

Bond premium amortization.   A premium on bonds acquired is charged against interest received over the life of the bonds. The bond account is credited and Interest Income is charged each period for the part of the premium that is written off. The investment, then, moves towards its maturity value, and interest is reported periodically at the amount actually earned — the interest collected decreased by that part of the premium considered to have been recovered. The reduction of bonds to face value by periodic charges to income is referred to as *bond premium amortization.*

Bond discount accumulation.   A discount on bonds acquired is added to bond interest received over the life of the bonds. The bond account is charged and Interest Income is credited each period for the part of the discount that is accumulated. Here, too, the investment moves toward its maturity value, and interest is reported periodically at the amount actually earned — the interest collected increased by that part of the discount considered realized. Increase of bonds to face value by periodic credits to income is called *bond discount accumulation.*

Methods of amortization and accumulation.   The *straight-line* method of amortization or accumulation provides for the recognition of an equal amount of premium or discount each period. Use of the *compound-interest* or *effective-rate* method requires that the effective earnings rate on the purchase of the bonds first be determined; interest income is then reported periodically at the effective rate, the difference between the amount earned and the amount actually received being recognized as an adjustment to the investment account. To illustrate, assume the purchase of 5-year bonds of $100,000, interest at 6% payable semi-annually, at a price of 104⅜. Reference to bond tables indicates a yield at this price of approximately 5%. The following tabulations show the differences in use of the two methods:

AMORTIZATION OF PREMIUM — STRAIGHT-LINE METHOD
$100,000 5-Year Bonds, Interest at 6% Payable Semiannually, Purchased at $104,375

Interest Payment	A Interest Received (3% of Face Value)	B Premium Amortization (1/10 x $4,375)	C Interest Income (A – B)	D Bond Carrying Value (D – B)
				$104,375.00
1	$3,000.00	$437.50	$2,562.50	103,937.50
2	3,000.00	437.50	2,562.50	103,500.00
3	3,000.00	437.50	2,562.50	103,062.50
4	3,000.00	437.50	2,562.50	102,625.00
5	3,000.00	437.50	2,562.50	102,187.50
6	3,000.00	437.50	2,562.50	101,750.00
7	3,000.00	437.50	2,562.50	101,312.50
8	3,000.00	437.50	2,562.50	100,875.00
9	3,000.00	437.50	2,562.50	100,437.50
10	3,000.00	437.50	2,562.50	100,000.00

AMORTIZATION OF PREMIUM — COMPOUND-INTEREST METHOD
$100,000 5-Year Bonds, Interest at 6% Payable Semiannually, Purchased at $104,375
To Yield Approximately 5%

Interest Payment	A Interest Received (3% of Face Value)	B Interest Income (2½% of Bond Carrying Value)	C Premium Amortization (A – B)	D Bond Carrying Value (D – C)
				$104,375.00
1	$3,000.00	$2,609.38 (2½% of $104,375.00)	$390.62	103,984.38
2	3,000.00	2,599.61 (2½% of $103,984.38)	400.39	103,583.99
3	3,000.00	2,589.60 (2½% of $103,583.99)	410.40	103,173.59
4	3,000.00	2,579.34 (2½% of $103,173.59)	420.66	102,752.93
5	3,000.00	2,568.82 (2½% of $102,752.93)	431.18	102,321.75
6	3,000.00	2,558.04 (2½% of $102,321.75)	441.96	101,879.79
7	3,000.00	2,546.99 (2½% of $101,879.79)	453.01	101,426.78
8	3,000.00	2,535.67 (2½% of $101,426.78)	464.33	100,962.45
9	3,000.00	2,524.06 (2½% of $100,962.45)	475.94	100,486.51
10	3,000.00	2,513.49 ($3,000 – $486.51)*	486.51	100,000.00

*2½% of $100,486.51 would be $2,512.16. However, use of 5% when the effective rate was not exactly 5% has resulted in a small discrepancy that requires compensation upon recording the final receipt of interest. The bond account is reduced to face value, interest income being reduced by the premium balance at the time of bond maturity.

The straight-line method of amortization offers a uniform interest amount for each period. The compound-interest method offers a uniform earnings rate based upon a declining investment balance; since each interest payment represents a partial return of the premium, the investment is reduced each period and earnings, in turn, are correspondingly less.

The use of the two methods when bonds are acquired at a discount is illustrated in the tables that follow. Here it is assumed that 5-year bonds of $100,000, interest at 4% payable semiannually, are purchased to yield 5%, or at a price as shown by bond tables of $95,623.93.

ACCUMULATION OF DISCOUNT — STRAIGHT-LINE METHOD
$100,000 5-Year Bonds, Interest at 4% Payable Semiannually, Purchased at $95,623.93

Interest Payment	A Interest Received (2% of Face Value)	B Discount Accumulation (1/10 x $4,376.07)	C Interest Income (A+B)	D Bond Carrying Value (D+B)
				$ 95,623.93
1	$2,000.00	$437.61	$2,437.61	96,061.54
2	2,000.00	437.61	2,437.61	96,499.15
3	2,000.00	437.61	2,437.61	96,936.76
4	2,000.00	437.61	2,437.61	97,374.37
5	2,000.00	437.61	2,437.61	97,811.98
6	2,000.00	437.61	2,437.61	98,249.59
7	2,000.00	437.61	2,437.61	98,687.20
8	2,000.00	437.61	2,437.61	99,124.81
9	2,000.00	437.61	2,437.61	99,562.42
10	2,000.00	437.58	2,437.58	100,000.00

ACCUMULATION OF DISCOUNT — COMPOUND-INTEREST METHOD
$100,000 5-Year Bonds, Interest at 4% Payable Semiannually, Purchased at $95,623.93
To Yield 5%

Interest Payment	A Interest Received (2% of Face Value)	B Interest Income (2½% of Bond Carrying Value)	C Discount Accumulation (B−A)	D Bond Carrying Value (D+C)
				$ 95,623.93
1	$2,000.00	$2,390.60 (2½% of $95,623.93)	$390.60	96,014.53
2	2,000.00	2,400.36 (2½% of $96,014.53)	400.36	96,414.89
3	2,000.00	2,410.37 (2½% of $96,414.89)	410.37	96,825.26
4	2,000.00	2,420.63 (2½% of $96,825.26)	420.63	97,245.89
5	2,000.00	2,431.15 (2½% of $97,245.89)	431.15	97,677.04
6	2,000.00	2,441.93 (2½% of $97,677.04)	441.93	98,118.97
7	2,000.00	2,452.97 (2½% of $98,118.97)	452.97	98,571.94
8	2,000.00	2,464.30 (2½% of $98,571.94)	464.30	99,036.24
9	2,000.00	2,475.91 (2½% of $99,036.24)	475.91	99,512.15
10	2,000.00	2,487.85 ($2,000+$487.85)*	487.85	100,000.00

*2½% of $99,512.15 would be $2,487.80. By earlier computations to the nearest cent, an element of error was introduced. Compensation for the error is made when the final receipt of interest is recorded. The bond account is raised to face value, interest income being increased by the discount balance at the time of bond maturity.

The compound-interest method offers a uniform earnings rate based upon a successively higher investment balance. Periodic earnings are composed of the cash received plus the increase that is considered to have taken place in the investment balance. As the investment balance goes up each period, earnings are correspondingly greater.

The compound-interest method may be favored by many businesses because of the greater accuracy it affords by recognizing interest at a constant rate.[1]   However, because of its simplicity, the straight-line procedure is frequently preferred except in those instances where large blocks of bonds are acquired at substantial premiums or discounts and use of the straight-line method would provide results that differ materially from the use of the compound-interest method. Straight-line amortization is accepted for income tax purposes. Use of the straight-line method is assumed in the remaining illustrations of this chapter.

Accounting for long-term investments in bonds

The entries for a long-term investment in bonds are illustrated in the example that follows. Assume that an investor acquires 6% bonds, face value $100,000, for $107,000, with interest payable semiannually on April 1 and October 1. Bonds are acquired on July 1, 1972, and mature on April 1, 1981. Books are to be adjusted and closed at the end of each calendar year.

A schedule may be prepared by the investor to summarize premium amortization and earnings over the period the bonds are to be held. This schedule can then be used in making periodic adjustments. The bond premium is to be spread over the period that bonds will be earning interest, July 1, 1972, to April 1, 1981, or 105 months. An amortization schedule is prepared as follows:

AMORTIZATION SCHEDULE — STRAIGHT-LINE METHOD

Period	A Interest Received (including adjustments for accruals)	Number of Months	Premium Amortization			E Bond Carrying Value (E−C)
			B Fraction of Premium to be Amortized	C Amount of Premium Amortization (B×$7,000)	D Interest Income (A−C)	
July 1 (acquisition date) to Dec. 31, 1972						$107,000
	$3,000	6	6/105	$ 400	$2,600	106,600
Year Ended Dec. 31, 1973	6,000	12	12/105	800	5,200	105,800
Year Ended Dec. 31, 1974	6,000	12	12/105	800	5,200	105,000
Year Ended Dec. 31, 1975	6,000	12	12/105	800	5,200	104,200
Year Ended Dec. 31, 1976	6,000	12	12/105	800	5,200	103,400
Year Ended Dec. 31, 1977	6,000	12	12/105	800	5,200	102,600
Year Ended Dec. 31, 1978	6,000	12	12/105	800	5,200	101,800
Year Ended Dec. 31, 1979	6,000	12	12/105	800	5,200	101,000
Year Ended Dec. 31, 1980	6,000	12	12/105	800	5,200	100,200
Jan. 1 to Apr. 1, 1981 (maturity date)	1,500	3	3/105	200	1,300	100,000
		105	105/105	$7,000		

---

[1]The Accounting Principles Board has recognized the compound-interest method as being theoretically sound and thus an acceptable method. The Board refers to this method as the *interest* method. *Opinions of the Accounting Principles Board, No. 12,* "Omnibus Opinion — 1967" (New York: American Institute of Certified Public Accountants, 1967), p. 194.

Entries for bond ownership in 1972 and 1973 appear below:

Transaction	Entry
JULY 1, 1972 Purchased 100, $1,000, 6% bonds of Hope Corp. at 106¾, bonds maturing on April 1, 1981. Interest is payable semiannually on April 1 and October 1. Payment was made as follows: Bonds of $100,000 at 106¾.... $106,750 Costs of purchase........... 250 Accrued interest, April 1– July 1.................. 1,500 $108,500	Investment in Hope Corp. 6's............. 107,000 Interest Income........ 1,500[1] Cash.............. 108,500
OCTOBER 1, 1972 Received semiannual interest.	Cash................. 3,000 Interest Income...... 3,000
DECEMBER 31, 1972 (a) To record accrued interest for 3 months, and (b) to amortize bond premium applicable to current year. Amortization: period held in current year, 6 months; total life of bond issue, 8¾ years or 105 months; current amortization, $\frac{6}{105}$ x $7,000, or $400 (or 6 x $66.66⅔, monthly amortization= $400).	(a) Accrued Interest on Investment in Bonds........... 1,500 Interest Income... 1,500 (b) Interest Income.... 400 Investment in Hope Corp. 6's.. 400
JANUARY 1, 1973 To reverse 1972 accrued interest.	Interest Income........ 1,500 Accrued Interest on Investment in Bonds. 1,500
APRIL 1, 1973 Received semiannual interest.	Cash................. 3,000 Interest Income...... 3,000
OCTOBER 1, 1973 Received semiannual interest.	Cash................. 3,000 Interest Income...... 3,000
DECEMBER 31, 1973 (a) To record accrued interest for 3 months, and (b) to amortize bond premium applicable to current year, $\frac{12}{105}$ x $7,000, or $800 (or 12 x $66.66⅔, monthly amortization= $800).	(a) Accrued Interest on Investment in Bonds........... 1,500 Interest Income... 1,500 (b) Interest Income.... 800 Investment in Hope Corp. 6's.. 800

Entries similar to those for 1973 will be made until 1980. The reversing entry required on January 1, 1981, and the entries on April 1, 1981, when the last interest payment is received, will be as follows:

Transaction	Entry
JANUARY 1, 1981 To reverse 1980 accrued interest.	Interest Income........ 1,500 Accrued Interest on Investment in Bonds 1,500

---

[1]As indicated in Chapter 6, payment for accrued interest can be recorded by a charge to an accrued receivable balance; this account would be closed when interest is collected.

Transaction	Entry

APRIL 1, 1981
(a) To record amortization for last 3-month period, $\frac{3}{105}$ x $7,000, or $200 (or 3 x 66.66\frac{2}{3}$, monthly amortization = $200), and (b) to record receipt of semiannual interest and principal amount.
	(a) Interest Income.... 200
	   Investment in
	     Hope Corp. 6's.. 200
	
	(b) Cash............. 103,000
	   I n v e s t m e n t i n
	     Hope Corp. 6's.. 100,000
	     Interest Income... 3,000

When bonds are acquired at a discount, the investment account is raised to face value by discount accumulation as illustrated below:

Transaction	Entry

OCTOBER 11, 1972
Purchased 100, $1,000, 5$\frac{1}{4}$% bonds of Atlas, Inc., at 96$\frac{1}{2}$, bonds maturing on March 1, 1979. Interest is payable semiannually on March 1 and September 1.
Payment was made as follows:
Bonds of $100,000 at 96$\frac{1}{2}$... $96,500.00
Costs of purchase.........   250.00
Interest, Sept. 1–Oct. 11,
40 days, at 5$\frac{1}{4}$% 583.33
 	
          $97,333.33
	Investment in Atlas,
	  Inc., 5$\frac{1}{4}$'s.......... 96,750.00
	Interest Income...... 583.33
	  Cash............ 97,333.33

DECEMBER 31, 1972
(a) To record accrued interest for 4 months, and (b) to accumulate bond discount applicable to current year. Accumulation: period held in current year, 3 months; total life of bond issue, 5$\frac{5}{12}$ years, or 65 months; current accumulation, $\frac{3}{65}$ x $3,250, or $150 (or 3 x $50, monthly accumulation = $150).
	(a) Accrued Interest
	    on Investment in
	    Bonds......... 1,750.00
	     Interest Income. 1,750.00
	
	(b) I n v e s t m e n t i n
	    Atlas, Inc., 5$\frac{1}{4}$'s.. 150.00
	     Interest Income 150.00

JANUARY 1, 1973
To reverse 1972 accrued income.
	Interest Income...... 1,750.00
	  Accrued Interest on
	  Investment in
	  Bonds........... 1,750.00

MARCH 1, 1973 Received semiannual interest.	Cash.............. 2,625.00 Interest Income.... 2,625.00
SEPTEMBER 1, 1973 Received semiannual interest.	Cash.............. 2,625.00 Interest Income.... 2,625.00

DECEMBER 31, 1973
(a) To record accrued interest for 4 months, and (b) to accumulate bond discount applicable to current year, $\frac{12}{65}$ x $3,250, or $600 (or 12 x $50, monthly accumulation = $600).
	(a) Accrued Interest on
	    Investment in
	    Bonds......... 1,750.00
	    Interest Income 1,750.00
	(b) I n v e s t m e n t i n
	    Atlas, Inc., 5$\frac{1}{4}$'s. 600.00
	    Interest Income. 600.00

It is necessary to set some arbitrary minimum time unit in the amortization of bond premium or the accumulation of bond discount. The month is used in the text as the minimum unit. Transactions occurring during the first half of the month are treated as though they were made at the beginning of the month; transactions occurring during the second half are treated as though made at the start of the following month. Use of a longer term, such as the quarter or half year, is possible, although this offers less accuracy than the use of a shorter time unit.

Amortization of bond premium and accumulation of bond discount are recognized in the foregoing examples at the end of the investor's fiscal period. It would be possible to recognize amortization or accumulation whenever interest is received. But it would still be necessary to bring the amortization or the accumulation up to date at the end of the year when accrued interest is recognized. Instead of making the adjustment several times a year and for fractional periods, the adjustment is more conveniently made for a full year at the end of each fiscal year, except for the first and last years that the bonds are held when fractional parts of a year are involved.

Bond disposition

Bonds may not always be held to maturity. They may be sold to another investor, they may be called in by the issuing company for redemption, or they may be turned in to the issuing company for conversion into another class of security. Each of these possibilities will be discussed in the following sections.

Sale of bonds prior to maturity. Sometimes bonds held as a long-term investment are sold prior to their maturity. The book value of the bonds must be determined as of the date of the sale. This requires bond premium or discount adjustment to the date of the sale. The difference between the book value on the date of sale and the cash proceeds from the sale represents the net gain or loss. To illustrate a sale, assume that the bonds of Atlas, Inc., in the previous example are not held until maturity, but are sold February 1, 1974, at 97 plus accrued interest. Entries in 1974 are:

Transaction	Entry	
JANUARY 1, 1974 To reverse 1973 accrued interest.	Interest Income....... 1,750.00 Accrued Interest on Investment in Bonds	1,750.00
FEBRUARY 1, 1974 To record accumulation of discount to date of sale: $\frac{1}{65}$ x $3,250, or $50. To record sale of bonds: (a) Accrued interest, September 1–February 1 ... $2,187.50	Investment in Atlas, Inc., $5\frac{1}{4}$'s............ 50.00 Interest Income..... (a) Cash............ 2,187.50 Interest Income	50.00 2,187.50

Transaction	Entry

(b) Book value of bonds:
Cost.................. $96,750.00
Plus discount accumulation
to date of sale:
   1972 $150.00
   1973 600.00
   1974   50.00   800.00
                   $97,550.00
Sales proceeds $97,000.00
Less costs of sale   200.00 96,800.00
Net loss.............. $ 750.00
	(b) Cash.......... 96,800.00
	   Loss on Sale of
	   Atlas, Inc., 5¼'s 750.00
	     Investment in
	     Atlas, Inc.
	     5¼'s........ 97,550.00

The two cash entries may be combined as a single compound entry. The bond interest income for January, 1974, is $487.50, consisting of interest received, $2,187.50, decreased by the interest relating to 1973, $1,750.00, and increased by discount accumulation for the current period, $50.00. This is the same as the monthly interest recognized in 1972 and 1973.

When bonds are acquired at a premium and bond interest is subject to federal income tax, the bondholder is permitted to report as income (1) the actual amount received or (2) the amount received less the amortization of bond premium. If the actual amount received is reported as income, the bondholder must use the original cost of the bonds as a basis for calculating the gain or the loss arising from the subsequent sale or redemption of the bonds; if income is reduced by amortization, bond cost less the amount of amortization becomes the basis for calculation of gain or loss on the ultimate disposal of the bond. In the case of state and municipal bonds whose interest is wholly tax exempt, federal tax laws require the amortization of any premium. Since the interest is nontaxable, the deduction for the amortization is not reflected on the return; however, the basis of the bonds is reduced by the premium amortization in calculating the gain or the loss on the sale of the bonds.

When bonds are acquired at a discount, the bondholder must report as income for tax purposes the interest actually received. Upon disposal of the bonds, he reports the difference between proceeds and cost as a gain or loss. The realization of a discount is thus recognized as a gain from the disposal of bonds rather than as interest income related to the holding period. Exception to this treatment is required for bonds issued after December 31, 1954, at a discount that aggregates ¼ of 1% or more per year on the redemption price; full or partial recovery of original issue discount on such issues is taxed as ordinary income. A further exception is made in the case of United States savings bonds issued at a discount; realization of the discount is taxed as ordinary income. A taxpayer reporting on the cash basis is allowed the option of recognizing such discount as income in the year of bond redemption or in annual increments according to bond redemption values. A taxpayer reporting on the accrual basis must recognize as income the annual increment in bond value each year.

When an investment in bonds consists of several purchases and some of the holdings are sold, tax laws call for the same rules that apply on the sale of stock. Unless the bonds can be identified as to lot and related cost, cost must be determined by the first-in, first-out rule, earliest cost thus being applied to sales proceeds in calculating the gain or loss.

Bond redemption prior to maturity. Bonds that are callable by the issuing company prior to their maturity generally provide for the payment of a premium to the bondholder in the event this option is exercised. To illustrate, bonds issued on January 1, 1971, and due on January 1, 1991, may provide a table of redemption values as follows:

Redeemable January 1, 1976, to December 31, 1980, at 105
Redeemable January 1, 1981, to December 31, 1985, at $102\frac{1}{2}$
Redeemable January 1, 1986, to December 31, 1990, at 101

When bonds are acquired at a premium, conservatism calls for an amortization policy that will prevent the bonds from being reported at more than their redemption values at the various call dates. To illustrate, assume in the example above that bonds of $10,000 are acquired for $10,800 on January 1, 1973. Regular premium amortization and accelerated amortization based upon bond redemption values of $10,500, $10,250 and $10,100, are compared below:

Regular Amortization	Accelerated Amortization
$800 ÷ 18 years = $44.44 per year (1973–1991)	($10,800 − $10,500) ÷ 3 years (1973–1975) = $100.00 per year
	($10,500 − $10,250) ÷ 5 years (1976–1980) = $ 50.00 per year
	($10,250 − $10,100) ÷ 5 years (1981–1985) = $ 30.00 per year
	($10,100 − $10,000) ÷ 5 years (1986–1990) = $ 20.00 per year

If regular amortization procedures are followed on the books of the investor, bond redemption prior to maturity will result in a recovery of cash that is less than bond carrying value and will require recognition of a loss that nullifies in part the earnings recognized in the past. Accelerated amortization reduces the investment to its redemption value; bond redemption values are used for income measurement purposes and the need for recognition of a loss upon redemption is avoided. Obviously, bonds reported at a discount, or bonds reported at a premium reduced by normal amortization to an amount that is not greater than redemption value, require no special treatment.

When bonds are called, Cash is debited for the call price received, the investment account is credited for the book value of the bonds called, and a gain or loss is reported for the difference. The contract with bond-holders normally provides for the payment of accrued interest to the bond call date. When bonds are called on a regular interest payment date, the bondholder will receive the call price plus interest for a full period. Interest income is credited for the interest received.

Bond conversion. When bonds are converted into another security, accounts are opened for the newly acquired security and the bond invest-ment balance is closed. The procedures that are followed by the investor are similar to those previously described for the exchange of stock for other securities. The newly acquired security is recorded at its market value, and the difference between this value and the book value of the bonds surrendered is reported as gain or loss. Before an exchange is recorded, the investment account should be brought up to date for dis-count accumulation or premium amortization. Interest collected at the time of the exchange is recorded as interest income.

To illustrate bond conversion, assume that the Carl Co. offers bond-holders 40 shares of Carl Co. common stock, par $25, in exchange for each $1,000 5% bond that they hold. An investor exchanges bonds of $10,000, book value as brought up to date, $9,850, for 400 shares of common stock having a market price at the time of exchange of $26 per share. The exchange is completed three months after an interest pay-ment date. The exchange is recorded as follows:

Cash...	125	
Investment in Carl Co. Common Stock............	10,400	
Investment in Carl Co. 5% Bonds...............		9,850
Gain on Exchange of Carl Co. Bonds............		550
Interest Income...............................		125

For federal income tax purposes the exchange of bonds for other securities or property results in gain or loss except for the following that are recognized as nontaxable: the exchange of bonds for other bonds of the same company that are considered substantially the same, and the conversion of bonds into stock in accordance with provisions of the bond indenture.

Bond valuation

The market value of bonds varies with changes in the financial strength of the issuing company, changes in the level of interest rates, and shrinkage in the remaining life of the issue. In the absence of material price declines, bonds held as long-term investments are reported on the balance sheet at book value. This book value approaches par as the bonds move closer to maturity. To this extent, then, the accounting can be considered to follow a similar change that is taking place on the market as the bond life is reduced and a correspondingly lower valuation is attached to the difference between the actual rate and the market rate of remaining interest payments. Although investments are properly reported at book value, parenthetical disclosure of the aggregate market value of the securities makes the financial statements more informative.

A material decline in bond value, however, as a result of unfavorable developments relating to the issuer cannot be ignored. Assume, for example, that the issuing company has found it impossible to meet redemption fund requirements, which suggests that it may have difficulties in paying off the obligation at its maturity. Even more serious, assume that there has been default on bond interest payments. When significant investment loss is indicated, entries to record the loss should be made. Such loss may be established by reference to current market quotations, by an investigation of prices at which similar bonds are sold, or by special appraisal of the assets that are pledged as security on the bonded indebtedness.

When bonds are purchased *flat,* that is, when interest on bonds is in arrears and one price is paid for the bonds together with all accrued and unpaid interest, this price is recorded as the bond investment cost. Any amounts subsequently received on the bonds, whether designated as payments of principal or defaulted interest, should be treated as a recovery of investment cost as long as there is uncertainty of ultimate recovery of more than the amount invested. No interest should be accrued on the bonds until solvency of the debtor is restored and the regular receipt of interest is assured. Such bonds are reported at their unrecovered cost with full information as to the nature of the investment.

Long-term notes and mortgages

Investments in long-term notes and mortgages have many characteristics in common with bond investments. During their lives they provide interest, and at their maturities they call for specified cash payments. Long-term notes and mortgages should be recorded at cost, or at their fair market value when acquired in connection with a sale of property. Any difference between an acquisition value and a maturity value calls for adjustments to income over the life of the investment. A note or mortgage may be acquired at a considerable discount when it involves a relatively large element of risk. Such acquisition raises the question of possible failure to recover the full amount of the obligation at maturity. When this possibility is foreseen, the investor may choose to carry the investment at its original cost. If full payment is received at maturity, the discount would be recognized as interest at that time. Notes and mortgages should be analyzed in terms of installment maturities; the part that is due within one year is reported as a current asset, the balance as a long-term investment.

Funds

Cash and other assets set apart for certain common purposes are called *funds, sinking funds*, or *redemption funds*. Some funds are to be used for specified current purposes such as the payment of expenses or the discharge of current obligations and are appropriately reported as current assets. Examples of these are petty cash funds, payroll funds, interest funds, dividend funds, and withholding, social security, and other tax funds. Other funds are accumulated over a long term for such purposes as the acquisition or the replacement of properties, the retirement of long-term indebtedness, the redemption of capital stock, or possible future contingencies and are properly considered noncurrent and reported under the investment heading. Examples of these are bond retirement funds, preferred stock redemption funds, pension funds, funds for the acquisition of land, buildings, and equipment, and funds to meet costs arising from accidents, fires, and other contingencies.

Establishment of fund

A fund may be established through the voluntary action of management or it may be established as a result of contractual requirements. It may arise from a single deposit or from a series of deposits, or it may be composed of the sum of the deposits plus the earnings identified with such deposits. The fund may be used for a single purpose, such as the retirement of bonds at maturity, or it may be used for several related purposes, such as the periodic payment of interest on bonds, the retirement of bonds at various intervals, and the ultimate retirement of the remaining bonded indebtedness.

When a fund is voluntarily created by management, control of the fund and its disposition is an arbitrary matter depending upon the wishes of management. When a fund is created through some legal requirement, it must be administered and applied in accordance therewith. Such a fund is generally administered by one or more trustees under an agreement known as a *trust indenture.*

Although a fund that is to be applied to the retirement of debt may be controlled by a trustee, it should not be viewed as a reduction in debt unless it has been specifically agreed that payment to the trustee frees the transferor from any further obligation. Normally, the trustee plan is simply an arrangement for debt liquidation, and losses from fund misappropriation or from declines in the values of fund assets do not relieve the corporation of responsibility for full payment. Under such circumstances the fund calls for the same accounting that would be followed for a fund controlled by its owner.

Fund accumulation

When a corporation is required by agreement to establish a fund for a certain purpose such as the retirement of bonds or the redemption of stock, the agreement generally provides that (1) fund deposits shall be fixed amounts or shall vary according to gross revenue, net income, or units of product sold, or (2) deposits shall be equal periodic sums which, together with earnings, will produce a certain amount at some future date. The latter arrangement is based on compound-interest factors, and compound-interest tables are used in determining the equal periodic deposits. Use of such a table, for example, indicates that a fund of $100,000, to be produced by a series of 5 equal annual deposits at 4% compounded annually, requires periodic deposits of $18,462.71. A schedule can be developed to show the hypothetical fund accumulation through deposits and earnings. Such a schedule is illustrated below:

FUND ACCUMULATION SCHEDULE

Year	Earnings on Fund Balance for Year	Amount Deposited in Fund	Total Increase in Fund for Year	Accumulated Fund Total
1		$18,462.71	$18,462.71	$18,462.71
2	$ 738.51	18,462.71	19,201.22	37,663.93
3	1,506.56	18,462.71	19,969.27	57,633.20
4	2,305.33	18,462.71	20,768.04	78,401.24
5	3,136.05	18,462.71	21,598.76	100,000.00

Assuming deposits at the end of each year, the table shows a fund balance at the end of the first year of $18,462.71 resulting from the first deposit. At the end of the second year the fund is increased by (1) earnings at 4% on the investment in the fund during the year, $738.51, and (2) the second deposit to the fund, $18,462.71. The total in the fund at this time is $37,663.93. Fund earnings in the following year are based on a total investment of $37,663.93 as of the beginning of the year.

The schedule is developed on the assumption of annual earnings of 4%. However, various factors, such as fluctuations in the earnings rate and gains and losses on investments, may provide earnings that differ from the assumed amounts. If the fund is to be maintained in accordance with the accumulation schedule, deposits may be adjusted for earnings that differ from estimated amounts. Smaller deposits, then, can be made in periods when earnings exceed the assumed rate; larger deposits are necessary when earnings fail to meet the assumed rate.

Accounting for funds

Fund transactions involving investments in stocks and bonds call for recording and valuation procedures as described in the preceding sections. When a fund is administered by the company, fund transactions may be recorded currently on the company records. When a fund is administered by a trustee, fund transactions should be summarized by the trustee and periodic reports submitted to the company. This information can then be recorded on the company books. The trustee should maintain records enabling him to report on his fund stewardship. Such records are best kept in double-entry form.

The example on pages 408–409 illustrates the accounting that may be employed when (1) information is recorded currently on the company's books, and (2) information is recorded at the end of the period on the company's books from summaries provided by separate books maintained by a trustee. The example assumes the establishment of a fund for the retirement of bonds and gives the entries for the fund accumulation in the first year and for debt retirement in the last year.

It should be observed that when separate books are maintained by a trustee, assets are balanced by a *company* account summarizing the trustee's accountability to the company. This account is credited for assets received from the company as well as for net asset increases resulting from earnings; it is charged for assets applied to the purpose for which the fund was established as well as for assets transferred to the company. The *fund* account on the company's books, in turn, reports the company's equity in the fund. This account is charged for assets transferred to the trustee and for net asset increases resulting from fund earnings; it is credited for assets applied to the purpose for which the fund was established and for the assets transferred to the company. The company account on the trustee's books and the fund account on the company's books are *reciprocal accounts* since the credit balance in the company account is equal to the debit balance in the fund account when both sets of books are up to date. When a company administers a fund but wishes to remove fund detail from the general ledger, a separate ledger can be provided in a form similar to that employed by the trustee.

In the example, the bond fund assets as shown on the company's books or as reported to the company by the trustee at the end of 1972 are as follows:

Bond fund cash.....................................	$44,950
Bond fund securities.................................	35,500
Accrued interest on bond fund securities................	225
Total..	$80,675

Bond fund income for 1972 is $875 and bond fund expense is $200; the difference, $675, represents the fund earnings. This amount is reported on the income statement as Other Revenue. A gain or a loss on the sale of fund securities would be recognized as another revenue or expense item or as an extraordinary item, depending upon its materiality. The individual assets in the fund would be reported under the investments heading on the balance sheet.

The foregoing illustration assumed purchase of securities other than bonds originally issued by the company. Bond fund cash is commonly used to purchase a company's own bonds. Such fund use frequently operates to support a firm market price for the issue since the company can enter the market whenever the market price makes retirement of the company's bonds attractive.

When a company retires its own bonds through bond fund cash, the liability is canceled, the fund cash account is credited, and a loss or gain on the retirement is recorded. For example, assume that the books of a company show bonds of $100,000 outstanding with an unamortized bond discount balance relating to this issue of $3,500. The company acquires and formally retires bonds with a face value of $20,000 at a cost of $19,500. The entry to record the bond retirement follows:

Bonds Payable...............................	20,000	
Loss on Bond Retirement.......................	200	
Bond Fund Cash........		19,500
Unamortized Bond Discount...................		700

To record bond retirement as follows:

Amount paid on retirement..	$19,500
Book value of bonds retired: face value of bonds, $20,000, less unamortized discount applicable to bonds, $700 . . .	19,300
Loss on retirement........	$ 200

When bonds are acquired by a trustee and kept "alive," such bonds are sometimes carried on the books the same as any other investment. The trustee records the bonds at cost, collects interest on the bonds and records collections as income, applies accumulation and amortization procedures in calculating effective earnings, and reports a gain or a loss

Transaction	Fund Transactions Recorded Currently on Company's Books
	Entry
1972: JUNE 30, 1972 The Powell Corporation made the first of a series of 20 equal semiannual deposits of $40,000 to bond fund.	Bond Fund Cash. . . . . 40,000 Cash. 40,000
JULY 6, 1972 Purchased bond fund securities for $35,750, which includes accrued interest of $150.	Bond Fund Securities. . 35,600 Bond Fund Income. . . . 150 Bond Fund Cash. . . . 35,750
DECEMBER 1, 1972 Received interest on bond fund securities, $900.	Bond Fund Cash. . . . . 900 Bond Fund Income. 900
DECEMBER 31, 1972 Paid bond fund custodian fees, $200.	Bond Fund Expenses. . 200 Bond Fund Cash. . . . 200
Made second deposit of $40,000 to bond fund.	Bond Fund Cash. . . . . 40,000 Cash. 40,000
To record accrued interest on bond fund securities and cash deposits, $225.	Accrued Interest on Bond Fund Securities. 225 Bond Fund Income. 225
To record amortization of premium on bond fund securities, $100.	Bond Fund Income. . . . 100 Bond Fund Securities 100

(a) To recognize bond fund income and expense.
(b) To close bond fund income and expense balances.
	(b) Bond Fund Income 875
	  Bond Fund Ex-
	    penses. 200
	  Income
	    Summary. 675

1981:
DECEMBER 31, 1981
Sold bond fund securities, book value after entries for amortization, $1,060,000, for $1,100,000, which includes accrued interest, $8,000; total proceeds were added to bond fund cash on hand on this date of $15,000.
	Bond Fund Cash. 1,100,000
	  Bond Fund Securities 1,060,000
	  Bond Fund Income. 8,000
	  Gain on Sale of Bond
	    Fund Securities. . . . 32,000

Paid bonded indebtedness from bond fund cash, $1,000,000.	Bonds Payable. . . . . . . 1,000,000 Bond Fund Cash. . . . 1,000,000
Transferred bond fund cash on hand after payment of bonds to cash account.	Cash. . . . . 115,000 Bond Fund Cash. . . . 115,000

(a) To recognize bond fund income or loss.
(b) To close nominal accounts relating to bond fund activities.
	(b) Bond Fund Income 8,000
	  Gain on Sale of
	    Bond Fund Secu-
	    rities. 32,000
	  Income
	    Summary. 40,000

Fund Transactions Recorded Currently on Trustee's Books

Entry on Corporation's Books			Entry on Trustee's Books		
Bond Fund — A. G. Shaw, Trustee.......	40,000		Cash................	40,000	
Cash.............		40,000	The Powell Corp....		40,000
			Investments in Securities................	35,600	
			Interest Income......	150	
			Cash.............		35,750
			Cash................	900	
			Interest Income....		900
			Expenses............	200	
			Cash.............		200
Bond Fund — A. G. Shaw, Trustee.......	40,000		Cash................	40,000	
Cash.............		40,000	The Powell Corp....		40,000
			Accrued Interest on Securities..........	225	
			Interest Income....		225
			Interest Income......	100	
			Investments in Securities........		100
(a) Bond Fund — A. G. Shaw, Trustee...	675		Interest Income......	875	
Bond Fund Expenses..........	200		Expenses..........		200
Bond Fund Inc.		875	The Powell Corp....		675
(b) Bond Fund Income	875				
Bond Fund Exp.		200			
Income Summary.....		675			
			Cash................	1,100,000	
			Investments in Securities........		1,060,000
			Interest Income....		8,000
			Gain on Sale of Securities..........		32,000
Bonds Payable.......	1,000,000		The Powell Corp......	1,000,000	
Bond Fund — A. G. Shaw, Trustee.....		1,000,000	Cash.............		1,000,000
Cash................	115,000		The Powell Corp......	115,000	
Bond Fund — A. G. Shaw, Trustee.....		115,000	Cash.............		115,000
(a) Bond Fund — A. G. Shaw, Trustee	40,000		Interest Income......	8,000	
Interest Income		8,000	Gain on Sale of Securities............	32,000	
Gain on Sale of Bond Fund Securities....		32,000	The Powell Corp....		40,000
(b) Interest Income...	8,000				
Gain on Sale of Bond Fund Securities......	32,000				
Income Summary.....		40,000			

on the resale of bonds to outsiders. The treatment of reacquired bonds as an investment results in periodic cash transfers to the trustee representing bond interest and permits fund accumulation in accordance with scheduled requirements. Interest paid by the corporation on its own bonds is counterbalanced by interest received by the trustee. Any difference between the book value of the liability and the amount paid for the bonds is recognized over the remaining life of the bonds by the entries for discount accumulation and premium amortization by the corporation and by the trustee.

The treatment of bond reacquisition as an investment is not supportable in theory. Reacquired bonds, even though in the hands of a corporate agent, cannot be considered an asset by the corporation. Such bonds are, in effect, evidence of debt retirement. Reacquired bonds may be sold and thus provide additional cash, but this is also true of unissued bonds; both reacquired and unissued bonds are no more than instruments that may be used in future borrowing.

The treatment of bond reacquisition as a retirement by an entry similar to that on page 407 may call for an increase in the deposit schedule to compensate for the loss of interest in the fund accumulation. The larger transfers to the fund, however, are accompanied by reduced interest payments in the absence of interest accruals on bonds reacquired by the trustee. If bonds are resold, the sale is treated just as an original issue, any premium or discount on the reissue being identified with the remaining life of the bond lot resold. The treatment of bond reacquisitions as bond retirement should be followed even though this calls for adjustments in a plan for systematic fund accumulation.

The accounting procedures described for the bond fund are applicable to the other investment funds mentioned earlier.

Preferred stock redemption funds

Funds are frequently established for the reacquisition and the retirement of preferred stock. Such funds may be established voluntarily or they may be required by the terms of the preferred stock issue. The preferred stock contract may indicate a stated redemption value or a scale of redemption values related to specified periods when the preferred stock may be called in by the corporation.

The transfer of cash to the stock redemption fund increases the balance in the fund; the reacquisition of the company's stock reduces this balance. The amount paid on the redemption of preferred stock may be more or less than the amount received on the original sale of the stock. The subject of stock redemption is discussed further in Chapter 20.

Miscellaneous Investments

Many assets could be named that are of an auxiliary character in terms of central business activities and are properly reportable under the investments heading. If such assets do not produce current interest, dividends, or other revenue, it is expected by management that they will ultimately have a favorable business effect in some other way. For example, a purchase of adjoining property is made in advance of needs because it is felt that such acquisition in the future will be possible only at considerably higher costs. Or a long-term loan is made to an old customer because it is believed that the loan will carry him through a financial crisis and he will continue as a profitable customer after the present strain has passed. Several investment items that are commonly found are considered in the remaining sections of this chapter.

Cash surrender value of life insurance

Many business enterprises carry life insurance policies on the lives of their executives. It is recognized that the business has a definite stake in the continuing services of its officers. In some cases the insurance plan affords a financial cushion in the event of the loss of such personnel. In other instances the insurance offers a means of purchasing a deceased owner's interest in the business, thus avoiding a transfer of such interest to some outside party or the need to liquidate the business in effecting settlement with the estate of the deceased.

Insurance premiums may consist of an amount for only insurance protection and the balance for a form of investment. The investment portion is manifest in a growing *cash surrender value* that is available to the insured in the event of policy surrender and cancellation. If this cash surrender value belongs to the business, it should be reported as an investment. Insurance expense for a fiscal period is the difference between the insurance premium paid and the increase in the cash surrender value of the policy. The increase in the cash surrender value is ordinarily relatively uniform after the first year of the policy. At the end of the first year there may be no cash surrender value, or, if there is such a value, it may be quite low because the insurance company must recover certain costs connected with selling and initiating the policy. The cost of life insurance to the business, then, may be considered higher during the first year of the policy than in later years because of the starting costs involved.

An insurance policy with a cash surrender value also has a *loan value*; this is the amount that the insurance company will permit the insured to borrow on the policy. When the insured uses the policy as a basis for a loan, the amount borrowed should be recorded as a liability and not as a reduction in the cash value. Such a loan may be liquidated by payments of principal and interest, or the loan may be continuing, to be applied against the insurance proceeds upon policy cancellation or ultimate settlement.

The loan that an insurance company will make on a policy is normally limited to the policy cash surrender value at the end of the policy year less discount from the loan date to the cash surrender value date. For example, assume a cash surrender value of $3,000 at the end of a fifth policy year. The maximum loan value on the policy at the beginning of the fifth policy year, assuming that the insurance premium for the fifth year is paid, is $3,000 discounted for one year. If the discount rate applied by the insurance company is 5%, the policy loan value is calculated as follows: $3,000 ÷ 1.05 = $2,857.14.

Although it is possible for the insured to recognize policy loan values instead of cash surrender values, the latter value is generally used.

The insured may authorize the insurance company to apply any dividends that may be declared upon insurance policies to the reduction of the annual premium payment or to the increase in insurance cash surrender value, or he may collect such dividends in cash. Dividends should be viewed as a reduction in the cost of carrying insurance rather than as a source of supplementary revenue. Hence, if dividends are applied to the reduction of the annual premium, Insurance Expense is simply debited for the net amount paid. If the dividend is applied to the increase in the policy cash surrender value or if it is collected in cash, it should still be treated as an offset to the periodic expense of carrying the policy; the policy cash surrender value or Cash, then, is charged and Insurance Expense is credited. After a number of years, the periodic dividends plus increases in the cash surrender value may exceed the premium payments, thus resulting in revenue rather than expense on policy holdings.

Collection of a policy calls for cancellation of any cash surrender balance. Collection of a policy upon death of the insured requires the recognition of an increase in capital represented by the difference between the insurance proceeds and the balances relating to the insurance policy. The nature of the insurance policies carried and their coverage should be disclosed by appropriate comment on the balance sheet.

For income tax purposes no deduction may be taken by an employer for the payment of life insurance premiums on officers or employees when the employer is directly or indirectly the policy beneficiary. The amount recovered on the surrender of an insurance contract represents taxable income to the extent that this exceeds total policy payments;

the policy here is viewed as an investment that has realized an amount exceeding its cost. However, amounts collected on a policy by reason of the death of the insured are not subject to income taxes.

The entries to be made for an insurance contract are illustrated in the example that follows. The Andrews Manufacturing Company insured the life of its president, W. E. Andrews, on October 1, 1970. The amount of the policy was $50,000; the annual premiums were $2,100. The following table gives for each of the first three policy years the gross premium, the dividend, the net premium, the increase in cash value, and the net expense for the insurance.

Year	Gross Premium	Dividend	Net Premium	Increase in Cash Value	Insurance Expense for Year
1	$2,100	—	$2,100	—	$2,100
2	2,100	—	2,100	$1,150	950
3	2,100	$272	1,828	1,300	528

The fiscal period for the company is the calendar year. Mr. Andrews died on July 1, 1973. The entries made in recording transactions relating to the insurance contract follow:

Transaction	Entry
OCTOBER 1, 1970 Paid first annual premium, $2,100.	Prepaid Insurance.... 2,100.00 Cash............. 2,100.00
DECEMBER 31, 1970 To record insurance expense for Oct. 1–Dec. 31: ¼ x $2,100, or $525.	Life Insurance Expense 525.00 Prepaid Insurance.. 525.00
OCTOBER 1, 1971 Paid second annual premium, $2,100. Premium..................... $2,100 Less cash surrender value........ 1,150 Net insurance charge.......... $ 950	Cash Surrender Value of Life Insurance (as of 10/1/72......... 1,150.00 Prepaid Insurance.... 950.00 Cash............. 2,100.00
DECEMBER 31, 1971 To record insurance expense for the year: ¾ x $2,100 (Jan. 1–Sept.30) $1,575.00 ¼ x $950 (Oct. 1–Dec. 31) 237.50 $1,812.50	Life Insurance Expense 1,812.50 Prepaid Insurance.. 1,812.50
OCTOBER 1, 1972 Paid third annual premium, $2,100. Premium.............. $2,100 Less: Cash surrender value credit............. $1,300 Dividend credit.... 272 1,572 Net insurance charge.......... $ 528	Cash Surrender Value of Life Insurance (as of 10/1/73......... 1,300.00 Prepaid Insurance.... 528.00 Cash............. 1,828.00
DECEMBER 31, 1972 To record insurance expense for the year: ¾x $950 (Jan. 1–Sept. 30)..... $712.50 ¼x $528 (Oct. 1–Dec. 31)..... 132.00 $844.50	Life Insurance Expense 844.50 Prepaid Insurance.. 844.50

Transaction	Entry
July 1, 1973 To record insurance expense for Jan. 1– July 1: ½ x $528, or $264.	Life Insurance Expense 264.00 Prepaid Insurance. . 264.00

July 1, 1973
To record cancellation of policy upon death
of insured:
  Amount recoverable on policy:
    Face of policy.............. $50,000
    Premium rebate for period
    July 1–Oct. 1 and current year
    dividend...................   735
                        ———————
                        $50,735
 	
  Cancellation of asset values:
    Cash surrender value........ $ 2,450
    Prepaid insurance..........   132
                        ———————
                        $ 2,582
 	
  Gain on policy settlement....... $48,153
	Receivable from Insur-
	  ance Company...... 50,735.00
	    Cash Surrender
	    Value of Life In-
	    surance Policy.... 2,450.00
	    Prepaid Insurance 132.00
	    Gain on Settlement
	    of Life Insurance
	    Policy.......... 48,153.00

It should be observed in the example that cash surrender value increases are recognized on the books whenever a premium is paid. The periodic insurance premium includes a charge for the increase in the policy cash surrender value but such increase actually becomes effective as of the end of the policy year. Hence, anticipation of the cash surrender value on the date of the premium payment needs to be accompanied by a notation as to the effective date of such value. Anticipation of the cash surrender value should also be disclosed in presenting this asset on the balance sheet. If loan values instead of cash surrender values were recognized, no notation would be required since the loan values become effective immediately upon meeting premium requirements for the policy year. Dividends in the example reduce the insurance charge of the period in which they are applied against a premium. Actually the dividend applied against the premium for the third year accrues at the end of the second year and could be considered as a correction in the expense of the second year. Dividends received in the period of policy termination are recognized as a part of policy proceeds in final settlement rather than as a correction of insurance expense. The procedures that are illustrated involve certain concessions in theoretical accuracy but are normally preferred because of their practicality.

Interests in real estate

Improved property purchased for supplementary income and possible price appreciation or for future use is shown under the investment heading. The expenses relating to such holdings should be deducted from any revenue produced by the property. Unimproved property is frequently acquired for possible future use or for sale. Land while unused makes no contribution to periodic revenue. This would suggest that any costs incident to its holding need not be deducted from current earnings but may be added to the investment balance. When the land is used for construction purposes or is sold, its cost will include all expenditures incident to its acquisition and holding. In reporting the land on the balance sheet, information should be provided in parenthetical or note form relative to any adjustments that may have been made to cost. Market or appraised values, when they are available, may also be reported parenthetically.

Advances

Advances to subsidiaries are considered long-term investments when there is no evidence to indicate that amounts advanced will be collected currently. Such advances are sometimes presented on the balance sheet as additions to the investment in stock. But advances should be reported separately since they represent claims against the subsidiary, while an investment in stock represents an ownership interest. Advances of a long-term character to other parties are also classified as investments.

Deposits

Deposits to guarantee contract performance, to maintain various memberships, or to secure certain privileges or services, if not recoverable currently, are usually reported as investment items.

Interests in partnerships

Interests in partnerships and joint ventures should be shown as investments on the books of the individual participants. An investment account is charged for the contribution made by the individual to the partnership. This account is charged for any further contributions and for profits of the partnership increasing the partner's individual interest; it is credited for withdrawals and for losses decreasing his interest.

The reciprocal nature of the investment balance on the partner's own books and the related interest on the partnership books is illustrated in the example that follows:

Transactions	Separate Books of Partner A	Partnership Books — Firm of A and B
Cash invested by partners: A.............. $20,000 B.............. 25,000	Investment in Firm of A and B......... 20,000 Cash...... 20,000	Cash....... 45,000 A, Capital....... 20,000 B, Capital....... 25,000

Transactions	Separate Books of Partner A		Partnership Books — Firm of A and B	
Cash withdrawals by partners for period: A.............. $ 2,500 B.............. 4,000	Cash........ 2,500 Investment in Firm of A and B.	2,500	A, Capital.... 2,500 B, Capital.... 4,000 Cash......	6,500
Net income of partnership for period, $12,000, divided between A and B in the income ratio of 2:3: A, ⅖ x $12,000.... $ 4,800 B, ⅗ x $12,000.... 7,200	Investment in Firm of A and B..... 4,800 Income from Part- nership ..	4,800	Income Summary .. 12,000 A, Capital.. B, Capital..	4,800 7,200

At the end of the period, the partnership books report net assets and partners' interests as follows:

Assets................ $50,500   A, Capital............ $22,300
                                    B, Capital............ 28,200

$50,500 $50,500

The separate books of A follow the changes in his interest in the partnership and report an investment balance of $22,300.

Interests in trusts and estates

An interest in a trust or an estate is reported as an investment on the beneficiary's books. The investment account is charged for any increases in this interest resulting from periodic net incomes and is credited for any decreases resulting from periodic net losses or asset distributions made to the beneficiary. Accounting for an interest in a trust or an estate, then, is similar to that for an interest in a partnership.

Investments on the Balance Sheet

Investments are generally reported on the balance sheet following the current asset classification. The investment section should not include temporary investments held as a ready source of cash. Headings should be provided for the different investment categories and individual investments reported within such groupings. Detailed information relative to individual investments may be provided in separate supporting schedules. Investment costs should be supplemented by market quotations offered in parenthetical or note form. Information concerning the pledge of investments as collateral on loans should be provided. When investments are carried at amounts other than cost, the valuation that is employed should be described.

In reporting funds that are to be applied to specific purposes or paid to specific parties, disclosure should be made by special note of the conditions relative to their establishment and ultimate application. A fund arrearage or other failure to meet contractual requirements should be pointed out; the demand to be made upon current assets by deposit requirements in the succeeding fiscal period should also be disclosed when material. Offset of a fund balance against a liability item is proper only when an asset transfer to a trustee is irrevocable and actually serves to discharge the obligation.

The investment section of a balance sheet might appear as follows:

Investments:
  Affiliated companies:
    Investment in Wilson Co., not consolidated, reported by the equity method (Investment consists of 90,000 shares representing a 90% interest acquired on July 1, 1969, for $1,500,000. Retained earnings of the subsidiary since date of acquisition have increased by $120,000; 90% of this amount, or $108,000, is identified with the parent company equity and has been recognized in the accounts.).. $1,608,000

    Advances to Wilson Co......................   115,000 $1,723,000

Miscellaneous stock investments, at cost (stock has an aggregate quoted market value of $112,000; stock has been deposited as security on bank loan — refer to notes payable, contra)..........................   100,000

Bond retirement fund in hands of trustee, composed of:
  Cash....................................... $ 15,000
  Stocks and bonds, at cost (aggregate quoted market value, $420,000)..........................   410,500
  Dividends and interest receivable................   4,500   430,000

Investment in land and unused facilities.............   65,000
Cash surrender value of life insurance carried on officers' lives.......................................   12,500

Total investments............................... $2,330,500

QUESTIONS

1. Distinguish between (a) secured and unsecured bonds, (b) collateral trust and debenture bonds, (c) guaranteed bonds and income bonds, (d) convertible bonds and callable bonds, and (e) coupon bonds and registered bonds.

2. What is meant by bond market rate, nominal rate, and effective rate? Which of these rates changes during the lifetime of the bond issue?

3. An investor purchases bonds of $100,000. Payment for the bonds includes charges for (a) a premium, (b) accrued interest, and (c) brokerage fees. How would each of these charges be recorded and what disposition would ultimately be made of each of these charges?

4. Distinguish between straight-line and compound-interest methods of bond premium amortization. What arguments can be offered in support of each method?

5. (a) What is meant by purchase of bonds *flat*? (b) What special accounting procedure should be followed for such an investment?

6. What purpose is served by using callable bonds? What effect does a call feature have upon the amortization of a bond premium?

7. What value is used to record stock obtained through conversion of an investment in bonds?

8. A. C. McArthur acquires a second-mortgage note, face value $10,000, for $6,000. McArthur feels that in view of the risks involved on this paper, any future collections of both principal and interest should be treated as reductions in the investment balance until he has recovered $6,000. Thereafter, any collections of principal and interest can be regarded as earnings on the investment. What would be your comment on McArthur's stand?

9. Name and describe five funds that would be listed as current assets and five that would be listed as investments.

10. What benefits are obtained from using an independent trustee to administer investment funds? Would the use of such a trustee affect the total assets reported on a company's books?

11. Because of favorable market prices, the trustee of Wilson Company's bond sinking fund invested the current year's contributions to the fund in the company's own bonds. The bonds are kept "alive" in the fund and are not canceled. The fund also includes cash and securities of other companies. What are the arguments for and against carrying these bonds as an investment on Wilson Company's balance sheet?

12. The Duane Co. has made certain major modifications in property that was leased for a ten-year period. The leasehold contract provides that in addition to the payment of monthly rents Duane Co. was to make monthly deposits to a sinking fund that will be used to restore the properties to their original condition upon termination of the leasehold. How would you record the payments required by the terms of the contract?

13. The Hillory Company is required by terms of a bond indenture to deposit with a bond fund trustee at monthly intervals amounts that are to be applied to the payment of semiannual bond interest and at annual intervals amounts that are to be applied to the payment of the bonds at their maturity. The company charges interest expense for the monthly deposits and a bond sinking fund for the annual deposits. Do you approve?

14. (a) Distinguish between life insurance cash surrender value and loan value. (b) How is the loan value on a life insurance policy calculated?

15. Under what circumstances would the cash surrender value of insurance policies be properly reported as a current asset rather than as a long-term investment?

16. The Melville Company collects in cash the dividends on the life insurance policies that it carries; the Nielson Company uses dividend credits to reduce the life insurance premiums that it pays; the Otto Corporation authorizes the insurance companies to apply dividend credits to the increase of policy cash surrender values. What entries will each company make in recognizing dividends?

17. Name ten items that are properly reported under investment heading on the balance sheet?

18. Indicate the balance sheet classification for each of the following:

(a) Land used as parking area for customers.
(b) United States Treasury Bonds to provide income for otherwise idle cash during the slack season.
(c) Land to provide for expansion program at least five years hence.
(d) A company's own bonds held in a bond retirement fund.
(e) Accrued interest on company's own bonds in bond retirement fund.
(f) Advance to a subsidiary company.
(g) Cash surrender value of insurance policy.
(h) A fund to be used to pay current bond interest.
(i) A preferred stock redemption fund.

19. Why would a manufacturing company invest funds in stocks, bonds and other securities? What are the criteria for classifying these investments as current or noncurrent assets?

EXERCISES

1. A $1,500, 5% bond, interest payable semiannually, was acquired on January 1, 1972. The bond matures on January 1, 1981. Using the bond table on page 391, determine the price to be paid for the bond assuming it is purchased on a basis to yield (a) 4%, (b) 6%.

2. Investment is made in a $1,000 bond, interest at 5%, payable semiannually, maturing 8 years from date of purchase. Using the bond table on page 391, calculate the exact yield on the bond assuming that it is purchased for (a) $1,020, (b) $975.

3. (a) Assume that $100,000 Valley School District 3½% bonds are purchased for $97,523.45. Interest is payable semiannually and the bonds mature in 10 years. The purchase price provides a yield of 3.8% on the investment. What entries would be made for the receipt of the first two interest payments, assuming discount accumulation on each interest date by (1) the straight-line method and (2) the compound-interest method?

(b) Assume that the amount paid for the bonds is $106,518.28, a price to yield 2.75% on the investment. What entries would be made upon receipt of the first two interest payments, assuming premium amortization on each interest date by (1) the straight-line method and (2) the compound-interest method?

4. On June 1, 1972, Thomas Kline purchases Dohr Company bonds, face value $10,000, for $10,500 plus accrued interest. Bonds pay interest at the rate of 6% semiannually on April 1 and October 1, and they mature on October 1, 1980. What are the entries that will be made on Kline's books to record (a) purchase of the bonds on June 1, (b) receipt of interest on October 1, and (c) adjustment for accrued interest at the end of the fiscal period, December 31, 1972? (Assume that entries for the amortization of bond premium are made by the straight-line method.)

5. J. A. Stark acquired $10,000 of Burgess Battery 5% bonds on July 1, 1970. Bonds were acquired at 95; they pay interest semiannually on April 1 and October 1, and they mature on April 1, 1974. The fiscal period for Stark is the calendar year; discount is accumulated on the bonds by the straight-line method. On March 1, 1973, Stark sold the bonds for 98½ plus accrued interest. Give the entry to record the sale of the bonds on this date.

6. On January 1, 1972, James Adair purchases $20,000 of Carlson Company 6% bonds at 108. Bonds are due on January 1, 1987, but can be redeemed by the company at earlier dates at premium values as follows:

>January 1, 1980, to December 31, 1983, at 103
>January 1, 1984, to December 31, 1986, at 101

What amortization amounts do you recommend that Adair recognize over the life of the bond issue?

7. Rhodes Inc., shows Feather Mills Co. bonds of $7,000 on its books at a book value of $6,250 on July 1, 1972. Each $1,000 bond is convertible into 20 shares of the issuing company's common stock, and Rhodes exchanges the bonds for stock on this date. Stock on the date of conversion is quoted at 48¾; accrued interest on bonds of $49 is received together with the stock. What entry would be made on Rhodes Inc., books to record the exchange?

8. Sinking fund tables show that 5 annual deposits of $18,097.48 accruing interest at 5% compounded annually will result in a total accumulation of $100,000 immediately after the fifth payment. (a) Prepare a fund accumulation schedule showing the theoretical growth of the fund over the 5-year period. (b) Give all of the entries that would appear on the books for the increases in the bond retirement fund balance for the first three years.

9. The Frick Company has accumulated a bond retirement fund that shows the following balances on September 1, 1972:

Cash.....................................	$ 110,000	
Securities...............................	1,395,000	$1,505,000

On this date securities were sold for $1,429,000 plus accrued interest, $15,200. Retirement fund cash was then applied to the retirement of bonds of $1,500,000 maturing on this date and accrued interest on the bonds of $22,500. The balance of the bond retirement fund cash was transferred to the cash account. Give the entries to record the above transactions.

10. Give the entries that would be made for each of the following bond retirement fund transactions, assuming that (1) transactions are recorded only on the books of the corporation, and (2) the transactions are recorded in a double-entry set of books maintained by the trustee and are summarized on the books of the corporation.

  (a) Cash is transferred to the bond retirement fund trustee, $96,000.
  (b) Securities are purchased out of bond retirement fund cash, $85,000.
  (c) Income is collected on bond retirement fund securities, $7,900.
  (d) Expenses are paid out of bond retirement fund cash, $550.
  (e) All of the bond retirement fund securities are sold for $91,000.
  (f) Bonds are redeemed at maturity date out of bond retirement fund cash, $100,000.
  (g) Remaining cash in bond retirement fund is deposited in general cash account.
  (h) Nominal accounts are closed.

11. On April 1, 1972, the Swenko Corporation invested plant expansion fund cash in bonds of the local municipality. The corporation paid $9,400 for ten $1,000, 5% bonds due in 10 years. Interest is payable semiannually on April 1 and October 1. (a) Give all of the entries that will be made on the company's books in 1972 as a result of the investment. (b) Indicate how the investment should be presented on the corporation's balance sheet at the end of 1972.

12. The Bloomington Corporation insured the life of its president for $50,000. The policy was effective on January 1, 1969, and premiums were payable on the first of each year beginning on this date. The following table gives the data for the policy for the first four years:

Year	Gross Premium	Dividend	Net Premium	Increase in Cash Value	Net Cost for Year
1	$2,000	——	$2,000	——	$2,000
2	2,000	——	2,000	$1,100	900
3	2,000	$266	1,734	1,250	484
4	2,000	266	1,734	1,350	384

The fiscal period for the company is the calendar year. The Bloomington Corporation paid the insurance premiums at the beginning of 1969, 1970, 1971, 1972. The president of the company died on July 1, 1972, and the face value of the policy and also $1,070 representing premium refund and current year dividend became recoverable as of this date. Give all of the journal entries, including the periodic adjustments, that would be made on the books of the company relative to the above data for the period 1969–1972.

13. Gibson and Howard joined in a partnership in January, 1972, and agreed to share net income in the ratio of 7:3. Changes in their interests in the firm during 1972 are summarized below. What entries would be made on the individual books of Gibson and Howard for the following changes in their respective interests in the firm?

Jan. 15. Cash invested in the firm by Gibson & Howard was $60,000 and $30,000 respectively.
Mar. 10. Gibson withdrew cash of $2,000 from the firm.
June 30. Partnership activities for the period January 15–June 30 were summarized and disclosed a net loss of $7,000.
July 15. Howard invested additional cash of $7,500 in the firm.
Dec. 31. Partnership activities for the period July 1–December 31 were summarized and disclosed a net income of $12,000.

14. In 1962 the Hagen Appliance Corporation purchased for $50,000 ten acres adjoining its manufacturing plant to provide for possible future expansion. From 1962–1972 the company paid $20,000 in taxes and $30,000 in special assessments. In 1972 it sold one half of the land for $75,000 and erected a building at a cost of $300,000 on the other half. The company books on December 31, 1972, show a "plant" account balance of $325,000. Give the journal entries to correct the accounts.

PROBLEMS

12-1. The Norge Co. acquired $20,000 of Maynard Sales Co. 7% bonds, interest payable semiannually, bonds maturing in 5 years. The bonds were acquired at $20,853, a price to yield approximately 6%.

Instructions: (1) Prepare tables to show the periodic adjustments to the investment account and the annual bond earnings, assuming adjustment by each of the following methods: (a) the straight-line method, and (b) the compound-interest method.

(2) Give entries for the interest receipts and adjustments for the first year of bond ownership, assuming use of (a) the straight-line method, and (b) the compound-interest method.

12-2. The Patton Mfg. Co. acquired $75,000 of Baco Co. 5% bonds, interest payable semiannually, at a price to yield 5¾%. The bonds have a remaining life of 9 years.

Instructions: (1) Using the bond table on page 391, determine the amount paid for the bonds.

(2) Prepare a table of discount accumulation by the compound-interest method for the first two years of ownership.

(3) Give the entries to be made by the investor for the bond purchase, the semiannual interest receipts, and the discount accumulation for the two-year period.

12-3. Demclo Products decided to issue $1,000,000 in 10-year bonds. The interest rate on the bonds is stated at 5%, payable semiannually. At the time the bonds were sold, the market rate had increased to 6%.

Instructions: (1) Using the bond table on page 391, determine the maximum amount an investor should pay for these bonds.

(2) Assuming that the amount in (1) is paid, compute the amount at which the bonds would be reported after being held for one year. Use two recognized methods of handling amortization of the difference in cost and maturity value of the bonds, and give support for the method you prefer in a brief statement.

12-4. On May 1, 1969, the Walston Co. acquired $20,000 of Ace Corp. 9% bonds at 97 plus accrued interest. Interest on bonds is payable semiannually on March 1 and September 1, and bonds mature on September 1, 1972.

On May 1, 1970, the Walston Co. sold bonds of $6,000 for 101 plus accrued interest.

On July 1, 1971, bonds of $4,000 were exchanged for 1,000 shares of Ace Corp. no-par common, quoted on the market on this date at 5¼. Interest was received on bonds to date of exchange.

On September 1, 1972, remaining bonds were redeemed.

Instructions: Give journal entries for 1969–1972 to record the foregoing transactions on the books of the Walston Co. including any adjustments that are required at the end of each fiscal year ending on December 31. (Show all calculations.)

12-5. The Phelps Aero Corp. made the following long-term bond investments during 1972:

Date of Purchase	Investment	Interest Payment Dates	Maturity Date	Check Issued in Payment of Investment (Includes Accrued Interest)
Mar. 1	$20,000 Pacific Corp. 5's	Mar. 1, Sept. 1	Mar. 1, 1982	$20,000
June 1	60,000 Lake County 3's	July 1, Jan. 1	Jan. 1, 1981	58,690
Sept. 1	20,000 Bay Utilities 4's	June 1, Dec. 1	June 1, 1975	20,365

Instructions: Give the entries to record the investments, the collections of interest in 1972, and also the adjustments that are required on December 31, 1972, the end of the company's fiscal year. Assume that entries for amortization and accumulation are made only at the end of the year.

12-6. Robb, Inc., completes the following transactions, among others, during 1972:

Apr. 1. Purchased $80,000 of Ames Aluminum Corporation First-Mortgage Bonds, maturity date August 1, 1977, interest 6% payable semiannually on February 1 and August 1, at 95½ plus brokerage costs of $400 and accrued interest.

Apr. 15. Purchased 500 shares of Hitchcock Industries, Inc., common, par $40, at $49.50 plus commissions of $210.

June 2. Received a common stock dividend on Hitchcock Industries, Inc., common of 1 share for every 5 shares held.

July 15. Was granted the right to purchase 1 share of stock at $42 for every 4 shares of Hitchcock Industries, Inc., stock held, the option expiring September 15. Stock had a market value of $50 ex-rights, and each right had a value of $2 on the date the rights were issued.

Aug. 1. Received semiannual interest on bonds held. (Bond discount accumulation by the straight-line method is recorded at the time interest is received.)

Aug. 4. Sold Ames Aluminum Corporation bonds of $20,000 at 98 and accrued interest, less brokerage costs of $50; also exercised option on stock rights on this date.

Dec. 10. Sold 500 shares of Hitchcock Industries, Inc., at 58 less commissions of $170. (The first-in, first-out method is used in calculating the cost of shares sold.)

Dec. 31. Adjusted the accounts relative to the foregoing.

Instructions: Journalize the foregoing transactions. (Show calculations.)

12-7. Data relative to the investments of Mercury, Inc., during 1972 follow:

Jan. 24. Purchased 300 shares of Aero common stock, $40 par, for $23,100.

Feb. 11. Purchased as a long-term investment $75,000 of Axle First-Mortgage Bonds, maturity date October 1, 1976, interest of 6% payable semi-annually on April 1 and October 1, at 104 plus brokerage of $360 and accrued interest.

Mar. 10. Received a cash dividend of 40 cents and stock dividend of 1 share for every 4 held on Aero common stock.

Apr. 1. Received semiannual interest on bonds held. (Bond premium amortization by the straight-line method is recorded at the time interest is received.)

June 10. Received a cash dividend of 40 cents on Aero common stock. Also was granted the right to purchase 1 share of stock at 65 for every 5 shares held, the option expiring July 1. Stock had a market value of $75 ex-rights, and each stock right had a market value of $2 on the date the rights were issued.

June 30. Sold 225 rights for $500 and exercised option on remaining rights.

Aug. 14. Purchased 200 shares of Aero common stock for $14,400.

Sept. 11. Sold $15,000 of Axle bonds at 102 and accrued interest less brokerage fees of $60.

Sept. 20. Received a cash dividend of 40 cents on Aero common stock.

Oct. 1. Received semiannual interest on bonds held.

Dec. 9. Received a regular cash dividend of 40 cents and an extra dividend of 20 cents on Aero common stock.

Dec. 28. Sold 500 shares of Aero common stock for $28,320. (The first-in, first-out method is used in calculating the cost of shares sold.)

Dec. 31. Adjusted the accounts relative to the foregoing.

Instructions: Journalize the foregoing transactions. (Show calculations.)

12-8. In auditing the books for the Hoffman Corporation as of December 31, 1972, before the accounts are closed, you find the following long-term investment account balance:

Investment in Corey Steel 6's (Maturity Date, May 1, 1978)

January 22, 1972 Bonds, $100,000 par, acquired at 103 plus accrued interest..... 104,350	March 10, 1972 Proceeds from sale of bonds, $20,000 par and accrued interest 22,000
	May 1 Interest received............... 2,400 November 1 Amount received on call of bonds, $20,000 par, at 102 and accrued interest...................... 22,800

Instructions: (1) Give the entries that should have been made relative to the investment in bonds, including any adjusting entries that would be made on December 31, the end of the fiscal year. (Assume bond premium amortization by the straight-line method.)

(2) Give the journal entries required at the end of 1972 to correct and bring the accounts up to date in view of the entries that were actually made.

12-9. The Wiley Corporation wishes to accumulate a fund of $75,000 over a 5-year period. Ten equal deposits are to be made at semiannual intervals, beginning on June 30, 1972, to accumulate to the desired balance after the deposit on December 31, 1976. It is assumed that the fund will earn 6% compounded semiannually (3% each six-month period). Fund tables show that deposits of $6,542.22 are required to provide the desired fund.

Instructions: (1) Prepare a table similar to that illustrated on page 405 to show the theoretical growth of the fund over the 5-year period.

(2) Give the entries to record the fund increases for deposits and for interest for the years 1972 and 1973.

12-10. On January 1, 1972, the books of the Kinkade Corporation reported a balance in a bond retirement fund of $310,000. Books of Sidney Sperry, trustee in charge of the bond retirement fund for the Kinkade Corporation, showed account balances as follows:

Cash.....................................	$ 11,500	
Securities.................................	295,000	
Accrued interest on fund securities...........	3,500	
The Kinkade Corporation....................		$310,000
	$310,000	$310,000

The following transactions took place in 1972:

(a) A deposit of $62,100 was made with the trustee.

(b) Securities were acquired at a cost of $63,250 that included accrued interest of $1,450.

(c) Interest of $17,900 was collected on interest dates on investments.

(d) Trustee's fees and other miscellaneous expenses paid were $1,215.

(e) All of the bond retirement fund securities were sold for $352,000 that included accrued interest of $3,200.

(f) Bonds of $340,000 were retired on their maturity date and remaining cash was returned by the trustee to the corporation.

Instructions: (1) Give the entries required on the separate books of the trustee to record the foregoing and to close the books upon termination of the trusteeship.

(2) Give any entries that would be made on the corporation books as a result of the foregoing.

12-11. Baker and Brown, Inc., maintains a bond redemption and interest fund. Bonds acquired by the trustee of the fund are immediately canceled. Six percent bonds of $1,000,000, interest payable semiannually on January 1 and July 1, were originally issued at face value. Bonds of $200,000 were retired prior to 1972. The bond fund on January 1, 1972, had a balance of $41,000, and transactions affecting the fund in 1972 are reported below. The trustee keeps no separate books, all fund transactions being reported on the company books.

Jan. 8   A deposit of $50,000 was made to the bond fund.
Mar. 16   Bonds of $40,000 were called at 102 plus accrued interest.
June 30   Interest checks for 6 months ending July 1 were mailed to bondholders.
July 8   A deposit of $80,000 was made to the bond fund.
Sept. 1   Bonds of $60,000 were purchased on the open market at 99 plus accrued interest.
Nov. 1   Bonds of $25,000 were purchased at 98 plus accrued interest.
Dec. 31   Interest checks for 6 months ending January 1 were mailed to bondholders.
Dec. 31   Trustee's fees and bond fund expenses for the year of $4,000 were paid.

Instructions: Journalize the foregoing transactions.

12-12. The DeVac Co. has established a pension plan for employees. At the end of each period, Pensions Expense is debited and Liability Under Pension Plan is credited for the estimated pension requirements. A pension fund is also maintained and is increased by semiannual deposits. Pension payments are recorded by charges to Liability Under Pension Plan and credits to Pension Fund Cash. The balance in the pension fund and changes in the fund for 1972 follow:

Fund balance, January 1:

Cash	$ 30,000
U.S. Treasury 5's, interest payable May 1 and November 1, due May 1, 1981 (acquired at face value)	180,000
Denny Co. First-Mortgage 6's, interest payable January 1 and July 1, due January 1, 1982 (face $60,000)	63,600
Accrued interest on U.S. Treasury 5's	1,500

The pension fund transactions for 1972 are as follows:

Jan. 20   Transferred cash of $73,000 to the pension fund.
Feb. 7   Purchased $65,000 of Riverdale County 4% bonds, interest payable April 1 and October 1, at 97 plus accrued interest. Bonds mature on April 1, 1976.
Apr. 1   Received semiannual interest on Riverdale County 4's.
May   2   Received semiannual interest on U.S. Treasury 5's.

June 30 Pension payments for 6 months amounted to $18,100.
July 1 Received semiannual interest on Denny Co. 6's.
July 1 Purchased an additional $50,000 of Riverdale County 4's, 1976 series, at 98½ plus accrued interest.
July 25 Cash of $70,000 was transferred to pension fund.
Sept. 25 Sold $20,000 of Denny Co. 6's for $23,100, which included accrued interest on the bonds to this date.
Oct. 1 Received semiannual interest on Riverdale County 4's.
Nov. 1 Received semiannual interest on U.S. Treasury 5's.
Dec. 31 Pension payments for 6 months amounted to $19,200.
      31 The balance of Liability Under Pension Plan was increased by $131,000 for the year.
      31 Received semiannual interest on Denny Co. 6's.

Instructions: Give the entries required for 1972 as a result of the above, including any adjustments that would be necessary at the end of the year. (Assume that straight-line accumulation and amortization procedures are followed with respect to all bonds in the pension fund, entries being made at the end of the year.)

12-13. During the course of the audit of the Harlan Lee Company, which closes its accounts on December 31, you examine the life insurance policies, premium receipts, and confirmations returned by the insurance companies in response to your request for information. You find that in 1972 the company had paid premiums on the life of the president, Harlen Lee, as shown below:

Sole Owner and Beneficiary	Face of Policy	Annual Billed Premium 1972	Cash Dividend Used to Reduce Premium	Annual Premium Date	Cash Surrender Value December 31 1972	1971
1. Harlen Lee Company..	$100,000	$2,500	$700	June 30	$32,000	$30,000
2. Dorothy Lee, wife of Harlan Lee.........	50,000	1,600	300	Sept. 30	15,000	14,000
3. Harlen Lee Company..	100,000	3,600	800	April 1	22,000	21,000

Instructions: (1) Prepare all of the journal entries required for the year 1972.
(2) What balances relating to these insurance policies would appear on the balance sheet prepared on December 31, 1972?

12-14. On March 1, 1970, Stanley and Thompson, Inc., insured each of its officers, H. E. Stanley and W. E. Thompson, for $200,000. Policies of $200,000 were taken out on each officer effective March 1, 1970, the annual premium on each policy was $6,300. Total cash surrender values for each policy were stated as follows: at the end of second policy year, $3,210; at the end of third policy year, $7,810.

The fiscal period for the company was the calendar year. Premium payments on the insurance policies were made by the company annually on March 1, 1970 through 1972. Dividend credits were applied against premium payments on each policy on March 1, 1972, of $770. Mr. Stanley died on September 1, 1972, and collection was made by the company of the face value of his policy together with a premium refund and dividends totaling $2,410.

Instructions: Give all of the journal entries, including the periodic adjustments, that would appear on the books of the company relative to the above data for the years 1970 to 1972.

12-15. During your audit of the 1972 financial statements of Longwood, Inc., you find a new account titled "Miscellaneous Assets." Your examination reveals that in 1972 Longwood, Inc., began investing cash in securities and the corporation's bookkeeper entered all transactions he believed related to investments in this account. Information summarized from the miscellaneous assets account appears below:

Longwood, Inc.

Information Summarized from
the Miscellaneous Assets Account

For Year Ended December 31, 1972

Date 1972		Folio	Debit	Credit
	Compudata common stock			
Mar. 31	Purchased 500 shares @ 48.........	CD	$24,000	
July 31	Received cash dividend of $2 per share.	CR		$ 1,000
July 31	Sold 100 shares @ 60..............	CR		6,000
Nov. 15	Pledged 100 shares as security for $4,000 bank loan payable February 15, 1973....................	CR		4,000
Nov. 30	Received 150 shares by donation from stockholder whose cost in 1965 was $10 per share..................	JE	1,500	
	Standard Atomic common stock			
Mar. 31	Purchased 900 shares @ 26.........	CD	23,400	
June 30	Received dividend ($.25 per share in cash and 1 share Standard Atomic preferred for each 5 shares common owned).......................	CR		225
	Standard Atomic preferred stock			
June 30	Received 180 shares as stock dividend on Standard Atomic common.....	MEMO		
July 31	Sold 80 shares @ 17..............	CR		1,360
	Interstate Airlines bonds (due November 30, 1982 with interest at 6% payable May 31 and November 30)			
June 30	Purchased 25 $1,000 bonds @ 102...	CD	25,625	
Nov. 30	Received interest due..............	CR		750
Nov. 30	Accumulated amortization..........	JE		25
Nov. 30	Sold 25 bonds @ 101..............	CR		25,250
	Other			
Dec. 29	Paid 1973 rental charge on safe deposit box used for investments.........	CD	35	
	Total.....................		$74,560	$38,610

All security purchases include brokers' fees, and sales are net of brokers' fees and transfer taxes when applicable. The fair market values (net of brokers' fees and transfer taxes) for each security as of the 1972 date of each transaction were:

Security	3/31	6/30	7/31	11/15	11/30
Compudata common..........	48		60	61¼	62
Standard Atomic common......	26	30			
Standard Atomic preferred.....		16⅔	17		
Interstate Airlines bonds.......		102			101

Instructions: Prepare a work sheet to distribute or correct each of the transactions entered in the miscellaneous assets account. Ignore income taxes in your solution. Formal adjusting entries are not required. Make separate entries for each transaction; do not combine adjustments. In addition to columns for entries in the miscellaneous assets account, the following column headings are recommended for your work sheet:

ADJUSTMENTS TO DISTRIBUTE AND CORRECT ITEMS ENTERED IN THE MISCELLANEOUS ASSETS ACCOUNT

Miscellaneous Assets Debit (Credit)	Investments Debit (Credit)	(Gain) Loss from Sale of Investments	(Income) from Dividends and Interest	Other Accounts	
				Name of Account	Debit (Credit)

(AICPA adapted)

chapter 13

land, buildings, and equipment - acquisition, use, and retirement

Land, buildings, and equipment is a classification heading for those tangible properties of a relatively permanent character that are used in the normal conduct of a business. Many other terms have been and are being used to describe such properties. *Fixed assets* has been frequently used in the past; however, it must be modified by *tangible* or *intangible* to distinguish between these two classes of assets. *Plant and equipment* is ambiguous because of the several connotations to the word "plant." Plant could mean only the buildings, or perhaps buildings and land. *Property, plant, and equipment* has been used by the Accounting Principles Board in its opinions. In this use, property means land, but in a more normal connotation, both plant and equipment are also property and this title is also ambiguous. The heading most commonly found on financial statements appears to be "Land, buildings, and equipment." This term is used throughout the text, and "property" is used as a general term referring to all three classes of items.

As in the case of other noncurrent assets, land, buildings, and equipment items do not turn over as frequently as current assets. Land, buildings, and equipment are acquired, used and retired. Although these properties as a class remain as long as the business continues, the individual items, with the exception of land, have limited service lives. The costs of buildings and equipment are assigned to operations by means of periodic depreciation charges. When an item is no longer of economic benefit to the business, its cost should have been fully absorbed through these periodic charges.

Composition of land, buildings, and equipment

Land refers to earth surface and includes building sites, yards, and parking areas. When natural resources in the form of mineral deposits, oil and gas wells, and timber are found on land, these are frequently reported separately. Buildings refer to improvements permanently affixed to land and include not only structures in the form of factories, office buildings, storage quarters, and garages, but also structure facilities and appurtenances such as loading docks, heating and air conditioning systems, and walks and drives. Equipment consists of a wide variety of items including factory machines, hand and machine tools, patterns and dies, store and office equipment, and motor vehicles and other transport equipment. Items in the equipment group are frequently referred to as *personal property* or *personalty* as distinguished from the land and buildings group referred to as *real property* or *realty*.

Capital and revenue expenditures

The proper treatment of expenditures incident to the acquisition and use of property presents many accounting problems. Expenditures for property are made in anticipation of their favorable effects upon operations. In recording such expenditures, it must be determined whether favorable effects are limited to the current period or whether they extend into future periods. The underlying concept involved is the "matching" principle already described. An expenditure that benefits only the current period is called a *revenue expenditure* and is recorded as an expense. An expenditure that benefits operations beyond the current period is called a *capital expenditure* and is recorded as an asset. A property expenditure that is recorded as an asset is said to be *capitalized*.

Income cannot be accurately measured unless expenditures are properly identified and recorded as revenue or capital charges. An incorrect charge to an equipment item instead of to expense, for example, results in the current overstatement of earnings on the income statement and the overstatement of assets and capital on the balance sheet. As the charge is assigned to operations in subsequent periods, earnings of such periods will be understated; assets and capital on the successive balance sheets will continue to be overstated, although by lesser amounts each year, until the asset is written off and the original error is fully counterbalanced. On the other hand, an incorrect charge to expense instead of to an equipment item results in the current understatement of earnings and the understatement of assets and capital. Earnings of subsequent periods will be overstated in the absence of charges for depreciation; assets and capital will continue to be understated, although by lesser amounts each year, until the original error is counterbalanced.

Although all property expenditures that will provide benefits beyond the current period should be capitalized, companies frequently adopt an arbitrary practice of charging expense for all expenditures that do not exceed a certain amount, perhaps $50 or $100. Such practice is adopted for the sake of expediency; the analysis of relatively small expenditures, as well as the application of depreciation procedures for them, is avoided. Adherence to such a practice is acceptable if it results in no material misstatement of property costs and periodic income.

Valuation of property accounts

Property items, just as all other facilities acquired by the business entity, are recognized initially at cost — the original bargained price for such resources. When payment for an asset is not made in the form of cash, the cash value of the consideration that is given in exchange must be established in arriving at cost. When it is not possible to arrive at a satisfactory cash value for the consideration that is transferred, the asset is reported at its present fair market value or, stated differently, the amount which would have been paid if it had been acquired in a cash transaction. A similar procedure is followed for assets acquired through gift or discovery.

The cost of property includes not only the original purchase price or equivalent value, but also the other expenditures required in obtaining and preparing it for the purpose for which it was acquired. Any taxes and duties, freight and cartage, and installation and other expenditures related to the acquisition are added to the original outlay.

Property items are presented on the balance sheet at cost less the portion of cost that has been assigned to past revenues. Land is normally considered to have an unlimited service life and, therefore, is properly reported at its original cost. In special cases where agricultural land may lose its fertility through use or erosion or a building site may lose its utility through physical or environmental changes, reductions in cost to reflect the decline in asset usefulness may be appropriate. Natural resources are subject to exhaustion and are normally reported at cost less the portion of cost related to resources that have been removed. All other property items are considered to have a limited service life and are normally reported at *cost less accumulated depreciation*. By *accumulated depreciation* is meant the portion of the asset cost that has been written off by periodic depreciation charges since the asset was acquired. The difference between asset cost and accumulated depreciation is referred to as the asset *book value*. Ordinarily no reference to market values or replacement values is made in presenting property on the balance sheet. However, there has been an increasing interest in reporting property items at their current values or at their costs adjusted for general price-level changes. These matters are discussed in later chapters.

Acquisition of property

There are a number of different ways in which property is acquired and each presents special problems relating to asset cost. The acquisition of properties is discussed under the following headings: (1) purchase for cash, (2) purchase on deferred payment plan, (3) exchange, (4) issuance of securities, (5) self-construction, and (6) gift or discovery.

Purchase for cash. Property that is acquired for cash is recorded at the amount of the cash outlay. Incidental outlays relating to its purchase or to its preparation for use are added to the original cost.

It was suggested in an earlier chapter that sound theory requires that discounts on purchases be regarded as reductions in costs: earnings arise from sales, not from purchases. In applying such theory, any available discounts on property acquisitions should be treated as reductions in asset cost. Charges resulting from failure to take such discounts should be reported as discounts lost or interest expense. The treatment of discounts on property acquisitions should not be affected by the exceptional practice that may be employed for reporting discounts on merchandise purchases. Reasons of expediency that may support the treatment of discounts on merchandise purchases as revenue are not applicable in accounting for property acquisitions.

A number of property items may be acquired for one lump sum. Some of the assets may be depreciable, others nondepreciable. Depreciable assets may have different useful lives. If there is to be an accountability for the assets on an individual basis, the total purchase price must be allocated among the individual assets. When part of a purchase price can be clearly identified with specific assets, such cost assignment should be made and the balance of the purchase price allocated among the remaining assets; when no part of the purchase price can be related to specific assets, the entire amount must be allocated among the different assets acquired. Appraisal values or other such evidence that is provided by a competent independent authority should be sought to support such allocation.

To illustrate the allocation of a joint asset cost, assume that land, buildings, and equipment are acquired for $80,000. Assume further that assessed values for the individual assets as reported on the property tax bill are considered to provide an equitable basis for cost allocation. The allocation is made as shown at the top of the following page.

An asset acquired in secondhand or used condition should be set up at its cost without reference to the balance that might be found on the seller's books. Expenditures to repair, recondition, or improve the asset before it is placed in use should be added to cost. It must be assumed that

	Assessed Values	Cost Allocation According to Relative Assessed Values	Cost Assigned to Individual Assets
Real properties:			
Land....................	$14,000	14,000/50,000 × $80,000	$22,400
Improvements (building)	30,000	30,000/50,000 × $80,000	48,000
Personal property (equipment).................	6,000	6,000/50,000 × $80,000	9,600
	$50,000		$80,000

the buyer knew that additional expenditures would be required when he made the purchase.

Purchase on deferred payment plan. When property is acquired on a deferred payment plan and interest is charged on the unpaid balance of the contract, such interest should be recognized as an expense. When a specific charge for interest is not made but the contract price exceeds the cash price at which the asset can be acquired, such excess should be regarded as the charge for deferring the payment. When a cash price is not quoted, the contract price on a deferred payment plan may still be considered to include a financing charge. In such a case, the difference between the contract price and an assumed cash price, regarded as the future payments discounted at an appropriate interest rate, would properly be recognized as interest.

Property may be acquired under a conditional sales contract whereby legal title to the asset is retained by the seller until payments are completed. The failure to acquire legal title may be disregarded by the buyer and the transaction recognized in terms of its substance — the acquisition of an asset and the assumption of a liability. The buyer has the possession and use of the asset and must absorb any decline in its value; title to the asset is retained by the seller simply as a means of assuring payment on the purchase contract. In reporting the asset on the balance sheet prior to full settlement, there should be disclosure by parenthetical remark or note that legal title to the asset still remains with the seller.

In order to conserve working capital and to obtain other benefits, business enterprises frequently lease certain properties and pay a periodic rental for the services derived from the use of the assets. When the lease provides an option for the lessee to buy the asset, the lease contract may actually represent a deferred purchase arrangement which would call for reporting both the asset and the lease obligation on the lessee's balance sheet.

Acquisition by exchange. When one asset is traded for another, the new asset should be recorded at the fair market value of the asset given up; any difference between the fair market value of the asset given up and its book value should be recognized as a gain or loss on the exchange. When a cash payment is required on the acquisition, the new asset should be recorded at the sum of the cash paid and the fair market value of the asset exchanged. Any trade-in allowance should be carefully examined to determine whether it fairly measures the value of the asset exchanged. The use of a trade-in allowance that is inflated to provide a price concession will result in the overstatement of the newly acquired asset and also in the subsequent overstatement of depreciation charges. The newly acquired asset should be recorded at no more than the cash price that would be paid in the absence of a trade-in.

To illustrate an exchange, assume that machinery with an original cost of $5,000 and a book value of $2,000 is accepted at $1,600 in part payment on new machinery priced at $6,000. The following entry is then made:

Machinery..	6,000	
Accumulated Depreciation — Machinery.............	3,000	
Loss on Trade of Machinery.......................	400	
Machinery.......................................		5,000
Cash...		4,400

If, in the foregoing example, the machinery could have been acquired at a cash price of $5,600, this value should have been used in recording the asset. Although the trade-in allowance on the old machinery was stated at $1,600, the asset had an actual worth of no more than $1,200; the loss on the exchange was $800, the difference between the actual value of the asset given up, $1,200, and its book value, $2,000.

It was assumed in the example that the asset was exchanged at the beginning of a fiscal period. When a depreciable asset is exchanged within a fiscal period, depreciation should be recognized to the time of the exchange, and the entry to record the exchange should recognize the book value of the asset as of that date.

For federal income tax purposes, no gain or loss is recognized on the exchange of property held for productive use or investment solely for property of a like kind.[1] The tax basis of the new asset is measured by the book value of the asset given up increased by any cash paid on the trade. To illustrate, in the example just given, the loss cannot be recognized for tax purposes; instead, the cost of the new machinery is regarded as $6,400, the book value of the asset exchanged, $2,000, plus the cash paid, $4,400. In determining taxable income, depreciation on the new

---

[1]This rule does not cover stock in trade or stocks, bonds, or other evidences of indebtedness or interest.

asset is calculated on $6,400. The loss on the old asset is thus recovered in the form of additional depreciation over the life of the new asset.

The income tax method for reporting an asset acquired in an exchange cannot be supported as a sound accounting procedure. The life cycle of an old asset has ended and past periods should have absorbed the cost of the asset; a new asset has been acquired and future periods should be charged with neither more nor less than its actual cost. The tax method is frequently applied in the accounts so that analysis and restatement of asset balances may be avoided in the preparation of income tax returns. However, such practice cannot be defended if it results in a material misstatement of assets and periodic income.

A loss or a gain would be recognized for tax purposes as well as for accounting purposes when an old asset is sold for cash and a new asset is acquired in an independent transaction.

Acquisition by issuance of securities. A company may acquire certain property in exchange for its own bonds or stock. When a market value for the securities can be determined, such value is assigned to the asset; in the absence of a market value for the securities, the fair market value of the asset would be sought.

Assets received in exchange for securities are properly valued at the par value of the securities only when the market value of the securities equals par value. If bonds or stock are selling at more or less than par value, the asset should be reported at such current cash value; bonds payable or capital stock should be credited at par and a premium or discount should be established for the difference. To illustrate, assume that a company issues bonds of $100,000 in acquiring land; the bonds are currently selling on the market at 95. An entry should be made as follows:

Land..	95,000	
Discount on Bonds Payable....................	5,000	
Bonds Payable.............................		100,000

Thus the value of the securities is set as of the time of the exchange and at a price that is established by market transactions.

When securities do not have an established market value, appraisal of the assets by independent authority may be required in arriving at an objective determination of their fair market value. If satisfactory market values cannot be obtained for either securities that are issued or the assets that are acquired, values as established by the board of directors may have to be accepted for accounting purposes. For example, assume that a corporation issues stock in payment for certain mining property. A market value cannot be established for the stock, and there are no means of arriving at a fair market value for the property received. If the board of directors values the property at $100,000, the property value and the issuing price of the stock are thereby set at this amount. Disclosure should be provided on the balance sheet of the source of the valuation. The assignment of values by the board of directors is normally not subject to challenge unless it can be shown that the board has acted fraudulently. Nevertheless, evidence should be sought to validate the fairness of original valuations, and if within a short time after an acquisition, the sale of stock or other information indicates that original valuations were erroneous, appropriate action should be taken to restate asset and owners' equity accounts.

When a purchase price is made up of both cash and securities, similar standards for valuing properties apply. Any security discounts or premiums should be accounted for separately. When an asset is purchased for a given down payment plus a series of non-interest-bearing notes whose face values provide for interest charges, the asset cost should not include such charges.

Property is frequently acquired in exchange for securities pursuant to a corporate merger or consolidation. When such combination represents the transfer of properties to a new owner, the combination is designated a *purchase* and acquired assets are reported at their cost to the new owner. But when such combination represents essentially no more than a continuation of the original ownership in the enlarged entity, the combination is designated a *pooling of interests* and accounting authorities have approved the practice of recording properties at their original book values as shown on the books of the acquired company.

The pooling concept has been widely used primarily because of its conservatism in reporting assets rather than its theoretical soundness. It is maintained that employing security market values as a basis for assigning costs to properties acquired has frequently led to the recognition of properties and invested capital at grossly inflated amounts. However, many accountants have challenged the exceptional treatment that disregards the value of the consideration given in exchange for assets and brings these on the books at the amounts reported on the books of the original owner. Two Accounting Research Studies, sponsored by the American Institute of Certified Public Accountants, have focused on this controversy. In Accounting Research Study No. 5, *A Critical Study of Accounting for Business Combinations*, the author recommends the abandonment of pooling of interests as currently practiced. In its place the purchase method is recommended. The authors of Accounting Research Study No. 10, *Accounting for Goodwill*, recommend the abandonment of pooling of interests as an acceptable accounting method. The AICPA

Committee on Accounting Procedure first made a distinction between purchase and pooling of interests accounting and defined the special criteria that would support the pooling of interests approach in 1957 in Accounting Research Bulletin No. 48. The Accounting Principles Board reaffirmed the distinction in 1965 in Opinion No. 6. With continuing criticism from many segments of the business community, the Accounting Principles Board in 1970 issued Opinion No. 16, which made some modifications in the rules governing the adoption of the pooling approach. It further indicated that where specific conditions were not met, the purchase method of accounting would have to be employed.[1]

Acquisition by self-construction. Sometimes buildings or equipment items are constructed by a company for its own use. This may be done to save on construction costs, to utilize idle facilities, or to achieve a higher quality of construction. When such construction takes place, a number of special problems arise in arriving at asset cost.

Overhead chargeable to self-construction. All costs that can be related to construction should be charged to the assets under construction. There is no question about the inclusion of charges that are directly attributable to the new construction. However, there is a difference of opinion regarding the amount of overhead that is properly assignable to the construction activity. Some accountants take the position that assets under construction should be charged with no more than the incremental overhead — the increase in a company's total overhead resulting from the special construction activity. Others maintain that overhead should be assigned to construction just as it is assigned to normal operations. This would call for the inclusion of not only the increase in overhead resulting from construction activities but also a pro rata share of the company's fixed overhead.

Those supporting charges for overhead limited to incremental amounts maintain that the cost of construction is actually no more than the extra costs incurred. Normal operations should receive no special favors as a result of construction. Management is aware of the cost of normal operations and decides to undertake a project on the basis of the added costs that are anticipated. Those taking the position that construction should carry a fair share of the fixed overhead maintain that this must be done if the full cost of the asset is to be reported. It is their view that construction is entitled to no special favors, and this practice

---

[1]The pooling of interests concept is discussed in greater detail in Chapter 16 and in *Advanced Accounting* by Simons and Karrenbrock.

should be followed even though general operations are relieved of a portion of the overhead that they would normally carry; overhead has served a double purpose during the construction period and this is properly reflected in reduced operating costs. The latter argument may be particularly persuasive if construction takes place during a period of subnormal operations and utilizes what would otherwise represent idle capacity cost, or if construction restricts production or other regular business activities.

It should be noted that the assignment to construction of normal overhead otherwise chargeable to current operations will increase net income during the construction period. The recognition of a portion of overhead is postponed and related to subsequent periods through charges in the form of depreciation.

Although there is theoretical support for the use of either position suggested, accountants generally lean toward charging construction with no more than the incremental overhead. Conservatism is frequently stated as a reason for such practice.

Saving or loss on self-construction. When the cost of self-construction of an asset is less than the cost to acquire it through purchase or construction by outsiders, such difference for accounting purposes is not a profit but a *saving*. The construction is properly reported at its actual cost. The saving will emerge as income over the life of the asset as lower depreciation is charged against periodic revenue. Assume, on the other hand, that the cost of self-construction is greater than bids originally received for such construction. There is generally no assurance that the asset under alternative arrangements might have been equal to that which was self-constructed, and in recording this transaction, just as in recording others, accounts should reflect those courses of action that were taken, not the alternatives that might have been selected. At the same time, if there is evidence indicating that cost has been materially excessive because of certain construction inefficiencies or failures, such excess is properly recognized as an extraordinary loss; subsequent periods should not be burdened with charges for depreciation arising from costs that could have been avoided.

Acquisition by gift or discovery. When property is received through donation by a governmental unit or other source, there is no cost that can be used as a basis for its valuation. Even though certain expenditures may have to be made incident to the gift, these are generally considerably less than the value of the property. Here cost obviously fails to provide a satisfactory basis for asset accountability as well as for future income measurement. In failing to recognize the property at the time of the donation, assets, as well as owners' equity, will be understated. In subsequent periods, periodic net income will be overstated through the failure to record depreciation and amortization on donated properties having a limited term of usefulness. These misstatements will be accompanied by misrepresentations of the company's earning power reflected in the earnings-to-assets and earnings-to-equity relationships.

To avoid the foregoing consequences, property acquired through donation should be appraised and recorded at its fair market value. A donation is the source of the owners' equity increase, therefore a donated capital balance is credited. To illustrate, if the Beverly Hills Chamber of Commerce donates land and buildings appraised at $50,000 and $150,000 respectively, the entry on the books of the donee would be:

Land..	50,000	
Buildings....................................	150,000	
Donated Capital — Acquisition of Land and Buildings...............................		200,000

Depreciation of an asset acquired by gift should be recorded in the usual manner, the value assigned to the asset providing the basis for the depreciation charge.

If a gift is contingent upon some act to be performed by the donee, the contingent nature of the asset and the capital item should be indicated in the account titles. Account balances should be reported "short" or a special note made on the balance sheet. When conditions of the gift have been met, both the increase in assets and in owners' equity should be recognized in the accounts and on the financial statements.

Discoveries of valuable natural resources may be made on land that is owned. The presence of valuable resources, not previously known, materially enhances the value of the land. As in the case of a gift, cost fails to provide a satisfactory basis for asset valuation and income measurement. Here, too, an appraisal of the land is appropriate, and it should be restated in terms of the estimated value of the discovered resources. In this case, a revaluation of land is the source of the capital increase; appraisal capital, then, is recognized equal to the asset increase, a credit being made to an account such as Appraisal Capital — Discovery Value of Natural Resources.

Interest during period of construction. In public utility accounting, interest during a period of building construction is recognized as a part of asset cost. This practice applies both to interest actually paid and to an implicit interest charge if the public utility uses its own funds. Interest, then, emerges as a charge for depreciation in the periods in which the properties are income-producing. Service rates established by regulatory bodies are based upon current charges and may provide for a recovery of past interest in this manner.

The practice of capitalizing interest has sometimes been carried into accounting for the industrial unit. Support for this practice is made on the grounds that cash raised through borrowing is employed for construction purposes; furthermore, if buildings were acquired through purchase, a charge for interest during construction would be implicit in the purchase price. On the other hand, it can be maintained that interest is a money cost, a cost that could have been avoided by raising cash through the sale of stock rather than through borrowing. Even in this case, however, it can be maintained that there is an implicit cost for the cash that is used. If the proceeds from the stock issue were invested rather than spent, additional earnings could have been realized.

If interest is to be capitalized, the amount should be limited to charges related to amounts borrowed applied to construction. Thus, construction may be charged for the full interest charges on temporary construction loans. However, when bonds are issued, the charge to construction should be limited to interest on that part of the bonds proceeds applied to construction. When interest payments are capitalized, it follows that similar treatment should be applied to interest adjustments for debt discount and premium amortization.

Other expenditures during periods of organization and construction. Some have maintained that all charges for interest, taxes, and general and administrative services during a period of organization and construction should be capitalized. Support for such procedure is based on the theory that future periods are benefited by necessary initial costs and it is unreasonable to assume that losses have been incurred before sales activities begin. If the practice of capitalizing such initial expenditures is followed, the asset should be reported as noncurrent and should be written off against revenues in some systematic manner. In reporting the asset on the balance sheet, a note should be provided describing the expenditures that are summarized therein. Initial costs of organization and construction should not be reported as a part of buildings and equipment. If this is done, the property items, as well as periodic depreciation charges, will be misstated.

Special problems relating to property acquisitions. Special accounting problems arise in recording the acquisition of certain property items. Attention is directed in the sections that follow to specific properties and the special problems relating thereto.

Land. Rights to land arising from *purchase* should be distinguished from rights under *leaseholds* and under *easements*. With a purchase, the buyer acquires title and ownership *in fee simple*, and the property is properly recognized as an asset. A leasehold provides rights for the *possession and profits* of land for a certain period. An easement provides rights for the *use* of land as in the case of rights-of-way or other special privileges. Recognition of asset balances for leaseholds and easements is limited to prepayments of rents and fees to the owners of land for the rights that were acquired unless the leasehold or easement is in substance a purchase.

When land is purchased, its cost includes not only the negotiated purchase price but also all other costs related to the acquisition including brokers' commissions, legal fees, title, recording, and escrow fees, and surveying fees. Any existing unpaid taxes, interest, or other liens on the property assumed by the buyer are added to cost.

Costs of clearing, grading, subdividing, landscaping, or otherwise permanently improving the land after its acquisition should also be treated as increases in the cost of land. When a site secured for a new plant is already occupied by a building that must be torn down, the cost of dismantling and removing the old structure less any recovery from salvage is added to land cost. If salvage exceeds the cost of razing buildings, such excess may be considered a reduction of land cost. Special assessments for certain local benefits, such as streets and sidewalks, lighting, and sewers and drainage systems, may be regarded as permanently improving land and thus chargeable to this asset. When expenditures are incurred for land improvements that have a limited life and require ultimate replacement as, for example, paving, fencing, and water and sewage systems, such costs should be summarized separately in an account entitled Land Improvements and written off over the estimated useful life of the improvements. The useful life of some improvements may be limited to the life of the buildings on the land; other improvements may have an independent service life.

Land qualifies for presentation in the land, buildings, and equipment category only when it is being used in the normal activities of the business. For example, land held for future use or for speculation should be reported under the investments heading; land held for current sale should be reported as a current asset. A descriptive account title should be used to distinguish land not used in normal operations from the land in use.

When land is acquired and held for future use or as a speculative venture, a question arises as to the proper treatment of the charges of carrying such property. Should expenditures for taxes and interest on mortgages, for example, be charged to periodic revenue or should these be added to the cost of the land? There is strong support for adding such charges to land. The buyer knows that costs will be involved in holding the land before it can be applied to the specific purpose for which it is acquired and makes the purchase with the expectation that the investment will yield benefits exceeding both the original cost and carrying charges. When carrying charges are capitalized, the full cost of the investment can be assigned to the purpose for which it is ultimately applied.

To illustrate, assume that in 1972 a company acquires land for expansion purposes although it does not expect to use the land until 1982. Cost of the land is $40,000; taxes and other carrying charges are estimated at $20,000 for the ten-year period. Under these circumstances, the company has actually made a decision to invest $60,000 in land instead of delaying action until some later date when efforts toward expansion might find circumstances less favorable. Or assume that in 1972 land is acquired as a speculative investment for $40,000 and that it is ultimately sold in 1982 for $75,000, carrying charges during the ten-year period having totaled $20,000. Here, too, the investment in land may be regarded as $60,000 and the gain as $15,000. The land represented, in effect, "goods in process" during the holding period; $75,000 is ultimately realized on an investment totaling $60,000. If carrying charges had been assigned to the periodic revenues, net income during the ten-year holding period would have been reduced by $20,000 and a gain of $35,000 would be reported on the sale of the property. The latter treatment fails to offer a satisfactory accounting for periodic earnings and for the gain emerging from the investment.

It is difficult to support capitalizing expenditures for carrying assets when market values fail to confirm increasing property values; here conservatism requires the treatment of such expenditures as charges to periodic revenues. The capitalization procedure is likewise inappropriate when land is used for such purposes as rental or farming and produces current revenue; expenditures under these circumstances should be treated as charges against such revenue.

Carrying charges on investments in land are sometimes recorded as expenses rather than as part of the cost of land. In reporting land held as an investment on the balance sheet, it is desirable to indicate in parenthetical or note form the cost procedure that is employed for the asset as well as its current fair market value when this can be supported by objective evidence.

For federal income tax purposes, taxes, interest on mortgages, and other carrying charges on unimproved and unproductive real property may be deducted as expenses or added to the cost of the property. The taxpayer may elect to capitalize carrying charges even though he has deducted such items in the past and such election is not binding on future expenditures.

Buildings. A purchase involving the acquisition of both land and buildings requires that the cost be allocated between the two assets. Allocable cost consists of the purchase price plus all charges incident to the purchase. The cost allocated to buildings is increased by expenditures for reconditioning and repairs in preparing the asset for use as well as by expenditures for improvements and additions.

When buildings are constructed, their cost consists of materials, labor, and overhead related to construction. Costs of excavation or grading and filling required for purposes of the specific project rather than for making land usable are charged to buildings. Charges for architects' fees, building permits and fees, workmen's compensation and accident insurance, fire insurance for the period of construction, and temporary buildings used in connection with construction activities, form part of the total building cost. Taxes on property improvements, as well as financing costs during a period of construction, are generally capitalized as a cost of buildings.

It was suggested earlier that when land and buildings are acquired and buildings are immediately demolished, the cost of demolishing buildings is added to land as a cost of preparing land for its intended use. However, the cost of demolishing buildings that have been previously occupied by the company requires different treatment. This is a cost that should be identified with the life of the original buildings. The recovery of salvage upon asset retirement serves to reduce the cost arising from the use of an asset and is frequently anticipated in calculating periodic charges for depreciation; a cost arising from asset retirement, however, serves to increase the cost of asset use but is seldom anticipated in developing periodic charges. When asset retirement costs are material and have not been anticipated, they require recognition as an extraordinary charge.

In many instances, careful analysis is required in determining whether an expenditure should be recognized as buildings or whether it should be identified with the land or machinery and equipment categories. For example, expenditures for sidewalks and roads that are part of a building program are normally reported as buildings, but these would be properly reported as land improvements when they improve land regardless of its use; expenditures for items such as shelving, cabinets, or partitions in the course of building construction are normally reported as buildings, but these would be properly reported as equipment items when they are movable, can be used in different centers, and are considered to have independent lives.   Particular care should be directed to the charges that will be made against revenues under different classification and recording alternatives.   Frequently alternative classifications can be supported and the ultimate choice will be a matter of judgment.

If depreciation on buildings is to be recognized satisfactorily, separate accounts should be maintained for each building with a different life as well as for those structural elements of a building that will require modification or replacement before the building is fully depreciated, such as loading and shipping quarters, storage facilities and garages.   Separate recording should also be extended to building equipment and appurtenances that will require replacement before the buildings are fully depreciated, such as boilers, heating and ventilating systems, plumbing and lighting systems, elevators, and wiring and piping installations.   The latter items are frequently summarized in an account titled Building Equipment or Building Improvements, but detailed records will be required in support of this balance because of the different service lives of the individual items.

Equipment.   Equipment covers a wide range of items that vary with the particular enterprise and its activities.   The discussion in the paragraphs that follow is limited to machinery, tools, patterns and dies, furniture and fixtures, motor vehicles, and returnable containers.

Machinery of the manufacturing concern includes such items as lathes, stamping machines, ovens, and conveyor systems.   The machinery account is charged for all expenditures identified with the acquisition and the preparation for use of factory machines.   Machinery cost includes the purchase price, taxes and duties on purchase, freight and drayage charges, insurance charges while in transit, installation charges, and expenditures for testing and final preparation for use.

Two classes of tools are employed in productive activities: (1) machine tools representing detachable parts of a machine, such as dies, drills, and punches; and (2) hand tools such as hammers, wrenches, and saws.   Both classes of tools are normally of small individual cost and are relatively short-lived as a result of wear, breakage, and loss.   Such factors frequently suggest that these items be accounted for as a single asset.   Replacement of these small tools may then either be charged directly to expense or added to the single asset account and written off by reasonable annual amortization charges.

Patterns and dies are acquired for designing, stamping, cutting, or forging out a particular object.   The cost of patterns and dies is either a purchase cost or a developmental cost composed of labor, materials, and overhead. When patterns and dies are used in normal productive activities, their cost is reported as an asset and this asset is written off over the period of its usefulness. When the use of such items is limited to the manufacture of a single job, their cost is recognized as a part of the cost of that job.

Furniture and fixtures include such items as desks, chairs, carpets, showcases, and display fixtures. Acquisitions should be identified with production, selling, or general and administrative functions. Such classification makes it possible to assign depreciation accurately to the different business activities. Furniture and fixtures are recorded at cost, which includes purchase price, taxes, freight, and installation charges.

Automobile and truck acquisitions should also be identified with production, selling, or general and administrative functions. Depreciation can then be accurately related to the different activities. Automotive equipment is recorded at its purchase price increased by any sales and excise taxes and delivery charges paid. When payment for equipment includes charges for items such as current license fees, personal property taxes, and insurance, these should be recognized separately as expenses relating to both the current and the future use of the equipment.

Goods are frequently delivered in containers that are to be returned and reused. Returnable containers consist of such items as tanks, drums, and barrels. Containers are depreciable assets used in the business and are included in the property group.

The investment credit. The Revenue Act of 1962, in order to encourage investment in productive facilities, permitted taxpayers to reduce their federal income taxes by an *investment credit* equal to a specified percentage of the cost of certain depreciable properties acquired after January 1, 1962. This act thus provided certain tax benefits as a stimulant to the economy. The investment credit has had a turbulent history both in politics and in accounting practice. The credit provisions were significantly amended in 1964; the credit was temporarily suspended in 1966 and suspended again in 1969 when the economy was in an inflationary period. The credit was reinstated in 1971.

Accounting for the credit has also been the subject of much controversy and change. Essentially, there are two methods that can be used to record the tax reduction: (1) The credit can be used to reduce the income tax charge for the year in which it is received, commonly referred to as the *flow-through method*, or (2) the credit can be used to reduce the cost of the asset, thus reducing the depreciation charges over the asset's useful life, commonly referred to as the *deferred method*.

To illustrate the two approaches, assume that a business acquired machinery in 1972 for $100,000. The asset has an estimated useful life of 10 years with no salvage value and is to be depreciated on a straight-line basis. Assume further that federal income taxes for 1972 are $40,000 reduced by an investment credit of $7,000 (7% of $100,000). Entries in 1972 would be made as follows:

Transaction	Assuming that the investment credit is treated as a reduction in asset cost (Deferred Method)		Assuming that the investment credit is treated as a reduction in taxes (Flow-Through Method)	

Purchase of machinery for $100,000	Machinery...... 100,000
	   Cash.........
		100,000	Machinery....... 100,000
			   Cash..........
				100,000

Recognition of income taxes, $40,000 less investment credit, $7,000.	Income Taxes... 40,000
	  Deferred
	    Investment
	    Tax Credit..
	  Income Taxes
	    Payable....
		
		7,000
		
		33,000
			Income Taxes.... 33,000
			  Income Taxes
			    Payable.....
				
				33,000

Amortization of deferred investment tax credit	Deferred
	  Investment
	  Tax Credit.... 7,000
	    Investment Tax
	     Credit Real-
	     ized ....
		
		7,000
			No entry	

The Accounting Principles Board favored the deferred method and approved it in Opinion No. 2. Lack of support for this view among many prominent accountants led to the issuance in 1964 of Opinion No. 4 in which the Board accepted both methods although still stating a preference for the deferred method. In 1968 a further attempt was made by the Accounting Principles Board to restore the deferred method approach as a single uniform method. Again, differences of opinion resulted in failure to adopt the original conclusions. In 1971, the Board once again made serious effort to restore the deferred method. However, they had to postpone such effort as a result of congressional action that permitted the taxpayer to choose the method to be used in recognizing the benefit arising from the credit.

Expenditures incurred during service life of property items

During the lives of property items, regular as well as special expenditures are incurred in their use. Certain expenditures are required to maintain and repair assets; others are incurred to increase their capacity or efficiency or to extend their useful lives. Each expenditure requires careful analysis to determine whether it should be assigned to revenue of the current period, hence charged to an expense account, or whether it should be assigned to revenue of more than one period, which calls for a charge to an asset account or to an accumulated depreciation account.

In many cases the answer may not be clear, and the procedure that is ultimately chosen may be a matter of judgment.

The terms maintenance, repairs, betterments, improvements, additions, and rearrangements are used in describing expenditures that are made in the course of asset use. These are described below.

Maintenance. Expenditures to maintain assets in fit condition to perform their work are referred to as *maintenance*. Among these are expenditures for painting, lubricating, and adjusting equipment. Maintenance items are ordinary and recurring and do not improve the asset or add to its life; therefore they are recorded as expenses.

Repairs. Expenditures to restore assets to a fit condition upon their breakdown or to restore and replace broken parts are referred to as *repairs*. When these expenditures are ordinary and benefit only current operations, they are charged to expense. When these are extraordinary and extend the life of the asset, they may be charged to the accumulated depreciation account. The depreciation rate is then redetermined in view of changes in the asset book values and estimated life. Charges for repairs that extend the useful life of the asset are made against the accumulated depreciation account to avoid a build-up of gross asset values. The book value of the asset will be the same regardless of whether the charge is made to the asset account directly or to the accumulated depreciation account.

Repairs involving the overhauling of certain assets are frequently referred to as *renewals*. Substitutions of parts or entire units are referred to as *replacements*. Minor renewals or part replacements may be regarded as ordinary repairs; major renewals or part replacements fall into the category of extraordinary repairs. When the component parts of an asset have different lives and are carried separately, a part replacement calls for entries to cancel the book value related to the old part and to establish the new. Replacement of an entire unit calls for similar entries.

Repairs arising from flood, fire, or other casualty require special analysis. An expenditure to restore an asset to its previous condition should be reported as a loss from casualties. An expenditure that improves or enlarges the asset should be added to the asset balance, while an expenditure that extends the original life of the asset should be treated as a reduction in the accumulated depreciation.

Betterments and improvements. Changes in assets designed to provide increased or improved services are referred to as *betterments* or *improvements*. Installation of improved lighting systems, heating systems, or sanitary systems, represent such betterments. Minor expenditures for betterments may be recorded as ordinary repairs. Major expenditures call for entries to cancel the book value related to the old asset and to establish the new, or entries to reduce the accumulated depreciation related to the original asset. The latter method is sometimes required when the cost of the item replaced is not readily separable from the whole unit.

Additions. Enlargements and extensions of existing facilities are referred to as *additions*. A new plant wing, additional loading docks, or the expansion of a paved parking lot, represent additions. Such expenditures are capitalized, and this cost is written off over the service life of the addition.

Rearrangements. Movement of machinery and equipment items and reinstallations to secure economies or greater efficiencies are referred to as *rearrangements*. Costs related to rearrangements should be assigned to those periods that will benefit from such changes. When more than one period is benefited, an asset account, appropriately designated to indicate the nature of the cost deferral, should be established and this balance allocated systematically to revenue. When rearrangements involve reinstallation costs, the portion of asset book value related to an original installation should be canceled and the cost of the new installation added to the asset and written off over its remaining life.

Establishment of allowance for repairs and parts replacements. When certain relatively large repair and parts replacement charges are expected at irregular intervals during the life of an asset, provision may be made to charge operations not only with a share of the original cost of the asset but also with a share of the total repair and replacement charges that are anticipated over the life of the asset. An expense account may be charged periodically and a repairs and replacements allowance account credited for the estimated repairs and replacements. If this is done, repairs and replacements, when incurred, are properly charged against the allowance. To illustrate, a new roof for a building does not increase the original estimated service of the building, but it may represent a relatively heavy charge if made against the revenue of a single fiscal period. If an allowance for repairs and replacements has been set up by periodic charges to operations, the expenditure for the new roof can be charged against this allowance. Each period is thus charged with its share of the charges of this kind, and an unreasonably large charge against the revenue of a single period is avoided. In preparing the balance sheet then, the building account would be reduced by both accumulated depreciation and the allowance for repairs and replacements. The allowance for repairs and replacements may be regarded as reflecting the above-normal depreciation of certain components of the property item.

If a business has a great many equipment items of different ages in service, total repairs and replacements charges may not vary significantly from period to period, and little may be gained by establishing an allowance. Charges that are made in recognizing an allowance for repairs and replacements are not deductible for income tax purposes; charges for repairs and replacements are deductible for tax purposes only when the expenditures are made.

It should be observed that irregular charges for major repairs and parts replacements are largely avoided when individual accounts are established for each separate component of an asset item that is deemed to have an independent life. Instead of a single depreciation rate applied to a composite asset, individual rates are applied to the separate asset components. Major expenditures during the life of the property item are reported as newly acquired asset components, and balances related to original components are canceled. Such procedure, although it may require considerable analysis and detailed records, has merit in achieving fairer assignments of expenses to revenue.

Property retirements

Properties may be retired by sale, trade, scrapping and removal, or abandonment. When properties are disposed of, both property and accumulated depreciation accounts are canceled and a gain or loss is recognized for the difference between the amount recovered on the asset and its book value.

In recording a disposal, it is necessary to consider the practice that has been adopted for recognizing depreciation for fractional periods. Various practices are employed including the following:

1. Depreciation is recognized on the asset from the time it is acquired to the time it is retired.
2. Depreciation is recognized at the annual rate on the beginning-of-year balance in the asset account plus or minus depreciation at one half the annual rate on the net additions or subtractions in the account for the year. The effect of this procedure is to recognize depreciation for one half year on all acquisitions and all retirements.
3. Depreciation is recognized at the annual rate on the beginning-of-year balance in the asset account. Thus, no depreciation is recognized on acquisitions during the year but depreciation for a full year is recognized on retirements.
4. Depreciation is recognized at the annual rate on the end-of-year balance in the asset account. Thus, depreciation is recognized for a full year on acquisitions during the year but no depreciation is recognized on retirements.

Methods (2), (3), and (4) are attractive because of their simplicity. However, method (1) provides greatest accuracy and its use is assumed unless some alternate policy is specifically stated. In applying method (1), depreciation, rather than being recognized on as short a period as a day or a week, would normally be calculated to the nearest month: no charge would be made for an asset that is used for less than half of a month; a charge for a full month would be recognized for an asset that is used for more than half of a month. This practice is assumed in the examples and problems in the text.

To illustrate the entries for asset retirement, assume that it is decided to sell certain machinery. The machinery was originally acquired on November 20, 1963, for $10,000 and had been depreciated at 10% per year. The asset is sold on April 10, 1972, for $1,250. The entries to record depreciation for 1972 and sale of the property item follow:

Depreciation Expense — Machinery..........	250.00	
Accumulated Depreciation — Machinery......		250.00
To record depreciation for three months in 1972:		
$10,000 × 10% × 3/12, or $250.00.		

Cash..	1,250.00	
Accumulated Depreciation — Machinery........	8,333.33	
Loss on Sale of Machinery...................	416.67	
Machinery...............................		10,000.00

To record sale of machinery:

Cost.............................	$10,000.00
Depreciation to date of sale:	
November 20, 1963–April 10, 1972	
(10% per year for 8-4/12 years).......	8,333.33
Asset book value....................	$ 1,666.67
Proceeds from sale..................	1,250.00
Loss on sale.......................	$ 416.67

The above entries can be combined in the form of a single compound entry as follows:

Cash..	1,250.00	
Depreciation Expense — Machinery...........	250.00	
Accumulated Depreciation — Machinery.......	8,083.33	
Loss on Sale of Machinery..................	416.67	
Machinery...............................		10,000.00

If a property item is scrapped or abandoned without cash recovery, a loss would be recognized equal to the asset book value; if the full cost of the asset has been written off, the asset and its offset balances would simply be canceled. If a property item is retired from active or standby service but is not immediately disposed of, asset and accumulated depreciation balances should be closed and the salvage value of the asset established as a separate asset.

In the examples in this chapter a difference between the amount recovered and the book value of a depreciable asset exchanged, sold, or scrapped, was recognized as a special gain or loss related to the current decision to dispose of the asset. Prior to 1966 such a difference was sometimes recognized as a prior period adjustment arising from a failure to measure depreciation accurately and was charged directly to Retained Earnings. The Accounting Principles Board in Opinion No. 9 has clearly stated that this is not to be regarded as a prior period adjustment as now defined. The Board maintains that economic events subsequent to the date of financial statements must of necessity enter into the elimination of any previously existing uncertainty; the disposal of the property item is no more than an element in the determination of the net income for the period in which the uncertainty is eliminated.[1]

Property damage or destruction. Special accounting problems arise when property is damaged or destroyed as a result of fire, flood, storm, or other casualty. When a company owns many properties and these are widely distributed, the company itself may assume the risk of loss. However, companies ordinarily carry insurance for casualties that may involve large sums.

When uninsured property items are damaged and expenditures are incurred in their restoration, such expenditures, if material, should be reported as an extraordinary loss. When uninsured properties are partly or wholly destroyed, asset book values should be reduced or canceled and an extraordinary loss recorded for such reductions. When property items are insured and these are damaged or destroyed, entries on the books must be made to report asset losses and also the insurance claims that arise from such losses.

The most common casualty loss incurred by a business is that from fire. Of all of the various types of protection offered by insurance, fire is the risk that is most widely covered. Because of the importance of fire insurance in business and because of the special accounting problems that arise in the event of fire, the remaining pages of this chapter are devoted to a detailed discussion of this matter.

Fire insurance. Fire insurance policies are usually written in $100 or $1,000 units for a period of one, three, or five years. Insurance premiums are normally paid in advance. The amount of the premium is determined by the conditions prevailing in each case.

---

[1] *Opinions of the Accounting Principles Board, No. 9*, "Reporting the Results of Operations" (New York: American Institute of Certified Public Accountants, December, 1966), par. 23-25.

The insurance contract may be canceled by either the insurer or the insured. When the insurance company cancels the policy, a refund is made on a pro rata basis. When the policyholder cancels the policy, a refund may be made on what is known as a "short-rate" basis that provides for a higher insurance rate for the shorter period of coverage.

A *coinsurance clause* is frequently written into a policy by the insurance companies to offset the tendency by the buyer to purchase only a minimum insurance coverage. A business with assets that are worth $100,000, for example, may estimate that any single loss could not destroy more than one half of these assets and might consider itself adequately protected by insurance of $50,000. With an 80% coinsurance clause, however, the business would have to carry insurance equal to 80% of the value of the property, or $80,000, to recover the full amount on claims up to the face of the policy. When less than this percentage is carried, the insured shares in the risk with the insurer.

To illustrate the calculation of the amount recoverable on a policy that fails to meet coinsurance requirements, assume the following: assets are insured for $70,000 under a policy containing an 80% coinsurance clause; on the date of a fire, assets have a fair market value of $100,000. Because insurance of only $70,000 is carried when coinsurance requirements are $80,000, any loss will be borne 7/8 by the insurance company and 1/8 by the policyholder; furthermore, whatever the loss, the maximum to be borne by the insurance company is $70,000, the face of the policy. The amount recoverable from the insurance company if a fire loss is $50,000, for example, is calculated as follows:

$$\frac{70,000 \text{ (policy)}}{80,000 \text{ (coinsurance requirement)}} \times \$50,000 \text{ (loss)} = \$43,750$$

The same calculations are made when the loss is greater than the face of the policy. Assume the facts that were given but a fire loss of $75,000. The amount recoverable from the insurance is calculated as follows:

$$\frac{70,000 \text{ (policy)}}{80,000 \text{ (coinsurance requirement)}} \times \$75,000 \text{ (loss)} = \$65,625$$

In the example above, application of the formula gives an amount that is still less than the face of the policy and hence fully recoverable. But if application of the formula results in an amount that exceeds the face value of the policy, the claim is limited to the latter amount. If, for example, the loss is $90,000, the following calculation is made:

$$\frac{70,000 \text{ (policy)}}{80,000 \text{ (coinsurance requirement)}} \times \$90,000 \text{ (loss)} = \$78,750$$

Recovery from the insurance company, however, is limited to $70,000, the ceiling set by the policy.

When the insurance coverage is equal to or greater than the percentage required by the coinsurance clause, the formula need not be applied since any loss is paid in full up to the face value of the policy. It is important to note that coinsurance requirements are based not on the cost or book value of the insured property but upon the actual market value of the property on the date of a fire. If coinsurance requirements are to be met, a rise in the value of insured assets requires that insurance coverage be increased.

The following general rules may be formulated:
1. In the absence of a coinsurance clause the amount recoverable is the lower of the loss or the face of the policy.
2. When a policy includes a coinsurance clause, the amount recoverable is the lower of the loss as adjusted by the coinsurance formula or the face of the policy.

Insurance policies normally include a *contribution clause* that provides that if other policies are carried on the same property, recovery of a loss on a policy shall be limited to the ratio which the face of the policy bears to the total insurance carried. Such a limitation on the amount to be paid eliminates the possibility of recovery by the insured of amounts in excess of the actual loss. When coinsurance clauses are found on the different policies, the recoverable amount on each is limited to the ratio of the face of the policy to the higher of (1) the total insurance carried, or (2) the total insurance required to be carried by the policy. To illustrate the limitations that are set by contribution clauses, assume a fire loss of $30,000 on property with a value of $100,000 on which policies are carried as follows: Co. A, $50,000; Co. B, $15,000; Co. C, $10,000.

(a) Assuming that policies have no coinsurance clauses, amounts that may be recovered from each company are as follows:

$$\text{Co. A: } \frac{50,000 \text{ (policy)}}{75,000 \text{ (total policies)}} \times \$30,000 \text{ (loss)} \qquad = \$20,000$$

$$\text{Co. B: } \frac{15,000 \text{ (policy)}}{75,000 \text{ (total policies)}} \times \$30,000 \text{ (loss)} \qquad = \quad 6,000$$

$$\text{Co. C: } \frac{10,000 \text{ (policy)}}{75,000 \text{ (total policies)}} \times \$30,000 \text{ (loss)} \qquad = \quad 4,000$$

Total amount recoverable $\qquad\qquad\qquad\qquad\qquad\qquad \$30,000$

(b) Assuming that each policy includes an 80% coinsurance clause, coinsurance requirements on each policy would exceed the total insurance carried and amounts that may be recovered from each company are as follows:

$$\text{Co. A: } \frac{50,000 \text{ (policy)}}{80,000 \text{ (coinsurance requirement)}} \times \$30,000 \text{ (loss)} = \$18,750$$

$$\text{Co. B: } \frac{15,000 \text{ (policy)}}{80,000 \text{ (coinsurance requirement)}} \times \$30,000 \text{ (loss)} = \quad 5,625$$

$$\text{Co. C: } \frac{10,000 \text{ (policy)}}{80,000 \text{ (coinsurance requirement)}} \times \$30,000 \text{ (loss)} = \quad 3,750$$

Total amount recoverable $\qquad\qquad\qquad\qquad\qquad\qquad \$28,125$

(c) Assuming that each policy includes a 70% coinsurance clause, total insurance carried exceeds coinsurance requirements on each policy and amounts that may be recovered from each company are the same as in (a).

(d) Assuming that coinsurance requirements are Co. A — none, Co. B — 70%, and Co. C — 80%, recovery on each policy is based on its relationship to the total insurance carried or the coinsurance requirement where this is higher, as follows:

$$\text{Co. A:} \quad \frac{50,000 \ (\text{policy})}{75,000 \ (\text{total policies})} \times \$30,000 \ (\text{loss}) \qquad = \$20,000$$

$$\text{Co. B:} \quad \frac{15,000 \ (\text{policy})}{75,000 \ (\text{total policies})} \times \$30,000 \ (\text{loss}) \qquad = \quad 6,000$$

$$\text{Co. C:} \quad \frac{10,000 \ (\text{policy})}{80,000 \ (\text{coinsurance requirement})} \times \$30,000 \ (\text{loss}) = \quad 3,750$$

Total amount recoverable $29,750

Accounting for fire losses. In the event that a fire occurs and books of account are destroyed, account balances to the date of the fire will have to be reconstructed from the best available evidence. As the first step in summarizing the fire loss, books as maintained or as reconstructed are adjusted as of the date of the fire. With accounts brought up to date, the loss may be summarized in a fire loss account. The fire loss account is charged for the book value of properties destroyed, and it is credited for amounts recoverable from insurance companies and amounts recoverable from salvage. The balance of the account is recognized as an extraordinary loss and is closed into the income summary account.

A number of special problems are encountered in arriving at the charges to be made to the fire loss account. When depreciable assets are destroyed, the book values of the properties must be brought up to date and these balances in total or in part then transferred to the fire loss account. When merchandise is destroyed, the estimated cost of the merchandise on hand at the time of the fire must be determined. If perpetual inventory records are available, the goods on hand may be obtained from this source. In the absence of such records, the inventory is generally calculated by the gross profit method. The inventory may be set up by a charge to the inventory account and a credit to the income summary account. The inventory total or portion destroyed may now be transferred to the fire loss account.

Insurance expired to the date of the fire is recorded as an expense. The balance in the unexpired insurance account is carried forward when policies continue in force and offer original protection on rehabilitated properties or newly acquired replacements. If a business does not plan to repair or replace the assets, it may cancel a part or all of a policy and recover cash on a short-rate basis. The difference between the unexpired insurance balance and the amount received on the short-rate basis is a loss from insurance cancellation brought about by the fire and is recorded as an addition to the fire loss balance.[1]

To illustrate the accounting for a fire loss, assume the facts that follow. J. J. Bailey, a retailer, suffers a fire loss after the close of business on March 31, 1972. Assets destroyed and amounts recoverable from insurance and salvage are summarized below:

Item	Loss — Book Values	Amount Recoverable
Inventory	Entire inventory, estimated to have a cost of $18,000.	Policy carried............ $12,500 Value of property at date of fire as agreed by insured and insurer............ 18,000 Salvage goods valued at... 1,400 Amount recoverable from insurance company: Full amount of policy... 12,500
Equipment	One third of equipment: Cost of equipment...... $15,000 Accumulated depr., 1/1/72.... $9,000 Add depr. at 10% for 3 months.... 375 9,375 Asset book value....... $ 5,625 Book value of portion lost: ⅓ × $5,625............ $ 1,875	Policy carried............ $ 6,000 Value of equipment at date of fire, as agreed by in- sured and insurer....... 7,800 Amount recoverable from insurance company: ⅓ × $7,800........... 2,600
Buildings	One fourth of buildings: Cost of buildings........ $32,000 Accumulated depr., 1/1/72.... $4,000 Add depr. at 2½% for 3 months.... 200 4,200 Asset book value....... $27,800 Book value of portion lost: ¼ × $27,800......... $ 6,950	Policy carried............ $35,000 Value of buildings at date of fire, as agreed by insured and insurer........... 32,000 Amount recoverable from insurance company: ¼ × $32,000......... 8,000

Entries for the fire loss are given on the following page. These are given in three groups: (1) entries that bring asset book values up to date so that the loss may be determined, (2) entries that record the assets lost, and (3) entries that record the amounts recoverable from salvage and due from the insurance companies. Explanations for the entries are not given; however, each entry requires an explanation accompanied by the data that were used in arriving at the reported amounts.

Entries to adjust the accounts and to record the fire loss may be transferred to the ledger, but nominal accounts may be left open and transactions for the remainder of the fiscal period recorded therein. At the end of the period, then, nominal accounts will reflect activities for

---

[1]Under policies written in some states, payment by the insurer on a policy may serve to cancel that portion of the policy paid by the insured. When this is the case, any unexpired insurance balance applicable to the portion of the policy paid should be written off as an addition to the fire loss account.

the entire period and statements can be prepared summarizing activities in the usual manner. Any differences that are found during the period between amounts originally stated to be recoverable from insurance and amounts actually recovered should be charged or credited to the fire loss account, thus correcting this balance to the loss actually sustained.

(1) Entries to Bring Asset Book Values up to Date

(a)	Income Summary........................	12,250	
	Inventory[1]............................		12,250
(b)	Inventory.............................	18,000	
	Income Summary......................		18,000
(c)	Depreciation Expense — Equipment...........	375	
	Accumulated Depreciation — Equipment.....		375
(d)	Depreciation Expense — Buildings.............	200	
	Accumulated Depreciation — Buildings.......		200

(2) Entries to Record Assets Lost by Fire

(e)	Fire Loss..............................	18,000	
	Inventory.............................		18,000
(f)	Fire Loss..............................	1,875	
	Accumulated Depreciation — Equipment.......	3,125	
	Equipment.............................		5,000
(g)	Fire Loss..............................	6,950	
	Accumulated Depreciation — Buildings.........	1,050	
	Buildings.............................		8,000

(3) Entries to Record Amounts Recoverable from Salvage and Due from Insurance Companies

(h)	Salvage Goods...........................	1,400	
	Fire Loss..............................		1,400
(i)	Recoverable from Insurance Companies........	12,500	
	Fire Loss..............................		12,500
(j)	Recoverable from Insurance Companies........	2,600	
	Fire Loss..............................		2,600
(k)	Recoverable from Insurance Companies........	8,000	
	Fire Loss..............................		8,000

The total amount recoverable from the insurance companies is $23,100 and this balance would be reported as a current asset if current settlement is anticipated. The fire loss account reports a debit balance of $2,325; this is the "Loss from Fire."

Because the insurance proceeds are based upon appraised values, insurance proceeds may exceed the book value of assets destroyed, resulting in a credit balance in the fire loss account. If the assets that are destroyed must be replaced at current market prices, such a credit

---

[1]It is assumed that the opening inventory balance is $12,250; this balance is closed to Income Summary. The inventory on the date of the fire is recorded in entry (b) by a charge to the asset and a credit to Income Summary; the credit represents a subtraction item from goods available for the period in arriving at the cost of goods sold. The inventory balance as of the date of the fire is transferred to the fire loss account in entry (e).

balance can hardly be viewed as indicating an economic gain. The credit balance may be designated for reporting purposes, "Excess of Insurance and Salvage over Book Value of Assets Lost by Fire."

QUESTIONS

1. Distinguish between the terms "plant," "property," "tangible fixed assets," and "intangible fixed assets."

2. Which of the following items are properly shown under the heading "Land, buildings, and equipment"?
- (a) Deposits on machinery not yet received.
- (b) Idle equipment awaiting sale.
- (c) Property held for investment purposes.
- (d) Land held for possible future plant site.

3. (a) Distinguish between capital expenditures and revenue expenditures. (b) Give five examples of each.

4. Which of the following items would be recorded as a revenue expenditure and which would be recorded as a capital expenditure?
- (a) Cost of installing machinery.
- (b) Cost of moving and reinstalling machinery.
- (c) Extensive repairs as a result of fire.
- (d) Cost of grading land.
- (e) Insurance on machinery in transit.
- (f) Bond discount amortization during construction period.
- (g) Cost of major overhaul on machinery.
- (h) New safety guards on machinery.
- (i) Commission on purchase of real estate.
- (j) Special tax assessment for street improvements.
- (k) Cost of repainting offices.

5. Indicate the effects of the following errors on the balance sheet and the income statement in the current year and in succeeding years:
- (a) The cost of a depreciable asset is incorrectly recorded as a revenue expenditure.
- (b) A revenue expenditure is incorrectly recorded as an addition to the cost of a depreciable asset.

6. The controller for the Alston Co. insists that since discounts received on merchandise purchases are treated as revenue, consistency requires that a similar practice be followed for discounts received on land and buildings and equipment acquisitions. Evaluate the controller's position.

7. The Robinson Co. trades an asset for a similar new one, the trade-in value of the old asset being less than its book value. (a) What is the disposition of this difference for income tax purposes? (b) Would you recommend similar treatment in the accounts? Explain.

8. What is meant by a business "pooling of interest"? How does this differ from a business "purchase"?

9. Whitehaven, Inc., decides to construct a building for itself and plans to use whatever plant facilities it has to further such construction. (a) What costs will enter into the cost of construction? (b) What two positions can the company take with respect to general overhead allocation during the period of construction? Evaluate each position and indicate your preference.

10. The Cranney Co. decides to construct a piece of specialized machinery using personnel from the maintenance department. Personnel were instructed to schedule their work so that all overtime hours were charged to the machinery. Evaluate the practice as it relates to the resulting cost of the machine.

11. When the Bowman Corporation finds that the lowest bid it can get on the construction of an addition to its building is $40,000, it proceeds to erect the building with its own workmen and equipment. (a) Assuming that the cost of construction is $35,000, how would you treat the savings? (b) Assuming the cost of construction is $50,000, how would you treat the excess cost?

12. The Parkinson Corporation acquires land and buildings valued at $250,000 as a gift from Industrial City. The president of the company maintains that since there was no cost for the acquisition, neither cost of the facilities nor depreciation needs to be recognized for financial statement purposes. Evaluate the president's position assuming (a) the donation is unconditional; (b) the donation is contingent upon the employment by the company of a certain number of employees for a ten-year period.

13. In the balance sheets of many companies, the largest classification of assets in amount is fixed assets. Name the items, in addition to the amount paid to the former owner or contractor, that may be properly included as part of the acquisition cost of the following property items: (a) land, (b) buildings, and (c) equipment.

14. Distinguish between (a) maintenance and repairs, (b) ordinary repairs and extraordinary repairs, (c) betterments and additions.

15. Machinery in the finishing department of the Washburn Co., although less than 50% depreciated, has been replaced by new machinery. The company expects to find a buyer for the old machinery, and on December 31 the machinery is in the yards and available for inspection. How should it be reported on the balance sheet?

16. (a) What is a coinsurance clause and why is it found in policies? (b) Prepare a formula, accompanied by a rule or explanation, for determining the liability of an insurance company when a coinsurance clause is included.

EXERCISES

1. Holand, Inc., acquires a machine that is priced at $2,400. Payment of this amount may be made within 60 days; a 2% discount is allowed if cash is paid at time of purchase. Give the entry to record the acquisition, assuming:

(a) Cash is paid at time of purchase.
(b) Payment is to be made at the end of 60 days.
(c) A deferred payment plan is agreed upon whereby a down payment of $200 is made with 12 payments of $200 to be made at monthly intervals thereafter.

2. The Henriksen Co. acquired land, buildings, and equipment items at a lump-sum price of $75,000. An appraisal of the assets at the time of acquisition disclosed the following values.

Land...	$20,000
Buildings..	30,000
Equipment..	40,000

What cost should be assigned to each asset?

3. A piece of equipment which cost $20,000 has a book value on December 31, 1972, of $8,000. It is traded in on new equipment, cost $25,000; $10,500 was allowed as the trade-in value, the balance being paid in cash.

(a) What entry is required to record the transaction?
(b) What is the cost basis of the new equipment for income tax purposes?

4. ABC Co. purchased a new milling machine. The following data relate to the purchase:

Invoice price of new machine to ABC Co. — $10,000.
Price of new machine with "no trade-in" deal — $9,200.
Terms of sale — 2%, 10 days, net 30 days on cash payment portion of purchase.
The ABC Co. received a trade-in allowance of $6,000 on a machine that cost $12,000 new and had a present book value of $4,000.
The Express Delivery Service charged ABC Co. $300 to deliver the machine.

Give the entry to record the acquisition of the new machine.

5. Downtown Stores acquires a delivery truck, making payment of $1,781.46, the payment being analyzed as follows:

Price of truck...	$2,208.00
Charges for extra equipment.........................	124.00
State sales tax, 3% of $2,332.00......................	69.96
Insurance for one year.................................	88.00
License and tax for remainder of 1972..................	41.50
	$2,531.46
Less trade-in allowed on old truck.....................	750.00
Cash paid...	$1,781.46

The old truck cost $2,000 and had a book value of $550 on the date of the trade. Give the entry to be made by Downtown Stores to record the exchange, assuming each of the following procedures:

(a) Any difference between the book value of the asset traded in and the trade-in allowance is recognized as an extraordinary gain or loss.

(b) Any difference between the book value of the asset traded in and the trade-in allowance is recognized as an adjustment in the basis of the new asset in accordance with income tax requirements.

6. The Broadway Co. enters into a contract with the Sharp Construction Co. for construction of an office building at a cost of $600,000. Upon completion of construction, the Sharp Construction Co. agrees to accept in full payment of the contract price Broadway Co. 6% bonds with a face value of $300,000 and common stock with a par value of $275,000. Broadway Co. bonds are selling on the market at this time at 95. How would you recommend that the building acquisition be recorded?

7. The Pentel Company acquired land in exchange for 5,000 shares of its common stock, par $10, and cash of $25,000. The land was recorded at $75,000. The auditor ascertains that the company's stock was selling on the market at $8 when the purchase was made. What correcting entry should be made?

8. The Milroy Corporation summarizes manufacturing and construction activities for 1972 as follows:

	On Product Manufacture	On Building Wing Construction
Materials.....................	$120,000	$24,000
Direct labor..................	105,000	30,000

Overhead for 1971 was 80% of the direct labor cost. Overhead in 1972 related to both product manufacture and construction activities totaled $91,500.

(a) Calculate the cost of the building addition, assuming that manufacturing activities are to be charged with overhead at the rate experienced in 1971 and that construction activities are to be charged with the excess.

(b) Calculate the cost of the addition if manufacturing and construction activities are to be charged with overhead at the same rate.

9. The following expenditures were incurred by the Vincent Co. in 1972: purchase of land, $90,000; land survey, $600; fees for search of title on land, $350; building permit, $250; temporary quarters for construction crews, $1,500; payment to tenants of old building for vacating premises, $2,000; razing of old building, $2,000; excavation for basement, $6,000; special assessment taxes for street project, $2,000; dividends, $5,000; damages awarded for injuries sustained in construction,

$4,200 (no insurance was carried; the cost of insurance would have been $200); interest on temporary construction loan, $3,000; costs of construction, $180,000, cost of paving parking lot adjoining building, $2,500; cost of shrubs, trees, and other landscaping, $1,500. What is the cost of the land and the cost of the building?

10. The Murray Motors Corp. acquired land and old buildings at a cost of $60,000. Delinquent taxes of $6,000 were paid, as well as attorney's fees of $2,000 for legal work in connection with the purchase of the property. Buildings were removed at a cost of $4,000, but $1,000 was realized from the sale of salvaged materials. From January 1 to April 1 buildings were constructed at a cost of $75,000. Buildings were occupied on April 1. Cost of insurance on buildings taken out on January 1 was $3,000 for a 3-year period. How could land and buildings be carried on the books at the end of the year?

11. The Morning Dairy Company bills its customers for milk bottles. During July the total amount billed for milk and bottles was $50,750. Of this amount, $3,500 was for the bottles. Bottles were returned by customers and customers were given credit for $2,750 on such returns. The cost of bottles not returned was determined to be $500. The cost of bottles is carried in a property account, "Containers."

Give the entries to record the transactions for July.

12. One of the most difficult problems facing an accountant is the determination of which expenditures should be deferred as assets and which should be immediately charged off as expense. What position would you take in each of the following instances?

    (a) Painting of partitions in large room recently divided into 4 sections.

    (b) Labor cost of tearing down wall to permit extension of assembly line.

    (c) Replacement of motor on machine. Life used to depreciate machine is 8 years. Machine is 4 years old. Replacement of the motor was anticipated when machine was purchased.

    (d) Cost of grading land prior to construction.

    (e) Assessment for street paving.

    (f) Cost of moving and reinstalling equipment.

    (g) Cost of tearing down an old building in preparation for new construction; old building is fully depreciated.

13. A fire insurance policy on buildings has a face value of $90,000 and an 80% coinsurance clause. Assuming that buildings have a fair value of $150,000 on the date of a fire, what amount will be recovered if the fire loss totals are: (a) $60,000; (b) $110,000; (c) $140,000?

14. The Browning Company purchased a building for $80,000 on August 1, 1964. Depreciation was recorded at 3% a year. On October 31, 1972, 50% of the building was destroyed. On this date the building had a fair market value of $100,000. A policy for $60,000 was carried on the building, the policy containing a 80% coinsurance clause. What entries would be made to record (a) the loss from destruction of the building, and (b) the amount due from the insurance company? (Assume that the company's fiscal period is the calendar year.)

15. Part of the buildings owned by the Wilcoxsen Manufacturing Co. are destroyed by fire. Buildings are carried on the books at a value of $80,000; their sound value on the date of the fire is established at $125,000. Assuming that insurance policies contain an 80% coinsurance clause, give the amounts recoverable from each insurance company in the following cases:

(a) One half of the buildings are destroyed.
   Policies are carried as follows: with A Co............... $50,000
                                    with B Co............... 25,000
(b) Buildings are wholly destroyed.
   Policies are carried as follows: with A Co............... $78,000
                                    with B Co............... 52,000
(c) Buildings are wholly destroyed; recoverable salvage is estimated at $11,000.
   Policies are carried as follows: with A Co............... $70,000
                                    with B Co............... 35,000

PROBLEMS

13-1. The following transactions were completed by the Northland Co. during 1972:

Mar. 1	Purchased real property for $89,750 which included a charge of $750 representing property taxes for March 1–June 30 that had been prepaid by the vendor Twenty percent of the purchase price is deemed applicable to land and the balance to buildings. A mortgage of $60,000 was assumed by the Northland Co. on the purchase.
Mar. 2–30	Previous owners had failed to take care of normal maintenance and repairs requirements on the building, necessitating current reconditioning at a cost of $8,300.
Apr. 1–May 15	Garages in the rear of the buildings were demolished, $500 being recovered on the lumber salvage. The company itself proceeded to construct a warehouse. The cost of such construction was $12,500 which was almost exactly the same as bids made on the construction by independent contractors. Upon completion of construction, city inspectors ordered extensive modifications in the buildings as a result of failure on the part of the company to comply with the Building Safety Code. Such modifications, which could have been avoided, cost $3,000.
Nov. 5–20	A fire of unknown origin destroyed the building show windows and entrance. The amount of the fire loss was estimated at $4,000, which included display merchandise of $750 and fixtures of $500, and the full amount of the loss was immediately

recovered from the insurance company. A new entrance and windows of modern design were completed at a cost of $6,800.

Dec. 29–31   The business was closed to permit taking the year-end inventory. During this period, required redecorating and repairs were completed at a cost of $600.

Instructions: Give journal entries to record each of the preceding transactions. (Disregard depreciation.)

13-2. On December 31, 1972, the Aerospace Co. shows the following account for machinery that it had assembled for its own use during 1972:

Machinery (Job Order #62)

Cost of dismantling old machine.....................	570	Cash proceeds from sale of old machine.................	500
Raw materials used in construction of new machine..	13,600	Depreciation for 1972, 10% of $34,620.................	3,462
Labor in construction of new machine................	9,800		
Cost of installation..........	1,400		
Materials spoiled in machine trial runs................	600		
Profit on construction........	6,900		
Purchase of machine tools....	2,250		

An analysis of the detail in the account discloses the following:

(a) The old machine, which was removed in the installation of the new one, had been fully depreciated.

(b) Cash discounts received on the payments for materials used in construction totaled $400 and these were reported in the purchases discount account.

(c) The factory overhead account shows a balance of $52,000 for the year ended December 31, 1972; this balance exceeds normal overhead on regular plant activities by approximately $2,900 and is attributable to machine construction.

(d) A profit was recognized on construction for the difference between costs incurred and the price at which the machine could have been purchased.

(e) Machine tools have an estimated life of 3 years; machinery has an estimated life of 10 years. The machinery was used for production beginning on September 1, 1972.

Instructions: (1) Set up machinery and machine tools accounts as they should appear at the end of 1972.

(2) Give individual journal entries that are necessary to correct the accounts as of December 31, 1972, assuming that the nominal accounts are still open.

13-3. The Walstead Company buys the land, building, and machinery of the Ryan Company for $35,000. The building and machinery are in very poor condition. It is expected that the building will be torn down and replaced, and that, before the machinery is used, expenditures of $5,000 will be required, after which the machinery will have a value of $25,000. The books of the Ryan Company show that the land cost $2,500 (present land values are estimated to be 10 times as great as when this land was acquired); the building cost $16,000 on which accumulated depreciation of $12,800 had been recognized; and the machinery cost $60,000, on which accumulated depreciation of $35,000 had been recognized.

Instructions: (1) Prepare the journal entries to record the purchase.

(2) Prepare the journal entry for the repair costs of $10,000 on the machinery.

13-4. The Mercury Company planned to open a new store. The company narrowed the possible sites to two lots and decided to take purchase options on both lots while they studied traffic densities in both areas. They paid $1,800 for the option on Lot A and $2,400 for the option on Lot B. After studying traffic densities, they decided to purchase Lot B. The company opened a single real estate account that shows the following:

Debits:	Option on Lot A.............................	$ 1,800
	Option on Lot B.............................	2,400
	Payment of balance on Lot B..................	40,000
	Title insurance..............................	700
	Assessment for street improvement..............	1,200
	Recording fee for deed........................	50
	Cost of razing old building on Lot B.............	3,000
	Payment for erection of new building............	100,000
Credit:	Sale of salvaged materials from old building.......	2,000

The salvage value of material obtained from the old building and used in the erection of the new building was $2,500. The depreciated value of the old building, as shown by the books of the company from which the purchase was made, was $12,000. The old building was razed immediately after the purchase.

Instructions: (1) Determine the cost of the land, listing the items that are included in the total.

(2) Determine the cost of the new building, listing the items that are included in the total.

13-5. The Ambassador Corporation was organized in June 1972. In auditing the books of the company, you find a land, buildings, and equipment account with the following detail:

Land, Buildings, and Equipment

Date	Item	Debits
1972		
June 8	Organization fees paid to the state....................	$ 1,000
16	Bond discount.......................................	2,400
16	Land site and old building...........................	250,000
30	Corporate organization costs.........................	2,500
July 2	Title clearance fees..................................	2,800
Aug. 28	Cost of razing old building...........................	4,000
Sept. 1	Salaries of Ambassador Corporation executives..........	10,600
Dec. 12	Stock bonus to corporate promoters, 2,000 shares of common stock, $10 par value............................	20,000

Date	Item	Debits
Dec. 15	Bond interest, six months............................	$ 2,000
15	County real estate tax................................	3,600
15	Cost of new building completed and occupied on this date.	620,000

An analysis of the foregoing account and of other accounts disclosed the following additional information:

(a) The building acquired on June 16, 1972, was valued at $35,000.

(b) The company paid $4,000 for the demolition of the old building, then sold the scrap for $200 and credited the proceeds to Miscellaneous Income.

(c) The company executives did not participate in the construction of the new building.

(d) Bonds with a face value of $100,000, and payable in 10 years, were sold to an underwriting syndicate at $97,600 to complete the financing of the new building.

(e) The county real estate tax was for the six-month period ended December 31, 1972, and was assessed by the county on the land.

Instructions: Prepare journal entries to correct the books of the Ambassador Corporation. Each entry should include an explanation.

13-6. The Triumph Company completed a program of expansion and improvement of its plant during 1972. You are provided with the following information concerning its buildings account:

(a) On October 31, 1972, a 30-foot extension to the present factory building was completed at a contract cost of $52,000.

(b) During the course of construction, the following costs were incurred for the removal of the end wall of the building where the extension was being constructed:

(1) Payroll costs during the month of April arising from employees' time spent in removal of the wall, $3,215.

(2) Payments to a salvage company for removing unusual debris, $520.

(c) The cost of the original structure allocable to the end wall was estimated to be $17,600, with accumulated depreciation thereon of $7,400; $3,926 was received by Triumph Company from the construction company for windows and other assorted materials salvaged from the old wall.

(d) The old flooring was covered with a new type long-lasting floor covering at a cost of $2,860.

(e) The interior of the plant was painted in new, bright colors for a contract price of $3,250.

(f) New and improved shelving was installed at a cost of $178.

(g) Old electrical wiring was replaced at a cost of $6,812. Cost of the old wiring was determined to be $3,100 with accumulated depreciation to date of $1,370.

(h) New electrical fixtures using flourescent bulbs were installed. The new fixtures were purchased on the installment plan; the schedule of monthly payments showed total payments of $6,200. which included interest and carrying charges of $480. The old fixtures were carried at a cost of $1,860, with accumulated depreciation to date of $796. The old fixtures had no scrap value.

Instructions: Prepare journal entries including explanations for the above information. Briefly justify the capitalization v. revenue decision for each item.

13-7. A building with a fair market value of $300,000 is insured under a policy containing a coinsurance clause. Determine the amount recoverable from the insurance company under each of the following assumptions:

	Amount of Loss	Face of Policy	Percentage Coinsurance Clause
(a)	$130,000	$225,000	75%
(b)	260,000	250,000	80
(c)	70,000	157,500	70
(d)	180,000	120,000	50
(e)	210,000	150,000	70
(f)	180,000	200,000	80
(g)	297,000	240,000	90
(h)	300,000	350,000	80

13-8. On March 1, 1970, the Mooney Co. took out a $90,000, 4-year fire insurance policy on a building that was completed at a cost of $160,000 at the end of June, 1954. The insurance policy contains an 80% coinsurance clause. Depreciation is calculated at 2½% annually. On July 5, 1972, the building was 50% destroyed by fire. The insurance company accepted a sound value for the property of $125,000 and agreed to make settlement on this basis. The fiscal period for the Mooney Co. is the calendar year.

Instructions: Prepare the journal entries necessary as of July 5, 1972, to summarize the foregoing information in the fire loss account and to close the account to Income Summary.

13-9. The Valley Manufacturing Company was incorporated on January 2, 1972, but was unable to begin manufacturing activities until July 1, 1972, when the new factory facilities were completed.

The land and building account at December 31, 1972, was as follows:

Date	Item	Amount
1972		
Jan. 31	Land and building....................................	$ 98,000
Feb. 28	Cost of removal of building.........................	1,500
May 1	Partial payment of new construction..................	35,000
May 1	Legal fees paid......................................	2,000
June 1	Second payment on new construction..................	30,000
June 1	Insurance premium...................................	1,800
June 1	Special tax assessment..............................	2,500
June 30	General expenses....................................	12,000
July 1	Final payment on new construction...................	35,000
Dec. 31	Asset write-up......................................	12,200
		$230,000
Dec. 31	Depreciation — 1972 at 1%..........................	2,300
	Account balance.....................................	$227,700

The following additional information is to be considered:

(a) To acquire land and building the company paid $48,000 cash and 500 shares of its 5% cumulative preferred stock, par value $100 per share.

(b) Cost of removal of old buildings amounted to $1,500 with the demolition company retaining all materials of the building.

(c) Legal fees covered the following:

Cost of organization..................................	$ 500
Examination of title covering purchase of land..........	1,000
Legal work in connection with construction contract.....	500
	$2,000

(d) Insurance premium covered premiums for three-year term beginning May 1, 1972.

(e) General expenses covered the following for the period from January 2, 1972 to June 30, 1972:

President's salary....................................	$ 6,000
Plant superintendent covering supervision of new building.	5,000
Office salaries.......................................	1,000
	$12,000

(f) The special tax assessment covered street improvements.

(g) Because of a general increase in construction costs after entering into the building contract, the Board of Directors increased the value of the building $12,200, believing such increase justified to reflect current market at the time building completed. Retained Earnings was credited for this amount.

(h) Estimated life of building — 50 years.
Write-off for 1972 — 1% of asset value (1% of $230,000 = $2,300).

Instructions: (1) Prepare entries to reflect correct land, buildings, and accumulated depreciation accounts at December 31, 1972. Post the entries for land and buildings to skeleton "T" ledger accounts or list them in a schedule.

(2) Show the proper presentation of land, buildings, and accumulated depreciation on the balance sheet at December 31, 1972.

(AICPA adapted)

13-10. In your examination of the financial statements of Gaar Corporation at December 31, 1972 you observe the contents of certain accounts and other pertinent information as follows:

Building

Date	Explanation	LF	Debit	Credit	Balance
12/31/71	Balance................	X	$100,000		$100,000
7/ 1/72	New boiler.............	CD	16,480	$ 1,480	115,000
9/ 1/72	Insurance recovery......	CR		2,000	113,000

Accumulated Depreciation — Building

Date	Explanation	LF	Debit	Credit	Balance
12/31/71	Balance — 15 years @ 4% of $100,000...........	X		$60,000	$ 60,000
12/31/72	Annual depreciation.....	GJ		4,440	64,440

You learn that on June 15 the company's old high-pressure boiler exploded. Damage to the building was insignificant but the boiler was replaced by a more efficient oil-burning boiler. The company received $2,000 as an insurance adjustment under terms of its policy for damage to the boiler.

The disbursement voucher charged to the building account on July 1, 1972, is reproduced below:

To: REX HEATING COMPANY
List price — new oil-burning boiler
   (including fuel oil tank and 5,000 gallons fuel oil)........ $16,000
Sales tax — 3% of $16,000............................. 480

   Total... $16,480

Less:
Allowance for old coal-burning boiler in building — to be removed at the expense of the Rex Heating Company...... 1,480

   Total price.................................... $15,000

In vouching the expenditure you determine that the terms included a 2% cash discount which was properly computed and taken. The sales tax and the fuel oil are not subject to discount.

Your audit discloses that a voucher for $1,000 was paid to Emment Co. on July 2, 1972, and charged to the repair expense account. The voucher is adequately supported and is marked "installation costs for new oil-burning boiler."

The company's fuel oil supplier advises that fuel oil had a market price of 16¢ per gallon July 1 and 18¢ per gallon December 31. The fuel oil inventory at December 31 was 2,000 gallons.

A review of subsidiary property records discloses that the replaced coal-burning boiler was installed when the building was constructed and was recorded at a cost of $10,000. According to its manufacturers the new boiler should be serviceable for 15 years.

In computing depreciation for retirements Gaar Corporation consistently treats a fraction of a month as a full month.

Instructions: Prepare the adjusting journal entries that you would suggest for the books of Gaar Corporation. The books have not been closed. Support your entries with computations in good form.

(AICPA adapted)

13-11. Ellford Corporation received a $400,000 low bid from a reputable manufacturer for the construction of special production equipment needed by Ellford in an expansion program. Because the company's own plant was not operating at capacity, Ellford decided to construct the equipment there and recorded the following production costs related to the construction:

Services of consulting engineer........................	$ 10,000
Work subcontracted.................................	20,000
Materials..	200,000
Plant labor normally assigned to production.............	65,000
Plant labor normally assigned to maintenance...........	100,000
Total...	$395,000

Management prefers to record the cost of the equipment under the incremental cost method. Approximately 40% of the corporation's production is devoted to government supply contracts which are all based in some way on cost. The contracts require that any self-constructed equipment be allocated its full share of all costs related to the construction.

The following information is also available:

(a) The above production labor was for partial fabrication of the equipment in the plant. Skilled personnel were required and were assigned from other projects. The maintenance labor would have been idle time of nonproduction plant employees who would have been retained on the payroll whether or not their services were utilized.

(b) Payroll taxes and employee fringe benefits are approximately 30% of labor cost and are included in manufacturing overhead cost. Total manufacturing overhead for the year was $5,630,000 including the $100,000 maintenance labor used to construct the equipment.

(c) Manufacturing overhead is approximately 50% variable and is applied on the basis of production labor cost. Production labor cost for the year for the corporation's normal products totaled $6,810,000.

(d) General and administrative expenses include $22,500 of executive salary cost and $10,500 of postage, telephone, supplies and miscellaneous expenses identifiable with this equipment construction.

Instructions: (1) Prepare a schedule computing the amount that should be reported as the full cost of the constructed equipment to meet the requirements of the government contracts. Any supporting computations should be in good form.

(2) Prepare a schedule computing the incremental cost of the constructed equipment.

(3) What is the greatest amount that should be capitalized as the cost of the equipment? Why?

(AICPA adapted)

13-12. A fire at the Roseville plant of Rose Distributors completely destroyed a building on July 1, 1972. The company had insured the building against fire with two companies under the following three-year policies:

Company	Face	Coinsurance Clause	Unexpired Premium 1/1/72	Date of Expiration
Metropolitan	$100,000	80%	$ 800	8/31/72
Universal	97,500	90%	1,200	8/31/72

An umpire set the insurable value at date of the fire at $325,000 and the loss at $315,000. In spite of this ruling, there proved to be no net salvage value recoverable from the building. The building was carried on the books of the corporation at a cost of $197,500 less accumulated depreciation charged to operations to date of fire of $37,500.

Instructions: (1) Compute the amount recoverable under each insurance policy and the total amount recoverable. You *must* set forth the formula which you use in making your computation.

(2) Compute the balance of the fire loss account after such of the above data as affect it have been recorded. Label clearly the various elements entering into your computation.   (AICPA adapted)

13-13. The ABC Corporation is a small manufacturing company producing a highly flammable cleaning fluid. On May 31, 1972, the company had a fire which completely destroyed the processing building and the in-process inventory; some of the equipment was saved.

The cost of the fixed assets destroyed and their related accumulated depreciation accounts at May 31, 1972 were as follows:

	Cost	Allowance
Buildings...............................	$40,000	$24,667
Equipment.............................	15,000	4,375

At present prices the cost to replace the destroyed property would be: building, $80,000; equipment, $37,500. At the time of the fire it was determined that the destroyed building was 62½% depreciated, and the destroyed equipment was 33⅓% depreciated. The insurable value of all the building and equipment was determined to be $75,000.

After the fire a physical inventory was taken. The raw materials were valued at $30,000, the finished goods at $60,000, and supplies at $5,000.

The inventories on January 1, 1972 consisted of:

Raw materials.......................................	$ 15,000
Goods in process....................................	50,000
Finished goods......................................	70,000
Supplies..	2,000
Total..	$137,000

A review of the accounts showed that the sales and gross profit for the last five years were:

	Sales	Gross Profit
1967....................................	$300,000	$ 86,200
1968....................................	320,000	102,400
1969....................................	330,000	108,900
1970....................................	250,000	62,500
1971....................................	280,000	84,000

The sales for the first five months of 1972 were $150,000. Raw materials purchases were $50,000. Freight on purchases was $5,000.

Direct labor for the five months was $40,000; for the past five years manufacturing overhead was 50% of direct labor.

Insurance on the property and inventory was carried with three companies. Each policy included an 80% coinsurance clause. The amount of insurance carried with the various companies was:

	Buildings and Equipment	Inventories
Company A...................	$30,000	$38,000
Company B...................	20,000	35,000
Company C...................	15,000	35,000

The cost of cleaning up the debris was $7,000. The value of the scrap salvaged from the fire was $600.

Instructions: (1) Compute the value of inventory lost.

(2) Compute the expected recovery from each insurance company.

(AICPA adapted)

chapter 14

land, buildings, and
equipment - depreciation
and depletion

In spite of expenditures for maintenance and repairs, the time ultimately comes when all building and equipment items can no longer make a favorable contribution to business activities and must be retired. The costs of these assets must be allocated to revenues over the limited duration of the assets' usefulness. *Depreciation* represents the decline in service potential of the asset that occurred during the period.

The Committee on Terminology of the American Institute of Certified Public Accountants has defined depreciation accounting as follows:

> *Depreciation accounting* is a system of accounting which aims to distribute the cost or other basic value of tangible capital assets, less salvage (if any), over the estimated useful life of the unit (which may be a group of assets) in a systematic and rational manner. It is a process of allocation, not of valuation. *Depreciation for the year* is the portion of the total charge under such a system that is allocated to the year. Although the allocation may properly take into account occurrences during the year, it is not intended to be a measurement of the effect of all such occurrences.[1]

It should be noted that the term "depreciation" is used in a specialized sense in accounting. It is the systematic allocation of cost in recognition of the exhaustion of asset life and is applicable only to those tangible assets that are used by the business. Depreciation is not used to designate a decline in market value as the term is popularly employed. Nor is the term used to designate the physical change in an asset, for an asset may show little physical decline in the early years and may have significant physical utility even at the time of its retirement. It is not used to designate the charge for using up wasting assets, which is termed *depletion*, nor to designate the allocation of costs over a period of time for

---

[1]*Accounting Terminology Bulletin No. 1*, "Review and Resumé" (New York: American Institute of Certified Public Accountants, 1953), par. 56.

limited-life intangible assets, which is termed *amortization*. Depreciation does not refer to a decrease in value assigned to marketable securities as a result of market decline, or to a decrease in value assigned to inventories as a result of obsolescence, spoilage, or other deterioration. The suggestion is frequently made that a term such as "property cost allocation" be used in place of "depreciation" to avoid any misinterpretation.

Factors determining the periodic depreciation charge

Three factors must be recognized in arriving at the periodic charge for the use of a depreciable property item: (1) *asset cost*, (2) *residual or salvage value*, and (3) *useful life*.

Asset cost. The *cost* of a property item includes all of the expenditures relating to its acquisition and preparation for use as described in Chapter 13. Expenditures considered to be related to revenues of future periods are thus capitalized and form the base for depreciation charges.

Residual or salvage value. The *residual* or *salvage value* of a depreciable asset is the amount which can reasonably be expected to be realized upon retirement of an asset. This may depend upon the retirement policy of the company as well as market conditions and other factors. If, for example, the company normally uses equipment until it is physically exhausted and no longer serviceable, the residual value, represented by the scrap or junk that may be salvaged, may be only nominal. But if the company normally trades its equipment after a relatively short period of use, the residual value, represented by the value in trade, may be relatively high. In some cases the cost of dismantling and removing an asset may equal or exceed the residual value. From a theoretical point of view, any estimated residual value should be subtracted from cost in arriving at the depreciable cost of the asset; on the other hand, dismantling and removal costs that are expected to exceed the ultimate salvage value should be added to the cost in arriving at the asset's depreciable cost.

In practice, both salvage values and dismantling and removal costs are frequently ignored in developing periodic depreciation charges. Disregard of these items is not objectionable when they are relatively small and not subject to reasonable estimate and when it is doubtful whether greater accuracy will be gained through such refinement of the depreciation estimate.

Useful life. Buildings and equipment items have a limited *useful life* as a result of certain *physical* and *functional* factors. The physical factors that move a property item towards its ultimate retirement are (1) *wear* *and tear*, (2) *deterioration and decay*, and (3) *damage or destruction.* Everyone is familiar with the processes of wear and tear that render an automobile, a typewriter, or furniture no longer usable. The deterioration and the decay of an asset through aging, whether the asset is used or not, is also well known. Finally, fire, flood, earthquake, or accident may reduce or terminate the useful life of an asset.

The functional factors that limit the life of a property item are (1) *inadequacy* and (2) *obsolescence.* An asset may lose its usefulness when, as a result of altered business requirements, it can no longer carry the productive load and requires replacement. Although the asset is still usable, its inadequacy for present purposes has cut short its service life. An asset may also lose its usefulness as a result of consumer demand for new and different products or services or as a result of technical progress and the availability of other assets that can be more economically employed. In such instances, obsolescence is the factor that operates to limit service life.

Depreciation accounting calls for the recognition of both the physical and functional factors that limit the useful life of an asset. Physical factors are more readily apparent than functional factors in predicting the asset life. But when certain functional factors hasten the retirement of an asset, these must also be recognized. Both physical and functional factors may operate gradually or may emerge in sudden fashion. Recognition of depreciation is usually limited to the conditions that operate gradually and are reasonably foreseeable. For example, a sudden change in demand for a certain product may make a property item worthless, or an accident may destroy a property item, but these are unforeseeable events that call for the recognition of extraordinary charges at the time they occur.

Since the service life of an asset is affected by maintenance and repairs, the policy that is operative with respect to these matters must be considered in estimating useful life. Low standards of maintenance and repair keep these charges at a minimum but may hasten the physical deterioration of the asset, thus requiring higher-than-normal allocations for depreciation. On the other hand, high standards of maintenance and repairs will mean higher charges for these items; but with a policy that prolongs the usefulness of assets, allocations for depreciation may be reduced.

The useful life of a property item may be expressed in terms of either an estimated *time* factor or an estimated *use* factor. The time factor may be a period of months or years; the use factor may be a number of hours of service or a number of units of output. The cost of the property item flows into production in accordance with the lapse of time or degrees of use. The rate of cost flow may be modified by other factors, but basically depreciation must be measured on a time or use basis.[1]

In arriving at the useful life of an asset, it is necessary to consider the *pattern of use* and focus upon how the asset's services are actually to be used over that life. Service cost is being matched against revenue. If the asset produces a varying revenue pattern, then the depreciation charges should vary in a corresponding manner. When depreciation is measured in terms of a time factor, the pattern of use must be estimated. Several somewhat arbitrary methods have come into common use. Each method represents a different pattern and is designed to make the time basis approximate the use basis. The time factor is employed in two general classes of methods, *straight-line depreciation* and *decreasing-charge depreciation*. When depreciation is measured in terms of a use factor, the units of use must be estimated. The depreciation charge varies periodically in accordance with the services provided by the asset. The use factor is employed in *service-hours depreciation* and in *productive-output depreciation*.

Recording depreciation

Periodic depreciation could be recorded by a charge to operations and a credit to the property item. Such practice would be consistent with that normally employed in the recognition of periodic charges for intangible assets and other costs. However, it is customary to report the reduction in a depreciable asset in a separate valuation account. When cost allocation is reported in a separate account, original cost, as well as that part of the cost already allocated to revenues, can be provided on the balance sheet. This practice also serves to emphasize the estimates inherent in the allocation process.

A variety of titles are used to designate the valuation balance, such as Accumulated Depreciation, Allowance for Depreciation, and Depreciation Allocated to Past Operations. The term Reserve for Depreciation has also been widely used, but since this title may suggest the existence of a fund available for asset replacement, its use has been discouraged.

A separate valuation account is maintained for each asset or class of assets requiring the use of a separate depreciation rate. When a subsidiary ledger is maintained for land, buildings, and equipment, such record

[1]Prior to 1962 the Internal Revenue Service in *Bulletin "F"* offered a compilation of different assets and their probable useful lives on a time basis as found by normal experiences in various industries to assist taxpayers in establishing appropriate depreciation rates. This publication was superseded in July, 1962, by *Revenue Procedure 62-21*. While the original publication listed depreciation guidelines for thousands of individual items, the present guidelines are limited to 75 broad classes of property items. A further modification of the present guidelines was made in 1971 when the Asset Depreciation Range (ADR) system was installed by the Treasury Department. Under this system, the life of each class of asset has a range 20% above and 20% below the guideline life. This latter modification adds flexibility to the allowed depreciation.

normally provides for the accumulation of depreciation allocations on the individual assets. Separate charges relating to individual property items in the subsidiary ledger support the land, buildings, and equipment balance in the general ledger; separate credits representing individual property item cost allocations in the subsidiary ledger support the accumulated depreciation balance in the general ledger.

When a property item consists of a number of units or structural elements with varying lives and such units are recorded separately, depreciation is recognized in terms of the respective lives of the different units. Retirement of an individual unit and its replacement by a new unit requires the cancellation of cost and accumulated depreciation balances related to the old unit and recognition of the new.

Methods of cost allocation

As mentioned earlier, there are a number of different methods for allocating the costs of depreciable assets. The method that is to be used in any specific instance is frequently a matter of judgment and should be selected to approximate most closely the actual pattern of use of the asset. The following methods are described in this chapter:

Time-factor methods
  1. Straight-line depreciation
  2. Decreasing-charge depreciation
    (a) Declining-balance method
    (b) Double-declining-balance method
    (c) Sum-of-the-years-digits method
Use-factor methods
  1. Service-hours depreciation
  2. Productive-output depreciation

Two other time-factor methods each providing for increasing charges, the *annuity method* and the *sinking fund method*, require the use of compound interest calculations. These methods are rarely encountered in practice and are beyond the scope of the present discussion.

The examples that follow assume the acquisition of a machine at a cost of $10,000 with a salvage value at the end of its useful life of $500. The following symbols are employed in the formulas for the development of depreciation rates:

C = Asset cost
S = Estimated salvage value
n = Estimated life in years, hours of service, or units of output
r = Depreciation rate per period, per hour of service, or per unit of output
D = Annual depreciation charge

Straight-line depreciation. *Straight-line* depreciation relates cost allocation to the passage of time and recognizes equal periodic charges over the life of the asset. The depreciation charge assumes equal usefulness per time period, and in applying this assumption the charge is not affected by asset productivity or efficiency variations. In developing the periodic charge, an estimate is made of the useful life of the asset in terms of months or years. The difference between the asset cost and residual value is divided by the useful life of the asset in arriving at the cost assigned to each time unit.

Using data for the machine referred to earlier and assuming a 10-year life, annual depreciation is determined as follows:

$$D = \frac{C - S}{n}, \text{ or } \frac{\$10,000 - \$500}{10} = \$950$$

The depreciation rate is commonly expressed as a percentage to be applied periodically to asset cost. The depreciation rate in the example is calculated as follows: $(100\% - 5\%) \div 10 = 9.5\%$. This percentage applied to cost provides a periodic charge of $950. The rate may also be expressed as a percentage to be applied to depreciable cost — cost less residual value. Expressed in this way the rate is simply the reciprocal value of the useful life expressed in periods, or r (per period) $= 1 \div n$. In the example, then, the annual rate would be $1 \div 10$, or 10%, and this rate applied to depreciable cost, $9,500, gives an annual charge of $950. A table to summarize the process of cost allocation follows:

Asset Cost Allocation — Straight-Line Method

End of Year	Debit to Depreciation	Credit to Accumulated Depreciation	Balance of Accumulated Depreciation	Asset Book Value
				$10,000
1	$ 950	$ 950	$ 950	9,050
2	950	950	1,900	8,100
3	950	950	2,850	7,150
4	950	950	3,800	6,200
5	950	950	4,750	5,250
6	950	950	5,700	4,300
7	950	950	6,650	3,350
8	950	950	7,600	2,400
9	950	950	8,550	1,450
10	950	950	9,500	500
	$9,500	$9,500		

It was indicated earlier that residual value is frequently ignored when this is only a relatively minor amount. If this were done in the example, a ten-year life would call for the use of a 10% rate; depreciation, then, would be recognized at $1,000 per year instead of $950.

In using the straight-line method, depreciation is a constant or fixed charge of each period. Net income measurements become particularly sensitive to changes in the volume of business activity: with above-normal activity, there is no increase in the depreciation charge; with below-normal activity, revenue is still charged with the costs of assets standing ready to serve. When the life of a property item is affected primarily by the lapse of time rather than by the degree of use, recognition of depreciation as a constant charge is particularly appropriate.

Straight-line depreciation is a widely used procedure. It is readily understood and frequently parallels observable asset deterioration. It has the advantage of simplicity and under normal property conditions offers a satisfactory means of cost allocation. By normal property conditions is meant (1) properties that have been accumulated over a period of years so that the total of depreciation plus maintenance is comparatively even from period to period, and (2) properties whose service potentials are being steadily reduced by functional as well as physical factors. The absence of either of these conditions may suggest the use of some method other than the straight-line method.

Decreasing-charge depreciation.   *Decreasing-charge* or *accelerated* depreciation methods also relate charges for depreciation to time. However, they provide for the highest depreciation charge in the first year of asset use and declining depreciation charges in ensuing years. Such plans are based largely on the assumption that there will be reductions in asset efficiency, output, or other benefits as the asset ages. Such reductions may be accompanied by increased charges for maintenance and repairs. Charges for depreciation decline, then, as the economic advantages afforded through ownership of the asset decline.

Declining-balance method.   The *declining-balance method* provides decreasing charges by applying a constant percentage rate to a declining asset book value. The rate to be applied to the declining book value in producing the estimated salvage value at the end of the useful life of the asset is calculated by the following formula:

$$r \text{ (rate per period applicable to declining book value)} = 1 - \sqrt[n]{S \div C}$$

Using the previous asset data and assuming a 10-year asset life, the depreciation rate is determined as follows:

$$1 - \sqrt[10]{500 \div 10,000} = 1 - \sqrt[10]{.05} = 1 - .74113 = .25887, \text{ or } 25.887\%$$

Dividing the estimated salvage value by cost in the formula above gives .05, the value that the salvage value at the end of 10 years should bear to cost. The tenth root of this value is .74113. Multiplying cost and the successive declining book values by .74113 ten times will reduce the asset to .05 of its cost. The difference between 1 and .74113, or .25887, then, is the rate of decrease to be applied successively in bringing the asset down to .05 of its original balance. Since it is impossible to bring a value down to zero by a constant multiplier, a residual value must be assigned to the asset in using the formula. In the absence of an expected residual value, a nominal value of $1 can be assumed for this purpose.

Depreciation calculated by application of the 25.887% rate to the declining book value is summarized in the table that follows:

Asset Cost Allocation — Declining-Balance Method

End of Year	Debit to Depreciation		Credit to Accumulated Depreciation	Balance of Accumulated Depreciation	Asset Book Value
					$10,000.00
1	(25.887% × $10,000.00)	$2,588.70	$2,588.70	$2,588.70	7,411.30
2	(25.887% × $ 7,411.30)	1,918.56	1,918.56	4,507.26	5,492.74
3	(25.887% × $ 5,492.74)	1,421.91	1,421.91	5,929.17	4,070.83
4	(25.887% × $ 4,070.83)	1,053.82	1,053.82	6,982.99	3,017.01
5	(25.887% × $ 3,017.01)	781.01	781.01	7,764.00	2,236.00
6	(25.887% × $ 2,236.00)	578.83	578.83	8,342.83	1,657.17
7	(25.887% × $ 1,657.17)	428.99	428.99	8,771.82	1,228.18
8	(25.887% × $ 1,228.18)	317.94	317.94	9,089.76	910.24
9	(25.887% × $ 910.24)	235.63	235.63	9,325.39	674.61
10	(25.887% × $ 674.61)	174.64	174.64	9,500.03	499.97
		$9,500.03	$9,500.03		

Instead of developing an exact rate that will produce a salvage value of $500, it is usually more convenient to approximate a rate that will provide satisfactory cost allocation; since depreciation involves an estimate, there is little assurance that rate refinement will produce more accurate results. In the previous illustration, the use of a rate of 25% is more convenient than 25.887%; differences are not material.

Double-declining-balance method. Federal income tax regulations provide that for certain assets, depreciation is allowed at a fixed percentage that is equal to double the straight-line rate. This is referred to as the *double-declining-balance method*. Although a residual value is not taken into account in employing this method as in other methods, depreciation charges should not be made after reaching the residual balance. The double-declining-balance method was initially introduced into the income tax laws in 1954. Since that time, this method has gained increased acceptability for both financial accounting as well as for tax reporting. The percentage is readily calculated as follows:

Estimated Life in Years	Straight-Line Rate	Double-Declining-Balance Rate
3	33⅓%	66⅔%
5	20	40
6	16⅔	33⅓
8	12½	25
10	10	20
20	5	10

Depreciation using the double-declining-balance method for the asset described earlier is summarized in the table that follows:

Asset Cost Allocation — Double-Declining-Balance Method

End of Year	Debit to Depreciation		Credit to Accumulated Depreciation	Balance of Accumulated Depreciation	Asset Book Value
					$10,000.00
1	(20% × $10,000.00)	$2,000.00	$2,000.00	$2,000.00	8,000.00
2	(20% × 8,000.00)	1,600.00	1,600.00	3,600.00	6,400.00
3	(20% × 6,400.00)	1,280.00	1,280.00	4,880.00	5,120.00
4	(20% × 5,120.00)	1,024.00	1,024.00	5,904.00	4,096.00
5	(20% × 4,096.00)	819.20	819.20	6,723.20	3,276.80
6	(20% × 3,276.80)	655.36	655.36	7,378.56	2,621.44
7	(20% × 2,621.44)	524.29	524.29	7,902.85	2,097.15
8	(20% × 2,097.15)	419.43	419.43	8,322.28	1,677.72
9	(20% × 1,677.72)	335.54	335.54	8,657.82	1,342.18
10	(20% × 1,342.18)	268.44	268.44	8,926.26	1,073.74
		$8,926.26	$8,926.26		

It should be noted that the rate of 20% is applied to the book value of the asset each year. In applying this rate, the book value after ten years exceeds the residual value by $573.74 ($1,073.74 − $500.00). This condition arises wherever residual values are relatively low in amount. One way to make the book value equal the residual value is to change from the double-declining-balance method to the straight-line method prior to the end of the asset's useful life. This change is permitted for tax purposes.[1]

---

[1]The optimal time to make the change is at the point when depreciation for the year using the straight-line method exceeds that computed using the double-declining-balance method. In the example that is given, this would occur after the sixth year of the asset's life.

At this point the book value is $2,621.44. After deducting the estimated residual value of $500, the amount to be depreciated over the remaining four years would be $2,121.44. This would amount to annual charges of $530.36, and for the seventh year would exceed the charge of $524.29 using the double-declining balance method. The table would be adjusted for years 7-10 to reflect the change as follows:

Asset Cost Allocation — Double-Declining-Balance Method With Change to Straight-Line Method in Seventh Year

End of Year	Debit to Depreciation	Credit to Accumulated Depreciation	Balance of Accumulated Depreciation	Asset Book Value
1–6	$7,378.56	$7,378.56	$7,378.56	$2,621.44
7	530.36	530.36	7,908.92	2,091.08
8	530.36	530.36	8,439.28	1,560.72
9	530.36	530.36	8,969.64	1,030.36
10	530.36	530.36	9,500.00	500.00
	$9,500.00	$9,500.00		

It may be observed that when a residual value is relatively high in amount, consistent use of the double-declining-balance method will produce an asset book value that is less than the estimated residual value. This possibility is not permitted in the tax laws by the provision that an asset cannot be depreciated below a reasonable residual value.

Sum-of-the-years-digits method. The *sum-of-the-years-digits method* provides decreasing charges by applying a series of fractions, each of a smaller value, to depreciable asset cost. Fractions are developed in terms of the sum of the asset life periods. Assuming the asset previously described has an estimated 10-year life, periodic charges are developed by the sum-of-the-years-digits method as follows:

	Reducing Weights	Reducing Fractions
First year	10	10/55
Second year	9	9/55
Third year	8	8/55
Fourth year	7	7/55
Fifth year	6	6/55
Sixth year	5	5/55
Seventh year	4	4/55
Eighth year	3	3/55
Ninth year	2	2/55
Tenth year	1	1/55
	55	55/55

Weights for purposes of developing reducing fractions are the years-digits listed in reverse order. The denominator for the fraction is obtained by adding these weights; the numerator is the weight assigned to the specific year. The denominator for the fraction can be obtained by an alternate calculation: the sum of the digits for the first and last years can be divided by 2 and multiplied by the number of years of asset life. In the example, the denominator can be determined as follows: $[(10 + 1) \div 2] \times 10 = 55$. Depreciation computed by the application of reducing fractions to depreciable cost is summarized in the table below.

Asset Cost Allocation — Sum-of-the-Years-Digits Method

End of Year	Debit to Depreciation		Credit to Accumulated Depreciation	Balance of Accumulated Depreciation	Asset Book Value
					$10,000.00
1	(10/55 × $9,500)	$1,727.27	$1,727.27	$1,727.27	8,272.73
2	(9/55 × $9,500)	1,554.55	1,554.55	3,281.82	6,718.18
3	(8/55 × $9,500)	1,381.82	1,381.82	4,663.64	5,336.36
4	(7/55 × $9,500)	1,209.09	1,209.09	5,872.73	4,127.27
5	(6/55 × $9,500)	1,036.36	1,036.36	6,909.09	3,090.91
6	(5/55 × $9,500)	863.64	863.64	7,772.73	2,227.27
7	(4/55 × $9,500)	690.91	690.91	8,463.64	1,536.36
8	(3/55 × $9,500)	518.18	518.18	8,981.82	1,018.18
9	(2/55 × $9,500)	345.45	345.45	9,327.27	672.73
10	(1/55 × $9,500)	172.73	172.73	9,500.00	500.00
		$9,500.00	$9,500.00		

Evaluation of decreasing-charge methods. Decreasing-charge methods can be supported as reasonable approaches to asset cost allocation when the benefits provided by a property item decline as it grows older. These methods, too, are suggested when a property item calls for increasing maintenance and repairs over its useful life. [1] When straight-line depreciation is employed, the combined charges for depreciation, maintenance, and repairs will increase over the life of the asset; when the decreasing-charge methods are used, the combined charges will tend to be equalized.

Other factors that may suggest use of a decreasing-charge method include: (1) the anticipation of a significant contribution in early periods with the extent of the contribution to be realized in later periods less definite; (2) the possibility that inadequacy or obsolescence may result in premature retirement of the asset; in the event of premature retirement, depreciation charges will have absorbed what would otherwise require recognition as a loss. Decreasing-charge methods are supported as conservative approaches to the cost allocation problem.

Decreasing-charge or accelerated methods are frequently used for income tax purposes. Although total depreciation over the asset life is no greater than that provided by alternative methods, the recognition of higher depreciation in the early years of an asset's life serves to postpone the income taxes that would otherwise be payable and thus provides interest-free working capital to the business. Many taxpayers use accelerated depreciation methods on their tax returns but straight-line depreciation on their books. This requires that income tax allocation adjustments be made on the books in view of the timing differences in recognizing depreciation charge.

Service-hours depreciation. *Service-hours* depreciation is based on the theory that purchase of an asset represents the purchase of a number of hours of direct service. This method requires an estimate of the life of the asset in terms of service hours. Depreciable cost is divided by total service hours in arriving at the depreciation rate to be assigned for each hour of asset use. The use of the asset during the period is measured, and the number of service hours is multiplied by the depreciation rate in arriving at the depreciation charge. Depreciation charges fluctuate periodically according to the contribution that the asset makes in service hours.

---

[1]The AICPA Committee on Accounting Procedure has stated, "The declining-balance method is one of those which meets the requirements of being 'systematic and rational.' In those cases where the expected productivity or revenue-earning power of the asset is relatively greater during the earlier years of its life, or where maintenance charges tend to increase during the later years, the declining-balance method may well provide the most satisfactory allocation of cost." The Committee would apply these conclusions to other decreasing-charge methods, including the sum-of-the-years-digits method, that produce substantially similar results. See: *Accounting Research Bulletin No. 44 (Revised),* "Declining-Balance Depreciation" (New York: American Institute of Certified Public Accountants, 1958), par. 2.

Using asset data previously given and an estimated service life of 20,000 hours, the rate to be applied for each service hour is determined as follows:

$$r \text{ (per hour)} = \frac{C - S}{n}, \text{ or } \frac{\$10,000 - \$500}{20,000} = \$.475$$

Allocation of asset cost in terms of service hours is summarized in the table below:

Asset Cost Allocation — Service-Hours Method

End of Year	Service Hours	Debit to Depreciation		Credit to Accumulated Depreciation	Balance of Accumulated Depreciation	Asset Book Value
						$10,000.00
1	1,500	(1,500 × $.475)	$ 712.50	$ 712.50	$ 712.50	9,287.50
2	2,500	(2,500 × $.475)	1,187.50	1,187.50	1,900.00	8,100.00
3	2,500	(2,500 × $.475)	1,187.50	1,187.50	3,087.50	6,912.50
4	2,000	(2,000 × $.475)	950.00	950.00	4,037.50	5,962.50
5	1,500	(1,500 × $.475)	712.50	712.50	4,750.00	5,250.00
6	1,500	(1,500 × $.475)	712.50	712.50	5,462.50	4,537.50
7	3,000	(3,000 × $.475)	1,425.00	1,425.00	6,887.50	3,112.50
8	2,500	(2,500 × $.475)	1,187.50	1,187.50	8,075.00	1,925.00
9	2,000	(2,000 × $.475)	950.00	950.00	9,025.00	975.00
10	1,000	(1,000 × $.475)	475.00	475.00	9,500.00	500.00
	20,000			$9,500.00	$9,500.00	

It is assumed above that the original estimate of service hours is confirmed and the asset is retired after 20,000 hours reached in the tenth year. Such precise confirmation would seldom be found in practice.

It should be observed that straight-line depreciation resulted in an annual charge of $950 regardless of fluctuations in productive activity. When asset life is affected directly by the degree of use, and when there are significant fluctuations in such use in successive periods, the service-hours method, which recognizes "hours used" instead of "hours available for use," normally provides the more equitable charges to operations.

Productive-output depreciation. *Productive-output* depreciation is based on the theory that an asset is acquired for the service that it can provide in the form of production output. This method requires an estimate of the total unit output of the property item. Depreciable cost divided by the total output gives the equal depreciation charge to be assigned for each unit of output. The measured production for a period multiplied by the depreciation charge per unit gives the charge to be made for depreciation. Depreciation charges fluctuate periodically according to the contribution that the asset makes in unit output.

Using the previous asset data and an estimated productive life of 2,500,000 units, the rate to be applied for each thousand units produced is determined as follows:

$$r \text{ (per thousand units)} = \frac{C - S}{n}, \text{ or } \frac{\$10,000 - \$500}{2,500} = \$3.80$$

Asset cost allocation in terms of productive output is summarized in the tabulation below:

Asset Cost Allocation — Productive-Output Method

End of Year	Unit Output	Debit to Depreciation		Credit to Accumulated Depreciation	Balance of Accumulated Depreciation	Asset Book Value
						$10,000
1	80,000	(80 × $3.80)	$ 304	$ 304	$ 304	9,696
2	250,000	(250 × $3.80)	950	950	1,254	8,746
3	400,000	(400 × $3.80)	1,520	1,520	2,774	7,226
4	320,000	(320 × $3.80)	1,216	1,216	3,990	6,010
5	440,000	(440 × $3.80)	1,672	1,672	5,662	4,338
6	360,000	(360 × $3.80)	1,368	1,368	7,030	2,970
7	280,000	(280 × $3.80)	1,064	1,064	8,094	1,906
8	210,000	(210 × $3.80)	798	798	8,892	1,108
9	120,000	(120 × $3.80)	456	456	9,348	652
10	40,000	(40 × $3.80)	152	152	9,500	500
	2,500,000		$9,500	$9,500		

Evaluation of use-factor methods. When quantitative uses of depreciable properties can be reasonably estimated and readily measured, the use-factor methods provide highly satisfactory approaches to asset cost allocation. Depreciation is a fluctuating charge that tends to follow the revenue curve: high depreciation charges are assigned to periods of high activity; low depreciation charges are assigned to periods of low activity. When the useful life of an asset is affected primarily by the degree of its use, recognition of depreciation as a variable charge is particularly appropriate.

However, certain limitations in the use of the use-factor methods need to be pointed out. Asset performance in terms of service hours or productive output may be difficult to estimate. Measurement solely in terms of such factors could fail to recognize special conditions that may be operative, such as increasing maintenance and repair costs as well as possible inadequacy and obsolescence. Furthermore, when service life expires even in the absence of use, a use-factor method may serve to conceal actual fluctuations in earnings; by relating periodic depreciation to the volume of operations, periodic operating results may be smoothed out, thus creating a false appearance of stability.

Group-rate and composite-rate methods

It was assumed in preceding discussions that depreciation is associated with individual property items and is applied to each separate unit. Such practice is commonly referred to as *unit depreciation*. Frequently, however, there may be certain advantages in associating depreciation with a group of properties and applying a single rate to the collective cost of the group. Group cost allocation procedures are referred to as *group depreciation* and *composite depreciation*.

Group depreciation. When useful life is affected primarily by physical factors, a group of similar items purchased at one time should have the same expected life, but in fact some will probably remain useful longer than others. In recording depreciation on a unit basis, the sale or retirement of an asset before or after its anticipated lifetime requires recognition of a gain or loss. Such gains and losses, however, can usually be attributed to normal variations in useful life rather than to unforeseen disasters and windfalls.

The *group-depreciation* procedure treats a collection of similar assets as a single group. Depreciation is accumulated in a single valuation account and the depreciation rate is based on the average life of assets in the group. Because the accumulated depreciation account under the group procedure applies to the entire group of assets, it is not related to any specific asset. Thus, there are no "fully depreciated" assets and the depreciation rate is applied to the cost of all assets remaining in service, regardless of age, in arriving at the periodic depreciation charge.

When an item in the group is retired, no gain or loss is recognized; the asset account is credited with the cost of the item and the valuation account is charged for the difference between cost and any salvage. With normal variations in asset lives, the losses not recognized on early retirements are offset by the continued depreciation charges on those assets still in service after the average life has elapsed.

To illustrate, assume that 100 similar machines having an average expected useful life of 5 years are purchased at a total cost of $200,000. Of this group, 30 machines are retired at the end of four years, 40 at the end of five years, and the remaining 30 at the end of the sixth year. Based on the average expected useful life of 5 years, a depreciation charge of 20% is reported on those assets in service each year. The charges for depreciation and the changes in the group asset and accumulated depreciation accounts are summarized at the top of the following page.

It should be noted that the depreciation charge is exactly $400 per machine-year. In each of the first four years, 100 machine-years of service are utilized, and the annual depreciation charge is $40,000. In the fifth year, when only 70 machines are in operation, the charge is $28,000. In the sixth year, when 30 units are still in service, a proportionate charge for such use of $12,000 is made. Under unit depreciation a

Asset Cost Allocation — Group Depreciation

End of Year	Debit to Depreciation (20% of Cost)	Asset			Accumulated Depreciation			Asset Book Value
		Debit	Credit	Balance	Debit	Credit	Balance	
		$200,000		$200,000				$200,000
1	$ 40,000			200,000		$ 40,000	$ 40,000	160,000
2	40,000			200,000		40,000	80,000	120,000
3	40,000			200,000		40,000	120,000	80,000
4	40,000		$ 60,000	140,000	$ 60,000	40,000	100,000	40,000
5	28,000		80,000	60,000	80,000	28,000	48,000	12,000
6	12,000		60,000	—	60,000	12,000	—	—
	$200,000	$200,000	$200,000		$200,000	$200,000		

loss of $12,000 would have been recognized at the end of the fourth year when 30 machines were scrapped prematurely. However, no charge for depreciation would have been recognized in the sixth year when the 30 machines remaining in service would have been fully depreciated.[1]

Application of the group depreciation procedure under circumstances such as the foregoing provides an annual charge that is more closely related to the quantity of productive facilities being used. Gains and losses due solely to normal variations in asset lives are not recognized, and operating results are more meaningfully stated. The convenience of applying a uniform depreciation rate to a number of similar items may also represent a substantial advantage.

Composite depreciation. The basic procedures employed under the group method for allocating the cost of substantially identical assets may be extended to include dissimilar assets. This special application of the group procedure is known as *composite depreciation.* The composite method retains the convenience of the group method, but because assets with varying service-lives are aggregated to determine an "average" life, it is unlikely to provide the reporting advantages of the group method.

A composite rate is established by analyzing the various assets or classes of assets in use and computing the depreciation as follows:

Asset	Cost	Residual Value	Depreciable Cost	Estimated Life in Years	Annual Depreciation
A	$ 2,000	$ 120	$ 1,880	4	$ 470
B	6,000	300	5,700	6	950
C	12,000	1,200	10,800	10	1,080
	$20,000	$1,620	$18,380		$2,500

Composite depreciation rate to be applied to cost: $2,500 ÷ $20,000, or 12.5%
Composite life of assets: $18,380 ÷ $2,500, or 7.35 years

---

[1]It should be observed that in the example the original estimates of an average useful life of 5 years is confirmed in the use of the assets. Such precise confirmation would seldom be the case. In instances where assets in a group are continued in use after their cost has been assigned to operations, no further depreciation charges would be recognized. On the other hand, where all of the assets in a group are retired before their cost has been assigned to operations, a special charge related to such retirement would have to be recognized.

It will be observed that a rate of 12.5% applied to the cost of the assets, $20,000, results in annual depreciation of $2,500. Annual depreciation of $2,500 will accumulate to a total of $18,380 in 7.35 years; hence 7.35 years may be considered the composite or average life of the assets. Composite depreciation would be reported in a single valuation account. Upon the retirement of an individual asset, the asset account is closed and the valuation account is charged with the difference between cost and residual value. As with the group procedure, no gains or losses are recognized at the time individual assets are retired.

After a composite rate has been set, it is ordinarily continued in the absence of significant changes in the lives of assets or asset additions and retirements having a material effect upon the rate. It is assumed in the preceding example that the assets are replaced with similar assets when they are retired. If they are not replaced, continuation of the 12.5% rate will misstate depreciation charges.

Appraisal, retirement, and replacement systems

The charge to operations for buildings and equipment use may be made on a basis other than the cost allocation processes described. Other systems that are sometimes employed include the following:

Appraisal systems. Asset accounts are charged for all expenditures relating to property acquisitions. At the end of each period assets are appraised, asset balances are reduced to the appraised values, and a charge is made to operations for such decrease. In appraising assets care must be exercised to assign values that reflect the portion of original cost that may reasonably be identified with remaining service utilities of the asset, not market values.

Retirement systems. Asset accounts are charged for all expenditures relating to property acquisitions. Whenever property items are retired, the asset accounts are credited for the full cost of properties retired and a charge is made to operations for such cost less any amounts recovered as salvage.

Replacement systems. Asset accounts are charged for expenditures relating to original property acquisitions. Whenever original property items are replaced, a charge is made to operations for the cost of replacements less any amounts recovered as salvage on the properties replaced.

Depreciation systems such as the foregoing can be considered acceptable only when the use of standard depreciation procedures involve serious practical difficulties, such as in estimating useful lives, in distinguishing between replacements and repairs, and in handling recording routines. Systems should be reviewed periodically to provide assurance that they result in fair charges to revenue and that they do not serve as means for income manipulation. The use of the above systems may be suggested in accounting for hand and machine tools of a manufacturing company, poles and related equipment of an electric utility, railroad ties of a railway, and dishes and silverware of a restaurant.

Allowable depreciation for federal income tax purposes

The Internal Revenue Code allows taxpayers to use any reasonable method for computing depreciation, with certain limitations. The Code specifically names the following methods as acceptable:

For all classes of depreciable property:

1. The straight-line method.
2. The declining-balance method, using an annual rate limited to one-and-one-half times the rate which would be applicable to the straight-line method unadjusted for salvage.

For property having a useful life of 3 years or more which is acquired new after December 31, 1953, methods (1) and (2) and also the following:

3. The declining-balance method, using an annual rate limited to double the straight-line rate unadjusted for salvage except that new realty (buildings) constructed after July 24, 1969, is limited to 150% of the straight-line rate.
4. The sum-of-the-years-digits method.
5. Any other consistent method, provided accumulated depreciation over the first two thirds of the useful life of the property does not exceed that obtained in (3) above.

A taxpayer acquiring tangible personal property having a useful life of at least six years may elect to deduct 20% of the cost of such property without regard to residual value in the year of acquisition in addition to the regular deduction for depreciation. This bonus first-year deduction must be subtracted from the cost of the asset in calculating periodic depreciation. A limitation of $10,000 in any one year is placed on the costs of property acquisitions used as a basis for the special deduction.

Depreciation is recognized as a deduction from ordinary income on the books and the tax return. Prior to the early 1960's, any excess of proceeds from the sale of the asset over book value was treated for tax purposes as a capital gain with its attendant lower tax rates. The incentive to the taxpayer, therefore, was to depreciate an asset as fast as possible for tax purposes and thus obtain the ordinary deduction from income. The gain on disposal could then be recognized as a capital gain. Such practice was denied in the early 1960's by depreciation recapture provisions in the tax laws. There are many facets to the regulations but, essentially, any gain on depreciable personal property and any gain on real property that can be related to the adoption of accelerated depreciation methods is now reportable as ordinary income rather than as capital gain.

Property records

Data concerning individual property items are required in accounting for past activities and in planning future activities. Such data are also required for insurance, tax, and other purposes. Data requirements can be met only by detailed records that are systematically and efficiently maintained. Such records are variously termed "Unit Property Records," "Property Ledger," and "Fixed Asset Control." They usually involve the controlling account principle, property items being summarized in the general ledger and detail being recorded in subsidiary ledger form. Subsidiary ledger records are maintained to provide the significant data for the individual property items.

Subsidiary records are commonly found in the form of a property register or a property file. When a property register is used, special sections are usually assigned to the assets of each department in order that depreciation charges may be accumulated departmentally. One line is provided for each asset, and significant information regarding the asset is reported in special columns. A register prepared in a form that summarizes periodic depreciation charges is generally referred to as a *lapsing schedule.* Individual assets are listed as they are acquired and periodic depreciation charges for the entire life of each depreciable asset are reported in a series of columns representing successive years. The charge for depreciation is readily determined by adding the charges appearing in the column for the particular year.

The use of a property file consisting of cards or separate sheets frequently provides a more flexible record than the register form since assets can be arranged in an order other than date of acquisition. One card or one sheet is provided for each asset, and all information with respect to the item is listed thereon. For buildings and equipment, this information usually includes the name of the asset, location, name of the vendor, guarantee period, insurance carried, date acquired, original cost, transportation charges, installation cost, estimated life, estimated residual value, depreciation rate, depreciation to date, major expenditures for repairs and improvements, and proceeds from final disposal. A property file may also be maintained on tabulating cards, magnetic tapes, or in the memory of an electronic computer. When the information is maintained and stored in this form, it may be sorted and used in making high speed calculations. The ease and convenience in which data may be handled has prompted many business units to adopt these information methods despite the high costs of such systems.

Disclosure of depreciation methods in financial statements

Because of the alternative methods that can be used in reporting depreciation, it is necessary that the method that is used be disclosed in the financial statements. Without such disclosure, the user of the statements might be misled in trying to compare the financial results of one company with another. In the past, companies have not been consistent in disclosing this information.

The Accounting Principles Board was concerned by the lack of information relative to depreciation precedures and in 1967 in Omnibus Opinion No. 12, they detailed the information they thought was pertinent to full disclosure. The Board concluded:

> Because of the significant effects on financial position and results of operations of the depreciation method or methods used, the following disclosures should be made in the financial statements or in notes thereto:
> a. Depreciation expense for the period,
> b. Balances of major classes of depreciable assets, by nature or function, at the balance sheet date,
> c. Accumulated depreciation, either by major classes of depreciable assets or in total, at the balance sheet date, and
> d. A general description of the method or methods used in computing depreciation with respect to major classes of depreciable assets.[1]

When changes in depreciation methods are made, the effects of these changes should be fully disclosed in the financial statements.

Depreciation accounting and property replacement

There has been a tendency on the part of many readers of financial statements to interpret depreciation accounting as somehow related to the accumulation of a fund for asset replacement. The use of such terms as "provision for depreciation" and "reserve for depreciation" has contributed much to such misinterpretation.

It has been pointed out that the charge for depreciation originates from the recognition of the movement of a property item towards ultimate exhaustion. The nature of this charge is no different from such as those that are made to recognize the expiration of insurance premiums or patent rights. It is true that revenue equal to or in excess of expenses for a period results in a recovery of such expenses; salary expense is thus

---

[1]*Opinions of the Accounting Principles Board, No. 12,* "Omnibus Opinion — 1967" (New York: American Institute of Certified Public Accountants, 1967), par. 5. Of the 600 companies included in the AICPA's 1968 *Accounting Trends & Techniques,* only 333 or 56 percent included information as to the depreciation method used in their 1967 reports. The effect of the requirement for disclosure is evidenced by the analysis of the 1968 financial reports; 503 of the 600 companies included information as to the method used.

recovered by revenue, as is insurance expense, patent amortization, and charges for depreciation. But this does not suggest that cash equivalent to the recorded depreciation will be available to meet the cost of property replacement. Resources from revenues may be applied to many uses: to the increase in receivables, inventories, or other working capital items; to the acquisition of property or other noncurrent items; to the retirement of debt or the redemption of stock; and to the payment of dividends. If a fund is to be available for the replacement of property items, this calls for special authorization by management. Such a fund is seldom found, however, because its establishment would have to promise earnings exceeding those that might accrue from other uses of capital.

Depletion

Natural resources, also called *wasting assets*, move towards exhaustion as the physical units representing such resources are removed and sold. The withdrawal of oil or gas, the cutting of timber, and the mining of coal, sulphur, iron, copper, or silver ore are examples of processes leading to the exhaustion of natural resources. The reduction in the cost or value of natural resources as a result of the withdrawal of such resources is referred to as *depletion*.

Depletion may be distinguished from depreciation in the following respects:

1. Depletion is recognition of the quantitative exhaustion taking place in a natural resource, while depreciation is recognition of the service exhaustion taking place in a building and equipment item.
2. Related to (1), depletion is recognized as the cost of the material that becomes directly embodied in the product of the company; through depreciation, the cost of an asset may be allocated to production but the asset itself does not become a part of the finished product.
3. Depletion involves a distinctive asset that cannot be directly replaced in kind upon its exhaustion; depreciation involves an asset that can generally be replaced upon its exhaustion.

The measurement of net income calls for the recognition of depletion. If the natural resource is sold directly upon its emergence or withdrawal, the recognition of depletion is, in effect, the recognition of cost of goods sold; if the natural resource is processed and stored before sale, depletion is initially recognized as a part of inventory cost.

When natural resources are acquired together with land for a lump sum, the total cost of the property must be allocated to the two property items. Separate accounts may be established for land and for the resources. The cost of the latter asset divided by the estimated quantity of resources that can profitably be removed gives the charge to be recognized for each unit removed, or the *unit depletion charge*. Depletion for the period is the measured number of units removed during the period multiplied by the unit depletion charge.

To illustrate, assume the following facts: Land containing natural resources is purchased at a cost of $5,500,000. The land has a value after resource exploitation estimated at $250,000; the natural resource supply is estimated at 1,000,000 tons. The unit depletion charge and the total depletion charge for the first year, assuming the withdrawal of 80,000 tons, are calculated as follows:

Depletion charge per ton: ($5,500,000 − $250,000) ÷ 1,000,000, or $5.25
Depletion charge for the first year: 80,000 tons × $5.25, or $420,000

When developmental costs, such as costs of drilling, sinking mine shafts, and constructing roads, are related to the exploitation of the resource, these should be added to the original cost of the property in arriving at the total cost subject to depletion. These costs may be incurred before normal activities begin. On the other hand, they may be continuing and therefore may call for estimates in arriving at a depletion charge that is to be used uniformly for all recoverable units.[1]

When costs will be required in restoring land for use after the resources are exhausted, these should also be added to depletable cost.

The charge for resource exhaustion is recorded by a debit to Depletion and a credit directly to the resource account or to Accumulated

---

[1] It should be observed that the capitalization of developmental costs is an application of the matching process that requires that costs incurred in anticipation of subsequent revenue be deferred. In practice, however, in view of a variety of special situations that are encountered by companies with wasting assets, practices ranging from the full capitalization of periodic developmental expenditures to the full assignment to current revenue of such expenditures are encountered. Support for charging current revenue for developmental costs is made on the grounds that such a practice affords the conservatism that is required in view of the general uncertainty of the benefits that the costs may provide. Because a number of companies report developmental costs as expenses, there is a need to review carefully the financial statements of companies with wasting assets if operating results are to be properly evaluated. The wide range of practices may be indicated by the following examples that are given in *Accounting Trends & Techniques:*

Continental Oil Company in its 1967 annual report to stockholders provides the following note:

"Intangible development costs applicable to productive oil or gas wells or to the opening of new coal mines are capitalized and amortized on a unit-of-production basis. Costs of additional mine facilities required to maintain production after a mine reaches the production stage, generally referred to as 'receding face costs', are charged to expense as incurred; however, costs of additional air shafts and new portals are capitalized and amortized. For federal income tax purposes, all of these costs are deducted as incurred."

United Park City Mines Company in its 1967 annual report provides the following note:

"The company's mining properties and claims are located in a mineralized area, but these properties and claims have not as yet been fully developed. It has been the company's practice to limit its development expenditures each year to funds currently available for this purpose. This has had the result of proving ore reserves only a few years ahead of mining operations and no reasonable estimates of ultimate ore reserves can be made at this time. No reasonable basis exists, therefore, on which to compute depletion and the company and its predecessors have consistently followed the practice of presenting their financial statements without deduction for depletion of mines and no such deduction is included in these financial statements. Statutory depletion is recognized for tax purposes."

Depletion. If an accumulated depletion account is established, it should be subtracted from the resource account in reporting the asset.

The charge for depletion, increased by labor and overhead relating to removal and processing, is reported in the cost of goods sold section of the income statement. If all of the units represented by the depletion charge are sold, depletion, labor, and overhead costs measure the cost of goods sold to be applied against revenue in arriving at gross profit on sales; if some of the units remain on hand, the total for depletion, labor, and overhead related to such units is recognized as inventory and subtracted from total costs in arriving at cost of goods sold. Depletion, therefore, is comparable to raw materials purchases in the summarizing of operations.

Revisions in the unit depletion charge often become necessary. Revisions are necessary when developmental costs differ significantly from original estimates and when estimates of the available unit supply change as a result of further discoveries or improved extraction processes. Revisions may also be required when changes in sales prices indicate changes in the number of units that can profitably be extracted.

In revising depletion charges, past charges would be allowed to stand; a current charge would be established by dividing the resource cost balance as found at the end of the year by the estimated remaining recoverable units as of the beginning of the year (units recovered during the year plus the estimated recoverable units at the end of the year). To illustrate, assume in the preceding example that additional developmental costs of $500,000 are incurred in the second year and recoverable units are estimated at 950,000 tons after second-year withdrawals of 100,000 tons. The depletion charge for the second year is then determined as follows:

Cost assignable to recoverable tons as of the beginning of the second year:

Original costs applicable to depletable resources.........	$5,250,000
Add additional costs incurred in the second year........	500,000
	$5,750,000
Deduct depletion charge for the first year..............	420,000
Balance subject to depletion.........................	$5,330,000

Estimated recoverable tons as of the beginning of the second year:

Number of tons withdrawn in the second year..........	100,000
Estimated recoverable tons as of the end of the second year	950,000
Total recoverable tons at the beginning of the second year	1,050,000

Depletion charge per ton for the second year: $5,330,000 ÷ 1,050,000, or $5.0762
Depletion charge for the second year: 100,000 × $5.0762, or $507,620

When buildings and improvements are constructed in connection with the exploitation of natural resources and their usefulness is limited to the duration of the project, it is reasonable to recognize depreciation on such properties on an output basis consistent with the charges to be recognized for the natural resources themselves. For example, assume that buildings are constructed at a cost of $250,000; the useful lives of the buildings are expected to terminate upon exhaustion of the natural resource consisting of 1,000,000 units. Under such circumstances, a depreciation charge of $.25 ($250,000 ÷ 1,000,000) should accompany the depletion charge that is recognized for each unit. When improvements provide benefits that are expected to terminate prior to the exhaustion of the natural resource, the cost of such improvements may be allocated on the basis of the units to be removed during the life of the improvements or on a time basis, whichever is considered to be more appropriate.

Depletion for tax purposes may differ from the amount reported on the books. Federal income tax laws permit the taxpayer to deduct annually a fixed percentage of gross income for depletion of oil and gas wells and minerals. Such *percentage* or *statutory depletion* is applicable only when it exceeds *cost depletion*. Under current law the depletion rate for oil and gas wells is 22 percent of gross income and varies on minerals from 5 percent to 22 percent of gross income, but such deduction cannot exceed 50 percent of the taxable income from the property calculated without regard to the charge for depletion. The taxpayer is permitted to take percentage depletion as long as properties are income producing; there is no limitation on the total allowable depletion, and the sum of periodic depletion deductions may ultimately far exceed property cost.

For income tax purposes, development costs may be deducted in the year incurred or they may be capitalized and written off over the estimated number of units of resources recoverable.

Dividends representing proceeds from wasting assets

When a company's stock in trade is its wasting assets, revenue represents a recovery of the cost of such wasting assets charged to operations, a recovery of other expenses, and earnings. When operations are to cease upon exhaustion of the resources, dividends need not be limited to net income but may be paid in amounts equal to such net income increased by the amount charged against revenue as depletion. To limit dividends to net income would be to retain the amount recovered from wasting assets, possibly in unproductive form, until the time the business is liquidated. In the absence of effective utilization of revenue proceeds for new properties or other productive purposes, such assets should be made available to stockholders. Amounts received by stockholders, then, would represent a distribution of earnings and in part a return of invested capital.

To illustrate the nature of the foregoing, assume that the Midas Mines Co. in 1972 issues capital stock in exchange for certain mineral properties valued at $100,000. During the course of the fiscal period, natural resources that cost $25,000 are sold for $50,000 and operating expenses of $10,000 are incurred. At the end of the period, the balance sheet reports the following:

Midas Mines Co.
Balance Sheet
December 31, 1972

Cash........................		$ 35,000	Liabilities...................		$ 5,000
Receivables.................		10,000	Capital stock...............		100,000
Mineral properties...	$100,000		Retained earnings...........		15,000
Less accumulated					
depletion........	25,000	75,000			
			Total liabilities and stock-		
Total assets.................		$120,000	holders' equity............		$120,000

Management here does not need to limit dividends to the retained earnings balance of $15,000 but may consider the limitation to be $40,000, or net income, $15,000, increased by the recovery of the asset depletion, $25,000. However, since revenue has not been fully realized in cash, and since some cash is required for a continuation of operations, dividends of a lesser amount would be in order. If a dividend of $28,000 is paid, it is regarded as representing first a distribution of earnings of $15,000, the balance a return of invested capital to owners. The return of invested capital is reported by a charge to a capital stock offset balance rather than by a charge to capital stock. The entry to record the $28,000 dividend distribution follows:

Retained Earnings..............................	15,000	
Capital Distributions to Stockholders..............	13,000	
Cash..		28,000

The stockholders' equity after the distribution would be reported as follows:

Capital stock......................................	$100,000
Less capital distributions to stockholders.................	13,000
Stockholders' equity.................................	$ 87,000

The distribution to stockholders of amounts equal to net income increased by the depletion charge is permitted by state laws. Such action is sanctioned on the theory that creditors are aware of the shrinking investment requirements that are peculiar to operations involving wasting assets not subject to replacement. As indicated in Chapter 11, when dividends are in part liquidating, stockholders should be informed of the portion of the dividend representing a distribution of corporate earnings and of the portion representing a return of invested capital.

QUESTIONS

1. There are several different methods that may be used to allocate the cost of property items against revenue. Wouldn't it be better to require all companies to use the same method? Discuss briefly.

2. The recognition of depreciation has no essential relation to the problem of replacement. Do you agree?

3. Distinguish between functional depreciation and physical depreciation of assets.

4. In what ways, if any, do accelerated methods of depreciation increase the flow of cash funds into a company?

5. After reading an article on the allocation of costs, the controller for a client corporation asks you to explain the following excerpt:

Depreciation may be either a fixed cost or a variable cost, depending on the method used to compute it.

6. The president of the Hathaway Co. recommends that no depreciation be recorded for 1972 since the depreciation rate is 5% per year and indexes show that prices during the year have risen by more than this figure. Evaluate this argument.

7. The policy of the Burke Co. is to recondition its building and equipment each year so that they may be maintained in perfect repair. In view of the extensive periodic costs involved in keeping the property in such condition, officials of the company feel that the need for recognizing depreciation is eliminated. Evaluate this argument.

8. The board of directors of Chambers, Inc., believes that it is proper to provide for depreciation when determining the results of operations. Because depreciation does not affect the cash position of the company, the board believes it can be disregarded in determining the amount of net income available for dividends. What condition might develop if the company follows this policy?

9. The Acme Manufacturing Company purchased a new machine that was especially built to perform one particular function on their assembly line. A difference of opinion has arisen as to the method of depreciation to be used in connection with this machine. Three methods are now being considered by the president of the company:

(a) The straight-line method.
(b) The productive-output method.
(c) The sum-of-the-years-digits method.

List separately the arguments for and against each of the proposed methods from both the theoretical and the practical viewpoints. In your answer, you need not express your preference and you are to disregard income tax consequences.

10. The president of the Tucker Co. objects to the use of straight-line depreciation on the grounds that sale of the asset at the end of the first year of its life would result in a loss significantly greater than the depreciation charge. The vice-president objects to the use of the straight-line method on the grounds that an appraisal of the asset at the end of the first year would hardly show a physical decline equal to the depreciation charge. Evaluate each position.

11. The certified public accountant is frequently called upon by management for advice regarding methods of computing depreciation. Although the question arises less frequently, of comparable importance is whether the depreciation method should be based on the consideration of the property items as units, as groups, or as having a composite life.

(a) Briefly describe the depreciation methods based on recognizing property items as (1) units, (2) groups, or (3) as having a composite life.
(b) Present the arguments for and against the use of each of these methods.
(c) Describe how retirements are recorded under each of these methods.

12. Buildings and equipment donated to corporations are recorded on the books at their fair market value and depreciation charges are based on such valuation. Discuss the accounting justification for (a) recording property received as a gift, and (b) recording depreciation based upon the values assigned to the donated property.

13. (a) Describe the allocation of plant charges to operations under (1) the appraisal system (2) the retirement system, and (3) the replacement system. (b) Do you recommend the use of such procedures?

14. (a) Define wasting assets. (b) Give five examples of wasting assets.

15. What are the similarities and the differences in recognizing depreciation on buildings and equipment and depletion on wasting assets?

16. Justify the practice, followed in the case of a company with wasting assets, of adding the charge for depletion to net income in arriving at the amount available for dividends.

EXERCISES

1. A machine is purchased at the beginning of 1972 for $19,500. Its estimated life is 6 years. Freight in on the machine is $400. Installation costs are $300. The machine is estimated to have a residual value of $1,000, and a useful life of 40,000 hours. It was used 5,000 hours in 1972.

  (a) What is the cost of the machine for accounting purposes?
  (b) Compare the depreciation charge for 1972 using (1) the straight-line method, and (2) the service-hours method.

2. Equipment costing $5,500 and having an estimated life of ten years was depreciated for five years using the sum-of-the-years-digits method and then sold for $1,250. Give the journal entry for the sale assuming that no residual value was recognized in computing depreciation.

3. Ewald Manufacturing Co. acquired machinery at a cost of $100,000. The asset had a 10-year life and a scrap value of $7,000. Depreciation was to be recorded at a rate that is double the straight-line rate. However, realizing that a continuation of depreciation at the same rate would require the recognition of a significant loss in the last year of asset life, the company decided to change to the straight-line method and write off the remaining asset book value over the remaining asset life beginning with the year in which the declining-balance method produced a smaller charge than such straight-line depreciation. Prepare a table listing annual depreciation charges and the accumulated depreciation for the 10-year period.

4. The Dimension Manufacturing Co. acquires a machine at a cost of $19,080 on March 1, 1966. The machine is estimated to have a life of 10 years except for a special unit that will require replacement at the end of 6 years. The asset is recorded in two accounts, $14,400 being assigned to the main unit, and $4,680 to the special unit. Depreciation is recorded by the straight-line method, salvage values being disregarded. On March 1, 1972, the special unit is scrapped and is replaced with a similar unit; the cost of the replacement at this time is $5,600, and it is estimated that the unit will have a residual value of approximately 25% of cost at the end of the useful life of the main unit. What are the depreciation charges to be recognized for the years 1966, 1972, and 1973?

5. The Diamond Co. records show the following assets:

	Acquired	Cost	Salvage	Estimated Useful Life
Machinery	7/1/71	$70,000	$5,000	10 years
Equipment	1/1/72	22,000	1,000	6 years
Fixtures	1/1/72	30,000	3,000	4 years

What is (a) the composite life of the assets and (b) the composite depreciation rate on assets?

6. The Hercules Co. obtains a lease for 25 years on a piece of land upon which it erects a building at a cost of $300,000 with an estimated life of 30 years. Buildings belong to the lessor at the end of the lease period. It also leases another piece of land for 20 years and erects a factory building at a cost of $210,000 with an estimated life of 15 years. What is the annual depreciation charge on each piece of property?

7. The Kennedy Mining Co. in 1969 paid $800,000 for property with a supply of natural resources estimated at 1,000,000 tons. The property was estimated to be worth $100,000 after removal of the natural resource. Developmental costs of $150,000 were incurred in 1970 before withdrawals of the resource could be made. In 1971, resources removed totaled 200,000 tons. In 1972 resources removed totaled 300,000 tons. During 1972 discoveries were made indicating that available resources subsequent to 1972 will total 1,500,000 tons, but these will require additional developmental costs of $220,000. What entries should be made to recognize depletion for 1971 and 1972?

PROBLEMS

14-1. The cost of a machine purchased by Midwest Badge, Inc., on April 1, 1972, is $50,000. It is estimated that the machine will have a $5,000 trade-in value at the end of its service life. Its life is estimated at 5 years; its working hours are estimated at 30,000, its production is estimated at 600,000 units. During 1972, the machine was operated 6,000 hours and produced 120,000 units.

Instructions: Compute the depreciation on the machine for 1972 by: (1) the straight-line method, (2) the service-hours method, (3) the productive-output method, (4) the sum-of-the-years-digits method, and (5) the double-declining-balance method.

14-2. A delivery truck was acquired by Allstate Bag, Inc., for $5,000 on January 1, 1971. The truck was estimated to have a 5-year life and a trade-in value at the end of that time of $500. Prepare tables reporting periodic depreciation and asset book value over the 5-year period, similar to those illustrated in the text, for each assumption below:

  (a) Depreciation is to be calculated by the straight-line method.
  (b) Depreciation is to be calculated by the sum-of-the-years-digits method.
  (c) Depreciation is to be calculated by applying a fixed percentage to the declining book value of the asset that will reduce the asset book value to its residual value at the end of the fifth year. (The fifth root of .10 = .631.)
  (d) Repair charges are estimated at $70 for the first year and are estimated to increase by $50 in each succeeding year; depreciation charges are to be made on a diminishing scale so that the sum of depreciation and estimated repairs is the same for each year over the life of the asset.

14-3. A company buys a machine for $2,400. The maintenance costs for the years 1970–1973 are as follows:

```
1970.........$ 50
1971..........  55
1972.........  650 (Includes $624 for cost of a new motor installed in
1973..........  70 December 1972.)
```

Instructions: (1) Assume that the machine is recorded in a single account at a cost of $2,400. No record is kept of the cost of the component parts. Straight-line depreciation is used and the asset is estimated to have a useful life of 8 years. It is assumed that there will be no residual value at the end of the useful life. What is the sum of the depreciation and maintenance charges for each of the first four years?

(2) Assume that the cost of the frame of the machine was recorded in one account at a cost of $1,800 and the motor was recorded in a second account at a cost of $600. Straight-line depreciation is used with a useful life of 10 years for the frame and 4 years for the motor. Neither item is assumed to have any residual value at the end of its useful life. What is the sum of depreciation and maintenance charges for each of the first three years?

(3) Evaluate the two methods.

14-4. The Westco Company had the following property transactions during the first two years of its operation:

Year	Property Acquired Cost	Estimated Life	Property Sold Cost	Year Acquired
1971	$210,000	12 years		
1972	72,000	12 years	$40,000	1971

Depreciation was recorded on the books of the company at one half of the full year's depreciation in the year of asset acquisition and at a full year's depreciation in the year of asset disposal. No residual value was recognized.

Instructions: Based upon the above information, show in T-account form the entries that would appear at the end of the two-year period in the accumulated depreciation account, assuming that depreciation is calculated by each of the following methods (show all calculations):

(1) Depreciation for the first one third of asset life is to be recorded at one and one-half times the straight-line rate; for the second one third, at the straight-line rate; and for the last one third, at one half of the straight-line rate.

(2) Depreciation is to be recorded on the asset declining balance at a rate that is double the straight-line rate.

14-5. The Atlas Steel Company changed the method of depreciation from double-declining balance to straight line for the year 1973 in order to fully depreciate the asset. Included in its assets was a machine that cost $100,000 in January 1967, and was being depreciated over a 10-year life. Salvage at the end of the 10 years was expected to be $2,000.

Instructions: (1) Compute the book value of the machine at the beginning of 1972.

(2) Give the entry to record the depreciation for 1972.

14-6. The Royal Mfg. Co. acquired 25 similar machines at the beginning of 1967 for $50,000. Machines have an average life of 5 years and no residual value. The group-depreciation method is employed in writing off the cost of the machines. Machines were retired as follows:

2 machines at the end of 1969   11 machines at the end of 1971
6 machines at the end of 1970   6 machines at the end of 1972

Instructions: Give the entries to record the retirement of machines and the periodic depreciation for the years 1967–1972 inclusive.

14-7. Economy Auto-Rent uses group depreciation for the automobiles that it employs in its business. Depreciation is based on a three-year life for the automobiles and an estimated trade-in value at the end of that time of 25% of cost. Automobiles are acquired for cash. Acquisitions for the years 1968–1972 are summarized below:

January, 1968 Purchased 20 automobiles for $62,000.
January, 1969 Purchased 6 automobiles for $18,100.
January, 1971 Purchased 2 automobiles for $6,600, trading in 2 automobiles acquired in 1968 and receiving a total trade-in allowance of $3,000.
January, 1972 Purchased 15 automobiles for $52,500, trading in 15 automobiles acquired in 1968 and receiving a trade-in allowance of $8,000.

Instructions: Give the entries to record the acquisitions of automobiles by purchase and trade and also the periodic depreciation for the years 1968–1972 inclusive.

14-8. Machines are acquired by Carnes, Inc., on March 1, 1972, as follows:

	Cost	Estimated Salvage Value	Estimated Life in Years
Machine 101	$27,000	$6,000	6
102	10,000	1,000	8
103	1,000	400	8
104	8,500	900	10
105	3,500	None	10

Instructions: (1) Calculate a composite depreciation rate for this group.
(2) Calculate the average life in years for the group.
(3) Give the entry to record the depreciation for the year ending December 31, 1972.

14-9. The Dennison Co. uses a certain hand tool in its manufacturing activities. On December 31, 1969, there were 400 such tools on hand at a cost of $4.65 each. Acquisitions and retirements in the years 1970–1972 follow:

	Acquisitions and Cost	Retirements and Retirement Proceeds
1970	200 @ $5.20	150 @ $.75
1971	190 @ 5.30	180 @ .80
1972	135 @ 5.50	195 @ .80

Retirements may be assumed to be on a first-in, first-out basis.

Instructions: Give all of the entries affecting the tools account for 1970, 1971, and 1972, assuming that:

(1) Operations are charged for the cost of tool retirements, less recovery on such units.

(2) Tools on hand at the end of each year are valued at 50% of cost.

(3) Operations are charged for the cost of periodic acquisitions equal to retirements, less recovery on the old units; any tools acquired in excess of retirements are reported as an increase in the asset balance; any deficiency in the acquisitions over retirements calls for an additional charge to operations for the shrinkage in the tools balance at original costs.

14-10. Miller Steel Products Company uses a number of electric cranes, each consisting of a chassis, motor, and truck. The crane chassis has a normal service life of 10 years, the truck lasts 5 years and must be overhauled at the end of every 3 years, and the motor normally requires a major overhaul at the end of every 2 years and must be replaced every 4 years.

The operating history of crane No. 315 is as follows:

Jan. 1963   Purchased crane for $70,000. Estimated cost of components: chassis, $35,000; truck, $25,000; motor, $10,000.

Dec. 1964   Overhauled motor at cost of $1,000.

Dec. 1965   Overhauled truck at cost of $3,000.

Dec. 1966   Replaced motor at cost of $10,200.

Dec. 1967   Overhauled motor at cost of $700; replaced truck at cost of $28,000.

Dec. 1969   Overhauled truck at cost of $3,300; replaced motor at cost of $11,000.

Dec. 1970   Overhauled motor at cost of $1,100.

Dec. 1972   Scrapped crane; proceeds from scrap was equal to the cost of dismantling and removing the asset.

The company depreciates its cranes at an average straight-line rate of 15% per year. The cost of motor and truck overhauls is charged to expense and the cost of replacing motors and trucks is charged against the accumulated depreciation account.

The assistant controller has suggested that the company revise its accounting procedure as follows: Separate property records would be maintained for motors, trucks, and chassis. Annual depreciation on each component would be computed by totaling the cost of the component and the estimated cost of the overhaul (in the case of motors and trucks) and dividing by the estimated service life. The cost of major overhauls would be charged against Accumulated Depreciation, and components would be retired from the property account with any gain or loss recorded at the time of replacement.

The controller feels that this procedure would not make any significant difference in the pattern of operating charges and asks the assistant to prepare a comparative history, using crane No. 315 as an example, showing the results under the company's present policy and the results under the assistant's suggested procedure.

Instructions: (1) Prepare a schedule summarizing the operating history of crane No. 315 if the company's present procedures are followed showing the total charge to expense for depreciation and repairs for each of the 10 years. Assume that any difference between asset cost and accumulated depreciation is added to or deducted from the depreciation charged in the tenth year.

(2) Prepare a similar schedule summarizing the operating history of crane No. 315 assuming that the company had followed the assistant's suggested procedure. Assume that the cost of the first overhaul is estimated as follows: motor, $1,000; truck, $3,000. Subsequent overhauls are estimated at the cost actually incurred in making the last previous overhaul. Include supporting schedules showing the computation of revised depreciation charges after the replacement of a component and the gain or loss at the time of retirement.

(3) Evaluate the two procedures and explain why you would or would not recommend that the assistant's suggestion be adopted.

14-11. At the close of each year the Pamper Co. determines the total cost of machinery in the assembly department and, without consideration of the acquisition date or life of the individual assets, applies a rate of 15% to the total cost in calculating depreciation for the year. At the end of 1971 it is decided that more satisfactory estimates for depreciation would be obtained by use of the straight-line method as applied to individual machines within the department. Data relative to the machines in the department on this date follow:

Machine	Date Acquired	Total Cost	Estimated Salvage Value	Estimated Life in Years
A	April 5, 1970	$26,500	$2,500	6
B	June 21, 1970	14,000	1,500	5
C	Sept. 28, 1971	8,000	1,000	7
D	Oct. 5, 1972	12,500	1,500	5

Instructions: (1) Determine (a) the balance in the accumulated depreciation account as of January 1, 1972, based upon use of the 15% depreciation rate, and (b) the balance as of January 1, 1972 if straight-line depreciation had been recorded. (Show calculations.)

(2) Give the journal entries (a) to adjust the accumulated depreciation account so that it shows depreciation as calculated on individual items and (b) to record the depreciation for 1972 on the revised basis. (Show calculations.)

14-12. The Dimension Corp. was organized on January 2, 1972. It was authorized to issue 80,000 shares of common stock, par $25. On the date of organization it sold 20,000 shares at par and gave the remaining shares in exchange for certain land bearing recoverable ore deposits estimated by geologists at 800,000 tons. The property is deemed to have a value of $1,500,000.

During 1972 mine improvements totaled $22,500. Miscellaneous buildings and sheds were constructed at a cost of $49,500. During the year 50,000 tons were mined; 4,000 tons of this amount were on hand unsold on December 31, the balance of the tonnage being sold for cash at $8 per ton. Expenses incurred and paid for during the year, exclusive of depletion and depreciation, were as follows:

Mining.	$151,750
Delivery.	15,000
General and administrative.	12,800

Cash dividends of $2 per share were declared on December 31, payable January 15, 1973.

It is believed that buildings and sheds will be useful only over the life of the mine; hence depreciation is to be recognized in terms of the mine output.

Instructions: Prepare an income statement and a balance sheet for 1972. Submit working papers showing the development of statement data. Disregard income taxes.

14-13. A depreciation schedule for auto trucks of the Way Mfg. Company was requested by an income tax revenue agent soon after December 31, 1972, showing the additions, retirements, depreciation, and other data affecting the taxable income of the company in the four-year period 1969 to 1972, inclusive. The following data were ascertained:

Balance of auto trucks account January 1, 1969:
Truck No. 1 purchased January 1, 1966, cost............... $6,000
Truck No. 2 purchased July 1, 1966, cost.................. 5,400
Truck No. 3 purchased January 1, 1968, cost.............. 4,800
Truck No. 4 purchased July 1, 1968, cost................. 5,000

Balance January 1, 1969............................. $21,200

The auto trucks accumulated depreciation account, previously adjusted by a revenue agent to January 1, 1969, and duly entered in the ledger, had a balance on that date of $7,760, this amount being depreciation on the four trucks from the respective dates of purchase, based on a five-year life. No charges had been made against this account prior to January 1, 1969.

Transactions between January 1, 1968, and December 31, 1972, and their record in the ledger were as follows:

(a) *July 1, 1969:* Truck No. 1 was sold for $2,000 cash. The entry made was a debit to Cash and a credit to Auto Trucks, $2,000.

(b) *January 1, 1970:* Truck No. 3 was traded for a larger one (No. 5), the agreed purchase price of which was $5,000. The Way Mfg. Company paid the automobile dealer $1,780 cash on the transaction. The entry was a debit to Auto Trucks and a credit to Cash, $1,780.

(c) *July 1, 1971:* Truck No. 4 was damaged in a wreck to such an extent that it was sold as junk for $50 cash. Way Mfg. Company received $950 from the insurance company. The entry made by the bookkeeper was a debit to Cash, $1,000, and credits to Miscellaneous Income, $50, and Auto Trucks, $950.

(d) *July 1, 1971:* A new truck (No. 6) was acquired for $6,500 cash and charged at that amount to the auto trucks account.

Entries for depreciation had been made at the close of each year as follows: 1969, $3,600; 1970, $3,000; 1971, $3,200; 1972, $4,000.

Instructions: (1) For each of the four years, calculate separately the increase or decrease in earnings arising from the company's errors in determining or entering depreciation or in recording transactions affecting trucks. Ignore any effect that income tax regulations concerning gain or loss on trade-ins may have on the earnings.

(2) Prove your work by one compound journal entry as of December 31, 1972; the adjustment of the auto trucks account is to reflect the correct balances assuming the books have not been closed for 1972.

(AICPA adapted)

14-14. The controller of the Johnson Manufacturing Co. asks for your advice and assistance as to whether the company should replace its "A" machines with new and advanced "B" machines which are capable of doubling the present annual capacity of the "A" machines. Annual finished production of the "A" machines is 2,500,000 good units. The increased production can be sold at the same profitable price.

The "A" machines are being depreciated by the Johnson Manufacturing Co. under the straight line method using a salvage value of 10% and a useful life of 8 years. The "A" machines cost the Johnson Manufacturing Co. $175,000 plus freight and insurance of $25,000. The raw materials as they are fed into the machines are subject to heavy pressure; because of this there is a 20% waste factor on an annual basis. The waste materials have no value and are scrapped for nominal value. Direct labor costs are equal to 60% of prime costs at the present time (labor and materials are considered prime costs). The company has been purchasing its raw materials in small lots at a cost of $50.00 per 1,000 units. Factory overhead, exclusive of depreciation, is applied to the manufacturing process at the rate of 20% of direct labor costs.

If the company purchases the "B" machines, certain economies will be gained. Material costs will decrease 20% because the company will be able to buy in larger quantities. In addition, the new machines have been perfected to such an extent that the waste factor will be reduced by 50%. However, because the "B" machine is much larger than the "A" machine, direct labor cost will be expected to increase by 20% of itself. Direct labor will continue to be 60% of prime cost before the increase of 20% in direct labor cost is applied. In addition to this, it is expected that the factory overhead rate will increase by 10% of itself. The life of the new machines is expected to exceed the life of the "A" machines by ¼, and the salvage value of the "B" machines will be in the same ratio as the salvage value of the "A" machines. The cost of the "B" machines, including freight and insurance of $35,000, will amount to $500,000. The company is aware of the fact that dismantling costs and installation costs will be involved, but it does not wish to consider this factor at the present time.

Instructions: (1) Prepare a statement of estimated cost comparisons on an annual basis. (Round to the nearest dollar.)

(2) List additional factors that should be considered in deciding upon the replacement.

(3) Comment briefly on the usefulness and validity of the comparisons made in part (1).

(AICPA adapted)

14-15. You are engaged in the examination of the financial statements of The Smoky Mountain Mfg. Company and are auditing the machinery and equipment account and the related depreciation accounts for the year ended December 31, 1972.

Your permanent file contains the following schedules:

Machinery and Equipment

	Balance 12/31/70	1971 Retirements	1971 Additions	Balance 12/31/71
1958–61	$ 8,000	$2,100	——	$ 5,900
1962	400	——	——	400
1963	——	——	——	——
1964	——	——	——	——
1965	3,900	——	——	3,900
1966	——	——	——	——
1967	5,300	——	——	5,300
1968	——	——	——	——
1969	4,200	——	——	4,200
1970	——	——	——	——
1971	——	——	$5,700	5,700
	$21,800	$2,100	$5,700	$25,400

Accumulated Depreciation

	Balance 12/31/70	1971 Retirements	1971 Provision	Balance 12/31/71
1958–61	$ 7,840	$2,100	$ 160	$ 5,900
1962	340	——	40	380
1963	——	——	——	——
1964	——	——	——	——
1965	2,145	——	390	2,535
1966	——	——	——	——
1967	1,855	——	530	2,385
1968	——	——	——	——
1969	630	——	420	1,050
1970	——	——	——	——
1971	——	——	285	285
	$12,810	$2,100	$1,825	$12,535

A transcript of the machinery and equipment account for 1972 follows:

1972	Machinery and Equipment	Debit	Credit
Jan. 1	Balance forward..................	$25,400	
Mar. 1	Burnham grinder.................	1,200	
May 1	Air compressor...................	4,500	
June 1	Power lawnmower................	600	
June 1	Lift truck battery................	320	
Aug. 1	Rockwood saw....................		$ 150
Nov. 1	Electric spot welder..............	4,500	
Nov. 1	Baking oven......................	2,800	
Dec. 1	Baking oven......................	236	
		$39,556	$ 150
Dec. 31	Balance forward.................		39,406
		$39,556	$39,556

Your examination reveals the following information:

(a) The company uses a ten-year life for all machinery and equipment for depreciation purposes. Depreciation is computed by the straight-line method. Six months' depreciation is recorded in the year of acquisition or retirement. For 1972 the company recorded depreciation of $2,800 on machinery and equipment.

(b) The Burnham grinder was purchased for cash from a firm in financial distress. The chief engineer and a used machinery dealer agreed that the practically new machine was worth $2,100 in the open market.

(c) For production reasons the new air compressor was installed in a small building that was erected in 1972 to house the machine and will also be used for general storage. The cost of the building, which has a 25-year life, was $2,000 and is included in the $4,500 voucher for the air compressor.

(d) The power lawnmower was delivered to the home of the company president for his personal use.

(e) On June 1 the battery in a battery-powered lift truck was accidentally damaged beyond repair. The damaged battery was included at a price of $600 in the $4,200 cost of the lift truck purchased on July 1, 1969. The company decided to rent a replacement battery rather than buy a new battery. The $320 expenditure is the annual rental for the battery paid in advance, net of a $40 allowance for the scrap value of the damaged battery that was returned to the battery company.

(f) The Rockwood saw sold on August 1 had been purchased on August 1, 1959 for $1,500. The saw was in use until it was sold.

(g) On September 1 the company determined that a production casting machine was no longer needed and advertised it for sale for $1,800 after determining from a used machinery dealer that this was its market value. The casting machine had been purchased for $5,000 on September 1, 1967.

(h) The company elected to exercise an option under a lease-purchase agreement to buy the electric spot welder. The welder had been installed on February 1, 1972 at a monthly rental of $100.

(i) On November 1 a baking oven was purchased for $10,000. A $2,800 down-payment was made and the balance will be paid in monthly installments over a three-year period. The December 1 payment includes interest charges of $36. Legal title to the oven will not pass to the company until the payments are completed.

Instructions: Prepare the auditor's adjusting journal entries required at December 31, 1972 for equipment and the related depreciation.

(AICPA adapted)

14-16. You are engaged in the examination of the financial statements of the Ute Corp. for the year ended December 31, 1971. The following schedules for the land, buildings, and equipment and related accumulated depreciation accounts have been prepared by the client. You have checked the opening balances to your prior year's audit working papers.

ASSETS

Description	Final 12/31/71	Additions	Retirements	Per Books 12/31/72
Land....................	$ 22,500	$ 5,000		$ 27,500
Buildings................	120,000	17,500		137,500
Machinery and equipment...	385,000	40,400	$26,000	399,400
	$527,500	$62,900	$26,000	$564,400

ACCUMULATED DEPRECIATION

Description	Final 12/31/71	Additions*	Retirements	Per Books 12/31/72
Buildings................	$ 60,000	$ 5,150		$ 65,150
Machinery and equipment...	173,250	39,220		212,470
	$233,250	$44,370		$277,620

*Depreciation expense for the year.

Your examination reveals the following information:

(a) All equipment is depreciated on the straight-line basis (no salvage value taken into consideration) based on the following estimated lives:

buildings, 25 years; all other items, 10 years. The company's policy is to take one-half year's depreciation on all asset acquisitions and disposals during the year.

(b) On April 1, the company entered into a ten-year lease contract for a die casting machine with annual rentals of $5,000 payable in advance every April 1. The lease is cancelable by either party (sixty days written notice is required) and there is no option to renew the lease or buy the equipment at the end of the lease. The estimated useful life of the machine is ten years with no salvage value. The company recorded the die casting machine in the machinery and equipment account at $40,400, the present discounted value at the date of the lease, and $2,020 applicable to the machine has been included in depreciation expense for the year.

(c) The company completed the construction of a wing on the plant building on June 30. The useful life of the building was not extended by this addition. The lowest construction bid received was $17,500 the amount recorded in the buildings account. Company personnel were used to construct the addition at a cost of $16,000 (materials, $7,500; labor, $5,500; and overhead, $3,000).

(d) On August 18, $5,000 was paid for paving and fencing a portion of land owned by the company and used as a parking lot for employees. The expenditure was charged to the land account.

(e) The amount shown in the machinery and equipment asset retirement column represents cash received on September 5 upon disposal of a machine purchased in July 1968, for $48,000. The bookkeeper recorded depreciation expense of $3,500 on this machine in 1972.

(f) Crux City donated land and building appraised at $10,000 and $40,000 respectively to the Ute Corporation for a plant. On September 1, the company began operating the plant. Since no costs were involved, the bookkeeper made no entry for the above transaction.

Instructions: Prepare the formal adjusting journal entries that you would suggest at December 31, 1972, to adjust the accounts for the above transactions. Disregard income tax implications. The books have not been closed. Computations should be rounded off to the nearest dollar.

(AICPA adapted)

chapter 15

land, buildings, and equipment - revaluations

It was indicated in the preceding chapters that land, buildings, and equipment items are recorded at cost, that estimates are made of the useful lives of these assets, and that schedules are developed for the reasonable and systematic allocation of property costs to periodic revenues. These are the normal procedures in accounting for land, buildings, and equipment. But during the course of their use, certain circumstances may suggest revisions in cost allocation plans and, in some instances, actual departures from cost for property valuation as well as for periodic allocations. These problems are considered in this chapter.

Revisions in estimates of property life

When a property item is retired, any errors in the estimates of life and residual value become evident, and recognition is made in the accounts at that time for any past over-depreciation or under-depreciation. If depreciation charges have been inadequate, the book value of the asset exceeds its residual value and a special loss is recognized; if depreciation charges have been excessive, the book value is less than residual value and a special gain is recognized.

It may become evident during the life of a property item that depreciation was incorrectly estimated and that periodic charges have been inadequate or excessive. It may be found that asset life has been reduced by physical declines that exceed original expectations or by inadequacy or obsolescence that could not have been foreseen, or that life has been prolonged by high standards of maintenance and repairs or the absence of certain anticipated declines in usefulness. Under these circumstances, two positions have been supported:

1. The book value is accepted as it stands and such remaining book value allocated over the estimated remaining life of the asset.

2. An entry is made to restate accumulated depreciation on the basis of present evidence, and depreciation charges for the remaining life of the asset is reported in accordance with such evidence.

To illustrate the alternate positions, assume that depreciation at 10% has been applied for a property item, cost $10,000 with an estimated life of 10 years. At the end of 5 years, when the book value of the asset is reduced to 50% of cost, it is determined that the asset has a remaining useful life of 10 years. If no change in prior depreciation is to be recognized in the accounts, the remaining asset cost is distributed over the remaining life or at the rate of 5% a year (50% ÷ 10). If a correction for past over-depreciation is to be recognized, the asset book value is increased to two thirds of original cost and depreciation for the remaining life of the asset is reported at 6⅔% a year (66⅔% ÷ 10).

The entries applying these two approaches would be as follows:

Approach 1	Approach 2
(No change in depreciation of prior periods)	(Change in depreciation of prior periods)

Entry at beginning of sixth year:

No entry	Accumulated Depreciation.... 1,667
	Restatement of Depreciation of Prior Periods...... 1,667
	To adjust depreciation for prior periods.

Entry at end of each of next ten years:

Depreciation Expense........ 500	Depreciation Expense......... 667
Accumulated Depreciation.. 500	Accumulated Depreciation.. 667
Book value of $5,000 divided by 10-year remaining life.	Cost of $10,000 divided by revised 15-year life.

The first position, which accepts existing book value as a basis for subsequent charges, has received wide support in practice. Those supporting this position maintain that cost once assigned to revenue is a permanent disposition of such cost and only unassigned cost is subject to future allocation. The restatement of accounts for depreciation recognized in prior periods is considered unacceptable since this will result in total depreciation charges over the life of the asset that will differ from original depreciable cost.

The American Accounting Association Committee on Concepts and Standards Underlying Corporate Financial Statements took this position as early as 1953. The Committee would permit the correction of past errors of a mechanical and nonjudgment character, and also the correction of judgment errors when new events of an unusual character and of significant potential effect on future income prove past judgments to have been erroneous. However, the Committee indicated that the reversal, revision, or reaccounting for past depreciation or amortization would open the doors to the possibility of manipulation in the reporting of periodic income.[1]

In 1966, in Opinion No. 9, the Accounting Principles Board also gave support to the first approach. It stated:

> Treatment as prior period adjustments should not be applied to the normal, recurring corrections and adjustments which are the natural result of the use of estimates inherent in the accounting process. For example, changes in the estimated remaining lives of fixed assets affect the computed amounts of depreciation, but these changes should be considered prospective in nature and not prior period adjustments.[2]

In 1970, the Accounting Principles Board in Opinion No. 20 re-affirmed the position that a change in the period of benefits or service and residual values should be regarded as a change in estimate that is a necessary consequence of periodic presentations of financial statements and not as a correction of errors of prior periods. The Board concluded,

> . . . the effect of a change in accounting estimate should be accounted for in (a) the period of change if the change affects that period only or (b) the period of change and future periods if the change affects both.[3]

Additional support for the first position is found in certain practical considerations. This is the general position that must be taken for income tax purposes; depreciation once allowed for tax purposes is not subject to revision. When depreciation is reported on the books in accordance with income tax requirements, special account analysis and restatement of depreciation data is unnecessary in preparing the tax returns.

Those taking the second position maintain that errors, no matter what their source, call for appropriate correction. The depreciation for each period should be the best estimate that can be made from the evidence at hand. Errors in past charges should not be corrected by compensating errors in subsequent charges; such a practice, it is maintained, serves only to distort measurements of the past, present, and future.

The weight of the arguments at the present time favors the first approach. With an annual review of the depreciation policy, it is maintained that the possibilities of material failures in recording appropriate charges for depreciation can be largely avoided.

Fully depreciated properties still in use

There are instances in which a fully depreciated asset may be continued in use. However, such continued use may involve extraordinary

---

[1] *Accounting and Reporting Standards for Corporate Financial Statements and Preceding Statements and Supplements,* Supplementary Statement No. 5 (1957 rev.; Madison, Wisconsin: American Accounting Association), p. 35.

[2] *Opinions of the Accounting Principles Board, No. 9,* "Reporting the Results of Operations" (New York: American Institute of Certified Public Accountants, 1966), par. 24.

[3] *Opinions of the Accounting Principles Board, No. 20,* "Accounting Changes" (New York: American Institute of Certified Public Accountants, 1971), par. 31.

maintenance and repair charges that suggest little or no contribution on the part of the asset itself. For example, a fully depreciated asset may be continued in use by a business unit because of inability to finance a replacement. Inefficiencies and extraordinary charges may actually make the use of such an asset more costly than a new machine. Under these circumstances no value can be assigned to the property item. Even when continued use of the asset may be considered to afford some contribution to revenues, the position taken by the Accounting Principles Board would preclude any adjustment for depreciation assigned to prior periods. Cost and accumulated depreciation balances for fully depreciated assets should not be offset until the property items are actually retired; the financial statements should provide parenthetical or note references to the fully depreciated assets that are still in use and are included in the account totals.

Changes in depreciation resulting from additions, betterments, and replacements

Depreciation charges may require revision during the life of building and equipment items as a result of additional expenditures related to these properties. Expenditures that enlarge or improve property items and that are reported as increases in the asset cost must be recognized in recording depreciation in subsequent periods. For example, assume that a machine with an estimated life of 20 years is acquired for $10,000. After the machine is used for 15 years, an expenditure of $2,000 is made that improves the machine but does not prolong its useful life. The entry for the betterment is:

Machinery..	2,000	
Cash..		2,000

Annual depreciation would now be calculated as follows:

Original asset:	$10,000 ÷ 20......................	$500
Betterment:	$ 2,000 ÷ 5......................	400
Revised annual depreciation........................		$900

Expenditures that rehabilitate certain assets or increase their service lives beyond original estimates, and are recorded by charges to the asset valuation account also affect the depreciation charges to be made in subsequent periods. To illustrate, assume in the previous example that the expenditure did not improve the asset but simply prolonged its remaining service life to 8 years. The expenditure to rehabilitate the asset is recorded as follows:

Accumulated Depreciation — Machinery............	2,000	
Cash..		2,000

Depreciation for the remaining life of the asset is determined as follows:

Asset cost.......................................	$10,000
Less accumulated depreciation, $7,500, reduced by $2,000 as a result of asset rehabilitation..........................	5,500
Book value to be written off during remaining 8 years......	$ 4,500

Revised annual depreciation: $4,500 \div 8$, or $562.50.

Expenditures for the replacement of certain property parts also affect subsequent depreciation. For example, assume that a machine that cost $10,000 has an estimated life of 10 years. After six years an important machine part, estimated to represent 25% of the original asset cost, is worn out and replaced. The cost of the new part is $2,800 and its usefulness will terminate with that of the machine. Entries to record the retirement of the old part and acquisition of the new one are as follows:

Accumulated Depreciation — Machinery............	1,500	
Loss on Retirement of Machine Parts...............	1,000	
Machinery....................................		2,500

Loss on asset retirement:		
Asset cost estimated at 25% of $10,000.......	$2,500	
Depreciation, 60% of cost................	1,500	
Loss...................................	$1,000	

Machinery.......................................	2,800	
Cash..		2,800

Depreciation for the remaining life of the asset is determined as follows:

Depreciation of original asset: ($10,000 − $2,500) \div 10	$ 750
Depreciation of new part: $2,800 \div 4...........	700
Revised annual depreciation.......................	$1,450

Departures from cost

As discussed in Chapter 1, and as indicated in the preceding chapters, accountants normally use the cost approach to asset valuation. However, departures from cost to estimates of current values are found in certain special instances. For example, current assets, such as marketable securities and inventories, are reported at less than cost when it is believed that realization of these assets may be limited to the lower amounts; long-term investments are reported at less than cost when there is evidence of a permanent decline in the value of these assets; and properties acquired through donation or discovery are reported at their fair market values in providing satisfactory bases for asset reporting and income measurement. However, these variations from cost have been the exception.

Although there has been little variation from the use of historical cost in the records, the level of discussion concerning modification of this principle continues to increase through the years. The principal reason for such interest has been the widely fluctuating value of the dollar as the economy in the United States has swung from a severe depression through periods of inflation and recession and more recently to an almost sustained inflation. In addition to these changes in the economy, there have been widely fluctuating values within certain industries that have reflected the dynamic aspect of expanding technology and significant changes in social structures and the environment.

These economic events give rise to two distinct kinds of value changes. One kind of change is the variation in the value of the dollar which is the unit used to measure every aspect of accounting in the United States. A second kind is a change, in a comparative sense, between specific segments of the economy. The latter occur as a result of such economic events as the favorable location of land due to freeway construction or industrial expansion, the scarcity of equipment because of high demands for an industry's end product, or the enhanced value of buildings because of changes in real estate areas. Valuation changes of the first kind have suggested *general price-level adjustments*, and of the second kind, *specific price-level* or *current value adjustments*.

General price-level adjustments. Adjustment for general price changes retains the basic concept of a cost-based system. The major objective of general price-level adjustments is to standardize the measuring unit and thus avoid the misleading comparisons that can arise from the application of a flexible measuring stick. Recognition of price-level changes involves the application of an overall general adjustment index to all aspects of the records in providing statements that reflect the current purchasing power of the monetary unit. Much attention has been given to this matter both in the United States and in some foreign countries where price fluctuations have been even more severe than those in the United States. In 1969, the Accounting Principles Board issued Statement No. 3, "Financial Statements Restated for General Price-Level Changes." This statement encouraged companies to issue supplemental financial statements adjusted for changes in the measuring unit.

Because of the special problems that arise in the preparation of statements adjusted for general price-level changes, this subject is treated in detail in Chapter 28.

Current value adjustments. The second kind of value change in reality encompasses the first, but goes beyond it. By adjusting asset cost to current values measured by some approach to market values, not only are adjustments made for general price-level changes, but also for comparative changes in the particular segment of the economy being evaluated. No longer is a cost base retained. Distinctions may be made between changes in the monetary unit itself and the comparative change, but many suggested approaches do not attempt to make this distinction. The most frequently mentioned approach to current values for land, building, and equipment items is *appraisal accounting* whereby appraisals are used to arrive at the current valuation of such assets. Appraisal accounting has a long history: it was widely used in the 1920's by company managements in their desire to report the increased value of their assets in a period of rapidly rising prices. Standards for appraisals were vague, and many analysts of the 1930 depression feel that the application of appraisal accounting was a significant factor in the subsequent economic decline.

Since the experience of the 1920's, the accounting profession as a body has been reluctant to accept appraisal valuations, especially if they were upward in direction. The Accounting Principles Board emphasized this point in 1965 in Opinion No. 6:

> The Board is of the opinion that property, plant and equipment should not be written up by an entity to reflect appraisal, market or current values which are above cost to the entity.[1]

The Board further emphasized this view by indicating that the proposals for general price-level adjusted supplemental statements were "not intended to represent appraisal values, replacement costs, or any other measure of current value."[2]

Even though these negative views have been strong, some companies have made appraisal adjustments under circumstances that they supported as exceptional. Because of this factor, the Accounting Principles Board and its predecessor committees have established guidelines to follow when property appraisals are recorded. Problems relating to the

---

[1]*Opinions of the Accounting Principles Board, No. 6,* "Status of Accounting Research Bulletins" (New York: American Institute of Certified Public Accountants, 1965), par. 17.

[2]*Statements of the Accounting Principles Board, No. 3,* "Financial Statements Restated for General Price-Level Changes" (New York: American Institute of Certified Public Accountants) par. 5.

use of appraisal values in the accounts are considered in the sections that follow.

Use of appraisal data

Appraisal values for property items may be required for credit, tax, insurance, sale, or merger purposes. On the other hand, such values may be sought under exceptional circumstances for use in the accounts. When appraisal values are to be employed, they should be provided by reliable independent appraisers.

Appraisals by professional engineers or appraisers normally afford data relative to the cost of reproducing individual assets as follows:

1. *Reproduction cost*, which is the present amount required to reproduce the property new.
2. *Sound value*, which is the remaining fractional life of the asset applied to reproduction cost. Sometimes sound value is expressed as a *condition percent*, which is the present percentage relationship of sound value to reproduction cost.

It may frequently be more informative to obtain data relative to replacement cost rather than reproduction cost. Replacement cost suggests the cost of replacing existing capacity rather than reproducing identical facilities.

The purpose of obtaining appraisal data may be to bring property items into agreement with current reproduction values and to recognize depreciation in subsequent periods in terms of such current reproduction values. The appraisal, then, involves a change in method from cost valuation and cost allocation to appraisal valuation and appraisal allocation. To illustrate such uses, assume the following: A property item was acquired at a cost of $600,000 and is being depreciated on an 8-year life or at a rate of $12\frac{1}{2}\%$. After being used for 4 years, the property is appraised at a reproduction cost of $1,000,000 and at a sound value of $600,000 or a condition percent of 60%.

Accumulated depreciation on asset cost is 50%. However, an asset decline to date of only 40% is indicated by the appraisal. If the latter decline measures primarily the physical deterioration of the asset, no change in original allocations may be indicated and future depreciation charges may be continued at $12\frac{1}{2}\%$. On the other hand, if the decline of 40% can be accepted as a measure of physical and functional decline, the appraisal may be regarded as indicating that past depreciation was excessive and that subsequent depreciation should be recognized at 10% per year. It has already been stated that a change in the depreciation rate of a property item should not be regarded as calling for a prior period adjustment in applying the standards as set by the Accounting Principles

Board in Opinions No. 9 and No. 20. However, recognition in the accounts of appraisal values involves not only a change in the valuation of a property item but also a change in depreciation in terms of such appraisal; this represents, in effect, a change in the method of reporting the property item and the related depreciation charge. Under the circumstances, it is assumed in the examples that follow that the change in method calls for (1) a restatement of the accumulated depreciation of the property account that is recognized as a special "cumulative effect" item in the period of appraisal, and (2) a restatement of the property item and related accumulation balance to reflect the effect of the appraisal.[1] The restatement of the accumulated depreciation is necessary to report the sound value at the date of the appraisal.

Any changes that are reported in the accounts for asset cost as well as for related depreciation charges must be disregarded for income tax purposes. For tax purposes the basis for depreciation continues to be original cost; the basis for computing gain or loss on the disposal of the property item is the asset book value stated in terms of such cost.

Property devaluation recorded in the accounts. A write-down of land, buildings, and equipment cost reduces the property item and is reported on the income statement as a special item arising from a change in accounting method. In the case of depreciable assets, devaluation generally affects both the asset and the related accumulated depreciation balances.

To illustrate the write-down of a depreciable asset, assume the following data for a company's buildings:

Cost	Asset Use to Date	Depreciation to Date	Accumulated Depreciation
$500,000	10 yrs.	20%	$100,000

An appraisal of buildings establishes a present reproduction cost of $300,000 and a sound value of $240,000, or 80% of the reproduction cost. Since the appraisal confirms a 20% decline in the asset in 10 years, no restatement of the past depreciation charges is required. In recording the appraisal decrease in the accounts, then, the changes are limited to the following:

	Cost	Asset Use to Date	Depreciation to Date	Accumulated Depreciation
Original cost balances................	$500,000	10 yrs.	20%	$100,000
Appraisal decrease...................	(200,000)			(40,000)
Balances, per appraisal..............	$300,000	10 yrs.	20%	$ 60,000

---

[1]The accounting procedures that are required in reporting a change in method are defined in Accounting Principles Board Opinion No. 20, "Accounting Changes," and were described in Chapter 3.

The entry to revalue the asset follows:

Accumulated Depreciation — Buildings..........	40,000	
Cumulative Effect on Prior Years of Changing to Appraisal Accounting for Buildings...........	160,000	
Buildings..................................		200,000

Assume in the preceding example that the appraisal establishes a reproduction cost for the asset of $300,000 but a sound value of only $225,000 or 75% of such reproduction cost, depreciation of 25% being related to asset use for 10 years. Here the appraisal indicates: (1) inadequate depreciation of $25,000 in the past in terms of cost; (2) a further reduction in the asset from a book value as restated of $375,000 to a sound value of $225,000. The changes are summarized below:

	Cost	Asset Use to Date	Depreciation to Date	Accumulated Depreciation
Original cost balances...............	$500,000	10 yrs.	20%	$100,000
Restatement of depreciation of prior periods.........................			5%	25,000
Cost balances as restated............	$500,000	10 yrs.	25%	$125,000
Appraisal decrease..................	(200,000)			(50,000)
Balances, per appraisal..............	$300,000	10 yrs.	25%	$ 75,000

The entries to accomplish these changes follow:

Transaction	Entry		
(1) To restate accumulated depreciation to 25% of cost, per appraisal.	Cumulative Effect on Prior Years of Changing to Appraisal Accounting for Buildings......................... Accumulated Depreciation—Buildings.	25,000	25,000
(2) To reduce asset and accumulated depreciation balances to a reproduction cost of $300,000, per appraisal.	Accumulated Depreciation—Buildings... Extraordinary Loss on Buildings Revaluation............................ Buildings.........................	50,000 150,000	200,000

Depreciation after the restatement of the accumulated depreciation balance would be recognized at $2\frac{1}{2}\%$ per year as established by the appraisal.

Quasi-reorganization. A situation may arise in which a company's properties were acquired at costs that do not permit earnings under current conditions. There may also be a deficit from previous operations or a retained earnings balance that is insufficient to absorb a reduction in the carrying value of the property items. Yet such a reduction may be warranted by current conditions and indeed may be necessary if the company is to be able to report profitable operations in future periods. The company erred in acquiring property which could not be employed profitably in the business, but it should be recognized that a mistake was made and that the future operations of the company should not be burdened with past mistakes.

Under such circumstances a company may elect to write down property items and to accompany such action with a restatement of the capital structure, eliminating the deficit that is found after the write-off. The elimination of a deficit through a restatement of invested capital balances that provides, in effect, a "fresh start" accounting-wise on the part of the corporation, is called a *quasi-reorganization* or *corporate readjustment*. The quasi-reorganization procedure does not require recourse to the courts as in formal reorganization procedures; there is no change in the legal corporate entity or interruption in business activity.

To illustrate the nature of a quasi-reorganization, assume that the Baldwin Corporation has suffered losses from operations for some time and both current and future revenues appear to be insufficient to cover the depreciation on properties that were acquired when prices were considerably higher than at present. The company decides upon a restatement of assets and also the restatement of paid-in capital to remove the deficit and make possible the declaration of dividends upon a return to profitable operations. A balance sheet for the company just prior to this action follows:

Baldwin Corporation
Balance Sheet
June 30, 1972

Current assets		$ 250,000	Liabilities		$ 300,000
Land, buildings,			Stockholders' equity:		
and equipment.	$1,500,000		Capital stock, $10 par,		
Less accumulated			100,000 shares .	$1,000,000	
depreciation	600,000	900,000	Less deficit	150,000	850,000
			Total liabilities and stock-		
Total assets		$1,150,000	holders' equity		$1,150,000

The quasi-reorganization is to be accomplished as follows:

1. Land, buildings, and equipment are to be reduced to their present sound value of $600,000 by reductions in the asset and accumulated depreciation balances of $33\frac{1}{3}\%$.
2. Capital stock is to be reduced to a par of $5, $500,000 in capital stock thus being converted into "additional paid-in capital."
3. The deficit of $450,000 ($150,000 as reported on the balance sheet increased by $300,000 arising from the write-down of land, buildings, and equipment) is to be applied against the capital from the reduction of the par value of stock.

Entries to record the changes follow:

Transaction	Entry
(1) To write down land, buildings, and equipment and accumulated depreciation balances by 33⅓%.	Retained Earnings (Deficit)............ 300,000 Accumulated Depreciation............. 200,000 Land, Buildings, and Equipment...... 500,000

(2) To reduce the capital stock balance from $10 par to $5 par and to establish paid-in capital from reduction in stock par value.	Capital Stock ($10 par, 100,000 shares). 1,000,000
	   Capital Stock ($5 par, 100,000
	      shares)...................... 500,000
	   Paid-In Capital from Reduction in
	      Stock Par Value.............. 500,000

(3) To apply the deficit after asset devaluation against paid-in capital from reduction in stock par value.	Paid-In Capital from Reduction in
	   Stock Par Value................ 450,000
	   Retained Earnings (Deficit)....... 450,000

The balance sheet after the quasi-reorganization is shown below.

Baldwin Corporation
Balance Sheet
June 30, 1972

Current assets..............		$ 250,000	Liabilities.................	$	300,000
Land, buildings,			Capital stock, $5 par, 100,000		
and equipment.	$1,000,000		shares...................		500,000
Less accumulated			Paid-in capital from reduc-		
depreciation...	400,000	600,000	tion in stock par value....		50,000
			Total liabilities and stock-		
Total assets...............		$ 850,000	holders' equity..........	$	850,000

Following the quasi-reorganization, the accounting for the operations of the company is similar to that for a new company. Earnings subsequent to the quasi-reorganization, however, should be accumulated in a *dated retained earnings* account. On future balance sheets, retained earnings dated as of the time of account readjustment will inform readers of the date of such action and of the fresh start in earnings accumulation.

The AICPA Committee on Accounting Procedure has recommended that a company electing to bring about a legitimate restatement of its assets, capital stock, and retained earnings through a quasi-reorganization, relieving future income or retained earnings of charges that would otherwise be made against these, should meet the following conditions:

1. It should make a clear report to stockholders of the proposed changes and should obtain their formal consent.

2. It should present a fair balance sheet with a reasonably complete restatement of values so that there will be no continuation of the circumstances that justify charges to invested capital.

3. Assets should be carried forward as of the date of the quasi-reorganization at fair and not unduly conservative amounts, determined with due regard for the accounting to be employed thereafter. Excessive write-downs

that will result in the overstatement of earnings or retained earnings on the ultimate realization of assets should be avoided.[1]

The Committee recognized that in some cases the fair value of an asset or the amount of potential losses or charges cannot be measured satisfactorily as of the date of a quasi-reorganization and estimates of asset and liability values will be required. In such cases, material differences between book values and ultimate realization or liquidation amounts that cannot be attributed to events or circumstances originating after the date of the readjustment should not be recognized as losses but should be reported as corrections identified with the readjustment.

Property appreciation recorded in the accounts. When appreciation is to be entered on the books, both the property and capital balances are increased. The capital increase, however, is still unrealized and must be designated as appraisal capital.

To illustrate the process of recording asset appreciation, assume that land, cost $50,000, is increased to an appraised value of $80,000. An entry is made as follows:

Land — Appraisal Increase	30,000	
Appraisal Capital — Land		30,000

Land would be reported on the balance sheet at its appraised value, $80,000. The appraisal capital should not be combined with other capital balances but should be reported separately on the balance sheet so that the reader of the statement is fully aware of the unrealized nature of such capital.

If the land is sold at a later date for $75,000, $25,000 of the recorded appreciation will have been realized. The gain is recognized and the appraisal capital is canceled by the following entry:

Cash	75,000	
Appraisal Capital — Land	30,000	
Land		50,000
Land — Appraisal Increase		30,000
Gain on Sale of Land		25,000

With this entry, all evidence of the appraisal is canceled, and the account balances are the same as though the asset had been carried at its cost, $50,000, and subsequently sold for $75,000.

As indicated earlier, appraisals of depreciable assets may indicate restatements in accumulated depreciation as well as increased reproduction costs. In recording devaluation, the effects of both the

---

[1]*Accounting Research Bulletin No. 43*, "Restatement and Revision of Accounting Research Bulletins" (New York: American Institute of Certified Public Accountants, 1953), Ch. 7, sect. A.

restatement in accumulated depreciation and the asset write-down were ultimately reflected in retained earnings. In recording appreciation, however, the restatement in accumulated depreciation is ultimately reflected in retained earnings, but the asset write-up calls for the recognition of appraisal capital. Entries, then, are required (1) to restate the accumulated depreciation in terms of cost, and (2) to record the appraisal increase in the asset and in the accumulated depreciation and also to report appraisal capital. Although appraisal increases may be reported directly in the asset and the accumulated depreciation accounts, it is normally desirable to report these in separate accounts. Cost data are thus preserved and are available in the preparation of income tax returns where the effects of appraisals are ignored. Subsequent entries that require information concerning both cost and appraisal increases can be more conveniently prepared.

To illustrate the foregoing, assume the following data for buildings:

Cost	Asset Use to Date	Depreciation to Date	Accumulated Depreciation
$200,000	20 yrs.	40%	$80,000

At this time an appraisal of the property shows it to have a reproduction cost of $320,000 and a sound value of only $160,000, 50% of its useful life having expired. The appraisal thus indicates (1) inadequate depreciation in the past in terms of cost of $20,000; (2) an increase in the asset from a book value as restated of $100,000 to a sound value of $160,000. These changes are summarized as follows:

	Cost	Asset Use to Date	Depreciation to Date	Accumulated Depreciation
Original cost balances................	$200,000	20 yrs.	40%	$ 80,000
Restatement of depreciation of prior periods..........................			10%	20,000
Cost balances as restated..............	$200,000	20 yrs.	50%	$100,000
Appraisal increase...................	120,000			60,000
Balances, per appraisal..............	$320,000	20 yrs.	50%	$160,000

Entries to record the appraisal follow:

Transaction	Entry		
(1) To restate accumulated depreciation to 50% of cost, per appraisal.	Cumulative Effect on Prior Years of Changing to Appraisal Accounting for Buildings............................ Accumulated Depreciation—Buildings	20,000	20,000
(2) To increase asset and accumulated depreciation balances to a reproduction cost of $320,000, per appraisal.	Buildings — Appraisal Increase........ Accumulated Depreciation of Buildings — Appraisal Increase......... Appraisal Capital — Buildings.......	120,000	60,000 60,000

Depreciation on property appreciation. As stated earlier, the Accounting Principles Board in 1965 in Opinion No. 6, specifically rejected the use of appraisal adjustments to "property, plant and equipment." However, they gave their support to an earlier position taken by the AICPA Committee on Accounting Procedure by concluding:

> . . . whenever appreciation has been recorded on the books, income should be charged with depreciation computed on the written up amount.[1]

The reasoning behind this requirement would appear to be that there should be consistency of treatment between the balance sheet and the income statement. To record depreciation at cost when appraisal values appear on the balance sheet would clearly violate such consistency.

Depreciation on appraised values is recorded by a charge to expense and credits to the accumulated depreciation accounts reporting depreciation on cost and on the appraisal increase. The entry to record depreciation may be accompanied by a second entry to recognize the portion of appraisal capital that may be regarded as realized through operations. This is done by a charge to appraisal capital and a credit to retained earnings. The reduction of the asset in terms of appraised values is thus accompanied by the realization of appraisal capital, and retained earnings is reported at the balance that would have been shown in the absence of an appraisal. To illustrate, assume that at the beginning of 1972, equipment acquired on January 1, 1969, is shown on the books at cost $100,000 less accumulated depreciation of $37,500 representing depreciation at $12\frac{1}{2}\%$ a year, or at a book value of $62,500. An appraisal on January 2, 1972, sets the reproduction cost of the equipment at $150,000 and its present sound value at 70% of this amount, or $105,000. Depreciation of 30% in 3 years reported by the appraisal indicates a depreciation rate of 10%. The entry to record the appraisal is as follows:

Transaction	Entry		
January 2, 1972 (1) To restate accumulated depreciation to 30% of cost, per appraisal.	Accumulated Depreciation—Equipment. Cumulative Effect on Prior Years of Changing to Appraisal Accounting for Equipment......................	7,500	7,500
(2) To increase asset and accumulated depreciation balances to a reproduction cost of $150,000 per appraisal.	Equipment—Appraisal Increase........ Accumulated Depreciation of Buildings —Appraisal Increase............... Appraisal Capital—Buildings........	50,000	15,000 35,000

Entries to record depreciation based on the appraisal values are then made periodically as shown on the following page.

---

[1] *Opinions of the Accounting Principles Board, No. 6, loc. cit.*

Transaction	Entry

December 31, 1972
(1) To record depreciation on appraised value of $150,000 at corrected rate of 10%, per appraisal.
	Depreciation Expense—Equipment....... 15,000
	   Accumulated Depreciation—Equip.... 10,000
	   Accumulated Depreciation of Equip. —
	     Appraisal Increase............... 5,000

(2) To record realization of appraisal capital of $50,000 at rate of 10%, consistent with reduction in the asset appraisal increase.	Appraisal Capital — Equipment......... 5,000 Retained Earnings................... 5,000

The first entry records depreciation on the appraised value. The second entry transfers appraisal capital to the retained earnings account. Appraisal capital then reflects the appraisal increase in the reduced book value of the asset, and retained earnings reports earnings based upon actual costs. Thus, the Retained Earnings balance is the same as though the appraisal had not been recorded. When the asset is fully depreciated, the entire balance in the appraisal capital account will have been transferred to retained earnings by the periodic entries. Upon disposal of the asset, accumulated depreciation balances are applied against their respective asset accounts.

Instead of periodic transfers from appraisal capital to retained earnings, transfers may be made to a special revenue account which is ultimately combined with other income data and carried to retained earnings. The special revenue account is recognized on the income statement as an adjustment to the summary of operations to compensate for depreciation that is recognized at more than cost. When such a procedure is followed, operations can be viewed in terms of depreciation calculated on appraisal values, but both final net income and retained earnings balances are developed in accordance with historical cost.

Some accountants object to the transfer of appraisal capital either directly or indirectly to retained earnings. They view appreciation procedures as similar to devaluation procedures and would regard both asset and capital changes as of a permanent nature. Appraisal balances in asset accounts would be recognized for all further asset accounting including periodic allocations to operations; appraisal capital would be viewed as permanent capital with neither utilization nor sale of the asset affecting this balance. In answering such objection, it may be maintained that the recognition of appraisal capital is required by the presence of income that has definitely accrued to the benefit of stockholders but has not yet been *realized*. The subsequent utilization or sale of the asset gives rise to income that would normally be recognized in accordance with the accepted principles of income realization. At that point the increase in capital is no longer due to a subjective appraisal estimate, but is the result of actual business transactions, thus justifying its reclassification as retained earnings.

Examples in the preceding sections have illustrated the procedures that are followed when property appreciation is reported in separate accounts, original asset and accumulated depreciation accounts continuing to report costs and retained earnings remaining unchanged. It should be observed that similar procedures can be followed in recording asset devaluation: reductions in asset and accumulated depreciation accounts can be reported by separate offset or negative account balances; the decrease in capital can be reported by a charge to a special devaluation capital account, retained earnings continuing to summarize activities reported in terms of cost.

Holding gains and losses. Recently, some writers have suggested that appraisal changes should be recognized as *holding gains or losses*.[1] The term signifies that gains or losses do occur while holding an asset during a period of price changes, and these gains and losses should be distinguished from those occurring as a result of normal operations. Views differ as to whether these holding gains and losses should be reported as a part of the stockholders' interest until they are realized through use or sale, or whether they should be reported in the income statement as a special form of income. In the first case, the accounting treatment for holding gains would be identical to that illustrated for appraisal capital with allocation of the holding gain being made to revenue as it was realized. In the second case, total income would include the unrealized gains and losses.

Support for the use of current values

The previous discussion in this chapter has distinguished between valuation adjustments for general price-level changes and those for current value changes. Although the accounting profession, through the Accounting Principles Board, is on record as being opposed to the presentation of current values on the general-purpose financial statements, there has been increasing demand for such information from many members of the accounting profession and from some businesses and investors. In 1962, Robert T. Sprouse and Maurice Moonitz in Accounting Research Study No. 3 took the following position:

> In the external reports, plant and equipment should be restated in terms of current replacement costs whenever some significant event occurs, such as a reorganization of the business entity or its merger

---

[1]One of the more influential sources for this approach was Edgar O. Edwards and Phillip W. Bell's *Theory and Measurement of Business Income*. The authors developed a theory of business income which incorporated these concepts.

with another entity or when it becomes a subsidiary of a parent company. Even in the absence of a significant event, the accounts could be restated at periodic intervals, perhaps every five years. The development of satisfactory indexes of construction costs and of machinery and equipment prices would assist materially in making the calculation of replacement costs feasible, practical, and objective.[1]

In 1964, an American Accounting Association Committee issued Supplementary Statement No. 1 to the 1957 Revision of *Accounting and Reporting Standards for Corporate Financial Statements*. The committee concluded that:

> Current cost be adopted immediately as the basis of valuation for land, buildings and equipment whenever the amounts involved are significant and the available measures of current cost are sufficiently objective.[2]

The Committee went on to recommend that the increase in valuation be reflected in holding gains and loss accounts with a distinction being made between the realized and the unrealized portions.

In 1966, another committee of the American Accounting Association issued *A Standard of Basic Accounting Theory* and reached a similar conclusion. It stated

> We . . . recommend that current costs be reported. There are many approaches to "current values," and we suggest that the approach that is most likely to meet the standards of accounting information . . . is current cost to replace the assets or services involved.[3]

Perhaps no general question in accounting has caused more clearly divided points of view than has that of the adoption of current values. The use of current values has been advocated for all assets, not just land, buildings, and equipment. However, because of the longer lives of these assets, more significant changes between cost and current values are usually evident for these items than for the more liquid assets.

Arguments for and against the use of current values

The following arguments are most frequently presented as support for the opposing points of view.

Arguments for the use of current values:

1. Readers of financial statements desire to compare the results of one company with that of another. Companies have widely varying mixes of assets acquired at different times; thus the cost bases differ between

---

[1] Robert T. Sprouse and Maurice Moonitz, *A Tentative Set of Broad Accounting Principles for Business Enterprises*, Accounting Research Study No. 3 (New York: American Institute of Certified Public Accountants, 1962), p. 34.

[2] "Accounting for Land, Buildings, and Equipment," Supplementary Statement No. 1, *Accounting Review*, Vol. XXXIX (July, 1964), p. 698.

[3] *A Statement of Basic Accounting Theory* (Evanston, Illinois: American Accounting Association, 1966), p. 34.

companies to the extent that it is difficult, if not impossible, for a reader to evaluate how effectively one company is using its assets as compared with another company or the industry.

2. Readers of financial statements have various decisions to make which require forecasting ability. Present investors decide whether to buy more shares or sell what they have. Failure to report current values may mislead the investor and he may make decisions under the circumstances that would not be in his best interests.

3. Depreciable assets must ultimately be replaced. Although depreciation is not intended to provide a replacement fund for retired assets, the property items used up must be replaced if the entity is to continue in operation at its same level. If the replacement cost of these assets has risen, the excess must be raised either by additional capital or by retention of a part of net income. Since replacement must be made at current costs, proper matching requires charges based upon current values.

Arguments against the use of current values:

1. There are many ways of measuring current values. This leads to a lack of objective measurement and the introduction of a wide variety of values that require differing interpretations.

2. Cost is highly objective and subject to little disagreement. Thus, it is highly verifiable. Market is subjective and thus open to disagreement.

3. The purpose of depreciation is to match cost that is expended against the revenue that is produced. No adjustment of cost is necessary to achieve this purpose.

4. Value changes occur continuously. Many difficulties would be encountered in making frequent adjustments to the asset and accumulated depreciation accounts.

5. Replacement of fully depreciated properties is a separate issue from determination of net income. Technological change makes exact replacement unlikely, and each replacement is a new decision based upon expectation of future revenues.

It is safe to assume that the discussion of current values and the merits of using current values, either as a *replacement* for cost or as an *addition* to cost in some form of multi-valued statement or supplementary report, will continue for many years to come.

Land, buildings, and equipment on the balance sheet

Land, buildings, and equipment frequently constitute a substantial portion of a company's total assets, and a separate listing on the balance sheet of the principal assets or groups of assets in this classification is normally desirable. Nondepreciable assets should not be combined with those that are subject to reductions for accumulated depreciation. Depreciable assets should be reported at their cost or other basis, and accumulated depreciation should be shown as subtractions from such amounts. The basis of an asset, whether cost or a value other than cost, should be disclosed. When there are significant differences in property costs and fair market values, it would be appropriate to disclose such differences by special note or parenthetical remark. When property is reported at an amount other than cost, the difference between the reported value and cost should be stated together with an explanation of the source of such value and the authority for reporting such value in the accounts. When only summaries of land, buildings, and equipment items are provided, detail may be offered on supporting schedules.

Land, buildings, and equipment may be presented on the balance sheet as follows:

Land, buildings, and equipment:		
Land, at cost of acquisition in 1953.......		$ 65,000
Buildings, at cost.....................	$320,000	
Less accumulated depreciation (calculated by the straight-line method)...........	125,000	195,000
Equipment at cost (balance includes $40,000 of fully depreciated items still in use)................................	$184,000	
Less accumulated depreciation (calculated by the sum-of-the-years-digits method)..	124,000	60,000
Tools, patterns, and dies, at inventory value		16,500
Total land, buildings and equipment.		$336,500

When appraisal increases have been recorded in the accounts, assets may be stated at appraised balances and costs reported parenthetically. It would be preferable, however, to offer information for both asset and accumulated depreciation balances in a form such as the following:

	Cost	Appraisal Increase	Book Value as Appraised	
Buildings.............	$100,000	$ 75,000	$175,000	
Less accumulated depreciation.............	40,000	30,000	70,000	
Balance..............	$ 60,000	$ 45,000		$105,000

QUESTIONS

1. What alternative procedures can you suggest that might be followed in the accounts upon determining that depreciation has been incorrectly estimated in past years? Evaluate each position.

2. How would you recommend that fully depreciated properties be carried in the accounts when they are still being used by the business?

3. What is the Accounting Principles Board's position on properly recording a change in depreciation rate?

4. Revision of past depreciation on properties and revision of account balances to conform to present replacement values of properties are two aspects of the same problem, the fair statement of balance sheet data. Do you agree?

5. List the factors that, alone or in combination, may cause the difference between the book value and the current value of the land, buildings, and equipment.

6. (a) When, in your opinion, would the recognition of a downward revision in the cost of property items be appropriate? (b) When would you support an upward revision?

7. Distinguish between (a) reproduction cost and sound value, (b) appraisal capital and retained earnings, (c) appreciation and devaluation.

8. How will changes from cost to appraisal values affect the charges to be recognized on asset use and disposal for income tax purposes?

9. The president of Parkhurst Corporation, your client, has asked you for an explanation of a "quasi-reorganization." He is unfamiliar with the procedure and is concerned that a competitor might have an advantage since undergoing a quasi-reorganization. Prepare a report for the president explaining the "quasi-reorganization." Your report should include the following parts:

    (a) Definition and accounting features of the procedure.
    (b) The purposes of the procedure and the conditions under which it should be considered.
    (c) The authorization necessary.
    (d) The disclosure required in the financial statements.
    (e) Does the competitor have an advantage? Discuss briefly.

10. Officials of the Palmer Corporation insist that the appreciation of land, buildings, and equipment should be recorded as an increase in paid-in capital since these properties were originally acquired in exchange for capital stock of the company. Evaluate this argument.

11. Assuming that appreciation is recorded in the accounts, what are the arguments in support of (a) depreciation in terms of cost and (b) depreciation in terms of appraised value?

12. Appraisal capital is a permanent addition to the stockholders' equity section; it can be reduced only if the company is sold. Evaluate this statement.

13. Describe a situation that could suggest the recognition of a holding loss on buildings.

14. Distinguish between realized and unrealized holding gains and losses.

15. Evaluate the arguments which are used to justify the use of current values on the financial statement.

16. Officers of the X Corporation feel that prices have reached a permanently higher level and thus insist that depreciation on building and equipment be recognized in terms of higher reproduction costs if current earnings are to be fairly stated. Officers of the Y Corporation feel that prices are too high and will ultimately decline and thus insist that current revenue be charged with a part of the cost of assets currently acquired if current earnings are to be fairly stated. How would you reply to each of these proposals?

17. Historical costs for land, buildings, and equipment are not relevant to the needs of the external investor. Evaluate this statement.

18. The management of Bowles Corporation suggests that depreciation on assets that have been written up be recorded on the higher values in order to assure the availability of funds for the replacement of such assets. In your opinion, is this practice necessary and sufficient in meeting the problem?

19. How are current values more subjective than historical costs?

EXERCISES

1. Equipment was acquired by the Curtis Construction Co. at a cost of $15,000. Depreciation on the asset was recorded by the straight-line method on the basis of an 8-year life and a $600 residual value. At the end of the sixth year, it was estimated that the asset could be used for another four years and would have a residual value as originally estimated. What are the entries required at the end of the sixth year?

2. Machinery was acquired by the Greendale Co. on July 1, 1969, at a cost of $40,000 and was depreciated by the straight-line method on an estimated 8-year life. On December 31, 1972, in reviewing account balances for purposes of making the adjustments for the past fiscal year, it was determined that the machinery will probably have a 10-year life. What entry would be made to record depreciation for 1972?

3. The Peerless Corporation owns office equipment costing $8,000 that has been used for 5 years and that has been reduced to a book value of $900, the estimated trade-in value at this time. Because of a shortage of new equipment for replacement, the company spends $2,100 overhauling the old equipment. It is assumed that this expenditure will prolong the life of the equipment by 3 years and that the trade-in value will remain the same. (a) What entry is made to record the expenditure? (b) What is the annual straight-line depreciation subsequent to the expenditure?

4. The Gardner Co. purchased land and an old building for $125,000. The land is estimated to be worth $100,000; the building is estimated to have a remaining life not to exceed 10 years. The building is used for 5 years and is then completely remodeled at a cost of $75,000. It is estimated that the building should have a life of 20 years from the date of such remodeling. Give the entries to be made for (a) purchase of the land and building, (b) periodic depreciation, (c) cost of remodeling the building, and (d) subsequent depreciation.

5. At the beginning of 1969 the Troy Company purchased machinery for $20,000. The machinery had an estimated life of 10 years. As of December 31, 1972, the same machinery had a replacement cost of $30,000. General prices have risen 20% in the 4-year period.

(a) How is the $10,000 increase divided between general and specific price rises?
(b) Show how the machinery and accumulated depreciation would be reported on the balance sheet at the end of 1972 using the following values:
(1) Original cost.
(2) Original cost adjusted for general price changes.
(3) Current values.

6. The Henry Co. shows property and stockholders' equity balances on January 1, 1972, as follows:

Property Accounts		Stockholders' Equity	
Buildings and equipment.	$1,650,000	Capital stock (100,000	
Accumulated depreciation	350,000	shares, $10 par).......	$1,000,000
	$1,300,000	Premium on capital stock	150,000
			$1,150,000
		Less deficit.............	300,000
		Total stockholders' equity	$ 850,000

On January 5, stockholders authorize that the property accounts be written down to their sound values as indicated by appraisal as follows:

Buildings and equipment...........................	$1,250,000
Accumulated depreciation..........................	280,000
	$ 970,000

They further authorize that the deficit after property restatement be applied against the premium on stock and any excess against the capital stock account; capital stock outstanding is to be changed from $10 par to no-par. Give the entries that are required in recording the quasi-reorganization.

7. Machinery, reported on the books at $45,000 with an accumulated depreciation of $12,000 and an estimated life of 15 years, was appraised on January 1 and found to have a reproduction cost new of $60,000 and an estimated total life of 20 years. What entries would be made to record the appraisal?

8. Machinery acquired on January 1, 1967, at a cost of $300,000 shows accumulated depreciation of $60,000 on January 1, 1972. On this date engineers and appraisers estimate that the machinery should have a remaining useful life of 25 years and a reproduction cost new of $450,000. (a) What entries should be made for the appraisal? (b) What entries should be made to record depreciation on this asset for the year 1972 if operations are charged with appraised values?

9. The Inland Marine Co. acquired buildings at the beginning of 1964 at a cost of $100,000 and is depreciating these on a 50-year basis. At the beginning of 1972 an appraisal indicates that the buildings have a reproduction cost of $200,000 and a sound value of $160,000 based on a 40-year life. The appraisal is recorded in the accounts, and depreciation for 1972 is recorded on the appraisal value. On January 3, 1973, the buildings are sold for cash, $175,000. What entries would be made on the books of the Inland Marine Co. for 1972 and 1973?

PROBLEMS

15-1. The information that follows summarizes transactions of the Rayson Mfg. Co. relating to the acquisition of a machine:

Jan. 5, 1965   Purchased machine for $25,000; was allowed a 2% discount for making cash payment. The machine is estimated to have a 5-year life; its residual value is estimated at $2,500.

Dec. 31, 1967   The estimated life of the machine is revised from 5 years to 8 years. The estimated residual value is the same.

Jan. 10, 1969   Costs of $3,300 are incurred in overhauling the machine at this point, and it is estimated that the machine will have a 10-year life as a result of the overhaul. Residual value on a 10-year life is estimated at only $800.

Apr. 4, 1972   The machine is sold for $4,500.

Instructions: Give all of the entries that would be made relative to machinery for the period 1965–1972, including the adjustments that are required at the end of each calendar year to recognized depreciation by the straight-line method.

15-2. The Rialto Corporation established a new assembly line for its major product in the fall of 1967 at a cost of $660,000. It was estimated to have a life of 10 years with no salvage value and was depreciated by the sum-of-the-years-digits method. In 1972, a special inspection of the line indicated it was still operating efficiently and would probably be satisfactory for another 8 years after remodeling at a cost of $90,000. The remodeling was completed during the fall of 1972.

Instructions: Give the entries to record depreciation for 1972 and for 1973 assuming that one-half year depreciation is recorded in the year of acquisition and one half in year of retirement. The same depreciation method will be used, and depreciation charges of prior periods are not to be restated.

15-3. Four machines are found in the shop of the York Engineering Co. at the beginning of 1972 as follows:

Machine	Date Acquired	Cost, Including Installation	Estimated Useful Life	Estimated Salvage Value
No. 1	Mar. 5, 1964	$12,000	10 yrs.	$ 900
No. 2	May 1, 1966	9,000	10 yrs.	600
No. 3	Aug. 20, 1968	11,200	10 yrs.	1,000
No. 4	Nov. 6, 1969	12,000	5 yrs.	1,200

During 1972 the following transactions relating to machines are completed:

Jan. 2 Machine No. 1, which had not been operating satisfactorily, was sold for $850. It was decided that the lives of Machines Nos. 2 and 3 probably would not exceed 8 years and that salvage values would be negligible and hence could be ignored.

Jan. 20 Machine No. 5 was purchased for cash at a cost of $12,000. The new machine is estimated to have a life of 10 years and no salvage value.

Feb. 28 Machine No. 4 was traded in for a larger machine costing $18,000. Machine No. 4 was accepted at a value of $7,600 for purposes of the trade-in, the balance of the purchase price being paid in cash. The new machine, to be referred to as Machine No. 6, is recorded at $18,000. It is estimated to have a life of 10 years and a trade-in value of $1,500 at that time.

Instructions: (1) Give the journal entries that are required for 1972, including the adjustments for depreciation by the straight-line method at the end of the year (depreciation is calculated to the nearest month).

(2) Prepare a schedule showing the cost, the accumulated depreciation, and the book value of machines on hand as of December 31, 1972.

15-4. The books of the Baher Manufacturing Co. were audited for the first time and the following account was found during the course of the audit in 1973:

Machinery

1971			1971		
May 8	Machine A	10,000	Dec. 31 Depreciation		2,500
8	Machine B	5,200	1972		
Sept. 26	Machine C	17,000	Mar. 20 Machine A		7,000
1972			Nov. 1 Machine B		—
Apr. 21	Machine D	4,800	Dec. 31 Depreciation		3,200
Nov. 1	Machine E	5,000			

An examination of the books and records revealed the following additional data concerning machinery: Machines A, B, C, and D were purchased for cash. Machines A and B proved inadequate. Machine A was sold for $7,000. Machine B was traded for Machine E. The purchase price of Machine E was $7,500; cash of $5,000 was paid for the new machine, an allowance of $2,500 being received on Machine B. All machines were estimated to have a 10-year life. Depreciation of machinery had been recorded on the basis of estimates by company engineers as follows:

		Depreciation	
Machine		1972	1971
A.........................		——	$1,000
B.........................		$ 400	500
C.........................		1,600	1,000
D.........................		750	——
E.........................		450	——
		$3,200	$2,500

Instructions: (1) Prepare the journal entries that should have been made to record properly the above transactions. (Assume that depreciation by the straight-line method is recorded to the nearest year, and an asset acquired by trade-in is reported at its regular purchase price.)

(2) Prepare the journal entries necessary in 1973 to correct the accounts in view of the entries actually made in prior years.

(3) Give the balances that are reported in the asset and accumulated depreciation accounts after these have been corrected, and list the detail for the individual machines making up such balances.

(4) Prepare the journal entry to record depreciation for 1973.

15-5. The Land-o-Lake Company has experienced several poor earnings years and has several assets on its books that are overvalued. It desires to revalue its assets downward and eliminate the deficit. At December 31, 1972, the company owns the following land, buildings and equipment:

	Cost	Accumulated Depreciation	Book Value	Current Value
Land.....................	$250,000	——	$250,000	$175,000
Buildings.................	375,000	$175,000	200,000	150,000
Machinery and equipment...	175,000	75,000	100,000	50,000
	$800,000	$250,000	$550,000	$375,000

The balance sheet on December 31, 1972, reported the following balances in the stockholders' equity section:

Common stock — 100,000 shares, $10 par..............	$1,000,000
Additional paid-in capital.........................	100,000
Retained earnings (deficit)........................	(175,000)
Total.......................................	$ 925,000

As part of the reorganization, the common stock is to be canceled and reissued at $5 par.

Instructions: (1) Prepare the journal entries to record the quasi-reorganization.

(2) Give the property section and equity section of the company's balance sheet as they would appear after the entries are posted.

15-6. The Halper Distributor Sales Co. owns real estate acquired at the beginning of 1960. Account balances for this asset on January 2, 1969, appear as follows:

Land..		$50,000
Buildings...................................	$45,000	
Less accumulated depreciation.................	20,000	25,000
		$75,000

An appraisal of this property as of January 2, 1969, indicated that the land was worth $85,000, that buildings had a reproduction cost, new, of $60,000, and a present sound value of $38,400. The appraisal is recorded in the accounts. On July 1, 1972, the company borrowed $50,000, issuing a 10-year note secured by a mortgage on the property; interest at 8% is payable annually on July 1. On October 1, 1972, the company sold the land and buildings for $120,000, the purchaser assuming the mortgage note and accrued interest and making payment in cash for the difference.

Instructions: (1) Prepare the entries to record the asset appraisal on January 2, 1969.

(2) Prepare the entries to record straight-line depreciation in the years 1969–1971.

(3) Prepare the entry to record the sale of property on October 1, 1972.

15-7. The following account balances relating to land, buildings, and equipment appear on the books of the Ardmore Corporation on December 31, 1971:

Land..	$150,000	
Building A.......................................	390,000	
Accumulated depreciation — building A.............		$ 97,500
Building B.......................................	300,000	
Accumulated depreciation — building B.............		37,500
Equipment.......................................	270,000	
Accumulated depreciation — equipment.............		135,000
Furniture and fixtures...........................	60,000	
Accumulated depreciation — furniture and fixtures....		60,000

Assets have been carried at cost since their acquisition. With the exception of Building B, completed on January 1, 1967, at a cost of $300,000, all of the assets were acquired on January 1, 1962. The straight-line method was used in recording depreciation; residual values were not recognized. The company now wishes to show land, buildings, and equipment items at their present sound values.

An appraisal firm submitted the following report on January 2, 1972:

	Replacement Value (New)	Present Depreciated Value
Furniture and fixtures..............	$ 75,000	$ 12,500
Equipment........................	330,000	110,000
Buildings: A, constructed 1/1/62.....	450,000	300,000
B, constructed 1/1/67.....	360,000	300,000
Land............................	250,000	

Instructions: (1) What is the estimated remaining life of each depreciable asset as determined from the appraiser's report?

(2) Prepare journal entries to give effect to appraisal values.

(3) Prepare the land, buildings, and equipment section of the balance sheet reporting appraisal values as of the date of the appraisal.

(4) Prepare the adjusting entries for depreciation at the end of 1972.

15-8. Right after its incorporation July 1, 1968, the Land Corporation acquired land, buildings, and equipment for cash as follows:

	Cost	Estimated Useful Life
Land.................................	$ 80,000	
Buildings............................	250,000	50 years
Equipment...........................	210,000	15 years
Office furniture and fixtures.............	24,000	12 years

On April 27, 1971, additional equipment was acquired at $75,000 less a 5% discount for cash payment. Cost of freight was $1,750. Installation of equipment was completed at the end of June at a cost of $9,500. This equipment is estimated to have a 10-year life.

At the beginning of 1972, an appraisal of property items was made by professional appraisers. While no change was indicated in the life of the assets, it was ascertained that reproduction costs of those assets acquired in 1968 had increased by the following percentages:

Land......................................	200%
Buildings.................................	80
Equipment................................	60
Office furniture and fixtures................	40

It was authorized that such appraisal increases be recorded in the accounts and that depreciation be recorded on the basis of appraisal values.

Instructions: (1) Prepare the journal entries relating to land, buildings, and equipment accounts for the period July 1, 1968, to December 31, 1972, including the entries for depreciation that are made at the end of each calendar year. (Assume that no changes are made in appraisal capital balances at the end of each year since dividends are to be limited to net income based on appraisal depreciation.)

(2) Give the information that will appear in the land, buildings, and equipment and the appraisal capital sections of the balance sheet prepared as of December 31, 1972.

15-9. ABC Corporation purchased a machine in 1970, trading in an older machine of a similar type. The old machine, which was acquired in 1957, had a cost basis of $77,250 but was written up $47,750 to $125,000 in 1961. Both the old and new machines have an estimated 20-year life, and reappraisal of the old machine did not affect its estimated life. ABC Corporation takes one-half year of depreciation in years of acquisition and disposal.

The terms of the purchase provided for a trade-in allowance of $25,000 and called for a cash payment of $125,000 or 12 monthly payments of $11,000 each. ABC chose the latter alternative. Other expenses incurred in connection with the exchange were as follows:

Payroll charges:
Removal of old machine.	$ 800
Repairs to factory floor.	700
Installation of new machine.	900

Invoices received:
Sales engineer who supervised installation: 40 hours @ $10 .	400
Hotels, meals, travel, etc., for sales engineer.	200
Freight-in — new machine.	1,100
Freight-out — old machine.	1,000

Instructions: (1) Prepare entries to reflect the exchange on the books of ABC on a basis acceptable for federal income tax purposes.

(2) Compute depreciation on the new machine for the years 1970, 1971, and 1972 using the basis you computed in part (1) assuming that depreciation is recorded by each of the methods stated below. (Assume that the special first-year write-off has been applied to other assets. Show all computations clearly labeled.)

(a) The straight-line method.
(b) The sum-of-the-years-digits method.
(c) The declining-balance method at twice the straight-line rate.

(AICPA adapted)

15-10. The Columbia Corporation had $105,000 of dividends in arrears on its preferred stock as of March 31, 1972. While retained earnings were adequate to meet the accumulated dividends, the company's management did not wish to weaken its working capital position. The management also realized that a portion of the fixed assets were no longer used or useful in their operation. Therefore, the following reorganization was proposed, which was approved by stockholders to be effective as of April 1, 1972:

(a) The preferred stock was to be exchanged for $300,000 of 5% debenture bonds. Dividends in arrears were to be settled by the issuance of $120,000 of $10 par value, 5% noncumulative preferred stock.
(b) Common stock was to be assigned a value of $50 per share.
(c) Goodwill was to be written off.
(d) Land, buildings, and equipment were to be written down, based on appraisal and estimates of useful value, by a total of $103,200, consisting of an $85,400 increase in accumulated depreciation and a $17,800 decrease in certain assets.

(e) Current assets were to be written down by $10,460 to reduce certain items to expected realizable values.

The condensed balance sheet as of March 31, 1972, was as follows:

Assets

Cash..		$ 34,690
Other current assets...........................		252,890
Land, buildings, and equipment................	$1,458,731	
Accumulated depreciation......................	512,481	
		946,250
Goodwill..		50,000
		$1,283,830

Liabilities and Stockholders' Equity

Current liabilities..	$ 136,860
7% Cumulative preferred stock ($100 par)*.................	300,000
Common stock (9,000 shares, no-par)......................	648,430
Premium on preferred stock...............................	22,470
Retained earnings..	176,070
	$1,283,830

*$105,000 dividends in arrears.

Instructions: (1) Prepare journal entries to give effect to the reorganization as of April 1, 1972. Give complete explanations with each entry and comment on any possible options in recording the reorganization.

(2) Prepare a balance sheet as of April 30, 1972, assuming that net income for April was $10,320 after provision for taxes. The operations resulted in a $5,290 increase in cash, a $10,660 increase in other current assets, a $2,010 increase in current liabilities, and a $3,620 increase in accumulated depreciation.

(3) In making an audit of the Columbia Corporation as of December 31, 1972, you find that the following items had been charged or credited directly to Retained Earnings during the nine months since April 1, 1972:

(a) A debit of $14,496 arising from an income tax assessment applicable to prior years.

(b) A credit of $20,387 resulting from a gain on the sale of equipment that was no longer used in the business. This equipment had been written down by a $10,000 increase in accumulated depreciation at the time of the reorganization.

(c) A debit of $7,492 resulting from a loss on fixed assets destroyed in a fire on November 2, 1972.

(d) A debit of $13,500 representing dividends declared on common and preferred stock.

For each of these items, state whether you believe it to be correctly charged or credited to Retained Earnings. Give the reasons for your conclusion. If the item is not handled properly, prepare the necessary correcting entry.

(AICPA adapted)

chapter 16

intangible assets

The term *intangible assets* is used in accounting to denote long-term property items without physical characteristics. From a strictly legal point of view, such assets as shares of stock, bonds, and claims against customers are regarded as intangibles. For the accountant, however, the term is limited to such properties as patents, copyrights, trademarks, franchises, leaseholds, and goodwill.

Intangible assets derive their values by affording special rights or advantages that are expected to contribute to the earnings of the business. Special rights contributing to earnings may be found, for example, in the ownership of patents; special advantages contributing to earnings may arise from the skill of employees, the ability of management, desirable location of the business, and good customer relationships — elements of a company's goodwill.

The "intangible assets" designation is perhaps unfortunate since it has contributed to a general misunderstanding of the nature of these assets and to the accounting treatment that should be accorded them. Mere physical existence does not affect an item's economic significance. A factory building about to be razed may be reported on the balance sheet at little or no value despite its massive physical dimensions. On the other hand, patents without physical qualities could be the most valuable property item owned by a company. Intangible assets, no less than tangible properties, require a full accounting.

Valuation of intangible assets at time of acquisition

In general, valuation for intangible assets should follow the standards employed for the tangible group. Intangible assets should be recorded at cost. Cost should include all expenditures related to the development or the purchase of the assets. When an intangible asset is acquired in exchange for an asset other than cash, the fair market value of the asset exchanged or that of the intangible asset, whichever is more clearly determinable, should be used to record the acquisition. When shares of stock or bonds are issued in exchange for an intangible asset, the fair market value of the securities issued or the intangible asset acquired should be determined in recording the exchange. When several intangible assets or a combination of tangible and intangible assets are acquired for a lump sum, this sum must be allocated to the individual assets in some equitable manner, normally on the basis of the relative market values of the individual assets acquired.

Costs are reported for intangible assets only when certain expenditures can be related to their acquisition. For example, no value should appear on the books for a franchise that is acquired without cost or for a company's goodwill developed internally over a period of years. But when an intangible asset without an accountable cost makes significant contribution to the earnings of a business, reference on the balance sheet to such right or advantage by means of a special note is appropriate.

Valuation of intangible assets subsequent to the time of acquisition

The subject of accounting for intangible assets subsequent to their acquisition has received wide attention. The costs of intangible assets have been charged off in many different ways. The process of assigning the costs of intangible assets to operations in a systematic manner is called *amortization*. Amortization is recorded by a charge to an expense account and a credit to the asset account or to an asset valuation account.

Intangible assets may be classified according to their expected periods of economic benefit. The terms of existence of certain intangible assets are limited by law, regulation, contract, or economic factors. The terms of existence of other intangible assets are not limited and the periods of their usefulness are indefinite or indeterminate. The Accounting Research Bulletins, in establishing standards for accounting for the cost of intangible assets, originally recognized two types of intangible assets: type (a) those with a limited term of existence, and type (b) those having no limited term of existence and no indication of limited life at the time of their acquisition. The cost of a type (a) intangible asset was assigned to revenue according to the estimate of its useful life. The cost of a type (b) intangible asset was generally carried forward until the time it appeared that its benefits would be of limited duration or that it no longer made a contribution to revenue. At this time, the cost of the asset either was assigned to revenue over the period of such remaining estimated life or was written off entirely. The accounting for a type (b) intangible asset was criticized because of the wide flexibility it afforded companies in the determination of net income.

In 1970 the Accounting Principles Board issued Opinion No. 17 on Intangible Assets, and made the following observation:

> Present accounting for goodwill and other unidentifiable intangible assets is often criticized because alternative methods of accounting for costs are acceptable. Some companies amortize the cost of acquired intangible assets over a short arbitrary period to reduce the amount of the asset as rapidly as practicable, while others retain the cost as an asset until evidence shows a loss of value and then record a material reduction in a single period. Selecting an arbitrary period of amortization is criticized because it may understate net income during the amortization period and overstate later net income. Retaining the cost as an asset is criticized because it may overstate net income before the loss of value is recognized and understate net income in the period of write-off.[1]

In answer to criticisms of past practice, the Board established a maximum amortization period for all intangible assets. The Board reasoned that few, if any, intangible assets last forever; that those intangible assets with an indeterminate life, such as goodwill, should be amortized over a limited term because their usefulness will almost surely eventually disappear. Factors that should be considered in estimating the useful lives of intangible assets include:

1. Legal, regulatory, or contractual provisions may limit the maximum useful life.
2. Provisions for renewal or extension may alter a specified limit on useful life.
3. Effects of obsolescence, demand, competition, and other economic factors may reduce a useful life.
4. A useful life may parallel the service life expectancies of individuals or groups of employees.
5. Expected actions of competitors and others may restrict present competitive advantages.
6. An apparently unlimited useful life may in fact be indefinite and benefits cannot be reasonably projected.
7. An intangible asset may be a composite of many individual factors with varying effective lives.[2]

Within these general guidelines for estimating a useful life for an intangible asset, the Board established a maximum amortization period of forty years for any intangible asset. If analysis indicated that the life of an intangible asset was likely to exceed forty years, the cost of the asset should be amortized over the maximum forty-year period and not some arbitrary shorter period. The Board also concluded that the straight-line method of amortization should be applied unless it could be shown that another systematic method would be more appropriate.[3]

---

[1]*Opinions of the Accounting Principles Board, No. 17,* "Intangible Assets" (New York: American Institute of Certified Public Accountants, 1970), par. 14.

[2]*Ibid.*, par. 27.

[3]*Ibid.*, par. 29 and 30.

A company should evaluate periodically the estimated life selected for each intangible asset to determine whether current events or circumstances warrant a revision of the original estimated lives. When a change is indicated, the original amortization plan may be modified in a manner similar to that described earlier for tangible assets. Thus, a change in the period of usefulness of an intangible asset would be recognized by an increase or a decrease in the rate of amortization for the remainder of the asset life. When a revised life for an intangible asset is indicated, this should not exceed forty years from the original date of acquisition. Under some conditions, a significant reduction in the unamortized cost of an intangible asset may be warranted. If such reduction is material, it may be reported as an extraordinary item.[1] However, if periodic reviews are made of the estimated future benefits of recorded intangible assets, the need for recognizing write-offs that would be regarded as extraordinary would be minimized.

Intangible assets subject to amortization are reported on the balance sheet at unamortized cost or at original cost less the amount reported in a valuation account summarizing past accumulated amortization. If an intangible asset is reported at a value other than cost, full information concerning such valuation should be provided. The periodic charge for amortization is reported as a manufacturing cost or as an operating expense depending upon the nature of the contribution made by the intangible asset.

Federal income tax regulations allow the taxpayer to write off the cost of an intangible asset by periodic charges when its term of existence is definitely limited in duration. Periodic deductions would be recognized for income tax purposes on patents, copyrights, leaseholds, licenses, franchises, and similar properties. Present income tax regulations do not allow a deduction for goodwill. However, upon the sale or termination of a business, a deduction would be allowed for the portion of the asset not realized.[2]

Accounting problems that are related to specific intangible assets are discussed in the sections that follow.

Identifiable intangible assets

Intangible assets may be divided between those assets that can be identified with a specific right or type of activity, and those assets that

[1]*Opinions of the Accounting Principles Board, No. 9,* "Reporting the Results of Operations" (New York: American Institute of Certified Public Accountants, 1966), par. 21. Also, *Opinions of the Accounting Principles Board, No. 17, op. cit.,* par. 31.

[2]The APB does not view the difference between accounting for goodwill for accounting purposes and for income tax purposes as a timing difference and hence observes that the allocation of income taxes under these circumstances is inappropriate. *Ibid.,* par. 30.

cannot be specifically identified and are regarded as related to the enterprise as a whole. The latter are generally designated as goodwill. Management involved in the purchase of a company carefully values all tangible assets as well as all intangible assets that can be identified. An amount paid on the purchase of a company that exceeds the sum of identifiable net assets is normally recorded as goodwill. The identifiable intangible assets will be discussed first in this chapter, followed by a discussion of goodwill.

Patents. A *patent* is an exclusive right granted by the government to an inventor enabling him to control the manufacture, sale, or other use of his invention for a specified period of time. The United States Patent Office issues patents which are valid for seventeen years from the date of issuance. Patents are not renewable although effective control of an invention is frequently maintained beyond the expiration of the original patent through new patents covering improvements or changes. The owner of a patent may grant its use to others under royalty agreements or he may sell it.

The issuance of a patent does not necessarily indicate the existence of a valuable right. The value of a patent stems from whatever advantage it might afford its owner in excluding competitors from utilizing a process that results in lower costs or superior products. Many patents cover inventions that cannot be exploited commercially and may actually be worthless.

Patents are recorded at their acquisition costs. When a patent is developed through company-sponsored research, its cost includes such items as legal fees, patent fees, the cost of models and drawings, and related experimental and developmental expenditures. When a patent is purchased, it is recorded at its purchase price by the new owner.

The validity of a patent may be challenged in the courts. The cost of successfully prosecuting or defending original infringement suits is regarded as a cost of establishing the legal rights of the holder and may be added to the other costs of the patent. In the event of unsuccessful litigation, the litigation cost, as well as other patent costs, should be written off as a loss.

Patent cost should be amortized over the useful life of the patent. The legal life of a patent is used for amortization only when the patent is expected to provide benefits during its full legal life. The useful life of a patent is usually much shorter than its legal life because of obsolescence and supersession. New and more efficient inventions or changes in demand for certain products may result in loss of patent value; processes developed by competitors that are sufficiently different to qualify as new inventions yet so similar to a company's own process as to destroy the economic advantages enjoyed through patent protection may also result in the loss of patent value. In some instances, the useful life of a patent is expressed in terms of productive output rather than in years, and cost is assigned to operations on the basis of units produced.

The classification of the charge for patent amortization depends upon the nature and the use of the patent. A charge for a patent that is used in the manufacturing process would be recognized as a manufacturing cost. A charge for a patent that is used in shipping department activities would be recognized as a selling expense.

Copyrights. *Copyrights* are exclusive rights granted by the federal government to the author or the artist enabling him to publish, sell, or otherwise control his literary, musical, or artistic works. The right to exclusive control is issued for a period of twenty-eight years with the privilege of renewal for another twenty-eight years. Copyrights, like patents, may be licensed to others or sold.

The cost assigned to a copyright consists of all of the charges relating to the production of the work, including those required to establish the right. When a copyright is purchased, the copyright is recorded at its purchase price.

The useful life of a copyright is generally considerably less than its legal life. The cost of a copyright may be amortized over the number of years in which sales or royalties can be expected, or cost may be assigned in terms of the estimated sales units relating to such rights. As a conservative measure, costs of a copyright are frequently written off against first revenues from the copyright.

Franchises. A *franchise* is a contract, often between a governmental unit and a private company, that gives the latter exclusive rights to perform certain functions or to sell certain products or services. The rights may be granted for a specified number of years or in perpetuity; in certain instances, the rights may be revoked by the grantor.

The cost of a franchise includes any sum that may be paid specifically for a franchise as well as legal fees and other costs incurred in obtaining it. Although the value of a franchise at the time of its acquisition may be substantially in excess of its cost, the amount recorded for this item should be limited to actual outlays. When a franchise is purchased from another company, the amount paid is recorded as franchise cost.

When a franchise has a limited life, its cost should be amortized over such limited life. When the life of a franchise can be terminated at the option of the granting authority, the cost is best amortized over a relatively short period. The cost of a perpetual franchise that appears to be of continuing economic value should be amortized over a period of forty years.

A franchise may require that periodic payments be made to the grantor. Payments may be fixed amounts or they may be variable amounts depending upon revenue, utilization, or other factors. Such payments should be recognized as charges to periodic revenue. When certain property improvements are required under terms of the franchise, the costs of the improvements should be capitalized and charged to revenue over the life of the franchise.

Trademarks and trade names. *Trademarks* and *trade names*, together with distinctive symbols, labels, and designs, are important to all companies that depend upon a public demand for their products. It is by means of such distinctive markings that particular products are differentiated from competing brands. In building up the reputation of a product, relatively large costs may be involved. The federal government offers legal protection for trademarks through their registry with the United States Patent Office. Prior and continuous use is the important factor in determining the ownership of a particular trademark. The right to a trademark is retained as long as continuous use is made of it. Protection of trade names and brands that cannot be registered must be sought in the common law. Distinctive trademarks, trade names, and brands can be assigned or sold.

When a trademark is developed, its cost includes developmental expenditures such as designing costs, filing and registry fees, and also expenditures for successful litigation in the defense of such right. When a trademark is purchased, it is recorded at its purchase price.

Even though the legal life of a trademark is not limited, the trademark cost is frequently amortized over a relatively short period on the theory that changes in consumer demand may limit its usefulness.

Research and development costs. Large enterprises engage in continuous research for the improvement of processes and formulas and the development of new and improved products. Expenditures for general research are frequently recorded as a part of regular manufacturing overhead, being regarded as a continuing charge of keeping abreast of current technological advance. When research is directed to particular improvements, it is appropriate to capitalize expenditures identified with such projects and report these on the balance sheet as research and development costs. When these activities are successful, costs as accumulated can be assigned to future periods that receive the benefits of such outlays. Expenditures on projects that are patentable are summarized and reported as patents; expenditures on projects that are not patentable but offer exclusive benefits may be summarized and reported as formulas or as special or secret processes. When activities directed to certain improvements prove unsuccessful, costs previously capitalized should be written off as a loss. Formulas and special processes are generally amortized over a relatively short period because any advantages offered through their possession may terminate at any time through discoveries by others.

Most companies follow the practice of charging all research expenditures to periodic revenue even though valuable rights are produced through research activities. When such practice is followed, the balance sheet fails to disclose the costs of special processes and improvements that will make significant contribution to future business revenue. The income statement fails to show the charges for processes and improvements that were developed in prior periods and reflects charges that are applicable to future periods.

The problem of recognition of recurring research and development costs has not been specifically dealt with in AICPA pronouncements. However, an American Accounting Association Committee in 1966 in *A Statement of Basic Accounting Theory* commented as follows:

> . . . Expenditures and other costs devoted to such activities as research and development . . . often involve an element of future usefulness and are examples of conversions that would be recognized as quantifiable and verifiable . . . Relevance demands that the best available techniques for allocating these expenditures to asset and expense categories should be utilized . . .[1]

For federal income tax purposes the taxpayer may elect to report research and experimental expenditures either as (1) expenses that are deductible in the year paid or incurred, or (2) deferred costs to be amortized over a period of sixty months or more beginning with the month in which benefits are first realized from such costs. When expenditures for research and development are deferred on the books but are reported as current expenses for income tax purposes, there will be timing differences between book income and taxable income requiring interperiod tax allocations.

Organization costs. In forming a corporation, certain expenditures are incurred including legal fees, promotional costs, stock certificate costs, underwriting costs, and incorporation fees. The benefits to be derived from these expenditures normally extend beyond the first fiscal period. Further, the recognition of such expenditures as expenses at the time of

---

[1]*A Statement of Basic Accounting Theory* (Evanston, Illinois: American Accounting Association, 1966), p. 35.

organization would commit the corporation to a deficit before it actually begins operations. These factors support the practice of recognizing the initial costs of organization as an intangible asset.

Expenditures relating to organization may be considered to benefit the corporation during its entire life. Thus, when the life of a company is not limited, there is support for carrying organization costs as an intangible asset for the maximum period of forty years. On the other hand, in the absence of a disposal value, these costs must be applied to revenue before the ultimate net income arising from business activities is determinable. This approach has led to the widespread practice of writing off organization costs within a relatively short period from the date of corporate organization.

It is sometimes suggested that operating losses of the first few years should be capitalized as organization costs or as goodwill. It is argued that the losses cannot be avoided in the early years when the business is being developed, and hence it is reasonable that these losses should be absorbed in later years. Although losses may be inevitable, they do not necessarily carry any service potential. To report these losses as intangible assets will result in the overstatement of assets and owners' equity. Such practice cannot be condoned.

Prior to 1954, organization costs of a corporation could not be written off for federal income tax purposes unless the life of a corporation was limited by its charter or articles of incorporation. Organization costs for a company with an indeterminate life were recognized as a deductible item only in the last year of the company's life. Since 1954, however, newly organized corporations may elect to amortize their organization costs. But such election applies only to organization costs incurred before the end of the taxable year in which the corporation began business. Furthermore, costs must be amortized over a period of not less than sixty months starting with the month in which the company begins business. Amortization of the costs of corporate reorganization or recapitalization is not permitted.

Leaseholds. *Leaseholds* are personal property interests representing rights to the use of land or realty for a specified term. These rights are granted by property owners in consideration of specified rents through terms of a tenure contract called a *lease*.

Recent years have witnessed a great increase in the use of the lease as a method of financing properties that are to be used in a business. In many cases, *sale-and-leaseback* arrangements are negotiated. Under such arrangements, a company normally acquires land and constructs buildings to meet its requirements, then sells the property to an investor and simultaneously leases it from the new owner. Occupancy and use of the property are continued without interruption. Such arrangements are entered into when they offer both investor and lessee financial and income tax advantages that are not found in alternative arrangements for the construction and use of facilities.

Leases are generally noncancelable and provide rights to the use of properties that are similar in many cases to those found in direct ownership of properties. This has raised the question as to whether fair presentation on the financial statements should provide for (1) the recognition of only the rentals that are paid periodically under terms of the lease, or (2) the recognition of the property rights acquired for the duration of the lease together with the related contractual obligation that is assumed in acquiring such rights. The second approach carries with it a related problem of the amounts to be recognized periodically as the expense of using the property as well as the expense of financing the acquisition. Normally companies have accounted for leases as a series of rental payments. This method has been seriously challenged in recent years, however, and there has been growing support for the recognition of a lease as an installment purchase of valuable property rights; in effect, the purchase of a property item. The alternate methods of accounting for a lease as described above are referred to as the *lease-rental* method and the *lease-purchase* method.

To illustrate the alternate methods and their effects upon the financial statements, assume the following:

A company enters into a noncancelable lease contract for the use of equipment. The contract calls for an annual rental of $50,000 for a ten-year period; at the end of this period the equipment reverts to the lessor. Rental payments are made at the beginning of each rental year.

Lease-rental method. If the lease is recognized as a lease-rental, an entry is made in each of the ten years as follows:

Lease-Rental Expense	50,000	
Cash		50,000

There is no recognition on the balance sheet of an asset for the rights acquired or a liability for the obligations assumed under the contract. However, when a lease involves material amounts and a long term, disclosure of the lease arrangement is made by a footnote.

Lease-purchase method. The lease-purchase method requires assigning a value to the lease. This value is reported as an intangible asset and also as a liability. The amount to be assigned to the lease is the discounted value at an appropriate interest rate of all future rents. For example, if

8% is considered a reasonable interest rate in the preceding example, the present value of 10 annual rents of $50,000, discounted at 8%, is computed as $362,344.40.[1]

The entry to record the lease would be:

Lease Rights................................	362,344.40	
Lease Obligation.........................		362,344.40

The lease rights account balance would be reported as an intangible asset on the balance sheet; the lease obligation account balance would be reported as a liability, the amount to be paid within one year being reported as a current liability, and the balance reported as a long-term liability.

Each of these account balances is reduced over the life of the lease. The asset, lease rights, should be amortized according to the same principles that govern the depreciation of tangible property. The life of the lease defines the term of amortization, and the pattern of usefulness should be used in selecting the method for assigning the asset cost to revenues. Assuming that the straight-line method is considered appropriate for amortization of the lease rights, an entry would be made each year as follows:

Amortization of Lease Rights..............	36,234.44	
Lease Rights............................		36,234.44

The liability, lease obligation, should be reduced each period by the lease payment less the interest for the period on the balance of the lease obligation. For example, the interest expense for the first year of the lease would be $24,987.55 ([$362,344.40 − $50,000] × .08), and the reduction of the obligation would be $25,012.45 ($50,000.00 − $24,987.55). The entry to record the lease payment for the first year would be as follows:

Lease Interest Expense....................	24,987.55	
Lease Obligation.........................	25,012.45	
Cash.................................		50,000.00

Since the balance of the lease obligation declines each year, the annual charge for lease interest will also decline. Interest expense for the second year would be $22,986.55 ([$312,344.40 − $25,012.45] × 8%); the reduction in the obligation would be $27,013.45 ($50,000 − $22,986.55).

---

[1] $362,344.40 is the present value of an annuity of 10 rents of $50,000 at interest of 8%, rents being payable at the beginning of each year. A full discussion of the computation of present values is described in Chapter 27 of *Advanced Accounting*, by Simons and Karrenbrock.

The net effect upon the annual income of the lease-purchase method as compared with the lease-rental method varies according to the amortization method used for the lease rights. This is illustrated for two of the more common amortization methods in the tabulation below.

Lease-Rental Method		Lease-Purchase Method						
		Total Expense Assuming Amortization Computed by Straight-Line Method			Total Expense Assuming Amortization Computed by Sum-of-the-Years-Digits Method			
Year	Expense	Amortization	Interest	Total	Amortization		Interest	Total
1	$ 50,000.00	1/10 $ 36,234.44	$ 24,987.55	$ 61,221.99	10/55	$ 65,880.80	$ 24,987.55	$ 90,868.35
2	50,000.00	1/10 36,234.44	22,986.55	59,220.99	9/55	59,292.72	22,986.55	82,279.27
3	50,000.00	1/10 36,234.44	20,825.48	57,059.92	8/55	52,704.64	20,825.48	73,530.12
4	50,000.00	1/10 36,234.44	18,491.52	54,725.96	7/55	46,116.56	18,491.52	64,608.08
5	50,000.00	1/10 36,234.44	15,970.84	52,205.28	6/55	39,528.48	15,970.84	55,499.32
6	50,000.00	1/10 36,234.44	13,248.52	49,482.96	5/55	32,940.40	13,248.52	46,188.96
7	50,000.00	1/10 36,234.44	10,308.39	46,542.83	4/55	26,352.32	10,308.39	36,660.71
8	50,000.00	1/10 36,234.44	7,133.06	43,367.50	3/55	19,764.24	7,133.06	26,897.30
9	50,000.00	1/10 36,234.44	3,703.69	39,938.13	2/55	13,176.16	3,703.69	16,879.85
10	50,000.00	1/10 36,234.44	....	36,234.44	1/55	6,588.08	....	6,588.08
	$500,000.00	10/10 $362,344.40	$137,655.60	$500,000.00	55/55	$362,344.40	$137,655.60	$500,000.00

It should be noted that the total charges against revenue over the life of the lease is the same regardless of the method that is used for reporting the lease. Only the pattern of annual charges varies with the method that is adopted.

Criteria for selection of lease method. It was indicated earlier that accounting for leases has been the subject of controversy for many years. Because of the wide increase in the use of leases as a means of financing the costs of assets and the questions arising with respect to the criteria that should determine the recognition of a lease as a rental or as an installment purchase, a research study on the subject of accounting for leases was authorized by the Accounting Research Division of the American Institute of Certified Public Accountants. The study, *Reporting of Leases in Financial Statements* by Dr. John H. Myers, was completed and published in 1962. In this study, Dr. Myers concluded that to the extent that leases give rise to property rights, these rights should be measured and incorporated in the balance sheet of the lessee. The majority of lease agreements, therefore, would call for accounting by the lease-purchase method.[1]

The Accounting Principles Board in Opinion No. 5 issued in 1964 did not concur with the conclusions of the research study. Support for the recognition of an asset and related liability, in the opinion of the Board, depends upon whether the lease can be supported as in substance

---

[1]John H. Myers, *Reporting of Leases in Financial Statements*, Accounting Research Study No. 4. (New York: American Institute of Certified Public Accountants, 1962).

a purchase of property.[1] The Accounting Principles Board recommended that accounting by the lease-purchase method be limited to those instances where a lease is noncancelable, or cancelable only upon the occurrence of some remote contingency, and one or more of the following conditions or circumstances indicate that the lease can be considered in substance a purchase:

1. The initial term is materially less than the useful life of the property, and the lessee has the option to renew the lease for the remaining useful life of the property at substantially less than the fair rental value; or
2. The lessee has the right, during or at the expiration of the lease, to acquire the property at a price which at the inception of the lease appears to be substantially less than the probable fair value of the property at the time or times of permitted acquisition by the lessee.
3. The property was acquired by the lessor to meet the special needs of the lessee and will probably be usable only for that purpose and only by the lessee.
4. The term of the lease corresponds substantially to the estimated useful life of the property, and the lessee is obligated to pay costs such as taxes, insurance, and maintenance, which are usually considered incidental to ownership.
5. The lessee has guaranteed the obligations of the lessor with respect to the property leased.
6. The lessee has treated the lease as a purchase for tax purposes.[2]

The Board also indicated that when the lessee and the lessor are related, the lease-purchase approach might be appropriate even in the absence of the above conditions.[3] The lease-purchase method of accounting for leases has been more widely used since the issuance of Opinion No. 5.

If a lease contract does not meet the criteria that qualify it for treatment as a lease-purchase, the APB indicates that financial statements should disclose sufficient information to enable the reader to assess the effect of the lease commitments on the financial position and operations, both present and prospective, of the lessee. The Board has stated that the disclosure should include in the statements or by accompanying notes all significant data including:

1. The minimum annual rentals.
2. The lease period.
3. Current year rental if significantly different from minimum rental.
4. Type of property leased.

---

[1]See *Opinions of the Accounting Principles Board, No. 5*, "Reporting of Leases in Financial Statements of the Lessee" (New York: American Institute of Certified Public Accountants, 1964). The Board in commenting upon the conclusions in Accounting Research Study No. 4 remarked, ". . . The Board agrees that the nature of some lease agreements is such that an asset and a related liability should be shown on the balance sheet, and that it is important to distinguish this type of lease from other leases. The Board believes, however, that the distinction depends on the issue of whether or not the lease is in substance a purchase of the property rather than on the issue of whether or not a property right exists. . . . " par. 5.

[2]*Ibid.*, par. 10 and 11.

[3]*Ibid.*, par. 12.

5. Obligations assumed or guarantees made in the lease agreement.
6. Other significant lease provisions such as restrictions on dividends or on other leasing or borrowing arrangements.[1]

The chief concern in this area is that financial statements can be misleading if lease contracts that are essentially equivalent to installment purchases are not reflected on the balance sheet. Assets and liabilities for companies that acquire properties by lease arrangements are not comparable with the assets and liabilities reported by companies that purchase properties and assume long-term indebtedness on such acquisitions. Lease-purchase accounting tends to record in a consistent manner essentially similar transactions for financing new acquisitions.

Relationship with treatment on lessor's books.   The importance of the proper recognition of a lease as a rental or purchase on the books of the lessee also applies to the recognition of a lease as a rental or sale on the books of the lessor. If the lease agreement can be regarded as a rental by the lessor, the periodic receipts are credited to Rental Income. However, if the lease is in substance a sale of assets, the difference between the present value of the lease payments and the cost identified with the assets leased should be recognized as income in the period of the lease agreement. Additional interest income is then reported over the term of the lease for the difference between the present value reported for the lease and the amounts ultimately collected. The two methods of accounting for leases by the lessor are referred to as (1) the *operating method* and (2) the *financing method*.

The Accounting Principles Board in Opinion No. 7, "Accounting for Leases in Financial Statements of Lessors," recognized the two general accounting methods for lessors. Major factors for selection of the method to be used by the lessors were given as follows:

1. The nature of the lessor's business activities. For example, the financing method would normally be suggested for the manufacturer who uses leases in the marketing of products and for the financial institution that uses leases of properties as a means of investing its financial resources.
2. The specific objectives of the leasing activity.
3. The term of the lease, including renewal options, in relation to the estimated useful life of the property.
4. The provisions relating to assumption of risks of ownership by the lessor. For example, the operating method would normally be suggested for the lessor who retains the usual rights of ownership, including servicing and maintenance of the property.[2]

---

[1]*Ibid.*, par. 16 and 17.

[2]*Opinions of the Accounting Principles Board, No. 7,* "Accounting for Leases in Financial Statements of Lessors" (New York: American Instititite of Certified Public Accountants, 1966), par. 7-9 and 12.

The Accounting Principles Board in Opinion No. 7 summarized its position on accounting for leases by the lessor as follows:

> The Board takes notice of a question that has been raised as to whether certain conclusions herein are inconsistent with conclusions in Opinion No. 5, "Reporting of Leases in Financial Statements of Lessee" — specifically, the question is whether leases accounted for on the financing method by lessors should be capitalized by lessees. . . . the Board considers the principal accounting problem of lessors to be the allocation of revenue and expenses to accounting periods covered by the lease in a manner that meets the objective of fairly stating the lessor's net income; the Board believes that this objective can be met by application of the financing method when circumstances are as described in the Opinion. As to the lessee, however, capitalization of leases, other than those which are in substance installment purchases of property, may not be necessary in order to state net income fairly since the amount of the lease rentals may represent a proper charge to income. There continues to be a question as to whether assets and the related obligations should be reflected in the balance sheet for leases other than those that are in substance installment purchases. The Board will continue to give consideration to this question.[1]

Special circumstances requiring recognition on the books of the lessee. There are other special circumstances under which a leasehold may call for entries on the lessee's books. These include the following:

1. A lessee may be required to pay a certain lump sum amount as advance rental or bonus at the time the lease is first negotiated. Such an amount is properly recognized as an asset that is to be assigned to the periods covered by the advance payment. Such assignment is made on the books by periodic charges to expense and credits to the asset.

2. An amount may be paid in obtaining an assignment of a lease from an original lessee, or a bonus may be paid to the original owner in obtaining a sublease. In either instance, costs of acquiring the lease should be recognized as an asset and amortized over the period of the sublease as an addition to the periodic lease charge.

3. A lessee may sublease the property to another party at a rental in excess of that payable under the original lease. If the payment of the rental under the sublease is adequately secured both by the earning power of the sublessee and by improvements made by the sublessee, the original lessee may show the leasehold on his books. The value at which the leasehold may be carried is the discounted value of the excess rentals receivable under the sublease. Under these circumstances the value of the leasehold must be amortized in some reasonable manner over the period covered by the sublease. This procedure may be particularly appropriate when a leasehold is to serve as the basis for obtaining credit.

Leasehold improvements. *Leasehold improvements* arise when property has been leased and additions, improvements, or alterations are

---

[1]*Ibid.*, par. 18.

made by the lessee. Improvements are usually identified with the original property and belong to the owner at the expiration of the lease. The lessee, however, enjoys the use of such improvements throughout the lease period. Under such circumstances, improvement costs are appropriately recorded by the lessee as leasehold improvements and are reported as an intangible asset.

Improvement costs should be written off to operations over the life of the benefits. This period is the length of the lease or the life of the improvement, whichever is shorter. If occupancy is terminated before improvement costs have been fully amortized, the unamortized balance must be written off as an extraordinary loss. When leaseholds include renewal options but renewal is uncertain, the life of improvements should be regarded as limited to the original lease period. However, when renewal options carry significant advantages and extension is highly probable, it would be appropriate to spread leasehold costs over the extended period.

It is sometimes provided that the lessor, upon the termination of the lease, shall pay a certain amount for leasehold improvements turned over to him. The amount to be paid may be an agreed price, the cost of the property less depreciation for the period, or the appraised value of the property at time of transfer. When such a payment is involved, the amount to be charged to revenue over the life of the lease is the cost of the improvements less the estimated amount recoverable upon termination of the lease.

Goodwill

Goodwill is generally regarded as the summation of all of the special advantages, not otherwise identifiable, related to a going concern. It includes such items as a good name, capable staff and personnel, high credit standing, reputation for superior products and services, and favorable location. Unlike most other assets, tangible or intangible, goodwill cannot be transferred without transferring the entire business.

From an accounting point of view, goodwill is recognized as the ability of a business to earn above-normal earnings with the identifiable assets employed in the business. By "above-normal earnings" is meant a rate of return greater than that normally required to attract investors into a particular type of business.

Valuation of goodwill. Goodwill is recorded on the books only when it is acquired by purchase or otherwise established through a business transaction. The latter condition includes its recognition in connection with a merger or a reorganization of a corporation, a purchase or a partial purchase of a business, or a change of partners in a partnership. Recognition only under such circumstances assures an objective approach to the valuation of goodwill. To permit the recognition of goodwill on the basis of judgment and estimates by owners and other interested parties would open the doors to all manner of abuse and misrepresentation. Goodwill reported on the balance sheet arises from a purchase or a contractual arrangement calling for its recognition; above-normal earnings can be pointed to by management and owners as evidence of the existence of additional goodwill that has not found expression in the accounts.

In the purchase of a going business, the actual price to be paid for goodwill usually results from bargaining and compromises between the parties concerned. A basis for negotiation in arriving at a price for goodwill normally involves the following steps:

1. Projection of the level of future earnings.
2. Determination of an appropriate rate of return.
3. Valuation of the net business assets other than goodwill.
4. Use of projected future earnings and rate of return in developing a value for goodwill.

Projection of the level of future earnings. Past earnings ordinarily offer the best basis upon which to develop a specific value for goodwill. However, it is not these past earnings but projected future earnings that are being purchased. In considering past earnings as a basis for projection into the future, reference should be made to earnings most recently experienced. A sufficient number of periods should be included in the analysis so that a representative measurement of business performance is available.

In certain instances, it may be considered necessary to restate revenue and expense balances to give effect to alternative depreciation or amortization methods, inventory methods, or other measurement processes that may be considered desirable in summarizing past operations. Extraordinary gains and losses which cannot be considered a part of normal activities would be excluded from past operating results. Such items would include gains and losses from the sale of investments and land, buildings, and equipment, gains and losses from the retirement of debt, and losses from casualties.

The normal earnings from operations should be analyzed to determine their trend and stability. If earnings over a period of years show a tendency to decline, careful analysis is necessary to determine whether such decline may be expected to continue. There may be greater confidence in possible future earnings when past earnings have been relatively stable rather than widely fluctuating.

Any changes in the operations of the business which may be antici-pated after the transfer of ownership should also be considered. The elimination of a division, the disposal of substantial property items, or the retirement of long-term debt, for example, could materially affect future earnings.

The normal earnings of the past are used as a basis for estimating earnings of the future. Business conditions, the business cycle, sources of supply, demand for the company's products or services, price structure, competition, and other significant factors must be studied in developing data that will make it possible to convert past earnings into estimated future earnings.

Determination of an appropriate rate of return. The existence of above-normal earnings, if any, can be determined only by reference to a normal rate of return. The *normal earnings rate* is that which would ordinarily be required to attract investors in the particular type of business being acquired. In judging this rate, consideration must be given to such fac-tors as money rates, business conditions at the time of the purchase, competitive factors, risks involved, entrepreneurial abilities required, and alternative investment opportunities.

In general, the greater the risk entailed in an investment, the higher the rate of return required. Because most business enterprises are subject to a considerable amount of risk, investors generally expect a relatively high rate of return to justify their investment. A long history of stable earnings or the existence of certain tangible assets that can be sold easily reduce the degree of risk in acquiring a business and thus reduce the rate of return required by a potential investor.

If goodwill is to be purchased, it should be looked upon as an invest-ment and must offer the prospect of sufficient return to justify the com-mitment. Special risks are associated with goodwill. The value of good-will is uncertain and fluctuating. It cannot be separated from the business as a whole and sold, as can most other business properties. Furthermore, it is subject to rapid deterioration and may be totally lost in the event of business sale or liquidation. As a result, a higher rate of return would normally be required on the purchase of goodwill than on the purchase of other business properties.

Valuation of net business assets other than goodwill. Because goodwill is associated with the earnings that cannot be attributed to a normal re-turn on identifiable assets, the ultimate evaluation of goodwill depends upon the valuation of those business properties that can be identified. In appraising properties for this purpose, current market values should be sought rather than the values reported in the accounts. Receivables should be stated at amounts estimated to be realized. Inventories and securities should be restated in terms of current market values. Land, buildings, and equipment items may require special appraisals in arriving at their present replacement or reproduction values. Intangible assets, such as patents and franchises, for example, should be included at their current values even though, originally, expenditures were reported as expenses or were reported as assets and amortized against revenue. Care should be taken to determine that liabilities are fully recognized. Assets at their current fair market values less the liabilities that are to be assumed provide the net assets total that, together with estimated future earnings, is used in arriving at a purchase price.

Use of projected future earnings and rate of return in developing a value for goodwill. A number of methods may be employed in arriving at a goodwill figure. Several of these will be described. Assume the following information for Company A:

Net earnings after adjustment and elimination of extraordinary and nonrecurring items:

1968	$140,000
1969	90,000
1970	110,000
1971	85,000
1972	115,000
Total	$540,000

Average net earnings 1968–1972 ($540,000 ÷ 5), $108,000.
Estimated future net earnings, $100,000.
Net assets as appraised on January 2, 1973, before recognizing goodwill, $1,000,000. (Land, buildings, equipment, inventories, receivables, $1,200,000; liabilities to be assumed by purchaser, $200,000.)

The average net earnings figure of $108,000 for the five-year period 1968–1972 was used in arriving at an estimate of the probable future net earnings. It is assumed that the prospective buyer after analyzing the assembled data concludes that future earnings may reasonably be estimated at $100,000 a year.

Capitalization of average net earnings. The amount to be paid for a business may be determined by capitalizing expected future earnings at a rate that represents the required return on the investment. Capitalization of earnings as used in this sense means calculation of the principal value that will yield the stated earnings at the specified rate. This is accomplished by dividing the earnings by the specified rate.[1] The

---

[1]This may be shown as follows: P = principal amount or the capitalized earnings to be computed; r = the specified rate of return; E = expected annual earnings. Then, $E = P \times r$, and $P = E \div r$.

difference between the amount to be paid for the business as thus obtained and the appraised values of the individual property items may be considered the price paid for goodwill.

If, in the example, a return of 8% was required on the investment and earnings were estimated at $100,000 per year, the business would be valued at $1,250,000 ($100,000 ÷ .08). Since net assets with the exception of goodwill were appraised at $1,000,000, goodwill would be valued at $250,000. If a 10% return was required on the investment, the business would be worth only $1,000,000. In acquiring the business for $1,000,000, there would be no payment for goodwill.

Capitalization of average excess net earnings. In the foregoing method, a single rate of return was applied to the earnings in arriving at the value of the business. No consideration was given to the extent to which the earnings were attributable to net identifiable assets and the extent to which the earnings were attributable to goodwill. It would seem reasonable, however, to expect a higher return on an investment in goodwill than on the other assets acquired. To illustrate, assume the following facts:

	Company A	Company B
Net assets as appraised..................	$1,000,000	$500,000
Estimated future net earnings............	100,000	100,000

If the estimated earnings are capitalized at a uniform rate of 8%, the value of each company is found to be $1,250,000. The goodwill for Company A is then $250,000, and for Company B, $750,000 as shown:

	Company A	Company B
Total net asset valuation (earnings capitalized at 8%).........................	$1,250,000	$1,250,000
Deduct net assets as appraised...........	1,000,000	500,000
Goodwill.............................	$ 250,000	$ 750,000

These calculations ignore the fact that the appraised value of the net assets identified with Company A exceeds that of Company B. Company A, whose earnings of $100,000 are accompanied by net assets valued at $1,000,000, would certainly command a higher price than Company B, whose earnings of $100,000 are accompanied by net assets valued at only $500,000.

Satisfactory recognition of both earnings and asset contributions is generally effected by (1) requiring a fair return on identifiable net assets, and (2) viewing any excess earnings as attributable to goodwill and capitalizing such excess at a higher rate that recognizes the degree of risk that characterizes goodwill. To illustrate, assume in the above cases that 8% is considered a normal return on identifiable net assets and that excess earnings are capitalized at 20% in determining the amount to be paid for goodwill. Amounts to be paid for Companies A and B would be calculated as follows:

	Company A	Company B
Estimated net earnings..................	$ 100,000	$ 100,000
Normal return on net assets:		
Company A — 8% of $1,000,000.......	80,000	
Company B — 8% of $ 500,000......		40,000
Excess net earnings.....................	$ 20,000	$ 60,000
Excess net earnings capitalized at 20%....	÷ .20	÷ .20
Value of goodwill.....................	$ 100,000	$ 300,000

	Company A	Company B
Value of net assets offering normal return of 8%............................	$1,000,000	$ 500,000
Value of goodwill, excess net earnings capitalized at 20%..................	100,000	300,000
Total net asset valuation	$1,100,000	$ 800,000

Number of years' purchase. Behind each of the capitalization methods just described, there is an implicit assumption that the superior earning power attributed to the existence of goodwill will continue indefinitely. The very nature of goodwill, however, makes it subject to rapid decline. A business with unusually high earnings may expect that competition from other companies will reduce earnings over a period of years. Furthermore, the high levels of earnings may frequently be maintained only by special efforts on the part of the new owners, and they cannot be expected to pay for something they themselves must achieve.

As the goodwill being purchased cannot be expected to last beyond a specific number of years, one frequently finds that payment for excess earnings is stated in terms of "years' purchase" rather than capitalization in perpetuity. For example, if excess annual earnings of $20,000 are expected and payment is to be made for excess earnings for a five-year period, the purchase price for goodwill would be $100,000. If the excess annual earnings are expected to be $60,000 and the payment is to be made for four years' excess earnings, the price for goodwill would be $240,000.

Calculation of goodwill in terms of number of years' purchase will yield results identical to the capitalization method when the number of years used is equal to the reciprocal of the capitalization rate. Payment for five years' earnings, for example, is equivalent to capitalizing earnings at a 20% rate ($1 \div .20 = 5$). Payment of four years' earnings is equivalent to capitalization at a 25% rate ($1 \div .25 = 4$).

The years' purchase method has the advantage of conceptual simplicity. It is related to the common business practice of evaluating investment opportunities in terms of their "payback period" — the number of years it is expected to take to recover the initial investment.

Present value method. The concept of the number of years' purchase can be combined with the concept of a rate of return on investment. The assumption here is that the excess earnings can be expected to continue for only a limited number of years, but an investment in these earnings should provide an adequate return, considering the risks involved. The amount to be paid for goodwill, then, is the discounted or present value of the excess earnings amounts that are expected to become available in future periods.

To illustrate the calculation of goodwill by the present value method, assume that the earnings of Company A exceed a normal return on the net identifiable assets used in the business by $20,000 per year. These excess earnings are expected to continue for a period of five years, and a return of 8% is considered necessary to attract investors in this industry. The amount to be paid for goodwill, then, may be regarded as the discounted value at 8% of five installments of $20,000 to be received at annual intervals. Present value tables may be used in determining the present value of the series of payments. The present value of 5 annual payments of $1 each, to provide a return of 8%, is found to be $3.992.[1] The present value of five payments of $20,000 each would then be calculated as $20,000 × 3.992, or $79,840.

It may be noted that the calculation of goodwill by the present value method, using a five-year period and an 8% return, produced approximately the same result as would have been obtained by purchasing four years' excess earnings, or by capitalizing these earnings at 25%. The years'-purchase method can be adjusted to provide for a return on investment by reducing the number of years' earnings below actual expectations. Similarly, the capitalization method can be adjusted to provide for the limited life-span of excess earnings by raising the capitalization rate above that normally considered appropriate. The principal advantage of the present value method is the explicit recognition of the anticipated duration of excess earnings together with the use of a realistic rate of return. Thus it focuses on the factors most relevant to the goodwill evaluation.

Implied goodwill. When a lump sum amount is paid for an established business and no explicit evaluation is made of goodwill as illus-

---

[1]The present value of an ordinary annuity of 5 rents at interest of 8% is required. The calculation of present values is described in *Advanced Accounting*, by Simons and Karrenbrock.

trated in the preceding section, goodwill may still be recognized. In such case the identifiable net assets require appraisal, and the difference between the full purchase price and the value of identifiable net assets can be attributed to the purchase of goodwill.

Failure to recognize the payment for goodwill separately may result in attaching this cost to identifiable assets and thus result in their overvaluation. If this cost is attributed to depreciable assets, the periodic depreciation charges and net income, as well as financial position, will then be misstated.

When capital stock is issued in exchange for a business, the value of the stock determines the consideration that is paid for the assets. Care must be exercised so that what in effect represents a discount on the stock is not reported as goodwill. For example, assume that a company exchanges 100,000 shares of common stock, par $10, and selling on the market at $7\frac{1}{2}$, for a business with assets appraised at $800,000 and liabilities of $200,000. The acquisition should be recorded as follows:

Assets.......................................	800,000	
Goodwill....................................	150,000	
Discount on Common Stock..................	250,000	
Liabilities...............................		200,000
Common Stock, $10 par...................		1,000,000

If the discount is not recognized and goodwill is established at $400,000, both assets and paid-in capital will be misstated.

The entry that is given above recognizes the exchange as a *purchase*. Not all exchanges are recognized in this manner. As indicated in an earlier chapter, under certain conditions the issuance of stock in exchange for the owners' equity in the net assets of a company is recognized as a *pooling of interests*. In applying this concept, the company issuing the stock reports the net asset balances at the same amounts previously reported. No changes to reflect current market values for property items are made and no additional intangible assets are recognized. The increase in net assets is accompanied by an increase in the stockholders' equity, and in certain instances this increase is recorded in the invested capital and retained earnings accounts at the same amounts previously reported. The Accounting Principles Board has been concerned that the pooling of interests method might not be fair and realistic in its application to certain combinations, and in Opinion No. 16, "Business Combinations," it established definite guidelines to govern the use of this method.[1]

---

[1] The subject of business combinations, including accounting by the pooling of interests method, is discussed fully in *Advanced Accounting* by Simons and Karrenbrock.

Adjustment of goodwill after acquisition. The amortization of goodwill, as well as of all other intangible assets, is now governed by APB Opinion No. 17. As indicated earlier in this chapter, a maximum period of forty years is used in the amortization of all intangible assets including goodwill. In some cases goodwill may be considered to have a measurable life that is less than forty years and the amortization period selected can be based upon this life.

Some accountants have suggested that goodwill should be written off immediately after acquisition. Justification for this action is given as follows:

1. Goodwill is not a resource or property right that is consumed or utilized in the production of earnings. It is the result of expectations of future earnings by investors and thus is not subject to normal amortization procedures.

2. Goodwill is subject to sudden and wide fluctuations. That value has no reliable or continuing relation to costs incurred in its creation.

3. Under existing practices of accounting, neither the cost nor the value of non-purchased goodwill is reported in the balance sheet. Purchased goodwill has no continuing, separate measurable existence after the combination and is merged with the total goodwill value of the continuing business entity. As such, its write-off cannot be measured with any validity.

4. Goodwill as an asset account is not relevant to an investor. Most analysts ignore goodwill when analyzing a company's status and operations.[1]

This position has consistently been rejected by the committees of the AICPA, and the lump-sum write-off of goodwill and other intangible assets is strongly discouraged.[2] In opposing the arbitrary write-off of goodwill or any other intangible asset, it can be maintained that asset and owners' equity balances are misstated and the ratio of earnings to owners' equity is distorted. Earnings thus appear to be more favorable than is actually the case as a result of this "conservative practice."

Intangible assets on the balance sheet

When a single long-term asset classification is given on the balance sheet, tangible and intangible asset subheadings should be provided and summaries developed for each group. When separate classifications are given for tangible and intangible assets, the intangible asset classification usually follows the tangible asset classifications. Each intangible asset

---

[1]George R. Catlett and Norman O. Olson, *Accounting for Goodwill*, Accounting Research Study No. 10 (New York: American Institute of Certified Public Accountants, 1968). The authors of this research study recommended the write-off of goodwill immediately upon acquisition.

[2]For example, see *Accounting Research Bulletin No. 43*, "Restatement and Revision of Accounting Research Bulletins" (New York: American Institute of Certified Public Accountants, 1953), Ch. 5, par. 9.

should be listed separately. If an intangible asset has been acquired for a consideration other than cash, disclosure should be made of the properties or securities exchanged and the data used in arriving at the original cost assigned to the asset. Disclosure should also be made of the valuation procedures that are employed for intangible assets subsequent to their acquisition.

Intangible assets as they might appear on the balance sheet follow:

Intangible assets:		
Goodwill, at cost less amortization on 25-year basis..................................	$220,000	
Licenses, at costs less amortization based on estimated useful lives....................	18,000	
Patents, acquired through issue of 12,000 shares of common stock with a market value of $12.50 per share and reported at such value, less amortization based on an estimated useful life of 10 years......................	107,500	
Leasehold, at present value of future minimum annual rentals; $20,000 for 15 years discounted at 7%.........................	194,910	540,410

QUESTIONS

1. What are the characteristics that distinguish intangible assets from tangible assets?

2. What reasons are offered in support of the position that all intangible assets have a limited life?

3. Under what circumstances would a reduction in an intangible asset properly be recorded as (a) an operating expense, (b) an extraordinary item?

4. Andrews Corporation reported the following item on its 1972 balance sheet at the end of 1972:

Intangible assets....................................... $1.00

What is the purpose of this type of disclosure? Do you agree with such practice?

5. (a) What items enter into the cost of a patent developed by a business? (b) What factors should be considered in establishing a schedule for amortization of patent cost?

6. What costs are included in the account, "Franchises"?

7. Attempts have been made to classify research and development costs in a way that might clarify those costs that should be capitalized and those that should be reported as expense. What classifications would you suggest, and what accounting treatment would you recommend for each classification?

8. (a) What items are normally considered to compose the organization costs of a company? (b) Would you approve the inclusion of the following items: (1) common stock discount; (2) first-year advertising costs; (3) first-year loss from operations?

9. (a) Define (1) leasehold, (2) leasehold improvements. (b) What factors need to be considered in the amortization of costs identified with these intangible assets?

10. The use of the lease-purchase method will always result in a lower net income balance than the lease-rental method. Do you agree? Explain fully.

11. The practice of using long-term leases as a method of financing land, building, and equipment acquisitions is well established. In many cases these lease arrangements represent, in substance, a purchase of the property, and the property and the obligations incurred should therefore be reported among the assets and liabilities of the lessee. What provisions of a long-term lease contract would you consider as support for recognizing the lease as the purchase of property?

12. What information about leases recognized in the accounts as lease rentals should be disclosed in the annual financial statements of the lessee?

13. The Bayes Co. leases its manufactured equipment to customers over a five-year period. What factors will determine the point of revenue recognition?

14. Distinguish between the operating method and the financing method for recording lease agreements on the lessor's books.

15. (a) Under what conditions may goodwill be reported as an asset? (b) The Barker Company engages in a widespread advertising campaign on behalf of new products, charging above-normal expenditures to goodwill. Do you approve of this practice?

16. Give four methods for arriving at a goodwill valuation, using estimated future earnings as a basis for such calculations.

17. The transactions that result in recording goodwill are primarily related to the acquisition and merger of companies. Describe an accounting method for recording such mergers that has eliminated the need for recognizing goodwill.

18. Wells, Inc., has valuable patent rights that are being amortized over their legal lives. The president of the company believes that such patents are contributing substantially to company goodwill and recommends that patent amortization be capitalized as company goodwill. What is your opinion of this proposal?

EXERCISES

1. The Holt Co. developed patents at a cost of $11,900, and patent rights were granted at the beginning of 1967. It is assumed that the patents will be useful during their full legal life. At the beginning of 1969, the company paid $4,500 in successfully prosecuting an attempted infringement of these patent rights. At the beginning of 1972, $18,000 was paid to acquire patents that could make its own patents worthless; the patents acquired have a remaining life of 15 years but will not be used. (a) Give the entries to record the expenditures relative to patents. (b) Give the entries to record patent amortization for the years 1967, 1969, and 1972.

2. The Brandeis Mfg. Co. was incorporated on January 1, 1972. In reviewing the accounts in 1973, you find that the organization costs account appears as follows:

Organization Costs

	Debit	Credit	Balance
Discount on common stock issued............	53,100		53,100
Incorporation fees........................	1,800		54,900
Legal fees relative to organization..........	14,100		69,000
Stock certificate cost.....................	4,000		73,000
Cost of rehabilitating building acquired at beginning of 1972 and estimated to have a remaining life of 10 years.................	48,000		121,000
Advertising expenditures to promote company products.............................	18,000		139,000
Amortization of organization costs for 1972, 20% of balance of organization cost (per board of directors' resolution)............		27,800	111,200
Net loss for 1972........................	30,000		141,200

Give the entry or entries required to correct the account.

3. The Industrial Development Co. constructs a building at a cost of $210,000, with an estimated life of 50 years, on property leased for a 30-year period at an annual rental of $15,000. (a) What are the entries in connection with the lease and the building amortization for the first year? (b) What entries would be made at the end of the twentieth year, assuming that the lessee and the lessor agree to cancel the original lease at this time? (c) What entries would be made at the end of the twenty-first year, assuming that the lessee and the lessor agree to an extension of the original lease for 10 years beyond its original life?

4. At the beginning of 1972, Sabin, Inc., acquired a 20-year lease on land and buildings from the Capital Development Co., a financing real estate company, at an annual rental of $20,000. Payment was made in

1972 of $40,000 representing rent for the first and last years of the lease. Modifications in the buildings were made by the lessee prior to occupancy at a cost of $52,000. Terms of the lease require that the buildings be restored to their original form by the lessee upon termination of the lease, and the cost of such changes is estimated at $26,000. (a) Give all of the entries that are required on the books of the lessee and of the lessor in 1972. (b) What items relative to the lease will appear on the balance sheets for the lessee and the lessor at the end of 1972?

5. Your client, a retailer, has recently taken occupancy of property under the terms of a 10-year renewable lease. In this connection, you note the following items of information:

(a) Annual rental under the lease is $15,000.
(b) Your client has made leasehold improvements at a cost of $80,000. Improvements have an estimated life of 30 years.
(c) The lease calls for removal of the improvements at the expiration of the lease. It is estimated that this will cost $20,000 net of salvage.

Describe fully the treatment of each of these items in the financial statements.

6. A factory building is leased by the Downey Company for 20 years at an annual rental of $200,000, payable at the beginning of each year. The present value of the future rentals at the beginning of the lease discounted at 7% is $2,267,119. (a) Assuming the use of the compound-interest method to reduce the liability, what entries are required in the first year to record the capitalization of the lease, the rental payment, and the amortization of the building using (1) the straight-line method and (2) the double-declining-balance method?

(b) What entry would be made for the rental payment if the Downey Company had not capitalized the lease?

(c) Prepare a table comparing the effect upon net income of using (1) the lease-purchase method, straight-line amortization; (2) lease-purchase method, double-declining balance method; and (3) the lease-rental method.

7. In analyzing the accounts of Feld's, Inc., in an attempt to measure goodwill, you find pretax earnings of $200,000 for 1972 after charges and credits for the items listed below. Land, buildings, and equipment are appraised at 50% above cost for purposes of the sale.

Depreciation of land, buildings, and equipment (at cost)....	$25,000
Special year-end bonus to president of company...........	10,000
Gain on sale of securities...............................	18,000
Gain on revaluation of securities........................	6,000
Write-off of goodwill...................................	50,000
Amortization of patents and leaseholds..................	30,000
Income tax refund for 1970.............................	8,000

What is the "normal" pretax earnings balance for purposes of your calculations?

8. The appraised value of net assets of the Holland Co. on December 31, 1972, was $80,000. Average net earnings for the past 5 years after elimination of extraordinary gains and losses were $13,500. Calculate the amount to be paid for goodwill under each of the following assumptions:

(a) Earnings are capitalized at 15% in arriving at the business worth.
(b) A return of 9% is considered normal on net assets at their appraised value; excess earnings are to be capitalized at 15% in arriving at the value of goodwill.
(c) A return of 12% is considered normal on net assets at their appraised value; goodwill is to be valued at 5 years' excess earnings.
(d) A return of 10% is considered normal on net identifiable assets at their appraised value. Excess earnings are expected to continue for 6 years. Goodwill is to be valued by the present value method using a rate of 12%. (The present value of 6 annual payments of $1 providing a return of 12% is $4.111.)

PROBLEMS

16-1. The Armstrong Company spent $72,000 in developing a product, a patent being granted January 10, 1964. The patent had an estimated useful life of 10 years. At the beginning of 1968 the company spent $9,000 in successfully prosecuting an attempted infringement of the patent. At the beginning of 1969, the company purchased for $25,000 a patent that was expected to prolong the life of its original patent by 5 years. On July 1, 1972, a competitor obtained rights to a patent which made the company's patent obsolete.

Instructions: Give all of the entries that would be made relative to the patent for the period 1964–1972, including entries to record patent cost, annual patent amortization, and ultimate patent obsolescence. (Assume that the company's accounting period is the calendar year.)

16-2. In your audit of the books of Mar-Dean Corporation for the year ending September 30, 1972, you found the following items in connection with the company's patents account:

(a) The company had spent $102,000 during its fiscal year ended September 30, 1971, for research and development costs and charged this amount to its patents account. Your review of the company's cost records indicated the company had spent a total of $123,500 for the research and development of its patents, of which $21,500 was spent in its fiscal year ended September 30, 1970, and had been charged to expense.
(b) The patents were issued on April 1, 1971. Legal expenses in connection with the issuance of the patents of $15,900 were charged to Legal and Professional Fees.

(c) The company paid a retainer of $7,500 on October 5, 1971, for legal services in connection with an infringement suit brought against it. This amount was charged to Deferred Costs.

(d) A letter dated October 15, 1972, from the company's attorneys in reply to your inquiry as to liabilities of the company existing at September 30, 1972, indicated that a settlement of the infringement suit had been arranged. The other party had agreed to drop the suit and to release the company from all future liabilities for $15,000. Additional fees due to the attorneys amounted to $600.

(e) The balance of the patents account on September 30, 1972, was $96,000. No amortization had been recognized on the patents for the fiscal year ended September 30, 1972.

Instructions: (1) From the above information prepare correcting journal entries as of September 30, 1972.

(2) Give the entry to record amortization on patents for the year ended September 30, 1972, assuming a life for patents of 17 years from the date of issuance.

16-3. In 1971, the Midland Company entered into a noncancelable lease for a new warehouse. The warehouse was built to the Midland Company's specifications and is in an area where rental to another lessee would be difficult. Rental payments are $125,000 a year for 10 years. The taxes and maintenance are to be paid by the Midland Company, and they have an option to purchase the property at the conclusion of the lease for a nominal amount. Assume that the cost of borrowing funds by the Midland Company is 8%.

Instructions: (1) Give the entry that should be made at the inception of the lease. (The present value of 10 rents of $1 at interest of 8%, the first rent payable at the beginning of the lease, is $7.2469)

(2) Give the entries that should be made for 1971 and 1972 relative to the amortization of the lease assuming: (a) the lease is amortized by the straight-line method; and (b) the lease is amortized by the double-declining-balance method.

16-4. The Fairview Company, a sole proprietorship, obtained a new building suitable for its operations by signing a long-term lease at the end of 1963. The lease covered a period of thirty years and provided for an annual cash rental of $35,000. Within a short time after signing the lease, rental values in the area began to rise very sharply. On December 31, 1968, the Fairview Company was incorporated and adopted the name of Fairview Corporation. In valuing the various assets taken over by the newly-created corporation, the directors obtained appraisals by competent and disinterested experts. A value of $200,000 was placed upon the leasehold.

You are engaged to audit the Fairview Corporation for the year ended December 31, 1972. You find that there has been no amortization of the leasehold but that an expenditure of $66,000 at the beginning of the year for additions and improvements on the leased property was charged to expense. In response to your questions concerning amortization of the leasehold, the client points out that a portion of the leased property was recently subleased at a monthly rental of $1,500 and that a recent appraisal of the property indicated that the leasehold was now worth more than the recorded amount of $200,000. To support this statement, he shows you a letter from a nationally known corporation offering to buy the lease for $250,000.

Instructions: State the position you would take with respect to the lease and give any adjusting entries that you consider appropriate.

16-5. The Anoka Corp. in considering acquisition of the Charnhill Company assembles the following information relative to the company.

Charnhill Company
Balance Sheet
December 31, 1972

Assets	Per Company's Books	As Adjusted by Appraisal and Audit
Current assets............................	$120,000	$115,000
Investments...............................	40,000	35,000
Land, buildings and equipment (net)..........	349,000	325,000
Goodwill..................................	80,000	80,000
	$589,000	$555,000
Liabilities and Stockholders' Equity		
Current liabilities..........................	$ 50,000	$ 50,000
Long-term debt...........................	260,000	260,000
Capital stock..............................	200,000	200,000
Retained earnings..........................	79,000	45,000
	$589,000	$555,000

An analysis of retained earnings discloses the following information:

	Per Company's Books	As Adjusted by Appraisal and Audit
Retained earnings, January 1, 1970...........	$ 64,200	$ 38,000
Add net income, 1970–1972*.................	50,800	43,000
Deduct dividends, 1970–1972................	(36,000)	(36,000)
Retained earnings, December 31, 1972.........	$ 79,000	$ 45,000
	$ 51,200	$ 56,000

*After loss on sale of assets in 1972.

Instructions: (1) Calculate the amount to be paid for goodwill, assuming that (a) earnings of the future are expected to be the same as average normal earnings of the past 3 years, and (b) 8% is accepted as a reasonable return on net assets other than goodwill as of December 31, 1972, and average earnings in excess of 8% are capitalized at 15% in determining goodwill.

(2) Give the entry on the books of the Anoka Corp., assuming purchase of the assets of the Charnhill Company and assumption of its liabilities on the basis as indicated in (1). Cash is paid for net assets acquired.

16-6. East Coast Industries, Inc., assembles the following data relative to the Cape Cod Corp. in determining the amount to be paid for the net assets and goodwill of the latter company:

Assets at appraised values (before goodwill)..............	$820,000
Liabilities..	360,000
Stockholders' equity................................	$460,000

Net earnings (after elimination of extraordinary items):

1968...............	$80,000
1969...............	62,000
1970...............	87,000
1971...............	85,000
1972...............	91,000

Instructions: Calculate the amount to be paid for goodwill under each of the following assumptions:

(1) Average earnings are capitalized at 15% in arriving at the business worth.

(2) A return of 12% is considered normal on net assets at appraised values; goodwill is valued at 5 years' excess earnings.

(3) A return of 14% is considered normal on net assets at appraised values; excess earnings are to be capitalized at 20%.

(4) Goodwill is valued at the sum of the earnings of the last 3 years in excess of a 10% annual yield on net assets at appraised values. (Assume that net assets are the same for the 3-year period.)

(5) A return of 10% is considered normal on net identifiable assets at their appraised values. Excess earnings are expected to continue for 10 years. Goodwill is to be valued by the present value method using a 20% rate. (The present value of 10 annual payments of $1 providing a return of 20% is $4.192.)

16-7. The Turpin Corporation is considering the acquisition of the assets and business of the Holt Corporation as of June 30, 1972. The Turpin Corporation is willing to pay the appraised value of the net identifiable assets of Holt plus a "reasonable amount" for goodwill. The net assets other than goodwill are appraised at $1,100,000 on June 30, 1972.

All-inclusive income statements prepared by the Holt Corporation show the following pretax income for the five years preceding the proposed acquisition:

Year Ending June 30	Pretax Income
1968	$ 20,000
1969	210,000
1970	180,000
1971	201,000
1972	224,000

Similar operating results are expected in the future except for the following items:

(a) A review of Holt Corporation accounting records reveals that building and equipment acquired in July, 1967, at a cost of $300,000 has been depreciated on a straight-line basis with a 20-year useful life and no estimated salvage value. This equipment was included in the appraisal of net tangible assets at a current value of $352,000. Company engineers estimate that the equipment will probably be retired with an estimated salvage value of $40,000 in approximately 12 years.

(b) Holt had been paying $15,000 per year in interest charges on bonds that were redeemed at a gain of $20,000 on June 30, 1972. Funds for bond retirement were provided by sale in June, 1972, of the company's Consumer Products division for $500,000. This division had constant losses of approximately $30,000 annually.

(c) Normal maintenance on building and equipment of Holt Corporation has been inadequate by approximately $14,000 annually.

Both parties agree that a return of 14% before taxes is normal on assets employed in the type of business engaged in by Holt Corporation. Earnings in excess of this amount are expected to continue for another 5 years but since there is less certainty about excess earnings, a return of 20% is considered reasonable for an investment in above-normal pretax earnings.

Instructions: Prepare a summary showing how the amount to be paid for goodwill of the Holt Corporation is determined using the present value method of calculating goodwill. (The present value of $1 per year for 5 years at 20% is approximately $3.)

16-8. Sorenson Manufacturing Corporation was incorporated on January 3, 1971. The corporation's financial statements for its first year's operations were not examined by a CPA. You have been engaged to examine the financial statements for the year ended December 31, 1972, and your examination is substantially completed. The trial balance at December 31, 1972, appears on the following page.

The following information relates to accounts that may yet require adjustment:

(a) Patents for Sorenson's manufacturing process were acquired January 2, 1972, at a cost of $68,000. An additional $17,000 was spent in December 1972, to improve machinery covered by the patents and charged to the patents account. Depreciation on fixed assets has been properly recorded for 1972 in accordance with Sorenson's practice which provides a full year's depreciation for property on hand June 30 and no depreciation otherwise. Sorenson uses the straight-line method for all depreciation and amortization.

(b) On January 3, 1971, Sorenson purchased two licensing agreements that were then believed to have unlimited useful lives. The balance in the licensing agreement No. 1 account includes its purchase price of $48,000 and expenses of $2,000 related to the acquisition. The balance in the licensing agreement No. 2 account includes its $48,000 purchase price and $2,000 in acquisition expenses, but it has been reduced by a credit of $1,000 for the advance collection of 1973 revenue from the agreement.

Sorenson Manufacturing Corporation
Trial Balance
December 31, 1972

Cash................................	11,000	
Accounts Receivable....................	42,500	
Allowance for Doubtful Accounts.........		500
Inventories...........................	38,500	
Machinery...........................	75,000	
Equipment...........................	29,000	
Accumulated Depreciation...............		10,000
Patents.............................	85,000	
Leasehold Improvements.................	26,000	
Prepaid Expenses......................	10,500	
Organization Expenses..................	29,000	
Goodwill.............................	24,000	
Licensing Agreement No. 1..............	50,000	
Licensing Agreement No. 2..............	49,000	
Accounts Payable......................		147,500
Deferred Credits......................		12,500
Capital Stock.........................		300,000
Retained Earnings, January 1, 1972.......	27,000	
Sales................................		668,500
Cost of Goods Sold.....................	454,000	
Selling and General Expenses.............	173,000	
Interest Expense.......................	3,500	
Extraordinary Losses...................	12,000	
	1,139,000	1,139,000

In December 1971, an explosion caused a permanent 60% reduction in the expected revenue-producing value of licensing agreement No. 1 and in January 1973, a flood caused additional damage that rendered the agreement worthless.

A study of licensing agreement No. 2 made by Sorenson in January 1972, revealed that its estimated remaining life expectancy was only 10 years as of January 1, 1972.

(c) The balance in the goodwill account includes (1) legal expenses of $16,000 incurred for Sorenson's incorporation on January 3, 1971, and (2) $8,000 paid January 15, 1972, for an advertising program that is expected to increase Sorenson's sales over a period of 3 to 5 years following the disbursement.

(d) The leasehold improvements account includes: (1) the $15,000 cost of improvements with a total estimated useful life of 12 years which Sorenson, as tenant, made to leased premises in January 1971; (2) movable assembly line equipment costing $8,500 which was installed in the leased premises in December 1972; and (3) real estate taxes of $2,500 paid by Sorenson in 1972 which, under the terms of the lease, should have been paid by the landlord. Sorenson paid its rental in full during 1972. A 10-year nonrenewable lease was signed January 3, 1971, for the leased building that Sorenson used in manufacturing operations.

(e) The balance in the organization expenses account properly includes costs incurred during the organizational period. The corporation has exercised its option to amortize organization costs over a 60-month period beginning January, 1971, for federal income tax purposes and wishes to amortize these costs for accounting purposes in the same manner.

Instructions: Prepare the journal entries required by the above information.

(AICPA adapted)

16-9. The Cripple Creek Sulphur Company, organized January 1, 1968, was formed to mine, refine, and sell sulphur. To that end it secured a 20-year lease on 500 acres of known sulphur deposits, referred to as Section A, and 500 acres of potential but undiscovered sulphur deposits, referred to as Section B. It was estimated after an engineers' survey that there were 5,000,000 tons of sulphur under Section A at the time of acquisition. Mine reports showed the number of tons taken out by years as follows: 1968, 250,000; 1969, 300,000; 1970, 500,000; 1971, 800,000; 1972, 1,000,000, of which 200,000 tons remained in stock pile.

The following statement is prepared by the company's bookkeeper:

Cripple Creek Sulphur Company
Balance Sheet
December 31, 1972

Cash........................	$ 500,000	Current liabilities, including in-	
Receivables.................	300,000	terest and taxes accrued.....	$ 150,000
Inventory of crude sulphur at		Bonds payable...............	300,000
cost of mining and extraction		Capital stock................	1,000,000
(market value $200,000)....	180,000	Retained earnings............	610,000
Leaseholds — at cost.........	600,000	Net income, 1972............	230,000
Section A.........$500,000			
Section B......... 100,000			
Land, buildings, and equipment	460,000		
Development — Section A....	200,000		
Prospecting — Section B......	50,000		
	$2,290,000		$2,290,000

This statement is correct and all accounting requirements have been met, except that the company has never provided for amortization or depletion, since, in the words of the company's president, "it had discovered from prospecting more new deposits than it had mined." Nor has provision been made for depreciation or obsolescence of land, buildings, and equipment acquired January 1, 1968, which are estimated to have a useful life greater than the 20-year period of the leases and a scrap value of $50,000.

The company had a survey made of Section B by competent engineers. This survey indicated sulphur deposits of 3,200,000 tons on January 1, 1972, which were estimated to have a fair value underground of 11 cents per ton. It was decided to increase the book value of the leasehold, now carried at $100,000, to that value. It was also decided that the company would charge the operations with depletion on the basis of the increased value although this would not affect the depletion deductible for tax purposes.

Of the total 1972 production of 1,000,000 tons, 400,000 tons were mined from Section B, all of which were sold in 1972. Prior to December 31, 1972, the bookkeeper had written down developmental costs for Section A by $50,000, charging this amount to Retained Earnings.

Instructions: (1) Prepare journal entries setting up the proper allowances and making necessary adjustments to other accounts.

(2) Prepare a columnar work sheet showing the changes caused by the adjustments.

(3) Prepare a final balance sheet.   (AICPA adapted)

16-10. During the course of your audit of a new client, Warehouse Company, for the year ended December 31, 1972, you learned of the following transactions between Warehouse Company and another client, Investment Company:

- (a) Warehouse Company completed construction of a warehouse building on its own land in June 1971, at a cost of $500,000. Construction was financed by a construction loan from the Uptown Savings Bank.
- (b) On July 1, 1971, Investment Company bought the building from Warehouse Company for $500,000 which Warehouse Company used to discharge its construction loan.
- (c) On July 1, 1971, Investment Company borrowed $500,000 from Uptown Savings Bank to be repaid quarterly over four years plus interest at 5%. A mortgage was placed on the building to secure the loan and Warehouse Company signed as a guarantor of the loan.
- (d) On July 1, 1971, Warehouse Company signed a noncancelable 10-year lease of the warehouse building from Investment Company. The lease specified that Warehouse Company would pay $65,000 per year for 10 years, payable in advance on each July 1, and granted an option, exercisable at the end of the 10-year period, permitting Warehouse Company to either (1) purchase the building for $140,000, or (2) renew the lease for an additional 15 years at $25,000 per year and purchase the building for $20,000 at the end of the renewal period. The lease specified that $10,650 of the annual payment would be for insurance, taxes, and maintenance for the following 12 months; if the lease should be renewed, $11,800 of each annual payment would be for insurance, taxes and maintenance.
- (e) The building has a useful life of 40 years and should be depreciated under the straight-line method (assume no salvage value).
- (f) Warehouse Company and Investment Company negotiated the lease to provide for a return of 6%. You determine that the present value of all future lease payments is approximately equal to the sales price and that the sale-and-leaseback transaction is in reality only a financing arrangement.

Instructions: For balance sheet presentation by Warehouse Company at December 31, 1972, prepare schedules computing the balances for the following items:

- (1) Prepaid insurance, taxes, and maintenance.
- (2) Warehouse building, less accumulated depreciation.
- (3) Current liabilities arising from the lease.
- (4) Long-term liabilities arising from the lease.   (AICPA adapted)

chapter 17

current and contingent liabilities

Liabilities are obligations arising from past actions or transactions to pay sums of money, to convey certain other assets, or to perform certain services. In an economic system based so largely on credit, many indications of debt will be found on the balance sheet. Most goods and services are purchased on account. Funds are borrowed from commercial banks for working capital purposes. Large sums are provided by bond issues to finance new buildings and equipment. During the life of such obligations, interest accrues as an additional liability. Taxes accrued but not yet due appear as liabilities until paid. Employees of the enterprise are creditors until they are paid for their services.

Liabilities of the business unit must be fully recognized and properly measured on the balance sheet if both the amounts owed and the owners' equity in business assets are to be reported accurately. In presenting liabilities, appropriate distinction must be made between current and noncurrent items if the company's working capital position is to be accurately defined.

Full recognition on the balance sheet of contingent liabilities, those liabilities that may materialize in the event of certain acts or circumstances, is also essential. If contingent liabilities become actual liabilities, creditor and ownership equities will change. Current payment will normally be required with a change in the status of the liability. Contingent liabilities, therefore, must be considered along with presently existing liabilities in arriving at conclusions concerning a company's ability to meet its financial commitments.

Valuation problems arise in the measurement of payables just as they do in the measurement of receivables. In reporting receivables, it was recognized that theoretical accuracy would require that these be reported at their present values. It was further observed that valuation accounts should be established for amounts estimated to be uncollectible and that further reductions should be recognized when receivables included finance and interest charges in their face amounts. In reporting payables, similar considerations apply. When properties, goods, or services are acquired at an amount that is payable at some future date, this amount may be regarded as composed of a purchase price and a charge for interest for the period of payment deferral. If determinable, an established exchange or purchase price may be used to arrive at the present value of the payable. In the absence of such a price, the present value of the payable should be determined by discounting the amount payable at an interest rate that is regarded as appropriate for the period that payment is deferred. The acquisition, then, is recorded by a debit to the account reporting the purchase at the amount computed, a debit to the discount on the payable, and a credit to the payable at its face amount. The discount is amortized over the life of the payable as a charge to interest expense; in preparing a balance sheet, any unamortized discount is reported as a direct subtraction from the payable. As indicated in the earlier section on receivables, the Accounting Principles Board in Opinion No. 21 has indicated that the discounting procedure is not regarded as appropriate in all instances, and exempts from such practice payables arising from creditors in the normal course of business that are due in customary trade terms not exceeding one year. It should further be observed that in the proper valuation of payables, deductions should be recognized for such items as discounts that can be anticipated in the course of settlement, and also for any finance or interest charges that are included in the face amounts of the payables.

Not all obligations are definite in amount at the time financial statements are prepared. For example, obligations that cannot be exactly determined include amounts to be paid under product service warranties and amounts to be paid under certain pension plan agreements. Even though the exact amounts to be paid are not determinable, proper matching of revenue and expenses, as well as the proper inclusion of all of the amounts owed by a business, requires that estimates of such obligations be made as accurately as possible.

This chapter considers the problems relating to the determination, measurement, and presentation of current liabilities as well as contingent liabilities. The problems relating to long-term liabilities are considered in the next chapter.

Current Liabilities

It was indicated in Chapter 2 that *current liabilities* are broadly defined to include (1) all obligations arising from operations related to the operating cycle, and (2) all other obligations that are to be paid within a year. These liabilities make a claim against resources classified as current. Current liabilities are subtracted from current assets in arriving at working capital.

Current liabilities that are definite in amount

Representative of current liabilities that are definite in amount and that are frequently found on the balance sheet include such items as notes and accounts currently payable, current maturities of long-term obligations, cash dividends payable, deposits and agency obligations, sales and use taxes, payroll taxes and income tax withholdings, liability under bonus agreements, and deferred revenues making claims on current assets. Some of the problems that arise in determining the balances to be reported for such items are described in the sections that follow.

Notes and accounts currently payable. Both notes and accounts that are currently payable originate from the purchase of goods and services and from short-term borrowings. Notes currently payable may include notes issued to trade creditors for the purchase of goods and services, notes issued to banks for loans, notes issued to officers and stockholders for advances, and notes issued to others for the purchase of equipment. Accounts currently payable may consist of a wide variety of items, including obligations to trade creditors for the purchase of goods and services, obligations for the purchase of property items and securities, credit balances in customers' accounts, customers' refundable deposits, advances from officers and stockholders, and guaranteed interest and dividends on securities of affiliated companies.

In presenting current payables on the balance sheet, it is normally desirable to classify notes and accounts in terms of their origin. Such presentation affords information concerning the sources of business indebtedness as well as the extent to which the business has relied upon each source in financing its activities.

In arriving at the total amount owed trade creditors, particular attention must be given to the purchase of goods and services at the end of the fiscal period. Both the goods and the services acquired, as well as the accompanying obligations, must be reported on the statements even though invoices evidencing the charges are not received until the following period.

Individual notes and accounts are frequently secured by the pledge of certain assets. Assets pledged may consist of marketable securities, notes receivable, accounts receivable, inventories, or land, buildings, and equipment items. The pledge of an asset limits the use or the disposition of the asset or its proceeds until the related obligation is liquidated. In the event of bankruptcy, the cash that is realized on a pledged asset must first be applied to the satisfaction of the related obligation. A liability is *partly secured* or *fully secured* depending upon whether the value of the pledged property is less than the amount of the obligation or whether such value is equal to or in excess of the obligation. It has already been stated that reference is made to a lien on an asset by a parenthetical remark in the asset section of the balance sheet. It is also desirable to provide a parenthetical remark in connection with the liability item that identifies the asset pledged and indicates its present market value.

There are many kinds of notes. However, two types frequently create difficulty in recording: (1) the note with no stated interest rate, and (2) the note that is discounted. An example of each of these types is included in the following paragraphs:

(1) Assume that equipment is purchased on terms calling for issue of a $10,000 non-interest-bearing note for one year. If the equipment and the related obligation are recorded at $10,000, this would fail to recognize the charge for interest implicit in the deferred payment arrangement and both asset and liability balances would be overstated. If money is worth 7% per year, the asset, as well as the liability, must be recognized at a cash-equivalent value of $9,345.79 ($10,000 ÷ 1.07). The following entry should be made:

Equipment..................................	9,345.79	
Discount on Notes Payable..................	654.21	
Notes Payable...........................		10,000.00

In reporting the note on the balance sheet prior to its payment, an adjustment should be made to recognize the accrual of interest at 7% on the amount of the debt of $9,345.79 to the date of the balance sheet. The accrual of interest is recorded by a debit to Interest Expense and a credit to Discount on Notes Payable. The balance of the discount on notes payable is subtracted from notes payable in reporting the liability on the balance sheet. A similar procedure would be required if a note provided for a nominal interest rate that was substantially lower than the current market rate.

(2) Assume that a company discounts a $10,000 one-year, non-interest-bearing note at the bank, receiving $10,000 less a discount of 7%, or $9,300. If the amount of the discount is recognized as prepaid interest and the note is recorded at $10,000, both asset and liability balances would be overstated: interest has not been paid in advance but is still to be paid; the obligation at the time of borrowing is no greater than the amount borrowed. The following entry should be made:

Cash.....................................	9,300.00	
Discount on Notes Payable..................	700.00	
Notes Payable...........................		10,000.00

In reporting the note on the balance sheet prior to its payment, an adjustment should be made to recognize the accrual of interest just as in the first example. However, a discount of 7% is, in effect, a charge for interest at the rate of 7.53% ($700 ÷ $9,300). The accrual of interest, then, is computed at 7.53% on the amount of the debt of $9,300 to the date of the balance sheet.

Current maturities of long-term obligations. Bonds, mortgage notes, and other long-term indebtedness are reported as current liabilities if they are to be paid within a twelve-month period. When only a part of a long-term obligation is to be paid currently, as in the case of bonds that are payable in a series of annual installments, the maturing portion of the debt is reported as current, the balance as noncurrent. But if the maturing obligation is payable out of a special retirement fund or if it is to be retired from the proceeds of a new bond issue or by conversion into capital stock, the obligation will not call for the use of current funds and therefore should continue to be listed as noncurrent. Reference to the plan for liquidation should be made parenthetically or by special note.

Dividends payable. A cash dividend that is declared by appropriate action of the board of directors is recorded by a charge to Retained Earnings and a credit to Cash Dividends Payable. The latter balance is reported as a current liability. The declaration of a dividend payable in the form of additional shares of stock is recorded by a charge to Retained Earnings and a credit to Stock Dividends Distributable. The latter balance is not recognized as a liability but is reported in the stockholders' equity section since it represents Retained Earnings in the process of transfer to paid-in capital.

A company with cumulative preferred stock outstanding may have sufficient retained earnings to legally declare a dividend but may fail to declare a dividend in order to preserve cash for other purposes. A liability is not recognized here, for dividends are not payable until formal action is taken by the corporate board of directors authorizing the distribution of earnings. Nevertheless, the amount of cumulative dividends unpaid should be reported on the balance sheet. This amount may be shown parenthetically in the stockholders' equity section following a description of the stock or it may be reported by a special note.

Deposits and agency obligations. Current resources of a company may include monies deposited with it and returnable to depositors, or monies that have been collected or otherwise accumulated and that are to be paid to third parties. A company may have received deposits as guarantees of contract performance; here a current liability needs to be recognized until the deposits are returned. In other instances, companies will make payroll deductions for such items as employees' income taxes, payroll taxes, insurance plans, or saving plans; here current liability balances to the third parties need to be recognized until payments are made and the company fulfills its responsibilities as an agent.

Sales and use taxes. With the passage of sales and use tax laws by state and local governments, additional duties are required of the business unit. Laws generally provide that the business unit must act as an agent for the governmental authority in the collection from customers of sales taxes on the transfers of tangible personal properties. Laws may also provide that the business unit is additionally liable for sales taxes or use taxes on goods that it buys for its own use. The buyer is responsible for the payment of sales taxes to the seller when both buyer and seller are in the same tax jurisdiction; however, the buyer is responsible for the payment of use taxes directly to the tax authority when the seller is outside the jurisdiction of such authority. Provision must be made in the accounts for the liability to the government for the taxes collected from customers and the additional taxes that the business must absorb.

Sales tax collections included in sales balance. The sales taxes payable are generally a stated percentage of sales. When the sales tax collections as well as sales are recorded in total in the sales account, it becomes necessary to divide this amount into its component parts, sales and sales taxes payable. For example, if the sales tax is 3% of sales, then the amount recorded in the sales account is equal to sales + .03 of sales, or 1.03 times the sales total. The amount of sales is obtained by dividing the sales account balance by 1.03, and 3% of the sales amount as thus derived is the tax liability. To illustrate, assume that the sales account balance is $100,000, which includes sales taxes of 3%. Sales, then, are $100,000 ÷ 1.03, or $97,087.38. The sales tax liability is then 3% of $97,087.38 or $2,912.62. The liability can also be determined by subtracting the sales figure, $97,087.38, from $100,000.00. To record the liability, Sales would be debited and Sales Taxes Payable would be credited for $2,912.62.

Sales tax collections recorded separately. Frequently the actual sales total and the sales tax collections are recorded separately at the time of sale. The sales taxes payable account then accumulates the sales tax liability. If sales tax collections are not exactly equal to the sales tax liability for the period as computed under the law, the payable account will require adjustment to bring it to the balance due. In making this adjustment a gain or a loss on sales tax collections is recognized.

Sales taxes or use taxes on acquisitions. The recognition in the accounts of obligations for sales taxes, use taxes, or for taxes on goods purchased by a business unit for its own use should be accompanied by charges to the asset or expense accounts in which the original purchases are recorded. For example, sales or use taxes on the purchase of furniture and fixtures are recorded as a part of the cost of this asset; sales or use taxes on the purchase of supplies representing selling expense would be recorded as selling expense.

Payroll taxes and income taxes withheld. Social security and income tax legislation impose four taxes based upon payrolls:

1. Federal old-age, survivors, disability, and hospital insurance
2. Federal unemployment insurance
3. State unemployment insurance
4. Income taxes withheld

Federal old-age, survivors, disability, and hospital insurance. The Federal Insurance Contributions Act (FICA), generally referred to as the federal old-age retirement legislation, provides for equal taxes on employer and employee to provide funds for federal old-age, survivors, disability, and hospital insurance benefits for certain individuals and members of their families. At one time only employees were covered by this legislation; however, coverage has now been broadened to include most individuals who are self-employed.

Provisions of the legislation provide for an equal matching of contributions by the employee and the employer. The contribution is based upon a tax rate applied to gross wages. The tax has gradually increased since the inception of the social security legislation to provide for increasing benefits. The tax rate is applied to all wages up to a designated maximum. This wage limit has also been raised through the years as the total cost of the program has increased.

Employers of one or more persons, with certain exceptions, come under the law. The amount of the employee's tax is withheld from the wage payment by the employer. The employer remits this amount together with his own tax. The employer is required to maintain complete records and submit detailed support for the tax remittance. He is responsible for the full amount of the tax even when he fails to withhold from employees amounts representing their contributions. Self-employed persons who carry on a trade or business are assessed tax rates somewhat higher than the employee rates but less than the sum of the employee and employer contributions.

Federal unemployment insurance. The Federal Social Security Act and the Federal Unemployment Tax Act (FUTA) provide for the establishment of unemployment insurance plans. Employers with covered workers employed in each of 20 weeks during a calendar year are affected.

Under present provisions of the law, the federal government taxes eligible employers on the first $4,200 paid to every employee during the calendar year at 3.2% but allows the employer a tax credit limited to 2.7% for taxes paid under state unemployment compensation laws. No tax is levied on the employee. When an employer is subject to a tax of 2.7% or more as a result of state unemployment legislation, the federal unemployment tax, then, is 0.5% of the wages. Payment to the federal government is required quarterly. Unemployment benefits are provided by the systems created by the individual states. Revenues of the federal government under the acts are used to meet the cost of administering state and federal unemployment plans as well as to provide supplemental unemployment benefits.

State unemployment insurance. State unemployment compensation laws are not the same in all states. In most states laws provide for taxes only on employers; but in a few states taxes are applicable to both employers and employees. Each state law specifies the classes of employees that are exempt, the number of employees that are required, or the amount of wages that must be paid before the tax is applicable, and the contributions that are to be made by employers and employees. The federal legislation now applies to all employers of one or more employees, a change from the previous legislation which applied only to employers of four or more persons. Exemptions are frequently similar to those under the federal act. Tax payment is generally required on or before the last day of the month following each calendar quarter.

Although the normal tax on employers may be 2.7%, states have merit rating or experience plans that provide for lower rates based upon employers' individual employment experiences. Thus employers with stable employment records are taxed at a rate in keeping with the limited amount of benefits required for their employees; employers with less satisfactory employment records contribute at a rate more nearly approaching 2.7% in view of the greater amount of benefits paid to their employees. Savings under state merit systems are allowed as credits in the calculation of the federal contribution, so that the federal tax does not exceed 0.5% even though payment of less than 2.7% is made by an employer entitled to a lower rate under the merit rating system.

Income taxes withheld. Federal income taxes on the wages of an individual are collected in the period in which the wages are paid. The "pay-as-you-go" plan requires employers to withhold income taxes from wages paid to their employees. Withholding is required not only of employers engaged in a trade or business, but also of religious and charitable organizations, educational institutions, social organizations, and governments of the United States, the states, the territories, and their agencies, instrumentalities, and political subdivisions. Certain classes of wage payments are exempt from withholding although these are still subject to income taxes.

An employer must meet withholding requirements under the law even if wages of no more than one employee are subject to such withholding. The amounts to be withheld by the employer are developed from formulas provided by the law or from tax withholding tables made available by the government. Withholding is based upon the length of the payroll period, the amount earned, and the number of withholding exemptions claimed by the employee. Taxes that are required under the Federal Insurance Contributions Act (both employees' and employer's portions) and income taxes that have been withheld by the employer are paid to the federal government at the same time. These combined taxes are deposited in an authorized bank quarterly, monthly, or quarter-monthly depending upon the amount of the liability. A quarterly statement must also be filed that provides a summary of all wages paid by the employer.

Accounting for payroll taxes and income taxes withheld. To illustrate the accounting procedures for payroll taxes and income taxes withheld, assume that in January, 1972, salaries for a retail store with 15 employees are $10,000. The state unemployment compensation law provides for a tax on employers of 2.7%. Income tax withholdings for the month are $1,020. Assume FICA rates are 5% for employer and employee. Entries for the payroll and the employer's payroll taxes follow:

Salaries..	10,000	
FICA Taxes Payable...........................		500
Employees Income Taxes Payable..............		1,020
Cash..		8,480

      To record payment of payroll of $10,000 after deduction of 5% for employees' contribution for federal old-age benefits and $1,020 for income tax withholdings.

Payroll Taxes Expense.........................	820	
FICA Taxes Payable...........................		500
State Unemployment Taxes Payable.............		270
FUTA Taxes Payable...........................		50

      To record the payroll tax liability of the employer:
      (1) Taxes under Federal Insurance Contributions Act — 5% of $10,000, or $500.
      (2) Taxes under state unemployment insurance legislation — 2.7% of $10,000, or $270.
      (3) Taxes under Federal Unemployment Tax Act — 0.5% (3.2% less credit of 2.7%) of $10,000, or $50.

When tax payments are made to the proper agencies, the tax liability accounts are debited and Cash is credited.

The employer's payroll taxes, as well as the taxes withheld from employees, are based upon amounts paid to employees during the period regardless of the basis employed for reporting income. When financial reports are prepared on the accrual basis, the employer will have to recognize both accrued payroll and the employer's payroll taxes relating thereto by adjustments at the end of the accounting period. In adjusting the accounts for accrued payroll, however, recognition of the amounts to be withheld for employees' taxes may be ignored. The entries recording the accrued payroll and the employer's payroll taxes may be reversed at the start of the new period. The next regular payment of wages can then be recorded in the usual manner, giving recognition to the employees' taxes based upon the entire payroll and the balances payable to employees; a second entry is made at this time recording the accrual of the employer's payroll taxes based upon the full amount of the payroll. The accrual of payroll and taxes at the end of the period as indicated provides accurate statements while deferring the analysis of payroll as to amounts payable to the government and to employees until the wage payment date.

Agreements with employees may provide for payroll deductions and employer contributions for other items such as group insurance plans, pension plans, savings bonds purchases, or union dues. Such agreements call for accounting procedures that are similar to those described for payroll taxes and income tax withholdings.

Liability under bonus agreements. Bonuses accruing to officers, managers, or employees at the end of a period are recorded by a charge to an expense account and a credit to an accrued liability account. Employee bonuses, even though they may be defined as a sharing of profits with the employees, are deductible expenses for purposes of income tax.

Special problems frequently arise in the computation of the amount of the bonus accruing to personnel. An agreement may provide for a bonus computed on the basis of gross revenue or sales or on the basis of earnings. When earnings are to be used, the computation will depend upon whether the bonus is based on: (1) income before deductions for bonus or income taxes, (2) income after deduction for bonus but before deduction for income taxes, (3) net income after deduction for income taxes but before deduction for bonus, or (4) net income after deductions for both bonus and income taxes. To illustrate the computations required in each case, assume the following: Parker Sales, Inc., gives the sales managers of its individual stores a bonus of 10% of store earnings.

Income for 1972 for store No. 1 before any charges for bonus or income taxes was $100,000. The income taxes were 40% of income before income taxes.

Let B = Bonus
T = Income Taxes

(1) *Assuming that the bonus is based on income before deductions for bonus or income taxes:*

$$B = .10 \times \$100,000$$
$$B = \$10,000$$

(2) *Assuming that the bonus is based on income after deduction for bonus but before deduction for income taxes:*

$$B = .10 \; (\$100,000 - B)$$
$$B = \$10,000 - .10B$$
$$B + .10B = \$10,000$$
$$1.10B = \$10,000$$
$$B = \$9,090.91$$

Calculation of the bonus may be proved as follows:

Income before bonus and income taxes............	$100,000.00
Deduct bonus................................	9,090.91
Income after bonus but before income taxes........	$ 90,909.09
Bonus rate..................................	10%
Bonus......................................	$ 9,090.91

(3) *Assuming that the bonus is based on income after deduction for income taxes but before deduction for bonus:*

$$B = .10 \; (\$100,000 - T)$$
$$T = .40 \; (\$100,000 - B)$$

Substituting for T in the first equation and solving for B:

$$B = .10 \; [\$100,000 - .40 \; (\$100,000 - B)]$$
$$B = .10 \; (\$100,000 - \$40,000 + .40B)$$
$$B = \$10,000 - \$4,000 + .04B$$
$$B - .04B = \$6,000$$
$$.96B = \$6,000$$
$$B = \$6,250$$

Substituting for B in the second equation and solving for T:

$$T = .40 \; (\$100,000 - \$6,250)$$
$$T = .40 \times \$93,750$$
$$T = \$37,500$$

Calculation of the bonus may be proved as follows:

Income before bonus and income taxes..............	$100,000
Deduct income taxes............................	37,500
Income after income taxes but before bonus..........	$ 62,500
Bonus rate....................................	10%
Bonus..	$ 6,250

(4) *Assuming that the bonus is based on net income after deductions for bonus and income taxes:*

$$B = .10 (\$100,000 - B - T)$$
$$T = .40 (\$100,000 - B)$$

Substituting for T in the first equation and solving for B:

$$B = .10 [\$100,000 - B - .40 (\$100,000 - B)]$$
$$B = .10 (\$100,000 - B - \$40,000 + .40B)$$
$$B = \$10,000 - .1B - \$4,000 + .04B$$
$$B + .1B - .04B = \$10,000 - \$4,000$$
$$1.06B = \$6,000$$
$$B = \$5,660.38$$

Substituting for B in the second equation and solving for T:

$$T = .40 (\$100,000 - \$5,660.38)$$
$$T = .40 \times \$94,339.62$$
$$T = \$37,735.85$$

Calculation of the bonus is proved in the following summary:

Income before bonus and income taxes............		$100,000.00
Deduct: Bonus....................	$ 5,660.38	
Income taxes.............	37,735.85	43,396.23
Net income after bonus and income taxes..........		$ 56,603.77
Bonus rate...................................		10%
Bonus..		$ 5,660.38

The bonus should be reported on the income statement as an expense before arriving at net income regardless of the method employed in its computation.

Other accrued liabilities. The accrued liabilities most commonly found were described on the preceding pages. Other accruals that may be found include obligations for salaries, interest, and rent. Frequently these miscellaneous accruals are combined and reported on the balance sheet classification as *other accrued liabilities.*

Deferred revenues making claim on current assets. Advances from customers for goods and services that are to be supplied in the future are recorded as liabilities. When significant costs are involved in meeting customer commitments and such costs are to be met from resources classified as current, the advances should be recognized as current liabilities. Tuition fees received in advance by a school and subscriptions received in advance by a publisher are current liabilities; advances received from customers on purchase orders are likewise current. When the services or the goods are applied to liquidation of the obligation, the difference between the amount of the advance that has now become revenue and the expenses that have been incurred in its realization is recognized as income.

Estimated current liabilities

The amount of an obligation is generally established by contract or accrues at a certain rate. There are instances, however, when an obligation clearly exists on a balance sheet date but the amount ultimately to be paid cannot be definitely determined. The fact that the amount to be paid is not definite does not mean that the liability can be ignored or even given a "contingent" status. Such claim must be estimated from whatever data are available. The amount to be paid in the form of income taxes, for example, must be estimated in preparing interim statements or statements at the end of the period if the tax return has not yet been prepared. Although the exact amount ultimately payable is not known, the obligation is unquestioned and requires recognition. Expenditures to arise from current operations and the realization of current revenue, as, for example, the cost of meeting guarantees for servicing and repairs on goods sold, also call for estimates. Here, uncertainty as to the amount to be expended is accompanied by the inability to identify the payees as well as to determine the time of payments; but the fact that there are charges yet to be absorbed is certain. Liabilities established to meet estimated charges arising from current activities are sometimes referred to as *operating reserves*. These liabilities generally call for current liquidation and hence are classified under the current heading.

Certain long-term liabilities also call for estimates. A self-administered pension plan calls for estimates as to the amount ultimately payable. Long-term guarantees and agreements calling for severance payments to employees also involve estimates.

Liabilities definite in existence but estimated in amount have in the past been designated as "reserves." However, it was pointed out in an earlier chapter that this practice is now discouraged and account titles should be used that indicate the exact nature of the item. The designation "Estimated Income Taxes Payable" is preferable to "Reserve for Income Taxes"; "Estimated Amounts Payable Under Retirement Plans" is preferable to "Reserve for Retirement Plans." When a separate "Reserves" heading is found in the liability section of a balance sheet, it is important to determine what practices were followed in classifying items. Sometimes such diverse items as asset valuation accounts, short and long-term liabilities, and appropriations of retained earnings are found under this heading. When this is the case, restatement of account groupings may be necessary in analyzing balance sheet position. Special investigation is necessary when account titles such as "General Reserve," "Special Reserve," and "Contingency Reserve" are listed in the "reserves" section on the balance sheet. Such designations offer no information as to the real nature of the account.

Representative of short-term liabilities that are estimated in amount and are frequently found on financial statements are the following:

Estimated tax liabilities, reporting the estimated income, state franchise, property, and other tax obligations.

Estimated liabilities on customer premium offers, reporting the estimated value of premiums or prizes that are to be distributed as a result of past sales or sales promotion activities.

Estimated liabilities under guarantees for service and replacements, reporting the estimated future claims by customers as a result of past guarantees of services or product or product part replacement.

Estimated liabilities on tickets, tokens, and gift certificates outstanding, reporting the estimated obligations in the form of services or merchandise arising from the receipt of cash in past periods.

Some of the problems arising in the development of the balances to be reported for these items are described in the sections that follow.

Estimated tax liabilities. Estimates are required for all taxes that are related to current operations but that are not finally known at the time financial statements are prepared. Estimates may thus be called for in the case of federal income taxes, state income or franchise taxes, real and personal property taxes, and various other licenses and fees. Tax rates may vary from year to year. Normally the best guide as to current tax rates is found in rates that were applicable in the preceding period. When legislative bodies are considering revisions in tax rates and their application, the best available information should be used in developing estimates. Not only may estimates have to be made relative to rates but also to the bases on which such rates are applicable. In the case of real and personal property taxes, for example, the valuation to be assigned to properties owned may have to be estimated in arriving at an estimated tax liability. In the case of income taxes, estimates of the income subject to taxes are required unless tax data are fully compiled before the financial statements are prepared.

Estimated taxes are recorded by debits to expense and credits to liability accounts. Liabilities are closed when the taxes are paid. Any difference between the amount paid and the obligation originally recognized may be reported in the expense account in the period of payment.

Real and personal property taxes. Real and personal property taxes are based upon the assessed valuation of properties as of a given date. This has given rise to the view held by courts and others that taxes accrue as of a given date. Generally the date of accrual has been held to be the date of property assessment. However, accounting treatment, in general, has been to charge taxes ratably over a tax year rather than to recognize these at the time the legal obligation arises.

Real and personal property taxes have been charged against the revenue of various periods, including (1) the year in which paid (cash basis), (2) the year ending on the assessment (or lien) date, (3) the year beginning on the assessment (or lien) date, (4) the calendar or fiscal year of the taxpayer prior to the assessment (or lien) date, (5) the calendar or fiscal year of the taxpayer including the assessment (or lien) date, (6) the calendar or fiscal year of the taxpayer prior to the payment date, (7) the year appearing on the tax bill, and (8) the fiscal year of the governing body levying the tax.

The Committee on Accounting Procedure of the AICPA in considering the various alternatives for tax accounting has suggested, "Generally, the most acceptable basis of providing for property taxes is monthly accrual on the taxpayer's books during the fiscal period of the taxing authority for which the taxes are levied." This would relate the tax charge to the period in which taxes provide benefits through governmental services. However, the Committee indicates that special circumstances may suggest the use of alternative accrual periods, and it concludes, "Consistency of application from year to year is the important consideration and selection of any of the periods mentioned is a matter for individual judgment."[1]

Accounting for taxes when accrual is made over the fiscal year of the taxing authority is illustrated in the example that follows. Assume that the accounting period for the Baldwin Co. is the calendar year. The fiscal year for the city in which this company is located begins on July 1 and ends on the following June 30. Real and personal property taxes are assessed in March, but bills are sent out in November covering the year ending June 30 of the following year. Tax payments in equal installments are due on December 10 and the following April 10. The Baldwin Co. accrues taxes on its books monthly in terms of the fiscal period of the governmental unit.

On July 1, 1972, the Baldwin Co. estimated total property taxes for the year July 1, 1972, to June 30, 1973, at $1,800. On November 4 the company received a tax bill for 1972–73 of $1,842. Entries to record the monthly tax charges and tax payments are shown on the following page.

It should be noted that when the actual tax charge became known in November, an adjustment was made for charges of previous months.[2]

---

[1]*Accounting Research Bulletin No. 43*, "Restatement and Revision of Accounting Research Bulletins" (New York: American Institute of Certified Public Accountants, 1953), Ch. 10, par. 13.

[2]An alternative treatment would apply the adjustment over the remaining months of the fiscal year of the taxing authority.

Transaction	Entry

AT THE END OF JULY, AUGUST, SEPTEMBER, OCTOBER:
Estimated taxes for 1972–73, $1,800.
Monthly accrual, $\frac{1}{12} \times$ $1,800, or $150.
	Property Taxes........ 150.00
	  Property Taxes
	    Payable......... 150.00

AT THE END OF NOVEMBER:
Amount of taxes for year..... $1,842.00
 	
Amount chargeable to date
4×$153.50 ($1,842÷12)..... $ 614.00
Accrual recognized to date
4×$150.00................ 600.00
 	
Tax deficiency — prior periods $ 14.00
Add accrual for November.... 153.50
 	
Total charge................ $ 167.50
	Property Taxes........ 167.50
	  Property Taxes
	    Payable......... 167.50

DECEMBER 10: Payment of first installment, 50% of $1,842, or $921, chargeable as follows: July–November (accrued)...... $767.50 December (current period)..... 153.50	Property Taxes Payable. 767.50 Property Taxes........ 153.50 Cash............... 921.00

AT THE END OF JANUARY, FEBRUARY, MARCH:
Monthly accrual.
	Property Taxes........ 153.50
	  Property Taxes
	    Payable......... 153.50

APRIL 10: Payment of second installment, 50% of $1,842, or $921, chargeable as follows: January–March (accrued)...... $460.50 April (current period)......... 153.50 May and June (prepaid)....... 307.00	Property Taxes Payable. 460.50 Property Taxes........ 153.50 Prepaid Property Taxes. 307.00 Cash............... 921.00

AT THE END OF MAY, JUNE:
Monthly amortization of prepaid property taxes.
	Property Taxes........ 153.50
	  Prepaid Property
	    Taxes........... 153.50

Estimated liabilities on customer premium offers. Many companies offer special premiums to those purchasing their products. Such offers to stimulate the regular purchase of certain products may be open for a limited time or they may be of a continuing nature. The premium is normally made available when the customer submits the required number of product labels, box tops, wrappers, or certificates. In certain instances the premium offer may provide for an optional cash payment.

If a premium offer expires at the end of the company's fiscal period, adjustments in the accounts are not required. Premium requirements are fully met and the premium expense account summarizes the full charge for the period. However, when a premium offer is continuing, an adjustment must be made at the end of the period to recognize the liability that is found in the continuing costs of the offer. Premium Expense is debited and an appropriate liability account is credited. The expense is thus charged to the period that benefits from the premium plan and current liabilities reflect the claim for premiums outstanding. If premium distributions are charged to expense, the liability balance may be reversed at the beginning of the new period.

To illustrate the accounting for a premium offer, assume the following: Walker Foods offers a set of breakfast bowls upon the receipt of 20 certificates, one certificate being included in each package of the cereal distributed by this company. The cost of each set of bowls to the company is $1. It is estimated that only 40% of the coupons will be redeemed. Transactions and entries are as follows:

Transaction	Entry		
1972 Premium purchases: 10,000 sets @ $1	Premiums — Bowl Sets. Cash	10,000	10,000
Sales: 400,000 packages @ $.60	Cash. . . . . Sales.	240,000	240,000
Premium claim redemptions: 120,000 certificates, or 6,000 sets @ $1	Premium Expense. . . . . Premiums— Bowl Sets.	6,000	6,000
DECEMBER 31, 1972 Coupons estimated redeemable in future periods: Total estimated redemptions — 40% of 400,000 . . . . 160,000 Redemptions in 1972 . . . . 120,000 Estimated future redemptions . 40,000 Estimated claim outstanding: 2,000 sets @ $1 . . . . $ 2,000	Premium Expense. . . . . . . Estimated Premium Claims Outstanding.	2,000	2,000
JANUARY 1, 1973 Reversal of accrued liability balance.	Estimated Premium Claims Outstanding. Premium Expense. . .	2,000	2,000

The balance sheet at the end of 1972 will show premiums of $4,000 as a current asset and estimated premium claims outstanding of $2,000 as a current liability; the income statement for 1972 will show premium expense of $8,000 as a selling expense.

Experience that indicates a redemption percentage that differs from the assumed rate will call for an appropriate adjustment in the subsequent period and the revision of future redemption estimates.

The estimated cost of the premiums may be shown as a direct reduction of sales by recording the premium claim at the time of the sale. This requires an estimate of the premium cost at the time of the sale. For example, in the previous illustration, the entry to be made at the time of the sale employing the sales reduction approach would be as follows:

```
Cash....................................  240,000
    Sales..................................              232,000
    Estimated Premium Claims Outstanding.....                8,000
```

The redemption of premium claims would call for charges to the liability account. Either the expense method or the sales reduction method is acceptable and both are found in practice.

Many organizations have adopted plans for the issuance to customers of trading stamps, cash register tapes, or other media redeemable in merchandise, premiums, or cash. The accounting that is followed will depend upon the nature of the plan. A business may establish its own plan, prepare its own stamps or other trading media, and assume redemption responsibilities. Under these circumstances, the accounting would parallel that just illustrated for specific premium offers. On the other hand, the business unit may enter into an agreement for a stamp plan with a trading-stamp company. The latter normally assumes full responsibility for the redemption of stamps and sells the trading stamps for a set unit price whether they are redeemed or not. The business would report stamps purchased as an asset and stamps issued as a selling expense; the trading-stamp company would recognize on its books the sale of stamps, purchase of premiums, distributions of premiums, and the estimated redemptions identified with stamps outstanding.

Estimated liabilities under guarantees for service and replacements. Some companies agree to provide free service on units failing to perform satisfactorily or to replace goods that are defective. When agreements involve only minor costs, it may be decided to recognize such costs in the periods in which they are incurred. When agreements involve significant future costs, estimates of such costs should be made. Such estimates are recorded by a charge to an expense account and a credit to a liability account. Subsequent costs of fulfilling guarantees are charged to the liability account. The anticipation of costs results in charges to the period that is credited for the revenue and in recognition of the obligation that is outstanding.

In certain cases customers are charged special fees for a service or replacement guarantee covering a specific period. In such cases, a customers' advances account is credited. Expenditures in meeting contract requirements are charged to expense, and the advances balance is recognized as revenue over the guarantee period. Recognition of revenue in excess of expenses indicates a profit on such service contracts; revenue that is less than expenses indicates a loss on such contracts. The customers' advances balance should be reported as a current liability in view of the claim that it makes upon current assets.

Estimated liabilities on tickets, tokens, and gift certificates outstanding. Many companies sell tickets, tokens, and gift certificates that entitle the owner to services or merchandise. For example, railroads issue tickets that are used for travel; local transit companies issue tokens that are good for fares; department stores sell gift certificates that are redeemable in merchandise.

When instruments redeemable in services or merchandise are outstanding at the end of the period, accounts should be adjusted to reflect the obligations under such arrangements. The nature of the adjustment will depend upon the entries that were originally made in recording the sale of the instruments.

Ordinarily, the sale of instruments redeemable in services or merchandise is recorded by a debit to Cash and a credit to a liability account. As instruments are redeemed, the liability balance is debited and Sales or an appropriate revenue account is credited. Certain claims may be rendered void by lapse of time or for some other reason as defined by the sales agreement. In addition, experience may indicate that a certain percentage of outstanding claims will never be presented for redemption. These factors must be considered at the end of the period. At this time, the liability balance is reduced to the balance of the claim estimated to be outstanding and a revenue account is credited for the gain that is indicated from forfeitures. If Sales or a special revenue account is originally credited on the sale of the redemption instrument, the adjustment at the end of the period calls for a charge to the revenue account and a credit to a liability account for the claim still outstanding.

Contingent Liabilities

Contingent liabilities represent possible future liabilities; certain acts or circumstances have created conditions that may result in liabilities in the event of future developments that are considered possible though not probable. The question of whether a liability is contingent or actual is not related to whether it involves an amount that is definite or indefinite; a definite amount may be involved, yet if the claim is uncertain, it is recognized as a contingent liability; an indefinite amount may be involved, but if the claim is certain, an actual liability, though estimated in amount, must be reported. Although a contingent liability involves no legal obligation on the date of the balance sheet, reference must be made to the possibility of such claim materializing in the future if the company's financial condition is to be fully shown. If a contingent liability should become an actual liability, the liability is reported in the accounts at the later date, and a charge is made to an asset account, to an expense or extraordinary loss account, or to Retained Earnings, whichever is considered to be appropriate under the circumstances.

Examples of the contingent liabilities that call for recognition on the balance sheet are described in the following paragraphs.

Notes receivable discounted and accounts receivable assigned. The discounting of customers' notes and the assignment of customers' accounts involve a liability on the part of the transferor for payment of the claim in the event that the original debtor fails to make settlement. In the event that a liability ultimately materializes and is paid, the payment gives rise to a claim against the original debtor. Failure to recover such a claim calls for the recognition of an expense, an extraordinary loss, or a charge to Retained Earnings, whichever is appropriate.

Accommodation endorsements. A party may become an accommodation endorser on a note by endorsing it for purposes of transfer. Such an endorsement creates a contingent liability as in the preceding case, and any ultimate payment on such an instrument should be treated as described above. If a person signs an accommodation note as maker, an entry should be made charging the party accommodated and crediting Notes Payable. These balances are closed if the accommodated party pays the notes at maturity; if the accommodation maker is required to pay the note, he will attempt to recover the amount paid from the party originally accommodated.

Lawsuits pending. When there is litigation relative to matters such as patent infringement, breach of contract, or additional income tax liability, and advice of legal counsel indicates doubt as to the outcome of the litigation, amounts that are claimed may be regarded as contingent liabilities. If counsel is of the opinion that current litigation will ultimately result in a judgment against the company, an estimate of the amount payable should be made. The liability is recognized and a charge is made to an expense account, to an extraordinary loss account, or to Retained Earnings, whichever is considered appropriate.

Additional taxes. Certain tax items may be under review by tax authorities, giving rise to the possibility of additional tax assessments. If an additional assessment is ultimately confirmed, the liability is recognized and a charge is made to an expense account, an extraordinary loss account, or Retained Earnings, whichever is considered appropriate.

Guarantee of debt service of affiliated companies. A company may guarantee the payment of interest and principal on long-term debt of affiliated companies. If this contingency materializes and payments are required, such payments will be accompanied by claims against the company whose obligations were assumed.

Customer service guarantees. In many instances, product or service guarantees may be considered of a contingent nature rather than indicating the recognition of a liability of a stated amount. If charges are subsequently incurred, these guarantees are recognized as expenses or as extraordinary losses.

Customer refund guarantees. Guarantees may be made to customers for refunds on goods purchased in the event of price declines or other specified contingencies. If conditions develop that call for customer reimbursements, these are recognized as expenses or as extraordinary losses.

Current Liabilities and Contingent Liabilities on the Balance Sheet

The nature of the detail to be presented for current liabilities depends upon the use that is to be made of the statement. A balance sheet prepared for stockholders might report little detail; on the other hand, creditors may insist on full detail concerning current debt.

Current assets are normally recorded in the order of their liquidity, and consistency would suggest that liabilities be reported in the order of their maturity. The latter practice may be followed only to the extent that it is practical; observance of such procedure would require an analysis of the different classes of obligations and separate reporting for classes with varying maturity dates. A bank overdraft should be listed first in view of the immediate demand that it makes on cash. In some cases a distinction is made between liabilities that have matured and are presently payable and others that have not matured though they are current.

Current liabilities should not be reduced by assets that are to be applied to their liquidation except for limited offset against tax liabilities as discussed in Chapter 2. Disclosure as to future debt liquidation, however, may be provided by appropriate parenthetical remark or note. Disclosure of liabilities that are secured by specific assets should also be made by parenthetical remark or note.

Contingent liabilities are generally reported on the balance sheet by means of (1) parenthetical remarks, (2) accompanying notes, or (3) descriptions under a special contingent liabilities heading. When the third method is used and amounts are indicated, the amounts are reported "short," that is, they are not included in the totals on the liability side since they have not been established as obligations on the balance sheet date. Contingent liabilities presented in a separate section of the balance sheet are preferably reported immediately after the current liabilities since these will normally require current liquidation if they materialize. When a lengthy explanation is required for a contingent liability, such an explanation is best provided by the second method.

The foregoing discussion dealt with contingent liabilities as of the balance sheet date. Business commitments that will result in liabilities in succeeding periods that are material in amount may also warrant disclosure. Commitments for the purchase of merchandise, services, and equipment, and for the construction, purchase, or lease of properties, for example, may warrant disclosure by special notes accompanying the balance sheet.

Current and contingent liabilities sections on a balance sheet prepared on December 31, 1972, might appear as shown below.

Liabilities

Current liabilities:			
Notes payable:			
Trade creditors...........................	$12,000		
Banks (secured by assignment of monies to become due under certain contracts totaling $36,000 included in asset section)...........	20,000		
Officers..................................	10,000		
Miscellaneous............................	2,500	$44,500	
Accounts payable:			
Trade creditors...........................	$30,500		
Credit balances in customers' accounts.........	1,250		
Miscellaneous............................	3,500	35,250	
Long-term debt installments due in 1973........		10,000	
Cash dividends payable......................		4,500	
Income taxes payable........................		6,000	
Accrued liabilities:			
Salaries and wages........................	$ 1,250		
Real and personal property taxes.............	1,550		
Miscellaneous accrued liabilities.............	1,400	4,200	
Other:			
Customer advances........................	$ 7,500		
Estimated repair costs on goods sold with service guarantees...............................	2,500	10,000	
Total current liabilities......................			$114,450
Contingent liabilities:			
Guarantors on employees' loans...............	$ 7,500		
Customers' drafts discounted..................	12,000		
Additional income tax assessments proposed by the Treasury Department for 1970 that have been protested by the company..............	4,500		
Total contingent liabilities....................	$24,000		

QUESTIONS

1. (a) Distinguish between current and noncurrent liabilities. (b) Indicate the major classifications for current liabilities.

2. Contingent claims require careful consideration in the evaluation of a company's working capital position. Explain.

3. What problems arise in the proper valuation of liabilities?

4. The use of present value techniques is increasing in accounting. Name five balance sheet liability accounts that suggest measurement by using present value techniques.

5. The Walker Co. issues a non-interest-bearing note due in one year in payment for equipment. Describe the accounting procedures that should be employed for the purchase.

6. Under what circumstances would an interest-bearing note be reported at an amount that is less than its maturity value?

7. The sales manager for the Midwest Sales Co. is entitled to a bonus of "$12\frac{1}{2}\%$ of profits." What difficulties may arise in the interpretation of this profit-sharing agreement?

8. As a result of rising materials and labor costs, the Peerless Corporation expects to suffer a significant loss on orders for merchandise that were accepted in 1972 but will not be produced and delivered until the middle of 1973. What accounting recognition would you recommend at the end of 1972 for the anticipated loss?

9. The Wilson Co. closes its plant in the month of July of each year but continues to pay its employees during this period. The company prepares quarterly statements and also statements for the year on December 31. What accounting procedures would you employ in recognizing the vacation pay for July?

10. Real estate taxes become a lien on the property owned by the Vernon Company on the assessment date in March, yet the company does not begin to accrue taxes on the books until July which is the beginning of the city's fiscal period. What is your comment on this practice?

11. (a) Define contingent liabilities. (b) Give five examples of contingent liabilities. (c) Indicate for each example in (b) the accounting treatment to be followed in the event that a liability actually arises from the item previously considered of a contingent nature.

12. The Zenith Corporation has appealed the decision of a lower court in a damage law suit. The lower court assessed the company $75,000 for damages. Payment has been deferred pending the results of the appeal.

The amount is not covered by insurance. Legal representatives of the company are convinced that the appeal will either reverse the lower courts ruling or substantially reduce the amount to be paid in settlement. How should the matter be disclosed in the year-end statements?

13. What methods may be employed on the balance sheet for the disclosure of contingent liabilities?

14. (a) When in your opinion would commitments for future expenditures call for special disclosure? (b) How would you recommend that such disclosure be made?

15. Where would each of the following items be reported on the balance sheet?

(a) Bank overdraft.
(b) Cash dividends declared.
(c) Dividends in arrears on preferred stock.
(d) Estimated income taxes.
(e) Insurance premiums received in advance for a 5-year period by an insurance company.
(f) Stamps that were issued and that are redeemable by customers for certain premiums.
(g) Deposits received in connection with meter installations by a public utility.
(h) Personal injury claim pending.
(i) Notes receivable discounted.
(j) Current maturities of a serial bond issue.
(k) Customer accounts with credit balances.
(l) Purchase money obligation maturing in five annual installments.
(m) Gift certificates sold to customers but not yet presented for redemption.
(n) Service guarantees on equipment sales.
(o) Accommodation endorsement on a note issued by an affiliated company.
(p) Contract entered into with contractors for the construction of a new building.
(q) Stock dividend payable.
(r) Accrued vacation pay.
(s) Strike settlement calling for retroactive wage payments.

EXERCISES

1. The following notes were issued by the Morning Co.:

(1) Note issued to purchase machinery. Face amount, $12,960; no stated interest rate; market rate of interest, 8%; term of note, one year; date of note, December 1, 1972.
(2) Note issued to bank for a cash loan. Maturity value of note, $5,000; bank discount rate, 9%; term of note, one year; date of note, November 15, 1972.

(a) Give the entries required at the time the notes were issued. (b) Give the adjusting entries required at December 31, 1972, to recognize the accrual of the interest on each note.

2. Total sales plus sales taxes for the Lincoln Electric Company in 1972 were $99,450; 60% of the sales are normally made on account. Prepare an entry summarizing this data for 1972 if the sales tax rate is 2%.

3. Thomas King, certified public accountant, has 3 employees. The weekly payroll is $400. Give the entries to record payment of the salaries if: (a) the employer is responsible for remitting 10% of the salaries quarterly to the federal government for federal insurance contributions, 5% being deducted from employees' salaries and 5% representing the employer's contribution; (b) the employer is responsible for remitting a total of 3.7% of the salaries quarterly to the state for unemployment and disability insurance, 1% being deducted from employees' salaries and 2.7% representing the employer's contribution; and (c) income tax withholdings are $65.

4. Shapiro Sales, Inc., has an agreement with its sales manager whereby the latter is entitled to 6% of company earnings as a bonus. Company income for a calendar year before bonus and income taxes is $90,000. Income taxes are 40% of income after bonus. Compute the amount of the bonus under each of the conditions below.

    (a) The bonus is calculated on income before deductions for bonus and income taxes.
    (b) The bonus is calculated on income after deduction for bonus but before deduction for income taxes.
    (c) The bonus is calculated on income after deduction for income taxes but before deduction for bonus.
    (d) The bonus is calculated on net income after deductions for both bonus and income taxes.

5. The Clarkson Company gives a bonus to its branch managers annually. The bonus for Branch A was calculated to be $11,320.75. The bonus agreement provided that each branch manager will receive a 10% bonus of the branch net income after deducting the bonus and also income taxes. The income tax rate is 40%. What was the income of Clarkson Co. before bonus and income tax deductions?

6. The Donahue Company provides a special bonus for its executive officers based upon income before bonus or income taxes. Income before bonus and income taxes for 1972 was $300,000. The income tax rate is 45% and the income tax liability for 1972 is $114,750. What was the bonus rate?

7. The Dahlberg Co. includes 1 coupon in each box of soap powder that it packs, 15 coupons being redeemable for a premium consisting of a kitchen utensil. In 1972, the Dahlberg Co. purchases 4,500 premiums at

75 cents, and sells 105,000 boxes of soap powder: 22,500 coupons are presented for redemption. It is estimated that 60% of the coupons issued will be presented for redemption. What entries would be made relating to the premium plan in 1972?

8. The Dublin Company was named the defendant in a property damage suit. The plaintiff is asking $300,000 in damages. The initial judgment was in favor of the plaintiff for $120,000 damages. The case, as of December 31, 1972, is being appealed by the Dublin Company, and the company's attorney feels there is a good chance for a reversal of the judgment. How should the claim be recorded in the books and reported in the company's financial statements at the end of 1972?

9. Prepare the current liabilities section of the balance sheet for the Romney Co. on December 31, 1972, from the information that appears below:

Notes payable: arising from purchases of goods, $32,600; arising from loans from banks, $10,000, on which marketable securities valued at $14,500 have been pledged as security; arising from advances by officers, $12,000.

Accounts payable: arising from purchases of goods, $31,000.

Cash balance with Farmers Bank, $5,500; cash overdraft with Merchants Bank, $3,200.

Dividends in arrears on preferred stock, $18,000.

Employees income taxes payable, $710.

First-mortgage serial bonds, $125,000, payable in semiannual installments of $5,000 due on March 1 and September 1 of each year.

Advances received from customers on purchase orders, $2,300.

Customers' accounts with credit balances arising from purchases returns, $1,200.

Estimated expenses of meeting guarantee for service requirements on merchandise sold, $2,700.

Estimated damages to be paid as a result of unsatisfactory performance on a contract, $1,600.

PROBLEMS

17-1. The Blaine Corp. has an agreement with its sales manager whereby the latter is entitled to 20% of the company's earnings as an annual bonus. Company income for a calendar year before computing the bonus and the income taxes is $105,000. Income taxes are 50% of the income after bonus.

Instructions: Compute the amount of the bonus and the income taxes, assuming each of the following conditions:

(1) The bonus is computed on the income before deductions for bonus and income taxes.

(2) The bonus is computed on the income after deduction for bonus but before deduction for income taxes. Prove your answer.

(3) The bonus is computed on the net income after deduction for income taxes but before deduction for bonus. Prove your answer.

(4) The bonus is computed on the net income after deductions for both bonus and income taxes. Prove your answer.

17-2. The real and personal property taxes paid by the Dettman Corp. for 1970–1971 were $5,210. The taxes cover the city's fiscal year which is July 1, 1970–June 30, 1971, and the company follows the policy of accruing taxes over the fiscal period of the taxing authority. The company has made property improvements and estimates the tax for 1971–1972 at $6,300. On October 31, 1971, the company receives its tax bill reporting a liability of $6,900. The assessment is protested. The company pays 50% of the tax bill on December 10, 1971. On March 20, 1972, the company is advised that its tax liability for 1971–1972 was reduced to $6,480. The balance of the amount due, $3,030, is paid on April 10, 1972.

Instructions: Give the entries relating to the property taxes that will appear on the books of the Dettman Corp. over the period July 1, 1971–June 30, 1972, including monthly adjustments that are required for the preparation of monthly financial statements.

17-3. The Minnesota Mills Corp. manufactures a cake mix that is packaged and sold. A cake knife is offered to customers sending in 2 box tops from these packages accompanied by a remittance of 50 cents. Data with respect to the premium offer are summarized below:

	1972	1971
Cake mix sales (60¢ per package).............	$216,000	$180,000
Cake knife purchases (70¢ per knife)..........	$ 11,200	$ 9,800
Number of knives distributed as premiums.....	12,500	7,500
Estimated number of knives to be distributed in subsequent periods......................	3,000	2,000
Mailing costs are 15¢ per cake knife.		

Instructions: (1) Give the entries that would be made in 1971 and 1972 to record product sales, premium purchases and redemptions, and year-end adjustments.

(2) List the account balances that will appear on the balance sheet and the income statement at the end of 1972 and 1971 as a result of the foregoing.

17-4. Richfield Services, Inc., sells a television warranty policy covering all parts and labor for $75 per year. Warranties begin as of the first of the month following issuance of the policy. Policies were first issued in September, 1971. In reviewing the records before closing the accounts for 1972, you find that revenues and expenses on such contracts have been recognized in 1971 and 1972 on the cash basis. The accounts show revenues and expenses for the two years as follows:

	Revenue		Expense	
	1971	1972	1971	1972
January....................		$ 5,100		$ 1,610
February..................		4,800		2,130
March.....................		4,650		1,900
April......................		4,200		2,350
May.......................		5,700		2,650
June......................		3,900		2,800
July.......................		2,100		1,910
August....................		2,700		3,000
September.................	$ 1,800	4,200		2,675
October...................	2,250	4,050	$ 1,100	3,250
November.................	3,600	3,600	850	3,315
December.................	4,200	3,600	1,375	3,100
	$11,850	$48,600	$ 3,325	$30,690

Instructions: (1) List monthly revenue, expense, and income balances for 1971 and 1972, assuming that proper recognition is given to deferred revenue on the service policies. (Submit working paper summaries that show the determination of the monthly income figures listed.)

(2) Assuming that financial statements are to be prepared for 1972 that report the earnings with appropriate recognition of deferred revenue at the beginning and the end of the period, give (a) the correcting entry to be made in recognition of the deferred revenue balance at the beginning of the year and (b) the adjusting entry to be made in recognition of the deferred revenue balance at the end of the year.

17-5. The Kohler Appliance Company sells color television sets with a three-year repairs warranty. The sales price for each set is $460. The average expense of repairing a set is $20. Research has shown that 10% of all sets sold are repaired in the first year, 15% in the second year, and 40% in the third year. The number of sets sold were as follows: 3,000 in 1970, 5,000 in 1971, and 6,000 in 1972. Total payments for repairs associated with the warranties were $5,500 in 1970, $14,500 in 1971, and $30,000 in 1972.

Sales were made on account evenly throughout the year. Sales taxes are charged at 4%. Income tax regulations provide that expenses in connection with warranties can be deducted for tax purposes only when paid.

Instructions: (1) Give the entries to record sales, the liability for warranties, and the payments made in connection with warranties for 1970, 1971, and 1972.

(2) What is the amount of the liability for warranties that would appear on the balance sheet for 1972? Test the reasonableness of this amount using the expected repair experience.

(3) Give the entries to record the deferred income taxes expense in 1970, 1971, and 1972 assuming a tax rate for each year of 45%.

17-6. The Pacific South Seas Company opened a plant on Kutaw Island on January 1, 1971. Many of the employees have been brought to the island for a two-year period, and the company has established the following vacation policy.

Under twelve months...................... no paid vacation
12–24 months............................ 2 weeks paid vacation
Over 24 months.......................... 4 weeks paid vacation

The average employee weekly pay is $350. Eight hundred employees were hired during 1971. The work force grew evenly throughout the year.

The company has had some past experience with employees under similar conditions. Analysis of this experience indicates that 50% of the employees resign within the first twelve months after hiring, and an additional 15% of those who remain twelve months resign and take their two weeks leave before the full two year period is completed.

Instructions: Based upon the above data:

(1) Compute the number of employees who will ultimately receive (a) 2 weeks paid vacation; and (b) 4 weeks paid vacation.

(2) Compute the total vacation pay that will be made to these employees.

(3) Compute the proper charge to vacation expense for (a) 1971, (b) 1972, and (c) 1973.

(4) Compute the proper liability for accrued vacation pay as of (a) December 31, 1971, and (b) December 31, 1972.

17-7. The following data are made available for purposes of stating the financial position of the Salt River Corp. on December 31, 1972.

Cash in bank..	$20,000
Petty cash, which includes IOU's of employees totaling $350 that are to be repaid to the petty cash fund............	1,000
Marketable securities, valued at $48,900, securities valued at $25,000 having been pledged on a note payable to the bank for $20,000, reported on the books at cost..............	46,100
Notes receivable, which have been reduced by notes discounted of $8,000 that are not yet due and on which the company is contingently liable........................	12,500
Accounts receivable, which include accounts with credit balances of $560 and past-due accounts of $2,650 on which a loss of 60% is anticipated.............................	34,700
Merchandise inventory, which includes goods held on a consignment basis, $1,800, and goods received on December 31, $2,600, neither of these items having been recorded as a purchase.......................................	29,600
Prepaid insurance, which includes cash surrender value of life insurance policies, $4,200........................	6,100
Rents paid in advance..................................	830
Furniture and fixtures, which include fixtures that were fully depreciated and that have just been scrapped, $4,500:	
Cost....................................... $16,000	
Accumulated depreciation................... 8,250	7,750

Notes payable, which are trade notes with the exception of a 6-month, $20,000 note payable to Commerce First National Bank on June 15, 1973...............................	$32,100
Accounts payable, which include accounts with debit balances of $675...	24,100
Miscellaneous accrued expenses, which include $4,000 representing estimated costs of premiums in connection with a special sales offer made in December...................	8,650
Long-term notes, which are payable in annual installments of $2,500 on February 1 of each year.....................	10,000
6% cumulative preferred stock, $15 par, on which dividends for 3 years are in arrears.............................	45,000
No-par common stock, 40,000 shares authorized and outstanding...	50,000
Retained earnings (debit balance).......................	(11,270)

The following data are not included in the above account balances:

(a) A suit has been filed against the company for $75,000; legal counsel has informed the company that while it is probable that the company will lose the suit, the award for damages will not be in excess of $20,000.

(b) There are product replacement guarantees outstanding that are estimated to result in costs to the company of $6,000.

Instructions: Prepare a classified balance sheet, including whatever notes are appropriate in support of balance sheet data.

17-8. As of January 1, 1963, Henry M. Garfield leased for 10 years a building to be used as a retail store. His lease provided that annual rent payment was to be based on gross sales. On sales up to $150,000 per year the rate was to be 3%. On any sales in excess of $150,000 per year, the rate was to be 2%. However, during the first 5 years of the term of the lease, the annual rental was to be a minimum of $4,000 per year, after which the minimum was to be increased by $12\frac{1}{2}\%$.

The lease further provided that if, in any one year, the rent based on sales did not equal the minimum annual rental, the minimum would be payable, but the amount paid solely as a result of such minimum could be applied in reduction of the next year's rent to the extent that the next year's rent exceeded the minimum for that year.

Gross sales by years, including 1972, were as follows:

1963...................	$ 96,000	1968.............	$141,000
1964...................	129,000	1969............	165,000
1965...................	148,000	1970............	142,000
1966...................	161,000	1971............	170,000
1967...................	124,000	1972............	197,000

Instructions: (1) Compute the amount of rent payable each year under the terms of the lease.

(2) Discuss the treatment in the financial statements of any amounts payable under the provision for payment of a minimum amount of rent.

(AICPA adapted)

17-9. The Four Star Mining Co. started mining in the current year on certain land leased from Tapps Realty Company.

The royalty provisions in the lease are as follows:

(a) Minimum annual royalty — $6,000, with minimum of $1,500 payable quarterly. Unearned minimum royalties may be recovered in any subsequent period from earned royalties in excess of minimum royalties. Minimum royalties of $18,000 were paid for the three years prior to the current year.

(b) Earned royalty — $.10 per ton shipped from the mine plus a per-ton amount equal to 2% of the amount that the market value of the ore at the mine exceeds $4 per ton.

Operations in the current year were as follows:

| | | Per Ton | |
| | Tons | Market Value | Freight from Mine |
Periods	Shipped	at Destination	to Destination
1st quarter	None	———	———
2d quarter	100,000	$10.50	$3.10
3d quarter	200,000	10.00	3.20
4th quarter	None	———	———
	300,000		

Instructions: Compute the amount of royalty to be paid to Tapps Realty Company for the current year and the amount of unearned minimum royalty at the end of the year.

(AICPA adapted)

17-10. The Miracle Radio Corporation, a client, requests that you compute the appropriate balance for its estimated liability for product warranty account for a statement as of June 30, 1972.

The Miracle Radio Corporation manufactures television tubes and sells them with a six-month guarantee under which defective tubes will be replaced without a charge. On December 31, 1971, the Estimated Liability for Product Warranty had a balance of $510,000. By June 30, 1972, this balance had been reduced to $80,250 by charges for estimated net cost of tubes returned which had been sold in 1971.

The company started out in 1972 expecting 8% of the dollar volume of sales to be returned. However, due to the introduction of new models during the year, this estimated percentage of returns was increased to 10% on May 1. It is assumed that no tubes sold during a given month are returned in that month. Each tube is stamped with a date at time of sale so that the warranty may be properly administered. The following table of percentages indicates the likely pattern of sales returns during the six-month period of the warranty, starting with the month following the sale of tubes.

Month Following Sale	Percentage of Total Returns Expected
First..	20
Second.....................................	30
Third......................................	20
Fourth through sixth — 10% each month	30
Total.................................	100

Gross sales of tubes were as follows for the first six months of 1972:

Month	Amount	Month	Amount
January..............	$3,600,000	April..........	$2,850,000
February.............	3,300,000	May...........	2,000,000
March...............	4,100,000	June...........	1,800,000

The company's warranty also covers the payment of freight cost on defective tubes returned and on new tubes sent out as replacements. This freight cost runs approximately 10% of the sales price of the tubes returned. The manufacturing cost of the tubes is roughly 80% of the sales price, and the salvage value of returned tubes averages 15% of their sales price. Returned tubes on hand at December 31, 1971, were thus valued in inventory at 15% of their original sales price.

Instructions: Using the data given, draw up a suitable working-paper schedule for arriving at the balance of the estimated liability for product warranty account and give the proposed adjusting entry. Assume that proper recognition of costs for financial accounting will be allowed for income tax purposes.

(AICPA adapted)

17-11. In January, 1973, you were examining the financial statements of Lang Manufacturing Company for the year ended December 31, 1972. Lang filed the necessary payroll tax returns for the first three quarters of 1972 and had prepared drafts of the returns scheduled to be filed by January 31, 1973.

The following information was available from the general ledger, copies and drafts of payroll tax returns and other sources:

General Ledger:

Account	Balance December 31, 1972	Composition of Balance
Wages (various expense accounts)	$121,800	12 monthly entries from payroll summaries.
Payroll Taxes Expense	7,488	FICA (5% of $103,000), $5,150; state unemployment tax (2.7% of $59,000), $1,593; federal unemployment tax (.5% of $59,000), $295; amounts withheld from employees for FICA tax in October and November and paid to depositary, $450.

Account	Balance December 31, 1972	Composition of Balance
Employees Payroll Taxes Payable	$2,285	December income tax, $1,530; October through December FICA, $755.
Employer's Payroll Taxes Payable	561	December FICA, $305; October through December state unemployment tax, $216; 1972 federal unemployment tax, $40 for last quarter.

Copies of 1972 Tax Returns:

	Totals for Year	First Three Quarters (Duplicate Copies of Returns)	Last Quarter (Pencil Draft)
Gross wages......................	$121,800	$95,870	$25,930
Wages taxable for FICA...........	103,000	87,900	15,100
FICA taxes.....................	10,300	8,790	1,510
Income taxes withheld.............	15,740	11,490	4,250
Wages taxable for state and federal unemployment tax..............	59,000	51,000	8,000
Total state unemployment tax (employer only).............	1,593	1,377	216
Total federal unemployment tax — employer only...........	295	255	40

Information from other sources:

(a) In August, 1972, six laborers were hired to tear down an old warehouse building located on the site where a new warehouse would soon be constructed. The laborers' 1972 wages totaling $1,000 were charged to the land and buildings account. Payroll taxes were not withheld.

(b) Included in a 1972 wages expense account is one month's salary of $1,400 paid to the president on December 30, 1972, for his 1971 vacation allowance.

(c) In December, 1972, a contractor was paid $2,000 for making repairs to machinery usually made by company employees and the amount was charged to Wages Expense. No payroll taxes were withheld and none were required.

Instructions: (1) Prepare a schedule presenting the computation of total taxable wages to be reported on the 1972 payroll tax returns for FICA and for state unemployment taxes.

(2) Prepare a schedule presenting the computation of the amounts (to the nearest dollar) that should be paid with each of the year-end payroll tax returns to be filed in January, 1973, for (a) FICA taxes and income taxes withheld, (b) state unemployment tax and (c) federal unemployment tax.

(3) Prepare a schedule to reconcile the differences between the amounts which should be paid with payroll tax returns to be filed in January, 1973 (as computed for "2") and the balances shown at December 31, 1972, in the related general ledger liability accounts.

(AICPA adapted)

17-12. The Novelties Co., Inc., is engaged in manufacturing and wholesaling two principal products. As their accountant, you have been asked to advise management on sales policy for the coming year.

Two different plans are being considered by management, either of which, they believe, will (1) increase the volume of sales, (2) reduce the ratio of selling expense to sales, and (3) decrease unit production costs. These proposals are as follows:

Plan 1 — Premium Stamp Books

It is proposed that each package of Product A will contain 8 premium stamps, and each package of Product B will contain 4 premium stamps. Premium stamp books will be distributed to consumers, and when a book is filled with stamps (100 stamps) it will be redeemed by the award of a cash prize in an amount indicated under an unbroken seal attached to the book at the time of distribution. Every 10,000 books distributed will provide for prizes in accordance with the following schedule.

Number of books	Prize for each	Total prizes
1	$150.00	$ 150
5	50.00	250
14	20.00	280
50	10.00	500
160	5.00	800
1,020	1.00	1,020
8,750	.40	3,500
10,000		$6,500

This schedule is fixed and not subject to alteration or modification. The cost of this plan will be as follows:

Books, including distribution cost..............$ 15 per 1000 books
Stamps.....................................$ 1 per 1000 stamps
Prizes.........,............................$650 per 1000 books

The premium stamp book plan will take the place of all previous advertising, and previously established selling prices will be maintained.

Plan 2 — Reduced Selling Prices

It is proposed that the selling price of Product A will be reduced by $8\frac{1}{3}\%$ and of Product B by 5% and to increase the advertising expenditures over those of the prior year. This plan is an alternative to Plan 1, and only one will be adopted.

Management has provided you with the following information as to the previous year's operations, and as to anticipated changes:

Prior year's operations:	Product A	Product B
Quantity sold.....................	200,000 units	600,000 units
Production cost per unit...........	$.40	$.30
Selling price per unit..............	$.60	$.40

Selling expenses were 18% of sales, of which one third was for advertising. Administrative expenses were 5% of sales.

	Product A	Product B
Expected changes:		
Increase in unit sales volume:		
Plan 1........................	50%	50%
Plan 2........................	40%	25%
Decrease in unit production cost:		
Plan 1........................	5%	10%
Plan 2........................	$7\frac{1}{2}\%$	$6\frac{2}{3}\%$
Advertising:		
Plan 1........................	None	None
Plan 2........................	8% of sales	7% of sales
Other selling expenses:		
Plan 1........................	15% of sales	12% of sales
Plan 2........................	12% of sales	12% of sales
Premium book expenses:		
Plan 1........................	As indicated	
Plan 2........................	None	None
Administrative expenses:		
Plan 1........................	4% of sales	4% of sales
Plan 2........................	Same dollar amount as prior year.	

Instructions: Prepare a schedule for submission to management comparing operations of the previous year with those under both proposed plans.

(AICPA adapted)

chapter 18

long-term liabilities

Long-term or *fixed liabilities* include all obligations that are not to be liquidated out of company resources classified as current. *Long-term debt* normally comprises the major element of a company's long-term liabilities. Such debt is found in the form of bonds, long-term notes, advances from affiliated companies, and long-term contract obligations. Other long-term liabilities include such items as deferred income taxes payable, product warranties extending beyond the current period, claims in litigation that are not expected to be settled currently, obligations under long-term deposits, deferred compensation agreements, pension and other employee benefits payable, and deferred revenues making no claim upon current resources.

Bonds payable

The power of a corporation to create bonded indebtedness is found in the corporation laws of the state and may be specifically granted by charter. In some cases formal authorization by a majority of stockholders is required before a board of directors can approve a bond issue.

Borrowing by means of bonds involves the issue of a number of certificates of indebtedness. Bond certificates may represent equal parts of the bond issue or they may be of varying denominations. Bonds of the business unit are commonly issued in $1,000 denominations, referred to as the bond face, par, or maturity value. Bonds may be unsecured or they may be secured by liens on real estate, equipment, or specific securities. An earlier discussion of long-term investments made reference to the various classes of bonds and their special features.

The group contract between the corporation and the bondholders is known as the *bond* or *trust indenture*. The indenture details the rights and obligations of the contracting parties, indicates the property that is pledged as well as the protection that is offered on the loan, and names the bank or trust company that is to represent the bondholders.

Bonds may be sold by the company directly to investors, or they may be underwritten by investment bankers or a syndicate. The underwriters may agree to purchase the entire bond issue or that part of the issue which is not sold by the company, or they may agree simply to manage the sale of the security on a commission basis.

Funds to meet short-term needs, such as the financing of inventories and receivables, are normally raised by the corporation through the issue of short-term notes. Funds to meet long-term needs, the acquisition of land, buildings, and equipment, for example, are normally raised by issuing bonds or capital stock. The issue of bonds instead of stock may be preferred by stockholders for the following reasons: (1) the charge against earnings for bond interest is normally less than the share of earnings that would otherwise be payable as dividends on a new issue of preferred stock or on the sale of additional common stock; (2) present owners continue in control of the corporation; and (3) bond interest is a deductible expense in arriving at taxable income while dividends are not.

But there are certain limitations and disadvantages of financing through bonds. Bond financing is possible only when a company is in a satisfactory financial condition and can offer adequate security to a new creditor group. Furthermore, interest must be paid regardless of the company's earnings and financial position. With operating losses and the inability of a company to raise sufficient cash to meet the periodic interest payments, bondholders may take legal action to assume control of company properties.

Recording the bond issue. It was indicated in Chapter 12 that the sales price of a bond depends upon the interest rate it offers as compared with the interest rate on the money market. The market rate of interest varies with the nature of the credit risk and the length of the loan and fluctuates constantly with changes in the supply of money and the demand for money. Bonds will sell at face value only when they offer interest equal to the market rate at the time of sale; they will sell at a premium when they pay more than the market rate and will sell at a discount when they pay less than the market rate. With the need for assigning an interest rate to bonds before they are actually sold, there is frequently a difference between the bond rate and market rate at the time of bond sale.

Although the investor usually records bonds at cost, the borrower normally records bonds at their face value — the amount that the company must pay at maturity. Hence, when bonds are issued at an amount other than face value, a bond discount or premium balance is established for the difference between the cash received and the bond face value. The discount or premium balance is written off to Bond Interest Expense over the life of the bond issue; periodic adjustments correct interest expense to the effective charge.

When bonds are issued in exchange for property, the transaction should be recorded at the cash price at which the bonds could be issued. The yield that the bonds would have to provide is used in calculating a cash price. When difficulties are encountered in arriving at a cash price, the market or appraised value of the property acquired would be used. A difference between the face value of the bonds and the cash value of the bonds or the value of the property acquired is recognized as bond discount or bond premium.

When an entire bond issue is not disposed of at one time, alternative accounting procedures can be employed: (1) entries may be made only when bonds are sold and issued; or (2) an entry may be made upon approval of the issue recording bonds authorized and bonds unissued, and entries made thereafter to report changes in the unissued balance. In employing the latter method, the bond authorization is recorded by a charge to an unissued bonds account and a credit to an authorized bonds account. The subsequent sale and issuance of bonds is recorded by a charge to Cash and a credit to the unissued bonds account. The amount of bonds issued is obtained by subtracting the unissued balance from the authorized balance.

In certain instances subscriptions are first obtained for bonds. Issue of the bond certificate is normally withheld until the full subscription price is collected.

To illustrate the entries for a bond issue, assume that a company is authorized to issue 6% debenture bonds of $500,000. Bonds of $300,000 are sold at 98 to investment bankers. Subscriptions for bonds of $100,000 at the same price are received from officers of the company who pay 25% of the subscription price. Collection is made from officers who have subscribed for bonds of $80,000 of the unpaid balance, and bonds that are fully paid for are issued. Entries are made as shown at the bottom of the following page.

In reporting bonds on the balance sheet, bonds subscribed should be added to the bonds issued balance. The amount unissued should be reported parenthetically or as a subtraction from an authorized balance. Unissued bonds indicate a possible source of funds through sale or through pledge as security on other independent loans. The result of the bond transactions in the example may be reported as follows:

Long-term debt:
6% Debenture bonds due March 1, 1982............ $380,000
Add bonds subscribed...........................   20,000

Bonds issued and subscribed....................... $400,000
(Bonds authorized but unissued, $120,000; $20,000
of this amount is reserved for bond subscribers.)

Bond Subscriptions Receivable is reported as a current asset when current collection is anticipated and cash is to become available as working capital. When bond proceeds are to be applied to some noncurrent purpose, neither the receivable nor the cash received from the issue of the bonds should be recognized as a current asset. For example, when terms of the bond issue require that bond proceeds be applied to the retirement of other debt or to the payment for buildings and equipment, claims against subscribers, as well as cash proceeds, should be reported as noncurrent items with appropriate disclosure of the manner in which the cash will ultimately be applied.

In the past, bond discount was frequently reported as a deferred charge and bond premium as a deferred credit. However, sound theory calls for relating bond discount and premium to the bonds payable account: a discount should be subtracted from bonds reported at par; a premium should be added to bonds reported at par.

Transaction	If authorized and unissued balances are not maintained	If authorized and unissued balances are maintained
Received permission to issue $500,000 6% debenture bonds (500 bonds, $1,000 face value).	No entry	Unissued Bonds........500,000 Authorized Bonds Payable.....500,000
Sold bonds of $300,000 to investment bankers at 98.	Cash.........294,000 Discount on Bonds Payable.6,000 Bonds Payable.....300,000	Cash...........294,000 Discount on Bonds Payable...6,000 Unissued Bonds.......300,000
Received subscriptions for bonds of $100,000 at 98 accompanied by 25% down payment. Received 25% of $98,000...........$24,500 Receivable—75% of $98,000............73,500 ⎯⎯⎯⎯⎯⎯ $98,000	Cash...........24,500 Bond Subscriptions Receivable....73,500 Discount on Bonds Payable.........2,000 Bonds Payable Subscribed......100,000	Cash...........24,500 Bond Subscriptions Receivable.....73,500 Discount on Bonds Payable...........2,000 Bonds Payable Subscribed........100,000
Received balance due on bonds of $80,000 subscribed for at 98—75% of $78,400, or $58,800.	Cash...........58,800 Bond Subscriptions Receivable........58,800	Cash............58,800 Bond Subscriptions Receivable.........58,800
Issued bonds of $80,000 to paid-up subscribers.	Bonds Payable Subscribed....80,000 Bonds Payable.......80,000	Bonds Payable Subscribed.....80,000 Unissued Bonds........80,000

The bond sales price determines the balance for the obligation to be reported at the time of the issue. As amortization of discount and premium balances is recorded, the obligation approaches its maturity amount. Amortization of a discount by charges to the bond interest expense account over the life of the issue raises interest expense to the effective amount and raises the book value of the obligation; periodic interest is viewed as the interest paid increased by the accrual of the discount to be paid at bond maturity. Amortization of a premium by credits to the bond interest expense account over the life of the issue reduces interest expense to the effective amount and reduces the book value of the obligation; periodic interest is viewed as the interest paid reduced by the return of a part of the premium originally advanced by the bondholders.

The sale of bonds normally involves costs for legal services, printing and engraving, taxes, and underwriting. These costs should be summarized separately as issuing costs and charged to revenue over the life of the bond issue. However, issuing costs are frequently treated as deductions from bond proceeds, thus increasing the discount or reducing the premium that is recognized on the bond issue.

Bond interest payments. When coupon bonds are issued, cash is paid by the company in exchange for interest coupons on the interest dates. Payments on coupons may be made by the company directly to bondholders, or payments may be cleared through a bank or other disbursing agent. Subsidiary records with bondholders are not maintained since coupons are redeemable by bearers. In the case of registered bonds, interest checks are mailed either by the company or its agent. When bonds are registered, the bonds account requires subsidiary ledger support. The subsidiary ledger shows holdings by individuals and changes in such holdings. Checks are sent to bondholders of record as of the interest payment dates.

When an agent is to make interest payments, the company normally transfers cash to the agent in advance of the interest payment date. Since the company is not freed from its obligation to bondholders until payment has been made by its agent, it records the cash transfer by a charge to Cash Deposited with Agent for Bond Interest and a credit to Cash. On the date the interest is due, the company charges interest expense and credits accrued interest. Upon receipt from the agent of paid interest coupons, a certificate of coupon receipt and appropriate disposal, or other evidence that the interest was paid, the company charges accrued interest and credits the cash deposited with agent for bond interest account.

Premium and discount amortization procedures. As in the case of investments, either the straight-line method or the compound-interest or effective-interest method may be used for amortization of bond premium or discount. The straight-line method calls for writing off an equal amount of premium or discount each period; this results in equal periodic interest charges. The compound-interest method calls for reporting interest at the effective rate provided by the bond issue, which rate must first be determined. This rate is then applied periodically to the bond carrying value in arriving at the charge to the interest expense account; the difference between the charge to expense and the amount paid is reported as a reduction in the premium or discount balance.

To illustrate the application of the straight-line and compound-interest methods of amortization, assume that 5-year bonds of $100,000, interest at 6% payable semiannually, are sold to yield 5%. This price as shown by bond tables is $104,376.03. The following tabulations show the differences in results through the use of the two methods:

AMORTIZATION OF PREMIUM — STRAIGHT-LINE METHOD
$100,000 5-Year Bonds, Interest at 6% Payable Semiannually,
Sold at $104,376.03

Interest Payment	A Interest Paid (3% of Face Value)	B Premium Amortization (1/10 × $4,376.03)	C Interest Expense (A−B)	D Unamortized Premium (D−B)	E Bond Carrying Value ($100,000 + D)
				$4,376.03	$104,376.03
1	$3,000.00	$437.60	$2,562.40	3,938.43	103,938.43
2	3,000.00	437.60	2,562.40	3,500.83	103,500.83
3	3,000.00	437.60	2,562.40	3,063.23	103,063.23
4	3,000.00	437.60	2,562.40	2,625.63	102,625.63
5	3,000.00	437.60	2,562.40	2,188.03	102,188.03
6	3,000.00	437.60	2,562.40	1,750.43	101,750.43
7	3,000.00	437.60	2,562.40	1,312.83	101,312.83
8	3,000.00	437.60	2,562.40	875.23	100,875.23
9	3,000.00	437.60	2,562.40	437.63	100,437.63
10	3,000.00	437.63	2,562.37	———	100,000.00

AMORTIZATION OF PREMIUM — COMPOUND-INTEREST METHOD
$100,000 5-Year Bonds, Interest at 6% Payable Semiannually,
Sold at $104,376.03 to Yield 5%

Interest Payment	A Interest Paid (3% of Face Value)	B Interest Expense (2½% of Bond Carrying Value)	C Premium Amortization (A−B)	D Unamortized Premium (D−C)	E Bond Carrying Value ($100,000+D)
				$4,376.03	$104,376.03
1	$3,000.00	$2,609.40 (2½% of $104,376.03)	$390.60	3,985.43	103,985.43
2	3,000.00	2,599.64 (2½% of $103,985.43)	400.36	3,585.07	103,585.07
3	3,000.00	2,589.63 (2½% of $103,585.07)	410.37	3,174.70	103,174.70
4	3,000.00	2,579.37 (2½% of $103,174.70)	420.63	2,754.07	102,754.07
5	3,000.00	2,568.85 (2½% of $102,754.07)	431.15	2,322.92	102,322.92
6	3,000.00	2,558.07 (2½% of $102,322.92)	441.93	1,880.99	101,880.99
7	3,000.00	2,547.02 (2½% of $101,880.99)	452.98	1,428.01	101,428.01
8	3,000.00	2,535.70 (2½% of $101,428.01)	464.30	963.71	100,963.71
9	3,000.00	2,524.09 (2½% of $100,963.71)	475.91	487.80	100,487.80
10	3,000.00	2,512.20 (2½% of $100,487.80)	487.80	———	100,000.00

The use of the straight-line and compound-interest methods when bonds are issued at a discount is illustrated below. Here it is assumed that 5-year bonds of $100,000, interest at 4% payable semiannually, are sold for $95,625, a price that provides a yield of approximately 5%.

AMORTIZATION OF DISCOUNT — STRAIGHT-LINE METHOD
$100,000 5-Year Bonds, Interest at 4% Payable Semiannually,
Sold at $95,625

Interest Payment	A Interest Paid (2% of Face Value)	B Discount Amortization (1/10 × $4,375)	C Interest Expense (A + B)	D Unamortized Discount (D − B)	E Bond Carrying Value ($100,000 − D)
				$4,375.00	$ 95,625.00
1	$2,000.00	$437.50	$2,437.50	3,937.50	96,062.50
2	2,000.00	437.50	2,437.50	3,500.00	96,500.00
3	2,000.00	437.50	2,437.50	3,062.50	96,937.50
4	2,000.00	437.50	2,437.50	2,625.00	97,375.00
5	2,000.00	437.50	2,437.50	2,187.50	97,812.50
6	2,000.00	437.50	2,437.50	1,750.00	98,250.00
7	2,000.00	437.50	2,437.50	1,312.50	98,687.50
8	2,000.00	437.50	2,437.50	875.00	99,125.00
9	2,000.00	437.50	2,437.50	437.50	99,562.50
10	2,000.00	437.50	2,437.50	——————	100,000.00

AMORTIZATION OF DISCOUNT — COMPOUND-INTEREST METHOD
$100,000 5-Year Bonds, Interest at 4% Payable Semiannually,
Sold at $95,625 to Yield Approximately 5%

Interest Payment	A Interest Paid (2% of Face Value)	B Interest Expense (2½% of Bond Carrying Value)	C Discount Amortization (B − A)	D Unamortized Discount (D − C)	E Bond Carrying Value ($100,000 − D)
				$4,375.00	$ 95,625.00
1	$2,000.00	$2,390.63 (2½% of $95,625.00)	$390.63	3,984.37	96,015.63
2	2,000.00	2,400.39 (2½% of $96,015.63)	400.39	3,583.98	96,416.02
3	2,000.00	2,410.40 (2½% of $96,416.02)	410.40	3,173.58	96,826.42
4	2,000.00	2,420.66 (2½% of $96,826.42)	420.66	2,752.92	97,247.08
5	2,000.00	2,431.18 (2½% of $97,247.08)	431.18	2,321.74	97,678.26
6	2,000.00	2,441.96 (2½% of $97,678.26)	441.96	1,879.78	98,120.22
7	2,000.00	2,453.01 (2½% of $98,120.22)	453.01	1,426.77	98,573.23
8	2,000.00	2,464.33 (2½% of $98,573.23)	464.33	962.44	99,037.56
9	2,000.00	2,475.94 (2½% of $99,037.56)	475.94	486.50	99,513.50
10	2,000.00	2,486.50 ($2,000 + $486.50)[1]	486.50	——————	100,000.00

Even though it is possible that bonds may be retired prior to their maturity dates, such retirement cannot ordinarily be anticipated. Amortization schedules, then, are normally developed in terms of the full life of the bond issue. Early bond retirement will call for a cancellation of the bond premium or discount relating to the remaining life of the issue.

The investor in bonds normally employs straight-line amortization as a practical matter. With the acquisition of a number of different issues,

---

[1] 2½% of $99,513.50 is $2,487.84. However, use of 5% when the effective rate was not exactly 5% has resulted in a small discrepancy that requires adjustment upon recording the final interest payment. On the final payment the discount balance is closed and interest expense is increased by this amount.

the purchases and sales within the bond life, and the relatively minor differences in straight-line and compound-interest procedures, application of the simpler method is justified. But these considerations are not relevant in the case of the bond issuer. Here only one or a few issues are involved and amortization schedules can be followed from the time of issuance of the bonds to their retirement. When large issues are involved, the difference between compound-interest amortization and straight-line amortization may be significant. Such circumstances support the use of the compound-interest method that provides for the accurate measure of expense in terms of a changing liability balance. Nevertheless, straight-line amortization is frequently found in practice and is accepted for income tax purposes. Remaining illustrations in this chapter assume the use of straight-line amortization.

Accounting for bonds payable. When bonds are sold by a company between interest dates, the bond price is increased by a charge for accrued interest to the date of sale. Accrued Interest on Bonds Payable may be credited for the interest received from the investor; when interest for the full period is paid, the accrued interest balance is closed and Interest Expense is charged for the difference. It is also possible to credit Interest Expense for the accrued interest received. Payment of interest is then charged in full to Interest Expense. The latter procedure is used in subsequent illustrations.

Entries for the amortization of bond premium or discount may be made (1) at the time of each interest payment or (2) only at the end of the company's fiscal period. Normally the latter procedure is more convenient since entries for amortization are made for the full year except for the first and the last years when fractional parts of a year may be involved.

The entries for issuance of bonds and the payment of interest are illustrated in the example that follows. Assume that the Crescent Corporation decides to issue bonds of $100,000. Bonds are dated September 1, 1972, pay interest at 6% semiannually on March 1 and September 1, and mature on September 1, 1982. Bonds are sold on December 1, 1972, at $94,150 plus accrued interest. The corporation adjusts and closes its books at the end of each calendar year. Since the bonds are issued on December 1, bonds have a life of only 9¾ years or 117 months. A schedule may be prepared to summarize discount amortization over the bond life. These data can then be used in making periodic adjustments.[1] The amortization schedule follows on the next page.

---

[1]Amortization procedures for bond discount are equally applicable to bond issue costs when these are carried separately.

AMORTIZATION SCHEDULE — STRAIGHT-LINE METHOD

Period	A Int. Paym't (Includ. Adj. for Accruals)	B Discount Amortization			C Interest Expense (A+B)	D Unamortized Discount (D−B)	E Bond Carrying Value ($100,000 −D)
		No. of Mos.	Fraction of Disc. to be Amortized	Amt. of Disc. Amortization			
						$ 5,850	$ 94,150
Dec. 1 (sales date)–Dec. 31, 1972	$ 500	1	1/117	$ 50	$ 550	5,800	94,200
Year Ended Dec. 31, 1973	6,000	12	12/117	600	6,600	5,200	94,800
Year Ended Dec. 31, 1974	6,000	12	12/117	600	6,600	4,600	95,400
Year Ended Dec. 31, 1975	6,000	12	12/117	600	6,600	4,000	96,000
Year Ended Dec. 31, 1976	6,000	12	12/117	600	6,600	3,400	96,600
Year Ended Dec. 31, 1977	6,000	12	12/117	600	6,600	2,800	97,200
Year Ended Dec. 31, 1978	6,000	12	12/117	600	6,600	2,200	97,800
Year Ended Dec. 31, 1979	6,000	12	12/117	600	6,600	1,600	98,400
Year Ended Dec. 31, 1980	6,000	12	12/117	600	6,600	1,000	99,000
Year Ended Dec. 31, 1981	6,000	12	12/117	600	6,600	400	99,600
Jan. 1–Sept. 1, 1982 (maturity)	4,000	8	8/117	400	4,400	——	100,000
		117	117/117	$5,850			

Entries on the corporation books in 1972 and 1973 follow:

Transaction	Entry
DECEMBER 1, 1972 Sold $100,000 of 6% bonds for $94,150, bonds maturing on September 1, 1982, 10 years from date of issue. Interest is payable semiannually on March 1 and September 1. Accrued interest received for the period September 1–December 1 is $1,500.	Cash.................. 95,650 Discount on Bonds Payable................. 5,850 Bonds Payable........ 100,000 Bond Interest Expense. 1,500
DECEMBER 31, 1972 (a) To record accrued interest for 4 months, and (b) to record amortization of bond discount applicable to current year. Amortization: bonds outstanding in current year, one month; total life of bond issue, 9¾ years or 117 months; current amortization, 1/117 of $5,850 = $50 (one month at $50).	(a) Bond Interest Expense............ 2,000 Accrued Interest on Bonds Payable.. 2,000 (b) Bond Interest Expense 50 Discount on Bonds Payable........ 50
JANUARY 1, 1973 To reverse 1972 accrued interest.	Accrued Interest on Bonds Payable.............. 2,000 Bond Interest Expense. 2,000
MARCH 1, 1973 Paid semiannual interest.	Bond Interest Expense... 3,000 Cash............... 3,000
SEPTEMBER 1, 1973 Paid semiannual interest.	Bond Interest Expense... 3,000 Cash............... 3,000
DECEMBER 31, 1973 (a) To record accrued interest for 4 months, and (b) to record amortization of bond discount applicable to current year, 12/117 of $5,850, or $600 (or 12 months at $50 a month, $600).	(a) Bond Interest Expense 2,000 Accrued Interest on Bonds Payable.. 2,000 (b) Bond Interest Expense 600 Discount on Bonds Payable........ 600

Bond reacquisition prior to maturity. Corporations frequently reacquire their own bonds on the market when prices or other factors make such action desirable. Reacquisition of bonds prior to their maturity calls for the recognition of a gain or a loss for the difference between the bond carrying value and the amount paid. Payment of accrued interest on bond reacquisition is separately reported as a charge to Bond Interest Expense.

When bonds are reacquired, amortization of bond premium, discount, and issue costs should be brought up to date. Reacquisition calls for the cancellation of the bond face value together with any related premium, discount, or issue costs as of the reacquisition date.

When bonds are reacquired and canceled, Bonds Payable is debited. When bonds are reacquired but are held for possible future reissue, Treasury Bonds instead of Bonds Payable may be debited. It has already been indicated that treasury bonds are simply evidence of a liability that has been liquidated. Although treasury bonds may represent a ready source of cash, their sale creates new creditors, a situation that is no different from the debt created by any other type of borrowing. Treasury bonds, then, should be recorded at their face value and subtracted from the bonds payable balance in reporting bonds issued and outstanding. If treasury bonds are sold at a price other than face value, Cash is debited, Treasury Bonds is credited, thus reinstating the bond liability, and a premium or a discount on the sale is recorded, the latter balance to be amortized over the remaining life of this specific bond group. While held, treasury bonds occupy the same legal status as unissued bonds and, when an account is carried for unissued bonds, can be recorded with them. At the maturity of the bond issue, any balance in a treasury bonds account or unissued bonds account is applied against Bonds Payable.

To illustrate bond reacquisition, assume in the preceding example for the Crescent Corporation, that bonds of $10,000 are reacquired at 98½ by the company on February 1, 1974. Entries at the time of bond reacquisition would be as follows:

Transaction	Entry		

FEBRUARY 1, 1974
To record reacquisition of own bonds:
(a) Amortization of discount on bonds of $10,000 to date of purchase, 1/117 of $585, or $5 (or 1/10 of monthly amortization of $50).
	(a) Bond Interest Expense..
	    Discount on Bonds
	      Payable..........
		5	5

(b) Payment of accrued interest, Sept. 1–Feb. 1, $10,000 at 6% for 5 months.	(b) Bond Interest Expense.. Cash..............	250	250

Transaction			Entry		
(c) Loss on bond retirement:			(c) Bonds Payable (or Trea-		
Bonds at face value...........		$10,000	sury Bonds).........	10,000	
Discount on bonds....	$585		Loss on Bond Retire-		
Less amortization to			ment..............	365	
date of purchase, 14			Cash..............		9,850
months at $5.........	70	515	Discount on Bonds		
			Payable..........		515
Book value of bonds..........		$9,485			
Amount paid on reacquisition..		9,850			
Loss on bond retirement......		$365			

For income tax purposes a gain on bond reacquisition is fully taxable and a loss is fully deductible.

Bond retirement at maturity. Most bond issues are payable at the end of a specified period. When bond discount or premium and issue cost balances have been satisfactorily amortized over the life of the bonds, bond retirement simply calls for a charge to the bonds payable account and a credit to Cash. Any bonds not presented for payment at their maturity date should be removed from the bonds payable balance and reported separately as Matured Bonds Payable; these are reported as a current liability except when they are to be paid out of a sinking fund. Interest does not accrue on matured bonds that have not been presented for payment.

If a bond fund is used to pay off a bond issue, any cash remaining in the fund may be returned to the cash account. Appropriations of retained earnings that may have been established during the life of the issue may be returned to retained earnings.

Serial bonds. Foregoing discussions were related to *term bonds*, or bonds with a single maturity date. *Serial bonds* provide for a series of principal payments on periodic due dates. For example, a $500,000 bond issue may provide that stated bond blocks of $25,000 are to be paid off at the end of each year for 20 years. This plan provides for the gradual liquidation of the debt.

The issuance of serial bonds eliminates the need for a bond sinking fund. When a sinking fund cannot produce earnings at a rate equivalent to that paid on the bond issue, serial bonds are advantageous to the issuing company. Here cash that would otherwise be deposited in the fund is applied directly to the retirement of debt, and the payment of interest relating to that portion of the debt is terminated.

Amortization procedures for serial bonds. When serial bonds are issued, the amortization schedule for bond premium or discount requires recognition of a declining debt principal. Successive bond years cannot be charged with equal amounts of premium or discount because of a shrinking debt and successively smaller interest payments.

Premium or discount on serial bonds may be amortized by a straight-line procedure or by a compound-interest procedure. The straight-line procedure is referred to as the *bonds-outstanding method* and calls for de-creases in the amortization schedule proportionate to the decrease in the loan balance. The compound-interest procedure requires that the effec-tive interest rate at which the bonds were issued be determined first. The charge for interest is then reported at the effective rate applied to the bond carrying value, the difference between the amount reported as expense and the amount of interest paid being reported as a reduction in the premium or discount balance.

Bonds-outstanding method. Amortization by the bonds-outstanding method is illustrated in the example that follows. Assume that bonds of $100,000, dated January 1, 1972, are issued on this date for $101,350. Bonds of $20,000 mature at the beginning of each year. The bonds pay interest of 5% annually. The company's accounting period ends on December 31; the accounting period and the bond year thus coincide. A table showing the premium to be amortized each year is developed as shown on the following schedule.

AMORTIZATION SCHEDULE — BONDS-OUTSTANDING METHOD

Year	Bonds Outstanding	Fraction of Premium to be Amortized	Annual Premium Amortization (Fraction × $1,350)
1972	$100,000	100,000/300,000 (or 10/30)	$ 450
1973	80,000	80,000/300,000 (or 8/30)	360
1974	60,000	60,000/300,000 (or 6/30)	270
1975	40,000	40,000/300,000 (or 4/30)	180
1976	20,000	20,000/300,000 (or 2/30)	90
	$300,000	300,000/300,000 (or 30/30)	$1,350

The annual premium amortization is found by multiplying the premium by a fraction whose numerator is the number of bond dollars outstanding in that year and whose denominator is the total number of bond dollars outstanding for the life of the bond issue. As bonds are re-tired, the amounts of premium amortization decline accordingly.

Periodic amortization may be incorporated in a table summarizing the interest charges and changes in bond carrying values as shown on the following page.

AMORTIZATION OF PREMIUM — SERIAL BONDS
BONDS-OUTSTANDING METHOD

Date	A Interest Payment (5% of Face Value)	B Premium Amortiza- tion	C Interest Expense (A−B)	D Principal Payment	E Bond Carry- ing Value Decrease (B+D)	F Bond Carrying Value (F−E)
Jan. 1, 1972						$101,350
Dec. 31, 1972	$5,000	$450	$4,550	$20,000	$20,450	80,900
Dec. 31, 1973	4,000	360	3,640	20,000	20,360	60,540
Dec. 31, 1974	3,000	270	2,730	20,000	20,270	40,270
Dec. 31, 1975	2,000	180	1,820	20,000	20,180	20,090
Dec. 31, 1976	1,000	90	910	20,000	20,090	———

Compound-interest method. Tables show that the above bonds were sold to yield approximately $4\frac{1}{2}\%$. Use of this rate results in the following interest charges and premium amortization:

AMORTIZATION OF PREMIUM — SERIAL BONDS
COMPOUND-INTEREST METHOD

Date	A Interest Payment (5% of Face Value)	B Interest Expense (4½% of Bond Carrying Value)	C Premium Amortiza- tion (A−B)	D Principal Payment	E Bond Carry- ing Value Decrease (C+D)	F Bond Carrying Value (F−E)
Jan. 1, 1971						$101,350.00
Dec. 31, 1971	$5,000.00	$4,560.75	$439.25	$20,000.00	$20,439.25	80,910.75
Dec. 31, 1972	4,000.00	3,640.98	359.02	20,000.00	20,359.02	60,551.73
Dec. 31, 1973	3,000.00	2,724.83	275.17	20,000.00	20,275.17	40,276.56
Dec. 31, 1974	2,000.00	1,812.45	187.55	20,000.00	20,187.55	20,089.01
Dec. 31, 1975	1,000.00	910.99[1]	89.01	20,000.00	20,089.01	———

The straight-line method of amortization provides for the recognition of uniform amounts of amortization in terms of the par value of bonds outstanding. The compound-interest method provides for the recognition of interest at a uniform rate on the declining debt balance.

Serial bond reacquisition prior to maturity. When serial bonds are reacquired prior to their maturities, it is necessary to cancel the unamortized premium or discount relating to that part of the bond issue that is liquidated. For example, assume the issuance of serial bonds previously described and amortization of the premium by the bonds-outstanding method as given on page 623. On April 1, 1973, $10,000 of bonds due January 1, 1975, and $10,000 of bonds due January 1, 1976, are reacquired at $100\frac{1}{2}$ plus accrued interest. The premium for the period January 1–April 1, 1973, relating to retired bonds affects bond interest for the current period and will be written off as an adjustment to expense. The balance of the premium from the retirement date to the

---

[1] $4\frac{1}{2}\%$ of $20,089.01 is $904.01. However, use of $4\frac{1}{2}\%$ when the effective rate was not exactly $4\frac{1}{2}\%$ has resulted in a small discrepancy that requires adjustment upon the final interest payment. On the final payment the premium balance is closed and interest expense is reduced by this amount.

respective maturity date of the series retired must be canceled. The premium balance relating to retired bonds is calculated as follows:

Premium identified with 1973: $\dfrac{20,000}{80,000}$ $\times$ $360.00 $\times$ 9/12 $=$ $ 67.50

Premium identified with 1974: $\dfrac{20,000}{60,000}$ $\times$ $270.00 $=$ 90.00

Premium identified with 1975: $\dfrac{10,000}{40,000}$ $\times$ $180.00 $=$ 45.00

Premium identified with retired bonds $202.50

Instead of the above procedure, the premium amortization per year on each $1,000 bond may first be calculated and this rate applied to bonds of each period that are canceled. The annual amortization rate per $1,000 bond is calculated as follows:

$$\dfrac{\$1,350\ (\text{total premium — life of bonds})}{300\ (\text{total \$1,000 bonds outstanding — life of bonds})} = \$4.50$$

The premium to be canceled may now be determined as follows:

Year	Number of $1,000 Bonds $\times$	Annual Premium Amortization per $1,000 Bond $\times$	Fractional Part of Year $=$	Total Premium Cancellation
1973	20	$4.50	9/12	$ 67.50
1974	20	4.50		90.00
1975	10	4.50		45.00
Premium identified with retired bonds....................				$202.50

Bonds, carrying value $20,202.50, are retired at a cost of $20,100 resulting in a gain of $102.50. Payment is also made for interest on bonds of $20,000 for three months at 5%, or $250. The entry to record the retirement of bonds and the payment of interest on the series retired follows:

Bonds Payable (or Treasury Bonds).......... 20,000.00
Premium on Bonds Payable................   202.50
Bond Interest Expense.....................   250.00
   Cash....................................   20,350.00
   Gain on Bond Retirement................   102.50

A revised schedule for the amortization of bond premium follows:

AMORTIZATION SCHEDULE — BONDS-OUTSTANDING METHOD
REVISED FOR BOND RETIREMENT

Year	Annual Premium Amortization per Original Schedule	Premium Cancellation on Bond Retirement	Annual Premium Amortization Adjusted for Bond Retirement
1972	$ 450.00		$ 450.00
1973	360.00	$ 67.50	292.50
1974	270.00	90.00	180.00
1975	180.00	45.00	135.00
1976	90.00		90.00
	$1,350.00	$202.50	$1,147.50

Serial bond amortization procedures when bond year and fiscal year do not coincide. When serial bond retirement dates do not agree with the company's fiscal year, the amortization schedule must provide for amortization other than for full annual periods. To illustrate, assume that $500,000, 5% serial bonds, dated March 1, 1972, are sold on April 1, 1972, at a discount of $35,000. Bonds of $100,000 mature on March 1 of each year. The discount should be amortized over 59 months. Assuming that the fiscal period for the issuer is the calendar year, an amortization schedule that uses *bond month-dollars* may be prepared as follows:

AMORTIZATION SCHEDULE WHEN BOND YEAR AND FISCAL YEAR
DO NOT COINCIDE — BONDS-OUTSTANDING METHOD

Year	Bonds Outstanding	Months Outstanding	Bond Month-Dollars (Months Times Bonds Outstanding)	Total Bond Month-Dollars	Fraction of Discount to be Amortized	Annual Discount Amortization (Fraction × $35,000)
1972	$500,000	9	$4,500,000	$ 4,500,000	45/175	$ 9,000
1973	500,000	2	1,000,000 ⎫	5,000,000	50/175	10,000
	400,000	10	4,000,000 ⎭			
1974	400,000	2	800,000 ⎫	3,800,000	38/175	7,600
	300,000	10	3,000,000 ⎭			
1975	300,000	2	600,000 ⎫	2,600,000	26/175	5,200
	200,000	10	2,000,000 ⎭			
1976	200,000	2	400,000 ⎫	1,400,000	14/175	2,800
	100,000	10	1,000,000 ⎭			
1977	100,000	2	200,000	200,000	2/175	400
		59		$17,500,000	175/175	$35,000

Bond redemption prior to maturity. Provisions of the bond indenture frequently give the issuer the option of calling bonds for payment prior to maturity. Ordinarily the call must be made on an interest payment date and no further interest accrues on the bonds not presented at this time. When only a part of the issue is to be retired, the bonds that are called may be determined by lot.

The inclusion of call provisions in the bond agreement is a feature favoring the issuer. The company is in a position to terminate the bond agreement and eliminate future interest charges whenever its financial position makes such action feasible. Furthermore, the company is protected in the event of a fall in the market interest rate by being able to retire the old issue from proceeds of a new issue paying a lower rate of interest. The bond contract normally requires payment of a premium if bonds are called. The bondholder is thus offered special compensation if his investment is terminated.

When bonds are called, the difference between the amount paid and the bonds redeemed together with related premium, discount, and issue cost balances is reported as a loss or a gain on retirement. To illustrate, assume that bonds of a corporation are callable at a 5% premium or at 105. Bonds of $20,000 are retired on this basis. At the time of call, bonds outstanding are shown at $100,000 with an unamortized discount on the issue of $2,500 and unamortized bond issue costs of $1,000. The following entry is made:

Bonds Payable (or Treasury Bonds)..............	20,000	
Loss on Bond Retirement.......................	1,700	
Cash.......................................		21,000
Discount on Bonds Payable....................		500
Unamortized Bond Issue Costs................		200

Any interest paid at the time of call is recorded as a charge to Bond Interest Expense.

Bond refunding. Cash for the retirement of a bond issue is frequently raised through the sale of a new issue. This is referred to as *bond refunding*; the original issue is said to be *refunded*. Bond refunding may take place when an issue matures. Bonds may also be refunded prior to their maturity when the interest rate has dropped and the interest savings on a new issue will more than offset the costs of retiring the old issue. To illustrate, assume that a corporation has outstanding 8% bonds of $1,000,000 callable at 102 and with a remaining 10-year term, and similar 10-year bonds can be marketed currently at an interest rate of only $6\frac{1}{2}\%$. Under these circumstances it would be advantageous to retire the old issue with the proceeds from a new $6\frac{1}{2}\%$ issue since the future savings in interest will exceed by a considerable amount the premium to be paid on the call of the old issue.

The desirability of refunding may not be so obvious as in the preceding instance. In determining whether refunding is warranted in marginal cases, careful consideration must be given to such factors as the different maturity dates of the two issues, possible future changes in interest rates, changed loan requirements, different indenture provisions, income tax effects of refunding, and legal fees, printing costs, and marketing costs involved in refunding.

When refunding takes place before the maturity date of the old issue, the problem arises as to how to dispose of the call premium and unamortized discount and issue costs of the original bonds. Three positions are taken with respect to disposition of these items:

1. Such charges are considered a loss on bond retirement.
2. Such charges are considered deferrable and to be amortized systematically over the remaining life of the original issue.
3. Such charges are considered deferrable and to be amortized systematically over the life of the new issue.

The first position views bond retirement in refunding the same as any other debt cancellation. Payment of bonds terminates the old bond contract and a loss emerges from such termination. The new bond issue is considered a new transaction with only its own costs assignable to future periods. Recognition of bond redemption charges as a loss finds support as a conservative measure and is also the required procedure for income tax purposes.

The second position views the charges arising from bond retirement as the price paid for the option of entering into a new and more attractive borrowing arrangement. Such charges, then, are properly deferred so that they may be identified with the periods receiving the benefits from refunding — the unexpired term of the original issue. The remaining periods covered by the original issue will still realize a savings through reduced interest charges counterbalanced only in part by the amortization of redemption charges.

The third position views the charges from bond retirement as related to the benefits that are found in the new arrangement and, therefore, as distributable over the entire life of the new issue even when this exceeds the life of the original bonds. The decision to refund the issue is made on the basis of the present arrangement as compared with the alternative borrowing plans that are available. Any charges relating to the new financing, then, should be absorbed over the full term of the new issue.

Under certain conditions, any one of these methods is considered acceptable by the Accounting Principles Board. Prior to 1966, the third method was not accepted as a reasonable alternative under any circumstances. However, in APB Opinion No. 6 the Board made the following statement:

> The third method, amortization over the life of the new issue, is appropriate under circumstances where the refunding takes place because of currently lower interest rates or anticipation of higher interest rates in the future. In such circumstances, the expected benefits justify spreading the costs over the life of the new issue, and this method is, therefore, acceptable.[1]

Although all of the methods have support in theory, it would seem that this is an area where, in the interest of comparability, accounting differences might be narrowed. The strongest argument can be made for the first position. Here redemption charges are viewed as a loss in terminating an agreement that is no longer favorable rather than as costs for entering into more advantageous loan arrangements. The old loan cycle has ended; a new loan cycle has begun. To capitalize redemption charges would lend support to similar capitalization of the

---

[1]*Opinions of the Accounting Principles Board, No. 6*, "Status of Accounting Research Bulletins" (New York: American Institute of Certified Public Accountants, 1965), par. 19.

unrecovered book value of assets and removal charges when assets are retired upon the acquisition of new assets. Either instance may be better viewed as a move into a new situation that calls for the immediate recognition of an extraordinary loss.[1]

Convertible bonds. Many variations of debt financing are being made available to creditors. Some of the more complex of these are in reality hybrid issues which involve elements of both debt and owners' equity. The issue of *convertible debt securities*, most frequently bonds, has become very popular. These securities are convertible into the common stock of the issuing company or an affiliate at a specified price and at the option of the holder. These securities usually have the following characteristics:

1. An interest rate that is lower than the issuer could establish for nonconvertible debt.
2. An initial conversion price that is higher than the market value of the common stock at time of issuance.
3. A callable option that is retained by the issuer.

The popularity of these securities may be attributed to the advantages to both the issuer and the holder. The issuer is able to obtain his financing at a lower interest rate because of the value of the conversion feature to the holder. Because of the call provision, the issuer is in a position to exert influence upon the holders to exchange the debt into equity capital if stock values increase; he has had the use of relatively low interest rate financing if stock values do not increase. On the other hand, the holder has the advantage of the security of a debt instrument that, barring default, assures him the return of his investment plus a fixed yield, and at the same time offers him an option to transfer his interest to equity capital should such transfer become attractive.

The accounting problems associated with this type of financing may arise at two points in time: (1) the time of issuance of the convertible debt, and (2) the time of debt conversion.

Accounting for convertible bonds at the time of original issuance. Differences of opinion exist as to whether convertible debt securities should be treated by the issuer solely as debt, or whether part of the proceeds received from the issuance of debt should be recognized as equity capital. One view holds that the debt and the conversion privilege are inseparably

---

[1] The American Accounting Association Committee on Concepts and Standards Underlying Financial Statements has supported the first position in its statement, *Accounting and Reporting Standards for Corporate Financial Statements, 1957 Revision*, page 7. It should be noted that for federal income tax purposes, unamortized discount and issue costs and redemption premium on bonds retired must be recognized in the year of bond retirement. When these charges are deferred on the books, the differences in book income and taxable income will call for the use of interperiod tax allocations.

connected, and therefore the debt and equity portions of the security should not be separately valued. The holder cannot sell part of the instrument and retain the other. An alternate view holds that there are two distinct elements in these securities and that each should be recognized in the accounts: that portion of the issuance price attributable to the conversion privilege should be recorded as a credit to paid-in capital; the balance of the issuance price should be assigned to the debt. This would decrease the premium otherwise recognized on the debt or perhaps result in a discount.

These views are compared in the illustration that follows. Assume 500 ten-year bonds, face value $1,000, are sold at 105. The bonds contain a conversion privilege that provides for exchange of a $1,000 bond for 20 shares of stock, par value $40. The interest rate on the bonds is 5%. It is established that without the conversion privilege, the bonds would sell at 96. The journal entries to record the sale of the issue under the two approaches follow.

Debt and Equity Not Separated			Debt and Equity Separated		
Cash............	525,000		Cash............	525,000	
Bonds Payable...		500,000	Discount on Bonds		
Premium on			Payable.........	20,000	
Bonds Payable.		25,000	Bonds Payable...		500,000
			Paid-In Capital Arising from Bond Conversion Privilege..		45,000

The periodic charge for interest will differ depending upon which method is employed. Under the first approach, the annual interest charge would be $22,500 ($25,000 paid less $2,500 premium amortization). Under the second approach, the annual interest charge would be $27,000 ($25,000 paid plus $2,000 discount amortization).

In 1969 the Accounting Principles Board in APB Opinion No. 14 reversed a stand taken in 1966 in APB Opinion No. 10 and stated that when convertible debt is sold at a price or with a value at issuance not significantly in excess of the face amount, " . . . no portion of the proceeds from the issuance . . . should be accounted for as attributable to the conversion feature."[1]

The Opinion stated that greater weight for this decision was placed upon the inseparability of the debt and the conversion option than upon the practical problems of valuing the separate parts. However, the practical problems are considerable and did have much to do with the

---

[1] *Opinions of the Accounting Principles Board, No. 14*, "Accounting for Convertible Debt and Debt Issued with Stock Purchase Warrants" (New York: American Institute of Certified Public Accountants, 1969), par. 12.

reinvestigation of the problem by the Accounting Principles Board. Separate valuation requires asking the question, How much would the security sell for without the conversion feature? In many instances this question would appear to be unanswerable. Investment banks responsible for selling such issues are frequently unable to separate the two features for valuation purposes. The cash that is required simply could not be raised, they contend, without the conversion privilege.

There would seem to be strong theoretical support for separating the debt and equity portions of the proceeds from the issuance of convertible debt. The conversion privilege does have a value, and this situation is only an example of the complex transactions that require special analysis for proper recording. Present practical considerations may make it difficult to always separate the debt and conversion privileges. This means that valuation techniques require additional study. In applying present guidelines, even when separate values are determinable, they are not recorded.

Accounting for convertible bonds at time of conversion. If conversion privileges of convertible debt are exercised, another valuation question must be answered by the issuer. Should the new stock be assigned a value equal to the current market value of the stock or to the carrying value of the bonds? In applying the first method, a gain or loss arising from the use of the current market values would have to be recognized in the accounts.

An increase in capital equal to the market value of the stock can be supported on the grounds that bondholders are actually paid an amount equal to the value of the stock given in exchange. The exchange of stock for bonds closes the transaction cycle relating to bonds and opens a new cycle relating to stock in which stock is recorded at the value that it would bring if sold on the open market. The gain or the loss is related to the bond issue since it arises from the termination of the bond contract. Neither advantage nor penalty is assigned to the new stock issue.

The assignment of the bond carrying value to the stock is supported on the theory that the company upon issuing the bonds is aware of the fact that bond proceeds may ultimately represent the consideration identified with stock. Thus, when bondholders exercise their conversion privileges, the value identified with the obligation is transferred to the security that replaces it.

To illustrate the entries for bond conversion, assume that 100 of the 500 bonds described on page 630 are converted. At the time of conversion there is an unamortized premium on the bond issue of $15,000. The common stock on this date is quoted at $55 per share.

If the market value of the stock is to be used in recording the issue of stock, the entry to record the conversion would be as follows:

Bonds Payable...............................	100,000	
Premium on Bonds Payable....................	3,000	
Loss on Bond Conversion......................	7,000	
Common Stock (2,000 shares, $40 par)........		80,000
Premium on Common Stock................		30,000

If the bond carrying value is to be used in recording the issue of stock, the entry would be as follows:

Bonds Payable...............................	100,000	
Premium on Bonds Payable....................	3,000	
Common Stock (2,000 shares, $40 par)........		80,000
Premium on Common Stock................		23,000

It should be observed that total capital is the same regardless of the value assigned to the stock. However, when market value was used in the first example, retained earnings of $7,000 became a part of the corporate paid-in capital.[1]

Bonds issued with stock purchase warrants attached. In addition to an increasing volume of convertible debt issues, bonds with detachable stock purchase warrants have been issued. Because the debt instrument and the warrant are separate, they can and do trade on the market separately. Unlike convertible debt, of which repayment is uncertain, the presumption in debt with detachable warrants is that the debt will be repaid upon maturity. The decision to exercise the warrants depends upon the movement of the stock market.

As with convertible bonds, there are two ways in which sales proceeds can be assigned: (1) full sales proceeds can be identified with the bonds with the warrants given no value; or (2) bonds and warrants can be assigned values based on the relative fair value of the debt security without the warrants and the value of the warrants themselves at time of issuance. To illustrate the latter method, assume the same example used in the discussion of convertible bonds except that stock warrants are substituted for the conversion feature: 500 ten-year bonds, face value $1,000, are sold at 105. Each bond is accompanied by one warrant that permits the holder to purchase 20 shares of stock, par value $40. Each bond without the warrant has a market value of $960, and each

---

[1]The American Accounting Association Committee on Concepts and Standards Underlying Corporate Financial Statements takes the first approach. The Committee recommends, "Any difference between the amortized amount of a liability as reflected in the accounts and the amount of assets released or equities created should be recognized as a gain or loss in the period of liquidation. When a liability is discharged by conversion to a stock equity, the market value of the liability is ideally the measure of the new equity created. However, if a reliable market price for the liability is not available, the market value of the stock issued may be used." *Accounting and Reporting Standards for Corporate Financial Statements and Preceding Statements and Supplements* (1957 rev.; Madison, Wisconsin: American Accounting Association), p. 7.

warrant has a market value of $90. The proceeds of $525,000 would be allocated $480,000 to the debt and $45,000 to the owners' equity.

In the above example, the sum of the market value for bonds and stock warrants equaled the issue price of the joint offering. Market imperfections rarely provide such perfect relationships. When such relationship is not found, sales proceeds should be allocated between the two securities on the basis of their relative market values at the time of their issuance.

In Opinion No. 14, the Accounting Principles Board accepted a separation between debt and owners' equity for this type of transaction and recommended the allocation method just illustrated.[1] The difference between this treatment and that given to convertible debt is the separateness of a warrant as compared with the singleness of convertible debt. The Opinion further states that other types of debt with somewhat unique provisions are to be analyzed in terms of the substance of the transaction and within the framework of this Opinion. The Board has stated, for example, that "when convertible debt is issued at a substantial premium, there is a presumption that such premium represents paid-in capital."[2] In special instances, then, the accounting for bonds with stock warrants attached could be supported for convertible debt issues.

Long-term purchase contracts

Real estate or other property is frequently acquired under contracts whereby payments are to be made over a number of years. Upon making the acquisition, the buyer should record the long-term obligation assumed. Thereafter, in making payments on the contract, the buyer should analyze each payment in terms of the portion representing interest and the portion representing a reduction in the amount owed.

To illustrate the accounting for a long-term purchase contract, assume that land is acquired for $100,000; $25,000 is paid at the time of purchase and the balance is to be paid in semiannual installments of $5,000 that are to include interest on the unpaid principal at 8%. Entries for the purchase and for the first and second payments on the contract follow:

Transaction	Entry		

JANUARY 2, 1972 Purchased land for $100,000 paying $25,000 down, the balance to be paid in semiannual payments of $5,000 that include interest at 8%.	Land.....................100,000
	  Cash...................
	  8% Land Contract Payable
		25,000
		75,000	

---

[1] *Opinions of the Accounting Principles Board, No. 14, op. cit.*, par. 16.
[2] *Ibid.*, par. 18.

Transaction	Entry

JUNE 30, 1972
Made first payment:
Amount of payment.............. $5,000
Amount representing interest, 4%
  of unpaid balance of $75,000.....   3,000
 	
Balance — reduction in principal... $2,000
	Interest Expense........... 3,000
	8% Land Contract Payable. 2,000
	  Cash.................. 5,000

DECEMBER 31, 1972
Made second payment:
Amount of payment.............. $5,000
Amount representing interest, 4%
  of unpaid balance of $73,000
  ($75,000 − $2,000)............   2,920
 	
Balance — reduction in principal... $2,080
	Interest Expense........... 2,920
	8% Land Contract Payable. 2,080
	  Cash.................. 5,000

In the preceding example, the contract specified both a purchase price and interest at a stated rate on the unpaid balance. Sometimes, however, a contract may simply provide for a series of payments without reference to interest or may provide for a stated interest rate that is unreasonable in relation to the market. The Accounting Principles Board identified this type of contract in Opinion No. 21, "Interest on Receivables and Payables," and stated that:

> In these circumstances, the note, the sales price, and the cost of the property, goods, or service exchanged for the note should be recorded at the fair value of the property, goods or services or at an amount that reasonably approximates the market value of the note, whichever is the more clearly determinable. That amount may or may not be the same as its face amount, and any resulting discount or premium should be accounted for as an element of interest over the life of the note. In the absence of established exchange prices for the related property, goods, or service or evidence of the market value of the note, the present value of a note that stipulates either no interest or a rate of interest that is clearly unreasonable should be determined by discounting all future payments on the notes using an imputed rate of interest. . . .[1]

To illustrate the recognition of interest as described above, assume that certain equipment is acquired at a price of $40,000; the down payment is $10,000, and the balance is payable in four equal annual installments of $7,500. Assume further that although there is no interest rate specified in the contract, it is fair to assume that the contract price involves implicit interest at 8%. The debt at the date of purchase, then, should be regarded as the discounted value at 8% of installments of $7,500 due in one, two, three, and four years. Present value tables may be used in calculating the present value of the debt which is found to be $24,840.75.[2] The obligation is recorded by a credit to contracts

---

[1] *Opinions of the Accounting Principles Board, No. 21, op. cit.*, par. 12.

[2] The debt is computed as the present value of an ordinary annuity of 4 rents $7,500 at interest of 8%.

payable for $30,000 and a charge to a discount on the payable for $5,159.25. The 8% rate is applied to the declining debt balance in subsequent periods in amortizing the debt discount. Entries for the acquisition of the property item, the periodic payments, and the recognition of interest over the life of the contract follow:

Transaction	Entry
JANUARY 2, 1972 Purchased equipment at a price of $40,000.00 paying $10,000.00 down, the balance in four equal installments of $7,500.00. It is assumed that interest at 8% is implicit in the purchase price and the obligation is recorded at its present value of $24,840.75.	Equipment..........34,840.75 Discount on Equipment Contract Payable... 5,159.25 Cash............. 10,000.00 Equipment Contract Payable........ 30,000.00

DECEMBER 31, 1972
Made first payment of $7,500.00.
Amortization of debt discount:
 8% of $24,840.75 (debt,
 $30,000.00 − $5,159.25), or $1,987.26.
	Equipment Contract
	 Payable.......... 7,500.00
	 Cash............ 7,500.00
	
	Interest Expense..... 1,987.26
	 Discount on
	  Equipment Con-
	  tract Payable.... 1,987.26

DECEMBER 31, 1973
Made second payment of $7,500.00.
Amortization of debt discount:
 8% of $19,328.01 (debt,
 $22,500.00 − $3,171.99), or $1,546.24.
	Equipment Contract
	 Payable.......... 7,500.00
	 Cash............ 7,500.00
	
	Interest Expense..... 1,546.24
	 Discount on
	  Equipment Con-
	  tract Payable.... 1,546.24

DECEMBER 31, 1974
Made third payment of $7,500.00.
Amortization of debt discount:
 8% of $13,374.25 (debt,
 $15,000.00 − $1,625.75), or $1,069.94.
	Equipment Contract
	 Payable.......... 7,500.00
	 Cash............ 7,500.00
	
	Interest Expense..... 1,069.94
	 Discount on
	  Equipment Con-
	  tract Payable.... 1,069.94

DECEMBER 31, 1975
Made final payment of $7,500.00.
Amortization of debt discount:
 balance, $555.81.[1]
	Equipment Contract
	 Payable.......... 7,500.00
	 Cash............ 7,500.00
	
	Interest Expense..... 555.81
	 Discount on
	  Equipment Con-
	  tract Payable.... 555.81

When a cash price is quoted for a property item, this amount may be used in recording the property item and in recognizing the present value of the debt. In such instances, the debt discount may be amortized either by (1) calculating the effective interest rate and applying this to the declining debt balance as in the previous example, or (2) developing fractions expressing the dollar debt for the period to the dollar debt for the life of the contract and applying such fractions to the debt discount.

[1] 8% of $6,944.19 (debt $7,500.00 − $555.81) is $555.54. Difference of $.27 is due to rounding off amounts.

To illustrate the second procedure, assume that in the preceding example the equipment is quoted at a cash price of $35,000. The equipment, then, would be reported at $35,000, cash would be credited for the down payment of $10,000, and a payable would be recognized for $30,000 less a discount of $5,000. Discount amortization may be calculated as follows:

Year	Liability Balance	Fraction of Discount to be Amortized	Annual Discount Amortization (Fraction × $5,000)
1972	$30,000	300/750	$2,000
1973	22,500	225/750	1,500
1974	15,000	150/750	1,000
1975	7,500	75/750	500
	$75,000	750/750	$5,000

In reporting a contract payable on the balance sheet, installments due within one year should be reported as a current liability and any remaining balance should be reported as a long-term liability. Unamortized debt discount should be reported as a deduction from the related liability account.

Accounting for pension plans

The number of pension plans has grown sharply over the last twenty-five years. The number of plans continues to grow and the amount of financial resources related to such plans continuously rises. Furthermore, this trend is accompanied by an increase in the variety and complexity of plans. In view of these factors, accounting for pensions has received constantly increasing attention by accounting authorities. Principal attention has been focused on the timing of costs that are to be recognized for pension plans. The timing of costs is of central importance because this factor affects the measurement of periodic net income.

The American Institute of Certified Public Accountants made its first references to accounting for pension plans in Accounting Research Bulletin No. 36 issued in 1948. Recommended procedures were modified and augmented in subsequent bulletins. In general, however, a wide degree of flexibility was permitted in assigning pension costs to operations. The AICPA recognized the growing significance of the problem and in 1965 published Accounting Research Study No. 8, *Accounting for the Cost of Pension Plans*. This work by Ernest L. Hicks attempted to catalog the different kinds of pension plans and the significant variations that were found and then made certain recommendations for achieving uniformity in accounting practices. The Accounting Principles Board acted on these recommendations and in 1966 issued Opinion No. 8, "Accounting for the Cost of Pension Plans." Although this opinion did not accept the full conclusions of the research study, it did make recommendations that significantly narrowed the range of practices applicable to accounting for pension plan costs.

The Accounting Principles Board defines a pension plan for purposes of its discussion and recommendations as:

> . . . an arrangement whereby a company undertakes to provide its retired employees with benefits that can be determined or estimated in advance from provisions of a document or documents or from the company's practices.[1]

References to pension plans thus would apply to both written plans and plans whose existence may be implied from well-defined, although perhaps unwritten, company policies. A company's informal policy of paying certain benefits to employees that it may select at its option at or after their retirement would not meet the requirements for classification as a pension plan.

Before proceeding with a discussion of accounting for pension plans, it is necessary to describe the different kinds of pension plans that are found and indicate the special terms that are used in such descriptions.

Kinds of plans. A company may establish a pension plan that is *funded* or one that is *unfunded*. Under a funded plan, the employer makes payments to a *funding agency* that is responsible for accumulating the assets for the payment of benefits under the plan. The funding agency may be an organization or an individual, such as a specific corporate or individual trustee or an insurance company, that provides for the accumulation of assets for the payment of benefits under the plan; on the other hand, it may be an organization, such as a specific insurance company, that provides facilities for the purchase of the benefits. The process of making payments to a funding agency is referred to as *funding*. An employer may establish a special fund for the purpose of paying benefits, but as long as the fund is under the control of the employer, it would be designated as unfunded.

The computation of the cost to provide benefits under a pension plan is a highly involved process. Actuaries must be consulted. A number of methods have been developed to determine pension cost, and a choice of the method to be employed will have to be made in arriving at the present value of the benefits to be paid under the plan and the periodic accounting charges that must be recognized. In making his computations, the actuary must recognize the *vested benefits* of certain employees — benefits that are not contingent upon any further services by such employees. He must arrive at estimates on a wide variety of elements that cause uncertainties, including interest on the return on funds

---

[1]*Opinions of the Accounting Principles Board, No. 8,* "Accounting for the Cost of Pension Plans" (New York: American Institute of Certified Public Accountants, 1966), par. 8.

invested, expenses of administering the plan, and the amount and the timing of benefits payable to presently retired employees, former employees whose benefits have vested, and present employees. "Interest" on pension fund investments is used in a broad sense to represent the return to be earned on funds invested to provide for future benefits and, in addition to interest on debt securities, would include dividends on equity securities, rentals on real estate, and realized and unrealized gains or losses on fund investments.

Basic position of the Accounting Principles Board. A wide variety of practices in accounting for pension costs were applied prior to the issuance of Accounting Principles Board Opinion No. 8. Practices ranged from the recognition of pension costs when actually paid to a full accrual of such costs employing actuarial valuations. Sometimes charges to operations varied with the earnings of the company; frequently charges were affected by the income or market gains on funds that were established for pensions. The disclosure that was provided by the financial statements relative to the nature and amounts involved in pension plans also varied widely. With the issuance of Accounting Principles Board Opinion No. 8, the basic position of the APB was well expressed in the following statement:

> The Board recognizes that a company may limit its legal obligation by specifying that pensions shall be payable only to the extent of the assets in the pension fund. Experience shows, however, that with rare exceptions pension plans continue indefinitely and that termination and other limitations of the liability of the company are not invoked while the company continues in business. Consequently, the Board believes that, in the absence of convincing evidence that the company will reduce or discontinue the benefits called for in a pension plan, the cost of the plan should be accounted for on the assumption that the company will continue to provide such benefits. This assumption implies a long-term undertaking, the cost of which should be recognized annually whether or not funded. Therefore, accounting for pension cost should not be discretionary.[1]

In applying this approach, funding provisions of a plan are not necessarily related to nor do they determine the periodic costs that are to be charged to operations. Furthermore, instead of pension cost assignments to operations on an arbitrary basis, such assignments should be made on an accrual basis. Such assignment will affect not only net income determinations but also the amount of the long-term liability that is to be recognized.

A number of actuarial methods have been developed for application to pension plans. Although these methods are designed primarily as funding techniques, many of these may also be employed in determining

[1]*Ibid.*, par. 16.

pension costs. In developing costs, two basic types of costs must be identified and given accounting recognition: (1) *normal cost*, and (2) *past service cost*.

Normal cost. The *normal cost* of a pension plan is the annual cost assigned under the actuarial cost method in use to years subsequent to the inception of a pension plan or to a particular valuation date. This is the cost that recognizes the benefits to employees that are based upon services currently performed.

The entries that are made for normal pension costs depend upon whether the plan is unfunded or funded.

Entries for the unfunded plan. Assume that a company upon its organization establishes an unfunded pension plan. Actuarial valuations indicate that the normal cost of the pension for the first year is $20,000. An entry is made as follows:

Pension Expense................................	20,000	
Liability Under Pension Plan..................		20,000

Assuming subsequent monthly payments to an employee upon his retirement, entries would be made as follows:

Liability Under Pension Plan...................	300	
Cash..		300

When a company adopts a pension plan but establishes its own pension fund for the benefits to be paid, the charge to operations and the credit to the pension liability account would still be made. The transfer of cash to the fund would be recorded by a charge to the fund and a credit to Cash. Earnings of the fund would be recorded by charges to the fund and credits to revenue. Benefits paid to a retired employee would be recorded by a charge to the liability for pensions and a credit to the fund.

Entries for the funded plan. Assume that a company upon its organization establishes a funded plan. Payments, then, are to be made to the funding agency, and the benefits ultimately to be paid to the retiring employees are made by such funding agency. Assuming, again, that the normal cost of the plan for the first year is $20,000, an entry to record the cost and the funding of such cost is as follows:

Pension Expense................................	20,000	
Cash..		20,000

Past service cost. A company, upon establishing a pension plan, may provide for the recognition of the services of the employees prior to the adoption of the plan. When recognition of past services is made that will affect the payment of benefits of the future, an additional cost, referred to as a *past service cost*, will be incurred.

A company, after the adoption of a plan, may provide for amendments to the plan that change the benefits to be paid to employees. This results in a change in the pension costs that have been identified with prior periods. The amendment of a plan, then, involves factors similar to those that apply to the recognition of services prior to the adoption of a plan, and the accounting for the change in prior service cost would be similar to that for past service cost.[1]

Past service cost is computed at one point in time and may involve significant amounts. One question that needs to be answered is how such costs should be assigned to operations. The Accounting Principles Board has provided a definite answer for this question. Accounting Principles Board Opinion No. 8 states:

> All members of the Board believe that the entire cost of benefit payments ultimately to be made should be charged against income subsequent to the adoption or amendment of a plan and that no portion of such cost should be charged directly against retained earnings.[2]

Support for this position can be made on the following grounds. All pension costs are costs of doing business and are incurred in contemplation of present and future benefits. They are generally part of union contract negotiations and are one component of the total wage agreement. Past services are used as a basis for determining initial coverage under the plan, but subsequent business policies, such as product pricing, must recognize the full pension costs to be absorbed by revenue.

In recognizing past service cost, a question arises with regard to the manner in which the cost should be assigned to present and future operations. There are at least three general views that have been expressed on this problem. One view holds that each year should be charged for an amount equal to that actually paid to the funding agency, essentially a cash approach. With a wide variety of funding arrangements available that provide for great flexibility in periodic payments, a cash approach could lead to wide year-to-year fluctuations in pension charges and thus serve to distort net income measurements. A second view supports the assignment of the cost in some ratable manner over an arbitrarily determined number of future years. Such an approach finds support in the Internal Revenue Code that permits a maximum annual deduction of 10% of the total of past period costs for qualified pension

---

[1]Prior service cost is the cost of the plan assigned to past periods including any remaining past service cost.

[2]*Opinions of the Accounting Principles Board, No. 8, op. cit.,* par. 17.

plans. Many of those supporting the second view would assign this cost over the remaining service lives of the employees or an even longer period. A third view holds that periodic charges to operations limited to interest on the unfunded prior service cost is adequate to meet, on a continuing basis, all benefit payments under a plan. Others would adjust such charges by increases when the charges will not be equal to at least the actuarially computed value of vested benefits found in the plan.

The Accounting Principles Board recognized the alternative views that were held and the various procedures that were found in practice. In concluding that "accounting costs should not be discretionary," it thus rejected the first view that would recognize cost in the periods it was actually funded. In commenting upon the second and third views it expressed a preference for the second. However, since there was significant support for the third view, and since both views could be applied in a variety of different ways, the Board provided for a range within which the assignment of charges could be regarded as acceptable. The range specifies "minimum" and "maximum" charges that take into consideration elements from both views. The minimum and maximum limitations for the charge for pensions are defined as follows:

Minimum. The annual provision for pension cost should not be less than the total of:
1. The normal cost.
2. An amount equivalent to interest on any unfunded prior service cost.
3. If indicated, a provision for vested benefits.

Maximum. The annual provision for pension cost should not be more than the total of:
1. The normal cost.
2. Ten percent of the past service cost (until fully amortized).
3. Ten percent of the amounts of any increases or decreases in prior service cost arising on amendments of the plan (until fully amortized).
4. Interest equivalents on the difference between provisions and the amount funded.

Entries for past service cost. To illustrate the accounting for past service cost, assume that past service cost is computed to be $160,000. Annual charges to operations are to be recognized at 10% of past service cost and such charges are to be funded. The entry to record the annual charge to operations and the transfer of cash to the funding agency is as follows:

Past Service Pension Expense..................... 16,000
    Cash..   16,000

Recognition of the liability for prior service cost. When pension plans are funded, the amount paid to the funding agency may not agree with the amount that is recognized as the charge and liability for the year. Under these circumstances, the Accounting Principles Board calls for the following procedure:

> The difference between the amount which has been charged against income and the amount which has been paid should be shown in the balance sheet as accrued or prepaid pension cost. If the company has a legal obligation for pension cost in excess of amounts paid or accrued, the excess should be shown in the balance sheet as both a liability and a deferred charge. Except to the extent indicated in the preceding sentences of this paragraph, unfunded prior service cost is not a liability which should be shown in the balance sheet.[1]

Disclosure of pension plans. The Accounting Principles Board is aware of the fact that pension plans are of great importance to the proper understanding of both financial position and the results of operations and that there is a need for the adequate disclosure of such plans. The Board has suggested that disclosure be made in financial statements or by notes as follows:

1. A statement that such plans exist, identifying or describing the employee groups covered.
2. A statement of the company's accounting and funding policies.
3. The provision for pension cost for the period.
4. The excess, if any, of the actuarially computed value of vested benefits over the total of the pension fund and any balance-sheet pension accruals, less any pension prepayments or deferred charges.
5. Nature and effect of significant matters affecting comparability for all periods presented, such as changes in accounting methods (actuarial cost method, amortization of past and prior service cost, treatment of actuarial gains and losses, etc.), changes in circumstances (actuarial assumptions, etc.), or adoption or amendment of a plan.[2]

Deferred income taxes payable

The nature of interperiod income tax allocation has been described in earlier sections of the text. The principle of interperiod tax allocation was recognized by the Committee on Accounting Procedure in Bulletin No. 43, but the Committee recognized an exception to such allocation when it could be presumed that ". . . particular differences between the tax return and the income statement will recur regularly over a com-

---

[1]*Ibid.,* par. 18. For a full discussion of accounting for pension plans, one should consult Accounting Research Study No. 8, *Accounting for the Cost of Pension Plans* (New York: American Institute of Certified Public Accountants, 1965), *Opinions of the Accounting Principles Board, No. 8, op. cit.,* and *Interpretation of Accounting for the Cost of Pension Plans* (New York: American Institute of Certified Public Accountants, 1971).

[2]*Ibid.,* par. 46.

paratively long period of time."[1] This led to varied interpretations and alternative procedures by different companies. The Accounting Principles Board in 1967 in Opinion No. 11, in seeking to extend the principle of tax allocation as well as to achieve uniformity in practice, modified the original position and concluded that ". . . comprehensive interperiod tax allocation is an integral part of the determination of income tax expense."[2] *Comprehensive income tax allocation* provides for a charge to income taxes expense that includes the effects of revenue and expense transactions included in the determination of pretax accounting income. Tax effects of differences in pretax accounting income and taxable income are recognized in the periods in which they arise and subsequently in the periods in which the differences are reversed. The comprehensive income tax approach is now employed in practice and this approach has been employed in the illustrations in the text.

In the case of most companies, the amount of income reported for tax purposes has been larger than that reported on the income statement. This has resulted in the recognition on the balance sheets of a great many companies of deferred income taxes payable. Furthermore, in applying the comprehensive approach, the balance reported for deferred income taxes payable on the balance sheets of many companies has been increasing in amount. In some instances, this balance has become one of the largest items reported within the liability section. The reason for such increasing balances is found in two primary practices that are employed for tax purposes: (1) the charge for depreciation of buildings and equipment is more than that recognized on the books; (2) income from installment sales is less than the income recognized on the books. New buildings and equipment are being acquired faster than old properties are being retired and, as a result, depreciation reported on the tax return continues to exceed the depreciation reported on the books; installment sales increase in volume and, as a result, income reported on the books continues to exceed income reported on the tax return. As long as there is growth in these areas, the amount reported for deferred income taxes payable will continue to rise.[3]

With the increase in the deferred taxes payable balance, many accountants have stated the view that when recurring differences between

---

[1]*Accounting Research Bulletin No. 43*, "Restatement and Revision of Accounting Research Bulletins" (New York: American Institute of Certified Public Accountants, 1953), Ch. 10, sect. B, par. 1.

[2]*Opinions of the Accounting Principles Board, No. 11*, "Accounting for Income Taxes" (New York: American Institute of Certified Public Accountants, 1967), par. 34.

[3]A national CPA firm analyzed the balance sheets of 100 corporations between the years 1954 and 1965 and found that almost one billion dollars of deferred taxes payable had been recorded. In the twelve-year period, however, only twenty million dollars, or 2% of this amount, had been paid. *Is Generally Accepted Accounting for Income Taxes Possibly Misleading Investors?* (New York: Price Waterhouse and Co., 1967).

pretax income and taxable income give rise to the indefinite postponement of tax payments or continuing tax reductions, allocation should not be recognized for such differences. These persons take the position that deferred taxes payable should be recognized only when there is a demonstrable probability that the taxes will be paid in the near future. This approach, referred to as *partial income tax allocation*, has been rejected by the Accounting Principles Board. The principal argument against partial income tax allocation is that taxes due on specific items are paid even though for given years more taxes may be accrued in total than are actually paid. This is referred to as the *roll-over* or *revolving* theory, and has been widely accepted by accountants as a reasonable description of what actually occurs.

Another area that has been the subject of debate by accountants is the tax rate that should be used in recognizing deferred income taxes — the current rate or the probable future rate. Those accountants who advocate the use of the current rate emphasize the tax effect of timing differences on income in the period in which the differences originate. The deferred taxes are determined on the basis of the tax rate in effect when the timing differences originate and are not adjusted for future changes. Amortization of the deferral is based upon the nature of the original transactions. This method is referred to as the *deferred method* and is the method prescribed by the Accounting Principles Board in Opinion No. 11.

Those accountants who advocate the use of the expected future rate place their emphasis upon the amount of taxes ultimately to be paid. As tax rates are changed, the amount of the liability is adjusted. Prior to APB Opinion No. 11, this method was acceptable and quite widely followed. It is referred to as the *liability method*. It was not considered by the Board as an acceptable alternative to the deferred method.

There has been some question as to where the deferred taxes payable account should be placed on the balance sheet. Some companies have placed it between the liabilities and owners' equity in a nondefined status. Others view it not as a liability but as a part of owners' equity. Still others would report it as an offset against other assets and liabilities as a "net of tax" computation. In 1967 in Opinion No. 11 the Accounting Principles Board concluded that deferred taxes are properly shown as a deferred item in the long-term liability section until a portion of the taxes become payable; any amount payable currently is reported under the current liability classification. If deferred taxes arise from installment sales and the installment contracts receivable are classified as a current asset, then the deferred taxes should also be reported as a current liability.

Deferred revenues

Deferred revenues arise upon the receipt of cash or the recognition of some other asset before the asset may be considered earned. Cash received or receivables recognized for goods, services, or benefits to be supplied in future periods call for credits to deferred revenue accounts until commitments are fulfilled. Normally costs are involved before revenues may be considered realized and the earnings from this source still remain to be determined.

It has already been indicated that when an obligation is to be liquidated through the use of existing current assets, it is properly reported as a current liability. The deferred revenues classification in the long-term liabilities section of the balance sheet, then, should be limited to obligations that will not claim existing current assets in their liquidation. When a deferred revenue item involves an obligation covering a number of years, the amount of the obligation to be satisfied through existing current assets may be reported as current and the balance may be reported under the deferred revenues heading. However, when a balance is related to a number of years but the claim that it makes against existing current assets is considered only minor and incidental, the entire balance may be reported under the long-term heading. For example, the entire amount of rents collected in advance under a long-term lease would generally be reported under the deferred revenues heading. Costs arising under such a claim will involve (1) depreciation related to leased properties and (2) periodic expenditures for such items as taxes, repairs, and insurance, but the portion of the latter group to be paid currently would normally not be considered sufficiently important to call for special recognition. Items that are usually reported under the deferred revenues heading include leasehold and rental advances, interest received in advance, premiums received on long-term insurance contracts, and fees received in advance on long-term service contracts.

Long-term liabilities on the balance sheet

In reporting long-term liabilities on the balance sheet, the nature of the liabilities, maturity dates, interest rates, methods of liquidation, conversion privileges, and other significant matters should be indicated. When assets have been pledged to secure a liability, full particulars of the pledge should be indicated in the description of the obligation. This may be accompanied by identification on the asset side of the balance sheet of the specific assets pledged. When an agreement with a creditor limits the ability of a company to pay dividends, such limitation should be disclosed.

The portion of serial bonds that is payable within one year is reported as a current liability. Other long-term debt maturing within one year should be reported as a current liability only if retirement will claim current assets. If the debt is to be paid from a bond retirement fund or is to be retired through some form of refinancing, it would continue to be reported as noncurrent with an explanation of the method to be used in its liquidation.

Unissued bonds and treasury bonds may be combined since they both represent potential sources of funds without further authorization of bonds or mortgaging of properties. These may be reported parenthetically after listing bonds outstanding or as a subtraction item from the total bonds authorized. There should be disclosure of any treasury or unissued bonds that have been pledged on loans.

Long-term obligations other than long-term debt are generally listed separately or are reported under an "Other liabilities" heading after the long-term debt classification. Deferred revenues are normally reported as the last liability classification. Contingent long-term debt, such as accommodation endorsements or guarantees of debt of affiliated companies, should be disclosed by parenthetical remarks in the liability section or by special notes.

Long-term liabilities may be reported on a balance sheet as of December 31, 1972, as follows:

Long-term debt:
20-year, 6% first-mortgage bonds outstanding, due January 1, 1984 . . . . $210,000
Less unamortized bond discount 4,500

$205,500

(Authorized and unissued 6% first-mortgage bonds, $40,000: pledged as security on short-term loans, $25,000; held in treasury, $15,000)

Serial 7% debentures, due May 1, 1974, to May 1, 1983, inclusive $100,000
Purchase money obligations payable 1974 to 1978 . . . . 55,000 $360,500

Deferred income taxes payable 25,000
Estimated employee retirement benefits and pensions payable — self-administered fund . 120,000
Deferred revenues:
Lease advances 50,000

Total long-term liabilities $555,500

QUESTIONS

1. What factors should be considered in determining whether cash should be raised by the issue of bonds or by the sale of additional stock?

2. Distinguish between:
   (a) Secured bonds and unsecured bonds.
   (b) Callable bonds and convertible bonds.
   (c) Registered bonds and coupon bonds.
   (d) Term bonds and serial bonds.

3. The compound-interest method of bond premium or discount amortization is not desirable because it results in higher net income than would be found with straight-line amortization. Under what conditions would this be true?

4. (a) What arguments can you offer for reporting discount on bonds payable and premium on bonds payable as deferred items? (b) What arguments can you offer for reporting these balances as bond valuation accounts?

5. The Southwest National Bank is the corporate disbursing agent for the interest and principal amounts on bonds issued by the Wain Co. What entries should be made on the Wain Co. books for (a) transfers of cash to the fiscal agent for interest and principal payments, (b) recognition of accrued interest and matured bonds, and (c) payments of interest and principal amounts by the fiscal agent?

6. The treasurer for the Gardner Co. proposes that treasury bonds be reported as an asset at the amount paid upon their acquisition. What reply would you make to this proposal?

7. (a) Describe the bonds-outstanding method for premium or discount amortization. (b) How does this method differ from the compound-interest method of amortization?

8. What is meant by refunding a bond issue? Why may refunding be advisable?

9. Describe three methods for disposing of charges related to bonds retired through refunding. Give arguments both for and against each method. Which method do you feel has the greatest merit?

10. (a) Why do companies find the issuance of convertible bonds a desirable method of financing? (b) What are the normal characteristics of convertible bonds?

11. Convertible bonds provide something extra over a regular bond. That "extra" is really part of the owners' equity of the company, and part of the bond proceeds should be allocated to the stockholders' equity. What are the chief arguments against this proposal?

12. What is the currently accepted accounting principle governing the issuance of convertible debt?

13. (a) What is the difference in the accounting treatment between convertible bonds and bonds issued with detachable stock warrants? (b) Do you think this difference is justified? Give your reasons.

14. The Young Company acquires machinery and equipment under a contract calling for payments of $10,000 for a ten-year period. The cash price for such equipment is $75,000. The equipment has an estimated useful life of 20 years. Describe fully the accounting for (a) the purchase of the asset, and (b) the payments over the period of the contract.

15. What balance sheet differences would you expect to find for a company that administers its own pension plan as compared with a company that transfers funds to an outside funding agency?

16. What are the principal accounting problems that relate to pension costs?

17. Define (a) normal costs, (b) past service costs, (c) vested benefits.

18. What portion of past service costs must be reported as a liability under current accounting principles?

19. Why are past service costs considered a charge against future earnings rather than an adjustment of past earnings?

20. What pension information should be disclosed in annual reports?

21. What is the difference in concept between the deferred method and the liability method of reporting income tax allocations?

22. When a company grows, all liabilities grow in amount. The growth of deferred taxes payable is no different than the growth in accounts payable. Do you agree?

23. Publishers of magazines conventionally solicit subscriptions for two to five years in advance. On their balance sheet a portion of such subscriptions is commonly shown as deferred revenue and placed between liabilities and stockholders' equity as a separate category.
   (a) How do you reconcile this practice with the fact that the balance sheet is practically universally understood to be a statement of assets, liabilities, and owners' equity? Explain fully the nature of the amount shown as deferred revenue in such a situation.
   (b) Discuss the major factors that should be considered in determining the portion of revenue that should be deferred on a five-year subscription.

24. Comment on the following presentations and indicate what corrections you would make:
   (a) Equipment, cost $100,000, on which installment notes of $90,000 are unpaid, is reported on the balance sheet at the company's net equity therein, $10,000.
   (b) Treasury bonds, face value $50,000, cost $56,000 are reported as an asset at cost on the balance sheet.
   (c) Advances from a subsidiary company are reported as a subtraction from the investment in the stock of the company in reporting the net investment in the subsidiary on the balance sheet.

EXERCISES

1. The Prince Co. has issued 10,000 shares of $100 par common stock. The company requires additional working capital and finds that it can sell 2,000 additional shares of common at $100, or it can issue $200,000 of 6% bonds at par. Earnings of the company before income taxes have been $80,000 annually, and it is expected that these will increase 30% (before additional interest charges) as a result of the additional funds. Assuming that the income tax rate is estimated at 50%, which method of financing would you recommend as a common stock-holder? Why? (Show calculations.)

2. (a) The Williams Corporation issues $100,000 of 6% debenture bonds on a basis to yield 7%, receiving $95,842. Interest is payable semiannually and the bonds mature in 5 years. What entries would be made for the first two interest payments, assuming discount amortization on interest dates by (1) the straight-line method and (2) the compound-interest method?

(b) If the sale is made on a 5½% yield, $102,160 being received, what entries would be made for the first two interest payments, assuming premium amortization on interest dates by (1) the straight-line method and (2) the compound-interest method?

3. On December 1, 1970, the Pilgrim Company issues 20-year bonds of $100,000 at 104. Interest is payable on December 1 and June 1 at 6%. On April 1, 1972, the Pilgrim Company retires 20 of its own $1,000 bonds at 98 plus accrued interest. The fiscal period for the Pilgrim Co. is the calendar year. What entries are made to record (a) the issuance of the bonds, (b) the interest payments and adjustments relating to the debt in 1971, (c) the retirement of bonds in 1972, and (d) the interest payments and adjustments relating to the debt in 1972?

4. The Sunshine Corporation issues $1,000,000 of serial bonds on January 1, 1972, bonds of $200,000 to be retired at the end of each year. Interest of 5% is to be paid annually. The issue is sold for $1,013,556, a price that will result in a 4½% yield. (a) Assuming premium amortization by the compound-interest method, prepare a table summarizing interest charges and bond carrying values for the 5-year period similar to that illustrated on page 624. (b) Prepare a similar table assuming premium amortization by the straight-line method.

5. Carnegie, Inc., issues $500,000 of serial bonds on January 1, 1970, bonds of $50,000 being redeemable annually beginning on January 1, 1971. Bonds are sold for $489,000. Interest at 6% is payable semi-annually on January 1 and July 1. On May 1, 1972, the bond series due on January 1, 1975, is retired at 99 plus accrued interest. What entry is made to record the bond retirement?

6. Randall Insurance decides to finance expansion of its physical facilities by issuing convertible debenture bonds. The terms of the bonds are: maturity date 20 years after May 1, 1971, the date of issuance; conversion at option of holder after 2 years, 40 shares of $25 par value stock for each $1,000 bond held; interest rate of 6% and call provision on the bonds of 103. The bonds were sold at 102. (a) Give the entry to record the sale of 1,000 bonds on July 1, 1972; interest payment dates are May 1 and November 1. (b) Assume the same condition as in (a) above, except that the sale of the bonds is to be recorded in a manner that will recognize a value that is related to the conversion privilege. The estimated sales price of the bonds without the conversion privilege is 98.

7. Campbell Rotary, Inc., requests advice from its attorneys concerning the issuing of equity capital and decides to issue $1,000,000 of 7½% bonds with detachable warrants. Each warrant can be used to acquire 3 shares of common stock, par value $25. It is estimated that without the warrants, the bonds would have sold at 95. The bond price with warrants attached will sell for 103. How should the bonds be recorded upon issuance?

8. Bill Harris is a holder of $20,000 of 10-year convertible bonds of the Gunnell Corporation that were issued by the company at 102. He has the option of converting each $1,000 bond into 10 shares of common stock, par value $100. The bond rate is 5% payable semiannually. The option is exercised by Harris 2½ years after the issuance of the bonds. (a) What entries are required on Harris' books and on the corporation's books to record the exchange in the absence of a market value for the stock? Premium amortization has been recorded to the conversion date. (b) If the stock had a market value of $120 per share at the time of exchange and this value is to be recognized, what entries would be made on the books of each party?

9. In reviewing the accounts of the Great Lakes Co. at the beginning of 1972, you find that on January 1, 1968, it had acquired machinery in exchange for its own 6% bonds with a par value of $100,000 that mature on January 1, 1978. You determine that the bonds had a market value on the date of exchange of $94,000; however, the machinery was recorded at par value of the bonds and depreciation was recognized for 1968 through 1972 at the rate of 4% annually. What compound entry would you make to correct the accounts?

10. The Warner Company calls in a $300,000 of 8% bond issue that is not due for 5 years and on which there is unamortized bond discount of $3,500. The call price is 103. The company then issues 10-year 7% refunding bonds of $350,000, which are sold at 98. (a) List the methods that might be used for the disposition of charges relating to the bonds retired and give the entries for refunding that would be made in each case. (b) Show in summary form the effect of each method upon income in the year of refunding.

11. Winsom, Inc., is offered certain equipment for cash of $40,000 or on a contract providing for a down payment of $15,000 and six semiannual installments of $5,000. Calculations indicate that the deferred payment plan involves implicit interest at the rate of approximately 10%. Equipment has an estimated life of twenty years. The equipment is purchased at the beginning of 1972 on the installment payment plan. Give the entries to be made in 1972 for the purchase, the semiannual payments on June 30 and December 31, and the depreciation on the equipment on December 31.

12. The Everett Company entered into a pension plan for its employees on January 1, 1971. An outside trustee was engaged and an actuarial analysis was made of the employees and their pension requirements under the pension fund contract. Past service costs were calculated to be $1,200,000. The funding provision called for paying this amount in five equal installments of $300,500 each. Everett Company elects to write off the past service costs according to the "maximum" provision of APB Opinion No. 8. Normal costs funded for both 1971 and 1972 were $75,000. What entries relating to the pension plan are required on Everett Company's books for 1971 and 1972?

PROBLEMS

18-1. Harris and Mace, Inc., was authorized to issue 8-year, $6\frac{1}{2}\%$ bonds of $1,000,000. The bonds are dated January 1, 1971, and interest is payable semiannually on January 1 and July 1. Checks for interest are mailed on June 30 and December 31. Bond sales were as follows:

    April 1, 1971 $500,000 at $98\frac{1}{2}$ plus accrued interest.
    July 1, 1972 $300,000 at 103.

On September 1, 1972, remaining unissued bonds were pledged as collateral on the issue of $166,000 of short-term notes.

Instructions: (1) Give the journal entries relating to bonds that would appear on the corporation's books in 1971 and 1972. (Straight-line amortization is used; an unissued bonds account is set up.)

(2) Show how information relative to the bond issue will appear on the balance sheet prepared on December 31, 1972. (Give balance sheet section headings and accounts and account balances appearing within such sections.)

18-2. The Bernham Corporation issued $200,000 of 6% bonds, interest payable semiannually, bonds maturing 4 years after issue. The bonds were sold at $193,126, a price to yield 7% on the issue.

Instructions: (1) Prepare tables to show the periodic adjustments to the discount account and the annual bond interest assuming adjustment by each of the following methods: (a) the straight-line method and (b) the compound-interest method.

(2) Give entries for the interest payment and the discount amortization for the first year of the bond issue assuming use of (a) the straight-line method and (b) the compound-interest method.

18-3. The Gellman Corporation received permission as of January 1, 1972, to issue 8% bonds of $6,000,000 maturing on January 1, 1982. The bonds are dated January 1, 1972, and interest is payable semiannually on January 1 and July 1. The bonds are callable at 103 plus accrued interest at any time after January 1, 1977.

On April 1, 1972, the corporation sold bonds of $2,500,000 at 104 plus accrued interest. Checks for interest were placed in the mail on June 30, 1972. The balance of the authorized issue was sold for cash on October 1, 1972, at 99 plus accrued interest.

The corporation's fiscal period ends on November 30. Interest on bonds was accrued to this date, and bond amortization entries for the past fiscal year were recorded.

Interest checks were mailed on December 31, 1972.

Instructions: (1) Give the journal entries relating to the bonds that appear on the books for the year 1972. (The straight-line method is used for amortization; authorized bonds are not recorded in the accounts.)

(2) Assuming that the bonds are called in on July 1, 1977, give the journal entries to record the payment of interest and the bond retirement on this date.

18-4. The Fowler Co. was authorized to issue $3,000,000 of 7% debentures on April 1, 1971. Interest on the bonds is payable semiannually on April 1 and October 1. Bonds mature on April 1, 1981.

The entire issue was sold on April 1, 1971, at 98 less costs of $20,000 involved on the issue. In 1972 bonds were purchased on the open market and retired as follows:

July 1 $600,000 at 98½ plus accrued interest.
November 1 $900,000 at 97 plus accrued interest.

Instructions: Give the journal entries, including any adjustments relating to the issuance of bonds and interest on the obligation, that are required for 1971 and 1972. (The company's fiscal period is the calendar year.)

18-5. The Hoffer Company issued 7% bonds of $3,000,000 at 97 plus accrued interest on April 1, 1971. The bond issue is dated January 1, 1971; interest is payable semiannually on January 1 and July 1. On January 1 of each year for 10 years, beginning January 1, 1972, bonds of $300,000 mature and are paid. The company's fiscal period is the calendar year.

Instructions: Give the required journal entries relating to the bond issue in 1971 and 1972. Assume that checks are issued on December 31 for all payments due January 1.

18-6. Hercules Powder Company issued $500,000 of 6% serial bonds for $489,800 on January 1, 1972. Bonds were scheduled for retirement as follows:

Date of Maturity	Amount Retired
January 1, 1975	$100,000
January 1, 1976	100,000
January 1, 1977	100,000
January 1, 1978	100,000
January 1, 1979	50,000
January 1, 1980	50,000

Instructions: (1) Prepare a table showing the discount amortization each year by the bonds-outstanding method. (The company's fiscal period is the calendar year.)

(2) Prepare a table showing the premium amortization assuming that the bonds are sold on April 1, 1972, at $517,460 plus accrued interest. Retirement dates remain the same as in (1).

(3) Give the journal entries that would be made in 1972 assuming that the bonds are sold as indicated in (2) above.

18-7. The Morris Company sold $1,500,000 of 6% debenture bonds on January 1, 1970, to an investment banking firm at 97½. The bonds have serial maturities; bonds of $300,000 are payable at annual intervals beginning on January 1, 1973. Interest is payable annually on January 1. Checks for principal and interest payments are mailed on December 31 of each year. On April 1, 1972, the company reacquired at 99 plus accrued interest bonds of $100,000 due January 1, 1973, and bonds of $100,000 due January 1, 1974. Bonds were formally retired.

Instructions: (1) Assuming discount amortization by the bonds-outstanding method and bond retirements as scheduled, prepare a table summarizing interest charges and bond carrying values for the bond life similar to that illustrated on page 624, supported by a schedule showing the calculation of amortization amounts.

(2) Prepare a similar table summarizing interest charges and bond carrying values for the bond life taking into consideration bond redemptions in advance of maturity dates as indicated.

(3) Record in journal form the retirement of bonds on April 1, 1972.

18-8. The balance sheet for the Lakeland Corp. on December 31, 1971, the close of the fiscal period, shows the following accounts:

Bond discount and issue costs..........................	$ 18,000
Accrued interest on bonds.............................	25,500
Bonds payable, due January 1, 1976, interest at 6% payable semiannually on January 1 and July 1................	850,000

On January 1, 1972, the following took place: cash of $975,000 was made available from the sale of $1,000,000 of 10-year, 5½% bonds to Alexander Underwriters. Cash from the new issue was used for retirement of the 6% bonds at a call price of 101 and for payment of accrued interest on this issue; the balance of cash was added to the general funds of the company. Interest on the new issue is payable January 1 and July 1.

Instructions: Give the entries that would appear on the books of the corporation relative to bonds and bond interest for the year 1972 under the following assumptions:

    (1) Unamortized discount and call premium on the old issue are not to be identified with future fiscal periods.

    (2) Unamortized discount and call premium on the old issue are to be amortized over the remaining life of the old issue.

    (3) Unamortized discount and call premium on the old issue are to be amortized over the life of the new issue.

18-9. The Douglas Company issued $10 million of 5% convertible bonds with interest payment dates of April 1 and October 1. The bonds were issued on July 1, 1967, and mature on April 1, 1987. The bond discount and issue expenses totaled $533,250. The bond contract entitles the bondholders to receive 25 shares of $15 par value common stock in exchange for each $1,000 bond. On April 1, 1972, the holders of bonds, face value $1,000,000, exercised their conversion privilege. On July 1, 1972, the Douglas Company reacquired bonds, paying the face value of $500,000 on the open market. The balances in the capital accounts as of December 31, 1971 were:

Common stock, $15 par, authorized 3 million shares, issued
   and outstanding, 250,000 shares.................... $3,750,000
Premium on common stock......................... 2,500,000

Market value of the common stock and bonds were as follows:

Date	Bonds (per $1,000)	Common Stock (per share)
April 1, 1972	$1,220	$48
July 1, 1972	1,250	50

Instructions: Prepare journal entries for each of the following transactions. (Use straight-line amortization for the bond discount and issue expenses.)

    (1) Issuance of the bonds on July 1, 1967.

    (2) Interest payment on October 1, 1967.

    (3) Interest accrual on December 31, 1967, including bond discount amortization.

    (4) Conversion of bonds on April 1, 1972. (Gain or loss on conversion should be recognized. Assume that interest and discount amortization are correctly shown as of April 1, 1972.)

    (5) Reacquisition and retirement of bonds on July 1, 1972. (Interest and discount amortization are correctly reported as of July 1, 1972.)

18-10. Upon inspecting the records of the Garrett Corporation you find that 6½% first-mortgage serial bonds were authorized and dated July 1, 1969, with interest payable semiannually. The issue was sold on October 1, 1969, at 98 plus accrued interest and less costs on the issue of $2,300. Bonds of $20,000 mature at annual intervals; the first maturity date is July 1, 1970. Bonds are callable on any interest payment date.

On January 1, 1972, the company called in the 1974 maturities at 103. The company maintained a single account for the bond issue, and on December 31, 1972, the close of an annual fiscal period, this account showed a balance of $116,350, and appeared as follows:

6½% First-Mortgage Serial Bonds

July 1, 1970 Retirement of 1970 maturities	20,000	Oct. 1, 1969 Proceeds from sale of bonds	196,950
July 1, 1971 Retirement of 1971maturities	20,000		
Jan. 1, 1972 Retirement of 1974 maturities	20,600		
July 1, 1972 Retirement of 1972 maturities	20,000		

Instructions: (1) Give the correcting journal entries as well as any adjusting entries required as of December 31, 1972. (Assume that the books for 1972 have not been closed. Further assume that bond discount and issue costs are combined. Give any schedules that may be required in developing the entries.)

(2) What account balances and amounts relating to the bond issue would appear on the balance sheet as of December 31, 1972, and on the income statement for the year ending December 31, 1972?

18-11. The Kern Construction Co. acquires equipment on January 2, 1972, on a contract calling for a cash payment of $30,000 and twelve semiannual payments of $4,000. It is assumed that interest at the rate of 12% is implicit in the deferred payments and the present value of the series of payments on this basis is calculated at $33,535. The equipment is estimated to have a life of 10 years with a residual value of 5% of cost; property items are depreciated by the sum-of-the-years-digits method.

Instructions: Give the entries in 1972 for (1) the purchase of the asset, (2) the semiannual payments on June 30 and December 31 recognizing implicit interest at 12%, and (3) depreciation for 1972.

18-12. The Dell Corporation has been following income tax allocation procedures for the past eight years. As of December 31, 1972, the deferred income taxes payable account had a credit balance of $320,000. This amount was accrued at a 48% rate.

Instructions: (1) Assume that in 1972, the rate decreased to 45%. Book income and taxable income were the same. What entry, if any, would be required using (a) the liability method, (b) the deferred method.

(2) Assume that in 1973, depreciation per books exceeded depreciation shown on the tax return by $30,000. Book income is $100,000. Assuming a 45% rate, what entry would be required to record income taxes if the deferred method were used?

(3) Assume that depreciation per books in 1974 was $20,000 less than that shown on the tax return. Book income is $75,000. Assuming a 45% rate, what entry would be required using the deferred method?

18-13. The Catalina Co. issued $1,000,000 of convertible 10-year debentures on July 1, 1971. The debentures provide for 6% interest payable semiannually on January 1 and July 1. Expense and discount in connection with the issue were $19,500 which is being amortized monthly on a straight-line basis.

The debentures are convertible after one year into 7 shares of the Catalina Co.'s $100 par value common stock for each $1,000 of debentures.

On August 1, 1972, $100,000 of debentures were turned in for conversion into common. Interest has been accrued monthly and paid as due. Accrued interest on debentures is paid in cash upon conversion.

Instructions: Prepare the journal entries to record the conversion, amortization and interest in connection with the debentures as of: August 1, 1972; August 31, 1972; and December 31, 1972 — including closing entries for end of year.   (AICPA adapted)

18-14. The Arden Company issued $3,000,000 of 8% first-mortgage bonds on October 1, 1964, at 96 and accrued interest. The bonds were dated July 1, 1964; interest payable semiannually on January 1 and July 1; redeemable after June 30, 1969; and to June 30, 1971, at 104, and thereafter until maturity at 102; and convertible into $100 par value common stock as follows:

Until June 30, 1969, at the rate of 6 shares for each $1,000 of bonds.
From July 1, 1969, to June 30, 1972, at the rate of 5 shares for each $1,000 of bonds.
After June 30, 1972, at the rate of 4 shares for each $1,000 of bonds.

Costs of the issue were $6,360 and are to be combined with the premium or discount, and the total is to be amortized over the life of the bonds from date of issue. The bonds mature in 10 years from their date. The company adjusts its books monthly and closes its books as of December 31 each year. It follows the practice of writing off all unamortized bond discount and issue costs in the period of bond retirement.

The following transactions occur in connection with the bonds:

(a) July 1, 1970 — $500,000 of bonds were converted into stock.
(b) December 31, 1971 — $500,000 face amount of bonds were reacquired at 99¼ and accrued interest. These were immediately retired.
(c) July 1, 1972 — The remaining bonds were called for redemption. For purpose of obtaining funds for redemption and business expansion, a $4,000,000 issue of 6% bonds was sold at 98¾. These bonds were dated July 1, 1972, and were due in 20 years.

Instructions: Prepare in journal form the entries necessary for the company in connection with the above transactions, including monthly adjustments where appropriate, as of the following dates:

(1) October 1, 1964   (3) July 1, 1970   (5) July 1, 1972
(2) December 31, 1964   (4) December 31, 1971

(AICPA adapted)

18-15. The Jarman Corporation adopted a pension plan for its employees on January 1, 1971. A trial balance of the records of the plan at December 31, 1972 follows:

	Debit	Credit
Cash..	$ 400	—
Investments (at cost).........................	3,400	—
Bone, equity.................................	—	$1,590
Cohan, equity................................	—	1,060
Dohler, equity...............................	—	850
Income from investments — received in 1972.......	—	300
	$3,800	$3,800

The following data pertain to the corporation's employees for 1972.

	Date Employed	Date Terminated	Salary Paid in 1972
Bone.....................	12/ 8/67	—	$17,900
Cohan...................	2/ 1/69	—	14,100
Dohler..................	12/ 8/69	4/ 9/72	3,500
Kolman.................	9/15/70	—	8,000
Jones...................	9/21/72	12/22/72	3,000
Lohman.................	5/ 6/72	—	5,500
			$52,000

The provisions of the plan include the following:

(a) The corporation shall contribute 10% of its net income before deducting income taxes and the contribution but not in excess of 15% of the total salaries paid to the participants in the plan who are in the employ of the corporation at year end. The employees make no contributions to the plan.

(b) An employee shall be eligible to participate in the plan on January 1 following the completion of one full year of employment.

(c) The corporation's contribution shall be allocated to the participants' equities on the following point system:
1. For each full year of employment — 2 points.
2. For each $100 of salary paid in the current year — 1 point.

(d) A participant shall have a vested interest of 10% of his total equity for each full year of employment. Forfeitures shall be distributed to the remaining participants in proportion to their equities in the plan at the beginning of the year. Terminated employees shall receive their vested interests at year end.

(e) Income from the plan's investments shall be allocated to the equities of the remaining participants in proportion to their equities at the beginning of the year.

The Jarman Corporation's net income in 1972 before income taxes and contribution to the plan was $73,250.

Instructions: (1) Prepare a schedule computing the corporation's contribution to the plan for 1972.

(2) Prepare a schedule computing the vested interests of the participants terminating their employment during 1972.

(*continued*)

(3) Prepare a schedule showing the allocation of the corporation's 1972 contribution to each participant.

(4) Prepare a schedule showing the allocation of the plan's 1972 income on investments and forfeitures by terminated participants.

(AICPA adapted)

18-16. Zakin Co. recently issued $1,000,000 face value, 5%, 30-year subordinated debentures at 97. The debentures are redeemable at 103 upon demand by the issuer at any date upon 30 days notice ten years after issue. The debentures are convertible into $10 par value common stock of the company at the conversion price of $12.50 per share for each $500 or multiple thereof of the principal amount of the debentures.

Assume that no value is assigned to the conversion feature upon issue of the debentures. Assume further that five years after issue, debentures with a face value of $100,000 and book value of $97,500 are tendered for conversion on an interest payment date when the market price of the debentures is 104 and the common stock is selling at $14 per share and that the company records the conversion as follows:

Bonds Payable	100,000	
Discount on Bonds Payable		2,500
Common Stock		80,000
Premium on Common Stock		17,500

Instructions: Do you agree with this entry? If not, prepare a correct one.

(AICPA adapted)

chapter 19

paid-in capital -
capital upon corporate formation

The corporation is an artificial entity created by law that has an existence separate from its owners and may engage in business within prescribed limits just as a natural person. The modern corporation makes it possible for large amounts of property to be assembled under one management. This property is transferred to the corporation by the individual owners because they believe the corporation will make effective and efficient use of it. In exchange for this property, the corporation issues ownership interests in the form of shares of stock. Managements elected by stockholders supervise the use, operation, and disposition of the property. Unless the life of the corporation is limited by law, it has perpetual existence.

Corporations have become the dominant form of organization in today's economy. Not only are they the major source of our national output, but they also provide the majority of employment opportunities. Accounting for corporations has become very important because of the division between ownership and management and the widespread holding of ownership securities.

Forming the corporation

Business corporations may be created under the corporation laws of any one of the fifty states or of the federal government. Since the states do not follow a uniform incorporating act, the conditions under which corporations may be created and under which they may operate are somewhat varied.

In most states at least three individuals must join in applying for a corporate charter. Application is made by submitting *articles of incorporation* to the secretary of state or other appropriate official. The articles must set forth the name of the corporation, its purpose and nature, the stock that is to be issued, those persons who are to act as first directors, and other data required by law. If the articles conform to the state's laws governing corporate formation, they are approved and are recognized as the *charter* for the new corporate entity.[1] Subscriptions to capital stock then become effective. A stockholders' meeting is called at which a code of rules or *bylaws* governing meetings, voting procedures, and other internal operations are adopted, A *board of directors* is elected, and the board appoints company administrative officers. Corporate activities may now proceed in conformance with laws of the state of incorporation and charter authorization. A complete record of the proceedings of both the stockholders' and the directors' meetings must be maintained in a *minutes book*.

Corporations are classified as *public* when they represent governmental subdivisions or government-owned units and as *private* when they are privately owned. The private group includes *nonstock* companies where operations are of a nonprofit nature and stock is not issued, as in the case of hospitals, charities, and religious organizations, and *stock* companies where operations are for profit and stock is issued as evidence of an ownership interest. Corporations are also classified as *domestic* and *foreign;* a corporation is termed domestic in the state of its incorporation and foreign in all other states. A corporation whose stock is widely held and is available for purchase is known as an *open corporation;* a corporation whose stock is held by relatively few individuals and is not available for purchase is called a *close corporation*.

Nature of capital stock

An ownership interest in a corporate entity is evidenced by shares of stock in the form of certificates. When a value is assigned to each share and is reported on the stock certificate, the stock is said to have a *par value;* stock without such an assigned value is called *no-par* stock.

Most companies generally issue a single class of stock. However, in assembling property for a corporation there would appear to be increasing advantages in issuing more than one kind of stock with varying rights and priorities. When a single class of stock is issued, shares are all alike and are known as *common stock*. When more than one class is issued, stock that is given certain preferences over the common issue is called *preferred stock*.

Because of the increased need for financial expansion, many other types of securities have been used. Some types have both debt and equity

---

[1]When stock of a corporation is to be distributed outside of the state in which it is incorporated, registration with the Securities and Exchange Commission may be required. The objective of such registration is to assure that all of the facts relative to the business and its securities will be adequately and honestly disclosed.

qualities and can be converted into straight equity securities at the option of the holders. The use of these securities changes as economic conditions change, and they increase in variety as the acquisition of new investment funds becomes more difficult.

Unless restricted or withheld by terms of the stock contract, certain basic rights are held by each stockholder that are exercised pro rata according to the number of shares he owns. These rights are as follows:

1. To share in distributions of corporate earnings.
2. To vote in the election of directors and in the determination of certain corporate policies.
3. To maintain one's proportional interest in the corporation through purchase of additional capital stock if issued, known as the *preemptive right*.
4. To share in distributions of cash or other properties upon liquidation of the corporation.

If preferred and common stocks are issued, the special features of each class of stock are stated in the articles of incorporation or in the corporation bylaws and become a part of the stock contract between the corporation and its stockholders. One must be familiar with the overall capital structure to understand fully the nature of the equity that is found in any single class of stock. Frequently the stock certificate describes the rights and restrictions relative to the ownership interest it represents together with those pertaining to other securities issued. Shares of stock represent personal property and may be freely transferred by their owners.

Legal or stated value of stock. When stock is issued by a corporation, a portion or all of the capital arising from the issue is designated *legal* or *stated capital*. State incorporation laws provide that dividends cannot reduce corporate capital below legal capital. Modern corporation laws normally go beyond these limitations and add that legal capital cannot be impaired by the reacquisition of capital stock. Creditors of a corporation cannot hold individual stockholders liable for claims against the company. But with a portion of the corporate capital restricted as to distribution, creditors can rely on the absorption by the ownership group of losses equal to the legal capital before losses are applied to the creditors' equity.

When shares have a par value, the legal or stated capital is normally the aggregate par value of all shares issued and subscribed. When shares are no-par, laws of certain states require that the total consideration received for the shares, even when they are sold at different prices, be recognized as legal capital. Laws of a number of states, however, permit the corporate directors to establish legal capital by assigning an arbitrary value to each share regardless of issue price, although in some instances the value cannot be less than a certain minimum amount. The value that is fixed by the board of directors or the minimum value required by law is known as the share's *stated value*.[1] No-par shares whose full proceeds must be regarded as legal capital are frequently referred to as *true* or *pure no-par stock* to distinguish these from no-par issues with a stated value.

The full amount invested by stockholders is recognized as *paid-in capital* or *invested capital*. The portion of the paid-in capital representing legal capital is reported as *capital stock;* any amount in excess of that portion designated as legal capital is reported as *additional paid-in capital, paid-in surplus*, or *capital surplus*.

Legal or stated capital arises from the issuance of capital stock. It may be increased by a stock dividend or by other appropriate action of the board of directors transferring additional paid-in capital or retained earnings to capital stock. It is decreased by the formal retirement of capital stock. It may also be decreased by action of the board of directors reducing the par or stated value of shares as permitted by law.

Par and no-par stock. When a corporation is authorized to issue capital stock with a par value, the incorporation laws of some states permit such issue only for an amount equal to or in excess of par. Par value may be any amount, for example, $100, $5, or 25 cents. An amount received on the sale of capital stock for an amount in excess of its par value is recorded as a premium; the premium is added to capital stock at par in reporting total paid-in capital.

In certain states corporations may be permitted to sell stock at a discount. Capital stock is still reported at par, but the discount is reported as a subtraction item in presenting paid-in capital. Persons subscribing

---

[1]Section 1900 of the California Corporations Code (as amended through 1969) provides, for example, as follows:

"Every stock corporation shall have a stated capital which shall be an amount made up of the sum of the following amounts, less the amounts of any reductions of stated capital made as authorized by this division:

(a) The aggregate par value of par value shares which have been issued from time to time, except that if par value shares have been issued as fully paid up for a consideration less than par pursuant to Section 1110, only the amount of the agreed consideration for such shares specified in dollars shall be credited to stated capital.

(b) The aggregate amount specified in dollars of the agreed consideration received or to be received by the corporation for all shares without par value which have been issued from time to time, except any portion of the consideration for such shares which has been expressly designated by the board of directors upon or prior to issue as paid-in surplus. In the absence of such designation by the board of directors, the entire amount of the consideration for shares without par value shall be credited to stated capital. . . .

(c) Such amounts as are transferred from surplus to stated capital upon declaration of a share dividend or by resolution of the board of directors."

Note that under California law, in certain instances a discount on stock with a par value is deductible from par in arriving at stated capital (see [a] above).

for stock at a discount fulfill their obligation to the corporation upon payment of the agreed price. However, the laws of the state may provide that if the assets of a corporation are insufficient to meet its obligations, creditors may hold stockholders personally liable for deficiencies up to the amounts of the discounts. Creditors are thus protected by the full legal capital as reported in the capital stock account.

Prior to 1912 corporations were permitted to issue only stock with a par value. In 1912, however, New York state changed its corporation laws to permit the issuance of stock without a par value, and since that time all other states have followed with similar statutory provisions. Today many of the common stocks, as well as some of the preferred stocks, listed on the large securities exchanges are no-par.

Use of no-par issues was originally encouraged on the grounds that: (1) such stock could be sold as "fully paid" without making the subscriber contingently liable to creditors as in the case of par stock issued at a discount; (2) investors would not be misled by a less-than-par "bargain" price, but in the absence of a value appearing on stock certificates would investigate the value of a stock; and (3) assets acquired in exchange for stock would be recorded at their actual worth rather than at inflated amounts set by the par of the stock as a means of enabling stockholders to avoid the contingent liability for the discount.

It is questionable whether investors have subjected no-par stock to closer investigation than stock with a par value. It is also questionable whether more satisfactory valuations have been applied to properties received in exchange for no-par stock as compared with stock with a par value. Moreover, certain undesirable practices have arisen in the treatment of the paid-in capital arising from the sale of no-par stock at more than its stated value: (1) this portion of paid-in capital has been reported on financial statements in a manner suggesting accumulated earnings rather than invested capital; (2) such paid-in capital has been used to absorb operating losses, the balance sheet thus failing to disclose operating deficits; and (3) such paid-in capital has been used as a basis for dividends without disclosure to stockholders that dividends under such circumstances represent no more than a return of original investment. A disadvantage in the issue of no-par stock has been that transfer fees, stock taxes, and other fees and taxes on no-par stock are frequently based on an arbitrary share value that may be grossly in excess of the issuing price or market price of the stock.

Preferred stock

When a corporation issues both preferred and common stock, the preference attaching to preferred stock normally consists of a prior claim to dividends.   A dividend preference does not assure stockholders of dividends on the preferred issue but simply means that dividend requirements must be met on preferred stock before anything may be paid on common stock.   Dividends do not legally accrue; a dividend on preferred stock, as on common stock, requires the legal ability on the part of the company to make such a distribution as well as appropriate action by the board of directors.[1] When the board of directors fails to declare a dividend at the time such action would be called for, the dividend is said to be *passed*.   Although preferred stockholders have a prior claim on dividends, such preference is usually accompanied by limitations on the amount of dividends they may receive.

Preferred stock is generally issued with a par value.   When preferred stock has a par value, the dividend preference is stated in terms of a percentage of par value.   When preferred stock is no-par, the dividend must be stated in terms of dollars and cents.   Thus holders of 5% preferred stock with a $50 par value are entitled to an annual dividend of $2.50 per share before any distribution is made to common stockholders; holders of $5 no-par preferred stock are entitled to an annual dividend of $5 per share before dividends are paid to common stockholders.

A corporation may issue more than one class of preferred stock. For example, preferred issues may be designated first preferred or second preferred with the first preferred issue having a first claim on earnings and the second preferred having a second claim on earnings. In other instances the claim to earnings on the part of several preferred issues may have equal priority, but dividend rates or other preferences may vary.   Holders of the common stock may receive dividends only after the satisfaction of all preferred dividend requirements.

Other characteristics and conditions are frequently added to preferred stock in the extension of certain advantages or in the limitation of certain rights.   Such factors may be expressed in adjectives modifying preferred stock, as *cumulative* preferred stock, *participating* preferred stock, *convertible* preferred stock, and *callable* preferred stock.   More than one of these characteristics may be applicable to a specific issue of preferred stock.

Cumulative and noncumulative preferred stock.   *Cumulative* preferred stock provides that whenever the corporation fails to declare dividends on this class, such dividends accumulate and require payment in the future before any dividends may be paid to common stockholders. For example, assume that a corporation has outstanding 100,000 shares

---

[1]Although a company can make no guarantee of dividends on its own stock, it can guarantee dividends on stock of another company. Hence, one may find a company guaranteeing dividends of another in consideration for certain services or properties.

of 6% cumulative preferred stock, $10 par. Dividends were last paid through December 31, 1969, and the company wishes to resume payments at the end of 1972. The company will have to declare dividends on preferred for three years, or $180,000, before it may declare any dividends on common stock. Preferred dividends on cumulative preferred stock that are passed are referred to as *dividends in arrears*. Although these dividends are not a liability until declared by the board of directors, this information is of importance to stockholders and other users of the financial statements. Disclosure of the amount of the dividends in arrears is made by special note on the balance sheet.

If preferred stock is *noncumulative*, it is not necessary to provide for dividends that were passed. A dividend omission on preferred stock in any one year means that it is irretrievably lost; dividends may be declared on common stock as long as the preferred stock receives the preferred rate for the current period. Preferred stock contracts normally provide for cumulative dividends. Courts have generally held that dividend rights on preferred stock are cumulative in the absence of specific conditions to the contrary.

Participating and nonparticipating preferred stock. *Participating* preferred stock receives the preferred rate and also shares dividends with common stock in accordance with certain participation features. Preferred stock may be *fully participating* and thus be entitled to dividends at a rate or at an amount per share equal to that paid to common after common is paid the preferred rate or amount, or it may be participating but limited to a certain maximum rate or amount. Since it is preferred stock, it still receives its regular dividend before amounts are available for common stock or for distribution on a participating basis. To illustrate, assume that a corporation has outstanding 5% fully participating preferred stock, par $100,000, and common stock, par $200,000. If dividends totaling $36,000 are to be distributed, dividends of 12% will be paid on both preferred stock and common stock. The apportionment is made as follows:

	Preferred ($100,000 par)	Common ($200,000 par)
To preferred, 5%................	$ 5,000	
To common, up to preferred rate, 5%.		$10,000
To all shares ratably, 7% (balance to be paid, $21,000 ÷ par value of all stock outstanding, $300,000).......	7,000	14,000
	$12,000	$24,000

If the preferred stock was limited in participation to a maximum of 8%, it would receive $8,000, and the common stock would receive the balance, or $28,000. When preferred stock is no-par, participation arrangements must be stated in dollar amounts rather than in percentages. A variety of participation arrangements are found on preferred issues.

When preferred stock is *nonparticipating*, dividends on this class are limited to the preferred rate or amount. Common stockholders may be paid any amount after payment of the preferred dividend for the current year. Preferred issues normally do not include participating features. Courts have generally held that preferred stock is nonparticipating when the stock contract does not specifically provide for participation.

Convertible preferred stock. Preferred stock is *convertible* when terms of the issue provide that it can be exchanged by its owner for some other security of the issuing corporation. Conversion rights generally provide for the exchange of preferred stock into common stock. Since preferred stock normally has a prior but limited right on earnings, large earnings resulting from successful operations accrue to the common stockholders. The conversion privilege gives the preferred stockholder the opportunity to exchange his holdings for stock in which his rights to earnings are not limited. In some instances, preferred stock may also be convertible into bonds. Here the investor has the option of changing his position from stockholder to that of a creditor. Convertible preferred issues have become increasingly popular in recent years.

The decision by a stockholder of when to convert preferred holdings into common stock is a difficult one and involves many factors including the time limitation, if any, on the conversion privilege, the relative dividend returns on common stock as compared with preferred stock, as well as other provisions that may be related to the two classes of securities.

Callable preferred stock. Preferred stock is *callable* when it can be called or redeemed at the option of the corporation. Many preferred issues are callable. The *call price* is usually specified in the original agreement and provides for payment of dividends in arrears as part of the repurchase price. When convertible stock has a call provision, the holder of the stock frequently is given the option of converting his holdings into common stock. The decision made by the investor will be based on the market price of the common stock.

Asset and dividend preferences upon corporate liquidation. Preferred stock is generally preferred as to assets upon corporate liquidation. Such a preference, however, cannot be assumed but must be specifically stated in the preferred stock contract. The asset preference for stock with a par value is an amount equal to par, or par plus a premium; in the absence of a par value it is a stated amount. Terms of the preferred contract may also provide for the full payment of any dividends in arrears upon liquidation, regardless of the retained earnings balance reported by the company. When this is the case and there are insufficient retained earnings or a deficit, such dividend priorities must be met from paid-in capital of the common issue; common stockholders receive whatever assets remain after settlement with the preferred group.

Common stock

Strictly speaking, there should be but one kind of common stock. Common stock represents the residual ownership equity and carries the greatest risk. In return for the risk that it carries, it ordinarily shares in earnings to the greatest extent if the corporation is successful. There is no inherent distinction in voting rights between preferred and common stocks. However, voting rights are frequently given exclusively to common stockholders as long as dividends are paid regularly on preferred stock; upon failure to meet preferred dividend requirements, special voting rights may be granted to preferred stockholders, thus affording this group a more prominent role in the management. In some states voting rights cannot be withheld on any class of stock.

Because of certain legal restrictions on preferred stock, some corporations have issued two types of common stock, known as Class A stock and Class B stock. One of the two types will have special preferences or rights that the other type does not have, such as dividend preferences or voting rights. The distinction between Class A and Class B stock, then, may be similar to that normally found between a company's preferred and common issues. The use of such classified common stocks has been so greatly abused that some stock exchanges have refused to list such issues, and this form of corporate financing has been largely discontinued.

Recording issuance of capital stock

The capital stock of a corporation may be authorized but unissued; it may be subscribed for and held for issuance pending receipt of cash on stock subscriptions; it may be outstanding in the hands of stockholders; it may be reacquired and held by the corporation for subsequent resale or bonus distribution; it may be canceled by appropriate corporate action. An accurate record of the position of the corporation as a result of the exchanges of property between stockholders and the corporation must be maintained in the accounts. Each class of stock requires separate accounting.

Recording the stock authorization. The *authorized capital stock* of a corporation is the maximum number of shares that can be issued under the conditions set by the charter. Application to the state is required in obtaining any change in the original authorization. The amount of stock authorized may be recorded by a memorandum entry and then reported in memorandum form in the capital stock account.

Recording the stock subscription. The agreement to purchase stock, known as a *subscription*, states the number of shares subscribed for, the subscription price, terms of payment, and other conditions of the transaction. This is a legally binding contract on the subscriber and the corporation. By express provisions, however, the contract may be binding only if the corporation receives subscriptions for a stated number of shares A subscription, while giving the corporation a legal claim for the contract price, also gives the subscriber the legal status of a stockholder unless certain rights as a stockholder are specifically withheld by law or by terms of the contract. Ordinarily stock certificates evidencing share ownership are not issued until the full subscription price has been received by the corporation.

Upon receiving subscriptions, Capital Stock Subscriptions Receivable is debited for the subscription price, Capital Stock Subscribed is credited for the amount that is to be recognized as capital stock when subscriptions have been collected, and an additional paid-in capital account is credited for the amount of the subscription price in excess of par or stated value.[1] When stock has a par value, such excess may simply be designated Premium on Capital Stock; when a stock is no-par with a stated value, the excess is designated Paid-In Capital from Sale of Capital Stock at More Than Stated Value. When no-par stock is without a stated value, Capital Stock Subscribed is credited for the full amount of the subscription. If the laws of the state of incorporation permit stock with a par value to be sold at a discount and subscriptions are received on such a basis, Capital Stock Subscriptions Receivable is debited for the subscription price, Discount on Capital Stock is debited for the discount, and Capital Stock Subscribed is credited for the stock par value. A special *subscribers journal* may be used in recording capital stock subscriptions.

Capital Stock Subscriptions Receivable is a controlling account, individual subscriptions being reported in the subsidiary *subscribers ledger*. Subscriptions Receivable is regarded as a current asset only when the corporation expects to collect the balance currently. This is normally

---

[1]The term "Capital Stock" is used in account titles in the text when the class of stock is not specifically designated. When preferred and common designations are given, these are used in the account titles.

the case.   When subscription amounts are due or are called for at different intervals, separate receivable or "call" balances may be established for amounts due on each collection date.   Balances currently receivable are recognized as current assets; remaining balances are regarded as noncurrent.   When subscription balances are to be collected only if cash is required and they are to be called for by the company, these balances may be appropriately considered a subtraction item in reporting paid-in capital.

Recording collection of subscriptions.   Subscriptions may be collected in cash or in other properties accepted by the corporation.   When collections are made, the appropriate asset account is debited and the receivable account is credited.   Credits are also made to subscribers' accounts in the subsidiary ledger.

Recording the issue of stock.   The issuance of stock is recorded by a debit to Capital Stock Subscribed and a credit to Capital Stock.   A *stockholders ledger* is controlled by the capital stock account; here separate accounts are maintained with each stockholder that report the number of shares issued.   The issuance of stock by the corporation calls for a credit to a stockholder's account for the shares issued.   A transfer of stock ownership is recorded by a charge to the account of the person making the transfer and a credit to the account of the person acquiring the stock; since capital stock outstanding remains the same after transfer of individual holdings, general ledger accounts are not affected.

A *stock certificate book* also reports shares outstanding.   Certificates in the book are usually serially numbered.   As certificates are issued, the number of shares issued is reported on the certificate stubs.   When ownership transfers, the original certificates submitted by the sellers are canceled and attached to the original stubs and new certificates are issued to the buyers.   Frequently a corporation will appoint banks or trust companies to serve as *registrars* and *transfer agents*.   These parties are assigned various responsibilities such as transferring stock certificates, maintaining the stockholders ledger, preparing lists of stockholders for meetings, and making dividend distributions.

Issue of capital stock illustrated

The examples presented on pages 670 and 671 illustrate the entries for the sale of stock when: (1) stock has a par value, (2) stock is no-par but has a stated value, and (3) stock is no-par and without a stated value. It is assumed that the Globe Corporation is granted permission to issue 10,000 shares of capital stock.

Transaction	Assuming stock is $10 par value
NOVEMBER 1 Received cash of $10,000 and equipment valued at $20,000 in exchange for 3,000 shares.	Cash.................. 10,000 Equipment.............. 20,000 Capital Stock......... 30,000

NOVEMBER 1–30
Received subscriptions for 5,000 shares at 12½ with 50% down payment, balance payable in 60 days.
	Capital Stock Subscriptions Receivable........ 62,500
	   Capital Stock Subscribed 50,000
	   Premium on Capital
	     Stock.............. 12,500
	
	Cash.................. 31,250
	   Capital Stock Subscriptions Receivable...... 31,250

DECEMBER 1–31
Received balance due on one half of subscriptions and issued stock to the fully paid subscribers, 2,500 shares.
	Cash.................. 15,625
	   Capital Stock Subscriptions Receivable...... 15,625
	
	Capital Stock Subscribed.. 25,000
	   Capital Stock......... 25,000

Stockholders' equity after the above transactions:	Stockholders' Equity
	Paid-in capital:
	  Capital stock, $10 par; authorized, 10,000 shares; issued and outstanding, 5,500 shares.... $55,000
	  Capital stock subscribed, 2,500 shares................. 25,000
	  Premium on capital stock....... 12,500
	
	  Total stockholders' equity...... $92,500

Subscription defaults

If a subscriber defaults on his subscription by failing to make a payment when it is due, the corporation may (1) return to the subscriber the amount paid, (2) return to the subscriber the amount paid less any reduction in price or expense incurred upon the resale of the stock, (3) declare the full amount that the subscriber has paid as forfeited, or (4) issue to the subscriber shares equal to the number paid for in full. The practice that is followed will depend upon the policy adopted by the corporation within the legal limitations set by the state in which it is incorporated. To illustrate the entries under the different circumstances mentioned, assume the subscription of $10 par capital stock at 12½. One subscriber for 100 shares defaults after making a 50% down payment. Defaulted shares are subsequently resold at 11. The entries to record the default by the subscriber and the subsequent resale of the defaulted shares would be made as follows:

Assuming stock is no-par but has a stated value of $10			Assuming stock is no-par and has no stated value		
Cash..................	10,000		Cash..................	10,000	
Equipment.............	20,000		Equipment.............	20,000	
Capital Stock........		30,000	Capital Stock.........		30,000
Capital Stock Subscriptions Receivable........	62,500		Capital Stock Subscriptions Receivable........	62,500	
Capital Stock Subscribed.............		50,000	Capital Stock Subscribed.............		62,500
Paid-In Capital from Sale of Capital Stock at More Than Stated Value..............		12,500			
Cash..................	31,250		Cash..................	31,250	
Capital Stock Subscriptions Receivable.....		31,250	Capital Stock Subscriptions Receivable.....		31,250
Cash..................	15,625		Cash..................	15,625	
Capital Stock Subscriptions Receivable.....		15,625	Capital Stock Subscriptions Receivable.......		15,625
Capital Stock Subscribed..	25,000		Capital Stock Subscribed..	31,250	
Capital Stock.........		25,000	Capital Stock.........		31,250
Stockholders' Equity			**Stockholders' Equity**		
Paid-in capital:			Paid-in capital:		
Capital stock, $10 stated value; authorized, 10,000 shares; issued and outstanding, 5,500 shares...................		$55,000	Capital stock, no-par; authorized, 10,000 shares; issued and outstanding, 5,500 shares		$61,250
Capital stock subscribed, 2,500 shares...................		25,000	Capital stock subscribed, 2,500 shares..................		31,250
Paid-in capital from sale of capital stock at more than stated value..............		12,500			
Total stockholders' equity......		$92,500	Total stockholders' equity.......		$92,500

(1) Assuming that the amount paid in is returned:

Capital Stock Subscribed.........................	1,000	
Premium on Capital Stock.......................	250	
Capital Stock Subscriptions Receivable............		625
Cash..		625
Cash..	1,100	
Capital Stock.....................................		1,000
Premium on Capital Stock......................		100

(2) Assuming that the amount paid in less the price reduction on the resale is returned:

Capital Stock Subscribed.........................	1,000	
Premium on Capital Stock.......................	250	
Capital Stock Subscriptions Receivable............		625
Payable to Defaulting Subscriber (payment withheld pending stock resale)........................		625
Cash..	1,100	
Payable to Defaulting Subscriber...................	150	
Capital Stock.....................................		1,000
Premium on Capital Stock.......................		250
Payable to Defaulting Subscriber...................	475	
Cash..		475

(3) Assuming that the full amount paid in is declared to be forfeited:

Capital Stock Subscribed.........................	1,000	
Premium on Capital Stock........................	250	
Capital Stock Subscriptions Receivable...........		625
Paid-In Capital from Forfeited Stock Subscriptions..		625
Cash..	1,100	
Capital Stock.................................		1,000
Premium on Capital Stock......................		100

(4) Assuming that shares equal to the number paid for in full are issued:

Capital Stock Subscribed.........................	1,000	
Premium on Capital Stock........................	125	
Capital Stock.................................		500
Capital Stock Subscriptions Receivable...........		625
Cash..	550	
Capital Stock.................................		500
Premium on Capital Stock......................		50

Recording authorized stock in the accounts

If it is desired to maintain a record of the stock authorized as well as unissued in the accounts, stock transactions may be recorded by an alternative method. Stock authorized, instead of being recognized by a memorandum entry, is recorded by a formal entry in which Unissued Capital Stock is debited and Authorized Capital Stock is credited. Subscriptions and payments are recorded as in the previous examples. The issue of stock, however, calls for a debit to Capital Stock Subscribed and a credit to Unissued Capital Stock. The balance in Authorized Capital Stock less the balance in Unissued Capital Stock gives the amount of stock issued at any time. The alternate procedure applied to the sale of $10 par capital stock in the example on page 670 follows:

Transaction	Entry		

NOVEMBER 1
 Received authorization to issue 10,000 shares of capital stock, par $10.
	Unissued Capital Stock..
	   Authorized Capital
	     Stock..............
		100,000	100,000

NOVEMBER 1
 Received cash of $10,000 and equipment valued at $20,000 in exchange for 3,000 shares.
	Cash................
	 Equipment...........
	   Unissued Capital
	     Stock..............
		10,000
		 20,000
			30,000

NOVEMBER 1–30
 Received subscriptions for 5,000 shares at 12½ with 50% down payment, balance payable in 60 days.
	Capital Stock Subscriptions Receivable..
	   Capital Stock Subscribed...........
	   Premium on Capital
	     Stock..............
		62,500	50,000
			 12,500

	Cash................ Capital Stock Subscriptions Receivable	31,250	31,250

Transaction	Entry		
DECEMBER 1–31 Received balance due on one half of the subscriptions and issued stock to the fully paid subscribers, 2,500 shares.	Cash................	15,625	
	Capital Stock Subscriptions Receivable		15,625
	Capital Stock Subscribed.............	25,000	
	Unissued Capital Stock............		25,000

Paid-in capital may be reported on the balance sheet in the same manner as shown on page 670.

The foregoing method can be used only for stock with a par or stated value; in these instances the valuation to be applied to the entire issue is known at the time of stock authorization. Since the first method illustrated on pages 670 and 671 is the simpler one and may be used for both par and no-par issues, its use is assumed in the remaining examples.

Sale of security units for a single sum

Corporations sometimes sell for a single-sum price *security units* consisting of two or more classes of securities. In recording sales of this kind, the sales proceeds must be allocated among the different issues. When a sale consists of two different securities and both have a known market value, the single sum may be allocated to the securities according to their relative market values. If only one of the securities has a known market value, the sales price of the other may be determined by subtracting the known value from the sales price of the unit. To illustrate, assume that 1 share of common stock, par $100, is offered with each $1,000, 6% bond at $1,050. If the common stock is selling for $80 per share, this value is assigned to common and the sales price applicable to the bonds is calculated as follows:

Unit price of $1,000 bond together with 1 share of common.. $1,050
Price identified with common share (market price)........... 80
Price identified with bond................................ $ 970

A discount should thus be identified with both the common shares and the bonds. The entry to record the sale of 100 units would be:

Cash.. 105,000
Discount on Common Stock.................... 2,000
Discount on Bonds Payable................... 3,000
   Common Stock, $100 par.................. 10,000
   Bonds Payable.......................... 100,000

If two kinds of stock are offered as a unit, the procedure is similar. For example, assume that 2 shares of common, par $25, are offered with 5 shares of preferred, par $100, at $550 per unit. If the preferred stock has a market price of $96 per share, the sales price applicable to common stock is calculated as follows:

Unit price of 5 shares of preferred and 2 shares of common....	$550
Price identified with 5 shares of preferred (market price, $96 x 5).	480
Price identified with 2 shares of common.....................	$ 70

The entry to record the sale of 100 units, consisting of 500 shares of preferred and 200 shares of common, at $550 per unit would be:

Cash..	55,000	
Discount on Preferred Stock.....................	2,000	
Preferred Stock, $100 par......................		50,000
Common Stock, $25 par.......................		5,000
Premium on Common Stock...................		2,000

If in the previous case the price charged for each unit had been $500, the common stock might have been designated a "bonus" and offered as an inducement on the purchase of preferred. The market price of the several issues should still be recognized, if determinable. Here the apportionment of proceeds would be made as follows:

Unit price of 5 shares of preferred and 2 shares of common....	$500
Price identified with 5 shares of preferred (market price, $96 x 5).	480
Price identified with 2 shares of common....................	$ 20

The entry to record the sale follows:

Cash..	50,000	
Discount on Preferred Stock.....................	2,000	
Discount on Common Stock.....................	3,000	
Preferred Stock, $100 par......................		50,000
Common Stock, $25 par.......................		5,000

If neither preferred nor common stock has a market price that can be applied in allocating the sales price, it may be necessary to charge the difference between the combined par values and the sales price to Discount on Preferred and Common Stocks. This balance should be reported as a subtraction item in presenting the invested capital of the corporation and should be closed when the sales price can be allocated to the individual securities. However, if the unit consists of bonds and stock and neither has a market value, it will be necessary to estimate the amount at which the bonds could be sold since the sale of bonds at a figure other than face value requires discount or premium amortization in measuring periodic income.

Capital stock issued for consideration other than cash

When capital stock is issued for consideration in the form of property other than cash or for services, particular care is required in recording the transaction. When, at the time of the exchange, stock is sold by the company for cash or is quoted on the open market at a certain price, such price can be used in recording the consideration received and the capital increase. When means for arriving at the cash value of the securities are not available, it will be necessary to arrive at a value for the consideration that was acquired.

It may be possible to arrive at a satisfactory valuation of property received in exchange for stock through an appraisal by a competent outside authority. But such a solution may not be available in arriving at a valuation for consideration in the form of certain services as, for example, promotional services in organizing the corporation.

Normally the board of directors is given the right by law to establish valuations for consideration other than cash that is received for stock. Such values will stand for all legal purposes in the absence of proof that fraud was involved in the action. [1] The assignment of values by the board of directors should be subject to particularly careful scrutiny. There have been instances where directors have assigned excessive values to the consideration for stock to avoid the recognition of a discount on the issue of stock or to improve the company's reported financial position. When the value of the consideration cannot be clearly established and the directors' valuations are used in reporting assets and invested capital, the source of the valuations should be disclosed on the balance sheet. When there is evidence that improper values have been assigned to the consideration received for stock, such values should be restated.

Stock is said to be *watered* when assets are overstated and capital items are correspondingly overstated. On the other hand, the balance sheet is said to contain *secret reserves* when there is an understatement of assets or an overstatement of liabilities accompanied by a corresponding understatement of capital. Such misstatements may be intentional or unintentional. The accountant cannot condone either overstatement or understatement of net assets and capital. It should be observed once more that any failures in accounting for assets are not limited to the balance sheet: the overstatement of assets will result in understatements of net income as asset cost is assigned to revenue; the understatement of assets will result in overstatements of net income as asset cost is assigned to revenue.

---

[1] Section 1112 of the California Corporation Code (as amended through 1969) provides, for example, as follows: "The board of directors shall state by resolution its determinations of the fair value to the corporation in monetary terms of any consideration other than money for which shares with or without par value are issued. In the absence of fraud in making the determination of value, it shall be conclusive."

Treatment of premium and discount on sale of capital stock

Amounts received on the sale of capital stock give rise to paid-in capital. When the amount received on the sale of stock is greater than the par or stated value assigned to the stock, the excess is recorded separately as a premium or special paid-in capital balance and is carried on the books as long as the stock to which it relates is outstanding. When stock is retired, the capital stock balance, as well as any related paid-in capital balance, must be canceled.

When capital stock is sold at less than par, a discount is recorded. As stated previously, such discount indicates a claim that may be made by creditors upon stockholders in the event the company becomes insolvent; from a going-concern point of view, however, the discount should be recognized as a subtraction item in presenting the company's paid-in capital. There have been cases in practice where discounts on stock have been applied directly against paid-in capital balances arising from stock premiums or other sources. In other instances, discounts have been recognized as intangible assets or deferred costs and have been written off against periodic revenue. Such practices are objectionable. The absorption of a discount by positive paid-in capital balances serves only to obscure the original stockholders' investment as well as the claim that may be made upon stockholders by creditors. An account balance reporting a discount on stock does not indicate the ownership of an asset. Write-off of the discount against revenue is even more objectionable, for this not only obscures significant information relative to the stockholders' equity but also distorts periodic income. The discount should be carried on the books as long as the capital stock to which it relates is outstanding.

Capital stock assessments

Laws of some states provide that a corporation requiring additional funds may levy assessments upon stockholders. Failure of a stockholder to comply with such special levies by the corporation may result in stock forfeiture. If stock was originally issued at a discount, an additional cash contribution is recognized as a reduction in the discount; if legal capital requirements were fully met by original investments, assessments represent further increases in corporate paid-in capital. A capital stock assessment and its subsequent collection are recorded as follows:

Capital Stock Assessments Receivable..............	50,000	
Discount on Capital Stock (or Paid-In Capital from Capital Stock Assessments)...............		50,000
Cash...	50,000	
Capital Stock Assessments Receivable...........		50,000

Issuance of capital stock in exchange for a business

A corporation, upon its formation or at some later date, may take over a going business, issuing capital stock in exchange for the properties that are acquired. In determining the amount of the stock to be issued for business assets, the fair market value of the stock, as well as the values of the properties acquired, must be considered. Frequently the value of the stock transferred by the corporation will exceed the value of the identifiable assets acquired because of the favorable earnings record of the business acquired. If the exchange is recognized as a purchase, the value of the stock in excess of the values assigned to identifiable assets is recognized as goodwill. On the other hand, if the exchange is recognized as a pooling of interests, neither the revaluation of assets nor the recognition of goodwill is recorded. Assets are stated at the amounts previously reported; stockholders' equity is increased by the amount of the net increase in assets.

Incorporation of a sole proprietorship or partnership

When a sole proprietorship or partnership is incorporated to secure the advantages of the corporate form of organization, the books of the old organization may be used after the changes that have taken place as a result of the incorporation are recorded, or a new set of records may be opened. The accounting procedure to be followed in each instance will be illustrated. Assume that Martin and Moore, partners who share earnings and losses in a ratio of 3:2 respectively, desire to retire from active participation in their business, and they form a corporation to take over partnership assets. The partnership balance sheet just before incorporation on March 15, 1972, follows:

Martin and Moore
Balance Sheet
March 15, 1972

Assets			Liabilities and Owners' Equity	
Cash..................		$ 8,600	Accounts payable...............	$12,000
Accounts receivable....	$15,000		Martin, capital.................	50,000
Less allowance for doubt-			Moore, capital.................	16,200
ful accounts.........	400	14,600		
Inventories............		20,000		
Equipment............	$50,000			
Less accumulated de-				
preciation — equip-				
ment..............	15,000	35,000		
Total assets...........		$78,200	Total liabilities and owners' equity	$78,200

The corporation is organized as the United Corporation and is authorized to issue 25,000 shares of no-par stock. Fifteen thousand shares are sold at $10. The corporation takes over partnership assets other than cash and assumes partnership liabilities in exchange for the remaining 10,000 shares. In taking over net assets, the corporation makes the following adjustments:

1. The allowance for doubtful accounts is increased to $1,000.
2. Inventories are recorded at their present market value of $23,500.
3. Equipment is recorded at its appraised value of $52,500.
4. Accrued expenses of $400 are recorded.

The 10,000 shares received by the partners are divided as follows: Martin, 7,500 shares; Moore, 2,500 shares. The cash of $8,600 is then withdrawn by the partners according to the balances remaining in their capital accounts.

If original books are retained. If the partnership books are retained, entries are first made to indicate the changes in assets, liabilities, and the partners' interests prior to incorporation. A revaluation account may be charged with losses and credited with gains resulting from revaluations, and the balance in this account may subsequently be closed into the capital accounts in the earnings distribution ratio. However, with relatively few changes in asset and liability balances, gains and losses may be reported directly in the capital accounts. In recording the issuance of stock in exchange for the partners' equities, the partners' capital accounts are charged and Capital Stock is credited. Subsequent corporate transactions are recorded in the old books that have become the records for the newly-formed corporation. The entries to record the incorporation follow:

Transaction	Entry		
(a) To record revaluation of assets upon transfer to United Corporation, the net gain from revaluation and adjustments of $20,000 being credited to Martin and Moore in the earnings distribution ratio of 3:2 respectively.	Inventories............	3,500	
	Equipment............	2,500	
	Accumulated Deprecia-		
	tion — Equipment...	15,000	
	Allowance for Doubt-		
	ful Accounts........		600
	Accrued Expenses....		400
	Martin, Capital......		12,000
	Moore, Capital......		8,000
(b) To record goodwill as indicated by excess of value of stock issued to partners over the appraised value of net assets transferred:	Goodwill..............	22,400	
	Martin, Capital......		13,440
	Moore, Capital......		8,960
Value of stock issued (10,000 shares at $10, price at which stock is currently being sold)......... $100,000			
Value of net assets transferred:			
Assets............. $90,000			
Less liabilities...... 12,400 77,600			
Goodwill credited to partners in earnings distribution ratio........ $ 22,400			

Transaction	Entry		
(c) To record distribution of capital stock according to agreement: Martin — 7,500 shares valued at $10 .... $ 75,000 Moore — 2,500 shares valued at $10 .... $ 25,000	Martin, Capital .... Moore, Capital .... Capital Stock	75,000 25,000	100,000
(d) To record distribution of cash in final settlement of partners' claims according to balances in capital accounts: Martin Moore Capital after adjustment .... $75,440 $33,160 Less payment in stock .. 75,000 25,000 Balance paid in cash ... $ 440 $ 8,160	Martin, Capital .... Moore, Capital .... Cash	440 8,160	8,600
(e) To record sale of 15,000 shares at $10.	Cash .... Capital Stock	150,000	150,000

A balance sheet for the corporation after the foregoing transactions is shown below:

United Corporation
Balance Sheet
March 15, 1973

Assets			Liabilities	
Cash		$150,000	Accounts payable	$ 12,000
Accounts receivable ...	$15,000		Accrued expenses	400
Less allowance for doubtful accounts ...	1,000	14,000		$ 12,400
Inventories		23,500	Stockholders' Equity	
Equipment		52,500	Capital stock, no-par, authorized	
Goodwill		22,400	and issued, 25,000 shares	250,000
			Total liabilities and stockholders'	
Total assets		$262,400	equity	$262,400

If new books are opened for the corporation. If new books are opened for the corporation, all of the accounts on the partnership books are closed and partnership assets and liabilities are recorded on the new records. In closing the partnership books, entries are made to record the transfer of assets and liabilities to the corporation, the receipt of capital stock, and the distribution of stock and cash in payment of partners' respective interests. If desired, it would be possible to record the revaluation of assets and the recognition of goodwill before recording the transfer of assets and liabilities. Entries to close the partnership books for Martin and Moore may be made as shown on the following page.

It may be mentioned that for federal income tax purposes, when individual owners of a business transfer assets and immediately after such a

Transaction	Entry		
To record the transfer of assets and liabilities to United Corporation, the difference between claim against vendee, $100,000 (10,000 shares of stock valued at $10), and book value of net assets transferred, $57,600, representing gain on sale of business of $42,400. The gain is distributed to partners in the ratio of 3:2 as follows: To Martin: ⅗ of $42,400...... $25,440 To Moore: ⅖ of 42,400...... 16,960 ——— $42,400	Receivable from United Corporation.......... Accounts Payable...... Allowance for Doubtful Accounts........... Accumulated Depreciation — Equipment.... Accounts Receivable.. Inventories......... Equipment.......... Martin, Capital...... Moore, Capital......	100,000 12,000 400 15,000	 15,000 20,000 50,000 25,440 16,960
To record the receipt of capital stock in payment of net assets transferred.	Stock of United Corporation................. Receivable from United Corporation.	100,000	 100,000
To record distribution of capital stock according to agreement.	Martin, Capital........ Moore, Capital........ Stock of United Corporation........	75,000 25,000	 100,000
To record distribution of cash in final settlement of partners' claims according to balances in capital accounts.	Martin, Capital........ Moore, Capital........ Cash..............	440 8,160	 8,600

The entries on the separate corporation books would be as follows:

Transaction	Entry		
To record acquisition of assets and liabilities from Martin and Moore.	Accounts Receivable.... Inventories........... Equipment........... Goodwill............. Allowance for Doubtful Accounts....... Accounts Payable.... Accrued Expenses.... Payable to Martin and Moore...........	15,000 23,500 52,500 22,400	 1,000 12,000 400 100,000
To record issuance of 10,000 shares of stock in payment of net assets acquired.	Payable to Martin and Moore............. Capital Stock........	100,000	 100,000
To record sale of 15,000 shares of stock for cash.	Cash................. Capital Stock........	150,000	 150,000

transfer have "control" of the corporation, no gain or loss is recognized on the transfer, and the basis for the property transferred is the same for the corporation as it was for the original owners. Depreciation, then, would continue to be reported in terms of cost to the original owners, and any gain or loss on the disposal of an asset would be recognized on the basis of original cost less depreciation previously allowed or allowable. Control is defined by the tax law as ownership of stock possessing at least 80 percent of the total voting power together with at least 80 percent of the total number of shares of all other classes of stock of the corporation.

QUESTIONS

1. Mark Jones has been operating a small machine shop for several months. His business has grown, and he has given some thought to incorporating his business. What advantages and disadvantages would there be to such a change?

2. What are the four basic rights of stockholders?

3. Distinguish between: (a) a domestic corporation and a foreign corporation, (b) a stock corporation and a nonstock corporation, (c) an open corporation and a close corporation.

4. (a) Define legal capital. (b) What limitations are placed upon the corporation by law to safeguard legal capital?

5. (a) Distinguish between par stock and no-par stock. (b) What classes of no-par stock may be found?

6. Name the advantages and the disadvantages applying to no-par stock as compared with par-value stock.

7. (a) What preferences are usually granted preferred stockholders? (b) What is redeemable preferred stock? (c) What is convertible preferred stock? (d) Distinguish between (1) cumulative and noncumulative preferred stock and (2) participating and nonparticipating preferred stock. (e) What limitations on stockholders' rights are generally found in preferred stock?

8. (a) Describe the method of accounting for the issuance of capital stock when authorized and unissued accounts are used. (b) Describe the method of accounting when these accounts are not used.

9. Indicate how the balance of each of the following accounts is reported on the balance sheet: (a) Capital Stock Subscriptions Receivable; (b) Capital Stock Subscribed; (c) Unissued Capital Stock; (d) Authorized Capital Stock.

10. Describe each of the following records: (a) minutes book, (b) subscribers ledger, (c) stockholders ledger, (d) stock certificate book.

11. Although subscriptions receivable are generally presented as an asset, the theoretical propriety of such presentation has been questioned and it has been suggested that they be treated as a subtraction item in reporting the stockholders' equity. What questions can you raise as to the general treatment and what support can you provide for the alternate presentation?

12. The Benson Co. treats proceeds from capital stock subscription defaults as miscellaneous income. Would you approve this practice?

13. (a) How should cash proceeds be assigned to individual securities when two different securities are sold for a single sum? (b) Would your answer differ if one of the securities is designated a bonus? Give reasons for your answer.

14. (a) What are "secret reserves"? (b) The treasurer of one of your clients is in favor of secret reserves as a means of achieving "balance sheet conservatism." What is your comment?

15. Evaluate the following statement: Capital stock is "watered" when it is sold at a price in excess of its book value.

16. The Paxton Co. issues 5,000 shares of common stock to persons organizing and promoting the company and another 20,000 shares in exchange for properties that are believed to have valuable mineral rights. The par value of the stock, $10 per share, is used in recording the consideration for the shares. Shortly after organization the company decides to sell the properties and use the proceeds for another venture. The property is sold for cash of $65,000. How would you record the sale of the properties?

17. The Warner Corporation issues 100,000 shares of common stock, $10 par value, in exchange for certain patents and secret processes. The board of directors authorizes that the assets acquired be reported at $1,000,000. Would you accept this valuation in auditing the financial statements for this company? Explain your position fully.

18. The Bailey Co. records the discount on common stock issued as organization cost and writes this balance off against periodic revenue. What objections do you have to this treatment?

19. (a) What is a capital stock assessment? (b) What entry is made upon the collection of such an assessment if (1) shares were originally issued at a discount and (2) shares were originally issued at par?

20. The Walsh Company acquires the assets of the Goodman Company in exchange for 10,000 shares of its common stock, par value $10. (a) Assuming that the appraised value of the property acquired exceeds the par value of the stock issued, how would you record the acquisition? (b) Assuming that the par value of the stock issued exceeds the appraised value of the property acquired, suggest different methods for recording the acquisition. What factors will determine the method to be used?

EXERCISES

1. The Dearden Company pays out dividends at the end of each year as follows: 1970, $75,000; 1971, $120,000; 1972, $280,000. Give the amount that will be paid per share on common and preferred stock for each year, assuming capital structures as follows:

(a) 250,000 shares of no-par common; 10,000 shares of $100 par, 7%, non-cumulative, nonparticipating preferred.

(b) 250,000 shares of $10 par common; 10,000 shares of $100 par, 7%, cumulative, fully participating preferred, dividends three years in arrears at the beginning of 1970.

(c) 250,000 shares of $10 par common; $15,000 shares of $100 par, 7%, cumulative, nonparticipating preferred, no dividends in arrears at the beginning of 1970.

(d) 250,000 shares of $10 par common; 10,000 shares of $100 par, 7%, noncumulative, preferred, participating up to 8%.

2. Morris, Inc., has 500,000 shares of no-par common and 300,000 shares of $50 par, 6% preferred outstanding. Preferred is cumulative. It also participates with common at the rate of fifty cents for every dollar paid to common after common receives $3 per share, but preferred participation is limited to a total of $5 per share. Give the amounts that would be paid on each share of preferred and common each year, assuming dividend distributions as follows: 1970, $500,000; 1971, $2,500,000; and 1972, $5,000,000.

3. The stockholders' equity for the Dodge Corporation on July 1, 1972, is as follows:

10,000 shares of no-par, $1 cumulative preferred, entitled upon involuntary liquidation to $20 per share plus dividends in arrears amounting to $8 per share on July 1, 1972	$185,000
90,000 shares of no-par common, $1 stated value.........	90,000
Paid-in capital from sale of common stock at more than stated value.....................................	200,000
Retained earnings.....................................	28,000
Total stockholders' equity.............................	$503,000

Give the amounts that would be paid to each class of stockholders if the company is liquidated on this date, assuming cash available for stockholders after meeting all of the creditors' claims is: (a) $170,000; (b) $240,000; (c) $300,000.

4. The Raydon Corporation was organized and immediately sold its authorized stock of 75,000 shares at $15. Assuming balances for the stockholders' equity as reported at the top of the following page, describe fully the stock which was sold in each case.

Case 1

Common stock...................................	$ 750,000
Premium on common stock.......................	375,000
	$1,125,000

Case 2

Common stock...................................	$ 375,000
Paid-in capital from sale of common stock at more than stated value..................................	750,000
	$1,125,000

Case 3

Preferred stock.................................	$ 225,000
Common stock..................................	270,000
Premium on preferred stock.....................	225,000
Premium on common stock......................	405,000
	$1,125,000

5. The Richmond Corporation is organized with authorized capital as follows: 20,000 shares of no-par common and 4,000 shares of 8% preferred, par $100. Give the entries that are required for each of the following transactions:

(a) Assets formerly owned by B. Cassie are accepted as payment for 8,000 shares of common stock. Assets are recorded at values as follows: land, $30,000; buildings, $35,000; inventories, $95,000.

(b) Remaining common stock is sold at $22.50.

(c) Subscriptions are received for 3,000 shares of preferred stock at 103. A 20% down payment is made on preferred.

(d) One subscriber for 300 shares of preferred defaults and his down payment is retained pending sale of this lot. Remaining subscribers pay the balances due and the stock is issued.

(e) Lot of 300 shares of preferred is sold at 101. Loss on resale is charged against the account of the defaulting subscriber, and the down payment less the loss is returned to him.

6. On January 1, 1972, Jensen Corporation received authorization to issue 100,000 shares of no-par common stock with a stated value of $10 per share. The stock was offered to subscribers at a subscription price of $50 per share. Subscriptions were recorded by a debit to Subscriptions Receivable and credits to Common Stock Subscribed and to an additional paid-in capital account. Subsequently a subscriber who had contracted to purchase 100 shares defaulted after paying 40% of the subscription price. Give four methods of accounting for the default, and give the journal entry to record the default under each method.

7. J. Luber subscribed to 100 shares of Kapp Industries no-par stock on July 30, at $35. A down payment of 20% was required, and he paid

50% of the remaining balance due on August 30. In September a business loss made it necessary for Luber to default on his subscription. The shares were then sold by the company at $30. (a) What rule for the default was applied if the amount of the refund was (1) $2,100, (2) $1,600, (3) None. (b) Give the journal entries on the books of the corporation for the subscription, for the subsequent payment on the subscription, and for the refund of $1,600 under the second assumption above.

8. Marshall, Inc., receives authorization to issue 10,000 shares of common stock, $50 par. Subscriptions are received for 6,000 shares at $60, cash is received in full, and the stock is issued. (a) What entries would be made if the unissued and authorized accounts are used in recording subscriptions? (b) Prepare the stockholders' equity section of the balance sheet after the foregoing transactions.

9. The trial balance for the Hopkins Corporation includes the following account balances: Unissued Stock, $275,000; Capital Stock Authorized, $1,000,000; Discount on Capital Stock, $30,000; Capital Stock Subscribed, $200,000; Deficit, $20,000. (a) Summarize the stockholders' equity as it would be reported on the balance sheet. (b) Assuming that the trial balance also reports receivables from subscribers at this date of $60,000, how much has been paid into the company by stockholders to date?

10. The Bloomington Co. issues 20,000 shares of preferred stock and 90,000 shares of common stock, each with a par value of $10, in exchange for properties appraised at $1,150,000. Give the entry to record the exchange on the books of the corporation assuming that:

(a) No price can be assigned at date of issuance to the preferred stock or common stock issues.
(b) Common stock is selling on the market at $10.50 per share; there was no preferred stock issued prior to this issue.
(c) Common stock is selling on the market at $10 per share; preferred stock is selling on the market at $15 per share.

11. Bonds of $1,000,000 are sold at 105, 5 shares of common stock, par $10, being offered as a bonus with each $1,000 bond. At the time the bonds are sold on this basis, stock is selling on the market at $12 per share. What entry would be made to record the sale of the bonds?

12. Bell, Inc., sells 2,000 shares of its 5% cumulative preferred stock, par $100, to an investment group for $230,000, giving 1 share of common stock, par $50, as a bonus with every 4 shares of preferred. The market value of the preferred stock immediately following the sale is $103 per share. What is the entry for the sale?

13. The ledger of Reynolds and Wilson shows the following data on December 31: assets, $78,000; liabilities, $30,000; Reynolds, capital, $19,100; Wilson, capital, $28,900. The partners decide to sell the business to Wards, Inc., in exchange for 3,500 shares of that corporation's $10 par common stock. The market value of the stock at this time is $14. The assets acquired are considered to be stated at their fair market values. (a) What entries are required (1) to record the purchase in the corporation accounts, (2) to close the partnership books, assuming earnings and losses are shared equally by the partners? (b) How many shares in the new corporation will be distributed to each partner?

14. A balance sheet for Roberts and Simmons, prepared on March 15, appears below. Partners share earnings and losses in the ratio of 3:1 respectively.

Assets			Liabilities and Owners' Equity	
Cash............		$ 2,000	Accounts payable..........	$ 5,100
Accounts receivable.	$ 6,200		Roberts, capital..........	22,500
Less allowance for			Simmons, capital.........	17,300
doubtful accounts	600	5,600		
Inventories........		10,300		
Equipment........	$30,000			
Less accumulated				
depreciation.....	8,000	22,000		
Goodwill..........		5,000		
			Total liabilities and owners'	
Total assets........		$44,900	equity.................	$44,900

An appraisal of the assets discloses the following current values:

Inventories... $13,800
Equipment.. 25,000

The Webster Co. issues 7,000 shares of $1 par common stock to the partners in exchange for partnership assets other than cash. The corporation also agrees to assume partnership obligations. On this date the corporation stock has a market value of $6 per share. In dissolving the partnership, Roberts agrees to take 4,000 shares and Simmons, 3,000 shares. The partnership cash is then appropriately divided between the partners. Give the entries to record the foregoing on the books of the partnership and on the new books of the corporation.

PROBLEMS

19-1. The Hollingsworth Co. was organized on April 10, 1972, and was authorized to issue stock as follows:

200,000 shares of no-par common stock with a stated value of $10
5,000 shares of $5\frac{1}{2}\%$ preferred stock with a par value of $100

Capital stock transactions through September 1, 1972, were as follows:

May 15   Subscriptions were received for 100,000 shares of common stock at $15 on the following terms: 10% was paid in cash at the time of subscription, the balance being payable in three equal installments due on the fifteenth day of each succeeding month.

June 1   All of the preferred stock was sold to an investment company for cash at $95 and stock was issued.

June 15   The first installment on subscriptions to 97,600 shares was collected. Terms of the subscription contract provided that defaulting subscribers have 30 days in which to make payment and obtain reinstatement; failure to make payment within the specified period will result in the forfeiture of amounts already paid in.

July 15   The second installment on common subscriptions was collected. Collections included receipt of the first and second installment on 400 shares from subscribers who defaulted on their first installment; however, subscribers to 500 shares defaulted in addition to subscribers already in default.

Aug. 15   The third installment on common subscriptions was collected. Collections included receipt of the second and third installment from subscribers to 400 shares who defaulted on their second installment. Stock certificates were issued to fully paid subscribers.

Sept. 1   Stock in default was sold to an investment company at 13.

Instructions: (1) Give the journal entries to record these transactions.
(2) Prepare a balance sheet summarizing the transactions above.

19-2. The Baxter and Bradford Co. was organized on September 2, 1972, with authorized capital stock as follows:

6% cumulative preferred, $100 par.................. 10,000 shares
Common, no-par.................................250,000 shares

Statutes of the state of incorporation provide that the board of directors may set a stated value on no-par stock, but that such stated value shall not be less than $10 per share. The board of directors set the stated value at this minimum.

During the remainder of 1972 the following transactions took place:

(a) Assets of Baxter and Bradford were taken over in exchange for 80,000 shares of common stock. Assets of the partnership were appraised as follows:

Merchandise inventory..................... $250,000
Equipment................................ 475,000

The excess of the stated value of the stock issued over the appraised value of tangible assets acquired was regarded as payment for goodwill.

(b) 3,000 shares of preferred stock were sold at par.

(c) 70,000 shares of common stock were sold at $11.

(d) Subscriptions were received for 50,000 shares of common at $12; the stock is to be paid for in two equal installments, 50% being paid on the date of subscription and 50% to be paid within 90 days from the date of subscription.

(e) By December 31, $120,000 had been collected from subscribers as second installments on common subscriptions, and stock fully paid for was issued.

Instructions: (1) Give the journal entries to record the foregoing transactions, assuming the use of unissued and authorized accounts.

(2) Give the journal entries to record the foregoing transactions, assuming that unissued and authorized accounts are not used.

(3) Give the stockholders' equity section of the balance sheet on December 31, 1972.

19-3. The balance sheet of the Martin Corporation prepared on April 30, 1972, showed the following information:

Current assets:

Subscriptions receivable — common stock......		$ 11,000
Subscriptions receivable — preferred stock.....		7,000

Capital stock:

Preferred — 5% cumulative, $40 par; authorized 4,000 shares; issued and outstanding, 1,300 shares................................	$ 52,000	
Subscribed, but not issued, 300 shares.........	12,000	$ 64,000
Common — no par or stated value; authorized 90,000 shares; issued and outstanding, 60,000 shares................................	$150,000	
Subscribed, but not issued, 5,000 shares........	15,000	165,000
Premium on preferred stock...................		5,000

Martin Corporation issues stock certificates only upon the full payment of subscriptions. Subscriptions were received for the preferred shares as follows:

1,100 shares......................................	at par
500 shares.......................................	at $50 per share

Instructions: Prepare entries for the transactions that are indicated by the foregoing data.

19-4. The Oliver Machine Co. was incorporated on January 20, 1972, with authorized common stock of $2,000,000 and 6% cumulative preferred stock of $450,000, each class with a par value of $50.

Subscriptions were received for 8,000 shares of common stock at $60 a share, to be paid in four equal installments on March 1, April 1, May 1, and June 1. The first installment was paid in full. Subscribers for 300 shares defaulted on the second installment, and the amounts already received from these subscribers were returned. The second, third, and fourth installments were paid in full on their due dates by the remaining subscribers, and the stock was issued.

During March, preferred stock was offered for sale at $65, 1 share of common stock being offered with each subscription for 10 shares of preferred. On this basis subscriptions were received for all of the preferred stock. Subscriptions were payable in two equal installments: the first was payable by the end of March and the second was payable at any time prior to June 15. The first installment was paid in full. By June 1, $234,000 had been received on the second installment, and stock was issued to the fully paid subscribers.

Instructions: (1) Journalize the above transactions.
(2) Prepare a balance sheet as of June 1 reflecting the foregoing.

19-5. You obtained the following information concerning the Morris Company's stockholders' equity balances as of December 31, 1972. The corporation was formed January 1, 1970.

(a) 500 shares of $50 par, 6% preferred stock were authorized; one half of the shares were sold at the beginning of 1970 at $65. The stock is preferred as to dividends and is callable at any time at $70 plus dividends in arrears.

(b) 10,000 shares of $100 par common stock were authorized; 60% of the shares were sold at the beginning of 1970 at $105. No dividends have been paid on common stock to date.

(c) Undistributed earnings of the Morris Company for the three years of its operations were as follows:

1970	$175,000
1971	75,000
1972	40,000

Instructions: Prepare the stockholders' equity section of the Morris Company balance sheet including any special notes required for full disclosure.

19-6. The Wyman Corporation was organized on September 1, 1972, with an authorized capital stock of 200,000 shares of 6% cumulative preferred with a $30 par value and 500,000 shares of no-par common with a $25 stated value. During the balance of the year the following transactions relating to capital stock were completed:

Oct. 1 Subscriptions were received for 300,000 shares of common stock at 40, payable $15 down and the balance in two equal installments due November 1 and December 1. On the same date 15,000 shares of common stock were issued to Jim Wyman in exchange for his business. Assets transferred to the corporation were valued as follows: land, $180,000; buildings, $210,000; equipment, $60,000; merchandise, $104,500. Liabilities of the business assumed by the corporation were: mortgage payable, $37,000; accounts payable, $10,500; accrued interest on mortgage, $450. No goodwill is recognized in recording the issuance of the stock for net assets.

Oct. 3 Subscriptions were received for 120,000 shares of preferred stock at $32, payable $12 down and the balance in two equal installments due on November 1 and December 1.

Nov. 1 Amounts due on this date were collected from all common and preferred stock subscribers.

Nov. 12 Subscriptions were received for 120,000 shares of common stock at $38, payable $15 down and the balance in two equal installments due December 1 and January 1.

Dec. 1 Amounts due on this date were collected from all common stock subscribers and stock fully paid for was issued. The final installment on
preferred stock subscriptions was received from all subscribers except
one whose installment due on this date was $6,000. State corporation
laws provide that the company is liable for the return to the subscriber
of the amount received less the loss on the subsequent resale of the
stock. Preferred stock fully paid for was issued.

Dec. 6 Preferred stock defaulted on December 1 was sold for cash at $27.
Stock was issued, and settlement was made with the defaulting subscriber.

Instructions: (1) Prepare journal entries to record the foregoing transactions.

(2) Prepare the paid-in capital section of stockholders' equity for the
corporation as of December 31.

19-7. A balance sheet for the Adler Co. on June 30, 1972, just before
liquidation, showed the following:

Assets		Liabilities and Stockholders' Equity	
Cash......................	$ 200,000	Liabilities.................	$1,225,000
Other assets...............	2,760,000	6% Cumulative preferred stock, $100 par, 8,000 shares issued and outstanding (amount to be paid upon liq-uidation, $100 per share plus dividends in arrears)........	800,000
		Common stock, no-par, 40,000 shares..................	1,000,000
		Premium on preferred stock..	25,000
		Retained earnings (deficit)...	(90,000)
Total assets................	$2,960,000	Total liabilities and stock-holders' equity..........	$2,960,000

No dividends on preferred or common shares had been paid since the
company was organized. Dividends in arrears on preferred shares on
June 30, 1972, amounted to $240,000.

All of the non-cash assets were sold to Morgan and Jones, Inc., at the
beginning of July for a cash consideration of $2,400,000. Cash was paid
to creditors and stockholders in final liquidation.

Instructions: (1) Give the entries that would be made to record the sale of
assets and the distribution of cash to the appropriate parties, closing the books
of the corporation.

(2) Prepare a summary reporting the amount paid per share to preferred
and to common stockholders in final liquidation.

19-8. Stein and Trueblood, partners, who share earnings and losses in a
ratio of 3:2 respectively, wish to retire from active participation in their
manufacturing business and decide to form a corporation to take over the

partnership assets. The partnership balance sheet prepared on March 1, 1972, appears below:

Assets			Liabilities and Owners' Equity	
Cash................		$ 26,000	Notes payable.................	$ 42,000
Notes receivable......		49,000	Accounts payable.............	80,000
Accounts receivable...		60,000	Stein, capital.................	75,000
Inventories..........		70,500	Trueblood, capital............	87,500
Land................		30,000		
Buildings	$50,000			
Less accumulated depreciation—buildings..............	32,000	18,000		
Machinery...........	$80,000			
Less accumulated depreciation — machinery...........	49,000	31,000	Total liabilities and owners'	
Total assets.........		$284,500	equity....................	$284,500

The partners, together with Baldwin and Casper who wish to join the new enterprise, agree to the following:

(a) The corporation shall be known as the Wonder Scope Company, and its authorized stock shall consist of $75,000 shares of common stock, $10 par, and 5,000 shares of 7% preferred stock, $100 par.

(b) Partnership assets other than cash are to be transferred to the corporation and the liabilities are to be assumed by the corporation. The corporation is to issue 1,500 shares of preferred stock in payment for net assets acquired. (It is assumed that the stock is worth par value.) The stock is to be divided equally between Stein and Trueblood, and the partnership cash is then to be withdrawn by the partners in settlement of their interests. Partnership properties other than land, buildings, and equipment are to be recorded on the corporation records at book value. Land, buildings, and equipment items are to be recorded at current sound values as follows:

Land....................................... $40,000

Buildings.................................... 22,000

Machinery................................... 30,000

(c) Baldwin will take charge of the organization of the corporation and will be allowed 2,000 shares of common stock in full payment for his services.

(d) Casper, who owns valuable patent rights, will be given 8,000 shares of common stock upon transfer of these rights to the corporation.

The Wonder Scope Company is incorporated on March 1 and the foregoing transactions are completed.

Instructions: (1) Prepare the entries to record the transfer of assets and liabilities to the corporation, and the distribution of stock and cash on the partnership books.

(2) Prepare the entries for the separate corporation books.

(3) Prepare a balance sheet for the corporation on March 1, 1972, after the foregoing transactions have been recorded.

19-9. Hoover, Ivan, and James, partners sharing earnings and losses 3:3:2 respectively, draw up the following partnership balance sheet on November 1, 1972:

Assets			Liabilities and Owners' Equity			
Cash........................		$ 31,450	Liabilities			
Accounts receivable...........		35,000	Notes payable................		$ 15,000	
Merchandise inventory.........		62,000	Accounts payable.............		21,400	
Furniture and fixtures..	$21,450					
Less accumulated depreciation — furniture and fixtures....	7,250	14,200	Total liabilities...............		$ 36,400	
			Owners' Equity			
			Hoover, capital......	$40,250		
			Ivan, capital........	35,000		
			James, capital.......	31,000	$106,250	
			Total liabilities and owners'			
Total assets.........		$142,650	equity......................		$142,650	

The partners incorporate on this date as HIJ, Inc., with an authorized capital stock as follows:

Preferred stock, 10,000 shares, $20 par
Common stock, 10,000 shares, $10 par

The partners agree to the following:

(a) Adjustments are to be made in asset values as follows:
    (1) An allowance for doubtful accounts is to be established at 4% of accounts receivable.
    (2) Furniture and fixtures are to be restated at present replacement cost of $25,000 less accumulated depreciation of 30% on replacement cost.
    (3) Expenses of $500 have been prepaid and are to be recognized as an asset.
(b) Each partner is to be paid for his partnership interest as follows, it being assumed that stock has a value equal to its par:
    (1) 1,200 shares of preferred are to be allowed to each partner.
    (2) Remaining capital interests are to be paid for with common stock, in even multiples of 100 shares, each partner to be paid cash for his capital balance in excess of the highest 100-share multiple that can be issued.

The above adjustments and transactions are completed and shares not required for the settlement of the partners' interests are immediately sold at par.

Instructions: (1) Give journal entries to record the incorporation, assuming that it is to be reflected on the partnership books, no new books being opened by the corporation.

(2) Prepare a balance sheet for the corporation. (Assume that transactions are completed on November 1.)

19-10. Howard and Sanders Electrical Contracting Co., a partnership, and Grover Wholesale Electricians' Hardware Co., a proprietorship, have agreed to transfer the assets and liabilities of their companies on November 1, 1972, to a newly chartered corporation, Major Electrical, Inc., in exchange for Major Electrical, Inc.'s stock.   The agreement provides:

(a) Preferred stock shall be issued at par value of $100 per share to each of the parties in exchange for his share of the net assets (assets minus liabilities) transferred to Major Electrical, Inc.   John Grover shall receive at least 900 shares of preferred stock and Bill Howard and Joe Sanders shall receive together a total of not more than 480 shares of preferred stock.   Cash shall be contributed to the companies by the respective parties or distributed by the companies to the parties to accomplish the proper net asset transfers.

(b) Common stock shall be issued in a total amount equal to the earnings expected to be contributed by the companies to Major Electrical, Inc., for the next five years to the extent that the earnings of each company respectively, based on the past three calendar years, exceed the average earnings of its industry.   The common stock shall be issued at par value of $10 per share to the owners of the companies in the ratio of the amount that each company's average earnings are expected to exceed the average industry earnings of the company with the lesser earnings.

Additional information includes the following:

(c) Trial balances at October 31, 1972, for both companies are given below.

Grover Hardware Co. and
Howard & Sanders Co.
Trial Balances
October 31, 1972

	Grover Hardware		Howard & Sanders	
Account Title	Debit	Credit	Debit	Credit
Cash..................................	17,000		20,700	
Accounts Receivable....................	43,000			
Allowance for Doubtful Accounts..........		3,000		
Inventory..............................	63,000		3,500	
Prepaid Expenses.......................	2,000		1,300	
Land, Buildings, and Equipment..........	44,000		26,000	
Accumulated Depr.—Buildings and Equip...		27,000		12,000
Accounts Payable......................		54,000		
Accrued Expenses Payable...............		4,000		
Deposit on Contract.....................				2,500
Grover, Capital........................		75,000		
Grover, Drawing.......................	5,000			
Howard, Capital.......................				11,300
Sanders, Capital.......................				7,700
Revenues..............................		200,000		70,000
Cost of Producing Revenues..............	160,000		31,000	
Howard, Salary........................			4,000	
Sanders, Salary........................			3,000	
Operating Expenses.....................	29,000		14,000	
	363,000	363,000	103,500	103,500

(d) Howard and Sanders maintain the partnership books on the cash basis of accounting and Grover maintains his proprietorship books on the accrual basis.   Major Electrical, Inc.'s books are to be maintained on the accrual basis.   Items not recorded on Howard and Sanders' books at October 31, 1972, follow:

Accounts receivable.............................	$20,300
Allowance for doubtful accounts...................	400
Unbilled contract in progress.....................	8,000
Prepaid expenses................................	1,200
Accounts payable................................	6,200
Accrued expenses payable........................	2,400

All accounts receivable are for jobs completed and billed. The unbilled contract in progress is for a $10,000 contract which was 80% complete and upon which a $2,500 deposit was paid to Howard and Sanders when the contract was signed. Cash payments for work on the contract to October 31, 1972, total $3,500 and were recorded on the partnership books as inventory. Accounts payable include $2,800 owed to Grover Wholesale Electricians' Hardware Co.

(e) The partnership agreement specified Bill Howard would receive a salary of $12,000 per year and share 60% of any profit or loss and Joe Sanders would receive a salary of $9,000 per year and share 40% of any profit or loss. Each partner will receive the same annual salary from the corporation.

(f) John Grover withdraws an amount each month from his proprietorship equal to a normal salary. Grover's annual salary from the corporation will be $15,000.

(g) Based on the past three years, John Grover could expect his proprietorship to earn an average of $39,000 per year for the next five years before any salary allowance with average expected sales of $600,000 per year. The industry average net income (after deducting all salaries and income taxes) for electrical hardware wholesalers for the next five years is expected to be 1.35% of sales.

(h) Based on the past three years, Bill Howard and Joe Sanders could expect their partnership to earn an average of $55,500 per year for the next five years before deducting partners' salaries with average expected revenues of $240,000 per year. The industry average net income (after deducting all salaries and income taxes) for electrical contractors for the next five years is expected to be 7.5% of sales.

(i) The parties expect the corporation to pay income taxes at an average of 40% during the next five years.

Instructions: (1) Complete a work sheet with the columnar headings indicated below to determine the opening account balances of Major Electrical, Inc., giving effect to the agreement to transfer the assets and liabilities and issue stock.

Your work sheet would include space to list the names of accounts followed by a pair of columns for each of the following headings:

Grover Hardware Trial Balance
Howard and Sanders Trial Balance
Grover Hardware Adjusting and Closing Entries
Howard and Sanders Adjusting and Closing Entries
Major Electrical, Inc., Opening Account Balances

(2) Prepare supporting schedules computing (a) any cash contributions or distributions necessary and preferred stock to be issued to each party and (b) the number of shares of common stock to be issued to each party. Formal adjusting and closing entries and formal financial statements are not required.

(AICPA adapted)

chapter 20

paid-in capital -
changes subsequent
to corporate formation

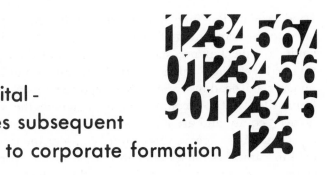

Corporate capital originates from different sources. These different sources need to be identified in providing information concerning the character of the stockholders' equity. These must also be known to determine the amounts that may legally be distributed as dividends. Corporate capital originates from three primary sources: (1) investments by those acquiring stock, (2) retention of net assets arising from earnings, and (3) recognition of appraisal values in the accounts.

1. *Investments by those acquiring stock*. Net assets received by the corporation in exchange for its stock are the source of the company's invested capital. Invested capital is divided into (a) an amount forming the corporate legal or stated capital, and (b) the balance not classified as legal capital. The amount of the investment representing the legal or stated capital is reported as *capital stock*. The balance is recognized as *additional paid-in capital* or *paid-in surplus*. Contributions of properties by outsiders may also be included in the additional paid-in capital grouping, although it would be possible to recognize these in a separate *donated capital* category.

2. *Retention of net assets arising from earnings*. Changes in net assets arising from the sale of goods and services give rise to earnings and losses that are summarized as *retained earnings*. When a portion of retained earnings is unavailable for dividends, it is referred to as *appropriated* or *reserved*; any balance is then regarded as *unappropriated* or *free*. A debit balance in retained earnings resulting from losses is termed a *deficit* and is subtracted from paid-in capital in arriving at the total corporate capital.

3. *Recognition of appraisal values in the accounts*. The recognition of appraisal values in the accounts gives rise to *appraisal capital* or *appraisal surplus*.

Individual accounts should be maintained in the ledger for each separate source of capital within each of the classifications listed. For example, separate accounts should be provided for preferred stock and for common stock, for a premium on preferred stock and for a premium on common stock, for a retained earnings appropriation related to a

695

bond redemption fund and for a retained earnings appropriation related to the acquisition of treasury stock. In reporting the stockholders' equity on the balance sheet, however, individual paid-in capital and retained earnings balances are frequently combined and presented under class headings. Whether reported separately or in combined form, the capital accounts simply designate the source of the stockholders' equity and are not related to specific assets.

Remaining pages of this chapter consider the transactions that affect paid-in capital balances after formation of the corporation. The next chapter considers those transactions that affect retained earnings and appraisal capital balances.

Capital stock reacquisition and retirement

A corporation may have the right to call certain classes of stock for redemption and may choose to exercise such right. In other cases, it may purchase stock on the open market and formally retire such shares. Whether obtained through call for redemption or through purchase on the market, retirement of stock at a cost that differs from the original issuance price presents special accounting problems.

It is agreed that the reacquisition and retirement of stock cannot be considered to give rise to income or loss. A company in issuing stock raises capital which it hopes to employ profitably; in reacquiring and retiring shares it reduces the capital that is to be employed in subsequent operations. Income or loss arises from the utilization of resources that have been placed in the hands of the corporation, not from capital transactions between the company and its stockholders. Notwithstanding agreement on this matter, there are still certain problems that arise in recording stock retirement.

If a class of stock is retired at the same amount originally recognized as capital stock upon its issuance, the capital stock account is debited and Cash is credited. All reference to the investment by the stockholders, then, is cancelled. However, when the purchase price of the stock retired exceeds the par or stated value of the stock, the excess must be assigned in some satisfactory manner to additional paid-in capital and retained earnings.

The Accounting Principles Board in Opinion No. 6 issued in 1965 commented upon the procedure to be followed when stock of a corporation is retired as follows:

> i *an excess of purchase price over par or stated value* may be allocated between capital surplus and retained earnings. The portion of the excess allocated to capital surplus should be limited to the sum of (a) all capital surplus arising from previous retirements and net "gains" on sales of treasury stock of the same issue and (b) the pro rata portion of capital

surplus paid in, voluntary transfers of retained earnings, capitalization of stock dividends, etc., on the same issue. For this purpose, any remaining capital surplus applicable to issues fully retired (formal or constructive) is deemed to be applicable pro rata to shares of common stock. Alternatively, the excess may be charged entirely to retained earnings in recognition of the fact that a corporation can always capitalize or allocate retained earnings for such purposes.

ii *an excess of par or stated value over purchase price* should be credited to capital surplus.[1]

The effects of these provisions are illustrated in the examples that follow. Assume that a corporation reports the following balances related to an issue of preferred stock:

Preferred stock outstanding, par $10, 10,000 shares........ $100,000
Premium on preferred stock..........................   10,000

(1) Assume that the corporation redeems and retires 2,000 shares, or 20%, of the preferred stock at $12.50 per share. Reductions are made in the preferred stock account for 2,000 shares, par $10, or $20,000, and in the premium on preferred stock for a pro rata share of the premium, 20% of $10,000, or $2,000, and the difference between the sum of these amounts and the amount paid is charged to Retained Earnings. The entry, then, is as follows:

Preferred Stock.................................   20,000
Premium on Preferred Stock....................   2,000
Retained Earnings.............................   3,000
    Cash......................................   25,000

If the alternate method indicated by the Accounting Principles Board is to be followed, the entire amount paid over par or stated value of the retired shares would be charged to Retained Earnings. In the example, then, the entry would be:

Preferred Stock.................................   20,000
Retained Earnings.............................   5,000
    Cash......................................   25,000

(2) Assume that the corporation redeems and retires the 2,000 shares of preferred stock at only $9.00 per share. Here the preferred stock account is reduced by the par value of the shares, $20,000, and the difference between the charge to Preferred Stock and the amount paid is credited to a paid-in capital account. The following entry is made:

Preferred Stock.................................   20,000
    Cash......................................   18,000
    Paid-In Capital from Preferred Stock Acquisition.   2,000

It would also be possible to reduce the premium on preferred stock for a pro rata share of the premium, $2,000, and report the paid-in capital

---

[1]*Opinions of the Accounting Principles Board, No. 6,* "Status of Accounting Research Bulletins" (New York: American Institute of Certified Public Accountants, 1965), par. 12 a.

from preferred stock reacquisition at the difference between the amount at which the preferred shares were originally issued and the amount that was paid on their retirement. The following entry can be made:

Preferred Stock..................................	20,000	
Premium on Preferred Stock....................	2,000	
Cash..		18,000
Paid-In Capital from Preferred Stock Reacquisition		4,000

If additional shares of preferred stock are subsequently retired at amounts in excess of par, the differences between the amounts paid and the par value of the preferred stock retired can be charged against the paid-in capital from the earlier preferred stock acquisition.

It should be observed that when stock is formally retired, there is a reduction in the corporate legal or stated capital. State laws normally do not bar the reduction of legal or stated capital when stock is issued subject to redemption and redemption is made at the price provided by terms of the stock issue.

Treasury stock

When a company's own stock, paid for and issued, is reacquired and held in the name of the company rather than formally retired, it is known as *treasury stock*. A company may acquire its own stock by purchase, by acceptance in satisfaction of a claim, or by donation from stockholders. Such shares may subsequently be sold or formally retired.

State laws vary widely in their regulations concerning treasury stock. In some states, the accounting for treasury stock is governed largely by statute. In other states, only general restrictions are applied. The accounting for treasury stock requires careful review of the state laws. State laws normally provide that the reacquisition of stock must serve some legitimate corporate purpose and must be made without injury or prejudice to the creditors or to the remaining stockholders. In almost every state, it is provided that the legal or stated capital of the corporation may not be reduced by such reacquisition.[1] Accordingly, purchases are limited to a company's retained earnings, or in some instances to the sum of its retained earnings and additional paid-in capital balances, and reduce the amount that would otherwise be available for distribution as

---

[1]Corporation laws of a few jurisdictions specifically provide that the purchase of treasury stock reduces the retained earnings balance. The purchase of shares thus has the same effect as a dividend. In California, for example, the purchase of shares is restricted to the amount of retained earnings and reduces this balance; the legal or stated capital remains the same even though there has been a decrease in the number of shares outstanding. If reacquired shares are retired, there are no changes in stated capital and retained earnings balances; if the shares are resold, the entire proceeds must be recognized as additional paid-in capital.

dividends. To illustrate the effects of such legislation, assume that the capital of a corporation is as follows:

Capital stock, $10 par, 100,000 shares outstanding. $1,000,000
Retained earnings   500,000

The company can declare dividends of $500,000 and creditors will continue to be safeguarded by the stockholders' investment of $1,000,000 as reported in the capital stock account. But assume the reacquisition by the company of a part of its outstanding stock for $400,000. If dividends of $500,000 were still permitted and were paid, protection to creditors would shrink to $600,000. With the company's ability to pay dividends reduced to $100,000 upon the purchase of treasury stock for $400,000, the original protection to the creditor group is assured; the sum of payments for treasury stock and dividends will not reduce net assets below the legal capital reported in capital stock, $1,000,000.

Despite the fact that the legal capital remains the same after a company has reacquired shares of its own stock, the treasury stock cannot normally be viewed as an asset but must be regarded as a reduction in corporate capital. A company cannot have an ownership interest in itself; treasury stock confers upon the corporation no dividend, voting, or subscription rights.

The AICPA has discouraged the recognition of treasury stock as an asset in the following statement issued in 1934 and accepted without change by the Accounting Principles Board in 1965:

> While it is perhaps in some circumstances permissible to show stock of a corporation held in its own treasury as an asset, if adequately disclosed, the dividends on stock so held should not be treated as a credit to the income account of the company.[1]

Although treasury stock has a number of similarities to unissued stock, there are some significant differences. Among these differences are the following: (1) stockholders' preemptive rights do not apply to treasury stock, (2) treasury stock may be reissued without authorization by stockholders, (3) having already been issued in accordance with legal requirements governing legal or stated capital, treasury stock may be reissued without the conditions that were imposed upon its original issue, for example, the discount liability on the original issue, and (4) treasury stock remains a part of legal capital in most states.

The sale of treasury stock increases the number of shares outstanding. However, the legal capital, remaining unchanged upon its purchase, is

---

[1]*Accounting Research Bulletin No. 43*, "Restatement and Revision of Accounting Research Bulletins" (New York: American Institute of Certified Public Accountants, 1953), Ch. 1, sect. A, par. 4. In 1970, 19 of the 600 companies listed in *Accounting Trends & Techniques* reported treasury stock as an asset. A bonus agreement that specifies that a liability to employees for a bonus that can be satisfied by issuing to the employees shares of company stock is an example where support is given for reporting treasury stock as an asset.

not increased through its sale. If treasury stock is to be retired, such retirement is formalized by the preparation of a certificate or notice of reduction that is filed with appropriate state officials. Upon the formal retirement of shares, these revert to the status of unissued shares and there is a reduction in the corporate legal or stated capital. It may be observed that for federal income tax purposes, treasury stock transactions provide no taxable gain or loss; stock reacquisition, as well as stock reissue or retirement, is regarded as a transaction related to a company's invested capital.

Purchase of treasury stock. A number of different methods for recording the purchase of treasury stock have been suggested. These methods are the products of two general approaches to the problem of treasury stock purchases:

1. The purchase of treasury stock may be viewed as the retirement of outstanding stock.
2. The purchase of treasury stock may be viewed as giving rise to a capital element whose ultimate disposition still remains to be resolved.

The two approaches are described in the following sections. Descriptions are accompanied by examples illustrating the different approaches.

First approach: Treasury stock purchase viewed as capital retirement (par or stated value method). The purchase of treasury stock may be regarded as the withdrawal of a group of stockholders calling for the cancellation of capital balances identified with this group. It follows that the sale of treasury stock represents the admission of a new group of stockholders calling for entries to give effect to the investment by this group. Thus, there are two separate transactions that must be recorded, the purchase and the sale.

When the purchase of stock is viewed as stock retirement, alternate methods may be employed in reporting the reduction in the capital stock balance: (1) the capital stock account may be charged directly; or (2) a treasury stock account may be charged and this balance treated as a subtraction item from capital stock; this procedure preserves capital at the legal or stated amount as reported by the capital stock account. The alternate methods are illustrated on pages 702 and 703. The transactions for each case are described on pages 700 and 701.

Treasury Stock Reported as a Reduction in Capital Stock:

Transaction (1): Treasury stock is acquired at a price that exceeds the original or stated value. Charges are made to capital stock and to additional paid-in capital and retained earnings balances applying the alternatives that were stated on pages 696 and 697.

Transaction (2): When the stock is sold at more than its par or stated value, Capital Stock is credited at par or stated value and Paid-In Capital from Sale of Treasury Stock at More Than Par or Stated Value is credited for the excess. When the stock is sold at less than par or stated value, Capital Stock is credited at par or stated value and a charge for the difference is made to any paid-in capital from earlier sales or retirements of treasury stock of the same class, or to Retained Earnings.

Treasury Stock Account Used to Report Reduction in Capital Stock:

Transaction (1): When treasury stock is acquired at a price that exceeds its par or stated value, a treasury stock account instead of capital stock may be charged for the amount of the reduction in the capital stock. The treasury stock account subtracted from the capital stock account reporting the amount issued then gives the capital stock outstanding. Charges to other paid-in capital and retained earnings balances would be made as described in the preceding section.

Transaction (2): When the treasury stock is sold, the treasury stock account is credited for the amount at which treasury stock is carried, and any difference between the sales price and the carrying amount is treated as described in the preceding section.

Second approach: Treasury stock purchase viewed as giving rise to capital element awaiting ultimate disposition (cost method). The purchase of treasury stock may be viewed as an application of cash to a capital purpose that has not been finally defined or consummated. Upon the purchase of treasury stock, a treasury stock account is charged for the cost of the purchase regardless of whether this cost is more or less than the original stock issue price. This balance is recognized as a negative stockholders' equity element that does not call for specific identification with paid-in capital or retained earnings at this time. If treasury stock is subsequently retired, the debit balance in the treasury stock account can be allocated to the appropriate equity balances as in the first approach. If the treasury stock is sold, the difference between the acquisition cost and the selling price is reported as an increase or decrease in stockholders' equity. It is the retirement or the sale of treasury stock that makes possible a determination of the effect of treasury stock transactions upon the elements of corporate capital.

The application of this approach is illustrated above. The transactions in the example are described below.

Transaction (1): When treasury stock is purchased, it is recorded at its cost regardless of whether this cost is more or less than the original stock issue price. In a presentation of corporate capital at this time, treasury stock, consisting of a cost unallocated as to the different capital elements, would normally be reported as a subtraction from the sum of paid-in capital and retained earnings.[1]

---

[1]"When a corporation's stock is acquired for purposes other than retirement (formal or constructive), or when ultimate disposition has not yet been decided, the cost of acquired stock may be shown separately as a deduction from the total of capital stock, capital surplus, and retained earnings or may be accorded the accounting treatment appropriate for retired stock . . . ." *Opinions of the Accounting Principles Board, No. 6, op. cit.,* par. 12 (b).

Transaction	First Approach: Treasury Stock Purchase Viewed as Capital Retirement
	Treasury Stock Purchase Reported as Reduction in Capital Stock

1971
Issue of stock, 10,000 shares, $10 par, at 15.
	Cash................ 150,000
	   Capital Stock........ 100,000
	   Premium on Capital
	    Stock............. 50,000

Net income for year, $30,000.	Income Summary...... 30,000 Retained Earnings.... 30,000

1972
(1) Reacquisition of 1,000 shares at 16.
	Capital Stock......... 10,000
	Premium on Capital
	   Stock*............. 5,000
	Retained Earnings...... 1,000
	   Cash.............. 16,000

(2) Sale of treasury stock at 20.	Cash................ 20,000
	   Capital Stock........ 10,000
	   Paid-In Capital from
	   Sale of Treasury Stock
	   at More Than Par.. 10,000

Stockholders' equity section after sale of treasury stock:	Stockholders' Equity
	Capital stock.......... $100,000
	Premium on capital
	  stock................ 45,000
	Paid-in capital from sale
	  of treasury stock at
	  more than par........ 10,000
	Retained earnings...... 29,000
	                $184,000

Transaction (2): When treasury stock is sold at more than its cost, Treasury Stock is credited at cost and Paid-In Capital from Sale of Treasury Stock at More Than Cost is credited. When the stock is sold at less than cost, Treasury Stock is credited at cost and a charge is made to any paid-in capital from earlier sales or retirements of treasury stock of the same class, or to Retained Earnings.

When retained earnings are restricted for dividend purposes while treasury stock is held, there are several ways such restrictions may be shown on the balance sheet. The most common are (1) as an appropriation of retained earnings, (2) as a parenthetical remark in the body of the statement, and (3) as a footnote. The restriction would be reported regardless of the method that had been used to record the purchase of the stock.

Evaluation of the two approaches to entries for treasury stock. The AICPA, through the Accounting Principles Board, has not expressed a preference between the two approaches of reporting treasury stock purchase.

The American Accounting Association Committee on Concepts and Standards Underlying Corporate Financial Statements would recognize the acquisition of treasury stock as equivalent to the retirement of such stock. The Committee has commented as follows:

First Approach: Treasury Stock Purchase Viewed as Capital Retirement		Second Approach: Treasury Stock Purchase Viewed as Giving Rise to Capital Element Awaiting Ultimate Disposition	
Treasury Stock Account Used to Report Reduction in Capital Stock			
Cash................	150,000	Cash................	150,000
Capital Stock........	100,000	Capital Stock........	100,000
Premium on Capital		Premium on Capital	
Stock.............	50,000	Stock.............	50,000
Income Summary.......	30,000	Income Summary......	30,000
Retained Earnings.....	30,000	Retained Earnings....	30,000
Treasury Stock..........	10,000	Treasury Stock.........	16,000
Premium on Capital		Cash..............	16,000
Stock*..............	5,000		
Retained Earnings.......	1,000		
Cash..............	16,000		
Cash................	20,000	Cash................	20,000
Treasury Stock........	10,000	Treasury Stock.......	16,000
Paid-In Capital from		Paid-In Capital from	
Sale of Treasury Stock		Sale of Treasury Stock	
at More Than Par....	10,000	at More Than Cost..	4,000
Stockholders' Equity		Stockholders' Equity	
Capital Stock..........	$100,000	Capital Stock..........	$100,000
Premium on capital		Premium on capital	
stock................	45,000	stock...............	50,000
Paid-in capital from sale of		Paid-in capital from sale	
treasury stock at more		of treasury stock at	
than par.............	10,000	more than cost........	4,000
Retained earnings......	29,000	Retained earnings......	30,000
	$184,000		$184,000

*As indicated earlier, the entire difference between the charge to Capital Stock and the amount paid can be charged to Retained Earnings.

The acquisition of its own shares by a corporation represents a contraction of its capital structure. However, statutory requirements are particularly restrictive in this area of corporate activity and, to an important degree, are controlling in the reporting of such transactions. Preferably, the outlay by a corporation for its own shares is reflected as a reduction of the aggregate of contributed capital, and any excess of outlay over the pro rata portion of contributed capital as a distribution of retained earnings. The issuance of reacquired shares should be accounted for in the same way as the issuance of previously unissued shares, that is, the entire proceeds should be credited to contributed capital.[1]

Although there is theoretical support for each of the approaches presented, laws of the states may take different views relative to the effects of treasury stock transactions upon corporate capital. It has already been indicated that the state laws generally provide that legal or stated capital is not reduced by the purchase by a company of its own shares. This provision is accompanied by restrictions on the availability of retained earnings and perhaps of additional paid-in capital for dividends. Upon the sale or retirement of treasury stock, some states cancel these restrictions, thus reinstating the reductions that were applied to specific

[1]*Accounting and Reporting Standards for Corporate Financial Statements and Preceding Statements and Supplements* (1957 rev.; Madison, Wisconsin; American Accounting Association), p. 7.

capital balances. Other states do not cancel such restrictions but require that if treasury stock is sold, the proceeds from the sale be recognized as an increase in additional paid-in capital, and if treasury stock is retired, a transfer be made from the legal capital to additional paid-in capital. When the procedures that have been illustrated in this chapter conflict with the legal requirements relative to the status of treasury stock and to the effects upon capital balances when treasury stock is sold or retired, the procedures may be modified to meet such requirements.[1]

Acquisition of no-par treasury stock. Previous illustrations assumed the purchase and sale of treasury stock with a par value. The purchase of stock with a stated value provides no new problems; the stated value instead of the par value is used in reducing capital stock or in reporting treasury stock. When there is no stated or par value and the capital stock account has been credited with the proceeds from stock issued at different prices, a special problem arises. Under these circumstances, the capital stock offset is usually considered to be either (1) the original issuing price of the particular lot reacquired, or (2) the weighted average price at which the stock of the company was originally sold. For example, assume that no-par stock has been issued as follows:

2,000 shares @ $18	$36,000
2,000 shares @ $20	40,000
1,000 shares @ $22	22,000
5,000 shares	$98,000

Assume that 1,000 shares are reacquired at $16.50. The acquisition is identified as the second lot sold, and treasury stock is to be recorded at the original issuing price. The following entry is made:

Treasury Stock	20,000	
Cash		16,500
Paid-In Capital from Capital Stock Reacquisition		3,500

Assume that treasury stock is to be recorded at the average issuing price. The average price per share is calculated as follows:

$98,000 (proceeds from sales) ÷ 5,000 (number of shares issued) = $19.60

The entry to record the acquisition would be:

Treasury Stock	19,600	
Cash		16,500
Paid-In Capital from Capital Stock Reacquisition		3,100

---

[1] In practice the cost method appears to be the preferred method for recording treasury stock. In 1970, 381 of the companies reported in *Accounting Trends & Techniques* used this approach and 107 used the par or stated value approach. *Accounting Trends & Techniques* (25th ed.; New York: American Institute of Certified Public Accountants, 1971), p. 151.

Conclusions relative to treasury stock transactions.   From the discussion of the treasury stock and the presentation of the different methods that may be followed when treasury stock is purchased, the current approaches may be summarized as follows:

1. Treasury stock is rarely includible as an asset on corporation books and does not qualify for dividends.
2. Neither gain nor loss can be recognized on the income statement relative to transactions in a company's own stock.
3. Retained earnings can be decreased as a result of capital transactions; however, retained earnings cannot be increased through such transactions.
4. In most states retained earnings equal to the cost of treasury stock is legally unavailable for dividends. This restriction on retained earnings is reported on the balance sheet by an appropriation of retained earnings, by parenthetical remark, or by footnote disclosure.
5. The total stockholder's equity is not affected by the method used; however, the amounts reported for paid-in capital and retained earnings can be affected by the recording procedure followed.

Donated stock

Treasury stock may be acquired by donation from the stockholders. Shares may be donated so that the company may raise working capital through their sale. In other instances shares may be donated so that the company may eliminate a deficit. Ordinarily, all of the stockholders participate in the donation, each party donating a certain percentage of his holdings so that relative interests in the corporation remain unchanged.

Donations of stock with a par value are sometimes found where large blocks of stock were originally issued in exchange for properties of uncertain values, for example, mining properties, patents, and leaseholds. Such stock, which is considered fully paid, may be resold at any price without involving the purchaser in a possible liability to creditors for the difference between par and a lower purchase price. Such a donation may represent a sacrifice on the part of the donors of the stock; frequently, however, it represents no more than return of a stock overissue. The issuance of an excessive number of shares of stock for properties and the subsequent donation of stock that may be sold without a discount liability has been referred to as the "treasury stock subterfuge."

In the absence of any cost, the acquisition of treasury stock by donation may be reported on the corporation books by a memorandum entry. Assuming that the assets of the company have been fairly valued, the sale of donated stock is recorded by a debit to Cash and a credit to Donated Capital. If assets of the company have been overvalued, however, it would be improper to recognize an increase in capital arising from the sale of donated shares. Under these circumstances, the sale price for the stock should be employed as a basis for restating the company assets and paid-in capital.

To illustrate the latter instance, assume that the Sunset Mining Co. is formed to take over the mining properties of partners Adams and Burke, and the corporation issues 10,000 shares of no-par stock to the partners in exchange for the properties. A value of $250,000 is assigned to the properties and an entry is made for the acquisition as follows:

Mining Properties............................	250,000	
Capital Stock.............................		250,000

Shortly after corporate formation, Adams and Burke donate 4,000 shares to the corporation, and the corporation sells these for $15 per share. If $15 can be regarded as a measure of the fair value of the stock exchanged for the properties, properties should be restated at $90,000, or $15 × 6,000, the number of shares actually exchanged for the properties. Upon the sale of the donated shares, then, entries should be made (1) to correct the property account and capital stock for both the stock overissue and the property overvaluation, and (2) to record the sale of the donated shares. These entries are:

Capital Stock...............................	160,000	
Mining Properties..........................		160,000
Cash..	60,000	
Capital Stock..............................		60,000

The balance sheet for the corporation would now show the following balances:

Cash..................	$60,000	Capital stock, no-par,	
Mining properties........	90,000	10,000 shares outstanding.................	$150,000

The membership of the AICPA has adopted the following rule relative to the donation of shares to an issuing company:

> . . . If capital stock is issued nominally for the acquisition of property and it appears that at about the same time, and pursuant to a previous agreement or understanding, some portion of the stock so issued is donated to the corporation, it is not permissible to treat the par value of the stock nominally issued for the property as the cost of that property. If stock so donated is subsequently sold, it is not permissible to treat the proceeds as a credit to surplus of the corporation.[1]

When stock is donated so that a company may cancel a deficit, the company should take formal action to retire donated shares. Upon such retirement, the capital stock is charged for the decrease in legal capital and additional paid-in capital is credited. The deficit can then be applied against the additional paid-in capital balance.

---

[1] *Accounting Research Bulletin No. 43, op. cit.*, Ch. 1, sect. A, par. 6.

Stock rights and options

As discussed in Chapter 11, a company may grant rights and options to buy its stock. Such grants generally arise under the following circumstances:

1. A company requiring additional capital may offer stockholders subscription rights to make the purchase of additional shares attractive to them.
2. A company may provide subscription rights with the issue of various classes of securities to promote the sale of these securities.
3. A company may offer promoters, officers, or employees special subscription rights or options as compensation for services or other contributions.

Rights to purchase are evidenced by certificates called *stock purchase warrants*. The rights enable their owners to purchase shares at a specified price. The period for exercise may or may not be limited. The rights have a value because of the difference between the exercise price of the right as compared with a higher market value for the security, either present or potential.

The accounting problems that are faced by the issuing company under each of the circumstances listed above are described in the following paragraphs.

Rights issued to stockholders as means of increasing invested capital. When rights are issued to stockholders, only a memorandum entry is made stating the number of shares that may be claimed under outstanding rights. This information is required so that the corporation may retain sufficient unissued or reacquired stock to meet the exercise of the rights. Upon surrender of the rights and payments as specified by the rights, the stock is issued. At this time a memorandum entry is made to record the decrease in the number of rights outstanding accompanied by an entry to record the stock sale. The entry for the sale depends upon the amount paid for the shares:

1. When the cash received in the exercise of rights is less than the required credit to Capital Stock, the difference must be charged to Retained Earnings; retained earnings are permanently capitalized under these conditions.
2. When the cash received is equal to the par or stated value of the stock or when no-par stock is without a stated value, Cash is debited and Capital Stock is credited.
3. When the cash received is more than the par or stated value of the stock, the excess is recorded as a credit to paid-in capital from the sale of stock at more than par or stated value.

Information concerning outstanding rights should be reported on the balance sheet so that the effects of the exercise of future rights may be ascertained.

Rights issued with various classes of securities to improve their marketability. When rights are issued with the sale of other securities, recognition of the rights in the entry to record the sale will depend upon whether a value can be related to these rights. When rights have no value on the date of sale, the full sales price is identified with the sale of the other securities. When the rights are exercised, the stock is recorded as described in the previous section; if the rights are not exercised and are allowed to expire, no entry is required since no value was originally assigned to the rights. When rights do have a market value upon issuance, the sales price should be allocated between the rights and the other securities issued. When the rights are exercised, the stock is recorded at the sum of the value assigned to the rights and the amount paid; if the rights are not exercised and expire, the value assigned to the rights should be transferred to a paid-in capital balance. The sale of securities accompanied by rights is illustrated in the examples that follow:

(1) Assume that the Matson Co. sells 1,000 shares of preferred stock at par, $50, and gives with this issue separate warrants enabling holders to subscribe to 1,000 shares of no-par common stock at $25 per share for a one-year period. Common stock has a stated value of $20 and is selling at this time for $22 per share. Since rights may be considered to have only speculative value at the time of the sale, the entry to record the sale of preferred stock and rights is:

Cash..	50,000	
Preferred Stock ($50 par, 1,000 shares)..........		50,000

In the succeeding year the value of the common stock rises above $25 per share and all of the rights are exercised. Issue of the stock upon exercise of the rights is recorded as follows:

Cash..	25,000	
Common Stock ($20 stated value, 1,000 shares)....		20,000
Paid-In Capital from Sale of Common Stock at		
More Than Stated Value....................		5,000

(2) Assume that the common stock is selling for $28 per share when the preferred stock is sold. Under these circumstances, it is reasonable to assume that the $50 sales price represents payment for two assets, a right worth $3 and a share of preferred stock worth $47. The following entry recognizes the sale of preferred stock and rights:

Cash..	50,000	
Discount on Preferred Stock......................	3,000	
Preferred Stock ($50 par, 1,000 shares)		50,000
Common Stock Rights Outstanding.............		3,000

Subsequent exercise of all of the rights and issue of the common stock at $25 is recorded as follows:

Cash..	25,000	
Common Stock Rights Outstanding	3,000	
Common Stock ($20 stated value, 1,000 shares)....		20,000
Paid-In Capital from Sale of Common Stock at		
More Than Stated Value....................		8,000

Assume, however, that the market value of the common stock falls below $25 per share and that the rights are not exercised. The following entry cancels the rights balance:

Common Stock Rights Outstanding 3,000
    Paid-In Capital from Unexercised Stock Rights . . .   3,000

Common Stock Rights Outstanding is a part of the paid-in capital of the company.

Rights or options issued as compensation for services. Compensation to promoters, officers, and other employees in the form of options to purchase stock or rights to subscribe for stock raises the following questions: (1) What amount shall be recognized as compensation? and (2) What periods shall be charged with such cost?

The fair market value of the shares granted under an option may vary considerably over the period of the option. This creates the problem of determining a date that may be used in measuring the cost of the compensation. The AICPA Committee on Accounting Procedure has pointed out that six dates may be considered for this purpose: (1) the date of the adoption of an option plan; (2) the date on which an option is granted to a specific individual; (3) the date on which the grantee has performed any conditions precedent to exercise of the option; (4) the date on which the grantee may first exercise the option; (5) the date on which the option is exercised by the grantee; and (6) the date on which the grantee disposes of the stock acquired. [1]

In reviewing each of these dates, the Committee concluded that, in most instances, the appropriate point for measuring the compensation and arriving at a valuation of the option agreement is the date on which the option is granted. This is the date on which the company acknowledges the claim and takes action that precludes any alternative use of the shares covered by the option. Dates prior to this time are not pertinent: plans calling for services are no more than proposed courses of action until services are formally recognized and the liability becomes effective. Dates after this time are not pertinent: changes in the values of the compensation award after its accrual are beyond the scope of the plan and represent matters of concern only to the grantee. Accordingly, the cost to be recognized for compensation is properly measured by the excess of the fair market value of the stock on date of grant over the price that must be paid for stock by the grantee. On the other hand, no cost would be recognized when the price that is to be paid by the grantee

---

[1]*Ibid.*, Ch. 13, sect. B, par. 6.

is equal to or in excess of the fair market value of the stock on the date of grant.[1]

The other date for valuing an option that has received strong support from some members of the accounting profession is the exercisable date, the date on which the grantee may first exercise the option. The argument supporting this view is that prior to the exercisable date, the employee has no right to exercise the option and thus is unable to appraise its value. The rights are given with the anticipation of a rise in market and if such condition does occur, the intended compensation is realized. A difficult measurement problem exists with the exercisable date, however, since the market price at the exercisable date is unknown until it is reached. Thus, the total amount of compensation is uncertain and it would be difficult to assign charges for compensation against revenue for the periods between the option date and the exercisable date. This difficulty has resulted in the rejection of this alternative.

Although the cost of the stock option is generally set at the date of the grant, the option may represent payment for services over an extended period. In accounting for the option, the period covered by the compensation must be determined and charges must be assigned to such period. For example, if options are granted in recognition of services performed currently, the cost of the option should be assigned to the current period; if options are related to current and future services, the cost should be related to present and future periods. When options represent payment for services that should be capitalized, charges should be made to the appropriate tangible or intangible asset accounts. Upon exercise of the options, the sum of the cash received and the value previously assigned to options represents the consideration related to the issue of the stock.

The Internal Revenue Code offers tax-favored treatment for certain employee stock options referred to as (1) *restricted stock options*, (2) *options under employee stock purchase plans*, and (3) *qualified stock options*. To qualify for special tax treatment, an option must include the following features:

1. It must be nontransferable.
2. An option price must be provided that is equal to or in excess of a stated percentage of the market price of the stock at the time of the grant — 85 percent under restricted stock options granted prior to 1964, 85 percent under employee stock purchase plans, and 100 percent under qualified stock options granted in 1964 and thereafter.
3. The option cannot be exercisable beyond a certain number of years.
4. The stock acquired under the option must be held for a certain period.

---

[1] It should be pointed out that in some instances stock option plans for officers and other employees may be established as means for raising capital or as inducements for securing stock ownership among the corporate personnel. Certain plans may include these purposes and also involve some degree of compensation. The AICPA Committee has observed, "Where the inducements are not larger per share than would reasonably be required in an offer of shares to all shareholders for the purpose of raising an equivalent amount of capital, no compensation need be presumed to be involved." *Ibid.*, Ch. 13, sect. B, par. 4.

An employee who is granted a stock option falling into one of the three classes named recognizes no taxable income when he exercises the option; furthermore, in selling the stock at more than the option price after holding it for a specified period, he is taxed on part or all of the gain at limited long-term capital gain rates. On the other hand, an employee who is granted a stock option that does not qualify for special tax treatment, upon exercising the option, must recognize ordinary income for the difference between the amount paid and the market value of the stock. The latter value then becomes the basis for the stock. Stock option plans in recent years have generally been designed to meet the requirements for tax-favored treatment.

Because of the tax factors, most options granted currently are stated at 100 percent of the market price of the stock as of the date of the grant, and no charge for compensation is recognized. Even when the percentage is less than 100 percent, companies seldom record compensation by taking the position that the difference is not material. Such accounting seems to ignore economic reality and is under study by the Accounting Principles Board. Value is assumed in the granting of these options. In many cases they are given and accepted in lieu of additional salary which would be diluted by taxes. There is a cost to existing stockholders attached to such options. If a significant increase in market price does occur, a potential dilution of equity occurs as a result of the issuance of additional shares. Of course, if the market declines, there is no benefit to the employee and the rights are not exercised.

Accounting for stock options is illustrated in the example that follows. Assume that on December 20, 1969, the board of directors of the Miller Co. authorizes the grant of nontransferable stock options to supplement the salaries of certain executives. Options permit the purchase of 10,000 shares of common stock at a price of $47.50. Stock is currently selling at $50. Options can be exercised beginning January 1, 1972, but only if executives are still in the employ of the company; options expire at the end of 1973. All of the options are exercised on January 15, 1972, when the stock is quoted on the market at $60.

The value of the stock options at the date of grant is determined as follows:

Market value of common stock on December 20, 1969,	
10,000 shares at $50	$500,000
Option price, 10,000 shares at $47.50	475,000
Value of stock options	$ 25,000

The following entries are made by the corporation to record the grant of the options, the annual accrual of option rights, and the exercise of the options.

Transaction	Entry
DECEMBER 20, 1969 Grant of nontransferable stock options.	(Memorandum entry) Granted nontransferable options to executives for the purchase of 10,000 shares of common at $47.50. Options are exercisable beginning January 1, 1972, providing officers are in the employ of the company on that date. Options expire on December 31, 1973. Value of options on December 20, 1969, is $25,000 (market value of stock, $500,000; option price, $475,000).

DECEMBER 31, 1970
To record compensation and option credit accrual for 1970: value of stock options, $25,000; period of services covered by plan, 1970 and 1971; cost assigned to 1970: ½ × $25,000, or $12,500.
	Executives Salaries..... 12,500
	   Credit Under Stock
	     Option Plan........ 12,500

DECEMBER 31, 1971
To record compensation and option credit accrual for 1971: ½ × $25,000, or $12,500.
	Executives Salaries..... 12,500
	   Credit Under Stock
	     Option Plan........ 12,500

JANUARY 15, 1972
To record exercise of stock options: cash received for stock, 10,000 shares at $47.50, or $475,000; par value of stock issued, 10,000 shares at $10, or $100,000.
	Cash................. 475,000
	Credit Under Stock Option Plan............ 25,000
	   Common Stock...... 100,000
	   Premium on Common
	     Stock............ 400,000

The accrued compensation reported in Credit Under Stock Option Plan is properly reported as a part of paid-in capital because it will be liquidated by the issue of stock. If options expire through a failure of employees to meet the conditions of the option or through changes in the price of the stock making exercise of options unattractive, the balance of the account should be transferred to a paid-in capital account that designates the capital increase arising from forfeitures of the accumulated stock option credits.

When option plans are operative, the financial statements should report the number of shares under option, option prices, the number of shares exercised, and the number of shares still exercisable.

The procedures that have been described for stock options representing compensation for services are also applicable when capital stock is employed as a means of compensation. The value of the stock should be established as of the date that the stock is granted to the employee, and the charge for compensation should be related to the periods covered by the compensation.

Stock conversions

Stockholders may be permitted by the terms of their stock agreement or by special action by the corporation to exchange their holdings for stock of other classes. In certain instances, the exchanges may affect only corporate paid-in capital accounts; in other instances, the exchanges may affect both paid-in capital and retained earnings accounts.

To illustrate the different conditions, assume that the capital of the Washington Corporation on December 31, 1972, is as follows:

Preferred stock, $100 par, 10,000 shares.	$1,000,000
Premium on preferred stock	100,000
Common stock, $25 stated value, 100,000 shares	2,500,000
Paid-in capital from sale of common stock at more than	
stated value	500,000
Retained earnings	1,000,000

Preferred shares are convertible into common shares at any time at the option of the shareholder.

Case 1: Assume that conditions of conversion permit the exchange of each share of preferred for 4 shares of common. On December 31, 1972, 1,000 shares of preferred stock are exchanged on the above basis. The amount originally paid for the preferred, $110,000, is now the consideration identified with 4,000 shares of common stock with a total stated value of $100,000. The conversion is recorded as follows:

Preferred Stock ($100 par, 1,000 shares)	100,000	
Premium on Preferred Stock	10,000	
Common Stock ($25 stated value, 4,000 shares) . .		100,000
Paid-In Capital from Conversion of Preferred		
Stock into Common Stock		10,000

Case 2: Assume that conditions of conversion permit the exchange of each share of preferred for 3 shares of common. The conversion of 1,000 shares of preferred stock for common stock calls for the transfer of the paid-in capital balances related to preferred stock to the common stock equity; the excess of the book value of preferred holdings over the stated value of the common stock issued in exchange is recognized as paid-in capital relating to the latter issue. The conversion is recorded by the following entry:

Preferred Stock ($100 par, 1,000 shares)	100,000	
Premium on Preferred Stock	10,000	
Common Stock ($25 stated value, 3,000 shares) .		75,000
Paid-In Capital from Conversion of Preferred		
Stock into Common Stock		35,000

Case 3: Assume that conditions of conversion permit the exchange of each share of preferred for 5 shares of common. In converting 1,000 shares of preferred for common, an increase in common stock of $125,000 must be recognized although it is accompanied by a decrease in the preferred equity of only $110,000; the increase in the legal capital related to the new issue can be accomplished only by a charge to retained earnings. The conversion, then, is recorded as follows:

Preferred Stock ($100 par, 1,000 shares)	100,000	
Premium on Preferred Stock	10,000	
Retained Earnings	15,000	
Common Stock ($25 stated value, 5,000 shares) .		125,000

The problems relating to the conversion of bonds for capital stock were described in Chapter 18. When either stocks or bonds have conversion rights, the company must be in a position to issue securities of the required class. Unissued or reacquired securities may be maintained by the company for this purpose. Detailed information should be given on the balance sheet relative to security conversion features as well as the means for meeting conversion requirements.

Recapitalizations

Corporate recapitalization occurs when an entire issue of stock is changed by appropriate action of the corporation. In some states recapitalizations including changes in the legal capital are possible by action of the board of directors and stockholders; in other states recapitalizations also require the approval of state authorities.

A common type of recapitalization is a change from par to no-par stock. If the capital stock balance is to remain the same after the change, the original capital stock account is closed and an account for the new issue is opened. Any premium relating to the original stock issue should be transferred to some other paid-in capital account appropriately labeled. If the capital stock balance is to exceed the consideration received on the original sale of the stock, a new capital stock account is credited for the value assigned to the new issue, original paid-in capital balances are closed, and the retained earnings account is charged for the difference. If the capital stock balance is to be reduced, the original account, as well as any premium account, is closed, a new capital stock account is credited for the value assigned to the new stock, and an appropriately titled additional paid-in capital account is credited for the difference.

To illustrate, assume capital for the Signal Corporation as follows:

Capital stock, $10 par, 100,000 shares...............	$1,000,000
Premium on capital stock...........................	100,000
Retained earnings.................................	250,000

Entries for each of the three possibilities are given below:

Case 1: Assume that the original stock is exchanged for no-par stock with a stated value of $10:

Capital Stock ($10 par, 100,000 shares).......	1,000,000	
Premium on Capital Stock.................	100,000	
Capital Stock ($10 stated value, 100,000 shares).................................		1,000,000
Paid-In Capital from Exchange of Par for No-Par Stock...........................		100,000

Case 2: Assume that the original stock is exchanged for no-par stock with a stated value of $12.50:

Capital Stock ($10 par, 100,000 shares).......	1,000,000	
Premium on Capital Stock.................	100,000	
Retained Earnings........................	150,000	
Capital Stock ($12.50 stated value, 100,000 shares)................................		1,250,000

Case 3: Assume that the original stock is exchanged for no-par stock with a stated value of $5:

Capital Stock ($10 par, 100,000 shares).......	1,000,000	
Premium on Capital Stock.................	100,000	
Capital Stock ($5 stated value, 100,000 shares)................................		500,000
Paid-In Capital from Reduction in Value Assigned to Capital Stock..............		600,000

Recapitalizations that involve changes in the stated values of no-par stock or changes from no-par stock to stock with a par value call for similar procedures.

Corporate recapitalization that is part of a plan for the elimination of a deficit is referred to as a *quasi-reorganization* and was described in Chapter 15.

Stock splits and reverse stock splits

When the market price of shares is high and it is felt that a lower price will result in a better market and a wider distribution of ownership, a corporation may authorize that the shares outstanding be replaced by a larger number of shares. For example, 100,000 shares of stock, par value $100, are called in and exchanged for 500,000 shares of stock, par value $20. Each stockholder receives 5 new shares for each share owned. The increase in shares outstanding in this manner is known as a *stock split* or *stock split-up*. The reverse procedure, replacement of shares outstanding by a smaller number of shares, may be desirable when the price of shares is low and it is felt that there may be certain advantages in having a higher price for shares. The reduction of shares outstanding by combining shares is referred to as a *reverse stock split* or a *stock split-down*.

After a stock split or reverse stock split, the capital stock balance remains the same; however, the change in the number of shares of stock outstanding is accompanied by a change in the par or stated value of the stock. The change in the number of shares outstanding, as well as the change in the par or stated value, may be recorded by means of a memorandum entry. However, it would normally be desirable to establish a new account reporting the nature and the amount of the new issue. In any event, notations will be required in the subsidiary stockholders ledger to report the exchange of stock and the change in the number of shares held by each stockholder.

Paid-in capital not designated as legal capital

Although it is common practice to report on the balance sheet a single value for additional paid-in capital, separate accounts should be provided in the ledger to identify the individual sources of such capital. Sources of additional paid-in capital and the accounts summarizing these are listed below.

Source	Additional Paid-In Capital Account
Sale of stock at more than par value	Premium on Capital Stock (or Paid-In Capital from Sale of Stock at More Than Par)
Sale of stock at more than stated value	Paid-In Capital from Sale of Capital Stock at More Than Stated Value
Stock subscription defaults resulting in forfeiture of amounts paid in	Paid-In Capital from Forfeited Stock Subscriptions
Assessments levied on stockholders	Paid-In Capital from Capital Stock Assessments (except where stock was originally sold at a discount and stock assessments are considered to be proper credits to such discount)
Reacquisition of stock at less than original sales price	Paid-In Capital from Capital Stock Reacquisition (or Paid-In Capital from Capital Stock Redemption)
Expiration of stock warrants or stock options	Paid-In Capital from Unexercised Stock Rights (or Paid-In Capital from Unexercised Stock Options)
Conversion of outstanding stock into a new issue with a smaller total par or stated value	Paid-In Capital from Conversion of Capital Stock
Reduction in corporate stated capital as a result of recapitalization	Paid-In Capital from Reduction in Value Assigned to Capital Stock
Sale of treasury stock at more than cost	Paid-In Capital from Sale of Treasury Stock at More Than Cost
Donation of stock or properties or forgiveness of corporate indebtedness by stockholders	Donated (or Paid-In) Capital from Contributions by Stockholders
Donation of properties or forgiveness of corporate indebtedness by governmental authorities or other outsiders	Donated (or Paid-In) Capital from Contributions by Governmental Authority (or others)

Charges should be made to additional paid-in capital balances only when (1) transactions may be regarded as reducing such balances, or

(2) there is an express authorization by the board of directors for such reduction. To illustrate (1) above, the redemption and retirement of a preferred stock issue may properly be recorded by cancellation of the preferred stock balance as well as any other paid-in capital balance relating to the original issue; all reference to paid-in capital relating to the preferred stock is thus canceled with the redemption of this class of stock. To illustrate (2) above, authorization by the board of directors for the capitalization of a portion of a particular paid-in capital balance would call for a reduction in the additional paid-in capital account and an increase in the capital stock account.

Additional paid-in capital balances should not be charged with losses whether from normal operations or from extraordinary sources, nor should such paid-in capital be used for the cancellation of a deficit in the absence of formal steps taken to effect a quasi-reorganization. The membership of the AICPA adopted the following rule on this matter:

> . . . Capital surplus, however created, should not be used to relieve the income account of the current or future years of charges which would otherwise fall to be made thereagainst. This rule might be subject to the exception that where, upon reorganization, a reorganized company would be relieved of charges which would require to be made against income if the existing corporation were continued, it might be regarded as permissible to accomplish the same result without reorganization provided the facts were as fully revealed to and the action as formally approved by the shareholders as in reorganization.[1]

The Chief Accountant of the Securities and Exchange Commission took a similar stand in the following statement:

> It is my conviction that capital surplus should under no circumstances be used to write off losses which, if currently recognized, would have been chargeable against income. In case a deficit is thereby created, I see no objection to writing off such a deficit against capital surplus, provided appropriate stockholder approval has been obtained. In this event, subsequent statements of earned surplus should designate the point of time from which the new surplus dates.[2]

The availability as a basis for dividends of paid-in capital that is not designated as legal capital depends upon the laws of the state of incorporation. In the absence of legal restrictions, such capital can be used as a basis for dividends. Laws may provide restrictions upon the use of all of the paid-in capital or upon the use of only certain kinds of paid-in capital. Separate accounts in the ledger summarizing paid-in capital by source make possible the ready determination of distributable capital. When capital other than retained earnings is used as a basis for

---

[1] *Accounting Research Bulletin No. 43, op. cit.*, Ch. 1, sect. A, par 2.
[2] "Treatment of Losses Resulting from Revaluation of Assets," *Accounting Series Releases*, Release No. 1 (Washington: United States Securities and Exchange Commission, 1937), p. 3.

dividends, stockholders should be informed by the corporation concerning the source of such distribution, since stockholders have the right to assume that dividends represent distributions of earnings unless they are notified to the contrary.

QUESTIONS

1. The controller for the Scott Co. contends that the redemption of preferred stock at less than its issuance price should be reported as an increase in retained earnings since redemption at more than issuance price calls for a decrease in retained earnings. How would you answer this argument?

2. Why might a company purchase its own stock?

3. What is the purpose of legislation limiting the purchase by a company of its own stock to its retained earnings balance?

4. The Waters Co. reports treasury stock as a current asset, explaining that it intends to sell the stock soon to acquire working capital. Do you approve of this reporting?

5. The Accounting Principles Board suggests alternate methods for the reacquisition and retirement by a company of its own shares at more than par or stated value. What are the alternate methods and what support can you give for each?

6. (a) Describe two approaches that may be taken in recording the reacquisition of treasury stock. (b) What are the entries in each case assuming that: (1) the stock is purchased at more than its par or stated value; (2) the stock is purchased at less than its par or stated value?

7. There is frequently a difference between the purchase price and the sales price of treasury stock. Why isn't this difference properly shown as an income statement item, especially in view of the APB opinions which restrict entries to Retained Earnings?

8. Retained earnings of the Saunders Co. equal to the amount paid on the acquisition of treasury stock cannot be used as a basis for dividends until treasury stock is sold. What accounting and reporting procedures may be followed by the company in giving effect to this requirement?

9. Describe in order of preference, alternative methods of accounting for the receipt and immediate disposition of donated treasury stock which was originally issued at its fair market value and had no aspects of a "treasury stock subterfuge."

10. Under what conditions, if any, should donated stock be recorded prior to its resale?

11. The Walsh Co. issues 10,000,000 shares of no-par common stock in exchange for certain mineral lands. Property is established on the books at $5,000,000. Shortly thereafter, stockholders donate to the corporation 20% of their shares. The stock is resold by the company at 10¢ per share. What accounting problems arise as a result of the stock donation and resale?

12. (a) What entries should be made on the books when stock rights are issued to stockholders? (b) What entries should be made when stock is issued on rights? (c) What information, if any, should appear on the balance sheet relative to outstanding rights?

13. (a) Define a stock option. What is a "qualified stock option"? (b) What are the circumstances that may suggest the issue of stock options?

14. Some users of accounting reports believe that earnings are overstated on certain income statements because of the currently accepted procedure for recording employee stock options. (a) Describe how the earnings may be overstated. (b) What alternative procedures would more satisfactorily match revenue and expense?

15. Preferred stockholders of the Burns Corporation exchange their holdings for no-par common stock in accordance with terms of the preferred issue. How should such conversion be reported on the corporation books?

16. Compare the objectives of a stock split with those of a conversion of stock.

17. The Mellon Corporation was formed in July, 1972. At date of incorporation it issued $1,000,000 of $100 par value common stock at par for cash. Operations during the remainder of 1972 resulted in net income of $75,000. At a directors' meeting in January, 1973, it was decided that $700,000 of contributed capital would be adequate to meet foreseeable operating needs and provide for reasonable expansion. The following individual suggestions were made to provide for the excess capitalization:

    (a) Reduce shares from $100 to $70 par value.
    (b) Invest $300,000 of excess cash in the company's own shares.
    (c) Distribute a cash dividend of $30 per share.
    (d) Resort to a quasi-reorganization and write down various assets by $300,000.

    In your opinion, how sound is each of these suggestions in accomplishing the desired purpose?

18. The accountant for the Walter Corporation closes stock discount and deficit account balances into paid-in capital from the sale of stock in excess of stated value and reports only the balance of the latter account on the balance sheet. Do you approve?

EXERCISES

1. The Livermore Co. has 20,000 shares of preferred stock outstanding; stock had been issued at par, $50. On June 1, 1972, the company redeemed and retired 1,500 shares of preferred stock at $52; on September 15, 1972, the company reacquired and retired 1,800 shares at $49. Give the entries to record the acquisition and the retirement of the preferred shares.

2. The capital accounts for the Western Co. were as follows on June 1, 1972:

Common stock, 80,000 shares, $15 par................. $1,200,000
Premium on common stock......................... 160,000
Retained earnings................................. 300,000

On this date the company purchased 4,000 shares of stock at $16; and in December of the same year it sold this stock at $19. (a) What entries should be made for the stock purchase and the sale if the purchase is viewed as a capital stock retirement and treasury stock is reported at par? (If alternate treatments are possible, justify your selection.) (b) What entries should be made for the stock purchase and the sale if the purchase is viewed as giving rise to a capital element awaiting ultimate disposition and treasury stock is reported at cost? (c) After the sale of the treasury stock, how does the stockholders' equity differ under the two methods?

3. The Boyer Company issued 20,000 shares of no-par stock at $35 and 40,000 shares at $50. The state in which Boyer is incorporated does not require any stated capital. During 1972, 4,000 shares were reacquired at $40. Assume that the treasury stock is to be carried at the weighted average price per share. Prepare the journal entry to record the reacquisition.

4. Stock outstanding of the Johnson Co. is no-par with a stated value of $25. Principal stockholders donated 15,000 shares of stock to the corporation. The shares were subsequently resold at $18. Give the entries to record the acquisition and the resale of the treasury stock. (Assume that corporation assets are properly valued.)

5. In your first audit of a mining company, you note the following facts with respect to its capital stock transactions:

Authorized capital consists of 5,000,000 shares of $1 par value common stock.

All of the shares were issued initially in exchange for certain mineral properties. The properties were recorded on the company books at $10,000,000.

Three million shares were received by the company as a donation shortly after incorporation and were sold immediately for cash of $4,500,000. This amount was recorded as a credit to paid-in capital.

(a) What values should be assigned to the mineral properties and the stockholders' equity? Discuss. (b) Prepare any required correcting entry.

6. The Lowell Co. issued $1,000,000 of 7% bonds at 103. With each subscription for a $1,000 bond it gave transferable warrants permitting the owner to subscribe for a one-year period to 6 shares of common stock with a par value per share of $75. (a) What entry would be made by the company for the sale of the bonds assuming that: (1) stock was selling at $70 per share on the date of the bond issue? (2) stock was selling at $90 per share on the date of the bond issue? (b) What entries would be made in (1) and (2) above, assuming that all of the rights are ultimately exercised? (c) What entries would be made in (1) and (2) above, assuming that only 70% of the rights are ultimately exercised?

7. Capital accounts for the Davidson Co. on December 31 are as follows:

Preferred stock, $25 par, 25,000 shares issued and outstanding........	$ 625,000
Premium on preferred stock........	31,250
Common stock, $5 par, 150,000 shares issued and outstanding........	750,000
Premium on common stock........	110,000
Retained earnings........	1,450,000

Preferred stock is convertible into common stock. Give the entry that is made on the corporation books assuming that 800 shares of preferred are converted under each assumption listed:

(a) Preferred shares are convertible into common on a share-for-share basis.
(b) Each preferred share is convertible into 8 shares of common.
(c) Each preferred share is convertible into 4 shares of common.

8. The Gilbert Co. has 18,000 shares of common stock, par $15, outstanding. Proceeds from the sale of the stock were $320,000 and this is reported in the paid-in capital balances. Give the entry that would be made on the company books for each assumption listed below.

(a) A recapitalization is effected, each stockholder receiving 3 shares of new no-par stock with a stated value of $5 for each share owned.
(b) A stock split is effected, each shareholder receiving 5 shares of new stock, par value $3, for each share owned.
(c) A recapitalization is effected, each shareholder receiving 2 shares of new $10 par value stock for each share owned.
(d) A recapitalization is effected, each shareholder receiving 1 share of new $10 par value stock for each share owned.

9. The Corless Co. reports its stockholders' equity as follows:

750,000 shares of common, $10 par.................	$7,500,000
Additional paid-in capital........................	530,000
Deficit...	(880,000)
Total stockholders' equity.......................	$7,150,000

The company wishes to cancel the deficit and is considering each of the possibilities listed below. Give the entries that would be required and prepare the stockholders' equity section for each assumption.

(a) Stockholders are to donate 25% of their shares to the company and these are to be formally retired.

(b) The par value of shares is to be reduced to $8.

(c) One new share of no-par stock is to be exchanged for each share of common stock outstanding and the legal capital for the company is to be restated at $7,150,000.

(d) One new share of no-par stock with a stated value of $20 is to be exchanged for every three shares of common.

10. From the following information, reconstruct the journal entries that were made by the Redco Corporation during 1972:

	Dec. 31, 1972		Dec. 31, 1971	
	Amount	Shares	Amount	Shares
Common stock..............	$150,000	7,500	$175,000	8,750
Premium on common stock...	45,000		62,500	
Paid-in capital from sale of treasury stock at more than cost.....................	—	—	1,000	200
Retained earnings...........	39,000	—	66,500*	—
Treasury stock..............	—	—	12,000	300

*Includes net income for 1971 of $30,000. There were no dividends.

Twelve hundred fifty shares of common stock that had been issued when the company was formed were purchased and retired during 1972. The cost method is used to record treasury stock transactions.

11. The Loring Steel Company wished to reduce the carrying value of its intangible assets from $200,000 to $1. To do this, the company decided to reduce the par value of its stock from $10 to $8 a share. The intangible assets could then be written off and the resulting deficit applied against the paid-in capital resulting from the recapitalization. On June 30, capital accounts for the corporation were:

Capital stock (150,000 shares).......................	$1,500,000
Premium on capital stock...........................	100,000
Retained earnings..................................	60,000

What entries would be made to reduce intangible assets to $1 following the plan given above?

12. The stockholders of the Trask Co. on December 24, 1966, approved a plan granting certain officers of the company nontransferable options to buy 50,000 shares of no-par common at $8 per share. Stock was selling at this time at $10 per share. The option plan provides that the officers must be employed by the company for the next five years, that options can be exercised after January 1, 1972, and that options will expire at the end of 1973. One of the officers who had been granted options for 10,000 shares left the company at the beginning of 1970; remaining officers exercised their rights under the option plan at the end of 1973. Give the entries that should be made on the books of the corporation at the end of each year for 1966–1973 inclusive. The market price of the stock at January 1, 1972, was $15 per share.

PROBLEMS

20-1. The accounts for the Jamison Products Co. at the beginning of 1972 showed the following issues of capital stock:

30,000 shares at $21.00	$630,000
7,000 shares at $25.00	175,000
3,000 shares at $23.00	69,000

During 1972 the company reacquired 3,000 shares at $20, and these were reissued at the beginning of 1973 at $26 per share.

Instructions: (1) Give the entries to record the acquisition and the reissue of treasury stock for each assumption listed below if the treasury stock purchase is viewed as capital retirement and the treasury stock account is charged at par, stated value, or average, whichever is appropriate.

(a) Assume that the stock has a $15 par value.
(b) Assume that the stock is no-par with a stated value of $20.
(c) Assume that the stock is no-par and without a stated value.

(2) Give the entries to record the acquisition and the resale of treasury stock for each assumption listed in (1) above if the treasury stock purchase is viewed as a capital element awaiting ultimate disposition and the treasury stock account is charged for the amount paid.

20-2. The Harmon Company has two classes of capital stock outstanding: 6%, $10 par preferred and $50 par common. During the fiscal year ending November 30, 1972, the company was active in transactions that affected the stockholders' equity. The following summarizes these transactions:

Type of Transaction	Number of Shares	Price per Share
(a) Issue of preferred stock	10,000	$12
(b) Issue of common stock	35,000	50
(c) Retirement of preferred stock	2,000	14
(d) Purchase of treasury stock — common (cost method)	5,000	60
(e) Stock split — common	2 for 1	
(f) Reissue of treasury stock	5,000	40

Balances of the accounts in the stockholders' equity section on November 30, 1971, were:

Preferred Stock — 50,000 shares.................... $ 500,000
Common Stock — 100,000 shares.................... 5,000,000
Premium on Preferred Stock........................ 200,000
Premium on Common Stock........................ 1,000,000
Retained Earnings................................ 520,000

Dividends were paid during the fiscal year on the common stock at $1 per share, and on 8,000 shares of preferred stock at the preferred rate. Net income for the year was $500,000.

Instructions: Based upon the above data, prepare the stockholders' equity section of the balance sheet as of November 30, 1972.

20-3. Transactions of the Flower Company during 1972, the first year of operations, that affected its stockholders' equity were as follows:
   (a) Sold 10,000 shares of 6% preferred stock, $10 par, at $14.
   (b) Sold 25,000 shares of $25 par common stock at $27.
   (c) Purchased and retired 4,000 shares of preferred stock at $15.
   (d) Purchased 3,000 shares of its own common stock at $29.
   (e) Sold 1,000 shares of treasury stock at $31.
   (f) Stockholders donated to the company 2,000 shares of common when shares had a market price of $30. One half of these shares were sold for $35.

No dividends were declared in 1972 and net income for 1972 was $75,000.

Instructions: (1) Record each of the above transactions. Assume that treasury stock acquisitions are recorded at cost.
   (2) Give the entries for (d) and (e) assuming that treasury stock acquisitions are reported as capital stock retirement.
   (3) Prepare the stockholders' equity section of the balance sheet assuming that treasury stock is recorded at cost and assuming that retained earnings restrictions are shown by parenthetical remarks.
   (4) Prepare the stockholders' equity section of the balance sheet assuming that treasury stock is recorded at par value and assuming that retained earnings restrictions are shown as appropriations.

20-4. The Redding Corporation was organized on October 1, 1970. It was authorized to issue stock as follows:

50,000 shares of 6% cumulative, nonparticipating preferred, $100 par.
100,000 shares of common, $10 par.

On October 1, 5,000 shares of the preferred stock were subscribed for at $108. On October 4, 90,000 shares of common stock were subscribed for at $15. Subscriptions on both common and preferred stock were payable 25% upon subscription, the balance in three equal installments due December 1, 1970, and February 1 and April 1, 1971: Defaults on the installment due December 1 were as follows: preferred, 50 shares; common, 1,000 shares. Subscriptions were received for defaulted stock as follows: preferred at $102; common at $12. Subscriptions on stock that was resold were payable 50% upon subscription, the balance in two equal installments due February 1 and April 1, 1971. Amounts paid in less losses on the resale of stock were returned to defaulting subscribers. The net loss from operations by the corporation for the 3-month period ended December 31, 1970, was $110,000.

In February 1971, the remaining common stock was sold for cash at $13. Cash was received in payment of remaining installments from all subscribers with the exception of one subscriber who was unable to pay his final 25% installment on the preferred. He issued to the corporation a note payable in January, 1972, for $13,500, the fourth installment owed. Stock was to be issued upon payment of the note. Stock was issued in April to all fully paid subscribers. The net loss from operations by the corporation for the year ended December 31, 1971, was $120,000.

On January 5, 1972, cash was received in payment of the note for $13,500, and stock was issued. In January, the stockholders agreed to the following: each share of common stock was to be exchanged for 2 shares of no-par common with a stated value per share of $3. The paid-in capital in excess of the stock par value created by the recapitalization was to be used in part to cancel the deficit arising from operations of past periods. The exchange was completed in February. The net income for the year ended December 31, 1972, was $150,000. On December 31 dividends were declared on preferred stock for the past 2¼ years, and a dividend of 20 cents a share was declared on the common stock.

Instructions: (1) Prepare journal entries for the transactions given above. (For annual net income or loss simply give the entry to close the income summary account to Retained Earnings.)

(2) Construct the stockholders' equity sections for the balance sheets as of (a) December 31, 1970, (b) December 31, 1971, and (c) December 31, 1972.

20-5. The balance sheet for the Dyer Corporation on December 31, 1971, is as follows:

Assets...		$750,000
Liabilities..		$410,000
Stockholders' equity:		
$1.00 Convertible preferred stock, $20 par...	$ 50,000	
Common stock, $10 par.....................	150,000	
Premium from original sale of common stock at $12..............................	30,000	
Retained earnings........................	116,000	
	$346,000	
Less treasury stock, common, 500 shares at cost	6,000	340,000
Total liabilities and stockholders' equity.................		$750,000

During 1972 the following transactions were completed in the order given:

(a) 750 shares of common stock were reacquired by purchase at $7. (Treasury stock is recorded at cost.)

(b) 150 shares of common stock were reacquired in settlement of an account receivable of $1,500.

(c) Semiannual cash dividends of 75 cents on common stock and 50 cents on preferred stock were declared and paid.

(d) Each share of preferred stock is convertible into 4 shares of common stock; 500 shares of preferred stock were turned in for common stock; accrued dividends totaling $100 were paid to preferred stockholders exchanging their holdings.

(e) The 900 shares of the common treasury stock acquired during 1972 were sold at $13. The remaining treasury shares were exchanged for machinery with a fair market value of $6,300.

(f) 3,000 shares of common stock were issued in exchange for land appraised at $39,000.

(g) Semiannual cash dividends of 75 cents on common stock and 50 cents on preferred stock were declared and paid.

(h) Net income was $35,000.

Instructions: (1) Give journal entries to record the transactions listed above. (For net income, simply give the entry to close the income summary account to Retained Earnings.)

(2) Prepare the stockholders' equity section of the balance sheet as of December 31, 1972.

20-6. Richard Walker, Inc., was organized on January 2, 1970, and was authorized to issue 75,000 shares of no-par stock. A stated value of $8 was assigned by the board of directors to each share, and shares were sold during 1970 as follows:

January 14	20,000 shares at	20
February 19	10,000 shares at	25
April 14	5,500 shares at	30

During 1970, the corporation paid regular quarterly dividends of $1 a share; the first quarterly dividend was paid to stockholders of record March 15 and the remaining dividends were paid at 3-month intervals thereafter. Dividends are paid on record date. Net income for the year was $375,000.

In 1971 the market price of its stock declined and the company reacquired its own stock as follows (treasury stock is recorded at cost):

April 12	1,500 shares at	25
May 10	2,500 shares at	21
June 20	5,000 shares at	20

The laws of the state provide that earnings equal to the amounts paid for treasury stock are not available for dividends; such restrictions are removed when treasury stock is sold and original invested capital restored. The company records such restrictions by appropriations of retained earnings.

In 1971 the company paid the first and second quarterly dividends of $1 to stockholders of record March 15 and June 15. The net income for the year was $45,000.

In 1972 business conditions improved and the company, in order to obtain funds for expansion purposes, resold the 5,000 shares of treasury stock acquired June 20, 1971, as follows:

February 5.................................2,000 shares at 34
June 1....................................3,000 shares at 40

The 2,500 shares of treasury stock acquired on May 10, 1971, were transferred to a creditor in settlement of a past-due account amounting to $75,600 on June 1, 1972. On this date stock had a market value of $78,000.

During 1972 the corporation paid regular dividends of 80 cents a share to stockholders of record March 15 and at quarterly intervals thereafter. A 40-cent extra dividend was paid on December 15. For the year, the company reported a net income of $240,000.

Instructions: (1) Prepare journal entries to record the above transactions. (For annual net income figures, simply give the entry to close the income summary account to Retained Earnings.)

(2) Construct the stockholders' equity section of the balance sheet as of December 31, 1970, December 31, 1971, and December 31, 1972.

20-7. James Marshall, Inc., reported a stockholders' equity on December 31, 1970, as follows:

Common stock, $25 par; 250,000 shares authorized:
   150,000 shares issued and outstanding; options to purchase 10,000 shares at $35 per share are held by officers, no value having been assigned to these options........ $3,750,000
Premium on common stock......................... 400,000
Retained earnings................................ 2,150,000

On May 31, 1971, the company issued bonds of $2,000,000 at par, giving with each $1,000 bond a warrant enabling the holder to purchase 4 shares of stock at $50 for a one-year period. Shares were selling for $46 at this time.

By December 31, 1971, 3,500 shares of stock had been issued to officers in connection with option agreements and 2,500 shares had been issued in connection with rights issued on the sale of bonds. Net income for 1971 was $315,000.

On January 15, 1972, the corporation issued rights to stockholders (1 right on each share) permitting holders to acquire for a 60-day period 1 share at $55 with every 8 rights submitted. Shares were selling for $59 at this time. All but 3,000 rights were exercised and the additional stock was issued.

By December 31, 1972, 2,500 shares of stock had been issued to officers in connection with option agreements and 2,500 shares had been issued in connection with rights issued on the sale of bonds. A special dividend of $2.00 per share was declared on December 31, 1972. Net income for 1972 was $650,000.

Instructions: (1) Give entries to record the foregoing transactions. (For net income, simply give the entry closing the income summary account to Retained Earnings.)

(2) Prepare the stockholders' equity section of the balance sheet on (a) December 31, 1971, and (b) December 31, 1972.

20-8. The board of directors of the King Production Co. adopted a stock option plan to supplement the salaries of certain executives of the company. Options to buy common stock were granted as follows:

		No. of Shares	Option Price	Price of Shares at Date of Grant
January 10, 1969	John Hancock......	75,000	16½	17
June 30, 1969	Donald Norton......	50,000	21	22
	Maynard Erickson...	20,000		

Options are nontransferable and can be exercised three years after date of grant providing the executive is still in the employ of the company. Options expire two years after the date they can first be exercised.

Maynard Erickson left the employ of the company at the beginning of 1971.

Stock options were exercised as follows:

		No. of Shares	Price of Shares at Date of Exercise
January 15, 1972	John Hancock...........	60,000	41
December 20, 1972	John Hancock...........	15,000	32
December 22, 1972	Donald Norton..........	50,000	28½

Stock of the company has a $10 par value. The accounting period for the company is the calendar year.

Instructions: Give all of the entries that would be made on the books of the corporation relative to the stock option agreement for the period 1969 to 1972 inclusive.

20-9. In April, 1972, The Henry Corporation stockholders approved the adoption of a "Deferred Compensation Plan for Officers and Key Employees" starting with the calendar year ending December 31, 1972. The Plan provides, among other things,

(a) that allotments to participants under the Plan shall consist of cash or of cash and common stock of The Henry Corporation;

(b) that the cash allotment shall be paid in the year in which allotted and that the balance of the participants' allotment shall be payable solely in common stock of The Henry Corporation;

(c) that the stock so allotted shall be treasury stock purchased by the corporation, and no authorized but unissued stock shall be used for purposes of the Plan;

(d) that during the calendar year the total amount to be set aside and credited to the Deferred Incentive Compensation Fund shall be determined by the board of directors but shall not exceed the following:

$.40 of the 1st $1.00 per share earned in excess of $1.50 per share,
$.30 of the 2d $1.00 per share earned in excess of $1.50 per share,
$.20 of the 3d and each succeeding $1.00 per share earned in excess
   of $1.50 per share,
or a proportionate amount of any fraction of a dollar.

Earnings per share shall be based on The Henry Corporation's net income after provision for federal income taxes (calculated at 52% less $5,500), but before the provision contemplated by this Plan and its tax effect, and on the average number of shares of common stock of the corporation outstanding during the calendar year (computed on an average monthly basis to the nearest 10 shares).

However, the maximum amount to be set aside from such earnings in excess of $1.50 per share for the purposes of this Plan shall not in any year exceed 18% of the net income for the year after federal taxes but before provision for deferred incentive compensation.

At December 31, 1972, the records of the corporation reflect the following data:

(a) On December 10, 1972, the board of directors approved a provision for deferred incentive compensation in the amount of $76,000 for the year ended December 31, 1972. Of this amount, 20% was to be paid in cash prior to December 31, 1972, and the balance set aside for stock allotment. (The cash portion was paid on December 29, 1972.)

(b) The condensed statement of income for the year ended December 31, 1972, follows:

Net sales.................................		$5,448,341
Cost and expenses:		
Cost of goods sold........................	$3,765,000	
Selling and administrative.................	799,000	
Provision for deferred incentive compensation.	76,000	4,640,000
Operating income.........................		$ 808,341
Provision for federal income taxes (52% less		
$5,500)................................		414,837
Net income..............................		$ 393,504

(c) Analysis of the common stock accounts show that there were 150,000 shares of common stock authorized at December 31, 1971 and 1972, and 140,000 shares issued and outstanding at December 31, 1971. On June 1, 1972, the corporation purchased in the open market 9,651 shares of its stock at an average price of $20.75 per share, which shares were held in the treasury at December 31, 1972. There were no other changes in common stock during the year.

(d) You are advised that the total provision for deferred incentive compensation in any year is an acceptable federal income tax deduction in the year provided, if in accordance with the terms of the Plan.

Instructions: Prepare a statement in good form showing the computations of the maximum amounts available for deferred incentive compensation as computed under the two limitations set forth in the Plan.   (AICPA adapted)

20-10. The president of Ronnico, Inc., F. A. Ronnie, is planning to retire. By agreement with the other stockholders of the company he will exchange his capital stock for non-voting preferred stock.

Ronnico, Inc., has no preferred stock in its capitalization. The capital stock is held as follows:

100 shares held by F. A. Ronnie, President
350 shares held by J. R. Stone, Executive Vice-President
150 shares held by M. A. Tall, Vice-President in Charge of Sales
150 shares held in the treasury of the company

750 shares, total capital stock issued

The stockholders' equity section of the company's balance sheet follows:

Capital stock ($100 par value)........................	$ 75,000
Premium on capital stock.............................	37,500
Retained earnings....................................	17,500
Total..	$130,000
Treasury stock, at cost..............................	10,000
Total stockholders' equity...........................	$120,000

Under terms of the agreement the company will be reorganized as follows:

(a) The treasury stock will be canceled.

(b) Two new issues will be authorized, common and 5% cumulative non-voting preferred. Both will be $100 par value per share.

(c) The stockholders will surrender their capital stock for cancellation and will receive the newly authorized issues as follows:
   (1) F. A. Ronnie will receive only preferred stock.
   (2) J. R. Stone will receive 60% of the common stock and the remainder of the preferred.
   (3) M. A. Tall will receive 40% of the common stock.

(d) The combined total number of shares of common and preferred stock outstanding after the exchange will be the same as the total number of shares authorized and outstanding before the transfer (after giving effect to the retirement of the treasury stock).

Instructions: (1) Prepare the journal entry to cancel the treasury stock account on the books of the company.

(2) Prepare a schedule computing the amount of each stockholder's equity in the company before the recapitalization.

(3) Compute the number of new common shares and new preferred shares to be issued.

(4) Prepare a schedule computing the number of shares of each type of newly issued stock that each stockholder must receive so that he will have the same equity in the company after the exchange as before the exchange.

(AICPA adapted)

20-11. You have just commenced your audit of Shaky Company for the year ended December 31, 1972. The president advises you that the company is insolvent and must declare bankruptcy unless a large loan can be obtained immediately. A lender who is willing to advance $450,000 to the company has been located, but he will only make the loan subject to the following conditions:

(a) A $600,000, 6% mortgage payable on the company's land and buildings held by a major stockholder will be canceled along with four months' accrued interest. The mortgage will be replaced by 5,000 shares of $100 par value, 6%, cumulative if earned, nonparticipating, preferred stock.

(b) A $450,000, 8% mortgage payable over 15 years on the land and buildings will be given as security on the new loan.

(c) On May 1, 1971, the company's trade creditors accepted $360,000 in notes payable on demand at 6% interest in settlement of all past-due accounts. No payment has been made to date. The company will offer to settle these liabilities at $.75 per $1.00 owed or to replace the notes payable on demand with new notes payable for full indebtedness over five years at 6% interest. It is estimated that $200,000 of the demand notes will be exchanged for the longer-term notes and that the remainder will accept the offer of a reduced cash settlement.

(d) A new issue of 500 shares of $100 par value, 5%, noncumulative, nonparticipating, preferred stock will replace 500 outstanding shares of $100 par value, 7%, cumulative, participating preferred stock. Preferred stockholders will repudiate all claims to $21,000 of dividends in arrears. The company has never formally declared the dividends.

(e) A new issue of 600 shares of $50 par value, class A common stock will replace 600 outstanding shares of $100 par value, class A common stock.

(f) A new issue of 650 shares of $40 par value, class B common stock will replace 650 outstanding shares of $100 par value, class B common stock.

The president of the Shaky Company requests that you determine the effect of the foregoing on the company and furnishes the following condensed account balances, which you believe are fairly presented:

Bank overdraft.	$ 15,000
Other current assets.	410,000
Land, buildings, and equipment.	840,000
Trade accounts payable.	235,000
Other current liabilities.	85,000
Contributed capital at more than par value.	125,000
Retained earnings deficit.	345,000

Instructions: (1) Prepare pro forma journal entries that you would suggest to give effect to the foregoing transactions as of January 1, 1973. Entries should be keyed to lettered information in order.

(2) Prepare a pro forma balance sheet for the Shaky Company at January 1, 1973, as if the recapitalization had been consummated.

(AICPA adapted)

chapter 21

retained earnings - earnings and earnings distribution

The difference between assets and liabilities is proprietorship or capital, the owners' equity in assets. In a sole proprietorship, a single capital account reports the owner's entire equity in assets resulting from investments, withdrawals, and earnings. In a partnership, capital balances for the individual partners normally report partners' full equities resulting from investments, withdrawals, and earnings. It has already been indicated that, because of the nature of the corporate form, it is necessary to distinguish between the capital originating from the stockholders' investment, designated as *paid-in* or *invested capital*, and the capital originating from earnings, designated as *retained earnings* or *earned surplus*.

Retained earnings is essentially the meeting place of the balance sheet accounts and the income statement accounts. In successive periods retained earnings are increased by earnings and decreased by dividends. As a result, the retained earnings balance represents the net accumulated earnings of the corporation. If the retained earnings account were affected only by earnings and dividends, there would be little confusion in its interpretation. But a number of factors tend to complicate the nature of retained earnings. Among these factors are: transactions between the corporation and its stockholders that affect retained earnings; stock dividends that result in transfers from retained earnings to paid-in capital; recapitalizations that result in transfers between retained earnings and capital stock; quasi-reorganizations and "fresh-start" retained earnings; legal restrictions upon retained earnings in protecting the stockholder and creditor groups; and contractual limitations upon the use of retained earnings for dividends. The nature of retained earnings is frequently misunderstood and this misunderstanding may lead to seriously misleading inferences in reading the balance sheet.

Source of retained earnings

Retained earnings is the terminus of all accounting for earnings. The retained earnings account is increased by net income from the activities of the business unit and is reduced by net loss from these activities. The retained earnings account is also affected by prior period adjustments.

Corporate earnings that are transferred to retained earnings originate from transactions with individuals or businesses outside of the company. No earnings are recognized in the construction of machinery or other plant items for a company's own use, even though the cost of such construction is below the price that would have to be paid outsiders for similar assets; self-construction at less than the asset purchase price is regarded simply as a savings in cost. No earnings are recognized on transactions with stockholders involving treasury stock; the purchase and sale of treasury stock are regarded as contractions and expansions of paid-in capital. The receipt of properties through donation and the recognition of appraisal increases in the accounts are not recognized as earnings; donations are regarded as giving rise to additional paid-in capital, while the appraisal increases are recognized as giving rise to a special unrealized capital element.

The earnings of a corporation may be distributed to the stockholders or they may be retained to provide for expanding operations. When earnings are retained, they may be appropriated so as to be reported as unavailable for dividend declaration. Appropriations may be returned to retained earnings after the purpose of the appropriation has been fulfilled. When operating losses or other charges to the retained earnings account produce a debit balance in this account, the debit balance is referred to as a *deficit*.

Dividends

Dividends are distributions to stockholders of a corporation in proportion to the number of shares that are held by the respective owners. Such distributions may take the form of (1) cash, (2) other assets, (3) evidences of corporate indebtedness, in effect, deferred cash dividends, and (4) shares of a company's own stock. All of these involve reductions in retained earnings except dividends in corporate liquidation, which represent a return to stockholders of a portion or all of the corporate legal capital and call for reductions in invested capital.

Use of the term *dividend* without qualification normally implies the distribution of cash, with accumulated earnings as the source of such a distribution. Dividends in a form other than cash should be designated by their special form, and dividends that are declared from a capital source other than retained earnings should carry a description of their special origin. The terms *property dividend, scrip dividend,* and *stock dividend* suggest distributions of a special form; designations such as *liquidating dividend, dividend distribution of paid-in capital,* and *stock dividend of appraisal increment* identify the special origin of the distribution.

"Dividends paid out of retained earnings" is an expression frequently encountered. Accuracy, however, would require the statement that dividends are paid out of cash, which serves to reduce retained earnings. Earnings of the corporation increase net assets and also the stockholders' equity. Dividend distributions represent no more than asset withdrawals and reduce net assets and the stockholders' equity.

Among the powers that are delegated by the stockholders to the board of directors is that of controlling the dividend policy. Whether dividends shall or shall not be paid, as well as the nature and the amount of dividends, then, are matters that the board determines. In declaring dividends, the board of directors must observe the legal requirements governing the maintenance of legal or stated capital. These requirements vary with the individual states. In addition, the board of directors must consider the financial aspects of dividend distributions — the company asset position, the present asset requirements, and the future asset requirements. The board of directors, then, must answer two questions: Do we have the legal right to declare a dividend? Is such a distribution financially advisable?[1]

When a dividend is legally declared and announced, its revocation is not possible. In the event of corporate insolvency prior to payment of

---

[1]Laws of the different states range from those making any part of capital other than that designated legal capital available for dividends to those permitting dividends only from retained earnings and under specified conditions. In most states dividends cannot be declared in the event of a deficit; in a few states, however, dividends equal to current earnings may be distributed despite a previously accumulated deficit. The availability of capital as a basis for dividends is a determination to be made by the attorney and not by the accountant. The accountant must report accurately the sources of each capital increase; the attorney investigates the availability of such sources as bases for dividend distributions.

An example of the nature of the provisions that may be found relating to dividends is the following taken from Sections 1500–1503 of the California Corporations Code (as amended through 1969):

"A stock corporation may declare dividends payable in cash or in property only as specified in one of the following subdivisions:

(a) Out of earned surplus.

(b) Out of net profits earned during the preceding accounting period, which shall not be less than six months nor more than one year in duration. The corporation may declare dividends out of such net profits despite the fact that the net assets of the corporation amount to less than the stated capital; but if the value of the net assets amounts to less than the aggregate amount of stated capital attributed to shares having liquidation preferences, because of depreciation, depletion, losses, or other cause, the corporation shall not declare dividends out of net profits pursuant to this subdivision except upon such shares, until the value of the net assets has been restored to the aggregate amount of the stated capital attributed to outstanding shares having liquidation preferences.

the dividend, stockholders have claims as a creditor group to the dividend, and as an ownership group to any assets remaining after all corporate liabilities have been paid. A dividend that was illegally declared is revocable; in the event of insolvency, such action is nullified and stockholders participate in asset distributions only after creditors have been paid in full.

The formal dividend announcement. Three dates are essential in the formal dividend statement: (1) date of declaration, (2) date of stockholders of record, (3) date of payment. Dividends are made payable to stockholders of record as of a date that follows the date of declaration and precedes the date of payment. The liability for dividends payable is recorded on the declaration date and is canceled on the payment date. No entry is required on the record date, but a list of the stockholders is made up as of the close of business on such date. These are the persons who are to receive dividends on the payment date. A full record of the dividend action must be provided in the minutes book.

Cash dividends. The most common type of dividend is a *cash dividend*. For the corporation, such dividends involve a reduction in retained earnings and in cash. A current liability for dividends payable is recognized on the declaration date; this is canceled when dividend checks are sent to stockholders. Entries to record the declaration and the payment of a cash dividend follow:

Retained Earnings.............................	100,000	
Cash Dividend Payable......................		100,000
Cash Dividend Payable........................	100,000	
Cash...		100,000

(c) Out of surplus arising from reduction of stated capital, subject to the provisions of chapter 5 of this part, or out of paid-in surplus; provided, that if any outstanding shares are entitled to preferential dividends, dividends may be paid pursuant to this division (c) only upon such shares.

Prior to or concurrently with the payment of dividends pursuant to this subdivision (c) the corporation shall give notice of their source to the shareholders receiving them.

A stock corporation shall not declare dividends payable in cash or in property when there is reasonable ground for believing that thereupon the corporation's debts and liabilities would exceed its assets, or that it would be unable to meet its debts and liabilities as they mature.

A stock corporation shall not declare dividends payable in cash or in property out of the mere appreciation in the value of its assets not yet realized, nor from earned surplus representing profits derived from an exchange of assets unless and until such profits have been realized or unless the assets received are currently realizable in cash.

A wasting asset corporation is a corporation engaged solely or substantially in the exploitation of mines, oil wells, gas wells, patents, or other wasting assets, or organized solely or substantially to liquidate specific assets.

A wasting asset corporation may distribute the net income derived from the exploitation of such wasting assets or the net proceeds derived from such liquidation without making any deduction or allowance for the depletion of the assets incidental to the lapse of time, consumption, liquidation, or exploitation, if adequate provision is made for meeting debts and liabilities and the liquidation preferences of outstanding shares and notice is given to shareholders that no deduction or allowance has been made for such depletion."

In declaring a dividend, the board of directors must consider the limitations set by the current position and the cash balance. For example, a corporation may have retained earnings of $500,000. If it has cash of only $150,000, however, cash dividends must be limited to this amount unless it converts certain assets into cash or borrows cash. If the cash required for regular operations is $100,000, the cash available for dividends is only $50,000. Although legally able to declare dividends of $500,000, the company would be able to distribute no more than one tenth of such amount at this time.

Scrip dividends. If a corporation has retained earnings that may be used as a basis for dividend declaration but does not have sufficient funds at the time for a cash dividend, it may declare a *scrip dividend* which consists of a written promise to pay certain amounts at some future date. The corporation can thus take regular dividend action although it is temporarily short of cash. Stockholders, in turn, are provided currently with instruments that they may sell for cash if they wish. Such dividends are rare.

Assume the declaration of a scrip dividend of $150,000, payable in six months together with interest at the rate of 6% for the period of payment deferment. The declaration is recorded as follows:

Retained Earnings............................	150,000	
Scrip Dividend Payable....................		150,000

When the scrip matures and scrip and interest payments are made, the entry is:

Scrip Dividend Payable......................	150,000	
Interest Expense.............................	4,500	
Cash.....................................		154,500

Property dividends. A distribution to stockholders that is payable in some asset other than cash is generally referred to as a *property dividend*. Frequently the asset to be distributed is certain securities of other companies that are owned by the corporation. The corporation thus transfers to its stockholders its ownership interest in such securities.

A property dividend avoids the need for selling assets to pay dividends. When the value of the property exceeds its cost, the corporation is not required to recognize a "gain" for income tax purposes. However, the individual stockholders are required to report dividend income equal to the fair market value of the asset acquired.

To illustrate the entries for a property dividend, assume that the State Oil Corporation owns 100,000 shares in the Valley Oil Co., cost $2,000,000, which it wishes to distribute to its stockholders. There are 1,000,000 shares of State Oil Corporation stock outstanding. Accordingly, a dividend of 1/10 of a share of Valley Oil Co. stock is declared on each share of State Oil Corporation stock outstanding. The entries for the dividend declaration and payment are:

Retained Earnings......................	2,000,000	
Dividend Payable in Stock of Valley Oil Co.		2,000,000
Dividend Payable in Stock of Valley Oil Co...	2,000,000	
Investment in Stock of Valley Oil Co.....		2,000,000

Stock dividends. A corporation may distribute to stockholders additional shares of the company's own stock. Such a distribution is known as a *stock dividend*. A stock dividend permits the corporation to retain within the business net assets produced by earnings while at the same time offering stockholders tangible evidence of the growth of their equity.

Reference to a stock dividend usually implies (1) the capitalization of retained earnings and (2) a distribution of common stock to common stockholders. Such distributions are sometimes referred to as *ordinary stock dividends*. In certain states, stock dividends may be effected by the capitalization of certain paid-in capital or appraisal capital balances. In certain instances, common or preferred stock is issued to holders of preferred stock or preferred stock is issued to holders of common stock. The latter distributions are sometimes referred to as *special stock dividends*.

A dividend makes a portion of retained earnings no longer available for distribution while raising the legal capital of the corporation. In recording the dividend, a charge is made to Retained Earnings and credits are made to appropriate paid-in capital balances. The stock dividend may be viewed as consisting, in effect, of two transactions: (1) the payment by the corporation of a cash dividend; and (2) the return of such cash to the corporation in exchange for capital stock.

In distributing stock as a dividend, the issuing corporation must meet legal requirements relative to the amounts to be capitalized. When stock has a par or a stated value, an amount equal to the value of the shares issued normally will have to be transferred to capital stock; when stock is no-par and without a stated value, the laws of the state of incorporation may provide specific requirements as to amounts to be transferred or they may leave such determinations to the corporate directors.

Although the minimum amounts to be transferred to legal or stated capital balances upon the issuance of additional stock are set by law, the board of directors is not prevented from going beyond legal requirements and authorizing increases in both capital stock and additional paid-in capital balances. For example, assume that $100 par stock was originally issued at $120. Legal requirements may call for the capitalization of no more than the par value of the additional shares issued. The board of directors, however, in order to preserve the paid-in capital relationship, may authorize a transfer from retained earnings of $120 per share; for every share issued, then, capital stock may be increased $100 and an additional paid-in capital balance $20. Or the board of directors may decide that the retained earnings transfer shall be made in terms of the fair value of shares which exceeds the legal value. Here, too, the credit to capital stock is accompanied by a credit to an additional paid-in capital account.

The Committee on Accounting Procedure of the AICPA, in commenting on the issuance by a corporation of its own common stock to its common stockholders, has indicated that proper corporate policy in certain situations would call for the capitalization of an amount that is equal to the fair value of shares issued. The Committee pointed out:

> . . . a stock dividend does not, in fact, give rise to any change whatsoever in either the corporation's assets or its respective shareholders' proportionate interests therein. However, it cannot fail to be recognized that, merely as a consequence of the expressed purpose of the transaction and its characterization as a *dividend* in related notices to shareholders and the public at large, many recipients of stock dividends look upon them as distributions of corporate earnings and usually in an amount equivalent to the fair value of the additional shares received. Furthermore, it is to be presumed that such views of recipients are materially strengthened in those instances, which are by far the most numerous, where the issuances are so small in comparison with the shares previously outstanding that they do not have any apparent effect upon the share market price and, consequently, the market value of the shares previously held remains substantially unchanged. The committee therefore believes that where these circumstances exist the corporation should in the public interest account for the transaction by transferring from earned surplus to the category of permanent capitalization (represented by the capital stock and capital surplus accounts) an amount equal to the fair value of the additional shares issued. Unless this is done, the amount of earnings which the shareholder may believe to have been distributed to him will be left, except to the extent otherwise dictated by legal requirements, in earned surplus subject to possible further similar stock issuances or cash distributions.[1]

However, the Committee indicated that certain circumstances would suggest that retained earnings be charged for no more than stock par, stated, or other value as required by law. The Committee stated:

> . . . Where the number of additional shares issued as a stock dividend is so great that it has, or may reasonably be expected to have, the effect of materially reducing the share market value, the committee believes that the implications and possible constructions discussed . . . are not likely to exist and that the transaction clearly partakes of the nature of a stock split-up. . . . Consequently, the committee considers that under such circumstances there is no need to capitalize earned surplus, other than

---

[1] *Accounting Research Bulletin No. 43*, "Restatement and Revision of Accounting Research Bulletins" (New York: American Institute of Certified Public Accountants, 1953), Ch. 7, par. 10.

to the extent occasioned by legal requirements. It recommends, however, that in such instances every effort be made to avoid the use of the word *dividend* in related corporate resolutions, notices, and announcements and that, in those cases where because of legal requirements this cannot be done, the transaction be described, for example, as a *split-up effected in the form of a dividend.*[1]

The Committee indicated that the majority of stock dividends would probably fall within the first category stated above, suggesting charges to retained earnings of amounts that exceed legal requirements. Although reluctant to name a dividend percentage that would require adherence to this practice, the Committee did suggest that in stock distributions involving the issuance of less than 20% to 25% of the number of shares previously outstanding, there would be but few instances where charges to retained earnings at the fair value of additional shares issued would not be appropriate.

The examples that follow illustrate the entries for the declaration and the issue of a stock dividend. Assume that the capital for the Bradford Co. on July 1 is as follows:

Capital stock, $10 par, 100,000 shares outstanding.	$1,000,000
Premium on capital stock.	100,000
Retained earnings.	750,000

The company declares a 10% stock dividend, or a dividend of 1 share for every 10 held. Shares are selling on the market on this date at $16 per share. The stock dividend is to be recorded at the market value of the shares issued, or $160,000 (10,000 shares at $16). The entries to record the declaration of the dividend and the issue of stock follow:

Retained Earnings.	160,000	
Stock Dividend Distributable.		100,000
Paid-In Capital from Stock Dividend.		60,000
Stock Dividend Distributable.	100,000	
Capital Stock, $10 par.		100,000

Assume, however, that the company declares a 50% stock dividend, or a dividend of 1 share for every 2 held. Legal requirements call for the transfer from retained earnings to capital stock of an amount equal to the par value of the shares issued, and the stock dividend is recorded at this value. Entries for the declaration of the dividend and the issue of stock follow:

Retained Earnings.	500,000	
Stock Dividend Distributable.		500,000
Stock Dividend Distributable.	500,000	
Capital Stock, $10 par.		500,000

---

[1]*Ibid.*, par. 11.

If in this case the board of directors wished to maintain invested capital balances in their original relationship, authorization could be made for capitalization of the issue at $11 per share. Entries to record the dividend declaration and stock issue would be:

Retained Earnings............................	550,000	
Stock Dividend Distributable.................		500,000
Paid-In Capital from Stock Dividend..........		50,000
Stock Dividend Distributable..................	500,000	
Capital Stock, $10 par......................		500,000

Fractional share warrants.   When stock dividends are issued by a company, it may be necessary to issue *fractional share warrants* to certain stockholders. For example, when a 10% stock dividend is issued, a stockholder owning 25 shares can be given no more than 2 full shares; however, the holdings in excess of an even multiple of 10 shares are recognized by the issue of a fractional share warrant for ½ share. The warrant for ½ share may be sold, or a warrant for an additional ½ share may be purchased so that a full share may be claimed from the company. In some instances the corporation may arrange for the payment of cash in lieu of fractional warrants or it may issue a full share of stock in exchange for warrants accompanied by cash for the fractional share deficiency.

Assume that the Miller Company in distributing a stock dividend issues fractional share warrants totaling 500 shares, par $50. The entry for the fractional share warrants issued would be as follows:

Stock Dividend Distributable.....................	25,000	
Fractional Share Warrants Issued...............		25,000

Assuming that 80% of the warrants are ultimately turned in for shares and that the remaining warrants expire, the following entry would be made:

Fractional Share Warrants Issued.................	25,000	
Capital Stock, $50 par		20,000
Paid-In Capital from Forfeitures of Fractional Share Warrants............................		5,000

Stock dividends on the balance sheet.   If a balance sheet is prepared after the declaration of a stock dividend but before issue of the shares, Stock Dividend Distributable is reported in the stockholders' equity section as an addition to Capital Stock Outstanding. By the declaration of the dividend, the corporation has reduced its retained earnings balance and is committed to the increase of capital stock. The stock that the corporation may still sell is limited to the difference between capital stock authorized and the sum of (1) capital stock issued, (2) capital stock subscribed, (3) stock reserved for the exercise of stock rights and stock options, and (4) stock dividends distributable.

Although a stock dividend can be compared to a stock split from the investors' point of view, its effects upon corporate capital differ from those of the stock split. A stock dividend results in an increase in the number of shares outstanding and in an increase in the capital stock balance, no change being made in the value assigned to each share of stock on the company records; the increase in capital stock outstanding is effected by a transfer from the retained earnings balance, retained earnings available for dividends being permanently reduced by this transfer. A stock split merely divides the existing capital stock balance into more parts with a reduction in the stated or legal value related to each share; there is no change in the retained earnings available for dividends, both the capital stock and the retained earnings balances remaining unchanged.

There have been suggestions that special disclosure be provided on the balance sheet when retained earnings has been reclassified as paid-in capital as a result of stock dividends, recapitalizations, or other actions. Information concerning the amount of retained earnings that was transferred to paid-in capital will contribute to an understanding of the extent to which business growth has been financed through corporate earnings. For example, assume the information for the Bradford Co. on page 739 and the transfer to paid-in capital of $500,000 as a result of the 50% stock dividend. The stockholders' equity may be presented in the following manner:

Paid-in capital:		
Capital stock, $10 par, 150,000 shares....	$1,500,000	
Premium on capital stock..............	100,000	$1,600,000
Retained earnings......................	$ 750,000	
Less amount transferred to paid-in capital		
by stock dividend...................	500,000	250,000
Total stockholders' equity...............		$1,850,000

Liquidating dividends. A corporation will declare a *liquidating dividend* when the dividend is to be considered a return to stockholders of a portion of their original investments. Such distributions by the corporation represent reductions of invested capital balances. Instead of actually charging capital stock and additional paid-in capital balances, however, it is possible to charge a separate account for the reduction in invested capital. This balance is subtracted from the invested capital balances in presenting the stockholders' equity on the balance sheet.

Corporations owning wasting assets may regularly declare dividends that are in part a distribution of earnings and in part a distribution of the corporation's invested capital. Entries on the corporation books for such dividend declarations should reflect the decrease in the two capital elements. This information should be reported to stockholders so that they may recognize dividends as representing in part income and in part a return of investment.

Dividends on preferred stock. When dividends on preferred stock are cumulative, the payment of a stipulated amount on these shares is necessary before any dividends may be paid on common. When the board of directors fails to declare dividends on cumulative preferred stock, information concerning the amount of dividends in arrears should be reported parenthetically or in note form on the balance sheet. Or retained earnings may be divided on the balance sheet to show the amount required to meet dividends in arrears and the balance that is free for other purposes. In this case retained earnings may be reported on the balance sheet in the following manner:

Retained earnings:
 Required to meet dividends in arrears on pre-
  ferred stock............................ $40,000
 Balance................................. 60,000

 Total retained earnings.................... $100,000

The board of directors may pay a portion of a cumulative preferred dividend or a portion of the total in arrears. For example, 2% may be paid annually on 7% cumulative preferred stock, allowing 5% to accumulate for future payment. Or a payment of $15 may be made on cumulative dividends in arrears of $50, leaving $35 still in arrears.

Dividends on no-par stock. Cash dividends on no-par stock must be expressed as certain amount per share since there is no par value upon which a percentage may be applied. Dividends on capital stock with a par value are often expressed in the same manner.

When no-par stock is outstanding and the corporation desires to transfer an amount from Retained Earnings to Capital Stock, there is no need to declare a stock dividend. The board of directors can simply take action to raise the stated value of the no-par stock. An entry such as the following is made:

Retained Earnings............................ 500,000
 Capital Stock.............................   500,000
  To raise $5 stated value on 100,000 shares of
  no-par stock to $10 in accordance with resolu-
  tion by board of directors.

Extraordinary dividend distributions. In the case of common stock, a corporation may establish a policy of *regular dividends* and may provide for greater payments when warranted through *extraordinary dividends* or *extra dividends*. For example, a corporation may have a regular rate of 50 cents a quarter or $2 a year per share on common stock. In a particular quarter it may wish to declare a dividend of 80 cents a share. Such a dividend may be expressed as a 50-cent regular dividend plus a 30-cent extra dividend.

Appraisal capital

The problems and the procedures involved in recording an increase in property after its valuation by independent appraisers and the use of this information in the accounts were described in Chapter 15. Charges to asset accounts for increases established by appraisal were accompanied by credits to appraisal capital accounts. Such capital is separately designated in the stockholders' equity section on the balance sheet. Readers of the statement are thus informed that property items are stated at amounts in excess of cost and that this action has resulted in an unrealized capital element.

Disposal of an asset that has been increased by appraisal results in cancellation of the asset balance at appraised value, cancellation of the related appraisal capital, and recognition of a gain or loss that is based upon cost.

When a depreciable asset is increased as a result of appraisal and when depreciation is reported on the basis of appraised value, transfers may be made periodically from appraisal capital balances to retained earnings. In applying this practice, appraisal capital reports no more than the appraisal increase still included in the net asset balance while retained earnings is raised by the portion of the appraisal increase that has been realized. When the asset is fully depreciated, the full amount of the appraisal capital will have been transferred to retained earnings. Appraisal capital shrinks only as the asset value from which it emerged shrinks. Entries that are made to record depreciation on property items at appraised values and to record the transfer of appraisal capital to retained earnings were previously described and illustrated on pages 525 and 526.

Appraisal capital should never be used to absorb operating losses or the write-down of properties other than those values representing the source of such appraisal increase. Appraisal capital, representing unrealized earnings, is not properly used as a basis for cash dividends; however, its use as a basis for stock dividends is permitted in some states.

Use of term "reserve"

It has already been indicated that the term "reserve" has been employed in a variety of different senses in accounting practice. It has been used in the following ways:

(1) *As a valuation account.* The reserve designation has been employed to report a valuation account related to a balance sheet item. For example, deductions may be required from the face amount of assets in arriving at the amounts that they are expected to realize, as in the case of marketable securities, receivables, or inventories. Deductions may also be required from the face amount of assets in the recognition of cost expirations, as in the case of assets subject to depreciation, depletion, or amortization. When such reductions are related to current revenues, expense accounts are charged and asset valuation accounts are credited. Valuation accounts are ultimately applied against the items to which they relate. The accounts receivable valuation account is used to absorb accounts that prove to be uncollectible; the property valuation account is applied against the property item when the latter is disposed of or scrapped. It was suggested earlier that a term such as "allowance" should be substituted for the term reserve in designating valuation accounts.

(2) *As an estimate of a liability of uncertain amount.* The reserve title has been employed to designate a liability of uncertain amount requiring an estimate. Estimates may be required for such items as unsettled claims for damages and injuries, premium claims outstanding, claims under guarantees for services and replacements, tax obligations, and obligations under pension plans. When such claims are related to current revenue, expense accounts are charged and liability accounts are credited. The liabilities are ultimately canceled through payment. Designation of the accounts in this class as "estimated liabilities" rather than as reserves would clarify the nature of the items presented.

(3) *As an appropriation of retained earnings.* The reserve title is used to indicate that retained earnings have been appropriated in accordance with legal or contractual requirements or as a result of authorization by the board of directors. The appropriation of retained earnings has no effect upon individual assets and liabilities nor does it change total capital; amounts are merely transferred from retained earnings to special retained earnings accounts and assets that might otherwise be distributed as dividends are thus kept within the business. The appropriation balance is no guarantee that cash or any other specific asset will be available in carrying out the purpose of the appropriation. Resources represented by retained earnings may have been applied to the enlargement of plant, to the increase of working capital, or possibly to the retire-

ment of corporate indebtedness. If assets are to be made available for a particular purpose, special action relative to asset use would be required. When the purpose of the appropriation has been served, the appropriation balance is returned to Retained Earnings.

It was indicated in an earlier chapter that the American Institute Committee on Terminology has held that the use of the term reserve to indicate the retention of assets comes closest to its popular meaning. Accordingly, the Committee has recommended that the term reserve be limited to appropriations of retained earnings and that any alternative use of the term on the financial statements be discontinued.[1]   The American Accounting Association Committee on Concepts and Standards Underlying Corporate Financial Statements, however, would abandon the use of the term in financial statements. The Committee has maintained that although accounting terminology would be improved if the term were limited to balances includible in capital, this would still leave unresolved the conflict between the general and the accounting connotations of the word.[2]   There can be little question that greater clarity in financial statement presentation would be promoted through abandonment of the term "reserve" and the adoption of more descriptive terminology.

Retained earnings appropriations

Appropriations of retained earnings may be classified under the following headings:

(1) *Appropriations to report legal restrictions on retained earnings.* Laws of the state of incorporation may require that a company, upon reacquiring its own stock, retain its earnings as a means of maintaining its legal capital. The restriction may be recognized in the accounts by the appropriation of retained earnings.

(2) *Appropriations to report contractual restrictions on retained earnings.* Agreements with creditors or stockholders may provide for the retention of earnings within the company to protect the interests of these parties and assure redemption of the securities they hold. The restriction may be indicated in the accounts by the appropriation of retained earnings.

(3) *Appropriations to report discretionary action by the board of directors in the presentation of retained earnings.* The board of directors may authorize that a portion or all of the retained earnings be presented in a manner

---

[1]*Accounting Terminology Bulletin No. 1* (New York: American Institute of Certified Public Accountants, 1953), par. 57–64.

[2]*Accounting and Reporting Standards for Corporate Financial Statements and Preceding Statements and Supplements*, Supplementary Statement No. 1 (1957 rev.; Madison, Wisconsin: American Accounting Association), p. 20.

that will disclose the actual use in the present or the planned use in the future of the resources represented by this part of the stockholders' equity. Discretionary action on the part of the board of directors may then be the basis for appropriations.

A number of appropriated retained earnings accounts and the purposes for which such balances are established are listed below:

Account	Purpose
(1) *Appropriations to report legal restrictions on retained earnings:* Retained Earnings Appropriated for Purchase of Treasury Stock	To retain earnings upon the reacquisition of stock so that resources of the business and the stockholders' equity may be maintained at original legal or stated balances.
(2) *Appropriations to report contractual restrictions on retained earnings:* Retained Earnings Appropriated for Redemption of Bonds Retained Earnings Appropriated for Bond Redemption Fund	To retain earnings so that resources may be available for the redemption of bonds or for transfer to a fund for bond redemption.
Retained Earnings Appropriated for Redemption of Preferred Stock Retained Earnings Appropriated for Preferred Stock Redemption Fund	To retain earnings so that resources may be available for the redemption of preferred stock or for transfer to a fund for stock redemption.
(3) *Appropriations to report discretionary action by the board of directors in the presentation of retained earnings:* Retained Earnings Appropriated for General Contingencies Retained Earnings Appropriated for Possible Inventory Decline Retained Earnings Appropriated for Self-Insurance	To retain earnings in the business so that resources may be available for use in meeting possible future losses.
Retained Earnings Appropriated for Increased Working Capital Retained Earnings Appropriated for Plant Expansion	To report that resources from earnings are to be applied or have been applied to some particular business purpose and thus are unavailable for dividends.

Appropriations relating to stock reacquisitions. A legal restriction upon retained earnings arising upon the reacquisition of the company's own stock is recorded by a charge to Retained Earnings and a credit to an appropriately titled appropriations account. Retained earnings thus replace the capital impairment arising from treasury stock acquisition.

The appropriated balance may be returned to retained earnings when the legal restriction is removed. To illustrate, assume that a corporation reacquires its own stock and subsequently resells this stock. Retained earnings of $100,000 are restricted by law from use for dividends during the period treasury stock is held. The entries for the appropriation and for its subsequent cancellation follow:

Retained Earnings.............................	100,000	
Retained Earnings Appropriated for Purchase of		
Treasury Stock...........................		100,000
Retained Earnings Appropriated for Purchase of		
Treasury Stock.............................	100,000	
Retained Earnings........................		100,000

Appropriations relating to bond redemption. A restriction upon retained earnings arising from a contract with creditors or stockholders is recorded by a charge to Retained Earnings and a credit to an appropriations account. When the restriction is removed, the appropriation is returned to retained earnings. To illustrate, assume that the corporation agrees to restrict retained earnings of $5,000,000 from dividend distribution during the full term of a bond issue. Entries when the loan is made and when it is liquidated follow:

Retained Earnings.........................	5,000,000	
Retained Earnings Appropriated for Redemp-		
tion of Bonds..........................		5,000,000
Retained Earnings Appropriated for Redemp-		
tion of Bonds...........................	5,000,000	
Retained Earnings......................		5,000,000

When the agreement with creditors provides for the periodic appropriation of earnings during the life of the obligation, entries similar to the first entry above would be made each period.

The appropriation of retained earnings may be accompanied by the segregation of assets in a special fund for retirement of the obligation at maturity. The establishment of the fund may be voluntary or it may be required by the bond indenture. A retained earnings appropriation that is accompanied by the segregation of assets in a special fund is said to be *funded*. This practice results not only in the limitation of dividends but also in the accumulation of resources to meet the obligation. Liquidation of the obligation by means of the redemption fund and the termination of the contract with creditors releases previously existing restrictions, and the appropriated retained earnings may be returned to a free status. It may be observed, however, that when proceeds from a bond issue are used for expansion purposes and when resources from profitable operations have been used to retire the bonds, the expansion has in effect been financed by earnings. Under these circumstances, the board of directors may choose to report retained earnings equivalent to the amount applied to expansion under the designation "Retained Earnings Appropriated for Plant Expansion," or it may choose to effect a permanent capitalization of such retained earnings by means of a stock dividend.

Appropriations relating to stock redemption. Retained earnings may be appropriated at regular intervals as part of a plan to retire preferred stock from resources arising from earnings. The appropriation of earnings may be required by the contract with stockholders or it may be voluntary and established at the discretion of the board of directors. Stock may be reacquired out of cash or out of a redemption fund previously established by transfers from cash. In either case, upon the retirement of outstanding stock, the board of directors may authorize the return of the appropriation balance to retained earnings. However, it should be observed that retained earnings now take the place of the capital stock equity previously reported. In recognition of this factor, the board of directors may choose to designate these earnings as applied to the retirement of a previously existing stockholders' equity; on the other hand, it may choose to effect a permanent capitalization of such retained earnings by means of a stock dividend.

Appropriations for possible future losses. Appropriations of retained earnings may be authorized by the board of directors in anticipation of possible future losses. Three examples of such appropriations are described in the following paragraphs: (1) the general purpose contingency appropriation, (2) the appropriation for possible inventory decline, and (3) the appropriation for self-insurance.

Appropriation for general contingencies. Company management may authorize that provision be made in the accounts for general undetermined contingencies. Such authorization calls for the appropriation of retained earnings to assure the availability of resources to absorb the losses if they materialize. The establishment of an asset valuation balance or a liability balance is not appropriate under these circumstances; the provision for contingencies is related to losses of the future that may or may not take place, not to losses of the past or of the present. In the event that the contingencies fail to materialize, the board of directors may authorize cancellation of the provision for contingencies, and the appropriated balance would then be returned to retained earnings. If the contingencies do materialize, the appropriated balance is still returned to retained earnings and the losses are assigned to the period in which they materialized.

To illustrate the foregoing, assume that management, in reviewing business conditions at the end of 1970, concludes that there may be a general business decline in the next year or two and authorizes that retained earnings of $500,000 be reported as an appropriation for general contingencies. In 1972 the company sells its marketable securities at a loss of $150,000. At the end of 1972, with prospects for business good, management decides that the provision for general contingencies is no longer required and should be canceled. The following entries record the appropriation for general contingencies, the recognition of the loss on the sale of the securities, and the return of the appropriation to retained earnings.

1970: Retained Earnings..........................	500,000	
Retained Earnings Appropriated for General Contingencies..........................		500,000
1972: Cash....................................	250,000	
Loss on Sale of Marketable Securities.........	150,000	
Marketable Securities.....................		400,000
Retained Earnings Appropriated for General Contingencies...........................	500,000	
Retained Earnings......................		500,000

It should be observed that the appropriation for general contingencies established at the end of 1970 can be viewed only as a part of retained earnings; neither asset shrinkage nor liability can be recognized at this date. Since such provision is part of retained earnings, it must be established not by a charge to revenue in 1970 but by a charge to Retained Earnings. If revenue were charged, income of $500,000 in 1970 would bypass recognition on the income statement and earnings for the year would be understated. Having established the appropriation by a charge to Retained Earnings, it would be improper to charge it for the losses resulting from the sale of securities in 1972. If this were done, losses of $150,000 in 1972 would bypass recognition on the income statement and earnings for the year would be overstated. Any loss is recognized in the period in which it is incurred. The appropriation for contingencies is returned to retained earnings when the losses have been incurred or when they are no longer in prospect. The return is made directly to retained earnings and not through a revenue account since no revenue is involved in the transfer.

Appropriation for possible inventory decline. When inventories are acquired in a high-price period, management may authorize that provision be made in the accounts for possible future inventory decline. Valuation accounts reducing inventory costs to a lower market are established by charges to current revenue; valuation accounts providing for inventory obsolescence, deterioration, and similar losses already incurred are also established by charges to current revenue. A provision for possible future inventory decline, however, cannot be viewed as an inventory valuation account but must be considered a part of retained earnings. Accordingly, an appropriation procedure similar to that for the general purpose contingency is required. An appropriation for possible inventory decline is established by a charge to Retained Earnings, and the appropriated balance is ultimately returned to Retained Earnings; no costs or losses should be charged to the appropriation, nor should any part of the appropriation be transferred to income. A loss on inventories requires separate recognition in the period in which it actually emerges.

The AICPA Committee on Accounting Procedure has considered the problems that arise in anticipating possible future losses and has cautioned against improper accounting treatment in these matters that may serve to arbitrarily reduce income or shift income from one period to another. The Committee has stated:

> . . . If a provision for a reserve, made against income, is not properly chargeable to current revenues, net income for the period is understated by the amount of the provision. If a reserve so created is used to relieve the income of subsequent periods of charges that would otherwise be made against it, the income of such subsequent periods is thereby overstated. By use of the reserve in this manner, profit for a given period may be significantly increased or decreased by mere whim. As a result of this practice the integrity of financial statements is impaired, and the statements tend to be misleading.
>
> The committee recognizes the character of the income statement as a tentative instalment in the record of long-time financial results, and is aware of the tendency to exaggerate the significance of the net income for a single year. Nevertheless, there still exists the responsibility for determining net income as fairly as possible by sound methods consistently applied and the duty to show it clearly. In accomplishing these objectives, it is deemed desirable to provide, by charges in the current income statement, properly classified, for all forseeable costs and losses applicable against current revenues, to the extent that they can be measured and allocated to fiscal periods with reasonable approximation.
>
> . . . The committee is . . . of the opinion that reserves such as those created:
>
> (a) for general undetermined contingencies, or
> (b) for any indefinite possible future losses, such as, for example, losses on inventories not on hand or contracted for, or
> (c) for the purpose of reducing inventories other than to a basis which is in accordance with generally accepted accounting principles, or
> (d) without regard to any specific loss reasonably related to the operations of the current period, or
> (e) in amounts not determined on the basis of any reasonable estimates of costs or losses
>
> are of such a nature that charges or credits relating to such reserves should not enter into the determination of net income.

Accordingly, it is the opinion of the committee that if a reserve of the type described . . . is set up:

(a) it should be created by a segregation or appropriation of earned surplus,

(b) no costs or losses should be charged to it and no part of it should be transferred to income or in any way used to affect the determination of net income for any year,

(c) it should be restored to earned surplus directly when such a reserve or any part thereof is no longer considered necessary, and

(d) it should preferably be classified in the balance sheet as a part of shareholders' equity.[1]

Appropriation for self-insurance. A company may face certain risks but may not obtain insurance on the theory that the assumption of these risks will prove less expensive in the long run than the cost of outside protection. When a company is self-insured, it may authorize that provision be made in the accounts in anticipation of the losses that may have to be absorbed.

Self-insurance that involves definitely accruing obligations requires the establishment of liabilities through charges to periodic revenues. However, a self-insurance plan related to losses or casualties that cannot be considered to accrue would call for appropriations of retained earnings; charges to revenue would be made only when the losses are actually incurred.

To illustrate, assume that a construction company decides to assume the risks for workmen's compensation. The company is satisfied that it can make reliable estimates of the amounts payable under compensation claims arising from employee accidents. Under these circumstances, the estimated amounts payable at the end of each period are recognized by a charge to an expense account and a credit to an estimated liability account; when payments are made in subsequent periods, the liability balance is charged and cash is credited. If payable estimates prove to be inadequate or excessive, correcting entries would be required. A fund may be established for payments to be made under the plan.

On the other hand, assume that a company with a number of branches throughout the country decides to act as self-insurer for any fire losses and authorizes that provision be made in the accounts for the losses that may have to be absorbed as a result of this policy. Fire loss cannot be considered to accrue; it is a contingency that may or may not occur. Until a fire occurs no loss has been incurred; the absence of a fire loss in one period does not increase the probability of such a loss in the next period. Under these circumstances, there is no support for the

---

[1]*Accounting Research Bulletin No. 43, op. cit.*, Ch. 6, par. 3, 4, 7, 8.

recognition in the accounts of either an asset valuation account or a liability account; any provision in the accounts for possible future losses would be regarded as an appropriation of retained earnings. Accounting for possible fire losses, then, would be similar to that employed for other contingencies. Appropriations arising from a policy of self-insurance must be established by a charge to Retained Earnings. Upon incurring a fire loss, a loss account is charged and the appropriate property accounts are credited. At the same time amounts in the appropriation account may be returned to retained earnings to absorb the losses that will be summarized in the latter account. When the appropriation account is credited for insurance premiums that would otherwise be paid and is charged for transfers to retained earnings based upon losses actually sustained, the balance in the account will measure the savings accruing to the company as a result of the self-insurance plan. The appropriation may be funded so that cash will be available for property replacement.

The two procedures described are illustrated below. It is assumed that a fund is maintained in each case to meet losses that emerge under the self-insurance plans.

Transaction	Self-Insurance Considered to Involve Accruable Losses		Self-Insurance Considered to Involve Nonaccruable Losses	

(a) Estimated liability under workmen's compensation self-insurance plan.
 	
(b) Retained earnings appropriation under fire loss self-insurance plan.
	(a)
	Workmen's Compensation....... 20,000
	Estimated
	  Claims Under
	  Workmen's
	  Compensation
	  Plan..........
		20,000	(b)
			Retained Earnings. 20,000
			Retained
			  Earnings
			  Appropriated
			  for Self-
			  Insurance —
			  Fire Loss......
				20,000

Establishment of fund to meet self-insurance plans.	Workmen's Compensation Fund.. 20,000 Cash..........	20,000	Property Replacement Fund...... 20,000 Cash..........	20,000

(a) Workmen's compensation paid, $15,000.
 	
(b) Fire loss: asset book value, $15,000; building replacement cost, $23,500, paid $15,000 from fund and $8,500 from regular cash balance.
	(a)
	Estimated Claims
	  Under
	  Workmen's
	  Compensation
	  Plan.......... 15,000
	Workmen's
	  Compensation
	  Fund........
		15,000	(b)
			Fire Loss........ 15,000
			Accumulated
			  Depreciation —
			  Buildings....... 6,500
			  Buildings......
				21,500
				
				Retained Earnings
				  Appropriated for
				  Self-Insurance —
				  Fire Loss....... 15,000
				  Ret. Earnings... 15,000
				Buildings........ 23,500
				  Prop. Replacement Fund.... 15,000
				  Cash.......... 8,500

It should be observed that self-insurance is simply a policy of "no insurance," since there is no indemnity in the event of loss. Management, in considering such a policy, should evaluate carefully such factors as the size of the organization and how this affects risk, the protective measures that are available in minimizing risk, and the probable savings that will accrue through such action. Self-insurance should be undertaken only when a company is financially prepared to assume the full responsibilities that are related to the risk-bearing role.

Appropriations to describe business purposes served by retained earnings. Corporate officials may authorize appropriations to show the use of retained earnings within the business. For example, assume that earnings are to be retained by a company to finance the expansion of plant facilities. Or assume that resources from earnings have already been applied to plant expansion. In either instance, instead of continuing to report undistributed profits in retained earnings, which may be interpreted by stockholders as amounts available for dividends, the company may authorize transfers from retained earnings to a special account that describes the utilization of earnings. A permanent increase in a company's working capital position may likewise suggest an appropriation of earnings. Such appropriations may be carried forward indefinitely. On the other hand, in view of the permanent commitment of assets, the company may choose to effect a permanent capitalization of retained earnings by means of a stock dividend.

Objections to appropriation procedures. The Committee on Concepts and Standards Underlying Corporate Financial Statements of the American Accounting Association has taken issue with the general practice of earmarking retained earnings through the appropriation procedure, pointing out that such practice may serve to confuse and mislead those using the financial statements. When earnings are retained, the objectives of such retention are best explained, in the opinion of the Committee, by narrative materials accompanying the statements. Managerial policy arises from a number of complex factors; the stockholders' equity section of the balance sheet is hardly the most practical vehicle for the description of such policy. In considering the problems presented by "reserves" and retained earnings, the Committee has recommended:

1. The term "reserve" should not be employed in published financial statements of business corporations.
2. The "reserve section" in corporate balance sheets should be eliminated and its elements exhibited as deduction-from-asset, or liability, or retained income amounts.
3. Appropriations of retained income should not be made or displayed in such a manner as to create misleading inferences.
(a) Appropriations of retained income which purport to reflect managerial policies relative to earnings retention are ineffective, and frequently misleading, unless all retained income which has in fact been committed to operating capital is earmarked. Partial appropriation fosters the implication that retained earnings not earmarked are available for distribution as dividends.

(b) Appropriations of retained income required by law or contract preferably should be disclosed by footnote. If required to be displayed as balance sheet amounts, such appropriations should be included in the proprietary section.

(c) Appropriations of retained income reflecting anticipated future losses, or conjectural past or present losses (when it is not established by reasonably objective evidence that any loss has been incurred) preferably should be disclosed by footnote. If displayed as balance sheet amounts, such appropriations should be included in the proprietary section.

(d) In any event, whenever appropriations are exhibited in a balance sheet, the retained income (excluding amounts formally capitalized) should be summarized in one total.

4. The determination of periodic earnings is not affected by the appropriation of retained income or the restoration of such appropriated amounts to unappropriated retained income.[1]

There can be little objection to the position taken by the American Accounting Association Committee.

Dated retained earnings

Any earnings after a corporate quasi-reorganization should be separately summarized and reported on the balance sheet as retained earnings dating from the time of such action. *Dated retained earnings* inform investors and others of the occurrence of a restatement of capital and the financial progress that has been made since that time.

The AICPA Committee on Accounting Procedure, in considering the problem of reporting dated retained earnings on the balance sheet, originally recommended that a dated balance be disclosed until the time that the date of quasi-reorganization was no longer considered to possess any special significance. In 1956 the Committee in a special bulletin indicated that dating would rarely, if ever, be of significance after a period of ten years, and under exceptional circumstances might be discontinued upon the conclusion of a shorter period.[2]

Financial statements prepared for the corporation

Transactions affecting the stockholders' equity have been described in this and the preceding two chapters. The persons who refer to the financial statements of a corporation must be provided with a full explanation of the changes that took place during the period in the individual balances that compose the stockholders' equity. In the remaining pages of this chapter, the financial statements for the General Manufac-

[1]*Accounting and Reporting Standards for Corporate Financial Statements and Preceding Statements and Supplements, op. cit.,* p. 19.

[2]*Accounting Research Bulletin No. 46,* "Discontinuance of Dating Earned Surplus" (New York: American Institute of Certified Public Accountants, 1956), par. 1 and 2.

turing Company are illustrated with special attention directed to the stockholders' equity section of the balance sheet. The statements are prepared as of December 31, 1972, and summarize the position of the company as of this date and operations for the year ending on this date.

The balance sheet. The balance sheet for the General Manufacturing Company as of December 31, 1972, is given on pages 756 and 757. Classifications and the presentation of financial data follow the standards that have been developed in the preceding chapters. The following matters deserve special attention:

1. The stockholders' equity is reported in terms of its source: (a) the amount paid in by stockholders; and (b) the amount representing earnings retained in the business.
2. The classes of capital stock are reported separately and are described in detail. Information is offered concerning the nature of the stock, the number of shares authorized, the number of shares issued, and the number of shares reacquired and held as treasury stock.
3. The capital items representing additional paid-in capital and retained earnings are reported in detail; when paid-in capital and appropriated retained earnings are composed of a great many items, related balances are frequently combined and reported in total on the balance sheet.
4. In complying with legal requirements, the company has reported retained earnings equivalent to the cost of the treasury stock held as an appropriation of retained earnings.

Reference is made at the bottom of the balance sheet to the notes that accompany the financial statement. This reference would also appear on the other financial statements prepared by the company.

The income statement. The income statement for the General Manufacturing Company is prepared in modified single-step form. The income statement for the year ended December 31, 1972, is illustrated on page 758.

With single amounts reported for sales and for cost of goods sold, special supporting schedules may be provided to offer an analysis of these balances in terms of the major divisions of the business or of the different product lines. With single amounts reported for selling, general and administrative, and other expenses, supporting schedules may be provided to indicate the individual items composing such totals.

Statements accounting for the changes in the stockholders' equity. Those who wish to be fully informed on the financial position and results of operations of the corporation require full information explaining the change in the stockholders' equity. When changes in paid-in capital have taken place, a *paid-in capital statement* may be prepared. This statement reports the paid-in capital balances at the beginning of the period and the changes that took place in these balances during the period as a

General
Balance
December

Assets

Current assets:

Cash on hand and on deposit..................		$ 55,000
U.S. Government securities at cost (market, $87,500).................................		86,000
Trade notes and accounts receivable — less allowance for doubtful accounts, $2,600............		180,000
Inventories:		
Finished goods............................	$ 190,000	
Goods in process..........................	200,000	
Raw materials and supplies.................	185,000	575,000
Loans, advances, and accrued income items......		20,000
Prepayments including taxes, insurance, and sundry current items.......................		14,500
Total current assets........................		$ 930,500
Investments:		
Fund consisting of U. S. Government securities to be used for property additions..............	$ 250,000	
Land held for future expansion...............	110,000	360,000
Land, buildings, and equipment:		
Land, buildings, and equipment, at cost.........	$1,235,000	
Less accumulated depreciation..............	580,000	655,000
Intangible assets:		
Patents, formulas, and goodwill — less amortization.....................................		120,000
Other assets:		
Advance payments on equipment purchase contracts.....................................	$ 25,000	
Bond issue costs............................	15,000	
Developmental costs.........................	62,500	102,500
Total assets................................		$2,168,000

The accompanying notes A through C are an integral part of this financial statement.

Manufacturing Company
Sheet
31, 1972

Liabilities

Current liabilities:

Notes and accounts payable..............................		$ 52,500
Income taxes payable....................................		12,000
Accrued payrolls, interest, and taxes......................		23,500
Serial debenture bonds due May 1, 1973..................		20,000
Customers' deposits and sundry items.....................		24,000
Total current liabilities...............................		$ 132,000

Long-term debt:

Twenty-year 7% first-mortgage bonds...........	$ 260,000	
Less unamortized discount on first-mortgage bonds.	10,000	
	$ 250,000	
Serial 7½% debenture bonds due May 1, 1974, to May 1, 1982, inclusive......................	180,000	430,000
Deferred leasehold revenue................................		160,000
Liability under pension plan (See Note A)..................		60,000
Contingent liabilities (See Note B)		
Total liabilities..		$ 782,000

Stockholders' Equity

Paid-in capital:

6% Preferred stock, $100 par value, cumulative, callable, 5,000 shares authorized and issued (See Note C).............................	$ 500,000	
No-par common stock, $5 stated value, 100,000 shares authorized, 60,000 shares issued; treasury stock, 5,000 shares — deducted below..	300,000	
	$ 800,000	

Additional paid-in capital:

From sale of common stock at more than stated value...............	$260,000		
From sale of treasury stock at more than cost.....................	16,000	276,000	
Total paid-in capital......................		$1,076,000	

Retained earnings:
Appropriated:

For purchase of treasury stock $40,000			
For contingencies.........	85,000	$125,000	
Unappropriated....................		225,000	
Total retained earnings......................		350,000	
		$1,426,000	
Less common treasury stock, at cost (5,000 shares acquired at $8).............................		40,000	
Total stockholders' equity.......................			1,386,000
Total liabilities and stockholders' equity..........			$2,168,000

(See page 761.)

General Manufacturing Company
Income Statement
For Year Ended December 31, 1972

Revenues:		
Sales..	$1,550,000	
Other income.............................	100,000	$1,650,000
Costs and expenses:		
Cost of goods sold...........................	$ 940,000	
Selling expense.............................	300,000	
General and administrative expense...........	125,000	
Other expense.............................	80,000	
Income taxes...............................	92,500	1,537,500
Income before extraordinary items...............		$ 112,500
Extraordinary items:		
Gain on sale of investments, net of income taxes applicable to gain.........................	$ 12,500	
Loss on sale of land, net of income tax credit applicable to loss.............................	5,000	7,500
Net income.................................		$ 120,000
Earnings per common share:[1]		
Income before extraordinary items.............		$1.50
Extraordinary items........................		.14
Net income................................		$1.64

Income statement

result of such transactions as the sale of capital stock, stock dividends, the retirement of stock, and the purchase and sale of treasury stock. The paid-in capital statement for the General Manufacturing Company for the year ended December 31, 1972, is shown on the opposite page.

The changes in retained earnings are summarized in the retained earnings statement. In some instances, it is necessary to recognize additional changes that took place such as those resulting from prior period adjustments, the acquisition of treasury stock, and transfers to paid-in capital. Frequently the retained earning statement is expanded to show changes in both unappropriated and appropriated balances. The statement then summarizes transfers from the unappropriated retained earnings account to accounts that report appropriations and also transfers from accounts that report appropriations to the unappropriated retained earnings account. When appraisal capital balances are reported on the balance sheet, any changes in these balances during the year may also be summarized by means of a special statement.

The form of statements reconciling paid-in capital, retained earnings, and appraisal capital vary greatly in practice. However, the following rules should be observed in their preparation:

---

[1]Preferred dividend requirements are subtracted from earnings to arrive at earnings related to common shares. This computation, as well as computations for more complex capital structures, are described in the following chapter.

General Manufacturing Company
Paid-In Capital Statement
For Year Ended December 31, 1972

	Preferred Stock	Common Stock	Additional Paid-In Capital[1]	Total
Paid-in capital, January 1, 1972......	$300,000	$300,000	$260,000	$ 860,000
Add: Increase from sale of 1,000 shares of preferred stock at the beginning of 1972 at par value..	200,000			200,000
Increase from sale of 25,000 shares of treasury stock, common, at the beginning of 1972, cost $20,000, for $36,000			16,000	16,000
Paid-in capital, December 31, 1972 ...	$500,000	$300,000	$276,000	$1,076,000

Paid-in capital statement

1. Paid-in capital, retained earnings, and appraisal capital changes should be summarized separately.
2. The beginning balances should be those reported on the balance sheet at the end of the preceding period; the changes that are stated should provide the balances that are reported in the balance sheet at the end of the current period.
3. Changes in balances that have taken place during the period should be classified and listed in some consistent manner.

The General Manufacturing Company's retained earnings statement for the year ended December 31, 1972, is illustrated on page 760.

Statement accounting for the changes in financial position. Reference was made in earlier chapters to the statement of changes in financial position that is required in offering a full reporting of a company's operations. This statement is prepared from comparative balance sheets as of the beginning and end of the period and summarizes the financing and investing activities that resulted in the change in financial position. The preparation of this statement is described and illustrated in Chapter 23.

Summary of significant accounting policies. In recent years, a number of companies have included a separate section with their financial statements describing the accounting policies that were followed in preparing the statements. Such disclosure makes it possible for the readers to use this information in their analyses of the financial statements.

---

[1]From sale of common stock at more than stated value.

General Manufacturing Company
Retained Earnings Statement
For Year Ended December 31, 1972

	Retained Earnings		
	Appropriated for Purchase of Treasury Stock	Appropriated for Contingencies	Unappropriated
Balances, January 1, 1972..	$60,000	$50,000	$202,500
Prior period adjustment — settlement of income tax claims for 1969 and 1970.			(25,000)
Balances, January 1, 1972, as adjusted	$60,000	$50,000	$177,500
Return to retained earnings of earnings previously restricted through ownership of treasury stock . . .	(20,000)		20,000
Retained earnings appropriated for contingencies.		35,000	(35,000)
Cash dividends:			
Preferred stock, $6 on 5,000 shares, $30,000.			
Common stock, $.50 on 55,000 shares, $27,500.			(57,500)
Net income for 1972			120,000
	$40,000	$85,000	$225,000

Retained earnings statement

The Accounting Principles Board has approved of this practice, and in April, 1972, they issued Opinion No. 22 which required such disclosure in statements issued after December 31, 1971. The Board stated:

> . . . . In general, the disclosure should encompass important judgments as to appropriateness of principles relating to recognition of revenue and allocation of asset costs to current and future periods; in particular, it should encompass those accounting principles and methods that involve any of the following:
>
> a. A selection from existing acceptable alternatives;
> b. Principles and methods peculiar to the industry in which the reporting entity operates, even if such principles and methods are predominately followed in that industry;
> c. Unusual or innovative applications of generally accepted accounting principles (and, as applicable, of principles and methods peculiar to the industry in which the reporting entity operates.)[1]

---

[1]*Opinions of the Accounting Principles Board, No. 22,* "Disclosure of Accounting Policies" (New York: American Institute of Certified Public Accountants, April 1972), par. 12.

Examples of disclosure of accounting policies required by this opinion would include, among others, those relating to depreciation methods, amortization of intangible assets, inventory pricing methods, research and development costs, the recognition of profit on long-term construction type contracts, and the recognition of revenue from leasing operations.[1]

The exact format of the section on disclosure of accounting policies was not specified by the Board. However, the Board felt that such disclosure would be particularly useful if it were included as a separate summary preceding the notes to the financial statement or as the initial note. A summary of the accounting policies followed in the preparation of the financial statements for the General Manufacturing Company is shown below. The notes for the financial statements for the company follow this summary.

General Manufacturing Company
Summary of Significant Accounting Policies
Year Ended December 31, 1971

1. Inventories are valued at cost or market, whichever is lower. Cost is calculated by the first-in, first-out method.
2. Depreciation is computed for both the books and the tax return by the double-declining balance method.
3. Intangible assets are being amortized over the period of their estimated useful lives; patents, 10 years; formulas, 8 years; and goodwill, 20 years.
4. Certain research and development costs in 1971 and 1972 related to new products that will be marketed beginning in 1973 have been deferred and will be charged to subsequent revenue.
5. The company leased Market Street properties for a 15-year period ending January 1, 1984. Leasehold payment received in advance is being recognized as revenue over the life of the lease.

General Manufacturing Company
Notes to Financial Statements — Year Ended December 31, 1972

Note A: The liability under the company pension plan has been calculated on the basis of actuarial studies.

Note B: The company is contingently liable on guaranteed notes and accounts totaling $40,000. Also, various suits are pending on which the ultimate payment cannot be determined. In the opinion of counsel and management, such liability, if any, will not be material. Retained earnings have been appropriated in anticipation of possible losses.

Note C: Preferred stock may be redeemed at the option of the board of directors at 105 plus accrued dividends on or before December 31, 1974, and at gradually reduced amounts but at not less than $102\frac{1}{2}$ plus accrued dividends after January 1, 1980.

---

[1]*Ibid.*, par. 13.

QUESTIONS

1. Accumulated earnings are in general supported by a cross section of all of the assets. Directors are criticized by stockholders for failure to declare dividends when accumulated earnings are present. Are these two statements related? Explain.

2. Which of the following transactions are a source of stockholders' equity? Indicate the class of stockholders' equity in each case.
- (a) Operating profits.
- (b) Cancellation of a part of a liability upon prompt payment of the balance.
- (c) Reduction of par value of stock outstanding.
- (d) Discovery of an understatement of income in a previous period.
- (e) Release of Retained Earnings Appropriated for Purchase of Treasury Stock upon the sale of treasury stock.
- (f) Issue of bonds at a premium.
- (g) Purchase of the corporation's own capital stock at a discount.
- (h) Increase in the company's earning capacity, taken to be evidence of considerable goodwill.
- (i) Construction of equipment for the company's own use at a cost less than the prevailing market price of identical equipment.
- (j) Donation to the corporation of its own stock.
- (k) Sale of land, buildings, and equipment at a gain.
- (l) Gain on bond retirement.
- (m) Revaluation of land, buildings, and equipment resulting in an increase in asset book value as a result of increase in asset replacement value.
- (n) Collection of stock assessments from stockholders.
- (o) Discovery of valuable resources on company property.
- (p) Conversion of bonds into common stock.
- (q) Conversion of preferred stock into common stock.

3. The following announcement appeared on the financial page of a newspaper:

"The Board of Directors of the Maxwell Co., at their meeting on June 15, 1972, declared the regular quarterly dividend on outstanding common stock of 50 cents per share and an extra dividend of $1 per share, both payable on July 10, 1972, to the stockholders of record at the close of business June 30, 1972."

(a) What is the purpose of each of the three dates given in the declaration? (b) When would the stock become "ex-dividend"? (c) Why is the $1 designated as an "extra" dividend?

4. Dividends are sometimes said to have been paid "out of retained earnings." What is wrong with this statement?

5. The directors of Lenox Corporation are considering the issuance of a stock dividend. They have asked you to discuss the proposed action by answering the questions below:

(a) What is a stock dividend? How is a stock dividend distinguished from a stock split: (1) from a legal standpoint? (2) from an accounting standpoint?

(b) For what reasons does a corporation usually declare (1) a stock dividend? (2) a stock split?

6. The Blattner Co. has 1,000,000 shares of no-par common outstanding. Dividends have been limited to approximately 20% of annual earnings, remaining earnings being used to finance expansion. With pressure from stockholders for an increase in dividends, the board of directors takes action to issue to stockholders an additional 1,000,000 shares, and the president of the company informs stockholders that the company will pay a 100% dividend in view of the conservative dividend policy in the past. What is your comment on this statement?

7. It has been recommended that the balance sheet maintain a permanent distinction between paid-in capital and retained earnings. How can such a distinction be maintained when action is taken to convert retained earnings into capital stock?

8. (a) What is a liquidating dividend? (b) Under what circumstances are such distributions made? (c) How would you recommend that liquidating dividends be recorded in the accounts of the corporation?

9. At the regular meeting of the board of directors of the May Corporation, a dividend payable in the stock of the June Corporation is to be declared. The stock of the June Corporation is recorded on the books of May Corporation at $87,000; the market value of the stock is $100,000.

The question is raised whether the amount to be recorded for the dividend payable should be the book value or the market value. (a) Discuss the propriety of the two methods of recording the dividend liability, including an analysis of the circumstances under which each might be acceptable. (b) The property dividend declaration might state that "corporate property is being distributed as a dividend," or it might state that "corporate property is being distributed in payment of the dividend liability." Discuss briefly the significance of the wording of the property dividend declaration and its effect on the stockholder who is receiving the dividend.

10. The Byron Corporation, acting within the law of the state of incorporation, paid a cash dividend to stockholders for which it debited Paid-In Capital from Sale of Stock at a Premium. A stockholder protested, saying that such a dividend was a partial liquidation of his holdings. Is this true?

11. What methods can be followed in reporting dividends in arrears on preferred stock on the balance sheet?

12. What objections would you raise for the use of appraisal capital (a) to absorb operating losses, (b) as a basis for cash dividends, and (c) as a basis for stock dividends?

13. (a) What criticisms have been made of the term "reserve"? (b) What position has been taken by the American Institute of Certified Public Accountants and by the American Accounting Association with respect to the use of the term? (c) What position would you take with respect to use of the term? What substitute terms would you employ?

14. Some of the following account titles use the term "reserve" improperly. For each account indicate (a) the proper account title, and (b) the heading under which it would appear in the balance sheet.

(1) Reserve for Contingencies
(2) Reserve for Doubtful Accounts
(3) Reserve for Possible Inventory Decline
(4) Reserve for Self-Insurance — Fire Loss
(5) Reserve for Bond Retirement
(6) Reserve for Income Taxes
(7) Reserve for Undeclared Dividends
(8) Reserve for Increased Investment in Land, Buildings, and Equipment
(9) Reserve for Depletion
(10) Reserve for Redeemable Coupons Outstanding
(11) Reserve for Repairs and Replacements
(12) Reserve for Purchase of Treasury Stock
(13) Reserve for Personal Injury Claims Pending
(14) Reserve for Unrealized Building Appreciation
(15) Reserve for Leasehold Amortization
(16) Reserve for Restoration of Properties upon Termination of Lease
(17) Reserve for Sales Discounts
(18) Reserve for Reduction of Inventory to Market
(19) Reserve for Vacation Pay for Employees.

15. What is meant by a funded appropriation?

16. A stockholder of Barker, Inc., does not understand the purpose of the Appropriation for Bond Redemption Fund that has been set up by periodic charges to Retained Earnings. He is told that this balance will not be used to redeem the bonds at their maturity. (a) What account will be reduced by the payment of the bonds? (b) What purpose is accomplished by the Appropriation for Bond Redemption Fund? (c) What dispositions may be made of the appropriation?

17. Management Research, Inc., has appropriated retained earnings of $5,000,000 over a five-year period for plant expansion. In the sixth year the company completes an expansion program at a cost of $6,500,000; such expansion is financed through company funds of

$4,500,000, and borrowed funds of $2,000,000. What disposition of the appropriation for plant expansion would you recommend?

18. Management of the Gilbert Co., considering the possibility of a strike by employees, authorized the establishment of an appropriation for contingencies at the end of 1971 by a charge to revenue. The strike was called in 1972, and company losses incurred to the date of the strike settlement were charged against the appropriation. The company management points out that it exercised good judgment in anticipating strike losses and providing a cushion for such losses. What criticism, if any, can you offer of the accounting procedures followed by the company?

19. (a) What is meant by self-insurance? (b) Describe the accounting procedures in considering possible future charges and in recognizing such charges when they occur assuming that (1) self-insurance is considered to involve accruable losses and (2) self-insurance is considered to involve nonaccruable losses.

20. The Clark Co. reports appropriations as a subtraction from net income at the bottom of the income statement. When an appropriation is canceled, it is reported as an addition to net income on the income statement. What objections would you raise to such a practice?

21. (a) Which of the following transactions change total stockholders' equity? (b) What is the nature of the change?
    (1) Declaration of a cash dividend.
    (2) Payment of a cash dividend.
    (3) Retirement of bonds payable for which both a redemption fund and an appropriation had been established.
    (4) Declaration of a stock dividend.
    (5) Payment of a stock dividend.
    (6) Conversion of bonds payable into preferred stock.
    (7) The passing of a dividend on cumulative preferred stock.
    (8) Donation by the officers of shares of stock.
    (9) Operating loss for the period.

22. How would you report the following items on the balance sheet: (a) dividends in arrears on cumulative preferred stock, (b) unclaimed bond interest and unclaimed dividends, (c) stock purchase rights issued but not exercised as of the balance sheet date, (d) stock that is callable at a premium at the option of the corporation?

EXERCISES

1. The retained earnings account for the Morris Company shows the following charges and credits. The bookkeeper was not aware of APB Opinion No. 9 concerning the recording of extraordinary items. Give whatever entries may be required to correct the account.

Retained Earnings

(a) Loss from fire...........	850		Jan. 1 Balance..........	75,200
(b) Write-off of goodwill.....	6,500	(g)	Premium on common stock	18,500
(c) Stock dividend.........	20,000	(h)	Stock subscription defaults	1,210
(d) Loss on sale of equipment.	6,900	(i)	Gain on retirement of pre-	
(e) Officers compensation re-			ferred stock at less than	
lated to income of prior			issuance price.........	3,600
periods — accrual over-		(j)	Gain on retirement of	
looked..............	45,000		bonds at less than book	
(f) Loss on retirement of pre-			value...............	2,150
ferred shares at more		(k)	Revaluation of buildings:	
than issuance price....	9,100		Over-depreciation of	
			prior periods.......	3,000
		(l)	Increase from appraisal	15,000
		(m)	Gain on life insurance	
			policy settlement......	2,200
		(n)	Refund of prior year's in-	
			come taxes..........	7,150

2. The balance sheet of the Racer Corporation shows the following:

Capital stock, $5 stated value, 20,000 shares issued and out-
standing... $100,000
Additional paid-in capital............................ 200,000
Retained earnings.................................... 175,000

A 25% stock dividend is declared, the board of directors authorizing a transfer from Retained Earnings to Capital Stock at the stock stated value. (a) Give entries to record the declaration and payment of the dividend. (b) What was the book value per share before the dividend declaration and after the issue of the dividend? (c) What was the effect of the issue of the stock dividend on the ownership equity of each stockholder in the corporation?

3. The capital accounts for the Rusk Co. on June 30, 1972, follow:

Capital stock, $20 par, 75,000 shares.................. $1,500,000
Premium on capital stock............................ 725,000
Retained earnings................................... 3,600,000

Shares of the company's stock are selling at this time at 36. What entries would you make in each case below?

(a) A stock dividend of 5% is declared and issued.
(b) A stock dividend of 100% is declared and issued.
(c) A 2-for-1 stock split is declared and issued.

4. The dividend declarations and distributions by the National Company over a three-year period are listed below. Give the entry required in each case.

July 1, 1970 Declared a 10% stock dividend on 1,000,000 shares of stock, par value $15. The stock was originally sold at $17, and Retained Earnings is to be charged for the stock dividend for an amount equal to the original stock issuance price.

July 15, 1970 Distributed the stock dividend declared on July 1, which included fractional warrants for 800 shares.

Sept. 1, 1970 500 shares were issued for fractional warrants; remaining fractional warrants expired.

July 1, 1971 Declared a scrip dividend of $2 per share, payable on January 1, 1972, with interest at the rate of 8%.

Jan. 1, 1972 Paid scrip dividend.

July 1, 1972 Declared a dividend of 1 share of Eastern Co. common stock on every share of National Company stock owned. Eastern Co. common stock is carried on the books of the National Company at a cost of $1.50 per share, and the market price is $2.00 per share.

July 15, 1972 Distributed Eastern Co. common stock to shareholders.

5. On October 31, 1972, the Board of Directors of the Paulson Construction Company declared a 6% common stock dividend to be paid on January 15, 1973, to shareholders of record December 6, 1972. Market value of the stock was $21.25 per share. Par value per share of stock was $4.00; 5,600 shares were issued and $8,500 was paid in lieu of fractional shares on the agreed payment date. (a) Prepare all of the required entries on October 31, 1972, December 6, 1972, and January 15, 1973. (b) What was the total amount of outstanding common stock prior to the declaration of the stock dividend?

6. Variety Chain Stores, Inc., with total assets of $500,000, capital stock outstanding of $260,000, and retained earnings of $65,000, sold five of its stores at their book value, $150,000. This cash is distributed to the present stockholders. What entry should be made?

7. As a result of an agreement with bondholders, the Randall Co. is required to appropriate earnings of $300,000 at the end of each calendar year for the years 1967–1971. At the beginning of 1972, upon liquidation of the bonded indebtedness, the retained earnings appropriation is canceled. This is followed by the declaration and the issue of a 40% common stock dividend on 200,000 shares of $10 par common stock outstanding. Retained Earnings is charged for the stock dividend at par. What entries are required for (a) periodic appropriations, (b) cancellation of the appropriation in 1972, and (c) capitalization of retained earnings by means of the stock dividend?

8. A physical inventory taken by the Farmer Co. on December 31, 1972, discloses goods on hand with a cost of $430,000; the inventory is recorded at this figure less an allowance of $18,000 to reduce it to the lower of cost or market. At the same time, the company authorizes that an appropriation for possible future inventory decline of $150,000 be established. (a) Give the entries to be made at the end of 1972 in recording the inventory and establishing the accounts as indicated. (b) Give the entries in 1973 to close the beginning inventory and balances established at the end of 1972, assuming that the estimated inventory decline does not materialize and that the inventory at the end of 1973 is properly reported at cost, which is lower than market. (c) Give the entries in 1973 to close the inventory and other account balances established at the end of 1972 if a decline in the value of the December 31, 1972 inventory of $80,000 is to be recognized; the inventory at the end of 1973 is properly reported at cost, which is lower than its market value at this date.

9. The Parker Co. reports appropriated retained earnings on its balance sheet at the end of 1972 at $435,000. Analysis of the account balances in support of this total discloses the following:

Reserve for contingencies — to meet estimated claims arising from damage suits in 1972 for which the company has been held to be liable..	$ 45,000
Reserve for self-insurance for fire loss — to meet possible fire losses as a result of self-insurance on this contingency....	40,000
Reserve for pensions — to meet estimated pension costs arising from contracts with employees.................	195,000
Reserve for revaluation of properties — arising from asset appraisal increases..................................	100,000
Reserve for possible declines on marketable securities — to meet possible future losses on marketable securities......	25,000
Reserve for property rehabilitation costs — to meet costs of rehabilitating plant at termination of lease in accordance with contractual requirements.......................	30,000

(a) Which of the above items, if any, would you exclude from the appropriated retained earnings classification? (b) State how you would classify such items, and what account title you would use.

10. List each error below and indicate how the item should have been recorded.

Retained Earnings

(a) Dividends declared to common stockholders.	(e) Appraisal of land, buildings, and equipment.
(b) Transfer to reserve for bond redemption fund.	(f) Net income for year.
	(g) Gain from sale of treasury stock.
(c) Sale of stock at a discount.	(h) Donation of land by governmental agency.
(d) Profit-sharing bonus to employees.	(i) Proceeds from life insurance policy on officer's life.

Additional Paid-In Capital

(j) Dividends declared to preferred stockholders.	(l) Gain on sale of investment in securities.
(k) Correction of error reducing net income of previous year.	(m) Reserve for bond redemption fund.
	(n) Premium from sale of bonds.
	(o) Gain on sale of property originally acquired by exchange for capital stock.

PROBLEMS

21-1. The stockholders' equity for the Morgan Co. on December 31, 1971, was as follows:

Stockholders' Equity

6% Preferred stock, $25 par, 20,000 shares authorized and issued (each share is callable at $27.50 and is convertible into 2 shares of common)..		$ 500,000
Common stock, $10 par, 75,000 shares issued..	$750,000	
Premium on common stock.................	250,000	1,000,000
Total paid-in capital.....................		$1,500,000
Retained earnings.......................		275,000
Total stockholders' equity................		$1,775,000

During 1972, the following transactions affected the stockholders' equity:

Jan.   2 7,000 shares of preferred stock were called in for retirement at $27.50 in accordance with call provisions of the preferred stock.

Mar.   2 4,000 shares of common stock were reacquired at $12; treasury stock is reported at cost.

Mar. 30 A 50¢ cash dividend was paid on common stock.

Apr. 20 Common stock reacquired on March 2 was sold at $13.

June 30 The semiannual dividend was paid on preferred stock.

July   1 4,000 shares of preferred stock were converted into common stock on a 2-for-1 basis in accordance with the conversion privilege of the preferred stock.

Sept. 30 A 50¢ cash dividend was paid on common stock, together with a 10% stock dividend. Common stock was selling on this date at $14 and retained earnings equal to the selling price of the stock issued were transferred to paid-in capital.

Dec. 31 The semiannual dividend was paid on preferred stock and a special dividend of $1 was paid on common stock.

Dec. 31 Net income for the year, $215,500, was transferred to retained earnings. (Debit Income Summary.)

Instructions: (1) Record in journal form the transactions given above.

(2) Prepare the stockholders' equity section of the balance sheet as of December 31, 1972.

21-2. The stockholders' equity for the Pace Co. on June 30, 1972, was as follows:

Cumulative 8% preferred stock, $50 par, 10,000 shares issued, dividends 5 years in arrears.................	$ 500,000
Common stock, $20 par, 80,000 shares issued..........	1,600,000
	$2,100,000
Less deficit from operations........................	300,000
Total stockholders' equity..........................	$1,800,000

On this date the following action was taken:

(a) Common stockholders turned in their stock and received in exchange new common stock, 1 share of the new stock being exchanged for every 4 shares of the old. New stock was given a stated value of $40 per share.

(b) One-half share of the new common stock was issued on each share of preferred stock outstanding in liquidation of dividends in arrears on preferred stock.

(c) The deficit from operations was applied against the paid-in capital arising from the common stock restatement.

Transactions for the remainder of 1972 affecting the stockholders' equity were as follows:

Oct. 1 5,000 shares of preferred stock were called in at $55 plus dividends for 3 months at 8%. Stock was formally retired.

Nov. 10 30,000 shares of new common stock were sold at 42.

Dec. 31 Net income for the six months ended on this date was $85,000. (Debit Income Summary.) The semiannual dividend was declared on preferred shares and a 50¢ dividend on common shares, dividends being payable January 20, 1973.

Instructions: (1) Record in journal form the transactions given above.

(2) Prepare the stockholders' equity section of the balance sheet as of December 31, 1972.

21-3. The Davis Co. was organized on January 2, 1971, with authorized stock consisting of 40,000 shares of 8% nonparticipating $100 par preferred, and 125,000 shares of no-par common. During the first two years of the company's existence, the following transactions took place:

1971

Jan. 2 Sold 5,300 shares of common stock at 8.

  2 Sold 2,600 shares of preferred stock at 108.

Mar. 2 Sold common stock as follows:

  5,100 shares at 11.

  1,200 shares at 12.

July 10 A nearby piece of land, appraised at $202,000, was acquired for 600 shares of preferred stock and 14,000 shares of common. (Preferred stock was recorded at 108, the balance being assigned to common.)

Dec. 16 The regular preferred and a 75¢ common dividend were declared.

  28 Dividends declared on December 16 were paid.

  31 The income summary account showed a credit balance of $52,000, which was transferred to retained earnings.

1972

Feb. 27 The corporation reacquired 6,000 shares of common stock at 9. (State law requires that an appropriation of retained earnings be made for the purchase price of treasury stock. Appropriations may be returned to retained earnings upon resale of the stock.)

June 17 Resold 5,000 shares of treasury stock at 10.

July 31 Resold all of the remaining treasury stock at 9½.

Sept. 30 The corporation sold 6,000 additional shares of common stock at 10½.

Dec. 16 The regular preferred dividend and a 40¢ common dividend were declared.

Dec. 28 Dividends declared on December 16 were paid.
    31 The income summary account showed a credit balance of $89,000, which was transferred to retained earnings.

Instructions: (1) Give the journal entries to record the foregoing transactions.

(2) Prepare the stockholders' equity section of the balance sheet as of December 31, 1972.

21-4. A condensed balance sheet for Nicholes, Inc., as of December 31, 1969, appears below:

Assets.................	$350,000	Liabilities...............	$ 80,000
		Preferred 7% stock, $100	
		par.................	50,000
		Common stock, $50 par...	100,000
		Premium on common stock	20,000
		Retained earnings.......	100,000
	$350,000		$350,000

Capital stock authorized consists of: 500 shares of 7% cumulative, non-participating preferred stock with a prior claim on assets, and 10,000 shares of common stock.

Information relating to operations of the succeeding three years follows:

	1970	1971	1972
Dividends declared on Dec. 20, payable on Jan. 10 of following year:			
Preferred stock.............	7% cash	7% cash	7% cash
Common stock.............	$1.00 cash 50% stock*	$1.25 cash	$1.00 cash
Net income for year...........	$45,000	$26,000	$34,000

*Retained earnings is reduced by the par value of the stock dividend.

1970: On July 1, land having a book value of $40,000 was appraised at $110,000. The board of directors authorized that the appraisal be recorded in the accounts.

1971: On February 12 accumulated depreciation was reduced by $24,000 following an income tax investigation. (Assume that this qualifies as a prior period adjustment.) Additional income taxes of $7,500 for prior years were paid. On March 3, 200 shares of common stock were purchased by the corporation at $53 per share; treasury stock is recorded at cost and retained earnings are appropriated equal to such cost.

1972: On August 10 all of the treasury stock was resold at $59 per share and the retained earnings appropriation was canceled. By vote of the stockholders on September 12, each share of the common stock was exchanged by the corporation for 4 shares of no-par common stock with a stated value of $15.

Instructions: (1) Give the journal entries affecting the capital accounts for the 3-year period ended December 31, 1972.

(2) Prepare the stockholders' equity section of the balance sheet as it would appear at the end of 1970, 1971, and 1972.

21-5. Accounts of the Pike Co. on December 31, 1972, show the balances listed below. From this data prepare the stockholders' equity section as it would appear on the balance sheet.

	Debit	Credit
Accumulated depreciation — buildings.....		$ 340,000
Accumulated depreciation of buildings — appraisal increase........................		85,000
Allowance for purchases discount..........	$ 3,000	
Appraisal capital........................		255,000
Authorized capital stock ($10)............		1,000,000
Bonds payable..........................		400,000
Bond retirement fund....................	140,000	
Buildings...............................	1,500,000	
Buildings — appraisal increase............	340,000	
Capital stock subscribed..................		50,000
Current assets..........................	960,000	
Current liabilities.......................		325,000
Customers deposits......................		25,000
Dividends payable — cash................		20,000
Income taxes payable....................		50,000
Paid-in capital from sale of treasury stock at more than cost.........................		33,000
Premium on capital stock.................		40,000
Retained earnings appropriated for contingencies.............................		120,000
Retained earnings appropriated for bond retirement fund........................		140,000
Retained earnings appropriated for purchase of treasury stock.......................		70,000
Stock dividend distributable..............		82,000
Treasury stock, 6,000 shares at cost........	70,000	
Unappropriated retained earnings..........		188,000
Unissued capital stock...................	210,000	
	$3,223,000	$3,223,000

21-6. The balance sheet of the Young Corporation on December 31, 1971, is shown on the following page.

The following transactions affecting the stockholders' equity were completed in 1972:

Jan. 10 2,000 shares of 7% preferred stock were sold at 14.

31 The following errors were discovered as of the end of 1971:
Merchandise inventory was understated by $3,000.
Depreciation had not been recorded on store furniture and fixtures. These had been purchased on April 1, 1969. Straight-line depreciation at 20% per year should be recognized.
Building repairs of $2,500 made at the end of the year were improperly capitalized.

Feb. 2 5,000 shares of no-par common stock were sold for cash at 30.

Mar. 31 A semiannual dividend of 40¢ was declared and paid on common stock.

May 16 2,000 shares of no-par common stock were issued to Keith Wilson in exchange for his going business. Assets taken over were recorded at the following values: land, $20,000; buildings, $25,000; merchandise inventory, $12,000; accounts receivable, $6,000. Accounts payable of $10,000 were assumed. Goodwill was recognized on the purchase equal to the difference between the net assets acquired and $72,000, the market value of the shares at the time of issue.

Aug. 15 600 shares of the company's own common stock were reacquired on the market for cash at 21. Stock was recorded at cost.

Sept. 30 A semiannual dividend of 25¢ and an extra dividend of 15¢ were declared and paid on common stock.

Oct. 3 The 600 shares of treasury stock were sold for cash at $24 per share.

Dec. 21 The 7% annual dividend on preferred stock was declared, payable January 12, 1973. The board of directors authorized an appropriation of retained earnings for property expansion of $40,000.

     31 After closing the accounts, the income summary account showed a credit balance of $83,000; this was transferred to retained earnings.

Young Corporation
Balance Sheet
December 31, 1971

Assets			Liabilities and Stockholders' Equity		
			Liabilities		
Cash		$ 29,500	Notes payable	$ 25,000	
Notes receivable		30,000	Accounts payable	12,000	
Accounts receivable (net)		40,000	Preferred dividends		
Merchandise inventory		40,000	payable	10,500	
Land		60,000	Mortgage payable	43,000	$ 90,500
Buildings	$81,500				
Less accumulated depr.	21,000	60,500	**Stockholders' Equity**		
			7% Preferred stock —		
Store furniture and fixtures		12,500	5,000 shares, $10 par	$ 50,000	
Organization costs		20,000	Common stock —		
			18,000 shares, $5		
			stated value	90,000	
			Additional paid-in		
			capital*	21,000	
			Retained earnings	41,000	202,000
			Total liabilities and		
Total assets		$292,500	stockholders' equity.		$292,500

*Additional paid-in capital on the balance sheet consists of paid-in capital from the sale of preferred stock at a premium, $6,000, and paid-in capital from the sale of common stock at more than stated value, $15,000.

Instructions: (1) Record the information above in journal entry form.

(2) Prepare the stockholders' equity section of the balance sheet and statements of paid-in capital and retained earnings for the year ended December 31, 1972.

21-7. The following accounts are taken from the ledger of Twede Co.

Retained Earnings Appropriated for Plant Expansion

	1972		
	Jan. 1 Balance		125,000
	Dec. 31		25,000

Retained Earnings Appropriated for Purchase of Treasury Stock

1972		1972	
July 1	42,000	Jan. 1 Balance	72,000
		Apr. 1	31,000

Unappropriated Retained Earnings

1972			
Apr. 1 Appropriated for purchase		Jan. 1 Balance................. 725,000	
of treasury stock.........	31,000	July 1 Appropriated for treasury	
Oct. 31 Preferred dividends.......	50,000	stock acquisitions......... 42,000	
31 Stock dividend on common		Dec. 31 Net income for 1972..... 210,000	
stock...................	200,000		
Dec. 31 Appropriated for plant ex-			
pansion.................	25,000		

Instructions: Prepare a retained earnings statement for 1972 in support of the retained earnings balance to be reported on the company's balance sheet at the end of the year.

21-8. The Board of Directors of the XYZ Corporation on December 1, 1972, declared a 2% stock dividend on the common stock of the corporation, payable on December 28, 1972, to the holders of record at the close of business December 15, 1972. They stipulated that cash dividends were to be paid in lieu of issuing any fractional shares. They also directed that the amount to be charged against Retained Earnings should be an amount equal to the market value of the stock on the record date multiplied by the total of (a) the number of shares issued as a stock dividend and (b) the number of shares upon which cash is paid in lieu of the issuance of fractional shares.

The following facts are given:

(a) At the dividend record date —

    (1) Shares of XYZ common issued................. 2,771,600

    (2) Shares of XYZ common held in treasury......... 1,000

    (3) Shares of XYZ common included in (1) held by persons who will receive cash in lieu of fractional shares.................................... 202,500

    (4) Shares of predecessor company stock which are exchangeable for XYZ common at the rate of $1\frac{1}{4}$ shares of XYZ common for each share of predecessor company stock (necessary number of shares of XYZ common have been reserved but not issued).. 600
Provision was made for a cash dividend in lieu of fractional shares to holders of 240 of these 600 shares.

(b) Values of XYZ common were:

    Par value...................................... $ 5

    Market value at December 1st and 15th (Bid)...... 21

                                          (Asked).... 23

    Book value at December 1st and 15th............ 16

    Capital value at December 1st and 15th........... 10

Instructions: Give journal entries and explanations to record the payment of the dividend. Assume no entry was made at the declaration date.

(AICPA adapted)

21-9. The following trial balance was taken from the books of the Welcome Manufacturing Company as of April 30, 1972:

	Debit	Credit
Cash..	$ 310,000	
Accounts Receivable......................	800,000	
Finished Goods on Hand..................	500,000	
Finished Goods Out on Consignment.......	100,000	
Raw Materials on Hand...................	750,000	
Land, Buildings, and Equipment...........	1,460,000	
Prepaid Expenses........................	5,400	
Sales Returns and Allowances.............	25,000	
Administrative Salaries...................	65,000	
Cost of Goods Sold.......................	2,350,000	
Travel Expenses.........................	30,030	
Interest Expense.........................	10,570	
Accounts Payable........................		$ 175,000
Notes Payable...........................		100,000
Accrued Payroll.........................		6,000
Accrued Interest Payable on 6% Bonds.....		10,000
Capital Stock — 6% Preferred.............		1,000,000
Capital Stock — Common.................		1,416,000
6% Bonds, due June 30, 1980.............		500,000
Sales....................................		2,500,000
Retained Earnings, December 31, 1971.....		520
Additional Paid-In Capital................		698,480
	$6,406,000	$6,406,000

The following transactions had been completed by the company:

(a) The company has purchased various lots of its $100 par value common stock, aggregating 840 shares, at an average price of $65.50 per share, for $55,020. In recording these transactions the company has canceled the stock certificates and charged the common stock account with the par value of $84,000 and credited the additional paid-in capital account with the difference of $28,980 between par and the cash paid therefor.

(b) Additional paid-in capital was previously credited with (1) a premium at $20 per share on 15,000 shares of common stock issued, and (2) adjustments arising from the appraisal of land, buildings, and equipment bought at a receivers' sale, $398,000.

(c) 6% bonds of the face amount of $250,000 falling due on December 31, 1978, were issued on January 1, 1954, at a 10% discount. To June 30, 1970, $16,500 of this discount had been charged against revenues and as of this date the entire issue of these bonds was retired at par and the unamortized discount charged to Additional Paid-In Capital.

(d) A new issue of $500,000, 6% ten-year bonds was effected as of July 1, 1970, at par. Expenses incurred with respect to this issue in the amount of $20,000 were charged to Additional Paid-In Capital.

Instructions: Prepare a balance sheet as of April 30, 1972, in which effect has been given to such changes as may be necessary in view of the treatment accorded by the company to the transactions described above.

(AICPA adapted)

21-10. You are a senior accountant responsible for the annual audit of Desco, Inc., for the year ended 12/31/72. The information available to you is presented below. You may assume that any pertinent information not presented below has already been checked and found satisfactory.

(a) Excerpts from trial balance 12/31/72.

	Debit	Credit
Retained earnings......................		$40,000
Allowance for inventory decline to market..		7,500
Capital stock (600 shares)...............		60,000

(b) The books have not been closed but all adjusting entries which the company expects to make have been posted. Their trial balance shows a $15,000 net income for the year.

(c) Selected ledger accounts.

Retained Earnings

8/ 6/72	CD62	160	12/31/71	Balance	52,960
10/10/72	J34	10,000	4/29/72	CR8	200
12/31/72	J40	3,000			

(*Note:* The balance at 12/31/71 agrees with last year's working papers and represents the net difference over the years between credits from the income summary account and debits for dividends.)

Allowance for Inventory Decline to Market

9/26/72	CD78	500	6/30/72	J19	5,000
			12/31/72	J40	3,000

(d) Analysis of selected cash receipts.

Date	Page	Account Credited	Explanation	Amount
4/29/72	8	Capital Stock	Sold $100 par stock @ $102	$10,000
		Retained		
		Earnings		200
10/10/72	20	Building	See J34	20,000

(e) Analysis of selected cash disbursements.

Date	Page	Account debited	Explanation	Amount
8/ 6/72	62	Retained Earnings	Freak accident to company truck not covered by insurance; repair by Doe & Co.	$ 160
9/26/72	78	Allowance for Inventory Decline to Market	Purchase of materials (X Co.) to be used on orders taken prior to 6/30/72; $500 is price increase since 6/30/72.	500
		Purchases		6,300

(f) Selected entries in general journal.

Date	Page	Entry and Explanation	Debit	Credit
6/30/72	19	Inventory Loss (Inc. Sum.)	5,000	
		Allowance for Inventory Decline to Market		5,000
		Provision voted by board of directors for estimated future price increases in materials needed to complete orders on hand. (*Note: Orders do not represent contractual obligations.*)		
10/10/72	34	Accumulated Depreciation	50,000	
		Retained Earnings	10,000	
		Building		60,000
		Sale of main office building, moved to rental quarters downtown. (See CR20)		
12/31/72	40	Retained Earnings	3,000	
		Allowance for Inventory Decline to Market		3,000
		Provision to value materials inventory at lower of cost or market in accordance with company pricing policy.		
		Cost...... $30,000		
		Market.... 28,000		
		$ 3,000		

Instructions: Prepare in good form:

(1) Schedule of recommended correcting entries to be placed on the books to state the stockholders' equity accounts in accordance with accepted accounting principles.

(2) Statement of retained earnings for 1972.

(3) Stockholders' equity section of balance sheet.

(AICPA adapted)

chapter 22

special measurements
based upon stockholders' equity

The financial statements of a corporation were illustrated in Chapter 21. The persons who refer to these statements are interested in certain special measurements that can be developed from the data concerning the stockholders' equity and the data concerning operations for the period. Two special measurements that are of particular interest are described in this chapter: (1) the *book value per share* as determined by an analysis of the stockholders' equity as reported on the balance sheet, and (2) the *earnings per common share* as determined by an analysis of the capital structure of the company and the net income as reported on the income statement.

Book value per share

The *book value per share* measurement is the dollar equity in corporate capital of each share of stock. It is the amount that would be paid on each share assuming that the company is liquidated and the amount available to stockholders is exactly the amount reported as the stockholders' equity.[1] The book value measurement is widely used as a factor in evaluating stock worth. Both single values and comparative values may be required, the latter to afford data relative to trends and growth in the stockholders' equity.

One class of outstanding stock. When only one class of stock is outstanding, the calculation of book value is relatively simple; the total stockholders' equity is divided by the number of shares of stock outstanding. When stock has been reacquired and a treasury stock balance is reported, this balance should be recognized as a subtraction item in arriving at the stockholders' equity, and the shares represented by the

---

[1]Financial analysts frequently follow the practice of subtracting any amounts that are reported for intangible assets from the total reported for the stockholders' equity in calculating share book value.

treasury stock should be subtracted from the shares issued in arriving at the shares outstanding. When shares of stock have been subscribed for but are unissued, capital stock subscribed should be included in the total for the stockholders' equity and the shares subscribed should be added to the shares outstanding. To illustrate, assume a stockholders' equity for the Moore Corporation as shown below.

Capital stock, $10 par, 100,000 shares issued, 5,000 shares reacquired and held as treasury stock (see below)...............		$1,000,000
Capital stock subscribed, 20,000 shares......		200,000
Additional paid-in capital................		350,000
Retained earnings:		
Appropriated.........................	$200,000	
Unappropriated.......................	450,000	650,000
		$2,200,000
Less stock reacquired and held as treasury stock, 5,000 shares, reported at cost......		75,000
Total stockholders' equity......................		$2,125,000

The book value per share of stock is calculated as follows:
$2,125,000 (total capital) ÷ 115,000 (shares issued, 100,000, plus shares subscribed, 20,000, minus treasury shares, 5,000) = $18.48.

More than one class of outstanding stock. When more than one class of stock has been issued, it is necessary to consider the rights of the different classes of stockholders. With preferred and common issues, for example, the prior rights of preferred stockholders must first be determined and the portion of the stockholders' equity related to preferred stockholders calculated. The preferred stockholders' equity when subtracted from the total stockholders' equity gives the equity related to the common stockholders. The preferred equity divided by the number of preferred shares gives the book value of a preferred share; the common equity divided by the number of common shares gives the book value of a common share.

The portion of the stockholders' equity related to preferred would be that amount distributable to preferred stockholders in the event of corporate liquidation and calls for consideration of the liquidation value and also the special dividend rights of the preferred issue.

Liquidation value. Preferred shares may have a liquidation value equal to par, to par plus a premium, or to a stated dollar amount. Capital equal to this value for the number of preferred shares outstanding should be assigned to preferred. A preferred call price that differs from the amount to be paid to preferred stockholders upon liquidation would not be applicable for book value computations; the call of preferred stock is not obligatory, hence call prices are not relevant in the apportionment of values between preferred and common stockholders.

Dividend rights. (1) Preferred stock may have certain rights in retained earnings as a result of special dividend privileges. For example, preferred shares may be entitled to dividends not yet declared for a portion of the current year, assuming liquidation; here a portion of retained earnings equal to the dividend requirements would be related to preferred shares. (2) Preferred stock may be cumulative with dividends in arrears. When terms of the preferred issue provide that dividends in arrears must be paid upon liquidation regardless of any retained earnings or deficit balance reported on the books, capital equivalent to the dividends in arrears must be assigned to preferred shares even though this impairs or eliminates the equity relating to common stockholders. When preferred stockholders are entitled to dividends in arrears only in the event of accumulated earnings, as much retained earnings as are available, but not in excess of such dividend requirements, are related to preferred stock. (3) Preferred stock may be participating. When retained earnings are subject to distribution on a participating basis, the portion distributable to preferred stock must be calculated and assigned to this equity.

The computation of book values for preferred and common shares is illustrated in the series of examples that follow. Examples are based upon the stockholders' equity reported by the Maxwell Corporation on December 31, 1972, which follows:

6% Preferred stock, $50 par, 10,000 shares.............	$ 500,000
Common stock, $10 par, 100,000 shares................	1,000,000
Retained earnings....................................	250,000
Total stockholders' equity...........................	$1,750,000

Example 1. Assume that preferred dividends have been paid to July 1, 1972. Preferred stock has a liquidation value of $52 and is entitled to current unpaid dividends. Book values on December 31, 1972, are developed as follows:

Total stockholders' equity...........................		$1,750,000
Equity identified with preferred:		
Liquidation value, 10,000 shares @ $52....	$520,000	
Current dividends, 3% of $500,000........	15,000	535,000
Balance — equity identified with common.............		$1,215,000
Book values per share:		
Preferred: $ 535,000 ÷ 10,000.....................		$53.50
Common: $1,215,000 ÷ 100,000...................		$12.15

Example 2. Assume that preferred stock has a liquidation value of $52. Preferred is cumulative with dividends 5 years in arrears that must be

paid in the event of liquidation. Book values for common and preferred shares would be developed as follows:

Total stockholders' equity.............................		$1,750,000
Equity identified with preferred:		
Liquidation value, 10,000 shares @ $52....	$520,000	
Dividends in arrears, 30% of $500,000......	150,000	670,000
Balance — equity identified with common.............		$1,080,000
Book values per share:		
Preferred: $ 670,000 ÷ 10,000.....................		$67.00
Common: $1,080,000 ÷ 100,000...................		$10.80

Example 3. Assume that preferred stock has a liquidation value equal to its par value. Preferred is cumulative with dividends 10 years in arrears that are payable in the event of liquidation even though impairing the invested capital of the common shareholders. Book values for common and preferred shares are developed as follows:

Total stockholders' equity.............................		$1,750,000
Equity identified with preferred:		
Liquidation value, 10,000 shares @ $50....	$500,000	
Dividends in arrears, 60% of $500,000......	300,000	800,000
Balance — equity identified with common.............		$ 950,000
Book values per share:		
Preferred: $800,000 ÷ 10,000.....................		$80.00
Common: $950,000 ÷ 100,000.....................		$ 9.50

Example 4. Assume that preferred stock has a liquidation value equal to its par value. Preferred stock participates ratably with the common stock after the common stock has received the preferred dividend rate. A preferred dividend of $1.50 has been paid for the first half of 1972 but no common dividends have been declared or paid.

The portions of the retained earnings relating to the preferred and common issues on December 31, 1972, are calculated as follows:

		Preferred	Common
Balance of retained earnings......................	$250,000		
Less balance of current dividend requirements on preferred, 6% of $500,000 for 6 months.............	15,000	$ 15,000	
	$235,000		
Less current dividend requirements on common, 6% of $1,000,000................................	60,000		$ 60,000
	$175,000		
Balance of retained earnings, distributable ratably to preferred and common, 11.6667% ($175,000, retained earnings available to both classes ÷ $1,500,000, par value of stock of both classes). Distributable to preferred, 11.6667% of $500,000.....	58,333	58,333	
Distributable to common, 11.6667% of $1,000,000..	$116,667		116,667
Totals to common and preferred...........................		$ 73,333	$176,667

Book values may now be developed as follows:

Total stockholders' equity......................		$1,750,000
Equity identified with preferred:		
Liquidation value, 10,000 shares @ $50....	$500,000	
Current dividends and retained earnings in		
participation with common (see page 781).	73,333	573,333
Balance — equity identified with common....		$1,176,667
Book values per share:		
Preferred: $ 573,333 ÷ 10,000.................		$57.33
Common: $1,176,667 ÷ 100,000...............		$11.77

The nature and the limitations of the share book value measurements must be appreciated in using these data. Share book values are developed from the net asset values as reported on the books. Furthermore, calculations require the assumption of liquidation in the allocation of amounts to the several classes of stock. Book values of assets may vary materially from present fair values or immediate realizable values. Moreover, book values of property items are stated in terms of the "going concern"; the full implications of a "quitting concern" approach would call for many significant changes in the values as reported by the books.

Earnings per share presentation on the income statement

The term *earnings per share* refers to the amount earned during a given period on each share of common stock outstanding. This information is used by investors in evaluating the results of operations of a business and in estimating earnings of the business in order to make investment decisions. This information is also used in judging the dividend policies of a company, the earnings per share being compared with the dividends per share for a period in determining the company's *payout percentage* or *payout ratio*.

Earnings per share data receive wide recognition in the annual reports issued by companies, in the press, and in financial reporting publications. This measurement is frequently regarded as an important determinant of the market price of the common stock. The American Institute of Certified Public Accountants has recognized the widespread use and importance attached to earnings per share data and has devoted considerable study to determine how this information might be presented on a consistent basis and in the most meaningful manner. In 1958, the Committee on Accounting Procedure in Bulletin No. 49, "Earnings per Share," offered certain guidelines for presenting such data. In 1966, the Accounting Principles Board in Opinion No. 9, "Reporting the Results of Operations," devoted the second part of the

Opinion to "Computation and Reporting of Earnings per Share," and in 1969, in Opinion No. 15, "Earnings per Share," it gave full attention to the calculation of earnings per share and to the presentation of such data. In the 1969 pronouncement, the APB reached the following conclusion:

> The Board believes that the significance attached by investors and others to earnings per share data, together with the importance of evaluating the data in conjunction with the financial statements, requires that such data be presented prominently in the financial statements. The Board has therefore concluded that earnings per share or net loss per share data should be shown on the face of the income statement. The extent of the data to be presented and the captions used will vary with the complexity of the company's capital structure. . . .

The Board further stated:

> The reporting of earnings per share data should be consistent with the income statement presentation called for by . . . Opinion No. 9. Earnings per share amounts should therefore be presented for (a) income before extraordinary items and (b) net income. It may also be desirable to present earnings per share amounts for extraordinary items, if any.[1]

The Accounting Principles Board in Opinion No. 15 has made recommendations for the calculation and presentation of earnings per share data under a variety of circumstances. Only the basic recommendations can be presented here. When the Opinion fails to state the specific procedures that are to be followed under special circumstances, the accountant will have to exercise judgment in developing presentations that can be supported within the recommended framework.

The many problems in developing earnings per share presentations arise because of the different securities that make up the capital structure of a company. In the last two decades a number of companies have issued new and unique securities. As a result of these developments, the accountant encounters a wide variety of complex capital structures that complicate earnings per share calculations and presentations.

Simple and complex capital structures. The capital structure of a company is regarded as *simple* when it consists of only common stock or includes no potentially dilutive convertible securities, options, warrants, or other rights that upon conversion or exercise could in the aggregate dilute earnings per share. In the case of the simple capital structure,

---

[1]*Opinions of the Accounting Principles Board, No. 15,* "Earnings per Share" (New York: American Institute of Certified Public Accountants, 1969), par. 12 and 13. A number of questions arose in the interpretation of APB Opinion No. 15, and in 1970 a guide to the application of this Opinion, "Computing Earnings per Share," was prepared by J. R. Ball and published by the AICPA.

earnings presentations can be developed directly from historical summaries of earnings for the period and the number of shares that were outstanding.

A capital structure is regarded as *complex* when it includes securities and rights that could have a dilutive effect upon earnings per common share. The complex structure calls for earnings per share presentations that will indicate the maximum possible dilution of earnings on a prospective basis. This requires a detailed analysis of the nature and terms of the items that compose the capital structure and also the adoption of certain assumptions with respect to the dilutive effects of such items.

Whether the capital structure is simple or complex, earnings per share data should be given for all periods covered by the income statement. When results of operations of a prior period have been restated as a result of a prior period adjustment, the earnings per share data given for the prior period should also be restated. The effect of the restatement, expressed in per share terms, should be disclosed in the year of the restatement.

The simple capital structure — computational guidelines. The simple capital structure calls for a single presentation on the face of the income statement that may be designated *earnings per common share.* The earnings per share computation presents no problem when only common stock has been issued and the number of shares outstanding has remained the same for the entire period. Here earnings divided by the number of shares outstanding gives the amount of earnings per common share. Frequently, however, consideration will have to be given to the following matters:

(1) When common shares have been issued or have been reacquired by a company during a period, the amount invested by stockholders has changed and such change has affected earnings. Under these circumstances, a weighted average for common shares outstanding should be computed. Earnings per share are computed by dividing earnings for the period by the weighted average of shares outstanding.

(2) When the number of common shares outstanding has changed during a period as a result of a stock dividend, a stock split, or a reverse split, recognition of such change must be made in arriving at the amount of earnings per share. In developing comparative data, recognition of equivalent changes in the common stock of prior periods is necessary. With the retroactive recognition of changes in the number of shares, earnings per share presentations for prior periods can be stated on a basis that is comparable with the earnings per share presentation for the current period.

(3) When a capital structure includes nonconvertible preferred stock, the claim of preferred stock should be deducted from net income and also from income before extraordinary items when such an amount appears on the income statement, in arriving at the earnings related to common shares. If preferred dividends are not cumulative, only the dividends declared on preferred stock during the period are deducted. If preferred dividends are cumulative, the full amount of dividends on preferred stock for the period, whether declared or not, should be deducted from income before extraordinary items in arriving at the earnings or loss balance related to the common stock. If there is a loss for the period, the amount of dividends on cumulative preferred stock for the period is added to the loss in arriving at the full loss related to the common stock.

To illustrate the computation of earnings per share for a simple capital structure for a comparative two-year period, assume the data that follow.

Summary of changes in capital balances

	6% Cumulative Preferred Stock $100 Par		Common Stock No Par		Retained Earnings
	Shares	Amount	Shares	Amount	
Dec. 31, 1970 Balances.........	10,000	$1,000,000	200,000	$1,000,000	$4,000,000
June 30, 1971 Issuance of 100,000 shares of common stock.......			100,000	600,000	
June 30, 1971 Dividend on preferred stock, 6%.............					(60,000)
June 30, 1971 Dividend on common stock, $.30.................					(90,000)
Dec. 31, 1971 Net income for year, including extraordinary gain of $75,000.....................					360,000
Dec. 31, 1971 Balances.........	10,000	$1,000,000	300,000	$1,600,000	$4,210,000
May 1, 1972 50% Stock dividend on common stock............			150,000	800,000	(800,000)
June 30, 1972 Dividend on preferred stock, 6%.............					(60,000)
Dec. 31, 1972 Net loss for year....					(75,000)
	10,000	$1,000,000	450,000	$2,400,000	$3,275,000

Number of common shares expressed as weighted average of current equivalent shares

1971: Jan. 1–June 30 200,000 × 150% (50% stock dividend in 1972) × 6/12 year.......	150,000	
July 1–Dec. 31 200,000 + 100,000 (sale of stock in 1971) × 150% (50% stock dividend in 1972) × 6/12 year.......	225,000	375,000
1972: Jan. 1–Dec. 31 300,000 × 150% (50% stock dividend in 1972) × 12/12 year......		450,000

Computation of earnings per share:

1971: Income before extraordinary gain....................... $285,000
      Deduct preferred dividend..............................   60,000

      Income after preferred dividend........................ $225,000
      Add extraordinary gain.................................   75,000

      Net income identified with common stock............... $300,000

      Earnings per common share before extraordinary gain,
        $225,000 ÷ 375,000.................................... $ .60
      Extraordinary gain, $75,000 ÷ 375,000..................   .20

      Total earnings per common share....................... $ .80

1972: Net loss for year...................................... $ 75,000
      Add cumulative preferred dividends.....................   60,000

      Loss identified with common stock...................... $135,000

      Loss per common share, $135,000 ÷ 450,000.............. $ .30

It would be inappropriate to report earnings per share on preferred stock in view of the limited dividend rights of such stock. In the case of preferred, however, it may be informative to indicate the number of times or the extent to which the dividend per share requirements were met. Such information should be designated as *earnings coverage on preferred stock* and in the example above would be computed as follows:

   1971: Earnings coverage on preferred stock, $360,000 ÷ $60,000
   (cumulative preferred requirements) = 6.00 times*

   1972: Earnings coverage on preferred stock, $75,000 ÷ $60,000
   (cumulative preferred requirements) = 1.25 times

   *Earnings coverage on preferred stock before extraordinary gain,
   $285,000 ÷ $60,000, or 4.75 times.

The complex capital structure — computational guidelines. Complex capital structures call for a dual presentation of earnings per share data on the face of the income statement: (1) a presentation based upon the number of common shares outstanding plus the shares represented by *common stock equivalents* — securities that are in substance common shares and that have a dilutive effect on earnings per share; (2) a second presentation based on the assumption that all of the contingent issuances of shares of common stock that would individually reduce earnings per share had taken place. The first presentation may be designated on the income statement as *earnings per common and common equivalent share*; the second may be designated as *earnings per common share — assuming full dilution*; for convenience in discussion, the two sets of data are referred to as *primary earnings per share* and *fully diluted earnings per share*. It should be recognized that the primary earnings per share for a complex structure with common stock equivalents is not the same as the basic earnings per share for a simple structure. APB Opinion No. 15 does not provide for an earnings per share figure for complex capital structures with common stock equivalents that is based solely upon common shares actually issued and outstanding.[1]

The difference between primary and fully diluted presentations indicates the maximum extent of dilution of earnings that is possible through the full conversion of securities that are not recognized as common stock equivalents. When a capital structure does not include common stock equivalents, the first presentation may be designated *earnings per common share — assuming no dilution*, and the second *earnings per common share — assuming full dilution*.

A schedule or note should be provided for a dual presentation that explains the bases upon which both primary and fully diluted earnings are calculated. Those issues that are included as common stock equivalents in arriving at primary earnings per share, as well as those issues that are included in the computation of fully diluted earnings per share, should be identified. All of the assumptions that were made and the resulting adjustments that were required in developing the earnings per share data should be indicated. Additional disclosures should be made of the number of shares of common stock issued upon conversion, exercise, or satisfaction of required conditions for at least the most recent annual fiscal period.[2]

Computation of dual earnings per share requires application of the procedures for the simple structure previously described as well as special analyses and additional computations that are described in the following sections. The first section describes the computation of primary earnings per share; the second section describes the computation of fully diluted earnings per share.

---

[1]Many accountants feel that this omission may result in the misinterpretation of the term "primary earnings per share." It may be noted that the Canadian Institute of Chartered Accountants issued a statement on earnings per share in 1970 rejecting a "primary earnings per share" presentation calling for the computation of common stock equivalents and recommended a "basic earnings per share" presentation computed in terms of the number of common shares actually outstanding. *CICA Handbook, Section 3500,* "Earnings per Share" (The Canadian Institute of Chartered Accountants, February, 1970).

[2]APB Opinion No. 15 also recognizes the need for special disclosure on the financial statements of the capital structure in view of the variety and complexity of securities that have been issued. The Board states that ". . . financial statements should include a description, in summary form, sufficient to explain the pertinent rights and privileges of the various securities outstanding. Examples of information which should be disclosed are dividend and liquidation preferences, participation rights, call prices and dates, conversion or exercise prices or rates, and pertinent dates, sinking fund requirements, unusual voting rights, etc." *Opinions of the Accounting Principles Board, No. 15, op. cit.,* par. 19.

Primary earnings per share. The computation of primary earnings per share requires an identification of those securities that qualify as common stock equivalents. A *common stock equivalent* is a security that is not in the form of common stock but one whose terms enable its holder to acquire common shares. Holders of these securities can expect to participate in the appreciation of the value of common stock that results primarily from present and potential earnings of the issuing company. The imminence of conversion is not a factor in the identification. A security that is identified as a common stock equivalent enters into the computation of primary earnings per share only if its effects on earnings are dilutive. Once a security is recognized as a common stock equivalent, it retains this status and it could enter into the computation of primary earnings per share in one period and not in another depending upon its dilutive effect. Common stock equivalents are composed of the securities described in the following paragraphs.

Convertible securities. A convertible security, whether bonds or preferred stock, which at the time of its issuance has terms that make it substantially equivalent to common stock is recognized as a common stock equivalent. The Accounting Principles Board has indicated that to meet this test, the cash yield of the convertible security at the time of its issuance must be significantly less than a comparable security without the conversion option.[1] To make the determination both simple and objective, the Board, after considering a number of alternatives, concluded that a convertible security should be recognized as a common stock equivalent if it has a cash yield based upon its market price of less than $66\frac{2}{3}\%$ of the bank prime interest rate at the time of its issuance. The identification of a convertible security as a common stock equivalent is made at the time of its issuance, and it retains this identity as long as it remains outstanding.

For example, assume that at December 31, 1972, the prime interest rate is $7\frac{1}{2}\%$. Twenty-year convertible debenture bonds with a stated interest rate of 6% are sold at a premium that provides a cash yield of only $4\frac{1}{2}\%$. Since the yield is less than $\frac{2}{3}$ of the bank prime rate of $7\frac{1}{2}\%$, or 5%, the bonds are recognized as a common stock equivalent. The bonds will retain this classification even though the future bank prime rate falls and the cash yield exceeds the $\frac{2}{3}$ ratio.

The computation of primary earnings per share when convertible securities are involved is shown in the example that follows. It is assumed that all issued and issuable shares were outstanding from the

---

[1]Cash yield as used in this opinion is the cash to be received annually expressed as a percentage of the market value of the security at the specified date. For example, a $1,000 bond paying interest at $4\frac{1}{2}\%$ and selling for 90 would have a cash yield of 5% ($\frac{45}{900} = 5\%$).

beginning of the period. Accordingly, any interest or dividends applicable to such convertible securities should not be deducted in computing primary earnings.

Summary of relevant information

Maturity value of convertible bonds.	$500,000
Net income for the year.	$ 83,000
Common shares outstanding.	100,000
Conversion terms of convertible bonds. . . . . . .80 shares for each $1,000 bond	

Primary earnings to be used in computing primary earnings per share

Actual net income.		$ 83,000
Add interest on convertible bonds, net of tax:		
Interest $500,000 at 6%.	$ 30,000	
Less income taxes (assuming 50% rate).	15,000	15,000
Total.		$ 98,000

Number of shares to be used in computing primary earnings per share

Actual number of shares outstanding.	100,000
Additional shares that are issued upon the assumed conversion of bonds, 500 × 80.	40,000
Total.	140,000

Computation of primary earnings per common share

Primary earnings.	$ 98,000
Number of shares related to primary earnings.	140,000
Primary earnings per common share, $98,000 ÷ 140,000.	$ .70

Stock options and warrants and their equivalents and stock purchase contracts. Stock options, warrants, and similar arrangements may provide no cash yield, but these have values because of the rights they offer for the acquisition of common shares at specified prices for an extended period. Other such items may have a low cash yield and may require the payment of cash upon their exchange for common shares; nevertheless, a significant part of their value is related to such exchange rights. These items are always to be regarded as common stock equivalents.

In determining the extent of dilution in earnings per share arising from options, warrants, and similar arrangements providing for the acquisition of common stock, the APB has stated that, except for a few special cases, computation of the number of common stock equivalent shares should be made by the *treasury stock method.* Earnings per share are computed as though these options and warrants were exercised at the beginning of the period or at time of issuance, if later, and as though the funds obtained thereby were applied to the reacquisition of common stock at the average market price of the stock for the period. The computation is necessary whenever the average market price of the stock obtainable exceeds the exercise price of the options or warrants.

To illustrate the use of the treasury stock method for computing common stock equivalent shares, assume the following data:

Summary of relevant information

Net income for the year (primary earnings).................	$ 92,800
Common shares outstanding.................................	100,000
Options outstanding to purchase equivalent shares............	20,000
Exercise price per share on options.........................	$ 2.00
Average market price for common shares....................	$10.00

Application of proceeds from assumed exercise of options outstanding to purchase treasury stock

Proceeds from assumed exercise of options outstanding, 20,000 × $2.00..	$ 40,000
Number of outstanding shares assumed to be repurchased with proceeds from options, $40,000 ÷ $10....................	4,000

Number of shares to be used in computing primary earnings per share

Actual number of shares outstanding...............		100,000
Additional shares issued:		
On assumed exercise of options..................	20,000	
Less assumed repurchase of shares from proceeds of options...................................	4,000	16,000
Total..		116,000

Computation of primary earnings per common share

Primary earnings......................................	$ 92,800
Number of shares related to primary earnings...............	116,000
Primary earnings per common share, $92,800 ÷ 116,000.......	.80

It is recognized that the funds becoming available from the exercise of options and warrants may be applied in a variety of different ways. However, the treasury stock method is regarded as offering a practical approach to the dilutive effect arising from the issuance of common stock at a price below the average market price.

A modification in the procedure described above must be observed. The APB has indicated that the treasury stock method may not adequately reflect potential dilution when options and warrants to obtain a substantial number of common shares are outstanding. Accordingly, it concluded that the treasury stock method be modified if the number of shares of stock obtainable upon exercise of outstanding warrants and options exceeds 20% of the number of shares outstanding at the end of the period for which the computation is being made. In these circumstances, aggregate proceeds from the options and warrants should be

applied in two steps: (1) as if the funds were first applied to the repurchase of outstanding common stock but not to exceed 20% of the outstanding stock, and (2) as if the balance of the funds were applied first to
reduce any short-term or long-term borrowings and any remaining funds
were invested in U.S. government securities or commercial paper with
appropriate recognition of any income tax effect. The results of the two
steps should be combined, and if the net effect is dilutive, it should enter
into the earnings per share computations.

To illustrate the computation of primary earnings per share under
such circumstances, assume the data that follow:

Summary of relevant information

Net income for the year.....................	$ 4,000,000
Common shares outstanding................	3,000,000
6% First-mortgage bonds outstanding.........	$ 5,000,000
Earnings per share before adjustment, $4,000,000 ÷ 3,000,000...........................	$1.33
Options outstanding to purchase equivalent shares.....................................	1,000,000
Limitation on assumed repurchase of shares, 3,000,000 × 20%.........................	600,000
Exercise price per share on options...........	$15
Market value per common share (average; also year-end).................................	$20

Application of assumed proceeds from exercise of options outstanding

Proceeds from assumed exercise of options outstanding, 1,000,000 × $15.................	$15,000,000
Applied toward repurchase of outstanding shares, 600,000 × $20...........................	12,000,000
Balance applied to retirement of 6% first-mortgage bonds...........................	$ 3,000,000

Primary earnings to be used in computing primary earnings per share

Actual net income.........................		$ 4,000,000
Add interest on 6% first-mortgage bonds, net of income taxes:		
Interest, $3,000,000 × 6%................	$ 180,000	
Less income taxes (assuming 50% rate)......	90,000	90,000
Total....................................		$ 4,090,000

Number of shares to be used in computing primary earnings per share

Actual number of shares outstanding..........		3,000,000
Additional shares issued:		
On assumed exercise of options.............	1,000,000	
Less assumed repurchase of outstanding shares from proceeds of options...............	600,000	400,000
Total....................................		3,400,000

Computation of primary earnings per common share

Primary earnings............................	$ 4,090,000
Number of shares related to primary earnings..	3,400,000
Primary earnings per common share, $4,090,000 ÷ 3,400,000............................	$1.20

Participating securities and two-class common stocks. Participating securities and two-class common stocks with participating features that enable their holders to share in the earnings potential of the issuing corporation on substantially the same basis as common stock, are recognized as common stock equivalents.

Contingent shares. Shares whose issuance depends merely upon the passage of time or shares held in escrow pending the satisfaction of conditions unrelated to earnings or market values, are recognized as common stock equivalents. If additional shares are issuable for little or no consideration after the satisfaction of certain conditions, they should be considered as outstanding when the conditions are met.

Fully diluted earnings per share. In calculating fully diluted earnings in the dual presentation of earnings per share, it is necessary to recognize all contingent issuances of common stock that individually would have decreased earnings per share and in the aggregate would have a dilutive effect although they do not qualify as common stock equivalents. All such issuances are assumed to have taken place at the beginning of the period or at the time the convertible security was issued, if later. The maximum potential dilution of current earnings per share on a prospective basis is thus determined.

Fully diluted earnings must be reported on the income statement for each period presented if (1) shares of common stock were issued during the period on conversion, exercise, or other contingent issuance, or (2) shares of common stock were contingently issuable at the close of any period presented and if primary earnings would have been reduced by 3% or more if such actual or contingent issues had taken place at the beginning of the period. The above contingencies may result from the existence of debt or preferred stock that is convertible into common stock but is not a common stock equivalent, options or warrants, or agreements for the issuance of common stock upon the satisfaction of certain conditions.

When primary earnings are diluted as a result of the inclusion of outstanding options and warrants, a modification in the application of the treasury stock method may be necessary for purposes of calculating the fully diluted earnings per share. To reflect maximum potential dilution, the market price of the common stock at the close of the period is used in computing the number of shares assumed to be reacquired if such market price is higher than the average price that had been used in computing primary earnings per share. Furthermore, common shares that are issued on the exercise of options or warrants during each period should be included in fully diluted earnings per share from the beginning of the period or the date of issuance of the options or warrants, if later; the computation for the portion of the period prior to the date of exercise should be based on market prices of the common stock when exercised.[1]

As indicated earlier, computations of fully diluted earnings should exclude those securities whose subsequent conversion, exercise, or other contingent issuance would increase the earnings per share amount or decrease the loss per share amount.

To continue with the example on page 791 and illustrate the computation of fully diluted earnings, assume that the following convertible security that did not qualify as a common stock equivalent had been outstanding during the year:

7½% Convertible bonds outstanding, issued at face value... $5,000,000
Each $1,000 bond is convertible into 60 shares of common stock.

Fully diluted earnings to be used in computing fully diluted earnings per share

Primary earnings (as computed earlier)...........		$4,090,000
Add interest on 7½% convertible bonds, net of tax:		
Interest, $5,000,000 × 7½%.................	$375,000	
Less income taxes (assuming 50% rate).........	187,500	187,500
Total.......................................		$4,277,500

Number of shares to be used in computing fully diluted earnings per share

Number of shares used in computing primary earnings per share (as computed earlier)...........	3,400,000
Additional shares issued on assumed conversion of convertible bonds, 5,000 × 60.................	300,000
Total.......................................	3,700,000

Computation of fully diluted earnings per common share

Fully diluted earnings...........................	$4,277,500
Number of shares to be used in computing fully diluted earnings per share.....................	3,700,000
Fully diluted earnings per common share, $4,277,500 ÷ 3,700,000.....................................	$1.16

[1]The APB indicates that fully diluted earnings per share computations should be made on the most advantageous conversion or exercise rights that become effective for a period limited to ten years from the close of the period; rights that are not effective after a ten-year period may be of only limited significance in decisions by investors and it is questionable whether they would be relevant to current operating results.

Primary and fully diluted earnings in the example would be reported on the income statement as shown below. This presentation would be accompanied by notes explaining the nature of the calculations.

Earnings per common and common equivalent share......... $1.20
Earnings per common share — assuming full dilution......... 1.16

Earnings per share presentations.   When earnings of a period include earnings before extraordinary items, earnings per share amounts would be presented for both earnings before extraordinary items and net income balances, both on a common equivalent share basis and on a fully diluted basis. It may also be desirable to present per share amounts for any extraordinary items.

In 1971, the Accounting Principles Board in Opinion No. 20, "Accounting Changes," recommended that the cumulative effect of a change in accounting principle be reported under a separate income statement heading between "extraordinary items" and "net income." The Board referred to earnings per share calculations and stated:

> The per share information shown on the face of the income statement should include the per share amount of the cumulative effect of the accounting change.[1]

APB Opinion No. 15 concludes with the following observation concerning the presentation of information concerning dividends per share:

> Dividends constitute historical facts and usually are so reported. However, in certain cases, such as those affected by stock dividends, or splits, or reverse splits, the presentation of dividends per share should be made in terms of the current equivalents of the number of common shares outstanding at the time of the dividend. . . . When dividends per share are presented on other than an historical basis, the basis of presentation should be disclosed.[2]

It is important that great care be exercised in interpreting earnings per share data regardless of the degree of refinement that is applied in the development of such data. These values are the products of the principles and practices employed in the accounting process and are subject to the same limitations as found in the net income measurement reported on the income statement.

---

[1]*Opinions of the Accounting Principles Board, No. 20,* "Accounting Changes" (New York: American Institute of Certified Public Accountants, 1971), par. 20.

[2]*Opinions of the Accounting Principles Board, No. 15, op. cit.,* par. 70.

QUESTIONS

1. Why is book value per share often a poor indicator of stock worth?

2. What adjustments are applied to the total stockholders' equity in computing book value per common share when there is more than one class of stock outstanding?

3. What kinds of decisions are influenced by the availability of book value per share computations?

4. The liquidation value of preferred stock is 100 and the call price is 105. Which value should be used in computing book value for preferred stock? Why?

5. Earnings per share computations have been receiving increased prominence on the income statement. How would an investor use such information to assist him in making investment decisions?

6. What computation is reported for preferred stock instead of earnings per share? Why is such a computation more appropriate?

7. What criteria determines the number of years for which earnings per share computations should be reported?

8. What distinguishes a simple from a complex capital structure?

9. How does the purchase of treasury stock affect the computation of earnings per share?

10. What constitutes a common stock equivalent for calculating primary earnings per share?

11. What is meant by "dilution of earnings per share"?

12. Under what circumstances should the earnings per share amounts for prior periods be recalculated for reporting earnings trends?

13. (a) Under what conditions is a convertible security recognized as a common stock equivalent?
(b) Under what conditions are stock options and warrants recognized as common stock equivalents?

14. What is the treasury stock method of accounting for outstanding stock options and warrants in computing primary earnings?

15. What modification to the treasury stock method is required if the number of shares obtainable from the exercise of outstanding options and warrants exceeds 20% of the number of shares outstanding?

16. Compare the concept of primary earnings per share with the concept of fully diluted earnings per share.

17. How is the treasury stock method for stock options and warrants modified in computing fully diluted earnings per share as compared with computing primary earnings per share?

18. Under what circumstances would the earnings per share computation for a complex capital structure be the same as for a simple capital structure?

19. What limitations should be recognized in using earnings per share data?

EXERCISES

1. The stockholders' equity of the Orderville Co. follows:

Authorized capital stock, $25 par, 100,000 shares.	$2,500,000
Unissued capital stock (20,000 shares).	500,000
Treasury stock (3,000 shares, at cost).	60,000
Additional paid-in capital.	145,000
Deficit.	300,000

Calculate the book value per share of stock outstanding.

2. The stockholders' equity of Stephens, Inc., on December 31, 1972, follows:

Common stock, 50,000 shares, $10 par.	$500,000
6% Preferred stock, 5,000 shares, $25 par.	125,000
Additional paid-in capital.	75,000
Retained earnings.	50,000
	$750,000

Calculate the book values per share of preferred stock and common stock under each of the following assumptions:

(a) Preferred stock is noncumulative and nonparticipating, callable at $30, and preferred as to assets at $27.50 upon corporate liquidation.

(b) Preferred stock is cumulative, nonparticipating, with dividends in arrears for 6 years; upon corporate liquidation, shares are preferred as to assets up to par, and must be paid any dividends in arrears before distributions may be made to common shares.

(c) Preferred stock is fully participating with common stock; upon corporate liquidation any distributions beyond stock par values are to be made ratably on preferred and common shares.

3. Calculate the weighted average number of shares outstanding for Nielson Construction Company assuming transactions in common stock occurred during the year as follows:

Date	Transactions in Common Stock	Number of Shares $10 Par Value
Jan. 1, 1972	Outstanding	16,000
Feb. 15, 1972	Issued for cash	3,200
April 1, 1972	Repurchased shares outstanding	(3,000)
June 1, 1972	Resold part of shares acquired April 1	1,400
Sept. 1, 1972	Issued in exchange for property	6,400
Dec. 1, 1972	25% stock dividend	25% of outstanding shares

4. The income statement for the Spencer Co. for the year ended December 31, 1972, shows the following:

Income before income taxes............................	$520,000
Income taxes......................................	260,000
Income before extraordinary item......................	$260,000
Add extraordinary gain from sale of Springfield branch store (net of income taxes)................................	160,000
Net income.......................................	$420,000

Calculate earnings per share amounts for 1972 under each of the following assumptions:

(a) The company has only one class of stock, the number of shares outstanding totaling 200,000.
(b) The company has shares outstanding as follows:
5% cumulative, nonparticipating preferred, $100 par, 10,000 shares; common, $25 par, 200,000 shares.

5. The Harris Manufacturing Company reports long-term debt and stockholders' equity balances at December 31, 1972, as follows:

Convertible 4% bonds (sold at par)....................	$ 500,000
Common stock, $25 par, 100,000 shares issued and outstanding..	2,500,000

Additional information is determined as follows:

Conversion terms of bonds............40 shares for each $1,000 bond	
Income before extraordinary gain — 1972..............	$ 80,000
Extraordinary gain.................................	10,000
Net income — 1972................................	$ 90,000

What are the primary earnings per share for the company for 1972 assuming that the tax rate is 50% and that the prime interest rate at the date the bonds were sold was $7\frac{1}{2}\%$? No changes occurred in the above debt and equity balances during 1972.

6. Options to purchase 2,000 common shares at $2 per share are outstanding. All of these options were outstanding during the entire year and are presently exercisable or will become exercisable within four years. The average market price of the company's common stock during the year was $10 and the price of the stock at the end of the year was $15. Compute the common stock equivalent shares that would be used in arriving at (a) primary earnings per share, and (b) fully diluted earnings per share.

7. Which of the following securities qualify as common stock equivalents for the purpose of computing primary earnings per share? Give reasons supporting each answer.

(a) Employee stock options to purchase 500 shares of common stock at 35 are issued. Current market price of the stock is 32.
(b) Warrants to purchase 2,000 shares at 28 are issued. Current market price of the stock is 32.
(c) 5% convertible bonds are sold: nominal rate, 5%; sales price, 95. The prime interest rate is 9%.
(d) 6% convertible preferred stock is sold at par. The prime interest rate is 8%.
(e) An agreement was made with management to issue 2,000 shares of stock if a 5% growth rate in income is reported for the current year.

PROBLEMS

22-1. The stockholders' equity for the Barker Company on December 31, 1972, follows:

5% Preferred stock, $50 par, 20,000 shares............	$1,000,000
Common stock, $20 par, 100,000 shares...............	2,000,000
Additional paid-in capital..........................	25,000
Retained earnings.................................	195,000
Total stockholders' equity.........................	$3,220,000

Instructions: Calculate the book values of preferred shares and common shares as of December 31, 1972, under each of the following assumptions:
(1) Preferred dividends have been paid to October 1, 1972; preferred shares have a call value of $55, a liquidation value of $52.50, and are entitled to current unpaid dividends.
(2) Preferred shares have a liquidation value of par; shares are cumulative, with dividends 3 years in arrears and fully payable in the event of liquidation.
(3) Preferred shares have a liquidation value of par; shares are cumulative, with dividends 5 years in arrears and fully payable in the event of liquidation.
(4) Preferred shares have been paid 5% in 1972 but dividends have not been paid on common; preferred is entitled to full participation ratably with common after common has been paid the preferred rate.

22-2. Transactions involving the common stock account of the Beardall Company during the two-year period, 1971 and 1972, were as follows:

January 1, 1971........	Balance: 30,000 shares of $50 par stock.
May 1, 1971...........	Sold 10,000 shares at $55.
June 1, 1971...........	Paid a cash dividend of $2.00 per share.
October 1, 1971........	Issued a 5% stock dividend.
December 1, 1971.......	Sold 30,000 shares at $60.
March 1, 1972.........	Purchased 3,000 shares as treasury stock.
May 1, 1972...........	Sold 1,000 shares of treasury stock.
June 15, 1972.........	Sold 20,000 shares at $75.
July 1, 1972...........	Issued a 2-for-1 stock split.
November 1, 1972.......	Formally retired 4,000 shares of treasury stock.
December 31, 1972......	Paid a cash dividend of $4.00 per share.

Beardall Company has a simple capital structure.

Instructions: Compute the weighted average number of equivalent common shares for 1971 and 1972 that are to be used for both book value and earnings per share computations at the end of 1972.

22-3. The following 1972 condensed financial statements for the Evans Corporation were prepared by the accounting department:

Evans Corporation
Income Statement
For Year Ended December 31, 1972

Sales..		$6,000,000
Cost of goods sold............................		5,000,000
Gross profit on sales...........................		$1,000,000
Less expenses:		
Selling......................................	$ 400,000	
Administrative...............................	400,000	
Interest expense.............................	40,000	840,000
Income from operations........................		$ 160,000
Income taxes.................................		80,000
Income before extraordinary item..............		$ 80,000
Extraordinary item:		
Gain on disposal of land net of income taxes applicable to gain........................		15,000
Net income.................................		$ 95,000

Evans Corporation
Balance Sheet (Condensed)
December 31, 1972

Assets...		$1,800,000
Current liabilities..................................		$ 800,000
8% Bonds, due December 31, 1977....................		500,000
Stockholders' equity:		
Common stock, par value, $2 per share. Authorized, 200,000 shares; issued and outstanding, 100,000 shares............		200,000
Retained earnings......................................		300,000
		$1,800,000

Instructions: Compute the earnings per share under each of the following assumptions:

(1) No change in the capital structure occurred in 1972.

(2) On December 31, 1971, there were 60,000 shares outstanding. On May 1, 1972, 30,000 shares were sold at par and on October 1, 1972, 10,000 shares were sold at par.

(3) On December 31, 1971, there were 75,000 shares outstanding. On July 1, 1972, the company issued a 33⅓% stock dividend.

22-4. The Supreme Block Company reported the following comparative balances in the stockholders' equity section of its balance sheets at the end of 1972.

	December 31, 1972	December 31, 1971	December 31, 1970
Preferred stock	$ 300,000	$ 200,000	$ 150,000
Premium on preferred stock	100,000	50,000	37,500
Common stock	1,020,000	1,020,000	750,000
Premium on common stock	250,000	250,000	230,000
Paid-in capital from sale of treasury stock at more than cost	25,000	15,000	15,000
Retained earnings— unappropriated	231,000	320,000	412,000
Retained earnings appropriated for contingencies	150,000	100,000	100,000
Total stockholders' equity	$2,076,000	$1,955,000	$1,694,500

The following transactions involving the stockholders' equity balances occurred during 1971 and 1972.

May 1, 1971 — Sold 10,000 shares of $10 par common stock for $12.

July 1, 1971 — Sold 2,500 shares of $20 par preferred stock for $25.

Nov. 1, 1971 — Issued a 20% stock dividend on common stock. The market price for common stock on this date was $12.

Dec. 31, 1971 — Paid cash dividends: 5% on preferred shares; $1 per share on common stock.

Dec. 31, 1971 — Net income for 1971 was $200,000 that included an extraordinary loss of $20,000.

Feb. 1, 1972 — Sold 5,000 shares of preferred stock for $30.

Mar. 1, 1971 — Split common stock on a 2-for-1 basis.

July 1, 1972 — Purchased 4,000 shares of common stock for $6.00 to be held as treasury stock.

Oct. 1, 1972 — Sold 4,000 shares of treasury stock for $8.50.

Dec. 31, 1972 — Paid cash dividends: 5% on preferred shares; $1 per share on common stock.

Dec. 31, 1972 — Net income for 1972 included an extraordinary gain of $40,000.

The Supreme Block Co. has a simple capital structure. The liquidation value of the preferred stock is $25.00.

Instructions: Compute the comparative book value per share and earnings per share amounts for 1971 and 1972.

22-5. The Tanner Manufacturing Co. reported the following changes in its stockholders' equity accounts during 1971 and 1972:

Date	Transaction	8% Cumulative Preferred Stock $50 Par		Common Stock No Par		Retained Earnings
		Shares	Amount	Shares	Amount	
Dec. 31, 1970	Balances..............	2,500	$125,000	40,000	$ 875,000	$1,860,000
May 1, 1971	Issuance of 10,000 shares of common stock			10,000	425,000	
Oct. 1, 1971	20% stock dividend on common stock........			10,000	500,000	(500,000)
Dec. 1, 1971	Repurchase of 2,000 shares of common stock			(2,000)	(80,000)	
Dec. 31, 1971	8% cash dividend on preferred stock........					(10,000)
Dec. 31, 1971	Net income for the year that includes an extra-ordinary loss of $40,000					190,000
Dec. 31, 1971	Balances..............	2,500	$125,000	58,000	$1,720,000	$1,540,000
Mar. 1, 1972	Sale of 2,000 shares of common treasury stock.			2,000	80,000	
July 1, 1972	3-for-1 split on common stock................			120,000		
Oct. 1, 1972	Repurchase of 500 shares of preferred stock	(500)	(25,000)			
Dec. 31, 1972	Net income for the year that includes an extra-ordinary gain of $30,000............					68,000
Dec. 31, 1972	8% cash dividend on preferred stock........					(8,000)
Dec. 31, 1972	Cash dividend on common, $.50............					(90,000)
Dec. 31, 1972	Balances.............	2,000	$100,000	180,000	$1,800,000	$1,510,000

Instructions: (1) Compute the comparative book value per common share for 1971 and 1972, assuming that preferred stock has a liquidating value of $53.

(2) Compute the following measurements for both 1971 and 1972.

(a) Weighted average of equivalent common shares.

(b) Earnings per common share.

(c) Earnings coverage on preferred stock.

22-6. Bills Company provides you with the following data at December 31, 1972:

Operating revenue.............................	$500,000
Operating expenses............................	$300,000
Income tax rate...............................	50%
Common stock outstanding during the entire year...	10,000 shares

On January 1, 1972, there were options outstanding to purchase 5,000 shares of common stock at $20 per share. During 1972, the average price per share was $25 but at December 31, 1972, the market price had risen to $30 per share. The balance sheet reports $100,000 of 6% non-convertible bonds at December 31, 1972. (Interest expense is included in operating expenses.)

Instructions: Compute for 1972:

(1) Primary earnings per share.

(2) Fully diluted earnings per share.

22-7. Data for the Chalmers Company at the end of 1972 are listed below. All bonds are convertible as indicated and were issued at their face amounts.

Description of Bonds	Amount	Date Issued	Prime Interest Rate on Date Issued	Conversion Terms
10-year, 5% convertible bonds	$ 500,000	6/30/71	7%	60 shares of common for each $1,000 bond
15-year, 5¼% convertible bonds	$1,000,000	1/1/72	8%	50 shares of common for each $1,000 bond
20-year, 5% convertible bonds	$ 400,000	6/30/72	7½%	80 shares of common for each $1,000 bond

Number of common shares outstanding at December 31, 1971	500,000
Net income for 1972 (after income taxes)................	$675,000
Income tax rate......................................	50%

Instructions: (1) Compute the primary earnings per share for 1972, assuming that no additional shares of common stock were issued during the year.

(2) Compute the fully diluted earnings per share for 1972 assuming that no additional shares of common stock were issued during the year.

(3) Compute both primary and fully diluted earnings per share for 1972 assuming that the 10-year bonds were converted on April 1, 1972, and that net income for the year was $684,375.

22-8. The balance sheet of the Sterns Company on September 30, 1972, has the following items on the credit side of the statement:

Current liabilities......................................	$103,732
Bonds payable..	300,000
Reserve for bond retirement............................	160,000
6% Cumulative preferred stock, $100 par value (entitled to $110 and accumulated dividends per share in voluntary liquidation and to $100 per share in involuntary liquidation). Authorized — 3,000 shares, issued — 2,000 shares, in treasury — 150 shares............................	185,000
Common stock, $100 par value, authorized — 10,000 shares, issued and outstanding — 4,000 shares................	400,000
Premium on preferred stock............................	10,000
Premium on common stock............................	67,300
Retained earnings.....................................	131,260

The company proposes to finance a plant expansion program by issuing an additional 2,000 shares of common stock. Common stockholders of record October 1, 1972, were notified that they will be permitted to subscribe to the new issue at $150 per share up to 50% of their holdings. The market value of the stock on October 1, 1972, was $172.50 per share. The stock goes ex-rights in the market on October 3, 1972.

Peter Singer owns 100 shares of the Sterns Company common stock that he purchased in 1970 for $16,431.20. He does not want to exercise his rights but wishes to sell them.

Instructions: (1) Calculate the book value of a share of common stock as of September 30, 1972. Preferred dividends have been paid or set up as payable through September 30, 1972.

(2) Compute the theoretical value of Peter Singer's rights as of October 1, 1972.

22-9. In the course of your audit of Mystic Company, you were requested to prepare comparative data from the company's inception to the present. Toward this end you determined the following:

(a) Mystic Company's charter became effective on January 1, 1968, when 1,000 shares of no-par common and 1,000 shares of 6% cumulative, nonparticipating preferred stock were issued. The no-par common stock was sold at its stated value of $150 per share, and the preferred stock was sold at its par value of $100 per share.

(b) Mystic Company was unable to pay preferred dividends at the end of its first year. The owners of the preferred stock agreed to accept one share of common stock for every twenty shares of preferred stock owned in discharge of the preferred dividends due on December 31, 1968. The shares were issued on January 2, 1969, which was also the declaration date. The fair market value was $120 per share for common on the date of issue.

(c) On April 30, 1970, Mystic Company paid a 10% stock dividend in preferred stock (one share for every ten shares held) to all common stockholders. The fair market value of preferred stock was $85 per share on that date of issue.

(d) Mystic Company acquired all of the outstanding stock of Homes Corporation on May 1, 1970, in exchange for 600 shares of Mystic Company common stock. The transaction was recorded as a purchase. Homes Corporation reported a net income of $12,000 for its fiscal year ended April 30, 1970, and had reported a net income of $15,000 per year in each of its two prior years.

(e) Mystic Company split its common stock 3-for-2 on January 1, 1971, and 2-for-1 on January 1, 1972.

(f) Mystic Company tendered an offer to convert 20% of the preferred stock to common stock on the basis of two shares of common for one share of preferred. The offer was fully accepted, and the conversion was made on July 1, 1972.

(g) The company reported the following in income statements for the years indicated:

Year	Operating Income (Loss)	Other Income	Income Taxes Expense	Net Income (Loss)
1968.........	$(9,600)			$(9,600)
1969.........	23,421		$ 4,146 (1)	19,275
1970.........	47,920 (2)		16,960	30,960
1971.........	60,221 (2)	$13,200 (3)	25,706 (4)	47,715
1972.........	57,365 (2)		23,615 (5)	33,750

Notes:

(1) After net operating loss deduction; tax rate is 30%.
(2) Includes net income of combined companies.
(3) Gain from sale of land.
(4) Includes $3,300 tax on gain from sale of land.
(5) Includes $2,580 income tax applicable to 1970.

(h) No cash dividends were paid on common stock until December 31, 1970. Cash dividends per share of common stock were paid as follows:

	June 30	December 31
1970..............		$3.19
1971..............	$1.75	2.75
1972..............	1.25	1.25

Instructions: (1) Prepare schedules which show the computation of:

(a) The number of shares of each class of stock outstanding on the last day of each year.
(b) The number of shares of common stock outstanding each year expressed as a weighted average of the current equivalent shares. (A current equivalent share is a share adjusted for stock splits.)
(c) Cash dividends paid on common stock.

(2) Prepare a five-year summary of financial statistics by years of "Net Income," "Earnings per Share" and "Dividends per Share" for common stock, and "Earnings Coverage" for preferred stock. The summary is to be included in the Mystic Company's annual report and should be properly footnoted. Supporting computations should be in good form. (Earnings coverage indicates the number of times preferred dividends were earned.)

(AICPA adapted)

22-10. On February 1, 1973, when your audit and report is nearly complete, the president of the Scooter Corporation asks you to prepare statistical schedules of comparative financial data for the past five years for inclusion in the company's annual report. Your working papers reveal the following information:

(a) Income statements show net income amounts as follows:

1968 — $20,000*
1969 — (17,000) (loss)
1970 — 30,000
1971 — 38,000
1972 — 42,000**

*Includes extraordinary gain of $8,000.
**Includes unfavorable income tax adjustment of $5,000 applicable to 1970.

(b) On January 1, 1968, there were outstanding 1,000 shares of common stock, par value $100, and 500 shares of 6% cumulative preferred stock, par value $50.

(c) A 5% dividend was paid in common stock to common stockholders on December 31, 1969. The fair market value of the stock was $150 per share at the time.

(d) Four hundred shares of common stock were issued on March 31, 1970, to purchase another company.

(e) A dividend of cumulative preferred stock was distributed to common stockholders on July 1, 1970. One share of preferred stock was distributed for every five shares of common stock held. The fair market value of the preferred stock was $55 per share before the distribution and $53 per share immediately after the distribution.

(f) The common stock was split 2-for-1 on December 31, 1971, and December 31, 1972.

(g) Cash dividends are paid on the preferred stock on June 30 and December 31. Preferred stock dividends were paid in each year except 1969; the 1969 and 1970 dividends were paid in 1970.

(h) Cash dividends on common stock are paid semiannually. Dividends paid per share of stock outstanding at the respective dates were:

	June 30	December 31
1968.............	$ .50	$ .50
1969.............	None	None
1970.............	.75	.75
1971.............	1.00	.50*
1972.............	.75	.75**

*After 2-for-1 split.
**Before 2-for-1 split.

Instructions: (1) In connection with your preparation of the statistical schedule of comparative financial data for the past five years:

(a) Prepare a schedule computing the number of shares of common stock and preferred stock outstanding as of the respective year-end dates.

(b) Prepare a schedule computing the current equivalent number of shares of common stock outstanding as of the respective year-end dates. The current equivalent shares means the number of shares outstanding in the respective prior periods in terms of the present stock position.

(c) Compute the total cash dividends paid to holders of preferred stock and to holders of common stock for each of the five years.

(2) Prepare a five-year summary of financial statistics to be included in the annual report. The summary should show by years "Net Income (or Loss)," "Earnings per Share of Common Stock," and "Dividends per Share of Common Stock." Include any explanatory footnotes considered necessary.

(AICPA adapted)

22-11. The controller of Lafayette Corporation has requested assistance in determining income, primary earnings per share and fully diluted earnings per share for presentation in the company's income statement for the ended September 30, 1970. As currently calculated, the company's net income is $400,000 for fiscal year 1969–1970. The controller has indicated that the income figure might be adjusted for the following transactions which were recorded by charges or credits directly to retained earnings (the amounts are net of applicable income taxes):

(a) The sum of $375,000, applicable to a breached 1976 contract, was received as a result of a lawsuit. Prior to the award, legal counsel was uncertain about the outcome of the suit.

(b) A gain of $300,000 was realized on the sale of a subsidiary.

(c) A gain of $80,000 was realized on the sale of treasury stock.

(d) A special inventory write-off of $150,000 was made, of which $125,000 applied to goods manufactured prior to October 1, 1969.

Your working papers disclose the following opening balances and transactions in the company's capital stock accounts during the year:

1. Common stock (at October 1, 1969, stated value $10, authorized 300,000 shares; effective December 1, 1969, stated value $5, authorized 600,000 shares):

   Balance, October 1, 1969 — issued and outstanding 60,000 shares.
   December 1, 1969 — 60,000 shares issued in a 2-for-1 stock split.
   December 1, 1969 — 280,000 shares (stated value $5) issued at $39 per share.

2. Treasury stock common:
   March 1, 1970 — purchased 40,000 shares at $38 per share.
   April 1, 1970 — sold 40,000 shares at $40 per share.

3. Stock purchase warrants, Series A (initially, each warrant was exchangeable with $60 for one common share; effective December 1, 1969, each warrant became exchangeable for two common shares at $30 per share):
   October 1, 1969 — 25,000 warrants issued at $6 each.

4. Stock purchase warrants, Series B (each warrant is exchangeable with $40 for one common share):
   April 1, 1970 — 20,000 warrants authorized and issued at $10 each.

5. First-mortgage bonds, $5\frac{1}{2}\%$, due 1985 (nonconvertible; priced to yield 5% when issued):

   Balance, October 1, 1969 — authorized, issued and outstanding — the face value of $1,400,000.

6. Convertible debentures, 7%, due 1989 (initially each $1,000 bond was convertible at any time until maturity into $12\frac{1}{2}$ common shares; effective December 1, 1969, the conversion rate became 25 shares for each bond):

   October 1, 1969 — authorized and issued at their face value (no premium or discount) of $2,400,000.

The following table shows market prices for the company's securities and the assumed bank prime interest rate during 1969–1970.

	Price (or Rate) at			Average for Year Ended September 30, 1970
	October 1, 1969	April 1, 1970	September 30, 1970	
Common stock	66	40	$36\frac{1}{4}$	$37\frac{1}{2}$*
First-mortgage bonds	$88\frac{1}{2}$	87	86	87
Convertible debentures	100	120	119	115
Series A Warrants	6	22	$19\frac{1}{2}$	15
Series B Warrants	–	10	9	$9\frac{1}{2}$
Bank prime interest rate	8%	$7\frac{3}{4}\%$	$7\frac{1}{2}\%$	$7\frac{3}{4}\%$

*Adjusted for stock split.

Instructions: (1) Prepare a schedule computing net income as it should be presented in the company's income statement for the year ended September 30, 1970.

(2) Assuming that net income after income taxes for the year was $540,000 and that there were no extraordinary items, prepare a schedule computing (a) the primary earnings per share, and (b) the fully diluted earnings per share which should be presented in the company's income statement for the year ended September 30, 1970. A supporting schedule computing the number of shares to be used in these computations should also be prepared. (Because of the relative stability of the market price for its common shares, the annual average market price may be used where appropriate in your calculations. Assume an income tax rate of 48% with no surcharge.)

(AICPA adapted)

22-12. The stockholders' equity section of Lowe Company's balance sheet as of December 31, 1972, contains the following:

$1.00 Cumulative convertible preferred stock (par value $25 a share; authorized 1,600,000 shares, issued 1,400,000, converted to common 750,000, and outstanding 650,000 shares; involuntary liquidation value, $30 a share, aggregating $19,500,000).............	$16,250,000
Common stock (par value $.25 a share; authorized 15,000,000 shares, issued and outstanding 8,800,000 shares)..	2,200,000
Additional paid-in capital.........................	32,750,000
Retained earnings................................	40,595,000
Total stockholders' equity........................	$91,795,000

On April 1, 1972, Lowe Company acquired the business and assets and assumed the liabilities of Diane Corporation in a transaction accounted for as a pooling of interests. For each of Diane Corporation's 2,400,000 shares of $.25 par value common stock outstanding, the owner received one share of common stock of the Lowe Company.

Included in the liabilities of Lowe Company are 5½% convertible subordinated debentures issued at their face value of $20,000,000 in 1971. The debentures are due in 1991 and until then are convertible into the common stock of Lowe Company at the rate of five shares of common stock for each $100 debenture. To date none of these have been converted.

On April 2, 1972, Lowe Company issued 1,400,000 shares of convertible preferred stock at $40 per share. Quarterly dividends to December 31, 1972, have been paid on these shares. The preferred stock is convertible into common stock at the rate of two shares of common for each share of preferred. On October 1, 1972, 150,000 shares and on November 1, 1972, 600,000 shares of the preferred stock were converted into common stock.

During July 1971, Lowe Company granted options to its officers and key employees to purchase 500,000 shares of the company's common stock at a price of $20 a share. The options do not become exercisable until 1973.

During 1972 dividend payments and average market prices of the Lowe common stock have been as follows:

	Dividend per Share	Average Market Price per Share
First quarter	$.10	$20
Second quarter	.15	25
Third quarter	.10	30
Fourth quarter	.15	25
Average for the year		25

The December 31, 1972, closing price of the common stock was $25 a share.

Assume that the bank prime interest rate was 7% throughout 1971 and 1972. Lowe Company's consolidated net income for the year ended December 31, 1972, was $9,200,000. The provision for income taxes was computed at a rate of 48%.

Instructions: (1) Prepare a schedule which shows the evaluation of the common stock equivalency status of the (a) convertible debentures, (b) convertible preferred stock, and (c) employee stock options.

(2) Prepare a schedule which shows for 1972 the computation of:

(a) The weighted average number of shares for computing primary earnings per share.

(b) The weighted average number of shares for computing fully diluted earnings per share.

(3) Prepare a schedule which shows for 1972 the computation to the nearest cent of:

(a) Primary earnings per share.

(b) Fully diluted earnings per share.

(AICPA adapted)

chapter 23

the statement of changes
in financial position

Financial reporting for the business unit consists of statements reporting financial position and the results of operations. The position of the business at a given time is reported on the balance sheet. The operations for a given period are reported on the income statement and on the funds statement. The income statement summarizes the revenues and expenses for the period and accounts for the change in retained earnings in successive periods. When there are further transactions that must be recognized in explaining the change in owners' equity, these would be reported in separate statements accompanying the income statement. The funds statement, on the other hand, offers a summary not only of the operations of the business but also of the financing and investing activities of the business for the period. It thus accounts for all of the changes in financial position as reported on successive balance sheets.

The funds statement has variously been referred to as *the statement of application of funds, the statement of sources and uses of funds, the source and application of funds statement, the statement of financial operations, and the statement of resources provided and applied.* In reporting funds flow, it is possible to adopt a funds concept that would provide for a limited recognition of financial changes or a funds concept that is broadened to cover all financial changes. The Accounting Principles Board in 1971 recommended that the broadened concept be adopted, and in applying such concept, that the funds statement be called the *statement of changes in financial position.*

To simplify reference to the statement, the term "funds statement" is used in the discussions that follow.

Increase in funds-flow reporting

A great deal of research has been directed in recent years to financial presentations — their form, their use, and their interpretation. Within this area, particular emphasis has been placed on funds-flow reporting. Although first efforts of the Accounting Principles Board were directed to the postulates and broad principles of accounting, early attention was also focused upon the presentation of funds-flow data. In 1961 the Director of Accounting Research authorized the publication of *"Cash Flow" Analysis and the Funds Statement*, Accounting Research Study No. 2, by Dr. Perry Mason. In 1963 the APB in Opinion No. 3 pointed to an increasing awareness by the different users of financial reporting of the value of funds-flow information and encouraged the presentation of a statement summarizing fund sources and uses. Since publication of this Opinion, there has been a substantial increase in the inclusion of funds-flow statements in annual reports, and in 1971 the APB issued Opinion No. 19 in which it concluded that information concerning the financing and investing activities of a business and the changes in its financial position for a period is essential in arriving at economic decisions concerning a business. Accordingly, it stated

> ... When financial statements purporting to present both financial position (balance sheet) and results of operations (statement of income and retained earnings) are issued, a statement summarizing changes in financial position should also be presented as a basic financial statement for each period for which an income statement is presented.

The funds statement was thus recognized as a third statement that was required in fully reporting the activities of the business unit.

The funds statement has a long history of use. Many companies prepared the statement for management purposes long before actually presenting this information to the external user. The definition for the term "funds," as well as the form for the presentation of fund sources and uses, has varied with different companies depending upon the use that was to be made of the statement.

Funds defined

One significant variation that is found in funds-flow reporting is the definition that is applied to the term "funds." The term has been defined in different ways and the definition determines the character and the form of the statement. Funds has most frequently been used to mean working capital, and in these instances the funds statement reports

---

[1]*Opinions of The Accounting Principles Board*, No. *19*, "Reporting Changes in Financial Position" (New York: The American Institute of Certified Public Accountants, 1971), par. 7.

financing and investing activities in terms of working capital. The funds statement thus provides a summary of the individual sources and uses of working capital and accounts for the change in working capital for the period. In its narrowest sense, funds has been used simply to denote cash, and a funds statement applying this concept simply provides a presentation of the individual sources and uses of cash for the period and the resulting change in the cash balance. Intermediate views would define funds as net monetary assets — current assets excluding inventory and prepaid items less current liabilities — all monetary assets, or simply cash and temporary investments combined. In applying the alternative definitions, the funds statement would report the sources and applications of such "funds" and reconcile their change in successive balance sheets. In practice, funds reporting generally employs the working capital or cash concept, and subsequent discussions will describe the preparation of funds statement when these concepts are adopted.

The broadened interpretation of funds

If the funds definitions were to be applied literally, a number of transactions involving highly significant information relative to financing and investing activities would be omitted from the funds statement and thus fail to be recognized by the user. For example, debt and equity securities may be issued in exchange for land and buildings; long-term investments may be exchanged for machinery and equipment; shares of stock may be issued in payment of long-term debt; properties may be received as gifts. These transactions carry significant implications in analyzing the change that has taken place in financial position even though they are not factors in reconciling the change in funds as commonly defined. This suggests that in order to make the funds statement more useful, the funds interpretation should be broadened to recognize transactions such as those mentioned. The broadened view, for example, would recognize the issuance of capital stock for a property item as funds provided by the issuance of stock offset by funds applied to the acquisition of the asset.[1] Because sources and applications from such transactions are equal in amount, the remaining items reported on the funds statement will still serve to reconcile the change in funds for the period. As indicated earlier, the broadened interpretation of funds has been recommended by the Accounting Principles Board, and such an interpretation is assumed throughout the chapter.

---

[1]It may be observed that this treatment requires adoption of the hypothesis that the transfer of an item in exchange or a gift provides the company with working capital or cash that is immediately applied to the acquisition of property, the liquidation of debt, or the retirement of capital stock.

Nature of the funds statement

The funds statement provides a summary of the sources from which funds became available during a period and the purposes to which funds were applied. An important part of the summary is the presentation of data concerning the extent to which funds were generated by income-oriented operations of the business. In addition to reporting funds provided by operations, funds inflow is also related to such sources as the sale of property items, the issuance of long-term obligations, and the issuance of capital stock. Funds outflow is related to such uses as the acquisition of property items, the retirement of long-term obligations, the reacquisition of outstanding stock, and the payment of dividends.

The funds statement can answer directly questions such as: What use was made of profits? How was expansion financed? Why aren't dividend payments larger in view of rising earnings? Why did cash or working capital go down even though there was a substantial profit? How was bonded indebtedness paid off even though there was a substantial loss? These questions require answers if the various users of financial statements are to be provided the means of fully evaluating the operations of the business unit and the management of its resources.

Use of the funds statement

The funds statement, although related to the balance sheet and the income statement, cannot be considered in any sense as a duplication or substitution for the other financial statements. The Accounting Principles Board, in Opinion No. 19, points out:

> The funds statement is related to both the income statement and the balance sheet and provides information that can be obtained only partially, or at most in piecemeal form, by interpreting them. An income statement together with a statement of retained earnings reports results of operations but does not show other changes in financial position. Comparative balance sheets can significantly augment that information, but the objectives of the funds statement require that all such information be selected, classified, and summarized in meaningful form. The funds statement cannot supplant either the income statement or the balance sheet but is intended to provide information that the other statements either do not provide or provide only indirectly about the flow of funds and changes in financial position during the period.[1]

To illustrate the special contribution that is made by the funds statement, consider the needs of a prospective creditor and the means for meeting these needs. An individual or group asked to make a long-term loan to a company is concerned with the company's proposed use of the

---

[1] *Opinions of the Accounting Principles Board, No. 19, op. cit,* par. 5.

loan, the ability of the company to meet the periodic interest payments on the loan, and the ability of the company ultimately to pay off the loan. Balance sheet analysis will provide answers to questions relative to the cash and near-cash items on hand, the working capital of the business — its amount and composition — present long-term indebtedness, and the implications on financial position if the loan is granted. Income statement analysis will provide answers to questions relative to the earnings of the company, the ability of earnings to cover current interest charges, and the implications as to earnings and interest charges if the loan is granted. The funds statement analysis will indicate the resources that were available to the company in the past and the uses that were made of such resources as well as the financing and investing implications if the loan is granted. Finally, funds data can be used in estimating the resources that will be generated in the future and the ability of the company to meet the added indebtedness.

It is obvious that in meeting the requirements of the user of financial statements, funds information will be most useful if offered in comparative form for two or more years. In many instances, the statement will prove particularly informative when prepared in cumulative form for a number of years. An additional statement that reports forecasted or budgeted funds-flow data may prove of equal or even greater value. Although suggestions have been made that the latter information be made available to the external user of financial information, such practice has not yet been adopted.

Funds statement applying different funds concepts

Regardless of how funds are defined, the funds statement is prepared from comparative balance sheets supplemented by explanations for the individual account balance changes. The preparation of the statement calls for the following steps:

1. The definition to be used for "funds" is selected.
2. The changes in each "non-funds" account on the comparative balance sheets are computed.
3. The changes in "non-funds" accounts are classified as sources or applications of funds, and the net increase or decrease arising from such changes is computed.
4. The "funds" accounts on the comparative balance sheets are listed and totaled; the net change in funds items found here should be the same as that computed in step (3).

To illustrate the process of analysis and the development of the funds statement applying the working capital and cash concepts, a relatively simple example will first be considered. Assume balance sheet information for the Parker Company as shown on page 814.

Assets	December 31, 1972	December 31, 1971
Cash...	$ 75,000	$100,000
Accounts receivable............................	170,000	110,000
Inventories....................................	195,000	160,000
Prepaid expenses..............................	10,000	20,000
Land...	160,000	160,000
Buildings and equipment........................	130,000	———
	$740,000	$550,000

Liabilities and Stockholders' Equity		
Accounts payable	$160,000	$100,000
Accrued expenses..............................	20,000	30,000
Long-term debt................................	80,000	100,000
Preferred stock................................	100,000	100,000
Common stock.................................	320,000	200,000
Retained earnings.............................	60,000	20,000
	$740,000	$550,000

Funds defined as working capital. When funds are defined as working capital, balance sheet changes must be analyzed in terms of their effects upon the working capital pool. Investigation of the balance sheet changes for the Parker Company for 1972 reveals the following:

The increase in buildings and equipment reflects funds applied to the purchase of buildings and equipment, $130,000.

The decrease in long-term debt reflects funds applied to the retirement of long-term debt, $20,000.

The increase in common stock reflects funds provided from the sale of shares, $120,000.

Retained earnings went up as a result of net income for the period. The increase in retained earnings, then, reflects funds provided, $40,000 — working capital provided through sales exceeding the working capital consumed through cost of goods sold and expenses.

The foregoing analysis indicates that funds of $160,000 were provided from operations and from the sale of common stock, and funds of $150,000 were applied to the acquisition of buildings and equipment and to the retirement of long-term debt, a net increase in funds of $10,000.

A statement for the Parker Company summarizing working capital changes for the year is given on the following page.

The funds statement shown is composed of two sections. The first section reports working capital inflow and outflow and the change in

Parker Company
Statement of Changes in Financial Position
For Year Ended December 31, 1972

Working capital was provided by:		
Operations during the period............................	$ 40,000	
Sale of common stock.................................	120,000	$160,000
Working capital was applied to:		
Acquisition of buildings and equipment...................	$130,000	
Retirement of long-term debt...........................	20,000	150,000
Increase in working capital..............................		$ 10,000

The increase in working capital is accounted for as follows:

Working Capital Items	Dec. 31, 1972	Dec. 31, 1971	Increase (Decrease)
Current assets:			
Cash.....................................	$ 75,000	$100,000	$(25,000)
Accounts receivable.....................	170,000	110,000	60,000
Inventories.............................	195,000	160,000	35,000
Prepaid expenses........................	10,000	20,000	(10,000)
Current liabilities:			
Accounts payable........................	160,000	100,000	(60,000)
Accrued expenses........................	20,000	30,000	10,000
Increase in working capital..................			$ 10,000

working capital for the period. The second section reports the individual changes within the working capital pool and summarizes and reconciles such changes with the change in working capital reported in the first section. Although working capital has increased by $10,000, which may be regarded as favorable, significant changes have taken place within the working capital pool which may not be similarly regarded, and the ratio of current assets to current liabilities has now changed from 3.0:1 to 2.5:1.

Instead of being prepared in two-section form, the statement may be limited to the presentation of the data in the first section and may refer to a separate supporting tabulation that offers a summary of the changes in the individual working capital items.

Funds defined as cash. When the funds concept is used to denote cash, balance sheet account changes require analysis in terms of their effects upon the movement of cash. Cash is used in the same sense as that employed for cash recognized as a current asset — cash on hand

and demand deposits in banks. The funds statement, then, describes the cash sources and cash uses and offers a reconciliation of the beginning and ending cash balances. Such a statement might be developed by simply classifying and summarizing cash receipts and disbursements as reported in the cash account. However, the statement is prepared to point out the broad sources and uses of cash, and such items as cash collected from customers, cash paid for merchandise, and cash paid for expenses are generally submerged in a cash-from-operations category. Such information can be developed from comparative balance sheets supplemented by operating detail.

A statement for the Parker Company giving effect to the cash concept follows.

Parker Company
Statement of Changes in Financial Position
For Year Ended December 31, 1972

Cash was provided by:			
Operations during the period:			
Income from operations........................		$ 40,000	
Items to be added to operating income:			
Decrease in prepaid expenses...................	$10,000		
Increase in accounts payable...................	60,000	70,000	
		$110,000	
Items to be deducted from operating income:			
Increase in accounts receivable.................	$60,000		
Increase in inventories.........................	35,000		
Decrease in accrued expenses...................	10,000	105,000	
Cash provided by operations....................		$ 5,000	
Sale of common stock..............................		120,000	$125,000
Cash was applied to:			
Acquisition of buildings and equipment..............		$130,000	
Retirement of long-term debt.......................		20,000	150,000
Decrease in cash.....................................			$ 25,000

The decrease in cash of $25,000 is the same as that reported on the comparative balance sheets.

When funds are defined as cash, the analysis of the balance sheet changes is similar to that employed in the previous example, but it must now be extended to include all of the working capital items except cash. A change in marketable securities is recognized as a source or an application of cash. Changes in other current assets and current liabilities that are related to operations are recognized by adjustments to net income. In the example, the following adjustments are required:

Accounts receivable increase — Net income is decreased since the cash receipts for goods and services sold were less than the revenue that was recognized in arriving at net income.

Inventory increase — Net income is decreased since purchases were greater than the charge made against revenue for cost of sales in arriving at net income.

Prepaid expense decrease — Net income is increased since the cash disbursements for expenses were less than the charges that were made against revenue for certain expenses in arriving at net income.

Accounts payable increase — Net income is increased since the cash disbursements for goods and services purchased were less than the charges that were made for these items in arriving at net income.

Accrued expense decrease — Net income is decreased since the cash disbursements for expenses were greater than the charges that were made against revenue for certain expenses in arriving at net income.

The cash-flow approach to the analysis of financial operations has received increasing attention in recent years. The statement is readily interpreted by the reader. It can be a highly useful tool for forecasting and planning of cash flow. However, a working capital analysis may still be required if questions are to be answered with respect to the effect of financial activities upon the working capital pool.

Analysis of account changes in preparation of funds statement

As indicated earlier, the preparation of the funds statement requires comparative balance sheet information supplemented by explanations for account changes. Examples in the preceding sections were relatively simple and changes in account balances defined fund sources and applications. Ordinarily, however, more complex circumstances are encountered and it is not possible to rely on the net change in an account balance for a full explanation of the effect of that item on a company's funds. To illustrate, assume that comparative balance sheets report a $50,000 increase in bonds payable. Without further investigation, this might be interpreted as a source of funds of $50,000. However, reference to the liability account may disclose that bonds of $100,000 were retired during the period while new bonds of $150,000 were issued. A further analysis of the transactions affecting the liability account may reveal that a call premium of $2,000 was paid on bonds retired and a discount of $7,500 was identified with the new issue. The funds statement, then, should report that funds were provided by the new issue of $142,500 and that funds were applied to retirement of the old issue of $102,000.

Decreases in noncurrent assets and increases in noncurrent liabilities and in owners' equity require analysis in calculating funds provided; increases in noncurrent assets and decreases in noncurrent liabilities and in owners' equity require analysis in calculating funds applied.

Remaining pages of this chapter describe the nature of the analysis that is required as well as the procedures that are employed in developing the funds statement.

Fund sources. The following examples indicate fund sources and suggest the nature of the analysis that is necessary in determining the actual amounts provided.

1. *Decreases in noncurrent asset accounts.* Balances in land, equipment, investment, and other noncurrent asset accounts may decrease as a result of assets sold, thus representing fund sources. However, an analysis of the transactions that account for each change is necessary; sale of investments at a gain, for example, provides funds that exceed the decrease in the asset account.

2. *Increases in noncurrent liabilities.* Balances in long-term notes, bonds, and other noncurrent liability accounts may increase as a result of amounts borrowed, thus representing fund sources. An analysis of the transactions that account for each change is necessary; issuance of bonds at a discount, for example, provides funds that are less than the increase in the bond account.

3. *Increases in owners' equity.* Capital stock balances may increase as a result of the sale of stock, thus representing fund sources. However, the amounts received for shares must be determined, for these may differ from the increases in the capital stock balances. When an increase in retained earnings cannot be explained solely by the net income for the period, an analysis of the retained earnings account is necessary. An increase in retained earnings resulting from profitable operations is recognized as a source of funds; a decrease in retained earnings resulting from cash dividends is separately recognized as an application of funds.

Fund applications. The following examples indicate fund applications and suggest the nature of the analysis necessary in determining the actual amounts applied.

1. *Increases in noncurrent assets.* Balances in land, buildings, patents, and other noncurrent asset accounts may increase as a result of the acquisitions of such items, thus representing fund uses. An analysis of transactions that account for the change is necessary; the amount paid for patents, for example, is greater than the increase in the patents account balance when the account is reduced during the period for patents cost amortization.

2. *Decreases in noncurrent liabilities.* The balances in mortgage, bond, and other noncurrent liability accounts may show decreases resulting from retirement of obligations, thus representing fund applications. An analysis of transactions that account for each change is necessary; the amount paid bondholders, for example, exceeds the decrease in the bonds account when a call premium is paid upon bond retirement.

3. *Decreases in owners' equity.* Capital stock balances may show decreases as a result of the acquisition of shares previously issued, thus representing fund applications. However, the amounts paid for reacquired shares must be determined, for these may differ from the decreases in the capital stock balances. When a decrease in retained earnings cannot be explained solely by a net loss for the period, an analysis of the retained earnings account is necessary. A decrease in retained earnings resulting from operations at a loss is recognized as an application of funds; a further decrease resulting from cash dividends is separately recognized as an application of funds.

Changes in noncurrent asset and liability balances and in the owners' equity account balances must be analyzed and recognized as described regardless of the definition that is employed for funds. When the concept of funds is narrowed, changes in certain current asset and current liability balances are also recognized in arriving at the amount of funds provided and applied.

Adjustments in developing amounts provided and applied. The preceding discussion has indicated that the changes in account balances require adjustment when they fail to report the amounts of funds actually provided or applied. When there are many adjustments or when adjustments are complex, use of working papers may facilitate the preparation of the funds statement. In employing working papers, special columns are provided for adjustments that modify account balance changes. The changes as adjusted may then be carried to columns summarizing fund sources and applications.

The adjustments that are required in developing funds data may be classified under three headings:

1. *Adjustments to cancel account changes that do not represent fund sources or applications.* Certain account changes may carry no funds-flow implications. For example, properties may have been appraised and the appraisal changes recorded in the accounts. Fully depreciated assets may have been applied against accumulated depreciation balances. Errors of prior periods may have been discovered requiring changes in property and owners' equity balances. Stock dividends may have been issued and retained earnings transferred to paid-in capital accounts. The foregoing items result in changes in account balances but such changes should be disregarded in reporting the flow of funds. When working papers are prepared, adjustments are made to cancel account changes that do not require recognition on the funds statement.

2. *Adjustments to report the individual fund sources and applications when several transactions are summarized in a single account.* The change in the balance of an account may result from funds provided by several different sources or applied to several different purposes, or from a combination of funds provided and applied. For example, the change in the land, buildings, and equipment balance may reflect funds applied to the construction of buildings and also to the purchase of equipment. The change in the bonds payable balance may reflect both funds applied to the retirement of an old bond issue and funds provided by a new issue. The change in the capital stock balance may reflect both funds provided by the issue of shares and funds applied to the reacquisition and retirement of shares. When working papers are prepared, adjustments are made to report separately the different fund sources and applications.

3. *Adjustments to report individual fund sources and applications when such information is reported in two or more accounts.* The amount of funds that are provided or applied as a result of a single transaction may be reflected in two or more accounts. For example, certain investments may have been sold for more than cost; the gain reported in net income and the decrease

in the investment account must be combined in arriving at the actual amount provided by the sale. Bonds may have been issued at a discount; the increase in the discount account balance must be applied against the increase in the bond account in arriving at the actual amount provided by the issue. Stock may have been retired at a premium; the decreases in the paid-in capital and retained earnings account balances must be combined in arriving at the actual amount applied to the retirement. When working papers are prepared, adjustments are made to combine related changes.

Retained Earnings is an example of an account that may be affected by all three types of adjustments. To illustrate, assume that a retained earnings account shows an increase for a year of $10,000. Inspection of the account discloses the following:

Retained Earnings

Mar. 1 Appropriation for bond sinking fund..........	20,000	Jan. 1 Balance................	200,000
July 10 Cash dividends..........	30,000	Dec. 31 Net income for the year..	60,000

Retained earnings was reduced by the appropriation for bond sinking fund. Although both retained earnings and the appropriated retained earnings balance show changes of $20,000, the changes are without funds significance. If working papers are prepared, the decreases in the account balances should be restored; the account changes are thus canceled and receive no recognition in developing the funds statement. Cash dividends of $30,000 are reported separately as funds applied. This leaves $60,000 in the retained earnings account to be reported as funds provided by operations.

If certain charges or credits that were recognized in arriving at net income carry no funds implications, the net income figure does not report the amount of funds actually made available by operations. For example, assume that depreciation of $20,000 is recorded in computing net income. The entry for depreciation, although representing a proper charge in arriving at net income, is without funds significance; its effects, therefore, should be canceled. Funds from profitable operations, then, consist of $60,000, as reported, plus $20,000. If working papers are prepared, the increase in accumulated depreciation is canceled and funds provided by operations are increased. To fully illustrate the nature of this adjustment, assume the following facts:

At the end of 1971, an attorney, in establishing a new office, invests cash of $15,000 and immediately acquires furniture and fixtures for $10,000. Furniture and fixtures are estimated to have a five-year life. Condensed comparative balance sheet and income statement data for 1971–1972 appear on the opposite page.

Although there were no operating activities in 1971, funds of $10,000 were applied to the acquisition of furniture and fixtures and working

	Dec. 31, 1972	Dec. 31, 1971
Working capital.......................................		$14,500	$ 5,000
Furniture and fixtures................................	$10,000		10,000
Less accumulated depreciation.......................	2,000	8,000	
Capital..		$22,500	$15,000
Fees — received in cash or recognized as receivables.........		$20,000	
Expenses — paid in cash or recognized as payables..........	$10,500		
— depreciation, recognized as reduction in furniture and fixtures balance.......................	2,000	12,500	
Net income...		$ 7,500	

capital changed from $15,000 to $5,000. In 1972, the income statement reported net income of $7,500 after a charge against revenue for depreciation of $2,000. However, operations provided working capital of $9,500 — fees providing working capital of $20,000 and expenses consuming working capital of $10,500. To arrive at the net increase in working capital, revenue representing working capital inflow is reduced only by those expenses that involve working capital outflow or, alternately, net income is raised by the charge for depreciation that involved no working capital outflow. Break-even operations would have recouped working capital equivalent to the reduction in the furniture and fixtures balance; profitable operations served to increase the working capital by both the charge for depreciation and the reported net income.

In calculating the funds provided by operations, net income must be increased by all changes that were recognized in arriving at net income from operations but that involved no working capital outflow. Net income is increased for such charges as depletion, depreciation of buildings and equipment items, and amortization of patents, research and development costs, leaseholds, bond payable discounts, and bond investment premiums. Net income must be decreased by all credits that were recognized in arriving at net income but that involved no working capital inflow. Net income is decreased for such items as the amortization of bond payable premiums and the accumulation of bond investment discounts. Any extraordinary gains and losses included in net income must be related to their particular sources; funds provided by operations are thus limited to amounts that are produced by normal and recurring activities.

Preparation of the funds statement — funds defined as working capital

In the examples given earlier, funds statements were prepared directly from comparative account balances. In the example that follows, comparative account balances require a number of adjustments and working papers are employed in developing the funds statement. In this section it is assumed that the funds are defined as working capital. The modifications in working papers and in statements when funds are defined as cash are illustrated in a later section.

Assume comparative balance sheets and supplementary data for Harper, Inc., as follows:

Harper, Inc.
Comparative Balance Sheet
December 31, 1972 and 1971

	December 31, 1972		December 31, 1971	
Current assets:				
Cash in banks and on hand.......		$ 59,350		$ 65,000
Accounts receivable (net).......		60,000		70,500
Accrued interest receivable......		250		2,400
Inventories..................		75,000		76,500
Prepaid operating expenses......		16,500	$211,100	12,000	$226,400
Building expansion fund investments (at cost)......................			10,000		106,000
Land, buildings, and equipment:				
Land..........................		$160,000		$ 75,000
Buildings.....................	$290,000		$225,000	
Less accumulated depreciation...	122,600	167,400	155,000	70,000
Machinery and equipment........	$132,000		$ 80,000	
Less accumulated depreciation...	32,800	99,200	34,000	46,000
Delivery equipment.............	$ 40,000		$ 38,800	
Less accumulated depreciation...	26,000	14,000	20,000	18,800
Office equipment................	$ 34,000		$ 26,000	
Less accumulated depreciation...	12,500	21,500	462,100	6,000	20,000	229,800
Patents..........................			35,000		40,000
Total assets.....................			$718,200		$602,200
Current liabilities:				
Income taxes payable............		$ 10,000		$ 9,500
Accounts payable................		86,000		81,200
Accrued salaries................		5,000		1,500
Dividends payable..............		4,400	$105,400		$ 92,200
Bonds payable....................	$ 60,000			
Less unamortized bond discount....	2,700	57,300		
Total liabilities.................			$162,700		$ 92,200
Stockholders' equity:				
Preferred stock.................		$140,000		$100,000
Common stock..................	$240,000			160,000
Less treasury stock at par.......	12,000	228,000		
Additional paid-in capital........		38,000		40,000
Retained earnings appropriated for building expansion.............				100,000
Retained earnings...............		149,500	555,500	110,000	510,000
Total liabilities and stockholders' equity......................			$718,200		$602,200

Supplementary data:

Changes in retained earnings during the year were as follows:

Balance, January 1, 1972....................................		$110,000
Increases:		
Net income...	$ 36,000	
Appropriation for building expansion returned to retained earnings..	100,000	136,000
		$246,000
Decreases:		
Cash dividends......................................	$ 12,000	
50% Stock dividend on common stock....................	80,000	
Prior period adjustment resulting from omission of charges for depreciation on certain office equipment items...............	3,500	
Acquisition of treasury stock for $15,000; par value of stock, $12,000, originally issued at premium of $2,000.....................	1,000	96,500
		$149,500

The income statement for 1972 summarizes operations as follows:

Income before extraordinary items..	$30,300
Add gain on sale of expansion fund investments..............................	6,500
	$36,800
Deduct loss on trade of delivery equipment..................................	800
Net income...	$36,000

Building expansion fund investments, cost $96,000, were sold for $102,500.

Delivery equipment was acquired at a cost of $6,000; $2,000 was allowed on the trade-in of old equipment that had a cost of $4,800 and a book value of $2,800, and $4,000 was paid in cash.

Fully depreciated buildings of $40,000 were demolished with no salvage value; new buildings were then constructed at a cost of $105,000.

Land was acquired for $85,000, the seller accepting in payment preferred stock, par $40,000, and cash of $45,000.

Machinery and equipment were overhauled and their lives extended at a cost of $16,500, the cost being charged to the accumulated depreciation account.

Amortization of patents cost and depreciation on buildings and equipment were reported as follows:

Buildings..	$ 7,600
Machinery and equipment..	15,300
Delivery equipment...	8,000
Office equipment...	3,000
Patents...	5,000
Total...	$38,900

Office equipment was acquired for cash, $8,000.

Machinery and equipment were acquired for cash, $52,000.

Ten-year bonds of $60,000 were issued at a discount of $3,000 at the beginning of the year; discount amortization for the year was $300.

Working papers for the preparation of the funds statement are given on pages 824 and 825.

		Balances		
	Item	Dec. 31, 1972	Dec. 31, 1971	
	Debits			
1	Cash in banks and on hand	59,350	65,000	1
2	Accounts receivable (net)	60,000	70,500	2
3	Accrued interest receivable	250	2,400	3
4	Inventories	75,000	76,500	4
5	Prepaid operating expenses	16,500	12,000	5
6	Building expansion fund investments	10,000	106,000	6
7	Land	160,000	75,000	7
8	Buildings	290,000	225,000	8
9	Machinery and equipment	132,000	80,000	9
10	Delivery equipment	40,000	38,800	10
11	Office equipment	34,000	26,000	11
12	Patents	35,000	40,000	12
13	Unamortized bond discount	2,700		13
14	Treasury stock, common, at par	12,000		14
15		926,800	817,200	15
16	Credits			16
17	Accumulated depreciation — buildings	122,600	155,000	17
18	Accumulated depreciation — machinery and equipment	32,800	34,000	18
19	Accumulated depreciation — delivery equipment	26,000	20,000	19
20	Accumulated depreciation — office equipment	12,500	6,000	20
21				21
22	Income taxes payable	10,000	9,500	22
23	Accounts payable	86,000	81,200	23
24	Accrued salaries	5,000	1,500	24
25	Dividends payable	4,400		25
26	Bonds payable	60,000		26
27	Preferred stock	140,000	100,000	27
28	Common stock	240,000	160,000	28
29	Additional paid-in capital	38,000	40,000	29
30	Retained earnings appropriated for building expansion		100,000	30
31	Retained earnings	149,500	110,000	31
32				32
33				33
34				34
35		926,800	817,200	35
36	Working capital provided by operations:			36
37	Income from operations			37
38	Add: Depreciation and patents cost amortization			38
39	Bond discount amortization			39
40	Loss on trade of delivery equipment			40
41	Gain on sale of building expansion fund investments			41
42	Funds applied to dividends			42
43	Funds applied to purchase of treasury stock, common			43
44	Funds provided by sale of building expansion fund investments			44
45	Funds applied to purchase of delivery equipment			45
46	Funds applied to construction of buildings			46
47	Funds applied to acquisition of land			47
48	Deduct: Preferred stock issued in part payment of land			48
49	Funds applied to overhauling machinery and equipment			49
50	Funds provided by issuance of bonds			50
51				51
52	Decrease in working capital			52
53				53

Inc.
Changes in Financial Position
December 31, 1972

	Net Changes		Adjustments		Funds		Working Capital		
	Debit	Credit	Debit	Credit	Applied	Provided	Increase	Decrease	
1		5,650						5,650	1
2		10,500						10,500	2
3		2,150						2,150	3
4		1,500						1,500	4
5	4,500						4,500		5
6		96,000	(g) 96,000						6
7	85,000			(k) 85,000					7
8	65,000		(i) 40,000	(j) 105,000					8
9	52,000				52,000				9
10	1,200		(h) 4,800	(h) 6,000					10
11	8,000				8,000				11
12		5,000	(n) 5,000						12
13	2,700		(p) 300	(o) 3,000					13
14	12,000			(f) 12,000					14
15									15
16									16
17	32,400		(n) 7,600	(i) 40,000					17
18	1,200		(n) 15,300	(m) 16,500					18
19		6,000	(n) 8,000	(h) 2,000					19
20		6,500	(e) 3,500						20
21			(n) 3,000						21
22		500						500	22
23		4,800						4,800	23
24		3,500						3,500	24
25		4,400						4,400	25
26		60,000	(o) 60,000						26
27		40,000	(l) 40,000						27
28		80,000	(d) 80,000						28
29	2,000			(f) 2,000					29
30	100,000			(b) 100,000					30
31		39,500	(a) 36,000	(c) 12,000					31
32			(b) 100,000	(d) 80,000					32
33				(e) 3,500					33
34				(f) 1,000					34
35	366,000	366,000							35
36									36
37				(a) 30,300					37
38				(n) 38,900					38
39				(p) 300		69,500			39
40			(a) 800	(h) 800					40
41			(g) 6,500	(a) 6,500					41
42			(c) 12,000		12,000				42
43			(f) 15,000		15,000				43
44				(g) 102,500		102,500			44
45			(h) 4,000		4,000				45
46			(j) 105,000		105,000				46
47			(k) 85,000						47
48				(l) 40,000	45,000				48
49			(m) 16,500		16,500				49
50				(o) 57,000		57,000			50
51			744,300	744,300	257,500	229,000	4,500	33,000	51
52						28,500	28,500		52
53					257,500	257,500	33,000	33,000	53

In preparing working papers, items appearing on the comparative balance sheet are listed in the first pair of columns. Individual current items may be reported at their net amounts since these are recognized as a part of the working capital and require no adjustment. However, separate recognition is made of land, buildings, and equipment cost and accumulated depreciation balances. Accumulated depreciation balances, instead of being reported as credit balances in the debit section, may be more conveniently listed with liability and owners' equity balances in the credit section. Similarly, negative long-term debt and negative owners' equity balances are separately recognized and more conveniently listed with assets in the debit section. Net changes in account balances appear in the second pair of columns. Increases in assets, decreases in liabilities, and decreases in owners' equity balances are reported in the debit column; decreases in assets, increases in liabilities, and increases in owners' equity balances are reported in the credit column. A pair of columns for adjustments is provided where change balances can be canceled or restated. After the adjustments have been recorded, adjusted balances are carried to the last two pairs of columns. Debit excesses in current asset and current liability items are reported in the working capital increase column; credit excesses are reported in the working capital decrease column. Remaining debit balances are reported in the funds applied column; remaining credit balances are reported in the funds provided column. The net effect of activities upon working capital is summarized in the funds columns and this change is carried to the working capital columns bringing the latter into balance.

In developing the working papers, it will normally prove most convenient to make required adjustments in the following order: (1) the retained earnings change balance should be cleared and in this process the income from ordinary operations and the extraordinary items should be separately reported; (2) when an extraordinary item is related to an asset or liability change, it should be combined with such change balance; (3) the income statement and other supplementary data given, as well as any remaining account change balances, should be reviewed to determine what additional adjustments are appropriate.

Explanations for individual adjustments that are recorded on the working papers for Harper, Inc., on pages 824 and 825 follow. The letter preceding each explanation corresponds with that used in reporting the elimination on the working papers.

(a) Net income included in the ending retained earnings balance is composed of income from operations and extraordinary items. The income from operations balance will require adjustment in arriving at the total funds provided by operations; the extraordinary items will require separate recognition as funds provided or applied or will be combined with other asset or liability change balances in arriving at the full amounts provided by or applied to the specific asset or liability items. Net income, then, is analyzed and is reported by an adjustment in compound form as follows:

Retained Earnings.............................	36,000	
Loss on Trade of Delivery Equipment..............	800	
Gain on Sale of Building Expansion Fund Investments.......................................		6,500
Funds Provided by Operations..................		30,300

"Funds provided by operations" is reported on a separate line below the comparative balance sheet detail. Since a number of adjustments may be required in arriving at the actual amount of funds provided by operations, adequate space should be allowed after this line for such adjustments. The extraordinary items are listed below the space allowed for the income adjustments. Additional items requiring recognition are listed after the extraordinary items.

(b) The transfer of retained earnings appropriated for buildings expansion to retained earnings has no funds significance and the changes in the account balances are canceled by the following adjustment:

Retained Earnings.............................	100,000	
Retained Earnings Appropriated for Building Expansion..................................		100,000

(c) The cash dividends reported in retained earnings are reported separately as an application of funds by the following adjustment:

Funds Applied to Dividends.....................	12,000	
Retained Earnings.............................		12,000

(d) The transfer of retained earnings to capital stock as a result of the common stock dividend has no funds significance and the changes in the account balances are canceled by the following adjustment:

Common Stock.................................	80,000	
Retained Earnings.............................		80,000

(e) The recognition that depreciation had been omitted on certain office equipment items in prior periods was recorded by a charge to retained earnings and a credit to accumulated depreciation of office equipment. The correction of earnings of prior periods has no funds significance and the changes in the account balances are canceled by the following adjustment:

Accumulated Depreciation — Office Equipment.....	3,500	
Retained Earnings.............................		3,500

(f) The acquisition of treasury stock, common, for $15,000 was recorded by a charge to treasury stock at par, $12,000, a charge to additional paid-in capital, $2,000, and a charge to retained earnings, $1,000. Funds applied to the acquisition of treasury stock are summarized by the following adjustment:

Funds Applied to Purchase of Treasury Stock, Common...	15,000	
Treasury Stock, Common (at par)..............		12,000
Additional Paid-In Capital....................		2,000
Retained Earnings.............................		1,000

Instead of recognizing the application of funds on a separate line, it would be possible to transfer charges from additional paid-in capital and retained earnings accounts to the treasury stock account; the sum of the charges to this account, $15,000, would then be extended to the funds applied column. Although such procedure may be followed whenever two or more balances account for a single source or application of funds, it is generally desirable to transfer related balances to a separate line where a full description of the transaction can be provided.

Charges to retained earnings of $136,000 and credits of $96,500, or net charges of $39,500, have canceled the retained earnings credit excess of $39,500 reported in the net changes column; fund sources and applications that were reflected in the retained earnings balance have been fully identified and given appropriate recognition.

(g) The sale of building expansion fund investments was recorded by a credit to the asset account at cost, $96,000, and a credit to an account reporting extraordinary gain. The gain is listed separately on the working papers as a result of the earlier recognition of the individual items comprising net income. Since the effect of the sale was to provide funds of $102,500, this is reported on a separate line and both the reduction in the investments balance and the extraordinary gain are canceled. The following adjustment is made:

Building Expansion Fund Investments............	96,000	
Gain on Sale of Building Expansion Fund Investments	6,500	
Funds Provided by Sale of Building Expansion Fund Investments.........................		102,500

(h) Delivery equipment was purchased for $6,000; $2,000 was allowed on the trade-in of old delivery equipment, cost $4,800, with a book value of $2,800, and $4,000 was paid in cash. The loss of $800 on the equipment traded in was recognized as an extraordinary loss. The loss is listed separately on the working papers as a result of the earlier recognition of the individual items comprising net income. Since the effect of the trade was to apply funds of $4,000, this is reported on a separate line and the changes in the delivery equipment balance and in the accumulated depreciation on delivery equipment are canceled together with the extraordinary loss. The following adjustment is made:

Funds Applied to Purchase of Delivery Equipment..	4,000	
Delivery Equipment (old).......................	4,800	
Accumulated Depreciation—Delivery Equipment..		2,000
Delivery Equipment (new)....................		6,000
Loss on Trade of Delivery Equipment...........		800

(i) The write-off of the cost of fully depreciated buildings against the accumulated depreciation is without funds significance, and the changes in the account balances are canceled by the following adjustment:

Buildings......................................	40,000	
Accumulated Depreciation — Buildings..........		40,000

(j) The buildings account reports a debit excess of $65,000 increased by the above adjustment of $40,000. The sum of the debits represents the cost of constructing buildings. The cost of new buildings is reported separately as an application of funds by the following adjustment:

Funds Applied to Construction of Buildings........	105,000	
Buildings......................................		105,000

This adjustment could be omitted and the $105,000 balance for buildings simply carried to the funds applied column. However, the adjustment is made in the interest of clarity; the account change is transferred to a separate line and a full description of the transaction is provided.

(k) and (l) Land was acquired at a price of $85,000; payment was made in preferred stock valued at par, $40,000, and cash, $45,000. Adjustments are made on the working papers as follows: (k) the increase in the land balance, $85,000, is reported separately as an application of funds; (l) the increase in the preferred stock balance, $40,000, is transferred to the section summarizing the acquisition of land and is reported as an offset to the charge recognized in (k) in arriving at the funds applied to the acquisition. The adjustments are:

Funds Applied to Acquisition of Land............	85,000	
Land..		85,000
Preferred Stock................................	40,000	
Preferred Stock Issued in Part Payment of Land..		40,000

(m) The cost of overhauling machinery and equipment that was charged to the accumulated depreciation balance is reported separately as an application of funds by the following adjustment:

Funds Applied to Overhauling Machinery and Equipment....................................	16,500	
Accumulated Depreciation — Machinery and Equipment..................................		16,500

(n) The changes in the accumulated depreciation accounts and in the patents account resulting from the recognition of depreciation and patents amortization are canceled, and funds provided by operations are increased by the charges against earnings that did not involve funds outflow by the following adjustment:

Accumulated Depreciation — Buildings............	7,600	
Accumulated Depreciation — Machinery and Equipment...................................	15,300	
Accumulated Depreciation — Delivery Equipment...	8,000	
Accumulated Depreciation — Office Equipment.....	3,000	
Patents......................................	5,000	
Income from Operations — Depreciation and Patents Cost Amortization........................		38,900

(o) Bonds payable was credited $60,000 and unamortized bond discount was charged $3,000 when bonds were issued. Funds provided by the bond issue are summarized by the following adjustment:

Bonds Payable.................................	60,000	
Unamortized Bond Discount...................		3,000
Funds Provided by Issuance of Bonds............		57,000

(p) The change in the bond discount account for discount amortization is canceled and funds provided by operations are increased by the charge against earnings that did not involve fund outflow by the following adjustment:

Unamortized Bond Discount......................	300	
Income from Operations — Bond Discount Amortization...............................		300

Office equipment of $8,000 and machinery and equipment of $52,000 were acquired during the year. No adjustments are made to the asset accounts since balances reflect only the single changes.

Adjusted balances, together with the additional data established on the working papers, are now extended to the funds and working capital columns and the working capital change is calculated. The funds statement is then prepared from the working papers.

A funds statement for Harper, Inc., would be prepared from the working papers as follows:

Harper, Inc.
Statement of Changes in Financial Position
For Year Ended December 31, 1972

Working capital was provided by:			
Operations during the period, exclusive of extraordinary items:			
Income from operations.....................		$ 30,300	
Add expenses not requiring outlay of working capital during the period:			
Depreciation and amortization............	$ 38,900		
Bond discount amortization..............	300	39,200	
Working capital provided by operations........		$ 69,500	
Sale of building expansion fund investments.......		102,500	
Issuance of bonds...........................		57,000	$229,000
Working capital was applied to:			
Acquisitions of land, buildings, and equipment:			
Land............................ $ 85,000			
Deduct preferred stock issued in part payment of land................ 40,000	$ 45,000		
Buildings....................................	105,000		
Machinery and equipment...................	52,000		
Office equipment..........................	8,000		
Delivery equipment........................	4,000	$214,000	
Overhauling machinery and equipment.........		16,500	
Purchase of treasury stock, common............		15,000	
Dividends...................................		12,000	257,500
Decrease in working capital.....................			$ 28,500

The decrease in working capital is accounted for as follows:

Working Capital Items	Dec. 31, 1972	Dec. 31, 1971	Increase (Decrease)
Current assets:			
Cash in banks and on hand................	$ 59,350	$ 65,000	$ (5,650)
Accounts receivable (net)..................	60,000	70,500	(10,500)
Accrued interest receivable................	250	2,400	(2,150)
Inventories..............................	75,000	76,500	(1,500)
Prepaid operating expenses...............	16,500	12,000	4,500
Current liabilities:			
Income taxes payable.....................	10,000	9,500	(500)
Accounts payable.........................	86,000	81,200	(4,800)
Accrued salaries.........................	5,000	1,500	(3,500)
Dividends payable........................	4,400	———	(4,400)
Decrease in working capital................			$(28,500)

The funds statement should begin with a summary of the funds related to normal operations. Income or loss before extraordinary items is listed. Those items reflected in this balance that did not require funds are added back while those items that did not provide funds are subtracted. The adjusted balance, representing funds provided by or applied to operations, is followed by any extraordinary items that represent direct sources or applications of funds. Remaining sources and applications of funds are then listed in arriving at the net fund changes for the period.

Some persons object to the presentation of funds provided by operations in the form just illustrated. This form, they maintain, implies that the depreciation of assets generates funds. Actually, it is revenue that provides funds but the income from operations balance fails to report the full amount provided because of charges for depreciation. This objection is overcome by listing the individual revenues and expenses but excluding items and amounts that do not involve current fund inflow or outflow.

Special problems. The analyses that are required in developing the funds statement may be simple or complex. In each instance where a noncurrent asset, a noncurrent liability, or an owners' equity account balance has changed, the question should be asked: Does this indicate a change in working capital? Frequently the answer to this question is obvious, but in some cases careful analysis is required. The following items suggest special analyses that may be required:

1. Assume that a company recognizes depreciation for tax purposes by the double-declining-balance method and reports depreciation on its books by the straight-line method. Periodically it recognizes the depreciation timing differences on its books by an entry charging Income Taxes Expense and crediting Deferred Income Taxes Payable that is reported as a long-term obligation. The additional charges to Income Taxes Expense did not reduce the amount of funds provided by operations; the increase in the long-term liability does not indicate that funds have been provided. Under these circumstances, the entry should be canceled so that the income figure will indicate the full working capital change arising from operations, and the long-term liability will indicate no funds recognition. In subsequent periods, when the deferred tax credit is applied to the reduction of the tax charge as a result of charges for depreciation on the books that exceed those on the tax return, such entry would also require cancelation in stating the funds-flow accurately.

2. Assume that retained earnings are reduced upon the declaration of a cash dividend that is payable in the following period. Declaration of the dividend has increased current liabilities and thus reduced working capital. Subsequent payment of the dividend will have no effect upon the amount of working capital, simply reducing both cash and the current liability. Declaration of a dividend, then, should be reported as funds applied. The reduction in working capital will be confirmed in the summary of working capital balances.

3. Assume that a long-term obligation becomes payable within a year, and requires change to the current classification. Such a change calls for a recognition of funds applied. The change in classification has resulted in a shrinkage of working capital; subsequent payment will have no effect upon the amount of working capital. The reduction in the long-term liability can be reported as "Funds applied to long-term obligations maturing currently." Working capital balances will confirm the reduction in working capital.

4. In the previous examples, prepaid expenses were classified as current assets and therefore treated as working capital items in the analysis of the change in working capital. Prepaid expenses are sometimes listed under a separate heading or reported with noncurrent assets. Such treatment calls for the special analysis of the prepaid expenses just as for other items classified as noncurrent, since their exclusion from the current group makes them part of the explanation for the change that took place in the current classification.

Alternative methods for developing statement. When the funds statement reports the changes in working capital, adjustments apply only to noncurrent assets and liabilities and to owners' equity balances. Since adjustments do not affect the working capital items, it is possible to substitute working capital totals for the individual items for each year on the working papers. With the working capital change already calculated and reported, there is no need for a special pair of columns for this purpose; the difference between funds provided and funds applied is ultimately reported as a balancing figure in the funds columns and reconciled with the working capital change already listed. Working papers may be further simplified by eliminating comparative balance sheet data and beginning with account balance changes as follows:

Item	Net Changes		Adjustments		Funds	
	Dr.	Cr.	Dr.	Cr.	Applied	Provided
Decrease in working capital.. (followed by changes in noncurrent asset, noncurrent liability, and owners' equity accounts)		28,500				
Decrease in working capital...					257,500	229,000
						28,500
					257,500	257,500

It may be possible in some instances to analyze changes in comparative balance sheets and prepare the funds statement without the use of working papers, as was done in the first part of the chapter. In other instances, it may be possible to arrive at fund changes by establishing several "T" accounts that will serve to control such an analysis; or it may be convenient to establish "T" accounts for all account balances reported at the beginning of the period and by the process of posting the changes in these accounts for the year, to list concurrently the funds provided and applied on a funds statement.

Preparation of the funds statement — funds defined as cash

If Harper, Inc., wishes to prepare a funds statement using the cash concept for funds, working papers would be prepared as illustrated on pages 834 and 835. Adjustments are the same as those described on pages 826–829 but are supplemented by adjustments to present operations and also dividends in terms of cash. Income from operations as previously adjusted is further adjusted for the differences that are found in working capital items other than cash. The charge for cash dividends is adjusted for the change in the dividends payable balance in arriving at the cash applied to dividends during the period. A statement of changes in financial position employing the cash concept for funds appears below.

Harper, Inc.
Statement of Changes in Financial Position
For Year Ended December 31, 1972

Cash was provided by:			
Operations during the period:			
Income from operations........................		$ 30,300	
Items to be added to operating income:			
Depreciation and patent cost amortization...	$ 38,900		
Bond discount amortization................	300		
Decrease in accounts receivable (net)........	10,500		
Increase in accounts payable..............	4,800		
Decrease in inventories...................	1,500		
Increase in accrued salaries..............	3,500		
Decrease in accrued interest receivable.......	2,150		
Increase in income taxes payable............	500	62,150	
		$ 92,450	
Item to be deducted from operating income:			
Increase in prepaid operating expenses......		4,500	
Cash provided by operations during the period......			$ 87,950
Sale of plant expansion fund investments...........			102,500
Issuance of bonds................................			57,000
			$247,450
Cash was applied to:			
Acquisitions of land, buildings, and equipment:			
Land......................................$ 85,000			
Deduct preferred stock issued in part			
payment of land................... 40,000	$ 45,000		
Buildings......................................	105,000		
Machinery and equipment......................	52,000		
Office equipment..............................	8,000		
Delivery equipment...........................	4,000	$214,000	
Overhauling machinery and equipment..............		16,500	
Purchase of treasury stock, common...............		15,000	
Dividends......................................		7,600	253,100
Decrease in cash.................................			$ 5,650

	Item	Balances Dec. 31, 1972	Balances Dec. 31, 1971	
	Debits			
1	Cash in banks and on hand	59,350	65,000	1
2	Accounts receivable (net)	60,000	70,500	2
3	Accrued interest receivable	250	2,400	3
4	Inventories	75,000	76,500	4
5	Prepaid operating expenses	16,500	12,000	5
6	Building expansion fund investments	10,000	106,000	6
7	Land	160,000	75,000	7
8	Buildings	290,000	225,000	8
9	Machinery and equipment	132,000	80,000	9
10	Delivery equipment	40,000	38,800	10
11	Office equipment	34,000	26,000	11
12	Patents	35,000	40,000	12
13	Unamortized bond discount	2,700		13
14	Treasury stock, common, at par	12,000		14
15		926,800	817,200	15
16	**Credits**			16
17	Accumulated depreciation — buildings	122,600	155,000	17
18	Accumulated depreciation — machinery and equip.	32,800	34,000	18
19	Accumulated depreciation — delivery equipment	26,000	20,000	19
20	Accumulated depreciation — office equipment	12,500	6,000	20
21				21
22	Income taxes payable	10,000	9,500	22
23	Accounts payable	86,000	81,200	23
24	Accrued salaries	5,000	1,500	24
25	Dividends payable	4,400		25
26	Bonds payable	60,000		26
27	Preferred stock	140,000	100,000	27
28	Common stock	240,000	160,000	28
29	Additional paid-in capital	38,000	40,000	29
30	Retained earnings appropriated for building expansion		100,000	30
31	Retained earnings	149,500	110,000	31
32				32
33				33
34				34
35		926,800	817,200	35
36	Cash provided by operations:			36
37	Income from operations			37
38	Add: Depreciation and patent cost amortization			38
39	Bond discount amortization			39
40	Decrease in accounts receivable (net)			40
41	Increase in accounts payable			41
42	Decrease in inventories			42
43	Increase in accrued salaries			43
44	Decrease in accrued interest receivable			44
45	Increase in income taxes payable			45
46	Deduct increase in prepaid operating expenses			46
47	Loss on delivery equipment			47
48	Gain on sale of building expansion fund investments			48
49	Cash applied to dividends			49
50	Cash applied to purchase of treasury stock, common			50
51	Cash provided by sale of bldg. expansion fund invest.			51
52	Cash applied to purchase of delivery equipment			52
53	Cash applied to construction of buildings			53
54	Cash applied to acquisition of land			54
55	Deduct: Pref. stock issued in part payment of land			55
56	Cash applied to overhauling machinery and equipment			56
57	Cash provided by issuance of bonds			57
58				58

Inc.
Statement of Changes in Financial Position
December 31, 1972

	Net Changes		Adjustments		Cash		
	Debit	Credit	Debit	Credit	Applied	Provided	
1		5,650				5,650	1
2		10,500	(r) 10,500				2
3		2,150	(w) 2,150				3
4		1,500	(t) 1,500				4
5	4,500			(u) 4,500			5
6		96,000	(g) 96,000				6
7	85,000			(k) 85,000			7
8	65,000		(i) 40,000	(j) 105,000			8
9	52,000				52,000		9
10	1,200		(h) 4,800	(h) 6,000			10
11	8,000				8,000		11
12		5,000	(n) 5,000				12
13	2,700		(p) 300	(o) 3,000			13
14	12,000			(f) 12,000			14
15							15
16							16
17	32,400		(n) 7,600	(i) 40,000			17
18	1,200		(n) 15,300	(m) 16,500			18
19		6,000	(n) 8,000	(h) 2,000			19
20		6,500	(e) 3,500				20
21			(n) 3,000				21
22		500	(x) 500				22
23		4,800	(s) 4,800				23
24		3,500	(v) 3,500				24
25		4,400	(q) 4,400				25
26		60,000	(o) 60,000				26
27		40,000	(l) 40,000				27
28		80,000	(d) 80,000				28
29	2,000			(f) 2,000			29
30	100,000			(b) 100,000			30
31		39,500	(a) 36,000	(c) 12,000			31
32			(b) 100,000	(d) 80,000			32
33				(e) 3,500			33
34				(f) 1,000			34
35	366,000	366,000					35
36							36
37				(a) 30,300			37
38				(n) 38,900			38
39				(p) 300			39
40				(r) 10,500			40
41				(s) 4,800			41
42				(t) 1,500			42
43				(v) 3,500			43
44				(w) 2,150		87,950	44
45				(x) 500			45
46			(u) 4,500				46
47			(a) 800	(h) 800			47
48			(g) 6,500	(a) 6,500			48
49			(c) 12,000	(q) 4,400	7,600		49
50			(f) 15,000		15,000		50
51				(g) 102,500		102,500	51
52			(h) 4,000		4,000		52
53			(j) 105,000		105,000		53
54			(k) 85,000				54
55				(l) 40,000	45,000		55
56			(m) 16,500		16,500		56
57				(o) 57,000		57,000	57
58			776,150	776,150	253,100	253,100	58

The working papers and the statement just illustrated reported the net amount of cash provided by operations. When a full explanation of the cash provided by operations is desired, this can be provided by applying adjustments to the individual revenue and expense items rather than to the net income balance. The operations section of the working papers will require expansion in developing this detail. The operations section of the working papers just illustrated can be expanded as shown below. Adjustment (a), instead of reporting the result of operations as summarized on the income statement, lists the individual revenue and expense items. The adjustments that are required in developing the cash flow from operations are then applied to the individual revenue and expense balances.

Item	Adjustments		Cash		
	Debit	Credit	Applied	Provided	
36 Cash provided by operations:					36
37 Sales		(a) 750,000			37
38 Add decrease in accounts receivable		(r) 10,500		760,500	38
39 Cost of goods sold	(a) 550,000				39
40 Deduct: Depr. of bldgs., mach. and equip., amort. of patents		(n) 27,900			40
41 Increase in accounts payable		(s) 4,800			41
42 Decrease in inventories		(t) 1,500	515,800		42
43 Selling and general expenses	(a) 146,400				43
44 Add increase in prepaid operating exp.	(u) 4,500				44
45 Deduct: Depr. of office and del. equip		(n) 11,000			45
46 Increase in accrued salaries		(v) 3,500	136,400		46
47 Other revenue — interest income		(a) 4,600			47
48 Add decrease in accrued int. rec.		(a) 2,150		6,750	48
49 Other expense — interest expense	(a) 3,900				49
50 Deduct bond discount amortization		(p) 300	3,600		50
51 Income tax	(a) 24,000				51
52 Deduct increase in income taxes payable		(x) 500	23,500		52
53 Gain on sale of building expansion fund investments		(a) 6,500			53
54 To cancel gain	(g) 6,500				54
55 Loss on trade of delivery equipment	(a) 800				55
56 To cancel loss		(h) 800			56

Cash made available through operations as summarized above may be presented on the statement as follows:

Cash was provided by:
  Operations:
    Receipts — Sales.......................... $760,500
                 Other revenue—interest income ...   6,750 $767,250

    Payments — Cost of goods sold.............. $515,800
                 Selling and general expenses...... 136,400
                 Other expense—interest expense...   3,600
                 Income taxes.................   23,500 679,300 $ 87,950

Special observations

The Accounting Principles Board in its latest pronouncement on the funds statement has recognized that the form, terminology, and content of the statement will not be the same for every company in meeting its objectives under different circumstances. Although recognizing the need for flexibility, the APB indicated that there was still a need for certain guides in the preparation of the statement and in its interpretation, which were set forth in its pronouncement. The attempt has been made in this chapter to apply such guides in funds-flow presentations.

Application of the broadened interpretation of funds. Alternate methods may be used for the presentation of exchanges interpreted as both financing and investing activities. For example, the acquisition of land for cash and capital stock may be presented as an application of funds for the full acquisition price less the value of the stock used in financing the acquisition. The difference, if any, would then represent the net amount of funds applied. On the other hand, it may be maintained that the issuance of stock should be reported as funds provided and the acquisition of land at the full acquisition price as funds applied. This would raise the totals for funds provided and applied but would not affect the increase or decrease in funds reported for the period. In the examples in this chapter, the financing and investing aspects of the transaction were related and the net effect on funds was reported. If the alternate approach is followed, there should be an appropriate note to indicate the relationship of the financing and investing activity, although these are reported separately as both funds provided and applied.

Use of cash-flow per-share computations. Accounting authorities, as well as the APB, have indicated serious concern that users of the statement properly interpret the data that it provides, particularly the data set forth as "funds provided by operations." Professor Perry Mason in Accounting Research Study No. 2 observed the widespread use in annual reports and other financial summaries of *cash-flow per-share* measurements that were calculated by dividing the sum of income and the charges for depreciation and depletion reported on the funds statement by the number of shares outstanding. Professor Mason cautioned that cash-flow comments and statistics should not be provided apart from or without reference to the funds statement. He further observed, "Isolated comments or statistics concerning cash flow should be avoided since they are generally meaningless and often misleading."[1] The APB also

---

[1] Perry Mason, *"Cash Flow" Analysis and the Funds Statement*, Accounting Research Study No. 2 (New York: American Institute of Certified Public Accountants, 1961), pp. 42–43, 90–91.

commented on the use of cash-flow measurements in Opinion No. 3 and in Opinion No. 19. In Opinion No. 3 the APB stated:

> Whether or not a cash distribution to shareholders is a return of capital or a distribution of earnings can be determined only by comparing the distribution with the amount of retained earnings available. No generalization or conclusion can be drawn as to the significance of the "cash flow" without reference to the entire flow of funds as reflected in the complete statement of source and application of funds. Adding back depreciation provisions to show the total funds generated from operations can be misleading unless the reader of financial statements keeps in mind that the renewal and replacement of productive facilities require substantial "cash outflow," which may well exceed the depreciation provisions. The "funds derived from operations" (cash flow) is one, but only one, of the important items in the statement, and its significance can be determined only by relating it to the other items.[1]

In Opinion No. 19 the Board comments:

> The amount of working capital or cash provided from operations is not a substitute for or an improvement upon properly determined net income as a measure of results of operations and the consequent effect on financial position. Terms referring to "cash" should not be used to describe amounts provided from operations unless all non-cash items have been appropriately adjusted. The adjusted amount should be described accurately, in conformity with the nature of the adjustments, e.g., "Cash provided from operations for the period" or "Working capital provided from operations for the period" as appropriate. The Board strongly recommends that isolated statistics of working capital or cash provided from operations, especially per-share amounts, not be presented in annual reports to shareholders. If any per-share data relating to flow of working capital or cash are presented, they should as a minimum include amounts for inflow from operations, inflow from other sources, and total outflow, and each per-share amount should be clearly identified with the corresponding total amount shown in the Statement.[2]

The Board in Opinion No. 19 indicates that the funds statement should be included as a basic statement in reporting for a business entity for fiscal periods beginning after September 30, 1971.

QUESTIONS

1. Describe the statement of changes in financial position. What information does it offer that is not provided by the income statement? What information does it offer that is not provided by comparative balance sheets?

---

[1]*Opinions of the Accounting Principles Board, No. 3*, "The Statement of Source and Application of Funds" (New York: American Institute of Certified Public Accountants, 1963), par. 14.
[2]*Opinions of the Accounting Principles Board, No. 19, op. cit.*, par. 15.

2. What different concepts for funds may be applied in preparing the statement of changes in financial position? Describe the statement under each of the different fund concepts. Which approach do you support?

3. Name a source of funds originating from a transaction involving (a) noncurrent assets, (b) noncurrent liabilities, (c) capital stock, (d) retained earnings. Name an application of funds identified with each group.

4. What three classes of adjustments are usually necessary in preparing the statement of changes in financial position?

5. Give five adjustments that are required to cancel account changes that have no effect upon funds.

6. Give five adjustments to summarize changes in two or more accounts in stating a single source or application of funds.

7. Give five examples where a single account change may provide a basis for recognizing both a source and an application of funds.

8. (a) What adjustments are applied to the operating income figure when the funds statement summarizes working capital flow? (b) What adjustments are applied to operating income when the funds statement summarizes cash flow?

9. The Warner Co. had its worst year in 1972, operations resulting in a substantial loss. Nevertheless, without the sale of property items, borrowing, or the issue of additional stock, the company's working capital increased significantly. What possible explanation can you suggest for such increase?

10. Indicate how each of the following would be reported on a funds statement assuming that funds are regarded as working capital.
   (1) Land and buildings are acquired for cash of 40% of the purchase price and a mortgage note for the balance.
   (2) Fully depreciated machinery is written off.
   (3) Long-term notes are due within the year and their classification is changed to current.
   (4) Capital stock is issued in exchange for land.
   (5) In an examination of past income tax returns, the government asserts certain tax deficiencies and these are recognized on the company books by charging retained earnings and crediting a current liability.

11. What uses might each of the following find for the cash-flow statement?

    (a) Manager of a small laundry.
    (b) Stockholder interested in regular dividends.
    (c) Banker granting short-term loans.
    (d) Officer of a labor union.

12. Would you support the inclusion of cash budgets in the annual financial reports? Give reasons for your answer.

13. A funds statement should be audited by public accountants. Give your conclusion and reasons for such conclusion.

EXERCISES

1. The balance sheet data of the Dangerfield Company at the end of 1971 and 1972 follow:

	1972	1971
Cash	$ 15,000	$ 25,000
Accounts receivable (net)	55,000	45,000
Merchandise inventory	70,000	40,000
Prepaid expenses	5,000	20,000
Buildings and equipment	90,000	70,000
Accumulated depreciation — buildings and equipment	(17,500)	(7,500)
Land	80,000	35,000
	$297,500	$227,500
Accounts payable	$ 60,000	$ 40,000
Accrued expenses	10,000	12,500
Notes payable — bank		45,000
Mortgage payable	35,000	
Capital stock, $10 par	185,000	140,000
Retained earnings (deficit)	7,500	(10,000)
	$297,500	$227,500

Land was acquired for $45,000 in exchange for capital stock, par $45,000, during the year; equipment of $25,000 was acquired for cash. Equipment costing $5,000 was sold for $2,000; book value of the equipment was $3,000 and the loss was reported as an extraordinary item in net income. Cash dividends of $10,000 were charged to retained earnings during the year; the transfer of net income to retained earnings was the only other entry in this account.

    Prepare the following statements without the use of working papers:

    (a) A statement of changes in financial position applying the working capital concept of funds.
    (b) A statement of changes in financial position applying the cash concept of funds.

2. From the information that follows, give the necessary adjustments to clear the changes in the accounts listed in preparing working papers for a statement of changes in financial position for 1972.

	Dec. 31, 1972	Dec. 31, 1971
Land...	$ 25,000	$ 40,000
Buildings......................................	100,000	100,000
Accumulated depreciation — buildings..................	68,500	62,500
Machinery.....................................	39,000	45,000
Accumulated depreciation — machinery.................	15,500	16,000
Delivery equipment.............................	18,000	15,000
Accumulated depreciation — delivery equipment..........	6,500	6,000
Tools...	14,000	12,000
Patents.......................................	3,500	4,500
Goodwill......................................	—	50,000
Discount on bonds payable.........................	—	6,000
Bonds payable..................................	—	100,000
Capital stock...................................	350,000	250,000
Treasury stock.................................	22,000	—
Retained earnings appropriated for bond retirement fund...	—	100,000
Retained earnings...............................	147,700	180,000

Retained Earnings

Stock dividend.................	100,000	Balance, Jan. 1, 1972...........	180,000
Premium on purchase of treasury stock, par $22,000............	8,000	Retained earnings appropriated for bond retirement fund......	100,000
Cash dividends.................	10,000		
Net loss for year...............	14,300		
Balance......................	147,700		
	280,000		280,000
		Balance, Dec. 31, 1972.........	147,700

The income statement reports depreciation of buildings, $6,000; depreciation of machinery, $4,000; depreciation of delivery equipment, $2,000; tools amortization, $4,000; patents amortization, $1,000; and bond discount amortization, $2,000. The income statement also reports the following:

Income before extraordinary items........................		$40,000
Extraordinary items:		
Gain on sale of land, cost $15,000, sold for $18,000.........	$ 3,000	
Gain on trade of delivery equipment, cost $4,000, book value $2,500, allowance of $3,200 being received on new equipment acquired at a cost of $7,000....................	700	3,700
		$43,700
Loss on scrapping machinery, cost $6,000, on which accumulated depreciation of $4,500 had been recognized..........	$ 1,500	
Goodwill written off...................................	50,000	
Unamortized discount, $4,000, and call premium, $2,500, on bond retirement..	6,500	58,000
Net loss...		$14,300

3. State how each of the following items will be reflected on the statement of changes in financial position if funds are defined as (1) working capital, (2) cash.

(a) Marketable securities were purchased for $12,000.

(b) Equipment, book value $7,000, was traded for new equipment costing $15,000; a trade-in value of $3,000 is allowed on the old equipment, the balance of the purchase price to be paid in twelve monthly installments.

(c) Buildings were acquired for $75,000, the company paying $40,000 cash and signing a 6% mortgage note payable in 5 years for the balance.

(d) Uncollectible accounts of $900 were written off against the allowance for doubtful accounts.

(e) Cash of $105,000 was paid on the purchase of business assets consisting of: merchandise, $40,000; furniture and fixtures, $10,000; land and buildings, $25,000; and goodwill, $30,000.

(f) A cash dividend of $5,000 was declared in the current period, payable at the beginning of the next period.

(g) An adjustment was made increasing Deferred Income Taxes Payable by $20,000.

(h) Accounts payable shows a decrease for the period of $15,000.

4. Give the adjustments needed for working papers for a statement of changes in financial position upon analyzing the following account:

Retained Earnings

1972			1972		
June 1	Stock dividend.........	200,000	Jan. 1	Balance..............	760,000
Aug. 5	Discount on sale of treas-		Mar. 20	Correction for error in	
	ury stock, par $150,000,			inventory at end of 1971.	15,000
	for $125,000...........	25,000			
Dec. 5	Cash dividends.........	50,000			
31	Appropriated for contin-				
	gencies..............	100,000			
31	Balance..............	400,000			
		775,000			775,000
			1973		
			Jan. 1	Balance..............	400,000

5. A summary of revenue and expense for the Carter Corporation for 1972 follows:

Sales.................................	$1,000,000
Cost of goods manufactured and sold........	600,000
Gross profit.............................	$ 400,000
Selling, general and administrative expenses..	200,000
Income before income taxes...............	$ 200,000
Income taxes...........................	90,000
Net income	$ 110,000

Net changes in working capital items for 1972 were as follows:

	Dr.	Cr.
Cash..	$26,000	
Trade accounts receivable (net)..............	50,000	
Inventories.................................		$15,000
Prepaid expenses (selling and general)...........	2,500	
Accrued expenses (75% of increase related to manu-		
facturing activities and 25% to general operating		
activities)..................................		8,000
Income taxes payable........................		12,000
Trade accounts payable......................		35,000

Depreciation on plant and equipment for the year totaled $140,000; 70% was related to manufacturing activities and 30% to general and administrative activities.

Prepare a summary of cash provided by operations for the year that shows revenue and expense detail.

PROBLEMS

23-1. Comparative balance sheet data for Cameron, Inc., follow:

Assets	Dec. 31, 1972	Dec. 31, 1971	Liabilities and Stockholders' Equity	Dec. 31, 1972	Dec. 31, 1971
Cash	$ 12,500	$ 30,000	Accrued expenses	$ 7,500	$ 5,000
Current receivables	60,000	50,000	Current payables	52,500	42,500
Inventory	75,000	62,500	Bonds payable	40,000	50,000
Prepaid expenses	12,500	10,000	Capital stock, at par	125,000	100,000
Land, buildings and			Additional paid-in capi-		
equipment	130,000	85,000	tal	15,000	10,000
			Retained earnings	20,000	5,000
Accumulated depr.	(30,000)	(25,000)			
Total	$260,000	$212,500	Total	$260,000	$212,500

Land and buildings were acquired in exchange for capital stock; the assets were recorded at $30,000, their appraised value. Equipment was acquired for $15,000 cash. Income from operations for the year transferred to retained earnings was $35,000; cash dividends accounted for the remaining change in retained earnings.

Instructions: Prepare the following (working papers are not required):

(1) A statement of changes in financial position applying the working capital concept of funds.

(2) A statement of changes in financial position applying the cash concept of funds.

23-2. Comparative balance sheet data for the firm of Allen and Cooper are given below.

Assets	Dec. 31, 1972	Dec. 31, 1971	Liabilities and Owners' Equity	Dec. 31, 1972	Dec. 31, 1971
Cash	$ 6,700	$ 3,600	Accrued expenses	$ 2,600	$ 2,200
Current receivables	8,800	10,500	Current payables	7,650	8,250
Inventory	45,000	33,000	Long-term note	6,000	
Prepaid expenses	1,200	2,200	Colin Allen, capital	20,550	22,550
Furniture and fixtures	23,500	16,000	Peter Cooper, capital	34,850	20,850
Accumulated depr.	(13,550)	(11,450)			
Total	$71,650	$53,850	Total	$71,650	$53,850

Income from operations for the year was $10,000 and this was transferred in equal amounts to the partners' capital accounts. Further changes in the capital accounts arose from additional investments and withdrawals by the partners. The change in the furniture and fixtures account arose from a purchase of additional furniture; part of the purchase price was paid in cash and a long-term note was issued for the balance.

Instructions: Prepare the following (working papers are not required):

(1) A statement of changes in financial position applying the working capital concept of funds.

(2) A statement of changes in financial position applying the cash concept of funds.

23-3. The O. K. Laundry reported a net income of $6,160 for 1972 but has been showing an overdraft in its bank account in recent months. The manager has contacted you as his auditor for an explanation. The following information was given to you for examination.

O. K. Laundry
Comparative Balance Sheet
December 31, 1972 and 1971

Assets	1972	1971
Cash..	$ (1,500)	$ 4,000
Accounts receivable.........................	6,000	$ 2,000
Inventory of laundry not picked up — at service value......	3,000	1,500
Prepaid insurance...........................	260	390
Total current assets.........................	$ 7,760	$ 7,890
Land.......................................	$ 25,000	$ 25,000
Building...................................	$ 50,000	$ 50,000
Less accumulated depreciation...............	(30,000)	(28,000)
Building — net book value..................	$ 20,000	$ 22,000
Equipment.................................	$ 74,500	$ 65,000
Less accumulated depreciation...............	(45,000)	(41,000)
Equipment — net book value...............	$ 29,500	$ 24,000
Total assets...............................	$ 82,260	$ 78,890
Liabilities and Stockholders' Equity		
Accounts payable...........................	$ 8,500	$ 6,000
Accrued taxes..............................	2,800	4,590
Accrued wages.............................	1,500	3,000
Notes payable — current portion............	3,000	2,000
Total current liabilities....................	$ 15,800	$ 15,590
Notes payable — long term.................	$ 21,000	$ 23,000
Capital stock..............................	$ 35,000	$ 30,000
Retained earnings..........................	10,460	10,300
Total stockholders' equity..................	$ 45,460	$ 40,300
Total liabilities and stockholders' equity......	$ 82,260	$ 78,890

You also determine the following:

Fully depreciated equipment was sold for $2,000; its cost was $5,000 and the gain was reported as an extraordinary item. Cash dividends of $6,000 were paid.

Instructions: Prepare the following (working papers are not required):

(1) A statement of changes in financial position applying the working capital concept of funds.

(2) A statement of changes in financial position applying the cash concept of funds.

23-4. The following data were obtained from the books and records of the Garrison Co.:

	Net changes in 1972	
	Debit	Credit
Current assets................................	$102,000	—
Land, buildings, and equipment (net)................	3,400	—
Current liabilities..................................	—	$ 51,000
Bonds payable.....................................	—	100,000
Bond discount.....................................	3,800	—
Preferred stock....................................	100,000	—
Common stock.....................................	—	50,000
Retained earnings..................................	—	38,200
Appraisal capital..................................	30,000	—
	$239,200	$239,200

Retained Earnings

Premium on retirement of preferred stock................	5,000	Balance, Jan. 1................	55,000
Stock dividend on common stock .	50,000	Net income (including gain on sale of land)................	103,200
Cash dividends paid during year..	10,000		

Ten-year bonds of $100,000 were issued on July 1, 1972, at 96. Proceeds were applied to the retirement of preferred stock. Land, cost $30,000 and recorded on the books at an appraised value of $60,000, was sold for cash of $70,000. The proceeds from the sale were applied to the construction of new buildings costing $72,000. Depreciation recorded for the year was $8,600.

Instructions: Prepare a statement of changes in financial position applying the working capital concept of funds (working papers are not required).

23-5. The following data were taken from the records of the Howard Co.

Balance Sheet Data

	December 31, 1972		December 31, 1971	
Current assets.............................		$165,200		$148,300
Land, buildings, and equipment.............	$100,500		$96,000	
Less accumulated depreciation.............	34,000	66,500	30,000	66,000
Investments in stocks and bonds............		32,000		35,000
Goodwill..................................		1		25,000
		$263,701		$274,300
Current liabilities.........................		$ 58,800		$ 43,300
Bonds payable.............................		—		50,000
Unamortized bond discount.................		—		(1,250)
Preferred stock ($100 par).................		—		50,000
Common stock ($10 par)...................		150,000		105,000
Additional paid-in capital..................		35,000		—
Retained earnings.........................		19,901		27,250
		$263,701		$274,300

Retained Earnings			
Premium on retirement of preferred stock.................	1,000	Balance........................	27,250
Cash dividends.................	17,500	Net income.....................	11,151

Income Statement Data for Year Ended December 31, 1972

Income before extraordinary items........................		$40,650
Add gain on trade of equipment..........................		1,500
		$42,150
Deduct: Loss on sale of investments......................	$ 2,500	
Loss on retirement of bonds......................	3,500	
Goodwill written off............................	24,999	30,999
Net income...		$11,151

Fully depreciated equipment, original cost $12,000, was traded in on new equipment costing $16,500; $1,500 was allowed by the vendor on the trade-in. One hundred shares of Brooks Co. preferred stock, cost $20,000, held as a long-term investment, were sold at the beginning of the year. Additional changes in the investments account resulted from the purchase of Cook Co. bonds. The company issued common stock in April, and part of the proceeds was used to retire preferred stock at 102 shortly thereafter. On July 1 the company called in its bonds outstanding, paying a premium of 5% on the call. Discount amortization on the bonds to the date of call was $250. Depreciation for the year on buildings and equipment was $16,000.

Instructions: Prepare working papers and a statement of changes in financial position applying the working capital concept of funds.

23-6. The following information is assembled for the Wood Corporation:

Balance Sheet Data

	December 31, 1972		December 31, 1971	
Cash (overdraft in 1971)..................		$ 38,625		$ (5,625)
Accounts receivable......................		62,000		95,500
Inventories.............................		73,250		50,000
Investments............................		12,000		27,000
Land, buildings, and equipment............	$130,000		$95,000	
Less accumulated depreciation............	21,500	108,500	20,000	75,000
Patents................................		—		35,000
		$294,375		$276,875
Accounts payable........................		$ 49,875		$ 49,375
Bonds payable..........................		50,000		20,000
Premium on bonds payable.................		2,375		—
Preferred stock, $100 par.................		—		50,000
Common stock, $10 par...................		150,000		100,000
Premium on common stock		20,000		
Retained earnings.......................		22,125		57,500
		$294,375		$276,875

Retained Earnings

1972			1972		
Oct. 15	Cash dividends..........	25,000	Jan. 1 Balance...............		57,500
Dec. 12	Premium on retirement of preferred stock.........	5,000			
Dec. 31	Net loss...............	5,375			

Income Statement Data for Year Ended December 31, 1972

Income before extraordinary items.......................		$29,475
Add gain on sale of investments..........................		3,250
		$32,725
Deduct:		
Loss on retirement of bonds.........................	$ 1,000	
Loss on disposal of equipment.......................	2,100	
Patents written off................................	35,000	38,100
Net loss...		$ 5,375

Equipment, cost $15,000, book value $3,000, was scrapped, salvage of $900 being recovered on the disposal. Additional equipment, cost $50,000, was acquired during the year. Securities, cost $15,000, were sold for $18,250; 7% bonds, face value $20,000, were called in at 105, and new 10-year, 5% bonds of $50,000 were issued at 105 on July 1. Preferred stock was retired at a cost of 110 while 5,000 shares of common stock were issued at $14. Depreciation on buildings and equipment for the year was $13,500.

Instructions: (1) Prepare working papers and a statement of changes in financial position applying the working capital concept of funds.

(2) Prepare a statement of changes in financial position applying the cash concept of funds.

23-7. A comparative balance sheet for the Johnson Company appears as follows:

	December 31	
	1972	1971
Cash...	$ 260,000	$ 175,000
Marketable securities.............................	140,000	90,000
Accounts and notes receivable, less allowance for doubtful accounts......................................	220,000	180,000
Inventories......................................	420,000	290,000
Investments in stock of other companies (at cost)........	240,000	335,000
Land, buildings, and equipment, less accumulated depreciation...	1,040,000	890,000
Patents...	65,000	70,000
Goodwill..	—0—	80,000
Unamortized bond issuance costs...................	21,600	30,000
	$2,406,600	$2,140,000
Accounts and notes payable........................	$ 215,000	$ 200,000
Miscellaneous accrued liabilities including taxes........	142,200	25,000
6% Mortgage bonds...............................	400,000	500,000
Preferred stock ($25 par, each share convertible into two shares of common stock).........................	210,000	250,000
Common stock ($10 par)...........................	482,000	350,000
Additional paid-in capital..........................	288,000	200,000
Retained earnings.................................	669,400	615,000
	$2,406,600	$2,140,000

The income statement reports the following:

Income Statement Data for Year Ended December 31, 1972

Income before extraordinary items......................		$ 88,800
Add gain on sale of Moore Co. stock...................		105,000
		$193,800
Deduct:		
Loss on sale of equipment...........................	$ 5,200	
Goodwill written off...............................	80,000	
Premium on retirement of bonds.....................	9,200	94,400
Net income...		$ 99,400

An analysis of balance sheet changes discloses the following:

(a) Stock of the Moore Co. reported as an investment at a cost of $95,000 was sold for $200,000.

(b) The patents had a remaining life of 14 years on December 31, 1971, and are being written off over this period.

(c) Mortgage bonds mature on January 1, 1982. On July 1, 1972, bonds of $100,000 were purchased on the market at $103\frac{1}{2}$ and formally canceled.

(d) The decrease in preferred stock outstanding resulted from the exercise of the conversion privilege by preferred stockholders.

(e) 10,000 shares of common stock were sold during the year at $18.

(f) Equipment that cost $92,000 and that had a book value of $12,000 was sold during the year for $6,800. Depreciation of $82,000 was reported for the year on buildings and equipment. Additional changes in the land, buildings, and equipment balance resulted from the purchase of equipment.

(g) Dividends paid during the year totaled $45,000.

Instructions: (1) Prepare working papers and a statement of changes in financial position applying the working capital concept of funds.

(2) Prepare a statement of changes in financial position applying the cash concept of funds.

23-8. Financial data for the Ogden Manufacturing Co. are presented on the opposite page.

Ten-year bonds of $50,000 had been issued on July 1, 1970, at 90. Additional ten-year bonds of $125,000 had been issued on July 1, 1972, at 94.

Machinery that was no longer required was sold for $7,000 in 1972; the machinery had an original cost of $13,000 and accumulated depreciation on the date of the sale totaled $5,000.

Fully depreciated storage quarters were dismantled during the year, and buildings, cost $2,000, were written off against the accumulated depreciation of buildings account. Investments in outside companies that cost $16,000 were sold at the beginning of the year for $18,500, and additional securities were subsequently acquired during the year. Additional capital stock was issued by the company during the year at 12 in order to raise working capital.

Ogden Manufacturing Co.
Comparative Balance Sheet
December 31, 1972 and 1971

	1972		1971	
Assets				
Cash....................................		$102,550		$ 45,000
Accounts receivable......................	$ 53,000		$ 27,625	
Allowance for doubtful accounts..........	2,500	50,500	2,125	25,500
Inventories.............................		48,000		32,000
Office supplies..........................		1,000		1,500
Miscellaneous prepaid expenses (sell. and gen.)		3,500		3,000
Investments in outside companies...........		27,000		20,000
Land..................................		60,000		25,000
Buildings..............................	$124,500		$ 90,000	
Less accumulated depreciation...........	40,000	84,500	36,000	54,000
Machinery.............................	$ 95,000		$ 75,000	
Less accumulated depreciation...........	44,000	51,000	40,000	35,000
Goodwill..............................				50,000
		$428,050		$291,000
Liabilities and Stockholders' Equity				
Accounts payable........................		$ 23,000		$ 25,000
Miscellaneous accrued expenses (sell. and gen.)		6,500		4,000
Income taxes payable.....................		20,000		10,000
Bonds payable...........................	$175,000		$ 50,000	
Less bond discount.....................	10,875	164,125	4,250	45,750
Capital stock ($10 par)..................		125,000		100,000
Additional paid-in capital................		35,000		30,000
Retained earnings.......................		54,425		76,250
		$428,050		$291,000

Ogden Manufacturing Co.
Condensed Income Statement
For Year Ended December 31, 1972

Sales...		$218,900
Less: Cost of goods sold (includes depreciation of machinery, $9,000, and depreciation of buildings, $6,000)....................	$118,000	
Selling, general, administrative, and other expenses..........	40,225	
Income taxes......................................	18,000	176,225
Income before extraordinary items.............................		$ 42,675
Add gain on sale of investments in outside companies.............		2,500
		$ 45,175
Less: Loss on disposal of machinery............................	$ 1,000	
Goodwill written off......................................	50,000	51,000
Net loss...		$ 5,825

Instructions: (1) Prepare working papers and a statement of changes in financial position applying the working capital concept of funds.

(2) Prepare working papers and a statement of changes in financial position applying the cash concept of funds and reporting revenue and expense detail.

23-9. The net changes in the balance sheet accounts of the Cramer Company for the year 1972 are shown below:

	Debit	Credit
Investments...............................		$25,000
Land.....................................	$ 3,200	
Buildings.................................	35,000	
Machinery................................	6,000	
Office equipment..........................		1,500
Accumulated depreciation:		
Buildings...............................		2,000
Machinery..............................		900
Office equipment........................	600	
Discount on bonds........................	2,000	
Bonds payable............................		40,000
Capital stock — preferred.................	10,000	
Capital stock — common...................		12,400
Premium on common stock.................		5,600
Retained earnings.........................		6,800
Working capital...........................	37,400	
	$94,200	$94,200

Additional information:

(a)

Income Statement Data for Year Ended December 31, 1972		
Income before extraordinary items................		$16,000
Add: Gain on sale of investments.................	$2,500	
Gain on sale of building....................	9,500	12,000
Net income......................................		$28,000

(b) Cash dividends of $18,000 were declared December 15, 1972, payable January 15, 1973. A 2% stock dividend was issued March 31, 1972, when the market value was $12.50 per share.

(c) The investments were sold for $27,500.

(d) A building which cost $45,000 and had a depreciated basis of $40,500 was sold for $50,000.

(e) The following entry was made to record an exchange of an old machine for a new one:

Machinery....................................	13,000	
Accumulated Depreciation — Machinery..........	5,000	
Machinery....................................		7,000
Cash..		11,000

(f) A fully depreciated office machine which cost $1,500 was written off.

(g) Preferred stock of $10,000 par value was redeemed for $10,200.

(h) The company sold 1,000 shares of its common stock (par value $10) on June 15, 1972 for $15 a share. There were 13,240 shares outstanding on December 31, 1972.

Instructions: Prepare a work sheet and a statement of changes in financial position for the year 1972.

(AICPA adapted)

23-10. The financial statements of Frank Manufacturing Corporation for 1972 and 1971 are shown below and on page 852. The corporation was formed on January 1, 1969.

Frank Manufacturing Corporation
Comparative Balance Sheet
December 31, 1972 and 1971

Assets	1972	1971	Increase (Decrease)
Current assets:			
Cash..	$ 33,500	$ 27,000	$ 6,500
Accounts receivable (net of allowance for doubtful accounts of $1,900 and $2,000)...................	89,900	79,700	10,200
Inventories (at lower of cost or market)..............	136,300	133,200	3,100
Prepaid expenses................................	4,600	12,900	(8,300)
Total current assets........................	$264,300	$252,800	$ 11,500
Investments:			
Land held for future plant site.....................	$ 35,000	—	$ 35,000
Land, buildings, and equipment:			
Land..	$ 47,000	$ 47,000	—
Buildings and equipment (net of accumulated depreciation of $155,600 and $117,000)..................	551,900	425,000	$126,900
Total land, buildings, and equipment...........	$598,900	$472,000	$126,900
Other assets:			
Organization expense.............................	$ 1,500	$ 3,000	$ (1,500)
Total assets......................................	$899,700	$727,800	$171,900
Liabilities and Stockholders' Equity			
Current liabilities:			
Accounts payable................................	$ 3,000	$ 7,800	$ (4,800)
Notes payable...................................	8,000	5,000	3,000
Mortgage.......................................	3,600	3,600	—
Accrued liabilities...............................	6,200	4,800	1,400
Income taxes payable............................	87,500	77,900	9,600
Total current liabilities......................	$108,300	$ 99,100	$ 9,200
Long-term liabilities:			
Notes payable...................................	—	$ 18,000	$(18,000)
Mortgage payable...............................	$ 70,200	73,800	(3,600)
Total long-term liabilities....................	$ 70,200	$ 91,800	$(21,600)
Deferred income—investment credit.................	$ 16,800	$ 18,900	$ (2,100)
Stockholders' equity:			
Capital stock; $1 par value; shares authorized, 300,000 in 1972 and 200,000 in 1971; shares issued and outstanding, 162,000 in 1972 and 120,000 in 1971.......	$162,000	$120,000	$ 42,000
Capital contributed in excess of par value............	306,900	197,900	109,000
Retained earnings appropriated for contingencies......	25,000	—	25,000
Retained earnings...............................	210,500	200,100	10,400
Total stockholders' equity.....................	$704,400	$518,000	$186,400
Total liabilities and stockholders' equity..............	$899,700	$727,800	$171,900

The following information was given effect in the preparation of the foregoing financial statements:

(a) The 10% stock dividend was distributed on August 1. The investment in land for a future plant site was obtained by the issuance of 10,000 shares of the corporation's common stock on October 1. On December 1, 20,000 shares of common stock were sold to obtain additional

Frank Manufacturing Corporation
Comparative Statement of Income and Retained Earnings
For Years Ended December 31, 1972 and 1971

	1972	1971	Increase (Decrease)
Sales..	$980,000	$900,000	$ 80,000
Cost of goods sold................................	540,000	490,000	50,000
Gross profit on sales..............................	$440,000	$410,000	$ 30,000
Selling and administrative expenses.................	(262,000)	(248,500)	(13,500)
Other income and deductions (net).................	(3,000)	(1,500)	(1,500)
Income before income taxes.......................	$175,000	$160,000	$ 15,000
Provision for income taxes........................	85,400	77,900	7,500
Net income......................................	$ 89,600	$ 82,100	$ 7,500
Retained earnings, January 1......................	200,100	118,000	82,100
10% Stock dividend distributed....................	(36,000)	—	(36,000)
Cash dividends paid..............................	(18,200)	—	(18,200)
Appropriation for contingent loss..................	(25,000)	—	(25,000)
Retained earnings, December 31....................	$210,500	$200,100	$ 10,400

working capital. There were no other transactions in 1972 affecting contributed capital.

(b) During 1972 depreciable assets with a total cost of $17,500 were retired and sold as scrap for a nominal amount. These assets were fully depreciated at December 31, 1971. The only depreciable asset acquired in 1972 was a new building which was completed in December; no depreciation was taken on its cost.

(c) When new equipment was purchased on January 2, 1971, for $300,000, the decision was made to record the resulting investment credit in a deferred income account with the benefit of the investment credit being allocated over the useful life of the machine by a reduction of the provision for income taxes. The income tax rate for 1971 and 1972 was 50%.

(d) In 1972 $10,000 was paid in advance on long-term notes payable. The balance of the long-term notes is due in 1973.

(e) An appropriation of retained earnings for a contingent loss of $25,000 arising from a law suit was established in 1972.

Instructions: Prepare a statement of changes in financial position and a schedule of changes in working capital for the year ended December 31, 1972. Supporting calculations should be presented in good form.

(AICPA adapted)

23-11. The president of Tuttle Specialties Company requests that you prepare a statement of changes in financial position for the benefit of the stockholders. Comparative trial balances for the company are presented on the opposite page.

Additional information is made available as follows:

(a)   Income Statement Data for Year Ended December 31, 1972

Income before extraordinary items.....................	$ 112,200
Deduct write-off of goodwill..........................	150,000
Net loss..	$ 37,800

Tuttle Specialties Company
General Ledger Post-Closing Trial Balances
For Years Ended December 31, 1972 and 1971

Debits	1972	1971	Increase (Decrease)
Cash...	$ 157,700	$ 100,400	$ 57,300
Certificates of deposit due March 31, 1972..........	175,000		175,000
Marketable securities.............................	100,100	262,100	(162,000)
Customers' notes and accounts receivable..........	390,000	327,300	62,700
Inventories.....................................	155,400	181,200	(25,800)
Investment in wholly owned subsidiary at equity in net assets...................................	140,000	190,400	(50,400)
Bond sinking fund...............................		62,200	(62,200)
Advance to suppliers.............................	137,500		137,500
Land, buildings, and equipment...................	2,138,600	1,952,600	186,000
Goodwill.......................................		150,000	(150,000)
Discount on bonds payable.......................		10,200	(10,200)
Total debits...............................	$3,394,300	$3,236,400	$157,900

Credits			
Notes receivable discounted......................	$ 100,000		$100,000
Accounts payable...............................	192,400	$ 147,600	44,800
Bank loans — current............................		70,000	(70,000)
Accumulated depreciation........................	510,000	359,700	150,300
Accrued payables...............................	47,100	72,300	(25,200)
Income and other taxes payable..................	128,700	25,500	103,200
Deferred income taxes payable...................	58,500	65,000	(6,500)
5% Mortgage bonds due 1980.....................		320,000	(320,000)
4% Serial bonds................................	100,000		100,000
Capital stock, $10 par value......................	1,110,000	900,000	210,000
Premium on capital stock........................	152,100		152,100
Retained earnings appropriated for the retirement of 5% mortgage bonds............................		62,200	(62,200)
Unappropriated retained earnings.................	995,500	1,214,100	(218,600)
Total credits..............................	$3,394,300	$3,236,400	$157,900

(b) An analysis of the unappropriated retained earnings account follows:

Retained earnings unappropriated, December 31, 1971.....		$1,214,100
Add transfer from appropriation for retirement of 5% mortgage bonds..............................		62,200
Total..		$1,276,300
Deduct: Net loss for year....................	$ 37,800	
Cash dividends.....................	90,000	
10% stock dividend.................	153,000	280,800
Retained earnings unappropriated, December 31, 1972.....		$ 995,500

(c) On January 2, 1972, marketable securities costing $162,000 were sold for $165,800. The proceeds from the sale of the securities, the funds in the Bond Sinking Fund, and the amount received from the sale of the 4% serial bonds were used to retire the 5% mortgage bonds at 102½.

(d) The company paid a stock dividend of 10% on stock outstanding at February 1, 1972. The market value per share at that date was $17.

(e) The company advanced $137,500 to a supplier on August 15 for the purchase of special machinery which is to be delivered in June 1973.

(f) Accounts receivable of $15,000 and $12,500 were considered uncollectible and written off against income in 1972 and 1971 respectively.

(g) The stockholders approved a stock option plan on September 1, 1972. Under the plan 100,000 shares of capital stock are reserved for issuance to key employees at prices not less than market value at the dates of grant. The options will become exercisable in three equal installments starting one year after the date of grant and will expire five years after the date of grant. At December 31, 1972, options were granted for 20,000 shares at $16 per share. The options are carried on a memo basis and are not recorded in the accounts.

(h) Extraordinary repairs of $12,500 to the equipment were charged to the accumulated depreciation account during the year. No assets were retired during 1972.

(i) The wholly owned subsidiary reported a loss for the year of $50,400. The loss was recorded by the parent.

Instructions: Prepare a statement of changes in financial position and a schedule of changes in working capital for year ended December 31, 1972. Supporting calculations should be presented in good form.

(AICPA adapted)

23-12. You have completed the field work in connection with your audit of The Delmar Corporation for the year ended December 31, 1972. You have decided to include a statement of changes in financial position in your long-form report. The following schedule shows the balance sheet accounts at the beginning and end of the year:

Debits	Dec. 31, 1972	Dec. 31, 1971	Increase (Decrease)
Cash	$ 282,400	$ 320,000	$ (37,600)
Accounts receivable	490,000	410,000	80,000
Inventory	695,000	660,000	35,000
Prepaid expenses	10,000	8,000	2,000
Investment in Subsidiary Co.	106,000	—	106,000
Cash surrender value of life insurance	2,100	1,800	300
Machinery	186,600	190,000	(3,400)
Buildings	566,500	507,500	59,000
Land	52,500	52,500	—
Patents	71,000	60,000	11,000
Goodwill	40,000	50,000	(10,000)
Bond expense	4,680	—	4,680
	$2,506,780	$2,259,800	$ 246,980

Credits			
Accrued taxes payable	$ 92,000	$ 80,000	$ 12,000
Accounts payable	301,280	280,000	21,280
Dividends payable	60,000	—	60,000
Bonds payable — 4%	125,000	—	125,000
Bonds payable — 6%	—	100,000	(100,000)
Allowance for doubtful accounts	45,300	40,000	5,300
Accumulated depreciation — building	407,000	400,000	7,000
Accumulated depreciation — machinery	141,000	130,000	11,000
Premium on bonds payable	—	1,600	(1,600)
Capital stock — no par	1,301,200	1,453,200	(152,000)
Additional paid-in capital	14,000	—	14,000
Retained earnings appropriated for plant expansion	10,000	—	10,000
Retained earnings	10,000	(225,000)	235,000
	$2,506,780	$2,259,800	$ 246,980

Statement of Retained Earnings Data

December 31, 1971	Balance (deficit).....................................	$(225,000)
March 31, 1972	Income for first quarter of 1972......................	25,000
April 1, 1972	Transfer from additional paid-in capital..............	200,000
	Balance...	—0—
December 31, 1972	Income for last three quarters of 1972.................	$ 80,000
	Dividend declared — payable January 21, 1973.........	(60,000)
	Appropriated for plant expansion.....................	(10,000)
	Balance...	$ 10,000

Your working papers contain the following information:

(a)   Income Statement Data for Year Ended December 31, 1972

Income before extraordinary items..............	$106,450	
Add gain on retirement of 6% bonds............	550	$107,000
Deduct loss on sale of machinery................		2,000
Net income.................................		$105,000

(b) On April 1, 1972, the existing deficit was written off against additional paid-in capital created by reducing the stated value of the no-par stock.

(c) On November 1, 1972, 8,000 shares of no-par stock were sold for $62,000. The board of directors voted to regard $6 per share as stated capital.

(d) A patent was purchased for $16,000.

(e) Machinery was purchased for $4,600 and installed in December, 1972. A check for this amount was sent to the vendor in January, 1973.

(f) During the year machinery which had a cost basis of $8,000 and on which there was accumulated depreciation of $5,000 was sold for $1,000. No other fixed assets were sold during the year.

(g) The 6%, 20-year bonds were dated and issued on January 2, 1960. Interest was payable on June 30 and December 31. They were sold originally at 104. These bonds were retired at 101 and accrued interest on March 31, 1972.

(h) The 4%, 40-year bonds were dated January 1, 1972 and were sold on March 31 at 97 and accrued interest. Interest is payable semiannually on June 30 and December 31. Expense of issuance was $1,020.

(i) The Delmar Corporation acquired 80% control in Subsidiary Co. on January 2, 1972 for $100,000. The income statement of Subsidiary Co. for 1972 shows a net income of $7,500.

(j) Extraordinary repairs to buildings of $7,000 were charged to accumulated depreciation — building.

Instructions: From the above information prepare a statement of changes in financial position and a schedule of working capital changes. A work sheet is not necessary, but the principal computations should be supported by schedules or skeleton ledger accounts.

(AICPA adapted)

23-13. The following schedule shows the account balances of the Relgne Corporation at the beginning and end of the fiscal year ended October 31, 1972:

Debits	October 31, 1972	Increase	Decrease	November 1, 1971
Cash..................................	$ 226,000	$176,000		$ 50,000
Accounts receivable......................	148,000	48,000		100,000
Inventories.............................	291,000		$ 9,000	300,000
Prepaid insurance.......................	2,500	500		2,000
Long-term investments at cost.............	10,000		30,000	40,000
Sinking fund............................	90,000	10,000		80,000
Land and building.......................	195,000			195,000
Equipment..............................	215,000	125,000		90,000
Discount on bonds payable................	8,500		500	9,000
Treasury stock at cost....................	5,000		5,000	10,000
Cost of goods sold.......................	539,000			
Selling and general expenses..............	287,000			
Income taxes...........................	32,000			
Loss on sale of equipment.................	1,000			
Capital gains tax........................	3,000			
Total debits.........................	$2,053,000			$876,000

Credits				
Allowance for doubtful accounts...........	$ 8,000	$ 3,000		$ 5,000
Accumulated depreciation — building......	26,250	3,750		22,500
Accumulated depreciation — equipment....	39,750	12,250		27,500
Accounts payable........................	55,000		5,000	60,000
Notes payable — current.................	70,000	50,000		20,000
Accrued expenses payable................	18,000	3,000		15,000
Taxes payable...........................	35,000	25,000		10,000
Unearned revenue.......................	1,000		8,000	9,000
Note payable — long-term................	40,000		20,000	60,000
Bonds payable — long-term...............	250,000			250,000
Common stock..........................	300,000	100,000		200,000
Retained earnings appropriated for sinking fund.............................	90,000	10,000		80,000
Unappropriated retained earnings.........	94,000		18,000	112,000
Paid-in capital in excess of par value.......	116,000	111,000		5,000
Sales..................................	898,000			
Gain on sale of investments...............	12,000			
Total credits.........................	$2,053,000			$876,000

The following information was also available:

(a) All purchases and sales were on account.
(b) The sinking fund will be used to retire the long-term bonds.
(c) Equipment with an original cost of $15,000 was sold for $7,000.
(d) Selling and general expenses includes the following expenses:

Expired insurance..	$ 2,000
Building depreciation.....................................	3,750
Equipment depreciation...................................	19,250
Doubtful accounts expense................................	4,000
Interest expense...	18,000

(e) A six-months note payable for $50,000 was issued towards the purchase of new equipment.
(f) The long-term note payable requires the payment of $20,000 per year plus interest until paid.
(g) Treasury stock was sold for $1,000 more than its cost.
(h) All dividends were paid by cash.

Instructions: (1) Prepare schedules computing: (a) collections of accounts receivable; (b) payments of accounts payable.

(2) Prepare a statement of changes in financial position applying the cash concept for funds. Supporting computations should be in good form.

(AICPA adapted)

23-14. You have been contacted by the president of the Boulder Company, Inc. This company has never retained the services of a public accountant, all financial statements and tax returns having been prepared by the comptroller.

The president is disturbed that the net working capital and cash balances at December 31, 1972, are substantially lower than those of the previous year despite the fact that the income for 1972 before taxes of $176,500 was $350,000.

You have been given the following financial statements and have satisfied yourself as to the correctness of the figures shown.

Boulder Company, Inc.
Comparative Balance Sheet
December 31, 1972 and 1971

	1972	1971	Increase or (Decrease)
Assets			
Cash in bank.............................	$ 42,000	$129,000	$(87,000)
Accounts receivable (net of allowance for doubtful accounts)..........................	133,000	85,500	47,500
Inventories...............................	192,000	152,500	39,500
Land, buildings, and equipment (net of accumulated depreciation).................	500,000	260,000	240,000
Deposits — utilities.......................	4,000	3,200	800
Prepaid expenses..........................	21,000	14,000	7,000
Total assets..............................	$892,000	$644,200	$247,800
Liabilities and Stockholders' Equity			
Accounts payable and accrued charges........	$263,000	$220,850	$ 42,150
Provision for income taxes.................	176,500	61,850	114,650
Mortgage payable.........................	—	125,000	(125,000)
Capital stock.............................	150,000	100,000	50,000
Retained earnings.........................	302,500	136,500	166,000
Total liabilities and stockholders' equity.......	$892,000	$644,200	$247,800

Boulder Company, Inc.
Statement of Retained Earnings
For Year Ended December 31, 1972

Balance, January 1, 1972.....................................	$136,500
Net income for the year.....................................	173,500
	$310,000
Dividends paid..	7,500
Balance, December 31, 1972..................................	$302,500

You also have obtained the following information:

(a) At December 31, the accumulated depreciation on fixed assets was $180,000 in 1972 and $160,000 in 1971. Machinery costing $20,000, which was one-half depreciated, was abandoned and written off in 1972. Manufacturing costs absorbed depreciation of $27,000 and selling and administrative expense absorbed $3,000.

(b) In 1972 sales were $3,300,000; cost of goods sold was $2,650,000 and selling and administrative expense (excluding taxes) was $290,000.

(c) On January 2, 1972, two insurance policies on material stored in a public warehouse were canceled. The unexpired premiums on these policies amounted to $2,000, and refund of this amount was received from the insurance company. Insurance charged to manufacturing expense was $4,000 and to selling and administrative expense $500 for the year. Other prepaid expense write-offs were $12,000 to manufacturing expense.

(d) The balance in the allowance for doubtful accounts at each year-end was 5% of the gross amount of receivables. Write-off of receivables amounted to $2,300 in 1972.

Instructions: (1) Prepare a statement reporting the changes in financial position that account for the decrease in working capital.

(2) Prepare a statement reporting the changes in financial position that account for the decrease in cash. Support this statement with details in good form showing how you arrived at cash required for sales, cost of goods sold, and expenses.

(AICPA adapted)

23-15. The comparative balance sheet for the Plainview Corporation is shown on the opposite page.

Your workpapers and other sources disclose the following additional information relating to 1972 activities:

(a) The retained earnings account was analyzed as follows:

Retained earnings, December 31, 1971		$758,200
Add net income		236,580
		$994,780
Deduct:		
Cash dividends	$130,000	
Loss on reissue of treasury stock	3,000	
10% stock dividend	100,200	233,200
Retained earnings, December 31, 1970		$761,580

You noted that the client's determination of net income complied with Opinion No. 9 of the Accounting Principles Board.

(b) On January 2, 1972, marketable securities costing $110,000 were sold for $127,000. The proceeds from this sale, the funds in the bond sinking fund, and the amount received from the issuance of the 8% debentures were used to retire the 6% mortgage bonds.

(c) The treasury stock was reissued on February 28, 1972.

(d) The stock dividend was declared on October 31, 1972, when the market price of Plainview Corporation's stock was $12 per share.

Plainview Corporation
Comparative Balance Sheet
December 31, 1972 and 1971

Assets	1972	1971	Increase (Decrease)
Cash...........................	$ 142,100	$ 165,300	$ (23,200)
Marketable securities (at cost)........	122,800	129,200	(6,400)
Accounts receivable (net)............	312,000	371,200	(59,200)
Inventories.......................	255,200	124,100	131,100
Prepaid expenses...................	23,400	22,000	1,400
Bond sinking fund..................		63,000	(63,000)
Investment in subsidiary (at equity)...	134,080	152,000	(17,920)
Land, buildings, and equipment (net).	1,443,700	1,534,600	(90,900)
Total assets......................	$2,433,280	$2,561,400	$(128,120)
Liabilities and Stockholders' Equity			
Accounts payable..................	$ 238,100	$ 213,300	$ 24,800
Notes payable — current............		145,000	(145,000)
Accrued payables..................	16,500	18,000	(1,500)
Income taxes payable..............	97,500	31,000	66,500
Deferred income taxes payable........	53,900	43,400	10,500
6% Mortgage bonds (due 1984).......		300,000	(300,000)
Premium on mortgage bonds.........		10,000	(10,000)
8% Debentures (due 1992)...........	125,000		125,000
Liabilities for estimated casualty losses.	74,000	85,000	(11,000)
Common stock, $10 par value........	1,033,500	950,000	83,500
Premium on common stock..........	67,700	51,000	16,700
Retained earnings..................	761,580	758,200	3,380
Treasury stock — at cost of $3 per share	(34,500)	(43,500)	9,000
Total liabilities and stockholders' equity	$2,433,280	$2,561,400	$ (128,120)

(e) On April 30, 1972, a fire destroyed a warehouse which cost $100,000 and upon which depreciation of $65,000 had accumulated. The deferred income taxes payable relating to the difference between tax and book depreciation on the warehouse was $12,700. The loss was charged to Liability for Estimated Casualty Losses.

(f) Building and equipment transactions consisted of the sale of a building at its book value of $4,000 and the purchase of equipment for $28,000.

(g) In 1972 a $30,000 charge was made to accumulated depreciation for excessive depreciation taken in prior years but disallowed by the Internal Revenue Service. A tax deficiency of $16,000 was paid and charged against deferred income taxes.

(h) Accounts receivable written off as uncollectible were $16,300 in 1971 and $18,500 in 1972. Expired insurance recorded in 1971 was $4,100 and $3,900 in 1972.

(i) The subsidiary, which is 80% owned, reported a loss of $22,400 for 1972.

Instructions: Prepare a formal statement of changes in financial position (working capital) for the year ended December 31, 1972. Include supporting schedules in good form.

(AICPA adapted)

chapter 24

financial statement analysis - use of comparative data

The analysis of financial data is directed to the requirements of the user of such information, and the nature of the analysis will depend upon the questions that are raised. The many groups on the outside who are interested in a company for a variety of reasons will normally find answers to their questions by analyzing the data provided by the general purpose financial statements and whatever additional financial data are made available in a company's annual report. For example, questions are raised concerning matters such as a company's sales and earnings and the trends for these items, the amount of working capital and the changes that took place in working capital, the relationship of earnings to sales, and the relationship of earnings to investments. These questions require analysis of the data reported on the income statement, the balance sheet, and the statement of changes in financial position. Internal management is also highly concerned with questions whose answers are provided by analyzing the general purpose financial statements. However, management also requires special information in setting policies and arriving at decisions for which they are responsible. Questions may arise on such matters as the performance of various company divisions, the return from sales of the individual products or product lines, and whether to make or to buy product parts or equipment. These questions can be answered only by establishing internal information systems that provide the data required for the special analyses.

The analyses of financial data that are described in this and in the following chapter are directed primarily to the questions that are raised by the groups on the outside who must generally rely on the financial reports issued by a company.

General objectives of financial analysis

The financial statements give vital information concerning the position of the business and the results of its operations. The many groups that are interested in financial data found in these statements include:

1. The owners — sole proprietor, partners, or stockholders.
2. The management.
3. The creditors.
4. Government — local, state, and federal (including regulatory, taxing, and statistical units).
5. Prospective owners and prospective creditors.
6. Stock exchanges, investment bankers, and stock brokers.
7. Trade associations.
8. Employees of the business and their labor unions.
9. The general public (including students and researchers).

Questions that are raised by these groups can generally be answered by means of analyses that develop comparisons and measure relationships of the data provided by the financial statements. The analyses will form the basis for the interpretations that are made and the conclusions that are reached by the user.

Analysis is generally directed toward reaching answers to three broad questions that are raised with respect to a business: (1) its liquidity, (2) its stability, and (3) its profitability.

To be liquid, a business must be able to meet its liabilities as they mature. The financial statements are analyzed to determine whether the business is currently liquid and whether it can retain its liquidity if it should experience a period of adversity. Such analysis includes studies of the relationship of current assets to current liabilities, the size and nature of the various creditor and ownership interests, the protection afforded the creditors and owners through the soundness of asset values, and the amounts and trends of periodic earnings.

Stability is measured by the ability of a business to meet interest and principal payment requirements on outstanding debt and also its ability to pay dividends to its stockholders regularly. In judging stability, data concerning operations and financial position require study. There must be a regular demand for the goods or services that are sold, and the margin on sales must be sufficient to cover operating expenses, interest, and dividends. There should be a satisfactory turnover of current assets and property items. All of the business resources should be productively employed.

Profitability is measured by the success of a business in maintaining a satisfactory dividend policy while at the same time being able to show a steadily increasing ownership equity. The nature and the amount of earnings, as well as their regularity and trend, are all significant factors in arriving at conclusions concerning profitability.

Although attention is normally directed to an evaluation of each of the foregoing matters, analysis must also serve the various groups that have individual questions of special interest. For example, owners are interested in the ability of the company to obtain additional capital for current needs and for possible expansion. Creditors are interested not only in the position of a business as a going concern but also in its position if it should be forced to liquidate.

The various groups that are interested in the facts of business have looked to the accountant, not only for general purpose statements concerning financial position and the results of operations, but also for the special analyses of financial data that they may require. They have regarded the accountant as best qualified to develop analytical data in view of his knowledge of the conventions and processes that are applied in developing the statements that form the basis for analysis. It is not uncommon for the accountant to submit, along with the regular financial statements, comprehensive analyses of significant financial information that will assist individuals in interpreting financial data and in reaching intelligent conclusions with respect to the business.

Preliminary study of financial statements

If analytical data are to be reliable, they must be developed from financial statements that properly exhibit business position and operations. As a first step, statements that are to be used as a basis for analysis should be carefully reviewed to determine whether they display any shortcomings or discrepancies. In the course of the examination, the following questions should be asked: Is there full disclosure of all relevant financial data? Have proper accounting principles and procedures been employed? Have appropriate and consistent bases for valuation been used? Are the data properly classified? When necessary, statements should be corrected so that they report the full financial story in conformance with accepted accounting principles.

Analytical procedures

Analytical procedures fall into two main categories: (1) comparisons and measurements based upon financial data for two or more periods, and (2) comparisons and measurements based upon the financial data of only the current fiscal period. The first category includes the preparation of comparative statements, the determination of ratios and trends for data on successive statements, and special analyses of changes in the balance sheet, income statement, and statement of changes in financial position. The second category includes the determination of current balance sheet and income statement relationships and special analyses of earnings and earning power. An adequate review of financial data usually requires both types of analysis.

The analytical procedures that are commonly employed are illustrated in this and the following chapter of the text. Although individual analyses will be presented in statement and tabular forms, such data are frequently reported in graphic form for more effective presentation of significant relationships. It should be emphasized that the analyses that are illustrated are simply guides to the evaluation of financial data. Sound conclusions can be reached only through the intelligent use and interpretation of such data.

Comparative statements

Financial data become more meaningful when they are compared with similar data for the preceding period or for a number of prior periods. Statements prepared in a form that reflects financial data for two or more periods are known as *comparative statements*. Annual data can be compared with similar data for prior years. Monthly or quarterly data can be compared with similar data for the previous months or quarters or with similar data for the same months or quarters of previous years. Accounting authorities have strongly encouraged the preparation of statements in comparative form. The Committee on Accounting Procedure of the AICPA in recommending that the use of comparative statements be extended, has commented:

> The presentation of comparative financial statements in annual and other reports enhances the usefulness of such reports and brings out more clearly the nature and trends of current changes affecting the enterprise. Such presentation emphasizes the fact that statements for a series of periods are far more significant than those for a single period and that the accounts for one period are but an instalment of what is essentially a continuous history.
>
> In any one year it is ordinarily desirable that the balance sheet, the income statement, and the surplus statement be given for one or more preceding years as well as for the current year. Footnotes, explanations, and accountants' qualifications which appeared on the statements for the preceding years should be repeated, or at least referred to, in the comparative statements to the extent that they continue to be of significance. If, because of reclassifications or for other reasons, changes have occurred in the manner of or basis for presenting corresponding items for two or more periods, information should be furnished which will explain the change. This procedure is in conformity with the well

recognized principle that any change in practice which affects comparability should be disclosed.[1]

The Accounting Principles Board in Statement No. 4 provides an extended discussion of comparative reporting and indicates that comparisons, whether they are made for the single enterprise or between two or more enterprises, are more informative and useful if the following conditions exist:

1. The presentations are in good form; that is, the arrangement within the statements is identical.
2. The content of the statements is identical; that is, the same items from the underlying accounting records are classified under the same captions.
3. Accounting principles are not changed or, if they are changed, the financial effects of the changes are disclosed.
4. Changes in circumstances or in the nature of the underlying transactions are disclosed.[2]

To the extent that the above criteria are not met, comparisons may be misleading. When comparisons are made for the single enterprise, the Accounting Principles Board would add the factors of consistency in practices and procedures and reporting periods that are of equal and regular lengths.

The number of companies submitting statements in comparative form has increased steadily in past years.[3]

Comparative statements — horizontal analysis. Operations and the financial position of a company may be viewed over a number of periods by preparing the financial statements in comparative form. The comparative statements may go beyond a simple listing of comparative values by offering analytical information in the form of dollar changes and percentage changes for the data that are presented. The absolute changes, together with the relative changes, are thus shown. The development of data measuring changes taking place over a number of periods is known as *horizontal analysis*. Horizontal analysis is illustrated in the comparative income statement on the opposite page. This statement reports income data for a three-year period together with the dollar changes and percentage changes for each item listed.

---

[1] *Accounting Research Bulletins No. 43*, "Restatement and Revision of Accounting Research Bulletins" (New York: American Institute of Certified Public Accountants, 1953), Ch. 2, par. 1–2.

[2] *Statements of the Accounting Principles Board, No. 4*, "Basic Concepts and Accounting Principles Underlying Financial Statements of Business Enterprises" (New York: American Institute of Certified Public Accountants, 1970), par. 95–99.

[3] In the AICPA list of 600 survey companies, the number of companies employing the comparative form for all of their customary certified statements was 543 in 1970 as compared with 256 in 1946. *Accounting Trends & Techniques* (25th ed.; New York: American Institute of Certified Public Accountants, 1971), p. 4.

Marshall Company
Condensed Comparative Income Statement
For Years Ended December 31, 1972, 1971 and 1970

	1972	1971	1970	Increase (Decrease) 1971–1972 Amount	Per-cent	1970–1971 Amount	Per-cent
Gross sales	1,500,000	1,750,000	1,000,000	(250,000)	(14%)	750,000	75%
Sales returns	75,000	100,000	50,000	(25,000)	(25%)	50,000	100%
Net sales	1,425,000	1,650,000	950,000	(225,000)	(14%)	700,000	74%
Cost of goods sold	1,000,000	1,200,000	630,000	(200,000)	(17%)	570,000	90%
Gross profit on sales	425,000	450,000	320,000	(25,000)	(6%)	130,000	41%
Selling expense	280,000	300,000	240,000	(20,000)	(7%)	60,000	25%
General expense	100,000	110,000	100,000	(10,000)	(9%)	10,000	10%
Total operating expenses	380,000	410,000	340,000	(30,000)	(7%)	70,000	21%
Operating income (loss)	45,000	40,000	(20,000)	5,000	13%	60,000	——
Other revenue items	85,000	75,000	50,000	10,000	13%	25,000	50%
	130,000	115,000	30,000	15,000	13%	85,000	283%
Other expense items	30,000	30,000	10,000	——	——	20,000	200%
Income before income taxes	100,000	85,000	20,000	15,000	18%	65,000	325%
Income taxes	30,000	25,000	5,000	5,000	20%	20,000	400%
Net income	70,000	60,000	15,000	10,000	17%	45,000	300%

The detail concerning cost of goods sold, operating expenses, and other revenue and expense items may be provided by expanding the statement or by preparing separate supporting schedules. A schedule reporting comparative cost of goods sold detail is illustrated below.

Marshall Company
Comparative Schedule of Cost of Goods sold
For Years Ended December 31, 1972, 1971 and 1970

	1972	1971	1970	Increase (Decrease) 1971–1972 Amount	Per-cent	1970–1971 Amount	Per-cent
Merchandise inventory, January 1	330,000	125,000	105,000	205,000	164%	20,000	19%
Purchases	895,000	1,405,000	650,000	(510,000)	(36%)	755,000	116%
Merchandise available for sale	1,225,000	1,530,000	755,000	(305,000)	(20%)	775,000	103%
Less merchandise inventory, December 31	225,000	330,000	125,000	(105,000)	(32%)	205,000	164%
Cost of goods sold	1,000,000	1,200,000	630,000	(200,000)	(17%)	570,000	90%

The effects of operations on financial position and the trends in financial position can be presented by means of a comparative balance sheet. Here, too, both dollar changes and percentage changes may be provided to show the absolute as well as the relative changes that have taken place. A comparative balance sheet for the Marshall Company for the three-year period, 1970–1972 inclusive, is illustrated below.

Marshall Company
Condensed Comparative Balance Sheet
December 31, 1972, 1971, and 1970

				Increase		(Decrease)	
				1971–1972		1970–1971	
	1972	1971	1970	Amount	Per-cent	Amount	Per-Cen*
Assets							
Current assets............	855,000	955,500	673,500	(100,500)	(11%)	282,000	42%
Investments..............	500,000	400,000	250,000	100,000	25%	150,000	60%
Land, buildings, and equipment (net)	775,000	875,000	675,000	(100,000)	(11%)	200,000	30%
Intangible assets..........	100,000	100,000	100,000	——	—	——	—
Other assets..............	48,000	60,500	61,500	(12,500)	(21%)	(1,000)	(2%
Total assets...............	2,278,000	2,391,000	1,760,000	(113,000)	(5%)	631,000	36%
Liabilities							
Current liabilities.........	410,000	546,000	130,000	(136,000)	(25%)	416,000	320%
Long-term liabilities – 6% bonds.................	400,000	400,000	300,000	——	—	100,000	33%
Total liabilities...........	810,000	946,000	430,000	(136,000)	(14%)	516,000	120%
Stockholders' Equity							
6% Preferred stock........	350,000	350,000	250,000	——	—	100,000	40%
Common stock............	750,000	750,000	750,000	——	—	——	—
Additional paid-in capital....	100,000	100,000	100,000	——	—	——	—
Retained earnings..........	268,000	245,000	230,000	23,000	9%	15,000	7%
Total stockholders' equity....	1,468,000	1,445,000	1,330,000	23,000	2%	115,000	9%
Total liabilities and stockholders' equity..........	2,278,000	2,391,000	1,760,000	(113,000)	(5%)	631,000	36%

Detail for the various asset, liability, and stockholders' equity categories may be provided by expanding the statement or by preparing separate supporting schedules as in the case of the income statement. A schedule reporting comparative current asset detail is given on the following page.

Changes in retained earnings over a number of periods may be viewed by means of a comparative retained earnings statement. A comparative retained earnings statement for the Marshall Company is also shown on the following page.

Marshall Company
Comparative Schedule of Current Assets
December 31, 1972, 1971, and 1970

	1972	1971	1970	Increase (Decrease)			
				1971–1972		1970–1971	
				Amount	Per-cent	Amount	Per-cent
Cash.....................	60,000	100,500	115,000	(40,500)	(40%)	(14,500)	(13%)
Marketable securities........	150,000	150,000	100,000	—	—	50,000	50%
Notes receivable............	50,000	40,000	10,000	10,000	25%	30,000	300%
Accounts receivable.........	380,000	350,000	328,500	30,000	9%	21,500	7%
Total receivables...........	430,000	390,000	338,500	40,000	10%	51,500	15%
Less allowance for doubtful accounts................	10,000	15,000	5,000	(5,000)	(33%)	10,000	200%
Net receivables.............	420,000	375,000	333,500	45,000	12%	41,500	12%
Merchandise inventory.......	225,000	330,000	125,000	(105,000)	(32%)	205,000	164%
Total current assets.........	855,000	955,500	673,500	(100,500)	(11%)	282,000	42%

Marshall Company
Comparative Retained Earnings Statement
For Years Ended December 31, 1972, 1971 and 1970

	1972	1971	1970	Increase (Decrease)			
				1971–1972		1970–1971	
				Amount	Per-cent	Amount	Per-cent
Retained earnings, Jan. 1....	245,000	230,000	240,000	15,000	7%	(10,000)	(4%)
Net income per income statement...............	70,000	60,000	15,000	10,000	17%	45,000	300%
Total....................	315,000	290,000	255,000	25,000	9%	35,000	14%
Dividends:							
Preferred stock............	21,000	21,000	15,000	—	—	6,000	40%
Common stock............	26,000	24,000	10,000	2,000	8%	14,000	140%
Total....................	47,000	45,000	25,000	2,000	4%	20,000	80%
Retained earnings, Dec. 31 ...	268,000	245,000	230,000	23,000	9%	15,000	7%

In viewing operations of a company, there is a need for interpreting operations in terms of their profitability and also in terms of their effect upon financial resources. A comparative statement of changes in financial position that provides absolute changes as well as percentage changes for the Marshall Company is illustrated on page 868.

The absolute changes reported on the comparative statements may suggest further investigation in arriving at fully informed judgments with respect to the changes. For example, the comparative statement of

Marshall Company
Condensed Comparative Statement of Changes in Financial Position
For Years Ended December 31, 1972, 1971 and 1970

| | 1972 | 1971 | 1970 | Increase (Decrease) | | | |
| | | | | 1971–1972 | | 1970–1971 | |
				Amount	Per-cent	Amount	Per-cent
Working capital was provided by:							
Operations during the period:							
Income from operations......	70,000	60,000	15,000	10,000	17%	45,000	300%
Add expenses not requiring outlay of working capital during the period:							
Depreciation..........	125,000	100,000	75,000	25,000	25%	25,000	33%
Working capital provided by operations................	195,000	160,000	90,000	35,000	22%	70,000	77%
Other assets..................	12,500	1,000	10,000	11,500	1,150%	(9,000)	(90%
Issuance of bonds............	——	100,000	100,000	(100,000)	(100%)	——	——
Issuance of preferred stock.....	——	——	100,000	——	——	(100,000)	(100%
Issuance of common stock......	——	——	250,000	——	——	(250,000)	(100%
Total....................	207,500	261,000	550,000	(53,500)	(20%)	(289,000)	(34%
Working capital was applied to:							
Dividends..................	47,000	45,000	25,000	2,000	4%	20,000	80%
Investments................	100,000	150,000	200,000	(50,000)	(33%)	(50,000)	(25%
Land, buildings and equipment..	25,000	300,000	100,000	(275,000)	(92%)	200,000	200%
Total....................	172,000	495,000	325,000	(323,000)	(65%)	170,000	52%
Increase (decrease) in working capital....................	35,500	(234,000)	225,000	269,500	——	(459,000)	(204%

changes in financial position shows that funds of $550,000 were made available during the three-year period through the issuance of bonds and preferred and common stock. During this same period, $450,000 was applied to investments. Investigation may indicate that the investments do not provide an adequate return on the capital provided by bondholder and stockholder groups. The statement also indicates that operations have provided significantly increasing amounts of working capital; it may be questioned whether such increases have been employed to the best advantage in view of the fact that net income for 1972 shows only a moderate increase over 1971.

The relative changes on the comparative statements may also suggest a need for further investigation in evaluating the changes. For example, the comparative schedule of current assets shows an increase in notes receivable for 1971 of $30,000. The indication that this is a 300% increase serves to emphasize the significance of the change. Investigation may disclose that collections on account are slow and that customers are postponing payments by the issuance of notes. The comparative income statement reports an increase in sales returns for 1971 of $50,000. This information becomes more meaningful when gross sales are shown to have increased by 75% for the year while sales returns have increased by 100%. Investigation of the causes for the disproportionate increase appears warranted. The income statement also shows that in 1971 net sales went up 74% while cost of goods sold went up 90%; in 1972 net sales went down 14% while cost of goods sold went down 17%. These data suggest that wholesale price changes are not promptly reflected in the company's sales prices, and further study of the cost-price relationship appears warranted. When absolute amounts or relative amounts appear out of line, conclusions, favorable or unfavorable, are not justified until investigation has disclosed all of the reasons for the changes.

Percentage changes in the previous examples were given in terms of the data for the year immediately preceding. With data covering more than two years, this procedure results in a changing base that makes the comparison of relative changes over a number of years difficult. When comparative data for more than two years are to be provided, it is generally desirable to develop all comparisons in terms of a base year. This may be the earliest year given, or some other year that is considered particularly appropriate. Each amount on the statement representing the base year is considered to be 100%. Each amount on all other statements is expressed as a percentage of the base-year amount. The set of percentages for several years may thus be interpreted as trend values or as a series of index numbers relating to the particular item. Assuming that the Marshall Company recognizes 1970 as the base year, comparative income statement data may be presented as shown on page 870.

When relationships for a certain base period can be regarded as "normal," a statement such as the one on page 870 serves as a clearer medium for interpretation than those previously illustrated. For example, the comparative income statement on page 865 shows that gross sales increased 75%, then decreased 14%; sales returns increased 100%, then decreased 25%. Analyses were based upon the data for the year immediately preceding. The illustration on page 870 shows that gross sales increased 75% and 50% in terms of 1970 amounts. It also shows that sales returns increased 100% and 50% as compared with 1970 amounts. It is thus shown that, while sales returns increased disproportionately as compared with sales in 1971, the increase was proportionate in 1972, both sales and sales returns increasing 50% in terms of 1970 data.

Analysis in terms of a base year is desirable, not only for the comparison of entire statements, but also for the comparison of various related

Marshall Company
Condensed Comparative Income Statement
For Years Ended December 31, 1972, 1971 and 1970

| | 1972 | 1971 | 1970 | Increase (Decrease) | | | |
| | | | | 1970–1972 | | 1970–1971 | |
				Amount	Per-cent	Amount	Per-cent
Gross sales................	1,500,000	1,750,000	1,000,000	500,000	50%	750,000	75%
Sales returns..............	75,000	100,000	50,000	25,000	50%	50,000	100%
Net sales..................	1,425,000	1,650,000	950,000	475,000	50%	700,000	74%
Cost of goods sold..........	1,000,000	1,200,000	630,000	370,000	59%	570,000	90%
Gross profit on sales........	425,000	450,000	320,000	105,000	33%	130,000	41%
Selling expense............	280,000	300,000	240,000	40,000	17%	60,000	25%
General expense...........	100,000	110,000	100,000	——	——	10,000	10%
Total operating expenses.....	380,000	410,000	340,000	40,000	12%	70,000	21%
Operating income (loss)......	45,000	40,000	(20,000)	65,000	——	60,000	——
Other revenue items.........	85,000	75,000	50,000	35,000	70%	25,000	50%
	130,000	115,000	30,000	100,000	333%	85,000	283%
Other expense items.........	30,000	30,000	10,000	20,000	200%	20,000	200%
Income before income taxes ...	100,000	85,000	20,000	80,000	400%	65,000	325%
Income taxes..............	30,000	25,000	5,000	25,000	500%	20,000	400%
Net income................	70,000	60,000	15,000	55,000	367%	45,000	300%

single items, ratios, and other pertinent data. Data expressed in terms of a base year are well adapted for graphic presentation.

Data expressed in terms of a base year are frequently useful for comparisons with series summarizing similar data that are provided by business or industry sources or by governmental agencies. When the series that is to be used for making comparisons does not employ the same base period, it will have to be restated. Such restatement calls for the expression of each value in the series as a percentage of the value for the period that is recognized as the base year.

To illustrate, assume that net sales data for the Marshall Company for 1970-1972 are to be compared with a sales index for its particular industry. The industry sales indexes are as follows:

	1972	1971	1970
(1963 − 1965 = 100).................	146	157	124

Recognizing 1970 as the base year, industry sales are restated as follows:

1970... 100
1971 (157 ÷ 124)... 127
1972 (146 ÷ 124)... 118

Industry sales and net sales for the Marshall Company can now be expressed in comparative form as follows:

	1972	1971	1970
Industry sales index....................	118	127	100
Marshall Company sales index..........	150	174	100

Instead of comparisons of the financial data of a company in terms of a base year, comparisons can be made in terms of averages of the data for a period of years. Averages are first computed. Deviations from the averages for the individual years are then developed and presented in both absolute amounts and percentages. Such presentations may be particularly useful in defining trends and pointing out significant deviations from such trends.

Changes in the preceding examples were expressed in the form of percentages. Changes can be expressed in the form of ratios instead of percentages. A 50% increase in an item results in the designation of a ratio to the base figure of 1.50; a 25% decrease in an item results in a ratio to the base figure of .75. Plus and minus designations are thus avoided. Use of ratios instead of percentages is illustrated in the statement that follows:

Marshall Company
Condensed Comparative Income Statement
For Years Ended December 31, 1972, 1971 and 1970

	1972	1971	1970	Increase (Decrease) 1970–1972 Amount	Ratio	Increase (Decrease) 1970–1971 Amount	Ratio
Gross sales................	1,500,000	1,750,000	1,000,000	500,000	1.50	750,000	1.75
Sales returns..............	75,000	100,000	50,000	25,000	1.50	50,000	2.00
Net sales..................	1,425,000	1,650,000	950,000	475,000	1.50	700,000	1.74
Cost of goods sold..........	1,000,000	1,200,000	630,000	370,000	1.59	570,000	1.90
Gross profit on sales........	425,000	450,000	320,000	105,000	1.33	130,000	1.41
Selling expense............	280,000	300,000	240,000	40,000	1.17	60,000	1.25
General expense...........	100,000	110,000	100,000	——	1.00	10,000	1.10
Total operating expenses.....	380,000	410,000	340,000	40,000	1.12	70,000	1.21
Operating income (loss)......	45,000	40,000	(20,000)	65,000	——	60,000	——
Other revenue items........	85,000	75,000	50,000	35,000	1.70	25,000	1.50
	130,000	115,000	30,000	100,000	4.33	85,000	3.83
Other expense items........	30,000	30,000	10,000	20,000	3.00	20,000	3.00
Income before income taxes..	100,000	85,000	20,000	80,000	5.00	65,000	4.25
Income taxes..............	30,000	25,000	5,000	25,000	6.00	20,000	5.00
Net income................	70,000	60,000	15,000	55,000	4.67	45,000	4.00

When a base figure is zero or is a minus value, it is possible to report a dollar change but the change cannot be expressed as a percentage. When a base figure is a positive value, however, a dollar change and also a percentage change can be stated. When ratio analysis is employed, ratios can be provided only when two positive values are given. The foregoing practices are illustrated in the examples below:

Net Income (Loss) for Year Ended December 31		Increase (Decrease)		
1972	1971	Amount	Percent	Ratio
$20,000	$ 0	$20,000	————	————
(2,000)	0	(2,000)	————	————
2,000	(5,000)	7,000	————	————
(10,000)	(5,000)	(5,000)	————	————
0	10,000	(10,000)	(100%)	————
(2,000)	10,000	(12,000)	(120%)	————
35,000	10,000	25,000	250%	3.50
8,000	10,000	(2,000)	(20%)	.80
10,000	10,000	————	————	1.00

Although comparisons in previous examples have been limited to annual data, it is frequently desirable to develop comparisons for shorter periods. It would be possible, for example, to prepare comparative statements for monthly or quarterly periods. Furthermore, in the case of earnings data, it may be desirable to compare a current month with the same month of preceding years, or cumulative data for the current year to date with cumulative data for the corresponding period of preceding years.

A number of companies have adopted the thirteen-month year, dividing the calendar year into thirteen equal periods of four weeks. Variations for the total number of days and number of Saturdays and Sundays found in the calendar months are thus eliminated in the development of comparative "monthly" statements. More reliable conclusions can be drawn from analyses developed from data for periods of comparable length.

Comparative statements — vertical analysis. Comparative data may include analyses in terms of percentages or ratios based upon the related data of each individual period. For example, in presenting comparative operating data, it may be desirable to show the relationship in each period of cost of goods sold, operating expenses, other revenue and expense items, and income taxes to sales. The development of data expressing relationships within a single period is known as *vertical analysis*. Vertical analysis as applied to the comparative data on the income statement for the Marshall Company is illustrated below. The net sales figure for each year is used as the base figure for that year and is expressed as 100%. The analysis can be expressed in the form of ratios rather than percentages. Net sales, then, would be expressed as 1.00 and revenue and expense items would be reported in terms of this base.

Marshall Company
Condensed Comparative Income Statement
For Years Ended December 31, 1972, 1971 and 1970

	1972		1971		1970	
	Amount	Percent	Amount	Percent	Amount	Percent
Gross sales..................	1,500,000	105.3%	1,750,000	106.1%	1,000,000	105.3%
Sales returns.................	75,000	5.3	100,000	6.1	50,000	5.3
Net sales....................	1,425,000	100.0%	1,650,000	100.0%	950,000	100.0%
Cost of goods sold............	1,000,000	70.2	1,200,000	72.7	630,000	66.3
Gross profit on sales..........	425,000	29.8%	450,000	27.3%	320,000	33.7%
Selling expense..............	280,000	19.7%	300,000	18.2%	240,000	25.3%
General expense.............	100,000	7.0	110,000	6.7	100,000	10.5
Total operating expenses.......	380,000	26.7%	410,000	24.9%	340,000	35.8%
Operating income (loss)	45,000	3.1%	40,000	2.4%	(20,000)	(2.1%)
Other revenue items..........	85,000	6.0	75,000	4.5	50,000	5.3
	130,000	9.1%	115,000	6.9%	30,000	3.2%
Other expense items..........	30,000	2.1	30,000	1.8	10,000	1.1
Income before income taxes	100,000	7.0%	85,000	5.1%	20,000	2.1%
Income taxes................	30,000	2.1	25,000	1.5	5,000	.5
Net income..................	70,000	4.9%	60,000	3.6%	15,000	1.6%

Although it may not be possible to specify a normal gross profit rate for the Marshall Company, it can be determined from the comparative income statement that a significant decline in the gross profit rate took place in 1971 with a partial recovery in 1972. This would suggest that an analysis be made of the causes for the increase in the cost of goods sold percentage. Notwithstanding the reduction in the gross profit rate, the net income percentage on each dollar of sales increased in 1971 and again in 1972. These increases resulted from reductions in the expense percentage per dollar of sales that more than compensated for the increases in the cost of goods sold percentage. The comparative statement points to certain relationships and trends that require further investigation in arriving at an explanation and an evaluation of the changes.

When supporting schedules are prepared for the detail relating to totals on the condensed income statement, individual items may be expressed in terms of net sales or in terms of the totals reported on the individual schedules. Sales salaries for the Marshall Company for 1972, for example, may be reported as a certain percentage of net sales of $1,425,000, with the selling expense schedule listing expenses adding up to 19.7%; or the salaries may be reported as a percentage of total selling expenses of $280,000, with the individual items on the schedule adding up to 100%.

Vertical analysis may also be employed in presenting a comparative balance sheet, a comparative statement of retained earnings, and a comparative statement of changes in financial position. On the balance sheet, individual items are expressed in terms of the total assets and the total liabilities and stockholders' equity; on the statement of retained earnings, individual items can be expressed in terms of the retained earnings balance at the beginning or at the end of the period; on the statement of changes in financial position, individual items are expressed in terms of total funds provided or total funds applied. Examples of these statements with percentage analyses for the Marshall Company are illustrated as follows:

Marshall Company
Condensed Comparative Balance Sheet
December 31, 1972, 1971 and 1970

	1972		1971		1970	
	Amount	Percent	Amount	Percent	Amount	Percent
Assets						
Current assets.................	855,000	38%	955,500	40%	673,500	38%
Investments..................	500,000	22	400,000	17	250,000	14
Land, buildings, and equipment						
(net)	775,000	34	875,000	37	675,000	38
Intangible assets	100,000	4	100,000	4	100,000	6
Other assets..................	48,000	2	60,500	2	61,500	4
Total assets...................	2,278,000	100%	2,391,000	100%	1,760,000	100%
Liabilities						
Current liabilities.............	410,000	18%	546,000	23%	130,000	7%
Long-term liabilities—6% bonds.	400,000	18	400,000	17	300,000	17
Total liabilities...............	810,000	36%	946,000	40%	430,000	24%
Stockholders' Equity						
6% Preferred stock............	350,000	15%	350,000	15%	250,000	14%
Common stock................	750,000	33	750,000	31	750,000	43
Additional paid-in capital......	100,000	4	100,000	4	100,000	6
Retained earnings	268,000	12	245,000	10	230,000	13
Total stockholders' equity.......	1,468,000	64%	1,445,000	60%	1,330,000	76%
Total liabilities and stockholders'						
equity.....................	2,278,000	100%	2,391,000	100%	1,760,000	100%

Marshall Company
Comparative Retained Earnings Statement
For Years Ended December 31, 1972, 1971 and 1970

	1972		1971		1970	
	Amount	Percent	Amount	Percent	Amount	Percent
Retained earnings, January 1....	245,000	100%	230,000	100%	240,000	100%
Net income per income statement.	70,000	29	60,000	26	15,000	6
Total........................	315,000	129%	290,000	126%	255,000	106%
Dividends:						
Preferred stock..............	21,000	9%	21,000	9%	15,000	6%
Common stock..............	26,000	11	24,000	10	10,000	4
Total.....................	47,000	20%	45,000	19%	25,000	10%
Retained earnings, December 31.	268,000	109%	245,000	107%	230,000	96%

Marshall Company
Condensed Comparative Statement of Changes in Financial Position
For Years Ended December 31, 1972, 1971 and 1970

	1972		1971		1970	
	Amount	Percent	Amount	Percent	Amount	Percent
Working capital was provided by:						
Operations during the period:						
Income from operations........	70,000	33.7%	60,000	23.0%	15,000	2.7%
Add expenses not requiring outlay of working capital during the period:						
Depreciation..............	125,000	60.3	100,000	38.3	75,000	13.6
Working capital provided by operations.................	195,000	94.0%	160,000	61.3%	90,000	16.4%
Other assets.....................	12,500	6.0	1,000	.4	10,000	1.8
Issuance of bonds.................	—	—	100,000	38.3	100,000	18.2
Issuance of preferred stock........	—	—	—	—	100,000	18.2
Issuance of common stock........	—	—	—	—	250,000	45.4
Total......................	207,500	100.0%	261,000	100.0%	550,000	100.0%
Working capital was applied to:						
Dividends......................	47,000	22.7%	45,000	17.2%	25,000	4.5%
Investments....................	100,000	48.2	150,000	57.5	200,000	36.4
Land, buildings and equipment....	25,000	12.0	300,000	115.0	100,000	18.2
Total.......................	172,000	82.9%	495,000	189.7%	325,000	59.1%
Increase (decrease) in working capital.	35,500	17.1	(234,000)	(89.7)	225,000	40.9
Total......................	207,500	100.0%	261,000	100.0%	550,000	100.0%

When a supporting schedule is prepared to show the detail for a group total, individual items may be expressed as a percentage of the base figure or as a percentage of the group total.

Both horizontal and vertical analyses are required if business trends and financial and operating relationships are to be fully understood.

Measurements used in horizontal analyses are frequently referred to as *trend ratios;* measurements used in vertical analyses are frequently referred to as *structural ratios.* When vertical relationships are expressed for a number of periods, analyses of both a horizontal and vertical character are provided.

Comparative statements when there have been accounting changes and prior period adjustments

The comparative statements that have been presented in the preceding pages of this chapter were based on the assumptions that there had been no changes in accounting principles or estimates and no prior period adjustments including corrections for the periods covered by the statements. When accounting changes or prior period adjustments have been made, special procedures are required in preparing comparative statements. The Accounting Principles Board in Opinion No. 20 has provided guidelines for the procedures to be followed under such circumstances, and these are summarized in the sections that follow.

Change in accounting principle. It was indicated in Chapter 3 that the Accounting Principles Board concluded that a change in accounting principle should be reported by a restatement of assets and liabilities accompanied by a special charge or credit reporting the cumulative effect of the change on past earnings that is to be recognized in arriving at net income for the period. With a change in accounting principle, earnings per share presentations both on a primary and a fully diluted basis on the income statement should be expanded to report (1) income before extraordinary items and the cumulative effect of a change in accounting principle, (2) extraordinary items, (3) cumulative effect of change in accounting principle, and (4) net income. Financial statements of prior periods included for comparative purposes would be presented as in the past. In addition to such data, the Board requires an accompanying presentation that reports net income before extraordinary items and net income together with related earnings per share amounts computed on a pro forma basis that assumes that the newly adopted principle had been applied in each of the periods presented on the income statement.[1]

Change in accounting estimate. It has already been indicated that a change in accounting estimate is accounted for in present and subsequent periods. Under these circumstances, the Board has indicated

---

[1]Reference was made in the footnote on page 75 to the recommendations of the Board indicating exceptional treatment in the form of retroactive adjustments for certain specified changes in principle. In these special cases, financial statements of all prior periods presented would be restated to reflect the retroactive application of the newly adopted principle.

that disclosure of the effects upon income and related earnings per share measurements should be provided for a change that affects several future periods, for example, a change in the service life of an asset, and also for other changes whose effects are limited to the current period, but only if these are material. Financial statements of prior periods that are included for comparative purposes are reported without change.

Prior period adjustment including the correction of an error in previously issued statements. A prior period adjustment including correction of an error in previously issued financial statements is recorded by a restatement of assets and liabilities and a charge or credit directly to the owners' equity for the cumulative effect of the adjustment on past earnings. In these circumstances, financial statements of all prior periods included for comparative purposes should be restated to reflect the retroactive application of the adjustment. Financial statements, then, will provide data that can satisfactorily be used in defining trends and in developing required analyses.

Changes in the reporting entity. The presentation of consolidated statements or combined statements in place of separate statements previously presented, or a change in the specific subsidiaries or business units included in consolidated or combined statements, represents a special type of accounting change that results in financial statements which are, in effect, those of a different reporting entity. The preparation of financial statements for a business combination considered to be a pooling of interests also represents an accounting change in response to a different reporting entity. In each of these circumstances, the Board states that the financial statements for the period in which the entity change is first reported should describe both the nature and the reason for the change. This explanation should be accompanied by a presentation reporting the effects of the change in reporting the entity upon income before extraordinary items and net income and the related earnings per share amounts for each period presented. In addition, financial statements of all prior periods presented for comparative purposes should be restated in terms of the accounting change that applies to the different reporting entity.

Changes for an initial public distribution of shares. Accounting Principles Board Opinion No. 20 states that financial statements for all prior periods presented may be restated retroactively in one specific instance. Assume, for example, that a company owned by a few individuals decides upon a public offering of its equity securities. When the enlarged entity is expected to apply accounting principles that differ from those previously used, potential investors will be better served by comparative financial statements for the past presented in terms of the principles that are expected to be applied in the future. In recognition of such a situation, the Board concludes,

> . . . financial statements for all prior periods presented may be restated retroactively when a company first issues its financial statements for any one of the following purposes: (a) obtaining additional equity capital from investors, (b) effecting a business combination, or (c) registering securities. This exemption is available only once for changes made at the time a company's financial statements are first used for any of those purposes and is not available to companies whose securities currently are widely held.[1]

Common-size statements

Comparative statements that give relationships of the individual items to the whole without giving dollar values are known as *common-size statements*. These relationships may be stated in terms of percentages or in terms of ratios. Common-size statements may be prepared for the same business as of different dates or periods or for two or more business units as of the same date or for the same period.

A common-size income statement for the Marshall Company is given at the top of the next page. The statement is prepared simply by reporting the percentage figures that were shown on the comparative income statement on page 873. A common-size statement comparing balance sheet data for the Marshall Company with that of the Norris Company is given at the bottom of the next page. This statement provides a comparison of the relationships of balance sheet items for the two companies. It is readily seen, for example, that the relationship of the stockholders' equity to total assets is approximately the same for each company. Although the percentage of current liabilities to total assets for the Norris Company is somewhat higher than that for the Marshall Company, the ratio of current assets to current liabilities for the Norris Company exceeds significantly that of the Marshall Company. It would thus appear that the Norris Company has the stronger working capital position. Further inquiry, however, is necessary. Reference to the items composing working capital may show that Norris Company current assets consist primarily of slow-moving inventories, whereas Marshall Company current assets consist primarily of cash and marketable securities, and inventories are only a small part of the total. It may be further disclosed that although the inventories of both companies are reported on

---

[1] *Opinions of the Accounting Principles Board, No. 20*, "Accounting Changes" (New York: American Institute of Public Accountants, 1971), par. 29.

Marshall Company
Condensed Common-Size Income Statement
For Years Ended December 31, 1972, 1971, and 1970

	1972	1971	1970
Gross sales.................................	105.3%	106.1%	105.3%
Sales returns..............................	5.3	6.1	5.3
Net sales.................................	100.0%	100.0%	100.0%
Cost of goods sold........................	70.2	72.7	66.3
Gross profit on sales......................	29.8%	27.3%	33.7%
Selling expense...........................	19.7%	18.2%	25.3%
General expense..........................	7.0	6.7	10.5
Total operating expenses...................	26.7%	24.9%	35.8%
Operating income (loss)..................	3.1%	2.4%	(2.1%)
Other revenue items.......................	6.0	4.5	5.3
	9.1%	6.9%	3.2%
Other expense items.......................	2.1	1.8	1.1
Income before income taxes...............	7.0%	5.1%	2.1%
Income taxes............................	2.1	1.5	0.5
Net income.............................	4.9%	3.6%	1.6%

Marshall Company and Norris Company
Condensed Common-Size Balance Sheet
December 31, 1972

	Marshall Company	Norris Company
Assets		
Current assets..............................	38%	64%
Investments................................	22	—
Land, buildings, and equipment (net)..........	34	35
Intangible assets............................	4	—
Other assets................................	2	1
Total assets.............................	100%	100%
Liabilities		
Current liabilities..........................	18%	20%
Long-term liabilities........................	18	12
Deferred revenues..........................	—	2
Total liabilities...........................	36%	34%
Stockholders' Equity		
Preferred stock............................	15%	—
Common stock.............................	33	46%
Additional paid-in capital....................	4	5
Retained earnings..........................	12	15
Total stockholders' equity...................	64%	66%
Total liabilities and stockholders' equity........	100%	100%

the last-in, first-out basis, this method was adopted by the Marshall Company some time prior to its adoption by the Norris Company, and, as a result, inventories of the Marshall Company reflect costs that are significantly lower than those of the Norris Company.

In preparing common-size statements for two companies, it is important that the financial data for each company reflect comparable price levels. Furthermore, it should be determined that financial data were developed in terms of comparable accounting methods, classification procedures, and valuation bases. Comparisons should be limited to companies that are engaged in similar activities. When financial policies of the two companies are different, such differences should be recognized in evaluating comparative reports. For example, one company may lease its properties while the other may purchase such items; one company may resort to financing by means of long-term borrowing while the other may rely primarily on funds supplied by stockholders and by earnings. Operating results for the two companies under these circumstances cannot be wholly comparable.

The above suggests that comparisons between different companies should be approached with care, and when comparisons are made, these should be viewed with a full understanding of the limitations inherent in them. Reference was made earlier to the criteria that the Accounting Principles Board has set if comparisons are to be most meaningful under any circumstances. The Board is aware of the fact that comparability between enterprises is more difficult to obtain than comparability within a single enterprise. Ideally, differences in companies' financial reports should arise from basic differences in the companies themselves or from the nature of their transactions and not from differences in accounting practices and procedures. The Board remarks, "One of the most important unsolved problems at present is the general acceptance of alternative accounting practices under circumstances which themselves do not appear to be sufficiently different to justify different practices."[1]

Statements reporting general price-level changes

Comparative statements of a company that are adjusted for changes in the general purchasing power of the dollar are referred to as *statements reporting general price-level changes*. The purchasing power of the dollar as of a certain base period is assigned an index of 100 and comparative statements are reported in terms of such base values. A dollar of uniform purchasing power is thus used in preparing the latest and prior years'

---

[1]*Statements of the Accounting Principles Board, No. 4, op. cit.*, par. 100–105.

reports and the effects of inflation or deflation are removed. The procedures employed in the preparation of statements reporting dollars of uniform purchasing power are described in detail in Chapter 28.

Statement accounting for variation in net income

As previously illustrated, the comparative income statement shows comparative balances, changes in individual revenue and expense items, and also changes in the net income. Comparative income statement data may be used in the preparation of a statement accounting for the variation in net income. Here comparative data are assembled and presented in a manner that calls attention to the various constituent factors that were responsible for the change in net income. A statement accounting for the increase in the net income for the Marshall Company for 1972 over 1971 may be prepared from comparative income statement data as follows:

Marshall Company
Statement Accounting for Variation in Net Income
1972 as Compared with 1971

Net income for year ended December 31, 1971.........................				$60,000
Net income was increased as a result of:				
Decrease in selling expenses				
1971...	$300,000			
1972...	280,000	$20,000		
Decrease in general expenses				
1971...	$110,000			
1972...	100,000	10,000		
Increase in other revenue items				
1972...	$ 85,000			
1971...	75,000	10,000	$40,000	
Net income was decreased as a result of:				
Decrease in gross profit on sales:				
Decrease in net sales				
1971.........................	$1,650,000			
1972.........................	1,425,000	$225,000		
Less decrease in cost of goods sold				
1971.........................	$1,200,000			
1972.........................	1,000,000	200,000	$25,000	
Increase in income taxes				
1972...	$ 30,000			
1971...	25,000	5,000	30,000	10,000
Net income for year ended December 31, 1972............................				$70,000

The statement shows that although reductions in net income resulted from a decrease in the gross profit on sales and an increase in income taxes, these were more than offset by a decrease in cost of goods sold, a decrease in operating expenses, and an increase in other revenue. It would appear, then, that increased operating efficiency was a significant factor in increasing net income.

The statement may be prepared in an alternate form as follows:

Marshall Company

Statement Accounting for Variation in Net Income

1972 as Compared with 1971

	1972	1971	Net Income Increase	Net Income Decrease
Sales (net)........................	$1,425,000	$1,650,000		$225,000
Cost of goods sold...............	1,000,000	1,200,000	$200,000	
Gross profit on sales.............	$ 425,000	$ 450,000		
Selling expense..................	$ 280,000	$ 300,000	20,000	
General expense.................	100,000	110,000	10,000	
Total operating expenses.........	$ 380,000	$ 410,000		
Operating income................	$ 45,000	$ 40,000		
Other net revenue items.........	55,000	45,000	10,000	
Income before income taxes......	$ 100,000	$ 85,000		
Income taxes...................	30,000	25,000		5,000
Net income.....................	$ 70,000	$ 60,000	$240,000	$230,000
Increase in net income...........		10,000		10,000
	$ 70,000	$ 70,000	$240,000	$240,000

Statement accounting for variation in gross profit

Since gross profit is so significant in determining earnings, special analyses may be directed to the factors that are responsible for the periodic changes in gross profit. If such analyses are to go beyond simply reporting the effects of changes in sales and in cost of goods sold on gross profit, information will be required concerning the changes in the number of units sold. With this information it is possible to determine the volume and the price factors that are responsible for the changes in sales and the changes in cost of goods sold. The summary that is given below indicates the volume and price variations that can be provided and the computations that they require.

Variations identified with the change in sales

1. *Variations arising from the change in sales volume.* To calculate the change in sales arising from the change in the sales volume, the change in volume is multiplied by the sales price for the preceding period.
2. *Variations arising from the change in sales price.* To calculate the change in sales arising from the change in the sales price, the volume of goods sold in the preceding period is multiplied by the change in sales price.

3. *Variations arising from the change in the joint sales price-volume factor.* Since the computation in (1) used the sales price of the preceding period as a base and the computation in (2) used the volume of goods sold in the preceding period as a base, a third price-volume factor must now be recognized to complete the explanation for the change in sales. The price-volume factor is computed by multiplying the change in sales volume by the change in sales price. An increase in both volume and price indicates an increase in sales; a decrease in volume or in price indicates a decrease in sales arising from the joint price-volume factor.

Variations identified with the change in the cost of goods sold

1. *Variations arising from the change in sales volume.* To calculate the change in cost of goods sold arising from the change in the volume of goods sold, the change in volume is multiplied by the cost price for the preceding period.
2. *Variations arising from the change in cost price.* To calculate the change in cost of goods sold arising from the change in the cost price, the change in price is multiplied by the volume of goods sold in the preceding period.
3. *Variations arising from the change in the joint cost price-volume factor.* Since the computation in (1) used the cost price of the preceding period as a base and the computation in (2) used the volume of goods sold at the preceding period as a base, a third price-volume factor is computed by multiplying the change in the volume of goods sold by the change in cost price. An increase in both volume and cost indicates an addition in cost of goods sold; a decrease in volume or in cost indicates a reduction in cost of goods sold arising from the joint price-volume factor.

To illustrate the nature of the calculations, assume the following gross profit data:

	1972		1971		Change
Sales..............	120,000 @ $10.00	$1,200,000	100,000 @ $9.50	$950,000	$250,000
Cost of goods sold...	120,000 @ $ 7.00	840,000	100,000 @ $7.25	725,000	115,000
Gross profit........		$ 360,000		$225,000	$135,000

The variation in gross profit can now be analyzed as follows:

Increase in sales:
Variation arising from increase in sales volume (20,000 × $9.50).... $190,000
Variation arising from increase in sales price (100,000 × $.50)..... 50,000
Variation arising from joint increase in sales volume and increase in sales price, (20,000 × $.50)................................ 10,000 $250,000

Less increase in cost of goods sold:
Variation arising from increase in cost volume (20,000 × $7.25)... $145,000
Variation arising from decrease in cost price (100,000 × $.25).. (25,000)
Variation arising from joint increase in volume and decrease in cost price (20,000 × $.25)................................ (5,000) 115,000

Increase in gross profit...................................... $135,000

The analysis will now be applied to the Marshall Company and the statement of the variation of gross profit will be illustrated in formal form. Assume that information concerning sales and costs for the Marshall Company are as follows:

	1972		1971		Change
Sales..............	20,000 @ $71.25	$1,425,000	25,000 @ $66.00	$1,650,000	$(225,000)
Cost of goods sold..	20,000 @ 50.00	1,000,000	25,000 @ 48.00	1,200,000	(200,000)
Gross profit........		$ 425,000		$ 450,000	$ (25,000)

Analysis of these data are summarized in the statement that follows.

Marshall Company
Statement Accounting for Variation in Gross Profit
1972 as Compared with 1971

Decrease in gross profit resulted from:

Decrease in net sales:

Decrease arising from decrease in number of units sold (5,000 × $66.00), in absence of change in sales price.................	$(330,000)	
Increase arising from increase in sales price (25,000 × $5.25), in absence of change in volume.............................	131,250	
Decrease arising from joint decrease in number of units sold and increase in sales price (5,000 × $5.25)...................	(26,250)	$225,000

Less decrease in cost of goods sold:

Decrease arising from decrease in number of units sold (5,000 × $48.00), in absence of change in cost price.................	$(240,000)	
Increase arising from increase in cost price (25,000 × $2.00), in absence of change in volume........................	50,000	
Decrease arising from joint decrease in number of units sold and increase in cost price (5,000 × $2.00)................	(10,000)	200,000
Decrease in gross profit.......................................		$ 25,000

The above analysis indicates that although sales went down $225,000, the decline would have been even greater were it not for the increases that were made in sales prices. The decreases in selling and general and administrative expenses for the year reported on the statement accounting for the variation in net income given on page 881 had been interpreted as evidence of increased operating efficiency. It would appear that this conclusion needs to be questioned in view of the analysis showing a significant reduction in the number of units sold. The gross profit analysis also shows that increases in sales prices exceeded the increased cost of goods sold, thus helping to maintain the gross profit at close to the total of the preceding year despite the reduction in sales. It thus appears that the increased net income for 1972 for the Marshall Company was the result of rising sales prices rather than greater managerial efficiency.

It was assumed that the Marshall Company sold a single commodity. If several commodities are sold, data would have to be assembled and separate schedules developed with respect to sales, sales prices, and costs for each. Analyses of the gross profit variations relating to each class of sales could then be prepared. When many commodities are sold and price changes are numerous, such refined analyses may become extremely complicated.

Although the analysis of gross profit variation may be of value to certain external groups, the analysis requires information concerning the change in the volume of sales that is not ordinarily found on the published financial statements. In some cases, such data may be provided in the annual reports. In other cases, information in the annual reports may have to be supplemented by reference to other sources, by special research and inquiry, or by estimates.

Break-even point analysis

Financial statements are frequently analyzed to arrive at the level of sales that will cover all of the expenses, referred to as the business unit's *break-even point*. At the break-even point operations of the business would result in neither income nor loss.

Measurement of a company's break-even point requires a determination of its *variable expenses*, those expenses that fluctuate with the volume of sales, and its *fixed expenses*, those expenses that remain constant regardless of the volume of sales. In a retail business, variable expenses include cost of goods sold, sales commissions, shipping supplies, and similar items that are affected by the volume of sales; fixed expenses include store depreciation, property taxes, administrative salaries, and similar items that are not affected by the volume of sales. In a manufacturing business, variable expenses include raw materials and direct labor; fixed expenses include depreciation of factory properties, factory management salaries, and similar items that are not affected by production volume. Selling and administrative expenses that fluctuate with sales would be recognized as variable; selling and administrative expenses that are not affected by sales would be recognized as fixed. Since income taxes apply only after the break-even point is reached, this charge would not be included for purposes of break-even point analysis. In disregarding income taxes, any earnings that may be designated in relationship to the break-even point would be before adjustment for income taxes.

If all expenses vary in direct proportion to sales and sales are made at a price in excess of such expenses, there is no break-even point, for income arises with the first sale. Whenever fixed expenses exist, however, sales must cover both variable and fixed expenses in reaching the break-even point. Stated differently, sales after covering variable expenses serve to absorb fixed expenses; the break-even point is reached when the excess of sales over variable expenses just equals the amount of fixed expenses. Income arises only when the sales figure exceeds the sum of the variable and fixed expenses.

The ratio of variable expenses to the sales dollar is commonly referred to as the *variable expense ratio*. The part of the sales dollar after deducting variable expenses that becomes available to cover fixed expenses and to provide earnings is referred to as *marginal income*. Marginal income expressed in terms of the sales dollar is called the *marginal income ratio* or the *profit-volume ratio*, commonly designated the *P/V ratio*. Marginal income that exceeds fixed expenses provides income. The amount by which total sales exceed sales at the break-even point is referred to as the *margin of safety*. The relationship of this excess to total sales is referred to as the margin of safety ratio, commonly designated the *M/S ratio*.

The break-even point can be arrived at by means of a chart or it can be arrived at mathematically. In either case, two amounts must be known: (1) the total fixed expenses of all categories — production, selling, and general and administrative; and (2) the relationship of variable expenses of all categories to the sales figure. The break-even point can be determined graphically by plotting fixed and variable expenses and sales information on a chart. When the maximum sales that can be achieved at full capacity or production are known, an analysis of income or loss at any sales level can be developed. To illustrate, assume the following for the Eastern Manufacturing Company:

(a) Variable expenses are 40% of sales.
(b) Total fixed expenses are $180,000.
(c) Maximum sales volume at full capacity is $500,000.

These data are plotted on the chart at the top of the opposite page.

The chart indicates that sales of $300,000 must be reached to break even; stated differently, 60% of full capacity must be achieved. This is the point where the total expense line and the sales line intersect. At this point variable expenses are $120,000 (40% of $300,000) and fixed expenses are $180,000.

The income or loss at different sales volumes can also be determined from the chart. The lower the sales figure below the break-even point, the greater the loss; the higher the sales figure above the break-even point, the greater the income. Sales of $250,000, for example, will result in a loss of $30,000 ($250,000 − [(40% of $250,000) + $180,000]); sales of $400,000 will produce income of $60,000 ($400,000 − [(40% of $400,000) + $180,000]). Maximum sales will result in income of $120,000 ($500,000 − [(40% of $500,000) + $180,000]). With sales at $400,000, a margin of safety of 25% would be achieved (sales in excess of sales at break-even point, $100,000 ÷ sales, $400,000).

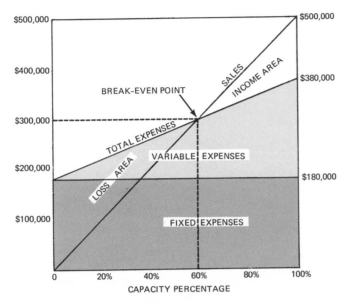

Break-even chart

The break-even chart can be constructed in a manner that shows readily the amount of marginal income at any sales volume. A graph prepared in an alternate manner, using the facts that were given in the foregoing example, follows:

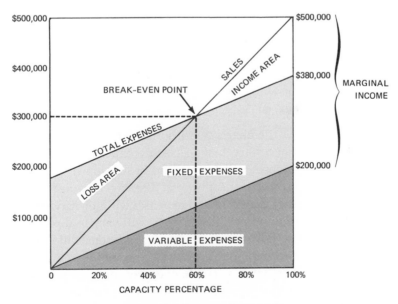

Break-even chart showing marginal income

If sales at the break-even point are to be arrived at mathematically, calculations are made in the following manner. Let S equal sales at the break-even point. Then S is equal to the sum of the variable expenses, which are 40% of sales, plus the fixed expenses of $180,000:

$$\begin{aligned} S &= .40S + \$180,000 \\ S - .40S &= \$180,000 \\ .60S &= \$180,000 \\ S &= \$300,000 \end{aligned}$$

The break-even point can also be calculated by employing the P/V ratio described earlier. The P/V ratio or the portion of the sales dollar available for meeting fixed expenses in the example above is .60 (sales, 1.00 − variable expenses, .40). The following calculation is made:

$$\begin{aligned} S &= \$180,000 \div .60 \\ S &= \$300,000 \end{aligned}$$

It should be noted that an increase in variable expenses or in fixed expenses or a decrease in sales price will raise the break-even point. On the other hand, a decrease in variable expenses or in fixed expenses or an increase in sales price will lower the break-even point. A change in the product sales mix, assuming that different products produce varying marginal income rates, will change the aggregate P/V ratio and thus also increase or decrease the sales volume necessary to break even.

Income or loss at different sales volumes can also be arrived at mathematically. The M/S and P/V ratios are employed and the following calculation is made:

$$\text{Sales} \times \text{M/S} \times \text{P/V}$$

To illustrate, assume that sales of $400,000 are expected by the company previously referred to. The M/S ratio is .25 ([sales, $400,000 − sales at break-even point, $300,000] ÷ sales, $400,000); the P–V ratio is .60 (sales, 1.00 − variable expenses, .40). The following calculation is made:

Income at $400,000 sales level = $400,000 × .25 × .60, or $60,000.

In developing the charts and also the measurements that have been illustrated, it is necessary first to classify expenses as fixed or variable. Semivariable expenses will have to be broken down into their fixed or variable components for this purpose. Break-even point analysis is based on the assumptions that the fixed expenses will not vary regardless of the level of sales and that variable expenses will vary in direct proportion to sales. Obviously, however, such exact conditions will seldom be found in practice. Fixed expenses may vary to some degree depending upon sales; on the other hand, variable expenses may not vary in direct proportion to sales. For example, economies of purchasing and production may serve to lower certain variable expenses; many expenses, both variable and fixed, may rise sharply upon reaching a certain volume and may contract markedly below a certain level. When actual conditions vary from the assumptions that are required in developing the break-even analysis, the limitations that are found in such measurement should be understood. It should be recognized that although the basic assumptions of break-even analysis may not hold over the entire potential volume of the company, they may be realistic over the normal or relevant range of production volume.

Many practical applications may be made of break-even analysis. Break-even information is useful in predicting the effect upon earnings of an increase or a decrease in sales volumes. For example, if it is predicted that operations of the Eastern Manufacturing Company, referred to on page 886, will reach 90% of capacity, income would be estimated at $90,000 ($450,000 − [$180,000 + 40% of $450,000]). This information may suggest future policy with respect to property acquisitions, loans, and dividend payments.

Break-even point analysis may be particularly valuable in making decisions concerning the expansion of building facilities. For example, assume that the Eastern Manufacturing Company, in view of operations at 90% capacity or sales at $450,000, considers an expansion in building facilities that will raise maximum sales possibilities to $800,000 but will raise fixed expenses to $240,000. Assume that variable expenses in either case are 40% of sales. The following calculations may be made:

	Under Present Conditions	Under Proposed Conditions
Sales at break-even point (S):	$S = .40S + \$180,000$, or $300,000	$S = .40S + \$240,000$, or $400,000
Income, assuming sales at 90% of present capacity or $450,000:	$450,000 − [(40% of $450,000) + $180,000], or $90,000	$450,000 − [(40% of $450,000) + $240,000], or $30,000
Sales necessary to reach income of $90,000 (S'):	$S' = .40S' + \$180,000 + \$90,000$, or $450,000	$S' = .40S' + \$240,000 + \$90,000$, or $550,000
Maximum income at full capacity:	$500,000 − [(40% of $500,000) + $180,000], or $120,000	$800,000 − [(40% of $800,000) + $240,000], or $240,000

In deciding whether expansion is warranted at this stage, the increased break-even point, the decreased earnings if sales remain $450,000, and the increased sales required to produce the same amount of earnings would be weighed against the increased sales and earnings potentials.

It is obvious that break-even point analysis is of great importance to management in arriving at many decisions involving production, sales promotion, pricing, and property expansion. However, break-even analysis is also important to the external user of financial information for the interpretations and conclusions that he is required to make. For example, a determination of the break-even point is certainly of high significance to the creditor and to the ownership groups in a period of economic decline; on the other hand, a determination of the limits upon earnings as established by break-even point analysis is equally important to these groups in a period of economic advance. It may not be possible to develop break-even analyses directly from the published financial statements. However, when such information is important to the external user but is not supplied by the company, he may use whatever relevant information is made available in the annual reports and supplement such data by reference to other sources, by special inquiry, or by estimates.

QUESTIONS

1. What groups may be interested in a company's financial statements?

2. Explain how an understanding of accounting assists in the analysis and interpretation of financial statements.

3. What are the factors that one would look for in judging a company's (a) liquidity, (b) stability, (c) profitability?

4. Distinguish between horizontal and vertical analytical procedures. What special purpose does each serve?

5. What type of information is provided by analysis of comparative changes in financial position that is not available from analysis of comparative balance sheets and income statements?

6. When data for more than two years are available, what are the advantages of developing comparisons in terms of the earliest year given? What are the advantages of developing comparisons in terms of the preceding year?

7. What are the relative advantages of changes reported as percentages as compared with changes reported as ratios?

8. Mention some factors that may limit the comparability of financial statements of two companies in the same industry.

9. What is meant by a *thirteen-month year*? What advantages and disadvantages can you suggest in the use of such a year for accounting purposes?

10. What is meant by a *common-size* statement? What are its advantages?

11. What factors may be responsible for a change in a company's net income from one year to the next?

12. What factors may be responsible for a change in a company's gross profit from one year to the next?

13. (a) The Marsh Co. reports an increase in gross profit in 1972 over 1971 of $60,000. What other information would be useful in the evaluation of this increase? (b) Give possible unfavorable factors that might accompany an increase in gross profit.

14. The Atlas Co. develops the following measurements for 1972 as compared with the year 1971. What additional information would you require before arriving at favorable or unfavorable conclusions for each item?

    (a) Net income has increased $70,000.
    (b) Sales returns and allowances have increased by $25,000.
    (c) The gross profit rate has increased by 5%.
    (d) Purchases discounts have increased by $5,000.
    (e) Working capital has increased by $85,000.
    (f) Accounts receivable have increased by $150,000.
    (g) Inventories have decreased by $100,000.
    (h) Retained earnings have decreased by $300,000.

15. What is meant by the joint sales price-volume factor? Why do total sales decline as a result of this factor if *either* sales price or sales volume declines?

16. Distinguish between fixed expenses and variable expenses.

17. (a) What is meant by a company's break-even point? (b) How is it calculated? (c) Suggest certain practical applications for external users that can be made of break-even point analysis.

18. (a) What is meant by the P/V ratio? (b) What is meant by the M/S ratio? (c) Define marginal income.

19. What are the basic assumptions that underlie a break-even chart? Are these assumptions realistic in relation to a company's operations?

20. Assuming the same total revenue and expense figures at full production for two companies, what factor will result in a lower break-even point for one company than for the other?

EXERCISES

1. Indicate the dollar change, the percentage change, and also the ratio that would be reported for each case below, assuming horizontal analysis:

Gain (loss) on sale of investments:

	1972	1971			1972	1971
(a)	$45,000	$20,000		(f)	$(30,000)	0
(b)	20,000	40,000		(g)	5,000	$(5,000)
(c)	30,000	0		(h)	(20,000)	5,000
(d)	0	40,000		(i)	(10,000)	(10,000)
(e)	(30,000)	10,000		(j)	20,000	20,000

2. Sales for the Fowler Company for a five-year period and an industry sales index for this period are listed below. Convert both series into indexes employing 1968 as the base year.

	1972	1971	1970	1969	1968
Sales of Fowler Company (in thousands of dollars)	$5,500	$6,160	$6,270	$5,445	$5,170
Industry sales index (1958–60 = 100)......	180	270	216	198	171

3. From the following data for Pritchett Importers, explain the causes for the reduction in net income supported by a detailed analysis of the causes for the change in gross profit.

		1972		1971
Sales	250,000 units @ $4.20	$1,050,000	200,000 units @ $4	$800,000
Cost of goods sold		700,000		400,000
Gross profit on sales		$ 350,000		$400,000
Operating expenses		150,000		100,000
Net income		$ 200,000		$300,000

4. Comparative data for the Weston Co. appear below:

	1972	1971
Sales..............................	$6,875,000	$5,000,000
Cost of goods sold....................	3,875,000	3,000,000
Gross profit on sales...................	$3,000,000	$2,000,000

(a) Assume that sales prices in 1972 average 25% above those for 1971. What part of the change in gross profit is due to changes in the sales volume, in the sales price, and in the gross profit rate?

(b) Assume, instead, that a single commodity is sold, and that the sales price of this commodity was $2.50 in 1971 and $2.75 in 1972. Prepare a statement analyzing the change in gross profit in terms of volume and price changes for both sales and costs.

5. It is determined that the variable expenses for the Henry Company are 60% of sales. Sales at capacity operations are $1,000,000. What are sales at the break-even point, assuming that total fixed expenses are (a) $150,000, and (b) $450,000?

6. The total fixed expenses for the Ashcraft Mfg. Co. are $150,000; variable expenses are 25% of the product sales price. Units sell for $5 each. (a) How many units must be sold for the company to break even? (b) How many units must be sold for the company to realize income before income taxes of $75,000?

7. The Maston Corporation shows the following results for 1972:

Sales.....................................		$500,000
Fixed expenses............................	$360,000	
Variable expenses.........................	100,000	460,000
Income before income taxes.................		$ 40,000

Operations during 1972 were at 80% of capacity. Management assumes that capacity can be increased 50% by building remodeling and enlargement, which will increase fixed expenses by $200,000 annually. Variable expenses are expected to remain at 20% of sales.

(a) Compute sales at the break-even point under both current and proposed conditions.
(b) Compute the pretax income at full capacity under both current and proposed conditions.
(c) Compute the sales necessary under the proposed plan to reach the equivalent of maximum pretax income under current conditions.

8. The Roy Co. has sales of $900,000, an M/S ratio of .40, and a P/V ratio of .30.

(a) What is the company's break-even point?
(b) What are the fixed expenses?
(c) What is the income before income taxes?

9. The Slack Corporation is operating at full capacity, selling 100,000 units annually for $10 each. Fixed expenses are $300,000 and the marginal income rate is 50%. Calculate the effect upon the break-even point and the maximum pretax income potential of each of the following independent alternatives proposed by the company's controller:

(a) Capacity is to be expanded by 20%. This will require an increase in fixed expenses to $400,000. Variable expenses per unit and sales prices will remain constant.
(b) Selling price per unit is to be raised to $12.50.

PROBLEMS

24-1. Operations of the Owens Co. for 1972 and 1971 are summarized below:

	1972	1971
Sales..................................	$260,000	$210,000
Sales returns..........................	10,000	10,000
Net sales..............................	$250,000	$200,000
Cost of goods sold.....................	180,000	120,000
Gross profit on sales..................	$ 70,000	$ 80,000
Selling and general expenses...........	65,000	50,000
Operating income......................	$ 5,000	$ 30,000
Other expense items...................	20,000	10,000
Income (loss) before income taxes......	$(15,000)	$ 20,000
Income taxes..........................		10,000
Net income (loss).....................	$(15,000)	$ 10,000

Instructions: (1) Prepare a comparative income statement showing dollar changes and percentage changes for 1972 as compared with 1971.

(2) Prepare a comparative income statement offering a percentage analysis of component revenue and expense items in terms of net sales for each year.

(3) Prepare a statement accounting for the variation in net income for 1972 as compared with 1971.

24-2. The financial position of Andersons, Inc., at the end of 1972 and at the end of 1971 are summarized below:

Assets	1972	1971
Current assets:		
Cash on hand and on deposit..................	$ 40,000	$ 50,000
U.S. Government securities, at cost.............	60,000	80,000
Notes and accounts receivable, less allowance....	300,000	240,000
Raw materials and supplies...................	300,000	200,000
Goods in process...........................	200,000	160,000
Finished goods.............................	450,000	300,000
Miscellaneous prepaid items.................	20,000	20,000
Total current assets..........................	$1,370,000	$1,050,000
Investments:		
Bond redemption fund.......................	$ 300,000	$ 200,000
Investment in properties not in current use......	250,000	250,000
Total investments...........................	$ 550,000	$ 450,000

(continued on next page)

	1972	1971
Land, buildings, and equipment at cost, less accumulated depreciation..........................	$ 720,000	$ 800,000
Intangible assets.............................	$ 120,000	$ 150,000
Other assets:		
Unamortized bond issue costs................	$ 24,000	$ 30,000
Machinery rearrangement costs..............	16,000	20,000
Total other assets.........................	$ 40,000	$ 50,000
Total assets................................	$2,800,000	$2,500,000

Liabilities

Current liabilities:

	1972	1971
Notes and accounts payable.................	$ 210,000	$ 140,000
Income taxes payable......................	40,000	20,000
Accrued payrolls, interest, and taxes...........	40,000	25,000
Cash dividends payable.....................	15,000	10,000
Miscellaneous payables.....................	5,000	5,000
Total current liabilities.....................	$ 310,000	$ 200,000
Long-term debt — 10-year first-mortgage bonds....	300,000	250,000
Estimated employee pensions payable...........	90,000	120,000
Deferred revenues..........................	10,000	20,000
Total liabilities............................	$ 710,000	$ 590,000

Stockholders' Equity

Paid-in capital:

	1972	1971
5% Preferred stock, $25 par.................	$ 500,000	$ 500,000
No-par common stock, $10 stated value........	500,000	500,000
Additional paid-in capital...................	650,000	650,000
Total paid-in capital.......................	$1,650,000	$1,650,000

Retained earnings:

	1972	1971
Appropriated..............................	$ 200,000	$ 160,000
Free.....................................	240,000	100,000
Total retained earnings.....................	$ 440,000	$ 260,000
Total stockholders' equity.....................	$2,090,000	$1,910,000
Total liabilities and stockholders' equity..........	$2,800,000	$2,500,000

Instructions: (1) Prepare a comparative balance sheet showing dollar changes and changes in terms of ratios for 1972 as compared with 1971.

(2) Prepare a common-size balance sheet comparing financial structure ratios for 1972 with those for 1971.

24-3. Financial statements for the Carter Mfg. Co. are given below and on pages 897 and 898.

Carter Mfg. Co.
Balance Sheet
December 31, 1972, 1971 and 1970

Assets	1972	1971	1970
Current assets....................	$1,200,000	$1,000,000	$ 700,000
Investments.......................	300,000	250,000	300,000
Land, buildings, and equipment (net)..	1,320,000	1,000,000	1,050,000
Intangible assets...................	180,000	150,000	150,000
Total assets......................	$3,000,000	$2,400,000	$2,200,000

Liabilities			
Current liabilities..................	$ 300,000	$ 400,000	$ 240,000
Long-term debt (5%)..............	300,000	200,000	200,000
Deferred revenues..................	10,000	40,000	20,000
Total liabilities...................	$ 610,000	$ 640,000	$ 460,000

Stockholders' Equity			
6% Cumulative, nonparticipating preferred stock, $50 par..............	$ 500,000	$ 500,000	$ 500,000
Common stock, $50 par.............	1,500,000	1,000,000	1,000,000
Additional paid-in capital...........	350,000	250,000	250,000
Retained earnings (deficit)..........	40,000	10,000	(10,000)
Total stockholders' equity...........	$2,390,000	$1,760,000	$1,740,000
Total liabilities and stockholders' equity	$3,000,000	$2,400,000	$2,200,000

Carter Mfg. Co.
Income Statement
For Years Ended December 31, 1972, 1971 and 1970

	1972	1971	1970
Gross sales.......................	$2,800,000	$2,400,000	$1,800,000
Sales returns.....................	100,000	80,000	50,000
Net sales.........................	$2,700,000	$2,320,000	$1,750,000
Finished goods inventory, Jan. 1.....	$ 320,000	$ 210,000	$ 220,000
Cost of goods manufactured........	1,840,000	1,630,000	1,230,000
Goods available for sale............	$2,160,000	$1,840,000	$1,450,000
Finished goods inventory, Dec. 31....	360,000	320,000	210,000
Cost of goods sold.................	$1,800,000	$1,520,000	$1,240,000
Gross profit on sales..............	$ 900,000	$ 800,000	$ 510,000

(continued on next page)

Selling expense.....................	$ 560,000	$ 480,000	$ 400,000
General and administrative expense...	180,000	160,000	150,000
Total operating expenses............	$ 740,000	$ 640,000	$ 550,000
Operating income (loss).............	$ 160,000	$ 160,000	$ (40,000)
Other revenue items................	40,000	40,000	30,000
	$ 200,000	$ 200,000	$ (10,000)
Other expense items................	40,000	20,000	10,000
Income (loss) before income taxes....	$ 160,000	$ 180,000	$ (20,000)
Income taxes......................	80,000	90,000	
Net income (loss).................	$ 80,000	$ 90,000	$ (20,000)

Carter Mfg. Co.
Schedule of Cost of Goods Manufactured
For Years Ended December 31, 1972, 1971 and 1970

	1972	1971	1970
Raw materials inventory, Jan. 1......	$ 210,000	$ 160,000	$ 180,000
Raw materials purchases............	1,080,000	920,000	600,000
	$1,290,000	$1,080,000	$ 780,000
Raw materials inventory, Dec. 31....	300,000	210,000	160,000
Cost of raw materials used...........	$ 990,000	$ 870,000	$ 620,000
Direct labor......................	500,000	440,000	360,000
Manufacturing overhead............	390,000	360,000	300,000
	$1,880,000	$1,670,000	$1,280,000
Goods in process inventory, Jan. 1....	250,000	210,000	160,000
	$2,130,000	$1,880,000	$1,440,000
Goods in process inventory, Dec. 31...	290,000	250,000	210,000
Cost of goods manufactured.........	$1,840,000	$1,630,000	$1,230,000

Carter Mfg. Co.
Retained Earnings Statement
For Years Ended December 31, 1972, 1971 and 1970

	1972	1971	1970
Retained earnings (deficit), Jan. 1....	$ 10,000	$ (10,000)	$ 10,000
Net income (loss) per income statement	80,000	90,000	(20,000)
	$ 90,000	$ 80,000	$ (10,000)
Cash dividends:			
Preferred stock...................	$ 30,000	$ 60,000	
Common stock...................	20,000	10,000	
Total..........................	$ 50,000	$ 70,000	
Retained earnings (deficit), Dec. 31...	$ 40,000	$ 10,000	$ (10,000)

Carter Mfg. Co.
Statement of Changes in Financial Position
For Years Ended December 31, 1972, 1971 and 1970

	1972	1971	1970
Working capital was provided by:			
Income from operations..................	$ 80,000	$ 90,000	$ (20,000)
Add expenses not requiring outlay of working capital:			
Depreciation........................	70,000	65,000	60,000
Increase in deferred revenues representing source of working capital.......		20,000	10,000
Total..........................	$150,000	$175,000	$ 50,000
Less revenues not representing source of working capital:			
Deferred revenues...................	30,000		
Working capital provided by operations..	$120,000	$175,000	$ 50,000
Issuance of bonds.....................	100,000		
Issuance of common stock..............	600,000		
Sale of investments...................		50,000	
	$820,000	$225,000	$ 50,000
Working capital was applied to:			
Dividends...........................	$ 50,000	$ 70,000	$ 40,000
Intangible assets......................	30,000		
Investments..........................	50,000		75,000
Land, buildings, and equipment........	390,000	15,000	110,000
Total..........................	$520,000	$ 85,000	$ 225,000
Increase (decrease) in working capital.....	$300,000	$140,000	$ (175,000)

Instructions: Prepare comparative statements for the three-year period showing dollar and percentage changes in terms of 1970, which is to be considered the base year.

24-4. (1) From the data for the Carter Mfg. Co. given in Problem 24-3, develop a comparative income statement for the three-year period, offering percentage analysis of component revenue and expense items in terms of net sales for each period.

(2) Prepare a comparative schedule of cost of goods manufactured for the three-year period in support of the comparative income statement, offering percentage analysis of component cost of goods manufactured items in terms of the total cost of goods manufactured for each year.

24-5. (1) From the data for the Carter Mfg. Co. given in Problem 24-3, prepare a condensed common-size balance sheet comparing financial structure percentages for the three-year period.

(2) What analytical conclusions can be drawn from this common-size statement?

24-6. From the data for the Carter Mfg. Co. given in Problem 24-3, prepare statements accounting for the variation in net income (1) for 1972 as compared with 1970, and (2) for 1972 as compared with 1971. (Use the form illustrated on page 881.)

24-7. Sales for Harper Mfg. Co. and its chief competitor, the Allen Company, and the sales index for the industry, are given below:

	1972	1971	1970	1969	1968
Sales of Harper Mfg. Co. (in thousands of dollars).	$6,500	$7,280	$7,735	$8,450	$8,385
Sales of Allen Company (in thousands of dollars).	$9,500	$9,690	$9,975	$9,785	$9,880
Industry sales index (1960 = 100).........	140	154	161	147	133

Instructions: (1) Convert the three series to index numbers using 1968 as the base year.

(2) Prepare a short report for the management of Harper Mfg. Co. summarizing your findings.

24-8. The Lloyd Corp., which sells a single commodity, shows the following operating results for a three-year period:

	1972	1971	1970
Sales......................	$6,200,000	$6,000,000	$4,500,000
Cost of goods sold...........	4,216,000	4,200,000	2,500,000
Gross profit on sales...........	$1,984,000	$1,800,000	$2,000,000
Operating expenses...........	1,400,000	1,400,000	1,200,000
Net income.................	$ 584,000	$ 400,000	$ 800,000

Sales prices of the commodity sold were as follows: in 1972, $2.50; in 1971, $2.40; in 1970, $2.25.

Instructions: Prepare statements for 1972 and 1971 analyzing the change in gross profit as compared with the year immediately preceding in terms of volume changes and price changes for both sales and costs.

24-9. Revenue and expense data of David & Paul, Inc., for 1972 and 1971 follow:

	1972	1971
Sales.....................................	$3,450,000	$2,000,000
Cost of goods sold......................	2,400,000	800,000
Gross profit on sales......................	$1,050,000	$1,200,000
Operating expenses......................	550,000	500,000
Net income...........................	$ 500,000	$ 700,000

Instructions: Prepare a statement analyzing the variation in gross profit, giving as much information as can be determined concerning factors responsible for the change, under each of the following assumptions:

(1) No data are available relative to price and volume changes.

(2) Sales prices in 1972 are 20% above sales prices in 1971.

(3) Total units sold in 1972 are 25% above total units sold in 1971.

24-10. Total fixed expenses for the Stratton Mfg. Co. are $350,000; the variable expenses are $300,000 at full capacity. The estimated sales price of goods sold at full capacity is $1,000,000. Assume that fixed expenses are constant and that variable expenses vary in direct proportion to sales. Assume an income tax rate of 45%.

Instructions: (1) Draw a chart showing the sales at the break-even point and the net income after income taxes on sales beyond the break-even point.

(2) Calculate sales at the break-even point, assuming estimates to be the same except that the total expenses of $650,000 at full capacity consist of fixed expenses, $450,000, and variable expenses, $200,000.

24-11. The following data are determined for the Waldron Co.: up to 40% activity or sales, the fixed expenses are $500,000; above 40%, the fixed expenses are $600,000. The variable expenses are estimated as follows:

Rate of Activity or Sales	Estimated Variable Expenses	Rate of Activity or Sales	Estimated Variable Expenses
10%	$300,000	60%	$620,000
20%	400,000	70%	740,000
30%	460,000	80%	775,000
40%	500,000	90%	790,000
50%	600,000	100%	800,000

The sales at 100% capacity are assumed to be $2,000,000.

Instructions: Construct a chart and determine the approximate break-even point.

24-12. The Tolboe Co. presents the following summary relating to current activities at capacity and estimated activities at capacity with proposed enlarged facilities:

	With Present Facilities		With Enlarged Facilities	
Sales		$1,000,000		$1,500,000
Fixed expenses	$450,000		$750,000	
Variable expenses	250,000	700,000	300,000	1,050,000
Income before income taxes		$ 300,000		$ 450,000

Instructions: (1) Calculate the sales that are required at the break-even point under present and under proposed conditions.

(2) Calculate the sales that are required under proposed conditions in reaching present income at full capacity.

(3) Calculate the result from operations under proposed conditions if sales do not exceed the present dollar amount.

24-13. The Jones Corporation, which has been operating at full capacity, shows the following results for 1972:

Sales..................................		$6,000,000
Fixed expenses........................	$3,000,000	
Variable expenses.....................	2,400,000	5,400,000
Income before income taxes..............		$ 600,000

Management assumes that sales can be increased 50% by improving and enlarging the plant. It is estimated that such a program will increase fixed expenses by 40%; however, variable expenses are expected to decrease about 15% in terms of sales as a result of the improved plant facilities, thus resulting in a P/V ratio of .75.

Instructions: (1) Calculate sales at the break-even point under present conditions and under proposed conditions.

(2) Calculate the sales necessary under proposed conditions if the current pretax income is to be maintained.

(3) Calculate the pretax income if operations under proposed conditions reach 80% of capacity.

(4) Calculate the maximum pretax income that can be realized under proposed conditions.

24-14. The Dawn Mining Company mines selum, a commonly used mineral. Following is the company's report of operations:

	1972	1971	Increase (Decrease)
Net sales.....................	$891,000	$ 840,000	$ 51,000
Cost of goods sold.............	688,500	945,000	(256,500)
Gross profit (loss).............	$202,500	$(105,000)	$307,500

The following information pertains to the company's operations:

(a) The sales price of selum was increased from $8 per ton to $11 per ton on January 1, 1972.

(b) New mining machinery was placed in operation on January 1, 1972, that reduced the cost of mining from $9 per ton to $8.50 per ton.

(c) There was no change in ending inventories which were valued on the lifo basis.

Instructions: Prepare an analysis accounting for the change in the gross profit of The Dawn Mining Company. The analysis should account for the effects of the changes in price, volume, and volume-price factors upon (1) sales and (2) cost of goods sold.

(AICPA adapted)

24-15. The president of the Redbrick Tile Company is concerned because his gross profit has decreased from $130,000 in 1971 to $87,960 in 1972. He asks you to prepare an analysis of the causes of change.

You find that the company operates two plants, each as a separate unit. Investigation reveals the following information:

Plant No. 1 (makes a variety of products)

	1972	1971
Sales....................................	$200,000	$300,000
Cost of sales..............................	160,000	210,000
Gross profit.............................	$ 40,000	$ 90,000

Plant No. 2 (makes only one product)

	1972 Amount	1972 Per Unit	1971 Amount	1971 Per Unit
Sales................	$112,200	$10.20	$100,000	$10.00
Cost of sales..........	64,240	5.84	60,000	6.00
Gross profit..........	$ 47,960	$ 4.36	$ 40,000	$ 4.00

Instructions: Prepare a detailed analysis of the causes for the change in gross profit for each of the plants to the extent that the above data permit such an analysis. Critical comment on the analysis is not required.

(AICPA adapted)

24-16. You are preparing your long-form report in connection with the audit of the City Gas Company at December 31, 1972. The report will include an explanation of the 1972 increase in operating revenues.

The following information is available from the company records:

	1971	1972	Increase (Decrease)
Average number of customers..	27,000	26,000	(1,000)
MCF sales..................	486,000	520,000	34,000
Revenue...................	$1,215,000	$1,274,000	$59,000

Instructions: To explain the 1972 increase in operating revenues, prepare an analysis accounting for the effect of changes in:
   (1) Average number of customers.
   (2) Average gas consumption per customer.
   (3) Average rate per MCF sold (MCF = thousand cubic feet).

(AICPA adapted)

24-17. A client has recently leased manufacturing facilities for production of a new product. Based on studies made by his staff, the following data have been made available to you:

Estimated annual sales....................	24,000 units	

	Amount	Per Unit
Estimated costs:		
Materials...............................	$ 96,000	$4.00
Direct labor...........................	14,400	.60
Overhead..............................	24,000	1.00
Administrative expense....................	28,800	1.20
Total................................	$163,200	$6.80

Selling expenses are expected to be 15% of sales and profit is to amount to $1.02 per unit.

Instructions: (1) Compute the selling price per unit.

(2) Project an income statement for the year.

(3) Compute a break-even point expressed in dollars and in units assuming that overhead and administrative expenses are fixed but that other expenses are fully variable.

(AICPA adapted)

24-18. The Clark Metals Co. manufactures three different models of a single product. The following data are available:

Model Number	Annual Sales Budget (Units)	Budgeted Unit Sales Price	Budgeted Sales Allowances for a Year
100.........................	30,000	$15.00	$1,260
200.........................	16,000	18.00	480
300.........................	10,000	25.00	410

1972 Estimates

Model Number	Quantity Budgeted for Production	Overall Estimated Expense per Unit		
		Total	Variable Expense	Fixed Expense
100.......	30,500	$15.072	$ 9.871	$5.201
200.......	15,000	17.335	10.250	7.085
300.......	10,000	23.756	15.436	8.320

Instructions: Prepare a schedule, supported by computations, showing the sales quantity and the sales dollar figure for each model necessary to enable the company to cover its expenses.

(AICPA adapted)

24-19. The president of Eastern Company wants guidance on the advisability of eliminating Product C, one of the company's three similar products, or investing in new machinery to reduce the cost of Product C in the hope of reversing Product C's operating loss sustained in 1972. The three similar products are manufactured in a single plant in about the same amount of floor space and the markets in which they are sold are very competitive.

Below is the condensed statement of operating income for the company and for Product C for the year ended October 31, 1972.

Eastern Company

Statement of Operating Income

For Year Ended October 31, 1972

	All Three Products	Product C
Sales...........................	$2,800,150	$350,000
Cost of goods sold:		
Raw materials...................	$ 565,000	$ 80,000
Labor:		
Direct.........................	1,250,000	150,000
Indirect (fixed expense)..........	55,000	18,000
Fringe benefits (15% of labor)......	195,750	25,200
Royalties (1% of Product C sales).....	3,500	3,500
Maintenance and repairs.............	6,000	2,000
Factory supplies....................	15,000	2,100
Depreciation (straight-line)..........	25,200	7,100
Electrical power....................	25,000	3,000
Scrap and spoilage.................	4,300	600
Cost of goods sold...............	$2,144,750	$291,500
Gross profit on sales..................	$ 655,400	$ 58,500
Selling, general and administrative expenses:		
Sales commissions..................	$ 120,000	$ 15,000
Officers salaries.	32,000	10,500
Other wages and salaries............	14,000	5,300
Fringe benefits (15% of wages, salaries,		
and commissions).................	24,900	4,620
Delivery expense....................	79,500	10,000
Advertising expense (variable)........	195,100	26,000
Miscellaneous fixed expenses..........	31,900	10,630
Total selling, general and administrative expenses.....................	$ 497,400	$ 82,050
Operating income (loss)...............	$ 158,000	$(23,550)

Instructions: (Disregard income taxes.) (1) Prepare a schedule showing the contribution of Product C to the recovery of fixed expenses (marginal income) for the year ended October 31, 1972. Assume that each element of expense is entirely fixed or variable within the relevant range and that the change in inventory levels has been negligible.

(2) Assume that in fiscal 1972 the variable expenses of Product C totaled $297,500 and that its fixed expenses amounted to $75,100. Prepare a schedule computing the break-even point of Product C in terms of annual dollar sales volume. Sales for 1972 amounted to $350,000.

(3) The direct labor expenses of Product C could have been reduced by $75,000 and the indirect labor expenses by $4,000 by investing an additional $340,000 (financed with 5% bonds) in machinery with a ten-year life and an estimated salvage value of $30,000 at the end of the period. However, the company would have been liable for total severance pay expenses of $18,000 (to be amortized over a five-year period), and electrical power expenses would have increased $500 annually.

Assuming the information given above in part (2), prepare a schedule computing the break-even point of Product C in terms of annual dollar sales volume if the additional machinery had been purchased and installed at the beginning of the year.

(AICPA adapted)

chapter 25

financial statement analysis - special measurements of liquidity and profitability

There are a great many special measurements that may be developed from financial statements and supplementary financial data. Such measurements may be divided into: (1) those that analyze financial position or the *liquidity and stability* of the firm, and (2) those that analyze operations or the *profitability* of the firm. Some of these measurements have special significance to particular groups, while others may be of general interest to all groups. Creditors, for example, are concerned with the ability of a company to pay its current obligations and seek information about the relationship of current assets to current liabilities. Stockholders are concerned with dividends and seek information relating to the earnings per share that will form the basis for dividend declarations. Management is concerned with the liquidity of the merchandise stock and seeks information relating to the number of times goods have turned over during the period. All parties are vitally interested in the profitability of operations and wish to be informed about the relationship of earnings to both liabilities and owners' equities.

A number of measurements developed from the financial data for a single period will be described and illustrated in this chapter. These measurements represent extensions of the vertical analysis procedure. Measurements will also be provided in comparative form and will therefore represent the further application of the horizontal procedure. The analyses that are described and illustrated in this chapter should not be considered all-inclusive; other ratios and measurements may be useful to the various groups, depending upon their particular needs. It should be emphasized again that sound conclusions cannot be reached from an individual ratio or measurement. But this information, together with adequate investigation and study, may lead to a satisfactory interpretation and evaluation of financial data. The analyses that will be presented are based upon the financial statements for the Marshall Company for 1970, 1971, and 1972 that were given in the preceding chapter.

Ratios and measurements developed from balance sheet data

A number of special analyses are developed from balance sheet data. Some of these are based upon current assets and current liabilities and have become generally accepted as measurements of the liquidity of the business unit. Other analyses are based upon noncurrent assets, noncurrent liabilities, and owners' equity, and offer measurements of certain significant relationships within these groups. Although many of the measurements are made directly from the balance sheet, some require the use of income statement data.

Current ratio. The comparison of current assets with current liabilities is regarded as a fundamental measurement of a company's liquidity. Total current assets divided by total current liabilities gives the ratio of current assets to current liabilities, variously referred to as the *current ratio* or the *working capital ratio*.

The current ratio is a valuable measure of the ability of a business unit to meet its current obligations. Since it is a measure of liquidity, care must be taken to determine that the proper items have been included in the current asset and current liability categories. In the past, a ratio of current assets to current liabilities of less than 2 to 1 for a trading or manufacturing unit has frequently been regarded as unsatisfactory. Because liquidity needs are different for different industries and companies, the recognition of any such arbitrary measure is now regarded as inappropriate. However, a comfortable margin of current assets over current liabilities does suggest that a company will be able to meet maturing obligations even in the event of an unfavorable turn in business conditions and losses in the realization of such assets as marketable securities, receivables, and inventories.

In considering current conditions, reference is frequently made to a company's *working capital*. In this text working capital is used to denote the excess of current assets over current liabilities. In some cases the term is used to indicate total current assets. When the term working capital is used to indicate total current assets, the term *net working capital* is used to indicate the excess of current assets over current liabilities. Because of the different uses of the term, the definition that is used for working capital should be ascertained in interpreting working capital analyses.

For the Marshall Company, working capital totals and current ratios for 1972 and 1971 are developed as follows:[1]

	1972	1971
Current assets.......................	$855,000	$955,500
Current liabilities....................	410,000	546,000
Working capital......................	$445,000	$409,500
Current ratio........................	2.1 : 1	1.8 : 1

Ratio calculations are sometimes carried out to two or more decimal places; however, ratios do not need to be carried out beyond one place unless some particularly significant interpretative value is afforded by the more refined measurement. The current ratio just given, as well as the other ratios to be described, can be expressed in terms of percentages. The ratios just given are expressed as percentages as follows:

	1972	1971
Current ratio........................	209%	175%

From the standpoint of liquidity it is more important to consider the ratio of current assets to current liabilities than the amount of working capital. For example, assume balance sheet data for Companies A and B as follows:

Company A: Current assets, $400,000; current liabilities, $50,000.
Company B: Current assets, $1,050,000; current liabilities, $700,000.

Both Company A and Company B have a working capital of $350,000, but Company A has a current ratio of 8:1 while Company B has a current ratio of 1.5:1. The short-term creditors of Company A are more certain of receiving prompt and full payment than those of Company B. On requests for short-term loans, bankers would probably be more favorable to Company A than to Company B.

It is possible, however, to overemphasize the importance of a high current ratio. Assume that a company is normally able to carry on its operations with current assets of $200,000 and current liabilities of $100,000. If the company finds itself with current assets of $500,000, current liabilities remaining at $100,000, its current ratio has increased from 2:1 to 5:1. The company may now have considerably more working capital than it actually requires. It should also be observed that certain unfavorable conditions may be accompanied by an improving ratio. For example, with a slowdown in business and postponement of programs

[1]Comparative data for more than two years are generally required in evaluating financial trends. Analyses for only two years are given in the examples in this chapter, since these are sufficient to illustrate the comparative procedures involved.

for advertising, research, and buildings and equipment repairs and replacements, a company's cash balance may rise. At the same time, slower customer collections may result in rising trade receivables, and reduced sales volume may result in rising inventories.

The amount of working capital required by a particular enterprise depends not only upon its size and its sales activity but also upon the character of its business. For example, a company that does business for cash and maintains a small inventory that turns over rapidly does not require as much working capital as a company with the same volume of business that sells goods on a credit basis and maintains a large inventory that turns over slowly. Working capital requirements may vary, too, depending upon the industry within which the enterprise is found. A construction company may require a large amount of working capital in financing construction activities; a public utility, on the other hand, may require only a small amount of working capital in its operations.

In analyzing working capital position, particular note should be taken of the valuation procedures used for the various assets and liabilities. Inventories reported on a last-in, first-out basis may be substantially below their market values during a period of rising prices; marketable securities reported at cost may be substantially below market; both receivables and payables reported at face or settlement amounts may be considerably above their present values. Special reference should also be made to estimated liabilities and to contingent liabilities in evaluating the effects of possible payment requirements that may differ from reported amounts.

Acid-test ratio. A test of a company's immediate liquidity is made by comparing the sum of cash, marketable securities, notes receivable, and accounts receivable, commonly referred to as the *quick assets*, with current liabilities. The total of the quick assets when divided by current liabilities gives the ratio of quick assets to current liabilities, known as the *acid-test ratio* or *quick ratio*. Considerable time may be required in the conversion of raw materials, goods in process, and finished goods into receivables and then receivables into cash. A company with a satisfactory current ratio may be in an unsatisfactory condition in terms of liquidity when inventories form a significant part of the current asset total. This is revealed by the acid-test ratio. In developing the ratio, close inspection must be given to the receivables and the securities that are included in the quick asset total. There may be instances where such items are actually less liquid than inventories.

Usually a ratio of quick assets to current liabilities of not less than 1 to 1 has been regarded as desirable. Again, however, special conditions applicable to the particular business must be evaluated. Questions such as the following should be considered: What is the composition of the quick assets? What special requirements are made by current activities upon these assets? How soon are the current payables due?

Acid-test ratios for the Marshall Company are computed as follows:

	1972	1971
Quick assets:		
Cash..........................	$ 60,000	$100,500
Marketable securities.........	150,000	150,000
Receivables (net).............	420,000	375,000
Total quick assets............	$630,000	$625,500
Total current liabilities.....	$410,000	$546,000
Acid-test ratio...............	1.5 : 1	1.1 : 1

Other measurements of working capital position. It may be desirable to develop other ratios in analyzing a company's working capital position. For example, it may be useful to show the relationship of total current assets to total assets, and of individual current assets such as receivables and inventories to total current assets. In the case of liabilities, it may be useful to show the relationship of total current liabilities to total liabilities, and of individual current liabilities to total current liabilities. Vertical analysis as applied to comparative statements in the previous chapter made available such data and also reported the changes and the trends in such relationships over a period of years.

The foregoing comparisons may provide information concerning the relative liquidity of total assets and the maturity of total obligations as well as the structure of working capital and shifts within the working capital group. The latter data are significant, since all of the items within the current classification are not equally current. What may be considered reasonable relationships in the analysis of the working capital position will depend upon the particular enterprise.

Analysis of receivables. There are special tests that may be applied in considering the liquidity of two significant working capital elements, receivables and inventories. In both cases, analysis is directed to evaluation of both the amount and the quality of the assets.

Accounts receivable turnover. The amount of receivables usually bears a close relationship to the volume of credit sales. The receivable position and approximate collection time may be evaluated by computing the *accounts receivable turnover*. This rate is determined by dividing net credit sales for the period by the average notes and accounts receivable from trade debtors. In developing an average receivables amount, monthly balances should be used if available; the average is computed from thirteen monthly balances, those of January 1, January 31, February 28, and the last day of each of the remaining months of the year.

Assume in the case of the Marshall Company that all sales are made on a credit basis, that receivables arise only from sales, and that receivable totals for only the beginning and the end of the year are available. Receivable turnover rates are computed as follows:

	1972	1971
Net credit sales.	$1,425,000	$1,650,000
Net receivables:		
Beginning of year.	$ 375,000	$ 333,500
End of year.	$ 420,000	$ 375,000
Average receivables.	$ 397,500	$ 354,250
Receivables turnover for year.	3.6	4.7

Number of days' sales in receivables. Average receivables are sometimes expressed in terms of the *number of days' sales in receivables*. The average time required to collect receivables is thus shown. For example, assume that a business has 300 business or sales days per year. Annual dollar sales are divided by 300 to find average daily sales. Average receivables divided by average daily sales then gives the number of days' sales in average receivables. The latter procedure for the Marshall Company is illustrated below:

	1972	1971
Average receivables.	$ 397,500	$ 354,250
Net sales on account.	$1,425,000	$1,650,000
Average daily sales on account (net sales on account ÷ 300).	$ 4,750	$ 5,500
Number of days' sales in average receivables.	84	64

The same measurements can be obtained by dividing the number of days representing the year by the receivable turnover rates. A comparable number of days for each year should be used in developing comparisons. Computations are generally based on the calendar year consisting of 365 days or a business year consisting of 300 days (365 days less Sundays and holidays).

In certain instances, instead of developing the number of days' sales in average receivables, it may be considered more useful to report the number of days' credit sales in receivables at the end of the period. Data in this form would be of special significance in evaluating current position and particularly the receivable position as of a given date. This information for the Marshall Company is presented below:

	1972	1971
Receivables at end of year	$420,000	$375,000
Average daily credit sales	$ 4,750	$ 5,500
Number of days' credit sales in receivables at end of year	88	68

What constitutes a reasonable number of days in receivables varies with the individual business. For example, if merchandise is sold on terms of net 60 days, 40 days' sales in receivables would not be unreasonable; but if terms are net 30 days, a receivable balance equal to 40 days' sales would indicate slow collections.

Sales activity just before the close of the period should be considered in interpreting the accounts receivable measurements. If sales are unusually light or heavy just before the end of the fiscal period, this affects total receivables as well as the measurements for which they are used. When such unevenness prevails, it may be better to analyze accounts receivable according to their due dates, as was illustrated in Chapter 7.

The problem of keeping accounts receivable at a minimum without losing desirable business is important. The company's investment in receivables usually does not provide revenue. The cost of carrying these accounts must be covered by the margin of profit made on sales. The longer the accounts are carried, the smaller will be the percentage return realized on invested capital. In addition, heavier bookkeeping and collection charges and increased bad debts must be considered.

To attract business, credit is frequently granted for relatively long periods. The element of cost involved in granting long-term credit should be recognized. Assume that a business has an average daily credit sales volume of $5,000 and the average amount of accounts receivable is $250,000. The latter figure represents the average daily credit business for 50 days. If collections and the credit period can be improved so that accounts receivable represent only 30 days' sales, then accounts receivable will be reduced to $150,000. Assuming a total cost of 8 percent to carry and service the accounts, the decrease in accounts of $100,000 would represent an annual savings of $8,000.

Analysis of inventories. Procedures similar to those for evaluating receivables may be employed in evaluating inventory position. Both the number of times the average inventory has been replenished during a fiscal period, known as the *inventory turnover*, and the average time to dispose of an inventory, known as the *number of days' sales in inventories*, may be computed from inventory and cost of goods sold data.

Inventory turnover. The amount of inventory carried in stock frequently bears a close relationship to the sales volume. The inventory position and the approximate disposal time may be evaluated by computing the inventory turnover. The inventory turnover is computed by dividing the cost of goods sold for the period by the average inventory. Whenever possible, monthly figures should be used in developing a representative average inventory balance.

Assume for the Marshall Company that inventory balances for only the beginning and the end of the year are available. Inventory turnover rates are computed as follows:

	1972	1971
Cost of goods sold......................	$1,000,000	$1,200,000
Merchandise inventory:		
Beginning of year.....................	$ 330,000	$ 125,000
End of year.........................	$ 225,000	$ 330,000
Average merchandise inventory............	$ 277,500	$ 227,500
Inventory turnover for year..............	3.6	5.3

Number of days' sales in inventories. Average inventories are sometimes expressed in terms of the number of days' sales in inventories. Information is thus afforded concerning the average time it takes to dispose of the inventory. The number of days' sales in inventories is calculated by dividing the average inventory by the average daily cost of goods sold. When an inventory turnover rate has been computed, the number of days' sales can be obtained by dividing the number of days in the year by the turnover rate for the year. The latter procedure for the Marshall Company is illustrated below:

	1972	1971
Inventory turnover for year.......................	3.6	5.3
Number of days' sales in average inventory (assuming a business year of 300 days).....................	83	57

In certain instances, instead of developing the number of days' sales in average inventories, it may be considered more useful to report the number of days' sales in inventories at the end of the period. The latter measurement is determined by dividing the ending inventory by the average daily cost of goods sold. This information would be helpful in evaluating the current asset position and particularly the inventory position as of a given date.

A company with departmental classifications for merchandise will find it desirable to support the inventory measurements for the company as a whole with individual measurements for each department since there may be considerable variation among departments. A company engaged in manufacturing may compute turnover rates for finished goods, goods in process, and raw materials. The finished goods turnover is computed by dividing the cost of goods sold by the average finished goods inventory. Goods in process turnover is computed by dividing the cost of goods manufactured by the average goods in process inventory. Raw materials turnover is computed by dividing the cost of raw materials used by the average raw materials inventory.

The same valuation methods must be employed for inventories in successive periods if measurements developed from inventory figures are to be comparable. Maximum accuracy in developing measurements is possible if information relating to inventories and cost of goods sold is available in terms of physical units rather than dollar costs.

The effect of seasonal factors on the size of inventories at the end of the period should be considered in the inventory analyses. Inventories may be abnormally high or low at the end of the period. Many companies adopt a fiscal year that ends when operations are at their lowest point. This is referred to as a *natural business year*. Inventories will normally be at their lowest point at the end of such a period. The organization is able to take inventory and complete year-end closing most conveniently. Under such circumstances, monthly inventory balances should be calculated by the gross profit method as illustrated in Chapter 10 in arriving at a representative average inventory figure.

With an increased rate of turnover of the stock of merchandise, the amount of investment necessary for a given volume of business is smaller, and consequently the rate of return on invested capital is higher. This conclusion assumes that the enterprise can acquire goods in smaller quantities sufficiently often at no price disadvantage. If merchandise must be bought in very large quantities in order to get favorable prices, then the savings on quantity purchases must be weighed against the additional investment and the increased costs of storage and other carrying charges.

The financial advantage of an increased turnover rate may be illustrated as follows. Assume that the cost of goods sold for a year was $1,000,000, and the average inventory at cost was $250,000; the rate of turnover, then, was 4 times. Assume, further, that through careful buying the same volume of business can be maintained with turnover of 5 times, or an average inventory of only $200,000. If interest on the money invested in carrying the inventory is 6 percent, the savings on $50,000 will be $3,000 annually. The above does not include possible advantages gained from a decrease in merchandise spoilage and obsolescence, savings in storage costs, insurance, and taxes, and a reduction in the risk of losses from price declines.

Inventory investments and turnover rates vary among different businesses. The facts of each business unit must be judged in terms of the financial structure and the operations of the particular unit. Each business must plan an inventory policy that will avoid the extremes of a dangerously low stock, which may impair sales volume, and an over-stocking of goods involving a heavy capital investment which is attended by dangers that the goods may become shopworn or obsolete, that prices may fall, and that difficulties may arise in meeting the obligations resulting from purchases.

Further analysis of current assets and current liabilities. Turnover analysis applied to the specific receivable and inventory items can be applied to total current assets and to working capital. Current asset turnover is calculated by dividing net sales by average current assets. Working capital turnover is calculated by dividing net sales by the average working capital. The turnover figures may be viewed as the number of times current asset or working capital is replenished, or alternatively, as the number of sales dollars emerging for every dollar invested in current assets or in working capital. Increases in the turnover rates would generally indicate more effective utilization of current assets or working capital.

Procedures similar to those used in analyzing specific assets may also be used in analyzing specific liabilities. An accounts payable turnover rate, for example, may be developed by dividing purchases by the average payables balance, or the number of days' purchases in accounts payable may be developed by dividing accounts payable by the average daily purchases. Analysis of liabilities in terms of due dates may assist management in its cash planning activities. Useful relationships may also be obtained by comparing specific assets or liabilities with other assets or liabilities or with asset or liability totals. For example, data concerning the relationship of cash to accounts payable and of cash to total liabilities may be useful.

Ratio of stockholders' equity to total liabilities. Instead of expressing stockholder and creditor equities in terms of total assets, equities may also be expressed in terms of each other. For example, stockholders may have a 60 percent interest in total assets and creditors a 40 percent interest. Here one can say that the ratio of the stockholders' equity to the creditors' equity is 1.5 to 1, or that the stockholders' equity is 150 percent of the total liabilities of the business.

Comparative data reporting stockholders' and creditors' equities in assets and the relationships of such equities to each other show the changes taking place in the sources of business capital. As the stock-holders' equity rises in relation to the total liabilities, the margin of protection to the creditor group goes up. From the stockholders' point of view, such an increase makes the organization less vulnerable to a decline in business and possible inability to meet obligations, and also serves to minimize the cost of carrying the debt.

However, it should not be overlooked that it is often advantageous to supplement funds invested by stockholders with a certain amount of funds provided by creditors. The use of borrowed funds is known as *trading on the equity* or *applying leverage*. It is assumed that the additional earnings accruing to the business through use of borrowed funds will exceed the interest charges for such use. When the rate earned on bor-rowed funds exceeds the rate paid on borrowings, the rate of return on the stockholders' equity rises and the stockholders realize a gain through trading on the equity; when the rate earned is less than that paid, the rate of return shrinks and the stockholders suffer a loss.

The effects of trading on the equity are illustrated in the example that follows. Assume that a company with 10,000 shares of stock outstanding is able to borrow $1,000,000 at 6 percent interest. The company esti-mates that pretax earnings will be $80,000 if it operates without the borrowed capital. Income taxes are estimated at 50 percent of earnings. The summary below reports the effects upon net income, assuming that borrowed capital earns (1) 10 percent, and (2) 4 percent.

	Results of Operations Without Borrowed Capital	Results of Operations If Borrowed Capital Earns 10%	Results of Operations If Borrowed Capital Earns 4%
Operating income..................	$ 80,000	$180,000	$120,000
Interest expense...................		60,000	60,000
Income before income taxes.........	$ 80,000	$120,000	$ 60,000
Income taxes at 50%..............	40,000	60,000	30,000
Net income.......................	$ 40,000	$ 60,000	$ 30,000
Number of shares outstanding.......	10,000	10,000	10,000
Earnings per share................	$4	$6	$3

For the Marshall Company, relationships of the stockholders' equity to total liabilities are calculated as follows:

	1972	1971
Stockholders' equity......................	$1,468,000	$1,445,000
Total liabilities..........................	$ 810,000	$ 946,000
Ratio of stockholders' equity to total liabilities	1.8 : 1	1.5 : 1

In analyzing the relationship of the stockholders' equity to total liabilities, particular note should be made of any lease arrangements that represent primarily financing devices. Both the property rights provided under the leases and the liabilities that accompany such rights would need to be considered in arriving at a full evaluation of the status of equities, the relationships of equities, and changes in such equities from period to period.

Ratio of land, buildings, and equipment to long-term debt. Comparisons may be made between land, buildings, and equipment and the total long-term debt. When property items are pledged on the long-term obligations, this ratio indicates the protection afforded to the long-term creditor group as well as the possibility for the expansion of long-term indebtedness on the basis of available security.

In the development of the ratio of land, buildings, and equipment to long-term debt, present sound values of the property items instead of book values should be used whenever available, since the protection to creditors, as well as the ability of the business to borrow, is based on the present market values of the properties pledged. If a bond retirement fund is maintained consisting of a company's own obligations that have been reacquired but not retired, this fund should be subtracted from the long-term debt in developing the ratio; a bond retirement fund consisting of other investments, however, would represent additional security on the indebtedness rather than a reduction in debt and should be added to land, buildings, and equipment for purposes of this ratio. Long-term creditors generally limit their loans to a certain percentage of the value of properties pledged, so that there may be an adequate margin of safety in the event of business failure and a need to apply the properties to the payment of the indebtedness.

For the Marshall Company, ratios of land, buildings, and equipment to long-term debt are as follows:

	1972	1971
Land, buildings, and equipment (net)	$775,000	$875,000
Long-term debt	$400,000	$400,000
Ratio of land, buildings, and equipment to long-term debt	1.9:1	2.2:1

Ratio of stockholders' equity to land, buildings, and equipment. The changes in the relationship of stockholders' equity to land, buildings, and equipment need to be considered in judging whether expansion is taking place through increases in the stockholders' equity or through borrowing. An increasing ratio indicates that property acquisitions are being financed through funds supplied by the sale of stock or the retention of earnings, and normally this would be looked upon favorably by the creditor group. A declining ratio indicates that the increase of properties has exceeded the expansion in stockholders' equity. This may suggest possible overexpansion, excessive use of credit, and greater vulnerability to financial difficulties in the event of a decline in business.

For the Marshall Company, ratios of stockholders' equity to land, buildings, and equipment are as follows:

	1972	1971
Stockholders' equity......................	$1,468,000	$1,445,000
Land, buildings, and equipment (net)......	$ 775,000	$ 875,000
Ratio of stockholders' equity to land, buildings, and equipment..................	1.9:1	1.7:1

Book value per share of stock. An important measurement of the stockholders' equity is afforded by a determination of the *book value per share*. This is the recorded dollar equity related to each share. The calculation of share book value was described in Chapter 22. It was indicated there that, when there is only one class of stock, book value per share is calculated by dividing the total stockholders' equity by the number of shares outstanding. When both common and preferred shares are outstanding, it is necessary to allocate the total stockholders' equity to the two classes of stock. Redemption or liquidation values and cumulative and participating features of the preferred issue must be considered in determining the portion of the stockholders' equity relating to preferred stock.

Both common and preferred stock of the Marshall Company are $10 par. The preferred stock is cumulative and nonparticipating, and no dividends are in arrears. The preferred stock has a liquidation value equal to its par value. The book values per share for common and preferred stock are computed as follows:

	1972	1971
Total stockholders' equity.................	$1,468,000	$1,445,000
Equity related to preferred shares..........	350,000	350,000
Equity related to common shares...........	$1,118,000	$1,095,000
Number of shares outstanding: Preferred....	35,000	35,000
Common....	75,000	75,000
Book value per share: Preferred...........	$10.00	$10.00
Common...........	$14.91	$14.60

Retained earnings are sometimes reduced by the amount of intangible assets reported on the balance sheet for the purpose of share book value calculations. Such a procedure would be appropriate when intangible assets are of doubtful value. Book value of the stock thus reported offers a more conservative measure of the stockholders' equity.

Other measurements of financial position. A number of measurements of financial position other than those already described are developed in specific instances. Among these might be mentioned the ratio of individual noncurrent assets to total assets of the business or to total assets of the group, and individual noncurrent liabilities to total liabilities of the business or to total liabilities of the group. Relationships such as the foregoing may be presented directly on comparative statements by means of vertical analysis procedures.

Ratios and measurements developed from income statement data

A number of special analyses are developed from income statement data. Many of these offer measurements of the profitability of operations. Others offer measurements of certain significant relationships relative to operating performance. Although some of these measurements are made directly from the income statement, others require the use of balance sheet data.

Ratio of net sales to total assets. Among the measurements that are developed from balance sheet and income statement data is the *ratio of net sales to total assets*, sometimes called the *assets turnover rate*. This ratio is calculated by dividing the net sales figure by the total assets that produced the sales. The resulting figure indicates the contribution that is made by total assets to sales. With comparative data, judgments can be made concerning the relative effectiveness of asset utilization. A ratio increase may suggest the better utilization of assets, although a point may be reached where there is a strain on assets and a company is unable to achieve its full sales potential. An increase in total assets when accompanied by a ratio decrease may suggest an overinvestment in assets or their inefficient use.

In developing the ratio, long-term investments should be excluded from the asset total when these make no contribution to sales. On the other hand, leased properties should be added to the asset total to permit comparability between companies that own their properties and those that lease them. If monthly figures for assets are available, they may be used in developing a representative average for total assets employed during the year. Sometimes the assets at the end of the year are used as a basis for the computation. When sales can be expressed in terms of units sold, ratios in terms of sales units to total assets offer more reliable guides to interpretation than sales dollars, since unit results are not affected by product sales prices.

Assume in the case of the Marshall Company that only asset totals for the beginning and end of the year are available and that sales cannot be expressed in terms of units. Ratios of net sales to total assets are computed as follows:

	1972	1971
Net sales..............................	$1,425,000	$1,650,000
Total assets (excluding long-term investments):		
Beginning of year.....................	$1,991,000	$1,510,000
End of year..........................	$1,778,000	$1,991,000
Average total assets.....................	$1,884,500	$1,750,500
Ratio of net sales to average total assets.....	0.8 : 1	0.9 : 1

Ratio of net sales to land, buildings, and equipment. Related to the ratio just described is the *ratio of net sales to land, buildings, and equipment*, sometimes referred to as the *property turnover* or the *fixed asset turnover*. Net sales, here, is divided by the investment in land, buildings, and equipment. The resulting measurement indicates how effectively these properties are utilized in terms of sales. With comparative data, judgments may be made concerning the relative efficiency of utilization of these assets and the effects on sales of increases or decreases in property totals. An increase in land, buildings, and equipment when accompanied by a ratio decrease may suggest overexpansion in property facilities.

Assume for the Marshall Company that balances at the beginning and end of the year are used in measuring the average investment in land, buildings, and equipment. Ratios of net sales to land, buildings, and equipment are computed as follows:

	1972	1971
Net sales..............................	$1,425,000	$1,650,000
Land, buildings, and equipment (net):		
Beginning of year.....................	$ 875,000	$ 675,000
End of year..........................	$ 775,000	$ 875,000
Average investment in land, buildings, and equipment............................	$ 825,000	$ 775,000
Ratio of net sales to average land, buildings, and equipment........................	1.7:1	2.1:1

When intangible assets and leased assets contribute significantly to sales, these should be combined with land, buildings, and equipment in establishing the base for this measurement.

It may be pointed out that with increasing price levels and an unchanged sales volume in terms of units sold, the ratio of sales to land, buildings, and equipment may show regular improvement because sales prices are increasing while property costs remain unchanged. In order to obtain a more meaningful ratio, the fair market values of property items rather than historical book values may be used.

Rate earned on total assets. The adequacy of earnings may be measured in terms of (1) the rate earned on sales, (2) the rate earned on total assets, and (3) the rate earned on the stockholders' equity. There should be an adequate rate of earnings in terms of each of the three standards if operating results are to be considered satisfactory. The rate earned on sales was measured in the preceding chapter where vertical analysis was applied to income statement data. The rate earned on total assets and on stockholders' equity are described in this and in the following section.

The *rate earned on total assets*, frequently referred to as the *asset productivity rate*, is found by dividing the net income for the year by the total assets employed in the production of net income. This rate measures the degree of efficiency in the use of the resources to generate net income. If total assets by months are available, they should be used in developing an average for the year. Frequently, however, the assets at the beginning of the year or the assets at the end of the year are used for the calculation. In some instances it may be desirable to limit net income to that resulting from trading operations by excluding revenue items arising from investments, such as interest, dividends, and rents. When this is the case, total assets should be reduced by the investments in developing the rate of earnings. Sometimes comparisons are developed for the rate of operating income to total assets or, perhaps, the rate of income before income taxes to total assets, so that rates of earnings are not affected by financial management items or by changes in income tax rates.

Rates earned on total assets for the Marshall Company are determined as follows:

	1972	1971
Net income	$ 70,000	$ 60,000
Total assets:		
Beginning of year	$2,391,000	$1,760,000
End of year	$2,278,000	$2,391,000
Average total assets	$2,334,500	$2,075,500
Rate earned on average total assets	3.00%	2.89%

Rate earned on stockholders' equity. Net income may be expressed as the *rate earned on the stockholders' equity* by dividing net income by the stockholders' equity. By excluding liabilities, a rate is computed that reflects the use of leverage to generate net income. In the development of this rate, it is preferable to use the average stockholders' equity for a year calculated from monthly data, particularly when significant changes have occurred during the year as a result of the sale of additional stock, the retirement of stock, the payment of dividends, and the accumulation of earnings. Sometimes the beginning or the ending stockholders' equity is used for the measurement.

For the Marshall Company, rates earned on the stockholders' equity are calculated as follows:

	1972	1971
Net income............................	$ 70,000	$ 60,000
Stockholders' equity:		
Beginning of year.....................	$1,445,000	$1,330,000
End of year..........................	$1,468,000	$1,445,000
Average stockholders' equity.............	$1,456,500	$1,387,500
Rate earned on average stockholders' equity.	4.81%	4.32%

As a company's liabilities increase in relationship to the stockholders' equity, the spread between the rate earned on stockholders' equity and the rate earned on total assets rises. The rate earned on the stockholders' equity is of interest to the investor who must reconcile the risk of a highly leveraged company with the potentially greater profitability.

Rate earned on common stockholders' equity. Earnings may be measured in terms of the residual common stockholders' equity. The *rate earned on the common stockholders' equity* is computed by dividing the net income after preferred dividend requirements by the equity of the common stockholders. The average equity for common stockholders should be determined, although the rate is frequently based upon the beginning or ending common equity.

In the case of the Marshall Company whose preferred stock is non-participating, preferred dividend requirements are limited to 6 percent. The rate earned on the common stockholders' equity, then, is calculated as follows:

	1972	1971
Net income.............................	$ 70,000	$ 60,000
Less dividend requirements on preferred stock	21,000	21,000
Net income related to common stockholders' equity................................	$ 49,000	$ 39,000
Common stockholders' equity:		
Beginning of year.....................	$1,095,000	$1,080,000
End of year..........................	$1,118,000	$1,095,000

	1972	1971
Average common stockholders' equity......	$1,106,500	$1,087,500
Rate earned on average common stockholders' equity..................................	4.4%	3.6%

Number of times bond interest requirements were earned. Earnings may also be measured in terms of (1) their relationship to bond interest requirements, (2) their relationship to preferred dividend requirements, and (3) their availability to common stockholders.

The number of times that earnings cover the bond interest is calculated by dividing income before any charges for bond interest or income taxes by the bond interest requirements for the period. The ability of the company to meet interest payments and the degree of safety afforded the bondholders are thus reported. The number of times interest charges were earned by the Marshall Company follows:

	1972	1971
Income before income taxes..................	$100,000	$ 85,000
Add bond interest (6% of $400,000)...........	24,000	24,000
Amount available in meeting bond interest requirements............................	$124,000	$109,000
Number of times bond interest requirements were earned.................................	5.2	4.5

Income before income taxes was used in the calculation above in view of the fact that income taxes apply only after bond interest is deducted and it is pretax income that affords the protection to the bondholder group. However, the calculation is frequently made in terms of net income after income taxes. The latter procedure is employed because it is easier to apply since it is based on the last figure on the income statement, it is consistent with other measurements employing net income, and it offers a more conservative approach in measuring the ability of the company to meet periodic interest requirements. For the Marshall Company, net income balances after income taxes were $70,000 for 1972 and $60,000 for 1971. These balances would be raised by interest requirements for each year of $24,000 and the sums divided by the periodic interest, resulting in times-interest-earned amounts for 1972 of 3.9 and for 1971 of 3.5.

In addition to calculations of interest coverage, calculations may be made of the number of times all fixed charges are covered in measuring a company's ability to meet its regularly recurring financial commitments such as management salaries, rents, taxes, and interest.

Number of times preferred dividend requirements were earned.
The number of times that earnings cover the preferred dividends is calculated by dividing net income for the year by the annual preferred
dividend requirements. For the Marshall Company, calculations are:

	1972	1971
Net income..................................	$ 70,000	$ 60,000
Preferred dividend requirements (6% of $350,000)	$ 21,000	$ 21,000
Number of times preferred dividend require-		
ments were earned.......................	3.3	2.9

The relationship of earnings to preferred dividend requirements may
also be indicated by dividing net income by the number of preferred
shares outstanding. It should be recognized that this calculation does
not show the amount of earnings to which preferred shares are entitled,
but simply the amount of earnings that are available in meeting preferred dividend requirements.

For the Marshall Company, earnings available in meeting preferred
dividend requirements are calculated as follows:

	1972	1971
Net income..................................	$ 70,000	$ 60,000
Number of shares of preferred outstanding.....	35,000	35,000
Income available in meeting preferred dividend		
requirements per share....................	$2.00	$1.71

Since preferred stock is 6%, $10 par, earnings required to cover pre-
ferred dividends are 60 cents per share.

Earnings per share on common stock. Earnings per share calculations were described in detail in Chapter 22. It will be recalled that the
Accounting Principles Board in Opinion No. 15 issued in 1969 indicated
that earnings per share data were of such importance to investors and
others interested in the results of a company's operations that such data
should be presented prominently on the periodic statements. In computing per share earnings on common stock, earnings are first reduced by
the prior dividend rights of preferred stock. Computations are made in
terms of the weighted average number of common shares and common
share equivalents for each period presented. When net income on the
income statement includes amounts for extraordinary items and for the
cumulative changes in accounting principles, earnings per share amounts
would be reported for each of these items as well as for the final net
income balance. When the capital structure of a corporation includes
no potentially dilutive convertible securities, options, warrants, or other
rights, a single presentation of earnings per share is appropriate; when

the capital structure includes potentially dilutive items, a dual presentation of earnings in the form of primary earnings per share and fully diluted earnings per share would be required.

In the case of the Marshall Company, it is assumed that no potentially dilutive items are present and earnings per share on common stock call for simple computations as follows:

	1972	1971
Net income.	$70,000	$60,000
Less dividend requirements on preferred stock. . . .	21,000	21,000
Income related to common stockholders' equity. . .	$49,000	$39,000
Number of shares of common stock outstanding. . .	75,000	75,000
Earnings per share on common stock.	$ .65	$ .52

Price-earnings ratio on common stock. The market price of common stock may be expressed as a multiple of its earnings to provide a means of evaluating the attractiveness of common stock as an investment. This measurement is referred to as the *price-earnings ratio* and is computed by dividing the market value per share of stock by the annual earnings per share. Instead of using the average market value of shares for the period covered by earnings, the latest market value is normally used. Assuming market values per common share of the Marshall Company at the end of 1972 of $10.00 and at the end of 1971 of $6.50, price-earnings ratios would be computed as follows:

	1972	1971
Market value per common share at end of year.	$10.00	$ 6.50
Earnings per share.	$ .65	$ .52
Price-earnings ratio.	15.4	12.5

As an alternative to the above, earnings per share can be presented as a percentage based on the market value of the stock. Care should be taken to indicate that the earnings rate thus computed is stated in terms of the increase in the stockholders' equity as a result of profitable operations and not in terms of dividends actually paid to stockholders.

Yield on common stock. A rate of return in terms of actual distributions to common stockholders may be provided. Such a rate, referred to as the *yield on common stock*, is found by dividing the annual dividends on a common share by the latest market value per common share. For the Marshall Company, the yield on the common stock is computed as follows:

	1972	1971
Dividends for year per common share.	$ .3467	$ .32
Market value per common share at end of year. . . .	$10.00	$ 6.50
Yield on common stock.	3.5%	4.9%

Distribution of earnings to creditor and ownership equities. Inasmuch as earnings are the ultimate source upon which the creditors and the owners of an enterprise must rely for a return of both principal and income, and because the different classes of security holders normally obtain different rates of return, a percentage analysis of the disposition of the earnings of a company may be of interest to all groups. In the case of the Marshall Company it is possible to prepare a summary of the distribution of earnings as follows:

	Equity Totals[1]		Equity Percentage		Amount of Earnings Paid or Accruing* on Equities		Percentage Distribution of Total Earnings Paid or Accruing* on Equities		Percentage Paid or Accruing* on Equities	
	1972	1971	1972	1971	1972	1971	1972	1971	1972	1971
Bondholders (6% long-term debt)...........	$ 400,000	$ 400,000	22%	22%	$24,000	$24,000	26%	29%	6.0%	6.0%
Preferred stockholders....	350,000	350,000	19%	19%	21,000	21,000	22%	25%	6.0%	6.0%
Common stockholders....	1,106,500	1,087,500	59%	59%	{26,000	24,000	28%	29%	2.3%[2]	2.2%
					{23,000*	15,000*	24%*	17%*	2.1%*	1.4%*
Total.................	$1,856,500	$1,837,500	100%	100%	$94,000	$84,000	100%	100%	5.1%	4.6%

Other measurements of operations. A number of other measurements of operations that are significant in various instances can be developed. Among these may be mentioned such ratios as gross profit to sales, operating income to sales, net income to sales, individual manufacturing costs to cost of goods manufactured, individual selling expenses and individual general and administrative expenses to the totals for these groups. These relationships are generally presented by means of comparative statements offering horizontal and vertical analyses of income statement data.

Interpretation of analyses

Analyses offered in Chapter 24 and in this chapter are developed to help the analyst arrive at certain conclusions with regard to the business. It has already been stated that these are merely guides to the intelligent interpretation of financial data.

All of the ratios and measurements need not be used, but rather only those that will actually assist the analyst in arriving at informed conclusions with respect to the questions that he would raise. The measurements that are developed need to be interpreted in terms of the conditions relating to the particular enterprise, the conditions relating to the

---

[1]Average equities for the year are indicated in this illustration. It would be possible to base analyses on equities as of the beginning of the year or on equities as of the end of the year.

[2]This percentage, while stated in terms of the common stockholders' equity as reported by the books, could be stated in terms of the par or stated value of the common stock or in terms of market value of the stock.

particular industry in which the enterprise is found, and the conditions relating to the general business and the economic environment within which the enterprise operates. If measurements are to be of maximum value, they need to be compared with similar data developed for the particular enterprise for past periods, with similar measurements for the industry as a whole that may be regarded as standard, and with pertinent data relating to general business conditions and business and price fluctuations as these affect the individual enterprise. Only through the intelligent use and integration of the foregoing sources of data can financial weaknesses and strengths be identified and reliable opinions be developed concerning business structure, operations, and growth.

QUESTIONS

1. Define working capital and appraise its significance.

2. Distinguish between the current ratio and the acid-test ratio. What are usually considered minimums for each ratio?

3. Balance sheets for the Blake Corporation and the Carlson Corporation each show a working capital total of $500,000. Does this indicate that the short-term liquidity of the Blake Corporation is approximately equal to that of the Carlson Corporation? Explain.

4. Define (a) quick assets, (b) price-earnings ratio.

5. (a) How is the accounts receivable turnover computed? (b) How would you interpret a rising accounts receivable turnover rate?

6. (a) How is the merchandise inventory turnover computed? (b) What precautions are necessary in arriving at the basis for the turnover calculation? (c) How would you interpret a rising inventory turnover rate?

7. (a) What is meant by "trading on the equity"? (b) Give figures to illustrate a gain accruing to owners through this practice.

8. The ratio of stockholders' equity to total liabilities offers information concerning the long-term liquidity of the business unit. Explain.

9. Give rules for computing share book values when a company has both common and preferred stock outstanding.

10. State the significance of each of the following measurements: (a) the ratio of land, buildings, and equipment to long-term debt, (b) the ratio of stockholders' equity to land, buildings, and equipment, (c) the ratio of sales to total assets, and (d) the ratio of sales to land, buildings, and equipment.

11. (a) What is meant by the "asset productivity rate"? (b) How is it calculated?

12. Indicate how each of the following measurements is calculated and appraise its significance:
- (a) The number of times bond interest requirements were earned.
- (b) The number of times preferred dividend requirements were earned.
- (c) The rate of earnings on the common stockholders' equity.
- (d) The earnings per share on common stock.
- (e) The price-earnings ratio on common stock.
- (f) The yield on common stock.

13. (a) Distinguish between the "natural business year" and the "thirteen-month year." (b) What advantages are found in the adoption of each for accounting purposes?

EXERCISES

1. The data that follow are taken from comparative balance sheets prepared for the Morgan Company:

	1972	1971
Cash	$ 28,000	$ 14,000
Marketable securities	10,000	20,000
Trade receivables (net)	50,000	45,000
Inventories	75,000	60,000
Prepaid expenses	2,000	1,000
Land, buildings, and equipment (net)	85,000	80,000
Intangible assets	20,000	25,000
Other assets	5,000	5,000
	$275,000	$250,000
Current liabilities	$100,000	$ 70,000

(a) From the data given, compute for 1972 and for 1971: (1) the working capital, (2) the current ratio, (3) the acid-test ratio, (4) the ratio of current assets to total assets, (5) the ratio of cash to current liabilities.
(b) Evaluate each of the above changes.

2. Statements for the Lunn Co. show the following balances:

	1972	1971	1970
Average receivables (net)	$ 50,000	$ 40,000	$ 30,000
Net sales	480,000	390,000	360,000

Give any significant measurements that may be developed in analyzing the foregoing, assuming a 300-day business year and assuming that approximately one third of the sales are for cash, the balance being on account. What conclusions may be made concerning the receivables if sales on account are made on a 2/30, n/60 basis?

3. The average inventory for the Lindbrook Company at cost is $50,000; sales for 1972 were made at 20% above cost and totaled $300,000. (a) What was the inventory turnover rate? (b) What is the average age of the inventory, assuming a 300-day year?

4. Operating statements for the Hull Sales Co. show the following:

	1972	1971	1970
Sales.	$110,000	$100,000	$ 80,000
Cost of goods sold:			
Beginning inventory	$ 30,000	$ 20,000	$ 10,000
Purchases	95,000	80,000	60,000
	$125,000	$100,000	$ 70,000
Ending inventory	50,000	30,000	20,000
	$ 75,000	$ 70,000	$ 50,000
Gross profit on sales	$ 35,000	$ 30,000	$ 30,000

Give whatever measurements may be developed in analyzing the inventory position at the end of each year. What conclusions would you make concerning the inventory trend?

5. The following data are taken from the Wills Corporation records for the years ending December 31, 1972, 1971, and 1970:

	1972	1971	1970
Finished goods inventory	$ 60,000	$ 30,000	$ 10,000
Goods in process inventory	50,000	50,000	50,000
Raw materials inventory	60,000	40,000	25,000
Sales	400,000	340,000	360,000
Cost of goods sold	225,000	230,000	210,000
Cost of goods manufactured	260,000	250,000	200,000
Materials used in production	150,000	130,000	120,000

Compute turnover rates for 1972 and for 1971 for (a) finished goods, (b) goods in process, and (c) raw materials.

6. The total purchases of goods by the Seiler Wholesale Company during 1972 were $390,000. All purchases were on a 2/10, n/30 basis. The average balance in the vouchers payable account was $44,200. Was the company prompt, slow, or average in paying for goods? How many days' average purchases were there in accounts payable, assuming a 300-day year?

7. The stockholders' equity of the Johnson Corporation on December 31, 1972, is as follows:

6% Preferred stock, $25 par	$ 500,000
Common stock, $20 par	1,000,000
Additional paid-in capital	200,000
Retained earnings	100,000

Compute the book value per share of both preferred and common stocks, assuming each of the following conditions. (Assume that dividends may legally be paid from additional paid-in capital.)

(a) Preferred stock is cumulative and nonparticipating, with no dividends in arrears.
(b) Preferred stock is cumulative and nonparticipating, and dividends are in arrears since January 1, 1971.
(c) Preferred stock is cumulative and fully participating, with no dividends in arrears.
(d) Preferred stock is cumulative and fully participating, and dividends are in arrears since January 1, 1971.

8. The balance sheets for the Wertz Company showed the following long-term debt and stockholders' equity balances at the end of each year:

	1972	1971
6% Bonds payable......................	$ 500,000	$ 500,000
6% Nonparticipating preferred stock, $100 par.................................	600,000	500,000
Common stock, $25 par.................	1,200,000	1,000,000
Additional paid-in capital...............	100,000	100,000
Retained earnings......................	300,000	100,000

Net income after income taxes was: 1972, $120,000; 1971, $90,000. Using the foregoing data, compute for each year:

(a) The rate of earnings on the total stockholders' equity at the end of the year.
(b) The number of times bond interest requirements were earned.
(c) The number of times preferred dividend requirements were earned.
(d) The rate earned on the common stockholders' equity.
(e) The earnings per share on common stock.

PROBLEMS

25-1. The balance sheet data for the Hayworth Corp. on December 31, 1972, are given below.

Assets		Liabilities and Stockholders' Equity	
Cash	$ 60,000	Notes and accounts payable ...	$ 75,000
Marketable securities	160,000	Income taxes payable	15,000
Notes and accounts receivable (net)	180,000	Accrued wages and interest ...	5,000
Inventories	300,000	Dividends payable	5,000
Prepaid expenses	10,000	Bonds payable	380,000
Bond redemption fund (securities of other companies) ...	150,000	Deferred revenues	20,000
Land, buildings, and equipment (net).....................	930,000	Common stock, $20 par	1,000,000
Intangible assets.............	200,000	Preferred stock, $20 par (nonparticipating, noncumulative)	200,000
Unamortized bond issue costs .	10,000	Retained earnings appropriated for plant expansion....	100,000
		Retained earnings..........	200,000
	$2,000,000		$2,000,000

Instructions: From the balance sheet data, compute the following:
(1) The amount of working capital.
(2) The current ratio.
(3) The acid-test ratio.
(4) The ratio of current assets to total assets.
(5) The ratio of stockholders' equity to total liabilities.
(6) The ratio of land, buildings, and equipment to bonds payable.
(7) The book value per share of preferred stock.
(8) The book value per share of common stock.

25-2. Comparative data for Stewart, Inc., for the three-year period 1970–1972 are presented below.

Income Statement Data

	1972	1971	1970
Net sales..........................	$1,200,000	$1,000,000	$ 800,000
Cost of goods sold...................	760,000	600,000	500,000
Gross profit on sales.................	$ 440,000	$ 400,000	$ 300,000
Selling, general, and other expenses....	350,000	300,000	290,000
Operating income...................	$ 90,000	$ 100,000	$ 10,000
Income taxes......................	45,000	50,000	5,000
Net income.......................	$ 45,000	$ 50,000	$ 5,000
Dividends paid....................	35,000	30,000	15,000
Net increase (decrease) in retained earnings........................	$ 10,000	$ 20,000	$ (10,000)

Balance Sheet Data

Assets	1972	1971	1970
Cash.............................	$ 60,000	$ 40,000	$ 50,000
Trade notes and accounts rec. (net) ...	400,000	320,000	250,000
Inventory (at cost).................	420,000	420,000	320,000
Prepaid expenses...................	30,000	10,000	20,000
Land, buildings, and equipment (net).	720,000	600,000	650,000
Intangible assets...................	100,000	100,000	100,000
Other assets......................	70,000	10,000	10,000
	$1,800,000	$1,500,000	$1,400,000

Liabilities and Stockholders' Equity	1972	1971	1970
Trade notes and accounts payable.....	$ 220,000	$ 150,000	$ 130,000
Wages, interest, dividends payable.....	45,000	25,000	15,000
Income taxes payable...............	45,000	50,000	5,000
Miscellaneous current liabilities.......	10,000	15,000	10,000
5% Bonds payable.................	300,000	300,000	300,000
Deferred revenues..................	10,000	10,000	10,000
6% Preferred stock, nonparticipating, $100 par......................	200,000	200,000	200,000
No-par common stock, $10 stated value.	500,000	400,000	400,000
Additional paid-in capital............	310,000	200,000	200,000
Retained earnings — appropriated....	80,000	60,000	60,000
Retained earnings — free...........	80,000	90,000	70,000
	$1,800,000	$1,500,000	$1,400,000

Instructions: (1) From the foregoing data, calculate comparative measurements for 1972 and 1971 as follows:

(a) The amount of working capital.
(b) The current ratio.
(c) The acid-test ratio.
(d) The trade receivables turnover rate for the year (all sales are on a credit basis).
(e) The average days' sales in trade receivables at the end of the year (assume a 300-day business year and all sales on a credit basis).
(f) The trade payables turnover rate for the year.
(g) The average days' purchases in payables at the end of the year.
(h) The inventory turnover rate.
(i) The number of days' sales in the inventory at the end of the year.
(j) The ratio of stockholders' equity to total liabilities.
(k) The ratio of land, buildings, and equipment to bonds payable.
(l) The ratio of stockholders' equity to land, buildings, and equipment.
(m) The book value per share of preferred stock.
(n) The book value per share of common stock.

(2) Based upon the measurements made in (1), evaluate the liquidity position of Stewart, Inc., at the end of 1972 as compared with the end of 1971.

25-3. (1) Using the comparative data for Stewart, Inc., (as given in Problem 25-2), compute comparative measurements for 1972 and 1971 as follows:

(a) The ratio of net sales to average total assets.
(b) The ratio of net sales to average land, buildings, and equipment.
(c) The rate earned on net sales.
(d) The gross profit rate on net sales.
(e) The rate earned on average total assets.
(f) The rate earned on average stockholders' equity.
(g) The number of times bond interest requirements were earned (before income taxes).
(h) The number of times preferred dividend requirements were earned.
(i) The rate earned on average common stockholders' equity.
(j) The earnings per share on common stock.

(2) Based upon the measurements made in (1), evaluate the profitability of Stewart, Inc., for 1972 as compared with 1971.

25-4. Using the comparative data for Stewart, Inc., as given in Problem 25-2, prepare a summary of the distribution of earnings for the three-year period similar to that illustrated on page 926. Measurements are to be based on equity totals as of the end of each year.

25-5. (1) Using the data for the Carter Mfg. Co. as given in Problem 24-3 on pages 896–898, compute comparative measurements for 1972 and 1971 as follows:

(a) The amount of working capital.
(b) The current ratio.

(c) The acid-test ratio.
(d) The current asset turnover rate.
(e) The finished goods inventory turnover rate.
(f) The raw materials inventory turnover rate.
(g) The number of days' sales in average finished goods inventory (assume a 300-day business year).
(h) The number of days' raw materials requirements in average raw materials inventory.
(i) The ratio of stockholders' equity to total liabilities.
(j) The ratio of land, buildings, and equipment to long-term debt.
(k) The book value per share of the preferred stock.
(l) The book value per share of the common stock.

(2) Based upon the measurements made in (1), evaluate the liquidity position of Carter Mfg. Co. at the end of 1972 as compared with the end of 1971.

25-6. (1) Using the data for the Carter Mfg. Co. as given in Problem 24-3 on pages 896–898, compute comparative measurements for 1972 and 1971 as follows:

(a) The ratio of net sales to average total assets (excluding long-term investments).
(b) The ratio of net sales to average land, buildings, and equipment.
(c) The rate earned on net sales.
(d) The gross profit rate on net sales.
(e) The rate earned on average total assets.
(f) The rate earned on average stockholders' equity.
(g) The number of times long-term debt interest requirements were earned (before income taxes).
(h) The number of times preferred dividend requirements were earned.
(i) The rate earned on average common stockholders' equity.
(j) The earnings per share on common stock.

(2) Based upon the measurements made in (1), evaluate the profitability of Carter Mfg. Co. for 1972 as compared with 1971.

25-7. Using the comparative data for the Carter Mfg. Co. as given in Problem 24-3 on pages 896–898, prepare a summary of the distribution of earnings for 1972 and 1971 similar to that illustrated on page 926. Measurements are to be based on equity totals as of the end of each year.

25-8. Inventory and receivable balances and also gross profit data for the Thorne Company appear below:

	1972	1971	1970
Balance sheet data:			
Inventory, December 31............	$ 80,000	$ 60,000	$ 40,000
Receivables, December 31..........	50,000	40,000	30,000
Income statement data:			
Net sales........................	$300,000	$270,000	$200,000
Cost of goods sold................	230,000	200,000	150,000
Gross profit on sales..............	$ 70,000	$ 70,000	$ 50,000

Instructions: Assuming a 300-day business year and all sales on a credit basis, compute the following measurements for 1972 and 1971.

(1) The receivables turnover rate.
(2) The average days' sales in receivables at the end of the year.
(3) The inventory turnover rate.
(4) The number of days' sales in the inventory at the end of the year.

25-9. Stockholders' equities for the Berg Corporation at the end of 1972 and 1971 were as follows:

	1972	1971
6% Preferred stock, $50 par and liquidating value	$100,000	$100,000
Common stock, $10 par.....................	350,000	300,000
Additional paid-in capital..................	500,000	400,000
Retained earnings.........................	50,000	100,000

Instructions: Compute the book value per share of both preferred stock and common stock at the end of 1972 and at the end of 1971, assuming the conditions that are stated in each case below. (Assume that dividends may legally be paid from additional paid-in capital.)

(1) Preferred is cumulative and nonparticipating; dividend requirements on preferred stock have been met annually.
(2) Preferred is cumulative and nonparticipating; the last dividend on preferred stock was paid for the year 1969.
(3) Preferred is cumulative and fully participating; dividend requirements on preferred stock have been met annually.
(4) Preferred is cumulative and fully participating; the last dividend on preferred stock was paid for the year 1969.

25-10. Stockholders' equities for the McDermitt Corporation at the end of 1972 and 1971 were as follows:

	December 31, 1972	December 31, 1971
6% Preferred stock, $100 par cumulative and nonparticipating.....	$1,000,000	$1,000,000
Common stock, $20 par..........	2,000,000	2,000,000
Additional paid-in capital........	150,000	150,000
Retained earnings (deficit).......	(50,000)	200,000

In event of liquidation, preferred shares are entitled to payment equal to par value and any amount of dividends in arrears.

Instructions: Compute the book value of preferred and common stocks at the end of 1972 and 1971 assuming:

(1) No dividends were paid on preferred stock for the year 1972.
(2) No dividends were paid on preferred stock since payment was made for the first quarter of 1968.

25-11. (a) For each of the following numbered items you are to select the letter items which indicate its effects on the corporation's statements. Indicate your choice by giving the letters identifying the effects which you select. If there is no appropriate response among the effects listed, leave the item blank. If more than one effect is applicable to a particular item, be sure to list *all* applicable letters. (Assume that the state statutes do not permit declaration of nonliquidating dividends except from earnings.)

Item	Effect
(1) Declaration of a cash dividend due in one month on noncumulative preferred stock.	A. Reduces working capital.
	B. Increases working capital.
	C. Reduces current ratio.
(2) Declaration and payment of an ordinary stock dividend.	D. Increases current ratio.
	E. Reduces the dollar amount of total capital stock.
(3) Receipt of a cash dividend, not previously recorded, on stock of another corporation.	F. Increases the dollar amount of total capital stock.
(4) Passing of a dividend on cumulative preferred stocks.	G. Reduces total retained earnings.
	H. Increases total retained earnings.
(5) Receipt of preferred shares as a dividend on stock held as a temporary investment. This was not a regularly-recurring dividend.	S. Reduces equity per share of common stock.
	T. Reduces equity of each common stockholder.
(6) Payment of dividend mentioned in (1).	
(7) Issue of new common shares in a 5-for-1 stock split.	

(b) The following are partially condensed financial statements.

X Corporation
Balance Sheet
December 31, 1972

Cash..	$ 63,000
Trade receivables, less estimated uncollectibles of $12,000........	238,000
Inventories...	170,000
Prepaid expenses...	7,000
Land, buildings, and equipment, cost less $182,000 charged to operations..	390,000
Other assets...	13,000
	$881,000
Accounts and notes payable — trade..........................	$ 98,000
Accrued liabilities..	17,000
Income taxes payable..	18,000
First-mortgage, 4% bonds, due in 1982.......................	150,000
$7 Preferred stock — no par value (entitled to $110 per share in liquidation); authorized 1,000 shares; in treasury 400 shares; outstanding 600 shares....................................	108,000
Common stock — no par; authorized 100,000 shares, issued and outstanding 10,000 shares stated at a nominal value of $10 per share..	100,000
Paid-in capital from sale of common stock at more than stated value.	242,000
Retained earnings appropriated for plant expansion.............	50,000
Retained earnings appropriated for cost of treasury stock........	47,000
Retained earnings..	98,000
Cost of 400 shares of treasury stock.........................	(47,000)
	$881,000

NOTES: (1) Working capital — 12/31/71 was $205,000. (2) Trade receivables — 12/31/71 were $220,000 gross, $206,000 net. (3) Dividends for 1972 have been declared and paid. (4) There has been no change in amount of bonds outstanding during 1972.

X Corporation

Income Statement

For Year Ended December 31, 1972

	Cash	Charge	Total
Gross sales................................	$116,000	$876,000	$992,000
Less: Sales discount......................	$ 3,000	$ 12,000	$ 15,000
Sales returns and allowances..........	1,000	6,000	7,000
	$ 4,000	$ 18,000	$ 22,000
Net sales.................................	$112,000	$858,000	$970,000
Cost of sales:			
Inventory of finished goods, January 1....		$ 92,000	
Cost of goods manufactured.............		680,000	
Inventory of finished goods, December 31.		(100,000)	672,000
Gross profit on sales......................			$298,000
Selling expenses..........................		$173,000	
General expenses.........................		70,000	243,000
Income from operations..................			$ 55,000
Other additions and deductions (net).......			3,000
Income before income taxes..............			$ 58,000
Income taxes (estimated)................			18,000
Net income..............................			$ 40,000

Instructions: For each item listed below select the best answer from the approximate answers. Indicate your choice by giving the appropriate letter for each. Give the calculations in support of each choice.

Items To Be Computed	Approximate Answers				
	(a)	(b)	(c)	(d)	(e)
(1) Acid test ratio............	3.2:1	2.3:1	2.9:1	2.4:1	3.07:1
(2) Average number of days' charge sales uncollected..	86	94	35	100	105
(3) Average finished goods turnover..................	7	10.1	10.3	9.7	6.7
(4) Number of times bond interest was earned (before taxes).................	6⅔	10⅔	7⅔	9⅔	20⅓
(5) Number of times preferred dividend was earned....	5.71	8.3	13.8	9.52	8.52
(6) Earnings per share of common stock.............	$4.00	$3.30	$3.58	$5.10	$5.38
(7) Book value per share of common stock..........	$33.80	$35.00	$49.80	$48.80	$53.20
(8) Current ratio............	3.6:1	1:2.7	2.7:1	4.2:1	1:3.6

(AICPA adapted)

25-12. Derr Sales Corporation's management is concerned over the corporation's current financial position and return on investment. They request your assistance in analyzing their financial statements and furnish the following statements:

Derr Sales Corporation
Statement of Working Capital Deficit
December 31, 1972

Current liabilities..............................		$223,050
Less current assets:		
Cash...	$ 5,973	
Accounts receivable, net.........................	70,952	
Inventory.....................................	113,125	190,050
Working capital deficit..........................		$ 33,000

Derr Sales Corporation
Income Statement
For Year Ended December 31, 1972

Sales (90,500 units)..	$760,200
Cost of goods sold...	452,500
Gross profit..	$307,700
Selling and general expenses, including depreciation of $22,980...	155,660
Income before income taxes.................................	$152,040
Income taxes...	76,020
Net income...	$ 76,020

Additional data:

Assets other than current assets consist of land, building, and equipment with a book value of $352,950 on December 31, 1972.

Sales of 100,000 units are forecasted for 1973. Within this relevant range of activity costs are estimated as follows (excluding income taxes):

	Fixed Costs	Variable Costs per Unit
Cost of goods sold..........................		$4.90
Selling and general expenses, including depreciation of $15,450....................	$129,720	1.10
Total.................................	$129,720	$6.00

The income tax rate is expected to be 50%. Past experience indicates that current assets vary in direct proportion to sales.

Instructions: (1) Assuming Derr Sales Corporation operates 300 days per year compute the following (show your computations):

(a) Number of days' sales uncollected.
(b) Inventory turnover.
(c) Number of days' operations to cover the working capital deficit.
(d) Return on total assets as a product of asset turnover and the net income ratio (sometimes called profit margin).

(*continued*)

(2) Management feels that in 1973 the market will support a sales price of
$8.30 at a sales volume of 100,000 units. Compute the rate of return on book
value of total assets after income taxes assuming management's expectations are
realized.

(3) Assuming sales of 100,000 units at a price of $8.30 per unit in 1973,
prepare an analysis of the variation in gross profit between 1972 and 1973.
Your analysis should show the effects of changes in 1973 in sales volume, sales
prices, and unit costs on gross profit.   (AICPA adapted)

25-13. Near the close of your audit, the Treasurer of Ezy Corporation,
your client, informs you that the company is planning to acquire the
ATU Corporation and requests that you prepare certain statistics for
1972 and 1971 from the following statements of ATU Corporation.

ATU Corporation
Balance Sheet
December 31, 1972 and 1971

Assets	1972	1971
Current assets:		
Cash	$ 1,610,000	$ 1,387,000
Marketable securities, at cost (market value $550,000)	510,000	
Accounts receivable, less allowance for doubtful accounts: 1972, $125,000; 1971, $110,000	4,075,000	3,669,000
Inventories, at lower of cost or market	7,250,000	7,050,000
Prepaid expenses	125,000	218,000
Total current assets	$13,570,000	$12,324,000
Land, buildings, and equipment, at cost:		
Land and buildings	$13,500,000	$13,500,000
Equipment	9,250,000	8,520,000
Total land, buildings, and equipment	$22,750,000	$22,020,000
Less accumulated depreciation	13,470,000	12,549,000
Total land, buildings, and equipment — net	$ 9,280,000	$ 9,471,000
Long-term receivables	$ 250,000	$ 250,000
Deferred charges	$ 25,000	$ 75,000
Total assets	$23,125,000	$22,120,000
Liabilities and Stockholders' Equity		
Current liabilities:		
Accounts payable	$ 2,950,000	$ 3,426,000
Accrued expenses	1,575,000	1,644,000
Income taxes payable	875,000	750,000
Current maturities on long-term debt	500,000	500,000
Total current liabilities	$ 5,900,000	$ 6,320,000
Other liabilities:		
5% Sinking fund debentures, due January 1, 1983 ($500,000 redeemable annually)	$ 5,000,000	$ 5,500,000
Deferred taxes on income, related to depreciation	350,000	210,000
Total other liabilities	$ 5,350,000	$ 5,710,000
Total liabilities	$11,250,000	$12,030,000

(continued on next page)

Stockholders' equity:
Capital stock:

Preferred stock, $1 cumulative, $20 par, preference on liquidation $100 per share (autho-
rized: 100,000 shares; issued and outstanding:
50,000 shares).......................... $ 1,000,000 $ 1,000,000

Common stock, $1 par (authorized: 900,000
shares; issued and outstanding: 1972, 550,000
shares; 1971, 500,000 shares).............. 550,000 500,000

Premium on common stock................... 3,075,000 625,000
Retained earnings.......................... 7,250,000 7,965,000

Total stockholders' equity................. $11,875,000 $10,090,000
Total liabilities and stockholders' equity........ $23,125,000 $22,120,000

ATU Corporation
Statement of Income and Retained Earnings
For Years Ended December 31, 1972 and 1971

	1972	1971
Revenues:		
Net sales.....................................	$48,400,000	$41,700,000
Royalties.....................................	70,000	25,000
Interest......................................	30,000	
Total...................................	$48,500,000	$41,725,000
Costs and expenses:		
Cost of sales.................................	$31,460,000	$29,190,000
Selling, general and administrative...........	12,090,000	8,785,000
Interest on 5% sinking fund debentures.......	275,000	300,000
Provision for income taxes...................	2,315,000	1,695,000
Total...................................	$46,140,000	$39,970,000
Net income...................................	$ 2,360,000	$ 1,755,000
Retained earnings, beginning of year...........	7,965,000	6,760,000
Total...................................	$10,325,000	$ 8,515,000
Dividends paid:		
Preferred stock, $1 per share in cash..........	$ 50,000	$ 50,000
Common stock:		
Cash — $1 per share.....................	525,000	500,000
Stock — (10%) — 50,000 shares at market value of $50 per share.................	2,500,000	
Total...................................	$ 3,075,000	$ 550,000
Retained earnings, end of year................	$ 7,250,000	$ 7,965,000

Additional information:

(a) The inventory at January 1, 1971, was $6,850,000.

(b) The market prices of the common stock at December 31, 1972 and 1971 were $73.50 and $47.75 respectively.

(c) The cash dividends for both preferred and common stock were declared and paid in June and December of each year. The stock dividend on common stock was declared and distributed in August 1972.

(d) Building and equipment sales and retirements during 1972 and 1971 were $375,000 and $425,000 respectively. The related accumulated depreciation amounts were $215,000 in 1972 and $335,000 in 1971. At December 31, 1970, the building and equipment asset balance was $21,470,000 and the related accumulated depreciation was $11,650,000.

Instructions: Prepare a schedule computing the following selected statistics for 1972 and 1971. The current equivalent number of shares outstanding as of the respective year-end dates should be utilized in computing per-share statistics. (The current equivalent shares means the number of shares outstanding in the prior period in terms of the present stock position.)

(1) At December 31:

  (a) Current ratio.
  (b) Acid-test (quick) ratio.
  (c) Book value per common share.

(2) Year ended December 31:

  (a) Gross margin rate.
  (b) Inventory turnover rate.
  (c) Times interest earned (before taxes).
  (d) Earnings per common share.
  (e) Common stock price-earnings ratio (end of year value).
  (f) Gross capital expenditures.

(AICPA adapted)

25-14. Ratio analysis is often applied to test the reasonableness of the relationships among current financial data against those of prior financial data. Given prior financial relationships and a few key amounts, a CPA could prepare estimates of current financial data to test the reasonableness of data furnished by his client.

Argo Sales Corporation has in recent prior years maintained the following relationships among the data on its financial statements:

Gross profit rate on net sales..........................	40%
Net profit rate on net sales...........................	10%
Rate of selling expenses to net sales....................	20%
Accounts receivable turnover.........................	8 per year
Inventory turnover..................................	6 per year
Acid-test ratio......................................	2 to 1
Current ratio.......................................	3 to 1
Quick-asset composition: 8% cash, 32% marketable securities, 60% accounts receivable	
Asset turnover......................................	2 per year
Ratio of total assets to intangible assets.................	20 to 1
Ratio of accumulated depreciation to cost of fixed assets..	1 to 3
Ratio of accounts receivable to accounts payable........	1.5 to 1
Ratio of working capital to stockholders' equity.........	1 to 1.6
Ratio of total debt to stockholders' equity..............	1 to 2

The corporation had a net income of $120,000 for 1972 which resulted in earnings of $5.20 per share of common stock. Additional information includes the following:

(a) Capital stock authorized, issued (all in 1964), and outstanding:
   Common, $10 per share par value, issued at 10% premium;
   Preferred, 6% nonparticipating, $100 per share par value, issued at a
   10% premium.
(b) Market value per share of common at December 31, 1972, $78.
(c) Preferred dividends paid in 1972, $3,000.
(d) Number of times interest earned in 1972, 33.
(e) The amounts of the following were the same at December 31, 1972 as at
   January 1, 1972. Inventory, accounts receivable, 5% bonds payable —
   due 1974, and total stockholders' equity.
(f) All purchases and sales were "on account."

Instructions: (1) Prepare in good form: (a) the condensed balance sheet, and (b) the condensed income statement for the year ending December 31, 1972, presenting the amounts you would expect to appear on Argo's financial statements (ignoring income taxes). Major captions appearing on Argo's balance sheet are: Current assets, Fixed assets, Intangible assets, Current liabilities, Long-term liabilities, and Stockholders' equity. In addition to the accounts divulged in the problem, you should include accounts for prepaid expenses, accrued expenses, and administrative expenses. Supporting computations should be in good form.

(2) Compute the following for 1972 (show your computations):
   (a) Rate of return on stockholders' equity.
   (b) Price-earnings ratio for common stock.
   (c) Dividends paid per share of common stock.
   (d) Dividends paid per share of preferred stock.
   (e) Yield on common stock.

(AICPA adapted)

chapter 26

statements from incomplete records

The procedures leading to the preparation of financial statements that have been applied in the preceding chapters are those required in a *double-entry system*. This is the characteristic system employed in practice and requires the analysis of each transaction in terms of debits and credits. Any set of procedures that does not provide for the analysis of each transaction in terms of double entry is referred to as a *single-entry system*.

Single-entry systems

Single-entry systems differ widely depending upon the needs of the organization and the originality of the person maintaining the system. Records that are found in a single-entry system may vary from a narrative of transactions recorded in a single journal, called a *daybook*, to a relatively complete set of journals and a ledger providing accounts for all significant items.

Single-entry procedures are frequently found in organizations whose activities do not warrant the employment of a bookkeeper. Such organizations include unincorporated retail businesses, professional and service units, and nonprofit organizations. Persons acting in a fiduciary capacity, such as estate executors and trust custodians, may also limit their record keeping to single-entry procedures. When double-entry records are not maintained, a professional accountant is normally engaged at different intervals to prepare financial statements, tax returns, and any other reports that may be required.

Records in single-entry systems

All of the variations of single entry encountered in practice cannot be described here. A characteristic single-entry system consists of the following records: (1) a daybook or general journal, (2) a cashbook, and (3) ledger accounts showing debtor and creditor balances. The simplest form of single-entry procedures consists of the daybook in which transactions are described in chronological order. No accounts are kept. At the other extreme of single-entry procedures, a number of journals may be maintained such as cash journals, sales and purchases journals, returns and allowances journals, and a general journal. Ledger accounts may be kept for debtors, creditors, and the owner, as well as for other significant items such as sales, purchases, and expenses.

Single-entry procedures commonly take the following form. A cashbook is maintained that shows all of the transactions affecting cash. Instead of naming accounts to be debited or credited as a result of cash receipts and disbursements, a description of the transaction is offered. Transactions not shown in the cashbook are recorded in a daybook in descriptive form. Whenever the account of a debtor, a creditor, or the owner is affected, attention is directed to the need for posting by indicating "dr" or "cr" before the amount. Offsetting debits or credits are not shown since accounts in the ledger are maintained only for customers, creditors, and the owner. At the end of the period reports may be limited to summaries of customer and creditor balances.

Preparation of financial statements from single-entry records

When records do not offer a complete summary of transactions, the preparation of accurate financial statements raises a number of special problems. These are discussed in the sections that follow.

Preparation of the balance sheet. When the ledger consists of account balances for only customers and creditors, the preparation of the balance sheet calls for reference to a number of different sources. Cash is reported at the balance shown in the cashbook after this figure has been reconciled with the totals of cash on hand and on deposit with the bank. Receivables and payables are summarized from the accounts maintained with debtors and creditors. Merchandise and supplies balances are found by taking inventories. Past statements, cash records, and other documents are reviewed in determining the book values of depreciable assets. Other assets and liabilities, including accrued and prepaid items, are determined by a review of the records, including invoices, documents, and other available sources offering evidence or information concerning transactions of the past, present, and future. The owner's capital balance in a double-entry system represents an amount arrived at by combining beginning capital, additional investments and withdrawals, and revenue and expense account balances; in single-entry, capital is simply the difference between the total reported for assets less the total reported for liabilities.

Determination of the net income or loss from comparative balance sheet data and cash summary. In the absence of revenue and expense accounts, net income may be calculated by the single-entry method. The owner's capital at the beginning of the period is subtracted from owner's capital at the end of the period. The difference is then increased for any withdrawals and decreased for any investments made by the owner during the period. Beginning and ending owner's capital balances are taken from the balance sheets prepared at the end of the previous period and at the end of the current period. Investments and withdrawals are ascertained from owner's capital and drawing accounts maintained in the ledger, or in the absence of these, from the cashbook and other memorandum records.

To illustrate the determination of the net income or loss, assume that the owner's capital is reported on comparative balance sheets as follows: January 1, $20,000; December 31, $30,000. In the absence of investments or withdrawals by the owner, it must be concluded that the net income for the year was $10,000. However, assume that the owner has invested $2,500 and has withdrawn $9,000 during the year. Net income is then computed as follows:

Owner's capital, December 31		$30,000
Owner's capital, January 1		20,000
Net increase in owner's capital		$10,000
Add excess of owner's withdrawals over investments:		
Withdrawals	$9,000	
Investments	2,500	6,500
Net income for the year		$16,500

Preparation of the income statement. A summary of the net income or loss calculated from comparative capital balances is generally inadequate. The owner needs detailed statements of operation in viewing past success or failure and in planning future activities. Creditors may insist upon such statements. In addition, revenue and expense data must be reported for income tax purposes.

An itemized income statement can be prepared by (1) rewriting transactions in double-entry form or (2) computing the individual revenue and expense balances by reference to cash receipts and disbursements and the changes in asset and liability balances. Obviously, little or nothing is saved by the adoption of a single-entry system if transactions are rewritten in double-entry form and posted to accounts. When the second procedure is followed, an analysis of all cash receipts and disbursements is required, unless this is already provided by special analysis columns in the cash journals. Cash receipts must be classified as: (1) receipts for goods sold for cash, (2) receipts of other revenue items, (3) collections on customers' accounts, (4) proceeds from the sale of assets other than merchandise, (5) amounts borrowed, and (6) investments by the owner. Cash payments must be classified as (1) payments for merchandise purchased for cash, (2) payments of other expense items, (3) payments on trade creditors' accounts, (4) payments for the purchase of assets other than merchandise, (5) loans paid off, and (6) withdrawals by the owner. These data, together with the data provided by the balance sheet, are used in the preparation of the income statement. Obviously, the accuracy of the income statement will depend upon the accuracy of the information that is used in computing revenue and expense items. The procedures that are followed in computing revenue and expense balances are illustrated in the sections that follow.

Sales. The amount to be reported for sales consists of the total of cash sales and sales on account. Sales are computed from the cash receipts analysis and comparative balance sheet data as follows:

Sales

Cash sales.		$ 7,500
Sales on account:		
Notes and accounts receivable at the end of the period.	$1,500	
Collections on notes and accounts receivable during the period	3,000	
	$4,500	
Deduct notes and accounts receivable at the beginning of the period.	2,000	2,500
Sales for the period.		$10,000

Notes and accounts receivable in the foregoing tabulation are limited to those arising from sales of merchandise.

Cost of goods sold. The inventory balance shown on the balance sheet prepared at the end of the preceding fiscal period is reported on the income statement as the beginning inventory.

The amount to be reported for purchases consists of the total of cash purchases and purchases on account. Purchases are computed from the cash payments analysis and comparative balance sheet data as follows:

Purchases

Cash purchases...............................		$1,500
Purchases on account:		
Notes and accounts payable at the end of the period	$2,500	
Payments on notes and accounts payable during the period...............................	5,000	
	$7,500	
Deduct notes and accounts payable at the beginning of the period...............................	3,500	4,000
Purchases for the period.......................		$5,500

Notes and accounts payable in the foregoing tabulation are limited to those arising from purchases of merchandise.

The inventory balance shown on the balance sheet at the end of the current period is reported on the income statement as the ending inventory.

Expense items. An expense balance is computed from the analysis of cash payments and comparative balance sheet data. The computation of an expense item is made as follows:

Expense Item

Cash payments representing expense................		$1,000
Add amounts not included in cash payments but to be charged to current period:		
Amount prepaid at the beginning of the period...	$250	
Amount accrued at the end of the period........	150	400
		$1,400
Deduct amounts included in payments but not to be charged to current period:		
Amount prepaid at the end of the period........	$200	
Amount accrued at the beginning of the period...	100	300
Expense for the period............................		$1,100

Revenue items. A revenue balance is computed from the analysis of cash receipts and comparative balance sheet data. The computation of a revenue item is made as follows:

Revenue Item

Cash receipts representing revenue..................		$ 800
Add amounts not included in cash receipts but to be credited to current period:		
Amount prepaid at the beginning of the period..	$300	
Amount accrued at the end of the period........	50	350
		$1,150
Deduct amounts included in receipts but not to be credited to current period:		
Amount prepaid at the end of the period........	$225	
Amount accrued at the beginning of the period...	175	400
Revenue for the period..........................		$ 750

Revenue and expense items requiring special analysis. The computation of certain revenue and expense items, such as doubtful accounts expense, sales discounts, and purchases discounts, requires special data in addition to the information offered by cash records and balance sheets. For example, assume sales data as follows:

Data from cash records:	
Cash sales..	$10,000
Collections on accounts receivable arising from sales......	42,000
Data from balance sheets:	
Accounts receivable at the beginning of the period.......	$14,300
Accounts receivable at the end of the period............	12,500
Supplementary data from special analysis of records:	
Accounts written off during the period.................	$ 600
Sales discounts allowed customers during the period......	850
Sales returns and allowances during the period..........	300

The supplementary data indicate that bad accounts of $600, sales discounts of $850, and sales returns and allowances of $300 are to be recognized. All of these amounts must be added to cash collections in arriving at gross sales, for there must have been sales equivalent to the reductions in accounts receivable from these sources. Gross sales for the period are computed as shown on page 948.

It may be noted that failure to recognize doubtful accounts, sales discounts, and sales returns and allowances will be counterbalanced by an understatement in gross sales. Although the omissions will have no effect upon the net income balance, revenue and expense balances will not be stated accurately.

Sales

Cash sales.		$10,000
Sales on account:		
Accounts receivable at the end of the period. . . .	$12,500	
Collections on accounts receivable.	42,000	
Accounts receivable written off	600	
Accounts receivable reduced by discounts	850	
Accounts receivable reduced by sales returns and		
allowances.	300	
	$56,250	
Deduct accounts receivable at the beginning of		
the period	14,300	41,950
Gross sales for the period		$51,950

When purchases discounts and purchases returns and allowances reduce accounts payable, the computation of purchases follows the procedure illustrated above. The purchases balance is increased by the total purchases discounts and purchases returns and allowances since there must have been purchases equivalent to the reductions in accounts payable from these sources.

The charge for depreciation or amortization to be recognized on the income statement requires special analysis of balance sheet as well as cash data. For example, assume no acquisition or disposal of property during the period and beginning and ending store furniture balances of $30,000 and $28,500. Depreciation is reported at $1,500, the net decrease in the asset account. Assume, however, that the following information is assembled at the end of a fiscal period:

Data from cash records:
    Payments for store furniture, including payments on notes
       arising from acquisition of store furniture. . . . . $ 2,500

Data from balance sheets:
    Store furniture at the beginning of the period $16,500
    Store furniture at the end of the period.   20,675
    Installment notes payable arising from acquisition of store
       furniture.   4,000

The charge for depreciation for the period is computed as shown on the opposite page.

The charge for depreciation developed from the cash records and balance sheet data should be confirmed by computations based upon the individual property items held. The inability to confirm the depreciation charge may indicate that property balances are not reported

Depreciation

Balance of store furniture at the beginning of the period....................................		$16,500
Add acquisitions of store furniture:		
Cash paid on acquisition of store furniture......	$2,500	
Amount owed at the end of the period on acquisition of store furniture.....................	4,000	6,500
Balance of store furniture before depreciation....		$23,000
Deduct balance of store furniture at the end of the period.......................................		20,675
Depreciation of store furniture for period..........		$ 2,325

accurately on the balance sheet. The following analysis is made to support the charge calculated above.

Property	Date Acquired	Cost	Accum. Depr. Prior Yrs.	Remaining Cost	Est. Life	Remaining Life from Beg. of Yr.	Depreciation Current Year
Store furn.	4/1/68	$24,000	$7,500	$16,500	12 yrs.	8¼ yrs.	$2,000
Store furn.	7/1/72	6,500	......	6,500	10 yrs.	......	325 (½ yr.)
		$30,500	$7,500	$23,000			$2,325

Preparation of the statement of changes in financial position.
Preparation of a statement of changes in financial position requires reference to the balance sheets at the beginning and end of the period, the income statement as developed by the analysis just described, and any other pertinent data relating to funds flow. These data are analyzed in accordance with the funds concept that is adopted for the presentation.

Preparation of financial statements from single-entry records illustrated

The example that follows illustrates the preparation from single-entry records of (1) a balance sheet, (2) a summary of net income by analysis of capital changes, (3) an income statement reporting revenue and expense detail and (4) a statement of changes in financial position. Wallace Ward does not maintain double-entry records. Balance sheet data, analyses of cash receipts and disbursements, and supplementary data required in the development of financial statements from the single-entry data are assembled at the end of 1972 as shown below.

Supplementary data developed from an analysis of business papers include the following:

(1) Purchases discounts of $600 were received on the payment of creditors invoices during the year. Sales returns and allowances amounted to $1,480.

(2) Furniture and fixtures were acquired during the year for cash, $3,500. Depreciation is recognized at 10% per year; one half of the normal rate is used for current acquisitions.

Comparative Balance Sheet Data

Assets	Dec. 31, 1972	Jan. 1, 1972
Cash.....................................	$ 5,200	$ 3,200
Notes receivable..........................	3,000	2,500
Accounts receivable.......................	4,500	6,000
Accrued interest income...................	50	150
Merchandise inventory....................	24,600	20,000
Supplies on hand.........................	600	400
Prepaid miscellaneous expense..............	———	100
Investments..............................	2,200	9,700
Furniture and fixtures (cost less accumulated depreciation)...........................	8,325	5,800
Total assets.........................	$48,475	$47,850

Liabilities		
Accounts payable.........................	$ 9,000	$ 7,500
Accrued salaries..........................	250	200
Accrued miscellaneous expense.............	150	———
Unearned rental income...................	125	150
Total liabilities.....................	$ 9,525	$ 7,850

Analyses of Cash Receipts and Disbursements

Balance, January 1, 1972......................			$ 3,200
Receipts:			
Cash sales.................................	$ 9,200		
Accounts and notes receivable arising from sales..	48,000		
From rental of store space..................	1,750		
From interest and dividends.................	400		
From sale of investments, cost $7,500..........	6,250	65,600	
			$68,800
Disbursements:			
Accounts payable arising from purchases.......	$40,000		
For salaries...............................	4,200		
For rent..................................	4,400		
For supplies..............................	1,000		
Acquisition of furniture and fixtures...........	3,500		
For miscellaneous expense...................	1,500		
Owner's withdrawals.......................	9,000	63,600	
Balance, December 31, 1972..................			$ 5,200

A balance sheet as of December 31, 1972, prepared from the foregoing data, is illustrated on the opposite page.

The net income or loss can be calculated from the comparative balance sheet data, and a summary of the investments and withdrawals by the owner is provided by the cash records, as shown on page 952.

Wallace Ward
Balance Sheet
December 31, 1972

Assets			Liabilities and Owner's Equity		
Current assets:			Current liabilities:		
Cash...............	$ 5,200		Accounts payable.....	$ 9,000	
Notes receivable......	3,000		Accrued salaries......	250	
Accounts receivable...	4,500		Accrued miscellaneous		
Accrued interest income............	50		expense..........	150	
Merchandise inventory.............	24,600		Unearned rental income............	125	$ 9,525
Supplies on hand.....	600	$37,950			
Investments		2,200	Wallace Ward, capital..		38,950
Furniture and fixtures (cost, less accumulated depreciation)........		8,325	Total liabilities and		
Total assets...........		$48,475	owner's equity.......		$48,475

An income statement with revenue and expense detail is shown below. Schedules in support of the balances reported on the income statement are included on pages 952 and 953.

Wallace Ward
Income Statement
For Year Ended December 31, 1972

Revenue from sales:				
Sales..	(A)	$57,680		
Less sales return and allowances................	(A-1)	1,480	$56,200	
Cost of goods sold:				
Merchandise inventory, January 1, 1972........			$20,000	
Purchases......................	(B)	$42,100		
Less purchases discount..........	(B-1)	600	41,500	
Merchandise available for sale.................			$61,500	
Less merchandise inventory, December 31, 1972..			24,600	36,900
Gross profit on sales............................				$19,300
Operating expenses:				
Salaries....................................	(C)	$ 4,250		
Rental expense..............................	(D)	4,400		
Supplies expense............................	(E)	800		
Depreciation expense — furniture and fixtures....	(F)	975		
Miscellaneous expense........................	(G)	1,750	12,175	
Operating income............................				$ 7,125
Other revenue items:				
Interest and dividend income.................	(H)	$ 300		
Rental income..............................	(I)	1,775	2,075	
Income before extraordinary item.................				$ 9,200
Extraordinary loss on sale of investments..........		(J)	1,250	
Net income.....................................				$ 7,950

Wallace Ward
Summary of Changes in Owner's Equity
For Year Ended December 31, 1972

Wallace Ward, capital, December 31, 1972...............		$38,950
Wallace Ward, capital, January 1, 1972 (assets, $47,850, less liabilities, $7,850).....................................		40,000
Net decrease in owner's equity..........................		$ (1,050)
Withdrawals by owner during year.......................		9,000
Net income for year..................................		$ 7,950

(A) Computation of sales:

Cash sales....................................			$ 9,200
Sales on account:			
Notes and accounts receivable, December 31....	$ 7,500		
Collections on notes and accounts.............	48,000		
(A-1) Sales returns and allowances.............	1,480		
	$56,980		
Deduct notes and accounts receivable, January 1	8,500	48,480	
Sales for the year............................		$57,680	

(B) Computation of purchases:

Purchases on accounts:		
Accounts payable, December 31...............		$ 9,000
Payments on account........................		40,000
(B-1) Discounts allowed on accounts payable....		600
		$49,600
Deduct accounts payable, January 1...........		7,500
Purchases for the year		$42,100

Computation of operating expenses:

(C) Salaries:

Payments for salaries.........................		$ 4,200
Add accrued salaries, December 31..............		250
		$ 4,450
Deduct accrued salaries, January 1.............		200
Salaries for the year.........................		$ 4,250

(D) Rental expense:

Payments for rent............................		$ 4,400

(E) Supplies expense:

Payments for supplies.........................		$ 1,000
Add supplies on hand, January 1................		400
		$ 1,400
Deduct supplies on hand, December 31..........		600
Supplies used during the year..................		$ 800

(F) Depreciation expense — furniture and fixtures:

Balance of furniture and fixtures, January 1........	$ 5,800	
Add cash paid on acquisition of furniture and fixtures	3,500	
Balance of furniture and fixtures before depreciation	$ 9,300	
Deduct balance of furniture and fixtures, Dec. 31..	8,325	
Depreciation of furniture and fixtures for the year .		$ 975

Depreciation charge is substantiated as follows:

Property	Date Ac- quired	Cost	Accum. Depr. Prior Yrs.	Remaining Cost	Est. Life	Remaining Life from Beginning of Year	Depreciation Current Year
Furniture and fixtures.	1968	$ 6,000	$2,100	$3,900	10 yrs.	6½ yrs.	$600
Furniture and fixtures.	1971	2,000	100	1,900	10 yrs.	9½ yrs.	200
Furniture and fixtures.	1972	3,500	......	3,500	10 yrs.	......	175 (½ yr.)
		$11,500	$2,200	$9,300			$975

(G) Miscellaneous expense:

Miscellaneous expense payments................	$ 1,500	
Add: Prepaid miscellaneous expense, January 1 ...	100	
Accrued miscellaneous expense, December 31	150	
Miscellaneous expense for the year..............		$ 1,750

(H) Computation of interest and dividend income:

Interest and dividend receipts..................	$ 400	
Add accrued interest income, December 31.......	50	
	$ 450	
Deduct accrued interest income, January 1.......	150	
Total interest and dividend income for the year . . .		$ 300

(I) Computation of rental income:

Rental receipts.................................	$ 1,750	
Add unearned rental income, January 1.........	150	
	$ 1,900	
Deduct unearned rental income, December 31.....	125	
Total rental income for the year................		$ 1,775

(J) Computation of loss on sale of investments:

Cost of investments sold.......................	$ 7,500	
Proceeds from sale............................	6,250	
Loss on sale of investments....................		$ 1,250

A statement of changes in financial position employing the working capital concept of funds can be prepared directly from comparative balance sheet and income statement data. Working capital was provided by operations and by the sale of investments; working capital was applied to the acquisition of furniture and fixtures and to withdrawals made by the owner. The statement follows:

Wallace Ward
Statement of Changes in Financial Position
For Year Ended December 31, 1972

Working capital was provided by:		
Operations during the period, exclusive of extraordinary item:		
Income from operations...........................	$9,200	
Add expenses not requiring outlay of working capital during the period:		
Depreciation...............................	975	
Working capital provided by operations.............		$10,175
Sale of investments................................		6,250
		$16,425
Working capital was applied to:		
Purchase of furniture and fixtures....................	$3,500	
Withdrawals by owner............................	9,000	12,500
Increase in working capital...........................		$ 3,925

The increase in working capital is accounted for as follows:

Working Capital Items	Dec. 31, 1972	Jan. 1, 1972	Increase (Decrease)
Current assets:			
Cash..............................	$ 5,200	$ 3,200	$2,000
Notes receivable......................	3,000	2,500	500
Accounts receivable...................	4,500	6,000	(1,500)
Accrued interest income..............	50	150	(100)
Merchandise inventory................	24,600	20,000	4,600
Supplies on hand.....................	600	400	200
Prepaid miscellaneous expense.........	——	100	(100)
Current liabilities:			
Accounts payable....................	9,000	7,500	(1,500)
Accrued salaries.....................	250	200	(50)
Accrued miscellaneous expense.........	150	——	(150)
Unearned rental income..............	125	150	25
Increase in working capital.............			$3,925

Work sheet for preparation of financial statements

In the preceding example, a balance sheet was prepared first. The income statement was then drawn up from special schedules that developed revenue and expense balances. The funds statement was prepared by analyzing balance sheet and income statement data. Such procedures are convenient under simple circumstances. However, when the preparation of the financial statements involves a number of special analyses and computations and when certain difficulties are anticipated, working papers may be employed in assembling the financial data.

The use of a work sheet for the preparation of a balance sheet and income statement in the previous example is illustrated on pages 956 and 957. Opening balances are listed in the first pair of columns. Summaries of the transactions for the year appear in the second pair of columns. Entries (A)–(J) record revenue and expense data previously developed by separate schedules and identified by the same letters. Entries (K), (L), and (M) record the purchase of furniture and fixtures, withdrawals by the owner, and the ending inventory. Adjusted account balances are carried to statement columns and statements are drawn up from the latter. Data on the work sheet should be traced to the statements presented on pages 951.

The use of working papers for the preparation of the statement of changes in financial position is not illustrated in view of the fact that sources and applications of funds are so readily identifiable.

Change from single entry to double entry

A business may find that single-entry procedures fail to meet its needs and may decide to change to double entry. Single-entry records may be converted to double entry by first drawing up a balance sheet as of the date of change. This statement is used as the basis for a journal entry establishing all of the asset, asset valuation, liability, and capital accounts. If additional accounts are to be added to a ledger already in use, accounts are opened and balances recorded for those items not included. If new books are to be used, accounts are opened and balances are recorded for all of the items reported in the opening journal entry.

Use of single-entry systems

Single entry is described here because it represents a system that the accountant may encounter when he is called upon to prepare financial statements, audit books and records, and prepare government informational reports and income tax returns. Many organizations, both profit and nonprofit, adopt single-entry procedures because of their simplicity and economy. Individuals who are required to maintain records of personal transactions for financial and tax purposes seldom maintain their records on a double-entry basis. In all such instances the type of analysis suggested in this chapter is followed in developing required financial data.

The adoption of single entry can be recommended only when an organization has few transactions and these are of a simple character.

Wallace
Work
For Year Ended

#	Account Title	Balance Sheet January 1, 1972 Debit	Credit	Transactions 1972 Debit	Credit	#
1	Cash	3,200		(A) 57,200	(B) 40,000	1
2					(C) 4,200	2
3				(H) 400	(D) 4,400	3
4					(E) 1,000	4
5				(I) 1,750	(G) 1,500	5
6					(K) 3,500	6
7				(J) 6,250	(L) 9,000	7
8	Notes Receivable	2,500		(A) 500		8
9	Accounts Receivable	6,000			(A) 1,500	9
10	Accrued Interest Income	150			(H) 100	10
11	Merchandise Inventory	20,000		(M) 24,600	(M) 24,600	11
12	Supplies on Hand	400		(E) 200		12
13	Prepaid Miscellaneous Expense	100			(G) 100	13
14	Investments	9,700			(J) 7,500	14
15	Furn. and Fix. Cost Less Accum. Depreciation	5,800		(K) 3,500	(F) 975	15
16	Accounts Payable		7,500		(B) 1,500	16
17	Accrued Salaries		200		(C) 50	17
18	Unearned Rental Income		150	(I) 25		18
19	Wallace Ward, Capital		40,000			19
20		47,850	47,850			20
21	Sales				(A) 57,680	21
22	Sales Returns and Allowances			(A) 1,480		22
23	Purchases			(B) 42,100		23
24	Purchases Discount				(B) 600	24
25	Salaries			(C) 4,250		25
26	Rental Expense			(D) 4,400		26
27	Supplies Expense			(E) 800		27
28	Depreciation Exp.—Furn. and Fix.			(F) 975		28
29	Accrued Miscellaneous Expense				(G) 150	29
30	Miscellaneous Expense			(G) 1,750		30
31	Interest and Dividend Income				(H) 300	31
32	Rental Income				(I) 1,775	32
33	Loss on Sale of Investments			(J) 1,250		33
34	Wallace Ward, Withdrawals			(L) 9,000		34
35				160,430	160,430	35
36						36
37	Net Income					37
38						38
39						39
40	Capital, December 31, 1972					40
41						41

Explanation of transactions and adjustments:

(A) Sales, $57,680: cash sales, $9,200 + collections on account, $48,000 + sales returns and allowances, $1,480 + increase in notes receivable, $500 − decrease in accounts receivable, $1,500.

(B) Purchases, $42,100: payments on account, $40,000 + purchases discount, $600 + increase in accounts payable, $1,500.

(C) Salaries, $4,250: payments, $4,200 + increase in accrued salaries, $50.

(D) Rental expense, $4,400: rental payments, $4,400.

(E) Supplies used, $800: payments $1,000 − increase in supplies inventory, $200.

(F) Depreciation expense — furniture and fixtures, $975 as calculated. (See page 953.)

Ward
Sheet
December 31, 1972

	Income Statement		Capital		Balance Sheet		
	Debit	Credit	Debit	Credit	Debit	Credit	
1							1
2							2
3							3
4							4
5							5
6							6
7					5,200		7
8					3,000		8
9					4,500		9
10					50		10
11	20,000	24,600			24,600		11
12					600		12
13							13
14					2,200		14
15					8,325		15
16						9,000	16
17						250	17
18						125	18
19				40,000			19
20							20
21		57,680					21
22	1,480						22
23	42,100						23
24		600					24
25	4,250						25
26	4,400						26
27	800						27
28	975						28
29						150	29
30	1,750						30
31		300					31
32		1,775					32
33	1,250						33
34			9,000				34
35							35
36	77,005	84,955					36
37	7,950			7,950			37
38	84,955	84,955					38
39			9,000	47,950			39
40			38,950			38,950	40
41			47,950	47,950	48,475	48,475	41

(G) Miscellaneous expense, $1,750: payments, $1,500 + decrease in prepaid miscellaneous expense, $100 + increase in accrued miscellaneous expense, $150.

(H) Interest and dividend income, $300: receipts, $400 − decrease in accrued interest income, $100.

(I) Rental income, $1,775: receipts, $1,750 + decrease in unearned rental income, $25.

(J) Loss on sale of investments, $1,250: cost of investments sold, $7,500 − proceeds from sale, $6,250.

(K) Purchase of furniture and fixtures, for cash, $3,500.

(L) Cash withdrawals by owner, $9,000.

(M) Merchandise inventory, December 31, $24,600.

Among the intrinsic shortcomings of single-entry procedures are the following factors:

1. A trial balance offering a check on the mathematical accuracy of posting is not available.
2. Preparation of the balance sheet from miscellaneous sources and memoranda may result in omissions and misstatements.
3. Detailed analysis of transactions is necessary in arriving at a summary of operations. Misstatements of assets and liabilities, particularly failures to report assets at properly depreciated or amortized balances, affect revenue and expense balances and may result in material misstatement of net income or loss.
4. There is failure to provide a centralized and coordinated accounting system subject to internal control and available for satisfactory and convenient audit by public accountants and Internal Revenue agents.

QUESTIONS

1. Distinguish between single-entry and double-entry procedures.

2. Describe the records and the nature of recording under typical single-entry bookkeeping.

3. What are the sources of information for balance sheet items when the single-entry plan is followed?

4. Distinguish between the manner in which the owner's capital balance is computed in a double-entry system as compared with a single-entry system.

5. John Day has his assets appraised at the end of each year and draws up a balance sheet using such appraisal values. He then calculates the change in capital for the year and adjusts this for investments and withdrawals in arriving at the net income or loss for the year. In your opinion, does this procedure provide a satisfactory measurement of earnings?

6. State how each of the following items is computed in preparing an income statement when single-entry procedures are followed and the accrual basis is used in reporting net income:

(a) Merchandise sales   (e) Insurance expense
(b) Merchandise purchases   (f) Interest income
(c) Depreciation on equipment   (g) Rental income
(d) Sales salaries   (h) Taxes

7. Single-entry systems are obsolete and have no place in modern business. Do you agree? Explain.

8. In developing the sales balance, the owner of a business recognizes cash collections from customers and the change in the receivables balance but ignores sales returns, sales allowances, and sales discounts. Indicate the effects, if any, that such omissions will have on net income.

9. Greater accuracy is achieved in financial statements prepared from double-entry data as compared with single-entry data. Do you agree?

10. Under what circumstances would you expect to find single-entry systems used?

11. Describe the procedure to be followed in changing from a single-entry system to double entry.

EXERCISES

1. Sales salaries are reported on the income statement for 1972 at $12,800. Balance sheet data relating to sales salaries are as follows:

	Jan. 1, 1972	Dec. 31, 1972
Prepaid salaries (advances to salesmen).	$ 250	—
Accrued salaries....................	800	$ 750

How much cash was paid out during 1972 for sales salaries expense?

2. Rental income is reported on the income statement for 1972 at $20,000. Balance sheet data relating to rental income are as follows:

	Jan. 1, 1972	Dec. 31, 1972
Unearned rental income............	$4,500	$4,800
Accrued rental income (delinquent rent)	400	650

How much cash was collected during 1972 for rental income?

3. Service fees collections in 1972 are $15,000; service fees income reported on the income statement is $14,000. The balance sheet prepared at the beginning of the year reported accrued service fees, $600, and unearned service fees, $450; the balance sheet at the end of the year reported accrued service fees, $850. What is the amount of unearned service fees at the end of the year?

4. Salary payments in 1972 were $14,000; salary expense reported on the income statement was $14,750. The balance sheet prepared at the beginning of the year reported salary advances, $400, accrued salaries, $600; the balance sheet at the end of the year reported salary advances, $450. What is the amount of accrued salaries at the end of the year?

5. On January 1 the capital of J. R. Adler was $2,400 and on January 31 the capital was $3,720. During the month Adler withdrew merchandise costing $150, and on January 25 he paid a $1,500 note payable of the business with interest at 8% for 3 months with a check drawn on his personal checking account. What was Adler's net income or loss for the month of January?

6. An analysis of the records of W. J. Arthur disclosed changes in account balances for 1972 and the supplementary data listed below. From these data, calculate the net income or loss for 1972.

Cash	$ 9,400 increase
Accounts receivable	1,500 decrease
Merchandise inventory	13,500 increase
Notes payable	8,000 increase
Accounts payable	2,500 increase

During the year Arthur borrowed $12,000 from the bank and paid off notes of $15,000 and interest of $750. Interest of $250 is accrued as of December 31, 1972.

In 1972 Arthur also transferred certain marketable securities that he owned to the business and these were sold for $6,300 to finance the purchase of merchandise.

Arthur made weekly withdrawals in 1972 of $200.

7. On December 31, 1972, Arnold Manufacturing Company showed the stockholders' equity on its balance sheet at $122,200. During 1972 the stockholders' equity was affected by: (1) an adjustment to retained earnings for an understatement of net income in 1971 of $1,200, (2) a dividend declared but not paid of $8,000, and (3) net income for 1972 of $9,420. The capital stock balance of $100,000 remained unchanged during the year. What was the retained earnings balance on January 1, 1972?

8. Total accounts receivable for the Power Sales Company were as follows: on January 1, $5,000; on January 31, $5,300. In January $8,000 was collected on accounts, $600 was received for cash sales, accounts receivable of $700 were written off as uncollectible, and allowances on sales of $200 were made. What amount should be reported for sales on the income statement for January?

PROBLEMS

26-1. The following data are obtained from a single-entry set of books kept by D. R. Summers, proprietor of a retail store:

	Mar. 31	Jan. 1
Notes receivable	$ 3,000	$1,000
Accounts receivable	5,000	4,000
Accrued interest on notes receivable	150	100
Merchandise inventories	2,400	4,000
Store equipment	2,850	3,000
Notes payable	1,250	1,800
Accounts payable	2,650	3,000
Accrued interest on notes payable	100	200

The cashbook shows the following information:

	Mar. 31	Jan. 1
Balance, January 1...........................		$ 3,000
Receipts: Accounts receivable.................	$7,500	
Notes receivable......................	2,400	
Interest on notes.....................	100	10,000
		$13,000
Payments: Accounts payable..................	$3,800	
Notes payable......................	3,200	
Interest on notes....................	200	
Operating expenses.................	1,900	
Withdrawals......................	1,000	10,100
Balance, March 31...........................		$ 2,900

The following supplementary information is available:

Accounts receivable of $250 were written off as uncollectible.
Allowances of $140 were received on merchandise purchases.

Instructions: (1) Compute the net income or loss for the three-month period by considering the changes in owner's capital.

(2) Prepare an income statement for the three-month period accompanied by schedules in support of revenue and expense balances.

26-2. The following information is obtained from the single-entry records of Wilford Harris:

	June 30	Jan. 1
Notes receivable.............................	$1,200	$2,000
Accounts receivable..........................	8,800	4,500
Accrued interest on notes receivable..............	80	100
Merchandise inventories.......................	1,000	3,800
Prepaid operating expenses.....................	220	250
Store equipment.............................	3,000	3,250
Notes payable..............................	1,200	1,000
Accounts payable............................	2,500	3,500
Accrued interest on notes payable................	50	30
Accrued operating expenses.....................	300	270

The cashbook shows the following:

Balance, January 1...........................		$1,500
Receipts: Accounts receivable..................	$4,800	
Notes receivable......................	1,500	
Interest income......................	200	6,500
		$8,000
Payments: Accounts payable...................	$5,200	
Notes payable......................	800	
Interest expense.....................	150	
Operating expenses...................	1,700	
Withdrawals.......................	600	8,450
Balance, June 30 — bank overdraft..............		$ (450)

Instructions: (1) Compute the net income or loss for the six-month period by considering the changes in the owner's capital.

(2) Prepare an income statement for the six-month period accompanied by schedules in support of revenue and expense balances.

26-3. Balance sheets for the Christopher Company prepared in 1972 report the following balances:

Assets	June 30	January 1
Cash.	$ 84,500	$ 23,000
Notes receivable	15,000	20,000
Accounts receivable	95,000	74,000
Merchandise inventories	150,000	160,000
Prepaid expenses.	10,000	12,000
Investments (at cost)	10,000	30,000
Buildings and equipment (net).	120,000	100,000
	$484,500	$419,000

Liabilities and Stockholders' Equity		
Notes payable.	$ 58,000	$ 55,000
Accounts payable.	75,000	60,000
Accrued interest on bank note.	450	————
Accrued expenses.	2,000	2,000
Bonds payable.	————	50,000
Common stock, $100 par.	150,000	100,000
Premium on common stock.	125,000	100,000
Retained earnings.	74,050	52,000
	$484,500	$419,000

An analysis of cash receipts and disbursements discloses the following:

Receipts		Disbursements	
Capital stock.	$ 75,000	Trade creditors—notes and ac-	
Trade debtors—notes and ac-		counts.	$210,000
counts.	230,000	Expenses.	70,000
Cash sales.	80,000	Dividends.	40,000
Notes receivable discounted:		Equipment.	28,000
face value, $20,000, proceeds. .	19,500	Bonds.	50,000
6% note issued to bank, dated			
March 31, 1972.	30,000		
Sale of investments.	25,000		

Instructions: (1) Prepare an income statement supported by schedules showing computations of revenue and expense balances for the six-month period ended June 30, 1972.

(2) Prove the net income or loss determined in part (1) by preparing a retained earnings statement.

26-4. A comparative balance sheet prepared from the single-entry records of Rice, Inc., follows:

Rice, Inc.
Comparative Balance Sheet
December 31, 1972 and 1971

	December 31, 1972		December 31, 1971	
Current assets:				
Cash..............................	$ 4,200		$ 3,300	
Accounts receivable...............	18,000		16,000	
Notes receivable..................	7,000		8,000	
Merchandise inventory	28,000		21,600	
Prepaid expenses..................	1,850		1,800	
Total current assets		$59,050		$50,700
Furniture and fixtures (net)		24,700		22,200
Total assets......................		$83,750		$72,900
Current liabilities:				
Accounts payable..................	$16,400		$15,200	
Notes payable–bank and trade creditors	12,000		8,500	
Accrued expenses.................	1,350		1,200	
Total liabilities..................		$29,750		$24,900
Stockholders' equity:				
Capital stock.....................	$50,000		$50,000	
Retained earnings (deficit)...........	4,000	54,000	(2,000)	48,000
Total liabilities and stockholders' equity..		$83,750		$72,900

Cash receipts and payments for 1972 are classified as follows:

Receipts:

Cash sales..	$ 6,000
Accounts receivable...............................	103,000
Notes payable (amount borrowed from bank)..........	7,500
	$116,500

Payments:

Accounts payable................................	$ 73,000
Notes payable...................................	6,200
Expenses..	23,900
Furniture and fixtures............................	4,500
Dividends.......................................	8,000
	$115,600

Instructions: (1) Compute the net income or loss for the year by considering the changes in retained earnings.

(2) Prepare an income statement for the year and schedules in support of revenue and expense balances.

26-5. Stokes and Henry operate a retail store, sharing profits equally. A balance sheet for the partnership on January 1, 1972, follows:

Assets		Liabilities and Owners' Equity	
Cash.	$ 260	Accounts payable.	$ 4,900
Notes receivable.	1,500	Accrued expenses.	260
Accounts receivable.	6,500	Stokes, capital.	6,900
Interest receivable.	40	Henry, capital.	6,700
Merchandise inventory.	7,000		
Prepaid expenses.	260		
Furniture and fixtures.	3,200	Total liabilities and	
Total assets.	$18,760	owners' equity.	$18,760

On December 31, 1972, asset and liability balances are:

Assets		Liabilities	
Notes receivable.	$ 2,000	Cash overdraft.	$ 200
Accounts receivable.	7,650	Notes payable.	2,500
Interest receivable.	50	Accounts payable.	7,100
Merchandise inventory.	8,000	Accrued expenses.	200
Prepaid expense.	300		$10,000
Furniture and fixtures.	4,000		
	$22,000		

Cash receipts and disbursements for the year were:

Receipts			Disbursements		
Investment by Stokes.		$ 800	Withdrawals by Stokes ($225		
Cash sales.		4,450	monthly).		$ 2,700
Receipts on accounts and			Withdrawals by Henry ($225		
notes.	$30,000		monthly).		2,700
Less discounts.	400	29,600	On accounts payable. . .	$22,300	
Interest on notes.		80	Less discounts.	500	21,800
Amount borrowed from bank on			Purchase of store fixtures on		
September 1; issued $2,500, 6%			July 1, 1972.		1,200
note due in one year.		2,500	Operating expenses.		9,490
		$37,430			$37,890

Accrued interest on the note payable of $50 is included in the accrued expenses total of $200 as of December 31.

Doubtful accounts written off during the year totaled $300.

Sales returns and allowances during the year were $600.

Instructions: (1) Prepare a work sheet for the preparation of a balance sheet and income statement.

(2) Prepare for the year ended December 31, 1972, (a) a balance sheet, (b) an income statement accompanied by a statement of changes in the partners' capitals, and (c) a statement of changes in financial position applying the working capital concept of funds.

26-6. Martin and James, partners, do not maintain double-entry records. In preparing statements for the year ended December 31, 1972, you assemble the data that follow.

A balance sheet as of December 31, 1971, showed the following balances.

Assets		Liabilities and Owners' Equity	
Cash........................	$ 6,025	Accounts payable..............	$ 4,800
Marketable securities (cost).....	3,600	Accrued taxes.................	250
Accounts receivable...........	10,515	Accrued miscellaneous expenses..	150
Allowance for doubtful accounts.	(650)	Notes payable.................	5,000
Merchandise inventory........	24,005	Martin, capital	14,450
Prepaid miscellaneous expenses..	115	James, capital.................	21,450
Supplies.....................	250		
Fixtures.....................	4,650		
Accumulated depreciation......	(2,410)	Total liabilities and owners'	
Total assets................	$46,100	equity...................	$46,100

Cash records for 1972 show the following:

Deposits:

Collections from customers..........................	$103,600
Investment by Martin...............................	6,000
Income from securities..............................	140
Sale of marketable securities, cost $3,600..............	4,000
	$113,740

Checks written:

Purchase of merchandise...........................	$ 77,200
Salaries..	6,880
Utilities..	800
Rent...	4,800
Supplies..	1,000
Fixtures..	4,000
Taxes..	1,240
Notes payable (includes interest of $180)..............	4,180
Miscellaneous expense..............................	6,300
Partners' salaries — Martin, $100 per week............	5,200
— James, $125 per week............	6,500
	$118,100

The following additional data are available:

Bank service charges during the year were $60.

Accounts receivable at the end of the year total $11,550. Accounts of $1,200 had been written off as worthless during the year; it is estimated that another $700 in accounts on hand at the end of the year will prove uncollectible.

Accounts payable on December 31, 1972, total $5,580. Purchases discounts of $1,440 had been taken during the year and merchandise of $1,580 had been returned to suppliers.

The merchandise inventory at the end of the year is $29,600; the supplies inventory is $215; and prepaid miscellaneous expenses are $210. Accrued taxes at the end of the year are $705, accrued salaries are $160, miscellaneous accrued expenses are $80, and accrued interest payable is $60.

Depreciation is recognized on the fixtures at the rate of 10% per year but only one half of this rate is applied on fixtures that are acquired during the year.

The partnership agreement provides that Martin and James are entitled to $100 and $125 per week respectively as salaries, and that any profits after salaries are to be divided equally.

Instructions: (1) Prepare a work sheet for the preparation of a balance sheet and income statement.

(2) Prepare for the year ended December 31, 1972, (a) a balance sheet, (b) an income statement accompanied by a statement of changes in the partners' capitals, and (c) a statement of changes in financial position applying the working capital concept of funds.

26-7. From the following data relative to the operation of the Garden Homes, Inc., during 1972, you are requested to prepare a schedule showing cash collections of rents for the year.

Gross potential rents.....................................	$211,688
Vacancies...	42,609
Space occupied by corporation for own use..............	4,925
Prepaid rent:	
Beginning of period...............................	302
End of period.....................................	984
Delinquent rent:	
Beginning of period...............................	377
End of period.....................................	79
Deposits (tenants) forfeited...........................	100
Refunds to tenants....................................	20
Uncollectible rents....................................	80

(AICPA adapted)

26-8. Buxby and Landon are partners in the operation of a retail store. They are concerned about the apparent discrepancy between their income and their volume of sales. Although they maintain incomplete accounting records, their experience in the business suggests to them that there is possible theft or larceny on the part of their staff.

The partners have asked you, in connection with your initial audit (covering the calendar year 1972), to apply such tests as you can to determine whether there is any indication of shortage. In the course of your investigation you obtain the following facts having a bearing on the problem:

(a) The physical inventory taken December 31, 1972, under your observation, amounted to $4,442 cost, $4,171 market. The inventory of December 31, 1971, was $6,256 cost, $6,013 market. It has been the firm's practice to value inventory at lower of cost or market, treating any loss or decline in market value as "other expense."

(b) Using the treatment of "loss or decline in market value" of inventory as mentioned in (a) above, the average gross profit in recent periods has been 35% of net sales. The partners inform you that this percent seems reasonable and that they expected the same result for 1972, since their markup percent was approximately the same as in the past.

(c) The December 31, 1971 balance sheet shows accounts receivable of $2,057. Notes payable to banks and trade accounts payable were combined on the December 31, 1971 balance sheet. They totaled $9,622. The firm records accounts payable at the net figure, as cash discounts are seldom missed. Purchases have been shown net in past income statements. Sales discounts have been treated as deductions from sales in the past.

(d) During 1972 accounts were written off in the amount of $216, and an account for $148 written off in 1971 was collected and recorded as a regular collection on account.

(e) Unpaid sales slips show that customers owed $3,246 on December 31, 1972.

(f) Unpaid invoices indicate that the firm owed trade creditors $5,027 at the end of 1972. Record of notes outstanding indicates that $3,000 was owed to banks on December 31, 1972.

(g) Sales returns amounted to $95 and purchase returns amounted to $272.

(h) Of the items in the cash records, the following are pertinent:

Receipts:

From customers (after $272 discounts).................	$49,851
From bank loan (net of 60-day, 6% discount)...........	2,970

Disbursements:

To trade creditors (after $916 cash discounts)...........	$38,970
To banks on loans.....................................	4,000
To customers for returned goods......................	72

Instructions: Compute the amount by which the physical inventory is short, assuming the gross profit rate of 35% is reasonable.

(AICPA adapted)

26-9. Paul Canby, a merchant, kept very limited records. Purchases of merchandise were paid for by check, but most other items of cost were paid out of cash receipts. Weekly the amount of cash on hand was deposited in a bank account. No record was kept of cash in the bank, nor was a record kept of sales. Accounts receivable were recorded only by keeping a copy of the sales ticket, and this copy was given to the customer when he paid his account.

Canby had started in business on January 1, 1972, with $20,000 cash and a building that had cost $15,000, of which one third was the value of the building site. The building depreciated 4% a year. An analysis of the bank statements showed total deposits, including the original cash investment, of $130,500. The balance in the bank per bank statement on December 31, 1972, was $5,300, but there were checks amounting to $2,150 dated in December but not paid by the bank until January. Cash on hand on December 31 was $334.

An inventory of merchandise taken on December 31, 1972, showed $16,710 of merchandise on a cost basis. Tickets for accounts receivable totaled $1,270, but $123 of that amount is probably not collectible. Unpaid suppliers' invoices for merchandise amounted to $3,780. During the year Canby had borrowed $10,000 from his bank, but he repaid by check

$5,000 principal and $100 interest. He has taken for personal expenses $4,800 from the cash collections. Expenses paid in cash were as follows:

Utilities.	$554
Advertising.	50
Sales help (part time).	590
Supplies, stationery, etc..	100
Insurance.	234
Real estate taxes.	350

Store fixtures with a list price of $7,000 were purchased early in January on a one-year installment basis. During the year, checks for the down payment and all maturing installments totaled $5,600. At December 31, the final installment of $1,525 remains unpaid. The fixtures have an estimated useful life of 10 years.

Instructions: Based on the above information, prepare an income statement for 1972, supported by all computations necessary to determine the sales and the purchases for the year. (AICPA adapted)

26-10. The Hardin Furniture Store (a sole proprietorship) did not have complete records on a double-entry basis. However, from an investigation of its records you have established the information shown below:

(a) The assets and the liabilities as of December 31, 1971, were:

	Debit	Credit
Cash.	$ 5,175	
Accounts receivable.	10,556	
Allowance for doubtful accounts.		$ 740
Fixtures.	3,130	
Accumulated depreciation — fixtures.		1,110
Prepaid insurance.	158	
Prepaid supplies.	79	
Accounts payable.		4,244
Accrued miscellaneous expenses.		206
Accrued taxes.		202
Merchandise inventory.	19,243	
Note payable.		5,000
Hardin, capital.		26,839

(b) A summary of the transactions for 1972 as recorded in the checkbook shows the following:

Deposits for the year (including the redeposit of $304 of checks charged back by the bank).	$83,187
Checks drawn during the year.	84,070
Customers' checks charged back by the bank	304
Bank service charges.	22

(c) The following information is available as to accounts payable:

Purchases on account during year.	$57,789
Returns of merchandise allowed as credits against accounts by vendors.	1,418
Payments of accounts by check	55,461

(d) Information as to accounts receivable shows the following:

Accounts written off....................................	$ 812
Accounts collected......................................	43,083
Balance of accounts December 31, 1972 (of this balance $700 is estimated to be uncollectible)......................	11,921

(e) Checks drawn during the year include checks for the following items:

Salaries...	$10,988
Rent..	3,600
Heat, light, and telephone............................	394
Supplies...	280
Insurance..	341
Taxes and licenses...................................	1,017
Drawings of proprietor...............................	6,140
Miscellaneous expense................................	769
Merchandise purchases...............................	2,080
Note payable.......................................	3,000
	$28,609

(f) Merchandise inventory December 31, 1972, was $17,807. Prepaid insurance amounted to $122 and supplies on hand amounted to $105 as of December 31, 1972. Accrued taxes were $216 and miscellaneous accrued expenses were $73 at the year end.

(g) Cash sales for the year are assumed to account for all cash received other than that collected on accounts. Fixtures are to be depreciated at the rate of 10% per annum.

Instructions: Prepare an income statement for the year ended December 31, 1972, and a balance sheet as of December 31, 1972.

(AICPA adapted)

26-11. The Braxton Printing Company is a proprietorship owned by Robert Braxton, who does not have the time to keep detailed accounting records. Mr. Braxton purchased the business on January 1, 1972. He asks you to prepare interim financial statements for the six months ended June 30, 1973, and he provides the following schedule:

	June 30, 1973	December 31, 1972
Cash.................................	$ 2,039	$ 1,650
Note receivable......................	600	—
Accounts receivable..................	1,700	1,300
Inventory...........................	3,140	2,370
Prepaid insurance....................	264	315
Equipment (original cost).............	10,200	8,600*
Total assets.......................	$17,943	$14,235
Accounts payable....................	$ 1,100	$ 890
Accrued expenses....................	100	55
Total liabilities....................	$ 1,200	$ 945

*As at January 1, 1972.

You are able to accumulate the following information:

(a) The schedule for December 31, 1972, was taken from the financial statements you prepared for Mr. Braxton as of that date.

(b) The cash balance of $2,039 was taken from the bank statement. The client's checkbook reveals the following:

Deposits:

Collections from customers............................	$25,025
Sale of equipment....................................	400
Loan from bank ($2,000, 4-month note due September 30, 1973)..	1,960
	$27,385

Withdrawals:

Payments to suppliers................................	$20,221
Insurance premiums..................................	264
Employee's salary....................................	775
Payment on Mr. Braxton's estimated income tax........	300
Purchase of equipment...............................	1,600
Withdrawn by Mr. Braxton as salary..................	2,400
Miscellaneous expenses, including rent................	1,436
	$26,996

(c) A check for $450 was received from a customer on June 30, 1973, and mailed to the bank on that day. The payment was deducted from the accounts receivable as of June 30 but not recorded in the checkbook or by the bank until July 2.

(d) Mr. Braxton excluded from accounts receivable $150 that he says is uncollectible. He estimates that the cost of this sale was $120.

(e) The note receivable is non-interest bearing and is due on September 1, 1973. It was accepted on May 1, 1973, from a delinquent account receivable.

(f) Printing equipment that was included in the original purchase price at $1,000 was sold for $400 on March 31. New equipment costing $1,600 was installed on April 1. All equipment has an estimated life of 10 years. Disregard salvage value of assets.

(g) Mr. Braxton hired an assistant on April 1, 1973, at a salary of $3,200 per year. (Disregard any payroll taxes.)

(h) An examination of insurance policies reveals the following:

Policy	Acquired	Term	Premium	Unexpired December 31, 1972
#2479	Jan. 1, 1972	3 years	$360	$240
C2160	June 1, 1972	1 year	180	75
831	April 1, 1973	1 year	72	
C2380	June 1, 1973	1 year	192	
			$804	$315

(i) The accrued expenses are miscellaneous public utility charges which you compute to be $70 at June 30. The $100 item at June 30 is an extra month's rent that Mr. Braxton paid in error. He listed the item when the landlord advised him of the overpayment.

Instructions: Prepare a work sheet that shows the account balances on December 31, 1972, the adjustments that are required in reporting revenue and expenses on an accrual basis for the six months ended June 30, 1973, the results of operations for the six months ended June 30, 1973, and the financial position at June 30, 1973. Formal journal entries and financial statements are not required.

(AICPA adapted)

26-12. The Valley Corporation is primarily a sales organization. The corporation has approximately 1,000 stockholders and its stock, which is traded "over-the-counter," sold throughout 1972 at about $7 a share with little fluctuation.

The Corporation's balance sheet at December 31, 1971, is shown below.

Valley Corporation
Balance Sheet
December 31, 1971

Assets

Current assets:		$ 4,386,040
Cash		
Accounts receivable	$3,150,000	
Less allowance for doubtful accounts	94,500	3,055,500
Inventories — at the lower of cost (first-in, first-out) or estimated realizable market		2,800,000
Total current assets		$10,241,540
Fixed assets — at cost	$3,300,000	
Less accumulated depreciation	1,300,000	2,000,000
Total assets		$12,241,540

Liabilities and Stockholders' Equity

Current liabilities:		
Notes payable due within one year		$ 1,000,000
Accounts payable and accrued liabilities		2,091,500
Income taxes payable		350,000
Total current liabilities		$ 3,441,500
Notes payable due after one year		4,000,000
Stockholders' equity:		
Capital stock — authorized 2,000,000 shares of $1 par value; issued and outstanding 1,000,000 shares	$1,000,000	
Additional paid-in capital	1,500,000	
Retained earnings	2,300,040	
Total stockholders' equity		4,800,040
Total liabilities and stockholders' equity		$12,241,540

Information concerning the corporation and its activities during 1972 follows:

(a) Sales for the year were $15,650,000. The gross profit percentage for the year was 30% of sales. Merchandise purchases and freight in totaled $10,905,000. It can be assumed that depreciation and other expenses do not enter into cost of goods sold.

(b) Administrative, selling and general expenses (including provision for state taxes) other than interest, depreciation, and provision for doubtful accounts amounted to $2,403,250.

(c) The December 31, 1972 accounts receivable were $3,350,000 and the corporation maintains an allowance for doubtful accounts equal to 3% of the accounts receivable outstanding. During the year $50,000 of 1971 receivables were deemed uncollectible and charged off to the allowance account.

(d) The rate of depreciation of fixed assets is 13% per annum and the corporation consistently follows the policy of taking one-half year's depreciation in the year of acquisition. The depreciation expense for 1972 was $474,500.

(e) The notes are payable in twenty equal quarterly installments commencing March 31, 1972, with interest at 5% per annum also payable quarterly.

(f) Accounts payable and accrued liabilities at December 31, 1972, were $2,221,000.

(g) The balance of the 1971 income tax paid in 1972 was in exact agreement with the amount accrued on the December 31, 1971 balance sheet.

(h) For purposes of the 1972 estimated income tax, the controller had made payments in 1972 totaling $350,000. It is estimated on the basis of income for 1972 that the income tax liability for the year will total $790,100. The balance of the tax is payable in 1973.

(i) During the second month of each quarter of the year, 1972 dividends of $.10 a share were declared and paid. In addition, in July, 1972, a 5% stock dividend was declared and paid.

Instructions: Prepare the following statements in good form, supported by well organized and detailed computations, for the year ended December 31, 1972:
(1) Balance sheet
(2) Income statement
(3) Statement of retained earnings   (AICPA adapted)

26-13. On January 3, 1972, Nolan-Paszkowski, Inc., was organized with two stockholders, Richard Nolan and Lynn Paszkowski. Richard Nolan purchased 500 shares of $100 par value common stock for $50,000 cash; Lynn Paszkowski received 500 shares of common stock in exchange for the assets and liabilities of a men's clothing shop that she had operated as a sole proprietorship. The balance sheet immediately after incorporation appears on the work sheet shown on the opposite page.

No formal books have been kept during 1972. The following data have been gathered from the checkbooks, deposit slips and other sources:

(a) Most balance sheet account balances at December 31, 1972, have been determined and recorded on the work sheet.

(b) Cash receipts for the year are summarized as follows:
Advances from customers............................ $ 700
Cash sales and collections on accounts receivable (after sales discounts of $1,520 and sales returns and allowances of $1,940)............................... 126,540
Sale of equipment costing $5,000 on which $1,000 of depreciation had accumulated.................... 4,500
                                                       $131,740

Nolan —
Work Sheet for Preparation of
For Year Ended

Item	Balance Sheet January 3, 1972	
	Debit	Credit
Cash..	50,000	
Accounts receivable.........................	12,400	
Merchandise inventory......................	23,000	
Prepaid insurance..........................	350	
Land......................................	15,000	
Buildings..................................	20,000	
Accumulated depreciation — buildings.........		7,000
Equipment.................................	8,000	
Accumulated depreciation — equipment........		2,400
Accounts payable...........................		17,300
Advances from customers....................		900
Salaries payable............................		600
Employees income taxes payable..............		450
FICA taxes payable.........................		100
Capital stock..............................		100,000
	128,750	128,750

(left page)

Paszkowski, Inc.
Accrual Basis Financial Statements
December 31, 1972

Summary and Adjusting Entries		Income Statement 1972		Balance Sheet December 31, 1972	
Debit	Credit	Debit	Credit	Debit	Credit
				18,700	
				24,500	
				200	
				15,000	
					8,679
					550
					1,595
					775
					190
					100,000

(right page)

(c) Cash disbursements for the year are summarized as follows:

Insurance premiums.	$ 825
Purchase of equipment.	18,000
Addition to building.	4,600
Cash purchases and payments on accounts payable (after purchases discounts of $1,150 and purchases returns and allowances of $1,800).	82,050
Remittance of payroll taxes (income taxes of $3,200 and FICA taxes of $1,250 — divided equally between employee withholdings and employer).	4,450
Net salaries paid to employees.	38,620
Utilities.	1,850
Dividends paid.	1,500
Total cash disbursements.	$151,895

(d) Dividends of $.75 per share were declared on June 30, September 30 and December 31.

(e) For tax purposes the depreciation expense for 1972 was: building $800, equipment $3,350. For financial accounting purposes the depreciation expense was: building $400, equipment $1,750.

(f) Doubtful accounts are estimated to be 1.2% of total sales for the year. The ending accounts receivable balance of $18,700 has been reduced by $650 for specific accounts which were written off as uncollectible.

(g) Annual income tax rates are 50% of taxable income. Assume that advances from customers are not included in taxable income.

Instructions: Complete a work sheet for the preparation of accrual basis financial statements with the columns and data as given on page 973. Formal financial statements and journal entries are not required.

(AICPA adapted)

26-14. Z. D. Danberry, who practices dentistry as a sole proprietor, recently filed as a candidate for mayor of his city. He has requested your assistance in preparing combined personal financial statements for himself and his wife. The statements are to show both the cost and estimated value bases. Your firm rendered an unqualified opinion on similar statements last year in connection with an examination conducted to support Mr. Danberry's application for a bank loan which was not made.

Mr. Danberry's bookkeeper has provided you with a trial balance listing the Danberrys' assets and liabilities on the cost basis at April 30, 1972, shown on work sheet on page 976. Your examination disclosed the following additional information:

(a) A summary of cash receipts and disbursements for the year ended April 30, 1972, follows:

Disbursements:

Personal expenditures, including personal life insurance premium.	$16,000
Purchase of Kindred Company 6% bonds at par.	8,000
Income taxes.	4,100
Interest on mortgage.	1,400

Disbursements (continued):

Mortgage principal amortization..........	$ 1,300	
Real estate taxes......................	900	$31,700

Receipts:

Withdrawals from Danberry's dental practice	$21,000	
Sale of Inco stock (purchased June 1, 1969, for $3,200; market value on April 30, 1971, $4,500)...............................	6,100	
Dividends on stock.....................	1,540	
Interest on bonds......................	240	28,880
Decrease in cash........................		$ 2,820

(b) The bonds were purchased on July 31, 1971. Interest is payable semi-annually on January 31 and July 31.

(c) In 1965 Danberry invested $10,000 to begin his dentistry practice and since has made additional investments. On April 2, 1972, Danberry was offered $31,000 for the net assets of his dental practice.

(d) Danberry owns 25% of the outstanding stock of the closely held corporation, Dental Supply, Inc.

(e) The April 30, 1972, statements of net assets of Danberry's dental practice and Dental Supply, Inc., both accompanied by unqualified opinions rendered by a CPA, were composed of the assets and liabilities as reported below.

	Danberry's Dental Practice	Dental Supply, Inc.
Current assets.....................	$ 6,000	$30,000
Noncurrent assets..................	36,000	70,000
Current liabilities.................	3,650	17,000
Long-term liabilities...............	16,350	35,000
Deferred credits...................	2,500	4,000

(f) Investments in marketable securities on April 30, 1972, were composed of the following:

	April 30, 1972 Latest Prices	
	Bid	Asked
Stocks:		
Steele, Inc............................	$15,100	$15,500
Gilliam Corp..........................	4,000	4,200
Bond:		
Kindred Company 6% bonds.............	7,800	7,900
	$26,900	$27,600

(g) The valuation (at 100% of fair market value) of other property owned by the Danberrys on April 30, 1972, was as follows:

Residence..	$60,000
Automobiles.......................................	4,300
Paintings...	14,500
Household furnishings..............................	7,600

There has been no appreciation during this or prior years in the value of automobiles or household furnishings.

(h) The accounts payable as of April 30, 1971, and April 30, 1972, represent liabilities for personal living costs.

(i) The Danberrys would have to pay a capital gains tax at an effective rate of 25% if the unrealized appreciation of the assets were realized. Decreases in asset values may be ignored in making this computation.

(j) Accrued income taxes payable of $2,225 as of April 30, 1972, represent the Danberrys' total tax liability.

Instructions: Complete a work sheet with the columns and data as given below, recording the necessary summary and adjusting entries for the year ended April 30, 1972. After all extensions, your work sheet will provide the data necessary for the preparation of financial statements on April 30, 1972, on the estimated value basis and should identify the individual changes in the various accounts. Formal financial statements and journal entries are not required.

Mr. and Mrs.
Work Sheet for Estimated Value
For Year Ended

	Assets and Liabilities	
Assets	Cost Basis April 30, 1972	Estimated Value Basis April 30, 1971
Cash.	3,300	6,120
Marketable securities.	23,000	21,400
Cash value of life insurance.	4,250	3,900
Net assets of Danberry's dental practice.	19,500	27,000
Interest in Dental Supply, Inc..	6,100	8,600
Residence.	50,000	55,600
Automobiles.	6,000	6,800
Paintings.	11,000	12,700
Household furnishings.	9,000	7,800
Total assets.	132,150	149,920
Liabilities		
Accounts payable.	3,100	2,850
Accrued income taxes payable.	2,225	1,900
Accrued income taxes on unrealized asset appreciation.	—	2,200
Mortgage payable.	34,000	35,300
Total liabilities.	39,325	42,250

(left page)

Z. D. Danberry
Basis Financial Statements
April 30, 1972

Summary and Adjusting Entries		Estimated Value Basis — April 30, 1972			
		Statement of Changes in Net Assets		Statement of Net Assets	
Debit	Credit	Debit	Credit	Debit	Credit

(right page)

(AICPA adapted)

chapter 27

errors and their correction

The accountant must be constantly aware of the possibilities of errors in recorded data. Errors can result from mathematical mistakes, the failure to apply appropriate accounting principles and procedures, or the misuse or omission of certain information. When the accountant discovers such errors, he must be able to analyze these in determining what action is appropriate under the circumstances. This calls for an understanding of the standards for a full and fair accounting as well as high judgment and skill in handling situations that indicate a failure to meet such standards. This chapter describes the errors that may be discovered and the corrections that are appropriate upon their discovery.

Preventing misstatements

A number of special practices are usually adopted by a business unit to insure accuracy in recording and summarizing business transactions. A prime requisite in achieving accuracy, of course, is the establishment of an accounting system that provides safeguards against both carelessness and dishonesty. Such a system should include orderly and integrated procedures and controls. Personnel should have well-defined responsibilities. An internal auditing staff may be established as a part of the accounting system to continuously reconcile and prove recorded data and also to evaluate information systems. Independent public accountants may be engaged to verify recorded data as a further means of insuring accounting accuracy.

Despite the accounting system that is established and the verification procedures that are employed, some misstatements will enter into the financial statements. Misstatements may be minor ones having little effect on the financial presentations; others may be of a major character, resulting in material misrepresentations of financial position and the results of operations. Misstatements may arise from intentional falsifications by employees or officers as well as from unintentional errors and omissions by employees.

Intentional misstatements. When misstatements result from intentional falsification of entries or records, the motive or motives may be: (1) to evade taxes; (2) to influence the market price of the company's securities; (3) to obtain favorable decisions by regulatory bodies; (4) to conceal the theft of cash, securities, merchandise, or other assets; (5) to conceal facts that may embarrass certain parties; or (6) to improve the company's ability to borrow. The best accounting system will not prevent misstatements that are made under the direction of management.

Unintentional misstatements. It would be impossible to offer a complete list of the misstatements that might arise unintentionally. Unintentional misstatements arise from clerical errors and omissions or from failures in the application of accounting principles. The most common misstatements include entries in the wrong customer or creditor accounts, entries in the wrong revenue and expense accounts, errors in counting and valuing inventories, errors in calculating depreciation and amortization, failures to distinguish properly between capital and revenue expenditures, and the omission of adjustments for prepaid and accrued items. These and other unintentional errors can be kept to a minimum through effective systems of internal control and satisfactory procedures for the audit and review of accounting data.

Errors are generally discovered at times when the periodic adjusting entries are being made, when an audit is being undertaken, when a business is to be sold, when a change of ownership is to be made in a partnership, when questions of taxation are to be decided, when heirs of an estate are to be satisfied, when a business is to be incorporated and shares are to be sold to outsiders, or when two or more business units are to be combined in a merger or consolidation.

Kinds of errors

There are a number of different kinds of errors. Some errors are discovered in the period in which they are made, and these are easily corrected. Others may not be discovered currently and are reflected on the financial statements until they are discovered. Some errors are never discovered; however, the effects of such errors are counterbalanced in subsequent periods and after this takes place, account balances are again accurately stated. Errors may be classified as follows.

Errors that are discovered currently in the course of the normal accounting procedures. Certain errors are of a clerical nature and are discovered in the course of the normal accounting processes. For example, an entry may be made that is not in balance and the entry is posted, an item may be posted to the wrong side of the account, an arithmetic mistake may be made in computing an account balance, an amount may be misstated or omitted in posting to a subsidiary ledger, or an account balance may be misstated or omitted in listing accounts on a trial balance or on a work sheet. Such errors, when not discovered during the period, will become evident at the end of the period in the regular course of summarizing operations. Errors are indicated when subsidiary account detail is not equal to the balance in the controlling account, when debit and credit totals on a trial balance are not equal, or when totals on a work sheet are not in balance. Normally the summarizing process points to the source of the error, and the error is readily corrected.

Errors limited to balance sheet accounts. Certain errors affect only the balance sheet accounts. For example, Marketable Securities may be debited instead of Notes Receivable, Interest Payable may be credited instead of Salaries Payable, or Prepaid Taxes may be debited instead of Accrued Taxes. In other instances, the acquisition of a property item on a deferred payment plan may be misstated, or the exchange of convertible bonds for stock may be omitted. Such errors are frequently discovered in the period in which they are made in the course of recording subsequent transactions in the accounts that are misstated, or in the course of reviewing preliminary summaries and statements. When the errors are discovered currently, entries are made to correct account balances. When the errors are not discovered until a subsequent period, corrections are made at that time. However, memorandum entries should be made on the books to indicate those accounts that were misstated so that the balance sheet data may be restated when the statement is to be presented in subsequent periods for analysis purposes or for comparative reporting.

Errors limited to income statement accounts. Certain errors affect only the income statement accounts. For example, Office Salaries may be debited instead of Sales Salaries, Purchases may be debited instead of Sales Returns, or Interest Income may be credited instead of Dividend Income. The discovery of the errors in the period in which they are made calls for the correction of the revenue and expense balances. However, if the errors are not discovered in the period in which they are made, net income will still be stated accurately; in closing the accounts at the end of the period, the balance sheet accounts remaining open are accurately stated and carried into the next period. If the errors are discovered in a subsequent period, no corrections are necessary. However, memorandum entries should be made on the books to indicate those accounts that were misstated so that the income statement data may be restated when the statement is to be presented in future periods for analysis purposes or for comparative reporting.

Errors affecting both income statement accounts and balance sheet accounts. Certain errors, when not discovered currently, result in the misstatement of earnings and thus affect both the income statement accounts and the balance sheet accounts. The balance sheet accounts are carried into the succeeding period; hence, an error made currently will affect earnings of the future when not detected. Such errors may be classified into two groups:

1. *Errors in earnings which, when not detected, are automatically counterbalanced in the following fiscal period.* Earnings on the income statements for two successive periods are inaccurately stated; certain account balances on the balance sheet at the end of the first period are inaccurately stated, but the account balances in the balance sheet at the end of the succeeding period are accurately stated. In this class are errors such as the misstatement of inventories and the omission of adjustments for prepaid and accrued items at the end of a period.

2. *Errors in earnings which, when not detected, are not automatically counterbalanced in the following fiscal period.* Account balances on successive balance sheets are inaccurately stated until the time entries are made that compensate for or correct the errors. In this class are errors such as the recognition of capital expenditures as revenue expenditures and the omission of charges for depreciation and amortization.

When errors in the last two groups are discovered, careful analysis is required in determining the action that is required to correct the account balances.

Determining the procedures to be employed in correcting the accounts

When it is discovered that an error in stating earnings of the past has been counterbalanced in subsequent periods, a memorandum entry is made to indicate the corrections required in the balance sheet and income statement in providing such presentations in the future. However, when errors of the past have not yet been counterbalanced, the accountant must decide upon the procedures that are appropriate under the circumstances. First, he must carefully analyze the errors and determine their effects upon the financial presentations in the present period and in subsequent periods. Then he must judge whether the errors are material in their effects and their correction can be justified as meeting the criteria of prior period adjustments. The answers to these questions will determine the course of the action, if any, that is warranted.

Errors that fail to meet the criteria as prior period adjustments. When it is discovered that errors of the past have an effect upon current or subsequent earnings but these are not judged material and thus fail to meet the criteria for prior period adjustments, the effects of such errors will have to be reflected in net income of the current period. The procedure for reporting the corrections within the current income statement may vary depending upon the nature of the item and the form of the disclosure that is regarded as appropriate. Assume, for example, that it is discovered that accrued sales salaries were understated at the end of the preceding period. It may be concluded that since the error does not have a material effect upon the expense item or net income, correction for the omission is not warranted; an overstatement in net income for the preceding period, then, is counterbalanced by an understatement in net income of the current period. In other instances, it may be suggested that a correction should be made to the account that is misstated and a special nominal account should be charged or credited to counterbalance the misstatement of earnings of the past. For example, assume that advances to employees were improperly recognized as salaries in the preceding period. The discovery of the error calls for a charge to an asset account and a credit to a nominal account that will be reported separately or combined with some other nominal account in summarizing operations. After nominal accounts are closed at the end of the period, real accounts are accurately stated and are carried forward to the next period.

Errors that warrant treatment as prior period adjustments. When errors are discovered that are judged to be material in effect and thus meet the criteria of prior period adjustments, corrections are made to the accounts that are misstated and the account summarizing prior period earnings is charged or credited directly for the misstatement of earnings of the past. For example, assume that it is discovered that the merchandise inventory at the end of the preceding period was overstated on the books of a corporation as the result of an error in the count and the error is regarded as material in effect; the error is corrected by a charge to Retained Earnings and a credit to the inventory balance. Assume that it is discovered that an omission was made in recording year-end sales on account in the previous period and the error is regarded as material in effect; the error is corrected by a charge to the accounts receivable account and a credit to Retained Earnings.

When the retained earnings statement shows corrections as prior period adjustments, disclosure should be provided by special note of the nature of the errors in previously issued statements and also the effects of such errors upon prior income, extraordinary items, and net income balances together with the related earnings per share amounts. It has already been indicated in earlier chapters that corporate annual reports generally provide comparative financial statements that report the financial position and the results of operations for the current period and for one or more preceding periods. In preparing comparative statements, these should be restated to report the retroactive application of corrections in the same manner as for all other prior period adjustments.

The remaining sections in this chapter are designed to describe and illustrate the procedures that are applied when corrections qualify as prior period adjustments. Accordingly, it is assumed that each of the errors named is material and calls for correction directly to the retained earnings account summarizing past earnings.

The analysis of errors of prior periods and their corrections illustrated

Before presenting a detailed review of errors of prior periods and their correction, a relatively simple example will be offered to suggest the nature of the correcting and reporting process.

Assume that the Webster Co. reports data on the financial statements at the end of 1971 as follows:

Income Statement For Year Ended December 31, 1971		Balance Sheet December 31, 1971		
Revenues	$500,000	Assets		$450,000
Expenses	380,000	Liabilities		$150,000
Income	$120,000	Stockholders' equity:		
Income taxes (50%)	60,000	Capital stock	$200,000	
Net income	$ 60,000	Retained earnings	100,000	300,000
		Total liabilities and stockholders' equity		$450,000

Retained Earnings Statement For Year Ended December 31, 1971	
Balance, January 1, 1971	$ 40,000
Net income for 1971	60,000
Balance, December 31, 1971	$100,000

Assume that in 1972, the Webster Co. found that year-end sales on account totaling $10,000 had been omitted in 1971. Upon recognizing the error, the company reported collections from such sales by charges to Cash and credits to Retained Earnings. As a result of the additional income related to 1971, the company prepared an amended income tax return for 1971 and was required to make an additional tax payment of $5,000. Financial statements at the end of 1972 reported the following:

Income Statement For Year Ended December 31, 1972		Balance Sheet December 31, 1972		
Revenues....................	$620,000	Assets.......................		$535,000
Expenses....................	460,000	Liabilities...................		$150,000
Income.....................	$160,000	Stockholders' equity:		
Income taxes................	80,000	Capital stock......	$200,000	
Net income.................	$ 80,000	Retained earnings.	185,000	385,000
		Total liabilities and stockholders' equity.........		$535,000

Retained Earnings Statement
For Year Ended December 31, 1972

Balance, January 1, 1972......		$100,000
Prior period adjustments:		
Increase in income for 1971.........	$10,000	
Less income taxes on additional income.	5,000	5,000
		$105,000
Net income for 1972..........		80,000
Balance, December 31, 1972...		$185,000

In preparing comparative statements, the income statement for 1971 should report an increase in sales of $10,000, an increase in income taxes of $5,000, and an increase in net income of $5,000. The retained earnings statement for 1971 should report an increase in net income for 1971 and a corresponding increase in the retained earnings total at the end of 1971. The balance sheet as of the end of 1971 should report an increase in accounts receivable of $10,000 an increase in income taxes payable of $5,000, and an increase in retained earnings of $5,000. With the statements for 1971 restated to reflect the retroactive application of the correction discovered in 1972, the statements for 1972 can be limited to financial operations of 1972. Comparative statements would be prepared as shown on page 984.

The example that follows further illustrates the analysis that is required upon the discovery of errors of prior periods and the entries that are made in correcting such errors.

Assume that the Monarch Wholesale Co. began operations at the beginning of 1971. An auditing firm is engaged for the first time in 1973.

Comparative Income Statement
For Years Ended
December 31, 1972 and 1971

	1972	1971
Revenues..........	$620,000	$510,000
Expenses..........	460,000	380,000
Income............	$160,000	$130,000
Income taxes.......	80,000	65,000
Net income........	$ 80,000	$ 65,000

Comparative Balance Sheet
December 31, 1972 and 1971

	1972	1971
Assets.............	$535,000	$460,000
Liabilities..........	$150,000	$155,000
Stockholders' equity:		
Capital stock......	$200,000	$200,000
Retained earnings.	185,000	105,000
	$385,000	$305,000
Total liabilities and stockholders' equity	$535,000	$460,000

Comparative Retained Earnings Statement
For Years Ended
December 31, 1972 and 1971

	1972	1971
Balance, January 1...	$105,000	$ 40,000
Net income.........	80,000	65,000
Balance, December 31	$185,000	$105,000

Before the accounts are adjusted and closed for 1973, the auditor reviews the books and accounts and discovers the following errors.

(1) *Understatement of merchandise inventory.* It is discovered that the merchandise inventory as of December 31, 1971, was understated by $1,000. The effects of the misstatement were as follows:

INCOME STATEMENT	BALANCE SHEET
For 1971: Cost of goods sold overstated (ending inventory too low)	Assets understated (inventory too low)
Net income understated	Retained earnings understated
For 1972: Cost of goods sold understated (beginning inventory too low)	Balance sheet items not affected, retained earnings understatement for 1971 being corrected by net income overstatement for 1972.
Net income overstated	

Since the balance sheet items at the end of 1972 were correctly stated, no entry to correct the accounts is required in 1973.

If the error had been discovered in 1972 instead of 1973, an entry could have been made to correct the account balances so that operations for 1972 might be reported accurately notwithstanding past errors. The beginning inventory would have to be increased by $1,000, the asset understatement, and Retained Earnings would have to be credited for this amount representing the income understatement in 1971. The correcting entry in 1972 would have been:

Merchandise Inventory.................................. 1,000
    Retained Earnings.................................... 1,000

(2) *Failure to record merchandise purchases.* It is discovered that purchases invoices as of December 28, 1971, for $850 were not recorded until 1972. The goods were included in the inventory at the end of 1971. The effects of the failure to record the purchases were as follows:

INCOME STATEMENT	BALANCE SHEET
For 1971: Cost of goods sold understated (purchases too low) Net income overstated	Liabilities understated (accounts payable too low) Retained earnings overstated
For 1972: Cost of goods sold overstated (purchases too high) Net income understated	Balance sheet items not affected, retained earnings overstatement for 1971 being corrected by net income understatement for 1972.

Since the balance sheet items at the end of 1972 were correctly stated, no entry to correct the accounts is required in 1973.

If the error had been discovered in 1972 instead of 1973, a correcting entry would have been necessary. In 1972 Purchases was debited and Accounts Payable credited for $850 for merchandise acquired in 1971 and included in the ending inventory of 1971. Retained Earnings would have to be debited for $850, representing the net income overstatement for 1971, and Purchases would have to be credited for a similar amount to reduce the purchases balance in 1972. The correcting entry in 1972 would have been:

Retained Earnings......................................	850	
Purchases...		850

(3) *Failure to record prepaid expense.* It is discovered that Miscellaneous General Expense for 1971 included taxes of $275 that should have been deferred in adjusting the accounts on December 31, 1971. The effects of the failure to record the prepaid expense were as follows:

INCOME STATEMENT	BALANCE SHEET
For 1971: Expenses overstated (miscellaneous general expense too high) Net income understated	Assets understated (prepaid taxes not reported) Retained earnings understated
For 1972: Expenses understated (miscellaneous general expense too low) Net income overstated	Balance sheet items not affected, retained earnings understatement for 1971 being corrected by net income overstatement for 1972.

Since the balance sheet items at the end of 1972 were correctly stated, no entry to correct the accounts is required in 1973.

If the error had been discovered in 1972 instead of 1973, a correcting entry would have been necessary. If prepaid taxes had been properly recorded at the end of 1971, this balance would have been transferred to the debit side of the expense account by a reversing entry at the beginning of 1972. The effect of the reversing entry would have to be recognized in preparing the correcting entry. Miscellaneous General Expense, then, would have to be debited for $275, the expense relating to operations of 1972, and Retained Earnings would have to be credited for a similar amount representing the net income understatement for 1971. The correcting entry in 1972 would have been:

Miscellaneous General Expense...........................	275	
Retained Earnings......................................		275

(4) *Failure to record accrued revenue.* Accrued interest on notes receivable of $150 was overlooked in adjusting the accounts on December 31, 1971. The revenue was recognized when the interest was collected in 1972. The effects of the failure to record the accrued revenue were as follows:

INCOME STATEMENT	BALANCE SHEET
For 1971: Revenue understated (interest income too low) Net income understated	Assets understated (accrued interest on notes receivable not reported) Net income understated
For 1972: Revenue overstated (interest income too high) Net income overstated	Balance sheet items not affected, retained earnings understatement for 1971 being corrected by net income overstatement for 1972.

Since the balance sheet items at the end of 1972 were correctly stated, no entry to correct the accounts is required in 1973.

If the error had been discovered in 1972 instead of 1973, an entry would have been necessary to correct the account balances. If accrued interest on notes receivable had been properly recorded at the end of 1971, this balance would have been transferred to the debit side of the interest income account by a reversing entry at the beginning of 1972. The effect of the reversing entry would have to be recognized in preparing the correcting entry. Interest Income, then, would have to be debited for $150, the amount to be subtracted from receipts of 1972, and Retained Earnings would have to be credited for a similar amount representing the net income understatement for 1971. The correcting entry in 1972 would have been:

Interest Income..	150	
Retained Earnings......................................		150

(5) *Overstatement of prepaid expense.* On January 2, 1971, $1,050 representing insurance for a three-year period was paid. The charge was made to the asset account, Prepaid Insurance. No adjustment was made at the end of 1971. At the end of 1972, the prepaid insurance account was reduced to the prepaid balance on that date, $350, insurance for two years, or $700, being charged to operations of 1972. The effects of the misstatements were as follows:

INCOME STATEMENT	BALANCE SHEET
For 1971: Expenses understated (insurance expense not reported) Net income overstated	Assets overstated (prepaid insurance too high) Retained earnings overstated
For 1972: Expenses overstated (insurance expense too high) Net income understated	Balance sheet items not affected, retained earnings overstatement for 1971 being corrected by net income understatement for 1972.

Since the balance sheet items at the end of 1972 were correctly stated, no entry to correct the accounts is required in 1973.

If the error had been discovered in 1972 instead of 1973, an entry would have been necessary to correct the account balances. Prepaid Insurance would have been decreased for the expired insurance of $350 and Retained Earnings would be debited for this amount representing the net income overstatement for 1971. The correcting entry in 1972 would have been:

Retained Earnings..................................	350	
Prepaid Insurance..................................		350

The expired insurance of $350 for 1972 would be recorded at the end of that year by an appropriate adjustment.

(6) *Failure to record prepaid revenue.* Fees received in advance for miscellaneous services of $175 as of December 31, 1971, and $225 as of December 31, 1972, were overlooked in adjusting the accounts on each of these dates. Miscellaneous Income had been credited when fees were received. The effects of the failure to recognize the prepaid revenue of $175 at the end of 1971 were as follows:

INCOME STATEMENT	BALANCE SHEET
For 1971: Revenue overstated (miscellaneous income too high) Net income overstated	Liabilities understated (unearned service fees not reported) Retained earnings overstated
For 1972: Revenue understated (miscellaneous income too low) Net income understated	Balance sheet items not affected, retained earnings overstatement for 1971 being corrected by net income understatement for 1972.

The effects of the failure to recognize the prepaid revenue of $225 at the end of 1972 were as follows:

INCOME STATEMENT	BALANCE SHEET
For 1972: Revenue overstated (miscellaneous income too high) Net income overstated	Liabilities understated (unearned service fees not reported) Retained earnings overstated

No entry is required in 1973 to correct the accounts for the failure to record the prepaid revenue at the end of 1971, the misstatement in 1971 having been counterbalanced by the misstatement in 1972. An entry is required, however, to correct the accounts for the failure to record the prepaid revenue at the end of 1972 if the net income for 1973 is not to be misstated. If the prepaid revenue had been recorded at the end of 1972, the balance in Unearned Service Fees would have been transferred to the credit side of the miscellaneous income account by a reversing entry at the beginning of 1973. This must be recognized in recording the correcting entry. Retained Earnings must be debited for $225, representing the net income overstatement for 1972, and Miscellaneous Income must be credited for the same amount, representing the revenue that is to be identified with 1973. The correcting entry is:

Retained Earnings..	225	
Miscellaneous Income....................................		225

If the failure to adjust the accounts for the prepaid revenue of 1971 had been recognized in 1972 instead of 1973, an entry similar to the one above would have been required in 1972 to correct the account balances. The entry at that time would have been:

Retained Earnings..	175	
Miscellaneous Income....................................		175

The unearned service fees of $225 as of the end of 1972 would be recorded at the end of that year by an appropriate adjustment.

(7) *Failure to record accrued expense.* Accrued sales salaries of $450 as of December 31, 1971, and $300 as of December 31, 1972, were overlooked in adjusting the accounts on each of these dates. Sales Salaries is debited for salary payments. The effects of the failure to record the accrued expense of $450 as of December 31, 1971, were as follows:

INCOME STATEMENT	BALANCE SHEET
For 1971: Expenses understated (sales salaries too low) Net income overstated	Liabilities understated (accrued sales salaries not reported) Retained earnings overstated
For 1972: Expenses overstated (sales salaries too high) Net income understated	Balance sheet items not affected, retained earnings overstatement for 1971 being corrected by net income understatement for 1972.

The effects of the failure to recognize the accrued expense of $300 on December 31, 1972, were as follows:

INCOME STATEMENT	BALANCE SHEET
For 1972: Expenses understated (sales salaries too low) Net income overstated	Liabilities understated (accrued sales salaries not reported) Retained earnings overstated

No entry is required in 1973 to correct the accounts for the failure to record the accrued expense at the end of 1971, the misstatement in 1971 having been counterbalanced by the misstatement in 1972. An entry is required, however, to correct the accounts for the failure to record the accrued expense at the end of 1972 if the net income for 1973 is not to be misstated. If the accrued expense had been recorded at the end of 1972, the balance in Accrued Salaries would have been transferred to the credit side of the sales salaries account by a reversing entry at the beginning of 1973. This must be recognized in recording the correcting entry. Retained Earnings must be debited for $300, representing the net income overstatement for 1972, and Sales Salaries must be credited for a similar amount, representing the amount to be subtracted from salary payments in 1973. The correcting entry is:

Retained Earnings....................................	300	
Sales Salaries....................................		300

If the failure to adjust the accounts for the accrued expense of 1971 had been recognized in 1972, an entry similar to the one above would have been required in 1972 to correct the account balances. The entry in 1972 would have been:

Retained Earnings....................................	450	
Sales Salaries....................................		450

The accrued salaries of $300 as of the end of 1972 would be recorded at the end of that year by an appropriate adjustment.

(8) *Failure to record depreciation.* Delivery equipment was acquired at the beginning of 1971 at a cost of $6,000. The equipment has an estimated five-year life, and depreciation of $1,200 was overlooked at the end of 1971 and 1972. The effects of the failure to record depreciation for 1971 were as follows:

INCOME STATEMENT	BALANCE SHEET
For 1971: Expenses understated (depreciation of delivery equipment too low)	Assets overstated (accumulated depreciation of delivery equipment too low)
Net income overstated	Retained earnings overstated
For 1972: Expenses not affected	Assets overstated (accumulated depreciation of delivery equipment too low)
Net income not affected	Retained earnings overstated

It should be observed that the misstatements arising from the failure to record depreciation are not counterbalanced in the succeeding year.

Failure to record depreciation for 1972 affected the statements as shown below:

INCOME STATEMENT	BALANCE SHEET
For 1972: Expenses understated (depreciation of delivery equipment too low)	Assets overstated (accumulated depreciation of delivery equipment understated)
Net income overstated	Retained earnings overstated

When the omission is recognized, Retained Earnings must be decreased by the net income overstatements of prior years and accumulated depreciation must be increased by the depreciation that should have been recorded. The correcting entry in 1973 for depreciation that should have been recognized for 1971 and 1972 is as follows:

Retained Earnings....................................... 2,400
    Accumulated Depreciation — Delivery Equipment.........   2,400

(9) Overstatement of prepaid revenue. Unearned Rental Income was credited for $375 representing revenue for December, 1972, and for January and February, 1973. No adjustment was made on December 31, 1972. The effects of the failure to adjust the accounts to show revenue of $125 for 1972 were as follows:

INCOME STATEMENT	BALANCE SHEET
For 1972: Revenue understated (rental income too low) Net income understated	Liabilities overstated (unearned rental income too high) Retained earnings understated

When the error is discovered in 1973, Unearned Rental Income is debited for $125 and Retained Earnings is credited for this amount representing the net income understatement in 1972. The following entry is made:

Unearned Rental Income................................ 125
    Retained Earnings....................................   125

(10) Failure to record merchandise sales. It is discovered that sales on account for the last week of December, 1972, for $1,800 were not recorded until 1973. The goods sold were not included in the inventory at the end of 1972. The effects of the failure to report the revenue in 1972 were as follows:

INCOME STATEMENT	BALANCE SHEET
For 1972: Revenue understated (sales too low) Net income understated	Assets understated (accounts receivable too low) Retained earnings understated

When the error is discovered in 1973, Sales is debited for $1,800 and Retained Earnings is credited for this amount representing the net income understatement for 1972. The following entry is made:

Sales.. 1,800
    Retained Earnings....................................   1,800

The analysis sheet on pages 992 and 993 summarizes the effects of the errors that are listed on pages 984–990. Effects on the financial statements are listed on the assumption that the errors were not discovered in 1971, 1972, or 1973. A plus sign (+) indicates an overstatement in the statement section; a minus sign $(-)$ indicates an understatement in the statement section.

Working papers to summarize corrections

It is assumed in the following sections that the errors previously listed are discovered in 1973 before the accounts for the year are adjusted and closed. Accounts are corrected so that revenue and expense accounts report the balances identified with the current period and asset, liability, and retained earnings accounts are accurately stated. Instead of preparing a separate entry for each correction, a single compound entry may be made for all of the errors that are discovered. The entry to correct earnings of prior years as well as to correct current earnings may be developed by the preparation of working papers. Assume the following retained earnings account for the Monarch Wholesale Co.:

Retained Earnings

Dec. 20, 1972 Dividends declared...	5,000	Dec. 31, 1971 Balance...........	12,000
Dec. 31, 1972 Balance...........	22,000	Dec. 31, 1972 Net income........	15,000
	27,000		27,000
		Jan. 1, 1973 Balance...........	22,000

The working papers to determine the corrected retained earnings balance on December 31, 1971, and the corrected net income for 1972 are shown on page 994.

The working papers indicate that Retained Earnings is to be decreased by $750 as of January 1, 1973. The reduction arises from the following:

Retained earnings overstatement as of Dec. 31, 1971:		
Retained earnings as originally reported..............	$12,000	
Retained earnings as corrected......................	10,800	$1,200
Retained earnings understatement in 1972:		
Net income as corrected...........................	$15,450	
Net income as originally reported...................	15,000	450
Retained earnings overstatement as of January 1, 1973....		$ 750

The following entry is prepared from the working papers to correct the account balances in 1973:

Retained Earnings......................................	750	
Unearned Rental Income................................	125	
Sales...	1,800	
Claim for Income Tax Refund — 1971....................	400	
Miscellaneous Income................................		225
Sales Salaries......................................		300
Accumulated Depreciation — Delivery Equipment.........		2,400
Income Taxes Payable — 1972........................		150

ANALYSIS SHEET TO SHOW EFFECTS

| | At End of 1971 | | | |
| | Income Statement | | Balance Sheet | |
	Section	Net Income	Section	Retained Earnings
(1) Understatement of merchandise inventory of $1,000 on December 31, 1971.	Cost of Goods Sold +	−	Current Assets −	−
(2) Failure to record merchandise purchases on account of $850 in 1971; purchases were recorded in 1972.	Cost of Goods Sold −	+	Current Liabilities −	+
(3) Failure to record prepaid taxes of $275 on December 31, 1971; amount was included as miscellaneous general expense.	General Expense +	−	Current Assets −	−
(4) Failure to record accrued interest on notes receivable of $150 on December 31, 1971; revenue was recognized on collection in 1972.	Other Revenue −	−	Current Assets −	−
(5) Failure to record reduction in prepaid insurance balance of $350 on December 31, 1971; insurance for 1971 was charged to 1972.	General Expense −	+	Current Assets +	+
(6) Failure to record unearned service fees; amounts received were included in Miscellaneous Income. On December 31, 1971, $175.	Other Revenue +	+	Current Liabilities −	+
On December 31, 1972, $225.				
(7) Failure to record accrued sales salaries; expense was recognized when payment was made. On December 31, 1971, $450.	Selling Expense −	+	Current Liabilities −	+
On December 31, 1972, $300.				
(8) Failure to record depreciation of delivery equipment. On December 31, 1971, $1,200.	Selling Expense −	+	Non-current Assets +	+
On December 31, 1972, $1,200.				
(9) Failure to record reduction in unearned rental income balance on December 31, 1972, $125. (It is assumed that the rental income for 1972 was recognized as revenue in 1973.)				
(10) Failure to record merchandise sales on account of $1,800 in 1972. (It is assumed that the sales for 1972 were recognized as revenue in 1973.)				

F ERRORS ON FINANCIAL STATEMENTS

| At End of 1972 | | | | At End of 1973 | | | |
| Income Statement | | Balance Sheet | | Income Statement | | Balance Sheet | |
Section	Net Income	Section	Retained Earnings	Section	Net Income	Section	Retained Earnings
Cost of Goods Sold —	+		No Effect				
Cost of Goods Sold +	−		No Effect				
General Expense —	+		No Effect				
Other Revenue +	+		No Effect				
General Expense +	−		No Effect				
Other Revenue —	−		No Effect				
Other Revenue +	+	Current Liabilities —	+	Other Revenue —	−		No Effect
Selling Expense +	−		No Effect				
Selling Expense —	+	Current Liabilities —	+	Selling Expense +	−		No Effect
	No Effect	Non-current Assets +	+		No Effect	Non-current Assets +	+
Selling Expense —	+	Non-current Assets +	+		No Effect	Non-current Assets +	+
Other Revenue —	−	Deferred Revenues +	−	Other Revenue +	+		No Effect
Sales —	−	Accounts Receivable —	−	Sales +	+		No Effect

Monarch Wholesale Co.
Working Papers for Correction of Account Balances
December 31, 1973

Explanation	Retained Earnings Dec. 31, 1971		Net Income Year Ended Dec. 31, 1972		Accounts Requiring Correction in 1973		
	Dr.	Cr.	Dr.	Cr.	Dr.	Cr.	Account
Reported retained earnings balance, Dec. 31, 1971		12,000					
Reported net income for year ended Dec. 31, 1972				15,000			
Corrections[1]:							
(1) Understatement of inventory on Dec. 31, 1971, $1,000		1,000	1,000				
(2) Failure to record merchandise purchases in 1971, $850	850			850			
(3) Failure to record prepaid taxes on Dec. 31, 1971, $275		275	275				
(4) Failure to record accrued interest on notes receivable on Dec. 31, 1971, $150		150	150				
(5) Failure to record insurance expense on Dec. 31, 1971, $350, insurance of $700 for 1971 and 1972 being charged to 1972	350			350			
(6) Failure to record unearned service fees:							
(a) On Dec. 31, 1971, $175	175			175			
(b) On Dec. 31, 1972, $225			225			225	Miscellaneous Income
(7) Failure to record accrued sales salaries:							
(a) On Dec. 31, 1971, $450	450			450			
(b) On Dec. 31, 1972, $300			300			300	Sales Salaries
(8) Failure to record depreciation of delivery equipment:							
(a) On Dec. 31, 1971, $1,200	1,200					1,200	Accumulated Depr. — Delivery Equip.
(b) On Dec. 31, 1972, $1,200			1,200			1,200	
(9) Failure to record rental income on Dec. 31, 1972, $125				125	125		Unearned Rental Income
(10) Failure to record merchandise sales in 1972, $1,800				1,800	1,800		Sales
	3,025	13,425	3,150	18,750	1,925	2,925	
Claim for income tax refund: 25% [$3,025 − ($13,425 − $12,000)][2]		400			400		Claim for Income Tax Refund — 1971
Income taxes payable: 25%.... [($18,750 − $15,000) − $3,150]				150		150	Income Taxes Payable — 1972
Corrected retained earnings balance, Dec. 31, 1971	10,800						
	13,825	13,825					
Corrected net income for 1972			15,450				
			18,750	18,750			
Net correction to retained earnings as of Jan. 1, 1973					750		Retained Earnings
					3,075	3,075	

[1]For a more detailed description of the individual errors and their correction, refer to pages 984–990

[2]For purposes of the example, the income taxes are assumed to be 25% of the reported net income In recent years the federal income tax on corporations has consisted of (1) a *normal rate* on all taxable income of 22%, and (2) a *surtax* on taxable income over $25,000 that has ranged from 26% to 30%. In some year an *additional surtax* has been applied to the total of the taxes calculated in (1) and (2).

The retained earnings account after correction will appear with a balance of $21,250, as follows:

Retained Earnings

Dec. 31, 1973 Corrections in net incomes of prior periods discovered during the course of the audit.....	750	Jan. 1, 1973 Balance............	22,000

The balance in Retained Earnings can be proved by reconstructing the account from the detail shown on the working papers. If the net incomes for 1971 and 1972 had been reported properly, Retained Earnings would have appeared as follows:

Retained Earnings

Dec. 20, 1972 Dividend declared...	5,000	Dec. 31, 1971 Corrected balance per working papers..	10,800
Dec. 31, 1972 Balance............	21,250	Dec. 31, 1972 Corrected net income for 1972 per working papers............	15,450
	26,250		26,250
		Jan. 1, 1973 Balance............	21,250

In the foregoing example, a corrected net income figure for only 1972 was required; hence any corrections in earnings for years prior to this date were shown as affecting the retained earnings balance as of December 31, 1971. Working papers on page 994 were constructed to summarize this information by providing a pair of columns for retained earnings as of December 31, 1971, and a pair of columns for earnings data for 1972. It may be desirable to determine corrected earnings for a number of years. When this is to be done, a pair of columns must be provided for retained earnings as of the beginning of the period under review and a separate pair of columns for each year for which corrected earnings are to be determined. For example, assume that corrected earnings for the years 1970, 1971, and 1972 are to be determined. Working papers for the correction of account balances would be constructed with headings as shown below. Corrections for the omission of accrued sales salaries for a four-year period would appear as follows:

Explanation	Retained Earnings Dec. 31, 1969		Net Income Year Ended Dec. 31, 1970		Net Income Year Ended Dec. 31, 1971		Net Income Year Ended Dec. 31, 1972		Accounts Requiring Correction in 1973		
	Dr.	Cr.	Dr.	Cr.	Dr.	Cr.	Dr.	Cr.	Dr.	Cr.	Account
Failure to record accrued sales salaries at end of:											
1969, $750	750			750							
1970, $800			800			800					
1971, $900					900			900			
1972, $625							625			625	Sales Salaries

The preparation of corrected financial statements

When only a few corrections are to be recognized, the restatement of the financial statements of prior periods may be a relatively simple matter. Corrections may be applied directly to the original balances reported on the financial statements in arriving at corrected statements. However, when many corrections are to be recognized, the use of a work sheet will facilitate the correction of the statements.

It is assumed that auditors for the Monarch Wholesale Co. are to prepare financial statements for 1973 and 1972 in comparative form. Statements for 1973 are prepared that reflect the corrections that have been described in the preceding section. However, statements for 1972 require restatement for purposes of the comparative reports. The preparation of corrected financial statements for the Monarch Wholesale Co. for 1972 is illustrated in the remaining pages of this chapter. The data affecting statements of 1972 that are to be recognized in correcting the statements follow:

1. Understatement of inventory on December 31, 1971, $1,000.
2. Failure to record merchandise purchases on account in 1971, $850.
3. Failure to record prepaid taxes on December 31, 1971, $275.
4. Failure to record accrued interest on notes receivable on December 31, 1971, $150.
5. Failure to record reduction in prepaid insurance balance on December 31, 1971, $350, insurance for 1971 being charged to 1972.
6. Failure to record unearned service fees:
   a. On December 31, 1971, $175.
   b. On December 31, 1972, $225.
7. Failure to record accrued sales salaries:
   a. On December 31, 1971, $450.
   b. On December 31, 1972, $300.
8. Failure to record depreciation of delivery equipment:
   a. On December 31, 1971, $1,200.
   b. On December 31, 1972, $1,200.
9. Failure to record reduction in unearned rental income balance on December 31, 1972, $125.
10. Failure to record merchandise sales on account in 1972, $1,800.
11. Establishment of Claim for Income Tax Refund — 25% of $1,600 decrease in earnings related to 1971, or $400.
12. Establishment of Income Taxes Payable — 25% of $600 increase in earnings related to 1972, or $150.

A work sheet for the preparation of the corrected statements for 1972 appears on pages 998–999. The corrected income statement and the corrected retained earnings statement are shown on page 997. The corrected balance sheet is given on page 1000. Work sheets and corrected statements for earlier years may be prepared in the same manner.

Monarch Wholesale Co.
Income Statement (Corrected)
For Year Ended December 31, 1972

Sales		$82,200	
Less sales discount		800	$81,400
Cost of goods sold:			
Merchandise inventory, January 1, 1972		$15,000	
Merchandise purchases		51,150	
Merchandise available for sale		$66,150	
Merchandise inventory, December 31, 1972		18,000	48,150
Gross profit on sales			$33,250
Operating expenses:			
Selling expenses:			
Sales salaries	$4,650		
Delivery expense	4,150	$ 8,800	
General expenses:			
Office and administrative salaries	$3,500		
Miscellaneous general expense	2,675	6,175	14,975
Operating income			$18,275
Other revenue and expense items:			
Interest income	$1,050		
Rental income	1,125		
Miscellaneous income	1,750	$ 3,925	
Interest expense		1,600	2,325
Income before income taxes			$20,600
Income taxes			5,150
Net income			$15,450

Monarch Wholesale Co.
Retained Earnings Statement (Corrected)
For Year Ended December 31, 1972

Retained earnings, January 1, 1972	$12,000
Deduct prior period adjustment — correction in net income for year ended December 31, 1971	1,200
Retained earnings as corrected, January 1, 1972	$10,800
Deduct dividends declared in 1972	5,000
	$ 5,800
Add net income for year ended December 31, 1972	15,450
Retained earnings, December 31, 1972	$21,250

	Item	Balances Before Corrections		
		Debit	Credit	
1	Cash	19,250		1
2	Accrued interest on notes receivable	650		2
3	Notes receivable	20,000		3
4	Accounts receivable	24,000		4
5	Merchandise inventory, December 31, 1971	14,000		5
6	Prepaid insurance	350		6
7	Prepaid taxes	325		7
8	Delivery equipment	6,000		8
9	Notes payable		6,500	9
10	Accounts payable		9,500	10
11	Accrued interest on notes payable		200	11
12	Unearned rental income		375	12
13	Capital stock, $10 par		40,000	13
14	Premium on capital stock		10,000	14
15	Retained earnings, December 31, 1971		12,000	15
16	Understatement of inventory, 12/31/71			16
17	Understatement of purchases in 1971			17
18	Understatement of prepaid taxes, 12/31/71			18
19	Understatement of accrued int. on notes receiv., 12/31/71			19
20	Overstatement of prepaid insurance, 12/31/71			20
21	Understatement of unearned service fees, 12/31/71			21
22	Understatement of accrued salaries, 12/31/71			23
23	Understatement of accumulated depreciation, 12/31/71			22
24	Claim for income tax refund			24
25	Dividends declared	5,000		25
26	Sales		80,400	26
27	Sales discount	800		27
28	Purchases	52,000		28
29	Sales salaries	4,800		29
30	Delivery expense	2,950		30
31	Office and administrative salaries	3,500		31
32	Miscellaneous general expense	2,750		32
33	Interest income		1,200	33
34	Rental income		1,000	34
35	Miscellaneous income		1,800	35
36	Interest expense	1,600		36
37	Income taxes	5,000		37
38	Merchandise inventory, 12/31/72 (Balance sheet)	18,000		38
39	Merchandise inventory, 12/31/72 (Income statement)		18,000	39
40	Unearned service fees			40
41	Accrued salaries			41
42	Accumulated depreciation — delivery equipment			42
43				43
44	Claim for income tax refund			44
45	Income taxes payable			45
46		180,975	180,975	46
47				47
48	Net income			48
49				49
50	Retained earnings			50
51				51

Wholesale Co.
Corrected Financial Statements
December 31, 1972

#	Corrections Debit	Corrections Credit	Income Statement Debit	Income Statement Credit	Retained Earnings Debit	Retained Earnings Credit	Balance Sheet Debit	Balance Sheet Credit	#
1							19,250		1
2							650		2
3							20,000		3
4	(10) 1,800						25,800		4
5	(1) 1,000		15,000						5
6							350		6
7							325		7
8							6,000		8
9								6,500	9
10								9,500	10
11								200	11
12	(9) 125							250	12
13								40,000	13
14								10,000	14
15						12,000			15
16		(1) 1,000							16
17	(2) 850								17
18		(3) 275							18
19		(4) 150							19
20	(5) 350								20
21	(6a) 175				1,200				21
22	(7a) 450								22
23	(8a) 1,200								23
24		(11) 400							24
25					5,000				25
26		(10) 1,800		82,200					26
27			800						27
28		(2) 850	51,150						28
29	(7b) 300	(7a) 450	4,650						29
30	(8b) 1,200		4,150						30
31			3,500						31
32	(3) 275	(5) 350	2,675						32
33	(4) 150			1,050					33
34		(9) 125		1,125					34
35	(6b) 225	(6a) 175		1,750					35
36			1,600						36
37	(12) 150		5,150						37
38							18,000		38
39				18,000					39
40		(6b) 225						225	40
41		(7b) 300						300	41
42		(8a) 1,200							42
43		(8b) 1,200						2,400	43
44	(11) 400						400		44
45		(12) 150						150	45
46	8,650	8,650	88,675	104,125					46
47			15,450			15,450			47
48			104,125	104,125					48
49					6,200	27,450			49
50					21,250			21,250	50
51					27,450	27,450	90,775	90,775	51

Monarch Wholesale Co.
Balance Sheet (Corrected)
December 31, 1972

Assets

Current assets:

Cash	$19,250	
Accrued interest on notes receivable	650	
Notes receivable	20,000	
Accounts receivable	25,800	
Claim for income tax refund	400	
Merchandise inventory	18,000	
Prepaid insurance	350	
Prepaid taxes	325	$84,775
Delivery equipment	$ 6,000	
Less accumulated depreciation — delivery equipment	2,400	3,600
Total assets		$88,375

Liabilities

Current liabilities:

Notes payable	$ 6,500	
Accounts payable	9,500	
Accrued interest on notes payable	200	
Accrued salaries	300	
Income taxes payable	150	
Unearned rental income	250	
Unearned service fees	225	
Total liabilities		$17,125

Stockholders' Equity

Paid-in capital:

Capital stock, $10 par	$40,000	
Premium on capital stock	10,000	$50,000
Retained earnings		21,250
Total stockholders' equity		71,250
Total liabilities and stockholders' equity		$88,375

QUESTIONS

1. Name three errors that are counterbalanced in the following period and do not require corrections if discovered after such time.

2. Name three errors that will not be counterbalanced in the following period and require corrections upon their discovery.

3. Name three errors that result in misstatements on the income statement but do not affect the balance sheet at the end of the current period.

4. Name three errors that result in misstatements on the balance sheet but do not affect the income statement at the end of the current period.

5. The controller for the Wellman Co. states: "The understatement of an expense in one year calls for an overstatement of the same expense in the following year even when the error is discovered; if this is not done, expense will bypass the income statement." Comment on this opinion.

6. Under what circumstances will the correction of an error not directly affect retained earnings?

7. State the effect upon net income in 1971 and 1972 of each of the following errors that are made at the end of 1971:
- (a) Accrued salaries are understated.
- (b) Accrued interest on notes receivable is understated.
- (c) Discount on notes payable is overstated.
- (d) Unearned rental income is understated.
- (e) Depreciation on an equipment item is overlooked.
- (f) Discount on notes receivable is overstated.
- (g) Accrued interest on notes payable is overstated.

8. State the effect of each of the following errors made in 1971 upon the balance sheets and the income statements prepared for 1971 and 1972:
- (a) The ending inventory is understated as a result of an error in the count of goods on hand.
- (b) The ending inventory is overstated as a result of the inclusion of goods acquired and held on a consignment basis.
- (c) A purchase of merchandise at the end of 1971 is not recorded until payment is made for the goods in 1972; the goods purchased were included in the inventory at the end of 1971.
- (d) A sale of merchandise at the end of 1971 is not recorded until cash is received for the goods in 1972; the goods sold were excluded from the inventory at the end of 1971.
- (e) Goods shipped to consignees in 1971 were reported as sales; goods in the hands of consignees at the end of 1971 were not recognized for inventory purposes; sale of such goods in 1972 and collections on such sales were recorded as credits to the receivables established with consignees in 1971.

EXERCISES

In solving the following exercises, assume that each correction qualifies as a prior period adjustment.

1. State the effect, if any, that each of the following errors of 1972 had on the statements prepared on December 31, 1972. Indicate the sections of the statements that are affected.
- (a) The adjustment for interest accrued on notes receivable was omitted.
- (b) The adjustment for service fees collected but not earned was omitted. Income was originally credited for collections.
- (c) No adjustment was made for rental income that was earned during 1972. Unearned Rental Income was originally credited for collections.
- (d) Depreciation of office furniture was omitted.

(*continued*)

(e) Merchandise received and on hand on December 31, 1972, was not included in the inventory figure, and no entry was made for the purchase until January 3, 1973.

(f) In December, 1972, an entry was made for a purchase of merchandise; the merchandise had not been received and was not included in the inventory of December 31, 1972, although the company had title to the goods.

(g) No adjustment was made for interest expense that should have been accrued.

2. Give the correcting entry that should be made in 1973 when each of the following errors is discovered:

(a) On December 19, 1972, a $20,000 non-interest-bearing note due in 60 days was received from a customer. The note was recorded at its face value, Interest Income was credited for $200, and the customer's account was credited for the difference.

(b) No adjustment was made on December 31, 1972, for the interest on a 90-day, 8%, $5,000 note receivable that is due on January 18.

(c) Accrued sales salaries of $400 were overlooked in adjusting the accounts at the end of 1972.

(d) During December, 1972, merchandise of $1,000 was received; this merchandise was included in the inventory, but no entry was made for the purchase until the invoice was received in January. At that time Purchases was debited.

(e) Prepaid Insurance was debited for $900, representing the premium for three years from October 1, 1972. No adjustment was made on December 31, 1972.

3. A condensed income statement for the year ended December 31, 1972, for Elliott Products shows the following:

Sales	$90,000
Cost of goods sold	60,000
Gross profit on sales	$30,000
Expenses	15,000
Net income	$15,000

An investigation of the records discloses the following errors in summarizing transactions for 1972:

1. Ending inventory was overstated by $4,100.

2. Accrued expenses of $600 and prepaid expenses of $1,000 were not given accounting recognition at the end of 1972.

3. Sales of $500 were not recorded although the goods were shipped and excluded from the inventory.

4. Purchases of $2,000 were made at the end of 1972, but were not recorded although the goods were received and included in the ending inventory.

5. A machine acquired on January 1, 1968, for $10,000 was sold on July 1, 1972, for $2,000; the credit for the sales proceeds was made to Sales. The machine had an estimated life of 5 years; no depreciation was recognized on the machine for 1972.

(a) Prepare a corrected income statement for 1972. (b) Give the correcting entries that are required in 1973.

4. The Bulson Co. reports net incomes for a three-year period as follows: 1970, $18,000; 1971, $7,500; 1972, $12,500.

In reviewing the accounts in 1973 after the books for the prior year have been closed, you find that the following errors have been made in summarizing activities:

	1970	1971	1972
Overstatement of inventories as a result of errors in count..........................	$1,600	$3,400	$1,800
Understatement of accrued advertising......	250	600	300
Overstatement of accrued interest income...	250	—	150
Omission of depreciation on property items still in use............................	900	600	750

(a) Prepare working papers summarizing corrections and reporting corrected net incomes for 1970, 1971, and 1972. (b) Give the entry to bring the books of the company up to date in 1973.

5. The Jenson Manufacturing Company has been in business since 1970 and produces a single product that is sold with a one-year warranty covering parts and labor. An audit is made of the company's records for the first time at the end of 1972 before the accounts for 1972 are closed, and it is found that charges for warranties have not been anticipated but have been recognized when incurred. The audit discloses the following data:

Year	Sales	Warranty Expense for Sales Made in 1970	1971	1972
1970	$ 600,000	$12,000	$14,000	
1971	800,000		20,000	$24,000
1972	1,200,000			32,000

The auditor decides that the company should have recognized the full expense for warranties in the year in which the sales were made. He recommends that charges for warranties should be recognized as a percentage of sales and that experiences of past years should be used in arriving at such a percentage. Earnings before correction have been as follows: 1970, $60,000; 1971, $85,000; 1972, $140,000.

(a) What earnings would have been reported if warranty costs had been anticipated and the percentage as calculated had been applied? (b) What correcting entry should be made as of December 31, 1972?

PROBLEMS

In solving the following problems, assume that each correction qualifies as a prior period adjustment.

27-1. The first audit of the books for the Quinn Corporation was made for the year ended December 31, 1972. In reviewing the books, the auditor discovered that certain adjustments had been overlooked at the end of 1971 and 1972, and also that other items had been improperly recorded. Omissions and other failures for each year are summarized below:

	December 31	
	1971	1972
Accrued sales salaries..........................	$ 900	$1,250
Accrued interest on investments.................	325	195
Prepaid insurance.............................	450	750
Advances from customers.......................	1,750	2,500
(Collections from customers had been included in sales but should have been recognized as advances from customers since goods were not shipped until the following year.)		
Equipment....................................	1,400	1,000
(Expenditures had been recognized as repairs but should have been recognized as cost of equipment; the depreciation rate on such equipment is 10% per year, but depreciation in the year of the expenditure is to be recognized at 5%.)		

Instructions: Prepare journal entries that will correct revenue and expense accounts for 1972 and that will record assets and liabilities that require recognition on the balance sheet as of December 31, 1972. Assume that the nominal accounts for 1972 have not yet been closed into the income summary account. Disregard effects of corrections on income tax.

27-2. Before the accounts of the Goodman Corporation are adjusted and closed for the annual fiscal period ended December 31, 1972, an examination of the company records by the auditor discloses the following facts. Give any correcting and adjusting entries called for by the information given. Disregard effects of corrections on income tax.

(a) Store supply inventories had been overlooked in adjusting the accounts in previous years. Store supplies on hand were: 1970, $450; 1971, $900. Store supplies on hand at the end of 1972 were $1,450.

(b) Accrued sales commissions due salesmen had been overlooked in adjusting the accounts at the end of 1970 and 1971. Accrued amounts were: 1970, $675; 1971, $730. Accrued commissions at the end of 1972 are $970.

(c) Checks totaling $650 issued to former employees in 1970 are still outstanding. Present whereabouts of such employees are unknown, and it is doubtful whether the checks will ever be presented for payment.

(d) Raw materials, cost $800, received on December 31, 1971, had been included in the physical inventory taken on that date; however, the purchase was recorded when the invoice was received on January 4, 1972.

(e) Five-year, 7% bonds of $500,000 were issued on January 1, 1969, bonds of $100,000 to be redeemed annually. Interest is payable annually on January 1. The bonds were sold at 94. One fifth of the discount had been amortized annually at the end of 1969, 1970, and 1971.

(f) In March, 1971, the company had received a 25% common stock dividend on 100 shares of Brookline, Inc., common acquired in 1970 at $150. The shares received as a stock dividend had been sold for cash in April, 1971, at $170 and a revenue account had been credited for the full proceeds.

27-3. The Hale Sales Co. has failed to recognize certain prepaid and accrued items in the years 1969–1972. The retained earnings account is as follows at the end of 1972:

Retained Earnings

Dividends, 1970...........	$12,000	Balance, December 31, 1969.....	$58,000
Dividends, 1971...........	14,800	Net income 1970.............	27,000
Dividends, 1972...........	21,200	Net income 1971.............	24,000
		Net income 1972.............	30,000

	End of			
	1969	1970	1971	1972
Prepaid expenses........................	$2,400	$2,600	$3,800	$4,800
Prepaid revenues........................		1,500	600	
Accrued expenses........................	6,000	5,500		6,500
Accrued revenues........................	200			400

Instructions: (1) Prepare working papers as illustrated on pages 994 and 995 to correct the retained earnings balance as of December 31, 1969, and to correct earnings for 1970, 1971, and 1972. Assume that an income tax rate of 25% applies to all years.

(2) Prepare a statement of retained earnings for the three-year period ending December 31, 1972, reporting corrected earnings.

(3) Give the entry that is required at the beginning of 1973 to correct the accounts assuming that the books are closed for 1972.

27-4. The auditors for the Stewart Co. in inspecting accounts on December 31, 1972, the end of the fiscal year, find that certain prepaid and accrued items had been overlooked in prior years and in the current year as follows:

	End of			
	1969	1970	1971	1972
Prepaid expenses........................	$ 650	$ 600	$ 750	$2,100
Accrued expenses........................	500	750	1,150	1,100
Prepaid revenues........................	170			420
Accrued revenues........................		100	150	200

Retained earnings on December 31, 1969, had been reported at $25,600; and net income for 1970 and for 1971 were reported at $10,200 and $13,250 respectively. Revenue and expense balances for 1972 were transferred to the income summary account and the latter shows a credit balance of $14,200 prior to correction by the auditors. No dividends had been declared in the three-year period.

Instructions: (1) Prepare working papers as illustrated on pages 994 and 995 to develop a corrected retained earnings balance as of December 31, 1969, and corrected earnings for 1970, 1971, and 1972. Disregard effects of corrections on income tax.

(continued)

(2) Prepare a corrected statement of retained earnings for the three-year period ending December 31, 1972.

(3) Give the entry or entries required as of December 31, 1972, to correct the income summary account and retained earnings account and to establish the appropriate balance sheet accounts as of this date.

27-5. An auditor is engaged by the Mantle Corp. in March, 1973, to examine the books and records and to make whatever corrections are necessary. The retained earnings account on the date of the audit is as follows:

Retained Earnings

Jan. 10, 1971 Dividends paid....	7,500	Jan. 1, 1970 Balance...........	41,000
Dec. 31, 1971 Net loss for year....	3,350	Dec. 31, 1970 Net income for year.	7,500
Jan. 10, 1972 Dividends paid....	7,500	Mar. 6, 1971 Premium on capital	
Dec. 31, 1972 Net loss for year....	8,150	stock.............	16,000

An examination of the accounts discloses the following:

(a) Dividends had been declared on December 15 in 1970 and 1971 but had not been entered in the books until paid.

(b) Improvements in buildings and equipment of $3,600 had been charged to expense at the end of April, 1969. Improvements are estimated to have an 8-year life. The company uses the straight-line method in recording depreciation.

(c) The physical inventory of merchandise had been understated by $1,200 at the end of 1970 and by $2,150 at the end of 1972.

(d) The merchandise inventories at the end of 1971 and 1972 did not include merchandise that was then in transit and to which the company had title. These shipments of $1,900 and $3,000 were recorded as purchases in January of 1972 and 1973 respectively.

(e) The company had failed to record accrued sales commissions of $1,050 and $900 at the end of 1971 and 1972 respectively.

(f) The company had failed to recognize supplies on hand of $750 and $950 at the end of 1971 and 1972 respectively.

Instructions: (1) Prepare working papers for the correction of account balances similar to those illustrated on pages 994 and 995, using the following columns (disregard effects of corrections on income tax):

Explanation	Retained Earnings Jan. 1, 1970		Net Income Year Ended Dec. 31, 1970		Net Income Year Ended Dec. 31, 1971		Net Income Year Ended Dec. 31, 1972		Accounts Requiring Correction in 1973		
	Dr.	Cr.	Dr.	Cr.	Dr.	Cr.	Dr.	Cr.	Dr.	Cr.	Account

(2) Journalize corrections required in March, 1973, in compound form.

(3) Prepare a statement of retained earnings covering the three-year period beginning January 1, 1970. The statement should report the corrected retained

earnings balance on January 1, 1970, the annual changes in the account, and the corrected retained earnings balances as of December 31, 1970, 1971, and 1972.

(4) Set up an account for retained earnings before correction, and post correcting data to this account from part (2) above. Balance the account, showing the corrected retained earnings as of December 31, 1972.

27-6. The statements below were prepared for the Ellsworth Company at the end of 1972.

Income Statement For Year Ended December 31, 1972			Balance Sheet December 31, 1972		
Sales		$75,000	Assets		
Cost of goods sold:			Cash		$17,500
Mdse. inv., Jan. 1	$24,000		Accounts receivable	$14,000	
Purchases	42,000		Less allow. for doubt. accts.	600	13,400
Mdse. available for sale	$66,000		Mdse. inventory		27,000
Deduct mdse. inv., Dec. 31	27,000	39,000	Delivery equipment		800
			Store equipment	$21,000	
Gross profit on sales		$36,000	Less accumulated depr.	7,000	14,000
Operating expenses:					
Selling expense	$18,000		Building	$55,000	
General expense	19,000	37,000	Less accumulated depr.	20,000	35,000
Operating loss		$ 1,000	Land		18,000
Other revenue and expense items:			Total assets		$125,700
Rental income	$ 4,650				
Misc. income	1,550		Liabilities		
			Accounts payable		$ 23,700
	$ 6,200				
Interest expense	700	5,500	Stockholders' Equity		
			Capital stock, $1 par	$50,000	
Net income		$ 4,500	Retained earnings	52,000	
			Total stockholders' equity		102,000
			Total liabilities and stockholders' equity		$125,700

During February, 1973, the following information is disclosed in connection with an audit of the books of the company:

(a) The merchandise inventory as of December 31, 1971, was overstated by $980.

(b) Merchandise in transit amounting to $1,870 was not included in the inventory of December 31, 1972, but the invoice had been entered in the purchases journal in 1972.

(c) On January 3, 1972, store equipment costing $6,000, with accumulated depreciation of $4,500, was sold for $1,000. Cash was debited and Store Equipment was credited for this amount.

(d) A truck was purchased on a conditional sales contract on December 30, 1972. The total purchase price was $2,500, but the purchase was recorded by a debit to Delivery Equipment and a credit to Cash for $800, the amount of the down payment.

(e) A check for $230 received from Kent Stevens on account had been deposited and then returned by the bank in December, 1972. No entry was made when the bank returned the check. The cash was collected from Stevens on January 20, 1973.

(f) A loss of $2,800 resulted from fire. The loss was not covered by insurance and was charged to General Expense in 1972.

(g) A part of the building was leased for $4,800 for 12 months ending April 30, 1973. The cash received was reported as income for 1972.

Instructions: (1) Prepare a work sheet for corrected financial statements for 1972. Disregard effects of corrections on income taxes.

(2) Prepare corrected financial statements.

27-7. The statements that follow were prepared for Fryer, Inc., at the end of 1972:

Income Statement For Year Ended December 31, 1972			Balance Sheet December 31, 1972		
Sales	$257,000			Assets	
Less sales discount	7,000	$250,000	Cash		$ 40,000
			Petty cash		200
			Accounts receivable		97,000
Cost of goods sold:			Mdse. inventory		70,000
Mdse. inv., Jan. 1	$ 73,000		Investment in bonds		10,000
Purchases	170,000				
			Total assets		$217,200
Mdse. available for sale	$243,000				
Less mdse. inv., Dec. 31	70,000	173,000			
Gross profit on sales		$ 77,000		Liabilities	
			Accounts payable		$ 35,000
			Bonds payable		98,000
Operating expenses:					
Selling expense	$ 30,000		Total liabilities		$133,000
General expense	32,000				
				Stockholders' Equity	
Total operating expenses		62,000	Capital stock, $5 par		$ 55,000
			Retained earnings		29,200
Operating income		$ 15,000			
Other revenue — interest			Total stockholders' equity		84,200
income		2,300			
Net income		$ 17,300	Total liabilities and stock-		
			holders' equity		$217,200

During January, 1973, the following facts were discovered:

(a) A 25% dividend in stock, payable on February 1, 1973, was declared on December 15, 1972. No entry had been made.

(b) Accrued expenses of $105 for utilities had not been included in the adjustments at the end of 1972.

(c) On January 2, 1972, a 5-year fire insurance policy was purchased for $1,500 and charged to General Expense. No adjustment was made at the end of 1972 for the unexpired insurance.

(d) Ten-year, 6% bonds of $100,000 par were issued at 98 on June 30, 1972. The bonds payable account was credited for the amount of cash received. The interest is payable annually on June 30. No adjustments were made at the end of 1972.

(e) 7% bonds, face value $10,000, had been purchased at face value on January 2, 1972. Interest is collected semiannually on January 1 and July 1. No adjustment for accrued interest was made at the end of 1972.

(f) The board of directors had authorized an appropriation of retained earnings of $10,000 for possible losses on damage suits at the end of 1972. No entry had been made.

(g) The petty cash fund, kept under the imprest system, had not been replenished at the end of the fiscal period. Payments had been made out of the fund as follows: $75 for General Expense and $65 for Selling Expense.

Instructions: (1) Prepare a work sheet for corrected financial statements for 1972. Disregard effects of corrections on income tax.

(2) Prepare corrected financial statements.

27-8. You have been engaged to review the records and prepare corrected financial statements for the Gable Corporation. The books of account are in agreement with the following balance sheet prepared on December 31, 1972:

Assets

Cash..	$ 5,000
Accounts receivable.........................	10,000
Notes receivable............................	3,000
Inventory...................................	25,000
	$43,000

Liabilities and Stockholders' Equity

Accounts payable............................	$ 2,000
Notes payable...............................	4,000
Capital stock...............................	10,000
Retained earnings...........................	27,000
	$43,000

A review of the books of the corporation indicates that the following errors and omissions had not been corrected during the applicable years:

December 31	Inventory Overvalued	Inventory Undervalued	Prepaid Expense	Prepaid Revenue	Accrued Expense	Accrued Revenue
1969	—	$6,000	$900	—	$200	—
1970	$7,000	—	700	$400	75	$125
1971	8,000	—	500	—	100	—
1972	—	9,000	600	300	50	150

The profits per books are: 1970, $7,500; 1971, $6,500; and 1972, $5,500. No dividends were declared during these years and no adjustments were made to retained earnings.

Instructions: Prepare a work sheet to develop the corrected profits for the years 1970, 1971, and 1972 and the adjusted balance sheet accounts as of December 31, 1972. Disregard effects of corrections on income tax.

(AICPA adapted)

27-9. You have been asked by a client to review the records of the Reardon Manufacturing Company, a small manufacturer of precision tools and machines. Your client is interested in buying the business and arrangements have been made for you to review the accounting records.

Your examination reveals the following:

(a) The Reardon Manufacturing Company commenced business on April 1, 1969, and has been reporting on a fiscal year ending March 31. The company has never been audited, but the annual statements prepared by the bookkeeper reflect the following income before closing and before deducting income taxes:

Year Ended March 31	Income Before Taxes
1970	$37,800
1971	56,200
1972	53,790

(b) A relatively small number of machines has been shipped on consignment. These transactions have been recorded as an ordinary sale and billed as such. On March 31 of each year, machines billed and in the hands of consignees amounted to:

1970	$ 6,110
1971	none
1972	5,343

Sales price was determined by adding 30% to cost.

(c) On March 30, 1971, two machines were shipped to a customer on a C.O.D. basis. The sale was not entered until April 5, 1971, when cash was received in the amount of $5,800. The machines were not included in the inventory at March 31, 1971.

(d) All machines are sold subject to a five-year warranty. It is estimated that the expense ultimately to be incurred in connection with the warranty will amount to ½% of sales. The company has charged an expense account for warranty costs incurred.
Sales per books and warranty costs were:

Year Ended March 31	Sales	Warranty Expense for Sales Made in 1970	1971	1972	Total
1970	$ 844,710	$ 680			$ 680
1971	905,000	320	$1,170		1,490
1972	1,604,110	290	1,450	$1,710	3,450

(e) A review of the corporate minutes reveals the manager is entitled to a bonus of ½% of the income before deducting income taxes and his bonus. The bonuses have never been recorded or paid.

(f) The bank deducts 6% on all contracts financed. Of this amount ½% is placed in a reserve to the credit of the Reardon Manufacturing Company which is refunded to Reardon as finance contracts are paid in full. The reserve established by the bank has not been reflected in the books of Reardon. The excess of credits over debits (net increase) to the reserve account with Reardon on the books of the bank for each fiscal year were as follows:

1970	$ 2,800
1971	3,750
1972	4,960
	$11,510

(g) Commissions on sales have been entered when paid. Commissions payable on March 31 of each year were:

1970... $ 1,200
1971... 700
1972... 960

(h) On May 17, 1971, the building was sold to an insurance company for $890,000. Its book value at the date of sale was $880,000.

Instructions: (1) Present a schedule showing the revised net income before income taxes for each of the years ended March 31, 1970, 1971, and 1972. Make computations to the nearest whole dollar.

(2) Prepare the journal entry or entries you would present the bookkeeper to correct the books. Assume the books have not yet been closed for the fiscal year ended March 31, 1972. Disregard correction of income taxes.

(3) Compute the purchase price. Your client will pay the amount of the corrected book value of the net assets at March 31, 1972 plus goodwill equal to two times the average profits before taxes in excess of a 6% return on the final capital. According to the books the net assets were $548,250 at March 31, 1972. Extraneous gains and losses are not to be considered in the calculation of average annual profits.

(AICPA adapted)

27-10. On January 10, 1973, the Racon Corporation engages you to adjust the books and prepare a balance sheet at December 31, 1972, that will conform with generally accepted accounting principles. You begin by preparing the following trial balance as of December 31, 1972, from the general ledger.

Cash..	16,000	
Accounts Receivable.........................	17,000	
Allowance for Doubtful Accounts..............		3,000
Inventories.................................	10,000	
Investments.................................	17,000	
Equipment..................................	148,000	
Accumulated Depreciation — Equipment........		5,000
Accounts Payable............................		6,000
Notes Payable..............................		14,000
Capital Stock...............................		75,000
Retained Earnings...........................		105,000
	208,000	208,000

Subsequent examination discloses the following:

(a) Cash:
   (1) The bank letter of confirmation shows a cash balance of $16,000 at December 31, 1972.
   (2) Examination of returned checks received with the January 15, 1973, cutoff statement reveals $3,000 of checks dated December 31, 1972. The checks were for unrecorded 1972 expenses.
   (3) The cash deposits made December 31, 1972, for $1,700 and January 2, 1973, for $900 were both recorded by the bank on January 3, 1973. The deposits were for unrecorded cash sales.
   (4) One of the checks returned January 15, 1973, dated December 31, 1972, for $300 for a 1972 expense was actually not written until January 3, 1973; the check was recorded as of December 31, 1972.

(b) Accounts receivable:

Analysis of accounts receivable reveals that with two exceptions all appeared collectible at December 31, 1972.

(1) The Ambrosia Butane Distributors had fallen into receivership and were expected to realize only 40 cents on the dollar. The December 31, 1972, balance was $5,000. On February 17, 1973, $4,000 was recovered.

(2) The Mercantile Association had not paid anything on its balance of $3,000 and this account was written off as uncollectible since Albert Wimberly, president of the Association, had informed your client in December, 1972, that it appeared impossible that current obligations could ever be met and that mortgage holders would probably absorb all asset proceeds in the event of liquidation. However, on March 2, 1973, ten days before issuance of your report, $1,500 was received as final settlement on this account.

(c) Allowance for doubtful accounts:

The $3,000 balance is the amount expected to absorb the loss on the Ambrosia Butane Distributors account.

(d) Inventories:

(1) Inventory in the amount of $9,000 is priced at net realizable value (regular sales price less marketing costs).

(2) Current cost of replacement of inventory mentioned in (1) above is $7,000.

(3) Estimated marketing costs are 10% of sales price.

(4) Goods are priced to return a 40% gross profit based on sales.

(5) Inventory in amount of $1,000 represents goods received on a consignment basis for which a liability has been recorded. These goods were priced at cost.

(e) Investments:

(1) $5,000 of the balance represents the cost of 1,000 shares of the Xelo Corporation, an unconsolidated subsidiary. Market value of these shares at December 31, 1972, was $1,700. The market is not expected to recover in the foreseeable future.

(2) $1,000 represents the cost of Brentlow, Incorporated bonds due August 1, 1992. Interest is payable February 1 and August 1 at 6%. The bonds were purchased at par, but would sell on the open market for $1,040.

(3) The remaining $11,000 represents the cost of temporary investments. Market value at December 31 was $10,400.

(f) Land, buildings, and equipment:

The balance in this account represents the cost of various equipment which was purchased at date of incorporation, January 1, 1971. One truck costing $6,000 was sold for $5,000 December 31, 1972, the proceeds being credited to accumulated depreciation.

(g) Accumulated depreciation:

(1) No entries have been made in this account except for the $5,000 realized from the sale of equipment.

(2) Equipment when purchased was expected to have a 10-year life with a 10% salvage value.

(3) You agree with the client to set up depreciation on a straight-line basis for book purposes and on a declining-balance method for federal income tax purposes. Proper depreciation was taken for tax purposes the previous year on a declining-balance method.

(h) Accounts payable:
The entire account of $6,000 is due to one creditor for consigned merchandise, $1,000 of which is still on hand.

(i) Notes payable:
The following is a trial balance of notes payable (interest payable semiannually on exact due dates):

Creditor	Date of Note	Interest Rate	Due Date	Amount
Brumalow and Breichour, Ltd.	1/1/72	6%	1/1/73	$ 5,000
Lawson Hickey, Incorporated	6/30/72	5%	*	4,000
Daniel Duncan	6/30/71	5%	6/30/73	5,000
				$14,000

*Principal payable in semiannual installments of $2,000 beginning December 31, 1973.

(j) Capital stock:
The following analysis was obtained:

Balance, January 1, 1972 (1,000 shares @ $100 par)......	$100,000
Deduct repurchase of 250 shares, still in treasury.........	25,000
Balance, December 31, 1972..........................	$ 75,000

(k) Retained earnings:
The following is an analysis of retained earnings since date of incorporation, per client's records:

Date	Explanation	Amount
1/1/71	Premium on stock sold (1,000 shares)	$ 10,000
12/31/71	Net loss for year	(15,000)
12/31/72	Loss on purchase of treasury stock	(2,000)
12/31/72	Net income for year	112,000
	Balance, December 31, 1972	$105,000

(l) You estimate the accrued federal income tax as of December 31, 1972, to be $17,043.40.

Instructions: Prepare a work sheet showing account balances per books, any adjustments you consider necessary, and adjusted balances. Also, indicate which balances you would consider to be current, which balances noncurrent, and which balances would be shown in the stockholders' equity section of the balance sheet. Prepare schedules of inventories, depreciation, and deferred taxes in good form. (Note: It is not necessary to prepare a formal balance sheet or journal entries for any adjustments you determine. Assume a 52% tax rate in calculating deferred taxes.)

(AICPA adapted)

27-11. The Karr-Turner Company is a partnership that has not maintained adequate accounting records because it has been unable to employ a competent bookkeeper. The company sells hardware items to the retail trade and also wholesales to builders and contractors. As the company's CPA, you have been asked to prepare the company's financial statements as of June 30, 1972.

Your work papers provide the following post-closing trial balance at December 31, 1971:

	Debit	Credit
Cash..................................	10,000	
Accounts Receivable.................	8,000	
Allowance for Doubtful Accounts..........		600
Merchandise Inventory................	35,000	
Prepaid Insurance...................	150	
Automobiles........................	7,800	
Accumulated Depreciation — Automobiles.........		4,250
Furniture and Fixtures................	2,200	
Accumulated Depreciation — Furniture and Fixtures.		650
Accounts Payable....................		13,800
Bank Loan Payable..................		8,000
Accrued Expenses...................		200
Karr, Capital......................		17,500
Turner, Capital....................		18,150
Total........................	63,150	63,150

You are able to collect the following information at June 30, 1972:

(a) Your analysis of cash transactions, derived from the company's bank statements and checkbook stubs, is as follows:

Deposits:

Cash receipts from customers.........................	$65,000
($40,000 of this amount represents collections on receivables including redeposited protested checks totaling $600)	
Bank loan, 1/2/72 (due 5/1/72, 5%).................	7,867
Bank loan, 5/1/72 (due 9/1/72, 5%).................	8,850
Sale of old automobile...............................	20
Total deposits....................................	$81,737

Disbursements:

Payments to merchandise creditors.....................	$45,000
Payment to Internal Revenue Service on Turner's 1972 declaration of estimated income taxes.................	3,000
General expenses....................................	7,000
Bank loan, 1/2/72.................................	8,000
Bank loan, 5/2/72.................................	8,000
Payment for new automobile.........................	2,400
Protested checks....................................	900
Karr, withdrawals...................................	5,000
Turner, withdrawals.................................	2,500
Total disbursements.............................	$81,800

(b) The protested checks include customers' checks totaling $600 that were redeposited and a $300 check from an employee that is still on hand.

(c) Accounts receivable from customers for merchandise sales amount to $18,000 and include accounts totaling $800 that have been placed with an attorney for collection. Correspondence with the client's attorney reveals that one of the accounts for $175 is uncollectible. Experience indicates that 1% of credit sales will prove uncollectible.

(d) On April 1 a new automobile was purchased. The list price of the automobile was $2,700 and $300 was allowed for the trade-in of an old automobile, even though the dealer stated that its condition was so poor that he did not want it. The client sold the old automobile, which cost $1,800 and was fully depreciated at December 31, to an auto wrecker for $20. The old automobile was in use up to the date of its sale.

(e) Depreciation is recorded by the straight-line method and is computed on acquisitions to the nearest full month. The estimated life for furniture and fixtures is ten years and for automobiles is three years. (Salvage value is to be ignored in computing depreciation. No asset other than the car in item (d) was fully depreciated prior to June 30, 1972.)

(f) Other data as of June 30, 1972, include the following:

Merchandise inventory	$37,500
Prepaid insurance	80
Accrued expenses	166

(g) Accounts payable to merchandise vendors total $18,750. There is on hand a $750 credit memorandum from a merchandise vendor for returned merchandise; the Company will apply the credit to July merchandise purchases. Neither the credit memorandum nor the return of the merchandise had been recorded on the books.

(h) Earnings and losses are divided equally between the partners.

Instructions: (1) Prepare a work sheet that provides, on the accrual basis, information regarding transactions for the six months ended June 30, 1972, the results of operations for the period, and the financial position of the partnership at June 30, 1972.

(2) Prepare an income statement for the six months ended June 30, 1972, and a balance sheet at June 30, 1972.

(AICPA adapted)

chapter 28

financial statements
reporting general
price-level changes

With the steady increase in the price level over a period of many years, there has been a growing awareness of the limitations in measurements that assume a stable monetary unit. Fluctuations in the general purchasing power of the dollar have made it difficult to interpret the dollar amounts reported on the conventional statements. The validity of the analytical data provided by such statements has been challenged. As a result, demands have been made that the accountant provide financial data that are restated in terms of the current general price level so that a company's position and progress may be viewed in proper perspective. The means of providing this information are considered in this chapter.

Background of the problem

In the fundamental accounting process, transactions are recorded in terms of the number of dollars exchanged. It is these dollar amounts representing diverse amounts of purchasing power that are reported in the conventional statements, sometimes referred to as *historical-dollar statements*. The primary reason for reporting original dollar amounts is the objectivity inherent in such procedure. If accountants were to depend upon the subjective judgments of appraisers in establishing values for property items on the financial statements, they would probably have to choose from a wide range of estimates. With a choice of alternative values, the doors would be opened to bias, errors, and even fraud. Reported values would be challenged; confidence in accounting reports would be undermined.

Although the historical cost concept provides objectivity in financial reporting, wide fluctuations in the general price level place severe limitations upon the validity and hence the usefulness of such reporting.

Cost must be expressed in monetary terms, and in unadjusted form this is likely to create misunderstandings. The dollar is an abstraction which has significance only in reference to a particular level of prices. A contemporary reader is likely to regard a dollar in terms of its general purchasing power currently rather than its general purchasing power at the time it was exchanged.

The distortion is increased when dollars of many different orders of purchasing power are added together to get a total or subtracted from each other to get a difference. An accountant would never think of adding 100 U.S. dollars to 100 British pounds to get 200 of something that is meaningful. He would first convert one of the figures to its exchange equivalent before proceeding with arithmetic operations. In the same way, the addition of the number of dollars expended many years ago for land, buildings, and equipment with the number of dollars expended currently for merchandise does not yield a meaningful total; similarly, the subtraction of a number of dollars for property acquired some time ago from the number of dollars realized currently on its sale fails to provide a meaningful difference. In each instance, the purchasing power involved in the dollars that are added or subtracted is not disclosed.

Suggested solutions

Possible methods of overcoming objections to financial statements based upon historical costs have come from many sources. Fundamentally, most of the suggestions by accounting authoritative bodies have not recommended the abandonment of present statements. Rather, they have recommended the use of supplementary statements or multi-column statements that would report the effects of general price-level changes on the account balances. The American Accounting Association in 1951 advocated the use of supplementary statements in which the historical cost figures would be adjusted for general price level changes. The Committee stated their conclusions as follows:

> Management may properly include in periodic reports to stockholders comprehensive supplementary statements which present the effects of the fluctuation in the value of the dollar upon net income and upon financial position.

> Such supplementary statements should be internally consistent; the income statement and the balance sheet should both be adjusted by the same procedures, so that the figures in such complementary statements are coordinate and have the same relative significance.

> Such supplementary statements should be reconciled in detail with the primary statements reflecting unadjusted original dollar costs, and should be regarded as an extension or elaboration of the primary statements rather than as a departure therefrom.

Such supplementary statements should be accompanied by comments and explanations clearly setting forth the implications, uses, and limitations of the adjusted data.[1]

The American Institute of Certified Public Accountants has also given close study to the problem of general price-level changes, and in 1963, the staff of the Accounting Research Division issued Accounting Research Study No. 6 and concluded in part:

> . . . The effects of price-level changes should be disclosed as a supplement to the conventional statements. This disclosure may take the form of physically separate statements, or of parallel columns in a combined statement, or of detailed supporting schedules (including charts and graphs), or some combination of these.
>
> In the supplementary data, all elements of the financial statements (e.g., balance sheet, income statement, analysis of retained earnings) should be restated by means of a single index of the general price level as of the balance-sheet date so that all the financial data will be expressed in terms of dollars of the same purchasing power.[2]

The Accounting Principles Board has not issued an Opinion on the subject of reporting the financial effects of price-level changes. However, in 1969 it issued Statement No. 3, "Financial Statements Restated for General Price-Level Changes." In this statement it "explains the effects on business enterprises and their financial statements of changes in the general purchasing power of money, describes the basic nature of financial statements restated for general price-level changes (general price-level financial statements) and gives general guidance on how to prepare and present these statements."[3] Although the Board observes that the presentation of price-level information is not mandatory, it states:

> Changes in the general purchasing power of money have an impact on almost every aspect of economic affairs, including such diverse matters as investment, wage negotiation, pricing policy, international trade, and government fiscal policy. The effects of changes in the general purchasing power of money on economic data expressed in monetary terms are widely recognized, and economic data for the economy as a whole are commonly restated to eliminate these effects. General price-level financial statements should prove useful to investors, creditors, management, employees, government officials, and others who are concerned with the economic affairs of business enterprises.[4]

---

[1]*Accounting and Reporting Standards for Corporate Financial Statements and Preceding Statements and Supplements*, "Supplementary Statement No. 2, Price Level Changes and Financial Statements" (1957 rev.; Madison, Wisconsin: American Accounting Association), p. 27.

[2]Accounting Research Division, *Reporting the Financial Effects of Price-Level Changes*, Accounting Research Study No. 6 (New York: American Institute of Certified Public Accountants, 1963), p. xi.

[3]*Statements of the Accounting Principles Board, No. 3*, "Financial Statements Restated for General Price-Level Changes" (New York: American Institute of Certified Public Accountants, 1969), par. 1.

[4]*Ibid.*, par. 6.

The Board goes on to conclude:

> The Board believes that general price-level financial statements or pertinent information extracted from them present useful information not available from basic historical-dollar financial statements. General price-level information may be presented in addition to the basic historical-dollar financial statements, but general price-level financial statements should not be presented as the basic statements. The Board believes that general price-level information is not required at this time for fair presentation of financial position and results of operations in conformity with generally accepted accounting principles in the United States.[1]

General price-level statements in which original dollar costs are restated in current dollar terms afford a means of disclosing the effects of price-level changes without giving up the objectivity inherent in the conventional statements. The restatement procedure is based on conversion of original dollar amounts to the purchasing power equivalent in current dollars by applying an objectively-determined measure of the change in the general purchasing power of the dollar. Restatement introduces no factor other than general price-level changes; the amounts reported are not intended to represent appraisal values, replacement costs, or any other measure of current value.

There have been some suggestions that the presentation of general price-level statements is not sufficient to solve the problem. The recognition of current values or replacement costs in the accounts, it has been suggested, would provide more meaningful statements of a company's worth and earnings. In 1966 an American Accounting Association Committee issued *A Statement of Basic Accounting Theory* in which it recommended that both historical cost data and current value or current cost data be provided in separate columns in financial statement presentations.[2] There are several ways of determining current values, including the use of market values and specific price-level indexes for given categories of goods and services. The possible increased use of current values in the financial statement presentations is being examined very carefully by the Accounting Principles Board. As with general price-level adjusted information, the presentation of current values is generally recommended for supplemental presentation.

Price-level indexes

The value or purchasing power of any monetary unit is inversely related to the price of the goods or services for which it can be exchanged. Over a period of time, the prices of specific goods or services will move

---

[1]*Ibid.*, par. 25.

[2]*A Statement of Basic Accounting Theory* (Evanston, Illinois: American Accounting Association, 1966), p. 30.

up or down depending upon their relative scarcity and desirability. In addition to such shifts among prices within a given price structure, there may be movements of the price structure for goods and services as a whole, referred to as *inflation* or *deflation*. It is the latter — the shifts in the general level of prices — that are the primary focus of this chapter.

The general level of prices cannot be measured in absolute terms, but the relative changes from time to time and the direction of change can be determined. To measure changes in the general price level, a sample of commodities is selected and the current prices of these items are compared with their prices during a base period. The prices during the base period are assigned a value of 100, and the prices of all other periods are expressed in percentages of this amount. The resulting series of numbers is called a *price-level index*.

Price-level indexes can be valuable aids in judging the extent of inflation or deflation. However, the limitations that are found in these measurements should be considered. In the first place, all price indexes are based upon a sampling process. Since all prices do not fluctuate in the same degree or direction, the selection of commodities to be included and their relative weights have important bearings on the computed values. In addition, improvements in the products that are included in the sample affect the general level of prices, but qualitative changes are difficult to measure.

Selecting an appropriate price-level index. Although no perfect means of measuring the changing value of the dollar has yet been devised, there are several readily-available indexes that provide reasonable estimates of the overall change in the dollar's general purchasing power. Among these are the Consumer Price Index and the Wholesale Price Index, both provided by the Bureau of Labor Statistics, and the GNP (Gross National Product) Implicit Price Deflator that is provided by the Department of Commerce. Annual averages of each of these indexes for the years 1941–1970 are listed on the opposite page.

Each of the three popular indexes exhibits a similar pattern of price-level change, but the indexes report different values. This is because each index is based upon the prices of a different group of items. Accountants have not reached agreement on the index that would be most suitable for accounting purposes.

The Staff of the AICPA Accounting Research Division in *Accounting Research Study No. 6* recommends use of the GNP Implicit Price Deflator. It observes:

> The only index currently compiled that is a measure of the general level of prices in the United States is the GNP Implicit Price Deflator.

PRICE-LEVEL INDEXES — USA

Year	Wholesale Price Index (1957–59 = 100)	Consumer Price Index (1957–59 = 100)	GNP Implicit Price Deflator (1958 = 100)
1941	47.8	51.3	47.2
1942	54.0	56.8	53.0
1943	56.5	60.3	56.8
1944	56.9	61.3	58.2
1945	57.9	62.7	59.7
1946	66.1	68.0	66.7
1947	81.2	77.8	74.6
1948	87.9	83.8	79.6
1949	83.5	83.0	79.1
1950	86.8	83.8	80.2
1951	96.7	90.5	85.6
1952	94.0	92.5	87.5
1953	92.7	93.2	88.3
1954	92.9	93.6	89.6
1955	93.2	93.3	90.9
1956	96.2	94.7	94.0
1957	99.0	98.0	97.5
1958	100.4	100.7	100.0
1959	100.6	101.5	101.6
1960	100.7	103.1	103.3
1961	100.3	104.2	104.6
1962	100.6	105.4	105.7
1963	100.3	106.7	107.1
1964	100.5	108.1	108.9
1965	102.5	109.9	110.9
1966	105.9	113.1	113.9
1967	106.1	116.3	117.3
1968	109.1	121.5	121.8
1969	106.5	127.7	128.1
1970	110.4	135.3	134.9

It is the only price index compiled in this country whose "universe" encompasses the entire economy. . . .

As a result of our investigation we are convinced that the GNP Implicit Price Deflators are reliable enough for accounting purposes. . . .[1]

The Accounting Principles Board in Statement No. 3 employs the GNP Deflator in illustrating the procedures for restating financial data for general price-level changes and recommends that this index should normally be used.[2]

Because there is a high degree of correlation among the three indexes, the choice of one rather than another would not be critical. However,

---

[1]Accounting Research Division, *op. cit.*, pp. 111–112.
[2]*Statements of the Accounting Principles Board, No. 3, op. cit.*, par. 30.

it is important that a general concensus be reached on the index that is to be used so that the choice is not left to the discretion of each company and so that index-adjusted statements of different companies can be regarded as comparable.

Effects of general price-level changes on monetary and nonmonetary items

In recognizing the effects of general price-level changes it is necessary to distinguish between *monetary items* and *nonmonetary items*. Monetary items are those assets and liabilities with dollar balances that are fixed by contract or otherwise and that do not change with a change in the general price level. All other items are nonmonetary.

Monetary assets include cash as well as such items as accounts receivable, notes receivable, long-term investments in bonds, cash surrender value of life insurance, and refundable deposits. Regardless of the changes that take place in the general price level, these balances are fixed and provide for the recovery of neither more nor less than the stated amounts. Monetary liabilities include such items as accounts payable, notes payable, refundable deposits, and accruals under pension plans. Regardless of the changes that take place in the price level, these balances are fixed and call for the payment of neither more nor less than the stated amounts. With asset and liability balances that do not respond to changes in the general price level, purchasing-power gains or losses are also related to these items — price-level gains or losses that are not disclosed in conventional reporting.

Nonmonetary assets include such items as inventories and supplies, prepaid expenses, land, buildings, and equipment, and intangible assets. The latter items derive their nonmonetary classification from the fact that with changes in the general price-level, the dollar amounts at which they are reported on the conventional financial statements will differ from the dollar resources they actually represent. On the other hand, nonmonetary liabilities include such items as deferred revenue, advances on sales contracts, and warranties on goods sold. The latter items derive their nonmonetary classification from the fact that with changes in the general price level, the dollar demands that they will actually make will differ from the dollar amounts that are reported on the conventional financial statements.[1]

---

[1]Ordinarily the stockholders' equity would be regarded as a nonmonetary item. However, an exception may be made with respect to the equity represented by nonconvertible, callable preferred stock. When preferred stock can be retired at a fixed-dollar amount, it is regarded as a monetary item. A comprehensive list of balance sheet items and their classification as monetary and nonmonetary items, together with an explanation of the reason for classification when needed, is given in Accounting Principles Board Statement No. 3, Appendix B.

The distinctions between monetary and nonmonetary items is not related to the current and noncurrent classifications used for assets and liabilities. For example, monetary assets include current assets such as accounts receivable and also noncurrent assets such as long-term investments in bonds; nonmonetary assets include current items such as inventories and supplies and noncurrent items such as land, buildings, and equipment. Monetary liabilities include current items such as accounts and notes payable and noncurrent items such as bonds payable; nonmonetary liabilities include current items such as advances on sales contracts and noncurrent items such as long-term sales warranties.

The difference between a company's monetary assets and its monetary liabilities is referred to as its *net monetary items*.[1]

With the number of dollars in monetary items remaining fixed and reflecting current dollars regardless of the change in the price level, general price-level gains and losses are associated with monetary items as follows:

During a period of *rising* prices:
    (a) a general price-level loss arises from holding monetary assets;
    (b) a general price-level gain arises from maintaining monetary liabilities.

Conversely, during a period of *declining* prices:
    (a) a general price-level gain arises from holding monetary assets;
    (b) a general price-level loss arises from maintaining monetary liabilities.

In any given period the gain or loss from holding monetary assets is offset by the loss or gain from maintaining monetary liabilities. The gain or loss for a period, then, depends upon whether a company's position in net monetary items is *positive* — monetary assets exceeding monetary liabilities; or *negative* — monetary liabilities exceeding monetary assets. Gains and losses are associated with a company's net monetary position as follows:

During a period of *rising* prices:
    (a) a general price-level loss arises from maintaining a positive position in net monetary items;
    (b) a general price-level gain arises from maintaining a negative position in net monetary items.

---

[1] "Net monetary items" should be distinguished from "net monetary assets" to which reference was made in preceding chapters. Net monetary assets is the difference between quick assets and current liabilities and is a measure of a company's liquidity; net monetary items is the difference between assets calling for receipt of a fixed number of dollars and liabilities calling for payment of a fixed number of dollars and is a measure of a company's net resources subject to gains and losses arising from general price-level changes.

During a period of *declining* prices:

    (a) a general price-level gain arises from maintaining a positive position in net monetary items;

    (b) a general price-level loss arises from maintaining a negative position in net monetary items.

Restating financial statements for general price-level changes

The process of restating financial statements for general price-level changes involves restating the dollar balances in conventional statements to the number of current dollars in equivalent current purchasing power. This requires a consideration of the relative purchasing power for each reported dollar amount.

Nonmonetary assets are generally reported on the financial statements at the number of dollars originally reported upon acquisition; nonmonetary liabilities are reported at the number of dollars originally received; and nonmonetary capital balances are stated at the number of dollars originally received from stockholders and accumulated through earnings. Restating these balances requires recognition of the change in the price level since the time each transaction within these groups took place. The monetary assets and liabilities state amounts that are recognized as representing current dollars. These items, therefore, do not require restatement.

A number of simple examples will be given to illustrate the restatement of financial data in terms of dollars of uniform purchasing power and to suggest the nature of the analysis afforded by such data. These examples will be followed by an extended illustration in which financial statements summarizing operations of successive periods are restated. In each of the examples in the section that follows, the activities of a company for the first year of its life are given. It is assumed in the examples that the general price level moves up evenly throughout the year and produces a 5 percent rise for the year.

Example 1 — Nonmonetary assets are held during the year. Assume that a company issues capital stock of $50,000 in exchange for land valued at $50,000. The company holds the land during the year without engaging in any other activities. A balance sheet prepared in conventional form at the end of the year will show both land and invested capital at their original amounts. In preparing a balance sheet expressing financial position in terms of the price level at the end of the year, however, land and capital stock will be reported as follows:

(1) Land, a nonmonetary asset, needs to be restated for the change in price level since its acquisition. Land with an acquisition cost of $50,000, is expressed in current dollars at $50,000 x 105/100, or $52,500.

...netary item, also requires restatement so
...ers' investment in terms of the current
...alance is expressed in current dollars at

...report resources and the stockholders'
...revailing at the end of the year follows.

...porting General Price-Level Changes

	Historical Amount	Conversion Factor	Restated Amount
...	$50,000	105/100	$52,500
..	$50,000	105/100	$52,500

...r the company prepared in conven-
...stockholders' equity balances at the
...balances at the beginning of the year.
...ative balance sheet expressed in terms of the purchasing power
of the dollar at the end of the year will also show account balances to
have remained unchanged. In preparing adjusted comparative data,
beginning balances must be updated or "rolled forward" so that they
are stated in a manner that will permit comparisons with the statements
prepared currently. Updating the balance sheet does not indicate that
earlier balances were misstated; it is simply a means of changing the form
of the information in terms of a later unit of measure. A balance sheet
comparing beginning and ending balances in dollars of uniform purchasing power follows.

Comparative Balance Sheet Reporting General Price-Level Changes

	Beginning of Year			End of Year	Increase (Decrease)
	Historical Amount	Conversion Factor	Restated Amount		
Land..................	$50,000	105/100	$52,500	$52,500	——
Capital stock............	$50,000	105/100	$52,500	$52,500	——

Conclusion. The comparative balance sheet shows that company
resources and the stockholders' equity have not changed during the year.
In the absence of monetary items, there has been neither price-level gain
nor loss arising from the decline in the purchasing power of the dollar in
the period of price-level advance.

Example 2 — Monetary and nonmonetary assets are held during the year.
Assume that a company issues capital stock of $100,000 in exchange for

cash of $25,000 and land valued at $75,000. The assets are held throughout the year without any accrual of revenue or expense. A balance sheet
prepared in conventional form at the end of the year will report assets
and stockholders' equity balances at their original amounts. However,
the company has suffered a decline in the purchasing power of its cash
holdings, and this decline will be revealed in the balance sheet restated
in terms of end-of-year dollars. A balance sheet expressing financial
position in terms of the price level at the end of the year will report the
following balances:

(1) Cash is a monetary asset, a resource of fixed-dollar amount, that
has not changed with the change in the purchasing power of the dollar.
The cash balance, then, is reported at $25,000.

(2) Land is restated in terms of the current price level at $75,000 x
105/100 or $78,750.

(3) Capital stock is restated in terms of the current price level at
$100,000 x 105/100, or $105,000.

(4) The stockholders' equity must be reported at a balance equal to
the sum of the assets as restated, or $103,750. With the original invest-
ment by stockholders expressed in terms of the current price level at
$105,000, a reduction in the stockholders' equity of $1,250 is indicated.
Since the company did not engage in operations during the year, the
reduction in the stockholders' equity must be recognized as a loss resulting from the decrease in the purchasing power of monetary assets held
during the year. This price-level loss is confirmed by a separate computation. In a period in which prices increased by 5%, the equivalent
number of dollars in terms of the end-of-year price level for monetary
assets of $25,000 held by the company throughout the year is $25,000 x
105/100, or $26,250; since monetary assets at the end of the year are
only $25,000, a loss of $1,250 was sustained. The loss can also be computed: $25,000 x 5/100, or $1,250.

A balance sheet prepared in terms of the price level at the end of the
year is given below. This is accompanied by a schedule reporting the
change in the stockholders' equity resulting from the change in the price
level during the year.

Balance Sheet at End of Year Reporting General Price-Level Changes

	Historical Amount	Conversion Factor	Restated Amount
Cash	$ 25,000		$ 25,000
Land	75,000	105/100	78,750
	$100,000		$103,750
Capital stock	$100,000	105/100	$105,000
Retained earnings (deficit)	——	(see schedule)	(1,250)
	$100,000		$103,750

Schedule Reporting General Price-Level Gain or Loss for Year

	Historical Amount	Conversion Factor	Restated Amount
Monetary assets at beginning of year.......	$ 25,000	105/100	$ 26,250
Monetary assets at end of year............			25,000
General price-level loss..................			$ 1,250

A comparative balance sheet prepared in conventional form will show no changes in the assets and in the stockholders' equity for the year. However, a comparative balance sheet adjusted for the purchasing power of the dollar shows that changes did take place. In preparing a comparative balance sheet, beginning balances are rolled forward to reflect dollars of purchasing power that are comparable with the dollars reported on the balance sheet at the end of the period. A balance sheet comparing the beginning and the ending balances in dollars of uniform purchasing power follows.

Comparative Balance Sheet Reporting General Price-Level Changes

	Beginning of Year			End of Year	Increase (Decrease)
	Historical Amount	Conversion Factor	Restated Amount		
Cash.................	$ 25,000	105/100	$ 26,250	$ 25,000	$(1,250)
Land.................	75,000	105/100	78,750	78,750	———
	$100,000		$105,000	$103,750	$(1,250)
Capital stock...........	$100,000	105/100	$105,000	$105,000	———
Retained earnings (deficit).............	———		———	(1,250)	$(1,250)
	$100,000		$105,000	$103,750	$(1,250)

Conclusion. Although no transactions took place during the year, the comparative balance sheet shows that there were decreases in company resources and in the stockholders' equity. These decreases resulted from a loss in the purchasing power of the monetary resources that were held during the period of price-level advance.

Example 3 — Monetary and nonmonetary assets are held and monetary liabilities are maintained during the year. Assume that a company issues capital stock of $75,000 in exchange for cash of $25,000 and land valued at $100,000 that is subject to a mortgage note of $50,000. The assets are held and the liability is maintained throughout the year without any accrual of revenue or expense. A balance sheet prepared in conventional form at the end of the year shows asset, liability, and stockholders' equity balances at their original amounts. However, in preparing a balance sheet in terms of the price level at the end of the year, balances would be as follows:

(1) Cash is reported at the balance on hand, $25,000.

(2) Land is restated in terms of the current price level at $100,000 x 105/100, or $105,000.

(3) The mortgage note is a monetary item, an obligation of fixed-dollar amount, that has not changed with the change in the purchasing power of the dollar. The mortgage note, then, is reported at $50,000.

(4) The capital stock balance is restated in terms of the current price level at $75,000 x 105/100, or $78,750.

(5) The stockholders' equity must be reported at an amount equal to the net assets as restated, or $80,000. With the original investment by stockholders expressed in terms of the current price level at $78,750, there has been an increase in the stockholders' equity of $1,250. Since there were no transactions during the year, the increase in the stock-holders' equity indicates a price-level gain from the increase in the pur-chasing power of the company's net monetary items during the year.

A balance sheet restated to report balances in terms of the price level prevailing at the end of the year and a schedule reporting the change in the stockholders' equity resulting from the change in the price level during the year follow.

Balance Sheet at End of Year Reporting General Price-Level Changes

	Historical Amount	Conversion Factor	Restated Amount
Cash..	$ 25,000		$ 25,000
Land..	100,000	105/100	105,000
	$125,000		$130,000
Mortgage note payable...................	$ 50,000		$ 50,000
Capital stock............................	75,000	105/100	78,750
Retained earnings.......................	———	(see schedule)	1,250
	$125,000		$130,000

Schedule Reporting General Price-Level Gain or Loss for Year

	Historical Amount	Conversion Factor	Restated Amount
Excess of monetary liabilities over monetary assets at beginning of year..............	$ 25,000	105/100	$ 26,250
Excess of monetary liabilities over monetary assets at end of year.....................			25,000
General price-level gain.................			$ 1,250

A comparative balance sheet prepared in conventional form will show asset, liability, and stockholders' equity balances as unchanged for the year. However, a comparative balance sheet expressed in terms of the purchasing power of the dollar at the end of the year shows that changes did take place. In preparing the comparative balance sheet, beginning asset, liability, and stockholders' equity balances are brought forward to express the price-level increase that took place during the year and are then compared with the ending balances. A comparative balance sheet reporting beginning and ending balances in dollars of uniform purchasing power follows.

Comparative Balance Sheet Reporting General Price-Level Changes

	Beginning of Year			End of Year	Increase (Decrease)
	Historical Amount	Conversion Factor	Restated Amount		
Cash....................	$ 25,000	105/100	$ 26,250	$ 25,000	$(1,250)
Land...................	100,000	105/100	105,000	105,000	
	$125,000		$131,250	$130,000	$(1,250)
Mortgage note payable...	$ 50,000	105/100	$ 52,500	$ 50,000	$(2,500)
Capital stock............	75,000	105/100	78,750	78,750	
Retained earnings	—		—	1,250	1,250
	$125,000		$131,250	$130,000	$(1,250)

Conclusion. Although no transactions took place during the year, the comparative balance sheet shows that there was an increase in the stockholders' equity. This increase resulted from a price-level gain identified with a financial position in which monetary liabilities exceeded monetary assets during the period of price-level advance.

Example 4 — Monetary assets are increased by proceeds from sale of property at the end of the year. Assume that a company issues capital stock of $75,000 in exchange for cash of $25,000 and land valued at $50,000. The land is sold at the end of the year for cash of $60,000. There are no other accruals of revenue or expense. A balance sheet prepared in conventional form will show an increase in assets of $10,000 accompanied by an increase in retained earnings of this amount. However, in preparing a balance sheet in terms of the price level at the end of the year, balances are reported as follows:

(1) Cash is reported at $85,000.

(2) The capital stock balance is restated in terms of the current price level as $75,000 x 105/100, or $78,750.

(3) The stockholders' equity must be reported at $85,000, the cash balance. Since the original investment by stockholders is $78,750, there has been an increase in the stockholders' equity for the year of $6,250. Two factors explain this change: (a) the sale of land, and (b) the change in the price level. The gain on the sale of land expressed in terms of the price level at the end of the period is $7,500 — the cost of the land in terms of the price level at the end of the year, $52,500, as compared with

sales price at that time of $60,000. However, there was a loss in purchasing power of $1,250 on the monetary assets of $25,000 held during the year. In reporting the stockholders' equity on the balance sheet, then, capital stock as restated is accompanied by retained earnings that summarizes the two factors responsible for the change in the stockholders' equity — the gain on the sale of land and the price-level loss.

A statement of income and retained earnings supported by a schedule to show the computation of the price-level loss, and a balance sheet follow.

Income and Retained Earnings Statement for Year
Reporting General Price-Level Changes

	Historical Amount	Conversion Factor	Restated Amount
Sale of land (at end of year)...............	$ 60,000	105/105	$ 60,000
Cost of land...........................	50,000	105/100	52,500
Gain on sale of land....................	$ 10,000		$ 7,500
Deduct general price-level loss (see schedule).			1,250
Retained earnings at end of year...........			$ 6,250

Schedule Reporting General Price-Level Gain or Loss for Year

	Historical Amount	Conversion Factor	Restated Amount
Monetary assets at beginning of year.......	$ 25,000	105/100	$ 26,250
Increase in monetary assets —			
from sale of land at end of year..........	60,000	105/105	60,000
			$ 86,250
Monetary assets at end of year............	$ 85,000		85,000
General price-level loss..................			$ 1,250

Balance Sheet at End of Year Reporting General Price-Level Changes

	Historical Amount	Conversion Factor	Restated Amount
Cash................................	$ 85,000		$ 85,000
Capital stock.........................	$ 75,000	105/100	$ 78,750
Retained earnings.....................	10,000		6,250
	$ 85,000		$ 85,000

If the factors responsible for the change in retained earnings are to be stated accurately, it is necessary to determine the dates on which monetary assets became available and were expended. In the example just given, it was stated that the sale of the property was made at the end of the year; therefore, no loss in the purchasing power of the monetary assets acquired through the sale required recognition. Assume, however, that the sale had been made at the beginning of the year and additional monetary assets of $60,000 were thus held during the year. The stock-holders' equity would still show an increase of $6,250 represented by the difference between the cash, $85,000, and the capital stock balance expressed at $78,750. In reporting the results of operations, however, the gain on the sale would be reported as $10,500, or sales price of the land, $60,000 x 105/100, less cost of the land, $50,000 x 105/100. This is accompanied by a price-level loss that is computed as follows: ($85,000 x 105/100) — $85,000, or simply $85,000 x 5/100, a loss of $4,250.

Assuming the facts originally given, a comparative balance sheet prepared in conventional form will show an increase in the stockholders' equity through earnings of $10,000. However, a comparative balance sheet expressed in terms of the purchasing power of the dollar at the end of the year will show an increase in the stockholders' equity of only $6,250. A balance sheet comparing beginning and ending balances in dollars of uniform purchasing power follows.

Comparative Balance Sheet Reporting General Price-Level Changes

	Beginning of Year			End of Year	Increase (Decrease)
	Historical Amount	Conversion Factor	Restated Amount		
Cash..................	$25,000	105/100	$26,250	$85,000	$58,750
Land.................	50,000	105/100	52,500	———	(52,500)
	$75,000		$78,750	$85,000	$ 6,250
Capital stock...........	$75,000	105/100	$78,750	$78,750	———
Retained earnings.......	———		———	6,250	$ 6,250
	$75,000		$78,750	$85,000	$ 6,250

Conclusion. The comparative balance sheet shows that the change in the financial position was not as favorable as that which would be shown on a similar statement prepared in conventional form. The gain on the sale of property when cost and sales price are expressed in terms of the purchasing power of the dollar at the end of the year was only $7,500. Furthermore, the increase in the stockholders' equity for the year after recognizing the price-level loss resulting from holding monetary assets in the period of price-level advance was limited to $6,250.

Example 5 — Monetary assets are increased as a result of operations during the year. Assume that a company receives cash of $25,000 on the sale of capital stock. Services are performed during the year resulting in net income of $10,000; earnings accrue evenly, and at the end of the year cash is $32,500 and accounts receivable are $2,500. A balance sheet prepared in conventional form will show increases in assets of $10,000 accompanied by an increase in retained earnings of this amount. In preparing a balance sheet restated in terms of current dollars, assets and stockholders' equity balances are reported as follows:

(1) Cash is reported at $32,500.

(2) Accounts receivable is a monetary asset, a resource of fixed-dollar amount, and is reported at $2,500.

(3) The capital stock balance is restated in terms of the current price level at $25,000 x 105/100, or $26,250.

(4) The stockholders' equity must be reported at an amount equal to the asset total, or $35,000. Since the original investment by stockholders in terms of the current price level is $26,250, there has been an increase in the stockholders' equity for the year of $8,750. Two factors account for this change: (a) operations for the year, and (b) the change in the price level. It was indicated earlier that the price level rose evenly throughout the year. Since earnings from operations accrued evenly during the year, the reported balance of $10,000 may be regarded as reflecting earnings from operations in terms of the average price level of the year, a level that is 2½% above that at the beginning of the year. This balance is adjusted to end-of-year dollars by the following computation: $10,000 x 105/102.5, or $10,244.[1] The price-level loss for the year consists of that sustained on the monetary assets held throughout the year as well as on the monetary assets that became available during the year. The price-level loss, then, is computed as follows: [($25,000 x 105/100) + ($10,000 x 105/102.5)] − $35,000, or simply, ($25,000 x 5/100) + ($10,000 x 2.5/102.5), a loss of $1,494.

A statement of income and retained earnings is shown below. A supporting schedule to show the price-level loss and a balance sheet are given on the opposite page.

Income and Retained Earnings Statement for Year
Reporting General Price-Level Changes

	Historical Amount	Conversion Factor	Restated Amount
Net income (realized evenly throughout year).	$ 10,000	105/102.5	$ 10,244
Deduct general price-level loss (see schedule).			1,494
Retained earnings at end of year...........			$ 8,750

A comparative balance sheet prepared in conventional form will show an increase in the stockholders' equity through earnings of $10,000. However, a comparative balance sheet prepared in terms of the current

---

[1] It may be observed that if the prices rose evenly during the year, the price rise for the first half-year would be 102.5/100 and the price rise for the second half-year would be 105/102.5; the rate of increase, then, in the second half of the year is not equal to that which took place in the first half of the year.

Schedule Reporting General Price-Level Gain or Loss for Year

	Historical Amount	Conversion Factor	Restated Amount
Monetary assets at beginning of year.......	$ 25,000	105/100	$ 26,250
Increase in monetary assets — from operations during the year.........	10,000	105/102.5	10,244
			$ 36,494
Monetary assets at end of year............	$ 35,000		35,000
General price-level loss.................			$ 1,494

Balance Sheet at End of Year Reporting General Price-Level Changes

	Historical Amount	Conversion Factor	Restated Amount
Cash.....................................	$ 32,500		$ 32,500
Accounts receivable......................	2,500		2,500
	$ 35,000		$ 35,000
Capital stock............................	$ 25,000	105/100	$ 26,250
Retained earnings.......................	10,000		8,750
	$ 35,000		$ 35,000

purchasing power of the dollar shows an increase in the stockholders' equity of only $8,750. A balance sheet comparing beginning and ending balances in dollars of uniform purchasing power follows.

Comparative Balance Sheet Reporting General Price-Level Changes

	Beginning of Year			End of Year	Increase (Decrease)
	Historical Amount	Conversion Factor	Restated Amount		
Cash..................	$25,000	105/100	$26,250	$32,500	$6,250
Receivables............	———		———	2,500	2,500
	$25,000		$26,250	$35,000	$8,750
Capital stock...........	$25,000	105/100	$26,250	$26,250	———
Retained earnings.......	———		———	8,750	$8,750
	$25,000		$26,250	$35,000	$8,750

Conclusion. The comparative balance sheet shows that the change in the financial position was not as favorable as that which would be shown on a similar statement prepared in conventional form. Although net income from sales when restated in terms of the price level of the end of the year was $10,244, the net increase in the stockholders' equity after recognizing the price-level loss from holding monetary assets in the period of price-level advance was limited to $8,750.

Example 6 — Monetary assets are increased as a result of the sale of goods during the year. Assume that a company acquires merchandise valued at

$100,000 in exchange for capital stock. One half of the merchandise is sold during the year for cash of $75,000; expenses of $15,000 are paid. Sales are made evenly and expenses are incurred evenly throughout the year. A balance sheet prepared in conventional form will show increases in assets of $10,000 accompanied by an increase in retained earnings of this amount. In preparing a balance sheet restated to report the financial position in terms of the current price level, assets and stockholders' equity balances are reported as follows:

(1) Cash is reported at $60,000.

(2) Merchandise on hand, a nonmonetary asset, is restated to reflect the change in the price level since its acquisition. Merchandise with an acquisition cost of $50,000, then, is restated in terms of the current price level at $500,000 x 105/100, or $105,000.

(3) The capital stock balance is restated in terms of the current price level at $100,000 x 105/100, or $105,000.

(4) The stockholders' equity must be reported at a balance equal to the asset total, or $112,500. Since the original investment by stockholders in terms of the current price level is $105,000, there has been an increase in the stockholders' equity for the year of $7,500. Two factors account for this change: (a) operations for the year, and (b) the change in the price level. It was indicated that sales were made evenly during the year, merchandise was acquired at the beginning of the year, and expenses were incurred evenly during the year. The sales balance is expressed at the average price level, cost of goods sold is expressed at the price level at the beginning of the year, and the expenses balance is expressed at the average price level. Net income, then, expressed in terms of the price level at the end of the period is computed as follows: ($75,000 x 105/102.5) − ($50,000 x 105/100) − ($15,000 x 105/102.5), or $8,963. A loss in purchasing power is sustained on monetary assets that become available and were held during the year. Monetary assets were accumulated evenly and reached a total of $60,000 at the end of the year; the $60,000 balance, then, may be regarded as expressing the average price level for the year, and the loss in purchasing power on monetary assets is computed as ($60,000 x 105/102.5) − $60,000, or simply $60,000 x 2.5/102.5, a loss of $1,463.

A statement of income and retained earnings supported by a schedule to show the price-level loss and a balance sheet are given at the top of the following page.

A comparative balance sheet prepared in conventional form will show an increase in the stockholders' equity through earnings of $10,000. However, a comparative balance sheet prepared in terms of the current purchasing power of the dollar shows an increase in the stockholders'

Income and Retained Earnings Statement for Year
Reporting General Price-Level Changes

	Historical Amount	Conversion Factor	Restated Amount
Sales.....................................	$ 75,000	105/102.5	$ 76,829
Cost of goods sold......................	50,000	105/100	52,500
Gross profit on sales....................	$ 25,000		$ 24,329
Expenses...............................	15,000	105/102.5	15,366
Income before adjustment for general price-level gain or loss......................	$ 10,000		$ 8,963
General price-level loss (see schedule).......			1,463
Retained earnings at end of year...........			$ 7,500

Schedule Reporting General Price-Level Gain or Loss for Year

	Historical Amount	Conversion Factor	Restated Amount
Monetary assets at beginning of year.......	—		—
Increase in monetary assets — from sales during the year..............	$ 75,000	105/102.5	$ 76,829
Decrease in monetary assets — from expenses during the year...........	15,000	105/102.5	15,366
			$ 61,463
Monetary assets at end of year............	$ 60,000		60,000
General price-level loss...................			$ 1,463

Balance Sheet at End of Year Reporting General Price-Level Changes

	Historical Amount	Conversion Factor	Restated Amount
Cash....................................	$ 60,000		$ 60,000
Merchandise on hand....................	50,000	105/100	52,500
	$110,000		$112,500
Capital stock............................	$100,000	105/100	$105,000
Retained earnings.......................	10,000		7,500
	$110,000		$112,500

equity of only $7,500. A balance sheet comparing beginning and ending balances in dollars of uniform purchasing power is given below.

Comparative Balance Sheet Reporting General Price-Level Changes

	Beginning of Year			End of Year	Increase (Decrease)
	Historical Amount	Conversion Factor	Restated Amount		
Cash..................	—		—	$ 60,000	$60,000
Merchandise on hand....	$100,000	105/100	$105,000	52,500	(52,500)
	$100,000		$105,000	$112,500	$ 7,500
Capital stock...........	$100,000	105/100	$105,000	$105,000	—
Retained earnings.......	—		—	7,500	$ 7,500
	$100,000		$105,000	$112,500	$ 7,500

Conclusion. The comparative balance sheet shows that the change in the financial position was not as favorable as that which would be shown on a similar statement prepared in conventional form. The increase in the stockholders' equity from earnings when revenues and expenses are expressed in terms of the price level at the end of the year was only $8,963. This was accompanied by a price-level loss from holding monetary assets in the period of price-level advance of $1,463, and the increase in the stockholders' equity was thus limited to $7,500.

Preparation of financial statements restated for general price-level changes illustrated

The illustration that follows indicates the basic procedures that are followed in restating financial statements in successive periods to reflect general price-level changes. The illustration covers operations of a company for the first two years of its life. Financial statements for the first and second years are provided in their conventional forms. Financial statements are restated at the end of the first year and at the end of the second year in terms of the price levels prevailing at each of these times.[1]

The illustration assumes the following:

(1) Price-level index numbers were:

At the time the business was formed. . 100
At the end of the first year. 104
At the end of the second year. 108

The price level rose evenly throughout each year. The average index for the first year, then, was 102; the average index for the second year was 106.

(2) Sales and purchases were made evenly and expenses were incurred evenly throughout each year.

(3) Inventories were valued at cost calculated by the first-in, first-out method.

(4) Dividends were declared and paid at the end of each year.

(5) Buildings had a useful life of 10 years and depreciation was recognized at $5,000 per year.

A comparative income and retained earnings statement reporting operations of the company for the first and second years and a comparative balance sheet reporting the financial position of the company upon its organization and at the end of the first and second years are given on the opposite page.

---

[1] The illustration is limited to the restatement of financial data presented on the income and retained earnings statement and on the balance sheet. In providing a full set of financial statements, a statement of changes in financial position would be required. However, the preparation of the latter statement from comparative balance sheets as restated presents no special problems.

Comparative Income and Retained Earnings Statement

	First Year	Second Year
Sales..	$300,000	$400,000
Cost of goods sold:		
Beginning inventory................................	$ 55,000	$ 65,000
Purchases..	200,000	280,000
Merchandise available for sale......................	$255,000	$345,000
Ending inventory..................................	65,000	80,000
Cost of goods sold................................	$190,000	$265,000
Gross profit on sales...............................	$110,000	$135,000
Expenses:		
Depreciation.....................................	$ 5,000	$ 5,000
Other expenses...................................	90,000	100,000
Total expenses...................................	$ 95,000	$105,000
Net income.......................................	$ 15,000	$ 30,000
Retained earnings at beginning of year..................	———	10,000
	$ 15,000	$ 40,000
Dividends paid....................................	5,000	10,000
Retained earnings at end of year.....................	$ 10,000	$ 30,000

Comparative Balance Sheet

	Beginning of Business	End of First Year	End of Second Year
Assets			
Cash...	$ 60,000	$ 30,000	$ 40,000
Accounts receivable...........................	—	40,000	50,000
Inventory......................................	55,000	65,000	80,000
Buildings (net)................................	50,000	45,000	40,000
Land...	35,000	35,000	35,000
Total assets...................................	$200,000	$215,000	$245,000
Liabilities			
Accounts payable.............................	$ 20,000	$ 25,000	$ 35,000
Mortgage payable............................	30,000	30,000	30,000
Total liabilities..............................	$ 50,000	$ 55,000	$ 65,000
Stockholders' Equity			
Capital stock.................................	$150,000	$150,000	$150,000
Retained earnings............................	—	10,000	30,000
Total stockholders' equity...................	$150,000	$160,000	$180,000
Total liabilities and stockholders' equity.......	$200,000	$215,000	$245,000

Preparation of statement of income and retained earnings restated for the general price-level changes at the end of the first year. A statement of income and retained earnings for the first year as restated at the end of the first year and a schedule reporting the price-level loss are given on page 1038.

Income and Retained Earnings Statement Restated for General Price-Level Changes
For First Year

	Historical Amount	Conversion Factor	Restated Amount
Sales..	$300,000	104/102	$305,882
Cost of goods sold:			
Beginning inventory............................	$ 55,000	104/100	$ 57,200
Purchases.....................................	200,000	104/102	203,922
Merchandise available for sale...................	$255,000		$261,122
Ending inventory..............................	65,000	104/102	66,275
Cost of goods sold............................	$190,000		$194,847
Gross profit on sales..............................	$110,000		$111,035
Expenses:			
Depreciation.................................	$ 5,000	104/100	$ 5,200
Other expenses...............................	90,000	104/102	91,765
Total expenses................................	$ 95,000		$ 96,965
Income before adjustment for general price-level gain or loss..	$ 15,000		$ 14,070
General price-level loss.............................	——		595
Net income after adjustment for general price-level loss..	$ 15,000		$ 13,475
Retained earnings at beginning of year...............	——		——
	$ 15,000		$ 13,475
Dividends paid....................................	5,000	104/104	5,000
Retained earnings at end of year....................	$ 10,000		$ 8,475

Schedule Reporting General Price-Level Gain or Loss
For First Year

	Historical Amount		Conversion Factor	Restated Amount
Net monetary items at beginning of year:				
Assets (cash)...........................	$60,000			
Liabilities (accounts payable and mortgage payable).............................	50,000	$ 10,000	104/100	$ 10,400
Increase in net monetary items during year:				
Sales..................................		300,000	104/102	305,882
		$310,000		$316,282
Decrease in net monetary items during year:				
Purchases..............................		$200,000	104/102	$203,922
Other expenses..........................		90,000	104/102	91,765
Dividends..............................		5,000	104/104	5,000
		$295,000		$300,687
				$ 15,595
Net monetary items at end of year:				
Assets (cash and accounts receivable)......	$70,000			
Liabilities (accounts payable and mortgage payable).............................	55,000	$ 15,000		15,000
General price-level loss...................				$ 595

Sales. Since sales were made evenly throughout the year, the sales balance reflects the average index for the year. To restate the sales balance to end-of-year dollars, it is multiplied by the ratio of the end-of-year index to the average index for the year.

Cost of goods sold. The inventory is reported on the first-in, first-out basis. Restatement of cost of goods sold to end-of-year dollars involves the following adjustments:

(1) The beginning inventory balance reports costs incurred when the business was organized and therefore reflects the index at the beginning of the year, 100. To restate the beginning inventory to end-of-year dollars, it is multiplied by the ratio of the end-of-year index to the index at the beginning of the year.

(2) Purchases were made evenly throughout the year. To restate the purchases balance to end-of-year dollars, it is multiplied by the ratio of the end-of-year index to the average index.

(3) In applying first-in, first-out, latest costs were assigned to the ending inventory. The ending inventory, then, may be regarded as composed of purchases of the current period. To restate the ending inventory to end-of-year dollars, it is multiplied by the ratio of the end-of-year index to the average index.[1]

Depreciation. Since the charge for depreciation represents the allocation of the cost of a property item to operations, the adjustment of the depreciation charge must be consistent with the adjustment applicable to the property item. To restate the buildings cost to end-of-year dollars, it is multiplied by the ratio of the end-of-year index to the index at the time the buildings were acquired, in this case the index at the beginning of the year, or 100; to restate the depreciation charge, it is similarly multiplied by the ratio expressing the price-level change since the date buildings were acquired. The charge for depreciation as restated can also be computed by applying the depreciation rate to the cost of the asset stated in terms of end-of-year dollars.

Other expenses. The other expenses were incurred evenly throughout the year. To restate the other expenses total to end-of-year dollars, it is multiplied by the ratio of the end-of-year index to the average index.

Income before adjustment for general price-level gain or loss. Revenue and expense items are summarized to arrive at the income for the year before adjustment for the general price-level gain or loss.

---

[1]When there is evidence that the ending inventory is composed of goods acquired within the last half of the year or the last quarter, the average index for such shorter period is properly applied in restating the inventory.

General price-level gain or loss. The income and retained earnings statement is supported by a schedule reporting the general price-level gain or loss from holding monetary assets and maintaining monetary liabilities in the period of changing prices. The schedule is developed as follows:

(1) The difference between the monetary assets and liabilities at the beginning of the period is restated to an end-of-year dollars balance.

(2) The net monetary items becoming available during the year are expressed in terms of end-of-year dollars. This amount is added to the beginning balance as adjusted.

(3) The actual monetary assets and the liabilities as of the end of the year are determined. The balance of net monetary items at the end of the year is compared with the sum of (1) and (2) above. In the example, net monetary items at the end of the year would have been $15,595 if the company had maintained its net monetary position during the period of rising prices; since net monetary items are only $15,000, a loss in purchasing power for the year of $595 was sustained.

The general price-level gain or loss is reported on the income and retained earnings statement, and the net income after adjustment for the gain or loss is determined.

Dividends. Dividends were declared and paid at the end of the year. The dividends paid balance, then, reflects end-of-year dollars and is reported without change.

Retained earnings at the end of the year. The dividends paid balance is subtracted from net income after adjustment for the general price-level loss in determining the retained earnings balance at the end of the first year in terms of year-end dollars.

Preparation of the balance sheet restated for the general price-level changes at the end of the first year. A balance sheet as restated at the end of the first year is given at the top of the opposite page. The following items should be noted:

Monetary assets. Monetary assets are reported without change.

Inventory. The ending inventory balance reflects the average index for the year. To restate this balance to end-of-year dollars, it is multiplied by the ratio of the end-of-year index to the average index. The dollar value for the inventory on the balance sheet must be the same as that reported in arriving at cost of goods sold on the income and retained earnings statement.

Buildings and land. Buildings and land accounts report dollar costs at the time that the assets were acquired. To restate buildings and land

Balance Sheet Restated for General Price-Level Changes
End of First Year

	Historical Amount	Conversion Factor	Restated Amount
Assets			
Cash.	$ 30,000		$ 30,000
Accounts receivable.	40,000		40,000
Inventory.	65,000	104/102	66,275
Buildings (net).	45,000	104/100	46,800
Land.	35,000	104/100	36,400
Total assets.	$215,000		$219,475
Liabilities			
Accounts payable.	$ 25,000		$ 25,000
Mortgage payable.	30,000		30,000
Total liabilities.	$ 55,000		$ 55,000
Stockholders' Equity			
Capital stock.	$150,000	(104/100)	$156,000
Retained earnings.	10,000		8,475
Total stockholders' equity	$160,000		$164,475
Total liabilities and stockholders' equity	$215,000		$219,475

balances to end-of-year dollars, these are multiplied by the ratio expressing the price-level change since the time they were acquired.

Liabilities. Liabilities are reported without change.

Stockholders' equity. Capital stock expressed in terms of original dollar investment is restated to end-of-year dollars. The retained earnings balance as summarized in terms of end-of-year dollars on the statement of income and retained earnings is added to the capital stock balances in arriving at the stockholders' equity. If comparable assumptions and procedures have been employed in developing balances on the income and retained earnings statement and the balance sheet, the statements will be complementary and recognition of the stockholders' equity will bring the balance sheet into balance. If the stockholders' equity is not equal to the difference between the assets and the liabilities, errors or inconsistencies are indicated, and these must be found and corrected.

Preparation of the comparative balance sheet restated for the general price-level changes at the end of the first year. A comparative balance sheet prepared in terms of the current price level is given at the top of page 1042. Opening balances are rolled forward to express current dollars that may be compared with closing balances reported in current dollars.

Preparation of the statement of income and retained earnings restated for the general price-level changes at the end of the second year. A statement of income and retained earnings as restated at the end

Comparative Balance Sheet Restated for General Price-Level Changes
End of First Year

| | Beginning of Business | | | End of First Year | Increase (Decreas |
	Historical Amount	Conversion Factor	Restated Amount		
Assets					
Cash.....................	$ 60,000	104/100	$ 62,400	$ 30,000	$(32,40(
Accounts receivable........				40,000	40,00(
Inventory.................	55,000	104/100	57,200	66,275	9,07!
Buildings (net)............	50,000	104/100	52,000	46,800	(5,20(
Land.....................	35,000	104/100	36,400	36,400	
Total assets...............	$200,000		$208,000	$219,475	$ 11,47!
Liabilities					
Accounts payable..........	$ 20,000	104/100	$ 20,800	$ 25,000	$ 4,20(
Mortgage payable.........	30,000	104/100	31,200	30,000	(1,20(
Total liabilities.............	$ 50,000		$ 52,000	$ 55,000	$ 3,00(
Stockholders' Equity					
Capital stock..............	$150,000	104/100	$156,000	$156,000	
Retained earnings.........				8,475	$ 8,47!
Total stockholders' equity....	$150,000		$156,000	$164,475	$ 8,47.
Total liabilities and stockholders' equity..........	$200,000		$208,000	$219,475	$ 11,47!

of the second year and a schedule reporting the price-level loss are given on the opposite page. The following items should be noted:

Income before adjustment for general price-level gain or loss. In developing the income and retained earning statement for the second year, sales, purchases, and other expense balances reflecting the average index for the year are multiplied by the ratio of the price-level index at the end of the second year to the average index for the second year. In developing cost of goods sold, the beginning inventory balance, stated at $65,000, that reflects acquisitions when the index was 102, must be adjusted to a dollar balance in terms of the price level at the end of the second year, 108, and hence is multiplied by 108/102; the ending inventory balance reflecting purchases during the second year is multiplied by the ratio of the index at the end of the second year to the average index for the second year, or 108/106. The charge for depreciation, reported in terms of asset cost, is multiplied by the ratio of the index at the end of the second year to the index at the date of asset acquisition, or 108/100. Revenue and expense balances are summarized to arrive at the income for the year before adjustment for the general price-level gain or loss.

General price-level gain or loss. The computation of the price-level gain or loss for the second year is made just as it was for the first year. Net monetary items available to the company during the second year are expressed in terms of end-of-year balances and are compared with

Income and Retained Earnings Statement Restated for General Price-Level Changes
For Second Year

	Historical Amount	Conversion Factor	Restated Amount
Sales...	$400,000	108/106	$407,547
Cost of goods sold:			
Beginning inventory...........................	$ 65,000	108/102	$ 68,824
Purchases....................................	280,000	108/106	285,283
Merchandise available for sale..................	$345,000		$354,107
Ending inventory.............................	80,000	108/106	81,509
Cost of goods sold............................	$265,000		$272,598
Gross profit on sales...........................	$135,000		$134,949
Expenses:			
Depreciation.................................	$ 5,000	108/100	$ 5,400
Other expenses...............................	100,000	108/106	101,887
Total expenses...............................	$105,000		$107,287
Income before adjustment for general price-level gain or loss...	$ 30,000		$ 27,662
General price-level loss (see schedule)..............	———		954
Net income after adjustment for general price-level loss......	$ 30,000		$ 26,708
Retained earnings at beginning of year.............	10,000	($8,475 × 108/104)	8,801
	$ 40,000		$ 35,509
Dividends paid................................	10,000	108/108	10,000
Retained earnings at end of year.................	$ 30,000		$ 25,509

Schedule Reporting General Price-Level Gain or Loss
For Second Year

		Historical Amount	Conversion Factor	Restated Amount
Net monetary items at beginning of year:				
Assets (cash and accounts receivable).........	$70,000			
Liabilities (accounts pay. and mortgage pay.)...	55,000	$ 15,000	108/104	$ 15,577
Increase in net monetary items during year:				
Sales.....................................		400,000	108/106	407,547
		$415,000		$423,124
Decrease in net monetary items during year:				
Purchases.................................		$280,000	108/106	$285,283
Other expenses............................		100,000	108/106	101,887
Dividends.................................		10,000	108/108	10,000
		$390,000		$397,170
				$ 25,954
Net monetary items at end of year:				
Assets (cash and accounts receivable).........	$90,000			
Liabilities (accounts pay. and mortgage pay.)..	65,000	$ 25,000		25,000
General price-level loss.......................				$ 954

the net monetary items actually found at the end of the second year. Such comparison indicates a further loss of purchasing power.

Retained earnings at the beginning of the year. All stockholders' equity balances expressed in terms of end-of-year dollars for the first year must be restated to end-of-year dollars for the second year. Retained earnings, then, as reported at the balance shown on the balance sheet at the end of the first year is updated to indicate its equivalent in dollars at the end of the second year.

Dividends. Dividends were declared and paid at the end of the year. The dividends paid balance, then, reflects end-of-year dollars and is reported without change.

Retained earnings at the end of the year. Having determined net income after adjustment for the general price-level change, this is increased by the beginning retained earnings balance as restated in end-of-year dollars and reduced by dividends to arrive at the ending retained earnings balance.

Preparation of the balance sheet restated for the general price-level changes at the end of the second year. A balance sheet at the end of the second year is given at the top of the opposite page. Monetary assets and liabilities are reported without change. The inventory acquired during the second year is raised to an end-of-year-dollars balance. Buildings and land reported at dollar amounts at the time the business was organized are adjusted for the change in the price level for the two-year period. Capital stock reported on the balance sheet at the end of the preceding period is updated to report current end-of-year dollars. The retained earnings balance as summarized in terms of end-of-year dollars on the statement of income and retained earnings is added to the capital stock balances in arriving at the stockholders' equity.

Preparation of comparative statements restated for the general price-level changes at the end of the second year. A comparative statement of income and retained earnings and a comparative balance sheet prepared at the end of the second year are given on pages 1045 and 1046. In preparing the comparative income and retained earnings statement, account balances reporting dollars at the end of the first year are rolled forward to express dollars of purchasing power at the end of the second year. Operations and changes in retained earnings for the two years can then be compared in terms of uniform dollars. The balance sheet for the preceding year is updated in a similar manner so that it may be compared with the current balance sheet.

General price-level restatements applied to inventories reported under alternative cost-flow assumptions

In the preceding illustration, inventories were reflected on a first-in, first-out cost-flow assumption and the implications of this procedure were

Balance Sheet Restated for General Price-Level Changes
End of Second Year

	Historical Amount	Conversion Factor	Restated Amount
Assets			
ash..	$ 40,000		$ 40,000
ccounts receivable.........................	50,000		50,000
ıventory...................................	80,000	108/106	81,509
ıilding (net)...............................	40,000	108/100	43,200
ınd.......................................	35,000	108/100	37,800
ɔtal assets.................................	$245,000		$252,509
Liabilities			
ccounts payable...........................	$ 35,000		$ 35,000
˹ortgage payable..........................	30,000		30,000
ɔtal liabilities.............................	$ 65,000		$ 65,000
Stockholders' Equity			
ıpital stock................................	$150,000	($156,000 × 108/104)	$162,000
ɔtained earnings............................	30,000		25,509
ɔtal stockholders' equity....................	$180,000		$187,509
ɔtal liabilities and stockholders' equity...........	$245,000		$252,509

ɔmparative Income and Retained Earnings Statement Restated for General Price-Level Changes
First and Second Years

	First Year				
	Restated to End of First Year	Con-version Factor	Restated to End of Second Year	Second Year	Increase (Decrease)
ˌles..............................	$305,882	108/104	$317,647	$407,547	$ 89,900
ɔst of goods sold:					
Beginning inventory...............	$ 57,200	108/104	$ 59,400	$ 68,824	$ 9,424
Purchases........................	203,922	108/104	211,765	285,283	73,518
Merchandise available for sale......	$261,122		$271,165	$354,107	$ 82,942
Ending inventory..................	66,275	108/104	68,824	81,509	12,685
Cost of goods sold.................	$194,847		$202,341	$272,598	$ 70,257
ˑoss profit on sales.................	$111,035		$115,306	$134,949	$ 19,643
˂penses:					
Depreciation.....................	$ 5,200	108/104	$ 5,400	$ 5,400	———
Other expenses...................	91,765	108/104	95,295	101,887	$ 6,592
Total expenses...................	$ 96,965	108/104	$100,695	$107,287	$ 6,592
come before adjustment for general price-level gain or loss.............	$ 14,070		$ 14,611	$ 27,662	$ 13,051
˘neral price-level loss...............	595	108/104	618	954	336
˘t income after adjustment for general price-level loss....................	$ 13,475	108/104	$ 13,993	$ 26,708	$ 12,715
˘tained earnings at beginning of year..	———		———	8,801	8,801
	$ 13,475		$ 13,993	$ 35,509	$ 21,516
ˌvidends paid.....................	5,000	108/104	5,192	10,000	4,808
˘tained earnings at end of year......	$ 8,475		$ 8,801	$ 25,509	$ 16,708

Comparative Balance Sheet Restated for General Price-Level Changes
End of Second Year

	Beginning of Business			End of First Year				Increase (Decrease)	
	Restated to End of First Year	Conversion Factor	Restated to End of Second Year	Restated to End of First Year	Conversion Factor	Restated to End of Second Year	End of Second Year	Beginning of Business to End of First Year	End of First Year to End of Second Year
Assets									
Cash	$ 62,400	108/104	$ 64,800	$ 30,000	108/104	$ 31,154	$ 40,000	$(33,646)	$ 8,846
Accounts receivable				40,000	108/104	41,538	50,000	41,538	8,462
Inventory	57,200	108/104	59,400	66,275	108/104	68,824	81,509	9,424	12,685
Buildings (net)	52,000	108/104	54,000	46,800	108/104	48,600	43,200	(5,400)	(5,400)
Land	36,400	108/104	37,800	36,400	108/104	37,800	37,800	—	—
Total assets	$208,000		$216,000	$219,475		$227,916	$252,509	$ 11,916	$ 24,593
Liabilities									
Accounts payable	$ 20,800	108/104	$ 21,600	$ 25,000	108/104	$ 25,961	$ 35,000	$ 4,361	$ 9,039
Mortgage payable	31,200	108/104	32,400	30,000	108/104	31,154	30,000	(1,246)	(1,154)
Total liabilities	$ 52,000		$ 54,000	$ 55,000		$ 57,115	$ 65,000	$ 3,115	$ 7,885
Stockholders' Equity									
Capital stock	$156,000	108/104	$162,000	$156,000	108/104	$162,000	$162,000	—	—
Retained earnings				8,475	108/104	8,801	25,509	$ 8,801	$ 16,708
Total stockholders' equity	$156,000		$162,000	$164,475		$170,801	$187,509	$ 8,801	$ 16,708
Total liabilities and stockholders' equity	$208,000		$216,000	$219,475		$227,916	$252,509	$ 11,916	$ 24,593

recognized in restating inventory and cost of goods sold balances. When other cost-flow assumptions are employed, restatements must be modified to recognize the costs reflected in the inventory balances as a result of the alternative assumptions. For example, with the first-in, first-out assumption, the inventory balance reports costs of the inventory in terms of most recent purchases, and accordingly the inventory is restated to the prevailing price level by applying an index expressing the price-level change from the time the goods were acquired. If the last-in, first-out procedure is employed, the inventory balance may report a number of cost layers, and different indexes must be applied to express the individual cost layers in terms of the prevailing price level.

To illustrate, assume price-level changes for a two-year period as given in the preceding illustration and a company that expresses inventories and costs during the first two years of its operations as follows:

	First Year	Second Year
Beginning inventory	$100,000	$120,000
Purchases	300,000	400,000
Goods available for sale	$400,000	$520,000
Ending inventory (lifo)	120,000	105,000
Cost of goods sold	$280,000	$415,000

Inventory balances and the cost of goods sold balances would be restated as follows:

	Historical Amount		Conversion Factor	Restated Amount	
First Year:					
Beginning inventory		$100,000	104/100		$104,000
Purchases		300,000	104/102		305,882
Goods available for sale		$400,000			$409,882
Ending inventory:					
Original balance	$100,000		104/100	$104,000	
First-year layer increase	20,000		104/102	20,392	
		120,000			124,392
Cost of goods sold		$280,000			$285,490
Second Year:					
Beginning inventory:					
Original balance	$100,000		108/100	$108,000	
First-year layer increase	20,000		108/102	21,176	
		$120,000			$129,176
Purchases		400,000	108/106		407,547
Goods available for sale		$520,000			$536,723
Ending inventory:					
Original balance	$100,000		108/100	$108,000	
First-year layer increase	5,000		108/102	5,294	
		105,000			113,294
Cost of goods sold		$415,000			$423,429

It should be observed that the inventory balance at the end of the first year was recognized as composed of two separate layers — a cost assigned to the original inventory balance and an incremental cost layer for the inventory increase for the year. The beginning cost is restated to report the change in the price level since the beginning of the year; the current cost layer is restated to report the difference between the end-of-year index and the average index for the year. The inventory at the end of the second year was recognized as composed of two layers — the cost assigned to the original inventory balance and a portion of the incremental cost related to the first year. The original cost is restated to report the change in the price level since the beginning of the first year; the incremental layer is restated to report the difference between the end-of-year index and the average index for the first year.

General price-level restatements applied to depreciable properties acquired at different times

In the illustration on pages 1036–1046, there was a single acquisition of depreciable property — the acquisition of buildings when the business was formed. When depreciable properties are acquired at different times, the restatement of depreciable properties becomes more involved. The acquisition dates for the individual property items must be determined and both property balances and depreciation charges must be restated to reflect price level changes since the various acquisition dates.

To illustrate, assume that the general price-level changes for a two-year period are the same as in the preceding illustration, and that a company purchases depreciable properties as follows:

Date of Acquisition	Asset	Cost	Useful Life
Beginning of first year	Building	$100,000	25 years
Middle of first year	Equipment	$ 61,200	6 years
Middle of second year	Furniture	$ 42,400	8 years

Assume that depreciation charges are calculated on the straight-line basis; salvage values are negligible and are not recognized. The cost of the property items would then be adjusted at the end of the first year as follows:

Asset	Historical Amount	Conversion Factor	Restated Amount
Building	$100,000	104/100	$104,000
Equipment	61,200	104/102	62,400
Total	$161,200		$166,400

The charges for depreciation may be obtained by applying depreciation rates to the restated costs. On the other hand, it is possible to compute depreciation charges by applying the individual conversion factors that are used in restating the property items to the depreciation charges based on cost. The latter procedure is illustrated below:

Asset	Historical Depreciation Charge	Conversion Factor	Restated Depreciation Charge
Building	$4,000 (1 yr.)	104/100	$4,160
Equipment	5,100 (½ yr.)	104/102	5,200
Total	$9,100		$9,360

In determining the balances for the property items to be reported on the balance sheet at the end of the first year, the individual conversion factors are applied to the separate acquisitions and to the related balances for accumulated depreciation. These balances at the end of the first year are derived as follows:

Asset	Historical Amount	Conversion Factor	Restated Amount	
Building cost	$100,000	104/100	$104,000	
Accumulated depreciation	4,000	104/100	4,160	$ 99,840
Net		$ 96,000		$ 62,400
Equipment cost	$ 61,200	104/102		
Accumulated depreciation	5,100	104/102	5,200	
Net		56,100		57,200
Total		$152,100		$157,040

At the end of the second year, depreciable assets would be restated as follows:

Asset	Historical Amount	Conversion Factor	Restated Amount
Building	$100,000	108/100	$108,000
Equipment	61,200	108/102	64,800
Furniture	42,400	108/106	43,200
Total	$203,600		$216,000

Depreciation for the second year would be computed as follows:

Asset	Historical Depreciation Charge	Conversion Factor	Restated Depreciation Charge
Building	$ 4,000 (1 yr.)	108/100	$ 4,320
Equipment	10,200 (1 yr.)	108/102	10,800
Furniture	2,650 (½ yr.)	108/106	2,700
Total	$16,850		$17,820

At the end of the second year, cost and accumulated depreciation balances would be restated as follows:

Asset	Historical Amount	Conversion Factor	Restated Amount
Building cost..................	$100,000	108/100	$108,000
Accumulated depreciation.....	8,000	108/100	8,640
Net........................	$ 92,000		$ 99,360
Equipment cost..............	$ 61,200	108/102	$ 64,800
Accumulated depreciation.....	15,300	108/102	16,200
Net........................	45,900		48,600
Furniture cost...............	$ 42,400	108/106	$ 43,200
Accumulated depreciation.....	2,650	108/106	2,700
Net........................	39,750		40,500
Total.................	$177,650		$188,460

Initial restatements

When general price-level statements are prepared from the time a company is formed, the restated balance for retained earnings can be fully supported. Retained earnings is the sum of the periodic retained earnings increases and decreases as summarized each year and rolled forward to reflect the periodic changes in the price level.

A special problem is encountered when a company has operated for a number of years and price-level statements are to be prepared for the first time. Asset, liability, and invested capital balances must be restated in terms of the prevailing price level. The retained earnings balance that is required to bring the balance sheet into balance represents the change in the stockholders' equity, including the effects of the changes in the general price-level since formation of the company.

In effecting the restatement of accounts for the first time, the question arises as to whether such restatement should be made from the date the company was formed or from an arbitrarily chosen later date. The Accounting Principles Board has taken the position that the restatement should be made from the date the company was formed or 1945, whichever is later. It observes:

> The precision of the measure of change in the general price level by any series of index numbers decreases over time because new commodities are continuously introduced and others disappear. No method has been devised to measure the percentage change in the general price level between two periods in which the bulk of commodities in each period are unique. A large portion of the dollar amount of current transactions involves goods and services that originated in discoveries and innovations that grew out of the war effort (World War II) and postwar developments. Consequently, comparison of current prices with prices during and prior to World War II would probably not be reliable enough for accounting purposes because of the dissimilarity of goods and services exchanged then and now. A cutoff date is therefore indi-

cated. The year 1945 is probably the earliest point that offers comparability of goods and services with later periods. All assets acquired, liabilities incurred, or owners' equity accumulated prior to 1945 should generally be treated as if they had originated during 1945.[1]

Special observations

The discussion and the examples on the preceding pages have provided the framework within which statements reporting general price-level changes are prepared. Certain observations need to be made relative to certain practices that may frequently be appropriate.

Alternate expression of conversion factors. In the examples in the chapter, conversion factors were expressed as fractions indicating the relationship of one index to another. Instead of expressing conversion factors as fractions, these can be stated as quotients of such fractions, the numerator of the fraction being divided by the denominator. A conversion factor of 105/100, then, can be stated as 1.05. With the price level moving up from a price index of 120.0 to a price index of 132.5, the conversion factor can be expressed as 132.5/120.0 or alternately as 110.4 (132.5 ÷ 120.0); with a price-level change from 88.2 to a current rate of 132.5, the conversion factor can be expressed as 132.5/88.2 or as 150.2 (135.2 ÷ 88.2). When the restatement process is a lengthy one but requires the use of relatively few conversion factors, it is generally convenient to prepare a table of values stated in quotients and apply such values to the individual items requiring restatement.

Use of the GNP Deflator. It should also be observed that in the examples, price indexes were given for the different points in time for which they were required, including the beginning of a current year and the end of a current year. Indexes provided by the Bureau of Labor Statistics are issued for each month. However, the GNP Deflator that will generally be used provides price indexes in terms of annual averages beginning with 1929 and also quarterly averages beginning with 1947. In the absence of end-of-year price-level measurements, the deflator for the last quarter of the year is normally used to approximate the price index at the end of the year.

Reporting price-level changes on the income statement and the balance sheet. The Staff of the Accounting Research Division in its examples in Accounting Research Study No. 6 reported the summary of operations on the income statement as "net profit or loss from operations," then added to this balance an amount for "inflation gain or loss"[2]

---

[1]*Statements of the Accounting Principles Board, No. 3, op. cit.*, Appendix C, par. 5.
[2]This is the term used originally to express "general price-level gain or loss,"

to arrive at net earnings for the period that was designated "net profit and net inflation gain or loss"; this analysis was carried to the balance sheet and retained earnings was reported in two parts: (1) the amount resulting from past operations after dividends; and (2) the "accumulated gain or loss on net monetary items," representing the total amount of inflation gains and losses recognized on prior income statements. The Accounting Principles Board also reports the general price-level gain or loss on the income statement as a special item but refers to the summary of operations and the price-level gain or loss as "net income"; retained earnings on the balance sheet is reported as a single item, no distinction being made between accumulated earnings and accumulated price-level gains and losses. This procedure has been followed in the illustrations in this chapter. If an analysis of the retained earnings balance is desired, operating data and price-level gains and losses as separately reported on the individual income statements would have to be summarized separately.

Price-level statements and financial analysis

The Staff of the Accounting Research Division of the AICPA summarizes the case for the preparation of price-level statements as a means for analyzing financial position and the results of business operations as follows:

> . . . if price-level changes can be measured in some satisfactory manner, and if the effects of those changes can be properly disclosed, the inferences that can be drawn from accounting data will be statistically more reliable. Specifically, for example, all the revenues and expenses in the earnings statement for any one year will be expressed in dollars of the same size and not in a mixture of dollars from different years. Similarly, the various balance-sheet items will all be expressed in terms of a common dollar. Since both the results of operations and financial position will be stated in terms of the same "common dollar," a calculation of a rate of return on invested capital can be made in which both numerator and denominator are expressed in the same units.
>
> Some inferences can be drawn in terms of the various groups interested in business activity. Investors and their representatives (e.g., management, including the board of directors) can tell whether the capital invested in the business has been increased or decreased as the result of all the policies followed and all the financial events that have taken place bearing on the business entity. More specifically, management and owners can tell if the dividend policy actually followed in the past has resulted in distributions out of economic or business capital, and, if not, what proportion of the earnings (adjusted for price-level changes) has in fact been distributed. With price-level adjusted data before them, the directors can tell if a proposed dividend will equal, exceed, or fall short of current earnings, or any other norm or standard they wish to use.
>
> Owners, management, and government can tell if taxes levied on income were less than pretax earnings, and if so, to what extent, and, if not, how much they exceeded pretax earnings. Creditors will be better

informed as to the buffer or cushion behind their claims. In addition, employees, as well as investors, and management will have a more reliable gauge of the rate of return to date on the capital employed, and will be able to use the information more intelligently to decide if the business entity has been profitable or not.

Financial statements fully adjusted for the effect of price-level changes will also reveal the losses or gains from holding or owing monetary items. All interested groups then have one important measure of the effect of a changing dollar on their position as debtors or creditors.

The Staff concludes:

... financial data adjusted for price-level effects provide a basis for a more intelligent, better informed allocation of resources, whether those resources are in the hands of individuals, of business entities, or of government.[1]

QUESTIONS

1. (a) Why do accountants prefer to report costs rather than market values in conventional statements? (b) Give three examples of the use of market values in conventional statements.

2. Compare the concept of reporting market values in the financial statements with the concept of restating original dollar costs for price-level changes.

3. What is meant by general price-level financial statements? Would you consider these as primary statements or supplementary statements? Why?

4. (a) Distinguish between monetary assets and nonmonetary assets. (b) Which of the following are monetary assets?

(1) Cash   (6) Buildings
(2) Investment in common stock   (7) Patents
(3) Investment in bonds   (8) Sinking fund—uninvested cash
(4) Merchandise on hand   (9) Sinking fund—investments in real estate
(5) Prepaid expenses   (10) Deferred developmental costs

5. Assume that a company holds property or maintains the obligation listed below during a year in which there is an increase in the price level. State in each case whether the position of the company at the end of the year is better, worse, or unchanged.

(a) Cash   (e) Accounts receivable
(b) Cash surrender value of life insurance (f) Notes payable
(c) Land   (g) Merchandise on hand
(d) Unearned subscription income   (h) Long-term warranties on sales

---

[1]Accounting Research Division, *op. cit.*, pp. 14–16.

6. Indicate whether a company gains or loses under each of the following conditions:

(a) A company maintains an excess of monetary assets over monetary liabilities during a period of general price-level increase.

(b) A company maintains an excess of monetary liabilities over monetary assets during a period of general price-level increase.

(c) A company maintains an excess of monetary assets over monetary liabilities during a period of general price-level decrease.

(d) A company maintains an excess of monetary liabilities over monetary assets during a period of general price-level decrease.

7. It has been suggested that although the stockholders' equity is nonmonetary in character, an exception should be made in the case of the equity of the preferred stockholders and this equity should be treated as a monetary item. Would you agree? Give your reasons.

8. Some have suggested that the restatement of accounting data to current dollars be limited to land, buildings, and equipment and to related depreciation charges. Would you defend or reject such a proposal? Give your reasons.

9. Describe the restatement of inventories in current dollars when inventories are reported (a) on a first-in, first-out basis; (b) on a last-in, first-out basis.

10. The most time-consuming step in the restatement of accounts to report general price-level changes is the "aging" of the depreciable property and the corresponding restatement of the periodic depreciation. What is meant by "aging" as used here? Do you agree with this statement?

11. What special procedures are required when price-level statements are prepared for the first time for a company that has operated for many years?

12. The effectiveness of management in maintaining the purchasing power of invested capital can be determined from general price-level financial statements prepared to supplement the conventional statements. Give four other purposes that may be served by such supplemental statements.

EXERCISES

1. Compute in each case below the general price-level gain or loss assuming that assets are held and liabilities are maintained during a period in which the general price level rises by 5%.

(a) Cash	$ 50,000
Current receivables	20,000
(b) Cash	100,000
Current payables	25,000
Long-term payables	55,000

(c) Cash..$ 25,000
    Land... 50,000
    Current payables.. 25,000
(d) Cash... 25,000
    Land and buildings.. 100,000
    Mortgage note payable... 40,000

2. Assume the same facts as in Exercise 1, but a general price-level decline of 5%. Compute the general price-level gain or loss in each case.

3. Assuming that prices rise evenly by 4% during a year, compute the amount of revenue stated in terms of end-of-year dollars in each of the following cases:

(a) Revenues of $1,000,000 were collected at the beginning of the year for services provided during the year.

(b) Revenues of $250,000 were collected at the beginning of each quarter for services provided during the quarter.

(c) Revenues of $250,000 were collected at the end of each quarter for services provided during the quarter.

(d) Revenues of $1,000,000 were collected at the end of the year for services provided during the year.

(e) Revenues of $1,000,000 were collected evenly throughout the year for services provided during the year.

4. A comparative income statement for the John Cannon Company for the first two years of operations appears below.

	Results of Operations			
	First Year		Second Year	
Sales......................		$750,000		$900,000
Cost of goods sold:				
Beginning inventory................	—		$300,000	
Purchases........................	$750,000		500,000	
Goods available for sales............	$750,000		$800,000	
Ending inventory..................	300,000	450,000	400,000	400,000
Gross profit on sales................		$300,000		$500,000
Operating expenses:				
Depreciation.....................	$ 30,000		$ 30,000	
Other...........................	240,000	270,000	350,000	380,000
Net income........................		$ 30,000		$120,000
Dividends.........................		15,000		30,000
Increase in retained earnings..........		$ 15,000		$ 90,000

Prepare a comparative income and retained earnings statement expressing items in dollars of purchasing power at the end of the second year, considering the following data:

(a) Prices rose evenly and index numbers expressing the general price-level changes were:

Beginning of first year............ 100
End of first year................. 110
End of second year............... 140

(*continued*)

(b) Sales and purchases were made and expenses were incurred evenly each year.
(c) Inventories were reported at cost using first-in, first-out pricing; average indexes for the year are applicable in restating inventories.
(d) Depreciation relates to equipment acquired at the beginning of the first year.
(e) Dividends were paid at the middle of each year.

5. Comparative balance sheet data for Egan Industries, Inc., since its formation appear below. The general price level during the two-year period went up steadily; index numbers expressing the general price-level changes are listed following the balance sheet. Restate the comparative balance sheet data in terms of the purchasing power at the end of the second year.

	End of First Year	End of Second Year
Cash.....................................	$ 62,500	$ 50,000
Receivables..............................	50,000	65,000
Land, buildings, and equipment (net)*	120,000	115,000
	$232,500	$230,000
Payables.................................	$ 62,500	$ 45,000
Capital stock............................	150,000	150,000
Retained earnings........................	20,000	35,000
	$232,500	$230,000

*Acquired at the beginning of the first year.

Price Level Index Numbers

At the beginning of the business..........	112
At the end of the first year..............	125
At the end of the second year............	140

6. The income statement for Bingham Products, Inc., is given below. Using the income statement together with the additional data provided, prepare an income statement that is restated in terms of end-of-year dollars accompanied by a schedule summarizing the general price-level gain or loss for the year.

Bingham Products, Inc.
Income Statement
For Year Ended December 31, 19--

Sales.....................................		$990,000
Cost of goods sold:		
Beginning inventory......................	$ 150,000	
Purchases...............................	900,000	
Goods available for sale.................	$1,050,000	
Ending inventory........................	450,000	600,000
Gross profit on sales....................		$390,000
Operating expenses......................		270,000
Income before income taxes		$120,000
Income taxes............................		60,000
Net income..............................		$ 60,000

The general price level rose evenly from 140 to 160 in the preceding year and from 160 to 200 in the current year. Sales and purchases were made evenly and expenses were incurred evenly during the year. The average index is regarded as applicable in stating inventories. All of the company's assets and liabilities, both at the beginning and at the end of the period, were classified as current; current assets were $600,000 and current liabilities were $200,000 at the beginning of the year.

PROBLEMS

28-1. The Taylor Co. began operations in 1947. At the end of 1970 it was decided to furnish stockholders with a balance sheet restated in terms of uniform 1970 dollars as a supplement to the conventional financial statements. This is the first time such a statement was prepared. The balance sheet prepared in conventional form at the end of 1970 was as follows:

Taylor Co.
Balance Sheet
December 31, 1970

Cash	$ 187,600	Accounts payable	$ 317,500
Accounts receivable	342,400	Mortgage note payable	450,000
Inventory	617,500	Bonds payable	1,250,000
Land	1,720,000	Capital stock	1,000,000
Building	2,350,000	Premium on capital stock	200,000
Less accumulated depr.	(705,000)	Retained earnings	1,295,000
		Total liabilities and	
Total assets	$4,512,500	stockholders' equity	$4,512,500

All of the stock was issued in 1947. Land was purchased subject to a mortgage note of $1,000,000 at the time the company was formed. The present building is being depreciated on a straight-line basis with a 40-year life and no salvage value. The bonds were issued in 1958. The company uses first-in, first-out in pricing inventories.

Instructions: Prepare a balance sheet for the Taylor Co. restated in terms of 1970 dollars. Use the GNP Deflator on page 1021 in making adjustments; assume that the index for each year is regarded as representative of the price level for the entire year.

28-2. An income statement for the Campbell Co. is given on page 1058. The following additional data are available:

(a) Price-level index numbers were as follows:

January 1	110
December 31	130

The price level rose evenly throughout the year.

Campbell Co.
Income Statement
For Year Ended December 31, 19--

Sales..		$480,000
Less sales discount and allowances..................		12,000
Net sales...		$468,000
Cost of goods sold:		
Inventory, January 1...........................	$110,000	
Purchases.....................................	240,000	
Goods available for sale.......................	$350,000	
Inventory, December 31........................	90,000	
Cost of goods sold............................		260,000
Gross profit on sales...............................		$208,000
Operating expenses:		
Depreciation..................................	$ 30,000	
Other operating expenses......................	100,000	
Total operating expenses......................		130,000
Income before income taxes......................		$ 78,000
Income taxes......................................		34,000
Net income..		$ 44,000

(b) Sales, sales discounts and allowances, purchases, and expenses took place evenly throughout the year.

(c) The inventory was valued at cost using the first-in, first-out method. The beginning inventory was acquired during the preceding period when the average price index was 100.

(d) The depreciation charge related to the following property items:

	Cost	Index Number at Date of Acquisition	Depreciation Rate
Building..................	$150,000	90	2½%
Equipment................	200,000	90	10 %
Equipment................	50,000	105	10 %
Equipment*...............	20,000	120	12½%

*Acquired on July 1 of the current year.

(e) Dividends were declared and paid at the end of the year.

(f) The balance sheet position of the company changed during the year as follows:

	January 1	December 31
Current assets................................	$160,000	$180,000
Building and equipment (net)..................	360,000	350,000
	$520,000	$530,000
Current liabilities............................	$ 39,000	$ 30,000
Paid-in capital...............................	300,000	300,000
Retained earnings............................	181,000	200,000
	$520,000	$530,000

Instructions: Prepare an income statement restated to report end-of-year dollars accompanied by a schedule summarizing the general price-level gain or loss for the year.

28-3. The income statement prepared at the end of the year for the Wilson Corporation follows:

Wilson Corporation
Income Statement
For Year Ended December 31, 19--

Sales...		$320,000
Less sales discount..........................		10,000
Net sales.....................................		$310,000
Cost of goods sold:		
Inventory, January 1.........................	$122,000	
Purchases...................................	200,000	
Goods available for sale......................	$322,000	
Inventory, December 31......................	120,000	
Cost of goods sold..........................		202,000
Gross profit on sales.........................		$108,000
Operating expenses:		
Depreciation................................	$ 15,000	
Other operating expenses....................	50,000	
Total operating expenses....................		65,000
Income before income taxes..................		$ 43,000
Income taxes................................		20,000
Net income..................................		$ 23,000
Dividends...................................		10,000
Increase in retained earnings................		$ 13,000

The following additional data are available:

(a) The price index rose evenly throughout the year from 120 on January 1 to 130 on December 31.

(b) Sales were made evenly throughout the year; expenses were incurred evenly throughout the year.

(c) The inventory was valued at cost using first-in, first-out pricing. The beginning inventory was acquired in the preceding period when the average index was 122.

(d) The depreciation charge related to the following items:

	Asset Cost	Index Number at Date of Acquisition	Depreciation Rate
Building..................	$75,000	95	3 %
Equipment................	80,000	95	12½%
Equipment................	20,000	98	12½%
Equipment*...............	1,500	120	16⅔%

*Acquired at the beginning of the current year.

(e) Semiannual dividends of $5,000 were declared and paid at the end of June and at the end of December.

(f) The balance sheet position for the company changed during the year as follows:

	January 1	December 31
Current assets.	$180,000	$186,500
Building and equipment (net)	120,000	106,500
	$300,000	$293,000
Current liabilities.	$ 55,000	$ 35,000
Capital stock.	200,000	200,000
Retained earnings.	45,000	58,000
	$300,000	$293,000

Instructions: Prepare an income statement in which items are stated in end-of-year dollars accompanied by a schedule summarizing the general price-level gain or loss for the year.

28-4. Financial statements are prepared for the Harold Co. at the end of each year in conventional form and also in price-level form. Balance sheet data summarized in conventional and in general price-level form at the end of 1971 are given below.

	Conventional Form		General Price-Level Form (Reporting Purchasing Power at End of Year)
Assets:			
Cash.		$ 23,000	$ 23,000
Current receivables.		70,000	70,000
Inventory.		105,000	106,500
Buildings and equipment.	$120,000		$153,600
Less accumulated depreciation.	48,000	72,000	61,440	92,160
Land.		50,000	64,000
Total assets.		$320,000	$355,660
Liabilities:			
Current payables.		$ 48,000	$ 48,000
Long-term obligations.		40,000	40,000
Total liabilities.		$ 88,000	$ 88,000
Stockholders' equity:			
Capital stock.		$150,000	$192,000
Retained earnings.		82,000	75,660
Total stockholders' equity.		$232,000	$267,660
Total liabilities and stockholders' equity.		$320,000	$355,660

Data from statements prepared in conventional form at the end of 1972 are given on the opposite page.

The following additional data are available at the end of 1972:

(a) Price-level index numbers were as follows for the year:

January 1 150
December 31 153

The price-level rose steadily during the year.

Balance Sheet		Income Statement	
Assets:		Sales.....................	$1,100,000
Cash.....................	$ 79,500	Cost of goods sold.........	600,000
Current receivables......	72,500	Gross profit on sales.......	$ 500,000
Inventory................	125,000	Operating expenses........	306,000
Buildings and equipment.	120,000		
Accumulated depreciation	(54,000)	Income before income taxes	$ 194,000
Land....................	50,000	Income taxes..............	90,000
	$393,000	Net income...............	$ 104,000
		Dividends................	20,000
Liabilities and stockholders' equity:		Increase in retained earnings	$ 84,000
Current payables........	$ 37,000		
Long-term obligations....	40,000		
Capital stock............	150,000		
Retained earnings.......	166,000		
	$393,000		

(b) Sales and purchases were made evenly and expenses were incurred evenly throughout the year.

(c) The first-in, first-out method was used to compute inventory cost.

(d) All of the land, buildings, and equipment were acquired when the company was formed.

(e) Dividends were declared and paid at the end of the year.

Instructions: Prepare in terms of end-of-year dollars: (1) an income and retained earnings statement accompanied by a schedule summarizing the general price-level gain or loss for 1972; (2) a balance sheet as of December 31, 1972.

28-5. Operations of the Hale Corporation for a two-year period after its organization are summarized on the comparative statements given on page 1062. Certain stockholders of the company request additional data that will enable them to judge the economic progress of the company during this period, and it is decided to prepare price-level statements for each year expressing the purchasing power of the dollar at the end of each year. The data and assumptions that are to be applied in the preparation of such statements follow:

(a) Price-level index numbers were:

Beginning of first year (at company formation)... 115

End of first year............................... 125

End of second year............................ 135

The price level rose evenly throughout each year.

(b) Sales, purchases, and expenses were made or incurred evenly throughout each year.

(c) The first-in, first-out method was used in calculating inventory cost.

(d) Dividends were declared and paid in the middle of each year.

(e) The mortgage note was paid off at the end of the second year.

(f) Buildings were depreciated at the rate of 4%.

Comparative Income Statement

	First Year		Second Year	
Sales		$1,000,000		$1,200,000
Cost of goods sold:				
Beginning inventory............	$180,000		$ 200,000	
Purchases....................	700,000		820,000	
Merchandise available for sale....	$880,000		$1,020,000	
Ending inventory..............	200,000	680,000	210,000	810,000
Gross profit on sales..............		$ 320,000		$ 390,000
Expenses (including depreciation)...		260,000		310,000
Net income.....................		$ 60,000		$ 80,000
Dividends......................		50,000		50,000
Increase in retained earnings.......		$ 10,000		$ 30,000

Comparative Balance Sheet

	Beginning of Business	End of First Year	End of Second Year
Assets:			
Cash..................................	$160,000	$110,000	$ 20,000
Accounts receivable.........................	—	150,000	150,000
Inventory..................................	180,000	200,000	210,000
Buildings (net)............................	250,000	240,000	230,000
Land......................................	60,000	60,000	60,000
Total assets.............................	$650,000	$760,000	$670,000
Liabilities:			
Accounts payable...........................	—	$100,000	$130,000
Mortgage note payable......................	$150,000	150,000	—
Total liabilities........................	$150,000	$250,000	$130,000
Stockholders' equity:			
Capital stock..............................	$500,000	$500,000	$500,000
Retained earnings..........................	—	10,000	40,000
Total stockholders' equity...............	$500,000	$510,000	$540,000
Total liabilities and stockholders' equity...........	$650,000	$760,000	$670,000

Price-level multipliers in ratio form are given below:

125/115....1.087	135/120....1.125
135/115....1.174	135/125....1.080
125/120....1.042	135/130....1.038

Instructions: (1) Prepare in terms of end-of-year dollars an income and retained earnings statement accompanied by a schedule summarizing the general price-level gain or loss, and a balance sheet for the first year.

(2) Prepare similar statements for the second year.

28-6. To obtain a more realistic appraisal of his investment, Walter Abbott, your client, has asked you to adjust certain financial data of the Global Company for price-level changes. On January 1, 1970, he invested $50,000 in the Global Company in return for 10,000 shares of common stock. Immediately after his investment the trial balance data appeared as follows:

	Dr.	Cr.
Cash and receivables................................	$ 65,200	
Merchandise inventory.............................	4,000	
Building...	50,000	
Accumulated depreciation — building................		$ 8,000
Equipment...	36,000	
Accumulated depreciation —equipment..............		7,200
Land..	10,000	
Current liabilities.................................		50,000
Capital stock, $5 par..............................		100,000
	$165,200	$165,200

Balances in certain selected accounts as of December 31 of each of the next three years were as follows:

	1970	1971	1972
Sales..	$39,650	$39,000	$42,350
Inventory....................................	4,500	5,600	5,347
Purchases....................................	14,475	16,350	18,150
Operating expenses (excluding depreciation)....	10,050	9,050	9,075

Assume the 1970 price level as the base year and that all changes in the price level take place at the beginning of each year. Further assume that the 1971 price level is 10% above the 1970 price level and that the 1972 price level is 10% above the 1971 level.

The building was constructed in 1966 at a cost of $50,000 with an estimated life of 25 years. The price level at that time was 80% of the 1970 price level.

The equipment was purchased in 1968 at a cost of $36,000 with an estimated life of ten years. The price level at that time was 90% of the 1970 price level.

The lifo method of inventory valuation is used. The original inventory was acquired in the same year the building was constructed and was maintained at a constant $4,000 until 1970. In 1970 a gradual buildup of the inventory was begun in anticipation of an increase in the volume of business.

Abbott considers the return on his investment as the dividend he actually receives. In 1970 and also in 1972 the Global Company paid cash dividends in the amount of $4,000.

On July 1, 1971, there was a reverse stock split-up of the company's stock in the ratio of one-for-ten.

Instructions: (1) Compute the 1972 earnings per share of common stock in terms of 1970 dollars.

(2) Compute the percentage return on the investment for 1970 and 1972 in terms of 1970 dollars.

(AICPA adapted)

28-7. You have been engaged by the Charlton Corporation since the fall of 1971 to translate the corporation's financial statements from historical costs to current or replacement costs for internal use. You assisted in the determination at December 31, 1971 and 1972 of the amounts listed in the Replacement Costs columns on the balance sheet given below.

One of the factors considered in determining replacement costs was an increase in the price level, which at December 31, 1972, was 104% of the price-level index at December 31, 1971. Management has now engaged you to translate Charlton Corporation's 1972 income statement from historical costs as it appears on the opposite page to current costs.

Charlton Corporation
Comparative Balance Sheet
December 31, 1971 and 1972

	Historical Costs		Replacement Costs	
	1971	1972	1971	1972
Assets				
Current assets:				
Cash............................	$ 238,500	$ 494,500	$ 238,500	$ 494,500
Receivables — net..................	581,500	760,850	581,500	760,850
Marketable securities................	27,500		28,600	
Inventories.......................	407,000	434,500	440,000	462,000
Prepaid expenses...................	5,500	11,000	5,500	11,000
Total current assets...............	$1,260,000	$1,700,850	$1,294,100	$1,728,350
Investment in affiliated company........	$ 440,000	$ 440,000	$ 660,000	$ 726,000
Long-term assets:				
Land...........................	$ 110,000	$ 105,000	$ 231,000	$ 231,000
Buildings and equipment.............	3,850,000	3,850,000	5,390,000	5,713,400
Accumulated depreciation...........	(1,925,000)	(2,117,500)	(2,695,000)	(3,142,370)
Long-term lease....................	540,000	480,000	567,000	529,200
Total long-term assets.............	$2,575,000	$2,317,500	$3,493,000	$3,331,230
Patents — net.......................	$ 395,000	$ 345,000	$ 495,000	$ 440,000
Total assets.........................	$4,670,000	$4,803,350	$5,942,100	$6,225,580
Liabilities				
Current liabilities:				
Accounts payable...................	$ 805,000	$ 709,400	$ 805,000	$ 709,400
Current portion of lease obligation.....	44,400	47,050	44,400	47,050
Total current liabilities.............	$ 849,400	$ 756,450	$ 849,400	$ 756,450
Long-term liabilities:				
5% Bonds payable, due 1981..........	$1,100,000	$1,100,000	$1,019,039	$1,025,181
Lease obligation....................	465,600	418,550	465,600	418,550
Deferred income taxes payable........	55,000	60,000	55,000	60,000
Estimated taxes on increases to replacement costs......................			591,005	645,524
Total long-term liabilities...........	$1,620,600	$1,578,550	$2,130,644	$2,149,255
Total liabilities......................	$2,470,000	$2,335,000	$2,980,044	$2,905,705
Stockholders' Equity				
Common stock — $100 par value.........	$1,650,000	$1,650,000		
Premium on common stock.............	330,000	330,000		
Retained earnings...................	220,000	488,350		
Total stockholders' equity..............	$2,200,000	$2,468,350	$2,962,056	$3,319,875
Total liabilities and stockholders' equity...	$4,670,000	$4,803,350	$5,942,100	$6,225,580

Charlton Corporation
Income Statement
For Year Ended December 31, 1972

	Historical Costs	
Sales.....		$7,999,750
Cost of goods sold:		
Inventories, January 1, 1972.....	$ 407,000	
Variable manufacturing costs.....	2,175,250	
Fixed manufacturing costs.....	825,000	
Depreciation.....	154,000	
Amortization of lease.....	60,000	
Amortization of patents.....	50,000	
Total.....	$3,671,250	
Less inventories, December 31, 1972.....	434,500	3,236,750
Gross profit on sales.....		$4,763,000
Operating expenses:		
Variable selling expenses.....	$1,375,000	
Fixed selling expenses.....	825,000	
Variable administrative expenses.....	275,000	
Fixed administrative expenses.....	1,650,000	4,125,000
Operating income.....		$ 638,000
Other revenue and expense items:		
Dividends received.....	$ 8,350	
Bond interest expense.....	(55,000)	
Lease interest expense.....	(27,950)	
Gain (loss) from sale of securities.....	1,500	
Gain from sale of land.....	7,000	(66,100)
Income before income taxes.....		$ 571,900
Income taxes.....		279,150
Net income.....		$ 292,750

The following information relative to current cost computations is also available:

(a) The general price level increased early in January 1972, to 104% of the 1971 price level.

(b) The marketable securities were sold August 17, 1972, for $29,000.

(c) Prepaid expenses are for prepaid variable manufacturing costs.

(d) Land purchased in 1965 for $5,000 was sold November 20, 1972, for $12,000. The land had a replacement cost of $10,500 at December 31, 1971.

(e) Replacement costs of the land and the building and equipment increased by amounts greater than the increase in the general price level. Depreciation on building and equipment is computed by the straight-line method at 5% of the 1972 replacement cost. The accumulated depreciation was increased by depreciation for 1972 plus an adjustment for prior years based on 1972 replacement cost of the building and equipment.

(f) Depreciation is allocated 80% to manufacturing operations and 10% each to fixed selling expenses and fixed administrative expenses and is included in the fixed selling and administrative expenses on the income statement.

(g) The long-term lease is for the use of manufacturing facilities during the period 1971 through 1980. The lease required the payment of $90,000 on January 1, 1971, and $75,000 on each January 1 through 1980. Charlton capitalized the lease at $600,000 and is amortizing it on a straight-line basis. The replacement cost for a comparable unexpired lease increased 5% each year for 1971 and 1972.

(h) The replacement cost of patents increased a total of $15,000 in 1972 and amortization amounted to $70,000 on a replacement cost basis.

(i) The 5% bonds were originally issued at par and are due December 31, 1981. At December 31, 1971, and December 31, 1972, these bonds were selling in the market to yield 6% interest. Interest is payable annually on December 31.

(j) The deferred income taxes payable result from differences in treatment of items for income tax and financial reporting purposes. Management would like to have income taxes in the current costs section of the income statement based on historical costs expressed in current dollars.

Instructions: Prepare an income statement that expresses all amounts in current costs and determines net income. Supporting schedules should be in good form. (In addition to income from transactions Charlton Corporation would also recognize gains from current cost valuations and from purchasing power gains on net debt on its current cost income statement, but these computations are not required.)

(AICPA adapted)

28-8. The Melgar Company purchased a tract of land as an investment in 1969 for $100,000; late in that year the company decided to construct a shopping center on the site. Construction began in 1970 and was completed in 1972; one third of the construction was completed each year. Melgar originally estimated the costs of the project would be $1,200,000 for materials, $750,000 for labor, $150,000 for variable overhead, and $600,000 for depreciation.

Actual costs (excluding depreciation) incurred for construction were:

	1970	1971	1972
Materials	$418,950	$434,560	$462,000
Labor	236,250	274,400	282,000
Variable overhead	47,250	54,208	61,200

Shortly after construction began, Melgar sold the shopping center for $3,000,000 with payment to be made in full on completion in December 1972. One hundred fifty thousand dollars of the sales price was allocated for the land.

The transaction was completed as scheduled and now a controversy has developed between the two major stockholders of the company. One feels the company should have invested in land because a high rate of return was earned on the land. The other feels the original decision was sound and that changes in the price level which were not anticipated affected the original cost estimates.

You were engaged to furnish guidance to these stockholders in resolving their controversy. As an aid, you obtained the following information:

(a) Using 1969 as the base year, price-level indexes for relevant years are: 1966 = 90, 1967 = 93, 1968 = 96, 1969 = 100, 1970 = 105, 1971 = 112, and 1972 = 120.

(b) The company allocated $200,000 per year for depreciation of fixed assets allocated to this construction project; of that amount $25,000 was for a building purchased in 1966 and $175,000 was for equipment purchased in 1968.

Instructions: (1) Prepare a schedule to restate in base year (1969) costs the actual costs, including depreciation, incurred each year. Disregard income taxes and assume that each price-level index was valid for the entire year.

(2) Prepare a schedule comparing the originally estimated costs of the project with the total actual costs for each element of cost (materials, labor, variable overhead, and depreciation) adjusted to the 1969 price-level.

(3) Prepare a schedule to restate the amount received on the sale in terms of base year (1969) purchasing power. The gain or loss should be determined separately for the land and the building in terms of base year purchasing power and should exclude depreciation.

(AICPA adapted)

28-9. Skadden, Inc., a retailer, was organized during 1966. Skadden's management has decided to supplement its December 31, 1969 historical dollar financial statements with general price-level financial statements. The following general ledger trial balance (historical dollar) and additional information have been furnished:

Skadden, Inc.
Trial Balance
December 31, 1969

	Debit	Credit
Cash and Receivables (net)...........................	540,000	
Marketable Securities (common stock)...................	400,000	
Inventory..	440,000	
Equipment...	650,000	
Accumulated Depreciation — Equipment................		164,000
Accounts Payable...................................		300,000
6% First-Mortgage Bonds, due 1987....................		500,000
Common Stock, $10 par.............................		1,000,000
Retained Earnings, December 31, 1968.................	46,000	
Sales...		1,900,000
Cost of Goods Sold.................................	1,508,000	
Depreciation.......................................	65,000	
Other Operating Expenses and Interest.................	215,000	
	3,864,000	3,864,000

(a) Monetary assets (cash and receivables) exceeded monetary liabilities (accounts payable and bonds payable) by $445,000 at December 31, 1968. The amounts of monetary items are fixed in terms of numbers of dollars regardless of changes in specific prices or in the general price level.

(b) Purchases ($1,840,000 in 1969) and sales are made uniformly throughout the year.

(c) Depreciation is computed on a straight-line basis, with a full year's depreciation being taken in the year of acquisition and none in the year of retirement. The depreciation rate is 10 percent and no salvage value is anticipated. Acquisitions and retirements have been made fairly evenly over each year and the retirements in 1969 consisted of assets purchased during 1967 which were scrapped. An analysis of the equipment account reveals the following:

Year	Beginning Balance	Additions	Retirements	Ending Balance
1967	——	$550,000	——	$550,000
1968	$550,000	10,000	——	560,000
1969	560,000	150,000	$60,000	650,000

(d) The bonds were issued in 1967 and the marketable securities were purchased fairly evenly over 1969. Other operating expenses and interest are assumed to be incurred evenly throughout the year.

(e) Assume that Gross National Product Implicit Price Deflators (1958 = 100) were as follows:

Annual Averages	Index	Conversion Factors (1969 4th Qtr. = 1.000)
1966	113.9	1.128
1967	116.8	1.100
1968	121.8	1.055
1969	126.7	1.014
Quarterly Averages		
1968 4th	123.5	1.040
1969 1st	124.9	1.029
2d	126.1	1.019
3d	127.3	1.009
4th	128.5	1.000

Instructions: (1) Prepare a schedule to convert the equipment account balance at December 31, 1969, from historical cost to general price-level adjusted dollars.

(2) Prepare a schedule to analyze in historical dollars the accumulated depreciation account for equipment for the year 1969.

(3) Prepare a schedule to analyze in general price-level dollars the accumulated depreciation account for equipment for the year 1969.

(4) Prepare a schedule to compute Skadden, Inc.'s general price-level gain or loss on its net holdings of monetary assets for 1969 (ignore income tax implications). The schedule should give consideration to appropriate items on or related to the balance sheet and the income statement.

(AICPA adapted)

appendix

specimen corporation statements

Statements of several well-known corporations are given on the pages that follow. Statements of financial position, operations, and changes in financial position, together with accompanying statement notes as presented in the corporate annual reports are reproduced. These statements illustrate practical applications of contemporary accounting standards and concepts.

A summary is presented preceding each set of statements pointing out matters of particular interest in viewing the statements. The forms, procedures, and items that are pointed out are not necessarily examples of good reporting or unsatisfactory reporting; rather, these are matters of interest that call for evaluation in terms of the accounting framework as a whole as developed in the text.

Reference to the statements and statement items may be made throughout the course as various phases of statement structure, form, and content are considered.

Statements are included for the following companies:

1. American Telephone and Telegraph
2. The Superior Oil Company
3. Twentieth Century-Fox Corporation
4. Southern Pacific Company
5. United States Steel Corp.
6. American Motors

American Telephone and Telegraph Company

The following features are of interest in reviewing the financial statements and accompanying notes taken from the annual report of American Telephone and Telegraph Company for 1971.

Three financial statements are presented: (1) Consolidated Statements of Income and Reinvested Earnings, (2) Consolidated Balance Sheet, and (3) Consolidated Statements of Changes in Financial Position.

Consolidated Statement of Income and Reinvested Earnings. The statement of income and reinvested earnings provides for a summary of net income and the changes in reinvested earnings in combined form. Net income data are presented under a series of revenue and expense designations. The resulting net income balance is increased by reinvested earnings reported at the beginning of the year as restated for a cumulative adjustment relating to a change in accounting method and is decreased by dividends and miscellaneous charges in arriving at the balance at the end of the year. An earnings per common share presentation is given immediately following the determination of net income.

Consolidated Balance Sheet. Plant and long-term investments are listed first in presenting assets, and stockholders' equity and long-term indebtedness are listed first in presenting liabilities and capital. Emphasis is then placed upon long-term assets and the means for their financing rather than upon working capital, an order of presentation that is typical for the balance sheets of public utility enterprises. It should be observed that current assets and current liabilities form only a small part of the respective asset and liability and capital totals.

Consolidated Statement of Changes in Financial Position. The statement of changes in financial position lists the sources and applications of working capital and the resulting change in working capital for the year. Changes in the individual current assets and current liabilities are listed in support of the net change in working capital reported for the year.

Notes to Consolidated Financial Statements. Notes to the financial statements first provide a summary of the accounting policies that were employed in preparing the statements. This summary includes the accounting policies adopted for consolidation, depreciation, capitalization of certain taxes and expenses, the investment credit, and research and fundamental development. Further notes offer descriptions of specific items reported on the statement of income and reinvested earnings and the statement of financial position. These include a summary of accounting for pension plans, the composition of "other income" in the summary of net income, and a listing of the investments that have not been consolidated and the accounting procedures that have been employed for these.

Report of Independent Certified Public Accountants

To the Share Owners of American Telephone and Telegraph Company: We have examined the consolidated balance sheet of American Telephone and Telegraph Company and its telephone subsidiaries as of December 31, 1971 and the related statements of income and reinvested earnings and changes in financial position for the year then ended. Our examination was made in accordance with generally accepted auditing standards, and accordingly included such tests of the accounting records and such other auditing procedures as we considered necessary in the circumstances. We previously examined and reported upon the consolidated financial statements of the Company and its telephone subsidiaries for the year 1970, which have been restated as described in note (a) to the financial statements. The financial statements of two telephone subsidiaries included in the consolidated financial statements for the year 1971 (constituting total assets of $7,960,911,000 and total operating revenues of $2,968,491,000 included in the consolidated totals) were examined by other auditors. The consolidated financial statements for the years 1971 and 1970 of Western Electric Company, Incorporated and Subsidiaries, the Company's principal nonconsolidated subsidiary (which statements reflect net income of $258,412,-000 and $253,447,000 included in consolidated net income for 1971 and 1970) were also examined by other auditors. The reports of other auditors have been furnished to us and our opinion expressed herein, insofar as it relates to the amounts included in the consolidated financial statements for subsidiaries examined by them is based solely upon such reports.

In our opinion, based upon our examination and the reports of other auditors, the consolidated financial statements on pages 26 to 32 present fairly the consolidated financial position at December 31, 1971 and 1970, the consolidated results of operations and the consolidated changes in financial position for the years then ended, of American Telephone and Telegraph Company and its telephone subsidiaries, in conformity with generally accepted accounting principles applied on a consistent basis.

LYBRAND, ROSS BROS. & MONTGOMERY

1251 Avenue of the Americas, New York, N.Y.
February 9, 1972

25

Consolidated Statements of Income and Reinvested Earnings

	Thousands of Dollars	
	Year 1971	Year 1970
OPERATING REVENUES		
Local service	$ 9,186,952	$ 8,455,967
Toll service	8,650,009	7,874,069
Miscellaneous	828,137	764,810
Principally from directory advertising		
Less: Provision for uncollectibles	154,333	139,965
Total operating revenues	18,510,765	16,954,881
OPERATING EXPENSES		
Maintenance	3,776,617	3,373,303
Depreciation	2,764,240	2,531,972
Portion of the cost of depreciable plant charged against		
current operations, approximately 5.2% in 1971 and 5.3% in 1970		
Traffic	1,586,748	1,469,573
Costs, principally operators' wages, incurred in the handling of messages		
Commercial	646,515	577,454
Primarily costs of local business office operations		
Marketing	806,766	754,845
Accounting	555,078	513,420
Research and fundamental development	133,963	120,358
Provision for pensions and other employee benefits (b)	1,221,957	1,018,993
Other operating expenses	900,214	786,051
Less: Expenses charged construction	317,501	277,595
Total operating expenses	12,074,597	10,868,374
Net operating revenues *(carried forward)*	$ 6,436,168	$ 6,086,507

26   *For notes, see page 30*